CONTEMPORARY LITERARY CRITICS

CONTEMPORARY
LITERARY CRITICS

SECOND EDITION

ELMER BORKLUND

St J
St James Press

Chicago and London

Published by
St. James Press
233 East Ontario Street
Chicago, Illinois 60611
U.S.A.

or

2-6 Boundary Row
London SE1 8HP
England

ISBN 0-912289-33-3

First published in the UK and USA in 1982

Preface to the First Edition

Contemporary Literary Critics is a descriptive reference guide to the work of 115 modern British and American critics, most of them still very much alive and flourishing. In order to hold this book down to a reasonable size, however, and to keep it reasonably within the limits of my own competence, I have not taken into account three worthy groups of writers: the aestheticians and professional philosophers (Susanne Langer and R.G. Collingwood, for example), even though they often make valuable observations about particular works and artists; the textual scholars and literary biographers, even though serious criticism obviously depends upon their achievements; and the continental critics (Erich Auerbach, for example, or, at the moment, Roland Barthes) whose work, even in translation, has already had an impact on the thinking of their Anglo-American counterparts. As for the critics I have included here, I am grateful to M.H. Abrams, Robert Martin Adams, F.W. Bateson, Wayne Booth, Martin Dodsworth and William Empson for looking over my initial list of candidates and giving me their recommendations. As it turned out, they usually agreed with each other; but no one adviser, probably, would be entirely happy with all of my choices: I am responsible for the final decisions and for what I have to say about each critic.

Anyone preparing a reference book of this sort has to live with the uncomfortable knowledge that his efforts may be misunderstood or abused. Partly to frustrate the impulse some readers might have to regard my comments as a substitute for the hard work of reading each critic complete and judging him by a wider range of standards than I generally apply here, I quote whenever possible, and often at great length. By doing so I hope to convey a sense of how each critic handles his texts and talks to his readers, even, sometimes, reasons with them. Nevertheless, the longest passages still appear out of context, and hence the bibliographies, which are designed to indicate the full range of each critic's work to date. For separately published critical books I have tried to make the listings complete; for uncollected essays and occasional reviews I have been generous but necessarily selective, as I also have been for publications in areas other than criticism and for studies of the critic *as* a critic (I have not listed studies, for example, of Auden and Eliot as poets or of E.M. Forster as a novelist). Over the past two years a few of the critics represented here have been writing their books faster than I could expand my comments, and thus in some instances the bibliographies are more up to date than my essays. I particularly regret not being able to describe very recent work by Walter Jackson Bate, Harold Bloom and John Holloway, among others.

Substantial quotations and bibliographies may reassure skeptical readers—up to a point. Although my primary aim has been to be descriptive, and fairly so, I have never hesitated to judge as well as describe when an important issue was at stake; and since the grounds for my judgments are not always apparent in each particular case, let me be explicit here: "critical pluralism," as it is now being called a little belatedly, seems to me to do the greatest possible justice to the diverse aims and methods of valid criticism. I have described this position in my remarks about Elder Olson and R.S. Crane, but once again, and very briefly: the crucial premise here is that the situations critics investigate are too complex to be encompassed by any one frame of reference. A literary work is a mental event for its author, a potential cause of similar or dissimilar events in the minds of his readers, an historically conditioned phenomenon, an embodiment of certain stylistic possibilities and ethical convictions, and so on. Each of these areas is perfectly suitable for investigation, but each can be adequately grasped only by the use of a limited set of principles and an appropriate methodology. As R.S. Crane demonstrates in *The Languages of Criticism and the Structure of Poetry*, the moral is that we should welcome as many frameworks or "languages" as there are "distinguishable major aspects in the construction, use, and appreciation of literary works." What we want to do with a text depends upon our immediate purposes and the power of our analytical tools. Intelligible discourse about literature or anything else depends, Crane continues, upon a finite conceptual scheme which

> delimits what the critic can say about any of the questions with which he may be concerned—and this for the simple reason that we can discuss only those aspects of existent objects which are represented or implied in the terms we select or have available

for the discussion: we cannot, for example, say anything about the specific forms of individual poems in a mode of criticism of which the distinctions used as principles in the argument pertain only to the poet's mind or to the constitution of his medium or to the psychology of his audience. We are thus committed, in any instance of coherent critical discourse, to a particular subject matter, which can be said to be of our own making, not in the sense that it may not correspond to something real, but in the sense that, by our choice of one rather than another possible set of definitions and hypotheses, we have decided what it is to be.

Pluralism is not a form of relativism: as Elder Olson points out, the men on the Tower of Babel were not talking nonsense to each other, they were simply talking in different languages. And of course once a critic has set his goal and selected his language we have a right (to quote Crane once more) to "hold him to the accepted canons of reasoning and hypothesis-making, as well as of common sense, that apply in any branch of inquiry dealing with particular things." Therefore in my own comments about each critic I have tried to indicate what he wants to do, what assumptions he makes about the nature and function of literature, and what he is able to accomplish, given his analytical tools. If I point out that a critic can do one thing but not another, I am by no means suggesting that what he can do is not worth doing or that a better critic would attempt more: the best critics are often those who have a sharp sense of their own limitations. Not all kinds of criticism seem to me to be equally worth doing, however, and if I have a bias it is against, for want of a more accurate term, "thematic" criticism, in which the critic is content merely to discover the presence of a moral or intellectual motif in a work or group of works. If a critic seems to me to write badly or reason ineptly, I have said so. And finally, I have made almost no historical generalizations about British and American criticism during the past fifty years or so: even if it were not too soon to do so pluralism compels us to recognize that critical terms are stipulative and mean only what the critic makes them mean within a given framework. When critics are as far apart as, say, Maud Bodkin and Northrop Frye, or John Crowe Ransom and I.A. Richards, it is worse than useless to believe that labels such as "myth criticism" or "the New Criticism" have any descriptive value.

It would have been impossible for me to undertake this project without the resources of the Regenstein Library of the University of Chicago and the courtesy of its staff. I am also grateful to a number of friends and colleagues: to Paul West for suggesting that a book about critics would make a sensible addition to the *Contemporary Writers* series, to Henry Sams for giving me the chance to teach criticism at Pennsylvania State University, to Dennis Marnon and John Shilts for their help with some of the bibliographies, to Albert Tsugawa for many conversations about critical problems, and to George Walsh and James Vinson of the St. James Press for their endless patience and aid. My greatest debts are to Maurice Cramer for many years of support, to the late David Farquhar, and to Elizabeth Borklund, to whose memory this book is dedicated.

ELMER BORKLUND

A Note to the Second Edition

I have added nine writers to this new edition of *Contemporary Literary Critics* (Terry Eagleton, Stanley Fish, Joseph Frank, Norman Holland, Edgell Rickword, C.H. Sisson, Barbara Herrnstein Smith, Ian Watt and Raymond Williams), brought the biographical and bibliographical information for writers included in the First Edition up to date, and commented on the important work some of them have done since 1977. If I were revising the Preface to the First Edition, I would remove the late Roland Barthes—now a household name—from his parenthetical position and replace him with Jacques Derrida, whose influence over the past few years has been remarkable, to the joy of some and the misery of others. I am indebted once more to George Walsh for his editorial aid, and especially to Daniel Kirkpatrick for his scrupulous attention to errors and omissions in the First Edition.

E.B.

M.H. Abrams
Robert Martin Adams
John W. Aldridge
Walter Allen
A. Alvarez
Quentin Anderson
Newton Arvin
Louis Auchincloss
W.H. Auden

Carlos Baker
Owen Barfield
Walter Jackson Bate
F.W. Bateson
John Bayley
Eric Bentley
Marius Bewley
R.P. Blackmur
Harold Bloom
Maud Bodkin
Wayne C. Booth
Malcolm Bradbury
Cleanth Brooks
Van Wyck Brooks
Kenneth Burke

Christopher Caudwell
Lord David Cecil
Richard Chase
Cyril Connolly
Malcolm Cowley
R.S. Crane
Frederick C. Crews
J.V. Cunningham

David Daiches
Donald Davie
C. Day Lewis
Denis Donoghue

Terry Eagleton
Leon Edel
T.S. Eliot
Richard Ellmann
William Empson
D.J. Enright
Martin Esslin

Francis Fergusson
Leslie Fiedler
Stanley Fish
E.M. Forster
Joseph Frank
G.S. Fraser
Northrop Frye

Dame Helen Gardner
Maxwell Geismar

Paul Goodman
Robert Graves

D.W. Harding
Barbara Hardy
Geoffrey H. Hartman
Ihab Hassan
Robert B. Heilman
Granville Hicks
E.D. Hirsch, Jr.
Norman Holland
John Holloway
Graham Hough
Irving Howe
Stanley Edgar Hyman

Randall Jarrell

Alfred Kazin
Hugh Kenner
Frank Kermode
Arnold Kettle
H.D.F. Kitto
G. Wilson Knight
L.C. Knights
Murray Krieger

Robert Langbaum
F.R. Leavis
Q.D. Leavis
Harry Levin
C.S. Lewis
R.W.B. Lewis
Robert Liddell
David Lodge
Percy Lubbock

F.O. Matthiessen
Mary McCarthy
Josephine Miles
J. Hillis Miller
Edwin Muir

Elder Olson

Roy Harvey Pearce
Morse Peckham
Richard Poirier
Ezra Pound
V.S. Pritchett

Philip Rahv
John Crowe Ransom
I.A. Richards
Edgell Rickword
Christopher Ricks

Mark Schorer

Delmore Schwartz	A.J.A. Waldock
Karl Shapiro	Austin Warren
C.H. Sisson	Robert Penn Warren
Barbara Herrnstein Smith	Ian Watt
James Smith	René Wellek
Stephen Spender	Paul West
George Steiner	Raymond Williams
	Edmund Wilson
Tony Tanner	W.K. Wimsatt
Allen Tate	Yvor Winters
Lionel Trilling	Virginia Woolf
John Wain	Philip Young

ABRAMS, M(eyer) H(oward). American. Born in Long Branch, New Jersey, 23 July 1912. Educated at Harvard University, Cambridge, Massachusetts, B.A. 1934, M.A. 1937, Ph.D. 1940; Cambridge University, England (Henry Fellow), 1934-35. Married Ruth Gaynes in 1937; has two children. Instructor, 1938-42, Research Associate, Psycho-acoustic Laboratory, 1942-45, Harvard University. Assistant Professor, 1945-47, Associate Professor, 1947-53, Professor of English, 1953-60, F.J. Whiton Professor, 1960-63, and since 1973 Class of 1916 Professor, Cornell University, Ithaca, New York. Since 1961, Advisory Editor, W.W. Norton, publishers, New York City. Fulbright Scholar, Royal University of Malta and Cambridge University, 1953; Roache Lecturer, Indiana University, Bloomington, 1963; Alexander Lecturer, University of Toronto, 1964; Fellow, Center for Advanced Study in the Behavioral Sciences, Palo Alto, California, 1967; Visiting Fellow, All Souls College, Oxford University, 1977. Recipient: Ford Fellowship, 1946; Rockefeller Fellowship, 1946; Phi Beta Kappa Christian Gauss Prize, 1954; Guggenheim Fellowship, 1957, 1960; James Russell Lowell Prize, 1972. D.H.L.: University of Rochester, New York, 1978; Northwestern University, Evanston, Illinois, 1981. Fellow, American Academy of Arts and Sciences and American Philosophical Society. Address: Department of English, Cornell University, Ithaca, New York 14850, U.S.A.

PUBLICATIONS

Criticism

> *The Milk of Paradise: The Effect of Opium Visions on the Works of De Quincey, Crabbe, Francis Thompson and Coleridge* (undergraduate thesis). Cambridge, Massachusetts, Harvard University Press, 1934.
> *The Mirror and the Lamp: Romantic Theory and the Critical Tradition.* New York and London, Oxford University Press, 1953.
> *A Glossary of Literary Terms.* New York, Rinehart, 1957; revised edition, 1971.
> "Belief and the Suspension of Disbelief," in *Literature and Belief*, edited by M.H. Abrams. New York, Columbia University Press, 1958.
> "The Correspondent Breeze: A Romantic Metaphor," revised version in *English Romantic Poets: Modern Essays in Criticism*, edited by M.H. Abrams. New York, Oxford University Press, 1960; revised edition, 1975.
> "Five Types of Lycidas," in *Milton's Lycidas: Tradition and Form*, edited by C.A. Patrides. New York, Holt Rinehart, 1961.
> "English Romanticism: The Spirit of the Age," in *Romanticism Reconsidered*, edited by Northrop Frye. New York, Columbia University Press, 1963.
> "Structure and Style in the Greater Romantic Lyric," in *From Sensibility to Romanticism: Essays Presented to Frederick A. Pottle*, edited by Frederick W. Hilles and Harold Bloom. New York, Oxford University Press, 1965.
> "Coleridge, Baudelaire, and Modernist Poetics," in *Immanente Aesthetik, Aesthetische Reflexion: Lyrik als Paradigma der Moderne*, edited by Wolfgang Iser. Munich, Wilhelm Fink, 1966.
> *Natural Supernaturalism: Tradition and Revolution in Romantic Literature.* New York and London, Norton, 1971.
> "What's the Use of Theorizing about the Arts?" in *In Search of Literary Theory*, edited by Morton W. Bloomfield. Ithaca, New York, Cornell University Press, 1972.
> "Coleridge and the Romantic Vision of the World," in *Coleridge's Variety*, edited by John Beer. London, Macmillan, 1974.
> "A Note on Wittgenstein and Literary Criticism," in *English Literary History* (Baltimore), 41, 1974.
> "Rationality and Imagination in Cultural History: A Reply to Wayne Booth," in *Critical Inquiry* (Chicago), 2, 1976.
> "The Limits of Pluralism II: The Deconstructive Angel," in *Critical Inquiry* (Chicago), 3, 1977.
> "Behavior and Deconstruction: A Comment on Morse Peckham's 'The Infinitude of Pluralism,' " in *Critical Inquiry* (Chicago), 4, 1977.
> "How to Do Things with Texts," in *Partisan Review* (Boston), 46, 1979.

"A Reply," in *High Romantic Argument: Essays for M.H. Abrams*, edited by Lawrence Lipking.   Ithaca, New York, and London, Cornell University Press, 1981.

Other

Editor, *Literature and Belief.*   New York, Columbia University Press, 1958.
Editor, *The Poetry of Pope.*   New York, Holt Rinehart, 1958.
Editor, *English Romantic Poets: Modern Essays in Criticism.*   New York, Oxford University Press, 1960; revised edition, 1975.
General Editor, *The Norton Anthology of English Literature.*   New York, Norton, 1962; revised edition, 1968, 1974, 1979.
Editor, with Jonathan Wordsworth and Stephen Gill, *William Wordsworth: The Prelude: 1799, 1805, 1850.*   New York, Norton, 1979.

CRITICAL STUDIES AND BIBLIOGRAPHY

J. Hillis Miller, "Tradition and Difference," in *Diacritics* (Ithaca, New York), 2, 1972.
Wayne C. Booth, "M.H. Abrams: Historian as Critic, Critic as Pluralist," in *Critical Inquiry* (Chicago), 2, 1976.
Wayne C. Booth, "History as Metaphor; or, Is M.H. Abrams a Mirror, or a Lamp, or a Fountain, or...?" in *High Romantic Argument: Essays for M.H. Abrams*, edited by Lawrence Lipking.   Ithaca, New York, and London, Cornell University Press, 1981.
Jonathan Culler, "The Mirror Stage," in *High Romantic Argument*, 1981.
Stuart A. Ende, "A Bibliography of M.H. Abrams," in *High Romantic Argument*, 1981.
Lawrence Lipking, "The Genie in the Lamp: M.H. Abrams and the Motives of Criticism," in *High Romantic Argument*, 1981.
Thomas McFarland, "A Coleridgean Criticism of the Work of M.H. Abrams," in *High Romantic Argument*, 1981.

*   *   *

In *The Mirror and the Lamp* M.H. Abrams observes that the crucial distinction between different modes of thinking lies in "the choice of initial premises (often, if I have not been mistaken, the analogical premises) of our reasoning, and the validity of the choice is measured by the adequacy of its coherently reasoned consequences in making the universe intelligible and manageable." In the humanities at least, no one method of inquiry can exhaust the complexities of its subject matter; and if this is true, then a critical system, like any other intellectual framework, is a kind of set or language game: the assumptions it employs, often unconsciously, determine what aspects of the subject it can grasp; its definitions and grammar generate an appropriate method of investigation and limit the range of criteria for judgment. Thus in his discussion of English Romantic theory Abrams is careful first of all to distinguish among the four different possibilities or "orientations" which have always been open to literary critics. Mimetic theory, such as Aristotle's, concentrates primarily on the work as an imitative representation of an objective, pre-existing reality; pragmatic criticism, such as Sidney's, emphasizes the effect the artist should strive to induce in his audience; objective criticism, versions of which appear in some extreme forms of modern criticism, isolates the work as a heterocosm, a complex, self-sufficient creation to be discussed only in its own terms. And a final mode, expressive criticism, such as that practiced by Wordsworth and Coleridge, deals primarily with the qualities of mind or soul supposed to be characteristic of the artist. (These languages are not, of course, rigidly exclusive: a pragmatic critic, for example, may well need to say something about appropriate formal qualities. The critic's overall purpose determines where we place him.)

The Mirror and the Lamp describes, within this larger "metacritical" context, the important shift in English critical theory from a primarily mimetic concern for the work as a kind of mirror reflecting external nature, to a primarily expressive mode of thinking which sees the mind of the artist as a kind of lamp, contributing its own essence to what it perceives. From this point of view, then, "the shift from neo-classical to romantic criticism can be formulated in a preliminary way as a radical alteration in the typical metaphors of critical discourse" (these metaphors are the "analogical premisses" referred to above.) Abrams' method is to scrutinize "the role in the history of criticism of certain more or less submerged conceptual models...in helping to select, interpret, systematize and evaluate the facts of art." The questions Romantic, "expressive" criticism raises and the conclusions it seeks are thus quite different from the questions and goals of the other modes.

The greater part of *The Mirror and the Lamp* traces this shift, a subject to which Abrams is able to bring a formidable amount of scholarly knowledge. For all his learning, however, Abrams seems unwilling to commit himself to a fixed conception of causation: the facts, the manifestations of the shift, are unmistakably there, but the causes of the shift may be complex beyond hope of recovery (thus at the very start of his argument Abrams reminds his readers of Aristotle's warning that an educated man, that is an experienced man, will look for precision only insofar as his subject matter permits). Given Abrams' skill in detecting recurrent metaphors and lines of action, he might be called a kind of "archetypal" critic, and this is in fact a label he seems willing to endure—provided it does not restrict him to "implications which are equally unnecessary and undesirable." He observes, characteristically, that there is no "rational need" to embrace Jung or the ingenious work of Maud Bodkin, which reduces literature to "mere variations upon a timeless theme" and thus has little value for a critic who must deal with the problems and powers of an individual text.

The shift from mimetic to expressive criticism at a particular moment in intellectual history leads to a problem which has concerned Abrams for some time: the question of poetic belief, the status and possible value of imaginatively generated statements that cannot be verified—and may well be discredited—by the increasingly prestigeful language of science. Can poetry still be defended as a mode of knowledge and source of value? In an important essay, "Belief and the Suspension of Disbelief," Abrams demonstrates that several tactics have been used to defend poetry against science. The critic may argue that a work is a self-contained second creation, non-referential and therefore subject only to the laws of its own being; or he may argue, with Whitehead and John Crowe Ransom, that the genuine work, while not factually true, nevertheless returns to us that vital, concrete fullness which science strips from experience. Or he may argue, as John Stuart Mill did, that poetic statements are revelations not of the real world, but of the speaker's feelings about that world, and thus constitute a kind of knowledge that still has powerful claims on our attention. Abrams' own position is essentially pragmatic: taking the climactic line of the *Paradiso*, "In His will is our peace," he maintains that

> the testimony of innumerable readers demonstrates that the passage can certainly be appreciated, and appreciated profoundly, independently of assent to its propositional truth. It touches sufficiently on universal experience—since all of us, whether Catholic, Protestant, or agnostic, know the heavy burden of individual decision—to enable us all to realize the relief that might come from saying to an infallible Providence, "Not my will, but Thine be done." This ability to take an assertion hypothetically, as a ground for imaginative experience, is one we in fact possess.

Here Abrams seems close to postulating a sort of general moral consensus, even among men who may be separated, at more particular levels of experience, by sharp doctrinal differences; and he also implies that this general moral sense is relatively fixed. Thus if the values embodied in a work are too special or idiosyncratic to touch our common humanity, the poetic effect will be impaired, as in fact it is, Abrams suggests, in a novel like *Aaron's Rod*.

If *The Mirror and the Lamp* deals primarily with the differences between Romantic theory and its predecessors, *Natural Supernaturalism* is designed to show the remarkable persistence of certain type-metaphors and archetypal actions, and to assert the essential continuity which exists between Christian concerns and the characteristic ventures of Romanticism. The background of scriptural metaphors and exegesis, Abrams argues, will prove "of repeated relevance to our understanding of the Romantic movement," since the Romantics revived these "ancient matters" in order to save the "cardinal virtues of their religious heritage" and thus make them "intellectually acceptable, as well as emotionally pertinent, for the time being." The archetypal Romantic plot—it may of course be an inner plot of meditation—fundamentally involves "the Neoplatonic paradigm of a primal unity and goodness, an emanation into multiplicity which is *ipso facto* a lapse into evil and suffering, and a return to unity and goodness." This familiar pattern of fall, quest, and return at a higher level of awareness Abrams demonstrates not by any special psychological apriorism but by solid argument and far ranging investigations into German philosophy of the period.

Abrams develops his metacritical position most fully in "What's the Use of Theorizing about the Arts?" Here he defends not poetry against science, but poetic theory against the attacks of some powerful, scientifically-minded analytic philosophers who maintain that coherent critical discourse is impossible. Like R.S. Crane, he argues that we should welcome a diversity of critical methods whose justification can only be pragmatic; we must accept the difficult conclusion, he maintains, that "once a concept or assertion has been adopted as the basis of a critical theory, its origin or truth-claim, whether empirical or metaphysical, ceases to matter, for its validity in this context is to be determined by its power of illumination when brought to bear in the scrutiny of works of art." Although critical languages should be subject to the general rules of common sense and sound hypothetical reasoning, "criticism must initiate its chief function where these simplified calculi [the precise sciences] stop; for the models of logic and scientific method achieve their extraordinary efficacy...by the device of systematically excluding just those features of experience that, humanly speaking, matter most."

As a critic of criticism then, Abrams is a pluralist or "pragmatist" in the usual sense: is he therefore a relativist? And as the historian of a particular period, is he also a pragmatist in the rather special sense of the term as it appears in *The Mirror and the Lamp*? That is, can he tell us anything about the human value of the tradition he has worked so carefully to define? As for relativism, no pragmatist has ever tried to maintain that all methods work equally well on all occasions. The value of a critical system lies in what it can tell us about a work viewed from a particular vantage point. As readers we are free to occupy the same point and judge, by perfectly ordinary, commonsense methods, the accuracy of what the critic has seen. The number, or rather the essential *kinds* of vantage points cannot be infinite—not even so radically "subjective" a critic as Barthes has proposed that. And as for critical judgments in the usual sense, Wayne Booth has recently argued at length, and persuasively, that "Abrams performs literary criticism through history—though he never quite tells us that he has done so":

> Abrams has described those moments in Romanticism when poets defined the universe, with their imagination, as essentially "friendly," in the precise sense that there was a natural marriage between the human spirit and the world it inhabits. And he leaves no doubt—though he says little directly about himself—that he clearly thinks their kind of hope, their faith in life and joy, can still be recommended, in some sense, even in our own blighted times. [*Natural Supernaturalism*] is his own (muted) theodicy, and those who think all theodicies by definition faulty are right in feeling challenged. In choosing our attitudes, the book implies, let us not pretend that rational defenses are all on the side of considering nature or the universe unfriendly to men, who are *essentially* alienated ....Showing us where we came from, demonstrating that it was a place of greatness in our past, transmitting forgotten connections that join us to the past, *Natural Supernaturalism* becomes a portrayal of who and where we are. It thus not only makes "extrinsic" criticism possible—because after all if one act of criticism is possible, the thing becomes possible. It makes life itself, in a post-Romantic age, tangibly, demonstrably livable.

This is high praise, as Booth intended it to be, but during the past few years it has become fashionable to question the very foundation of the kind of criticism which Abrams—and Booth—practice. In a 1972 review of *Natural Supernaturalism*, J. Hillis Miller also praised the book, calling it an achievement in "the grand tradition of modern humanistic scholarship, the tradition of Curtius, Auerbach, Lovejoy, C.S. Lewis"; but then, following Jacques Derrida, he went on to argue that Abrams' premises and by implication the premises of every major British and American critic of the twentieth century are based on fundamentally mistaken views of language and interpretation. Thanks to Nietzsche, we now know that "there is no 'correct' interpretation," since the very act of reading is "never the objective identifying of a sense but the importation of meaning into a text which has no meaning 'in itself.'" By the late 1970s the lines were firmly drawn: on one side are the "conservative" critics, such as Abrams, Booth and E.D. Hirsch, for whom there can be rational consensus about the determinate meaning of a literary text; on the other, Derrida and his American sympathizers, Paul de Man, Geoffrey Hartman and Miller himself (the challenges which Harold Bloom and Stanley Fish pose to the conservative critics are based on quite different principles). Given his view of the false metaphysics underlying our traditional, "logocentric" view of language and the universe, Derrida (in Abrams' patient summary) undermines "the possibility of understanding language as a medium of decidable meanings." His theories eventuate in "a radical scepticism about our ability to achieve a correct interpretation, proposing instead that reading should free itself from illusory linguistic constraints in order to become liberated, creative, producing the meanings that it makes rather than discovers." But such a position, Abrams warns, is "suicidal" since it is "self-reflexive," in that Derrida's "subversive process destroys the possibility that a reader can interpret correctly either the expression of his theory or the textual interpretations to which it is applied." This is not a clash of rival critical approaches—nothing, for example, like the opposition between the Neo-Aristotelians and the New Critics during the 1940's: what is at stake here is something much more basic. Derrida and his followers have made a decisive break with what Abrams eloquently defines as the entire Western "humanistic paradigm of reading and writing," in which

> the writer is conceived, in Wordsworth's terms, as "a man speaking to men." Literature, in other words, is a transaction between a human author and his human reader. By his command of linguistic and literary possibilities, the author actualizes and records in words what he undertakes to signify of human beings and actions and about matters of human concern, addressing himself to those readers who are competent to understand what he has written. The reader sets himself to make out what the author has designed and signified, through putting into play a linguistic and literary expertise that he shares with the author. By approximating what the author undertook to signify the reader understands what the language of the work means.

The "deconstructive" criticism of the opposing camp, he concludes, "has nothing whatever to do with the common experience of the uniqueness, the rich variety, and the passionate human concerns in works of literature, philosophy or criticism."

ADAMS, Robert Martin. Formerly Robert Martin Krapp. American. Born in New York City, 27 November 1915. Educated at Columbia University, New York City, B.A. 1935 (Phi Beta Kappa), M.A. 1937, Ph.D. 1942. Served as a captain in the United States Air Force, 1943-46: Bronze Star. Married Elaine Rosenbloom (divorced, 1957), 1 son; married Janet Malkin. Instructor in English, University of Wisconsin, Madison, 1942-43; Instructor and Assistant Professor, Rutgers University, New Brunswick, New Jersey, 1947-50; Assistant Professor and Professor of English, Cornell University, Ithaca, New York, 1950-68. Since 1968, Professor of English, University of California at Los Angeles. Recipient: *Hudson Review* Fellowship in Criticism, 1956; Guggenheim Fellowship, 1960. Address: 813 Waldo Street, Santa Fe, New Mexico 87501, U.S.A.

PUBLICATIONS

Criticism

> *Ikon: John Milton and the Modern Critics.* Ithaca, New York, Cornell University Press, 1955.
> *Strains of Discord: Studies in Literary Openness.* Ithaca, New York, Cornell University Press, 1958.

Stendhal: Notes on a Novelist.   New York, Noonday Press, and London, Merlin Press, 1959.
Surface and Symbol: The Consistency of James Joyce's Ulysses.   New York, Oxford University Press, 1962.
James Joyce: Common Sense and Beyond.   New York, Random House, 1966.
Nil: Episodes in the Literary Conquest of the Void During the Nineteenth Century.   New York, Oxford University Press, 1966.
Proteus, His Lies, His Truth: Discussions of Literary Translation.   New York, Norton, 1973.
"Precipitating Eliot," in *Eliot in His Time*, edited by A. Walton Litz.   Princeton, New Jersey, Princeton University Press, and London, Oxford University Press, 1973.
"The Sense of Verification: Pragmatic Commonplaces about Literary Criticism," in *Myth, Symbol, and Culture*, edited by Clifford Geertz.   New York, Norton, 1974.
"Transparency and Opaqueness," in *Novel* (Providence, Rhode Island), 7, 1974.
The Roman Stamp: Frame and Façade in Some Forms of Neo-Classicism.   Berkeley and London, University of California Press, 1974.
"Hades," in *James Joyce's Ulysses*, edited by Clive Hart and David Haymen.   Berkeley and London, University of California Press, 1974.
Afterjoyce: Studies in Fiction After Ulysses.   New York and London, Oxford University Press, 1977.
"Religion of Man, Religion of Woman," in *Art, Politics, and Will: Essays in Honor of Lionel Trilling*, edited by Quentin Anderson, Stephen Donadio and Steven Marcus.   New York, Basic Books, 1977.
Badmouth: Fugitive Papers on the Dark Side.   Berkeley and London, University of California Press, 1977.
"Dynamic Duos," in *Sewanee Review* (Tennessee), 86, 1979.
"What Was Modernism?" in *Hudson Review* (New York), 31, 1978.
"On the Bulk of Ben," in *Ben Jonson's Plays and Masques*, edited by Robert Martin Adams.   New York, Norton, 1979.
"Authenticity—Codes and Sincerity—Formulas," in *The State of the Language*, edited by Leonard Michaels and Christopher Ricks.   Berkeley and London, University of California Press, 1980.
The Lost Museum: Glimpses of Vanished Originals.   New York, Viking Press, 1981.

Other

Liberal Anglicanism 1636-1947: An Historical Essays (as Robert Martin Krapp).   Ridgefield, Connecticut, Acorn Press, 1944.

Editor, *Circe*, by Giovanni Battista Gelli, translated by Thomas Brown.   Ithaca, New York, Cornell University Press, 1963.
Editor and translator, *Red and Black*, by Stendhal.   New York, Norton, 1969.
Editor and translator, *The Prince*, by Machiavelli.   New York, Norton, 1977.
Editor, *Ben Jonson's Plays and Masques*.   New York, Norton, 1979.
Editor, *The Egoist*, by Meredith.   New York, Norton, 1979.

*   *   *

"It is only through the vigilant, the militant use of our critical faculties," Robert Martin Adams maintains, "that we can confer any real benefit on the authors whom we love." This might stand as the motto for Adams' own work, for behind his learning and sophistication there is always a kind of energy and sense of enjoyment which has all but vanished from modern criticism. And while Adams' taste is catholic and acute, it is also clear that he is most attracted to a certain kind of artist, anxious to pay tribute and communicate his enthusiasm, and determined to protect the qualities he most admires from inflexible and misapplied criticism. The primary value of art lies in the challenge it poses to complacency: "I mean simply and seriously," Adams asserts, "that literature by its very nature is committed to questioning yesterday's assumptions and today's commonplaces"; and as a corollary he adds that "one prime aim of scholarship is to promote uncertainty." Again, " 'I come to disquiet' says a writer like Gide. And he is right."

Adams' first book, *Ikon: John Milton and the Modern Critics*, introduces most of his characteristic concerns. The immediate purpose here is to question the versions of Milton which some influential modes of modern criticism have proposed. These conceptions, he argues,

> no longer offer a fruitful multiplicity but a blurred confusion and sometimes a downright contradiction. Each of these images is rooted in philosophical presuppositions, with which it is often useful to quarrel....If I interpret the contemporary prospect correctly it calls out, not for more seed and energetic cultivation, but for a firm hand on the pruning shears.

Thus he devotes one essay to challenging the assumption of some of the New Critics that *Comus* should be read as a closely-woven metaphysical lyric, thereby neglecting the "larger architecture" of the poem as a dramatic structure made for a specific occasion. In another essay he demonstrates the confusion introduced into discussions of *Paradise Lost* by critics eager to reduce Satan to an archetypal figure. In short, *Ikon* offers the reader a catalogue of the distortions and contradictions which modern criticism has fostered; but at the same time Adams also provides more appropriate ways of dealing with *Comus*, the figure of Satan, Milton's habits of revision, or whatever the topic may be (and it should be noted that his characterization of Milton's verse style is as informed and helpful as readers will find anywhere). His methods for correcting the partial views of other critics are diverse and flexible; he is uncommitted to any one mode of argument, bringing forward whatever seems relevant— classical learning, precise textual knowledge, even that most formidable of weapons, shrewd common sense. The image of Milton which finally emerges is convincing and of central importance in understanding Adams' general position:

> Milton-wrote for the morally committed reader...but he also wrote from beliefs which constantly surpassed or evaded the formal categories of his art, so that his great literary achievements, like those of Ibsen and Flaubert, Euripides and Swift, end rather in a stalemate than a fully resolved stasis. The antinomy on which Milton's work centers undergoes a full exploration, not a full resolution; we admire not the formal perfection with which a conclusion is worked out, but the truth and energy with which a conflict is explored down to its last grinding incompatibility.

While there is no reason to question his sensitivity to works which confirm rather than disquiet and which rest comfortably in conventional, well-made forms, Adams is temperamentally most intrigued by the tensions which this view of Milton suggests. Throughout his criticism he has tried to rescue the disturbing and restless writers he most admires from the simplification—or scorn—of complacent formal analysis which presupposes that "a work of art which is not ultimately unified thematically, ideologically, emotionally, imagistically, and on the narrative level—or which does not at least do its best to be unified in some or all of these ways—must remain diffuse and undirected. Conflicts must be resolved...so that a mere 'end' can be elevated to the dignity of a 'conclusion.' " But the novels of Stendhal, for example, "are not written to fill out certain patterns or achieve certain structural, textural, or verbal relations; they engage in a special kind of freedom and open possibility which is incompatible with the security of a fixed structure....Reading the novels of Stendhal is like riding a surfboard—one is not exactly oblivious of the past or the future, but they do not help much to balance the perilous present." Thus "literary experience which does not fit into systems is 'wrong' only if we are more interested in systems than in literature." Clearly there are works which by design include "a major unresolved conflict with the intent of displaying its unresolvedness" and thus can hardly be judged failures if there is a purpose for their "openness." (Adams is perfectly aware of—but quite untroubled by—what Yvor Winters called the fallacy of imitative form: the "fallacy," for example, of letting a work remain formless simply because its subject matter is a certain kind of disorder). The would-be critic should remember that it is no more probable that an elaborate over-all pattern exists (especially when one already has a number of other, perhaps lesser patterns) than that it does not. Even the most elaborately minded author may be unwilling or unable to maintain consistently all the levels of structure for which he has occasional uses. He may even find it aesthetically advantageous, now and then, to do what is (in isolation) structurally anomalous.

Adams is unwilling to legislate the "proper" uses of openness but suggests that "without putting a premium on novelty or magnitude as such, one may attribute value to any work of art which helps man to see experience from a new point of view or to see further into it than an old point of view has allowed him. This is no negation of formalism, but a supplement to it." The ultimate test of such works seems to be that they "extend experience instead of compacting it." A paradox remains, but one which could be resolved only at the cost of simplifying both literature and criticism: "And yet, why else does the continuing effort of criticism, comparison and judgment go on, if not to enable us to absorb even the great disquieter, the most mercurial and destructive of writers?"

Stendhal and Joyce strongly attract Adams' own restless intelligence. The games Stendhal plays, the ways in which he frustrates conventional expectations naturally appeal to those happy few who have "flexible, alive imaginations." In fact Adams' impassioned defense of Beylism is finally an argument for a way of living, not merely for the appreciation of unconstrained literary techniques: "a part of life is an art just as much as art formally defined. The self is or can be an artificial creation, not a discovery but a creation, which man is capable of directing, controlling, and adapting to the ends he selects for himself." For those capable of such self-creation Beylism suggests "a whole series of resilient resources." *James Joyce: Common Sense and Beyond* is a patient but far from oversimplified introduction which more than replaces Harry Levin's standard volume, while *Surface and Symbol* is, in comparison with *Strains of Discord* and *Stendhal*, essentially pre-critical. By examining the uses Joyce makes of raw materials around him and by asking which elements add to the realistic surface of the novel and which are pressed into symbolic service, Adams attempts to "discover what the object was made with as a step toward deciding how it should be looked at and (perhaps) what it should be measured with."

Nil is loosely structured and speculative, quickly sketching the ways in which a number of nineteenth century writers tried to express the sense of vacuums, abysses and emptiness, inner and outer, which leads to our own "void-haunted, void-fascinated age." If we ever see how we got here, Adams suggests, "we may know a little better where we are." The survey is inconclusive, perhaps inevitably so, since "even the history of other men's adventures into non-being defies regularity and method." *Proteus, His Lies, His Truth* is also discursive, a brilliantly conducted tour ending with a predictably gloomy commonplace: exact equivalences are hardly to be expected, since translation is "always a compromise, and great art is rarely a compromise." Yet even here there are prizes for the sensitive and the alert: "the chief reward of studying translations [is] an augmented sense of suspicion, including suspicion of one's own assumptions and responses."

In *The Roman Stamp* Adams traces some of the ways in which artists seeking—or forging—their own identities have turned to the image of Rome:

> for self-creators in the name of Rome, the city is an occasion if not a downright pretext. There are energies within them that Rome releases. Perhaps indeed only Rome could have released them, or only in the particular direction they took. But the men are not passive, plastic wax on which Rome printed its masculine stamp. Quite the contrary, they demanded to be influenced, required it. If Rome had not been handy they would have found something else—or perished from exasperation at the lack of it. The Roman stamp may well be a seal, an impression, but it is also an imperious stamp of the foot, a military "no" to the life of nature as given. In saying this "no," in various tones of voice, various figures over the ages drew upon Rome as a repertoire of attitudes, a set of stylistic devices, embodied in myth, history, architecture, religion, ethics—whatever.

Although some writers are included here, most of the figures are visual artists and architects —Mantegna, Palladio, Canova, and Piranesi, among others. Adams concludes (or rather doesn't conclude) that regarding the making of self-hood,

If one were writing the appropriately endless book on this theme, one could trace some roots of the development in the works of the romantics, Parnassiens, and Symbolists, in the time-attitudes of Schopenhauer and Spengler (not to mention Proust), in the work of the Cubists and the Cambridge anthropologists, in the paintings of Gustave Moreau, the drawings of Odilon Redon, the Hellenic illuminism of Hölderlin, in the "perennial philosophy" of the occultists, worshipers of Isis or thrice-great Hermes, who lie in the background of so much symbolist theory. One could press on to qualify, restrict, extend one's generalizations...to no fixed term. It's not the "disappearance of the object" [in modern art] that one would be tracing but its suffusion with plenitude of shapes or contexts so rich and deep that no "self" can be conceived capable of absorbing, containing, or stopping them. The world then appears an animated, aggressive arabesque, an infinity of self-extending patterns and self-defeated meanings, before which the minds [sic] stands only as victim.

All that, however, is something else again.

That "something else" leads, in *Afterjoyce*, to Adams' extremely sophisticated record of the ways the prose fiction of "modernism" is an "indicator particularly sensitive to the drifts and waverings of the imagination." As before, Joyce is the commanding figure, in some respects the instigator of modernism, who "prompts and provokes an d pre-empts, incites and forbids and interacts with the subtlest and most ambitious minds of the age." *Ulysses* and *Finnegans Wake* put an end forever to the assumption that the central values of conventional fiction—"mimetic solidity, stylistic transparency, consecutive narration, psychological insight, and moral authority within a middle-class framework"—are the only correct ones. "After Joyce" it obviously was—and still is—possible to write traditional novels, but in perspective they now seem only "one alternative among many, and the least adventurous." By exploiting "gaps, unexpressed implications and unresolved ironies" and constructing texts which "give way beneath the reader's feet," Joyce created what amounts to the basic repertoire of modernism:

> if we deliberately widen our perspective to see Joyce's work in context, I think we will find it peculiarly representative, in its dealing with surfaces, of two widespread, multiform trends that look more contradictory than they are. These are the rejection of representation in favor of overt artifice; and the rejection of artifice in favor of vision. Both involve an act of penetration, of seeing through surfaces. In the first place one gets rid of detailed descriptions, pictorial specificity, and that close imitation of surfaces which aims at achieving a persuasive sense of "truth to life." The work of art is an artificial arrangement which calls attention by its very exaggerations and formal structuring to the controlling mind of the artist. The artist is not nature's faithful hound, appealing to his audience to agree that he has followed her successfully; all she provides for him are a few commonplace materials, the more common the better, out of which he makes an artificial cosmos. It is then up to the audience to enter this new cosmos and appreciate its faceted and intricate structure, if they are able to do so. But the next stage is to transcend artifice as well, to push through artifice as easily as artifice had pushed away imitation, and to the same effect, of entering so far as possible the presence of pure vision—vision as an act wholly stripped of particular experience.

Although Adams mistrusts generalizations and is far too alert to the differences among the writers he considers to settle for anything like a conventional account of "influences," he does provide here a guide to the ways "writers of importance in many different tongues over many years...responded in highly individual ways to the different varieties of Joycean stimulus." The strategies he finds in Joyce and then illustrates in the work of Woolf, Nabokov, Faulkner, Beckett and Carlo Emilio Gadda (with brief glances at Döblin and Broch) are sometimes characterized as "post-modern," but he demonstrates so convincingly the continuing presence of Joyce that any distinction between modern and post-modern seems artificial. At the end of a 1978 essay, "What Was Modernism?" Adams observes "it's much easier...to say where and how modernism started than where it ended, or if it has: the central and hardest problem is always the closest, the problem of 'now' ":

> We seem neither to have pushed beyond the innovations of modernism nor to have

rejected them decisively. Primitivism no longer seems like a spacious new dimension of art, sex as a theme offers no larger perspectives than leit-motifs and montage as techniques. A lot of play continues to be made with varieties of illusionism, including the manipulation and disintegration of surface: in that sense and perhaps a few others, modernism can be thought of as pushing forward, though its heroic days are certainly over.

"I see no signs," he concludes, that the power of modernism has been "supplanted by any other major unit of cultural energy." And at the end of *Afterjoyce* he speculates that

> the current phrase "post-modern" signifies plainly that we are still forced to define ourselves in relation to the old modernist impulse, even though we know it's no longer ours, and haven't the faintest idea of what has succeeded it, or will do so. When the new age comes along, if it's really going to be new, it will no doubt announce itself as decisively as *The Waste Land* and *Ulysses* announced the advent of that cycle whose brass and iron ages we are, as it seems to me, now experiencing.

Depressing enough. But in *Bad Mouth*, Adams replaces brass and iron with images of rags, garbage and filth. Not primarily a "literary" study, *Bad Mouth* is a short, arresting inquiry into the "hateful and negative side of the imagination." The "lacerating and deliberately offensive mode in art and literature," he observes, "which used to be very much a minority mode, very much an occasional and subordinate effect within a larger composition, is now predominant." The "art of modern living," he goes on, "is the art of washing clean with dirty water"; but if the very language with which we "measure clean and dirty is itself in question—then what?" Language has always had the function of revealing reality *and* the function of protecting us from an unmediated glimpse of ourselves and our fate:

> In our own day, it's a particular function of language to shield us as best it can from the intolerable glare of Nothing and Nonbeing....As atmospheric gasses soften the otherwise intolerable rays of the sun, so the gasses of language protect the psyche from what it can't bear to contemplate steadily.

And yet the language of modern art and modern life, so preoccupied with lies, invective and obscenity, seems to protect us less and less. Why is this so? Again Adams is wary of generalizations, but remarks that it would be

> ridiculous to exclude from a discussion of the increasing autonomy of the ugly the possibility that the world really is getting uglier from year to year....Civilization rises out of a mound of garbage, into which it is continually subsiding. But in this flashy, fashionable observation, it seems clear, an attitude is expressed, rather than a set of facts. Man has been excreting and polluting for a good while now: much modern awareness of this distressing condition seems forced and *voulu*. We wouldn't emphasize civilization as an affair of tatters and dreck if we hadn't first decided that we ourselves are compounded of tatters and dreck—that laying claim to this inauthentic and corrupt status is the most authentic option open to us.

Mass society gives us a sense that "our identities have been contaminated if not crushed altogether."

Is any remission possible? On the whole it seems not, except for the grim satisfaction we may take in being honest and recording what we must be honest about, an activity which turns out to provide a measure of satisfaction:

> Robert Burton, anatomizing melancholy three and half centuries ago, reported sagely that the best cure of the condition was identical with its most frequent cause: study. The slip-slop of documents, the throb of accumulating particulars, the restless rhythm of the hobby horse are sovereign. Action, action, more and more action. Like pebbles rolling over and over in a tumbler, the samples of ugly that one has accumulated may take on,

14

from one another, a smoother gloss, a deeper luster. Or if that hope is delusive, activity that delays for a while recognition of its own futility may not be altogether futile.

Bad Mouth is an ominous, all too convincing book; and yet even so, there is a vitality and consoling authority about Adams' glistening style. "I confess to a faith," he remarks, "that some pretty heavy thought...can be put into bouyant packages."

ALDRIDGE, John W(atson).   American.   Born in Sioux City, Iowa, 26 September 1922. Educated at the University of Chattanooga, Tennessee, 1940-43; Breadloaf School of English, Vermont, Summer 1942; University of California at Berkeley, B.A. 1947. Served in the United States Army, 1943-45: Bronze Star. Married Leslie Felker in 1954 (marriage dissolved, 1968); Alexandra Bertash, 1968; has five children. Lecturer in Criticism, 1948-50, and Assistant Professor of English, 1950-55, University of Vermont, Burlington; Christian Gauss Lecturer in Criticism, Princeton University, New Jersey, 1953-54; Member of the Literature Faculty, Sarah Lawrence College, Bronxville, New York, The New School for Social Research, New York City, and Professor of English, Queens College, New York City, 1956-57; Berg Professor of English, New York University, 1957-58; Fulbright Lecturer, University of Munich, 1958-59, and the University of Copenhagen, 1962-63; Writer-in-Residence, Hollins College, Virginia, 1960-62. Since 1964, Professor of English, University of Michigan, Ann Arbor. Book Critic, *New York Herald Tribune Book Week*, 1965-66, and *Saturday Review*, New York City, 1970-72; Member of the Staff, Bread Loaf Writers Conference, 1966-69; Special Adviser for American Studies, American Embassy, Bonn, 1972-73. Rockefeller Humanities Fellow, 1976-77. Address: 1050 Wall Street, Ann Arbor, Michigan 48105, U.S.A.

PUBLICATIONS

Criticism

> *After the Lost Generation: A Critical Study of the Writers of Two Wars*.   New York, McGraw Hill, 1951; London, Vision Press, 1959.
> *In Search of Heresy: American Literature in the Age of Conformity*.   New York, McGraw Hill, 1956.
> *Time to Murder and Create: The Contemporary Novel in Crisis*.   New York, McKay, 1966.
> *The Devil in the Fire: Retrospective Essays on American Literature and Culture, 1951-1971*.   New York, Harper's Magazine Press, 1972.
> "Wright Morris Country" and "The American Novelist and the Contemporary Scene: A Conversation Between Wright Morris and John W. Aldridge," in *Wright Morris: Critical Views and Responses*, edited by Robert E. Knoll.   Lincoln, University of Nebraska Press, 1977.
> "An Interview with Norman Mailer," in *Partisan Review* (Boston), 47, 1980.

Novel

> *The Party at Cranton*.   New York, McKay, 1960; London, Constable, 1961.

Other

In the Country of the Young (social commentary).   New York, Harper's Magazine Press, 1970.

Editor, *Critiques and Essays on Modern Fiction, 1920-1951.*   New York, Ronald Press, 1952.
Editor, *Discovery 1.*   New York, Pocket Books, 1953.
Editor, *Selected Stories*, by P.G. Wodehouse.   New York, Random House, 1958.

*   *   *

When it first appeared in 1951, *After the Lost Generation* created something of a stir, for several reasons worth noting. Aldridge provided detailed criticism of the promising new novelists who had started publishing at the close of World War II; he raised an issue not much in vogue at the time (the evaluation of fiction in terms of its expressed values rather than its purely formal virtues); and his tone was strikingly, sometimes comically abrasive. Indeed, Aldridge found so little to admire that he often seemed to be writing—as Wilde said of Henry James—from a painful sense of duty. It is his stand concerning values, however, which has remained the most important element in his thinking and is best summarized, perhaps, in a passage he cites (although not with complete approval) from Ortega y Gasset: "Talent is but a subjective disposition that is brought to bear upon certain material. The material is independent of individual gifts; and when it is lacking, genius and talent are of no avail."

The relationship between fiction and the basic values of society—part of the "material" Ortega refers to—is a vital one for Aldridge, since the creation of fiction is itself fundamentally a process of "assigning values to human experience." If a society is corrupt (and Aldridge obviously hates the "general debility" of the times we live in), then the artist has little chance of creating something that has positive significance. At one point in *In Search of Heresy* he goes so far as to assert "I had perhaps better make it clear that I am concerned...with the kind of orthodoxy which, because it is backed by religious principles and the social code of manners, helps to make possible the delineation of scene and character in fiction. I do not say that such an orthodoxy is right or wrong in any sense save the aesthetic." In light of his later work, however, it is impossible to believe that Aldridge is willing to accept *any* code of values simply because it can provide a basis for fiction.

In *After the Lost Generation* Aldridge scrutinized the work of Hemingway, Fitzgerald and Dos Passos, the novelists who had testified most eloquently to the collapse of values in our time. The writers who emerged in the 1940's inherited the same sense of despair but could hardly go on repeating the same disillusionments indefinitely. The alternatives, as Aldridge defined them, were to assert the need for belief, "even though it is upon a background in which belief is impossible," to escape into journalism, or to cultivate those few remaining areas, mainly homosexuality and race relations, not yet exhausted by earlier novelists. For a few writers the pursuit of "pure technique" seemed to be a possibility. With these options in mind, Aldridge examined the new work of Vance Bourjaily, Norman Mailer, John Horne Burnes, Irwin Shaw, Merle Miller, Gore Vidal, Paul Bowles, Truman Capote and Frederick Buechner. His verdicts were, of course, overwhelmingly negative—and he has not mellowed over the years or regretted his youthful "idealism": if he were writing the book now, he has said recently, he would find even less to praise.

In Search of Heresy deals primarily with the impasse facing writers who were unable to find any release from the increasing conformity of American society in the late 1950's (it is characteristic here that Aldridge should use David Riesman's *The Lonely Crowd* as a key text, with its documentation of the shift in American character from autonomy to other-directedness). For the novelists at least—and Aldridge wisely has never ventured beyond fiction in his criticism—"the possibility for action beyond conformism has been cut down to nothing." But clearly conformity cannot be conformity to nothing, and here Aldridge's position has to be inferred: it is not the lack of values in general he deplores so much as the lack of those values he can personally approve of. In *After the Lost Generation* he makes this crucial admission:

It is true that today people everywhere are asking to be reassured and comforted. It is also true that in the last several years no work of fiction of genuine quality has been able to do either. That fact may indicate not only that a successful affirmative writing cannot be produced without affirmative experience but that the values that most people wish to see affirmed are really false and unworthy. It seems to me that the best literature in America will continue to be negative as long as the couhtry's values are such that no writer of honesty or insight can possibly take them seriously.

Until we somehow acquire a healthy new set of "positive" values, our literature seems doomed to repetition or conformity to the wrong values; our best literature will continue to be "negative" or, at most, offer pure displays of heroic individualism, a quality Aldridge cherishes but never really defines. The true individualist appears to be the man who "holds a dogmatic belief in his supreme power as an individual and a complete contempt for everything which stands in the way of its exercise." This tells us relatively little but it may explain why Aldridge can single out for praise Norman Mailer's *An American Dream* and *Why Are We in Vietnam?* The rest of Aldridge's recent criticism comes perilously close to empty rhetoric. Although his range is extremely narrow, his logic frequently obscure and his tone gratuitously unpleasant, he may deserve a place in the history of modern criticism for his cranky insistence that it is positive values, after all, which lie at the heart of literary experience.

ALLEN, Walter (Ernest). British. Born in Birmingham, England, 23 February 1911. Educated at the University of Birmingham, B.A. (honours) in English 1932. Married Peggy Yorke Joy in 1944; has four children. Assistant Master, King Edward's Grammar School, Aston, Birmingham, 1934; Visiting Professor of English, University of Iowa, Iowa City, 1935; Features Editor, Cater's News Service, Birmingham, 1935-37; Assistant Technical Officer, Wrought Light Alloys Development Association, Birmingham, 1943-45; Margaret Pilcher Visiting Professor, Coe College, Cedar Rapids, Iowa, 1955-56; Assistant Literary Editor, 1959-60, and Literary Editor, 1960-62, *New Statesman*, London; Visiting Professor of English, Vassar College, Poughkeepsie, New York, 1963-64, University of Kansas, Lawrence, and University of Washington, Seattle, 1967; Professor and Chairman of English Studies, New University of Ulster, Coleraine, 1967-73; Berg Professor of English, New York University, 1970-72; Visiting Professor, Dalhousie University, Halifax, Nova Scotia, 1973-74; C.P. Miles Professor of English, Virginia Polytechnic Institute and State University, Blacksburg, 1974-75. Fellow, Royal Society of Literature, 1960. Address: 6 Canonbury Square, London N1 2AU, England.

PUBLICATIONS

Criticism

Arnold Bennett. London, Home and Van Thal, 1948; Denver, Swallow, 1949.
Reading a Novel. London, Phoenix House, and Denver, Swallow, 1949; revised edition, Phoenix House, 1956, 1963.
Joyce Cary. London, Longman, 1953; revised edition, 1963, 1971.
The English Novel: A Short Critical History. London, Phoenix House, 1954; New York, Dutton, 1955.
Six Great Novelists: Defoe, Fielding, Scott, Dickens, Stevenson, Conrad. London, Hamish Hamilton, 1955; Folcroft, Pennsylvania, Folcroft Editions, 1969.

The Novel Today.   London, Longman, 1955; revised edition, 1960; Folcroft, Pennsylvania, Folcroft Editions, 1969.

George Eliot.   New York, Macmillan, 1964; London, Weidenfeld and Nicolson, 1965.

Tradition and Dream: The English and American Novel from the Twenties to Our Time.   London, Phoenix House, 1964; as *The Modern Novel in Britain and the United States*, New York, Dutton, 1964.

"The Comedy of Dickens," in *Dickens, 1970: Centenary Essays*, edited by Michael Slater.   London, Chapman and Hall, and New York, Stein and Day, 1970.

Some Aspects of the American Short Story (lecture).   London, Oxford University Press, 1973.

"Narrative, Distance, Tone and Character," in *The Theory of the Novel: New Essays*, edited by John Halperin.   London and New York, Oxford University Press, 1974.

The Short Story in English.   London and New York, Oxford University Press, 1980.

Novels

Innocence Is Drowned.   London, Joseph, 1938.
Blind Man's Ditch.   London, Joseph, 1939.
Living Space.   London, Joseph, 1940.
Rogue Elephant.   London, Joseph, and New York, Morrow, 1946.
Dead Man over All.   London, Joseph, 1950; as *Square Peg*, New York, Morrow, 1951.
All in a Lifetime.   London, Joseph, 1959; as *Threescore and Ten*, New York, Morrow, 1959.

Other

The Black Country (topography).   London, Elek, 1946.
The Festive Baked-Potato Cart and Other Stories (juvenile).   London, Muller, 1948.
The British Isles in Colour.   London, Batsford, and New York, Viking Press, 1965.
The Urgent West: An Introduction to the Idea of the United States.   London, Baker, 1969; as *The Urgent West: The American Dream and Modern Man*, New York, Dutton, 1969.
Transatlantic Crossing: American Visitors to Britain and British Visitors to America in the Nineteenth Century.   London, Heinemann, and New York, Morrow, 1971.

Editor, *Writers on Writing.*   London, Phoenix House, 1948; as *The Writer on His Art*, New York, McGraw Hill, 1949.
Editor, *The Roaring Queen*, by Wyndham Lewis.   London, Secker and Warburg, and New York, Liveright, 1973.

*   *   *

Literary histories are by definition critical insofar as they employ principles of selection and causation, but Walter Allen, who is justly admired for his comprehensive historical surveys of fiction, is critical in a more direct sense as well. "The reviewer's job," he maintains, "is to read a novel, find out what the author has set out to do, estimate how far he has succeeded, decide whether his intentions were worth while, and report his conclusions to his readers." Allen does precisely this in his own work, in addition to supplying such social and cultural information as may be useful. Quite sensibly following the example of E.M. Forster and others before him, he refuses to commit himself to a formal theory of the novel:

If our notions of what a novel ought to be prevent us from seeing the virtues of a work which does not fit into them, so much the worse for our notions of the novel. In art we have to put up with what we are given, and it is the artist who is the dictator, not the critic. The critic who attempts to survey the course of English fiction during its two hundred and fifty years of life cannot take up a rigid position, if he hopes to say anything to the point on the individual works which make up his subject.

Nevertheless Allen has set up some general guidelines, implicitly following the traditional distinctions between artist, work and intended effect.

Fictions of all sorts share with the novel an appeal to our primitive desire to discover what happens next. "For me," Allen writes, "the novel is a broadly realistic representation of man's life in society which is also a criticism of life and society." The great concern of the English novel in particular has been the "education of men and women, in the sense of their learning to distinguish, through their involvement in society, the true from the false both in themselves and in the world around them." For the novelist writing is a process of self-exploration, an almost obsessive activity carried out with little or no thought for the audience and sustained by the joyous energy which is characteristic of artistic creation:

> Part of the impulse that drives the novelist to make his imitation world must always be sheer delight in his own skill in making; part of the time he is, as it were, taking the observed universe to pieces and assembling it again for the simple and naive pleasure of doing so. He can no more help playing than a child can. And there is this further to be noted. The child cannot help but play, but how he plays is not under his conscious control....In play the child symbolizes, by the way he arranges his toys and so on, his emotional relation to the universe. In play he creates a personal myth.

Every novel, then, is "an extended metaphor of the author's view of life." For the audience, of course, the novel is not merely a symbolic statement of the author's view of life: it has the primary function of engaging and enlarging the reader's human sympathies. On several occasions Allen has praised Lionel Trilling's well-known claim that

> For our time the most effective agent of the moral imagination has been the novel...its greatness and practical usefulness lie in its unremitting work of involving the reader himself in the moral life, inviting him to put his own motives under examination, suggesting that reality is not as his conventional education has led him to see it....It was the literary form to which the emotions of understanding and forgiveness were indigenous, as if by definition of the form itself.

Traditionally the novel has been concerned with faithfully rendering the surface of life as a way of arousing our interest, which is why Allen is willing to discount Tolkien and Hesse, for example, as novelists, and why he tends to be uneasy with a mixed work such as *Ulysses* ("Whether it is a whole or a magnificent ruin I do not yet know"). But finally the illusion of reality exists for the purpose of revealing character. Thus Allen comments

> In *Moll Flanders* more than any other of his fictions Defoe is revealed as the first wholly unambiguous instance in our literature of that interest in character itself, that obsession to impart character, which Virginia Woolf found the distinguishing mark of the novelist. In this respect, if in no other, Defoe is the archetypal novelist.

As Forster maintains in *Aspects of the Novel*, action is the chief object of the drama; but the novelist is after something else, the disclosure of the secret, hidden life of his characters which gives us the sense of a more comprehensive humanity. There are unmistakable echoes of Forster in *Reading a Novel* and *The English Novel*, and echoes of Eliot and Richards as well.

An example of Allen's typical procedure will be of help here. William Golding receives four pages in a three hundred and fifty page survey of the modern novel. After examining *The Lord of the Flies* Allen turns to *Pincher Martin*:

> On a superficial reading, *Pincher Martin* relates a sailor's struggle for survival, as, after his ship has been torpedoed, he scrabbles for existence on an almost bare rock in mid Atlantic. It is all extraordinarily vivid, rendering in precise details the degradation to an animal level, or at least a level at which blind instinctual craving takes over completely. A

more careful reading reveals that Martin is dead, drowned, before he is cast up on the rock, and that his sojourn on the rock, in which he lives through his past life, before he is finally reduced to a mass of cringing, beaten flesh, is a sojourn in purgatory. It represents a confrontation with the facts and consequences of his life of selfishness. The hero's very name is significant. All Martins in the Royal Navy are nicknamed "Pincher" and the slang term "to pinch" means to steal, to convert to one's own use what is another's.

And he concludes about Golding's art in general:

Powerful as they are, Golding's novels seem to me to have the weakness normal to and perhaps inevitable in allegorical fiction. At the same time he is a genuinely religious novelist with a vision, based on the concept of original sin, of the horrifying thinness of civilization....He uses his great gifts of imagination and narrative to force us to accept, as part of the truth about man and his nature, the realities summed up in our time in the hysterical nastiness of Nazism and concentration camps. These, for many of us, are the most baffling phenomena of our century....There is, however, a danger here: the acceptance of the evil displayed in the phenomena as being *the* fundamental truth about man. It is, it seems to me, a danger most carefully to be guarded against. I am bound to say that for me the general effect of Golding's novels suggests that he has not done so. The very intransigence of his work compels protest against it.

Everything that matters to Allen is here—the attention to action as it reveals character, the qualification about departure from naturalism, the unequivocal final judgment. This is the method he applies to George Eliot, Arnold Bennett, Joyce Cary and literally hundreds of other British and American novelists in *The English Novel*, *The Modern Novel* and *The Urgent West*. As for the "moral" standard behind his verdicts, the reader can only work inductively and point to no more, finally, than Allen's generous good sense, tact and lack of dogmatism. The evaluating adjectives come thick and fast but the reader usually finds himself prepared to accept the advice of so amiable a guide.

What Allen has set out to do, then, he has done thoroughly. But there are other questions one may be inclined to ask: for whom are such works intended and what is their final value? *Reading a Novel* is clearly a popular work, meant for an audience with little or no university training; *The English Novel* and *The Modern Novel* seem designed for more sophisticated readers. But regardless of our training, if we read fiction for the pleasure of finding out what happens next, and if we are moved by the vivid rendering of character to broad human sympathy and understanding, then these second-hand accounts of Defoe and Golding and all the rest may do the novel a real disservice. It is not only in poetry that the heresy of paraphrase is something to think about.

ALVAREZ, A(lfred).   British.   Born in London, 5 August 1929. Educated at Oundle School, Northamptonshire; Corpus Christi College, Oxford (Senior Research Scholar, 1952-53, 1954-55). B.A. 1952, M.A. 1956; Princeton University, New Jersey (Proctor Visiting Fellow, 1953-54). Married Ursula Barr in 1956 (marriage dissolved, 1961), one son; Anne Adams, 1966, one son and one daughter. Gauss Lecturer, Princeton University, 1957-58; Visiting Professor, Brandeis University, Waltham, Massachusetts, 1960, and State University of New York, Buffalo, 1966. Editor, *Journal of Education*, 1957; Drama Critic, *New Statesman*, London, 1958-60. Since 1956, Advisory Poetry Editor, *The Observer*, London, and since 1965, Advisory Editor, Penguin Modern European Poets in Translation. Recipient: Rockefeller Fellowship, 1955; D.H. Lawrence Fellowship, 1958; Vachel Lindsay Prize (*Poetry*, Chicago), 1961. Address: The Observer, 8 St. Andrews Hill, London EC4V 5JA, England.

PUBLICATIONS

Criticism

> *The Shaping Spirit: Studies in Modern English and American Poets*.   London, Chatto
> and Windus, 1958; as *Stewards of Excellence: Studies in Modern English and American
> Poets*, New York, Scribner, 1958.
> *The School of Donne*.   London, Chatto and Windus, 1961; New York, Pantheon Books,
> 1962.
> *Under Pressure: The Artist and Society: Eastern Europe and the U.S.A.*   London,
> Penguin, 1965.
> *Beyond All This Fiddle: Essays 1955-1967*.   London, Allen Lane, 1968; New York,
> Random House, 1969.
> *Samuel Beckett*.   London, Fontana, and New York, Viking Press, 1973.

Verse

> *(Poems)*.   Oxford, Fantasy Press, 1952.
> *The End of It*.   Cambridge, Massachusetts, privately printed, 1958.
> *Twelve Poems*.   London, The Review, 1968.
> *Lost*.   London, Turret Books, 1968.
> *Penguin Modern Poets 18*, with Roy Fuller and Anthony Thwaite.   London, Penguin,
> 1970.
> *Apparition*.   Brisbane, University of Queensland Press, 1971.
> *The Legacy*.   London, Poem-of-the-Month Club, 1972.
> *Autumn to Autumn and Selected Poems 1953-1976*.   London, Macmillan, 1978.

Novels

> *Hers*.   London, Weidenfeld and Nicolson, 1974; New York, Random House, 1975.
> *Hunt*.   London, Macmillan, 1978; New York, Simon and Schuster, 1979.

Other

> *The Savage God: A Study of Suicide*.   London, Weidenfeld and Nicolson, 1971; New
> York, Random House, 1972.

> Editor, *The New Poetry: An Anthology*.   London, Penguin, 1962; revised edition, 1966.

*   *   *

In *The Shaping Spirit* Alvarez provides sound general essays on a number of modern British
and American poets and repeats the familiar argument, first suggested by F. W. Bateson, about
the different ways in which these poets have used the "English" language. That language is a
reservoir, a medium in which the best British poets have floated with ease, whereas Eliot,
Pound and Stevens had to start from scratch, literally constructing a new, personal language
not readily available to potential followers. "Eliot uses tradition," Alvarez observes; "Yeats is in
it." And Pound is at his best when "most actively putting the strengths of another language into
English—which is something quite different from the moment when he tries to write English
and fails." The issue at stake is the continuity of poetic language: are the impressive but quite
special verbal worlds of Eliot and Pound "fertile enough" for other poets? The answer appears

to be no, and Alvarez concludes with the predictable assertion that British poets have had to "worry less" about their "basic values" and their "literary manners," while the American imagination has had to deal with "a profound sense of alienation, so that it becomes directed solely towards the discovery of the artist's moral identity."

The School of Donne is a more specialized work, a useful contribution to the history of literary styles and the shifts in taste which make up an important part of that history. When Alvarez searches for the essential characteristic of Donne's style (going considerably beyond the commonplaces about "metaphysical" conceits) it turns out to be the forceful display of a certain kind of sensibility which enlists formal learning to reinforce highly personal statements: "Donne is not interested in Aquinas's or Aristotle's ideas *for themselves*; he is merely using them to give weight to his own arguments." The "school of Donne" refers to men who were rarely professional poets but who shared a common social and intellectual background and circulated their verses privately, among themselves. Consciously or not, they replaced "formality by personal sincerity and wrote in a deliberately off-hand manner for the pleasure of their intimate friends." At its best, then, this new realism "altered the language of poetry because for the first time a writer was dealing in compelling personal terms with the intellectual adult's full experience in all its immediacy." Alvarez supports these generalizations well enough, although the reader may sometimes wonder if Donne's peers were quite so impressionable. *The School of Donne* ends with an account of the corrupting excesses of metaphysical wit and the decisive attacks on the imagination made by Bacon, Hobbes and the Royal Academy.

Alvarez' popular study of suicide and literature, *The Savage God*, is a disturbing, suggestive, inconclusive book. It begins with a sympathetic essay on Sylvia Plath and the period leading up to her suicide, then seeks for some adequate causal explanations. This involves an interesting review of changing attitudes toward suicide, from classical times to the present, but there are no real answers: it may be impossible, finally, to account for the suicide of the ordinary suffering wretch in terms which have much relevance for a Sylvia Plath or John Berryman or Randall Jarrell. What we have then is a catalog of possibilities, each of which turns out to be a "fallacy" for "devaluing an act that cannot be denied or reversed." This ultimate existential gesture seems to mock any attempts at rationalization. Alvarez does try, however, to establish some general connections between the "extremity" of modern life and the poetry of Sylvia Plath, Berryman, Lowell, and Ted Hughes, all of whom he defends energetically:

> out of their private tribulations [the best modern artists] have invented a public language which can 'comfort guinea pigs who do not know the cause of their death.' That is, I think, the ultimate justification of the highbrow arts in an era in which they themselves seem less and less convinced of their claims to attention and even to existence. They survive morally by becoming, in one way or another, an imitation of death in which their audience can share. To achieve this the artist, in his role of scapegoat, finds himself testing out his own death and vulnerability for and on himself.

The final section of *The Savage God* opens dramatically with the revelation that Alvarez himself once attempted suicide. His account is moving but again inconclusive, or perhaps simply unconvincing because he tries to force an inexplicable gesture into the service of "maturity." Alvarez tells us that before his attempt he had not faced unhappiness as a basic condition of life: "instead, I had 'problems.' Which is an optimistic way of putting it, since problems imply solutions, whereas unhappiness is merely a condition of life you must live with, like the weather." Once he accepted the conclusion that there could be no answers, "even in death," he no longer cared whether he was happy or unhappy: " 'problems' and the 'problem of problems' no longer existed. And that in itself is already the beginning of happiness":

> It seems ludicrous now to have learned something so obvious in such a hard way, to have had to go almost the whole way into death to grow up. Somewhere I still feel cheated and aggrieved, and also ashamed of my stupidity. Yet, in the end, even oblivion was an experience of a kind. Certainly, nothing has been quite the same since I discovered for myself, in my own body and on my own nerves, that death is simply an end, a dead end, no more, no less. And I wonder if that piece of knowledge isn't itself a form of death....After that, the episode lost its power. It became just so much dead history, a

gossipy, mildly interesting anecdote about someone half forgotten. As Coriolanus said, "There is a world elsewhere."

Samuel Beckett reads a little like an assignment dutifully carried out (while not exactly misleading, Alvarez' common sense approach hardly does justice to the perversities and complexities of an artist like Beckett); and *Beyond All This Fiddle*, a collection of later reviews and essays, is also disappointing, save for one piece, "Beyond the Gentility Principle," in which Alvarez takes issue with the "flatness" of the Movement in British poetry during the fifties and early sixties. But more depressing than his haste and occasional superficiality are the hints that Alvarez may be on the verge of agreeing with Marshall McLuhan: the modern world is a post-literate, image-dominated global village in which poetry is threatened "in the same way as the platypus is." Of all creatures it is the least threatened by the H-bomb: "It has reached that point of minimum survival where almost nothing can make any difference to it."

ANDERSON, Quentin. American. Born in Minnewaukan, North Dakota, 21 July 1912; son of the writer Maxwell Anderson. Educated at Dartmouth College, Hanover, New Hampshire, 1931-32; Columbia University, New York City, B.A. 1937, Ph. D. in English 1953; Harvard University, Cambridge, Massachusetts, M.A. 1945. Married Margaret Pickett in 1933 (divorced, 1946), one daughter; Thelma Ehrlich in 1947, two sons. Instructor and Assistant Professor, 1939-55. Associate Professor, 1955-61, Professor of English, 1961-78, Julian Levi Professor of Humanities, 1978-81, and since 1981 Professor Emeritus (currently Special Lecturer in English), Columbia University; also, Fellow, National Humanities Center, 1979-80, and New York Institute for the Humanities, 1981-82. Fulbright Lecturer in France, 1962-63; Visiting Professor, University of Sussex, Brighton, 1966-67; Senior Fellow, National Endowment for the Humanities, 1973. Address: 423 Hamilton Hall, Columbia University, New York, New York 10027, U.S.A.

PUBLICATIONS

Criticism

The American Henry James. New Brunswick, New Jersey, Rutgers University Press, 1957; London, Calder, 1958.
"George Eliot in *Middlemarch*," in *The Pelican Guide to English Literature 6*, edited by Boris Ford. London, Penguin, 1958.
The Imperial Self: An Essay in American Literary and Cultural History. New York, Knopf, 1971.
"On the Middle of the Journey," in *Art, Politics, and Will: Essays in Honor of Lionel Trilling*, edited by Quentin Anderson, Stephen Donadio and Steven Marcus. New York, Basic Books, 1977.
"Property and Vision in 19th-Century America," in *Virginia Quarterly Review* (Charlottesville), 54, 1978.
"John Dewey's American Democrat," in *Daedalus* (Cambridge, Massachusetts), 108, 1979.
"Notes on the Responsibility of the Critic," in *Partisan Review* (Boston), 47, 1980.

Other

Editor, *Selected Short Stories*, by Henry James.   New York, Rinehart, 1950; revised
edition, 1957.
Editor, with Joseph A. Mazzeo, *The Proper Study: Essays on Western Classics*.   New
York, St. Martin's Press, 1962.
Editor, with Stephen Donadio and Steven Marcus, *Art, Politics, and Will: Essays in
Honor of Lionel Trilling*.   New York, Basic Books, 1977.

*   *   *

While *The American Henry James* and *The Imperial Self* both have clear implications for
conventional literary criticism, what Quentin Anderson is attempting here is nothing less than
the articulation of a dominant type of consciousness in American literature and American
society itself. Although separated by nearly fifteen years, the two studies form one continuous
argument in which Anderson proposes that Emerson, Henry James and Whitman should be
understood as representative figures in the struggle, or at least the contrast, between the kind of
ego which defines itself in terms of social roles and communal bonds and the kind of ego which
tries to incorporate the entire world within itself. The premisses of Anderson's thesis are
psychological, and the psychology is more or less Freudian in its view of the development of the
ego. The differentiated self insists on discovering an objective world of meaning and purpose:
the insistence may be sheer human presumption, as Freud maintains, but nevertheless the self
makes its demands; it attempts to fill the void between heaven and earth with goals and values,
preferably those which will give some dignity to the human enterprise. At times the self will find
satisfaction in society, in the historical moment and generational order it inherits; at other
times, when it judges these resources inadequate, the ego tries to assimilate the faltering world
and make itself the "arbiter of value and truth." Thus Anderson argues that early in the
nineteenth century the American ego imperiously "assumed psychic burdens because outer
supportive structures of custom and institutions had disappeared or lost imaginative authority....The idea of community was dying in [Emerson] and his fellows" and the "representative
power of the Christian story had altogether vanished." In short, Americans seem to have
suffered "a punishing psychic blow in the generation of Emerson's youth, to have lost the
assurance provided by their sense of the presence of leaders and an instituted order." But the
self will not tolerate such disappointments; if the world fails it, it will defensively employ what
Anderson calls the "bootstrap myth"—the strategy which is "what is most American in us
all"—and place the source of authority and validation squarely within the self. The history of
nineteenth century American thought is therefore in part the history of withdrawal from
communal life, but not a denial of the values which collective life once embodied:

The most percipient members of the generation from which the transcendentalists
emerged tried to maintain, by individual and endlessly recapitulated assertion, the moral
and religious sanctions which, for their fathers and grandfathers, had been institutionalized. They tried to stuff into the self what the society had ceased adequately to represent
....Emerson tried, in a more literal way than we acknowledge, to be his own church and
state. He tried to do for himself what church and state had done for his long line of
preacher ancestors. This is an attempt even more radical than it at first appears.

This is the imperial self, although Anderson's alternate term for it, the "hypertrophied self"
reveals more clearly his opinion of the ego's new claims to authority. His comparison at one
point of Emerson with Wordsworth, who never lost his sense of the objective existence of
natural powers outside himself, is crucial in this respect: "Wordsworth lost both his parents
early and Emerson lost his father; both men might have been expected to project parents into
their work. Wordsworth did; Emerson did not. In him the family constellation falls back into
the self. Why? We must conclude that it was through simple necessity, a desperate need to find
emotional lodgment in a world shot through with the terror of death." And this falling back
into the self represents for Anderson a "redisposition of emotional forces in the face of
threatening change. It is founded on, but must not be confused with, a regression to the infantile
stage in which the world and the self are coterminous." The qualification is vital here, for while

Anderson sees the hypertrophied self as regressive, infantile and finally pathological, he refuses to dismiss the power or appeal of its manifestations. Thus he is highly critical, for example, of Frederick Crews, who tries to explain Hawthorne in purely orthodox Freudian terms. The wound and the bow of Edmund Wilson's thesis, the psychic trauma and the artistic strength, are inseparable; and while Emerson, James and Whitman found a mode of incorporating the world which may amount to what Freud would call a delusional remolding of reality, "it was a delusion inextricably wound in the coils of their power." Moreover it was a delusion which many Americans were eager to accept:

> What I have spoken of as a regression proceeds outward to cultural innovation. Emerson's efforts to unite the fruits of infantile fantasy with adult demands proved extraordinarily successful in the sense that it met matching demands in his audience ...they wanted what he wanted; the freedom to imagine themselves as possessed of a power literally realizable by no man, and openly fantasied by most people only when they are infants.

Anderson's final judgment of the artistic results of imperial selfhood emerges unmistakably when he observes that "in such art the world has been moved into the self....These playlands of the imagination were great fun to explore, but they altogether lacked what a form such as tragedy provides, a recognition that life is actually open-ended."

In *The Imperial Self* Anderson demonstrates the workings of the hypertrophied ego in Emerson, with his incorporation of church and state, in Henry James, with his all-devouring consciousness, and in Whitman, the "prime poet of uncreation" who is intent on "dissolving the stable world of identities and relationships." Hawthorne represents the contrasting view that men are "fostered in a net of relations, finding their meaning and value only through those relations. This is a thumping commonplace or an heroic achievement, depending on what you love and what moves you." For Anderson, of course, the confirmation of society is an heroic act. It is one of the ironies of modern criticism, then, that he has devoted his career to the imperial selves of American literature rather than to those writers who have opposed self-absorption: Hawthorne, Cooper, Melville, Twain, Faulkner, Hemingway—these are the artists, Anderson confesses, who comprise the tradition that "engages my sympathies." Anderson long ago passed beyond the boundaries of academic criticism into a kind of speculative psychohistory, but he is well aware of his position and regards it as an implied rebuke to the narrowness of those modern critics who have "cut art off from the messiness of lives and the incoherence of history" and thus become the "emotional collaborators" of Emerson and the other imperial selves. Contemporary criticism has no vocabulary, he suggests, for dealing with, say, Whitman, who is trying to alter our consciousness while we are busy "trying to cobble his esthetic objects into independent entities." What Anderson is calling for in this difficult, densely reasoned book is a new way of regarding a persistent strain in American consciousness and a mode of criticism which can deal with it.

The same argument is implicit in *The American Henry James* but seems to have gone unnoticed, possibly because the particular thesis of this earlier book outraged critics who had grown up quoting T.S. Eliot's remark that James had a mind too fine to be violated by ideas. James himself had declared that he intended to be endlessly analytic and supersubtle, that nothing was to be taken as his last word about anything, and that he had a horror of generalizations; he had always been faintly contemptuous of his father's and brother's philosophizing and as a young man had remarked that the habit of allegorizing was a good way to ruin both a story and a moral. Now Anderson had the audacity to announce that after all, Henry James was a thinker who had a "secret relation to a body of thought: his father's combination of philosophy and psychology." James is our "domestic Dante," doing for his father's Swedenborgianism what Dante had done for Aquinas. The arguments are too complex to summarize here, but briefly, Anderson wishes to prove that James fully accepted his father's view of human nature: greed and self-righteousness are the cardinal sins, but love can redeem us. *The American Henry James* has been ridiculed rather than read and dismissed because it unsettles some conveniently settled opinions, but like *The Imperial Self* it deserves much more attention than it has received.

25

ARVIN, (Frederick) Newton. American. Born in Valparaiso, Indiana, 23 August 1900. Educated at Harvard University, Cambridge, Massachusetts, B.A. 1921. Associate Editor, *The Living Age*, New York, 1925-26. Instructor, 1922-25, 1926-28, Assistant and Associate Professor, 1928-40, and Professor of English, 1940-60, Smith College, Northampton, Massachusetts. Visiting Lecturer, Ohio State University, Columbus, 1951, and Harvard University, 1952-53. Director, Yaddo Corporation, 1939-51. Recipient: Guggenheim Fellowship, 1935; National Book Award, 1951; National Institute of Arts and Letters Award, 1951. Member, National Institute of Arts and Letters. *Died in 1963.*

PUBLICATIONS

Criticism

Hawthorne. Boston, Little Brown, 1929; London, Noel Douglas, 1930.
Whitman. New York, Macmillan, 1938.
Herman Melville. New York, Sloane, and London, Methuen, 1950.
Longfellow: His Life and Work. Boston, Little Brown, 1963.
American Pantheon, edited by Daniel Aaron and Sylvan Schendler, with a Memoir by Louis Kronenberger. New York, Delacorte Press, 1966.

Other

Editor, *The Heart of Hawthorne's Journals*. Boston, Houghton Mifflin, 1929.
Editor, *Hawthorne's Short Stories*. New York, Knopf, 1946.
Editor, *The Selected Letters of Henry Adams*. New York, Farrar Straus, 1951.

*   *   *

Hawthorne, the first of Newton Arvin's literary biographies, is the least impressive of his books. He is perfectly aware of the problems which confront the biographer who cares about the integrity of what his author has written ("without setting up any mystical dualism between 'the man' and 'the poet,'" he observes in his later study of Whitman, "we have always to remember how far the creative artist is from being completely absorbed and limited by the profane individual of biography"); and he accepts the principle that art must be more philosophic than history, that it must embody meanings with generalizing power far greater than the personal circumstances which initiated them. The problem is that Arvin seems unable to give any plausible reasons for the source of the pattern he finds in Hawthorne's novels and tales. As a young boy Hawthorne settled into "a solitude and inaction no less cloistral than that of his mother": eventually he fell victim to "a dualism which was to molest him to the end, shunning the ordinary occupations, the grand typical experiences of human life, when what he wanted most to do was to translate them into art." The need to withdraw produced that deep sense of guilt which is the true theme of his fiction. Obsessed with "the punishment which is visited upon the solitary," he became convinced that he was "committing the unpardonable sin in thus arrogating to himself a right and rank above or aside from those of other men." The archetypal sin in Hawthorne's life and art thus turns out to be pride: "it was the tragedy of every life in which the self is not brought into right relation with what lies beyond it; the essential tragedy of pride." This is a causal explanation of sorts, perhaps, but hardly a compelling one; the problem is that the reader never has any sense of why the process of withdrawal began in the first place. We may never "know" such things with any certainty, of course, but surely it is one of the functions of the shrewd literary biographer to speculate when the evidence is inconclusive. Moreover, *Hawthorne* is badly marred by Arvin's style, with its inflations and circumlocutions and dreary rhetorical questions to the reader. It may be foolish to generalize about durable style, but prose such as this could never have had much appeal:

> At one time the fishing village of Swampscott, over beyond Marblehead, knew him well; the old salts in Mr. Bartlett's store, spinning their yarns about cruises against the French and expeditions against cod, smelling strongly of rum and tar, were images of an unmistakable substantiality; a certain fresh-visaged maiden behind the counter of a little notion store, whom he had first seen on the bridge near King's Beach, is said to have made Hawthorne's heart flutter for a few days with a quite terrestrial excitement.

Possibly the high seriousness of Writing A Book bemused the young Arvin; it is worth noting, at any rate, that the prose of his shorter pieces and reviews is direct and graceful, quite free from the mannerisms which damage *Hawthorne* and, to a lesser extent, *Whitman* and *Longfellow*.

Whitman is something of an oddity. Evidently prompted by Arvin's political hopes for the future, the book is essentially a determined attempt to make Whitman's views fully compatible with socialism ("it is clear that the next inevitable step in human history is the establishment and construction of a socialist order"). Arvin offers a minutely detailed account of the poet's responses to the issues of the period; and while Whitman the man may have been obtuse or wrong or inconsistent from time to time, *Leaves of Grass* "belongs among a handful of books of the nineteenth century that reach out...and demand for their full realization in experience, even for their full understanding, an equalized and unified society." At best *Whitman* provides some useful documentation of the poet's political opinions and his hit-or-miss relationship to the science of the time.

Longfellow is painful to read and must have been even more painful to write. Arvin seems to have no real enthusiasm for the man or his work, and if there were any interesting complexities in Longfellow's character, they pass unnoticed here. Yet Arvin insists on reporting all the facts and doggedly analyzes one faded piece after another. Fortunately *Herman Melville* is a splendid success by any standards. The opening chapters provide exactly what *Hawthorne* had lacked, a firm grasp of the ways in which Melville's early circumstances determined his basic attitudes (particularly towards authority: Arvin makes a strong case for a painful and unresolved Oedipal situation). In his long chapter on *Moby Dick*, arguably the finest account we have of that novel, Arvin isolates four levels of meaning, partly akin to those "planes of significance" Dante is supposed to have identified for his patron: the literal, the psychological, the moral and the mythic. He explores the relationships existing between the levels but never reduces them to mere projections of Melville's own personal suffering and is equally convincing when he describes the grim, anti-climactic years following *Moby Dick*. Fully aware of Melville's diminished powers, Arvin patiently traces something which *is* of critical interest, the complex theme of philosophical acceptance which gradually develops from *Clarel* onwards. *Herman Melville* is a model of what critical biography at its best can do.

AUCHINCLOSS, Louis (Stanton). American. Born in Lawrence, New York, 17 September 1917. Educated at Groton School, Connecticut, graduated 1935; Yale University, New Haven, Connecticut, 1935-38; University of Virginia Law School, Charlottesville, L.L.B. 1941; admitted to the New York Bar, 1941. Served in the United States Naval Reserve, 1941-45: Lieutenant. Married Adèle Lawrence in 1957; three sons. Associate Lawyer, Sullivan and Cromwell, New York, 1941-51. Associate, 1954-58, and since 1958 Partner, Hawkins, Delafield and Wood, New York. Since 1966, President of the Museum of the City of New York. Trustee, Josiah Macy Jr. Foundation, New York; Member of the Executive Committee, Association of the Bar of New York City. D.Litt.: New York University, 1974; Pace College, New York, 1979. Member, American Academy. Address: 1111 Park Avenue, New York, New York 10028, U.S.A.

Criticism

Edith Wharton. Minneapolis, University of Minnesota Press, 1961.
Reflections of a Jacobite. Boston, Houghton Mifflin, 1961; London, Gollancz, 1962.
Ellen Glasgow. Minneapolis, University of Minnesota Press, 1964.
Pioneers and Caretakers: A Study of 9 American Women Novelists. Minneapolis,
    University of Minnesota Press, 1965; London, Oxford University Press, 1966.
Motiveless Malignity. Boston, Houghton Mifflin, 1969; London, Gollancz, 1970.
Henry Adams. Minneapolis, University of Minnesota Press, 1971.
Edith Wharton: A Woman in Her Time. New York, Viking Press, 1971; London,
    Joseph, 1972.
Reading Henry James. Minneapolis, University of Minnesota Press, 1975.

Novels

The Indifferent Children (as Andrew Lee). New York, Prentice Hall, 1947.
Sybil. Boston, Houghton Mifflin, 1951; London, Gollancz, 1952.
A Law for the Lion. Boston, Houghton Mifflin, and London, Gollancz, 1953.
The Great World and Timothy Colt. Boston, Houghton Mifflin, 1956; London, Gol-
    lancz, 1957.
Venus in Sparta. Boston, Houghton Mifflin, and London, Gollancz, 1958.
Pursuit of the Prodigal. Boston, Houghton Mifflin, 1959; London, Gollancz, 1960.
The House of Five Talents. Boston, Houghton Mifflin, 1960; London, Gollancz, 1961.
Portrait in Brownstone. Boston, Houghton Mifflin, and London, Gollancz, 1962.
The Rector of Justin. Boston, Houghton Mifflin, 1964; London, Gollancz, 1965.
The Embezzler. Boston, Houghton Mifflin, and London, Gollancz, 1966.
A World of Profit. Boston, Houghton Mifflin, 1968; London, Gollancz, 1969.
I Come as a Thief. Boston, Houghton Mifflin, 1972; London, Weidenfeld and Nicolson,
    1973.
The Partners. Boston, Houghton Mifflin, and London, Weidenfeld and Nicolson, 1974.
The Winthrop Covenant. Boston, Houghton Mifflin, and London, Weidenfeld and
    Nicolson, 1976.
The Dark Lady. Boston, Houghton Mifflin, and London, Weidenfeld and Nicolson,
    1977.
The Country Cousin. Boston, Houghton Mifflin, and London, Weidenfeld and Nicol-
    son, 1978.
The House of the Prophet. Boston, Houghton Mifflin, and London, Weidenfeld and
    Nicolson, 1980.
The Cat and the King. Boston, Houghton Mifflin, 1981.

Short Stories

The Injustice Collectors. Boston, Houghton Mifflin, 1950; London, Gollancz, 1951.
The Romantic Egoists: A Reflection in Eight Minutes. Boston, Houghton Mifflin, and
    London, Gollancz, 1954.
Powers of Attorney. Boston, Houghton Mifflin, and London, Gollancz, 1963.
Tales of Manhattan. Boston, Houghton Mifflin, and London, Gollancz, 1967.
Second Chance. Boston, Houghton Mifflin, 1970; London, Gollancz, 1971.

Play

   The Club Bedroom (produced New York, 1967).

Other

   Richelieu.   New York, Viking Press, 1972; London, Joseph, 1973.
   A Writer's Capital (autobiography).   Minneapolis, University of Minnesota Press, 1974.
   Persons of Consequence: Queen Victoria and Her Circle.   New York, Random House, and London, Weidenfeld and Nicolson, 1980.
   Life, Law, and Letters: Essays and Sketches.   Boston, Houghton Mifflin, 1979; London, Weidenfeld and Nicolson, 1980.

   Editor, *An Edith Wharton Reader.*   New York, Scribner, 1965.
   Editor, *The Warden, and Barchester Towers*, by Trollope.   Boston, Houghton Mifflin, 1966.
   Editor, *Fables of Wit and Elegance.*   New York, Scribner, 1975.

BIBLIOGRAPHY

   Jackson R. Bryer, *Louis Auchincloss and His Critics: A Bibliographical Record.*   Boston, Hall, 1977.

                              *   *   *

   The literary criticism of Louis Auchincloss is relaxed, unpretentious, impressionistic, even a little innocent in its directness and untroubled conviction that the novelist's job, after all, is "to entertain as well as instruct." He started relatively late as a novelist himself (he has also pursued a full-time career as a successful lawyer) and even later as a critic, reaching this entirely conventional definition of the artist's function in his own good time. Looking back on the reading he was able to do in the Navy during World War II he confesses that "it took a world conflagration to teach me what books were for." Presumably Auchincloss writes his own novels to please and instruct and his literary criticism is best seen as an informal tribute to those writers who have instructed and pleased him. Thus he has written on at least three occasions about Edith Wharton, whose complex attitude towards her social world comes closest, perhaps, to his preoccupations. Auchincloss is particularly skilful in detecting the tensions between Mrs. Wharton's needs as a spirited, independent woman who wanted her freedom and her awareness that the alternatives to a civilized code are frequently more painful than the conformity which the code exacts. The drama which makes her best work a kind of genteel *Civilization and Its Discontents* has attracted Auchincloss repeatedly—almost, it seems, as if he envied life for creating a character he would have enjoyed conjuring up.
   The same concerns also account for his continuing interest in Henry James, although there is possibly some inconsistency between his expectations that a writer should "instruct" and his claim (in *Reflections of a Jacobite*) that "despite all the chatter of the last twenty years about James as a moralist or philosopher or social commentator, there is not a phrase in all his published notebooks to indicate that he ever had anything in mind in his writing but to translate little patches of anecdote in terms of his individual aesthetic." Elsewhere Auchincloss is more insistent that the writer counter-balance his desire to instruct with his obligation to entertain. "The pity of it!" he exclaims about George Eliot: "That a writer with the power of characterization of a Thackeray, the narrative skill of a Trollope, the satirical eye of a Jane Austen and the descriptive ease of a Scott, should have wrecked her work with a foolish didacticism!" He is flexible enough, however, to welcome what James was suspicious of, the Russian novelists and their "great fluid puddings." Quite sensibly he refuses to choose between James' formal perfection and the teeming abundance of Dostoyevsky or Tolstoy. "I cannot imagine two

novels more different than *The Brothers Karamazov* and *The Ambassadors*," he concludes, "nor can I imagine two novels more admirable. It is idle to choose between them for one always has both." But given his sensitivity to James, the sketchy inadequacy of the recent *Reading Henry James* comes as a great disappointment. There is nothing new here, nothing beyond the usual commonplaces, save for one chapter in which he proposes a way of distinguishing between major and minor James by looking at preliminary remarks in the *Notebooks*. Surprisingly enough he seems troubled and uncertain about James' ambiguous effects. Thus while he finds that ambiguity may be suitable for a ghost story (the ghosts in *The Turn of the Screw* may be real *or* imagined) he is bothered by the complexities of "Madame de Mauves":

> I cannot determine just what it is that James is saying about [her]. Is she a foolish romantic girl who turns perversely frigid when she finds that the world is not the fairy tale that she has imagined it? Or is she, like Isabel Archer, the finest type of American woman, something too exquisite for an ancient and corrupted civilization to appreciate it? But I forget my questions in the beautiful mood and setting of the story.

Or again:

> But just what James means us to learn from Roderick [Hudson's] sorry case is harder to tell. Was Rowland wrong to have taken him from home and exposed him to the temptations of Rome? Would Roderick not have tired even more quickly of his subdued betrothed, Mary Garland, had he remained in Northampton? And are we to suppose that Roderick would have been "all right" had he never met Christina? Is *she* the villainess, pure and simple?

Does Auchincloss really want something "pure and simple"? *Roderick Hudson* and "Madame de Mauves" are both early works and Auchincloss seems to be suggesting that the ambiguities are a sign of James' immaturity. But later on he seems completely unaware of the far more profound and unsettling ambiguities of the novels he so admires, *The Portrait of a Lady*, *The Wings of the Dove*, and *The Golden Bowl*.

Reflections of a Jacobite is something of a miscellany, with subjects ranging from Thackeray and Meredith to Saint-Simon and the Newport diaries of George Templeton Strong; but the nine studies which make up *Pioneers and Caretakers* are governed, at least provisionally, by a thesis. Women, Auchincloss argues, have always been the "true conservatives," the guardians of society:

> A notable thing about our women writers is that they have struck a more affirmative note than the men. Their darkness is not as dark as that of Dreiser or Lewis or Faulkner or O'Neill, which is not to say that they see America less clearly, but that they may see it more discriminatingly. They have a sharper sense of their stake in the national heritage, and they are always at work to preserve it. They never destroy; they want the clean sweep.

This works well enough for Sarah Orne Jewett, some parts of Edith Wharton, and for Ellen Glasgow, Willa Cather and Elizabeth Madox Roberts; it seems less pertinent for Katherine Anne Porter, Jean Stafford, Carson McCullers and Mary McCarthy. But the individual chapters are so pleasantly appreciative that the reader soon forgets the initial proposition. The book stops rather than arriving at any conclusions, a sign, perhaps, that like some other critics, Auchincloss feels "the increasingly classless nature of our society" resists dramatic representation.

Motiveless Malignity also has a thesis: as time went on Shakespeare's sense of the "perverse and irrational in human nature" deepened. Thus *Othello* "reduces itself in the end to a picture of a man destroying his own happiness—perversely, madly, as men do." Shakespeare's suspicion that "many of our mortal ills are caused by a 'motiveless malignity' became confirmed with middle age. Does Macbeth really want to be King of Scotland? Does Lear really want to banish Cordelia? Does Coriolanus want to cause civil war? Do the Trojans care about keeping Helen? Or is there in all of these tragedies a deeper motivation, the human impulse toward self-destruction? But as in *Pioneers and Caretakers* there are no sustained arguments or elaborate proofs. This is gentlemanly, amateur Shakespeare criticism; the observations are left at the level of individual perceptions, often quite suggestive and fresh, to be developed or not, as the reader sees fit.

AUDEN, W(ystan) H(ugh). American. Born in York, England, 21 February 1907; emigrated to the United States in 1939; naturalized, 1946. Educated at St. Edmund's School, Grayshott, Surrey; Gresham's School, Holt, Norfolk; Christ Church (exhibitioner), Oxford, 1925-28. Served for the Loyalists in the Spanish Civil War; with the Strategic Bombing Survey of the United States Army in Germany during World War II. Married Erika Mann in 1935. Schoolmaster, Larchfield Academy, Helensburgh, Scotland, and Downs School, Colwall, near Malvern, Worcestershire, 1930-35; Co-Founder of the Group Theatre, 1932; worked with the G.P.O. Film Unit, 1935; travelled extensively in the 1930's, in Europe, Iceland, and China; taught at St. Mark's School, Southborough, Massachusetts, 1939-40, American Writers League School, 1939, New School for Social Research, New York, 1940-41, 1946-47, University of Michigan, Ann Arbor, 1941-42, Swarthmore College, Pennsylvania, 1942-45, Bryn Mawr College, Pennsylvania, 1943-45, Bennington College, Vermont, 1946, and Barnard College, New York, 1947; Neilson Research Professor, Smith College, Northampton, Massachusetts, 1953; Professor of Poetry, Oxford University, 1956-61. Editor, Yale Series of Younger Poets, 1947-62. Member of the Editorial Board, *Decision* magazine, 1940-41, and *Delos* magazine, 1968. Recipient: King's Gold Medal for Poetry, 1936; Guggenheim Fellowship, 1942; American Academy of Arts and Letters Award of Merit Medal, 1945, Gold Medal, 1968; Pulitzer Prize, 1948; Bollingen Prize, 1954; National Book Award, 1956; Feltrinelli Prize, 1957; Guinness Award, 1959; Poetry Society of America Droutskoy Gold Medal, 1959; National Endowment for the Arts grant, 1966; National Book Committee National Medal for Literature, 1967. D.Litt.: Swarthmore College, 1964. Member, American Academy of Arts and Letters, 1954; Honorary Student, Christ Church, Oxford, 1962. *Died 29 September 1973.*

PUBLICATIONS

Criticism

"Criticism in a Mass Society," in *The Intent of the Critic*, edited by Donald A. Stauffer. Princeton, New Jersey, Princeton University Press, 1941.

"Squares and Oblongs," in *Poets at Work: Essays Based on the Modern Poetry Collection at the Lockwood Memorial Library, University of Buffalo*, edited by Charles D. Abbott. New York, Harcourt Brace, 1948; reprinted in part in *The Dyer's Hand*, 1963.

The Enchafèd Flood; or, The Romantic Iconography of the Sea. New York, Random House, 1950; London, Faber, 1951.

Making, Knowing and Judging. Oxford, Clarendon Press, 1956; reprinted in *The Dyer's Hand*, 1963.

The Dyer's Hand and Other Essays. New York, Random House, 1962; London, Faber, 1963.

Louis MacNeice: A Memorial Lecture. London, Faber, 1963.

Selected Essays. London, Faber, 1964.

Worte und Noten: Rede zur Eröffnung der Salzburger Festspiele 1968. Salzburg, Festungsverlag, 1968.

Secondary Worlds. London, Faber, and New York, Random House, 1969.

Forewords and Afterwords, edited by Edward Mendelson.   New York, Viking Press, and London, Faber, 1973.

The English Auden: Poems, Essays and Dramatic Writings, edited by Edward Mendelson.   London, Faber, 1977; New York, Random House, 1978.

Verse

Poems.   N.p, S.H.S. (Stephen Spender), 1928.

Poems.   London, Faber, 1930; revised edition, 1933.

The Orators: An English Study.   London, Faber, 1932; revised edition, 1934, 1966; New York, Random House, 1967.

Poem.   Bryn Mawr, Pennsylvania, Frederic Prokosch, 1933.

Two Poems.   Bryn Mawr, Pennsylvania, Frederic Prokosch, 1934.

Poems (includes *The Orators* and *The Dance of Death*).   New York, Random House, 1934.

Our Hunting Fathers.   London, Frederic Prokosch, 1935.

Sonnet.   London, Federic Prokosch, 1935.

Look, Stranger!   London, Faber, 1936; as *On This Island*, New York, Random House, 1937.

Spain.   London, Faber, 1937.

Letters from Iceland, with Louis MacNeice.   London, Faber, and New York, Random House, 1937.

Selected Poems.   London, Faber, 1938.

Journey to a War, with Christopher Isherwood.   London, Faber, and New York, Random House, 1939; revised edition, Faber, 1973.

Ephithalamion Commemorating the Marriage of Giuseppe Antonio Borghese and Elisabeth Mann.   New York, privately printed, 1939.

Another Time: Poems (includes *Spain*).   New York, Random House, and London, Faber, 1940.

Some Poems.   London, Faber, 1940.

The Double Man.   New York, Random House, 1941; as *New Year Letter*, London, Faber, 1941.

Three Songs for St. Cecilia's Day.   New York, privately printed, 1941.

For the Time Being.   New York, Random House, 1944; London, Faber, 1945.

The Collected Poetry of W.H. Auden.   New York, Random House, 1945.

Litany and Anthem for St. Matthew's Day.   Northampton, St. Matthew's, 1946.

The Age of Anxiety: A Baroque Eclogue (produced New York, 1954).   New York, Random House, 1947; London, Faber, 1948.

Collected Shorter Poems 1930-1944.   London, Faber, 1950.

Nones.   New York, Random House, 1951; London, Faber, 1952.

Mountains.   London, Faber, 1954.

The Shield of Achilles.   New York, Random House, and London, Faber, 1955.

The Old Man's Road.   New York, Voyages Press, 1956.

Reflections on a Forest.   Greencastle, Indiana, DePauw University, 1957.

Goodbye to the Mezzogiorno (bilingual edition).   Milan, All'Insegno del Pesce d'Oro, 1958.

W.H. Auden: A Selection by the Author.   London, Penguin-Faber, 1958; as *Selected Poetry*, New York, Modern Library, 1959.

Homage to Clio.   New York, Random House, and London, Faber, 1960.

W.H. Auden: A Selection, edited by Richard Hoggart.   London, Hutchinson, 1961.

Elegy for J.F.K., music by Igor Stravinsky.   New York, Boosey and Hawkes, 1964.

The Common Life (in German, translated by Dieter Leisegang).   Darmstadt, J.G. Bläschke Verlag, 1964.

The Cave of Making (in German, translated by Dieter Leisegang).   Darmstadt, J.G. Bläschke Verlag, 1965.

Half-Way.   Cambridge, Massachusetts, Lowell-Adams House Printers, 1965.

About the House.   New York, Random House, 1965; London, Faber, 1966.

The Twelve, music by William Walton.   London, Oxford University Press, 1966.

Marginalia.   Cambridge, Massachusetts, Ibex Press, 1966.

Collected Shorter Poems, 1927-1957.   London, Faber, 1966; New York, Random House, 1967.

River Profile.   Cambridge, Massachusetts, Laurence Scott, 1967.

Selected Poems.   London, Faber, 1968.

Collected Longer Poems.   London, Faber, 1968; New York, Random House, 1969.

Two Songs.   New York, Phoenix Book Shop, 1968.

A New Year Greeting, with *The Dance of the Solids*, by John Updike.   New York, Scientific American, 1969.

City Without Walls and Other Poems.   London, Faber, 1969; New York, Random House, 1970.

Natural Linguistics.   London, Poem-of-the-Month Club, 1970.

Academic Graffiti.   London, Faber, 1971; New York, Random House, 1972.

Epistle to a Godson and Other Poems.   London, Faber, and New York, Random House, 1972.

Auden/Moore: Poems and Lithographs, edited by John Russell.   London, British Museum, 1974.

Poems, lithographs by Henry Moore, edited by Vera Lindsay.   London, Petersburg Press, 1974.

Thank You, Fog: Last Poems.   London, Faber, 1974.

The Collected Poems of W.H. Auden, edited by Edward Mendelson.   London, Faber, and New York, Random House, 1976.

"In the Year of My Youth," in "W.H. Auden's 'In the Year of My Youth' " by Lucy S. McDiarmid, in *Review of English Studies* (Oxford), 29 n.s., 1978.

Recordings: *Reading His Own Poems*, Harvard Vocarium, 1941; *Reading from His Works*, Caedmon, 1954; *Auden*, Argo, 1960; *Selected Poems*, Spoken Arts, 1968.

Plays

The Dance of Death (produced London, 1934; as *Come Out into the Sun*, produced Poughkeepsie, New York, 1935; as *The Dance of Death*, produced New York, 1936).   London, Faber, 1933; in *Poems*, 1934.

The Dog Beneath the Skin; or, Where Is Francis?, with Christopher Isherwood (produced London, 1936; revised version, produced New York, 1947).   London, Faber, and New York, Random House, 1937.

No More Peace! A Thoughtful Comedy, with Edward Crankshaw, adaptation of the play by Ernst Toller (produced London, 1936; Poughkeepsie, New York, and New York City, 1937).   New York, Farrar and Rinehart, and London, Lane, 1937.

The Ascent of F6, with Christopher Isherwood (produced London, 1937; New York, 1939).   London, Faber, 1936; revised edition, New York, Random House, and Faber, 1937.

On the Frontier, with Christopher Isherwood (produced Cambridge, 1938; London, 1939).   London, Faber, 1938; New York, Random House, 1939.

The Dark Valley (broadcast, 1940).   Published in *Best Broadcasts of 1939-40*, edited by Max Wylie, New York, Whittlesey House, and London, McGraw Hill, 1940.

Paul Bunyan, music by Benjamin Britten (produced New York, 1941; Aldeburgh, Suffolk, 1976).   London, Faber, 1976.

The Duchess of Malfi, music by Benjamin Britten, adaptation of the play by John Webster (produced New York, 1946).

The Knights of the Round Table, adaptation of the work by Jean Cocteau (broadcast, 1951; produced Salisbury, Wiltshire, 1954; New York, 1979).   Published in *The Infernal Machine and Other Plays*, by Jean Cocteau, New York, New Directions, 1963.

The Rake's Progress, with Chester Kallman, music by Igor Stravinsky (produced Venice, 1951; New York, 1953; London, 1962).   London and New York, Boosey and Hawkes, 1951.

Delia; or, A Masque of Night, with Chester Kallman (libretto), in *Botteghe Oscure XII* (Rome), 1953.

The Punch Revue (lyrics only) (produced London, 1955).

The Magic Flute, with Chester Kallman, adaptation of the libretto by Schikaneder and Giesecke, music by Mozart (televised, 1956).   New York, Random House, 1956; London, Faber, 1957.

The Play of Daniel (narration only) (produced New York, 1958; London, 1960).   Editor, with Noah Greenberg, New York, Oxford University Press, 1959; London, Oxford University Press, 1960.

The Seven Deadly Sins of the Lower Middle Class, with Chester Kallman, adaptation of the work by Brecht, music by Kurt Weill (produced New York, 1959; Edinburgh and London, 1961).   Published in *Tulane Drama Review* (New Orleans), September 1961.

Don Giovanni, with Chester Kallman, adaptation of the libretto by Lorenzo da Ponte, music by Mozart (televised, 1960).   New York and London, Schirmer, 1961.

The Caucasian Chalk Circle (lyrics only), with James and Tania Stern, adaptation of the play by Brecht (produced London, 1962).   Published in *Plays*, London, Methuen, 1960.

Elegy for Young Lovers, with Chester Kallman, music by Hans Werner Henze (produced Stuttgart and Glyndebourne, Sussex, 1961).   Mainz, B. Schotts Söhne, 1961.

Arcifanfarlo, King of Fools; or, It's Always Too Late to Learn, with Chester Kallman, adaptation of the libretto by Goldoni, music by Dittersdorf (produced New York, 1965).

Die Bassariden (The Bassarids), with Chester Kallman, music by Hans Werner Henze (produced Salzburg, 1966; Santa Fe, New Mexico, 1968; London, 1974).   Mainz, B. Schotts Söhne, 1966.

Moralities: Three Scenic Plays from Fables by Aesop, music by Hans Werner Henze. Mainz, B. Schotts Söhne, 1969.

The Ballad of Barnaby, music by Wykeham Rise School Students realized by Charles Turner (produced New York, 1970).

Love's Labour's Lost, with Chester Kallman, music by Nicholas Nabokov, adaptation of the play by Shakespeare (produced Brussels, 1973).

The Entertainment of the Senses, with Chester Kallman, music by John Gardner (produced London, 1974).   Included in *Thank You, Fog*, 1974.

The Rise and Fall of the City of Mahogonny, with Chester Kallman, adaptation of the opera by Brecht.   Boston, Godine, 1976.

Screenplays (documentaries, in verse): *Night Mail*, 1936; *Coal Face*, 1936; *The Londoners*, 1938.

Radio Writing: *Hadrian's Wall*, 1937 (UK); *The Dark Valley*, 1940 (USA); *The Rocking-Horse Winner*, with James Stern, from the story by D.H. Lawrence, 1941 (USA); *The Knights of the Round Table*, from a work by Jean Cocteau, 1951 (UK).

Television Writing: (with Chester Kallman): *The Magic Flute*, 1956 (USA); *Don Giovanni*, 1960 (USA).

Other

Education Today—and Tomorrow, with T.C. Worsley.   London, Hogarth Press, 1939.
A Certain World: A Commonplace Book.   New York, Viking Press, 1970; London, Faber, 1971.

Editor, with Charles Plumb, *Oxford Poetry 1926*.   Oxford, Blackwell, 1926.

Editor, with C. Day-Lewis, *Oxford Poetry 1927*.   Oxford, Blackwell, 1927.
Editor, with John Garrett, *The Poet's Tongue: An Anthology*.   London, G. Bell, 2 vols., 1935.
Editor, *The Oxford Book of Light Verse*.   Oxford, Clarendon Press, 1938.
Editor, *A Selection from the Poems of Alfred, Lord Tennyson*.   New York, Doubleday, 1944; as *Tennyson: An Introduction and a Selection*, London, Phoenix House, 1946.
Editor, *The American Scene, Together with Three Essays from "Portraits of Places,"* by Henry James.   New York, Scribner, 1946.
Editor, *Slick But Not Streamlined: Poems and Short Pieces*, by John Betjeman.   New York, Doubleday, 1947.
Editor, *The Portable Greek Reader*.   New York, Viking Press, 1948.
Editor, with Norman Holmes Pearson, *Poets of the English Language*.   New York, Viking Press, 5 vols., 1950; London, Eyre and Spottiswoode, 5 vols., 1952.
Editor, *Selected Prose and Poetry*, by Edgar Allan Poe.   New York, Rinehart, 1950.
Editor, *The Living Thoughts of Kierkegaard*.   New York, McKay, 1952; as *Kierkegaard*, London, Cassell, 1955.
Editor, with Marianne Moore and Karl Shapiro, *Riverside Poetry 1953: Poems by Students in Colleges and Universities in New York City*.   New York, Association Press, 1953.
Editor, with Chester Kallman and Noah Greenberg, *An Elizabethan Song Book: Lute Songs, Madrigals and Rounds*.   New York, Doubleday, 1955; London, Faber, 1957.
Editor, *The Faber Book of Modern American Verse*.   London, Faber, 1956; as *The Criterion Book of Modern American Verse*, New York, Criterion Books, 1956.
Editor, *Selected Writings of Sydney Smith*.   New York, Farrar Straus, 1956; London, Faber, 1957.
Editor, *Van Gogh: A Self-Portrait: Letters Revealing His Life as a Painter*.   Greenwich, Connecticut, New York Graphic Society, and London, Thames and Hudson, 1961.
Editor, with Louis Kronenberger, *The Viking Book of Aphorisms: A Personal Selection*. New York, Viking Press, 1962; as *The Faber Book of Aphorisms*, London, Faber, 1964.
Editor, *A Choice of de la Mare's Verse*.   London, Faber, 1963.
Editor, *The Pied Piper and Other Fairy Tales*, by Joseph Jacobs.   New York, Macmillan, and London, Collier Macmillan, 1963.
Editor, *Selected Poems*, by Louis MacNeice.   London, Faber, 1964.
Editor, with John Lawler, *To Nevill Coghill from Friends*.   London, Faber, 1966.
Editor, *Selected Poetry and Prose*, by George Gordon, Lord Byron.   New York, New American Library, 1966; London, New English Library, 1967.
Editor, *Nineteenth Century British Minor Poets*.   New York, Delacorte Press, 1966; as *Nineteenth Century Minor Poets*, London, Faber, 1967.
Editor, *G.K. Chesterton: A Selection from His Non-Fiction Prose*.   London, Faber, 1970.
Editor, *A Choice of Dryden's Verse*.   London, Faber, 1973.
Editor, *George Herbert*.   London, Penguin, 1973.
Editor, *Selected Songs of Thomas Campion*.   London, Bodley Head, 1974.

Translator, "On Poetry," in *Two Addresses*, by St.-John Perse.   New York, Viking Press, 1961.
Translator, with Elizabeth Mayer, *Italian Journey 1786-1788*, by Goethe.   London, Collins, and New York, Pantheon Books, 1962.
Translator, with Leif Sjöberg, *Markings*, by Dag Hammarskjöld.   New York, Knopf, and London, Faber, 1964.
Translator, with Paul B. Taylor, *Völupsá: The Song of the Sybil*, with an Icelandic Text edited by Peter H. Salus and Paul B. Taylor.   Iowa City, Windhover Press, 1968.
Translator, *The Elder Edda: A Selection*.   London, Faber, and New York, Random House, 1969.
Translator, with Elizabeth Mayer and Louise Bogan, *The Sorrows of Young Werther, and Novella*, by Goethe.   New York, Random House, 1973.

Translator, with Leif Sjöberg, *Evening Land/Aftonland*, by Pär Lagerkvist.   Detroit, Wayne State University Press, 1975.
Translator, with Paul Taylor, *Norse Poems*.   London, Athlone Press, 1981.

CRITICAL STUDIES AND BIBLIOGRAPHY

Monroe K. Spears, "Operas, Criticism, and Rites of Homage," in *The Poetry of W.H. Auden: The Disenchanted Island*.   New York, Oxford University Press, 1963.
Cleanth Brooks, "Auden as a Literary Critic," in *A Shaping Joy: Studies in the Writer's Craft*.   New York, Harcourt Brace, and London, Methuen, 1971.
Barry C. Bloomfield and Edward Mendelson, *W.H. Auden: A Bibliography, 1924-1969*.   Charlottesville, University of Virginia Press, 1972.
George Woodcock, "Auden—Critic and Criticized," in *Sewanee Review* (Tennessee), 82, 1974.
W.H. Auden: A Tribute, edited by Stephen Spender.   London, Weidenfeld and Nicolson, and New York, Macmillan, 1975.
Charles Osborne, *W.H. Auden: The Life of a Poet*.   New York, Harcourt Brace, 1979; London, Eyre Methuen, 1980.
Humphrey Carpenter, *W.H. Auden: A Biography*.   London, Allen and Unwin, and Boston, Houghton Mifflin, 1981.
Edward Mendelson, *Early Auden*.   New York, Viking, and London, Faber, 1981.

*   *   *

Apparent inconsistencies in Auden's thinking have always been a problem for critics, especially at the start of the 1940's, when it seemed impossible to reconcile his earlier liberalism with his emerging Christian orthodoxy. Yet consistency was as much a virtue for Auden as it is for these usually unsympathetic bystanders: "Every work of a writer should be a first step," he maintained, "but this will be a false step unless, whether or not he realizes it at the time, it is also a further step. When a writer is dead, one ought to be able to see that his various works, taken together, make one consistent *oeuvre*." Of course hindsight is easy now that the *oeuvre* is complete, but as early as 1939 Auden had provided alert readers a way of understanding where he had been and where he was likely to go next:

> the basic problem is man's anxiety in time; e.g., his present anxiety over himself in relation to his past and his parents (Freud), his present anxiety over himself in relation to his future and his neighbors (Marx), his present anxiety over himself in relation to eternity and God (Kierkegaard).

The liberal humanism Auden and his friends inherited gave way under the pressure of political events during the early 1930's: Marxism might explain—as *laissez-faire* apologists could not—depressions, strikes and hunger marches, but the evil of fascism was another matter, all the more shocking. Auden recalls, since "this utter denial of everything that liberalism had ever stood for was arousing wild enthusiasm not in some remote and barbaric land outside the pale, but in one of the most highly educated countries in Europe." With the rise of Nazism he concluded that "it was impossible any longer to believe that the values of liberalism were self-evident. Unless one was prepared to take a relativist view that all human values are a matter of personal taste, one could hardly avoid asking the question: 'If, as I am convinced, the Nazis are wrong and we are right, what is it that validates our values and invalidates theirs?'" For Auden, who was also experiencing a personal crisis of some sort ("I was forced to know in person what it is to feel oneself the prey of demonic powers...stripped of self-control and self-respect"), the answer was provided by Christian doctrine. In retrospect, then, his development was neither quixotic nor particularly mysterious. Commitment to transcendent goals in no way absolves us from caring about suffering here and now or the responsibility of working for the "Just City." Freud's diagnosis of "evil" (intolerable repression and lack of self-knowledge) is not necessarily opposed to Marx's diagnosis (unequal distribution of wealth and the exploitation of alienated workers); nor do they prevent the subsuming Christian diagnosis that the causes of disorder lie deeper, in man's fall from grace and continued misdirection of his will.

The cornerstones of Christian doctrine, Free Will and Incarnation, are articles of faith, not metaphors to be translated into the terms of secular humanism. For Auden, as for Eliot, a statement such as Arnold's, that the important thing for a Christian is the imitation and not the incarnation of Christ, is simply heretical. According to Auden, polytheism is aesthetic and "frivolous" because it is based on the assumption that human life is meaningless: "The whims of the gods and, behind them, the whim of the Fates, are the ultimate arbiters of all that happens. [Polytheism] is immediately frivolous because it is ultimately in despair." The coming of Christ, however, altered all this: "If the Fall made man conscious of the difference between good and evil, then the Incarnation made him conscious of the difference between seriousness and frivolity." What is serious is not the uniqueness of the individual or his gifts, but what we have in common: free will and the responsibility for choosing what reason and revelation disclose. The only serious matter is *what* we choose to love—ourselves, our neighbors, or God; the crucial issue for Auden, as it was for Dante, is how we direct our wills, what we love, with what intensity and for what reasons. In one of his last essays, "Words and the Word," Auden summarizes the meaning of the Incarnation and the consequences it has for a Christian conception of art:

> Man was created by God as a culture-making creature, endowed with imagination and reason, and capable of artistic fabrication and scientific investigation, so to say that Christ calls art into question does not mean that it is forbidden to a Christian as it is to a Platonist, only that the nature of the imagination and the function of the artist are seen otherwise than they were in pre-Christian times. In a magicopolytheistic culture all events are believed to be caused by personal powers who can be understood and to some extent controlled by speech, and the nearest that men can come to the concept of necessity is in the myth of the Fates who determine events by whim; in such a culture, therefore, poets are the theologians, the sacred mouthpieces of society....That to which the imagination responds with excitement, namely, the manifestly extraordinary and powerful, is identified with the Divine. The poet is one whose words are equal to his divine subjects, which can happen only if he is divinely inspired. The coming of Christ in the form of a servant who cannot be recognized by the eye of flesh and blood, only by the eye of faith, puts an end to all such claims. The imagination is to be regarded as a natural faculty the subject of which is the phenomenal world, not its creator.

Auden is therefore forced to conclude that art and science are secular activities, "that is to say, small beer"—however much this may irritate romantics and liberals (Harold Bloom, for example, one of the chief defenders of romanticism at the moment, finds *Secondary Worlds* a "bad book" simply because it is anti-romantic: "I find it bad for my character. On a higher level the experience of reading Auden then becomes rather like reading Kilmer's *Trees*: 'Poems are made by fools like me,' yes, and by Dante, Milton, Blake and Homer, but only God can make primary worlds.") Equally abrasive, but perfectly consistent, are Auden's qualifications concerning the powers of art:

> The world about us is, as it has always been, full of gross evils and appalling misery, but it is a fatal delusion and a shocking overestimation of the importance of the artist in the world, to suppose that by making works of art, we can do anything to eradicate the one or alleviate the other. The political and social history of Europe would be what it has been if Dante, Shakespeare, Goethe, Titian, Mozart *et al.*, had never existed. Where social evils are concerned, the only effective weapons are two, political action and straight reportage of the facts, journalism in the good sense. Art is impotent. The utmost an artist can hope to do for his contemporary readers is, as Dr. Johnson said, to enable them a little better to enjoy life or a little better to endure it.

But despite these essential qualifications, Auden still has a good deal to say about creativity and the function of art. In his earlier criticism he had maintained that the poet creates in order to satisfy a desire to determine his own activity: his ego "seeks constantly to assert its own autonomy by doing something which is completely arbitrary, a pure act of choice....The chief satisfaction of the creative act is the feeling that it is quite gratuitous." In his later criticism, however, Auden borrows (and changes the meaning of) Coleridge's terms, the Primary and Secondary Imagination, and defines the creative act as the poet's irresistible response to the numinous or the sacred. Confronted by such a manifestation, the Primary Imagination "has no choice but to respond....The response of the imagination to such a presence or significance is a passion of awe"; the Secondary Imagination, however, is active rather than passive:

> To the Primary Imagination a sacred being is that which it is. To the Secondary Imagination a beautiful form is as it ought to be, an ugly form as it ought not to be. Observing the beautiful, it has the feeling of satisfaction, pleasure, absence of conflict ....It approves of regularity, of spatial symmetry and temporal repetition, of law and order; it disapproves of loose ends, irrelevance and mess.

Thus

> the impulse to create a work of art is felt when, in certain persons, the passive awe provoked by sacred beings or events is transformed into a desire to express that awe in a rite of worship or homage, and to be fit homage, this rite must be beautiful...exhibiting, for example, balance, closure and aptness.

Art is no longer gratuitous activity: a poem is a verbal rite whose formal beauty Auden goes on to discuss in terms of an elaborate analogy to forms of social organization. A crowd is an accidental aggregate without order or purpose; a society is a system whose members are intent simply on maintaining themselves; but a community is comprised of members united by the love of something beyond themselves. By analogy,

> the subject matter of a poem is comprised of a crowd of recollected occasions of feeling, among which the most important are recollections of encounters with sacred beings or events. This crowd the poet attempts to transform into a community by embodying it in a verbal society.

Moreover, all poets hold three articles of faith in common: they believe that the historical world of unique persons and events exists and that this existence is good; they believe that although it was created good, the historical world is also a fallen world, full of "unreason and disorder"; and they believe that the historical world is redeemable. Every poem attempts to present "an analogy to that paradisal state in which Freedom and Law, Systems and Order are united in harmony." Thus a successful poem suggests an analogy to that sacred goodness which reconciles, unites and redeems—but an analogy only, not an equivalent or a substitute: aesthetic experience is misleading if it implies that since all is well inside the verbal society whose end is to praise the created world, all is well in the historical world. But, as Auden warns, "all is not well there."

   This analogy to order and goodness raises the question of the function of art. Poetry may help us better to enjoy or endure life, to remind us of true perfection, and to "provide us with some kind of revelation about our life which will show us what life is really like and free us from...self-deception." By telling us the truth, art may "disenchant and disintoxicate." But the depiction of evil poses a serious moral problem:

> It is necessary that we know about evil in the world...[and] this knowledge it is one of the duties of the historian to impart. But the poet cannot get into this business without defiling himself or his audience. To write a play, that is to construct a secondary world, about Auschwitz, for example, is wicked: author and audience may try to pretend that they are morally horrified, but in fact they are passing an evening together, in the aesthetic enjoyment of horrors.

This distinction between the poet and the historian is a source of tension in Auden's criticism. Present in every human being, he argues, is the desire to know the world as it truly is and the desire to fashion a secondary world which will be free from pain and death. The historian pursues the truth, the poet makes his visionary realms; but "the Historian cannot function without some assistance from the Poet, nor the Poet without some assistance from the Historian." Thus, "as in any marriage, the question who is to command and who is to obey is the source of constant quarrels." The conflict is within the poet himself, of course, which leads Auden to differentiate between Prospero-dominated poets, who are impelled to tell the truth and bear witness to unfreedom and disorder, and Ariel-dominated poets who fabricate worlds and offer unmixed satisfaction. But whatever the poet's inclination, his fundamental duty, as Auden puts it in "Precious Five," is to "bless what there is for being." Like the rest of us, poets have a basic obligation to regard this world "with a happy eye/But from a sober perspective."

The literary criticism of a major poet always has a pertinence beyond its intrinsic worth. It may provide a useful account of his sources and values, as the criticism of Yeats and Eliot does; or like the criticism of Wallace Stevens, it may reveal more directly habits of mind which are sometimes puzzling in their compressed, purely poetic manifestations. Auden's criticism does these things as well but also has a claim on our attention as the most comprehensive Christian view of poetry any modern artist has proposed.

Auden's most elaborate single work of criticism, however, does not depend on the Christian assumptions of the later essays. A free-wheeling investigation of certain key-images in Romantic poetry (chiefly the sea and the quest voyage as they appear in such diverse artists as Coleridge, Lewis Carroll and Rimbaud), *The Enchafèd Flood* is one of the few successful works of archetypal criticism we have. Summary is not easy, but basically Auden argues that the Romantic poet has lost faith in society; instead of the "Just City," what exists is rather the "Trivial Unhappy Unjust City, the desert of the average from which the only escape is to the wild, lonely, but still vital sea." In turn this leads to further distinctions between the Classical Hero, the Romantic Hero and the Christian Hero, whose inward quest is difficult or impossible to render dramatically. The Romantic rebellion is over, of course, but the courage of the doomed Romantic voyager is exemplary: "we are less likely to be tempted by Promethean pride: we are far more likely to become cowards in the face of the tyrant who would compel us to lie in the service of the False City."

BAKER, Carlos (Heard).   American. Born in Biddeford, Maine, 5 May 1909. Educated at Dartmouth College, Hanover, New Hampshire, B.A. 1932 (Phi Beta Kappa); Harvard University, Cambridge, Massachusetts, M.A. 1933; Princeton University, New Jersey, Ph.D. 1940. Married Dorothy Thomasson Scott in 1932; has three children. English Teacher, Thornton Academy, Saco, Maine. 1933-34, and Nichols School, Buffalo, New York, 1934-36. Instructor, 1938-42, Assistant Professor, 1942-46, Associate Professor, 1946-51, Professor of English, 1951-53, Chairman of the Department of English, 1952-58, 1974-75, Woodrow Wilson Professor, 1954-77, and since 1977 Professor Emeritus, Princeton University. Fulbright Lecturer, Oxford University, 1957-58, and Centre Universitaire, Nice, 1958. Recipient: Guggenheim Fellowship, 1965, 1967. Litt D.: Dartmouth College, 1957. Address: 34 Allison Road, Princeton, New Jersey 08540, U.S.A.

PUBLICATIONS

Criticism

Shelley's Major Poetry: The Fabric of Vision.   Princeton, New Jersey, Princeton University Press, and London, Oxford University Press, 1948.
Hemingway: The Writer as Artist.   Princeton, New Jersey, Princeton University Press, 1952.

Verse

Shadow in Stone.   Hanover, New Hampshire, Printer's Devil Press, 1930.
A Year and a Day.   Nashville, Tennessee, Vanderbilt University Press, 1963.

Novels

A Friend in Power.   New York, Scribner, and London, Faber, 1958.
The Land of Rumbelow: *A Fable in the Form of a Novel*.   New York, Scribner, 1963;
    London, Eyre and Spottiswoode, 1964.
The Gay Head Conspiracy: *A Novel of Suspense*.   New York, Scribner, 1973.

Short Stories

The Talismans and Other Stories.   New York, Scribner, 1976.

Other

Ernest Hemingway: *A Life Story*.   New York, Scribner, and London, Collins, 1969.

Editor, *The American Looks at the World*   New York, Harcourt Brace, 1944.
Editor, with Willard Thorpe and Merle Curti, *American Issues*.   Philadelphia, Lippin-
    cott, 2 vols., 1941; revised edition, 2 vols., 1955.
Editor, *The Prelude, with a Selection from the Shorter Poems and the Sonnets and the
    1800 Preface to Lyrical Ballads*, by Wordsworth.   New York, Rinehart, 1948.
Editor, *Selected Poetry and Prose*, by Shelley.   New York, Modern Library, 1951.
Editor, with others, *The Major English Romantic Poets*: *A Symposium in Reappraisal*.
    Carbondale, Southern Illinois University Press, 1957.
Editor, *Hemingway and His Critics*: *An International Anthology*.   New York, Hill and
    Wang, 1961.
Editor, *Ernest Hemingway*: *Critiques of Four Major Novels*.   New York, Scribner, 1962.
Editor, *Poems and Selected Letters*, by Keats.   New York, Scribner, 1962.
Editor, *Coleridge*: *Poetry and Prose*.   New York, Bantam, 1965.
Editor, with others, *Modern American Usage*, by Wilson Follett.   New York, Hill and
    Wang, and London, Longman, 1966.
Editor, *Ernest Hemingway*: *Selected Letters 1917-1961*.   New York, Scribner, and
    London, Granada, 1981.

*   *   *

In the hermeneutic tradition "criticism" and "interpretation" have different senses which help considerably in sorting out some basic problems of literary theory. As E.D. Hirsch presents the argument in *Validity in Interpretation*, meaning refers to the determinate sense an utterance has for those who share a common language. This meaning may be complex, it may carry a host of implications, but it is determinate, unless we wish to take the extreme position that we ourselves bring the meaning to the words: in short, meaning is what the author intended. Significance, on the other hand, refers to what we make of the meaning, how we relate it to our own scheme of values. Thus when we interpret we try to recover the author's meaning; when we criticize, we make a statement about the value of the author's meaning. The lesson is that many pointless controversies could be avoided if we would only be aware of what kind of statement we are making or responding to in a given instance. Consensus about meaning is usually possible, although often difficult; consensus about significance, "critical" agreement, is impossible as long as different people hold different values. These basic distinctions make it easier to characterize more precisely the work of academic critics such as Carlos Baker: strictly speaking his books on Shelley and Hemingway are interpretive rather than critical, yet they demonstrate clearly the ways in which responsible criticism depends upon careful interpretation.

In *Shelley's Major Poetry* Baker provides a detailed survey of the poet's "developing thought as it bears upon and is reflected in the individual poems" from 1812 through 1822. Shelley's fluctuating reputation indicates our failure to see that he is "primarily a philosophical and psychological poet with a strong if unorthodox ethical bias [and] an almost single-minded devotion to a set of esthetic ideals." To stress his purely lyrical qualities is rather like "trying to give an audience the central idea of *The Tempest* by quoting, without further comment, the song 'Full Fathom Five.'" Shelley is in fact a "stringently self-disciplined ethical and metaphysical thinker who employed the lyric as a servant to his own particular kind of white magic." His poetry displays "a striking combination of objective philosophical and psychological interests and a heavy dependence on antecedent literature"—all claims which Baker is prepared to substantiate in full detail. For Shelley philosophical intent takes precedence over concern for formal perfection:

> Though his medium was poetic, and often succeeds as such, his laws were those of the philosopher, the psychologist, the seer, and the prophet, and it is to these laws rather than those of his chosen medium that he primarily conforms, both by preference and by inner constitution.

Shelley was not a craftsman "in the sense of being interested deeply in...finer details of structure and texture." Of course we may find this deplorable and argue that poetry can never be truly philosophical and that the poet should always be in command of his medium; but responsible readers will take the trouble to see what Shelley was trying to do before they decide it was not worth doing or accuse him of failing to do something he never intended. This is interpretation in the strict sense: a rigorous, informed effort to determine what an author's words may validly be construed to mean and imply.

As for Shelley's development, Baker demonstrates that he moved from an early belief in the inevitability of moral progress to a belief in the need for heroic individual action and finally to a much more pessimistic view (in *The Triumph of Life*) that the "meretricious and the mundane" tragically frustrate growth and perfection. What remains constant is the ideal goal of self-realization and the freedom achievable only through love; and while altruism cannot be imposed from without, Shelley saw poetry as a means of embodying the principles men ought to live by. Baker's arguments are convincing, although readers may sometimes feel that the intellectual coherence is his rather than Shelley's. He concludes that

> to achieve a balanced and judicious estimate of the only really important aspect of Shelley, his career as a writer, in the midst of these periodic jostlings and fluctuations, one needs, above all, to understand his premises, his aims, and his achievements, and to keep as clear as may be from [extremes].

This judicious balance is in fact what *Shelley's Major Poetry* establishes. A genuine critical issue remains, of course, and an important one: the worth and relevance of Shelley's ideas; but at least the critic who struggles with that problem, if he has read Baker, will be dealing with a real body of statements. And if he wishes to conclude that Shelley is a bad poet because he wrote "The Indian Serenade," he will also be saying something important about the depth of his own knowledge and his right to be taken seriously.

Ernest Hemingway: A Life Story, like Blotner on Faulkner and Edel on James and Thompson on Frost, is a massive official biography which seems determined to give us every recoverable fact about the author's life. It is not critical; it is not a "thesis" biography, as Baker himself admits; it attempts to set the record straight, nothing more. *Hemingway: The Writer as Artist* is also interpretive rather than critical. Here Baker carefully pieces together Hemingway's "practical esthetic" and examines each of the major novels in painstaking detail. His argument is essentially an expansion of Geoffrey Brereton's assertion that what makes a book like *Death in the Afternoon* memorable is Hemingway's "obstinate devotion to the fact and its accompanying sensation." The vivid sense of fact which is typical of Hemingway at his best depends, as Baker shows, on an intense concern for place and scene; and for an account of Hemingway's skill in evoking the appropriate emotion Baker turns to Eliot's notion of the "objective correlative." Baker rightly emphasizes Hemingway's claim that "all good books are alike in that they are truer than if they really happened and after you are finished reading one you will find that all that happened to you and afterwards it belongs to you.... If you can get so that you can give that to people, then you are a writer." And again, "a writer's problem does not change. It is always how to write truly and having found out what is true to project it in such a way that it becomes part of the experience of the person who reads it." The reader's sense of direct experience is not, of course, an end in itself. Finding out what is true involves judgment, not merely sensation, and this leads directly to Hemingway's code of behavior—stoicism, bravery and grace under pressure. Baker is a trustworthy guide here, if more diffuse and considerably less stylish than Philip Young in *Ernest Hemingway: A Reconsideration.* Hemingway admired *The Writer as Artist* although (as Baker dutifully reports) he also said it was "a hard book and makes too much, as many critics do, of the symbolism.... No good writer ever prepared his symbols ahead of time and wrote his book around them, but out of a good book which is true to life symbols may arise and be properly explored if not overemphasized." In fact Baker is usually moderate and sensible in his reading of the novels. Internal coherence, consistency of tone, the art which conceals art—these are the standards which he appeals to. Hemingway could hardly have hoped for a more patient interpreter. The final act of criticism is left up to the reader, and perhaps rightly so.

BARFIELD, (Arthur) Owen. British. Born in London, 9 November 1898. Educated at Highgate School, London; Wadham College, Oxford, B.A. (first-class honours in English) 1921, B. Litt. 1922, Bachelor of Civil Law 1934. Served in the Royal Engineers, 1917-18: Second Lieutenant. Married Matilda Dovie in 1923; has two children. Partner, Barfield and Barfield, solicitors, London, 1934-59. Visiting Professor, Drew University, Madison, New Jersey, 1964-65, 1972-73, and Brandeis University, Waltham, Massachusetts, 1965-66. Since 1954, Chairman, International Help for Children; since 1960, Honorary Treasurer, the Anthroposophical Society in Great Britain. Fellow, Royal Society of Literature. Address: Hartley, near Dartford, Kent, England.

Publications

Criticism

Poetic Diction: A Study in Meaning. London, Faber, 1928; revised edition, with preface added, 1952; New York, McGraw Hill, 1964.
"Poetic Diction and Legal Fiction." in *Essays Presented to Charles Williams*, edited by C.S. Lewis. London, Oxford University Press, 1947.
"Imagination and Inspiration," in *Interpretation: The Poetry of Meaning*, edited by Stanley Romaine Hopper and David L. Miller. New York, Harcourt Brace, 1967.
What Coleridge Thought. Middletown, Connecticut, Wesleyan University Press, 1971; London, Oxford University Press, 1972.

The Rediscovery of Meaning and Other Essays.   Middletown, Connecticut, Wesleyan
   University Press, 1977.

Other

The Silver Trumpet: A Tale (juvenile).   London, Faber and Gwyer, 1925; Grand Rapids,
   Michigan, Eerdmans, 1968.
History in English Words.   London, Methuen, and New York, Doran, 1926; revised
   edition, Methuen, 1933; London, Faber, 1954; Grand Rapids, Michigan, Eerdmans,
   1967.
Law, Association and the Trade Union Movement.   London, Threefold Commonwealth
   Research Group, 1938.
Romanticism Comes of Age.   London, Anthroposophical Publishing Company, 1944;
   revised edition, London, Rudolf Steiner Press, 1966; Middletown, Connecticut, Wes-
   leyan University Press, 1967.
"Greek Thought in Greek Words," in *Essays and Studies*, n.s. 3.   London, Wyman, 1950.
This Ever Diverse Pair (as G.A.L. Burgeon: anecdotes, facetiae).   London, Gollancz,
   1950.
Saving the Appearances: A Study in Idolatry.   London, Faber, 1957; New York, Har-
   court Brace, 1965.
"The Meaning of the Word 'Literal,' " in *Metaphor and Symbol*, edited by L.C. Knights
   and Basil Cottle.   London, Faber, Butterworth, 1960.
Worlds Apart (A Dialogue of the 1960's).   Middletown, Connecticut, Wesleyan Uni-
   versity Press, and London, Faber, 1963.
Unancestral Voice.   Middletown, Connecticut, Wesleyan University Press, and London,
   Faber, 1965.
Introduction to *Light on C.S. Lewis*, edited by Joycelyn Gibb.   London, Bles, 1965; New
   York, Harcourt Brace, 1965.
Speaker's Meaning.   Middletown, Connecticut, Wesleyan University Press, 1967; Lon-
   don, Rudolf Steiner Press, 1972.
Mark vs. Tristram: Correspondence Between C.S. Lewis and Owen Barfield, edited by
   Walter Hooper.   Cambridge, Massachusetts, Lowell House Printers, 1967.
History, Guilt, and Habit (lectures).   Middletown, Connecticut, Wesleyan University
   Press, 1979.

Editor, *Anthroposophy*, by Rudolf Steiner, translated by V.C.B..   London, Anthroposophical Publishing Company, 1961.

Translator, with Edith Rigby, *Man and Animal: Their Essential Differences*, by Herman
   Poppelbaum.   London, Anthroposophical Publishing Company, and New York,
   Anthroposophic Press, 1931.
Editor and translator, *The Case for Anthroposophy*, by Rudolf Steiner.   London,
   Rudolf Steiner Press, 1970.
Translator, with Charles Davy (revised translation), *Guidance in Esoteric Training*, by
   Rudolf Steiner.   London, Rudolf Steiner Press, 1972.

CRITICAL STUDY

Robert J. Reilly, *Romantic Religion: A Study of Barfield, Lewis, Williams and Tolkien.*
   Athens, University of Georgia Press, 1971.

*   *   *

In his partly autobiographical introduction to the augmented edition of *Romanticism
Comes of Age*, Owen Barfield recalls that

the first serious thing that happened to my mind was (at the age of about twenty-one) a sudden and rapid increase in the intensity with which I experienced lyric poetry. This was a fact. It was something I could not successfully convict myself, though I tried hard to do so, of believing because I wanted to believe it. It was something that kept on actually happening to me...and in the intellectual vacuum created by my scepticism (I had been brought up as an agnostic) it was a conspicuous object to which I was not sorry to turn my attention. I began instinctively to investigate it, and the method I adopted, so far from drying up the sources of delight, seemed rather to refresh them.

As for the effect of these experiences, "Something happened: one felt wise. This was a fact." *Poetic Diction* and to a lesser extent *History in English Words* are the initial results of Barfield's attempt to explain the nature of this new "wisdom" and to fill the intellectual vacuum with a positive philosophy. A practicing lawyer until his retirement (law, Barfield has said, is the point where life and logic meet), he wrote very little until 1957; and what he has written since then has only an indirect bearing on literature in the narrower sense. Nevertheless, *Poetic Diction* is a remarkable book. As Howard Nemerov observed in his introduction to the belated American edition, "among the few poets and teachers of my acquaintance who do know *Poetic Diction* it has been valued not only as a secret book, but nearly as a sacred one."

Poetic Diction turns directly to the problem of aesthetic response, relying heavily on romantic theory and the teachings of Barfield's mentor, the anthroposophist Rudolf Steiner. Individual words and words in combination have the power to produce, in a receptive intelligence, a particular kind of pleasure. (Barfield is quite aware that the sound of words may also affect the "aesthetic imagination" but limits himself here entirely to verbal meaning). In responding to poetic meaning, Barfield continues.

> I am impressed not merely by the *difference* between my consciousness and the consciousness of which [the poem is] the expression, but by something more. I find that, in addition to the moment or moments of aesthetic pleasure in appreciation, I gain from [it] a more permanent boon. It is as though my own consciousness had actually been expanded.... Now my normal everyday experience, as a human being, of the world around me depends entirely on what *I* bring to the sense-datum from within; and the absorption of this metaphor into my imagination has enabled me to bring more than I could before. It has created something in me, a faculty or part of a faculty, enabling me to observe what I could not hitherto observe. This ability to recognize significant resemblances and analogies, considered as in action, I shall call *knowledge*.... The elements in poetic diction which are most conducive to it are, as we shall see, metaphor and simile.

The wisdom gained is, in Shelley's words, the knowledge of previously "unapprehended relations of things," an increased awareness of the intricate interrelationships existing in nature and between man and nature. The imagination grasps connections which reflect the very structure of nature: reality itself is a realm of interlocking correspondences. The mechanical distinction between a perceiving subject and an observed object falsifies and misleads: knower and known are both interpenetrating parts of an organic whole.

At an earlier state in the evolution of consciousness men intuited their proper relationship to nature. Their unconscious participation in the whole expressed itself in the very formation of language, in which words were not abstract markers but rather "flashing iridescent shapes like flames—ever-flickering vestiges of the slowly evolving consciousness beneath them." Thus words were at first "figurative" or "translucent" ("prevaricate," for example, is derived from the Latin verb which means "to plough in crooked lines"); they were based on a feeling for the relatedness of phenomena which has been destroyed by the rise of science and the triumph of abstraction:

> But we, in the development of consciousness, have lost the power to see this [unity]. Our sophistication, like Odin's has cost us an eye; and now it is the language of poets, in so far as they create true metaphors, which must restore this unity conceptually, after it has been lost from perception. Thus the "before-unapprehended" relations of which Shelley spoke, are in a sense "forgotten" relationships.

Since words have lost their original power it is now the poet's responsibility to recreate meaning—that is, to reveal the organic structure of reality—by overt metaphor which will communicate "participant knowledge." Thus the source of Barfield's early wisdom was the "analogy-perceiving, metaphor-creating imagination"; aesthetic pleasure is the sign of an expanding consciousness. But it is not only man who is served by the imagination: phenomena themselves are "incomplete" until we apprehend them rightly. True knowledge, then, "so far from being a mental copy of events and processes outside the human being, inserts the human being right into these processes, of whose development it is itself the last stage."

This evolutionary view of human consciousness suggests another version of man's fall from grace and the pride of intellect. In a sense this is what Barfield intends, and the fall is still a fortunate one, preparing the way for a final integration. The purpose of evolution is to return man to his original state of relatedness but at a higher level of awareness: "That the whole of humanity should eventually acquire such a consciousness is the entelechy of the earth-evolution as a whole." Reintegration is not automatically assured, however, since men have free will and may choose to follow exclusively the ways of abstraction and conceptualization:

> We may very well compare the self of man to a seed. Formerly, what is now the seed was a member of the old plant, and, as such, was wholly informed with a life not wholly its own. But now the pod or capsule has split open, and the dry seed has been ejected. It has attained to a separate existence. Henceforth one of two things may happen to it: either it may abide alone, isolated from the rest of the earth growing dryer and dryer, until it withers up altogether; or, by uniting with the earth, it may blossom into a fresh life of its own.

The imagination is an instrument of evolution; and just as "the study of law was once a valuable exercise for other purposes besides the practice of law, so today the study of poetry and of the poetic element in all meaningful language is a valuable exercise for other purposes than the practice or better enjoyment of poetry."

In his later books Barfield has traced the rise of western conceptualization and, most recently, explored the unity of Coleridge's thought (Goethe and Coleridge are for him the two philosophers whose organicism anticipates most clearly Steiner's system). And while it is unlikely that many of his readers will accept as literal truth Barfield's anthroposophical position, *Poetic Diction*, scattered passages in *Saving the Appearances* and his one essay in "practical" criticism, "The Form of Hamlet" (in *Romanticism Comes of Age*), are richly suggestive. At the very least Barfield's work is a fascinating testimony to the continuity of romantic thought and its faith in the restorative powers of poetry.

BATE, Walter Jackson. American. Born in Mankato, Minnesota, 23 May 1918. Educated at Harvard University, Cambridge, Massachusetts, B.A. 1939, M.A. 1940, Ph.D. 1942. Assistant Professor, 1946-49, Associate Professor, 1949-56, Chairman of the Department of English, 1955-62, Professor of English, 1956-62, Abbott Lawrence Lowell Professor of Humanities, 1962-79, and since 1979 Kingsley Porter University Professor, Harvard University. Recipient: Phi Beta Kappa Christian Gauss Prize, 1956, 1964; Harvard Faculty Prize, 1964; Pulitzer Prize for Biography, 1964, 1978; National Book Award, 1978. Litt. D.: Rutgers University, New Brunswick, New Jersey, 1979. Member, American Academy of Arts and Sciences. Address: 3 Warren House, Harvard University, Cambridge, Massachusetts 02138, U.S.A.

PUBLICATIONS

Criticism

Negative Capability: *The Intuitive Approach in Keats* (undergraduate thesis).   Cambridge, Massachusetts, Harvard University Press, 1939.
The Stylistic Development of Keats.   New York, Modern Language Association, 1945; London, Routledge, 1958.
From Classic to Romantic: *Premises of Taste in Eighteenth-Century England*.   Cambridge, Massachusetts, Harvard University Press, 1946.
The Achievement of Samuel Johnson.   New York, Oxford University Press, 1955.
Prefaces to Criticism.   New York, Doubleday, 1959.
John Keats.   Cambridge, Massachusetts, Harvard University Press, 1963.
Coleridge.   New York, Macmillan, 1968; London, Weidenfeld and Nicolson, 1969.
The Burden of the Past and the English Poet.   Cambridge, Massachusetts, Harvard University Press, 1970; London, Chatto and Windus, 1971.
Samuel Johnson.   New York, Harcourt Brace, 1977; London, Chatto and Windus, 1978.

Other

Editor, *Criticism*: *The Major Texts*.   New York, Harcourt Brace, 1952; revised edition, 1970; abbreviated edition as *Prefaces to Criticism*, New York, Doubleday, 1959.
Editor, *Selected Writings*, by Edmund Burke.   New York, Modern Library, 1960.
Editor, *Keats*: *A Collection of Critical Essays*.   Englewood Cliffs, New Jersey, Prentice Hall, 1964.
Editor, with others, *The Yale Edition of the Works of Samuel Johnson*.   New Haven, Connecticut, Yale University Press, Vols. 2-5, 1963, 1969.
Editor, *Essays from the Rambler, Adventurer, and Idler*, by Samuel Johnson.   New Haven, Connecticut, Yale University Press, 1968.

*   *   *

Walter Jackson Bate's repeated use of two key terms, "formative" and "centrality," clearly indicates his fundamental sympathy with the classical conception of art and its relationship to the proper end of human activity. *Prefaces to Criticism* has a premise, he admits at once, "though one so general that I hope it is unable to be doctrinaire. The premise is that the first justification of criticism is to bring into focus and emphasize the function of the arts and, indeed, of the humanities in general." Criticism itself must remain humanistic, "bearing in mind the larger claims of human nature, in their full variety"; and for this conception of human nature Bate returns to the broad common ground shared by the founders of the classical tradition. Despite the crucial differences between them, Humphrey House has argued, Plato and Aristotle directed their thought towards practical goals

and their speculation was never far removed from the business of teaching. The overriding concern of the Academy was the discussion of the "good life," as it is livable by man, on earth, in a society of his fellow-men. All subdivisions of human thought and activity were related to this primary ethical purpose, and all had their bearing on the political context in which ethical purposes were necessarily realized. The vision of human life as a whole was never lost sight of, and all special subjects were related to it. The individual was seen ideally as a balanced, mature person exercising all his powers harmoniously and at full stretch, and such exercise was impossible except in a political organization of the state which allowed and fostered it. The main business of the Academy was to teach men to be good men in the fullest sense, and good citizens...poetry was never thought of in isolation; it was something in which all men shared, an activity of public importance, to be interpreted as part of the means by which the whole human personality was both educated and controlled.

Men are born with the capacity to reason, to know the order of the objective world around them,w men. The purpose of human life is to maximize and maintain these uniquely human characterrmonious and productive relationships with their felloistics. Thus when human nature is completed or fulfilled, wisdom and virtue are inseparable; and it is in terms of this end—the happiness proper to man *qua* man—that art must be defended or rejected. The Aristotelian tradition argues that by imitating what is universal (what we come to know as probable or necessary in life) and by strengthening the emotional responses appropriate to a given situation, art is directly "formative." To quote Humphrey House once more, art

> arouses the emotions from potentiality to activity by worthy and adequate stimuli; it controls them by directing them to the right objects in the right way; and exercises them...as the emotions of the good man would be exercised [in life]. When they subside to potentiality again...it is a more "trained" potential than before. Our responses are brought nearer to those of the good and wise man.

Conceptions of art—and criticism—which keep this purpose in mind have what Bate calls "centrality."

The classical ideal, however, with its emphasis on the general and its appeal to our rationally governed emotions, is in direct opposition to the "Romantic" as Bate defines it:

> a turning away, in whatever direction, from the classical standard of ideal nature, and from the accompanying conviction that the full exercise of ethical reason may grasp that objective ideal. In more or less degree, [romanticism] substitutes for these premises the belief that such truth is to be realized primarily in or through the particular, and that this truth is to be realized, appreciated, and declared in art by the response to that particular of some faculty or capacity in man which is imaginative and often emotional rather than "rational," and which therefore inclines to be somewhat individualistic and subjective in its working.

As the title suggests, *From Classic to Romantic* analyzes the forces at work during this period of transition in England. The extreme development and in some instances rigid overinterpretation of classical principles brought about an inevitable reaction:

> The closing years of the [eighteenth century] were accordingly characterized by a general conviction decidedly different from that which it had inherited: a conviction that the essential nature of man was not reason...but that it consisted, in effect, either of a conglomeration of instincts, habits, and feelings, or else as German subjectivism was beginning to illustrate, of an ego which creates and projects its own world, and which has little real hope of knowing anything else.

(The crucial assumption here, that such one-sidedness will call forth its opposite, derives from Bate's acknowledged mentor, Alfred North Whitehead; indeed, *From Classic to Romantic* may properly be seen as a working out of certain aspects of *Science and the Modern World.* Contemporary British aesthetics served as "the main foundation for many of the familiar tenets of English romantic poets and critics"and behind the aesthetics lies the determining force of British empirical psychology:

> by encouraging aesthetics to take the subjective activity of the mind as the starting point of any investigation, British associationism opened the door even more widely for an inevitable individualistic relativism. In doing so, it substantiated a tendency which was to be even more characteristic of the romantic thought of the [nineteenth] century: a tendency to emphasize the fundamental importance of individual feeling or sentiment.

Twenty-five years later Bate regretted his emphasis on psychological theory—"so much else also enters into the picture"—but nevertheless it remains for him one of the chief causes of the emergence of romanticism.

Romanticism is thus a potent form of anti-rationalism, in turn creating its own extremes and imbalances. But it is a primary concern with Bate, here and elsewhere, to argue that the typically British genius for compromise enabled the great Romantic poets to avoid excessive emotionalism and relativism. They never lost sight of the purpose of art, as Bate makes clear in *The Burden of the Past*:

> Accordingly, the arts had the highest possible justification. In short, a new life was given, whatever the difference in vocabulary, to the old classical conviction of the formative or educative power of art; and not merely because art can reveal, suggest, or convey truth but because—as it reaches through symbols and varieties of expression to the "whole man," as Coleridge said—it also reawakens and intensifies the "germinal powers of growth and development" in the reader or audience.

Even so, Bate has some misgivings: "In common with much other nineteenth and twentieth-century art, many of even the most successful examples admittedly lack a certain moral centrality which is familiar in so much classical, Renaissance, and even neo-classical art.... It may be questioned whether this centrality has really been found.".

A striking passage from Whitehead suggests Bate's fundamental procedure in his justly admired studies of Johnson, Coleridge and Keats. There is no substitute, Whitehead suggests, "for the direct perception of the concrete achievement of a thing in its actuality. We want concrete fact with a high light thrown on what is *relevant to its preciousness*." Thus Bate wishes to define as precisely as possible the struggles and accomplishments of each writer and to determine the value of their hard-won victories. *The Achievement of Samuel Johnson* describes fully the ordeals Johnson faced, but Bate asserts that "the gain of dwelling on the more painful details of Johnson's life is not that they furnish the seed from which his final character develops. The real point in stressing them is precisely because they did not do so." Once again the emphasis is classical: art—and the art of criticism—ought to be more philosophic than history. Thus Johnson's great theme is neither vanity nor despair, but rather that "human fulfillment—the developing and completing of human nature—arises from awareness, from going beyond the slavery of our own subjective cage, however painful the impulses, habits, and stock responses that control us, into a rounded, charitable, and vital grasp of persisting forms and principles." At the heart of Johnson's work, then, lies "the greatest of classical discoveries and generalizations":

> It is the discovery that human nature is able to remake and remould itself, and that this recreation—this liberating and educating or leading out of human potentiality—can be carried through, not by denying or cutting off impulses, but rather by constantly broadening and enriching the quality of the *objects* to which they are reaching.

In like fashion Bate deals with Coleridge's intellectual development and his poetry in the context of that artist's compulsions and problems, employing the method which he defends most clearly in the later *John Keats*:

> *Endymion* is indeed of the first importance in the story of Keats' life. Yet two qualifications face us at the start. Each is a by-product of the very special way in which the poem was written; and in giving us this reminder, biography can possibly aid criticism, dissuading it from doomed ingenuity and the irritabilities of superfluous debate. Formalists may feel that an artist's intention is irrelevant. But form, in the concrete individual work, can never itself be explained solely by formal criteria.

John Keats is a massive, full length biography but no less critical than *Coleridge* or *The Achievement of Samuel Johnson*. There are expert contextual analyses of the poems and more than a suggestion that the example of the artist's struggles as well as his accomplishments may have a formative effect:

The life of Keats provides a unique opportunity for the study of literary greatness and of what permits or encourages its development. The interest is thus deeply human and moral.... For, to begin with, we have to do with a type of genius that...quickly acquires a personal relevance to a wide variety of readers. We find the steady growth of qualities of both mind and character that are equally appropriate to other forms of achievement.... We have a natural hunger to learn what qualities of mind or character, and what incidents in a man's life, encourage—or at least permit—an achievement so compelling when, at the same time, so little is apparently given at the start. This same appeal explains the fascination with which the life of Lincoln, to jump to a superficially different realm, still continues to be scanned and reinterpreted. Whatever our usual preoccupations, in approaching such figures we become more open to what Johnson thought the first aim of biography—to find what can be "put to use."

Bate follows Keats' astonishing development poem by poem, week by week, day by day when the facts permit. Like the other great English Romantics, Keats made his own "break-through,"although from what to what is best defined in Bate's most suggestive book thus far, *The Burden of the Past and the English Poet*.

The "burden" of the title refers to the poet's overwhelming awareness of the achievements of those who came before him. The basic question is as obvious as it is profound: what is there left to do? "Would that I had phrases that are not known," an Egyptian scribe complained in 2000 B.C., "utterances that are strange, in a new language that has not been used, free from repetition, not an utterance which has grown stale, which men of old have spoken." Bate limits himself primarily to the eighteenth century, however, since this was "the first period in modern history to face the problem of what it means to come *immediately* after a great creative achievement." There are different kinds of strategies for coping with the past, but in the end the problem is always inescapably personal:

the essential problem—the real anxiety—lay elsewhere, as David Hume had said, and it had to do with the artist's relation to his own art. It had to do with what the artist would least care to dwell on publicly if he were trying either to begin or even maintain his way, and with what is even now—in the second half of the twentieth century—not openly declared but surrounded with a protective fog of other considerations: that is, the nakedness and embarrassment (with the inevitable temptations to paralysis or routine imitation, to retrenchment or mere fitful rebellion) before the amplitude of what two thousand years or more of art had already been able to achieve.

The major Romantic poets also faced the past in various ways and tried to meet the conflicting demands to be both "original" and yet "sincere." For Keats, for example, there was the "archetypal method of modern poetry itself," the "profound opening up for literary treatment of the 'inner life' of the individual...the 'untrodden region of the mind.' " But whatever his particular solution, the great poet wins his victories by accepting rather than denying the past; according to his strength he finds there the proper stimulus—and the joy of entering what Keats called the "immortal free-masonry" of art. Properly approached the past will provide that liberating vision of greatness which Whitehead speaks of:

The fine remark of Whitehead keeps recurring to us: "Moral education is impossible apart from the habitual vision of greatness." For the ideal of greatness, as the Greeks discovered, is ultimately self-corrective in its effect as well as self-impelling. This is especially true when presented with the compelling power of a concrete example...[and] as the attraction persists, it can lead us to discover what is more fundamental. And since the example has not been merely recognized in an abstract way but is actually caught and followed through a process of identification, the further discoveries to which it persuades us are made freshly, creatively, and through our own direct experience.

The classical argument of Bate's critical biographies and historical overviews is finally something of an implicit rebuke to our own age, which has too often refused the vision of greatness and forfeited the power of centrality.

BATESON, F(rederick) (Noel) W(ilse). British. Born in Styal, Cheshire, 25 December 1901. Educated at Charterhouse, London; Trinity College, Oxford, B.A. 1924, B. Litt. 1926, M.A. 1927; Harvard University, Cambridge, Massachusetts (Commonwealth Fellow), 1927-29. Married Jan Chancellor in 1931; has two children. Editor, *Cambridge Bibliography of English Literature*, 1930-40; Lecturer, Workers' Education Association, 1935-40; Statistical Officer, Buckinghamshire War Agriculture Executive Committee, 1940-46; Agriculture Correspondent, *The Observer* and *The New Statesman*, both London, 1944-48. University Lecturer, 1946-60, and Special University Lecturer, 1960-68, Oxford University, and Fellow and Tutor in English Literature, 1946-69, and since 1969 Emeritus Fellow, Corpus Christi College, Oxford. Visiting Professor, University of Minnesota, Minneapolis, 1936, Cornell University, Ithaca, New York, 1955, University of California at Berkeley, 1958, and Pennsylvania State University, 1960, 1962, 1964. Founder and Editor, then Advisory Editor, *Essays in Criticism*, Oxford, 1951-78; General Editor, *Longman Annotated Poets Series*, London. *Died in 1978.*

PUBLICATIONS

Criticism

English Comic Drama, 1700-1750. Oxford, Clarendon Press, 1929; New York, Russell and Russell, 1963.
English Poetry and the English Language: An Experiment in Literary History. Oxford, Clarendon Press, 1934; revised edition, New York, Russell and Russell, 1961; Oxford, Clarendon Press, 1973.
English Poetry: A Critical Introduction. London, Longman, 1950; revised edition, 1966; New York, Russell and Russell, 1966.
Wordsworth: A Re-Interpretation. London, Longman, 1954.
A Guide to English Literature. London, Longman, and New York, Doubleday, 1965; revised edition, with Harrison T. Meserole, as *A Guide to English and American Literature*, London, Longman, 1976.
"Literary History: Non-Subject *Par Excellence*," in *New Literary History* (Charlottesville, Virginia), 2, 1970.
Essays in Critical Dissent. London, Longman, 1972.
The Scholar-Critic: An Introduction to Literary Research. London, Routledge, 1972.
"Could Chaucer Spell?" in *Essays in Criticism* (Oxford), 25, 1975.
"Criticism's Lost Leader," in *The Literary Criticism of T.S. Eliot: New Essays*, edited by David Newton-De Molina. London, Athlone Press, 1977.
"The Scrutiny Phenomenon," in *Sewanee Review* (Tennessee), 85, 1977.
"The Analysis of Poetic Texts: Owen's 'Futility' and Davie's 'The Garden Party,' "in *Essays in Criticism* (Oxford), 29, 1979.

Other

Mixed Farming and Muddled Thinking: An Analysis of Current Agricultural Policy. London, Macdonald, 1946.
Brill: A Short History. Brill, Buckinghamshire, The Brill Society, 1966.

Editor, *The Works of Congreve: Comedies: Incognita: Poems.* London, Davies, and New York, Minton Balch, 1930.
Editor, *The Beggar's Opera*, by John Gay. London, Dent, 1934.
Editor, *The Cambridge Bibliography of English Literature.* London, Cambridge University Press, 4 vols., 1940; New York, Cambridge University Press, 4 vols., 1941.

Editor, *Towards a Socialist Agriculture: Studies by a Group of Fabians*. London, Gollancz, 1946.

Editor, *Epistles to Several Persons*, by Pope, in *The Twickenham Pope*, vol. 3. London, Methuen, and New Haven, Connecticut, Yale University Press, 1951; revised edition, 1961.

Editor, *Selected Poems of William Blake*. London, Heinemann, and New York, Macmillan, 1957.

Editor, *Essays on English Literature*, by Matthew Arnold. London, University of London Press, 1965.

Editor, with N.A. Joukovsky, *Alexander Pope: A Critical Anthology*. London, Penguin, 1971.

Editor, *The School for Scandal*, by Sheridan. London, Benn, 1979.

CRITICAL STUDIES AND BIBLIOGRAPHY

A.D. Barker, "F.W. Bateson: A Checklist," in *Essays in Criticism* (Oxford), 29, 1979.

John Barnard, "F.W. Bateson, Pope, and Editing," in *Essays in Criticism* (Oxford), 29, 1979.

Valentine Cunningham, "F.W. Bateson: Scholar, Critic, and Scholar-Critic," in *Essays in Criticism* (Oxford), 29, 1979.

René Wellek, "The Literary Theories of F.W. Bateson," in *Essays in Criticism* (Oxford), 29, 1979.

*   *   *

Where a writer's emphasis will fall, F.W. Bateson observed in 1934, "is partly a matter of temperament (Leavis is a natural critic and I am a natural historian); and while Bateson has in fact devoted much of his career to matters of scholarship and literary history, he is pre-eminently a "scholar-critic," convinced that history and criticism at their best are complementary disciplines. Their proper relationship is the primary subject of *English Poetry and the English Language* and *English Poetry: A Critical Introduction*, both of which should in turn be read as parts of a continuing effort to settle two larger issues: the differences between prose and poetry and the connections between poetry and the ordinary language of a living, changing society. The various distinctions Bateson proposes lead directly to the more complicated question of making value judgments.

The argument of both books rests fundamentally on Ferdinand de Saussure's distinction between *langue* (the general language system, the meanings and grammar which fund the basic processes of communication within a society) and *parole* (the specific language occasion, the special choices and formations which constitute an individual utterance). Bateson goes further and proposes that poetry itself is a kind of *parole*, a patterned way of actualizing possibilities, a smaller language within the body of shared meanings. As such it may have its own preferred diction and construction, in short a style—although that word will not quite do for what Bateson has in mind. The most memorable works, he maintains, are those in which there has been the greatest degree of coincidence between the literary language and the language spoken by the original audience. (He notes that "a poetry which is coextensive with the language in which it was written has always been extremely rare. Dryden was the last English poet whose verse even approached such a condition." Yet in 1934 he felt that we were "on the verge of such a poetry at this moment" and suggested that the early Auden might be our Dryden. It could not be Yeats, in any event, and certainly not Eliot: "The one is an Irishman, the other an American, and the language they maltreat with such masterly virtuosity is not exactly English, but a sweeter and less stubborn instrument, a *dead* language. Eliot inquired from me, through a 'mutual friend,' for an example of what I meant in his work. I offered *Ash-Wednesday*, with its over-use of participles and its avoidance of main verbs." Deliberate outrageousness is sometimes part of Bateson's rhetoric as a critic, but this is not an example: he means what he says here.

Ordinary language is not fixed, of course. It changes, its denotations and connotations shift about, its very conception of itself alters from period to period; and behind the changes, finally, are larger social forces: "the prime mover...[is] always from a change in society to a change in the language: and then, only then, to a change in the poetry." The problem facing the student of English poetry thus becomes one of determining the significant phases of the English language—and English society itself. How are we to know what constitutes a "period"? In the *Critical Introduction* Bateson proposes the following divisions:

> Parallel with the six consecutive poetic schools—Anglo-French, Chaucerian, Renaissance, Augustan, Romantic and Modern—our hypothesis requires six distinguishable social orders whose basic incentives will provide a poetic context in the central line of evolution of each school. In terms of the source of the ultimate social influence a tabulation that recommends itself to me is:
> (i) The Period of Lawyers' Feudalism (Henry II—Edward III).
> (ii) The Local Democracy of the Yeomanry (Edward III—Henry VII).
> (iii) The Centralized Absolutism of the Prince's Servants (Henry VII—Cromwell).
> (iv) The Oligarchy of the Landed Interests (Charles II—George III).
> (v) The Plutocracy of Business (George III—George V).
> (vi) The Managerial State (George V—?).

The historian must be able to uncover the shared values and common goals beneath the welter of particular social phenomena:

> The formula that we need must be one that defines the human motives that controlled the social behaviour of [the] dominant group.... My conclusion, therefore, is that the social content of poetry must not be identified with the concrete particulars of everyday life. There is no reason why teapots, Proportional Representation and the Crystal Palace should not be introduced into a poem, but again there is no reason why they should be. The imprint of the social order must be looked for at a higher level of abstraction, and to the casual reader it may easily not be visible at all. It will normally be concerned with the basic incentives, the prime mover, that a particular society offers its members.

In English Renaissance poetry, for example, Bateson believes that "the centre of interest seems to lie in the variations round the theme of a precarious mystical individualism." (Both *English Poetry and the English Language* and the *Critical Introduction* contain several chapters devoted to the various poetic schools and representative individual works.

The literary historian is concerned with the recovery of meaning and the language-context in which the work first appeared. For Bateson the isolated work can never be an object of genuine knowledge: poetic meaning subsists only in a "poet-reader relationship." The task is to understand the terms of that realationship during a given period, but by this standard Bateson concluded (in 1950) that there has been "no good history of English poetry." In part this is inevitable:

> A history is only possible if there is an organic relationship between the component parts, and there is no such relationship between Old English poetry, and that of the present day, or indeed between any two periods of English poetry, except where one school immediately preceded or succeeded another.... English poetry in its entirety, like the English town or the English character, is too wide a field for profitable historical treatment.

Of course there can be *histories*, discerning accounts of particular periods: but even here there is probably not much work which lives up to Bateson's demands. The reason may be simply that the true historian, in his sense, needs to know a great deal more than he usually does.

The literary critic, on the other hand, is concerned with comparative value judgments. To use the hermeneutical terms developed by E.D. Hirsch in *Validity in Interpretation* (and which Bateson adopts in *The Scholar-Critic*), the historian or scholar interprets, recovering the "meaning-then" of a work, while the critic judges "significance," which involves relating the meaning to a particular set of values. Of course value-then may not be value-now, but at least the critic should be aware of what constituted value-then. Thus for Bateson the critic seems to have three responsibilities: to ascertain value-then, to judge how well a given work uses various linguistic devices to embody a social meaning, and to propose value-now. This last activity inescapably makes the critic something of a moralist, although Bateson tends to be evasive here: "The critic in this role is a moralist—a reputable occupation, no doubt, but one that is extraordinarily difficult to combine with either the writing or reading of poetry, except perhaps in some oblique or metaphorical manner." When he deals with texts from an earlier period the critic runs the risk of translating the original meaning and significance into the alien terms of a modern context. Thus "the special use of literary history to the literary critic is to preserve him from eccentricity and private meanings. A poem that is misunderstood inevitably stimulates the wrong emotional responses, and, though the reader may prefer his own meaning, the misinterpretation will always tend to sentimentalize or vulgarize its essential human significance." Over the years Bateson has devoted much of his energy to sharp attacks on naive history, irrelevancies such as the relationship of linguistics and certain bibliographical methods to criticism, and irresponsible, that is *context-less* criticism.

Bateson draws an equally important distinction between prose and poetry. Prose denotes as it unfolds; it is useful because it names, defines and makes propositions. But it is purely a means to an end—its terms are not in themselves memorable. Once the end has been achieved and the information conveyed, the prose, as Valéry puts it, disappears, and rightly so. Of course prose should be logical and precise, but it should not draw attention to itself. Poetry, however, denotes and connotes: it too unfolds in time but it also uses a complex of means to give the illusion of a completed whole suspended in the reader's mind:

> The positive function of the various formal devices of poetry—metre, alliteration, metaphor, verbal repetition, etc.—is to ensure that the poem achieves a unity of impression. They are all fundamentally "esemplastic," to use Coleridge's word. The continuous verbal links, interconnections and references back (i) prevent the reader from relegating to his memory the beginning of the poem before he has reached its end, and (ii) are continual reminders that each sentence in the poem must be read against a background of awareness of the whole poem in all its semantic complexity. Without realizing what is happening we find ourselves forced, in fact, to retain the whole poem in our consciousness all through the process of reading it.

The means of poetry are in themselves memorable as well as functional. Furthermore, the implication is that the poem brings about a fusion on a more complex level as well. Because it is metaphorical, poetry "facilitates a commentary on human behaviour which is more effective, more concentrated, more 'intense,' than common speech can provide." The following passage from "Gray's 'Elegy' Reconsidered" (now included in the *Critical Introduction*) illustrates these propositions clearly:

> The central section on the village Hampdens, Miltons and Cromwells—in my own opinion the best passage in the poem—is a continuous expanded paradox. The concept of a "village Hampden" appears to be a contradiction in terms (How can you be a national hero *and* unknown outside your own village?) Its resolution, carrying with it the implication that the smaller unit is at least as favourable a soil for the display of moral grandeur, shows Gray equally in the central social tradition of his time. The *Elegy*, in addition to all the other things that it is, was a tract for the times. It was a plea for decentralization, recalling the overurbanized ruling class to its roots in a rural society based upon the benevolent despotism of the manor house.

At its best poetry is nothing less than "the point of maximum consciousness, the synthesis of a particular social order, in which that society achieves its most significant self-expression—and ultimately its historical meaning." (Since prose is neither esemplastic nor essentially metaphorical, Bateson has little interest in the novel or the drama, "including poetic drama"—although elsewhere he finds that Acts IV and V of *Antony and Cleopatra* are "the highwater mark perhaps of English poetry.")

It is possible for the responsible critic, aided by the historian, to recover the original poet-reader relationship and to pass judgment on the technical success of a poem; but what value can the poem have now, in a different time and place? The problem, in short, seems to be an implied relativism. And Bateson does in fact state that "the criteria of interpretation and evaluation can never, it is true, be absolutely authoritative, if only because the subjects who contribute to the intersubjective interpretation or judgment are always changing, just as the society to which they owe their allegiance is constantly evolving. But a measure of literary agreement is possible." If so, what are the grounds of such agreements, however limited? Here Bateson is rather less clear. In *The Scholar-Critic* he has recently maintained that the first question of criticism is not, what is good literature that reflects such and such a society, but "What constitutes a Good Society? In the *Critical Introduction* he had maintained that "man, the political animal, is most himself in a selfless service to the community," yet surely we are not to conclude that all communities are of equal worth or that all societies deserve the selfless service of their members—unless we are complete cultural relativists. Bateson is no relativist, of course: his ideal society seems to be the *well-managed* democracy which provides maximum equality for its members. There is at least a suggestion that certain values transcend particular times and places in his observation that "some such concept of civilization therefore underlies and authenticates the competent Reader's response. We read in order to become more civilized, more humane, more useful because more perceptive citizens. And the refusal to separate meaning from significance is at the heart of the special 'esemplastic' contribution that literature makes to life." Thus it seems fair and reasonable to infer Bateson's general position regarding values from an aside he makes in connection with a particular dispute between philologists and critics: "The ideals of democracy provide a criterion to which reference can always be made."

BAYLEY, John (Oliver). British. Born in England, 27 March 1925. Educated at Eton College, Buckinghamshire; New College, Oxford, B.A. (first-class honours in English) 1950. Served in the Grenadier Guards and in Special Intelligence, 1943-47. Married the novelist Iris Murdoch in 1956. Member, St. Antony's and Magdalen Colleges, Oxford, 1951-55, Lecturer and Fellow, New College, Oxford, 1955-74, and since 1974 Fellow of St. Catherine's College, Oxford, and Warton Professor of English Literature, Oxford University. Recipient: Heinemann Literary Award, 1971. Fellow, Royal Society of Literature, 1972. Address: Cedar Lodge, Steeple Aston, Oxford, England.

PUBLICATIONS

Criticism

The Romantic Survival: A Study in Poetic Evolution.   London, Constable, 1957; New York, Basic Books, 1959.
The Characters of Love: A Study in the Literature of Personality.   London, Constable, 1960; New York, Basic Books, 1961.
"Keats and Reality," in *Proceedings of the British Academy 48.*   London, Oxford University Press, 1963..
Tolstoy and the Novel.   London, Chatto and Windus, 1966; New York, Viking Press, 1967
Introduction to *Jude the Obscure*, by Thomas Hardy.   New York, Heritage Press, 1969.
"The Pastoral of Intellect," in *Critical Essays on George Eliot*, edited by Barbara Hardy. London, Routledge, 1970.

Pushkin: A Comparative Commentary.   London, Cambridge University Press, 1971.
"Character and Consciousness," in *New Literary History* (Charlottesville, Virginia), 5, 1974.
Introduction to *Far from the Madding Crowd*, by Thomas Hardy.   London, Macmillan, 1974.
"Time and the Trojans," in *Essays in Criticism* (Oxford), 25, 1975.
"Only Critics Can't Play," in *W.H. Auden: A Tribute*, edited by Stephen Spender. London, Weidenfeld and Nicolson, and New York, Macmillan, 1975.
The Uses of Division: Unity and Disharmony in Literature.   London, Chatto and Windus, and New York, Viking, 1976.
An Essay on Hardy.   London, and New York, Cambridge University Press, 1978.
"Under Cover of Decadence," in *Vladimir Nabokov: A Tribute*, edited by Peter Quennell. London, Weidenfeld and Nicolson, 1979; New York, Morrow, 1980.
Shakespeare and Tragedy.   London, and Boston, Routledge, 1981.

Verse

El Dorado: The Newdigate Prize Poem, 1950.   Oxford, Blackwell, 1951.

Novel

In Another Country.   London, Constable, and New York, Coward McCann, 1955.

Editor, *The Portable Tolstoy.*   New York, Viking, and London, Penguin, 1978.

*   *   *

In *The Romantic Survival* John Bayley develops a conception of romanticism which extends well beyond the usual references to an historical period and characteristic subject-matter or style. His first step, however, is historical: he reminds us that for the English romantic poets the imagination was a vital power which partly creates the world we perceive, capable of reconciling man and nature and healing that division between subject and object fostered by eighteenth century psychology and science. Thus self-consciousness and a sense of obligation weigh heavily on the serious artist working after Wordsworth and Coleridge—"the self-consciousness of the poet about why and how he wrote poetry, the responsibility of the poet towards [his] new duties." The later English poets often failed to live up to the high demands of their calling as prophets and unacknowledged legislators: in Tennyson and Arnold, for example, "the grand idea of poetry as an all-embracing and unifying influence ...had already tacitly been given up. Before ugliness and *Philistinism* (Arnold's new-coined word) the Romantic Imagination was in retreat. It found itself unable to contain and absorb such things." The job was taken over by the novelists, with their firmer grasp of social realities and their gentler demands on their readers (after all, it was easier to enjoy passively the narratives of Scott than to join in the mental explorations of *The Prelude*). Meanwhile, the French poets were proudly justifying the isolation of the artist and his contempt for society; and thus for the Symbolists and their English followers at the close of the century, "ethical irresponsibility, or rather subsuming ethics and aesthetics under the same range of responses" was a natural enough consequence. Romanticism comes to rest unexpectedly in *The Renaissance*, whose conclusion Pater at first suppressed, fearful of its effect on the morals of young men. The emergence of Hulme, Eliot, and to some extent Pound therefore constitutes a kind of counter-reformation which rejects the claims of the individual imagination and calculating hedonism. Here Bayley observes that

[Eliot's] insistence on unified sensibility should be seen as part of the movement towards classicism which Hulme had begun; and it is difficult not to feel that beside the creative imagination whose enormous, if disorderly, cult in the nineteenth-century had produced so much, both Eliot's famous phrase and Hulme's Fancy seem as concepts rather devitalized and prim.

But while he may have relatively little taste for the classical dryness of Eliot, Bayley is not primarily an apologist for romanticism. Whether writing about Chaucer or Auden or Pushkin, he is mainly concerned with defining the strengths and weaknesses of a mode of creation which may appear at any time in history.

Bayley maintains that despite Eliot's influential classicism and the anti-romantic tendency of modern criticism in general, Yeats, Auden and Dylan Thomas "constitute the greatest and most interesting exponents of a new sort of romantic revival [in whose work] the original vitality and breadth of the movement have been restored." The weaknesses of romanticism as Bayley defines it are the inherent weaknesses of a radically individual and hence egotistical way of conceiving reality: "Crudely speaking, the criterion of romantic success is to imagine a world different from anyone else's" Thus Yeats' world merely *seems* to be the same world in which we fall in love and make revolutions:

> His vision and his poetry are equally artificial, equally the product of the will.... In his desire for romantic wholeness of vision and poetic personality Yeats is prepared to throw over the whole romantic conception of the ideal, and the spontaneous overflow. It follows from his idea of the inflexible wholeness of artificiality that there must be nothing *outside* poetry which either causes its flow or prevents it.... How could the poetry be anywhere *outside* the poet? It is an inflexible application of the romantic egoism that the poet's universe must be purely his own.

Past and present exist for Yeats only so that he "may perceive how to fasten on to the contrast and make poetry out of it":

> There are no mysteries, no profundities outside [the circle of Yeats' art] which...poetry can touch but not transmute; nothing which poetry must seek to become part of, rather than to absorb into itself.... Yeats, as we have said, brings Romanticism back to earth, but he pays the price of making himself and his poetry the measure of all things. So, it may be argued, do all romantic poets, but never before with Yeats's self-conscious deliberation.

In this respect, and despite obvious differences in range and tone. Auden and Yeats are both essentially romantics, devouring egotists, tricking out their autistic worlds with semblances of people, ideas and events:

> Now Auden's own poetic vision, where it is most effective and compelling, seems to owe much to Yeats's example.... Auden succeeds just as effectively as Yeats in endowing the apparent trivialities of life with a mysterious significance, a kind of esoteric harmony, and this vision is just as uncommitted to an allegiance *outside its own existence as poetry* as is Yeats's own. This particular romantic survival, in fact, depends on the poet's success in creating a world constructed of simple, recognizable materials—friends, houses, careers, cars, gasometers, the Communist Party—but transformed by a fine conspiracy of style and manner into something *eo ipso*, an aesthetic world in which, as Auden puts it, "what delights us is just that it neither is nor could possibly become one in which we could breathe or behave." Auden, like Yeats, has read all the latest theories, and is able to absorb a great deal more contemporary detail into his private magical universe. But it is a universe of essentially the same kind, insulated, unique, and founded on the same original rejection by the Symbolists of the nineteenth-century material world in favour of a mind-created structure.

Parts of Bayley's argument may be checked against the reader's own sense of cultural history, but his assertions concerning Auden and Yeats are difficult to deal with critically. They remain precisely that—assertions which are simply proposed rather than argued or proved. After quoting part of "The Gyres" for example, with its references to Empedocles, Hector and Troy, Bayley states that

The effect of incantation is obvious and superb. The identity of Empedocles, and why his influence should have been so unsettling, remain unimportant. The forces that threaten to destroy us are of an august kind, Yeats seems to be saying, and we should have enough sense of style to find that consoling. None the less, it is a long way from the world of Hector to the world of Hitler: we are not Housman's "Spartans on the sea-wet rock," and we are not the tragic heroes and heroines whom Yeats invokes as models of decorum when times are bad.

And again after quoting the well known stanza from "Lapis Lazuli" in which Yeats proclaims that "Hamlet and Lear are gay." Bayley concludes that

Our individual lives, in the midst of the twentieth century, do not seem much related to this. They are complex, difficult, random, perhaps horrifying, certainly concerned with issues which appear to demand some other response than tragic gaiety. Yeats's "acceptance" of life, in fact, often seems very much like a renunciation—where poetry is concerned—of what actually happens in life.

Are the obvious implications of such observations reasonable? Is it really "true" that for many readers Yeats' world is not their world and that his responses are so irrelevant or inadequate? If we happen to feel otherwise, what kinds of arguments can we use? In short, it is hard to see how Bayley's often quite subtle and ingenious assertions might convince anyone not already prepared to accept them. He does relatively little to compel us to feel the lines his way.

Romantic egotism is no less important in *The Characters of Love*. For Bayley love is the joyous sense of another person's uniqueness, the delight we take purely in the fact of his existence. But it is not love merely as a subject to write about that concerns Bayley here: he argues that if a writer is to create memorable characters *he* must love them in this way; he must accept their individuality gladly, as a parent rejoices in the individuality of his children. "Real" characters are not projections of his own ego or parts to be manipulated into some pleasing aesthetic design. And it is this kind of love—the love which Dickens and Scott have for their characters—which seems to be disappearing from modern fiction:

What I understand by an author's love for his characters...is analogous to our feelings towards those we love in life; and an intense interest in their personalities combines with a sort of detached solicitude, a respect for their freedom. This might be—indeed should be—a truism, but I suppose it to be one no longer. The writers whom we admire today do not appear to love their characters, and the critics who appraise their books show no sign of doing so either.

Thus Proust is just as romantic—that is, just as egotisical—as Yeats. The pejorative implications of the term are now much stronger than they were in *The Romantic Survival*. If we assume that love is the basis of morals, then inadequate artistry is a kind of inadequate morality. In any event, Bayley examines in detail *Troilus and Criseyde, Othello* and *The Golden Bowl* and argues that they succeed because Chaucer, Shakespeare and James create their characters with love and allow them complex individuality.

Bayley is frankly nostalgic for the older way of creating character but admits that it may be impossible to approach human nature as Scott did, now that there is a "total absence of agreement about what people are really like and how they can be portrayed." (This may be true, but it may also be true that having absorbed Marx and Freud we know only too well what people are like and are properly suspicious of sentimentality.) At the very center of Bayley's position, underlying his admirable charity towards human beings, is a belief in "nature" which is virtually the same as that of classical humanism—and implies many of the same standards for the artist who attempts to imitate nature:

"Nature" suggests an almost involuntary fidelity to what is constant in human types and human affairs; to the repetition of birth and death, joy and sorrow; to the humours of men and women and the peculiarities that are at once recognized as universal. It implies a lack of pretension—the author gets no particular credit for his awareness of Nature though he may get credit for portraying it well.

Perhaps "nature" in this sense no longer exists for us either, but Bayley ends *The Characters of Love* on a note of hope as well as charity:

> as long as human beings accept one another with love their artists will try to embody that love in the representation of men and women and of the external world. And when we look back on the living persons who have been created by the great artists of our language, from Chaucer to Henry James, it is surely desirable from time to time—instead of submitting them to the solvents of our local consciousness and our immediate preoccupations with value and meaning—to emphasize and salute them for what they are and to respond to them as they deserve.

Tolstoy appears briefly in *The Characters of Love* as another example of the artist who loves his characters, a point which is equally important in *Tolstoy and the Novel*:

> Indeed we might make a distinction, in the context of Russian and Western literature, between the author who writes about himself and his experiences, and the author who *exists*. Gide writes about himself; Tolstoy writes about himself; but with the former we feel the will to create and impose upon us the idea of a unique and significant person; with the latter, only the transparent statement of an existence.... [Tolstoy] plays out in himself, and on his scale, the most inevitable of human dramas. He *is* the state of our existence.

But this is clearly a more complex case of egotism: on closer examination Tolstoy seems no less egotistical than Proust or Yeats but somehow manages to escape the limitations of romanticism ("how" he does this is unexplained and perhaps inexplicable):

> Tolstoy's world is in the fullest sense that of the solipsistic consciousness, and that of external inevitability. In how many Tolstoyan novelists (Hemingway is one example) are we not aware of the primacy of the first consideration—"all that exists is but me"—and the total neglect of the second? The more we read Tolstoy the more we become aware of the clear and harmonious relation of the two kinds of cognition, and the sense of liberation—of his world and hence of ourselves—that follows from it. The greatest art is something of a trick—the happy yet laborious coincidence that constitutes a trick.

Just as Tolstoy becomes the subject of an extended study, so Pushkin, who appeared briefly in *Tolstoy and the Novel* as another "sympathetic genius," becomes in turn the subject of detailed analysis. The audience here, however, is much more specialized—in fact Bayley seems to be addressing mainly those students who are learning Russian in order to read Pushkin. *Pushkin* is much less speculative than its predecessors but its conclusions are the familiar ones: "like Shakespeare," Pushkin is "Protean"; his genius is "generous and unportentous":

> The technical seriousness of Babel, the personal obsession of Kafka and Genet, the yet more claustrophobic self-obsession of Hemingway—all display prose as a means to find the writer's self, and all possess the concomitant inability to allow the reader to manoeuvre on his own. He must either identify with the author or get out. But prose fiction for Pushkin is a liberating because a genuinely impersonal instrument, taking for granted the neutral existence of everything to which it gives artifice, proportion, and accord: it can never create its own exclusive world of style.

In *Tolstoy and the Novel* Bayley gives us his clearest statement thus far of the novel's primary function: "No one who is not interested in himself can be interested in a great novel, and in Tolstoy we experience in greater measure than in any other novelist the recognition of ourselves that leads to increased self-knowledge." If this is the case, then it is easy enough to see why and how romanticism falls short: when we go to works of fiction to learn about ourselves we should find there other complex and independent beings and not merely the disguised projections of a powerful creating ego.

The problem of egotism continues to engage Bayley—"obsess" would really be a better word—in *The Uses of Division* and *An Essay on Hardy*, both of them highly idiosyncratic and personal books. In the latter Bayley refers, with obvious approval, to some passages from John Fowles' "Notes on an Unfinished Novel":

> The story I am telling is all imagination. These characters I create never existed outside my own mind. If I have pretended until now to know my characters' minds and innermost thoughts it is because I am writing in...a convention universally accepted at the time of my story: that the novelist stands next to God. He may not know all, yet he tries to pretend that he does. But I live in the world of Alain Robbe-Grillet and Roland Barthes.
>
> We...know that a genuinely created world must be independent of its creator; a planned world (a world that fully reveals its planning) is a dead world.

That phrase, "a planned world...is a dead world," might well serve as a motto for these recent books, and for almost all of Bayley's earlier criticism: in *The Uses of Division* he is interested in the ways in which unresolved tensions within writers are reflected in their works and give readers a liberating sense of freedom from a totally planned design; in *An Essay on Hardy* he is concerned primarily with the ways that writer achieved greatness "without any of the creator's egocentric energy and will to power."

Bayley opens *The Uses of Division* with an engaging admission:

> Authors a critic has been especially familiar with over a number of years may have led him to adopt certain principles of understanding, standards and controls which make more clear aspects of their genius or areas of their work, and which in turn help him to judge other kinds and degrees of achievement. The clue that has come up constantly during my study and enjoyment of the writers who figure in this book is that of the involuntary divisions, amounting to a total disunity, which seems to characterize the reality of their art, and to make them what they are.

The lines are drawn almost immediately. On one side we have the tyrannizing creator who has palpable designs upon us, strictly controlling our responses. He may be a dazzling craftsman, but he gives us totally planned structure in which "there is nothing unsettled or left over to give the whole job a saving instability, to invite by reticence or irresolution participation in the processes of genius." Proust, not surprisingly, is the primary example:

> It may be that ultimately, with Proust, we feel we are not in the world of a great transforming spirit of the imagination, like those as diverse as Tolstoy or Hardy or Racine, but what amounts to a brilliant *translator*...or memoirist, Saint-Simon of the self, whose powers were made for this job alone and not for any complex and irresolute interplay between spirit and the world.

On the other side we have Jane Austen (who is both "moralist and anarch"), Dickens and Kipling (sometimes), Tolstoy, and as always for Bayley, Keats and Shakespeare. The writers he values most, then, are the ones whose own uncertainties and divisions allow their readers to move into new, free spaces:

> The point would be how such a literature works on us, and how we work upon it, finding what accident rather than intention put there, and perceiving ourselves how contradictions enlarge and emancipate the world of experience it offers.

Whether Bayley means simply emancipation *from* rigid patterns and palpable designs, or has some more positive conception of freedom in mind, is not clear.

A systematic study of this kind of literature would be fascinating (as Robert Martin Adams, for example, has demonstrated in *Strains of Discord*), but it is here that Bayley's own unwillingness to construct a "planned" critical world—and thus possibly a dead one—will disappoint many, perhaps most, of his readers. He certainly disappointed Wayne Booth, a critic who does not really like prolonged instability (see *A Rhetoric of Irony*) and ambiguity (see *The Rhetoric of Fiction*). In a no-nonsense review of *The Uses of Division* Booth complained that Bayley offers us at least seventeen kinds of tensions or "divisions": there are (in his summary) tensions between a tightly structured plot and richly imagined details seeking their freedom; between aspects of an author's genius and what his social self will accept; between parts willed by the conscious artist and parts dictated by instinct, and so on. Seven types or seventeen types, what matters is that Bayley has failed to define and organize his terms and categories and so has produced what appears to be a "sheer muddle," an "engaging but finally incoherent monologue." Moreover, according to Booth,

> Rival voices are not allowed a hearing; their very existence is implicitly denied. The book is written as if for the first time in human history a critic had chosen to probe the true diversities and complexities of authors and works. It ignores even the many partisans of freedom of the past few decades who have taken the case for disunity immeasurably farther than does Mr. Bayley.

The last point is very well taken. In Robinson Crusoe-like fashion, Bayley raises problems which Richards and Empson and Cleanth Brooks had faced many years before (the problems, that is, of "irony" and ambiguity, or more accurately multiple meanings within an utterance which conflict with rather than support each other). They might have helped Bayley, and in any event a nod in their direction would have been a pleasant gesture. The problem of Bayley's refusal to be systematic is more complicated, as the next book indicates.

An Essay on Hardy is a kind of luminous fog, an elegant and utterly sincere tribute to a problematic writer whose world Bayley has entered into more completely than any other critic before him. Hardy, he tell us, often gives the impression of "a man who would rather be silent than speak," and perhaps he hopes we will think of Karl Kraus, and of his remark that no truly honest man would be a writer. This means—this may mean—that the man who sees clearly and dispassionately sees too much to settle for verbal forms which seem to fix, define and exclude. In any event, a few passages will show the essential similarity between this book and the earlier criticism:

> But when [Hardy's] characters bumble, his text bumbles too; he does not in the least mind falling flat, if there is no occasion for rising, *and in life as he saw it there seldom is.*

> However sensational their contrivances, and their vocabulary, we can feel beneath the text the philosophy of *He Never Expected Much*. Nor should the reader expect too much, *for what is true of life must also be true of art.*

> Something resembling weakness is indeed a key factor in Hardy's text; its manifestations baffling but also, deep down, reassuring. It seems part of an admission that for a dealer in words life must be talked about, but that talking about it won't do much good.

> Throughout his work, the ways in which we are absorbed into it, moved, delighted, are never co-ordinated, never really unified.

> His vision refused to go past appearances, was stubbornly unsynthesising.

> Hardy always sought to "give shape and coherence to a series of seemings," as he said in the Preface to *Jude*, yet he also knew that what remains is the seemings themselves, *endowed with the immutable authority of fact, of things that were and are.*

I have emphasized those phrases which indicate a central problem in all of Bayley's criticism and which may be even more clearly demonstrated in another instance. He speaks with approval of the ways in which component parts of Hardy's prose "seem unconscious of each other's presence." Even his syntax often "seems not to know what other clauses and phrases are about"; and Bayley then gives us a passage which begins: "Standing in the centre, the sky overhead was met by a circular horizon of fern: this grew nearly to the bottom of the slope and then abruptly ceased." What will seem to many readers inattentiveness and grammatical vagueness becomes, in Bayley's view, an effective artistic embodiment of an attitude towards the world. The problem, in short, is what Yvor Winters long ago called "the fallacy of imitative form": does an artist have the right to make his manner follow his matter, when that matter is the randomness of things and the contingency of life? For Winters, of course, the answer is no. Bayley is perfectly well aware of the problem (Winters is one of the very few critics he mentions, even in passing)—and utterly untroubled by it. So much so that he is willing to let his own criticism mirror some of the same uncertainty and division present in his chosen writers. Booth called Bayley's judgments "gratuitous, undefended and cocksure," but while they may be "undefended," they are hardly gratuitous and certainly not cocksure: Bayley's tone is consistently elliptical and reticent. Perhaps this is what Booth meant when he called *The Uses of Division* an "incoherent monologue." In fact monologue is a good word, but it might be more accurate still to think of Bayley's recent criticism as a gentle, unassuming monologue, overheard from a distance.

BENTLEY, Eric (Russell).   American.   Born in Bolton, Lancashire, England, 14 September 1916. Educated at Bolton School; Oxford University, B.A. 1938, B.Lit. 1939; Yale University, New Haven, Connecticut, Ph.D. 1941. Married Maja Tschernjakow (marriage dissolved); Joanne Davis in 1953; has twin sons. Taught at Black Mountain College, North Carolina, 1942-44, and University of Minnesota, Minneapolis, 1944-48; Brander Matthews Professor of Dramatic Literature, Columbia University, New York, 1952-69; Charles Eliot Norton Professor of Poetry, Harvard University, Cambridge, Massachusetts, 1960-61. Since 1974, Katharine Cornell Professor of Theatre, State University of New York at Buffalo. Drama Critic, *New Republic*, New York, 1952-56. Recipient: Guggenheim Fellowship, 1948, 1967; Rockefeller grant, 1949; National Institute of Arts and Letters grant, 1953; Longview Award, for criticism, 1961; Ford grant, 1964; George Jean Nathan Award, for criticism, 1967. D.F.A.: University of Wisconsin, Madison; D.Litt.: University of East Anglia, Norwich, 1979. Address: 194 Riverside Drive, New York, New York 10025, U.S.A.

PUBLICATIONS

Criticism

The Playwright as Thinker: A Study of Drama in Modern Times.   New York, Reynal and Hitchcock, 1946; as *The Modern Theatre: A Study of Dramatists and the Drama,* London, Hale, 1948.
Bernard Shaw: A Reconsideration.   New York, New Directions, 1947; London, Hale, 1950; revised edition as *Bernard Shaw, 1856-1950*, New Directions, 1957; as *Bernard Shaw*, London, Methuen, 1967.
In Search of Theatre.   New York, Knopf, 1953; London, Dobson, 1954.
The Dramatic Event: An American Chronicle.   New York, Horizon Press, and London, Dobson, 1954.
What Is Theatre? A Query in Chronicle Form.   New York, Horizon Press, 1956; London, Dobson, 1957.
The Life of the Drama.   New York, Atheneum, 1964; London, Methuen, 1965.
The Theatre of Commitment and Other Essays on Drama in Our Society.   New York, Atheneum, 1967; London, Methuen, 1968.
What Is Theatre? Incorporating "The Dramatic Event"and Other Reviews 1944-1967.   New York, Atheneum, 1968; London, Methuen, 1969.

Theatre of War: Comments on 32 Occasions. New York, Viking Press, and London, Eyre Methuen, 1972.

The Brecht Commentaries 1934-1980. New York, Grove Press, and London, Eyre Methuen, 1981.

Plays

A Time to Live, and A Time to Die, adaptations of plays by Euripides and Sophocles (produced New York, 1967). New York, Grove Press, 1967.

Sketches in *DMZ Revue* (produced New York, 1968).

The Red White and Black, music by Brad Burg (produced New York, 1970). Published in *Liberation* (New York), May 1971.

Are You Now or Have You Ever Been: The Investigation of Show-Business by the Un-American Activities Committee, 1947-1958 (produced New Haven, Connecticut, 1972; Birmingham, 1976). New York, Harper, 1972.

The Recantation of Galileo Galilei: Scenes from History Perhaps (produced Detroit, 1973). New York, Harper, 1972.

Expletive Deleted (produced New York, 1974). Published in *Win* (New York), 6 June 1974.

From the Memoirs of Pontius Pilate (produced Buffalo, 1976).

As You Know (produced New York, 1973; Birmingham, 1976; London, 1977).

From the Memoirs (produced New York, 1976).

Rallying Cries: Three Plays. Washington, D. C., New Rupublic Books, 1977.

Larry Parks' Day in Court (produced New York, 1979).

Other

A Century of Hero-Worship: A Study of the Idea of Heroism in Carlyle and Nietzsche, with Notes on Other Hero-Worshipers of Modern Times. Philadelphia, Lippincott, 1944; as *The Cult of the Superman*, London, Hale, 1947.

Editor, *The Importance of "Scrutiny": Selections from "Scrutiny," A Quarterly Review, 1932-1948.* New York, G.W. Stewart, 1948.

Editor and Part Translator, *From the Modern Repertory.* Bloomington, Indiana University Press, series 1 and 3, 1949, 1965; Denver, University of Denver Press, series 2, 1952.

Editor, *The Play: A Critical Anthology.* New York, Prentice Hall, 1951.

Editor, *Shaw on Music.* New York, Doubleday, 1955.

Editor and Part Translator, *The Modern Theatre.* New York, Doubleday, 6 vols., 1955-60.

Editor and Part Translator, *The Classic Theatre.* New York, Doubleday, 4 vols., 1958-61.

Editor and Translator, *Let's Get a Divorce and Other Plays.* New York, Hill and Wang, 1958.

Editor and Part Translator, *Works of Bertolt Brecht.* New York, Grove Press, 1962-.

Editor and Part Translator, *The Genius of the Italian Theatre.* New York, New American Library, 1964.

Editor, *The Storm over "The Deputy."* New York, Grove Press, 1964.

Editor, *Songs of Bertolt Brecht and Hanns Eisler....* New York, Oak Publications, 1966.

Editor, *The Theory of the Modern Stage: An Introduction to Modern Theatre and Drama.* London, Penguin, 1968.

Editor and Part Translator, *The Great Playwrights: Twenty-Five Plays with Comments by Critics and Scholars.* New York, Doubleday, 2 vols., 1970.

Translator, *The Private Life of the Master Race*, by Bertolt Brecht. New York, James Laughlin, 1944.

Translator, *Parables for the Theatre*: *The Good Woman of Setzuan, and the Caucasian Chalk Circle*, by Bertolt Brecht.   Minneapolis, University of Minnesota Press, 1948; revised edition, 1965.

Translator, *Orpheus in the Underworld* (libretto) by Hector Cremieux and Ludovic Halévy.   New York, Program Publishing Company, 1956.

Recordings (all Folkways): *Bentley on Brecht*; *Brecht Before the Un-American Committee*; *A Man's A Man* (Spoken Arts); *Songs of Hanns Eisler*; *The Exception and the Rule*; *The Elephant Calf*, *Bentley on Biermann*; *Eric Bentley Sings The Queen of 42nd Street*.

*   *   *

In his first book of dramatic criticism, *The Playwright as Thinker*, Eric Bentley is concerned primarily with the rise of naturalism and the shifting fortunes of tragedy and comedy in the modern theatre. Strengthened by the growth of a middle class and "democratic reformism," naturalism or "realism" ("the conquest of a great area of human experience previously ignored...if not altogether taboo in art") abandoned the elevated style for "simple and colloquial discourse"and embraced "all writing in which the natural world is candidly represented": its precursors are Balzac, Flaubert and the Goncourts, its official spokesman Zola, and its success, of course, phenomenal. Without naturalism, as Bentley points out, there would have been no Ibsen or Shaw, no Chekov or Odets; but the triumph of naturalism also provoked one of those reactions which are as predictable in critical histories as they are in physics. Thus Rémy de Gourmont proclaimed, in 1891, that naturalism was finished: "Villiers de l'Isle-Adam is our Flaubert! Laforgue and Mallarmé are our masters." And without the rear-guard actions of these writers there would have been no Yeats, Claudel or Cocteau. Admitting some oversimplification here, Bentley ranges one set of terms on the side of naturalism (slice of life, social, political, propagandist, objective) and another set on the side of anti-naturalism (fantasy, individualism, aesthetic, poetic, subjective).

The distinctions between tragedy and comedy are no less important in *The Playwright as Thinker*, but here Bentley is less prepared to generalize. Although he makes a number of shrewd suggestions in passing, he is reluctant to theorize beyond a certain point:

Tragedy is a topic that easily lures us into talking nonsense. On this subject even more than on others the critic tends to generalize from a favorite example or merely to play high-minded cadenzas. The trouble always is that tragedy has been a different thing for every major practitioner. And if anything is more elusive than a correct description of the tragic it is a correct description of the comic.

And again, after examining some varieties of comedy, Bentley observes that

discussions of Shaw, Wilde, and Pirandello can go on indefinitely. Would it help us nearer to a definition of comedy than we were at the beginning of the chapter? If one cannot say *a priori* what comedy is, if it is hard to reach more than platitudinous definitions by generalizing about all known schools of comedy, we might doubt whether the exact study of particular comedies is of much assistance either. Obviously such a study cannot enable us to characterize *other* works. The question is rather what it reveals in particular comedies that superficial acquaintance would not reveal. In the present instance four analyses—correlated with other knowledge—have suggested some notions about comedy, notions which might plausibly be considered either too tentative to be of use. Detailed study of particular works naturally calls attention from generic to individual qualities, the only consolation being that greatness in art always takes an individual—a unique—form. One would never study the variety of religious experiences if one felt that one already had a good definition of religion. Having studied those varieties, one is less prepared to define religion than ever.

The arguments therefore tend to be historical rather than theoretical at this point in Bentley's thinking. He traces the rise of a "middle" genre, bourgeois tragedy, examines the important differences between Ibsen and Wagner, and concludes that one line of development leads to

Shaw (who is to comedy what Ibsen is to tragedy) while another leads to the pale experiments of Maeterlinck and Andreyev. Bentley does not labor the distinctions, however, nor does he force individual works to serve as examples of some overriding dialectical force at work in the history of the drama: his aim is to illuminate the "real identity"of the best playwrights and the kind of greatness which takes on "individual form." Thus the title of the book is misleading if it suggests that he is preoccupied with the presence of "ideas" in modern drama. Nevertheless,

> although the "theatre of ideas " has been developed chiefly since Hebbel, in a broader sense the playwright has always been a thinker, a teacher, or, in modern jargon, a propagandist. Born out of Greek religion, reborn out of medieval catholicism, Occidental drama has almost never rid itself of its admonitory tone and its salvationist spirit.

Yet at the same time the mere presence of serious thought has no necessary relationship to dramatic excellence: "What offers itself as theatre must submit to be judged as theatre and not appeal to a higher court." This seems to suggest the existence of some principles intrinsic to dramatic effectiveness, but the argument goes no further.

Twenty years later, however, in his finest book, *The Life of the Drama*, Bentley attempts nothing less than a comprehensive theory of the drama in general and the psychological causes of our continuing susceptibility to its basic forms. *The Life of the Drama* is Aristotelian in spirit, then, and often in detail as well. For Bentley, as for Aristotle, art is imitative; it engages our interest and causes pleasure simply because "pleasure resides in the act of recognition." The various dramatic forms or genres may be differentiated according to their proper subject matters and their differing powers to move us in distinct and definable ways. We have an "insatiable appetite" for knowledge, for learning by imitation and recognition, for discovering the hidden lives of others; we insist that our own lives be dramatic, as our dreams and fantasies attest. Restless and easily bored, we want to be "caught up in someone else's excitement" and the root of our responsiveness lies in an innate tendency to violence and aggression:

> if you wish to attract the audience's attention, be violent; if you wish to hold it, be violent again. It is true that bad plays are founded on such principles, but it is not true that good plays are written by defying them.... To be human is to revel in mishaps and disasters.... The psychology is sound and each man is a human being—a specimen of human psychology—before he is a scholar and a gentleman.

This emphasis on aggression is not particularly Aristotelian, but like Aristotle once again, Bentley insists on the primacy of plot, that rational arrangement of irrational matter, the "rearrangement of the incidents in the order most calculated to have the right effect." The "final cause," in Aristotelian terms, is the intended effect, that for which everything exists. Just as Aristotle specifies the constituent parts of tragedy—plot, agents (in their moral and intellectual capacities) and diction—so Bentley devises his kindred categories of plot, character, thought (the "ideas" in a work and not Aristotle's term for the reasoning characteristic of a particular agent), dialogue and enactment (the psychological mechanisms of role-playing, substitution and identification). Aristotle considers only tragedy (though there are some significant references in passing to comedy, the subject of another, lost treatise); Bentley develops fully a theory of five genres: melodrama is a primitive form of tragedy which exaggerates the incidents of the plot and the differences between "good" and "bad" characters and has as its proper end the evoking of fear (which is a form of self-pity), whereas farce is a primitive form of comedy, based on the free play of aggression and the therapeutic acting out of our "most treasured, unmentionable wishes":

> while defining melodrama as savage and infantile, I have sought also to defend it as an amusing and thrilling emanation of a natural self which we do well not to disown. And I follow Aristotle, rather than Plato, on the question of violence in art, concluding that melodrama, far from tending to make Hitlers of us, affords us, insofar as it has any effect at all, a healthy release, a modest catharsis. Much the same can be said of farce, except that the principle motor of farce is not the impulse to flee (or Fear), but the impulse to attack (or Hostility). In music, says Nietzsche, the passions enjoy themselves. In melodrama fear enjoys itself, in farce hostility enjoys itself.

Tragedy, on the other hand, forces the audience to confront the radically painful, the chaos and "purposelessness of life":

> tragedy cannot be contained within any philosophy: it is not even existentialist—it is existential. What the Restoration did to Shakespeare was to accommodate him to a philosophy. The happy ending to *Lear* makes sense. Sense is *exactly* what it makes. Shakespeare's play does not make sense. Sense is exactly what it does not make: it is an image of the nonsensical life we live, the nonsensical death we die.

Thus tragedy embodies a view of life Bentley himself seems to accept; but while it may be existential, tragedy is not despairing, partly because there is dignity in the virtue of endurance and partly because the act of giving form to the formless and sense to the senseless produces a kind of transcendence:

> Tragedy embodies an experience of chaos, and the only cosmos that the tragic poet can guarantee to offset it with is the cosmos of his tragedy with its integration of plot, character, dialogue and idea.... [The] aesthetic transcendence of suffering, disorder, and meaninglessness has a moral value. It signifies courage, which one might call the tragic virtue. And there is an element of wisdom in tragedy. Giving up the universe as an insoluble riddle...there is some wisdom in this. And there is more in acceptance of mystery.

Pure tragedy, however, may be impossible in an unheroic age: tragicomedy, to which Bentley devotes his final chapter, is our characteristic mode. And while it can be differentiated from comedy and tragedy, it is, like those major forms, "a way of trying to cope with despair, mental suffering, guilt and anxiety"; and like them it has the "same heuristic intent: self-knowledge." With its more disturbing appeal to comic *and* tragic emotions tragicomedy may come closer to the nihilism which seems to be the logical consequence of existentialism. But once again, art and nihilism are fundamentally opposed:

> All art is a challenge to despair, and the type of tragicomedy I am describing [in Beckett] has addressed itself to the peculiarly harrowing, withering despair of our epoch. Whatever one may say of it, one cannot say it does not get down to bedrock.... But precisely in this it is reassuring. Nothing less drastic would have given us any comfort, for we would not have believed it, any more than we believe bishops and politicians.... The appeal of that comedy which is infused with gloom and ends badly, that tragedy which is shot through with a comedy that only makes the outlook still bleaker, is that it holds out to us the only kind of hope we are in a position to accept.

In a handsome tribute to a fellow critic Bentley once observed that Stark Young was

> utterly a part of the theatrical occasion. In each article he tells you about it, yet as one civilized person to another, what it looked like, how it unfolded, what is essential to it, what considerations it leads to outside itself.... Simple as a prescription: rare as a fact; and hard to do.

Bentley's own practical criticism deserves the same praise for the same reasons. The best of it now appears in *In Search of Theatre*, in which he records his tour of theatres in Berlin, Paris and elsewhere, shortly after the end of World War II; if his later collections, *The Dramatic Event* and *What Is Theatre?* are less interesting is simply because his subject here, American drama during the late 50's and early 60's, is so dreary. Even when his targets are easy ones, however, Bentley is a stylish and entertaining critic. James Agate, Kenneth Tynan, Stark Young (in spite of Bentley's generosity), John Simon—the competition is not very impressive: Bentley is the only recent theatre critic who belongs in the company of Beerbohm and Shaw.

BEWLEY, Marius. American. Born in St. Louis Missouri, 23 January 1918. Educated at St. Louis University, B.A. 1938; Downing College, Cambridge, B.A. 1940, M.A. 1946, D. Phil. 1956. Assistant Professor of English, Catholic University of St. Louis, 1953-59; Visiting Assistant Professor, Wellesley College, Massachusetts, 1959-60; Assistant Professor, Connecticut College for Women, New London, 1960-61; Associate Professor, 1961-63, and Professor, 1963-66, Fordham University, New York; Professor of English, Rutgers University, New Brunswick, New Jersey, 1967-73. Member, Editorial Board, *The Hudson Review*, New York, 1966-73. Recipient: Rockefeller Foundation grant, 1952; American Council of Learned Societies Fellowship, 1958. *Died 24 January 1973.*

PUBLICATIONS

Criticism

The Complex Fate: Hawthorne, Henry James and Some Other American Writers. London, Chatto and Windus, 1952; New York, Grove Press, 1954.
The Eccentric Design: Form in the Classic American Novel. London, Chatto and Windus, and New York, Columbia University Press, 1959.
Masks and Mirrors: Essays in Criticism. New York, Atheneum, and London, Chatto and Windus, 1970.

Other

Editor, *Selected Poetry*, by John Donne. New York, New American Library, 1966.
Editor, *The English Romantic Poets: An Anthology with Commentaries.* New York, Modern Library, 1970.

*   *   *

In "A New Kind of Poetry?" one of the essays included in his last collection, *Masks and Mirrors*, Marius Bewley carefully distinguishes his critical approach from the preferred methods of the "'American auxiliaries...of such English critics as Eliot, Leavis, Empson, and Richards" which "rapidly proceeded to Alexandrian excess":

The justified word, as these critics understood it, was a complex organism perfectly adjusted to the particular poetic environment in which it lived and fed and bred. Unfortunately, the Alexandrian critics of America were inclined to stop here, and they began to talk rather too much about the "autonomy" of a given poem. But this was a conviction the English critics were not inclined to share. If they believed that the poem had to be read and evaluated in terms of its own verbal being, and not as a surrogate for social history, economic motives, archetypal patterns, or Freudian analysis, they continued to recognize that words and poems had responsibilities beyond themselves: responsibilities to meanings at many different levels—meanings *outside* the poem which were nevertheless relevant to the poem, to the reader who *remade* it in reading it, and was in turn altered by his reading; and meanings to the spirit of the age, which helped to make it, and which it helped to make. For the most part English criticism resisted the Alexandrian concentration of focus and exclusiveness of purpose that the American critics of that day rejoiced in, and for whom the justified word had pretty much become the antinomian word which could do no evil.

The British critic Bewley has uppermost in mind, of course, is his mentor, F.R. Leavis. And although Leavis and Bewley can be painstakingly close readers when it suits their purposes, they are primarily concerned with placing the writer under consideration in terms of an essential line of continuity, the "tradition" of excellence, as they define it, in poetry and fiction: the novelists in the "great tradition" of the English novel, for example, are (for Leavis) Jane Austen, Dickens, George Eliot, James, Conrad and Lawrence. But there is rarely any concern for overt influence. Tradition is a term of broad approval referring to certain moral characteristics which appear in particular works, no matter how they arrived there. F.R. Leavis' well-known benediction of Jane Austen is typical of this approach:

> As a matter of fact, when we examine the formal perfection of *Emma*, we find that it can be appreciated only in terms of the moral preoccupations that characterize the novelist's peculiar interest in life. Those who suppose it to be an "aesthetic matter," a beauty of "composition" that is combined, miraculously, with "truth to life," can give no adequate reason for the view that *Emma* is a great novel, and no intelligent account of its perfection of form. It is in the same way true of the other great English novelists that their interest in their art gives them the opposite of an affinity with Pater and George Moore; it is, brought into an intense focus, an unusually developed interest in life. For, far from having anything of Flaubert's disgust or disdain or boredom, they are all distinguished by a vital capacity for experience, a kind of reverent openness before life, and a marked moral intensity.

"Moral intensity," "maturity"—these and a half-dozen or so related phrases are the points of reference: if a writer manifests the proper qualities, he is admitted to the tradition; if not, he is dismissed harshly—the *Scrutiny* critics are nothing if not fiercely protective. Thus the standards invoked are derived from moral principles "outside" literature, as they must be, and as such are exemplary: it is hard to be against maturity and moral intensity and fine critical intelligence. But if both Jane Austen and D.H. Lawrence are to be regarded as mature writers, then the meaning of the phrase clearly needs closer definition than these critics provide. In any event, a few typical passages from Bewley will indicate his allegiance to the kind of argument favored by Leavis and his followers. Defending Wallace Stevens against charges or irresponsibility, for example, Bewley writes

> If the meaning in Stevens' poetry is again submitted to some scrutiny here, it is certainly not in the belief that anything surprisingly new can be said; but the substance of Stevens' poetry can be discussed in terms that incorporate it more firmly in a traditional context, and I think that is important: for Stevens's poetry has been too much discussed in terms of relativism, misology, Hedonism—even Bergsonianism. If several of these terms can be justified—and of course they can—the result is nevertheless that of dislodging Stevens' poetry from the tradition in which it seems to me most richly assimilable.

The proper context here turns out to be that established by Coleridge's insistence on the importance of the imagination. Or again, while admitting that the surface of Robert Lowell's verse is often "disagreeable," Bewley argues that his poetry still

> gives evidence of an unusual integrity. It proves, I think, that the sense of function...of the American poet, is not wholly, and in all cases, a product of America's material activity. Among its deeper historical roots one may point to the New England puritanism of the seventeenth century, which regarded logic and rhetoric as a means of knowing and communicating Divine Truth. It is under the banner of logic and rhetoric, although these are subsumed in the name of poet, that Mr. Lowell undertakes his work. And it makes little difference from the viewpoint of his intention that the logic is often elusive and the rhetoric unappealing. No poet could well conceive of a greater function than this religious onslaught on Truth, and it is...a function made wholly valid by the tradition from which Mr. Lowell emerges.

Bewley is a sharp and often quite precise critic of poetry, but his primary achievement is the attempt he makes, in *The Complex Fate* and *The Eccentric Design*, to do for American fiction what Leavis has done for the English novel in *The Great Tradition*. In characteristically broad final terms, then, he proposes that "Cooper, Hawthorne, Melville, and James form a line in American writing based on a finely critical consciousness of the national society."

For Bewley, as for Leavis and Lionel Trilling, the novel's basic subject is "man in society": its "texture" is necessarily "the manners and conventions by which social man defines his own identity." As Henry James had maintained in his classic study of Hawthorne as an American writer, the novelist finds his bearings and his subject in the shared understandings and expectations which constitute a complex, established culture; and it was precisely such a culture that Hawthorne lacked, to the detriment of his art. Unable to rely on a dense social medium for the embodiment of his most serious concerns, the novelist will be forced (Bewley concludes) to "make abstractions...the controlling factor in the motives and organization of his work":

> This should not surprise us, given the conditions under which the American writer had to create. Jane Austen, to take the ideal example, was able to move progressively into her values in the course of any given novel, to reveal them in the very circumstances of her story, in the reflection of her characters' speeches, or the way they wore their inherited manners. Her values *pre-existed* in the materials and conditions of her art, even if it took her genius to reveal them.... Her judgments and insights have the sureness and strength that come from the corroboration of traditional sanctions. But the American novelist had only his *ideas* with which to begin: ideas which, for the most part, were grounded in the great American democratic abstractions. And he found that these abstractions were disembodied, that there was no social context in which they might acquire a rich human relevance. For the traditional novelist, the universal and the particular come together in the world of manners; but for the American artist there was no social surface responsive to his touch.

American novelists were forced to become Symbolists, "metaphysical novelists"; and while Bewley does not question the native genius of some of these writers any more than James had questioned Hawthorne's fundamental gifts, the absence of a sustaining tradition exacts its price:

> Because the American tradition provided its artists with abstractions and ideas rather than with manners, we have no great characters, but great symbolic personifications and mythic embodiments that go under the names of Natty Bumpo, Jay Gatsby, Huckleberry Finn, Ahab, Ishmael—all of whom are strangely unrelated to the world of ordinary passions and longings, for the democrat is at last the loneliest man in the universe. The great American novelists can, in their way, give us Lear, and make a decent attempt to Hamlet; but Othello, and even Romeo, are beyond their range.... As artists they are thinkers and a species of metaphysician.

The great tradition of the American novel is for these reasons a lesser thing than the great English tradition which extends from Jane Austen through D.H. Lawrence. Given all the "terrible deprivations of [the] stark American condition," how could it be otherwise?

Since American novelists have tended to be Symbolists, the critical task is to discover what their novels are symbolic *of*. For Bewley the American writer has had two primary themes: "his own unhappy plight" as a struggling artist and, more important, the various "tensions" which accompany the complex fate of being an American in the nineteenth century, tensions which

> took on many forms concurrently: it was a opposition between tradition and progress, or between the past and present or future; between America and Europe, liberalism and reaction, aggressive acquisitive economics and benevolent wealth.

Since these conflicts usually appear in disguised form in American fiction and since it is crucial to his argument to prove that they are characteristically American, Bewley devotes the first section of *The Eccentric Design* to a discussion of their presence in the political thinking of Jefferson, Adams and Hamilton. When he uncovers these same themes and conflicts in Cooper and James he is often convincing; when he turns to Melville the argument is strained and grotesque:

> At bottom [Melville's torment] is an inability to keep the terms of good and evil distinct from each other; and it comes about because the democrat, in the beginning making a close identification between God and democratic society, later carries this spurious identification over to the defects and failures of democracy. When the human perfectibility that God seemed to promise when he crowned the great American experiment with brotherhood from sea to shining sea conspicuously fails, the disillusioned democrat proceeds from his earlier faith...either to cynicism or hatred, and God is cast in the role of the great betrayer.

There are arguments of the same sort in *The Complex Fate*, which deals mainly with the similarities between Hawthorne and James: both writers had to cope with the central problem of their separateness from the old world; and although James escaped in time to nurture his genius abroad, it was Hawthorne who "literally gave James a tradition"—a sense of society, admittedly undeveloped, which was to be crucial when James dramatized the differences between America and Europe. Bewley demonstrates in detail (and for the first time) the vital impact *The Blithedale Romance* had on James' finest American novel, *The Bostonians*, and finds decisive traces of Hawthorne in late James as well (in the connections, for example, between *The Marble Faun* and *The Wings of the Dove*). And he demonstrates the similar ways in which the two novelists handle the discrepancy between "appearance and reality" in human behavior and the consequences this has for one of their major common concerns, "the difficulty of knowing evil."

Masks and Mirrors is something of a miscellany, ranging from discussions of Donne's lingering Catholicism to the social idealism of the Oz books, but it is also Bewley's best work by far: in this last collection, published three years before his untimely death, he found his independence as a critic and resisted the temptation to indulge in broad moral generalizations. The essays here are flexible and undogmatic, still alert to the "traditional" excellence of the writer or work under consideration but equally willing to consider other sources of failure and success.

BLACKMUR, R(ichard) P(almer). American. Born in Springfield, Massachusetts, 21 January 1904. Self-educated. Married Helen Dickson in 1930 (divorced, 1951). Free-lance writer and critic until 1940. Resident Fellow, 1940-43, 1946-48, Hodder Fellow, 1944, Member of the Institute for Advanced Study, 1944-45, Associate Professor, 1948-51, and Professor of English, 1951-65, Princeton University, New Jersey. Fellow of Christ's College, Cambridge, and Pitt Professor of American History and Institutions, Cambridge University, 1961-62. Library of Congress Fellow in American Letters. Member of the Editorial Board, *Hound and Horn* magazine, 1928-29. Recipient: Guggenheim Fellowship, 1936, 1937. Litt.D.: Rutgers University, New Brunswick, New Jersey, 1958; M.A.: Cambridge University, 1961. Member, National Academy of Arts and Sciences. *Died 2 February 1965.*

PUBLICATIONS

Criticism

The Double Agent: Essays in Craft and Elucidation.   New York, Arrow Editions, 1935.
The Expense of Greatness.   New York, Arrow Editions, 1940.
The Lion and the Honeycomb: Essays in Solicitude and Critique.   New York, Harcourt Brace, 1955; London, Methuen, 1957.

Language as Gesture: Essays in Poetry. New York, Harcourt Brace, 1952; London, Allen and Unwin, 1954; shortened version, as *Form and Value in Modern Poetry*, New York, Doubleday, 1957.

Anni Mirabiles, 1921-1925; Reason in the Madness of Letters. Washington, D.C., Library of Congress, 1956; reprinted in *A Primer of Ignorance*, 1967.

Eleven Essays in the European Novel. New York, Harcourt Brace, 1964.

A Primer of Ignorance, edited by Joseph Frank. New York, Harcourt Brace, 1967.

Henry Adams, edited by Veronica A. Makowsky. New York, Harcourt Brace, and London, Secker and Warburg, 1980.

Verse

A Funeral for a Few Sticks. Lynn, Massachusetts, Lone Gull Press, 1927.

From Jordan's Delight. New York, Arrow Editions, 1937.

The Second World. Cummington, Massachusetts, Cummington Press, 1942.

The Good European and Other Poems. Cummington, Massachusetts, Cummington Press, 1947.

The Poems of R.P. Blackmur. Princeton, New Jersey, Princeton University Press, 1978.

Other

For Any Book. Privately printed, 1924.

T.S. Eliot. Portland, Maine, Hound and Horn, 1928.

Dirty Hands; or, The True-Born Censor. Cambridge, England, Minority Press, 1930; Folcroft, Pennsylvania, Folcroft Editions, 1976.

Psyche in the South. Tryon, North Carolina, Tryon Pamphlets, 1934.

New Criticism in the United States. Tokyo, Kenkyusha, 1959; Folcroft, Pennsylvania, Folcroft Editions, 1975.

Editor, *The Art of the Novel: Critical Prefaces*, by Henry James. New York, Scribner, 1934.

Editor, *The Wings of the Dove*, by Henry James. New York, Dell, 1958.

Editor, *Washington Square, and The Europeans*, by Henry James. New York, Dell, 1959.

Editor, *The American*, by Henry James. New York, Dell, 1960.

Editor, *American Short Novels.* New York, Crowell, 1960.

Editor, *The Tragic Muse*, by Henry James. New York, Dell, 1961.

CRITICAL STUDIES

Delmore Schwartz, "The Critical Method of R.P. Blackmur," in *Poetry* (Chicago), 53, 1938.

Stanley Edgar Hyman, "R.P. Blackmur and the Expense of Criticism," in *The Armed Vision: A Study in the Methods of Modern Literary Criticism.* New York, Knopf, 1948.

R.W.B. Lewis, "Casella as Critic: A Note on R.P. Blackmur," in *Kenyon Review* (Gambier, Ohio), 13, 1951.

Hugh Kenner, "Inside the Featherbed," in *Gnomon: Essays on Contemporary Literature.* New York, McDowell Obolensky, 1958.

Joseph Frank, "R.P. Blackmur: The Later Phase," in *The Widening Gyre: Crisis and Mastery in Modern Literature.* New Brunswick, New Jersey, Rutgers University Press, 1963.

René Wellek, "R.P. Blackmur Re-Examined," in *Southern Review* (Baton Rouge, Louisiana), 7, 1971.

Russell Fraser, "R.P. Blackmur: The Politics of a New Critic," in *Sewanee Review* (Tennessee), 87, 1979.

*   *   *

"A Critic's Job of Work," the essay which concludes R.P. Blackmur's first collection, *The Double Agent*, is the best place to begin if one is determined to make plain sense of this complex, often obscure and uneasy defender of modernism when it was still modern. Poetry, he asserts,

> names and arranges, and thus arrests and transfixes its subject in a form which has a life of its own forever separate but springing from the life which confronts it. Poetry is life at the remove of form and meaning; not life lived but life framed and identified. So the criticism of poetry is bound to be occupied at once with the terms and modes by which the remove was made and with the relation between—in the ambiguous stock phrase—content and form; which is to say with the establishment and appreciation of human or moral value.

How he makes this jump from formal analysis to moral evaluation is never indicated, but from the beginning of his career Blackmur was preoccupied with moral judgment and not merely the kind of close reading for which he is probably best remembered now: "value" and "form" are terms of equal importance in his critical vocabulary. The problem of understanding these two central concerns is complicated from the start, however, because Blackmur never defined with any precision what he meant by "form." In his early essays he often means nothing more than literary convention (as, for example, in "Herman Melville: A Putative Statement"); in his later essays he seems to mean something close to Croce's "theoretic form." "One of my clichés," Blackmur observes,

> is from Croce where he says that poetry gives to feelings theoretic form. Theory is primarily a way of looking at things, especially a fruitful way; it need not be a world view. Form I take it here means the limits by which we determine the identity of a thing; the identification may be false or incomplete. Though Croce might have rejected the expansion, I should like to make his words read: The novel gives theoretic form to life—especially to the behavior that is our life in motion.

This helps, a little; but when he concludes that the form of *Anna Karenina* (and by implication all great novels) is "an image of the theoretic form of the soul" the meaning is sacrificed, as it so often is, for the sake of an oracular effect. Form is obviously something valuable (in one of his best early essays he is eloquent about the lack of form in Lawrence), and it is quite possible that Blackmur usually means what James meant in his preface to *Roderick Hudson*: form is that illusion of a complete whole brought about by careful selection and arrangement. Still, the absence of any fixed definition is a serious obstacle for readers not properly attuned to Blackmur's indirections. In any event, whatever it is which differentiates one form from another, a work also depends upon smaller units, individual words and words in particular combinations, which demand the closest possible scrutiny. Here Blackmur is at his best: he has a healthy respect for the kind of scholarship which establishes verbal meaning and he is willing to accept I.A. Richards' broad claim that poetry at its best is "man's chief co-ordinating instrument"; but he also demands that criticism always be

> confronted with examples of poetry, and I want it so for the very practical purpose of assisting in pretty immediate appreciation of the use, meaning, and value of the language in that particular poetry. I want it to assist in doing for me what it actually assists Mr. Richards in doing, whatever that is, when he is reading poetry for its own sake.

It is Blackmur's scrupulous attention to diction and metaphor which distinguishes his classic attack on E.E. Cummings' "sentimental denial of the intelligence" and supports his equally influential defense of Wallace Stevens. Yet the precision which makes these early essays so valuable is always in the service of a larger, overall judgment which is often as severe as the verdicts passed by Yvor Winters or F.R. Leavis. In short, Blackmur's essays are never simply exercises in explication: what he strives for is a sense of the writer's conformity to a certain set of expectations he had not yet made clear. Thus his claim at the end of "A Critic's Job of Work," that his own approach "does not tell the whole story either" and that the reader is "conscientiously left with the poem and the real work yet to do," is not entirely accurate. Final judgments abound in *The Double Agent* and *The Expense of Greatness*, but to understand Blackmur's conception of the ultimate value of literature and the grounds of these judgments the reader must turn to "Language as Gesture," "The Lion and the Honeycomb" and the four lectures which make up *Anni Mirabiles*.

Nearly all of Blackmur's reflections about literature and language might be considered as variations on Ezra Pound's assertion that literature is "language charged with meaning to the utmost degree." So charged, language becomes "gesture," the "outward and dramatic play of inward and imagined meaning." The language of literature is not the language of abstraction but an "act of the whole mind" and "one of our skills of notation of the incarnation of the real into the actual." As "gesture," language is not simply the description of meaning; it embodies and recreates meaning in a verbal object. As Blackmur recognizes, his position is thus very close to Kenneth Burke's more "intellectual" thesis that

> the language of poetry may be regarded as symbolic action. The difference between Mr. Burke and myself is that where he is predominantly concerned with setting up methods for analyzing the actions as they are expressed in the symbol, I choose to emphasize the created or dead-end symbol.... Mr. Burke legislates; I would judge.

If the language of successful poetry actually embodies meaning, this is partly because of the additional intensity provided by rhythm and metre:

> Poetry is as near as words can get to our behavior; near enough so that the words sing, for it is when words sing that they give that absolute moving attention which is beyond prose powers.

Such movement may cause a "shudder of recognition"—the recognition, presumably, of truth in its full complexity. "Style," Blackmur continues, "is the quality of the act of perception but it is mere play and cannot move us much unless married in rhythm to the urgency of the thing perceived." Commenting on two lines from "The Dry Salvages," Blackmur observes

> The two together make an image, and in their pairing reveal, by self-symbol declare, by verse and position unite, two halves of a tragic gesture.
>
> > The salt is on the briar rose,
> > The fog is in the fir trees.
>
> I do not see that any other illustration is needed of how behavior gets into the words of the full mind and how, a little beyond the time that it is there, it sings.

But those who do not hear an enchanting tune may require another illustration, or better yet, a definition of exactly *how* rhythm may express the nature of its subject matter. The possibilities for this are distinctly limited, as critics from Dr. Johnson onwards have pointed out.

The aesthetic shudder of recognition which accompanies our perception of fully embodied meaning is not, of course, an end in itself. The question remains, in Richards' language, what this complex instrument is for; and it is this question which becomes the main topic of *Anni Mirabiles*. The arguments here are essentially expansions of a theme Blackmur had implied before but first expressed directly in a 1942 essay on Yeats: "To create greatly is to compass great discorder." In "The Techniques of Trouble," the second section of *Anni Mirabiles*, he states flatly that "Great literature—great art of any kind—finds techniques for dealing with the trouble otherwise provided." What gives literature its particular urgency now is the increasing chaos of modern civilization:

Do we not have a society in which we see the attrition of law and rational wisdom and general craft? Do we not have an age anti-intellectual and violent, in which there is felt a kind of total responsibility to total disorder?... It is a world alive and moving but which does not understand itself.

More specifically,

The anarchy of our artists is in response to facts as well as in evasion of facts. The two great external facts of our time are the explosion of populations and the explosions of new energies. The two great internal facts of our time are the recreation of the devil (or pure behavior) in a place of authority and the development of techniques for finding destructive troubles in the psyche of individuals.

Not only did we live in a time of proliferating troubles after the first World War,

We lived also in a time when we were learning a whole set of techniques for finding—even creating—trouble: new ways of undermining personality and conviction and belief and human relation. I myself can remember when the Oedipus complex was a shuddering shock and a neurosis was a ravening worm. It was not till later that we had the law of uncertainty in mathematical physics, which broke the last healthy remnants of moral determinism. But we had psychology which dissolved the personality into bad behavior, we had anthropology which dissolved religion into a competition, world- and history-wide, of monsters, and we had psychiatry which cured the disease by making a monument of it and sociology which flattened us into the average of a lonely crowd. We had thus the tools with which to construct the age of anxiety out of the older debris.

Such knowledge has tended to "dissolve the sense of moral experience"; the techniques for defining trouble in some ways increase the prevalence of the very troubles they seek to understand. Some literature—the literature of surrealism and anarchy which Blackmur deplores—has succumbed to the pressures of disorder: but there is another tradition, Blackmur states, that of "bourgeois humanism," which still values the authority of the "rational imagination" (a crucial term which is left undefined). This is the tradition which informs *Ulysses, The Waste Land, The Magic Mountain, The Tower* and the other modern works which "come as near masterpieces as our age provides." While Blackmur never pauses to offer a formal definition of bourgeois humanism, it is not difficult to deduce a fairly consistent meaning from the contexts of his particular discussions (the most revealing in this respect is his own identification with Serenus Zeitbloom, the narrator of Mann's *Dr. Faustus*, in the essay on that novel reprinted in *Eleven Essays in the European Novel*). The essence of such humanism is secular; its main tenet is the priority of reason and the natural connection between knowledge and virtue. To understand fully is to open the possibilities for right action. Thus

the devil and the techniques are the slow form of population and energy explosions. But if we let this relation transpire in the mind we see we have the power to cope with the facts themselves; for we then behold the nature of our troubles in what used to be called the unity of apperception. To say this is to involve bourgeois humanism once again.

Commenting on the value of *Ulysses*, for example, Blackmur is able to conclude that

The sharp difference between the situation of the dadaists and that of Joyce is that where the one prevented masterpieces at all costs the other is the theme of one of the greatly ordered masterpieces of all literature. The one has forgotten its ancestry and feels itself wholly bastardised, the other springs from a full bourgeois humanism of which it has lost nothing still alive and to which it adds its own innermost life. Shakespeare, the Bible, and Aristotle are all at work here, as is also all the working of June 16, 1904, in the city of Dublin, all working together into an order of the rational imagination.

At its best art offers "an irregualar metaphysic for the control of man's irrational powers." Proper criticism of modern literature is thus criticism of modern life itself: "It is therefore worthwhile considering the usefulness of a sequence of rational and critical judgments upon the art of our time as an aid in determining the identity, the meaning in itself, of present society." Thus Blackmur has from the start argued for critical pluralism and the use of the "flexible and diverse intelligence" Arnold so admired in Montaigne. And he has spoken sharply against criticism which uses literature for ulterior purposes which "deliberately expands the theoretic phase of every practical problem," and which tends to be concerned exclusively with verbal techniques. Yet if modern critics are guilty of this last excess, how could it have been otherwise, considering the nature of modern literature and the rise of a new, semi-literate audience which must be taught how to grasp complex verbal structures?

> The general poetry at the center of our time takes the compact and studiable conceit of Donne with the direct eccentricity, vision, and private symbolism of Blake; takes from Hopkins the incalculable and unreliable freedom (which cost him so much, too) of sprung rhythm, and the concentration camp of the single word; and from Emily Dickinson takes spontaneous snatched idiom and wooed accidental inductableness. It is a Court poetry, learned at its fingertips and full of a decorous willfulness called ambiguity. It is, in a mass society, a court poetry without a court.

Blackmur may never have lost faith in the importance of literature and just evaluation, but his characteristic tone in later years was that of a weary priest guarding an already half-forgotten religion. Alfred Alvarez' tribute is very much to the point here:

> All that purity and concentration and effort are somehow without much hope; [*Anni Mirables*] reads like an epitaph upon a tradition. Certainly, the times and styles were already changing before he died. He belonged to a period of high cosmopolitan sophistication in America which is now [1967] in eclipse. For the moment, the fashion is for what he called "that easiest of reservoirs, spontaneity," and the influence is with the tradition of the "barbarians," Whitman and Pound. He recognized this and didn't like it much.

BLOOM, Harold.   American.   Born in New York City, 11 July 1930. Educated at Cornell University, Ithaca, New York, B.A. 1951; Yale University, New Haven, Connecticut, Ph.D. 1955; Cambridge University (Fulbright Fellow), 1954-55. Married Jeanne Gould in 1958; has two children. Instructor, 1955-60, Assistant Professor, 1960-63, Associate Professor, 1963-65, Professor of English, 1965-74, and since 1974, DeVane Professor of the Humanities, Yale University. Visiting Lecturer, Hebrew University, Jerusalem, 1959; Visiting Professor, Bread-loaf Summer School, Vermont, 1965, 1966; Visiting Fellow, Society for the Humanities, Cornell University, 1968-69. Editor, The Romantic Tradition in American Literature series, Arno Press, New York. Recipient: John Addison Porter Prize, 1956; Guggenheim Fellowship, 1962; Newton Arvin Award, 1967; Poetry Society of America Melville Cane Award, 1970. D.H.L.: Boston College, 1973. Address: 179 Linden Avenue, New Haven, Connecticut 06511, U.S.A.

PUBLICATIONS

Criticism

Shelley's Mythmaking.   New Haven, Connecticut, Yale University Press, 1959.

The Visionary Company: A Reading of English Romantic Poetry.   New York, Double-
 day, 1961; London, Faber, 1962; revised edition, Ithaca, New York, Cornell University
 Press, 1971.
Blake's Apocalypse: A Study in Poetic Argument.   New York, Doubleday, and London,
 Gollancz, 1963.
The Poetry and Prose of William Blake (commentary only), edited by Daniel Erdman.
 New York, Doubleday, 1965.
Yeats.   New York, Oxford University Press, 1970; London, Oxford University Press,
 1972.
The Ringers in the Tower: Studies in Romantic Tradition.   Chicago and London,
 University of Chicago Press, 1971.
"The Native Strain: American Orphism," in *Literary Theory and Structure: Essays
 Presented to William K. Wimsatt*, edited by Frank Brady, John Palmer, and Martin
 Price.   New Haven, Connecticut, and London, Yale University Press, 1973.
The Anxiety of Influence: A Theory of Poetry.   New York, Oxford University Press,
 1973; London, Oxford University Press, 1975.
A Map of Misreading.   New York, Oxford University Press, 1975.
Kabbalah and Criticism.   New York, Seabury Press, 1975.
Figures of Capable Imagination.   New York, Seabury Press, 1976.
Poetry and Repression: Revisionism from Blake to Stevens.   New Haven, Connecticut,
 and London, Yale University Press, 1976.
Wallace Stevens: The Poems of Our Climate.   Ithaca, New York, and London, Cornell
 University Press, 1977.
"The Breaking of Form," in *Deconstruction and Criticism: Harold Bloom, Paul de Man,
 Jacques Derrida, Geoffrey H. Hartman, J. Hillis Miller.*   New York, Seabury Press,
 1979; London, Routledge, 1980.
"Lying Against Time," in *Oxford Literary Review*, 3, 1979.
"The White Light of Tropes: An Essay on John Hollander's 'Spectral Emanations,' " in
 Kenyon Review (Gambier, Ohio), 1 n.s., 1979.
"Freud's Concepts of Defense and Poetic Will," in *The Literary Freud: Mechanisms of
 Defense and the Poetic Will*, edited by Joseph H. Smith.   New Haven, Connecticut,
 and London, Yale University Press, 1980.
"Agon: Revisionism and Critical Personality," in *Raritan* (New Brunswick, New Jersey),
 1, 1981.

Novel

The Flight from Lucifer: A Gnostic Fantasy.   New York, Farrar Straus, and London,
 Faber, 1980.

Other

Editor, with John Hollander, *The Wind and the Rain: An Anthology of Poems for Young
 People.*   New York, Doubleday, 1961.
Editor, *English Romantic Poetry: An Anthology.*   New York, Doubleday, 1961; revised
 edition, 2 vols., 1963.
Editor, with Frederick W. Hilles, *From Sensibility to Romanticism: Essays Presented to
 Frederick A. Pottle.*   New York, Oxford University Press, 1965.
Editor, *The Literary Criticism of John Ruskin.*   New York, Doubleday, 1965.
Editor, *Selected Poetry*, by Percy Bysshe Shelley.   New York, New American Library,
 1966.
Editor, *Romanticism and Consciousness: Essays in Criticism.*   New York, Norton, 1970.
Editor, *Marius the Epicurean*, by Walter Pater.   New York, New American Library,
 1972.

Editor, *Selected Poetry*, by Samuel Taylor Coleridge.   New York, New American Library, 1972.

Editor, with others, *The Oxford Anthology of English Literature*.   New York, Oxford University Press, 2 vols., 1973.

Editor, *Selected Writings*, by Walter Pater.   New York, New American Library, 1974.

Editor, with Adrienne Munich, *Robert Browning: A Collection of Critical Essays*.   New York, Prentice Hall, 1979.

CRITICAL STUDIES

William H. Pritchard, "The Hermeneutical Mafia; or, After Strange Gods at Yale," in *Hudson Review* (New York), 28, 1975.

Leon Wieseltier, "Summoning Up the Kabbalah," in *New York Review of Books*, 19 February 1976.

Jerome J. McGann, "Formalism, Savagery, and Care; or, The Function of Criticism Once Again," in *Critical Inquiry* (Chicago), 2, 1976.

Frank Lentricchia, "Harold Bloom: The Spirit of Revenge," in *After the New Criticism*. Chicago and London, University of Chicago Press, 1980.

Denis Donoghue, "Harold Bloom," in *Ferocious Alphabets*.   Boston, Little Brown, and London, Faber, 1981.

*   *   *

"Northrop Frye has recently said that all selective approaches to tradition invariably have some ultracritical joker in them": since Harold Bloom has reminded his readers of Frye's warning he presumably recognizes that it may be applied to his own work as well. Thus while we can take his detailed examinations of Blake, Shelley, Yeats and Wallace Stevens simply as extended commentary and exegesis, it is important to understand that from the beginning of his career Bloom has been attempting something much more ambitious and problematic. In effect he has proposed a sophisticated redefinition of the Romantic tradition in English poetry and sought to defend his poets against the determined anti-romanticism which dominated literary criticism during the first half of this century. The joker in Bloom's pack is a particular kind of secular humanism but it is hardly "ultracritical"—unless one is prepared to accept Frye's claim that value judgments themselves have no place in literary criticism.

The reconstruction and defense begins with *Shelly's Mythmaking*, in which Bloom uses as his heuristic device (and thereby upset a number of conventional Shelley scholars) Martin Buber's distinction between the "I-It" and "I-Thou" attitudes. Very briefly, the I-It attitude refers to our usual treatment of objects and other persons simply as objects, to be used as need dictates. The I-Thou attitiude, however, refers to our sense of others as existences in themselves; it involves a moral, reciprocal relationship, a true encounter with the other in himself and with the creator of our common being: "every particular *Thou* is a glimpse through to the eternal *Thou*." Authentic existence is a "meeting" for Buber, although we cannot sustain our true encounters. As Bloom explains it,

Buber acknowledges that every "particular *Thou*, after the relational event has run its course, is *bound* to become an *It*," but he counters this by asserting that every "particular *It*, by entering the relational event, *may* become a *Thou*." As befits a theologian, Buber's conclusion is moral: "Without *It* man cannot live. But he who lives with *It* alone is not a man."

The I-Thou attitude also characterizes primitive mythic thinking, in which the phenomena of nature are encountered in their fulness of being; it persists in some varieties of religion and philosophy and also becomes "a certain kind, and tradition, of poetry." Thus Bloom argues that Shelley's "To Night" is an example of "primitive mythopoeic poetry, in which the poet enters into a relationship with a natural Thou, the relationship itself constituting the myth." The "Thou's" of "Mont Blanc," the "Hymn to Intellectual Beauty" and the "Ode to the West

Wind" are all "glimpses through to the Eternal Thou which comprehends them." The tragedy is that we cannot continue at this level of relationship:

> This horrible paradox is at the heart of Shelley's central myth, the burden of which is the defeat of, the unmaking of myth. The means and the end are irreconcilable; and this holds true whether the relational event, the means of good, is a poem or a lovers' confrontation.

The reason for this failure is not entirely clear, but it may be nothing more—and nothing less—than "something recalcitrant, something hardened in the human spirit...predisposed toward the condition of Itness, something that makes us prone to welcome experience at the price of relationship." As C.S. Lewis suggested, this sounds rather like original sin, but Bloom typically rejects any Christian translation of Shelley. Whatever the cause, this movement from I-It to I-Thou and the tragic counter-movement back to I-It form the dramatic basis for many individual poems and for Shelley's career as a whole: the myth of relationship reaches its climax in "Prometheus Unbound" and his final, unfinished poem, "The Triumph of Life," records the inevitable failure:

> The final aspect of Shelley's mythopoeia is that the myth, and the myth's maker, are fully conscious of the myth's necessary defeat. There are no Thou's of relationship in "The Triumph of Life"; the poem commemorates the triumph of the "It" of experience.

The inability to read Shelley properly is in itself a kind of moral shortcoming:

> If Shelley's poetry dies in our age it will not be because we have read it and found it wanting but because we have allowed ourselves to be persuaded into not reading it at all. Critics as eminent as Eliot, Leavis, Tate, Brooks, and Ransom, among others, have assured us that the bulk of it is not good poetry.... On their authority (though, it must be granted, not at their advice) a generation has chosen to condemn a poet while remaining largely ignorant of his works....
>
> If, in poetry, it is improper or impossible to affirm that in our best moments we can, and ought to, pass from I-It to I-Thou, from the world of phenomenal objects of the scientists to the world in which Nature wears a human face, the world of Blake and Shelley, then Tate [as a typical modern critic of Shelley] is justified in his pronouncement. But more than Spenser and the romantics, more indeed than some very good poetry will be swept away if we honor Tate's assertion. When Thou has altogether become It, irredeemably, and the poet, like the scientist, dwells in the world of experience alone, we shall suffer more of the lovelessness and overanxiousness of Coleridge's crowd [in the "Dejection" ode] than we do even at present.

In *Shelley's Mythmaking* Bloom begins to define the Romantic tradition, which he now extends from Blake and his precursors (Milton and Spenser, primarily) to Wallace Stevens and his successors; in *The Visionary Company*, or rather in the crucial introduction, "Prometheus Rising," which Bloom has added to the revised edition, we have his fullest statement of the nature of this tradition. Romanticism began as an apocalyptic poetry, fed by revolutionary hopes for the literal regeneration of man and society; but with the failure of the French Revolution and the repressive countermeasures provoked in England, it seemed to "idealists of every sort...that a new energy had been born into the world and then had died in its infancy." The quest for renewal, rather than dying out, however, became an individual, internalized quest; and while Romanticism was in some important respects a new movement, for Bloom it also has vital connections with the tradition of Protestant dissent and the "nonconformist vision that descended from the Left Wing of England's Puritan movement":

> There is no more important point to be made about English Romantic poetry than this one, or indeed about English poetry in general, particularly since it has been deliberately obscured by most modern criticism. Though it is a displaced Protestantism astonishingly transformed by different kinds of humanism or naturalism, the poetry of the English Romantics is a kind of religious poetry, and the religion is in the Protestant line,

though Calvin and Luther would have been horrified to contemplate it. Indeed, the entire continuity of English poetry that T.S. Eliot and his followers attacked is a radical Protestant or displaced Protestant tradition. It is no accident that the poets deprecated by the New Criticism were Puritans, or Protestant individualists, or men of that sort breaking away from Christianity and attempting to formulate personal religions in their poetry. This Protestant grouping begins with aspects of Spenser and Milton, passes through the major Romantics and Victorians, and is clearly represented by Hardy and Lawrence [and Yeats and Stevens] in our own century. It is also no accident that the poets brought into favor by the New Criticism were Catholics or High Church Anglicans—Donne, Herbert, Dryden, Pope, Dr. Johnson, Hopkins in the Victorian period, Eliot and Auden in our own time. Not that literary critics have been engaged in a cultural-religious conspiracy, but there are at least two main traditions of English Poetry, and what distinguishes them are not only aesthetic considerations but conscious differences in religion and politics. One line, and it is the central one, is Protestant, radical, and Miltonic-Romantic; the other is Catholic conservative, and by its claims, classical.

"The central desire of Blake and Wordsworth, and of Keats and Shelley," Bloom concludes, "was to find a final good in human existence itself": and this is basically the key statement of his "ultracritical" appeal. Romanticism becomes synonymous with secular, humanistic individualism; it manifests itself in imaginative acts of the mind, to use one of Bloom's favorite phrases from Stevens, searching for "what will suffice." But the quest may not go beyond experience: it must discover a final good *in* experience (hence Bloom's dismissal of Eliot and Auden, especially when they deny that poetry can become a substitute for religion).

With all its impressive command of the minutiae of Yeats scholarship and criticism, the burden of *Yeats* is moral as well. Yeats is a troublesome figure for Bloom, a great poet in many obvious ways, but also one whose final attitude was anti-humanistic. The last poems in *Under Ben Bulben* represent, for Bloom, an "abuse" of the Romantic tradition. The basis for Bloom's rejection here is, finally, his aversion to any highly deterministic point of view. "Yeats knew himself to be the heir of a great tradition in poetry, of the visionaries who have sought to make a more human man, to resolve all the sunderings of consciousness through the agency of the imagination"; but for Bloom, to be fully human means to be free, and it is precisely this freedom which the Yeats of *A Vision* and the later poetry denies. "That so great and unique a poet abdicated the idea of man to a conception of destiny," Bloom concludes, "'is not less than tragic." Merely to repeat Bloom's conclusions, however, is misleading: his readings of individual poems are as full and open as any we are likely to have. The polemical Bloom is usually kept apart from Bloom the patient explicator (his well-known aside, for example, that Eliot and Pound may prove to be the "Cowley and Cleveland of this age" is not typical and his defense of Romanticism does not prevent him from being fully sensible of the virtues of the Augustans).

The later essays in *The Ringers in the Tower* and *The Anxiety of Influence* are considerably more difficult, partly because Bloom unwisely affects the prophetic manner himself, but mainly because there has been a complicated shift away from the opposition between Catholicism and Dissent to Freud, for whom religious attitudes are, of course, symptoms to be accounted for in terms of a purely naturalistic model of human nature. Thus Bloom now asserts that "True poetic history is the story of how poets as poets have suffered from other poets, just as any true biography is the story of how anyone suffered his own family—or his own displacement of family into lovers and friends." The Romantic poet is still a rebel, he still engages in a quest for love which is perhaps doomed to failure—but according to Freud these are activities which mark the differentiation and development of every ego. By definition poets and non-poets alike participate in the Freudian "family romance":

> Freud thought all men unconsciously wish to beget themselves, to be their own fathers in place of their phallic fathers, and so "rescue" their mothers from erotic degradation... The poet, if he could, would be his own precursor, and so rescue the Muse from her degradation.

The argument here is not simply metaphorical: Bloom insists that his "revisionary ratios," or the ways in which poets deal with their precursors, have "the same function in intra-poetic relations that defense mechanisms have in our psychic life." Thus in *The Anxiety of Influence* and *A Map of Misreading* he attempts to identify the tactics the poet uses to cope with his artistic father, just as the non-poet, if he is to survive, must struggle to incorporate the authority of the father and find a substitute for the mother—a costly and never entirely successful undertaking. But successful or not, there are six kinds of strategies, each with a grandly obscure name: Clinamen, Tessera, Kenosis, Daemonization, Askesis and Apophrades. As Bloom summarizes his position:

> Poetic influence—when it involves two strong, authentic poets—always proceeds by a misreading of the prior poet, an act of creative correction that is actually and necessarily a misrepresentation. The history of fruitful poetic influence...is a history of anxiety and self-saving caricature, of distortion, of perverse, wilful revisionism without which modern poetry as such could not exist.

Poetry and Repression, *Figures of Capable Imagination*, and to some extent Bloom's massive study of Wallace Stevens are applications of this theory of poetic warfare, in which the strong young poet, or "ephebe," rises up against the father figure or "precursor." In *Kabbalah and Criticism*, however, Bloom extends his terminology and introduces a third warring party, the strong reader or critic. Freud disappears for the moment, to be replaced by the Kabbalah, which Bloom calls here "the classic paradigm upon which Western revisionism in all areas was to model itself" ("revisionism" means the assertion of independence. In 1981, it should be noted, Freud reappears: "I return obsessively," Bloom observes in "Agon: Revisionism and Critical Personality," to what "seem radically incompatible paradigms for poems and interpretations: Gnostic catastrophe creations [primarily Lurian Kabbalahism] and Freud's conflicts of heightened emotional ambivalence"). The new vocabulary is a maddening distraction, however, rather than an aid for understanding revisionism: Zinzum, Tikkum, Shevirat ha-kelim, Sefirot, Behinot and a host of others make Clinamen and other members of the modest sextet in *A Map of Misreading* seem homely and almost useful by comparison. As an exposition of the Kabbalah, the book is worse than useless, as Leon Wieseltier demonstrates in his long, indispensable essay, cited in the bibliography above. Wieseltier concludes that "everywhere [Bloom] looks—and he looks everywhere—he finds influence and imbroglios. This is glaringly apparent in his exploitation of the Kabbalah, whose conformity to his theory is purchased only at the price of a gross distortion." This hardly matters from Bloom's point of view, since the strong reader, like the strong poet, must deliberately misread his precursors in order to assert his own individuality and achieve "self-reliance" (Emerson's term now begins to appear frequently in Bloom's criticism). Beyond the thicket of terminology, then, there is this new element in Bloom's thinking. In *The Anxiety of Influence* and *A Map of Misreading*, the combat was between ephebe and precursor. Now that combat is joined by the strong reader, the "you" of the following passage:

> To see the history of poetry as an endless, defensive civil war, is to see that every idea of history relevant to the history of poetry must be a *concept of happening*. That is, when you *know* the influence relation between two poets, your knowing is a conceptualization, and your conceptualization (or misreading) is itself an event in the literary history you are writing. Indeed, your *knowledge* of the later poet's misprison of his precursor is exactly as crucial a concept of happening or historical event as the poetic misprison was. Your work as an event is no more or less privileged than the later poet's event of misprison in regard to the earlier poet. Therefore the relation of the earlier to the later poet is exactly analogous to the relation of the later poet to yourself. The ephebe's misreading of the precursor is the paradigm for your misreading of the ephebe. But this is the relation of every text to every reader whatsoever. The same figurations of belatedness govern revisionary reading as govern revisionary writing.

Even more radically, "the true poem is the critic's mind." Thus Bloom concludes, "and so I propose the unhappy formula that *reading is always a defensive process*, a process that I believe becomes severely quickened when we read poems." (And he also adds, "Some of the consequences of what I am saying dismay even me.")

The consequences for literary history, at least, are disastrous. In 1981 Bloom asserted that "there is no language *of criticism* but only of an individual critic, because I again agree with Rorty [Richard Rorty, in his recent, majesterial study, *Philosophy and the Mirror of Nature*] that a theory of strong misreading denies that there is or should be any common vocabulary in terms of which critics can argue with one another." Further more, "I neither want nor urge any 'method' of criticism. It is no concern of mine whether anybody else ever comes to share, or doesn't, my own vocabulary or revisionary ratios, of crossings, of whatever." These last two passages come from Bloom's 1981 essay, "Agon: Critical Revisionism and Critical Personality," and call into question the claim, made a year earlier by an unfriendly critic, Frank Lentricchia, that

> no theorist writing in the United States today has succeeded, as Bloom has, in returning poetry to history; he has managed better than most to move beyond the New Critical concern with the isolated, autonomous monad and the poststructuralist tendency to dissolve literary history into a repetitious synchronic rhetoric of *aporia*.

In a sense, Bloom has returned poetry to history, or at least to an atomized, violent kind of history which aggressively challenges Eliot's and some of the New Critics' conception of tradition. (For Bloom, of course, Eliot is a weak reader, and a weak poet because he does not wrestle with Dante, Donne and the French Symbolists. It might just as well be argued that Eliot—and M.H. Abrams—are the precursors against whom the ephebe Bloom has been struggling for a long time.) In any event, the kind of history Bloom has in mind is a very selective kind. As Denis Donoghue has recently pointed out,

> Bloom presents literary history since the Enlightenment as one story and one story only, a struggle of gods and demiurges, fathers and sons. The character of the struggle issues from a primal scene of obsession, trespass, defense and revenge. The basic story shows how a son survives and grows by killing his father. The story is mythic, it has nothing to say of time, history, society, manners, morals, beginnings or ends.... Bloom's interest in the poet's words expires with the disclosure of their plot...[his] practical criticism is indifferent to the structure, internal relations, of the poem, or to its diction, syntax, meters, rhythm, or tone: it is concerned chiefly to isolate the primal gesture which the critical paradigm has predicted. Like Desdemona, Bloom understands a fury in the words, but not the words; a fury of revisions, swervings, evasions, directed upon the precursor poem and, even more tellingly, away from it.

And of course, Donoghue continues, Bloom also has a stake in the game: "He is interested in exercising his will upon the work, so that it may become, however compromised by that attention, a part of his future."

It seems quite possible that Bloom intends what he has to say about poets and critics to apply to all of us, weak and strong alike. In *The Anxiety of Influence* he remarked, in passing, that "every poet begins (however 'unconsciously') by rebelling more strongly against the consciousness of death's necessity than all other men and women do." And in " 'To Reason With a Later Reason': Romanticism and the Rational" (reprinted in *The Ringers in the Tower*), he observes that "the whole enterprise of Romanticism, as I understand it, was to show the power of mind over a universe of death." A bit later he wondered

> Is Romanticism after all only the waning out of the Enlightenment, and its prophetic poetry and illusory therapy, not so much a saving fiction as an unconscious lie against the difficult human effort of holding the middle ground between instinctual existence and all mortality?

We may all be headed for an entropic state, bereft of illusions and too belated to think of making vain attempts to be strong once again.

BODKIN, (Amy) Maud.   British.   Born in Chelmsford, Essex, 30 March 1875.   Educated at University College of Wales, Aberystwyth, B.A. 1901. *Died in 1967.*

PUBLICATIONS

Criticism

Archetypal Patterns in Poetry: Psychological Studies of Imagination.   London, Oxford University Press, 1934; New York, Vintage, 1958.
The Quest for Salvation in an Ancient and a Modern Play.   London and New York, Oxford University Press, 1941.
"The Philosophical Novel," in *The Wind and the Rain* (London), 2, 1942.
Studies of Type-Images in Poetry, Religion, and Philosophy.   London and New York, Oxford University Press, 1951.

CRITICAL STUDY

Stanley Edgar Hyman, "Maud Bodkin and Psychological Criticism," in *The Armed Vision: A Study in the Methods of Modern Literary Criticism.*   New York, Knopf, 1948.
Irene Helen Zagorski, *Maud Bodkin's Journal and Her Psychology of Literary Response.*   Unpublished Doctoral Dissertation.   Syracuse, New York, Syracuse University, 1978.

*   *   *

There seem to be two primary reasons why a critic may be interested in the recurring plot and character types we call myths or "archetypes": like Northrop Frye he may use them as a way of classifying literary works without committing himself to any very definite theory as to how they enter the works, or like Maud Bodkin he may believe that these patterns are literally inherited and therefore somehow functional parts of human nature. Thus to read Miss Bodkin properly readers should have some knowledge of Jung and his disagreement with Freud concerning the nature and purpose of art (for Jung the best places to start are the essays in *Modern Man in Search of a Soul*; for Freud, the relevant essays in Trilling's *The Liberal Imagination* and Ernest Jones' *Hamlet and Oedipus*).

Freud and Jung agree that works of art originate in the artist's unconscious but differ importantly in their conceptions of the potential value of the work. For Freud art is a kind of daydreaming, a form of wishful thinking which compensates for some lack in the dreamer's waking life; but for Jung the images an artist produces are drawn from the collective unconscious of the race and have the power to assist in the complex series of adjustments to reality which life and growth depend upon. As Miss Bodkin summarizes it,

> [Freudians maintain] that the integrating or synthetic power—which is conceived as pertaining to the conscious ego, not at all to the unconscious id—is not in psychoanalytic practice found susceptible of direct influence. The most that can be done is to remove hindrances by making the patient more aware of himself; he must then be left to achieve his own adaptation to life. Jung would agree that the analyst's task is to help the patient to self-awareness, and that he himself must achieve readaptation. The difference between the two schools lies in Jung's belief that a synthetic or creative function does pertain to the unconscious—that within the fantasies arising in sleep or waking life there are present indications of new directions or modes of adaptation, which the reflexive self, when it discerns them, may adopt, and follow with some assurance that along these lines it has the backing of unconscious energies.

Art has origins which are collective as well as private, but Freud is unable to deal with its "public" significance because "the postulates within which he works require that later and higher products of the life process be explained in terms of the elements present at the beginning." The Freudian view of art is therefore reductive and guilty of the genetic fallacy, of evaluating an entity in terms of its productive causes. But for Jung art is the instrument of a "nature" which is purposeful, which strives to correct imbalances and bring about a fully integrated, heightened consciousness. Why should nature have this goal? In a moving passage from his autobiography Jung admits that "this question strikes at the core of the problem and I cannot easily answer it. It is a confession of faith." Remembering a visit to the plains of East Africa, Jung continues, "I had the feeling of being the first man, the first being to know that all this *is*....In the very moment in which I knew it, the world came into existence, and without this moment, it would never have been. All nature seeks this purpose, and finds it fulfilled in man and only in the most differentiated, the most conscious man." For Freud such talk of purpose is mere vanity and human presumption: we are simply here, left with the painful task of making the short term best of a bad job, threatened by destructive forces within and without; the consolations of art are illusory. For Jung the function of art is similar to that of religion. All human achievement involves maximizing one set of capacities at the expense of another set (the West, for example, has exploited the rational rather than the intuitive power of the mind); inevitably we become "one sided," but nature, seeking to restore wholeness, uses the artist and the prophet to produce compelling images of the energies we have neglected. Thus Miss Bodkin observes that in writing of man's "search for a soul"

> Jung has described the archetypes as "psychic organs," that may become "atrophied," but whose right functioning is necessary to mental and spiritual health. Such an organ would be the archetype of saving wisdom, appearing as the image of deliverer, or guide, in time of need. "The archetypal image of the wise man, the saviour or redeemer," Jung has written, "is awakened whenever the times are out of joint," when "conscious life is characterized by onesidedness."

In this special sense, then, the value of a given work is relative to the requirements of a particular time and place. But for Miss Bodkin, if not for all Jungians, the power of a work does not reside simply in the kind of image it presents. Thus after examining the dream of a patient undergoing analysis—a dream which seems to express the rebirth pattern present in *The Rime of the Ancient Mariner*—she observes the dream is inert, without the capacity to move anyone but the dreamer, whereas Charles Lamb's initial response to Coleridge's poem anticipated what John Livingston Lowes calls "the experience of thousands." A work of art is more than the pattern it contains because the poet has at his disposal resources of euphony and rhythm whose "evocative power" embodies the mythic content in a vivid and pleasurable manner. Miss Bodkin is therefore fairly close to the kind of critical pluralism recommended by R.S. Crane when she admits that "the images studied...in any particular instance of their occurrence in poetry can be considered either as related to the sensibility of a certain poet, and a certain age and country, or as a mode of expressing something potentially realizable in human experience of any time or place." Her preferred critical "language," to use Crane's term, is simply that of archetypal detection; she is under no illusions about its capacity to account for everything worth knowing about a particular work.

She begins *Archetypal Patterns in Poetry* with an ingenious argument to explain why we are responsive to the pattern of the classical tragedy. In *Oedipus*, for example, there is a conflict between the community suffering from the plague and the assertive protagonist whose actions have caused the plague. Each member of the audience, however, feels within himself the same tension between individual and communal claims:

> every individual must in some degree experience the contrast between a personal self—a limited ego, one among many—and a self that is free to range imaginatively through all human achievement. In infancy and in the later years of those who remain childish, a comparatively feeble imaginative activity together with an undisciplined instinct of self-assertion may present a fantasy self—the image of an infantile personality—in conflict with the chastened image which social contacts, arousing the instinct of submission, tend to enforce. In the more mature mind that has soberly taken the measure of the

personal self as revealed in practical life, there remains the contrast between this and the self revealed in imaginative thought....The experience of tragic drama both gives in the figure of the hero an objective form to the self of imaginative aspiration, or to the power-craving, and also, through the hero's death, satisfies the counter movement of feeling toward the surrender of personal claims and the merging of the ego within a greater power—the "community consciousness."

This "felt release...would seem to constitute that element of religious mystery—of purgation and atonement—traditionally connected with the idea of tragedy." Nevertheless, tragedy expresses only one important part of the whole range of human concerns; and here it is useful to turn to the conception of myth Northrop Frye develops in *Fables of Identity*. Primitive man found himself cast adrift in a natural world whose cyclic processes controlled his existence and suggested a series of crucial analogies between dawn, spring, and birth; between noon, summer, and maturity; and finally between night, winter, and death. The function of myth and religion is to put man into some sort of intelligible relationship with this cyclic movement; just as there is another dawn and another spring, so there is hope for rebirth or human continuance in one form or another. We may imagine a circle: at the top is summer and fulness of being, at the bottom, winter and darkness. Myth and ritual encompass both zenith and nadir: literature is a kind of displaced mythology and thus we may uncover a part of the cyclic pattern in any work we examine. The action of tragedy moves downward, the action of comedy upward, toward rebirth or restoration. Miss Bodkin finds the archetype of rebirth at work in *The Rime of the Ancient Mariner*, for example, and then goes on to discuss the basic images of the heroic man, woman, and the devil or evil in the epic patterns of Vergil, Dante and Milton:

> for the knowledge of the recurrences, the rhythms and seasons of life—a knowledge almost essential to the attitudes of courage and patience in misfortune and of temperance in prosperity—we depend upon participation in a moral and psychological tradition conveyed through the great images of tragic poetry and myth....The emotional significance of such images comes to inhere in the words used by the poet alike for the rhythms of nature and of human life....All poetry, laying hold of the individual through the sensuous resources of language, communicates in some measure the experience of an emotional but supra-personal life...[and] affords us a means of increased awareness, and of fuller expression and control, of our own lives in their secret and momentous obedience to universal rhythms.

The presence of such patterns is not limited, of course, to classical tragedy and the epic, as Miss Bodkin attempts to demonstrate in her references to *Orlando, Women in Love* and *The Waste Land*. In a separate monograph, *The Quest for Salvation in an Ancient and a Modern Play*, she examines in detail the parallels between the *Oresteia* of Aeschylus and T.S. Eliot's *The Family Reunion*:

> In the play of Eliot the same theme of wisdom, salvation, through suffering, is wrought out in terms of present-day life and of new psychological insight. We are shown personal despair and impotence—outcome of evil relationship blindly suffered and reproduced— transformed in a moment of understanding and of personal relationship sacramentally complete. Within that completeness is integrated the outcome of suffering mind and body have endured—all the groping exploration and self-probing achieved under the driving torment of those Furies known at last as ministers of salvation, the Eumenides.

In *Archetypal Patterns* Miss Bodkin had made the obvious extension of the rebirth archetype to the figure of Christ; but at that time she decided that she would "maintain this [mythic] view of the Gospel story, valuing it as poetry rather than in direct relation to history": she was content to accept Santayana's definition of religion as poetry in which one happens to believe. In her last book, however, *Studies of Type-Images in Poetry, Religion, and Philosophy*, she has clearly moved to a theistic if not unequivocally Christian position. She felt impelled, she tells us,

> to carry further what I had essayed to do in *Archetypal Patterns in Poetry*. If in the writing and reading of such poetry such patterns and images are operative, equally they

must be present in those religious and philosophic writings not named as poetry where men express their vision or theory of human capacity and the human condition, its origin and meaning. For those of us who cannot accept the dogmas of any religion as uniquely revealed by God, faith may be possible that the more universal ideas or patterns underlying these doctrines are God-given, their evolution into greater clarity and relevance to life part of the divine intention for man. In this faith the attempt, however inadequate as it may be, to trace such patterns in world-literature and relate them to present need becomes part of our duty to God.

She writes now as one who "maintains, though not easily, faith in the existence of God" and a divine plan. This final study traces the images of God present in works from Plato through Schweitzer and Martin Buber, and examines the image of the Sage as it recurs in a wide range of contexts. And she concludes that

I have not thought of this realization of the archetype as a meeting simply of subjective human need and objective traditional image. I have assumed, with Jung, that the individual mind brings to the encounter a creative activity, and that creative activity went into the fashioning of the image in the past. But also, I have believed that in the encounter there is co-operation of an influence, termed by the philosopher Whitehead, the Divine persuasion, and, by theologians, the Grace of God.

The works of the imagination are now quite literally the messengers of Grace.

BOOTH, Wayne C(layson).   American.   Born in American Fork, Utah, 22 February 1921. Educated at Brigham Young University, Salt Lake City, Utah, B.A. 1944; University of Chicago, M.A. 1947, Ph.D. 1950. Served in the United States Army, 1944-46. Married Phyllis Barnes in 1946; has 2 children. Instructor, University of Chicago, 1947-50; Assistant Professor, Haverford College, Pennsylvania, 1950-53; Professor of English and Chairman of the Department, Earlham College, Richmond, Indiana, 1953-62. George M. Pullman Professor of English, 1962-70, and since 1970 Distinguished Service Professor, University of Chicago (Dean of the College, 1964-69; Chairman, Committee on Ideas and Methods, 1972-75; Chairman, Board of University Publications, 1974-75, 1979-80). Fellow of the School of Letters, Indiana University, 1962; Christian Gauss Lecturer in Criticism, Princeton University, New Jersey, 1974; Phi Beta Kappa Visiting Scholar, 1977-78; Beckman Lecturer and Visiting Professor, University of California, Berkeley, 1979; Professor, The School of Criticism, University of California at Irvine, 1979. Trustee, Earlham College, 1965-75. Co-Editor, *Critical Inquiry*, Chicago; Member, Editorial Board, *Novel*; *Philosophy and Rhetoric*; and *Scholia Satyrica*. Member, National Executive Committee, College Conference on Composition and Communications, 1952-56; Member, National Advisory Council, Danforth Foundation Associates Program, 1963-69; Member, Commission on Literature, National Council of Teachers of English, and National Council on Religion and Higher Education, 1967-70; Member, Executive Council, 1973-76, and President, 1980-82, Modern Language Association of America. Recipient: Guggenheim Fellowship, 1956, 1969; Christian Gauss Award, Phi Beta Kappa, 1962; David H. Russell Award, National Council of Teachers of English, 1966; Quantrell Prize for Undergraduate Teaching, University of Chicago, 1972; American Academy of Arts and Sciences Fellowship, 1972; National Endowment for the Humanities Fellowship, 1975; Rockefeller Foundation Fellowship, 1981. Litt.D.: Rockford College, Illinois, 1965; St. Ambrose College, Davenport, Iowa, 1971; University of New Hampshire, Durham, 1977. Address: Department of English, University of Chicago, Chicago, Illinois 60637, U.S.A.

PUBLICATIONS

Criticism

The Rhetoric of Fiction.   Chicago and London, University of Chicago Press, 1961.
"The Use of Criticism in the Teaching of English," in *College English* (Chicago), 27, 1965.
Introduction to *The Idea of the Humanities and Other Essays Critical and Historical*, by
  R.S. Crane.   Chicago and London, University of Chicago Press, 2 vols., 1967.
Introduction to *Robert Liddell on the Novel.*   Chicago and London, University of
  Chicago Press, 1969.
Now Don't Try to Reason with Me: Essays and Ironies for a Credulous Age.   Chicago
  and London, University of Chicago Press, 1970.
"Kenneth Burke's Way of Knowing," in *Critical Inquiry* (Chicago), 1, 1974.
A Rhetoric of Irony.   Chicago and London, University of Chicago Press, 1974.
"Irony and Pity Once Again: Thaïs Revisited," in *Critical Inquiry* (Chicago), 2, 1975.
"M.H. Abrams: Historian as Critic, Critic as Pluralist," in *Critical Inquiry* (Chicago), 2,
  1976.
"The Limits of Pluralism I: 'Preserving the Exemplar'; or, How Not to Dig Our Own
  Graves," in *Critical Inquiry* (Chicago), 3, 1977.
"Form in *The Works of Love*," and "The Writing of Organic Fiction: A Conversation
  Between Wayne C. Booth and Wright Morris," in *Conversations with Wright Morris:
  Critical Views and Responses*, edited by Robert E. Knoll.   Lincoln, University of
  Nebraska Press, 1977.
"Metaphor as Rhetoric: The Problem of Evaluation," and "Ten Literal 'Theses,' " in
  Critical Inquiry (Chicago), 5, 1978.
Critical Understanding: The Powers and Limits of Pluralism.   Chicago and London,
  University of Chicago Press, 1978.
" 'The Way I Loved George Eliot': Friendship With Books As A Neglected Critical
  Metaphor," in *Kenyon Review* (Gambier, Ohio), 2 n.s., 1980.
"History as Metaphor: or, Is M.H. Abrams a Mirror, or a Lamp, or a Fountain, or...?" in
  High Romantic Argument: Essays for M.H. Abrams, edited by Lawrence Lipking.
  Ithaca, New York, and London, Cornell University Press, 1981.

Other

"Is There Any Knowledge That a Man Must Have?" in *The Knowledge Most Worth
  Having*, edited by Wayne C. Booth.   Chicago and London, University of Chicago
  Press, 1967.
Modern Drama and the Rhetoric of Assent.   Notre Dame, Indiana and London, Univer-
  sity of Notre Dame Press, 1974.

CRITICAL STUDY

John Ross Baker, "From Imitation to Rhetoric: The Chicago Critics, Wayne C. Booth,
  and *Tom Jones*," in *Novel* (Providence, Rhode Island), 6, 1973.

                         *   *   *

Like his mentor, R.S. Crane, Wayne Booth is a "Chicago" critic, a "Neo-Aristotelian" critic,
or as he would prefer to be called, a critical pluralist. Since this position is far from being
generally understood, however, some careful distinctions are in order if readers are to appreciate the full value of *The Rhetoric of Fiction* and *A Rhetoric of Irony*.
   The Aristotelian conception of art as essentially imitative or representational rests on a

broad definition of man and the proper end of human life. That end is happiness, but happiness for man *qua* man, involving the pleasures which result from exercising our unique characteristics as creatures capable of reason (the ability to abstract and deliberate) and morality (the capacity—and the desire—to live in harmonious relationship with our fellow men). Thus the most important question an Aristotelian can ask about art is what contribution it may make to the goals of life itself (the doctrine of art as irrational or gratuitous activity or mere self-expression makes no sense inside this particular philosophic framework). Booth's position concerning the value of art is indicated most clearly, perhaps, in *A Rhetoric of Irony*, when he observes that "for me, one good reading of one good passage is worth as much as anything there is, because the person achieving it is living life fully in that time....Perhaps I should just add that I do not see how any such person can prove to be useless in the world." Genuine aesthetic experience means, at least for the duration of that experience, the sharing of a perspective, a meeting of minds. "I have always assumed," Booth continues, that it is "good for two minds to meet in symbolic exchange." Unlike philosophical propositions or moral injunctions, a work of art is "*a living out* of how some problems of life can be represented." The firmly Aristotelian basis of Booth's thinking in this respect is apparent in a central passage from *Modern Dogma and the Rhetoric of Assent*:

> We must finally ask ourselves whether a creature made through assent, a rational animal—that is, a man who can find his "self" only through his communal building of selves, who can find his life, in fact, only by losing himself back into the society of selves that made him—whether such a man can finally withhold assent to the nature of things.

One of the ways in which we learn to assent is through our symbolic exchanges with each other; and assent—wisdom, the acceptance of the "proffered gifts" of existence, call it what you will—is a fundamental human gesture: "The great original choice between being and nothingness was, and eternally is, a fantastic, incomprehensible act of assent rather than denial: the universe is, nothingness is not." Thus art, as a vivid kind of prospective sharing or communing, assists us in the job of becoming fully human—even when a given work questions what we accept as true:

> from birth our primary movement is toward the world, to grasp it, assenting to and taking on other selves, new truths, the whole world. Our withdrawals and rejections come always in the light of some affirmation that has been denied or is being threatened. If man is essentially a rhetorical animal, his essential human act is that of making himself a self, in the symbolic communion with his fellows; that is, each of us makes himself or herself by assenting to and incorporating whoever and whatever represents life at its most immediate and persuasive. Our negatives are learned as we discover violations of our affirmings.

In his most recent book, *Critical Understanding* (primarily about the epistemological problems involved in establishing a genuine "pluralism of pluralisms" which is not simply a disguised form of monism or relativism), Booth reiterates this crucial point. There is a vital connection, as before, between understanding, virtue and human fulfillment: "understanding," he writes, "is a supreme value," and understanding, for Booth, is nothing less than "*the goal, process, and result whenever one mind succeeds in entering another mind or, what is the same thing, whenever one mind succeeds in incorporating any part of another mind.*" It is art, once again, which can powerfully stimulate and heighten this process of "understanding," which is by no means, as Booth goes on to demonstrate, a kind of mindless submission to the artist.

The artist, as a kind of calculating craftsman, makes his analogues of natural processes and forms, reflecting in these "imitations" the same forces of cause and effect, necessity and probability which govern the "real" world (including, of course, the world of human behavior). Thus art is more philosophic than history, as Aristotle maintains, because it reveals how the world actually runs. Coming to know the "meanings of things" is a source of pleasure, and so too is the experience of closure, unity, order, balance, in short all the qualities which constitute "beauty" for this approach to the nature of art. From Aristotle onwards these two terms, pleasure and knowledge, dominate the history of western criticism and its persistent attempts to justify the existence of art.

Just as natural phenomena occur in groups or classes, so most imitative works occur as members of pre-existing types ("we experience every work under the aspect of its implied general kind, or genre"). The Aristotelian discrimination among forms rests on a precise recognition of the ways in which differing literary kinds are intended to move the audience (the work is judged by its actual effect, of course, and not by some extrinsic evidence as to its "intention"). The process of criticizing is the process of experiencing the work as openly and fully as possible and then of devising an interpretive hypothesis as to the nature of the whole. The critic asks how well the artist has chosen and embodied his means, relative to his given end. And in criticism, as in the sciences, interpretive hypotheses demand flexibility and the kind of intelligence which comes only from broad experience. The model of the poor critic is the man who concludes sadly that *Oedipus* is an unsuccessful comedy.

The question, "What is a work of art?" is misleadingly reductive. Obviously it is many things: it exists as something in itself, as a constituted form, and it exists in a series of complex relationships with everything else around it. Ideally, R.S. Crane argues, we should have as many modes or "languages" of criticism as there are ways in which the work exists. In practical terms, then, we may discuss the work as an instance of a particular literary kind; moving further "outside" the work, we may consider it as an example of this artist's characteristic sensibility, conditioned, in part, by the conventions of the time; and finally we may consider the work as a force potentially affecting an audience in terms of the values we accept or deplore. Of these various dimensions, then, only the last is "rhetorical": the critic is concerned here with the power the work has to move us in a certain determinate way.

Booth's concern for effect makes possible his two primary achievements in *The Rhetoric of Fiction*. First, he examines the generally inadequate terminology which has characterized a good deal of criticism since Henry James (simplistic conceptions of "objectivity," for example, the artificial distinction between showing and telling, the conception of "pure" art and the hypostatization of one aspect of fiction as *the* essential characteristic of all fiction). And second, he demonstrates that there has been a historical shift away from the author's direct, explicit control of his readers' responses. In many modern works the intended effect is far from obvious, largely because the implied author has disappeared from the narrative and been replaced by a persona who may or may not be a reliable guide to our proper response. Interpretation becomes increasingly problematic: "whenever an impersonal author asks us to infer subtle differences between his narrator's norms and his own, we are likely to have trouble." The importance of this shift for Booth requires some careful consideration of his position concerning the morality of art.

Booth quotes with approval Jean-Louis Curtis' remarks that "if you destroy the notion of choice it is art that is annihilated." To choose, for an Aristotelian, is to choose for a purpose; the purpose which governs artistic choices is intended effect; effect in turn means evoking a particular sequence of particular emotions; and emotional responses rest, finally, on prior moral judgments. We cannot feel pity or anger or jealousy or whatever unless we have already placed the object of our response in terms of moral norms and expectations. In short, the entire system depends on the belief in objective, definable goods and the possibility of consensus. We will feel pity, for example, only if a character approaches or excels the norm; we respond quite differently to the spectacle of a wicked man suffering or prospering. It is in this sense, then, that Aristotelianism is far from being simply "formalistic." The good man should feel certain emotions on certain occasions—he *should* pity undeserved misfortune. Thus the properly made work of art strengthens our capacity for right response. As critics we may be content to observe that the means the artist has chosen are superbly fitted to his end; but as moralists, as citizens, we may wish to question the appropriateness of that end. From an ethical point of view some responses *are* clearly more important than others.

A "pure" rhetoric, then, would limit itself to the discussion of means, of the ways in which artists as diverse as Boccaccio, Fielding, Jane Austen and Céline have in fact achieved their ends; and in this respect Booth has given us the most important discussion of fictional techniques that we have. But the difficulties some readers have had with the conclusion of the *Rhetoric* indicate that Booth is not entirely concerned with matters of execution. The ambiguities which "unreliable" narrators foster are responsible for some "extraordinary delights"—and for some "critical troubles" as well. Few of us can be happy, Booth argues, with *The Turn of the Screw*, in which "we cannot decide whether the subject is two evil children as seen by a naïve, well-meaning governess or two innocent children as seen by a hysterical, destructive governess." Works such as James' "The Pupil" and Joyce's *Portrait of the Artist as a Young Man* leave us with real dilemmas for right response: Joyce's Stephen can hardly be a vain, self-indulgent young prig *and* a heroic figure of the artist. Of course we might argue that since life is deeply ambiguous and conclusive judgments virtually impossible, these works approach the true goal of imitative art. But Booth is unwilling to go quite this far: the last decades, he maintains, have produced an audience that has been "thrown off-guard by a barrage of ironic works.... In short we have looked for so long at foggy landscapes in misty mirrors that we have come to *like* fog. Clarity and simplicity are suspect; irony reigns supreme." And he concludes that "impersonal narration has raised moral difficulties too often for us to dismiss moral questions as irrelevant to technique." There may be a limit, he proposes, to what we should praise simply on the grounds that it has been fully rendered.

Booth has quite properly denied the implications his conclusions raise, however faintly, of formal or informal censorship (his position regarding censorship is developed in "Censorship and Values in Fiction," reprinted in *Now Don't Try to Reason with Me*). If some readers continue to be disturbed by the shifting argument of the last pages of the *Rhetoric* they should at least recognize that the "shift" is one an Aristotelian—and not just an Aristotelian critic— must make. Booth has returned the question of art to the context of the question, what kind of moral world do we wish to inhabit? Thus after pointing out the fully-realized excellence of *Lear* and a couplet by Pope

> I am his Highness' dog at Kew;
> Pray tell me, sir, whose dog are you?

Booth admits (in *A Rhetoric of Irony*) that "I simply cannot, try as I will, claim that the total picture of man and his universe implied in Pope's couplet is as interesting, as comprehensive, as true, as important, as the picture I get from *Lear*. But again, if you disagree with me, where are we to turn for genuine grounds of debate? Obviously we can turn only to other disciplines, many of which we will find plagued by the dogma that value judgments are essentially indefensible." Wherever we turn, he concludes, "we open up problems of value theory that some would say cannot be reasonably argued and that all would agree are not specific to 'literary criticism.' " That value judgments can be reasonably considered and held is precisely the point of *Modern Dogma and the Rhetoric of Assent*; and while that complex and eloquent book is not primarily a work of "literary criticism," it is indispensable reading for anyone interested in Booth's position—and in problems of valuation in general.

A Rhetoric of Irony is a more specialized book. Here Booth argues that irony is not, of course, a "genre" but a device which writers can use to further many different kinds of effects. A "stable" irony is one which demands that we reject the overt meaning of a statement ("Ignore the hungry and they'll go away") and reconstruct a new meaning which represents the author's "real" message. Since this reconstruction involves the collaboration of an alert reader, stable ironies provide a pleasure of their own; they "force us into hierarchical participation and hence make the results more actively our own." If they succeed, they succeed "more strongly than any literal statement can do" and create "a density and economy impossible in any literal mode." In "unstable" ironies, however, there is no real message: "The author—insofar as we can discover him, and he is often very remote indeed—refuses to declare himself, however subtly, for *any* proposition, even the opposite of whatever proposition his irony vigorously denies." As one might predict, Booth has rather less taste for such ironies, but it is not simply a matter of taste or moral concern. There is a logical problem here as well, since the nihilistic views which such ironies usually seem to support contradict the very definition of art as something to be understood and shared. After a brief consideration of Beckett (whom he genuinely admires), Booth concludes that "it seems likely that in all 'infinitely unstable' works that succeed, the same paradoxical communings will be found. The dramatic path of author and audience is somehow shared."

In the preface to *A Rhetoric of Irony* Booth remarks, "I have heard it said that the two standard tutorial questions of Oxford are 'What does he mean?' and 'How does he know?' " "I doubt the report," he goes on; "no university could be that good." Booth's own criticism embodies just these virtues: he asks (often with devastating results) what other critics know and how they claim to know it—what kinds of logic they use to reach what they *tell* us they know—and is scrupulous in constructing his own arguments. What he claims to know he states clearly and in such a way that his readers know why his position might reasonably be held. In short, he reasons with his readers. This might seem to be the beginning of critical wisdom, but anyone familiar with the oracular manner of many modern critics and their disdain for argument should be able to appreciate the value—it is hard not to say the unique value—of Booth's accomplishments.

BRADBURY, Malcolm (Stanley). British. Born in Sheffield, Yorkshire, 7 September 1932. Educated at West Bridgford Grammar School; University College of Leicester, B.A. in English 1953; Queen Mary College, University of London, M.A. in English 1955; Indiana University, Bloomington, 1955-56; University of Manchester, 1956-58, Ph.D. in American Studies 1963. Married Elizabeth Salt in 1959; has two children. Staff Tutor in Literature, Extra-Mural Department, University of Hull, Yorkshire, 1960-61; Lecturer in English, University of Birmingham, 1961-65. Lecturer in English, 1965-67, Senior Lecturer, 1967-69, Reader, 1969-70, and since 1970 Professor of American Studies, University of East Anglia, Norwich. Visiting Fellow, All Souls College, Oxford, 1969; Visiting Professor, University of Zurich, 1972. Member of the Committee of the British Association for American Studies. Recipient: British Association for American Studies Junior Fellowship, 1958; American Council of Learned Societies Fellowship, 1965; Heinemann Award, 1976. Address: 14 Heigham Grove, Norwich NR4 7TJ; or Lockington House Cottage, Lockington, near Driffield, East Yorkshire, England.

PUBLICATIONS

Criticism

Evelyn Waugh. Edinburgh, Oliver and Boyd, 1964.
What Is a Novel? London, Arnold, 1969.
"Introduction: The State of Criticism Today," in *Contemporary Criticism*, Stratford-Upon-Avon Studies 12, edited by Malcolm Bradbury and David Palmer. London, Arnold, and New York, St. Martin's Press, 1970.
The Social Context of Modern English Literature. Oxford, Blackwell, and New York, Schocken Books, 1971.
Possibilities: Essays on the State of the Novel. London and New York, Oxford University Press, 1972.
"The Cities of Modernism" and "London 1890-1920"; "The Name and Nature of Modernism" and "Movements, Magazines and Manifestos," with James McFarlane; "The Introverted Novel," with John Fletcher, in *Modernism 1890-1930*, edited by Malcolm Bradbury and James McFarlane. London, Penguin, 1976.
"The Outland Dart: American Writers and European Modernism," in *Proceedings of the British Academy* (London), 63, 1977.
"Preface" and "Putting in the Person: Character and Abstraction in Current Writing and Painting," in *The Contemporary English Novel*, edited by Malcolm Bradbury and George Palmer. London, Arnold, 1979; New York, Holmes and Meier, 1980.
"How I Invented America," in *Journal of American Studies* (Cambridge, England), 14, 1980.

Verse

Two Poets, with Allan Rodway.   Nottingham, Byron Press, 1966.

Plays

Between These Four Walls, with David Lodge and James Duckett (produced Birmingham, 1963).
Slap in the Middle, with David Lodge, David Turner, and James Duckett (produced Birmingham, 1965).

Radio Plays: *This Sporting Life*, with Elizabeth Bradbury, from the novel by David Storey, 1974; *Patterson*, with Christopher Bigsby, 1981.

Television Plays: *The After Dinner Game*, with Christopher Bigsby, 1975; *The Enigma*, from the story by John Fowles, 1980; *Standing In for Henry*, 1980.

Novels

Eating People Is Wrong.   London, Secker, and Warburg, 1959; New York, Knopf, 1960.
Stepping Westward.   London, Secker, and Warburg, 1965; Boston, Houghton Mifflin, 1966.
The History Man.   London, Secker, and Warburg, 1975; Boston, Houghton Mifflin, 1976.

Short Stories

Who Do You Think You Are? Stories and Parodies.   London, Secker and Warburg, 1976.

Other

Phogey! How to Have Class in a Classless Society.   London, Parrish, 1960.
All Dressed Up and Nowhere to Go: The Poor Man's Guide to the Affluent Society.
London, Parrish, 1962.

Editor, *E.M. Forster: A Collection of Critical Essays.*   Englewood Cliffs, New Jersey, Prentice Hall, 1966.
Editor, *Pudd'nhead Wilson, and Those Extraordinary Twins*, by Mark Twain.   London, Penguin, 1969.
Editor, *E.M. Forster: A Passage to India: A Casebook.*   London, Macmillan, 1970.
Editor, with David Palmer, *Contemporary Criticism.*   London, Arnold, 1970; New York, St. Martin's Press, 1971.
Editor, with Eric Mottram, *U.S.A.*, in *The Penguin Companion to Literature 3.*   London, Allen Lane-Penguin Press, and New York, McGraw Hill, 1971.
Editor, with David Palmer, *The American Novel and the Nineteen Twenties.*   London, Arnold, 1971.
Editor, with James McFarlane, *Modernism 1890-1900.*   London, Penguin, 1976.
Editor, *The Novel Today: Contemporary Writers on Modern Fiction.*   Manchester, Manchester University Press, and Totowa, New Jersey, Rowman and Littlefield, 1977.

Editor, with David Palmer, *The Contemporary English Novel*.   London, Arnold, 1979; New York, Holmes and Meier, 1980.
Editor, with Howard Temperley, *An Introduction to American Studies*.   London, Longman, 1981.

*   *   *

"The only real justification for criticism's existence," Malcolm Bradbury observes in the first essay of *Possibilities*, is that "openness of sympathy" which can illuminate the formal structures of literature; and literature, like the other arts, has as its justification the "power...to know and interpret the world and also to act as an humane influence on it." No one is likely to dispute these broad generalizations, but what gives Bradbury's work its particular interest is the sharpness of his practical criticism and his determination to find a poetics of the novel which will permit the openness and flexibility fiction demands. The chief influence at work here is the pluralism of the late R.S. Crane (who shares the dedication of *Possibilities* with David Lodge); but Bradbury's partial use of Crane leads to an impasse which pluralism is designed to prevent. (For a full statement of this position the reader should turn to *The Languages of Criticism and the Structure of Poetry*, but very briefly, Crane argues that no single critical approach or "language," with its necessarily limited vocabulary and means of argument, can discuss a given work in all its dimensions. We may be concerned with the style and meaning of a work as an individual instance of a literary kind; we may wish to discuss it in its relationship to the artist's sensibility or to the historical period which in part shaped it; or we may wish to examine it in terms of the values we hold or deplore. Each line of inquiry is valid and potentially important for certain purposes, but no one method will encompass the work itself *and* its multiple relationships.

Modern criticism of the novel began as a kind of poor relation of modern criticism of a particular kind of poetry (or it might be more accurate to say that for some modern critics fiction itself is a poor relation of poetry). If the New Critics turned their attention to a novel, they were likely to "poetize" it, that is, to apply the methods and criteria which seemed to work so well for Donne and Eliot. But novels are not simply failed poems; they have their own special powers and require a poetics which starts by recognizing the equal claims of a Jane Austen or Joyce. As to the essential nature of fiction, Bradbury agrees with Ian Watt and other recent critics that the novel has always had a basic commitment to the realistic portrayal of men living in society:

To deal with the novel form head-on, you have to come to terms with its sheer contingency and looseness, with the fact that novels cannot be possessed, in a single critical instant, as complete wholes; with the novel's traditionally large dependence on social experience, its tendency to explore and substantiate by the making of worlds containing likely persons and places and causal sequences; with its disposition to represent personages; with its narrative passion; and above all with its need to establish its credit with a reader on the basis of some form of recognition, some basic appeal to veracity.

Compared to the established genres of poetry and drama the novel is to some extent "formless." This is the price it pays for its empiricism; but formal characteristics are precisely what traditional poetics have always depended upon.

Readers familiar with R.S. Crane's work will anticipate easily enough the problem Bradbury faces. The novel cannot be a "genus" or "form" if we use those terms with any precision. To some extent we may talk about characteristic subject matter, typical means of presentation and even about appropriate kinds of diction in the novel, but the determining factor in the discrimination among forms, for an Aristotelian critic, is overall effect, the end for which everything else has been chosen. Here Bradbury has little to say—yet he persists in talking about species and forms of fiction. Divergence from Crane is not the point here: the problem is rather that Bradbury seems unable thus far to come up with anything which could make a unified poetics possible. "Openness" and "realism" are hardly generic terms; and if Bradbury is willing to go so far as to admit that "no generic theory can let us define closely the kind of matter [the novel] is likely to imitate, nor the kind of effect it is likely to produce," what is to serve as the basis for an a-generic poetics? And in fact when Bradbury does try to propose a basis, he becomes extremely general and vague:

> From the point of view of a poetics, then, a more profitable approach is surely to propose that novels are distinguishable and have much in common with each other, even over an extended chronological period; that while they have no *typical* action (as does tragedy), there are typical compositional problems, recurrent practices, definable options; and that these characteristics are particular derivatives of their fictive nature, their character as prose, and their length, or epic dimension.

Without further definition and specification it is hard to see how such a poetics could possibly

> allow for the book's referential dimension as an account of life, its rhetorical dimension as a species of language, its sociological dimension as an exploration and crystallization of a cultural situation, its philosophical dimension as a mode of thought, its stylistic dimension as a species of formed cultural gesture, and its psychological or mythic dimension as an exploration of individual or broadly social psychic experience.

These quotations are drawn from *Possibilities*, but the same problems return in Bradbury's valuable survey of modern criticism which serves as the introduction to *Contemporary Criticism*. Here he concludes that in view of the various approaches criticism offers at the moment, "we might therefore assume that the ideal state of affairs in criticism is a kind of pluralistic one in which questions of all these orders can be raised to get a 'total' view. But of course the problem with such pluralism is that the poetics do not always prove consistent one with another." The obfuscating word here, "consistent," reveals Bradbury's final rejection of the kind of pluralism Crane recommends. Different systems may validly differ from each other without being inconsistent or contradictory—unless, of course, we feel that we have a master language which can discuss with equal cogency everything these different approaches attend to. The lack of "agreement" between, say, F.R. Leavis and Northrop Frye, is neither surprising nor disturbing. As Elder Olson once remarked, the men on the Tower of Babel were not talking nonsense to each other, they were speaking different languages. Yet Bradbury seems unwilling to settle for pluralism; he has unfulfilled yearnings for *a* poetics of fiction, and the burden now is upon him. Some years ago Isaiah Berlin revived Archilochus' aphorism that the fox knows many things, the hedgehog one big thing. Bradbury is a fox who wants to be a hedgehog. In all fairness it is important to add that as a fox Bradbury is one of the very best critics now writing about modern British fiction. His longer study of Evelyn Waugh and especially his essays on Angus Wilson, Irish Murdoch and John Fowles have exactly that sympathy and undogmatic intelligence he requires of criticism, unspoiled by an premature appeals to a mysterious, unifying poetics.

BROOKS, Cleanth. American. Born in Murray, Kentucky, 16 October 1906. Educated at Vanderbilt University, Nashville, Tennessee, B.A. 1928; Tulane University, New Orleans, M.A. 1929; Exeter College, Oxford (Rhodes Scholar), 1929-32, B.A. (with honours) 1931, B.Litt. 1932. Married Edith Amy Blanchard in 1934. Professor of English, Louisiana State University, Baton Rouge, 1932-47. Professor, 1947-60, Gray Professor of Rhetoric, 1960-75, and since 1975, Gray Professor of Rhetoric Emeritus, Yale University, New Haven, Connecticut. Visiting Professor, University of Texas, Austin, 1941, and University of Southern California, Los Angeles, 1953. Editor, with Robert Penn Warren, *Southern Review*, Baton Rouge, Louisiana,

1935-41. Fellow, Library of Congress, Washington, D.C. 1951-62; Cultural Attaché, American Embassy, London, 1964-66; Fellow, National Humanities Center, North Carolina, 1980-81. Recipient: Guggenheim Fellowship, 1953, 1960. D.Litt.: Upsala College, East Orange, New Jersey, 1963; University of Kentucky, 1963; University of Exeter, 1966; Washington and Lee University, Lexington, Virginia, 1968; Tulane University, New Orleans, 1969; University of the South, Sewanee, Tennessee, 1975; Newberry College, Newberry, South Carolina, 1979; L.H.D.: St. Louis University, Missouri, 1968; Centenary College, Shreveport, Louisiana, 1972; Oglethorpe University, Atlanta, Georgia, 1976; St. Peter's College, Jersey City, New Jersey, 1978; Lehigh University, Bethlehem, Pennsylvania, 1980. Member, American Academy of Arts and Sciences; National Institute of Arts and Letters. Address: 70 Ogden St., New Haven, Connecticut 06511, U.S.A.

PUBLICATIONS

Criticism

Modern Poetry and the Tradition.   Chapel Hill, University of North Carolina Press, 1939; London, Editions Poetry London, 1948.
"The Poem as Organism: Modern Critical Procedure," in *English Institute Annual 1940*.   New York, Columbia University Press, 1941.
"The New Criticism and Scholarship," in *Twentieth-Century English*, edited by W.S. Knickerbocker.   New York, Philosophical Library, 1946.
"Literary Criticism," in *English Institute Essays 1946*.   New York, Columbia University Press, 1947.
Poetry in the Age of Anxiety (lecture).   Charlottesville, University of Virginia Press, 1947.
The Well Wrought Urn: *Studies in the Structure of Poetry*.   New York, Harcourt Brace, 1947; London, Dobson, 1949.
"The Quick and the Dead: A Comment on Humanistic Studies," in *The Humanities*: *An Appraisal*, edited by Julian Harris.   Madison, University of Wisconsin Press, 1950.
"Irony as a Principle of Structure," in *Literary Opinion in America,*, vol.2, edited by Morton Dauwen Zabel.   New York Harper and Row, revised edition, 1951.
Poems of Mr. John Milton: The 1645 Edition with Essays in Analysis, with John Edward Hardy.   New York, Harcourt Brace, 1951; London, Dobson, 1959.
"Metaphor and the Function of Criticism," in *Spiritual Problems in Contemporary Literature*, edited by S.R. Hopper.   New York, Harper, 1952.
"A Note on the Limits of 'History' and the Limits of 'Criticism,' " in *Sewanee Review* (Tennessee), 61, 1953.
Literary Criticism: *A Short History*, with W.K. Wimsatt.   New York, Knopf, and London, Routledge, 1957.
"Implications of an Organic Theory of Poetry," in *Literature and Belief*, edited by M.H. Abrams.   New York, Columbia University Press, 1958.
"Literary Criticism: Poet, Poem, and Reader," in *Varieties of Literary Experience*, edited by Stanley Burnshaw.   New York, Columbia University Press, 1962.
The Hidden God: *Studies in Hemingway, Faulkner, Yeats, Eliot, and Warren*.   New Haven, Connecticut, and London, Yale University Press, 1963.
William Faulkner: *The Yoknapatawpha Country*.   New Haven, Connecticut, and London, Yale University Press, 1963.
"Metaphor, Paradox, and Stereotype in Poetic Language," in *British Journal of Aesthetics* (London), 5 1965.
The Poetry of Tension (lecture).   St. Johns, Newfoundland, Memorial University, 1971.
A Shaping Joy: *Studies in the Writer's Craft*.   New York, Harcourt Brace, and London, Methuen, 1971.

"T.S. Eliot as Modernist Poet," in *Literary Theory and Structure*: *Essays Presented to William K. Wimsatt*, edited by Frank Brady, John Palmer, and Martin Price.   New Haven, Connecticut, and London, Yale University Press, 1973.

"A Conversation with Cleanth Brooks," with Robert Penn Warren, in *The Possibilities of Order*: *Cleanth Brooks and His Work*, edited by Lewis P. Simpson.   Baton Rouge, Louisiana State University Press, 1976.

"Allen Tate and the Nature of Modernism," in *Southern Review* (Baton Rouge, Louisiana), 12, 1976.

"Walker Percy and Modern Gnosticism," in *Southern Review* (Baton Rouge, Louisiana), 13, 1977.

William Faulkner: *Toward Yoknapatawpha and Beyond*.   New Haven, Connecticut, and London, Yale University Press, 1978.

"The New Criticism," in *Sewanee Review* (Tennessee), 87, 1979.

"A Form of Thanks," in *Eudora Welty*: *Critical Essays*, edited by Peggy Whitman Prenshaw.   Jackson, University of Mississippi Press, 1980.

Other

The Relation of the Alabama-Georgia Dialect to the Provincial Dialects of Great Britain.   Baton Rouge, Louisiana State University Press, 1935.

Understanding Poetry: *An Anthology for College Students*, with Robert Penn Warren.   New York, Holt, 1938; revised edition, 1950, Holt Rinehart, 1960.

Understanding Fiction, with Robert Penn Warren.   New York, Crofts, 1943; revised edition, Appleton Century Crofts, 1959; shortened version, as *The Scope of Fiction*, 1960.

Understanding Drama, with Robert B. Heilman.   New York, Holt, 1945; London, Harrap, 1947; revised edition, Holt Rinehart, 1960.

Modern Rhetoric: *With Readings*, with Robert Penn Warren.   New York, Harcourt Brace, 1949; revised edition, 1958, 1970.

Fundamentals of Good Writing: *A Handbook of Modern Rhetoric*, with Robert Penn Warren.   New York, Harcourt Brace, 1950; London, Dobson, 1952; revised edition, Dobson, 1956.

General Editor, with David Nicol Smith, *The Percy Letters*.   Baton Rouge, Louisiana State University Press, 6 vols., 1944-61.

Editor, with John Edward Hardy, *Poems*: *The 1645 Edition*, by John Milton.   New York, Harcourt Brace, 1951.

Editor, with Robert Penn Warren, *An Anthology of Stories from the Southern Review*, Baton Rouge, Louisiana State University Press, 1953.

Editor, *Tragic Themes in Western Literature*.   New Haven, Connecticut, and London, Yale University Press, 1955.

Editor, with Robert Penn Warren and R.W.B. Lewis, *American Literature*: *The Makers and the Making*.   New York, St. Martin's Press, 2 vols., 1973.

Editor, *The Correspondence of Thomas Percy and William Shenstone*.   New Haven, Connecticut, and London, Yale University Press, 1977.

CRITICAL STUDIES

R.S. Crane, "The Critical Monism of Cleanth Brooks," in *Critics and Criticism*: *Ancient and Modern*, edited by R.S. Crane and others.   Chicago and London, University of Chicago Press, 1952.

The Possibilities of Order: *Cleanth Brooks and His Work*, edited by Lewis P. Simpson.   Baton Rouge, Louisiana State University Press, 1976.

*   *   *

The basic principles of Cleanth Brooks' literary criticism derive mainly from I.A. Richards' distinctions between science and poetry and between the "poetry of exclusion" and the "poetry of synthesis," whose defining characteristic is irony. These distinctions, which in turn derive from Coleridge, play a vital role in Richards' defense of poetry as a species of knowledge—a concern no less central to Brooks' criticism, although his claims for poetry tend to be less sweeping. The position involves one of the commonplaces of modern criticism: with the rise of science it became increasingly apparent that the statements of poetry are wrong or irrelevant if they are taken as accurate descriptions of the natural world. As "referential language" poetry is useless, but as "emotive language" it has its own special powers. For Richards the "truth" of poetry is primarily a matter of self-consistency and coherence: "That is 'true' or 'internally necessary' which completes or accords with the rest of the experience." Thus Brooks observes that

> the "truth" of *Robinson Crusoe* or of *King Lear* [for Richards], in short, has nothing to do with objective truth. The "effects of the narrative" which determine the "acceptability" of the "things we are told" are psychological effects. The happy ending supplied by Nahum Tate for *Lear* is "false" because it is at odds with the rest of the play; the play as a whole is "true" only in virtue of giving rise to the proper psychological effects, in helping us, that is, to "order our attitudes to one another and to the world." That is why "we need no beliefs" in order to read *King Lear*. Indeed, Richards goes much further and writes that "we must have [no beliefs] if we are to read *King Lear*"; for beliefs, with their claim to objective truth, would disturb the self-contained coherence, the "internal necessity" which is the only "truth" that Richards will allow to the play. Such was Richards' solution to the conflict of science and poetry: it is as drastic as it is neat.

While Brooks largely accepts the crucial distinction between science and poetry he also finds it necessary to supplement Richards' drastic solution with the additional argument, drawn from Whitehead or more probably John Crowe Ransom, that the language of science is necessarily the language of abstraction; it excludes connotations and local differences. As Whitehead points out in *Science and the Modern World*, the picture of existence offered by science is an impoverished one, stripped of the concreteness and vivid immediacy which form the very grounds of aesthetic appreciation and moral discrimination. At his best the poet is able to restore the qualities science dismisses. Thus Ransom argues that "in all human history the dualism between science and art widens continually by reason of the aggressions of science. As science more and more completely reduces the world to its types and forms, art, replying, must invest it again with body." And thus after examining closely some lines from the "Ode on a Grecian Urn," Brooks argues that like other poets, Keats is "really building a more precise sort of language...by playing off the connotations and denotations of words against each other so as to make a total statement of a great deal more accuracy than is ordinarily attained." He concludes (in *The Well Wrought Urn*) that a successful poem "is not only the linguistic vehicle which conveys the thing communicated most 'poetically,' but that it is also the sole linguistic vehicle which conveys the thing communicated accurately. In fact, if we are to speak exactly, the poem itself is the *only* medium that communicates the particular 'what' that is communicated." There are complex perceptions and delicately adjusted states of mind, "attitudes," as Richards calls them, which can be realized only by the resources of poetic language.

Brooks accepts with no qualifications the separation Richards makes between weak, reductive poetic statements uncomplicated by irony and the higher "poetry of synthesis" leading to that fulfilled consciousness Richards calls, rather oddly, "sincerity." Brooks writes that such sincerity

> reveals itself as an unwillingness to ingore the complexity of experience. The poet attempts to fuse the conflicting elements in a harmonious whole. And here one may suggest a definition of wit. Wit is not merely an acute perception of analogies; it is a lively awareness of the fact that the obvious attitude toward a given situation is not the only possible attitude. Because wit, for us, is still associated with levity, it may be well to state it in its most serious terms...it is possible to describe it as merely the poet's refusal to blind himself to multiplicity which exists.

95

Wit is not simply a kind of adornment; it is, rather, a quality of the mature, competent mind, a "cognitive principle," as W.K. Wimsatt calls it, operating by means of irony, paradox and metaphor. For Brooks a good poem is of course an organic whole in Richards' sense and a particular *context* which determines the nature of its parts in an important way:

> The context endows the particular word or image or statement with significance. Images so charged become symbols; statements so charged become dramatic utterances. But there is another way in which to look at the impact of the context upon the part. The part is modified by the pressure of the context. Now the *obvious* warping of a statement by the context we characterize as "ironical." To take the simplest instance, we say "this is a fine state of affairs," and in certain contexts the statement means quite the opposite of what it purports to say literally. This is sarcasm, the most obvious kind of irony. Here a complete reversal of meaning is effected: effected by the context, and pointed, probably, by the tone of voice. But the modification can be most important even though it falls far short of sarcastic reversal...[it] can be effected by the skillful disposition of the context. Gray's *Elegy* will furnish an obvious example.

> > Can storied urn or animated bust
> > Back to its mansion call the fleeting breath?
> > Can Honour's voice provoke the silent dust,
> > Or Flatt'ry soothe the dull cold ear of death?

> In its context, the question is obviously rhetorical. The answer has been implied in the characterization of the breath as fleeting and of the ear of death as dull and cold. The form is that of a question, but the manner in which the question has been asked shows that it is no true question at all.

Irony in this very broad sense of contextual "warping" is the essential characteristic of poetry: "the truth which the poet utters can be approached only in terms of paradox." The statements of science must be purged of connotations and contradictions:

> What indeed would be a statement wholly devoid of an ironic potential—a statement that did not show any qualification of the context? One is forced to offer statements like.... "The square on the hypotenuse of a right triangle is equal to the sum of the squares on the two sides." [Such meaning]...is unqualified by any context...[and is] properly abstract.

The basis for judging one poem, or poet, superior to another follows naturally:

> We shall probably not be able to do better than to apply T.S. Eliot's test: does the statement seem to be that which the mind of the reader can accept as coherent, mature, and founded on the facts of experience? We raise such further questions as these: Does the speaker seem carried away with his own emotions? Does he seem to oversimplify the situation? Or does he, on the other hand, seem to have won to a kind of detachment and objectivity? In other words, we are forced to raise the question as to whether the statement grows properly out of a context; whether it is "ironical"—or merely callow, glib, and sentimental. I have suggested elsewhere that the poem which meets Eliot's test comes to the same thing as I.A. Richards' "poetry of synthesis"—that is, a poetry which does not leave out what is apparently hostile to its dominant tone, and which, because it is able to fuse the irrelevant and discordant, has come to terms with itself and is invulnerable to irony.

This complex but still unified ironic vision is the sign of the most successful poetry—and of the mature comprehension of life itself; the means of establishing such a vision is primarily the metaphor which fuses its terms into a new whole. This element of fusion or reconciliation, derived again from Coleridge's conception of the imagination, is of major importance for both Richards and for Brooks, who concludes that

> The essential structure of a poem...resembles that of architecture or painting: it is a pattern of resolved stresses.... In a unified poem the poet has "come to terms" with his experience. The poem does not merely eventuate in a logical conclusion.... It is "proved" as a dramatic conclusion is proved: by its ability to resolve the conflicts which have been accepted as the *données* of the drama.

Since this capacity to recognize complexities and synthesize the conflicting elements of experience is a power no less crucial to our survival than the powers of exact measurement and description, Richards concludes that the loss of poetry would be a "biological calamity" for the human race. Brooks is more cautious:

> [metrical pattern and metaphor] function in a good poem to modify, qualify and develop the total attitude which we are to take in coming to terms with the total situation. If the last sentence seems to take a dangerous turn toward some special "use of poetry"—some therapeutic value for the sake of which poetry is to be cultivated—I can only say that I have in mind no special ills which poetry is to cure.

Elsewhere Brooks limits himself to the conventional observation that poetry can help us to understand ourselves and to conceive more vividly the reality of each other's existence—no more than this, possibly because of Brooks' Christian commitments, which separate his thinking, like that of Eliot and Auden, from the unrelenting naturalism of Richards.

Thus equipped Brooks examines the course of English poetry and finds that with the rise of science and the discrediting of the imagination, poetry from Dryden onwards exhibits little of the wit, irony and paradox which characterize the best Elizabethan and Metaphysical verse. The Romantics inherited a mistrust of wit (as well as an inadequate theory of metaphor as mere ornament) and devised for themselves a mistaken belief in the inherent "poetry" of certain subjects whose simple presence in a poem secures the proper effect. In an important sense, then, the Romantic "revolution" was abortive, whereas now (Brooks maintains in *Modern Poetry and the Tradition*), in the poetry of Eliot and Yeats and such younger men as Auden, Ransom and Warren, we have a "powerful restatement" of the Elizabethan view of the poet and his "superior power to reconcile the irrelevant or apparently warring elements of experience." The great strength of modern poetry lies in the fact that it attempts "a complete liberation of the imagination": compared to the poetry of Donne and Eliot most nineteenth century efforts are simply "immature" (it should be noted, however, that Brooks' criticism of Romantic poetry has always been more temperate than that of Tate or Eliot: in a judicious "Retrospective Introduction" to *Modern Poetry*, for example, he admits that he had underestimated the Romantic conception of metaphor and adds that if he were to write the book now he would "want to lay more stress on the extent to which Eliot, Yeats, and the other modern poets have built upon the Romantic tradition and incorporated structural devices that are a part of the general Romantic inheritance").

In *The Well Wrought Urn* Brooks selects ten poems, ranging from "The Canonization" to "Among School Children," and reads them as if they were all metaphysical lyrics by Donne, testing, in effect, for the presence of irony, which he now regards as the determining power behind all complex poetic structures (how much he leaves out to reach this conclusion readers may judge by turning to R.S. Crane's typical job of overkill, "The Critical Monism of Cleanth Brooks"). *Modern Poetry* and *The Well Wrought Urn* exerted a good deal of influence during the 1940's and 50's, partly because Brooks writes persuasively and partly because the views developed there, simplified and copiously illustrated, form the basis of *Understanding Poetry*, the anthology-cum-commentary which taught generations of American college students (such generations take only four years) what to look for and care about in poems.

The relatively uncomplicated lectures which make up most of *A Shaping Joy* and *The Hidden God* are less important from the point of view of critical theory. The former is something of a miscellany; in the latter Brooks argues that Hemingway, Faulkner, Yeats and Robert Penn Warren exhibit "approximations" of doctrinal points and are finally "to be understood only by reference to Christian premises." *The Yoknapatawpha Country* is a minutely detailed reconstruction of the world Faulkner gradually built up in his fiction, but Brooks' conservative values are very much at work here as well. He is far from treating the novels as self-contained ironic structures. *Literary Criticism: A Short History* (in which Brooks is responsible for five of the thirty-two chapters) is a major achievement by any standards. Neither short nor simply historical, it provides the fairest and most informed account of the development of critical theories we are likely to have for a very long time to come.

BROOKS, Van Wyck. American. Born in Plainfield, New Jersey, 16 February 1886. Educated at Harvard University, Cambridge, Massachusetts, B.A. 1907. Married Eleanor Kenyon Stimson in 1911 (died, 1946), two children; Gladys Rice Billings in 1947. Worked in England, 1907-1909, 1913-14; worked on *Standard Dictionary, Collier's Encyclopedia*, and *World's Work*, New York, 1909-10; Instructor in English, Stanford University, California, 1910-13; Associate Editor, *Seven Arts*, New York, 1916-17, and *Freeman*, New York, 1920-24; Contributing Editor, *The New Republic*, New York, 1941-45. Recipient: *Dial* Award, 1923; Pulitzer Prize for History, 1936; National Institute of Arts and Letters Gold Medal, 1946. Litt.D: Harvard University; Columbia University, New York; Boston University; Bowdoin College, Brunswick, Maine; Dartmouth College, Hanover, New Hampshire; Northwestern University, Evanston, Illinois; Union College, Schenectady, New York; Northeastern University, Boston. Member, Royal Society of Literature, and American Philosophical Society; Fellow, American Academy of Arts and Letters. *Died 2 May 1963.*

PUBLICATIONS

Criticism

The Wine of the Puritans: A Study of Present-Day America. London, Sisley's, 1908; New York, Mitchell Kennerley, 1909.
The Soul: An Essay Towards a Point of View. San Francisco, privately printed, 1909.
The Malady of the Ideal: Obermann, Maurice de Guérin and Amiel. London, Fifield, 1913; Philadelphia, University of Pennsylvania Press, 1947.
America's Coming-of-Age. New York, Huebsch, 1915; as *Three Essays on America*, New York, Dutton, 1934.
Letters and Leadership. New York, Huebsch, 1918.
The Ordeal of Mark Twain. New York, Dutton, 1920; London, Heinemann, 1922; revised edition, New York, Dutton, 1933; London, Dent, 1934.
The Pilgrimage of Henry James. New York, Dutton, 1925; London, Cape, 1928.
Emerson and Others. New York, Dutton, and London, Cape, 1927.
Sketches in Criticism. New York, Dutton, 1932; London, Dent, 1934.
Makers and Finders: A History of the Writer in America, 1800-1915:
    The Flowering of New England: 1815-1865. New York, Dutton, and London, Dent, 1936.
    New England: Indian Summer: 1865-1915. New York, Dutton, 1940; London, Dent, 1941.
    The World of Washington Irving. New York, Dutton, 1944; London, Dent, 1945.
    The Times of Melville and Whitman. New York, Dutton, 1947; London, Dent, 1948.
    The Confident Years: 1885-1915. New York, Dutton, and London, Dent, 1952.
On Literature Today. New York, Dutton, 1941.
Opinions of Oliver Allston. New York, Dutton, 1941; London, Dent, 1942.
A Chilmark Miscellany. New York, Dutton, 1948.
The Writer in America. New York, Dutton, 1953.
From a Writer's Notebook. New York, Dutton, and London, Dent, 1958.

The Dream of Arcadia: American Writers and Artists in Italy, 1760-1915.   New York,
Dutton, and London, Dent, 1958.

Verse

Verses by Two Undergraduates, with John Hall Wheelock.   Cambridge, Massachusetts,
privately printed, 1905.

Other

John Addington Symonds: A Biographical Study.   New York, Mitchell Kennerley, and
London, Grant Richards, 1914.
The World of H.G. Wells.   New York, Mitchell Kennerley, and London, T. Fisher
Unwin, 1915.
The Life of Emerson.   New York, Dutton, 1932; London, Dent, 1934.
Scenes and Portraits: Memories of Childhood and Youth.   New York, Dutton, and
London, Dent, 1954.
John Sloan: A Painter's Life.   New York, Dutton, and London, Dent, 1955.
Helen Keller: Sketch for a Portrait.   New York, Dutton, and London, Dent, 1956.
Days of the Phoenix: The Nineteen-Twenties I Remember.   New York, Dutton, and
London, Dent, 1957.
Howells: His Life and World.   New York, Dutton, 1959.
From the Shadow of the Mountain: My Post-Meridian Years.   New York, Dutton, 1961;
London, Dent, 1962.
Fenollosa and His Circle, with Other Essays in Biography.   New York, Dutton, 1962.
An Autobiography.   New York, Dutton, 1965.

Editor, *History of a Literary Radical and Other Essays*, by Randolph Bourne.   New
York, Huebsch, 1920.
Editor, *Journal of the First Voyage to America*, by Christopher Columbus.   New York,
Boni, 1924.
Editor, with others, *American Caravan*.   New York, Macaulay, 1927.
Editor, *The Journal of Gamaliel Bradford, 1883-1932*.   Boston, Houghton Mifflin,
1934.
Editor, *The Letters of Gamaliel Bradford, 1918-1931*.   Boston, Houghton Mifflin, 1934.
Editor, *The Roots of American Culture and Other Essays*, by Constance Rourke.   New
York, Harcourt Brace, 1942.
Editor, *A New England Reader*.   New York, Atheneum, 1962.

Translator, *The Flame That Is France*, by Henry Malherbe.   New York, Century, 1918.
Translator, *The Story of Gotton Connixloo, Followed by Forgotten*, by Camille Mayran.
New York, Dutton, 1920.
Translator, *Jean Jacques Rousseau*, by Henri Frédéric Amiel.   New York, Huebsch,
1922.
Translator, with Eleanor Stimson Brooks, *Some Aspects of the Life of Jesus from the
Psychological and Psycho-Analytic Point of View*, by Georges Berguer.   New York,
Harcourt Brace, and London, Williams and Norgate, 1923.
Translator, *Henry Thoreau: Bachelor of Nature*, by Léon Bazalgette.   New York, Har-
court Brace, 1924; London, Cape, 1925.
Translator, with Eleanor Stimson Brooks, *Summer*, by Romain Rolland.   New York,
Holt, 1925; London, Butterworth, 1927.
Translator, *Mother and Son*, by Romain Rolland.   New York, Holt, 1927; London,
Butterworth, 1928.

Translator, *The Road*, by André Chamson.   New York, Schribner, 1930.
Translator, *Roux the Bandit*, by André Chamson.   New York, Scribner, 1929.
Translator, *The Crime of the Just*, by André Chamson.   New York, Scribner, 1930.
Translator, *Philine, from the Unpublished Journals of Henri-Frédéric Amiel*.   Boston, Houghton Mifflin, 1930; London, Constable, 1931.
Translator, with Charles Van Wyck Brooks, *The Private Journal of Henri-Frédéric Amiel*.   New York, Macmillan, 1935.
Translator, *Paul Gauguin's Intimate Journals*.   New York, Crown, 1936.

CRITICAL STUDIES

F.W.Dupee, "The Americanism of Van Wyck Brooks," in *Partisan Review* (New York), 6, 1939.
Stanley Edgar Hyman, "Van Wyck Brooks and Biographical Criticism," in *The Armed Vision: A Study in the Methods of Modern Literary Criticism*.   New York, Knopf, 1948.
James R. Vitelli, *Van Wyck Brooks*.   New York, Twayne, 1969.
William Wasserstrom, *The Legacy of Van Wyck Brooks: A Study of Maladies and Motives*.   Carbondale, Southern Illinois University Press, 1971.

*   *   *

Hostile and sympathetic critics alike are usually quick to point out the curious fact that there were really two Van Wyck Brookses: Brooks from 1908 to 1925, the radical analyst of American life, intent on demonstrating how an inadequate culture means an inadequate literature; and Brooks the reactionary, equally intent, from 1932 until his death in 1963, on denouncing modernism and idealizing much of the American past he once scorned. Granted that the division is real enough, it is still possible to see a certain coherence in Brooks' work, although it exists at a level so general it does little to explain or justify his particular inconsistencies and contradictions. What remains constant is best indicated by an important passage from the early *Malady of the Ideal*, where Brooks asserts that

life ought to be of such a character that every personality can be free to realize itself. And it is only by the study of personality that we can understand the obstructions that exist in the world and the methods of removing them.

Self-fulfillment is the goal, but can be realized only in the context of a "human" society which is an "all-embracing organism." Thus Brooks devotes much of his early criticism to an analysis of how American culture has made full personal development impossible. Compared to the ideal society America is still in its "Darwinian" stage: self-assertion, not self-fulfillment dominates our lives, accumulation rather than maturity is the guiding principle of national consciousness—all because of the unrestrained individualism which results from secularized Puritanism:

So it is from the beginning that we find two main currents in the American mind running side by side but rarely mingling—a current of overtones and a current of undertones— and both equally unsocial: on the one hand the transcendental current, originating in the piety of the Puritans, becoming philosophy in Jonathan Edwards, passing through Emerson, producing the fastidious refinement and aloofness of the chief American writers, and resulting in the final unreality of most contemporary American culture; and on the other hand the current of catch-penny opportunism, originating in the practical shifts of Puritan life, becoming a philosophy in Franklin, passing through the American humorists, and resulting in the atmosphere of our contemporary business life.

American literature has suffered because of this split, torn between stark realism and practicality and the "vaporous idealism" which developed as a weak counterstatement ("When Americans are idealists," Brooks observes in *The Wine of the Puritans*, "they are, by reaction, impossible idealists!—utterly scorning the real and useful and the practical.") Density, weight and richness are missing; and although Thoreau, Emerson, Poe and Hawthorne may be "possessions forever," Brooks continues,

> this does not alter the fact that if my soul were set on the accumulation of dollars not one of them would have the power to move me from it. And I take this to be a suggestive fact. Not one of them, not all of them, have had the power to move the soul of America from the accumulation of dollars; and when one has said this, one has arrived at some sort of basis for literary criticism.

This "basis," however, rests on a more fundamental belief in the relationship between the writer and his culture. All vital relationships, for Brooks, are reciprocal: "the mind can work healthily only when it is essentially in touch with the society of its own age." Poe, for all his gifts,

> having nothing in common with the world that produced him, constructed a little parallel world of his own, withered at the core, a silent comment. It is this that makes him so sterile and inhuman; and he is himself, conversely, the most menacing indictment of a society which is not also an all-embracing organism.

Yet in 1915 Brooks also felt that America was coming of age: there was "something vibrating in the air"—the promise of a new socialist basis for society which would replace competition with cooperation. And "if it is for the State to weed out the incentives to private gain, it is for us meanwhile simultaneously to build up other incentives to replace them." "We" here means the artists and critics who are the "path-finders of society; to [us] belongs the vision without which the people perish." Given these principles Brooks' early work fell into place readily: in *The Wine of the Puritans* he begins his attack on Puritanism; in *America's Coming-of-Age* he makes his full statement concerning the divisions in American life and its consequences for our literature; and in the lesser-known *Letters and Leadership* he deplores the intellectuals who have lost their calling and surrendered their humane values. Here he concludes that "we find no principle of integrity at work in any department of our life."

The final part of the crucial quotation from *The Malady of the Ideal*, that it is only by the study of personality that we can understand the "obstructions" in American life that prevent self-realization, accounts for Brooks' intention in *The Ordeal of Mark Twain* and *The Pilgrimage of Henry James*. As James Vitelli has pointed out, for Brooks "the critic becomes a kind of therapist; he aims at the removal of obstructions to fulfillment"; and as William Wasserstrom has observed, in another recent and sympathetic study, "the books on Mark Twain and James would exhibit the consquences of lowbrow debasement of spirit in American literature...Mark Twain the infernal lowbrow and James the expurgated highbrow were victims of a civilization which it was Brooks's holy mission to reform." By staying home and giving in to the values of a commercial culture Twain ruined his talent and ended his career in despair and bitter pessimism; by leaving America and thus denying himself a vital, sustaining relationship with his culture Henry James ruined his talent, producing work which was increasingly unreal and inconsequential. Their fates provide a critical lesson for the would-be writer now:

> Read, writers of America, the driven, disenchanted, anxious faces of your sensitive countrymen; remember the splendid parts your confrères have played in the human drama of other times and other peoples, and ask yourselves whether the hour has not come to put away childish things and walk on the stage as poets do.

The Twain book still seems to enjoy some respect but *The Pilgrimage of Henry James* is by any standards a wretched job of thesis-mongering and distortion. Stanley Edgar Hyman's sharp verdict is hard to dispute:

> Even if [the absurdity of the book] had not been an inevitable result of an aesthetic deficiency, it would have been an inevitable result of the assumption underlying the book, that James killed his talent by cutting his native roots, which required Brooks to find James's work progressively deteriorating, just as a comparable assumption about the social destruction of Twain required him to overestimate Twain's potential enor-

mously. The method is still biographical, but it is less social, less psychoanalytic, less productive of insights into the work, and, in the last analysis, relatively pointless.

As for Brooks' supposedly pioneering use of Freud, Wasserstrom has demonstrated convincingly that Brooks knew next to nothing about Freud or Jung and drew his psychology—without acknowledgment—from a popular work of the time, Bernard Hart's *The Psychology of Insanity*.

By 1925 Brooks had completed two of the three books which were to make his case complete. Twain and James represent opposing but equally destructive alternatives facing the American artist, but in Whitman he had found the "rudiments of a middle tradition":

> Whitman—how else can I express it?—precipitated the American character. All those things that had been separate, self-sufficient, incoordinate—action, theory, idealism, business—he cast into a crucible; and they emerged, harmonious and molten, in a fresh democratic ideal, based on the whole personality. [Whitman gave America] a *focal point*...[and the] sense of something organic in American life.

There is an ancedote, now confirmed by Malcolm Cowley, that once Brooks heard about Whitman's homosexuality he quickly replaced Whitman with Emerson (if the story is true—if Brooks had to be *told* about Whitman's homoeroticism—then it says something fatal about his capacity to read with any sensitivity). A book on Emerson was planned or partly written by the mid-1920's but interrupted by a long period of serious mental illness, in part brought on, perhaps, by the impasse Brooks had created: it was impossible for the artist to stay in America and it was impossible for him to leave.

In any event, the book on Emerson appeared in 1932 and opened the last phase of Brooks' career. Apparently cured of his own problems (which Jung diagnosed as "chronic melancholia") he now offered a cure for American letters: it seems that after all there was a "usable past" for the American writer in the New England culture which had flowered with Emerson and was—prior to the Civil War—truly "organic." For the next twenty-five years Brooks labored on the massive, five-volume *Makers and Finders*, in which he attempts to redeem the past he had once dismissed. His sentimental acceptance of the past, Edmund Wilson observed, "involves what amounts to an abdication of the critic"; and commenting on the first four volumes Hyman wrote that "they have no point of view, no standards, no depth, no ideas, and boundless love for everyone without distinction."

These verdicts are probably just, but from the point of view of critical theory it is worth noting Brooks' defense of *Makers and Finders* (now reprinted in *The Writer in America*). "What makes literature great," he asserts, "is the quality of its subject matter...together with as much formal virtue as a writer is able to compass." For Brooks the proper subject matter means the ideas characteristic of "primary literature"—affirmations of man's freedom and essential goodness in direct opposition to the fashionable pessimism of Eliot, Joyce and Kafka. But more important than his wholesale rejection of modernism is Brooks' emphasis on tradition. Like Eliot he believes that the mature artist must work with a sense of the past if the "continuity of greatness" is to be maintained. "It was to make this clear," he explains, "that I wrote *Makers and Finders*, hoping to connect the literary present with the past, reviving that special kind of memory that fertilizes the living mind and gives it the sense of a base on which to build." It is not Eliot's critical position which Brooks deplored: Eliot's mistake was in leaving America and turning his back on what the American past, properly understood, had to offer.

While admitting that Brooks suffered from a "sheerly emotional incapacity to anchor his thought in the firm and convincing ground of textual analysis," Wasserstrom also maintains that before Brooks abandoned the role of radical critic "he imposed his stamp on two generations of reformist literary men, on Mumford, Cowley, Waldo Frank, Matthew Josephson, Granville Hicks, Newton Arvin—above all on F.O. Matthiessen." But even as an "influence" Brooks' importance may be questionable. Which works by these particular critics have proved to be of any lasting interest? Newton Arvin's *Melville*, certainly, a study distinguished by the kind of close reading Brooks was incapable of, Matthiessen's *American Renaissance*, and, perhaps, Cowley's *Second Flowering*. And while *American Renaissance* may owe something to Brooks, Matthiessen's best work is in fact quite opposed to Brooks' thinking. Vitelli's conclusions are not encouraging:

How Brooks asserted his leadership is not so clear, and less certainty prevails in assessing the nature of his leadership. He provided American critics with no coherent set of ideas about literature; no distinct techniques for the analysis and judgment of a poem or a novel; no clear criteria, even, on how to judge an artist's success or failure.

BURKE, Kenneth (Duva). American. Born in Pittsburgh, Pennsylvania, 5 May 1897. Educated at Peabody High School, Pittsburgh; Ohio State University, Columbus, 1916-17; Columbia University, New York, 1917-18. Married 1) Lily Mary Batterham in 1919 (divorced); 2) Elizabeth Batterham in 1933; five children. Research Worker, Laura Spelman Rockefeller Memorial, New York, 1926-27. Music Critic, *Dial*, New York, 1927-29, and *The Nation*, New York, 1934-35. Editor, Bureau of Social Hygiene, New York, 1928-29. Lecturer, New School for Social Research, New York, 1937; University of Chicago, 1938, 1949-50; Bennington College, Vermont, 1943-61; Princeton University, New Jersey, 1949, 1975; Kenyon College, Gambier, Ohio, 1950; Indiana University, Bloomington, 1953, 1958; Drew University, Madison, New Jersey, 1962, 1964; Pennsylvania State University, University Park, 1963; Regents Professor, University of California at Santa Barbara, 1964-65; Lecturer, Central Washington State University, Ellensburg, 1966; Harvard University, Cambridge, Massachusetts, 1967-68; Washington University, St. Louis, 1970-71; Wesleyan University, Middletown, Connecticut, 1972; University of Pittsburgh, 1972. Recipient: *Dial* Award, 1928; Guggenheim Fellowship, 1935; National Institute of Arts and Letters grant, 1946, and Gold Medal, 1975; Princeton Institute for Advance Study Fellowship, 1949; Stanford University Center for Advanced Study in the Behavioral Sciences Fellowship, 1957; Rockefeller grant, 1966; Brandeis University Creative Arts Award, 1967; National Endowment for the Arts Award, 1968; National Medal for Literature, 1981. D.Litt.: Bennington College, 1966; Rutgers University, New Brunswick, New Jersey, 1968; Dartmouth College, Hanover, New Hampshire, 1969; Fairfield University, Connecticut, 1970; Northwestern University, Evanston, Illinois, 1972; University of Rochester, New York, 1972. Member, American Academy of Arts and Letters; American Academy of Arts and Sciences. Address R.D. 2, Andover, New Jersey 07821, U.S.A.

PUBLICATIONS

Criticism

> *Counter-Statement.* New York, Harcourt Brace, 1931; revised edition, Berkeley, University of California Press, and London, Cambridge University Press, 1968.
> *The Philosophy of Literary Form: Studies in Symbolic Action.* Baton Rouge, Louisiana State University Press, 1941; revised edition, New York, Random House, 1957; London, Peter Smith, 1959.
> *Language as Symbolic Action: Essays on Life, Literature, and Method.* Berkeley, University of California Press, and London, Cambridge University Press, 1966.
> "Dramatism," under "Interaction," in *International Encyclopedia of the Social Sciences*, vol. 7. New York, Macmillan-The Free Press, 1968.
> "As I Was Saying," in *The Michigan Quarterly Review* (Ann Arbor), 11, 1972.
> *Dramatism and Development* (lecture). Worcester, Massachusetts, Clark University, 1972.
> "Dancing with Tears in My Eyes," in *Critical Inquiry* (Chicago), 1, 1974.
> "Above the Over-Towering Babble," in *Michigan Quarterly Review* (Ann Arbor), 15, 1976.

"Post-Poesque Derivation of a Terministic Cluster," in *Critical Inquiry* (Chicago), 4, 1977.

"(Nonsymbolic) Motion/(Symbolic) Action," in *Critical Inquiry* (Chicago), 4, 1978.

"Methodological Repression and/or the Strategies of Containment," in *Critical Inquiry* (Chicago), 5, 1978.

"Theology and Logology," in *Kenyon Review* (Gambier, Ohio), 1 n.s., 1979.

Verse

Book of Moments: Poems 1915-1954.   Los Altos, California, Hermes, 1955.

Collected Poems 1915-1967.   Berkeley, University of California Press, and London, Cambridge University Press, 1968.

Novel

Towards a Better Life, Being a Series of Epistles or Declarations.   New York, Harcourt Brace, 1931; revised edition, Berkeley, University of California Press, and London, Cambridge University Press, 1966.

Short Stories

The White Oxen and Other Stories.   New York, Boni, 1924.

The Complete White Oxen: Collected Shorter Fiction.   Berkeley, University of California Press, 1968.

Other

Permanence and Change: An Anatomy of Purpose.   New York, New Republic, 1935; revised edition, Los Altos, California, Hermes, 1959.

Attitudes Toward History.   New York, New Republic, 2 vols., 1937; revised edition, Los Altos, California, Hermes, 1959.

A Grammar of Motives.   New York, Prentice Hall, 1945; London, Dobson, 1947.

A Rhetoric of Motives.   New York, Prentice Hall, 1950; London, Bailey Brothers and Swinfen, 1955.

The Rhetoric of Religion: Studies in Logology.   Boston, Beacon Press, 1961.

Translator, *Death in Venice*, by Thomas Mann.   New York, Knopf, 1925.

Translator, *Genius and Character*, by Emil Ludwig.   New York, Harcourt Brace, 1927; London, Cape, 1930.

Translator, *Saint Paul*, by Emile Baumann.   New York, Harcourt Brace, 1929.

Critical Studies and Bibliography

William H. Rueckert, *Kenneth Burke and the Drama of Human Relations.*   Minneapolis, University of Minnesota Press, 1963.

Armin and Mechtchild Frank, "The Writings of Kenneth Burke: A Checklist," in *Critical Responses to Kenneth Burke: 1924-1966*, edited by William H. Rueckert.   Minneapolis, University of Minnesota Press, 1969.

Armin Frank, *Kenneth Burke*. New York, Twayne, 1969.

Howard Nemerov, "Everything, Preferably All at Once: Coming to Terms with Kenneth Burke," in *Sewanee Review* (Tennessee), 79, 1971.

René Wellek, "Kenneth Burke and Literary Criticism," in *Sewanee Review* (Tennessee), 79, 1971.

Wayne C. Booth, "Kenneth Burke's Way of Knowing," in *Critical Inquiry* (Chicago), 2, 1974; expanded version as "Kenneth Burke's Comedy: The Multiplication of Perspectives," in *Critical Understanding: The Powers and Limits of Pluralism*. Chicago and London, University of Chicago Press, 1979.

Fredric R. Jameson, " The Symbolic Inference; or, Kenneth Burke and Ideological Analysis," in *Critical Inquiry* (Chicago), 4, 1978.

*   *   *

After making some typically unorthodox remarks about Keats and his relationship to the Grecian Urn, Kenneth Burke draws back for a moment and confesses

I grant that such speculations interfere with the symmetry of criticism as a game. (Criticism as a game is best to watch, I guess, when one confines himself to the single unit, and reports on its movement like a radio commentator broadcasting the blow-by-blow description of a prizefight.) But linguistic analysis has opened up new possibilities in the correlating of producer and product—and these concerns have such important bearing upon the matters of culture and conduct in general that no sheer conventions or ideals of criticism should be allowed to interfere with their development.

This aside indicates as well as any brief passage can the nature of Burke's thinking and the reasons why his work so often bewilders and angers conventional critics and scholars, such as René Wellek, with their orderly procedures and judicious vocabularies. Burke has never been restrained (his mind, as Howard Nemerov observes, "cannot stop exploding"); he has never respected the usual notions of what a literary critic ought to do or obeyed the rules which keep English departments safe, respectable places. For nearly fifty years he has been engaged in a massive attempt to say everything possible about culture and conduct, using not only the resources of "linguistic analysis," but of Marx, Veblen, Freud and a host of other theorists as well. The result is now a body of work which in sheer size and complexity is unmatched by the efforts of any critic since Coleridge. Neat summaries are impossible, the usual categories are too small—at best these remarks may serve as a modest introduction to Burke's persistent concern with language as symbolic action and with the curative powers of art.

Like Santayana and Richards, Burke begins with the conviction that the proper basis of aesthetics is no longer metaphysics but a firmly naturalistic psychology. His aim, as he states at the opening of *The Philosophy of Literary Form*, is to devise a reasoned method for dealing with literature as symbolic action, that is, as a kind of incipient behavior for artist and audience alike which will serve as "equipment for living." We may invent "god-terms" to console ourselves or justify our actions, but ultimately there is no appeal beyond our own resources as we huddle together, "nervously loquacious, at the edge of the abyss." We may start, then, with Burke's psychological "Definition of Man," first proposed in *The Rhetoric of Religion* and now considerably expanded as the opening chapter of *Language as Symbolic Action*. The first of the four clauses asserts that man is a *symbol-making animal*, by which Burke means what most philosophers since Aristotle mean when they define man as rational," as capable of abstraction and generalization. Thinking and symbolizing are inseparable elements of our basic attempt to encompass the situations we are thrust into. So much is obvious, Burke admits,

But can we bring ourselves to realize just what that formula implies, just how overwhelmingly much of what we mean by "reality" has been built up for us through nothing but our symbol systems? Take away our books, and what little do we know about history, biography, even something so "down to earth" as the relative position of seas and continents? What is our "reality" for today (beyond the paper-thin line of our own particular lives) but all this clutter of symbols about the past combined with whatever things we know mainly through maps, magazines, newspapers, and the like about the present?... And however important to us is the tiny sliver of reality each of us has experienced firsthand, the whole overall "picture" is but a construct of our symbol systems. To meditate on this fact until one sees its full implications is much like peering over the edge of things into a ultimate abyss. And doubtless that's one reason why, though man is typically the symbol-using animal, he clings to a kind of naive verbal realism that refuses to realize the full extent of the role played by symbolicity in his notions of reality.

Man is also *the inventor of the negative*—a somewhat indirect way of expressing the other half of the classical definition of man as a political (and thus potentially "moral") animal. In nature there are no negatives; everything "is simply what it is and as it is." But man is free to choose his ends and means and thus is moral, capable of living in harmony with his fellowmen, obeying or refusing to obey the thou-shalt-nots of communal life. Once out of the state of nature, obviously, man is *separated from his natural condition by instruments of his own making*. And finally, man is *goaded by the spirit of hierarchy*, a proposition which needs some further explication, as does its "wry codicile": man is *rotten with perfection*. To be goaded by the spirit of hierarchy means to be "moved by a sense of order." The natural world is hierarchically arranged in terms of increasing levels of complexity; the social world too is grounded in a sense of order, a pervasive set of understandings governing behavior and asserting "higher" and "lower" values. Under this clause, Burke continues,

> would fall the incentives of organization and status. In my *Rhetoric of Motives*, I tried to trace the relation between social hierarchy and mystery, or guilt. And I carried such speculations further in my *Rhetoric of Religion*. Here we encounter secular analogues of "original sin." For, despite any cult of good manners and humility, to the extent that a social structure becomes differentiated, with privileges to some that are denied to others, there are conditions for a kind of "built in" pride. King and peasant are "mysteries" to each other. Those "Up" are guilty of not being "Down," those "Down" are certainly guilty of not being "Up."

The sense or order is fundamental, though particular "orders" will obviously differ from culture to culture; and when there is a hierarchy there is always the possibility—or for Burke the certainty—of pride, of rise and fall. Thus he has attempted nothing less than a complete naturalistic translation of the Christian vocabulary of sin, guilt and redemption. William Rueckert's admirable summary of Burke's position should be quoted in full:

> Whether fact or myth, Burke says, both the Garden of Eden story and its sequel, the story of Christ, the sacrificial redeemer, are true in "essence," for they state, in narrative terms, certain essential truths about the human condition. By reducing both stories to the level of naturalistic discourse and explaining them in terms of the biological-neurological norms, Burke accepts the essential truths while rejecting both the doctrines and the organization (church) with which the stories are associated. The Garden of Eden, for example, has its biological analogue in the womb; there "food simply descends benignly...and the organism has but to open itself and receive the bounty. There is no competition here. The organism...thrives by pure receptivity. It is truly at one with its environment...[for] the separation of the part from the whole...has not yet taken place."... The Fall and expulsion from Eden have their biological and neurological analogues in the birth trauma and the agent's capacity for reason and social intercourse. The separation of the part from the whole, however, does not occur as a result of pride and original sin; it is natural and inevitable: man is not expelled because of original sin, but is expelled into it, for implicit in the nature of reason and the relationship between individual and society is the potential for "sin." Reason itself, man's neurological inheritance, is the very factor which causes the "categorial guilt" or "original sin" from which all men naturally suffer. Man "falls" every time he follows the impulse towards abstraction which reason and language make possible, and conceives of ideals ("god-terms") which are incapable of being perfectly realized. Man is naturally of "guilt-laden substance"...guilt as a permanent part of man's condition makes purification and

redemption a continuous necessity, for, if unrelieved, guilt fragments and corrodes the self. The secular analogue for Christ, the sacrificial redeemer, is symbolic action.

The verb "goad" is an important one for Burke: he assumes that there is an inherent drive in human nature towards the relief of tension and the transcendence of problems; we are by nature impelled to strive for a "synthesis atop the antithesis by the organizing of a unifying attitude." The concluding paragraph of *A Rhetoric of Motives* makes the point eloquently:

> But since, for better or worse, the mystery of the hierarchy is forever with us, let us, as students of rhetoric, scrutinize its range of entrancements, both with dismay and in delight. And finally let us observe, all about us, forever goading us, though it be in fragments, the motive that attains its ultimate identification in the thought, not of the universal holocaust, but of the universal order—as with the rhetorical and dialectic symmetry of the Aristotelian metaphysics, whereby all classes of beings are hierarchically arranged in a chain or ladder or pyramid of mounting worth, each kind striving towards the *perfection* of its kind, and so towards the kind next above it, while the strivings of the entire series head in God as the beloved cynosure and sinecure, the end of all desire.

But the final part of Burke's definition—man is "rotten with perfection"—also makes it clear that he is no naive optimist: there may be an inherent drive towards order but there is also a stubborn tendency to complete any line of action once begun. Thus one can become a "perfect villain," like Iago, or like Hitler find the "perfect enemy." Each of the defining clauses has its dark side. We may make our symbols ineptly, misuse our freedom and build a culture badly at odds with the chances for a good life. Perhaps in keeping with the miseries of recent history Burke's optimism now seems a bit more tentative, at least if we may generalize from a 1972 essay, "As I Was Saying":

> Everywhere I look, I encounter situations that make me feel sick and tired. I still think of life as a pilgrimage. In this respect I am like the mediaeval Christians. But whereas with them it was a pilgrimage towards a somewhere, now it is a pilgrimage towards nowhere.
> My novel, *Towards a Better Life*, was a ritual tragically inaugurating a theory of comedy. In my *Grammar of Motives* I hit upon the slogan, "smiling hypochondriasis." Later, in studying the nature of order, I became more and more involved in the conviction that order places strong demands upon a sacrificial principle (involving related motives of victimage and catharsis). Thus, while still opting for comedy, I became fascinated by the symbolism of ritual pollution in tragedy. But during the last couple of years my engrossment has shifted to the evidences of material pragmatic pollution in technology. I loathe the subject, even as I persist in wondering what can possibly be done about it. Men victimize nature, and in so doing they victimize themselves. This, I fear, is the ultimate impasse.

With these distinctions in mind we may return to Burke's conception of literature as symbolic action. Words are symbolic because they are not the things they represent; but they are also "symbolic of" important psychological operations. At the beginning of *The Philosophy of Symbolic Form* Burke states categorically that

> Critical and imaginative works are answers to questions posed by the situation in which they arose. They are not merely answers, they are *strategic* answers, *stylized* answers.... So I should propose an initial working distinction between "strategies" and "situation," whereby we think of poetry (I here use the term to include any work of critical or imaginative cast) as the adopting of various strategies for the encompassing of situation. These strategies size up the situations, name their structure and outstanding ingredients, and name them in a way that contains an attitude towards them.

And near the conclusion of this crucial long essay he writes

> Where our resources permit, we may piously encourage the awesome, and in so encom-

passing it, make ourselves immune (by "tolerance," as the word is used of drugs, by Mithridatism). Where our resources do not permit, where we cannot meet such exacting obligations, we may rebel, developing the stylistic antidote that would cancel out an overburdensome awe. And in between these extremes, there is the wide range of the mean, the many instances in which we dilute, attenuate, mixing the ingredient of danger into a recipe of other, more neutral ingredients, wide in their scope and complexity, a chart that concerns itself with the world in all its miraculous diverse plenitude. And for this plenitude of the Creation, being very thankful.

For Burke the poet expresses himself symbolically in order to ease the tensions of living ("The symbol-using animal experiences a certain kind of 'relief' in the mere act of converting any inarticulate muddle into the orderly terms of a symbol-system"). Thus Coleridge, for example, in *The Rime of the Ancient Mariner*, symbolically expresses and to some extent works out the anxieties caused by his marital difficulties and drug addiction: the poem is a partial unburdening. But for Burke, as for Freud, the unburdening is rarely direct and explicit. Like the dream of a patient undergoing analysis it is far more likely to be disguised by the fundamental processes of condensation and displacement, two tactics the critic must be able to recognize and translate: "cryptography is all," Burke asserts at one point. He is quite aware that concern with the poet's life runs counter to many of the principles of modern criticism and grants that

> If a critic prefers to so restrict the rules of critical analysis that these private elements are excluded, that is his right. I see no formal or categorial objection to criticism so conceived. But if his interest happens to be in the structure of the poetic act, he will use everything that is available—and would even consider it a kind of vandalism to exclude certain material that Coleridge has left, basing such exclusion upon some conventions as to the ideal of criticism. The main ideal of criticism, as I conceive it, is to use all that there is to use.

But if a poem like the *Rime* is something Coleridge put together, as Burke sees it, in order to keep from falling apart, the process by no means stops there:

> Many of the things that a poet's work does for *him* are not things that the same work does for *us*.... But my position is this: If we try to discover what the poem is doing for the poet, we may discover a set of generalizations as to what poems do for everybody.

The critic's approach should be comprehensive and frankly pragmatic: "We cannot understand a poem's structure without understanding the function of that structure. And to understand its function we must understand its purpose"—a purpose which for Burke is purgative and curative, for both poet and audience. By successfully encompassing a situation, symbolic action effects a kind of restoration, a "rebirth," to use one of his favorite terms. For Burke, as for a number of other critics, tragedy (and the primitive ritual force behind it) is therefore the archetypal literary form. To sum up, the ideal critic is able to consider the work as a *dream* (as the disguised expression of the poet's burden), as *prayer* (a curious way of referring to the work as a public act, capable of effecting a similar catharsis for the audience) and as *chart* ("the realistic sizing-up of situations that is sometimes explicit, sometimes implicit, in poetic strategies").

The importance of purgation leads to further problems which Burke explores in "The Thinking of the Body" (now reprinted in *Language as Symbolic Action*). The nature of the pollution is of course crucial, but since it usually involves what Burke calls the "fecal motive," the Demonic Trinity of urination, elimination and orgasm, it is almost certain to appear in highly indirect forms. Once again the critic must be an expert detective and decoder. But whether we are dealing with prayer, dream or chart, or with the Demonic Trinity, or with any of the other terms Burke delights in setting up, the approach is still pragmatic: what does the poem do for the artist and for the audience, and what must we do to illuminate the symbolic action involved? *A Grammar of Motives* provides the terms for which Burke is perhaps best known: the "pentad" of act, scene, agent, agency (the means or instruments the agent uses), purpose, and the intricate "ratios" or connections which may exist between these elements. These are the fundamental terms for a "dramatistic" analysis, but to state them so generally gives no indication, of course, of the complexities which a particular analysis may involve.

In *Counter-Statement* Burke examines symbolic action in terms of the formal arrangements which engage the audience's attention and arouse their expectations (the idea of art as catharsis is implied rather than clearly worked out in this early work). As he notes, the conception is similar to Eliot's notion of the "objective correlative." The artist creates a symbol which expresses—and eases—his own burdens, yet

> such utterance is obviously but one small aspect of self-expression. And, if it is a form of self-expression to utter our emotions, it is just as truly a form of self-expression to provoke emotion in others, if we happen to prefer such a practice, even though the emotions aimed at were not the predominant emotions of our own lives. The maniac attains self-expression when he tells us that he is Napoleon; but Napoleon attained self-expression by commanding an army. And, transferring the analogy, the self-expression of the artist *qua* artist, is not distinguished by the uttering of emotion. If, as humans, we cry out that we are Napoleon, as artists we seek to command an army.

In order to control and manipulate his army, however, the artist needs more than a personal "symbolic form" for his problems; he must devise an effective "technical form" which will arouse and satisfy "certain potentialities of appreciation which would seem to be inherent in the very germ-plasm of man." Form is "the creation of an appetite in the mind of the auditor, and the adequate satisfying of that appetite." We are peculiarly sensitive to matters of arrangement—rhythm, closure, balance, unity in variety and so on—and since "every dissonant chord cries out for resolution" what is involved here is not primarily the appeal of the subject matter (a factor, of course, since words are referential, but more properly investigated by what Burke calls the "psychology of information"); rather it is the power of formal arrangements themselves (which Burke classifies in "Lexicon Rhetoricae") to give the satisfaction he designates "eloquence" or "beauty" and to provoke the accompanying emotion, "exaltation." But even in these early "aesthetic" essays Burke anticipates his later concern for the psychological usefulness of the symbol as technical form. After discussing the various functions of such symbolic form Burke concludes, "we might summarize the entire list by saying that the Symbol appeals either as the orienting of a situation, or as the adjustment to a situation, or as both." Starting out in the late 1920's and early 1930's Burke was acutely sensitive to our "technological psychosis," our naive optimism and faith in science, and our suicidal overemphasis of the profit motive and the purely competitive aspects of work ("Would that I could say 'How different are the times now,'" Burke observed in 1952). At its best art may keep a society from relentlessly following its own "perfection," from becoming "too hopelessly itself." The splendid essay "Thomas Mann and André Gide" illustrates clearly the practical applications of Burke's arguments here.

The late R.S. Crane maintained that no one critical language (roughly "frame of reference," or Burke's "terministic screen") can possibly exhaust the complexities of a work considered in itself *and* in its multiple relationships to artist and audience. The moral, Crane concluded, is that "we ought to have at our command as many different critical methods as there are distinguishable major aspects in the construction, appreciation and use of literary works." While there are some important similarities between Burke and Crane, the crucial difference is that in Crane's terms Burke is trying to encompass everything—"preferably all at once," as Nemerov remarked. The question is finally how well he succeeds in making his eclectic methods do justice to the range of problems he is intent on solving. Yet pluralism is not the same as relativism: Burke may use a bewildering array of tools for the analysis of symbolic action but his aim has always been to understand how such action can implement a better life. The matter of comparative value judgements, however, presents some serious difficulties. As early as 1935 a friendly critic, R.P. Blackmur, pointed out that Burke's method works as well for trash as it does for Shakespeare. "When I got through wincing," Burke recalls,

> I had to admit that Blackmur was right.... [But] you can't properly put Marie Corelli and Shakespeare apart until you have first put them together. First genus, than differentia. The strategy in common is the genus. The *range* or *scale* or *spectrum* of particularizations is the differentiae.

But the problem remains: after spending a lifetime putting things together, can Burke really account for the nature of individual excellence?

This summary sketch, besides leaving out a good deal, gives no sense whatsoever of the eloquence or insights—or the occasional near-madness and opacity—which have always characterized Burke's thinking. He must be read slowly, carefully, and at length, without fixed preconceptions as to what a critic *ought* to talk about. Only then will a responsible reader be in any position to judge the controversy which surrounds him or to ponder Wayne Booth's recent claim (made in 1974) that Burke is "without question the most important living critic."

CAUDWELL, Christopher. Pseudonym for Christopher St. John Sprigg. British. Born in Putney, London, 20 October 1907. Educated at Ealing Priory School (Benedictine), London. Worked for the *Yorkshire Post* and later as editor of *British Malaya*. Formed an aeronautical publishing company and published designs in *Automobile Engineer*. Founder, *Aircraft Engineering*. Joined the Communist Party in 1935 (Poplar Branch) and the International Brigade in 1936. *Killed in the battle of the Jarama River, Spain, 12 February 1937.*

PUBLICATIONS

Criticism

> *Illusion and Reality: A Study of the Sources of History.*   London, Macmillan, 1937; New
>   York, Macmillan, 1947.
> *Studies in a Dying Culture.*   London, Lane, 1938; New York, Dodd Mead, 1958.
> *Further Studies in a Dying Culture*, edited by Edgell Rickword.   London, Lane, 1949;
>   New York, Dodd Mead, 1958.
> *The Concept of Freedom*, edited by George Thomson.   London, Lawrence and Wishart,
>   1965; reprints most of *Studies* and *The Crisis in Physics*.
> *Romance and Realism: A Study in English Bourgeois Literature.*   Princeton, New
>   Jersey, Princeton University Press, 1970.

Verse

> *Poems.*   London, Lane, 1939.

Novels

> *Crime in Kensington* (as Christopher St. John Sprigg).   London, Eldon Press, 1933; as
>   *Pass the Body*, New York, Dial Press, 1933.
> *Fatality in Fleet Street* (as Christopher St. John Sprigg).   London, Eldon Press, 1933.
> *The Perfect Alibi* (as Christopher St. John Sprigg).   London, Eldon Press, and New
>   York, Doubleday, 1934.

Death of an Airman (as Christopher St. John Sprigg).   London, Hutchinson, 1934.
Death of a Queen (as Christopher St. John Sprigg).   New York, Nelson, 1935.
The Corpse with the Sunburned Face (as Christopher St. John Sprigg).   London, Nelson, and New York, Doubleday, 1935.
This Is My Hand.   London, Hamish Hamilton, 1936.
The Six Queer Things (as Christopher St. John Sprigg).   London, Jenkins, and New York, Doubleday, 1937.

Other

The Airship: Its Design, History, Operation, and Future.   London, Sampson Low, 1931.
Fly with Me: An Elementary Textbook on the Art of Piloting, with Henry D. Davis.   London, John Hamilton, 1932.
British Airways.   London and New York, Nelson, 1934.
Great Flights.   London, Nelson, 1935.
Let's Learn to Fly.   London, Nelson, 1937.
The Crisis in Physics, edited by H. Levy.   London, Lane, 1939; New York, Dodd Mead, 1951.
The Breath of Discontent: A Study in Bourgeois Religion.   New York, Oriole Editions, n.d.
Consciousness: A Study in Bourgeois Psychology.   New York, Oriole Editions, n.d.
Liberty: A Study in Bourgeois Illusion.   New York, Oriole Editions, n.d.
Men and Nature: A Study in Bourgeois History.   New York, Oriole Editions, n.d.
Reality: A Study in Bourgeois Philosophy.   New York, Oriole Editions, n.d.

Editor, *Uncanny Stories*.   London, Nelson, 1936.

CRITICAL STUDIES

Stanley Edgar Hyman, "Christopher Caudwell and Marxist Criticism," in *The Armed Vision: A Study in the Methods of Modern Library Criticism*.   New York, Knopf, 1948; all later editions drop this chapter.
G.M. Matthews and others, "The Caudwell Discussion," in *Modern Quarterly* (London), 6, new series, 1951.
David Margolies, *The Function of Literature: A Study of Christopher Caudwell's Aesthetics*.   New York, International Publishers, and London, Lawrence and Wishart, 1969.
Samuel Hynes, Introduction to *Romance and Realism: A Study in English Bourgeois Literature*.   Princeton, New Jersey, Princeton University Press, 1970.

*   *   *

Any just account of Christopher Caudwell's critical position—and as a Marxist he has usually been dismissed rather than dealt with fairly—must begin with his conception of freedom, "the most important of all generalized goods." As Engels defines it, freedom is the recognition of necessity; and necessity, in turn, is necessity as the thorough-going naturalist sees it when he considers the proper end of human life. Man, Caudwell asserts, is "always struggling to make environment conform to instinct, consistency to beauty, and necessity to desire—in a word, to be free." Freedom is "always a specific struggle with Nature...always relative to the success of the struggle":

How are we to judge whether a given society is more highly developed than another? Is it a question of biological evolution? Fisher has pointed out that there can be only one definition of "fitness" justified by biological considerations, and that is increase of numbers at the expense of the environment, including other species. In man this increase must depend on the level of economic production—the more advanced this is, the more man will dominate his environment.

In the state of nature man is not free; he is subject to the laws of nature, the slave of his instincts and the endless work their gratification demands. The basis of true freedom lies rather in man's association with his fellow man, in the cooperative division of labor which is the very foundation of society. To Margaret Fuller's fatuous announcement that she accepted the universe Caudwell retorts "but man does *not* accept the Universe, for the Universe does not accept him. He must *change* it under penalty of extinction. And he can only change it in association." In summary, then, association makes it possible for man to acquire mastery over Nature

> through becoming actively conscious of its necessity and his own. This association of itself *necessarily* imposes certain restrictions, conventions and obligations, such as those of good behavior, language and mutual aid. But all these things are not fetters on the free instincts...they are the instruments by which instinctive man realizes his freedom. The view of reality which is science, the canons of feeling which are art and ethics, are imposed on the instincts from without; none the less they are not fetters, distortions, inhibitions or sublimations. They are the means by which instinct realizes its freedom because they give it understanding of Nature's necessity and its own and therefore are—since Nature will not yield to a mere wish—the only means by which the will can actively realize itself.

The freedom we think we want, the unconditional individualism and dream of "one man producing the phenomena of the world," is precisely that, a dream, an empty illusion fostered by the exploitation of another's labor.

These definitions rest, of course, on Caudwell's total commitment to Marxism and the ideal of freedom for which he finally gave his own life. At an early stage in history man did in fact practice a kind of primitive communism, based on the division of labor. There were functional roles but no classes; property and the means of production were held in common. But with the development of society the group which gains control of the economic machinery also gains control of the labor of others. Caudwell does not idealize primitive communism: it was a necessary stage of social evolution, just as bourgeois capitalism is another stage, though to those who live during each period the present historical moment seems a fixed "reality." Bourgeois consciousness, like all consciousness (except Marxist consciousness), is a social product and in this case involves a radical failure to grasp the proper end of human life, freedom, once again, in its final definition as "man's realization of all his instinctive powers." But of course this means the freedom of *all* members of society—as much freedom as the work required to control nature permits—and not merely the empty idleness of those who happen to control the means of production. Thus the inability of even well-meaning artists and intellectuals like Shaw, Freud, H.G. Wells and a host of others to realize the true nature of freedom provides the basis of attack in most of the essays collected in *Studies in a Dying Culture* and *Further Studies in a Dying Culture*. Analyzing D.H. Lawrence's "regressive" tendencies, for example, Caudwell observes

> One will not believe freedom and happiness can only be found through social relations, by co-operating with others to change them, but there is always something one can do, fly to Mexico, find the right woman or the right friends, and so discover salvation. One will never see the truth, that one can find salvation for oneself by finding it for all others at the same time.

By definition the dying culture cannot maintain itself: bourgeois capitalism, with its uncoordinated advances in science and technology, is constantly revolutionizing its own basis, giving rise to the contradictions—wars and recurring economic crises—which prepare the way for a truly free, just and humane society:

> The movement forward from bourgeois culture to communism is also a movement back to the social solidarity of primitive communism, but one which includes and gathers up all the development of the interim, all the division of labour which has made possible an

increase in freedom, individuation and consciousness. It is a movement back to collectivism and integrity of a society without coercion, where consciousness and freedom are equally shared by all.

Therefore Caudwell is concerned with science and art because as social products they can have "only one goal, that of freedom." Apparently following I.A. Richards' influential distinction between the language of science and the emotive language of poetry, Caudwell defines science as the cognition of outer necessity. The statements of science are "abstract," "perceptual," deliberately stripped of value judgments and emotional connotations. The statements of art, on the other hand, are statements "about" reality but colored by our emotions and wishes. The language of poetry is the language of affect, and "it is precisely because [such] language express feeling, is a judging as well as a picturing of parts of reality, that it is valuable." This leads directly to Caudwell's conception of the purpose of art (again reminiscent of Richards and, surprisingly enough, of Santayana):

> It is plain that poetry may be judged in different ways; either by the importance of the manifest content, or by the vividness of the affective colouring. To a poet who brings a new portion of external reality into the ambit of poetry, we feel more gratitude than to one who brings the old stale manifest contents....Old poets we shall judge almost entirely by their affective tone; their manifest contents have long belonged to our world of thought....From new poets we demand new manifest contents and new affective colouring, for it is their function to give us new emotional attitudes to a new social environment. A poet who provides both to a high degree will be a good poet....But the manifest content is not the purpose of the poem. The purpose is the specific emotional organization directed towards the manifest content and provided by the released affects....Poetry soaks external reality—nature and society—with emotional significance. This significance, because it gives the organism an appetitive interest in external reality, enables the organism to deal with it more resolutely, whether in the world of reality or of phantasy....
>
> [Art] remoulds external reality nearer to the likeness of the genotype's instincts....Art becomes more socially and biologically valuable and greater art the more that remoulding is comprehensive and true to the nature of reality, using as its materials the sadness, the catastrophes, the blind necessities, as well as the delights and pleasures of life. An organism which thinks life is all "for the best in the best possible of worlds" will have little survival value. Great art can thus be great tragedy, for here, reality at its bitterest...is yet given an organization, a shape, an affective arrangement which expresses a deeper and more social view of fate.

Art is an "illusion" in several distinct though related ways. It is an illusion in the sense of being a kind of compensatory activity, yet as Caudwell points out, today's wishful thinking may become tomorrow's reality. Art is also an illusion if it is based on an empty dream, like the hollow individualism of D.H. Lawrence. Art is an illusion in the sense that we knowingly and willingly accept a representation of reality as "real" for the time being and for the sake of the emotional response it may arouse. And finally art is an illusion in the sense that it is a carefully arranged "mock world":

> Art is therefore affective experimenting with selected pieces of external reality. The situation corresponds to a scientific experiment. In this a selected piece of external reality is set up in the laboratory. It is a mock world, an imitation of that part of external reality in which the experimenter is interested....[As in art] there is a "fake" piece of the world, detached so as to be handled conveniently, and illusory in this much, that it is not actually what we meet in real life, but a selection from external reality arranged for our own purposes. It is an "as if."

Even so, as Caudwell admits, this is not an exhaustive view of art. He recognizes but is not concerned with aesthetics or the "logic" of art:

> It is the essential task of aesthetics to rank Herrick below Milton, and Shakespeare above either, and to explain in rich and complex detail why and how they differ. But such

113

an act implies a standard...which is not scientific...but aesthetic. This is the logic of art.

The critic's task, if not the aesthetician's, may be deduced from these various meanings of "illusion." He may investigate what dream the work of art proposes for the world of action; he may investigate the relationship between the consciousness the work expresses and the general social consciousness of the times; and he may investigate the construction of the mock world and the emotional response which it is designed to evoke. Some of these activities are demonstrated briefly in *Illusion and Reality* and at greater length in *Romance and Realism* (which also deals with the novel, a form treated very hastily in *Illusion and Reality*). In both works Caudwell divides the social history of England into separate stages (nine of them, in *Illusion and Reality*), corresponding to the economic development of the country, from the period of "Primitive Accumulation, 1550-1600," to "The Final Capitalistic Crisis, 1930-?" It should be pointed out that if Caudwell's history is sometimes faulty or downright wrong, or if his correlations between particular works and general social consciousness are unconvincing, the *principle* of historical interpretation along Marxist lines is not necessarily discredited. A more accomplished historian and critic—a George Lukács, for example—might do the same kind of job persuasively.

For Caudwell the origins of art and its ultimate function are finally inseparable. As heightened, communal language in which men expressed their fears and hopes, poetry was an illusion in one of the senses already discussed. Work was necessary—work, for example, to bring about the harvest which was "illusory" in the sense of not yet accomplished:

> Thus the developing complex of society, in its struggle with the environment, secretes poetry as it secretes the technique of harvest, as part of its non-biological and specifically human adaptation to existence....The tool adapts the hand to a new function....The poem adapts the heart to a new purpose, without changing the eternal desires of men's hearts. It does so by projecting man into a world of phantasy which is superior to his present reality precisely because it is a world of superior reality...whose realisation demands the very poetry which phantastically anticipates it. Here is room for error, for the poem proposes something whose very reason for poetical treatment is that we cannot touch, smell or taste it yet....[Such primitive art] sweetens work and is generated by the needs of labour.

And since work will always be necessary, even in the classless society, presumably art will always have this power to sweeten labor as well as propose ideals. For Caudwell art is much more than simple propaganda, "rhymed economics," as he scornfully calls it, to make the proletariat conscious of its goal.

How valid or relevant is the criticism scattered throughout *Illusion and Reality, Romance and Realism,* and the posthumous essays? Only as valid, obviously, as the view of history and freedom which determines such criticism, just as bourgeois capitalism determines its superstructures. History may demonstrate that capitalism is capable of surviving any number of "final" crises and that the insoluble contradictions of life turn out to be not social injustices but overpopulation, pollution and the exhaustion of natural resources. For all its talk of material determinism, Caudwell's Marxism is utopian, optimistic, and therefore perhaps tragically irrelevant.

CECIL, Lord (Edward Christian) David (Gascoyne). British. Born in England, 9 April 1902. Educated at Eton College, Buckinghamshire; Christ Church, Oxford. Married Rachel MacCarthy in 1932; has three children. Fellow of Wadham College, Oxford, 1924-30, and of New College, Oxford, 1939-69 (now Honorary Fellow), and Goldsmith's Professor of English Literature, Oxford University, 1948-69. Trustee, National Portrait Gallery, 1937-51; President,

The Poetry Society, London, 1947-48; Rede Lecturer, Cambridge University, 1955. Litt. D.: University of Leeds, 1950; LL.D.: University of Liverpool, 1951; University of St. Andrews, 1951; D.Lit.: University of London, 1957; D.Litt.: University of Glasgow, 1962. Companion of Honour, 1949; Companion of Literature, Royal Society of Literature, 1972. Address: Red Lion House, Cranborne, Wimborne, Dorset, England.

PUBLICATIONS

Criticism

Sir Walter Scott. London, Constable, 1933.
Early Victorian Novelists: Essays in Revaluation. London, Constable, 1934; Indianapolis, Bobbs Merrill, 1935; reprinted with a new preface as *Victorian Novelists*, Chicago, University of Chicago Press, 1958.
Jane Austen. London, Cambridge University Press, 1935; New York, Macmillan, 1936; reprinted in *Poets and Story-Tellers*, 1949.
Hardy the Novelist: An Essay in Criticism. London, Constable, 1943; Indianapolis, Bobbs Merrill, 1946.
Antony and Cleopatra (lecture). Glasgow, University Press, 1944; reprinted in *Poets and Story-Tellers*, 1949.
"The Poetry of Thomas Gray," in *Proceedings of the British Academy 31.* London, Oxford University Press, 1945; reprinted in *Poets and Story-Tellers*, 1949.
Poets and Story-Tellers: A Book of Critical Essays. London, Constable, and New York, Macmillan, 1949.
Reading as One of the Fine Arts: An Inaugural Lecture. Oxford, Clarendon Press, 1949; reprinted in *The Fine Art of Reading*, 1957.
Walter de la Mare. London, Oxford University Press, 1951; reprinted in *The Fine Art of Reading*, 1957.
Walter Pater: The Scholar-Artist (lecture). London, Cambridge University Press, 1955; reprinted in *The Fine Art of Reading*, 1957.
The Fine Art of Reading and Other Literary Studies. London, Constable, and Indianapolis, Bobbs Merrill, 1957.
A Portrait of Jane Austen. London, Constable, 1978; New York, Hill and Wang, 1979.

Other

The Stricken Deer; or, The Life of Cowper. London, Constable, 1929; Indianapolis, Bobbs Merrill, 1930.
The Young Melbourne and the Story of His Marriage with Caroline Lamb. London, Constable, and Indianapolis, Bobbs Merrill, 1939.
Two Quiet Lives: Dorothy Osborne, Thomas Gray. London, Constable, and Indianapolis, Bobbs Merrill, 1948.
Lord M; or, The Later Life of Lord Melbourne. London, Constable, and Indianapolis, Bobbs Merrill, 1954.
Max: A Biography (of Max Beerbohm). London, Constable, 1964; Boston, Houghton Mifflin, 1965.
Visionary and Dreamer: Two Poetic Painters: Samuel Palmer and Edward Burne-Jones. London, Constable, 1969; Princeton, New Jersey, Princeton University Press, 1970.
The Cecils of Hatfield House. London, Constable, and Boston, Houghton Mifflin, 1973.
Library Looking Glass: A Personal Anthology. London, Constable, 1975; New York, Harper, 1977.

Editor, *An Anthology of Modern Biography.*   London, Nelson, 1936.
Editor, *The Oxford Book of Christian Verse.*   Oxford, Clarendon Press, 1940.
Editor, with Allen Tate, *Modern Verse in English, 1900-1950.*   London, Eyre and Spottiswoode, and New York, Macmillan, 1958.
Editor, *The Bodley Head Max Beerbohm.*   London, Bodley Head, 1970.
Editor, *English Short Stories of My Time.*   London, Oxford University Press, 1970.
Editor, *A Choice of Tennyson's Verse.*   London, Faber, 1971.

*   *   *

In the prefatory note to *Early Victorian Novelists* Lord David Cecil states his purpose clearly enough: he loves his novelists and wants others to love them too; and as a means to this end he plans to "discriminate and, as far as it is in my power, to illuminate the aesthetic aspects of [these] novels which can still make them a living delight to readers." But it will take a supersubtle and generous reader to discover what Lord David means by "aesthetic" or what the sources of delight may be. The aesthetic aspects have nothing to do with form, since he tells us that the Victorian novel, while "vital," and "imaginative," is "inevitably stained by immaturity and inefficiency and ignorance." Dickens, for example, "cannot construct"; his books "have no organic unity." Thackeray, "like all Victorian novelists, is a very uncertain craftsman." Still, these novelists have a redeeming virtue: "Apart from anything else, they tell a story so well." Or again, Dickens "may not construct his story well: but he tells it admirably." And these novelists also have the capacity to create characters in the classical manner: "Essential human nature—this is always Jane Austen's preoccupation.... These spinsters and curates have the universal significance of the scheme of values in whose light they are presented to us." What does it mean to tell a story well or to tell it badly? What problems does the novelist face in the creation of character and plot? And why are we so moved by his successes? It is all a delightful mystery, or a "miracle": "Miss Bates [in *Emma*] is a bore exactly like a hundred bores we fly from everyday. Only—we find ourselves hanging on her words; by a delightful miracle she has been made entertaining. Jane Austen could perform miracles upon even less promising material." No doubt she could and did; and no doubt Lord David loves her for it. But here, as elsewhere, love is not always enough.
  Scattered throughout the lectures which make up *Early Victorian Novelists, Poets and Story-Tellers, The Fine Art of Reading* and the study of Hardy there are a number of respectable critical commonplaces and even a familiar definition:

Art is not like mathematics or philosophy. It is a subjective, sensual, and highly personal activity in which facts are the servants of fancy and feeling; and the artist's aim is not truth but delight.

But the commonplaces remain inert; they are not earned or gainfully employed. The hard questions are not for us:

Of all [Gray's] work, his light verse appears the most inspired. How far this means that it is also the most precious is a different question. A very big one too: it opens the whole question as to whether comic art can of its nature be equal in significance to grave art, whether the humorist's view of things is always comparatively speaking, a superficial view. This takes us into deep waters; too deep to be fathomed in the brief close of an essay like the present.

Or again:

A work of art is certainly not delightful in proportion as it mirrors a delightful phase of experience. This is a dark and paradoxical mystery, in whose shadow lurks the whole question of the fundamental significance of art. It is not for me to propose a final answer to a riddle from which the wisest of mankind have recoiled baffled.

In short, Lord David is an unrepentant impressionist. "I like to think," he writes, "that I have a spiritual predecessor at Oxford in Pater, unworthy to follow him though I may be; and to fancy that his shade, with its pensive glance and ghostly moustache, sometimes leaves its sequestered haunt in his panelled rooms at Brasenose to hover benignly near me." There is nothing wrong with impressionistic criticism if, as is often the case with Pater, the impressions are new or finely expressed; but it is difficult to imagine that Lord David's essays could disclose anything a moderately sensitive reader might not see for himself. His descriptive powers are not remarkable:

> Each [novelist] has his characteristic, unforgettable scenery: Dickens' London, hazed with fog, livid with gaslight, with its shabby, clamorous, cheerful streets, its cozy and its squalid interiors, its stagnant waterside; and the different London of Thackeray: the west end of London on a summer afternoon, with its clubs and parks and pot-houses, mellow, modish, and a little dusty, full of bustle and idleness; and Mrs. Gaskell's countryside, so pastoral and sequestered and domesticated; and the elemental moorland of the Brontës.

and as for his powers of generalization:

> in every country, every walk of life Dickens strikes a responsive chord in the hearts of mankind. And especially in England. The English, the kindly, individualistic, illogical, sentimental English, are, more than other people, touched by impulsive benevolence, instinctive good nature, set a value on homely satisfactions. More than any other people they are repelled by the ruthless and impersonal—in thought or religion or administration or economics—by the ruthless and impersonal tyranny of church or class or state. Nor have they much perception of those purely intellectual values, that Dickens' view of life overlooks. In fact they find expressed in him with all the eloquence of genius, their deepest feelings, their controlling convictions....It is no wonder that to him, as to no other of their novelists, they have given their hearts.

But finally it is Lord David's complacency which should dismay anyone who feels that literature is something more than a source of delight and that criticism can be a serious and responsible undertaking:

> [Jane Austen's vision] is a profound vision. There are other views of life and more extensive; concerned as it is exclusively with personal relationships, it leaves out several important aspects of experience. But on her own ground Jane Austen gets to the heart of the matter; her graceful unpretentious philosophy, founded as it is on an unwavering recognition of fact, directed by an unerring perception of moral quality, is as impressive as those of the most majestic novelists. Myself I find it more impressive. If I were in doubt as to the wisdom of one of my actions I should not consult Flaubert or Dostoievsky. The opinion of Balzac or Dickens would carry little weight with me: were Stendhal to rebuke me, it would only convince me I had done right: even in the judgment of Tolstoy I should not put complete confidence. But I should be seriously upset, I should worry for weeks and weeks, if I incurred the disapproval of Jane Austen.

Weeks and weeks, dear reader!

CHASE, Richard (Volney). American. Born in Lakeport, New Hampshire, 12 October 1914. Educated at Dartmouth College, Hanover, New Hampshire, B.A. 1937; Columbia University, New York City, Ph.D. 1946. Instructor in English, Columbia University, 1939-45, and Connecticut College for Women, New London, 1945-49; Assistant Professor, Associate Professor, and Professor, Columbia University, 1949-62. Recipient: Guggenheim Fellowship, 1948; National Institute of Arts and Letters Award, 1953. *Died in 1963*.

PUBLICATIONS

Criticism

Quest for Myth.   Baton Rouge, Louisiana State University Press, 1949.
Herman Melville: A Critical Study.   New York, Macmillan, 1949.
"Art, Nature, Politics," in *Kenyon Review* (Gambier, Ohio), 12, 1950.
Emily Dickinson.   New York, Sloane, 1951; London, Methuen, 1952.
Walt Whitman Reconsidered.   New York, Sloane, and London, Gollancz, 1955.
The American Novel and Its Tradition.   New York, Doubleday, 1957; London, G. Bell, 1958.
Walt Whitman.   Minneapolis, University of Minnesota Press, 1961.

Other

The Democratic Vista: A Dialogue on Life and Letters in Contemporary America.   New York, Doubleday, 1958.

Editor, *The Complete Tales of Uncle Remus*.   Boston, Houghton Mifflin, 1955.
Editor, *Melville: A Collection of Critical Essays*.   Englewood Cliffs, New Jersey, Prentice Hall, 1962.

*   *   *

If there is a dominant characteristic of modern criticism it is probably what all the historians and anthologists have pointed out by now: a primary interest in "the text itself" as an aesthetic object to be scrutinized in terms of principles drawn from a special concern for the powers of "poetic" language and metaphor. And if there is a significant counter-tendency it may be the archetypal or myth criticism provoked by detailed verbal analysis and its frequent companion, "narrow,"—that is, conservative—social values. Encouraged by the prospects for myth criticism in the late 1940's Richard Chase announced that "we are close to one of those crucial opportunities which excite our times: the opportunity to recapture, in the name of the natural, something apparently beyond the pale." Chase, or at least the early Chase, is the very model of the myth critic, although the label is finally of little use: it would be as misleading to group together Chase, Maud Bodkin and Northrop Frye as it would be to concentrate on the similarities between Eliot and Richards.

Quest for Myth offers an historical review of theories of myth and develops an eclectic theory of its own in which myth and "literature" are in many ways synonymous. For Chase mythic thinking is still "dynamic and operative"; myth is not simply a term for discarded religious beliefs or primitive science:

> The central premise of this book is that *myth is literature and therefore a matter of aesthetic experience and the imagination*, a truth that literary critics should have affirmed long ago. The first critical step toward an understanding of mythological literature is to rescue myth from those who see it only as the means and end of philosophy, religious dogma, psychoanalysis, or semantics.

By "aesthetic" Chase seems to mean roughly what Dewey (whom he quotes) meant when he spoke of the spontaneous delight men take in telling stories. Mythology, he concluded, "is much more an affair of the psychology that generates art than an effort at scientific and philosophical explanation." And while Chase wishes to preserve an aesthetic dimension for myth—and literature—he is no less interested than philosophers or psychoanalysts have been in arriving at a functional definition. Borrowing here and there from modern anthropology Chase emphasizes the differences between religion and magic as fundamental mental phenomena: religion expresses man's sense of the outer world which controls him; magic expresses his desire to control these forces for his own ends. The function of myth and literature is therefore "Promethean":

> we pointed out that the clash between magic and religion in primitive society was psychologically a clash between the ego, which desires to envelop and coerce the objective world, and gods and spirits, those objectively conceived powers which seek to coerce man and nature. And we suggested that myth was that kind of poetry which reconciles these opposing forces "by making them interact coercively toward a common end."

In summary,

> myth is an aesthetic device for bringing the imaginary but powerful world of preternatural forces into a manageable collaboration with the objective facts of life in such a way as to excite a sense of reality amenable to both the unconscious passions and the conscious mind....If these observations are sound, any narrative or poem which reaffirms the dynamism and vibrancy of the world, which fortifies the ego with the impression that there is a magically potent brilliancy or dramatic force in the world, may be called a myth.

Vibrancy, magically potent brilliancy: these terms are vague to the point of uselessness, but apart from vagueness myth criticism such as Chase's usually suffers from two other serious limitations. It results in a definition so broad that it becomes impossible to find any literature which is not "mythic." And in itself, far from being able to deal with aesthetic experience, the mythic approach can do nothing, as Jung once pointed out, to discriminate between Dante and H. Rider Haggard. Myth criticism easily turns into a kind of special pleading: a work of art is good *because* it contains a mythic theme and hence mythic efficacy.

Chase's quick accounts of Enlightenment and Romantic attitudes towards myth are helpful up to a point, but he fails to do anything with two crucial figures, Nietzsche and Jung (each of whom receives three brief references to Max Müller's nine). He seems unaware of Maud Bodkin's pioneering work and equally unaware of Joseph Campbell's important applications of Jung in *The Hero with a Thousand Faces* (also published in 1949). This last omission is particularly damaging since Chase is searching for the same basic pattern which Campbell isolates clearly as the "monomyth": the hero's withdrawal from the ordinary world, his struggle with supernatural powers, and his return home with boons to bestow on his unheroic fellowmen. In the final section of *Quest for Myth* Chase attempts to deal with the mythic power of Donne's "Epithalamion made at Lincolnes Inn," Wordsworth's "Resolution and Independence" (and part of *The Prelude*) and Auden's "In Sickness and in Health." Again his terms are so extremely general that any poem which involves a "resolution" of sorts apparently becomes the coequal of any other.

Herman Melville is also mythic in its approach but here Chase's ultimate purpose seems to be cultural or frankly political. Melville, he maintains, is one of our fathers: "he stood opposed to the social pieties of transcendentalism very much as we must now [1949] oppose the progressive liberalism which was born fifteen or twenty years ago":

> One may distinguish between "liberal" and "progressive." Melville was a liberal in questions of politics, morals, and religion. But he was a progressive only in a very limited sense of the word. To be sure, he wanted to progress, to improve his lot; but he did not believe that progress was the principle of the universe or that man could do anything which would make progress inevitable—and he had a name for the pious and irresponsible progressive: he called him "the confidence man."...In sloughing off a facile idea of progress, Melville accepted what that sloughing-off implied: a tragic view of life. No

119

view of life can protect itself against the attritions of history if it cannot see man's lot as a tragedy.

And as Melville's personal myth is the symbolic search for a father ("not God but a cultural ideal") so this is America's primary myth as well:

> The myth has two central themes: the Fall and the Search, the Search for what was lost in the Fall or for the earthy and possible substitutes for what was lost. The idea of the Fall was Melville's instinctive image of his own fate and the fate of his family....The myth of the Fall seemed to be also an American myth, a so-far undefined legend of the Promethean nation which had revolted and fled from the high tyranny of British rule, an Ishmaelite nation cast out by Europe to wander in the wilderness, a nation betrayed by the Old World as a father might betray a son....The question Melville asks is: Will America turn out to be the true Prometheus who successfully opposes the will of Zeus, redeems Zeus with the Promethean creativity, and so leads man along the path of growth toward a higher culture?

Chase forces the Prometheus myth into alignment with the Oedipus myth as well:

> The "Prometheus complex" and the Oedipus complex have much in common, and Melville's vision of life makes use of many specifically Oedipean themes: the fear of castration (symbolized by cannibalism, decapitation, the injured leg, the horror of women), homoeroticism, narcissism, incest, and paricide. Ultimately, as we have noticed, Melville's vision seeks to delineate a Promethean king-hero who is less like our ususal conception of Prometheus than he is like the Oedipus of Sophocles. Most of Melville's protagonists are Prometheus-like men shown in the act of failing to become the American Oedipus—that fully moral, fully wise, and fully tragic American who in Melville's books always strides just beyond the horizon, just beyond our ken....The true Prometheus is...in a state of becoming Oedipus.

Chase reads each of Melville's works in this light, but once again his generalizations are hopelessly broad (Melville's basic philosophical theme becomes "the quest of consciousness for reality," something which might be said of almost any writer) and his particular interpretations wildly excessive ("The real theme of *Billy Budd* is castration and cannibalism, the ritual murder and eating of the Host"). But Chase's studies of Emily Dickinson and Walt Whitman are surprisingly free from such speculations. He sees Dickinson as critical of the superficialities of her culture but quickly adds that this is true of most writers, and he treats Whitman in quite conventional terms as a "comic poet...radical idealist...and profound elegist" ("comic," of course, in the sense of being assured and hopeful). But as competent conventional introductions to these poets both books have been more than superseded by the work of Gay Wilson Allen and Thomas Johnson.

The American Novel and Its Tradition, Chase's best-known book, attempts to define the "tradition" as that of the romance ("although most of the great American novels are romances, most of the great English novels are not"). Romance signifies

> besides the more obvious qualities of the picturesque and the heroic, an assumed freedom from the ordinary novelistic requirements of verisimilitude, development, and continuity; a tendency towards melodrama and idyl; a more or less formal abstractness and, on the other hand, a tendency to plunge into the underside of consciousness.

The romance has a particular power to "express dark and complex truths unavailable to realism." The American novel therefore tends to "rest in contradictions and among extreme ranges of experience"; it has been "stirred by the aesthetic possibilities of radical forms of alienation, contradiction, and disorder." Armed with this thesis Chase then discusses Brockden Brown, Hawthorne, Cooper, Melville, Twain, Norris and Faulkner, and more briefly, James and Fitzgerald. As might be expected, the arguments are less convincing when Chase takes up James and post-Civil War realism.

For whatever reasons, by 1958 Chase seems to have lost interest in a purely mythic approach to literature. One of the characters in his dialogue, *The Democratic Vista*, refers to "a touching and delirious book by Joseph Campbell," and another, who speaks for Chase himself, adds that the mythic approach to history is "a sort of Sargasso Sea for the beguiled to float about in." "Don't you think," he concludes, "that for some writers, myth became in the 1940's and '50's a substitute for the Stalinism on which they had been brought up but which they could no longer accept?"

CONNOLLY, Cyril (Vernon). British. Born in Coventry, Warwickshire, 10 September 1903. Educated at Eton College, Buckinghamshire; Balliol College, Oxford (Brackenbury Scholar). Married Dierdre Craig in 1959. Founding Editor, *Horizon*, London, 1939-50; Literary Editor, *The Observer*, London, 1942-43; Columnist for the *Sunday Times*, London, 1951-74. Fellow, and Companion of Literature, 1972, Royal Society of Literature; C.B.E. (Commander, Order of the British Empire), 1972; Chevalier, Legion of Honor. *Died 26 November 1974.*

PUBLICATIONS

Criticism

Enemies of Promise. London, Routledge, 1938; Boston, Little Brown, 1939; revised edition, New York, Macmillan, 1948; Routledge, 1949.
The Unquiet Grave: A Word Cycle by Palinurus. London, Horizon, 1944; revised edition, London, Hamish Hamilton, and New York, Harper, 1945; 2d revised edition, London, Hamish Hamilton, 1951.
The Condemned Playground: Essays 1927-1944. London, Routledge, 1945; New York, Macmillan, 1946.
Ideas and Places. London, Weidenfeld and Nicolson, and New York, Harper, 1953.
Enemies of Promise and Other Essays: An Autobiography of Ideas. New York, Doubleday, 1960.
Previous Convictions. London, Hamish Hamilton, 1963; New York, Harper, 1964.
The Modern Movement: 100 Key Books from England, France and America, 1880-1950. London, Deutsch, 1965; New York, Atheneum, 1966.
The Evening Colonnade. London, David Bruce and Watson, 1973; New York, Harcourt Brace, 1975.

Novel

The Rock Pool. Paris, Obelisk Press, and New York, Scribner, 1936; London, Hamish Hamilton, 1947.

Other

The Missing Diplomats. London, Queen Anne Press, 1952.

121

Les Pavillons: French Pavilions of the Eighteenth Century, with Jerome Zerbe.   London, Hamish Hamilton, and New York, Macmillan, 1962.
Bond Strikes Camp (on James Bond).   London, Shenval Press, 1963.
A Romantic Friendship: The Letters of Cyril Connolly to Noel Blakiston, edited by Noel Blakiston.   London, Constable, 1975.

Editor, *Horizon Stories*.   London, Faber, 1943; augmented edition, New York, Vanguard Press, 1946.
Editor, *Great English Short Novels*.   New York, Dial Press, 1953.
Editor, *The Golden Horizon*.   London, Weidenfeld and Nicolson, 1953; New York, University Books, 1956.

Translator, *Put Out the Light*, by Vercors.   London, Macmillan, 1944; as *Silence of the Sea*, New York, Macmillan, 1944.
Translator, *Ubu Rex* and *Ubu Cuckholded*, by Alfred Jarry, in *The Ubu Plays*, edited by Taylor.   London, Methuen, 1968.

*   *   *

"It is closing time in the gardens of the west," "The great marquee of European civilization in whose yellow light we all grew up and read or wrote or loved or travelled has fallen down"— these dying falls and a good many others like them confirm Cyril Connolly's description of himself as a man haunted by "the sense of evanescence" and driven by "an obsession with *tout ce qui resumait en ce mot: chute.*" Like Proust, however, Connolly enjoyed his obsession hugely and exploited it brilliantly for well over thirty years.

Time is the constant enemy: "The supreme liberty," Connolly maintains in *The Unquiet Grave*,

> is liberty from the body, the last freedom is freedom from time; the true work of art the one which the seventh wave of genius throws far up the beach where the under-tow of time cannot drag it back. When all the motives that lead artists to create have fallen away, and the satisfaction of vanity and the play-instinct been exhausted, there remains the desire to construct that which has its own order, as a protest against the chaos to which all else appears condemned. While thought exists, words are alive and literature becomes an escape, not from, but into living.

This last phrase, *into* living, takes on particular significance for readers familiar with a central later essay, "Beyond Believing," now reprinted in *Previous Convictions*. Here Connolly asserts that the natural condition of created things is one of "undiluted ecstasy":

> Self-consciousness is the consequence of some imperceptible deviation in biological process, a deviation spreading like a ladder in a stocking which cannot now be halted.
> Very small organisms have no fear or knowledge of death which, in a cell, is synonymous with parturition, and quite large organisms have no feeling of pain. It was not obligatory that there should be any disturbance of the primal ecstasy according to whether one ate or was eaten....The indifference to death of some large creatures...remains otherwise inexplicable. "Man has created death" because he has watched man die. Even so, assuming that natural, even violent death could be a part of our ecstasy as human beings or that our awareness of it can add meaning and poetry to life, such noble exits can be the reward only of a Sophocles or Goethe, for in our time and place so full a life...is seldom attainable. The happiest creatures are those which live out their brief existence in instinctive harmony with the universe, unconscious of their role in it. But since self-consciousness has arisen, we must stake all on developing it to the ultimate moment when we shall have completely understood our environment, for to understand may be to change it, to find a way of reducing death (so nearly a blessing, and the source of all our dignity and tragedy) to something we can bear.

Consciousness means a fall from grace, but there are some compensations. For Connolly art and love can provide moments when we seem to return to primal contentment with an awareness of our happiness which is impossible without consciousness. Thus he continues

> I believe in two wholly admirable human activities, guilt-free, unpunished, two ends in themselves equally rewarding: the satisfaction of curiosity (acquirement of knowledge) and mating of like minds (friendship and mutual attraction) with the apprehension of beauty in so far as it be not included in the other two.

"Would you die for your country?" an imaginary interrogator interrupts:

> "I have so many countries."
> "Would you die for Queen and country?"
> "Not if I could help it. I regard it as my duty to cling to consciousness until the last possible moment."
> "Duty to yourself?"
> "Duty to my consciousness."
> "As an artist?"
> "Certainly."
> "As an artist, forgive me, you don't write much?"
> "And I compose, paint, sculpt even less, but I am an artist all the same."
> "What then is Art?"
> "Art is the conscious apprehension of the unconscious ecstasy of all created things."

Art matters, then, because it provides such victories over time as we are capable of and because at its best it restores the feeling of "equilibrium," as Connolly calls it in *The Unquiet Grave*, which is "that sensation of harmony with the universe, of accepting life and being part of nature which we experience in childhood and which afterwards we discover through love, artistic creation, the pursuit of wisdom, through mystical elation or luminous calm." Proust, Pater, the echoes of Forster and Bloomsbury: the sources and parallels here are less important than the eloquent use Connolly makes of them.

All of these passages suggest a kind of hedonism, and in fact Connolly quoted, on several occasions and with obvious approval, Sainte-Beuve's remark, "L'epicureisme bien compris est la fin de tout." But Connolly's epicureanism is neither mindless nor selfish. Despite references to his youthful "left-wing militancy," and despite his observation that "the defeat of the Spanish republic shattered my faith in political action," there is a persistent strain of qualified optimism in most of what he wrote. "In the love of truth which leads to a knowledge of it," he asserted in 1938—when the prospects were hardly encouraging—"lies not only the hope of humanity but its safety":

> Deep down we feel that, as every human being has a right to air and water, so has he a right to food, clothing, light, heat, work, education, love and leisure. Ultimately we know the world will be run, its resources exploited and its efforts synchronized on this assumption. A writer can help to liberate that knowledge and to unmask those pretenders which accompany all human plans for improvement....A writer must be a lie-detector who exposes fallacies in words and ideals before half the world is killed for them.

The great artists have in common "a sense of perfection and a faith in human dignity, combined with a tragic apprehending of our moral situation, and our nearness to the Abyss."

This earnest pursuit of Connolly's principles and commitments is partly misleading, however—an essay like "Beyond Believing" is an important but rare exception to his usual critical manner. The scores of short reviews which make up his five books are not essays in applied aesthetics but quick, shrewd, elegant appreciations of the writers he happens to like, as rereadable as Edmund Wilson's journalism from the same period. It is simply that the grounds of Connolly's appreciations require some definition if the reader is to grasp the unity of his work.

One of these volumes, however, *Enemies of Promise*, deserves separate attention. Addressing himself to the problem of "how to write a book which lasts ten years" he makes his well-known distinction between the two styles which have dominated English prose: the vernacular, the realistic mode of "rebels, journalists, common sense-addicts and unromantic observers of human destiny," and the Mandarin, which is "artificial" but

> at its best yields the richest and most complex expression of the English language. It is the diction of Donne, Browne, Addison, Johnson, Gibbon, de Quincey, Landor, Carlyle and Ruskin as opposed to that of Bunyan, Dryden, Locke, Defoe, Cowper, Cobbett, Hazlitt, Southey and Newman. It is characterised by long sentences with many dependent clauses, by the use of the subjunctive and the conditional, by exclamations, interjections, quotations, allusions, metaphors, long images, Latin terminology, subtlety and conceits. Its cardinal assumption is that neither the writer nor the reader is in a hurry, that both are in possession of a classical education and a private income. It is Ciceronian English.

Social changes and the overdevelopment of one mode or the other lead to revolt and counter-reaction. "I do not say that one [style] is better than the other," Connolly explains:

> there is much to admire in both; what I have claimed is a relationship between them, a perpetual action and reaction; the realists had it their way in the years before the war; from 1918 to 1928, the period of Joyce, Proust, Valéry, Strachey, Woolf, the Sitwells, and Aldous Huxley, the new Mandarins reigned supreme, while from 1928 to 1938 the new realists have predominated. The deflationary activities of the Cambridge critics (Richards, Leavis) have replaced the inflationism of Bloomsbury.

Thus the writer who wants his prose to last is advised to synthesize the best qualities of the realists and the Mandarins. But whatever style he aims for, the young writer faces those "enemies of promise" which threaten every artist. Early success, the pressure to write too much too quickly, sexual and political enticements—the list is familiar enough. For Connolly himself the enemy was always journalism: the short space of a Sunday column or *Horizon* editorial rarely gave him much breathing space and the larger audience he wrote for after *Horizon* stopped publication needed oversimplifications, or so he seems to have felt. Given other circumstances he might have written at greater length about fewer matters, but it is pointless to speculate, and a little ungrateful as well: we have *Enemies of Promise*, *The Condemned Playground*, *Ideas and Places*, *Previous Convictions* and *The Evening Colonnade* and should be sensible enough to take them on their own considerable merits.

COWLEY, Malcolm. American. Born in Belsano, Pennsylvania, 24 August 1898. Educated at Peabody High School, Pittsburgh; Harvard University, Cambridge, Massachusetts (Editor, *The Advocate*, 1919), A.B. (cum laude) 1920 (Phi Beta Kappa); University of Montpellier, Diplome 1922. Served in the American Ambulance Service in France, 1917, and the United States Army, 1918; Office of Facts and Figures, Washington, D.C., 1942. Married Muriel Maurer (second wife) in 1932; one son, Robert. Associate Editor, *Broom* magazine, New York, 1923; Literary Editor, *New Republic*, New York, 1929-44. Visiting Professor: University of Washington, Seattle, 1950; Stanford University, California, 1956, 1959, 1960-61, 1965; University of Michigan, Ann Arbor, 1957; University of California, Berkeley, 1962; Cornell University, Ithaca, New York, 1964; University of Minnesota, Minneapolis, 1971; University of Warwick, England, 1973. Since 1948 Literary Adviser, The Viking Press, New York. Director of the Yaddo Corporation. Recipient: Levinson Prize, 1927, and Harriet Monroe Memorial Prize, 1939 (*Poetry*, Chicago); National Institute of Arts and Letters grant, 1946; National Endowment for the Arts grant, 1967; Signet Medal, 1976. Litt.D.: Franklin and Marshall College, Lancaster, Pennsylvania, 1961; Colby College, Waterville, Maine, 1962; University of

Warwick, Coventry, 1975. President, 1956-59, 1962-65, National Institute of Arts and Letters; Chancellor, American Academy of Arts and Letters, 1967-76. Address: Sherman, Connecticut 06784, U.S.A.

PUBLICATIONS

Criticism

Exile's Return: A Narrative of Ideas. New York, Norton, 1934; London, Cape, 1935; revised edition, as *Exile's Return: A Literary Odyssey of the 1920's*, Norton, 1951; London, Bodley Head, 1961.
The Literary Situation. New York, Viking Press, 1954.
Think Back on Us...A Contemporary Chronicle of the 1930's, edited by Henry Dan Piper. Carbondale and Edwardsville, Southern Illinois University Press, and London, Feffer and Simons, 1970.
A Many-Windowed House: Collected Essays on American Writers and American Writing. Carbondale and Edwardsville, Southern Illinois University Press, and London, Feffer and Simons, 1970.
A Second Flowering: Works and Days of the Lost Generation. New York, Viking Press, and London, Deutsch, 1973.
—And I Worked at the Writer's Trade: Chapters of Literary History. New York, Viking Press, 1978.

Verse

Blue Juniata. New York, Cape and Smith, 1929.
The Dry Season. New York, New Directions, 1941.
Blue Juniata: Collected Poems. New York, Viking Press, 1968.

Other

Black Cargoes: A History of the Atlantic Slave Trade, 1518-1865, with Daniel P. Mannix. New York, Viking Press, 1962; London, Longman, 1963.
The Faulkner-Cowley File: Letters and Memories, 1944-1962. New York, Viking Press, and London, Chatto and Windus, 1966.
The Dream of the Golden Mountains: Remembering the 1930's. New York, Viking Press, 1980.
The View from 80. New York, Viking Press, 1980.

Editor, *Adventures of an African Slaver, Being a True Account of the Life of Captain Theodore Canot*, by Brantz Mayer. London, Routledge, 1928.
Editor, *After the Genteel Tradition: American Writers since 1910*. New York, Norton, 1937; revised edition, Carbondale, Southern Illinois University Press, 1964.
Editor, with Bernard Smith, *Books That Changed Our Minds*. New York, Doubleday, 1940.
Editor, *The Portable Hemingway*. New York, Viking Press, 1944.
Editor, with Hannah Josephson, *Aragon: Poet of the French Resistance*. New York, Duell, 1945; as *Aragon: Poet of Resurgent France*, London, Pilot Press, 1946.
Editor, *The Portable Faulkner*. New York, Viking Press, 1946; revised edition, 1966; London, Chatto and Windus, 1967.

Editor, *The Portable Hawthorne*.   New York, Viking Press, 1948; revised edition, 1969;
  London, Penguin, 1969.
Editor, *The Complete Poetry and Prose of Walt Whitman*.   New York, Pellegrini, 1948;
  as *The Works of Walt Whitman*, New York, Funk and Wagnalls, 1968.
Editor, *Stories*, by F. Scott Fitzgerald.   New York, Scribner, 1951.
Editor, *Great Tales of the Deep South*.   New York, Lion Library, 1955.
Editor, *Writers at Work: The "Paris Review" Interviews*.   New York, Viking Press, and
  London, Secker and Warburg, 1958.
Editor, *Leaves of Grass, The First (1855) Edition*, by Walt Whitman.   New York, Viking
  Press, 1959.
Editor, with Robert Cowley, *Fitzgerald and the Jazz Age*.   New York, Scribner, 1966.
Editor, with Howard E. Hugo, *The Lessons of the Masters: An Anthology of the Novel
  from Cervantes to Hemingway*.   New York, Scribner, 1971.
Editor, *Walt Whitman*, edited by Mark Van Doren.   New York, Viking Press, 1974; as
  The Portable Walt Whitman, New York, Penguin, 1977.

Translator, *On Board the Morning Star*, by Pierre MacOrlan.   New York, Boni, 1924.
Translator, *Joan of Arc*, by Joseph Delteil.   New York, Minton, 1926.
Translator, *Variety*, by Paul Valéry.   New York, Harcourt Brace, 1928.
Translator, *Catherine-Paris*, by Marthe Bibesco.   New York, Harcourt Brace, 1928.
Translator, *The Green Parrot*, by Marthe Bibesco.   New York, Harcourt Brace, 1929.
Translator, *The Sacred Hill*, by Maurice Barrès.   New York, Macauley, 1929.
Translator, *The Count's Ball*, by Raymond Radiguet.   New York, Norton, 1929.
Translator, *Imaginary Interviews*, by André Gide.   New York, Knopf, 1944.
Translator, with James R. Lawler, *Leonardo Poe Mallarmé*, by Paul Valéry.   Princeton,
  New Jersey, Princeton University Press, 1972.

CRITICAL STUDY AND BIBLIOGRAPHY

Philip Young, "For Malcolm Cowley: Critic, Poet, 1898—," in *Southern Review* (Baton
  Rouge, Louisiana), 9, new series, 1973.
Diane U. Eisenberg, *Malcolm Cowley: A Checklist of His Writings*.   Carbondale,
  Southern Illinois University Press, 1975.

*   *   *

At the conclusion of *A Second Flowering*, looking back over a career which spans more than
fifty years, Malcolm Cowley admits he has some misgivings:

In later years I have wondered whether certain types of criticism are possible except in
relation to authors of one's own age group. Those types are not the highest ones, I
suspect; they do not often lead to universal principles and they are not as persuasive in
the classroom as the reinterpretation of an older work for a new age. The text of the older
work remains and every critic has the privilege of reading it attentively. But there are
values in the text, there are images and associations, that can be grasped intuitively by
those who grew up at the same time as the author; "empathy" is the abused word.

To some extent the limitations he suggests are real enough: unlike his friend Kenneth Burke, he
has never sought "universal principles"; he has never allied himself with any critical school; in
some ways he seems to operate without any discernible "method." But the very lack of
dogmatism and the fact that he shared so intensely the world of the writers who made the
literature of the 1920's give his work a special value. Critics who did not experience that earlier
world, he continues, "sometimes offer reinterpretations—I have read them by the dozen—that
are inspired, compelling, and completely wrong in their sense of values."
Such principles as Cowley does recognize are unremarkable:

I believe that the first of [the critic's] functions is to select works of art worth writing about, with special emphasis on works that are new, not much discussed, or widely misunderstood....His second function is to describe or analyze or reinterpret the chosen works as a basis for judgments which can sometimes be merely implied. In practice his problem may be to explain why he enjoys a particular book, and perhaps to find new reasons for enjoying it, so as to deepen his readers' capacity for appreciation.

And in an age which has taken criticism with astonishing seriousness Cowley has actually proposed humility ("I do not believe," he states, "that criticism is one of the major arts....Therefore a critic cannot afford to be arrogant. He is dealing in most cases with better works [than] he has proved his capability of writing.") As for method:

> I always start and end with the text itself, and am willing to accept the notion of the textual or integral critics that the principle value of a work lies in the complexity and unity of its internal relations. But I also try to start with a sort of innocence, that is, with a lack of preconceptions about what I might or might not discover.

Yet he is never content simply to deepen the reader's appreciation of a single text:

> What I read after the text itself are other texts by the same author. It is a mistake to approach each work as if it were an absolutely separate production, a unique artifact, the last and single relic of a buried civilization. Why not approach it as the author does? It seems to me that any author of magnitude has his eye on something larger than the individual story or poem or novel. He wants each of these to be as good as possible, and self-subsistent, but he also wants it to serve as a chapter or aspect of the larger work that is his lifetime's production, his *oeuvre*. This larger work is also part of the critic's subject matter.

Sympathy, openness, a concern for the writer's work as a whole: again, these are broad commonplaces; but what makes Cowley's criticism so attractive is the extent of his sympathy and his unfailing willingness to place himself completely at the service of the text and the reader's increased enjoyment. These virtues remain constant throughout the shorter pieces which make up *Think Back on Us*, the longer retrospective essays of *A Many-Windowed House* and *A Second Flowering*, and the two collections which fall someplace between criticism and social history, *Exile's Return* and *The Literary Situation*.

The best of Cowley's short pieces from *The New Republic* are now collected in *Think Back on Us*. "Pieces," he comments, "will do for want of a better word":

> some of them are essays, some are reports, some are editorial pontifications, but more are unabashed book reviews—and why not? The relatively short book review was my art form for many years; it became my blank-verse meditation, my sonnet sequence, my letter to distant friends, my private journal. I did not fall into the illusion that it was a major form; no, it was dependent for its subject matter on the existence of novels or plays or poems worth writing about.

Rather than starting with any preconceived ideas or standards, he recalls,

> I had nothing but a pretty wide range of interests and a few presuppositions: as notably that literature is a part of life, not subordinate to other parts, such as politics and economics, but intimately affected by them and sometimes affecting them in turn. All the parts were interwoven, I believed, in the web of history. That was a serviceable belief, but only as a background for opinions about the book at hand. Those I must find by going deeper into the book and into myself. What was the author really saying, as opposed to what he intended and appeared to say? What light did he cast on the drama of our times?

Inevitably, a good many of these pieces are dated by now, but a good many more are as worth reading as Edmund Wilson's work for the same magazine. After fifteen years at *The New Republic*, as Henry Dan Piper has noted, Cowley was free to turn to longer essays. There are no real changes, though the short review is now replaced by the various introductions and extended discussions gathered together in *A Many-Windowed House*. Readable as these are, however, Cowley's finest criticism appears in *A Second Flowering*, in which he sums up his final views of the writers of the 1920's. There is an introductory essay in which Cowley defines the importance of the First World War for writers born around the turn of the century; there is a moving memoir of Hart Crane; there are balanced appreciations of Hemingway, early and late, Dos Passos, Cummings, Fitzgerald and Wolfe; and finally there is the pioneering essay on the unity of Faulkner's work, "The Yoknapatawpha Story," which played a major role in calling attention to Faulkner's greatness. The liabilities are simply that by now much of what Cowley observed first-hand has been taken over, repeated and expanded by several generations of academic critics. Cowley is pefectly aware of this:

> Once I was proud of [these essays] for laying bare new beds of ore, but now the ore has been mined and smelted by others. Rereading those studies before filing them away, I felt myself sinking back into the magma of history. I wonder if anyone else has had the experience of writing about the same group of authors at intervals during half a century....One starts by trying to predict the nature of books that are still to be written...[and] ends with a retrospect of amazing careers that assume new shapes and meanings. One starts by speaking *for* the youngest writers and ends by speaking *to* them, from a point one hopes is not too distant for the voice to carry.

A Second Flowering is Cowley's finest book, but *Exile's Return* is still his best known. These partly autobiographical chapters are designed as a "literary odyssey," and rereading them over again in the 1950's Cowley observed that "the story they tell seems to follow the old pattern of alienation and reintegration, or departure and return." In retrospect the story seems to have distinct stages. The writers of Cowley's generation were uprooted from rural, unsophisticated America at the end of the nineteenth century first by their college experiences; the war completed their education:

> "You could not go back": the country of [the writer's] boyhood was gone and he was attached to no other.
> And that, I believe, was the final effect on us of the war; that was the honest emotion behind a pretentious phrase like "the lost generation." School and college had uprooted us in spirit: now we were physically uprooted, hundreds of us, millions, plucked from our own soil as if by a clamshell bucket and dumped, scattered among strange people.

After the war the young writers of this generation (which Cowley maintains should be called "lucky" rather than "lost") either stayed abroad or returned to America, only to separate themselves from the mainstream of national life by gathering together in the Greenwich Villages of the 1920's. Whatever the important differences between them, most of the best writers and artists struggled to believe in art as a way of life. The illusions ended with the Crash, Cowley argues, and the symbolic figure of the whole explosive decade becomes Harry Crosby, whose life

> included practically all the themes I have been trying to develop—the separation from home, the effect of service in the ambulance corps, the exile in France, then other themes, bohemianism, the religion of art, the escape from society, the effort to defend one's individuality even at the cost of sterility and madness, then the final period of demoralization when the whole philosophical structure crumbled after its greatest outpouring of luxuries, its longest debauch.

Those who survived the Crash returned to the realities of American life, and this, Cowley concludes, was the real homecoming:

> During the years when the exiles tried to stand apart from American society they had pictured it as a unified mass that was moving in a fixed direction and could not be turned aside by the efforts of any individual. The picture had to be changed after the Wall Street Crash, for then the mass seemed to hesitate like a cloud in a crosswind. Instead of being fixed, its direction proved to be the result of a struggle among social groups with

different aims and of social forces working against one another. The exiles learned that the struggle would affect everyone's future, including their own. When they took part in it, on one side or another (but usually on the liberal side); when they tried to strengthen some of the forces and allied themselves with one or another of the groups, they ceased to be exiles. They had acquired friends and enemies and purposes in the midst of society, and thus, wherever they lived in America, they had found a home.

The Literary Situation, which continues the odyssey into the mid-1950's, is much less interesting than its predecessors largely because the writers under examination here are so much duller than the best writers of the 1920's—as Cowley himself realizes:

> The recent period [roughly from 1940-54] has been a sort of interval or interregnum. One is impressed by the generally high technical level of writing in all fields. The poets have been erudite and generally honest, the novelists have been skilled and sensitive, but only the critics have seemed to know where they are going; most of the others wrote as if they were waiting for something or someone to give their work a definite direction. Mere talent has been relatively common; it was conviction and character that were needed.

The writers of the 40's and 50's may have been skilled and sensitive, the writers of the 30's may have been more realistic and led more orderly lives; but if American literature did have a second flowering it was during those brief years between the Armistice and the Crash to which Cowley remains the one indispensable guide.

CRANE, R(onald) S(almon).   American.   Born in Tecumseh, Michigan, 5 January 1886. Educated at the University of Michigan, Ann Arbor, B.A. 1908; University of Pennsylvania, Philadelphia, Ph.D. 1911. Married Julia L. Fuller in 1917; 2 children. Instructor in English, 1911-15, Assistant Professor, 1915-20, and Associate Professor, 1920-24, Northwestern University, Evanston, Illinois; Associate Professor, 1924-25, Professor, 1925-50, Chairman of the Department, 1935-47, Distinguished Service Professor, 1950-51, and Professor Emeritus, 1951-1967, University of Chicago. Visiting Professor and Alexander Lecturer, University of Toronto, 1952; Visiting Professor, Cornell University, Ithaca, New York, 1952-53, 1957, Carleton College, Northfield, Minnesota, 1953, University of Oregon, Eugene, 1954, Stanford University, California, 1954-55, and Indiana University, Bloomington, 1955-56. Editor, *Modern Philology*, Chicago, 1930-52. L.H.D.: University of Michigan, 1941. *Died in 1967.*

PUBLICATIONS

Criticism

> Foreword to "Two Essays in Practical Criticism," by Norman Maclean and Elder Olson, in *University Review* (Kansas City), 8, 1942.
> "I.A. Richards and the Art of Interpretation," "The Critical Monism of Cleanth Brooks," "English Neoclassical Criticism: An Outline Sketch," and "The Concept of Plot and the Plot of *Tom Jones*," in *Critics and Criticism: Ancient and Modern*, edited by R.S. Crane and others.   Chicago and London, University of Chicago Press, 1952.
> *The Languages of Criticism and the Structure of Poetry*.   Toronto, University of Toronto Press, 1953.
> *The Idea of the Humanities and Other Essays Critical and Historical*.   Chicago and London, University of Chicago Press, 2 vols., 1967.

Other

The Vogue of Guy of Warwick from the Close of the Middle Ages to the Romantic Revival. Cambridge, Massachusetts, Modern Language Association, 1915.
The Vogue of Medieval Chivalric Romance During the English Renaissance. Menasha, Wisconsin, Banta, 1916.
The Bibliography of Gray. Chicago, Bibliographical Society of America, 1918.

Editor, with William Frank Bryan, *The English Familiar Essay: Representative Texts.* New York, Ginn, 1916.
Editor, *New Essays*, by Oliver Goldsmith. Chicago, University of Chicago Press, 1927.
Editor, with F.B. Kaye and Moody Prior, *A Census of British Newspapers and Periodicals, 1620-1800.* Chapel Hill, University of North Carolina Press, 1927; London, Holland Press, 1966.
Editor, *A Collection of English Poems, 1660-1800.* New York, Harper, 1932.
Editor, with others, *A Documentary History of Primitivism and Related Ideas.* Baltimore, Johns Hopkins Press, 1935.
Editor, *English Literature, 1660-1800: A Bibliography of Modern Studies.* Princeton, New Jersey, Princeton University Press, 1950.
Editor, with others, *Critics and Criticism: Ancient and Modern.* Chicago and London, University of Chicago Press, 1952.

CRITICAL STUDIES

John Crowe Ransom, "Humanism at Chicago," in *Kenyon Review* (Gambier, Ohio), 14, 1952.
Eliseo Vivas, "The Neo-Aristotelians of Chicago," in *Sewanee Review* (Tennessee), 61, 1953.
W.K. Wimsatt, Jr., "The Chicago Critics: The Fallacy of the Neoclassic Species," in *The Verbal Icon: Studies in the Meaning of Poetry.* Lexington, University of Kentucky Press, 1954.
John Holloway, "The New and the Newer Criticism," in *The Charted Mirror: Literary and Critical Essays.* London, Routledge, 1960; New York, Horizon Press, 1962.
Wayne C. Booth, "Ronald Crane and the Pluralism of Discrete Modes," in *Critical Understanding: The Powers and Limits of Pluralism.* Chicago and London, University of Chicago Press, 1979.

*   *   *

The criticism of R.S. Crane is so closely reasoned and its implications so far reaching that a tolerably useful description is particularly difficult. One possible approach, however, is to consider his work as a sustained reply to I.A. Richards' well-known assertion (made in 1927) that two thousand years of critical speculation had produced little more than

a few conjectures, a supply of admonitions, many acute isolated observations, some brilliant guesses, much oratory and applied poetry, inexhaustible confusion, a sufficiency of dogma, no small stock of prejudices, whimsies and crotchets, a profusion of mysticism, a little genuine speculation, sundry stray inspirations, pregnant hints and random *aperçus....*

"Of such as these," Richards concluded, "it may be said without exaggeration, is extant critical theory composed." As Crane observes, there are several ways of responding to this aggressive half-truth. We may become completely skeptical about criticism as a discipline in which there can be rational consensus and therefore genuine knowledge: at best criticism is simply the record of sensitive or imaginative or otherwise striking subjective reactions. Or we may become dogmatic and assert—as Richards himself did—that a new set of principles will bring order out of the "chaos of critical theory."

Crane rejects these versions of dogmatism and scepticism and proposes instead a program of critical pluralism. The primary subject matter of criticism is the artistic work itself, but the crucial premise here is that the reality criticism investigates is too complex to be encompassed by any one frame of reference. The question is, what aspect of the total situation do we wish to consider; and this, Crane argues, involves a practical rather than a theoretical decision:

> Shall I use this or some other alternative framework, applicable to the same sphere of objects but constituting them as different kinds of things, for the inquiries I wish to pursue? Shall I, in criticism, for instance, employ a language which will necessarily lead me to dwell on characteristics that relate poetry to other things or a language which will necessarily cause me to emphasize characteristics peculiar to poetry or to one or another of its kinds? The issue, plainly, cannot be decided by an appeal to facts, for it is equally true that poetry is organically connected with everything else in life and that it is something with a distinctive reality of its own. I cannot, however, use the same conceptual language to exhibit both the organic interconnections and the specific differences; hence I must choose; but I can justify my choice only by arguing, and possibly persuading others to agree with me, that by means of the particular framework I have selected certain important questions about poetry...can be answered which I could not even raise, much less answer intelligently, in a framework of the other sort. There is thus a strict relativity, in criticism, not only of questions and statements to frameworks, but also of frameworks to ends, that is, to the different kinds of knowledge about poetry we may happen at one time or another or for one or another reason, to want.

Here Crane is indebted to the distinction his colleague Richard P. McKeon makes between literal and dialectical modes of inquiry. In "The Philosophic Bases of Art and Criticism" (now reprinted in *Critics and Criticism: Ancient and Modern*), McKeon states that the basic question among opposing critical systems

> is, perhaps, whether one discusses art adequately by discussing something else or by discussing art, for, in the former case, oppositions turn on what precise subject other than art should be discussed and, in the latter case, on what art itself is. The theories which have been based on the assumption that the meaning of art is explained best, or solely, by means of other phenomena have recently, as in the past, borrowed the principles and terminology of aesthetics and criticism from some fashionable science, from semantics, psychoanalysis, or economics, from sociology, morals or theology. The art object and the art experience are then nothing in themselves, since they are determined by circumstances and require, like the circumstances which determine them, biological, social, psychological, or historical principles of explanation. The theories which have been based on the assumption that aesthetic phenomena should be analyzed separately, whatever the complexities of the relations in which the aesthetic object or experience is involved, have sought principles in the construction and unity of the art object viewed in terms of expression (in which experience and intention are matched by form), composition (in which details are organized in form), or communication (in which emotion is evoked by form).

Each mode—the literal, which discusses the nature of the object itself, and the dialectical (or "analogical"), which discusses the object in its various relationships—has its inherent powers and limitations, and therefore McKeon concludes that "in application and precept, modes of criticism thus differently oriented will select different points of excellence in the work of the artist and indicate different objectives to be urged on his attention."

Within these two primary modes of discourse, however, lie possibilities for a great many diverse critical "languages," each attending to different aspects of its subject matter and each inherently limited by its principles and terms. Intelligible discourse about literature or anything else, Crane points out, rests upon a finite conceptual scheme which

> delimits what the critic can say about any of the questions with which he may be concerned—and this for the simple reason that we can discuss only those aspects of existent objects which are represented or implied in terms we select or have available for

131

the discussion: we cannot, for example, say anything about the specific forms of individual poems in a mode of criticism of which the distinctions used as principles in the argument pertain only to the poet's mind or to the constitution of his medium or to the psychology of his audience. We are thus committed, in any instance of coherent critical discourse, to a particular subject matter, which can be said to be of our own making, not in the sense that it may not correspond to something real, but in the sense that, by our choice of one rather than another possible set of definitions and hypotheses, we have decided what it is to be.

And when we consider the validity and meaning of a given critical statement it follows that "we must first reconstruct the underlying and often only partly explicit conceptual scheme in which the statement appears." Pluralism is not in any sense a form of intellectual relativism, nor can it tolerate, as an alternative to simple skepticism or dogmatism, any version of eclecticism. Principles and terms are functional only within a given kind of discourse; thus a coherent "synthesis" of different languages (such as Stanley Edgar Hyman proposes in *The Armed Vision*) is a logical impossibility.

The critic's initial choice of a conceptual language may come about as the result of his training or temperament or simply his awareness that particular occasions (different teaching situations, for example) require that he emphasize one aspect of his subject matter rather than another (once he has made his choice we have the right, of course, to "hold him to the accepted canons of reasoning and hypothesis-making, as well as of common sense, that apply in any branch of inquiry dealing with particular things"). As Crane's student, Elder Olson, observes, the men on the Tower of Babel were not talking nonsense to each other, they were simply speaking in different languages; and Crane himself concludes that the only adequate way of dealing with critical diversity (that same diversity which Richards condemns as "chaos") is to recognize and in fact welcome "a plurality of distinct critical methods—each of them valid or partially valid within its proper sphere" and then to ascertain "what a given critic is doing, and why, before attempting either to state the meaning or judge the truth or falsity of his conclusions or to compare his doctrines with those of other critics."

Near the end of *The Languages of Criticism and the Structure of Poetry* Crane observes that ideally, we ought to have as many different critical methods as there are "distinguishable major aspects in the construction, appreciation, and use of literary works." And in a footnote to this passage he remarks that he has discussed "some of the practical consequences of this view in an essay, to be published soon, entitled, 'Questions and Answers in the Teaching of Literature.'" The essay was not published until fifteen years later, but when it did appear (in the second volume of *The Idea of the Humanities*) it proved to be admirably specific. Here Crane isolates five "major distinguishable aspects" we may consider when we examine any particular work. In the first place,

> We may ask questions...that depend for their content and for the data of their answers, merely on a consideration of literary works, irrespective of their specific kinds, in their common aspect as verbal compositions. This is the distinctive sphere of *explication de textes*, in its various lexicographical, syntactical, prosodical, logical, and stylistic applications. We may call this, for short, the criticism of elements and devices.

The characteristics of a work are never present, however, simply for their own sake,

> but ultimately for the sake of what is done with them in the making of concrete literary wholes. Therefore the criticism of elements needs to be completed and reoriented, for any given work, by a second kind of criticism—that of structure or form. By form I simply mean the overall principle, whatever it may be, that makes of the materials of a work a single definite thing. It is the aspect of literary works which comes into view when we ask ourselves not simply what the meanings and dictional devices are, and what are the immediate effects they produce, but why these meanings and devices and local effects are appropriate in the work (if they do indeed belong) and how, and how well, they function artistically with respect to one another and the whole.

On other occasions we may be interested in a work as the manifestation of the artist's general sensibility; we may therefore wish to consider works as "the creative acts of men endowed by nature and education with certain qualities of soul or literary personality or 'vision,' which, as reflected in texts, are capable of stimulating responses not entirely to be accounted for by strictly formal considerations" and ask questions appropriate to literary history. This Crane calls the "criticism of circumstances," and he adds that

> A useful kind of training in literary history, I have often thought, would be one in which we first brought our students to recognize that *Lycidas, An Elegy Written in a Country Churchyard, In Memoriam,* and *The Waste Land* are all works having essentially the same poetic form, and then asked them to consider how far and in what ways the striking differences among the four are to be accounted for by differences in the genius and "vision" of their writers, and how far and in what ways by differences in the conventions of subject matter, language, and technique which depend on the fact that the first poem was published in 1638, the second in 1751, the third in 1856, and the fourth in 1922.

And finally there are questions of evaluation:

> They are the questions that give us what may be called the criticism of moral, social, political, and religious values; and they pertain to that aspect of literary works which is called to mind whenever we consider literature or poetry in the context of education or of the particular goods we are interested in realizing in the society of our time; they are concerned, in short, with the functions of literary works over and above the requirements of formal or qualitative excellence or the satisfaction of contemporary tastes.

Each of these different kinds of inquiries addresses itself to different aspects of the work and each will therefore require different principles, terminologies and procedures.

While aim or purpose constitutes one of the determinants of a critical language, the other determinant, method, is no less important. In *The Languages of Criticism and the Structure of Poetry* Crane distinguishes between a "matter of fact" method and the "abstract" method favored by most critics. The matter of fact method

> seeks to render an account of empirically distinguishable literary phenomena in terms of their essential and distinctive causes of production. Its starting-point is always some literary form or actuality that has been and hence can be achieved by art...and its procedure consists in reasoning back from this to the necessary and sufficient conditions of its existence or of its existence in the best possible state.

The abstract method, on the other hand,

> is that "other scientific method"—to quote Hume again—"where a general abstract principle is first established, and is afterwards branched out into a variety of inferences and conclusions" which are then made to apply to the immediate subject in hand. Its starting-point is always something laid down as a basic truth from which, if it is granted, consequences can be inferred by logical equation and opposition that are assumed to be appropriate in some way to literature or poetry through one or another or some combination of its causes in the minds or creative processes of writers, in the language they use, in the things or actions they represent, or in the effects their works are capable of having on readers. The essential first step is therefore to fix upon some kind of general structure discernible in things or actions or mental faculties or symbolic expressions ...which can then be taken as a model or analogue in the discussion and which, being simpler or better known than poetry, can be used to supply the critic with principles and distinctions wherewith to mark off poetry from other things or to assimilate it to them and ultimately to make statements about the structures and values of individual poems.

The affinities between the literal mode of criticism and the matter of fact method on the one hand, and between analogical criticism and the abstract method on the other, are apparent.

As a critic of criticism, then, Crane is a pluralist; as a practicing critic he is intent on exploring the possibility of extending the principles and method of the one great literal system we have in our tradition, the *Poetics* of Aristotle. Crane's preference here is partly a matter of temperament (he admits to a "fascinated distrust" of the abstract method) and partly the result of his conviction that the powers of the literal mode have been badly neglected. Only the literal mode, he maintains, can give us "a method of isolating and defining those principles of structure in individual poems which distinguish them from other poems and determine thus in highly specific ways what their distinctive elements are and the artistic reasons that justify the particular configurations we observe them to have." The elaborate interpretation and extension of Aristotle which Crane and his students undertook at the University of Chicago during the 1930's and 40's are too complicated to summarize here (readers should consult the second chapter of *The Languages of Criticism and the Structure of Poetry* and Elder Olson's essay, "The Poetic Method of Aristotle"), but Crane finally concludes that if we are really interested in the nature and powers of individual works we must be able to answer certain basic Aristotelian questions, considering as precisely as possible "what kind of human experience is being imitated, by the use of what possibilities of the poetic medium, through what mode of representation, and for the sake of evoking and resolving what particular sequence of expectations and emotions relative to the successive parts of the imitated object." But convinced as he is that the Aristotelian mode can answer certain fundamental questions no other system can begin to pose, Crane remains faithful to the principles of pluralism:

> Of the truth about literature, no critical language can ever have a monopoly or even a distant approach to one; and there are obviously many things the language I have been speaking of cannot do. It is a method not at all suited, as is criticism in the grand line of Longinus, Coleridge, and Matthew Arnold, to the definition and appreciation of those general qualities of writing—mirroring the souls of writers—for the sake of which most of us read or at any rate return to what we have read. It is a method that necessarily abstracts from history and hence requires to be supplemented by other very different procedures if we are to replace the works we study in the circumstances and temper of their times and see them as expressions and forces as well as objects of art. It is a method, above all, that completely fails, because of its essentially differentiating character, to give us insights into the larger moral and political values of literature or into any of the other organic relations with human nature and human experience in which literature is involved.

Recognition of Crane's value as a critic has been slow in coming, partly, perhaps, because of the tone of some of his early pieces. While the later Crane is perfectly serious about the ethics of pluralism, some of his earlier essays (and those of his students, Elder Olson and W.R. Keast) are ill-tempered and manage to suggest that the critical languages of Empson, Richards, Cleanth Brooks and R.B. Heilman, among others, are not worth taking up in the first place. The unpopular implication seems to be that only the Aristotelian mode is intellectually respectable, and that is by no means the conclusion Crane has in mind. More to the point are those objections levelled against the Aristotelian system itself, namely that the doctrine of art as imitation is too restricting, that these critics falsely hypostatize literary kinds or genres, and that they base their poetics on an inadequate scheme of the human emotions (which should of course be the very foundation of any system which emphasizes the importance of final cause or overall emotional effect). This last objection seems to me the most serious. Crane rarely moves beyond tragedy (or failed tragedy) and those venerable terms, pity and fear; and Elder Olson, after discussing Yeats' "Sailing to Byzantium," concludes that the effect of the poem is something that, "in the absence of a comprehensive analysis of the emotions, we can only call a kind of noble joy or exaltation." That "comprehensive analysis" has yet to be undertaken by an Aristotelian critic, though in theory at least it should be perfectly possible for him to take over an adequate psychology already worked out by others. Intelligent division of labor, as Crane repeatedly points out, is the very condition of knowledge about complex subjects. As for the doctrine of art as imitation, Crane is careful to maintain that a distinction exists

> between works, on the one hand, in which the formal nature is constituted of some particular human activity or state of feeling qualified morally and emotionally in a certain way, the beautiful rendering of this in words being the sufficient end of the poet's efforts, and works, on the other hand (like the *Divine Comedy*, *Absalom and Achito-*

phel, Don Juan, 1984, etc.), in which the material nature is "poetic" in the sense that it is made up of parts similar to those of imitative poems and the formal nature is constituted of some particular thesis, intellectual or practical, relative to some general human interest, the artful elaboration and enforcement of this by whatever means are available and appropriate being the sufficient end of the poet's efforts.

In other words, there are works which are primarily mimetic and works which are primarily didactic. And as for the false hypostatization of literary kinds, Crane is equally careful to maintain that generic distinctions are basically heuristic:

> for the "Aristotelian" critic, definitions of kinds are causal formulas inductively derived from an inspection, in "poetic" terms, and his use of them in practical criticism is essentially as heuristic devices for discovering what are the relevant questions to be asked about the individual works he proposes to study. There is no implication, either, that poetic kinds can ever be completely enumerated or always differentiated accurately from each other—and not only because new species are constantly emerging but because, when we go beyond such obvious extremes of form as tragedy and comedy, their bounds are often divided only by thin partitions.

Whatever one may feel about the strengths and limitations of the Aristotelian mode of criticism, there can hardly be real debate about the value of pluralism itself, as formulated by McKeon and Crane and as developed more recently by Elder Olson and Wayne Booth. No other approach does comparable justice to the diversity of the works we value or the critical languages we use to talk about them.

CREWS, Frederick C(ampbell). American. Born in Philadelphia, Pennsylvania, 20 February 1933. Educated at Yale University, New Haven, Connecticut, B.A. 1955; Princeton University, New Jersey, Ph.D. 1958. Married Elizabeth Peterson in 1959; has two children. Instructor in English, 1958-60, Assistant Professor, 1960-63, Associate Professor, 1963-66, and since 1966 Professor, University of California, Berkeley. Fulbright Lecturer, University of Turin, Italy, 1961-62; Fellow, Center for Advanced Study in the Behavioral Sciences, 1965-66. Recipient: Ford Grant, 1962; University of California research fellowship, 1965; American Council of Learned Societies fellowship, 1965; Guggenheim Fellowship, 1969-70. Address: 636 Vincente Avenue, Berkeley, California 94707, U.S.A.

PUBLICATIONS

Criticism

The Tragedy of Manners: Moral Drama in the Later Novels of Henry James (undergraduate prize essay). New Haven, Connecticut, Yale University Press, 1957.
E.M. Forster: The Perils of Humanism. Princeton, New Jersey, Princeton University Press, and London, Oxford University Press, 1962.
The Sins of the Fathers: Hawthorne's Psychological Themes. New York and London, Oxford University Press, 1966.

"Literature and Psychology," in *Relations of Literary Study*, edited by James Thorpe. New York, Modern Language Association, 1967.
Out of My System: Psychoanalysis, Ideology, and Critical Method.   New York and London, Oxford University Press, 1975.

Other

The Pooh Perplex: A Freshman Casebook (parodies).   New York, Dutton, 1963; London, Barker, 1964.
The Patch Commission (satire).   New York, Dutton, 1968.
The Random House Handbook.   New York, Random House, 1974; revised edition, 1977, 1980.

Editor, *Great Short Works of Nathaniel Hawthorne*.   New York, Harper, 1967.
Editor, with Orville Schell, *Starting Over: A College Reader*.   New York, Random House, 1970.
Editor, *Psychoanalysis and Literary Process*.   Cambridge, Massachusetts, Winthrop, 1970.

*   *   *

Frederick Crews' first book, *The Tragedy of Manners*, is a perfectly respectable study, but as an undergraduate thesis it is the sort of venture which probably meant a good deal more to its writer than it can possibly mean now to his readers. Crews argues that throughout his career Henry James dramatized his "values" in terms of the social behavior of his characters. The typical Jamesian protagonist has

> an aesthetic sense of Life's vastness and diversity, and he prizes this vision above every other goal. He will do anything to preserve it. In practice this means he will look for a measure of validity in every attitude that he meets, including those of his worldly enemies. His point of view...thus seems near to a Christian one, for it counsels a tolerance that borders on Christian love. However, the hero does not love his neighbor for Jesus' sake but for the sake of filling his own consciousness with truth.... [He] is characterized above all by magnanimity. He believes in everything as a part of Life but in nothing as a final version of it.

Isabel Archer is clearly the heroine of *Portrait of a Lady*, but even in this relatively early and straightforward novel there is some "ambiguity" (by which Crews seems to mean the kind of complex rendering which prevents unqualified moral judgments): Isabel is not entirely admirable nor her antagonists entirely detestable. And in the later novels which are Crews' chief concern "the moral question becomes more complex as naïveté comes less and less to be regarded as a virtue in itself." The very purity of Isabel's intentions and, in *The Ambassadors*, of Lambert Strether's refusal to "get anything for himself" out of his mission, involves these characters in a tragic denial of future possibilities. Strether's renunciation is

> the perfect, necessary conclusion to the gradual extension of his awareness. Again we arrive at the supreme Jamesian irony, that a full appreciation of Life is incompatible with the everyday business of living. Strether, like Hyacinth [in *The Princess Casamassima*] refuses to save himself....His vision is worth its price.

The question is whether we can be as sure as Crews seems to be here that for James the vision is really worth what it costs. In *The Wings of the Dove*, Crews argues, Merton Densher's renunciation is "equivalent to salvation"; but in *The Golden Bowl* Maggie Verver "effects a compromise between her ideals and her social duty, and hence is able to become an agent of positive good." Finally, among other developments James was gradually emancipating himself from black-versus-white contrasts of values. It became increasingly difficult for us to make simple moral judgments about a given character, for the author took great care to present both sides of the questions with the sympathy they deserved, and to present his drama only as it was seen by the participants. His aim was rather to increase the feeling of genuine life in his novels than to reduce his own moral awareness to that of his characters.

These observations are just and familiar enough by now, but Crews also seems anxious to see in the late James a kind of resolution of earlier problems *and* to preserve the fine air of complexity and uncertainty which is undeniably present. The problem is that he has not defined "manners" or "ambiguity" with enough precision to allow further argument nor raised the basic "moral" questions about James' technique which Wayne Booth explores so fully in *The Rhetoric of Fiction.*

The Perils of Humanism is a much more interesting undertaking. Crews uses as his point of departure Forster's admission that he is "what my age and upbringing have made me," that is, in Crews' well-documented argument, a liberal humanist, "a kind of lapsed Victorian of the upper middle class, whose intellectual loyalties have remained with the Cambridge he first knew in 1897." Crews locates the sources of Forster's values in the social and to a lesser extent the religious views of his mother's family and in his Cambridge friendships with Goldsworthy Lowes Dickinson and others. Yet while Crews is obviously sympathetic with Forster's humanism he values even more Forster's increasing capacity to question his own beliefs, or at least to sense their limitations. As Forster matured he became more skeptical. Thus the characters in his last novel, *A Passage to India*—"a solid masterpiece of pessimism"—do their best,

> but it is very little—not because they are exceptionally weak, but simply because they are human. Forster implies that we ourselves, his readers, are equally blocked off from meaning. We cannot fall back on reason and the visible world....Nor can we assert with humanistic piety that our whole duty is to love one another; this, too, proves more difficult than we might have gathered from Forster's previous books. What finally confronts us is an irreparable breach between man's powers and his needs.... Humanistic tolerance and sympathy remain the cardinal Forsterian virtues, but they lead to no splendid reward and must simply be exercised in the absence of any better way of getting along.

The Sins of the Fathers is virtually a repudiation of the careful academic approach Crews employed in his first two studies. The basis is now wholly Freudian, but in order to understand fully what Crews is attempting, the reader should first consult a 1970 essay, "Anaesthetic Criticism" (now reprinted in *Out of My System*). Recognizing here that the application of psychoanalytic principles will be called "antihumanistic" by the critical establishment, Crews maintains that it is necessary to pose a further question:

> What is meant by humanism? The humanism that purports to defend classical and Judaeo-Christian values by cherishing the texts in which those values supposedly reside is indeed jeopardized by extra-literary knowledge, but such a humanism amounts to little more than the confusion of a book list with an education, and its practical results are hardly worth preserving. Suppose, however, that humanism were taken to mean a concern for knowing (and protecting) man as an evolved species, embarked on a unique and possibly self-abbreviated experiment in the substitution of learning for instinct. In that case there would be no need to build walls between one discipline and all others out of fear that the alleged autonomy of one's speciality might be challenged.

Man is a creature whose cultural advances vitally depend on a period of prolonged infancy and childhood, a postponement of sexual gratification, and

> the diversion of part of this heightened sexuality into substitutive aims and bonds. The delay and detour of instinctual discharge, while not in themselves an explanation of man's capacity to form concepts and modify his behavior experientially, are almost certainly preconditions for it; yet this same interference with animal function dooms

man to self-disgust and neurosis, even making normal mating a precarious achievement
for him. Each individual must recapitulate for himself, as if it had never been done
before, the species' accommodation to social discipline, and this accommodation is
always grudging, never finally settled before the moment of death. A true appreciation of
man's works would take note of the renunciations and risks they inevitably entail.

Only psychoanalysis, Crews asserts, "has registered the psychic costs involved in man's pro-
longed dependency and his improvising of culture out of thwarted desire." Following Ernst
Kris rather than Freud himself Crews agrees that art is a "regression in the service of the ego."
The artist

> is someone who provisionally relaxes the censorship regnant in waking life, forgoes
> some of his society's characteristic defenses, and allows the repressed a measure of
> representation...in disguised and compromised form. His social role and his own equili-
> brium dictate a sign of victory for the ego, if not in "happy endings" then in the triumph
> of form over chaos, meaning over panic, mediated claims over naked conflict, purpose-
> ful action over sheer psychic spillage.

The great work of art, far from being mere fantasy or regressive indulgence, courts "engulfment
in order to recreate the conditions of a human order." Since the artist shares in the general
human problem of adjusting impulse to cultural demands we are by definition open to the
powers of art:

> Since our common plight is to be forever seeking acquittal from the fantasy-charges we
> have internalized as the price of ceasing to be infants, we share an eagerness for
> interpsychic transactions that seem to promise such an acquittal, or at least an abate-
> ment of guilt by means of establishing a confessional bond. Rather than being merely an
> unconscious release within the author or a similar release within the reader, literary
> process establishes a transitory complicity between the two.

Crews is very much concerned in this extraordinary essay with calling into question those
fashionable modes of criticism which have a falsely "elevated" view of art. Because of the
painful "complicity" art demands, such criticism welcomes the chance to evade the disturbances involved in genuine response and prefers to regard the work as somehow "autonomous"
(Northrop Frye's claim that "poetry can only be made out of other poems" is an extreme
instance of this tendency). Literary education conducted along these lines grows intolerant
toward "students who want to come to grips with their deepest responses":

> The cardinal features of professional critical training as most of us know it are a
> suppression of affect and a displacement of attention from artistic process onto motifs,
> genres, literary history...and the busywork of acquiring the skills and attitudes needed
> for circumspect research.

And if we accept the Freudian model, then

> we can see that much "impersonal" literary criticism and theory tends to isolate and
> redouble the defensive activity in literature while ignoring its barely mastered elements
> of fantasy, desire and anxiety. A criticism that explicitly or implicitly reduces art to some
> combination of moral content and abstract form and genre conventions is literally an
> anaesthetic criticism.

Assuming that Crews means exactly what he says here, it is obvious that he would have to
condemn as "anaesthetic" his own mannerly investigations of the "moral content" in Henry
James and E.M. Forster. With their particular sexual problems Forster and James would in
fact be easy targets for the amateur Freudian in search of "barely mastered elements of fantasy,
desire and anxiety."
   The argument of *The Sins of the Fathers* now becomes a good deal easier to trace. Crews
maintains that modern criticism has been anxious to "depart from the emotional texture of

Hawthorne's imagination" and to convert Hawthorne into a writer whose primary virtues are aesthetic or didactic. Yet as Crews points out, when Hawthorne's "submerged intensity and passion are ignored," he becomes a "very boring writer." The proper way to approach Hawthorne is to search for the personal predicaments which find disguised expression in his fiction; and as for the exact nature of those predicaments,

> Psychoanalysis invariably shows that an obsession with incest and its prevention, and indeed a general concern with sin and guilt as Hawthorne displays, stem from an incomplete resolution of early Oedipal feelings....In point of fact, sexual anxiety is the dominant tendency of the entire imaginative record he has left us.

At every moment in his fiction and on one level or another Hawthorne is engaged in "a death-struggle against the conscious emergence of patricidal and incestuous thoughts." A story such as "The Maypole of Merry Mount," for example, is "profoundly typical" of all Hawthorne's plots: "inadmissable fantasies are unleashed in an inhibited, decadent form and then further checked by a resurgence of authority." Granted that in purely aesthetic terms Hawthorne is frequently inept, what accounts for the apparently lasting appeal of his work? Crews seems to suggest an answer when he observes that Hawthorne's culturally forbidden impulses (which of course we share) "reach a point of catharsis after giving simultaneous and balanced voice to outrage and confession."

If the reader finds "Anaesthetic Criticism" and *The Sins of the Fathers* outrageous perhaps he should ask himself if he is not protesting too much—and for the very reason Crews has outlined: fear of emotional disturbance. But the argument need not be decided on a theoretical level; the test here is the test for any interpretive hypothesis: by employing psychoanalytic principles are we able to account for aspects of a work which have resisted explanation before?

> Thus the validation of a psychoanalytically oriented criticism rests on whether, at its best, it can make fuller sense of literary texts than could the most impressive instances of a rival criticism .
>
> The likelihood of this result rests on the psychoanalytic anticipation that even the most anomalous details in a work will prove psychically functional. Being at the bottom a theory of how conflicting demands are adjusted and merged, psychoanalysis is quite prepared for literature's mixed intentions, dissociations of affect from ideological content, hints of atonement for uncommitted acts, bursts of vindictiveness and sentimentality, and ironies that seem to occupy some middle ground between satire and self-criticism.

Nevertheless, in the past few years Crews seems to have become increasingly uneasy about the application of the psychoanalytic method to literature. "The essential fact is inescapable," he argues in "Reductionism and Its Discontents" (reprinted in *Out of My System*): "methodological provisos alone cannot ensure that a reductive style of interpretation won't result in reductionalist criticism." And he concludes—rather suprisingly—that any critic tempted by psychoanalysis

> would be well advised not only to seek out the most defensible and unmechanistic concepts within the system but also to think unsparingly about what is provincial and intolerant in that system. If he understands that Freudian reasoning ascribes key significance to its favorite themes, and that its supple rules of interpretation make the discovery of those themes a foregone conclusion; if he sees that the method tends to dichotomize between manifest and latent content even when the border between them is undiscernible; if he knows that psychoanalysis can say nothing substantial about considerations that fall outside an economics of desire and defense; and if he admits that it has a natural penchant for debunking—for sniffing out erotic and aggressive fantasies in the "purest" works and for mocking all pretentions to freedom from conflict—the critic may be able to borrow the clinical outlook without losing his intellectual independence and sense of proportion. He could hardly be blamed if, after weighing all these hazards, he decided to exchange Freud, for, say, Fredson Bowers. But if not—if he recognized that Freud in his questionable manner grasped some essential truths about motivation—he

would at least see his rhetorical task in a clear light. He would realize, that is, that in order to communicate with other readers he must look past psychoanalysis and establish a common ground of literary perception.

Making us choose between Freud and Fredson Bowers involves more than a little reductionism as well, or so one might argue. In any event, Crews now seems likely to return to the kind of criticism he practised before, when writing about James and Forster.

CUNNINGHAM, J(ames) V(incent). American. Born in Cumberland, Maryland, 23 August 1911. Educated at St. Mary's College, Kansas, 1928; Stanford University, California, A.B. 1934, Ph.D. 1945. Married 1) the poet Barbara Gibbs in 1937 (divorced, 1942); 2) Dolora Gallagher in 1945 (divorced, 1949); 3) Jessie MacGregor Campbell in 1950; one daughter. Instructor, Stanford University, 1937-45; Assistant Professor, University of Hawaii, Honolulu, 1945-46, University of Chicago, 1946-52, and University of Virginia, Charlottesville, 1952-53. Professor of English, 1953-76, and since 1976, University Professor, Brandeis University, Waltham, Massachusetts. Visiting Professor, Harvard University, Cambridge, Massachusetts, 1952, University of Washington, Seattle, 1956, Indiana University, Bloomington, 1961, University of California, Santa Barbara, 1963, and Washington University, St. Louis, 1976. Recipient: Guggenheim Fellowship, 1959, 1967; National Institute of Arts and Letters grant, 1965; National Endowment for the Arts grant, 1966; Academy of American Poets Fellowship, 1976. Address: Department of English, Brandeis University, Waltham, Massachusetts 02154, U.S.A.

PUBLICATIONS

Criticism

Woe or Wonder: The Emotional Effect of Shakespearean Tragedy. Denver, University of Denver Press, 1951.
Tradition and Poetic Structure: Essays in Literary History and Criticism. Denver, University of Denver Press, 1960; includes *Woe or Wonder.*
"The Problem of Form," in *The Journal of John Cardan, Together with The Quest of the Opal and The Problem of Form.* Denver, Swallow, 1964.
The Collected Essays of J.V. Cunningham. Chicago, Swallow, 1977.
Dickinson: Lyric and Legend. Los Angeles, Sylvestre and Orphanos, 1980.
"My Fires Are Met: Sappho, Longinus, and the Rhetorical Tradition," in *Antaeus* (New York), 40-41, 1981.

Verse

The Helmsman. San Francisco, Colt Press, 1942.
The Judge Is Fury. New York, Swallow Press-Morrow, 1947.
Doctor Drink: Poems. Cummington, Massachusetts, Cummington Press, 1950.
Trivial, Vulgar and Exalted: Epigrams. San Francisco, Poems in Folio, 1957.
The Exclusions of a Rhyme: Poems and Epigrams. Denver, Swallow, 1960.
To What Strangers, What Welcome: A Sequence of Short Poems. Denver, Swallow, 1964.

Some Salt: Poems and Epigrams.... Madison, Wisconsin, Perishable Press, 1967.
The Collected Poems and Epigrams of J. V. Cunningham. Chicago, Swallow Press, and
   London, Faber, 1971.

Other

The Quest of the Opal: A Commentary on "The Helmsman." Denver, Swallow, 1950.

Editor, *The Renaissance in England.* New York, Harcourt Brace, 1966.
Editor, *The Problem of Style.* Greenwich, Connecticut, Fawcett, 1966.
Editor, *In Shakespeare's Day.* Greenwich, Connecticut, Fawcett, 1970.

Translator, *An Essay on True and Apparent Beauty*, by Pierre Nicole. Los Angeles,
   University of California Library, 1950.

BIBLIOGRAPHY AND CRITICAL STUDY

Charles Gullans, *A Bibliography of the Published Writings of J. V. Cunningham.* Los
   Angeles, University of California Library, 1973.
Raymond Oliver, " 'The Scholar Is a Mere Conservative': The Criticism of J.V. Cun-
   ningham," in *Southern Review* (Baton Rouge, Louisiana), 15, 1979.

*   *   *

With characteristic bluntness J.V. Cunningham asserts that he prefers "the common or
garden variety" definition of poetry. The honorific definitions claim too much, he argues at the
opening of *Tradition and Poetic Structure*, and deliver too little:

> I mean by poetry what everyone means by it when he is not in an exalted mood, and when
> he is not being a critic, a visionary, or a philosopher. I mean by poetry what a man means
> when he goes to a bookstore to buy a book of poems as a graduation gift, or when he is
> commissioned by a publisher to do an anthology of sixteenth century poems. Poetry is
> what looks like poetry. It is metrical composition.

A poem is an ordered system of propositions expressed in metrical language:

> I take *proposition* in a more general sense than is usual; a proposition is a determinate
> relationship of signs forming an element in a composition consisting of successive
> elements of this nature. Thus an algebraic equation is a proposition, and that equation
> subjected to a successive series of transformations would constitute a system of proposi-
> tions. The syllogism in logic is of the same order, as is a piece of music in so far as the
> musical signs are grouped into elements, for example, into what are called phrases. Of
> the same order is a recorded game of chess, in which the elements, of course, are the
> distinct moves: P-K4, P-K4....Consequently there is an exact analogy between poetry
> and chess, since they are things of the same kind.

The comparison is "exact": just as an individual game of chess is the articulation of certain
possibilities permitted by the rules of the game, so an individual poem is an utterance which is
fundamentally ordered by the meanings and expectations the writer shares with his audience:

> It follows, then, that the poetry of a given time and place will tend to deal with those
> areas of experience which convention and history have assigned to writing in meter. In
> brief, a poem is the sort of thing that poets write, and what they write is the sort of thing

their society has come to regard as poetry....What the society regards as poetry is what I mean by tradition. What it regards as poetry will furnish the rules of the game.

Cunningham thus commits himself to a position which has been developed more recently by Northrop Frye: literature imitates not life, but other works of literature. Perception is always conditioned since the poet, like anyone else, learns to experience "life" as it is defined and sanctioned by the conventional modes of perception surrounding him. The sonnet, for example, is not an external principle of classification; it is rather "a principle operative in the production of works":

> [a literary form] is a scheme of experience recognized in the tradition and derived from prior works and from the description of those works extant in the tradition. It is, moreover, a scheme that directs the discovery of material and detail and it orders the disposition of the whole.

Anyone who has had experience with creative writing courses will recognize the powerful half-truth involved here. But there is of course a logical problem as well: how are we to account for the emergence of new forms or traditions? Here Cunningham is more reasonable than Frye:

> What a writer finds in real life is to a large extent what his literary tradition enables him to see and to handle [but it] may be conceded that experience is sometimes obtrusively at odds with tradition. We can see that it is, for we can see how tradition has been modified to render it more supple to experience. But the one term is always tradition, not unalterable but never abandoned, as, of course, the other term is always experience. The one is form, method, a way of apprehending; the other is matter, realization, and what is apprehended.

This view of tradition has obvious consequences for criticism, since, quite simply, the reader must be learned enough to know what the text meant to its contemporary audience:

> A work of art is the embodiment of an intention. To realize an intention in language is the function of the writer. To realize from language the intention of the author is the function of the reader or the critic, and his method is historical or philological interpretation.

To take one clear example from Cunningham's first book, *Woe or Wonder*: the phrase "Ripeness is all" has come to mean to T.S. Eliot and other untutored souls many fine, noble and profound things. By citing scripture, Seneca, ,Bishop Latimer, a 1560 *Art of Rhetoric* by Thomas Wilson and other passages from Shakespeare, Cunningham is able to claim quite plausibly that the phrase means simply "the fruit will fall in its time, and man dies when God is ready." But this example comes from *Woe or Wonder* and the reader who is dealing only with *Tradition and Poetic Structure* is obliged to conclude that Cunningham has evaded the major question: what is the status of these uninstructed interpretations? What about the reader who approaches *Hamlet* not with an awareness of the Donatan tradition behind Elizabethan tragedy but fresh, say, from the study of Coleridge or Henry James? What about the reader who fails to see how the *Romance of the Rose* shapes the "realistic" Prologue to the *Canterbury Tales*? If Cunningham is correct, most modern readings are doomed attempts to play one game by the rules of another. In *Woe or Wonder* he faces the problem directly in a passage which must be quoted in full:

> The modern meaning [of "Ripeness is all"] is one that is dear to us and one that is rich and important in itself. It would be a natural to ask, Need we give it up? I see no reason why we should give up the meaning: maturity of experience is certainly a good, and the phrase in a modern context is well enough fitted to convey this meaning. But it is our phrase now, and not Shakespeare's, and we should accept the responsibility for it. The difference in meaning is unmistakable: ours looks toward life and his looks towards death; ours finds its locus in modern psychology and his in Christian psychology. If we are secure in our own feelings we will accept our own meanings as ours, and if we have

any respect for the great we will penetrate and embrace Shakespeare's meaning as his. For our purpose in the study of literature...is not in the ordinary sense to further the understanding of ourselves. It is rather to enable us to see how we could think and feel otherwise than as we do....In fact, the problem that is here raised with respect to literature is really the problem of any human relationship: Shall we understand another on his terms or on ours?

In the Appendix to *Woe or Wonder* he concludes that responsible reading is finally a kind of moral activity (the influence of Yvor Winters is probably at work here as it is elsewhere in Cunningham):

For the understanding of an author in the scholarly sense involves the exercise under defined conditions of the two fundamental principles of morality in the Western tradition: 1) the principle of dignity, or of responsibility to the external fact, in the special form of respect for another person as revealed in his works; and 2) the principle of love, the exercise of sympathetic insight, or of imaginative transformation....The historical [approach] is that of respect by which we recognize otherness: to this the various historical disciplines are subsidiary. The aesthetic is that act of sympathy by which we realize the other and make it our own.

In *Woe or Wonder* Cunningham examines the proper end or intended effect of tragedy as the Elizabethans themselves defined it; in *Tradition and Poetic Structure* he makes the distinctions discussed above and applies them to several "traditions" in English poetry from Chaucer to Wallace Stevens. It is impossible not to be impressed by his scholarship and sensitivity but it is also impossible, finally, not to be irritated by his manner. His discriminations are frequently elliptical, his arguments so abrupt at times that he gives the impression of being impatient with critical discourse (the reader may test the fairness of these observations by considering the essay "Classical and Medieval: Statius, On Sleep"). Yet these two books of criticism are distinguished works, and if the reader finds himself growing impatient he might remember that as a first-rate poet Cunningham has had other things on his mind during the past twenty-five years.

DAICHES, David. British. Born in Sunderland, County Durham, 2 September 1912. Educated at George Watson's College, Edinburgh; University of Edinburgh, M.A. (first-class honours) 1934; Balliol College, Oxford (Elton Exhibitioner and Andrew Bradley Fellow, 1936-37), M.A. 1937, D.Phil. 1939. Married Isobel J. Mackey in 1937; has three children, Assistant in English, University of Edinburgh, 1935-36; Assistant Professor, University of Chicago, 1937-43; served in the British Information Services, 1943; Second Secretary, British Embassy, Washington, D.C., 1944-46; Professor, Cornell University, Ithaca, New York, 1946-51; University Lecturer in English, Cambridge University, 1951-61, and Fellow of Jesus College, Cambridge, 1957-62. Dean of the School of English Studies, 1961-68, and since 1961 Professor, University of Sussex, Brighton. Visiting Professor of Criticism, Indiana University, Bloomington, 1956-57; Elliston Lecturer, University of Cincinnati, Spring 1960; Whidden Lecturer, McMaster University, Hamilton, Ontario, 1964; Hill Foundation Visiting Professor, University of Minnesota, Minneapolis, Spring 1966; Ewing Lecturer, University of California at Los Angeles, 1967; Carpenter Memorial Lecturer, Ohio Wesleyan University, Delaware, Ohio, 1970. Litt.D.: Brown University, Providence, Rhode Island, 1964; Dr. honoris causa: Sorbonne, Paris, 1973; Ph.D.: Cambridge University. Fellow, Royal Society of Literature. Address: Downsview, Wellhouse Lane, Burgess Hill, Sussex, England.

PUBLICATIONS

Criticism

The Place of Meaning in Poetry.   Edinburgh, Oliver and Boyd, 1935; Folcroft, Pennsyl-
vania, Folcroft Editions, 1969.
New Literary Values: *Studies in Modern Literature*.   Edinburgh, Oliver and Boyd, 1936;
Freeport, New York, Books for Libraries Press, 1968.
Literature and Society.   London, Gollancz, 1938; New York, Haskell House, 1970.
The Novel and the Modern World.   Chicago, University of Chicago Press, 1939; revised
edition, London, Cambridge University Press, 1960.
Poetry and the Modern World: *A Study of Poetry in England Between 1900 and
1939*.   Chicago, University of Chicago Press, 1940.
Virginia Woolf.   New York, New Directions, 1942; London, Editions Poetry London,
1945; revised edition, New Directions, 1963.
Robert Louis Stevenson.   New York, New Directions, and Glasgow, MacLellan, 1947.
A Study of Literature for Readers and Critics.   Ithaca, New York, Cornell University
Press, and London, Oxford University Press, 1948.
Robert Burns.   New York, Rinehart, 1950; London, G.Bell, 1952; revised edition,
London, Deutsch, 1966, and New York, Macmillan, 1967.
Willa Cather: *A Critical Introduction*.   Ithaca, New York, Cornell University Press,
1951.
Stevenson and the Art of Fiction.   New York, privately printed, 1951.
Walt Whitman: *Man, Poet, Philosopher*.   Washington, D.C., Library of Congress, 1955;
reprinted in *Literary Essays*, 1956.
Critical Approaches to Literature.   Englewood Cliffs, New Jersey, Prentice Hall, and
London, Longman, 1956.
Literary Essays.   Edinburgh, Oliver and Boyd, 1956; New York, Philosophical Library,
1957.
Milton.   London, Hutchinson, 1957; revised edition, Hutchinson, and New York,
Norton, 1966.
Robert Burns.   London, Longman, 1957.
The Present Age: *After 1920*.   London, Cresset Press, 1958; as *The Present Age in British
Literature*, Bloomington, Indiana University Press, 1958.
Two Studies: *The Poetry of Dylan Thomas*; *Walt Whitman, Impressionist Poet*.   Lon-
don, privately printed, 1958; Folcroft, Pennsylvania, Folcroft Editions, 1970.
A Critical History of English Literature.   New York, Ronald Press, and London, Secker
and Warburg, 2 vols., 1960.
George Eliot: *Middlemarch*.   London, Arnold, and Great Neck, New York, Barron's
Educational Series, 1963.
Carlyle and the Victorian Dilemma.   Edinburgh, Carlyle Society, 1963.
English Literature.   Englewood Cliffs, New Jersey, Prentice Hall, 1964.
Time and the Poet.   Cardiff, University of Wales Press, 1965.
"Myth, Metaphor and Poetry," in *Essays by Divers Hands* (London), 33, 1965; reprinted
in *More Literary Essays*, 1968.
More Literary Essays.   Chicago, University of Chicago Press, and Edinburgh, Oliver
and Boyd, 1968.
The Teaching of Literature in American Universities.   Leicester, Leicester University
Press, 1968.
Some Late Victorian Attitudes.   New York, Norton, and London, Deutsch, 1969.
Sir Walter Scott and His World.   New York, Viking Press, and London, Thames and
Hudson, 1971.
Robert Burns and His World.   London, Thames and Hudson, 1971; New York, Viking
Press, 1972.
Robert Louis Stevenson and His World.   London, Thames and Hudson, 1973; New
York, Scribner, 1977.

"What Was the Modern Novel?," in *Critical Inquiry* (Chicago), 1, 1975.
James Boswell and His World.   London, Thames and Hudson, and New York, Scribner, 1976.
Shakespeare: *Julius Caesar*.   London, Evans, 1976.

Other

The Book of Jonah: *William Tindale's Version*: *A Jewish Tribute*.   London, Jewish Religious Union, 1937.
The King James Version of the English Bible: *An Account of the Development and Sources of the English Bible of 1611, with Special Reference to the Hebrew Tradition*. Chicago, University of Chicago Press, 1941.
Two Worlds: *An Edinburgh Jewish Childhood*.   New York, Harcourt Brace, 1956; London, Macmillan, 1957.
The Paradox of Scottish Culture: *The Eighteenth-Century Experience*.   London, Oxford University Press, 1964.
Scotch Whisky: *Its Past and Present*.   London, Deutsch, 1969; New York, Macmillan, 1970; revised edition, London, Fontana, 1976, and Deutsch, 1978.
A Third World (autobiography).   Brighton, Sussex University Press, 1971.
Charles Edward Stuart: *The Life and Times of Bonnie Prince Charlie*.   London, Thames and Hudson, 1973; as *The Last Stuart*: *The Life and Times of Bonnie Prince Charlie*, New York, Putnam, 1973.
Was: *A Pastime from the Time Past*.   London, Thames and Hudson, 1975.
Moses: *Man in the Wilderness*.   London, Weidenfeld and Nicolson, 1975; as *Moses*: *Man and His Vision*.   New York, Praeger, 1975.
Glasgow.   London, Deutsch, 1977.
Scotland and the Union.   London, Murray, 1977.
Edinburgh.   London, Hamilton Hamish, 1978.
Literary Landscapes of the British Isles: *A Narrative Atlas*, with John Flower.   New York, Paddington Press, 1979; London, Bell and Hyman, 1980.

Editor, with William Charvat, *Poems in English, 1930-1940*.   New York, Ronald Press, 1950.
Editor, *A Century of the Essay, British and American*.   New York, Harcourt Brace, 1951.
Editor, with others, *The Norton Anthology of English Literature*.   New York, Norton, 2 vols., 1962; revised edition, 1974.
Editor, *White Man in the Tropics*: *Two Moral Tales*, by Joseph Conrad and Robert Louis Stevenson.   New York, Harcourt Brace, 1962.
Editor, *The Idea of a New University*: *An Experiment in Sussex*.   London, Deutsch, 1964; Cambridge, Massachusetts Institute of Technology Press, 1970.
Editor, *Wuthering Heights*, by Emily Brontë.   London, Penguin, 1965.
Editor, *Kenilworth*, by Sir Walter Scott.   New York, Limited Editions Club, 1966.
Editor, *The Penguin Companion to English Literature I*: *Britain and the Commonwealth*. London, Allen Lane, 1971.
Editor, with others, *Literature and Western Civilization*.   London, Aldus Books, 6 vols., 1972-75.
Editor, *The Selected Poems of Robert Burns*.   London, Deutsch, 1979.
Editor, *Andrew Fletcher of Saltoun*: *Selected Political Writings and Speeches*.   Edinburgh, Scottish Academy Press, 1979.

*   *   *

The atmosphere of "left-wing euphoria" which David Daiches recalls from his Oxford days of the mid-1930's had important consequences for his own early and in many ways most interesting literary criticism. In *New Literary Values*, published when he was 24, Daiches speaks confidently of the critic's "duty" to define the right relationship between literature and culture; a year later, in *Literature and Society*, written for Gollancz's Left Book Club, he speaks again of the critic's "special responsibility as the guardian of culture in a changing—some would say a disintegrating—world," and continues:

> It is only in a humanist philosophy that literature can be seen as a human activity with a function and a value of its own in society. The literary critic is therefore *in his capacity as critic* interested in social questions to this extent: he is bound to be opposed to a civilisation in which the economic organisation is such that the lust for wealth on the part of a large number of those who control affairs...brings about an inevitable distortion of human values. The honest critic cannot help seeing that there are certain types of social and economic organisations under which experience itself becomes increasingly standardised and superficial.... The literary critic has a right to protest if he finds himself in the midst of a system whose contradictions are resulting in increasing dislocation and anomaly, where reality is obscured by a fog of catch-words and moral platitudes, and the experience of different classes is so diverse in every way that the artist has to decide which kind of life is "truer" and is prevented from seeing life whole.

Literature and criticism are concerned with "practical issues"—the activities "prompted by our more insistent humanitarian impulses"—and hence the true critic realizes that

> the study of history will enable us to understand and so to control the world into which we are born (and a proper study of history necessitates the study of past literature); that the reading, with understanding, of poetry and imaginative writing generally will give us an insight into the mind of man...without which we can have no real knowledge of the motives that impel him to act...[and] that the communal enjoyment of music or painting or drama can produce a sense of fellowship that will enable the most diverse types of people to understand and cooperate with each other to a degree and in a manner otherwise hardly possible.

"Art as such can only exist," Daiches maintains in *The Novel and the Modern World*, "when values are conventional" (that is, when the artist accepts the established values of his society). But since contemporary society suffers from the "drying-up of traditional sources of value and the consequent decay of uniform belief," the artist's "*raison d'être* is threatened." During periods which call into doubt the "public truth to which civilized activity as a whole is anchored" the artist will fall silent, content himself with "imitation and preservation...but not creation," or, like the typical modern artist, speak only on behalf of his private truths:

> In the past the emergence of this problem has meant the virtual cessation of literary activity until a new stability arose to replace the old and a new community of belief emerged to provide a basis on which the artist might build. The only reason why the same result has not followed the post-Victorian disintegration seems to be that by now literary communication had reached such a degree of subtlety and sophistication that it became possible to compensate for the lack of community of belief by new techniques of expression. Various means were discovered of making a highly individual standard of value appear to the reader, for the time being, a natural objective standard.... New developments in psychology arrived very opportunely and encouraged writers to beg the question of value by confining their world to the limits of an individual mind and assessing value solely in terms of the consciousness of that mind.

The artists Daiches examines in *The Novel and the Modern World* are thus in an important sense decadent artists (although Daiches does not use that term himself), and the question therefore arises, can any work written during a period of breakdown have much permanent value? Must literature criticize as well as reflect the society it springs from? Here Daiches is a little evasive: "the greatest works are those which, while fulfilling all the formal requirements, most adequately reflect the civilization of which they are a product." The problem is that

Daiches is never clear as to what the "formal requirements" of the novel are or what "adequate" reflection involves. Nevertheless, he is able to conclude that "there will always be aspects of human character and emotion as an illumination of which the decadent bourgeoisie, the struggling proletariat, the atrophied landed gentry, and similar phenomena of civilization will always be adequate myths long after these phenomena have passed away." Joyce, for example, illustrates with such "brilliance and subtlety and with such formal perfection" the bourgeois life of his times that *Ulysses* is "one of the great novels of civilization." But Daiches soon drops these larger issues and concentrates primarily on the techniques of modern fiction which somehow "compensate" for or beg the question of real communal values.

Daiches had completed at least some parts of *The Novel and the Modern World* before coming to America for a long period of teaching—a period he records with a good deal of spirit and frankness in *A Third World*. Arriving at the University of Chicago in 1937 he soon found himself engaged in a "curious on-going debate" with R.S. Crane over the latter's "two modes" of criticism:

> The two modes were Aristotelian or "meroscopic" and Platonic or "holoscopic." The former, concerning itself with the "meros" or part rather than the "holos" or whole, examined the given literary work as a unique and individual artefact, discovered its principle of order, and described it in terms that revealed that principle. The holoscopic method, on the other hand, took the whole universe into its area of discourse and discussed a literary work in a free-ranging manner which could include the realms of ethics, politics and biography. [Crane] felt that the Platonic or holoscopic method...had had its day and that its widespread application obscured the true nature and individuality of works of literature.... The trouble was, that I myself had just finished an essay (which later became the first chapter of my book, *The Novel and the Modern World*) that implicitly denied his basic distinction between Aristotelian and Platonic [approaches] in that it tried to establish a relationship between the principles of formal organisation as well as the other characteristics of a work on the one hand and social and intellectual history on the other.

Daiches admits that the Chicago experience sharpened his wits and "implicitly stigmatized my fondness for wide-ranging literary discussion as a confusion of disciplines." But he did not become a convert to Crane's position or to the formalism of the New Critics: the completed *Novel and the Modern World*—as well as his later criticism—is eclectic and unapologetically "holoscopic" (or "analogical," to use Crane's later and preferred term). In another sense, however, Daiches did absorb perhaps the most valuable lesson Crane's work has to offer, namely that a literary work exists in a diversity of modes and relationships and that no one critical language can possibly do justice to the entire complex. What is required, then, is not relativism but a rigorous and intelligent pluralism. Daiches puts these matters his own way in a 1950 essay, "The 'New Criticism': Some Qualifications":

> Our research for "criteria which make possible judgments about literary worth"...if pursued with a disinterested desire to find out what a work of literary art really is rather than with a desire to find merely a consistent method, will eventually turn up the fact that literary discourse is by its very nature several kinds of discourse at once. A poem is a structure with "internal consistency," but it is also often a fascinating record of the poet's mind, a period-piece reflecting with moving brilliance the climate of an age, and a story.... In appreciating a work of art, we have only one ear cocked for "internal consistency," for the purely "formal" aspect. And often when such consistency has been demonstrated we do not read the work with any richer enjoyment.

Daiches is a good deal less optimistic than Crane, however, about the capacities of criticism:

> On the level of aesthetic theory, it may be possible to construct a set of valid general principles, but practical criticism, criticism designed to demonstrate the nature and quality of a work and so to increase understanding and appreciation, must always be fragmentary, indirect, approximate, and can never be a complete and wholly satisfactory description of what in fact takes place in the work of art.

For Daiches it is finally the experience of the work which matters most:

> In the last analysis, the test of [a work's] value can be judged only by the receiver, and judged by him on some kind of "affective" theory.... Literature exists to be read and enjoyed, and criticism, at least in its pedagogical aspect, exists in order to increase awareness and so to increase enjoyment. The purely philosophical critic may entertain himself by trying to isolate the quiddity of poetry...but the "appreciative" critic will use any means at his disposal—analytic, descriptive, histrionic, yes, even historical—to arouse alert interest, to produce that communicative impact without which all further critical discussion is useless.

Thus Daiches is, or clearly has become, an "appreciative" critic. And by 1950 or thereabouts something also seems to have changed his other interests: for whatever reasons, the social concerns so important in his first books have virtually disappeared. The revised version of *The Novel and the Modern World*, for example, is almost entirely a study of literary techniques, prefaced by a vaguely pious invocation to "love":

> Throughout all these novelists the question "How is love possible in a world of individuals imprisoned by their own private and unique consciousness?" is asked and probed in a great variety of ways. Loneliness is the great reality, love the great necessity: how can these two be brought together? The more public and social the world, the less real it is likely to be, so neither the earlier public view of significance nor the earlier confidence in the role of society can be maintained. Much modern fiction is the charting of a way out of solipsism.

For a number of years Daiches' patient, sympathetic study of Virginia Woolf was by far the best introduction to her work available, but by now it has been replaced by more informed and specialized studies. The same fate has overtaken *The Novel and the Modern World* and *Poetry and the Modern World* (which he has wisely never had reprinted), while the occasional pieces collected in *Literary Essays* and *More Literary Essays* are usually too general to be of much interest. For this reason the longer study of Burns and the short pieces on Scott and Hugh MacDiarmid—figures not often taken up by other academic critics—are of more value. Daiches is a thoroughly respectable, genteel critic, well informed, in an old-fashioned way, supremely self-confident and a little condescending. He seems content now to "place" literary works—primarily for the benefit of students in survey courses. There are no more tensions, no real problems, in short no apparent euphoria for the writer and certainly none for the reader.

DAVIE, Donald (Alfred).   British.   Born in Barnsley, Yorkshire, 17 July 1922. Educated at Barnsley Grammar School; St. Catharine's College, Cambridge, B.A. 1947, M.A. 1949, Ph.D. 1951. Served in the Royal Navy, 1941-46. Married Doreen John in 1945; three children. Lecturer in English, 1950-57, and Fellow of Trinity College, 1954-57, Dublin University; Lecturer in English, 1958-64, and Fellow of Gonville and Caius College, 1959-64, Cambridge University; Professor of English, 1964-68, and Pro-Vice-Chancellor, 1965-68, University of Essex, Wivenhoe; Professor of English, Stanford University, California, 1968-78. Since 1978, Andrew W. Mellon Professor of Humanities, Vanderbilt University, Nashville. Visiting Professor, University of California, Santa Barbara, 1957-58; British Council Lecturer, Budapest, 1961; Elliston Lecturer, University of Cincinnati, 1963. Recipient: Guggenheim Fellowship, 1973, D.Litt.: University of Southern California, Los Angeles, 1978. Honorary Fellow, St. Catharine's College, Cambridge, 1973; Fellow, American Academy of Arts and Sciences, 1973; Honorary Fellow, Trinity College, Dublin, 1978. Address: 4400 Belmont Park Terrace, Nashville, Tennessee 37235, U.S.A., or, 31 Fore Street, Silverton, Exeter, Devon, England.

Criticism

Purity of Diction in English Verse. London, Chatto and Windus, 1952; New York, Oxford University Press, 1953.
Articulate Energy: An Inquiry into the Syntax of English Poetry. London, Routledge, 1955; New York, Harcourt Brace, 1958.
The Heyday of Sir Walter Scott. London, Routledge, and New York, Barnes and Noble, 1961.
"Ezra Pound's *Hugh Selwyn Mauberley*," in *The Pelican Guide to English Literature 7*, edited by Boris Ford. London, Penguin, 1961.
"The Poetry of Sir Walter Scott," in *Proceedings of the British Academy 47*. London, Oxford University Press, 1962.
The Language of Science and the Language of Literature, 1700-1740. New York and London, Sheed and Ward, 1963.
Ezra Pound: Poet as Sculptor. London, Routledge, and New York, Oxford University Press, 1964.
"Yeats, The Master of a Trade," in *The Integrity of Yeats*, edited by Denis Donoghue. Cork, Mercier Press, 1964.
"Tolstoy, Lermontov, and Others," in *Russian Literature and Modern English Fiction*, edited by Donald Davie. Chicago and London, University of Chicago Press, 1965.
"A New Aestheticism? A. Alvarez Talks to Donald Davie," in *The Modern Poet: Essays from "the Review,"* edited by Ian Hamilton. London, Macdonald, 1968.
Thomas Hardy and British Poetry. New York, Oxford University Press, 1972; London, Routledge, 1973.
Pound. London, Fontana, 1975; New York, Viking Press, 1976.
The Poet in the Imaginary Museum: Essays of Two Decades, edited by Barry Alpert. Manchester, Carcanet Press, 1976; New York, Persea Press, 1977.
A Gathered Church: The Literature of the English Dissenting Interest 1700-1930. London, Routledge, and New York, Oxford University Press, 1978.
Trying to Explain. Ann Arbor, University of Michigan Press, 1979; Manchester, Carcanet, 1980.
"A Puritan's Empire: The Case of Kipling," in *Sewanee Review* (Tennessee), 87, 1979.
"Winters and Leavis: Memories and Reflections," in *Sewanee Review* (Tennessee), 87, 1979.
"English and American in 'Briggflatts,' " in *British Poetry Since 1970: A Critical Survey*, edited by Peter Jones and Michael Schmidt. New York, Persea Press, and London, Carcanet, 1980.
"Personification," in *Essays in Criticism* (Oxford), 31, 1981.

Verse

(*Poems*). Oxford, Fantasy Press, 1954.
Brides of Reason. Oxford, Fantasy Press, 1955.
A Winter Talent and Other Poems. London, Routledge, 1957.
The Forests of Lithuania, adapted from a poem by Adam Mickiewicz. Hessle, Yorkshire, Marvell Press, 1959.
A Sequence for Francis Parkman. Hessle, Yorkshire, Marvell Press, 1961.
New and Selected Poems. Middletown, Connecticut, Wesleyan University Press, 1961.
Events and Wisdoms: Poems 1957-1963. London, Routledge, 1964; Middletown, Connecticut, Wesleyan University Press, 1965.
Poems. London, Turret Books, 1969.
Essex Poems 1963-1967. London, Routledge, 1969.

Six Epistles to Eva Hesse.   London, London Magazine Editions, 1970.
Collected Poems, 1950-1970.   London, Routledge, and New York, Oxford University Press, 1972.
Orpheus.   London, Poem-of-the-Month Club, 1974.
The Shires: Poems.   London, Routledge, 1974; New York, Oxford University Press, 1975.
In the Stopping Train and Other Poems.   Manchester, Carcanet Press, 1977; New York, Oxford University Press, 1980.
Three for Water-Music.   Manchester, Carcanet Press, 1981.

Other

Editor, *The Victims of Whiggery*, by George Loveless.   Hobart, Tasmania, privately printed, 1946.
Editor, *The Late Augustans: Longer Poems of the Later Eighteenth Century.*   London, Heinemann, and New York, Macmillan, 1958.
Editor, *Poems: Poetry Supplement.*   London, Poetry Book Society, 1960.
Editor, *Poetics Poetyka.*   Warsaw, Panstwowe Wydawn, 1961.
Editor, *Selected Poems of Wordsworth.*   London, Harrap, 1962.
Editor, *Russian Literature and Modern English Fiction: A Collection of Critical Essays.*   Chicago, University of Chicago Press, 1965.
Editor, with Angela Livingstone, *Pasternak.*   London, Macmillan, 1969.
Editor, "Thomas Hardy Issue" of *Agenda* (London), Spring-Summer 1972.
Editor, *Augustan Lyric.*   London, Heinemann, 1974.
Editor, *Collected Poems*, by Yvor Winters.   Manchester, Carcanet Press, 1978; Chicago, Swallow, 1980.

Translator, *The Poetry of Dr. Zhivago.*   Manchester, Manchester University Press, and New York, Barnes and Noble, 1965.

*   *   *

No matter what subtleties of poetic language Donald Davie may seem intent on pursuing, his basic critical position is firmly classical, moral, even Aristotelian. At the start of his first book, *Purity of Diction in English Verse*, he assets flatly that "all poets when they write have one purpose. They want to create an effect upon the mind of the reader." "Effect" here means the kind of pleasure which the artist may evoke by making choices among the possibilities open to him: "good diction," for example, "comes from making a selection from the language on reasonable principles and for a reasonable purpose." And while kinds of diction will vary from genre to genre, "according to the effect the poet wishes to produce," the critic is always concerned with determining, in each specific instance, "what moral value can be derived from this effect, by the reader who enjoys it." The poems he is about to examine, Davie maintains, are in fact morally valuable, "otherwise I should not care to write of them." Fourteen years later, in a Postscript to a new edition of *Purity of Diction*, he remarks that it seems to him "a vulgar streak shows up where I declared myself indifferent to any poem or poetic effect that cannot be shown to be 'moral'. Nowadays this strikes me as strident and silly." But this verdict is surely too harsh, and in any event the tendency of *Articulate Energy* and *Thomas Hardy and British Poetry* is hardly less moral than that of *Purity of Diction*.

Davie makes several important distinctions between poetry, verse, language and diction. The great poet is above the law: "one feels that Hopkins could have found a place for every word in the language if only he could have written enough poems. One feels the same about Shakespeare." But the lesser poet, the creator of verse, uses a limited range of language or "diction"; with them one feels that "a selection has been made and is continually being made, that words are thrusting at a poem and being fended off from it, that however many poems these poets wrote certain words would never be allowed." *Purity of Diction* attempts to define the real if lesser pleasures provided by some eighteenth century poets and those effects—ultimately moral—to which "most readers of today are blind."

Pure diction is "chaste" diction, that is diction which carefully and deliberately adheres to the cultivated, urbane conversational style of a given period:

> A chaste diction is "central," in Arnold's sense: it expresses the feeling of the capital, not the provinces. And it can do this because it is central in another way, central to the language, conversational not colloquial, poetic not poetical. The effect is a valuable urbanity, a civilized moderation and elegance; and this is the effect attainable, as I think, by Goldsmith, and not by Shakespeare.

When the center failed, when money and power replaced taste and judgment, the poet could no longer be sure of his audience; and when he lost confidence in his public, the nineteenth century poet "was thrown back upon confidence in himself. When this confidence, too, was shaken, it marked itself as hysterical arrogance. This is one way of describing the Romantic Revival." Thus Hopkins, for example, although he is a great poet in Davie's view, is also to some extent "decadent" because of his "self-regarding ingenuity"; he does not use his special rhythms to "catch the movement of living speech." And to have no respect for language, Davie concludes, is "to have no respect for life." (In all fairness it should be emphasized that his view of the Romantics is a good deal more complex than these quotations suggest).

Purity of diction also depends upon what Davie calls economy of metaphor. Again, the great poet creates new metaphors and thus "enlarges" the language. The lesser poet, however, does more than merely reproduce the tone of the center: he "enlivens" the dead metaphors which lie at the root of all language and thus purifies the dialect of the tribe. Davie takes the following lines (describing Cowley)

> To him no author was unknown,
> Yet what he wrote was all his own;
> Horace's wit and Virgil's state,
> He did not conceal, but emulate!
> And when he would like them appear,
> Their garb, but not their clothes, did wear.

and argues that "it had not occurred to the reader that the distinction between 'garb' and 'clothes' was so fine yet so definite. It is forced on his attention in a way that is salutary.... It purifies the spoken tongue, for it makes the reader alive to nice meanings." To attain such diction "is a moral achievement, a product of integrity and equilibrium in the poet, in some sense, perhaps, a manifestation of the Aristotelian mean." In short,

> We are saying that the poet who undertakes to preserve or refine a poetic diction is writing in a web of responsibilities. He is responsible to past masters for conserving the genres and the decorums which they have evolved. He is responsible to the persons or the themes on which he writes, to maintain a consistent tone and point of view in his dealings with them. He is responsible to the community in which he writes, for purifying and correcting the spoken language.

Clearly then, something valuable has been lost to English poetry since the time of Johnson. But it is equally clear that purity of diction will be possible only under certain cultural conditions. There is no center to modern life, although there be may be various competing centers, each with its own range of diction. It would seem to follow logically, then, that the modern poet, unless he is one of those great poets who enlarge the language, is condemned to a kind of decadence. Yet Davie admits that *Purity of Diction* was also intended as a kind of manifesto, justifying his own poetry and the poetry of Charles Tomlinson, Kingsley Amis, Philip Larkin and others loosely associated with "The Movement" in recent British poetry. These poets express "an originally passionate rejection...of all the values of Bohemia":

> We asserted that in London, in the 1940s and 1950s, [Bohemia] was no haven but a

quicksand; and if shunning the metropolis made us provincials, we were ready to take that risk, as William Cowper and William Wordsworth had taken it.

But of course provincialism, as Davie would probably admit, is simply another kind of decadence. *Purity of Diction* leaves unresolved many of the problems it raises, to be taken up again in *Thomas Hardy and British Poetry*.

A striking passage in *Purity of Diction* anticipates much of the argument Davie develops in his next book, *Articulate Energy*:

> It will be doubtful whether after all Mr. Eliot has purified the language as Dr. Johnson did, or whether any poet in the Symbolist tradition can do so. Finally, of course, one cannot avoid the fact that the poet's churches are empty, and the strong suspicion that dislocation of syntax has much to do with it. After all, there is no denying that modern poetry is obscure and that it would be less so if the poets adhered to the syntax of prose.
>
> Changes in linguistic habit are related to changes in man's outlook and hence, eventually, to changes in human conduct. Language does not merely reflect such changes; a change in language may precede the other changes, and even help to bring them about. To abandon syntax in poetry is not to start or indulge a literary fashion; it is to throw away a tradition central to human thought and conduct, as to human speech.

Thus there may be some ominous connection between Pound's authoritarianism and his dislocation of syntax:

> It would be too much to say that this is the logical end of abandoning prose syntax. But at least the development from imagism in poetry to fascism in politics is clear and unbroken. From a similar conviction about language and poetry Eliot has developed, not quite so obviously, to Royalism and Anglo-Catholicism. And yet it is impossible not to trace a connection between the laws of syntax and the laws of society.... One could almost say...that to dislocate syntax in poetry is to threaten the rule of law in the civilized community.
>
> Once one has seen this connection between law in language and law in conduct, observations about the nature of language take on an awful importance, and one comes to see potential dangers in attitudes which seemed innocuous.

In *Articulate Energy* Davie traces the declining role played in poetry by "syntax," which, as "the very nerve of poetry," is "above all an instrument of articulation, a way of establishing relationships, like the harmonies of music and equations of algebra." At fault here are those varieties of Symbolist aesthetics which maintain that the poem is somehow autonomous, that there is a difference between the function of syntax in prose as the logicians and grammarians understand it and the syntax the modern poet feels he is free to use or abandon. Davie's approach is indirect, at least to begin with. He demonstrates that Hulme's position would "banish syntax from poetry"; that Susanne Langer's position would empty syntax of its propositional force; and that Fenollosa's position, while there is a good deal to be said for it, would reject as " 'unpoetic' the greater part of what has been most admired in the poetry of the sixteenth and seventeenth centuries." Davie then proceeds to establish his own sophisticated conception of the role syntax plays in poetry, basing his subtle distinctions once again on the various kinds of pleasure syntax may afford. Returning to his attack on the modern disregard for logical articulation he argues that such poetry is in effect renouncing faith in the power of the mind itself:

> Systems of syntax are part of the heritable property of past civilization, and to hold firm to them is to be traditional in the best and most important sense. This seems ungracious to both Pound and Eliot, who have both insisted upon the value of the European civilized tradition, and have tried to embody it in their poems. Nevertheless it is hard not to agree with Yeats that the abandonment of syntax testifies to a failure of the poet's nerve, a loss of confidence in the intelligible structure of the conscious mind, and the validity of its activity.

The impulse behind *Articulate Energy* is, as Davie admits, conservative; but it is a "rational conservatism" which offers some startling insights into the ways in which modern poetic theory and practice have gone astray:

> A poetry in which the syntax articulates only "the world of the poem" is said to be "pure," "absolute," "sheer," "self-sufficient." Wordsworth's poems are "impure" because they have about them the smell of soil and soiled flesh, the reek of humanity. Their syntax is not "pure" syntax because it refers to, it mimes, something outside itself and outside the world of its poem, something that smells of the human, of generation and hence of corruption. It is my case against the symbolist theorists that, in trying to remove the human smell from poetry, they are only doing harm. For poetry to be great, it must reek of the human, as Wordsworth's poetry does. This is not a novel contention; but perhaps it is one of those things that cannot be said too often.

In his recent book, *Thomas Hardy and British Poetry*, Davie proposes that the most influential figure in British poetry for the past fifty years has been Hardy, and not Pound, Eliot, Yeats or Lawrence. Davie values Hardy because of the latter's "scientific humanism"—however qualified that humanism is by his grim naturalism—and the "liberalism" it seems to lead to. The argument is a very curious one:

> On every page, "Take it or leave it," he seems to say; or, even more permissively, "Take what you want, and leave the rest." This consciousness of having imposed on his reader so little is what lies behind Hardy's insistence that what he offers is only a series of disconnected observations, and behind his resentment that he should be taken as having a pessimistic design upon his reader.... It is on this basis—his respect of the reader's rights to be attentive or inattentive as he pleases—that one rests the claim for Hardy as perhaps the first and last "liberal" in modern poetry.

Hardy's poetry "opens a window on a world where liberalism may yet be a passion—as, one likes to believe, it always has been in the laboratories." Thus Hardy stands in violent contrast to those modern poets who have sought to remake the world rather than accept it on its own terms:

> [Pound, Eliot, Hopkins, Yeats] claim, by implication or else explicitly, to give us entry through their poems into a world that is true and more real than the world we know from statistics or scientific induction or common sense. Their criticism of life is radical in that they refuse to accept life on the terms in which it offers itself, and has to be coped with, through most of the hours of every day. In their poems, quotidian reality is transformed, displaced, supplanted; the alternative reality which their poems create is offered to us as a superior reality.... [But Hardy's poems] instead of transforming and displacing quantifiable reality or the reality of common sense, are on the contrary just so many glosses on that reality, which is conceived of as unchallengeably "given" and final. This is what makes it possible to say (once again) that he sold the vocation short, tacitly surrendering the proudest claims traditionally made for the act of the poetic imagination. Whether this was inevitable, given his intellectual convictions and the state of the world in his time, is an interesting question.

Davie's answer is no less interesting. By seeming to accept too much and demand too little, Hardy and his heirs—poets like Larkin and Davie himself—do diminish the role of the poet; unlike Pound or Lawrence they do not expect to be taken as prophets and seers. And yet Davie argues that by definition prophetic poetry is in fact inferior poetry:

> The prophet is above being fair-minded—judiciousness he will leave to someone else. But the poet will absolve himself from none of the responsibilities of being human.... And being human involves the responsibility of being judicious and fair-minded. In this way the poet supports the intellectual venture of humankind, taking his place along with...the scholar and the statesman and the learned divine.

The argument is now frankly political or moral. Recent history has proved that the authoritarian alternatives to social democracy in Britain—"mean-spirited as that undoubtedly is"—are "too costly in terms of human suffering for any man of humane feeling, least of all a poet, to find them real alternatives any longer." And it is in fact the spirit of decent, unheroic social democracy which Hardy and his heirs embody. The difficult question of "influence" is therefore a major one and Davie wisely limits his claims: "the Hardyesque tone in so much British writing is the result of social and political circumstances, which bear in upon and condition writers who perhaps are not directly influenced by Hardy's poems at all." There is a final point to be made here: however modest and realistic the "content" of his poetry may be, Hardy has not compromised the eternal responsibility of the artist to make his work as finely as he can. At its best Hardy's poetry gives us the sense of a man "making what hard stay he can against the temporal flux, and (if he is a technological man) using his technological symmetries and precisions to serve that perennial need."

In light of the argument running throughout his work against certain kinds of modernism, Davie's interest in Pound is unexpected. He devotes the kind of patient attention to Pound which suggests he thinks his subject is worth taking with the utmost seriousness. And yet Pound does not speak for any cultural center; his diction is not pure; he has abandoned many of the principles of prose syntax; he is an irascible and frequently inhumane prophet. Perhaps this is the answer: Pound is the supreme example of what can go wrong when a poet fancies himself above everyday humanity. His "disastrous career" has made it impossible for us "any longer to exalt the poet into a seer." Again it seems that the only honorable role left to the poet in the modern world is the one exemplified by Hardy. Alfred Alvarez once complained about the unexciting "gentility" of the poets Davie sees as Hardy's rightful heirs, and Davie, who is an infinitely finer critic in all the ways which matter, replied simply that "what is derided as 'gentility' can be glossed as 'civic sense' or 'political responsibility.' "

DAY LEWIS, C(ecil). Pseudonym: Nicholas Blake. British. Born in Ballintubber, Ireland, 27 April 1904. Educated at Sherborne School, Dorset; Wadham College, Oxford, M.A. Served as an Editor in the Ministry of Information, London, 1941-46. Married Constance Mary King in 1928 (divorced, 1951); Jill Balcon in 1951; four children. Taught at Summerfields School, Oxford, 1927-28; Larchfield, Helensburgh, 1928-30; Cheltenham College, Gloucestershire, 1930-35; Professor of Poetry, Oxford University, 1951-56; Norton Professor of Poetry, Harvard University, Cambridge, Massachusetts, 1964-65. Clark Lecturer, 1946, and Sidgwick Lecturer, 1956, Cambridge University; Warton Lecturer, British Academy, London, 1951; Byron Lecturer, University of Nottingham, 1952; Chancellor Dunning Lecturer, Queen's University, Kingston, Ontario, 1954; Compton Lecturer, University of Hull, Yorkshire, 1968. Director of Chatto and Windus Ltd., publishers, London, 1954-72. Member of the Arts Council of Great Britain, 1962-67. Honorary Fellow, Wadham College, Oxford, 1968. D.Litt.: University of Exeter, 1965; University of Hull, 1969; Litt.D.: Trinity College, Dublin, 1968. Fellow, 1944, Vice-President, 1958, and Companion of Literature, 1964, Royal Society of Literature; Honorary Member, American Academy of Arts and letters, 1966; Member, Irish Academy of Letters, 1968. C.B.E. (Commander, Order of the British Empire), 1950. Poet Laureate, 1968. *Died 22 May 1972.*

PUBLICATIONS

Criticism

A Hope for Poetry. Oxford, Blackwell, 1934; with *Collected Poems*, New York, Random House, 1935.
Revolution in Writing. London, Hogarth Press, 1935; New York, Random House, 1936.
Poetry for You: A Book for Boys and Girls on the Enjoyment of Poetry. Oxford, Blackwell, 1944; New York, Oxford University Press, 1947.
The Poetic Image. London, Cape, and New York, Oxford University Press, 1947.
Enjoying Poetry: A Reader's Guide. London, National Book League, 1947.
The Colloquial Element in English Poetry. Newcastle upon Tyne, Literary and Philosophical Society, 1947.
The Poet's Task: An Inaugural Lecture Delivered Before the University of Oxford on 1 June 1951. Oxford, Clarendon Press, 1951; Folcroft, Pennsylvania, Folcroft Editions, 1970.
The Grand Manner. Nottingham, University of Nottingham Press, 1952.
The Lyrical Poetry of Thomas Hardy. London, Oxford University Press, 1953; Folcroft, Pennsylvania, Folcroft Editions, 1970.
Notable Images of Virtue: Emily Brontë, George Meredith, W.B. Yeats. Toronto, Ryerson Press, 1954; Folcroft, Pennsylvania, Folcroft Editons, 1969.
The Poet's Way of Knowledge. London, Cambridge University Press, 1957.
The Lyric Impulse. Cambridge, Massachusetts, Harvard University Press, and London, Chatto and Windus, 1965.
A Need for Poetry? Hull, University of Hull Press, 1968.
On Translating Poetry: A Lecture. Abingdon-on-Thames, Berkshire, Abbey Press, 1970.

Verse

Beechen Vigil and Other Poems. London, Fortune Press, 1925.
Country Comets. London, Martin Hopkinson, 1928.
Transitional Poem. London, Hogarth Press, 1929.
From Feathers to Iron. London, Hogarth Press, 1931.
The Magnetic Mountain. London, Hogarth Press, 1933.
Collected Poems, 1929-1933. London, Hogarth Press, 1935; with *A Hope for Poetry*, New York, Random House, 1935.
A Time to Dance and Other Poems. London, Hogarth Press, 1935.
Noah and the Waters. London, Hogarth Press, 1936.
A Time to Dance, Noah and the Waters and Other Poems, with an Essay, Revolution in Writing. New York, Random House, 1936.
Overtures to Death and Other Poems. London, Cape, 1938.
Poems in Wartime. London, Cape, 1940.
Selected Poems. London, Hogarth Press, 1940.
Word over All. London, Cape, 1943; New York, Transatlantic, 1944.
(*Poems*). London, Eyre and Spottiswoode, 1943.
Short Is the Time: Poems, 1936-1943 (includes *Overtures to Death* and *Word over All*). New York, Oxford University Press, 1945.
Poems, 1943-1947. London, Cape, and New York, Oxford University Press, 1948.
Collected Poems, 1929-1936. London, Hogarth Press, 1954.
Selected Poems. London, Penguin, 1951; revised edition, 1957, 1969.
An Italian Visit. London, Cape, and New York, Harper, 1953.
Collected Poems. London, Cape-Hogarth Press, 1954.

Christmas Eve. London, Faber, 1954.
The Newborn: D.M.B., 29th April, 1957. London, Favil Press of Kensington, 1956.
Pegasus and Other Poems. London, Cape, 1957; New York, Harper, 1958.
The Gate and Other Poems. London, Cape, 1962.
Requiem for the Living. New York, Harper, 1964.
On Not Saying Anything. Cambridge, Massachusetts, privately printed, 1964.
A Marriage Song for Albert and Barbara. Cambridge, Massachusetts, privately printed,
   1965.
The Room and Other Poems. London, Cape, 1965.
C. Day Lewis: Selections from His Poetry, edited by Patric Dickinson. London, Chatto
   and Windus, 1967.
Selected Poems. New York, Harper, 1967.
The Abbey That Refused to Die: A Poem. County Mayo, Ireland, Ballintubber Abbey,
   1967.
The Whispering Roots. London, Cape, 1970; as *The Whispering Roots and Other
   Poems*, New York, Harper, 1970.
Going My Way. London, Poem-of-the-Month Club, 1970.
The Poems of C. Day Lewis, 1925-1972, edited by Ian Parsons. London, Cape-Hogarth
   Press, 1977.
Posthumous Poems. Andoversford, Whittington Press, 1979.

Recording: *Poems*, Argo, 1974.

Novels

The Friendly Tree. London, Cape, 1936; New York, 1937.
Starting Point. London, Cape, 1937; New York, 1938.
Child of Misfortune. London, Cape, 1939

Novels (as Nicholas Blake)

A Question of Proof. London, Collins, and New York, Harper, 1935.
Thou Shell of Death. London, Collins, 1936; as *Shell of Death*, New York, Harper,
   1936.
There's Trouble Brewing. London, Collins, and New York, Harper, 1937.
The Beast Must Die. London, Collins, and New York, Harper, 1938.
The Smiler with the Knife. London, Collins, and New York, Harper, 1939.
Malice in Wonderland. London, Collins, 1940; as *Summer Camp Mystery*, New York,
   Harper, 1940.
The Case of the Abominable Snowman. London, Collins, 1941; as *Corpse in the
   Snowman*, New York, Harper, 1941.
Minute for Murder. London, Collins, 1947; New York, Harper, 1948.
Head of a Traveller. London, Collins, and New York, Harper, 1949.
The Dreadful Hollow. London, Collins, and New York, Harper, 1953.
The Whisper in the Gloom. London, Collins, and New York, Harper, 1954.
A Tangled Web. London, Collins, and New York, Harper, 1956.
End of Chapter. London, Collins, and New York, Harper, 1957.
A Penknife in My Heart. London, Collins, and New York, Harper, 1958.
The Widow's Cruise. London, Collins, and New York, Harper, 1959.
The Worm of Death. London, Collins, and New York, Harper, 1961.
The Deadly Joker. London, Collins, 1963.
The Sad Variety. London, Collins, and New York, Harper, 1964.
The Morning after Death. London, Collins, and New York Harper, 1966.

The Nicholas Blake Omnibus (includes *The Beast Must Die, A Tangled Web, A Penknife in My Heart*). London, Collins, 1966.
The Private Wound. London, Collins, and New York, Harper, 1968.

Other

Dick Willoughby (juvenile). Oxford, Blackwell, 1933; New York, Random House, 1938.
Imagination and Thinking, with L. Susan Strebbing. London, British Institute of Adult Education, 1936.
We're Not Going to Do Nothing: A Reply to Mr. Aldous Huxley's Pamphlet "What Are You Going to Do about It?" London, Left Review, 1936; Folcroft, Pennsylvania, Folcroft Editons, 1970.
The Otterbury Incident (juvenile). London, Putnam, 1948; New York, Viking Press, 1949.
The Buried Day (autobiography). London, Chatto and Windus, and New York, Harper, 1960.
Thomas Hardy, with R.A. Scott-James. London, Longman, 1965.

Editor, with W.H. Auden, *Oxford Poetry 1927*. Oxford, Blackwell, 1927.
Editor, with others, *A Writer in Arms*, by Ralph Fox. London, Lawrence and Wishart, 1937.
Editor, *The Mind in Chains: Socialism and the Cultural Revolution*. London, Muller, 1937; Folcroft, Pennsylvania, Folcroft Editions, 1972.
Editor, *The Echoing Green: An Anthology of Verse*. Oxford, Blackwell, 3 vols., 1937.
Editor, with Charles Fenby, *Anatomy of Oxford: An Anthology*. London, Cape, 1938.
Editor, with L.A.G. Strong, *A New Anthology of Modern Verse 1920-1940*. London, Methuen, 1941.
Editor, with others, *Orion: Volume II* and *Volume III*. London, Nicholson and Watson, 1945, 1946.
Editor, *The Golden Treasury of the Best Songs and Lyrical Poems in the English Language*, by Francis Turner Palgrave. London, Collins, 1954.
Editor, with John Lehmann, *The Chatto Book of Modern Poetry, 1915-1955*. London, Chatto and Windus, 1956.
Editor, with Kathleen Nott and Thomas Blackburn, *New Poems 1957*. London, Joseph, 1957.
Editor, *A Book of English Lyrics*. London, Chatto and Windus, 1961; as *English Lyric Poems, 1500-1900*, New York, Appleton Century Crofts, 1961.
Editor, *The Collected Poems of Wilfred Owen*. London, Chatto and Windus, 1964; revised edition, New York, New Directions, 1964.
Editor, *The Midnight Skaters: Poems for Young Readers*, by Edmund Blunden. London, Bodley Head, 1968.
Editor, *The Poems of Robert Browning*. Cambridge, Limited Editions Club, 1969; New York, Heritage Press, 1971.
Editor, *A Choice of Keats's Verse*. London, Faber, 1971.
Editor, *Crabbe*. London, Penguin, 1973.

Translator, *The Georgics of Virgil*. London, Cape, 1940; New York, Oxford University Press, 1947.
Translator, *The Graveyard by the Sea*, by Paul Valéry. London, Secker and Warburg, 1947.
Editor, *The Aeneid of Virgil*. London, Hogarth Press, and New York, Oxford University Press, 1952.
Translator, *The Eclogues of Virgil*. London, Cape, 1963; with *The Georgics*, New York, Doubleday, 1964.
Translator, with Mátyás Sárközi, *The Tomtit in the Rain: Traditional Hungarian Rhymes*, by Erzsi Gazdas. London, Chatto and Windus, 1971.

Geoffrey Handley-Taylor and Timothy d'Arch-Smith, *C. Day-Lewis: The Poet Laureate: A Bibliography*.   London and Chicago, St. James Press, 1968.
Joseph N. Riddel, *C. Day Lewis*.   New York, Twayne, 1971.

*   *   *

In one of his last and most useful essays, "To Criticize the Critic," T.S. Eliot discriminates among four kinds of literary critics: there is the Professional Critic, like Sainte-Beuve, whose criticism is his only title to fame; there is the "Critic with Gusto," like Saintsbury, the "advocate of the author whose work he expounds"; there is the Academic or Theoretical Critic, like Empson or Richards; and finally there is the critic like Eliot himself, "whose criticism may be said to be a by-product of his creative activity":

> Particularly, the critic who is also a poet. Shall we say, the poet who has written some literary criticism? The condition of entrance into this category is that the candidate should be known primarily for his poetry, but that his criticism should be distinguished for its own sake, and not merely for any light it may throw upon its author's verse. And here I put Samuel Johnson and Coleridge; and Dryden and Racine in their prefaces; and Matthew Arnold with reservations; and it is into this company that I must shyly intrude.

Clearly Day Lewis belongs in this category as well. His criticism is an outgrowth of his poetic development over forty years, and what Eliot says of his own criticism, that "both in my general affirmations about poetry and in writing about authors who had influenced me, I was implicitly defending the sort of poetry that I and my friends were writing," is no less true for Day Lewis. Whether or not his criticism also has some intrinsic value is another question.

A Hope for Poetry, first published in 1934, springs from Day Lewis' belief that "some of the post-war writers, notably W.H. Auden and Stephen Spender, are true poets having more in common than mere contemporaneousness" (this group should also include Louis MacNeice and of course Day Lewis himself). The proper ancestors of these poets are not the genteel Georgians, but Hopkins, Wilfred Owen and Eliot: Hopkins matters because of his intensity and technical experiments; Owen, "the servant of common honesty," matters because of his determination to "tell the factual, un-'poetical' truth"; and Eliot was important, briefly, and apart from decisive efforts on behalf of the metaphysical poets and the Symbolists, because he "detected the death-will in western civilization before it rose to the surface in the disillusionment of the later war years." For Day Lewis "The Waste Land" is primarily a "social document"; after his conversion to Anglo-Catholicism Eliot renounced any claim to leadership. "We see Mr. Prufrock now," Day Lewis concludes, "like most converts, meticulous over points of ritual, very severe and aloof in tone, repenting profusely for a viciousness that had never, may be, broken the bounds of phantasy." Hardy is not mentioned at all, although he was a major influence on the early Auden; Yeats' poetry is "too personal in idiom, too insulated to allow an easy communication of its powers"; and for some undisclosed reason Day Lewis dismisses the importance of D.H. Lawrence as a poet. This is not very accurate literary history, but what matters is that Day Lewis and perhaps some of his contemporaries believed it was true for them.

Surveying the work of his generation, Day Lewis concludes that despite the discouraging power of mass culture and positivism, there "does seem to be an increase in what we may call vitality." The hope for poetry, however, is basically part of a larger revolutionary hope for a just society and that necessary change of heart Auden invoked in his early poetry. The poet today, Day Lewis maintains,

> is as it were starting again at the beginning. His starting point, therefore, is love. We shall not begin to understand post-war poetry until we realise that the poet is appealing above all for the creation of a society in which the real and living contact between man and man may again become possible. That is why, speaking from the living unit of himself and his friends, he appeals for the contraction of the social group to a size at which human

contact may again be established and demands the destruction of all impediments to love.

The claims on the young poet are difficult and conflicting:

On the one hand the Communist tells him that he is no better than a dope-peddler unless he "joins the revolution," that he is unhappy and ineffective because he is trying to live in two worlds at once.... On the other hand, the bourgeois critic rebukes him for allowing a sympathy with Communism which drives him into a kind of writing that at any rate sounds very like propaganda.

Both parties are right, up to a point, yet

the bourgeois critic must remember that there is no reason why poetry should not also be propaganda; the effect of invocation, of poetry, and of propaganda is to create a state of mind; and it is not enough to say that poetry must do unconsciously what propaganda does consciously, for that would be to dismiss all didactic poetry from that of the Bible downwards.

A Hope for Poetry is dated, but as an indication of how some of the younger poets saw themselves during the 1930's it has a certain documentary value. Day Lewis' position was to change over the years—the young Communist became in time the Poet Laureate—but one element in his thinking remains constant, and that is his conviction that poetry is fundamentally a matter of inspiration:

The poet is an artificer by profession, a poet by divine accident. The pure spirit that comes to possess him, for one minute it may be in twenty years, comes from regions over which he has no control. Between visits there is nothing he can do but work at his profession, so that, when next an angel arrives, he can better accommodate him.

He maintains much the same thing thirty years later, in *The Lyric Impulse*. The language of *A Hope for Poetry* may seem mystical, finally, but Day Lewis' conception of the poetic impulse is clearly psychological, as *The Poetic Image* makes clear.

As a verbal picture colored by the passions of the poet, the poetic image is for Day Lewis virtually synonymous with simile and metaphor: "every image recreates not merely an object but an object in the context of an experience, and thus an object as part of a relationship." Despite I.A. Richards' influential claim a few years before that there is no special aesthetic sense, Day Lewis argues that there *is* something unique about poetic experience, and that the accompanying pleasure leads to "revelation" and a "furtherance of life." There is a fundamental human need for the proper expression of relationships between things and feelings which "compels the poet to metaphor." But he does not create the pattern of relationship his metaphors reveal; the pattern is objectively there, if we have eyes to see:

There is a most remarkable weight and unanimity of evidence, both in the verse and the critical writings of English poets, that poetry's truth comes from the perception of a unity underlying and relating all phenomena, and that poetry's task is the perpetual discovery, through its imaging, metaphor-making faculty, of new relationships within this pattern, and the rediscovery and renovation of old ones. Because the pattern is constantly changing, no poetic image ever achieves absolute truth; because it is infinitely extended, the poet has always the sense of "something evermore about to be."

Once again, as in *A Hope for Poetry*, Love is the central term—the kind of love felt by the poet for things outside himself. Simile and metaphor are "signs of sympathy":

The poet's task...is to recognize pattern wherever he sees it, and to build his perceptions into a poetic form which by its urgency and coherence will persuade us of their truth. He is in the world, we may say, to bear witness to the principle of love, since love is as good a word as any for that human reaching-out of hands towards the warmth in all things, which is the source and passion of his song. Love is this to him first; he apprehends it as a kind of necessity by which all things are bound together and in which, could the whole pattern be seen, their contradictions would appear reconciled.

All of Day Lewis' arguments here rest on his acceptance of the Jungian conception of the collective unconscious, that vast store of literally inherited symbols which the poet is compelled to evoke and give persuasive aesthetic form as a way of correcting a culture which has gone astray and become "one-sided." Here *The Poetic Image* relies heavily and explicitly on Maud Bodkin's *Archetypal Patterns in Poetry*: our responsiveness to certain images, especially those of rebirth and renewal, is ultimately founded on the human need for continuity. Poetic synthesis and communal solidarity are aspects of the same drive towards total coherence. "Look inward," Day Lewis advises the young poet, "but outwards too no less steadily; for the virtues that unite mankind in families and societies are themselves variations of that single theme which also unifies your disjointed memories and warring moods to make a poem." *The Poetic Image* is a graceful and often eloquent book, but for a full understanding of archetypal theory and its implications for practical criticism the reader must turn to Maud Bodkin, Joseph Campbell and Jung himself.

The Lyric Impulse is an altogether weaker affair. In his sympathetic study of Day Lewis Joseph Riddel observes, tactfully, that it is a "strikingly casual book...almost completely void of intellectual tension." Commenting on the relationship of *The Lyric Impulse* to the kind of poetry Day Lewis was writing at the end of his career, Riddel continues:

Because it follows Day Lewis' last three volumes of poems rather than emerging from the immediacy of their creation, its argument is a kind of afterthought and apology. Or rather, we find in it the ultimate emergence of the residual conviction that earlier had prevented him, on the one hand, from embracing a Marxist poetics and, on the other, from any kind of experimental daring. As such, the book is an unimpassioned and direct plea for another countercurrent in modern poetry: a return, as it were, to the primal origins of poetry in song and a repudiation of the self-conscious, intellectual tradition of modern poetry to which Day Lewis had earlier been party.... The gist of Day Lewis' argument in *The Lyric Impulse* is that the history of poetry, especially its recent history, has been a progressive movement away from the root of the poetic "impulse," the lyric or "singing" line.... Although he claims to be speaking about genre, he is really speaking about a mystique of ecstasy, or about inspiration as the muse. Spontaneity, youthfulness, innocence, renewal—these are the lyric qualities.

A Hope for Poetry has a certain historical interest; *The Poetic Image* is a pleasant introduction to archetypal criticism; *The Lyric Impulse* partly justifies the kind of poetry Day Lewis eventually wanted to write: for these reasons some knowledge of his criticism may be useful. But it would be unrealistic to make any larger claims for it.

DONOGHUE, Denis. Irish. Born in Tullow, Ireland, 1 December 1928. Educated at University College, Dublin, B.A. 1949, M.A. 1952, Ph.D. 1957. Married Frances P. Rutledge in 1951; has eight children. Administrative Officer, Irish Department of Finance, Dublin, 1951-54; Music Critic, *Irish Times*, Dublin, 1957. Assistant Lecturer, 1954-57, College Lecturer, 1957-64, and Professor of Modern English and American Literature, 1965-79, University College, Dublin. Since 1979, Henry James Professor of English and American Letters, New York University. Director of the Yeats International Summer School, Dublin, 1960; Visiting Scholar, University of Pennsylvania, Philadelphia, 1962-63; University Lecturer and Fellow of King's College, Cambridge, 1964-65. Member of the Board, Abbey Theatre, Dublin. Recipient: American Council of Learned Societies Fellowship, 1963. M.A.: Cambridge University, 1965.

Address: Department of English, New York University, 19 University Place, New York, New York 10003, U.S.A.

PUBLICATIONS

Criticism

> *The Third Voice: Modern British and American Verse Drama*.   Princeton, New Jersey, Princeton University Press, 1959.
> "Yeats and Modern Poetry," in *The Integrity of Yeats*, edited by Denis Donoghue. Cork, Mercier Press, 1964; Folcroft, Pennsylvania, Folcroft Editions, 1971.
> *Connoisseurs of Chaos: Ideas of Order in Modern American Poetry*.   New York, Macmillan, 1965; London, Faber, 1966.
> *The Ordinary Universe: Soundings in Modern Literature*.   New York, Macmillan, and London, Faber, 1968.
> *Jonathan Swift: A Critical Introduction*.   London, Cambridge University Press, 1969.
> *Emily Dickinson*.   Minneapolis, University of Minnesota Press, 1969.
> *William Butler Yeats*.   New York, Viking Press, 1971; as *Yeats*, London, Fontana, 1971.
> *Thieves of Fire*.   London, Faber, 1973; and New York, Oxford University Press, 1974.
> *The Sovereign Ghost: Studies in Imagination*.   Berkeley and Los Angeles, University of California Press, 1976; London, Faber, 1978.
> "Eliot and the Criterion," in *The Literary Criticism of T.S. Eliot: New Essays*, edited by David Newton-De Molina.   London, Athlone Press, 1977.
> "Radio Talk," in *The State of the Language*, edited by Leonard Michaels and Christopher Ricks.   Berkeley and Los Angeles, University of California Press, 1980.
> *Ferocious Alphabets*.   Boston, Little Brown, and London, Faber, 1981.

Other ·

> Editor, *The Integrity of Yeats*.   Cork, Mercier Press, 1964; Folcroft, Pennsylvania, Folcroft Editions, 1971.
> Editor, with J.R. Mulryne, *An Honoured Guest: New Essays on W.B. Yeats*.   London, Arnold, 1965; New York, St. Martin's Press, 1966.
> Editor, *Swift Revisited*.   Cork, Mercier Press, 1968.
> Editor, *Jonathan Swift: A Critical Anthology*.   London, Penguin, 1971.
> Editor, *Memoirs*, by W.B. Yeats.   London, Macmillan, 1972; New York, Macmillan, 1973.

*   *   *

"Most good poets write plays," Denis Donoghue observes at the opening of *The Third Voice*, "bad plays. One thinks of Wallace Stevens, of Auden, of William Carlos Williams. Yeats is the greatest exception, thus providing a shadowy continuity with Ibsen, whose own theatre-poetry Yeats was very slow to acknowledge." He then proceeds to support this depressing thesis, arguing from a position which is basically if not consistently Aristotelian. Poetic drama is not to be defined by a particular range of subject matter or even by the presence of verse rather than prose; a drama is "poetic" when it manifests those virtues of unity, magnitude and economy which the Aristotelian critic expects of any successful work, regardless of its mode of representation: "A play is poetic, then, when its concrete elements (plot, agency, scene, speech, gesture) continuously exhibit in their internal relationships those qualitites of mutual coherence and illumination required of the words of a poem." (This definition is obviously a very broad one; a novel may be just as poetic as any poem or play, given these standards, and indeed "poetic" easily becomes a synonym here for artistic worth in general.) In the *Poetics* Aristotle maintains that since human happiness and misery take the form of action, the chief object of imitation in the drama must be a certain kind of action or plot, a sequence of causally related events having a convincing beginning, middle and end. But the plot does not exist for its own sake—it exists rather as the chief means the artist has for moving his audience in a specific, determinate way. Thus the intended effect governs the selection and development of plot, just as the plot then determines suitable agents and diction. In this strict sense, however, Donoghue fails to be Aristotelian enough: while he stresses the primacy of plot, he has nothing to say about different final causes, or overall intended effects, and thus lacks any means of distinguishing not only between the drama and other modes of imitation, but between different genres within the field of drama. To such objections Donoghue might well reply, of course, that formal analysis cannot handle those larger questions of themes and sensibility which are finally his major concern as a critic. Nevertheless his flirtation with Aristotelian terms in often misleading.

Modern poets have failed, Donoghue argues (and his arguments are detailed and convincing, particularly in the case of T.S. Eliot), largely because they have so little concern for the construction of their plots:

> The dramatist who has started as a poet or a novelist is often loath to concede that words alone are not enough. His natural impulse is to trust the words to carry all his burdens: action, plot, agency, gesture, and more than these.... His hope, in fact...is to deduce a play from a poem.... The appropriate corrective, of course, is Aristotle, recalling the implication in the tangled *Poetics* that a play is not in the first instance—to use Francis Fergusson's gloss—"a composition in the verbal medium"—...[but] a sequence of acts, whose nature is indicated partly by words, partly by gestures, partly by the "context of situation," partly by the "scene" itself.

Yet if the modern poet fails to construct sound and moving plots it is not entirely his fault. The modern world itself seems to have lost those codes which might support a line of action. If we no longer agree about the nature of heroism we can hardly make heroic plots—the argument by now is a very familiar one:

> The ages which have produced the greatest drama...are those which offer to the poet a seasoned code: drama would seem to depend on such a code for clarity and form. It matters little whether it is a code for the realisation of good or evil. The important thing is that it shall tell the dramatist how people behave.... By adhering strictly to the code the dramatist exhibits a "representative" action. [Allen Tate] also argued that with the disappearance of general patterns of conduct the power to depict action that is both single and complete also disappears. The dramatic genius of the poet is held to short flights, and the dramatic lyric is a fragment of a total action which the poet lacks the means to delineate.

In *Hamlet*, for example, there is a "reciprocal relation obtaining between the society and its drama":

> No confident feeling of this kind arises from the plays of Yeats or of Eliot. Can we not say this—that our theatre is full of individual insights, "characteristically" partial images of man, insights all the more extreme because they feel themselves caught in a trap? What we lack is an image of man, in the medium of theatre, which we can acknowledge as somehow representative, somehow central.

Until society changes, each dramatist can only make the best of a bad job. But even under ideal circumstances, of course, poetic drama will not write itself. We still need "the kind of insight that might emerge from the juxtaposition of Aristotle and Coleridge":

> For us Aristotle would endorse the primacy of plot.... He could warn us, graciously, that the determining fact about a play is that one thing is represented as happening after another.... In turn, Coleridge would define, with solicitude, the role of language in drama. And perhaps a third force, which we will call Kenneth Burke, might persuade both critics to assign a more creative role to the *scene* in which an *act* is performed.

This basic concern for the "values" which underlie a work of art is important in *Connoisseurs of Chaos* as well. Examining Bryant's "Thanatopsis," Donoghue notes the conventional pieties of the poem but observes that it also contains a darker strain of feeling:

> The shuddering...owes nothing to Wordsworth, Milton, Blair, or Cowper and every-thing to Bryant's American sensibility, which drains the hymn until it is a revery. To go through Bryant's poems is to see him wavering with some distress between two traditions—an English tradition, strong in its purposes, and an American tradition just barely emerging into form. "The figure a poem makes" in American literature is a question mark.

(Like many of Donoghue's generalizations this claim is broad enough to raise some questions. The reader may wonder, for example, if uncertainty about basic values was a specifically American characteristic during the nineteenth century.) In any event, Poe is the archetypal questioner, and "when we think of answers we think of Emerson." But the cost may have been too great: in order to come to terms with evil and an indifferent nature Emerson and his successors succumbed to what Donoghue calls elsewhere the "Circe of transcendence." By seeking to convert everything into the stuff of contemplation and thus making consciousness the end of existence, the poems of Wallace Stevens, for example, "leave out too much." Mark Twain—at least the Twain of "The Mysterious Stranger"—recognized the limits of trans-cendentalism:

> The chief difference between Emerson and Mark Twain is that for Emerson there is always a middle term to mediate between polarities; in Twain there is no middle term. Emerson says, in fact, "Nature is thoroughly mediate. It is made to serve." He means that it is the middle term between God and man, it is made by God to serve man. Mark Twain vetoes this function; nature is not mediate. In the resultant chasm man must do the best he can, which will turn out to be nothing.

"The terms of our discussion are order and chaos": but these terms are so large that they encourage a host of broad, familiar generalizations about Whitman, Melville, Dickinson, Frost and several more modern figures. Donoghue has a remarkable gift for graceful characterization of an artist's overall sensibility, but *Connoisseurs of Chaos* suffers from the inherent limitations of thematic criticism. For the purpose of these discussions it seems irrelevant that Frost was a poet rather than a novelist or philosopher; what matters is point of view and not formal excellence (hence the odd chapter on Frederick Goddard Tuckerman). There is no sense of concrete wholes: Stevens, once again, seems to have written one vast poem, any phrase of which may be called to witness regardless of its original function as part of a single work intended to achieve a specific effect.

In his discussion of Frost Donoghue praises the "plenitude of fact, of event, of plot" of one poem, " 'Out, Out'—. " Continuing this line of argument he opens *The Ordinary Universe* with a plea for the proper "plenitude of fact"—and of plot and character as well. The term may sound Aristotelian but once more Donoghue is concerned with themes and sensibilities and not with formal achievements. The heirs of Emerson and the Symbolists have taken the last step of making consciousness the final good of existence, and while Donoghue does not deny the value of consciousness he wishes to see it as "an instrument in the service of something other than itself": "Is it unfair to say," he asks, "that modern literature is written 'as if' there were nothing; nothing, that is, but consciousness; no value in the given, the finite, only in personal ascrip-tion?" Of course the answer is yes, no, and maybe: yes if you select some writers, no if you select others, and maybe—*perhaps* modern literature on the whole tends towards solipsism. The exceptions are important and the terms at least as unwieldy as "order and chaos." But clearly the writers Donoghue values most are those who remain faithful to the ordinary universe of facts and persons. While a novel like *To the Lighthouse* is filled with "the buzz of sensibility without an adequate commitment to story and event," the middle novels of Henry James "commit themselves to time, place, event, to the finite, the realm of action as the scene of disclosed value." And as for the existence of others: "A writer who assents to the Person does so not as a casual acknowledgement but as part of that larger, more inclusive assent which is a reverence for life." Donoghue discusses a good many modern writers in these terms, evidently

163

convinced that such concern for objectivity and moral relationships is rare in modern criticism;
he has observed, he tells us, that "most critics of modern literature assume that the poem's
attitudes are beyond dispute." Once again it all depends on which critics you choose. For every
Northrop Frye there is a Dr. Leavis. As for any single conclusion, "there is none." Yet
Donoghue is willing to venture that "one of the few generalizations we make of contemporary
literature is that the private and public worlds are now deemed to have nothing whatever to do
with each other.... There is nothing left but the 'universe within,' the little world made cunningly
of our own fantasies."

Thieves of Fire is a more rewarding book, partly because of its conciseness and partly
because he explicitly limits himself to the kind of inquiry thematic criticism is best able to
handle:

> I am interested in these writers chiefly for the light they cast upon a certain kind of
> imagination. Sometimes I describe that imagination by contrasting it with another kind
> which acts upon a different faith; the same procedure holds on those occasions, too; my
> aim is not to do full justice to the several writers [Milton, Blake, Melville and Lawrence]
> or to register the diversity of their works but to call them as witnesses to a particular
> character of the imagination.

The "Promethean" imagination strives ambitiously for greater goods; but like the gift of fire,
the rewards may be ambiguous, bearing the taint of stolen treasure and involving the recipient
in the guilt attached to them. Translated into literary terms, this usually means that increased
consciousness brings increased burdens as well as benefits. "The poet of *Paradise Lost*," for
example, is "bound to concern himself with...the cost of knowledge, the nature of poetic
inspiration, the no-man's-land between earth and heaven, earth and hell. Promethean fire."
Prior to his discussion of his chosen writers, however, Donoghue makes a basic distinction
which illuminates much of his critical thinking to date:

> I am describing two types of imagination, featuring two different attitudes to expe-
> rience.... The easiest paradigm comes from sculpture, where the artist working directly
> upon his materials is a concentrated image of man dealing with his experience. Adrian
> Stokes has provided the terms of two different artistic procedures, and they chime
> exactly with the two attitudes I am describing. He distinguishes between the motives
> involved in carving and in modelling, where carving is concerned with the release of
> significance deemed already to exist, imprisoned in the stone, and modelling is a more
> drastic process by which the sculptor imposes his meaning upon the stone. In carving the
> artist assumes that the block of stone contains within itself the form invented for it by
> nature; the artist's desire is merely to liberate that form.... In modelling, on the other
> hand, the artist gives the stone his own truth, or what he insists is his own truth; the truth
> of the stone as a different truth is not acknowledged.

In *The Ordinary Universe*, as Donoghue admits, his preference was for the objective carvers
and their fidelity to fact rather than for the Promethean modellers, who also have some kinship
with the transcendental egotists he had worried about in *Connoisseurs of Chaos*. In *Thieves of
Fire* Lawrence becomes the archetypal Promethean egotist:

> He quarrelled with life not because it refused to admit desire but because it would not
> tolerate the endlessness of desire. He quarrelled with the available forms of fiction
> because, doing so much, they did not do everything.... The myth of Prometheus answers
> to this pattern of feeling when it is interpreted as testifying to the endlessness and the
> namelessness of man's desires.

At this point Faust rather than Prometheus might seem the more appropriate mythic figure;
and of course the Faustian or Promethean impulse may characterize politicians, philosophers,
chefs, critics and critics of critics, as well as poets.

In the Preface to *The Sovereign Ghost* Donoghue provides a convenient summary statement
about the relationship of this book to his earlier criticism:

In *The Ordinary Universe* I looked at certain works which, running against the modern grain, acknowledge the validity of common experience as a force with which the imagination deals on terms pretty nearly equal. The imagination does not insist on its rights at the expense of nature, the world, or reality.... In *Thieves of Fire* I looked somewhat nervously at certain writers whose imaginations are intransigent, peremptory, strident in the presence of common experience and received poetic forms. In the present book I try to deal with some of the questions raised by the imagination itself, its character and relations, the claims regularly made on its behalf, the problems it poses.

Donoghue's continuing theme, then, is the shaping power of the imagination and its relationship to the world of stubborn realities. His rather neutral description of *The Sovereign Ghost*, however, is somewhat misleading, since he is very much concerned not simply to describe the imagination but to defend it as the "essential power" of the human mind:

why essential? Not merely (though this would be cause enough) because it is all we have, but because it is the only force that has the slightest chance of coping with the vast miscellany of arbitrary and ordained events which constitute the occasions of our experience.

And again, even more forcefully: "The essential power of imagination, a quality of spirit, is the power of making fictions and making sense of life by that means. Fiction is the most available form of freedom, freedom of feeling and action." This emphasis places Donoghue squarely in the tradition of Coleridge and the "sceptical" romantics, Santayana and Wallace Stevens, whom he quotes with increasing frequency (the title of the book comes from Stevens, as does the phrase "ferocious alphabets," which becomes the title of his most recent study). It is still possible to find a few poets concerned with the imagination, he observes, "but they rarely construe it as the essential power." Among the critics, even I.A. Richards, who devoted a major book to the imagination (*Coleridge on Imagination*), reduced the faculty to a biological mechanism "without mystery or privilege." It is the structuralists, however, whom Donoghue is most interested in opposing here. The argument is a long and complex one, but basically Donoghue objects to the view which makes language itself a determining force, prior in importance to the creative speech of the individual. The structuralists "would displace man from the creative center of experience and make him rather a function of certain governing systems or [linguistic] codes." The "I" of Roland Barthes, for example, is "merely the sum of occasions" which the codes have provided. We no longer create, in this view: we do not speak language but, in Heidegger's well-known phrase, language speaks us. The threat to our image of man is a serious one: we are the prisoner of the codes, and possibly Donoghue means us to think of another well-known passage, this time from Nietzsche, and protest against its implications: "We have to cease to think if we refuse to do it in the prison-house of language; for we cannot reach further than the doubt which asks whether the limit we see is really a limit."

Donoghue continues his opposition to the structuralists (and now the post-structuralists, as represented by Jacques Derrida) with commanding authority and wit in his most impressive book to date, *Ferocious Alphabets*. Donoghue begins with the argument that conversation is the "privileged mode of language." Following Plato (in the *Phaedrus*) he maintains that only in the active cooperation of two concerned parties is the truth gained, and more important, mutually shared. The position is as much ethical as it is philosophical:

What happens in a conversation? Each person describes or tries to make manifest his own experience: the other, listening, cannot share the experience, but he can perceive it, as if at a distance.... What makes a conversation memorable is the desire of each person to share experience with the other, giving and receiving.... The perfect companion in speech, as Barthes says in *Fragments d'un discours amoureux*, is the one who constructs around you the greatest possible resonance; friendship is a space with "total sonority." Such words as *communion, company, community* and *communication* testify to that resonance, or rather the desire for it; they try to extend the range of a voice, making it reach the other.

Donoghue then divides a number of influential writers and thinkers into two groups, according to the ways in which they honor or reject this goal of communion. On one side are the "epireaders" of literature (here he selects Gerard Manley Hopkins, Georges Poulet, Kenneth Burke, Paul Ricoeur, Richard Poirier and, rather surprisingly, Harold Bloom), for whom writing is also a form of ethical activity respecting the individual voice:

> Epireading is not willing to leave the written words as it finds them on the page; the reader wants to restore the words to a source, a human situation involving speech, character, personality, and destiny construed as having a personal form.... The only requirement in epireading is that reading be construed as a personal encounter, the reader enters into a virtual relation with the speaker. Knowledge arises in the sense of coming to know a person, rather than in the sense of discovering a secret.

On the other side are the "graphireaders," represented by Mallarmé, Derrida, Roland Barthes, Paul de Man, and Lucette Finas. Like the structuralists of *The Sovereign Ghost*, their concern is with the impersonal force—and tyranny—of linguistic forms, not with individual creative meaning. What makes Paul de Man, for example, a graphireader?

> One: he refuses to admit that the work of art is made by an artist who has chosen, from among the linguistic materials available, the particular components he needs. Two: he ascribes to Language the life an epireader would ascribe to the artist. And as a result he transfers to an examination of linguistic tropes the interest an epireader would bring to an examination of the artist's attitudes and gestures. Three: when he moves from a consideration of Language to a consideration of voice or speech, the movement is made with reluctance amounting to distress.

Is it necessary to choose between these two kinds of readers? Perhaps not, in theory, but in practice Donoghue chooses Burke over Derrida "because I prefer to live in conditions as far as possible free, unprescribed, undogmatic. Burke would let me practice a mind of my own; Derrida would not." The conclusion of *Ferocious Alphabets* (the title refers to the competing systems of modern "reading") is frankly, joyously polemical:

> What is the point of writing these sentences in *Ferocious Alphabets*? Only this: I detest the current ideology which refers, gloatingly, to the death of the author, the obsolescence of self, the end of man, and so forth.... The imagination is real; that is, we have a faculty it is reasonable to call mind, and the mind acts in conditions of such freedom as it needs.

EAGLETON, Terry (Francis).   British.   Born in Salford, Lancashire, 22 February 1943. Educated at De La Salle College, Salford, and Trinity College, Cambridge, 1961-64, B.A. 1964, Ph.D., 1969. Married Rosemary Galpin; has 2 children. Research Fellow and Tutorial Fellow, Jesus College, Cambridge, 1964-69. Since 1969, Fellow and Tutor in English, Wadham College, Oxford. Visiting Professor, University of Odensk, Denmark, 1975, University of California at San Diego, 1976, University of Iowa, Iowa City, 1977, and Cornell University, Ithaca, New York, 1980. Address: Wadham College, Oxford University, Oxford OX1 3BD, England.

PUBLICATIONS

Criticism

> *Shakespeare and Society: Critical Studies in Shakespearean Drama.*   London, Chatto
>   and Windus, and New York, Schocken, 1967.
> *Exiles and Émigrés: Studies in Modern Literature.*   London, Chatto and Windus, and
>   New York, Schocken, 1970.
> *Myths of Power: A Marxist Study of the Brontës.*   London, Macmillan, and New York,
>   Harper, 1975.
> *Criticism and Ideology: A Study in Marxist Literary Theory.*   London, New Left Books,
>   1976.
> *Marxism and Literary Criticism.*   London, Methuen, and Berkeley, University of Cali-
>   fornia Press, 1976.
> "Ideology, Fiction, Narrative," in *Social Text* (Madison, Wisconsin), 2, 1979.
> "Text, Ideology, Realism," in *Literature and Society: Selected Papers from the English
>   Institute*, edited by Edward W. Said.   Batimore and London, Johns Hopkins Press,
>   1980.
> *Walter Benjamin; or, Towards a Revolutionary Criticism.*   London, New Left Books,
>   1981.
> "The Idealism of American Criticism," in *New Left Review* (London), 127, 1981.

Other

> *The New Left Church.*   London, Sheed and Ward, 1966.
> *The Body as Language: Outline of a "New Left" Theology.*   London, Sheed and Ward,
>   1970.

> Editor, *Directions: Pointers for the Post-Conciliar Church.*   London, Sheed and Ward,
>   1968.
> Editor, with Brian Wicker, *From Culture to Revolution: The Slant Symposium.*   Lon-
>   don, Sheed and Ward, 1968.

*   *   *

Who are the major Marxist aestheticians of the twentieth century? Terry Eagleton asks this
question in his most recent book, *Walter Benjamin or Towards a Revolutionary Criticism*, and
promptly gives this forthright answer: "Lukács, Goldmann, Sartre, Caudwell, Adorno, Mar-
cuse, Della Volpe, Macherey, Jameson, Eagleton." Perhaps this is not the way academic writers
are supposed to talk, but neither is it really immodest or unjustified, since more than any other
British or American critic, Eagleton has been intent on using Marxism as a way of forging a
genuine "science of the text" which will transcend the ideological distortions of other systems.
    Eagleton never mentions Marxism by name in his first book, *Shakespeare and Society*, but
its presence can be felt there nonetheless. Although modern psychology and sociology have
taught us there can be no simple dividing line between society and the individual, it is still
possible, Eagleton argues here, to see in our time as in Shakespeare's time a "repressive
mechanism" which "*by definition* threatens individual authenticity" (that "mechanism" is of
course the class system fostered by capitalism). In this book, Eagleton goes on,

> I try to show the tension in some of Shakespeare's plays between the self as it seems to a
> man in its personal depth, and as it seems in action, to others, as part of and responsible
> to a whole society. Shakespeare lives the experience, both of breakdown and of healing,
> in an intense form: the effort to reconcile spontaneous life and social responsibility is,
> with him, a persistent concern.

He then examines the fatal divisions between individualism and social responsibility in *Troilus*, *Hamlet*, *Macbeth* and *Antony and Cleopatra* and concludes that in the world of these plays there can be no solution or "healing." In the world of the visionary late comedies, however, he finds "a deep sense of the connectedness of lives":

> Personal life is not independent of the community; it is derived from it, and survives only in terms of it. Similarly, the community survives only in terms of the personal lives which create and sustain it; the life of a whole society is dependent for its quality on the lives of particular individuals within it, individuals who focus and embody common feelings.

What permits this new synthesis or fusion is the presence of "Grace" and "Virtue":

> Grace, for the Christian, means that personal authenticating of the law which binds together the community, in a way which makes it natural and spontaneous to act responsibly; to have grace is to make the law part of one's own life so that one's most authentic self-expression is in terms of others, in terms of society. Virtue is the habit of goodness, good actions spontaneously done without hesitation.

Eagleton concludes his chapter on the comedies with a question which was clearly important to him at the time: "Whether this kind of exploration can be done only within a Christian context, whether grace and virtue must be accepted in a specific sense, remains controversial." By "specific sense" here Eagleton apparently means the literal sense or *truth* of Christian doctrine; and there seems to be no doubt that in his next two books he was able to accept as complementary the truths of both Christian doctrine and Marxism. In *The New Left Church* he states flatly

> If Christ is the meaning of community, to create community now in the world is to be in touch with the reality of history in the Marxist sense of "reality", in contact with the definitive, significant direction of that history. When the Christian does good—creates community—he is progressive, bearing the meaning of history in him and enacting it, as the Marxist who builds community within capitalism is progressive.

The program of Marxism, he concludes in *The Body as Language*, is

> nothing less than the total abolition of the alienations between man and man, man and his world, man and himself. With the emergence of captialism came a massive and widespread extension of social communications, a definitive transformation of human and natural relations causing profound dislocation and estrangement. The surmounting of these estrangements—the construction of human community—is the project of revolutionary socialism; it is also, I suggest, the project of the Christian church. It seem to me that the church has no proprietary revolutionary strategy of its own; nor can it offer any 'third way' between revolution and reaction. It must opt for one or the other, and that option is, in the end, the sole test of its contemporary relevance.

This is so forcefully put that the abrupt and complete disappearance of all references to Christian doctrine and the church in Eagleton's subsequent criticism is all the more striking. It may indicate a loss of personal faith—and in any event was decisive enough to permit him to refer to *The Body as Language* recently as merely "a minor curio of the Marxist-theological tradition."

In *Exiles and Émigrés* Eagleton takes up the puzzling question of why it is that the most significant writers in twentieth century English literature were a Pole (Conrad), three Americans (James, Pound and Eliot), two Irishmen (Joyce and Yeats), and one Englishman from the hardly less remote world of the working class, D.H. Lawrence. The great English writers of the nineteenth century were great because they had the combination of sympathetic understanding and critical distance to grasp their world as a totality:

> It is part of the genius of poets like Blake and Wordsworth, or novelists like Dickens and George Eliot, that they are able to fuse the profoundest in inwardness with the specific life of their own times with a capacity to generalise that life into the form of a complete

vision.... The Romantic poet or the great realist novelist writes out of a relationship of intricately detailed intimacy with his society; yet he is also able to grasp that society as a totality, in a way which one might have expected to be genuinely available only to an outsider free of its most immediate pressures.... At the height of their developments, both realism and Romanticism were able to discover...a point of balance at which inwardness could combine with an essential externality to produce great art.

This capacity to grasp and totalize society was precisely what English life in the early years of the twentieth century and especially after the first World War did not permit: as social tensions increased and class lines hardened, there developed on the one hand the "lower middle-class novel" of Gissing, Bennett, Wells and Orwell, and on the other hand the "upper-class novel" of Forster and Woolf:

The lower middle-class novel was in general *passively* related to its society: it was a sympton of oppression and frustration, but could not itself transcend the direct pressures of that experience to evaluate it as a whole. The upper-class novel, by contrast, was trapped, not within the crippling limits of routine existence, but within a world so partial, rarified and fragmentary that it could express little more than the relatively untypical living of a rootless, dispossessed sector of the dominant social class.

Moreover, the impoverishment of native English literature at this time comes from factors which Eagleton calls "structural rather than accidental," and by "structural" he means the repressive economic structure fostered by capitalism. The "outsiders," however, the exiles and émigrés, had some independence: they were able to escape restrictive class ideologies and had other resources which gave them at least a degree of genuine detachment and sympathetic penetration.

Criticism and Ideology is a full-fledged, fully committed Marxist analysis of the ideological basis of literature, tortuously written and stridently aggressive at times (Eagleton has particularly harsh things to say about F.R. Leavis and Raymond Williams, who stop short of "revolutionary socialism"). By ideology Eagleton means, of course, the whole set of "ideas, values and feelings by which men experience their societies at various times." The crucial point is that ideologies belong to the superstructure of society and not to the real base, the hard economic facts concerning the means of production, distribution of wealth and class structure present during a given time. In capitalist society these facts must be hidden or masked by the official ideologies of the time, which in turn permeate every aspect of cultural life, including literature and the way we talk about it. Marxism, however, puts itself in a privileged position: it springs from but is not trapped or deluded by history; it somehow knows better than other views of life which are merely ideological. But on what basis does it see and know more about the true nature of things? Unlike some Marxists, Eagleton at least raises this critical question:

It is the task of Marxist criticism...to recognize its own historical determinants, but to demonstrate that its validity is not identical with them. In the case of Marxism, however, this demonstration is especially difficult. For historical materialism stands or falls by the claim that it is not only not an ideology, but that it contains a scientific theory of the genesis, structure and decline of ideologies. It situates itself, in short, outside the terrain of competing "long perspectives" in order to theorize the conditions of their very possibility. This, doubtless, seems a somewhat unfair, deftly convenient advantage to claim over the adherents of such alternative methods.

There is a poignancy about that dying fall of a phrase, "somewhat unfair," and possibly Eagleton intends this note of uncertainty. But he does not really answer the question or even return to it in *Criticism and Ideology*: all one can say, perhaps, is that a belief in the privileged objectivity of Marxism is precisely that, an article of faith or belief, though not necessarily wrong for that reason.

In any event, a true "science of the text" would presuppose a systematic inquiry into the various ways in which ideologies condition literary works—an extremely complex matter for Eagleton, who steadfastly refuses to make the usual Marxist reduction of texts to mere "reflections" or "expressions" of prevailing ideologies. Nor does he pretend to be establishing such a science himself, in *Criticism and Ideology*. In the long chapter here called "Categories for a Materialist Criticism," he explores in general terms the shifting relations between "overde-termined" texts (texts, that is, which result from a multiplicity or "causes") and five major determinants: societal modes of production, societal ideology, literary modes of production, authorial ideology and aesthetic ideology. Fully worked out, of course, a science of texts would be of great value to Marxists, since literature itself, according to Eagleton,

> is the most revealing mode of experiential access to ideology that we possess. It is in literature, above all, that we observe in a peculiarly complex, coherent, intensive and immediate fashion the workings of ideologies in the textures of lived experience of class-societies. It is a mode of access more immediate than that of science, and more coherent than that normally available in daily living itself. Literature presents itself in this sense as 'midway' between the distancing rigour of scientific knowledge and the vivid but loose contingencies of the 'lived' itself. Unlike science, literature appropriates the real as it is given in ideological forms, but does so in a way which produces the illusion of the spontaneously, unmediatedly real.... Like private property, the literary text thus appears as a 'natural' object, typically denying the determinants of its productive process. The function of criticism is to refuse the spontaneous presence of the work—to deny that 'naturalness' in order to make its real determinants appear.

The most difficult problem Eagleton has had to consider in his work thus far follows directly from the relationshiip between the descriptive findings of such a science and the question which has always concerned traditional criticism most, namely the matter of intrinsic literary value. A science of texts might be admirably descriptive, demonstrating the unexpected ways in which ideologies inhere in texts from the past. It could very probably alert us to the hidden forms ideologies are assuming at the present time. But could any text, from this point of view, have continuing value for the future, when the long history of human exploitation and alienation is finally over? Are texts destined to wither away with the state and Marxism itself, once the truly just, classless society is established? How will such a society value literature? At the end of *Criticism and Ideology* Eagleton faces the issue, but his answer, if it can be called an answer, is shrouded in self-defeating prose:

> Literature is a peculiar mode of linguistic organization which, by a particular 'distur-bance' of conventional modes of signification, so foregrounds certain modes of sense-making as to allow us to perceive the ideology in which they inhere. Such foregrounding is at once constructed artifice and experiential enticement swallowing the reader into a play of signs which is seductive in proportion to its 'unnaturalness'. The text is a theatre which doubles, prolongs, compacts and variegates its signs, shaking them free from single determinants, merging and eliding them with a freedom unknown to history, in order to draw the reader into deeper experiential entry into the space thereby created.

The phrase "play of signs" suggests a certain debt to Jacques Derrida (whose radical scepticism, however, Eagleton now rejects) and especially to Roland Barthes, for whom literature ought to provide a kind of blissful, creative free fall through texts from which authorial meanings and intentions have been detached. The nature of Eagleton's "space" is far from clear, but the phrase "unknown to history" takes us closer to his meaning, which is simply that we are in no position as yet to know what the new society will be like and are thus wise to remain "silent" about its aesthetic—and moral—values:

> Men do not live by culture alone: far from it. But the claim of historical materialism is that, in effect, they will. Once emancipated from material scarcity, liberated from labour, they will live in a play of their mutual significations, move in the ceaseless 'excess' of freedom.... Yet if Marxism has maintained a certain silence about aesthetic value, it may well be because the material conditions which would make such a discourse fully possible do not as yet exist. The same holds true for 'morality':if Marxism has little directly to say about the 'moral', one reason for this obliquity is that one does not engage in moral debate with those for whom morality can only mean moralism.... It is, perhaps,

in the provisional, strategic silence of those who refuse to speak 'morally' and 'aesthetically' that something of the true meaning of both terms is articulated.

Criticism and Ideology, Eagleton explains in the preface to *Walter Benjamin or Towards a Revolutionary Criticism*, was a "theoretical" work, written at a time when Marxist criticism "had little anchorage in Britain" and there was a need to "systematize the categories necessary for a 'science of the text.' " "I would still defend the principle of that project," he goes on, "but it is perhaps no longer the focal concern of Marxist cultural studies. Partly under the pressure of global capitalist crisis, partly under the influence of new themes and forces within socialism, the centre of such studies is shifting from narrowly textual or conceptual analysis to problems of cultural production and the political use of artefacts." Though hardly a revolutionist's handbook, Eagleton's most recent work, inspired by the quixotic mixture of idealism and Marxism in the esoteric criticism of Walter Benjamin, is intended to be a "practical" study. Instead of worrying about theoretical issues, Eagleton suggests, the Marxist critic now has other possibilities to consider:

> There is...an alternative narrative to Caudwell on Donne and Kristeva on Mallarmé—to that academicist project, encircled by strange cross-currents of Stalinism and idealism, that has passed for a 'Marxist aesthetics'. There are also those astonishing moments in post-revolutionary Russia when at the Moscow State Theatre you might find Meyerhold at work on a play with music by Shostakovitch, script by Shklovsky, Mayakovsky or Tretyakov, film-effects by Eisenstein, designs by Tatlin.... Or the moment of Erwin Piscator in the 1920s at the SPD theatre in Berlin, where you might find him directing a play in which Brecht had a hand, with music by Eisler or Weill, film-effects by Grosz, stage designs by Moholy-Nagy, Otto Dix or John Heartfield.

The proper job now of the Marxist critic is "to actively participate in and help direct the cultural emancipation of the masses":

> the organizing of writers' workshops, artists' studios and popular theatre; the transformation of the cultural and educational apparatuses; the business of public design and architecture; a concern with the quality of quotidian life all the way from public discourse to domestic 'consumption': in short all of the projects on which Lenin, Trotsky, Krupskaya, Lunacharsky and others of the Bolsheviks were intensively engaged remain, for all the differences of historical situation, the chief responsibilities of a revolutionary cultural theory.

To what extent is Eagleton hopeful about the future of revolutionary socialism? It is not easy to tell at the moment, but perhaps the following, rather subdued passage from this recent book will provide as much of an answer as a future-oriented philosophy of history like Marxism will tolerate:

> Nobody becomes a socialist simply because he or she is convinced by the materialist theory of history or moved by the persuasive elegance of Marx's economic equations. Ultimately, the only reason for being a socialist is that one objects to the fact that the great majority of men and women in history have lived lives of suffering and degradation, and believes that this may conceivably be altered in the future.

EDEL, (Joseph) Leon. American. Born in Pittsburgh, Pennsylvania, 9 September 1907. Educated at McGill University, Montreal, B.A. 1927, M.A. 1928; University of Paris, Docteur-ès-Lettres, 1932. Served in the United States Army, 1943-47: First Lieutenant, Bronze Star.

Married Roberta Roberts in 1950. Instructor, McGill University, 1927-38; Assistant Professor, Sir George Williams College, Montreal, 1932-34; Visiting Professor, 1950-52, Associate Professor, 1954-55, Professor, 1955-66, and Henry James Professor of English and American Letters, 1966-73, now Emeritus, New York University. Since 1971, Citizens Professor of English, University of Hawaii, Honolulu. Christian Gauss Lecturer in Criticism, Princeton University, New Jersey, 1952-53; Visiting Professor, Indiana University, Bloomington, 1954-55, and University of Hawaii, 1955, 1969-70; Alexander Lecturer, University of Toronto, 1955-56; Visiting Professor, Harvard University, Cambridge, Massachusetts, 1959-60, Center for Advanced Study, Wesleyan University, Middletown, Connecticut, 1965, and University of Toronto, 1967. President of the United States Center of P.E.N., 1957-59. Recipient: Guggenheim Fellowship, 1936, 1937, 1965; Bollingen Foundation Fellowship, 1958-61; National Institute of Arts and Letters Grant, 1959, and Gold Medal, 1976; Pulitzer Prize in Biography, 1963; National Book Award for Non-Fiction, 1963; American Academy of Arts and Letters Grant, 1972; National Arts Club Gold Medal, 1981. Litt.D.: McGill University, 1972; Union College, Schenectady, New York, 1972. Member, American Academy of Arts and Letters, and American Academy of Arts and Sciences; Fellow, Royal Society of Literature; Honorary Member, William Allen White Psychoanalytic Society. Address: Department of English, University of Hawaii, Honolulu, Hawaii 96822, U.S.A.

PUBLICATIONS

Criticism

Henry James: Les Années Dramatiques.   Paris, Jouve, 1931; Folcroft, Pennsylvania, Folcroft Editions, 1969.
The Prefaces of Henry James.   Paris, Jouve, 1931; Folcroft, Pennsylvania, Folcroft Editions, 1970.
James Joyce: The Last Journey.   New York, Gotham Book Mart, 1947.
Henry James: The Untried Years 1843-1870.   Philadelphia, Lippincott, and London, Hart Davis, 1953.
The Psychological Novel: 1900-1950.   Philadelphia, Lippincott, and London, Hart Davis, 1955; as *The Modern Psychological Novel*, New York, Grove Press, 1959; revised edition, New York, Grosset and Dunlap, 1964.
Literary Biography: The Alexander Lectures, 1955-56.   Toronto, University of Toronto Press, London, Hart Davis, and New York, Doubleday, 1957.
Willa Cather: The Paradox of Success.   Washington D.C., Library of Congress, 1960.
Henry James: The Conquest of London 1870-1881.   Philadelphia, Lippincott, and London, Hart Davis, 1962.
Henry James: The Middle Years 1882-1895.   Philadelphia, Lippincott, and London, Hart Davis, 1962.
The Age of the Archive.   Middletown, Connecticut, Wesleyan University Center for Advanced Study, 1966.
Henry James: The Treacherous Years 1895-1901.   Philadelphia, Lippincott, and London, Hart Davis, 1969.
Henry D. Thoreau.   Minneapolis, University of Minnesota Press, 1970.
Henry James: The Master 1901-1916.   Philadelphia, Lippincott, and London, Hart Davis, 1972.
"Biography: A Manifesto," in *Biography: An Interdisciplinary Quarterly* (Honolulu, Hawaii), 1, 1978.
"The Figure Under the Carpet," in *Telling Lives: The Biographer's Art*, edited by Marc Pachter.   Washington, D.C., New Republic Books, 1979.
Bloomsbury: A House of Lions.   Philadelphia, Lippincott, and London, Hogarth, 1979.

Other

Willa Cather: A Critical Study, by E.K. Brown (completed by Leon Edel).   New York, Knopf, 1953.

Editor, *The Ghostly Tales of Henry James*.   New Brunswick, New Jersey, Rutgers University Press, 1949.
Editor, *The Complete Plays of Henry James*.   Philadelphia, Lippincott, and London, Hart Davis, 1949.
Editor, *Selected Fiction*, by Henry James.   New York, Dutton, 1953.
Editor, *Selected Letters of Henry James*.   New York, Farrar Straus, 1955; London, Hart Davis, 1956.
Editor, *The Portrait of a Lady*, by Henry James.   Boston, Houghton Mifflin, 1956.
Editor, *The Future of the Novel: Essays on the Art of Fiction*, by Henry James.   New York, Vintage, 1966; as *The House of Fiction: Essays on the Novel*, London, Hart Davis, 1957.
Editor, *The American Essays*, by Henry James.   New York, Vintage, 1966.
Editor, with Dan H. Laurence, *A Bibliography of Henry James*.   London, Hart Davis, 1957; revised edition, 1961.
Editor, with Ilse D. Lind, *Parisian Sketches: Letters to the New York Tribune, 1875-1876*, by Henry James.   New York, New York University Press, 1957; London, Hart Davis, 1958.
Editor, with Gordon Ray, *Henry James and H.G. Wells: A Record of Their Friendship, Their Debate on the Art of Fiction, and Their Quarrel*.   Urbana, University of Illinois Press, and London, Hart Davis, 1958.
Editor, with others, *Masters of American Literature*.   Boston, Houghton Mifflin, 1959.
Editor, *The Sacred Fount*, by Henry James.   London, Hart Davis, 1959.
Editor, *Roderick Hudson*, by Henry James.   New York, Harper, 1960; London, Hart Davis, 1961.
Editor, *Guy Domville*, by Henry James.   Philadelphia, Lippincott, 1960; London, Hart Davis, 1961.
Editor, *The Tragic Muse*, by Henry James.   New York, Harper, 1960.
Editor, *Watch and Ward*, by Henry James.   New York, Grove Press, and London, Hart Davis, 1960.
Editor, *The Ambassadors*, by Henry James.   Boston, Houghton Mifflin, 1960.
Editor, *The Complete Tales of Henry James*.   Philadelphia, Lippincott, and London, Hart Davis, 12 vols., 1962-1964.
Editor, *The American*, by Henry James.   New York, New American Library, 1963.
Editor, *Henry James: A Collection of Critical Essays*.   Englewood Cliffs, New Jersey, Prentice Hall, 1963.
Editor, *French Poets and Novelists*, by Henry James.   New York, Grosset and Dunlap, 1964.
Editor, *The Diary of Alice James*.   New York, Dodd Mead, 1964; London, Hart Davis, 1965.
Editor, with others, *Literary History and Literary Criticism*.   New York, New York University Press, 1965.
Editor, *The Henry James Reader*.   New York, Scribner, 1965.
Editor, *The Spoils of Poynton*, by Henry James.   London, Hart Davis, 1967.
Editor, *The American Scene*, by Henry James.   Bloomington, Indiana University Press, and London, Hart Davis, 1968.
Editor, *Henry James: Letters: 1843-1875*.   Cambridge, Massachusetts, Belknap Press, and London, Macmillan, 1974.
Editor, *Henry James: Letters: 1875-1883*.   Cambridge, Massachusetts, Belknap Press, 1975; London, Macmillan, 1978.
Editor, *The Twenties: From Notebooks and Diaries of the Period*, by Edmund Wilson.   New York, Farrar Straus, and London, Macmillan, 1975.
Editor, *The Thirties: From Notebooks and Diaries of the Period*, by Edmund Wilson.   New York, Farrar Straus, and London, Macmillan, 1980.

Editor, *Henry James: Letters: 1883-1895.*   Cambridge, Massachusetts, Belknap Press, 1980; London, Macmillan, 1981.

*   *   *

Anyone interested in Henry James, or in human nature, should read Leon Edel's massive biography, and having done so, should then consider the ethical and critical problems it raises. Assuming for the moment that those two kinds of questions can be separated, what are the ethics of such relentless and triumphantly successful spying on one of God's spies? James himself had no doubts: he often requested—often enough in vain— that the recipient of a letter "burn this" and tried to render his correspondents the same courtesy. As Edel tells us in *Literary Biography*, James

> had his correspondence of forty years heaped upon a great roaring fire in his garden at Lamb House, in Sussex, and watched its progress from paper to ash. Like his own character in *The Aspern Papers* he could boast "I have done the great thing."... It is quite clear that Henry James, warming his hands by the fire of Lamb House, would have exclaimed with Dickens who lit a similar blaze at Gad's Hill: "Would to God every letter I have ever written were on that pile." But think of the irony: while Dickens and James, both prolific letter writers, burned letters that would have illuminated many other lives and done service in other biographies, they could do little about those which illuminate their own and which today turn up in such numbers.

Irony indeed. In *The Aspern Papers* Miss Bordereau, if not James himself, calls the prying editor a "publishing scoundrel"; and in a later story another ambitious would-be biographer does "the real right thing"—after a few warning appearances by the ghost of his subject, an artist who, like James, felt that the writer "is what he *did*." Ideally, society should be the "land of consideration." Theodora Bosanquet recalls that James' utopia was a realm of privacy and freedom in which no one was responsible "for anyone else or for anything else save his own civilized behavior." But if Edel has seen any ghosts during the forty-odd years he has been pursuing James, he has not been frightened.

In the course of his biography Edel uncovers James' strange and finally tragic relationship (or lack of relationship) with Constance Fenimore Woolson, his homoerotic attachment to Hendrik Christian Andersen and other young men, and a host of matters James would have been horrified to see handed about for inspection. Given the detective skills and increasing frankness of modern biographers it is hardly surprising that Auden asked his friends to burn any letters they might have from him or that George Orwell and T.S. Eliot requested their executors *not* to cooperate with any prospective "biografiend," as Joyce called the breed. Considering the depressing impertinences of Robert Craft, Robert Sencourt and T.S. Matthews, perhaps D.J. Enright is right when he states that it is better for the artist to insist that his biography be written "as expeditiously as possible—and by a fellow-writer." A fellow-writer and a friend, preferably, but even this is no guarantee. If Boswell doesn't tell us about Dr. Johnson urging Mrs. Thrale to whip his bare back, then someone else will. The moral seems obvious: the artist must expect that anything he does or does not do will sooner or later be common knowledge. The great writer and his audience, the rest of us with our family and friends, everyone is the victim of that venerable psychoanalytic gag: if you walk down the Ringstrasse with someone, then obviously you're having an affair; if you go walking there alone—well, the meaning of that is sadly clear too. As James observed about the unspecified horrors of *The Turn of the Screw*, silence can be more provocative than disclosure.

The high moral tone of these remarks is no doubt too high for this world, but the critical problems raised by literary biography are clear enough. Since Aristotle it has been common practice to justify art as a source of legitimate pleasure and knowledge not easily come by elsewhere. Poetry is more philosophic than history: the artist takes historical or imagined particulars and makes them represent the universal, the necessary and the probable in human affairs. As early as 1865 James had criticized Dickens for failing in this respect:

> Mr. Dickens is a great observer and a great humorist, but he is nothing of a philosopher. Some people may hereupon say, so much the better; we say, so much the worse. For a

novelist very soon has need of a little philosophy. In treating of Micawber, and Boffin, and Pickwick, *et hoc genus omne*, he can, indeed, dispense with it, for this—we say with all deference—is not serious writing. But when he comes to tell the story of a passion, a story like that of Headstone and Wrayburn, he becomes a moralist as well as an artist. He must know *man* as well *men*, and to know man is to be a philosopher.... [All] his humor, all his fancy, will avail him nothing if, out of the fulness of his sympathy, he is unable to prosecute those generalizations in which alone consists the real greatness of a work of art.

Edel is certainly aware of the problem, but no matter how conscious he may be of the issues at stake, the effect of his biography is to dissolve James' work back into the stream of his life, to turn art back into history and thereby impair for many of his readers its proper generalizing force. And at times it almost seems as if art, for Edel, exists to serve biography: "To read between the lines of the best literature," he writes, "can indeed be one of the most absorbing pursuits in the world: to catch the flickering vision behind the metaphor, to touch the very pulse of the hand that holds the pen—that is what the biographer attempts." There is an equally revealing passage in *The Psychological Novel*:

> In *Honeycomb*, the third chapter or volume of her *Pilgrimage*, Dorothy Richardson's heroine, Miriam Henderson, makes a discovery while she is reading a book. It is that "I don't read books for the story, but as a psychological study of the author." Books come to mean to her "not the people in the books, but knowing, absolutely, everything about the author.... In life everything was so scrappy and mixed up. In a book the author was there in every word."

But knowing the pattern of an individual life, Edel suggests, is not an end in itself. Just as art may serve the ends of biography, so biography in turn may serve still larger ends. Thus at the conclusion of *Literary Biography* Edel observes that the biographer "throws open a window upon *a* life and thereby opens it upon life itself. Endless are the views and vistas. And I would say that we could sum up the process of gaining such a view in three simple words: understanding, sympathy, illumination." But surely if we have to go to the writer's *life* for "understanding, sympathy, illumination," then he has failed in his primary responsibility as an artist.

All biography is critical in the sense that it assumes principles of causation and selection, and here Edel is Freudian in an orthodox and uncomplicated way. The artist creates because he is driven to compensate for some lack in his "real," everyday life. Thus Edel observes that James dealt with the "frustrations of his juniorhood"—his sense of inferiority to his older and more outgoing brother William—by fashioning a fictional world "based on the realities around him in which older brothers were vanquished, fathers made to disappear, mothers put in their place." The biographer, like the analyst, seizes upon dreams, slips of the tongue or pen, and related phenomena as a means of getting at the situation for which the artistic symbol is a disguise or compensation. Attempting to account for James' celibacy, for example, Edel speculates about James' interpretation of his parents' relationship and concludes that as a child the novelist came to see marriage as a threat to life itself. Supporting this argument he then turns to a list of names James jotted down in his notebooks many years later, a list in which he included the word "Ledward"

> and then, as was often his custom, he improvised several variants, apparently as they came into his mind: "Ledward—Bedward—Deadward." This appeared to be a casual rhyming of led-bed-dead. It was, in fact, a highly-condensed statement...of the theme of "De Grey," "Longstaff," *The Sacred Fount* or that story of Merimée's he had liked so much as a youth, "La Vénus d'Ille." To be led to the marriage bed was to be dead.

Henry James accordingly chose the path of safety. He remained celibate. This suggests that in some way James was "neurotic," but Edel refuses to concede this and follows Lionel Trilling's well-known argument that the artist is not possessed by but rather possesses his subject:

> Art is the result not of calm and tranquility.... It springs from tension and passion, from a

state of disequilibrium in the artist's being.... The psychoanalyst, reading the pattern of the work, can attempt to tell us what was wrong with the artist's mental or psychic health. The biographer, reading the same pattern in the larger picture of the human condition, seeks to show how the negatives were converted into positives.... [These works by Proust, Virginia Woolf and Joyce] are the triumphs of art over neurosis, and of literature over life.

Some readers have complained that the Freudian emphasis of *Henry James: The Untried Years* vanishes in the later volumes of Edel's biography, but this is only to be expected: once a causal pattern has been detected in the writer's childhood, there is no reason for a Freudian to search for other factors. At most the biographer will call attention to new disguises for old problems.

Edel maintains that the novel has always been "psychological," but in *The Psychological Novel* he is mainly concerned with the special means some modern artists have devised to give the illusion of an apparently unmediated glimpse into the actual workings of the mind. He discusses Joyce, Proust and Dorothy Richardson in some detail and traces their indebtedness to "those creators of the intellectual atmosphere"—primarily Bergson and William James—"in which the novel of subjectivity came into being." Edel's comments on technique are sound as far as they go, which is not very far at all (here the reader interested in the complex implications of modern fictional techniques should consult Wayne Booth's *The Rhetoric of Fiction*). Edel's brief attempts at literary history are equally sketchy. Modern psychological novelists, he asserts, are "children of the romantic century":

> rationalism and reason had long before yielded to introspection and feeling. If classicism was intellect and repose, romanticism was self-absorption and flux. The romantic hero began by contemplating his heart; he ended by contemplating his mind. And he discovered that heart, symbol of feeling and perception, and mind, symbol of thought and reason, could be closely related.

And yet these heirs of romanticism were also the exponents of a new kind of realism more "real" than the objective naturalism of Wells, Bennett and Galsworthy. Left at this level of generalization "realism" and "romanticism," like most of Edel's purely critical distinctions, are of limited value.

ELIOT, T(homas) S(tearns).   British.   Born in St. Louis, Missouri, U.S.A., 26 September 1888; naturalized, 1927. Educated at Smith Academy, St. Louis, 1898-1905; Milton Academy, Massachusetts, 1905-06; Harvard University, Cambridge, Massachusetts (Editor, *Harvard Advocate*, 1909-10; Sheldon Fellowship, for study in Munich, 1914), 1906-10, 1911-14, B.A. 1909, M.A. 1910; The Sorbonne, Paris, 1910-11; Merton College, Oxford, 1914-15. Married Vivienne Haigh-Wood in 1915 (died, 1947); Esmé Valerie Fletcher, 1957. Teacher, High Wycombe Grammar School, Buckinghamshire, and Highgate School, London, 1915-17; clerk, Lloyds Bank, London, 1917-25; Editor, later Director, Faber and Gwyer, later Faber and Faber, publishers, London, 1926-65. Assistant Editor, *The Egoist*, London, 1917-19; Founding Editor, *The Criterion*, London, 1922-39. Clark Lecturer. Trinity College, Cambridge, 1926; Charles Eliot Norton Professor of Poetry, Harvard University, 1932-33; Page-Barbour Lecturer, University of Virginia, Charlottesville, 1933; Theodore Spencer Memorial Lecturer, Harvard University, 1950. President, Classical Association, 1941, Virgil Society, 1943, and Books Across the Sea, 1943-46. Resident, Institute for Advanced Study, Princeton University, New Jersey, 1950; Honorary Fellow, Merton College, Oxford, and Magdalene College, Cambridge. Recipient: *The Dial* Award, 1922: Nobel Prize for Literature, 1948; The Order of Merit, 1948; New York Drama Critics Circle Award, 1950; Hanseatic Goethe Prize, 1954; Dante Gold Medal, Florence, 1959; Order of Merit, Bonn, 1959; American Academy of Arts and Sciences

Emerson-Thoreau Medal, 1960. Litt.D.: Columbia University, New York, 1933; Cambridge University, 1938; University of Bristol, 1938; University of Leeds, 1939; Harvard University, 1947; Princeton University, 1947; Yale University, New Haven, Connecticut, 1947; Washington University, St Louis, 1953; University of Rome, 1958; University of Sheffield, 1959; LL.D.: University of Edinburgh, 1937; St. Andrews University, 1953; D.Litt.: Oxford University. 1948; D.Lit.: University of London, 1950; Docteur-ès-Lettres, University of Aix-Marseille, 1959; University of Rennes, 1959; D.Phil.: University of Munich, 1959. Officer, Légion d' Honneur. Honorary Member, American Academy of Arts and Letters; Foreign Member, Accademia dei Lincei, Rome, and Akademie der Schönen Künste. *Died 4 January 1965.*

PUBLICATIONS

Criticism

> *Ezra Pound: His Metric and Poetry.*   New York, Knopf, 1918; reprinted in *To Criticize the Critic and Other Writings,* 1965.
> *The Sacred Wood: Essays on Poetry and Criticism.*   London, Methuen, 1920; New York, Knopf, 1921; reprinted in part in *Selected Essays,* 1932.
> *Homage to John Dryden: Three Essays on Poetry of the Seventeenth Century.*   London, Hogarth Press, 1924; included in *The Hogarth Essays,* New York, Doubleday, 1928; reprinted in *Selected Essays,* 1932.
> *Shakespeare and the Stoicism of Seneca* (lecture).   London, Oxford University Press, 1927; reprinted in *Selected Essays,* 1932.
> *For Lancelot Andrewes: Essays on Style and Order.*   London, Faber and Gwyer, 1928; New York, Doubleday, 1929; reprinted in part in *Selected Essays,* 1932.
> *Dante.*   London, Faber, 1929; reprinted in *Selected Essays,* 1932.
> *Selected Essays 1917-1932.*   London, Faber, and New York, Harcourt Brace, 1932; revised edition, Harcourt Brace, 1950; Faber, 1951.
> *John Dryden: The Poet, The Dramatist, The Critic.*   New York, Terence and Elsa Holliday, 1932.
> *The Use of Poetry and the Use of Criticism: Studies in the Relation of Criticism to Poetry in England.*   London, Faber, and Cambridge, Massachusetts, Harvard University Press, 1933.
> *After Strange Gods: A Primer of Modern Heresy.*   London, Faber, and New York, Harcourt Brace, 1934.
> *Elizabethan Essays.*   London, Faber, 1934; reprinted in part as *Essays on Elizabethan Drama,* New York, Harcourt Brace, 1956; as *Elizabethan Dramatists,* Faber, 1963.
> Introduction to *Selected Poems,* by Marianne Moore.   New York, Macmillan, and London, Faber, 1935.
> *Essays Ancient and Modern.*   London, Faber, and New York, Harcourt Brace, 1936; reprinted in part in *Selected Essays,* 1950.
> Introduction to *Nightwood,* by Djuna Barnes.   New York, Harcourt Brace, 1937; London, Faber, 1950.
> "A Note on Two Odes of Cowley," in *Seventeenth Century Studies Presented to Sir Herbert Grierson.*   Oxford, Clarendon Press, 1938.
> *Points of View,* edited by John Hayward.   London, Faber, 1941; Westport, Connecticut, Hyperion Press, 1979.
> *The Classics and the Man of Letters* (lecture).   London and New York, Oxford University Press, 1942.
> *The Music of Poetry* (lecture).   Glasgow, University Press, 1942; reprinted in *On Poetry and Poets,* 1957.
> *What Is a Classic?* (lecture).   London, Faber, 1945; reprinted in *On Poetry and Poets,* 1957.
> *On Poetry* (lecture).   Concord, Massachusetts, Concord Academy, 1947.

Milton (lecture).   London, Oxford University Press, 1947; New York (unauthorized edition), 1965; reprinted in *On Poetry and Poets*, 1957.

From Poet to Valéry (lecture).   New York, Harcourt Brace, 1948; reprinted in *To Criticize the Critic and Other Writings*, 1965.

The Aims of Poetic Drama (lecture).   London, Poets' Theatre Guild, 1949.

Poetry and Drama (lecture).   Cambridge, Massachusetts, Harvard University Press, and London, Faber, 1951.

American Literature and the American Language (lecture).   St. Louis, Washington University, 1953; reprinted in *To Criticize the Critic and Other Writings*, 1965.

The Three Voices of Poetry (lecture).   London, Cambridge University Press, 1953; New York, Cambridge University Press, 1954; reprinted in *On Poetry and Poets*, 1957.

Religious Drama, Mediaeval and Modern (lecture).   New York, House of Books, 1954.

The Literature of Politics (lecture).   London, Conservative Political Centre, 1955; reprinted in *To Criticize the Critics and Other Writings*, 1965.

The Frontiers of Criticism (lecture).   Minneapolis, University of Minnesota Press, 1956; reprinted in *On Poetry and Poets*, 1957.

On Poetry and Poets.   London, Faber, and New York, Farrar Straus, 1957.

Introduction to *The Art of Poetry*, by Paul Valéry.   New York, Pantheon Books, and London, Routledge, 1958.

George Herbert.   London, Longman, 1962; in *British Writers and Their Work 4*.   Lincoln, University of Nebraska Press, 1964.

To Criticize the Critic and Other Writings.   London, Faber, and New York, Farrar Straus, 1965.

Verse

Prufrock and Other Observations.   London, The Egoist, 1917.

Poems.   Richmond, Surrey, Hogarth Press, 1919.

Ara Vos Prec.   London, Ovid Press, 1920; as *Poems*, New York, Knopf, 1920.

The Waste Land.   New York, Boni and Liveright, 1922; Richmond, Surrey, Hogarth Press, 1923.

Poems 1909-1925.   London, Faber and Gwyer, 1925; New York, Harcourt Brace, 1932.

Journey of the Magi.   London, Faber and Gwyer, and New York, William Edwin Rudge, 1927.

A Song for Simeon.   London, Faber and Gwyer, 1928.

Animula.   London, Faber, 1929.

Ash-Wednesday.   New York, Foundation Press, and London, Faber, 1930.

Marina.   London, Faber, 1930.

Triumphal March.   London, Faber, 1931.

Sweeney Agonistes: Fragments of an Aristophanic Melodrama.   London, Faber, 1932.

Words for Music.   Bryn Mawr, Pennsylvania, privately printed, 1935.

Two Poems.   Cambridge, privately printed, 1935.

Collected Poems 1909-1935.   London, Faber, and New York, Harcourt Brace, 1939.

Old Possum's Book of Practical Cats.   London, Faber, and New York, Harcourt Brace, 1939.

The Waste Land and Other Poems.   London, Faber, 1940; New York, Harcourt Brace, 1955.

East Coker.   London, New English Weekly, 1940.

Later Poems, 1925-1935.   London, Faber, 1941.

The Dry Salvages.   London, Faber, 1941.

Little Gidding.   London, Faber, 1942.

Four Quartets.   New York, Harcourt Brace, 1943; London, Faber, 1944.

A Practical Possum.   Cambridge, Massachusetts, privately printed, 1947.

Selected Poems.   London, Penguin, 1948; New York, Harcourt Brace, 1967.

The Undergraduate Poems of T.S. Eliot.   Cambridge Massachusetts (unauthorized edition), 1949.

Poems Written in Early Youth, edited by John Hayward.   Stockholm, privately printed, 1950; London, Faber, and New York, Farrar Straus, 1967.

The Cultivation of Christmas Trees.   London, Faber, 1954; New York, Farrar Straus, 1956.

Collected Poems 1909-1962.   London, Faber, and New York, Harcourt Brace, 1963.

The Waste Land: A Facsimile and Transcript of the Original Drafts Including the Annotations of Ezra Pound, edited by Valerie Eliot.   London, Faber, and New York, Farrar Straus, 1971.

Plays

The Rock: A Pageant Play (produced London, 1934).   London, Faber, and New York, Harcourt Brace, 1934.

Murder in the Cathedral (produced Canterbury and London, 1935; New York, 1936).   London, Faber, and New York, Harcourt Brace, 1935; revised edition, as *The Film of Murder in the Cathedral*, with George Hoellering, 1952.

The Family Reunion (produced London, 1939; New York, 1947).   London, Faber, and New York, Harcourt Brace, 1939.

The Cocktail Party (produced Edinburgh, 1949; London and New York, 1950).   London, Faber, and New York, Harcourt Brace, 1950; revised edition, 1950.

The Confidential Clerk (produced Edinburgh and London, 1953; New York, 1954).   London, Faber, and New York, Harcourt Brace, 1954.

The Elder Statesman (produced Edinburgh and London, 1958).   London, Faber, and New York, Farrar Straus, 1959.

Collected Plays: Murder in the Cathedral, The Family Reunion, The Cocktail Party, The Confidential Clerk, The Elder Statesman.   London, Faber, 1962; as *The Complete Plays*, New York, Harcourt Brace, 1969.

Other

Thoughts after Lambeth.   London, Faber, 1931.

Charles Whibley: A Memoir (lecture).   London, Oxford University Press, 1931.

The Idea of a Christian Society.   London, Faber, 1939; New York, Harcourt Brace, 1940.

Reunion by Destruction: Reflections on a Scheme for Church Union in South India, Addressed to the Laity.   London, Council for the Defence of Church Principles, 1943.

Die Einheit der Europäischen Kultur.   Berlin, Carl Habel, 1946.

A Sermon Preached in Magdalene College Chapel.   Cambridge, privately printed, 1948.

Notes Towards the Definition of Culture.   London, Faber, 1948; New York, Harcourt Brace, 1949.

The Complete Poems and Plays.   New York, Harcourt Brace, 1952; London, Faber, 1969.

The Value and Use of of Cathedrals in England Today (lecture).   Chichester, Friends of Chichester Cathedral, 1952.

An Address to Members of the London Library.   London, London Library, 1952; Providence, Rhode Island, Providence Athenaeum, 1953.

Selected Prose, edited by John Hayward.   London, Penguin, 1953.

Geoffrey Faber 1889-1961 (address).   London, Faber, 1961.

Knowledge and Experience in the Philosophy of F.H. Bradley (doctoral dissertation).   London, Faber, and New York, Farrar Straus, 1964.

Selected Prose, edited by Frank Kermode.   London, Faber, and New York, Harcourt Brace, 1975.

Editor, *Selected Poems*, by Ezra Pound.   London, Faber and Gwyer, 1928; revised edition, London, Faber, 1949.

Editor, *A Choice of Kipling's Verse*.   London, Faber, 1941; New York, Scribner, 1943.

Editor, *Introducing James Joyce*.   London, Faber, 1942.

Editor, *Literary Essays of Ezra Pound*.   London, Faber, and New York, New Directions, 1954.

Editor, *The Criterion 1922-1939*.   London, Faber, and New York, Barnes and Noble, 18 vols., 1967.

Translator, *Anabasis: A Poem*, by St.-John Perse.   London, Faber, 1930; revised edition, New York, Harcourt Brace, 1938, 1949, Faber, 1959.

CRITICAL STUDIES AND BIBLIOGRAPHY

F.O. Matthiessen, *The Achievement of T.S. Eliot: An Essay on the Nature of Poetry*. London and New York, Oxford University Press, 1935; revised edition, 1947.

John Crowe Ransom, "T.S. Eliot: The Historical Critic," in *The New Criticism*.   New York, New Directions, 1941.

Yvor Winters, "T.S. Eliot; or, The Illusion of Reaction," in *The Anatomy of Nonsense*. New York, New Directions, 1943.

M.C. Bradbrook, "Eliot's Critical Method," in *T.S. Eliot: A Study of His Writings by Several Hands*, edited by B. Rajan.   London, Dobson, 1947.

Donald Gallup, *T.S. Eliot: A Bibliography*.   London, Faber, 1952; revised edition, Faber, and New York, Harcourt Brace, 1969.

Eliseo Vivas, "The Objective Correlative of T.S. Eliot," in *Creation and Discovery: Essays in Criticism and Aethetics*.   New York, Noonday Press, 1955.

René Wellek, "The Criticism of T.S. Eliot," in *Sewanee Review* (Tennessee), 64, 1956.

Herbert Howarth, *Notes on Some Figures Behind T.S. Eliot*.   Boston, Houghton Mifflin, 1964.

Fei-Pai Lu, *T.S. Eliot: The Dialectical Structure of His Theory of Poetry*.   Berkeley and London, University of California Press, 1965.

F.R. Leavis, "T.S. Eliot as Critic," in *Anna Karenina and Other Essays*.   London, Chatto and Windus, 1967; New York, Pantheon Books, 1968.

John D. Margolis, *T.S. Eliot's Intellectual Development, 1922-1939*.   Chicago, University of Chicago Press, 1969.

James Smith, "Notes of the Criticism of T.S. Eliot." in *Essays in Criticism* (Oxford), 22, 1972.

Lyndall Gordon, *Eliot's Early Years*.   New York, Oxford University Press, 1977.

David Newton-De Molina, editor, *The Literary Criticism of T.S. Eliot: New Essays*. London, Athlone Press, 1977.

Edward Lobb, *T.S. Eliot and the Romantic Critical Tradition*.   London, Kegan Paul, 1981.

*   *   *

T.S. Eliot's position as the most influential man of letters during the first half of this century now seems beyond dispute. Fully understood or not, his opinions, like his poems, were reverently received and endlessly quoted; and in America at least, his highly personal view of literary history came to dominate the university teaching of English literature in an unprecedented manner. Thus while the sharp decline in his reputation which began almost immediately after his death may or may not be permanent, it remains true that if we are to grasp what happened in criticism between the two World Wars, we must come to terms with Eliot's thinking. And as soon as we attempt to do so, there is a fundamental problem. To borrow an apt image Charles Rycroft uses in asking a similar question about Freud: does the body of Eliot's work represent an edifice or a quarry; is it a capacious, well-reasoned point of view which can be applied to new situations, or is it merely a heap of striking judgments, memorable phrases and impressive-sounding terms? Eliot himself seems to have had no illusions." I am not a systematic thinker," he wrote privately to Paul Elmer More in 1934, "if indeed I am a thinker at all. I depend upon intuitions and perceptions; and although I may have some skill in the barren game of controversy, [I] have little capacity for sustained, exact, and closely knit argument and reasoning." And on at least two public occasions he was equally frank. "The best of my *literary* criticism," he told an audience in 1956

> —apart from a few notorious phrases which have had a truly embarrassing success in the world—consists of essays on poets and poetic dramatists who had influenced me. It is a by-product of my private poetry-workshop: or a prolongation of the thinking that went into the formation of my own verse.... My criticism has this in common with that of Ezra Pound, that its merits and its limitations can be fully appreciated only when it is considered in relation to the poetry I have written myself.

A few years later he observed (in "To Criticize the Critic"):

> So far as I can judge...it is my earlier essays which have made the deeper impression. I attribute this to two causes. The first is the dogmatism of youth.... When we are young, we are confident in our opinons, sure that we possess the whole truth; we are enthusiastic, or indignant. And readers, even mature readers, are attacted to a writer who is quite sure of himself. The second reason for the enduring popularity of some of my early criticism is less easily apprehended, especially by readers of a younger generation. It is that in my earlier criticism...I was implicitly defending the sort of poetry that I and my friends wrote. This gave my essays a kind of urgency, the warmth of appeal of the advocate, which my later, more detached and I hope more judicial essays cannot claim. I was in reaction, not only against Georgian poetry, but against Georgian criticism.

And he concludes

> I prophesy that if my phrases are given consideration, a century hence, it will be only in their historical context, by scholars interested in the mind of my generation.
> What I wish to suggest...is that these phrases may be accounted for as being conceptual symbols for emotional preferences. Thus, the emphasis on tradition came about, I believe, as a result of my reaction against the poetry, in the English language, of the nineteenth and early twentieth centuries, and my passion for the poetry, dramatic and lyric, of the late sixteenth and early seventeenth centuries.

Eliot's various qualifications should not be discounted, although his modesty here, as always, is a complicated matter. But it should also be noted that those who complain about the shifts in his judgments or the inconsistency of his terms often employ a kind of rigor which completely misses the heuristic value of his observations and would in fact demolish most critical systems. Ultimately, readers will have to make up their own minds, but I should say at the outset of this sketch that I find a good deal of consistency in Eliot's thinking and a pervasive emotional unity which it would be unreasonable to deny.

Shortly after his official conversion in 1928 ("the Christian scheme seemed the only possible scheme which found a place for values I must maintain or perish"), Eliot announced that his position was "classicist in literature, royalist in politics, and anglo-catholic in religion." He came to regret the categorical flatness and quotability of these phrases, but nevertheless they provide a valuable summary of his basic concerns. As John Margolis' careful study, *T.S. Eliot's Intellectual Development, 1922-1939*, now demonstrates, Eliot's stand had been prepared for earlier—at least as early as 1916, when he had maintained (in the syllabus for an Oxford Extention course in Modern French Literature) that

> The beginning of the twentieth century has witnessed a return to the ideals of classicism. These may roughly be characterized as *form* and *restraint* in art, *discipline* and *authority* in religion, *centralization* in government.... The classicist point of view has been defined essentially as a belief in Original Sin—the necessity for austere discipline.

There are a number of sources which might be used to explain Eliot's position (his debts to Irving Babbitt and T.E. Hulme have been documented by a number of critics) but perhaps the most concise is the 16th Canto of the *Purgatorio*. Here Dante asks Mark the Lombard to account for the presence of evil in this world: do the stars determine our actions or are we responsible for what we do? Mark replies that basically we are responsible, having been given free will and reason to tell right from wrong; but he adds that the soul is weak and easily distracted in this fallen world. Hence we need the strong supporting authority of the state and the true Church. This is the "catholic" position which Eliot had fully accepted by 1928: "man is man," he wrote in the following year,

> because he can recognise supernatural realities, not because he can invent them. Either everything in man can be traced as a development from below, or something must come from above. There is no avoiding that dilemma: you must be either a naturalist or a supernaturalist. If you remove from the word "human" all that the belief in the supernatural has given to man, you can view him finally as no more than an extremely clever, adaptable, and mischievous little animal.

In short, if we are to amount to anything as citzens and children of God we need the guidance of temporal and sacred authority; if we are to amount to anything as artists we need the authority of "tradition."

The crucial text here is the 1919 essay, "Tradition and the Individual Talent." Tradition, he maintains,

> cannot be inherited, and if you want it you must obtain it by great labour. It involves, in the first place, the historical sense, which we may call nearly indispensable to anyone who would continue to be a poet beyond his twenty-fifth year; and the historical sense involves a perception, not only of the pastness of the past, but of its presence; the historical sense compels a man to write not merely with his own generation in his bones, but with a feeling that the whole of the literature of Europe from Homer and within it the whole of the literature of his own country has a simultaneous existence and composes a simultaneous order.... The poet must be very conscious of the main current, which does not at all flow invariably through the most distinguished reputations.... He must be aware that the mind of Europe—the mind of his own country—a mind which he learns in time to be much more important than his own private mind—is a mind which changes, and that his change is a development which abandons nothing *en route*.

And he concludes that

> No poet, no artist of any sort, has his complete meaning alone. His significance, his appreciation is the appreciation of his relation to the dead poets and artists. You cannot value him alone; you must set him, for contrast and comparison, among the dead. I mean this as a principle of aesthetic, not merely historical, criticism. The necessity that he shall conform, that he shall cohere, is not onesided: what happens when a new work of art is created is something that happens simultaneously to all the works of art that preceded it. The existing monuments form an ideal order among themselves, which is modified by the introduction of the new (the really new) work of art among them. The existing order is complete before the new work arrives; for order to persist after the supervention of novelty, the *whole* existing order must be, if ever so slightly, altered; and so the relations, proportions, values of each work of art toward the whole are readjusted; and this is conformity between the old and the new.... And the poet who is aware of this will be aware of great difficulties and responsibilities.

Of course this "ideal order" exists not in some Platonic heaven, but in the mind and memory of the ideal reader—and critic. To take one brief example: the reader who recognizes that the 1929 poem "Animula" is in part based on the 16th Canto of the *Purgatorio* already knows something of the way in which Eliot's poem is to be understood; but it is also true that his complex appreciation of the passage from Dante will never again be the same. The poet who refuses to submit to the discipline of tradition, who will not learn how past masters have handled comparable problems, is like the defiant individualist who decides that he alone is best able to determine his temporal and spiritual welfare. The difference between the classical and the romantic, then, is simply the difference for Eliot between "the complete and the fragmentary, the adult and the immature, the orderly and the chaotic."

Eliot's "impersonal" theory of poetry follows naturally enough from all this. In the same key essay, "Tradition and the Individual Talent," he makes his notorious comparison between the mind of the artist and a catalytic agent:

> [when oxygen and sulphur dioxide] are mixed in the presence of a filament of platinum, they form sulphurous acid. This combination takes place only if platinum is present; nevertheless the newly formed acid contains no trace of platinum, and the platinum itself is apparently unaffected: has remained inert, neutral, and unchanged. The mind of the poet is the shred of platinum. It may partly or exclusively operate upon the experience of man himself; but, the more perfect the artist, the more completely separate in him will be the man who suffers and the mind which creates; the more perfectly will the mind digest and transmute other passions which are its material.... What happens is a continual surrender of himself as he is at the moment to something which is more valuable. The progress of an artist is a continual self-sacrifice, a continual extinction of personality.

For Eliot, as for most "classical" critics, art is more philosophic than history. The artist must transform his "personal and private agonies" into "something rich and strange, something universal and impersonal"; he must take "genuine and substantial human emotions, such emotions as observation can confirm, typical emotions, and give them artistic form." The end of poetry, he had observed in *The Sacred Wood*, is "a pure contemplation from which all accidents of personal emotion are removed." The artist achieves this impersonality partly by submitting to tradition and partly by hitting upon what Eliot calls in another famous phrase a proper "objective correlative." In "Hamlet" he assets that

> the only way of expressing emotion in the form of art is by finding an "objective correlative"; in other words, a set of objects, a situation, a chain of events which shall be the formula of that *particular* emotion; such that when the external facts, which must terminate in sensory experience, are given, the emotion is immediately evoked.... The artistic "inevitability" lies in this complete adequacy of the external to the emotion; and this is precisely what is deficient in *Hamlet*.

Thus Eliot (following J.M. Robertson) argues that Shakespeare the man suffered from Oedipal feelings, but that the Hamlet story could not encompass his anxieties. Because Hamlet is dominated by inexpressible emotions which are "excessive" in relation to the actual events of the play, we rightly find his actions incomprehensible at certain crucial points. The doctrine of the objective correlative may have some value as an after-the-fact critical tool, but as an account of what happens during the creative process it is surely the most vulnerable of Eliot's contentions: few artists can ever have begun with a disembodied "feeling" whose symbolic equivalent they then searched for. Nevertheless, Eliot's intention is clear enough; he wishes to preserve the impersonality of poetry and still make room for its therapeutic function—for both the artist (who feels "a sudden relief from an intolerable burden") and the audience, as this passage from "Baudelaire" implies:

> It is not merely in the use of imagery of common life, not merely in the use of imagery of the sordid life of a great metropolis, but in the elevation of such imagery to the *first intensity*—presenting it as it is, and yet making it represent something much more than itself—that Baudelaire has created a mode of release and expression for other men.

This passage should also remind readers that the poet is not simply "traditional." What he has to contribute as an individual is "the sense of his own time." And equally important for Eliot, the poet is a kind of guardian of the language, keeping it "pure" and yet "close to the speech of his time."

At his best the poet fuses thought and feeling at the moment of creation. After quoting passages from Lord Herbert of Cherbury and Tennyson, Eliot contends that the difference between the two poets is not simply one of degree:

It is something which had happened to the mind of England between the time of Donne or Lord Herbert and the time of Tennyson and Browning; it is the difference between the intellectual poet and the reflective poet. Tennyson and Browning are poets, and they think; but they do not feel their thought as immediately as the odour of a rose. A thought to Donne was an experience; it modified his sensibility. When a poet's mind is perfectly equipped for its work, it is constantly amalgamating disparate experience; the ordinary man's experience is chaotic, irregular, fragmentary. The latter falls in love, or reads Spinoza, and these two experiences have nothing do with each other, or with the noise of the typewriter or the smell of cooking; in the mind of the poet these experiences are always forming new wholes.

We may express the difference by the following theory: The poets of the seventeenth century, the successors of the dramatists of the sixteenth, possessed a mechanism of sensibility which could devour any kind of experience.

"What I see, in the history of English poetry," Eliot concluded, is "the splitting up of personality."

Eliot's conception of the end or purpose of poetry is rather more difficult to isolate. There are hints and suggestions in the early essays but no reasonably clear statement until 1933 and the conclusion to *The Use of Poetry and the Use of Criticism*:

I have insisted rather on the variety of poetry, variety so great that all the kinds seem to have nothing in common except the rhythm of verse instead of the rhythm of prose; and that does not tell you very much about all poetry. Poetry is of course not to be defined by its uses. If it commemorates a public occasion, or celebrates a festival, or decorates a religious rite, or amuses a crowd, so much the better. It may effect revolutions in sensibility such as are periodically needed; it may help to break up the conventional modes of perception and valuation which are perpetually forming and make people see the world afresh, or some new part of it. It may make us from time to time a little more aware of the deeper, unnamed feelings which form the substratum of our being, to which we rarely penetrate; for our lives are mostly an evasion of ourselves, and an evasion of the visible and sensible world. But to say all this is only to say what you know already, if you have felt poetry and thought about your feelings.

But it was not until 1951, in "Poetry and Drama," that he settled the matter once and for all:

it is ultimately the function of art, in imposing a credible order upon ordinary reality, and thereby eliciting some perception of an order *in* reality, to bring us to a condition of serenity, stillness, and reconciliation; and then leave us, as Virgil left Dante, to proceed toward a region where that guide can avail us no farther.

The implications of this simile are unmistakable: just as Dante's salvation cannot be brought about by Virgil alone—that is, by reason and art alone—but needs the final gifts of grace and revelation, so poetry, or culture in the broadest sense, is no substitute for religion. Poetry may console us, but it will not save us.

The responsibilities of criticism follow logically from Eliot's conception of tradition and the orthodoxy of the writer under consideration. As early as 1929 Eliot admitted that he could not in practice "separate my poetic appreciation from my personal beliefs," and in fact some of the most important later essays are written for fellow-believers who will not be disturbed by an observation such as this:

The World is trying the experiment of attempting to form a civilized but non-Christian mentality. The experiment will fail; but we must be very patient in awaiting its collapse; meanwhile redeeming the time: so that the Faith may be preserved alive through the dark ages before us; to renew and rebuild civilization, and save the World from suicide.

In general Eliot remains faithful to the broad definition of criticism he had proposed in 1923: "the elucidation of works of art and the correction of taste." He returns to these phrases in one of his last important lectures, "The Frontiers of Criticism":

Among all this variety, we may ask, what is there, if anything, that should be common to all literary criticism? Thirty years ago, I asserted that the essential function of criticism was "the elucidation of works of art and the correction of taste." That phrase may sound somewhat pompous to our ears in 1956. Perhaps I could put it more simply, and more acceptably to the present age, by saying "to promote the understanding and enjoyment of literature."... To understand a poem comes to the same thing as to enjoy it for the right reasons. One might say that it means getting from the poem such enjoyment as it is capable of giving.... It is certain that we do not fully understand a poem unless we enjoy it; and on the other hand, it is equally true that we do not fully enjoy a poem unless we understand it. And that means, enjoying it to the right degree and in the right way, relative to other poems.

The Aristotelian echoes here are deliberate: the good man enjoys doing good for the right reasons; he is the man who knows precisely what he is doing, bringing the full weight of his experience to bear upon each decision. The qualifications are much the same for the kind of Christian humanism which builds on this classical foundation. Poetry has special powers, but it is part of life; our judgments can never be simply technical or historical: "The greatness of literature," Eliot concludes, "cannot be determined solely by literary standards; though we must remember that whether it is literature or not can be determined only by literary standards." For these reasons, perhaps, he is a critic essentially without heirs. A preference for Donne rather than Milton, a dislike of romanticism, a hope for the revival of poetic drama or the use of terms such as the objective correlative or the dissociation of sensibility: these are not what matter. What does matter is the faith that makes judgments possible. Predictions are always risky, but it seems unlikely that criticism in the future will ally itself with the principles of Christian humanism. The future may not bring a Christian civilization, as Eliot himself recognized. And in that event, he once said, "I am not interested in the future."

ELLMANN, Richard. American. Born in Highland Park, Michigan, 15 March 1918. Educated at Yale University, New Haven, Connecticut, B.A. 1939, M.A. 1941, Ph.D. 1947; Trinity College, Dublin, B.Litt. 1947. Served in the United States Navy and the Office of Strategic Services, 1943-45. Married Mary Donahue in 1949; has three children. Instructor in English, 1942-43, 1947-48, and Briggs Copeland Assistant Professor of English Composition, 1948-51, Harvard University, Cambridge, Massachusetts; Professor of English and Franklin Bliss Snyder Professor, Northwestern University, Evanston, Illinois, 1951-68; Professor of English, Yale University, 1968-70. Since 1970, Fellow of New College, Oxford, and Professor of English Literature, Oxford University. Frederick Ives Carpenter Visiting Professor, University of Chicago, 1959, 1968; Woodruff Visiting Professor, Emory University, Atlanta, Georgia, 1973, 1974, 1975, 1981. Recipient: Rockefeller Fellowship, 1946; Guggenheim Fellowship, 1950, 1957, 1970; *Kenyon Review* Fellowship in Criticism, 1955; National Book Award, 1960; Fellowship, 1956, 1960, and Senior Fellowship, 1966-72, School of Letters, Indiana University, Bloomington. M.A.: Oxford University, 1970. Fellow of the American Academy of Arts and Letters and the Royal Society of Literature. Fellow of the British Academy, 1979. Address: New College, Oxford, England.

PUBLICATIONS

Criticism

Yeats: The Man and the Masks. New York, Macmillan, 1948; London, Macmillan,
    1949.
The Identity of Yeats. New York, Oxford University Press, and London, Macmillan,
    1954; revised edition, New York, Oxford University Press, 1964; London, Faber, 1965.
James Joyce. New York and London, Oxford University Press, 1959.
Eminent Domain: Yeats among Wilde, Joyce, Pound, Eliot and Auden. New York,
    Oxford University Press, 1967; London, Oxford University Press, 1970.
Literary Biography (lecture). Oxford, Clarendon Press, 1971.
Ulysses on the Liffey. New York, Oxford University Press, and London, Faber, 1972.
Golden Codgers: Biographical Speculations. New York and London, Oxford Univer-
    sity Press, 1973.
The Consciousness of Joyce. New York, Oxford University Press, and London, Faber,
    1977.
"A Late Victorian Love Affair," in *Oscar Wilde: Two Approaches*, with W.J. Espey. Los
    Angeles, Clark Memorial Library, University of California, 1977.
"How Wallace Stevens Saw Himself," in *Wallace Stevens: A Celebration*, edited by Frank
    Doggett and Robert Buttel. Princeton, New Jersey, Princeton University Press, 1980.

Other

Wilde and the Nineties: An Essay and an Exhibition, with E.D.H. Johnson and Alfred L.
    Bush, edited by Charles Ryskamp. Princeton, New Jersey, Princeton University
    Library, 1966.

Editor, *My Brother's Keeper: James Joyce's Early Years*, by Stanislaus Joyce. New
    York, Viking Press, and London, Faber, 1958.
Editor, *The Symbolist Movement in Literature*, by Arthur Symons. New York, Dutton,
    1958.
Editor, with Ellsworth Mason, *The Critical Writings of James Joyce*. New York, Viking
    Press, and London, Faber, 1959.
Editor and Translator, *Selected Writings of Henri Michaux*. New York, New Direc-
    tions, 1960.
Editor, *Edwardians and Late Victorians*. New York, Columbia University Press, 1960.
Editor, *A Portrait of the Artist as a Young Man*, by James Joyce. New York, Viking
    Press, 1964; London, Cape, 1968.
Editor, with Charles Feidelson, Jr., *The Modern Tradition: Backgrounds of Modern
    Literature*. New York, Oxford University Press, 1965.
Editor, *The Letters of James Joyce*, vols. 2 and 3. New York, Viking Press, and London,
    Faber, 1966.
Editor, *Giacomo Joyce*, by James Joyce. New York, Viking Press, and London, Faber,
    1968.
Editor, *The Artist as Critic: Critical Writings of Oscar Wilde*. New York, Random
    House, 1969; London, W.H. Allen, 1970.
Editor, *Ulysses*, by James Joyce. London, Penguin, 1969.
Editor, *Oscar Wilde: A Collection of Critical Essays*. Englewood Cliffs, New Jersey,
    Prentice Hall, 1969.
Editor, with Robert O'Clair, *The Norton Anthology of Modern Poetry*. New York,
    Norton, 1973.
Editor, *Selected Letters of James Joyce*. London, Faber, 1975; New York, Viking Press,
    1976.
Editor, *The New Oxford Book of American Verse*. London and New York, Oxford
    University Press, 1976.

*   *   *

Taken together, Richard Ellmann's two books on Yeats correct the tendency studies of that poet have had to be either purely critical or factually biographical, "with no bridge between them." In *Yeats: The Man and the Masks*, which is primarily biographical, Ellmann concentrates on "beginnings, efforts, forays," and tries to "represent as fully as possible the development of Yeats' mind":

> We shall ask how he became a symbolist poet and why he adopted an Irish subject matter; we shall try to determine what lay behind his interests in occultism and in nationalism, and how these interests affected his work. The notion is sometimes advanced nowadays that a poet's development can be traced in terms of the literary tradition alone; but whether we would or not, we shall be driven to answer many questions which seem at first to be beyond the literary pale: what was his family like? where was he reared and educated? why did he form certain friendships and not others? what effect did his long, frustrated love affair have upon him? how did his marriage alter his work?

But the emphasis here is not especially "psychological": Ellmann does not search for one grand determining principle in the poet's life or suggest that his poems be judged in terms of their private origins. Based on some "50,000 pages of unpublished manuscripts," *The Man and the Masks* is an indispensable foundation for Yeats studies of virtually any sort. *The Identity of Yeats*, on the other hand, is largely a work of explication in which Ellmann is intent on revealing the pattern in Yeats' poetry as a whole—although given the twistings and turning of Yeats' career, "dialectical principle" is a more apt term than "pattern":

> I sometimes think that we could try to codify the laws that govern the complexities of Yeats' poetry. Every poem offers alternative positions. While the choice between them may surprise us, we can be sure it will be based upon a preference for what is imprudent, reckless, contrary to fact, but that in so choosing the poet does not act out of folly but out of understandable passion. The alternative is never completely overwhelmed, but remains like the other side of the moon, or, to use another of Yeats' images, like some imprisoned animal, ready to burst out again with its message of common sense or of renunciation of the world.... The poem ends not in a considered conclusion, but in a kind of breathlessness, a break through from the domain of caution and calculation to that of imprudence and imagination; the poem gathers its strength from putting down one view with another, from saying, against the utmost opposition, what must be said.

The basic principle of Yeats' poetry, which Ellmann calls a principle of "affirmative capability," demands that "the more sharply we represent the contradictions of life, the more urgently we invoke a pattern of the reality which must transcend or include them." As for Yeats' significance now, Ellmann maintains that the principle of affirmative capability is "particularly suited to a time when there is no agreement over ultimate questions, when we are not even sure exactly what we think on matters that are so crucial and yet so obscure." There are other reasons too for regarding Yeats as "the dominant poet of our time," but on the whole Ellmann assumes rather than argues for Yeats' commanding importance. Towards the end of *The Identity of Yeats*, however, he does make at least one clear evaluative statement:

> In modern poetry Yeats and T.S. Eliot stand at opposite poles. For while both see life as incomplete, Eliot puts his faith in spiritual perfection, the ultimate conversion of sense to spirit. Yeats, on the other hand, stands with Michelangelo for "profane perfection of mankind," in which sense and spirit are fully and harmoniously exploited.... He presents this faith with such power and richness that Eliot's religion, in spite of its honesty and loftiness, is pale and infertile in comparison.

Yeats is also the central figure in *Eminent Domain*. Here Ellmann considers the problem of "influence" in modern poetry, having in mind something more complex, of course, than mere passive absorption by one writer of another's themes or techniques:

That writers flow into each other like waves, gently rather than tidally, is one of those decorous myths we impose upon a high-handed, even brutal procedure. The behavior, while not invariably marked by bad temper, is less polite. Writers move in upon other writers not as genial successors but as violent expropriators, knocking down established boundaries to seize by the force of youth, or of age, what they require.... What occurs then is not the assertion of a single sovereignty but of conflicting sovereignties which now encroach and now are encroached upon, like Italian city states in Malatesta's time.

As a young man Yeats helped himself to what he needed from Oscar Wilde; later on, Pound, Eliot, Joyce and (what seems at first an improbable claim) Auden took what they needed from Yeats. As Eliot puts it, rather more bluntly than Ellmann, lesser poets borrow, great poets steal—usually for purposes entirely their own. *Eminent Domain* is a generally persuasive exercise in the kind of sophisticated literary history Harold Bloom was to call for a few years later, in *The Anxiety of Influence*, although Ellmann characteristically avoids any "causal" explanations whereas Bloom welcomes speculation about the oedipal resentment younger poets always feel toward their "fathers."

Ellmann's massive biography of Joyce is probably definitive, and like his work on Yeats is now an indispensable source for any future criticism. He had access to everyone and everything connected with Joyce and faithfully reports it all, no matter how trivial it seems. In many ways Joyce's life was fairly uneventful, but as Ellmann points out, rarely has a major artist ever been so dependent upon the details of daily living. Joyce's great achievement, in fact, is his celebration of the "ordinary":

Whether we know it or not, Joyce's court, like Dante's or Tolstoy's, is always in session. The initial and determining act of judgment in his work is the justification of the commonplace. Other writers had labored tediously to portray it, but no one really knew what the commonplace was until Joyce had written.... Joyce was the first to endow an urban man of no importance with heroic consequence.... Bloom is a humble vessel elected to bear and transmit unimpeached the best qualities of the mind. Joyce's discovery, so humanistic that he would have been embarrassed to disclose it out of context, was that the ordinary is the extraordinary.

Occasionally Ellmann suggests that the finished work may be a disguised projection of private problems: about *Portrait* and *Ulysses*, for example, he observes that in both

Joyce seem to reconstitute his family relationships, to disengage himself from the contradictions of his view of himself as a child and to exploit them, to overcome his mother's conventionality and his father's rancour, to mother and father himself, to become, by the superhuman effort of the creative process, no one but James Joyce.

But this sounds more like Leon Edel on Henry James and is not really typical of Ellmann's procedure. Once again Ellmann tends to assume rather than demonstate his subject's importance, with less justification than before, perhaps, since there are still intelligent readers around who are not wholly convinced that Joyce managed to transform the mundane so miraculously. Perhaps no critic can explain *how* an artist makes this transformation, but for a much sharper discussion of Joyce's use of literal fact readers should consult Robert Martin Adams' *Ulysses: Surface and Symbol*.

Although not so dreary as its title might suggest, *Golden Codgers* is a miscellany, the most interesting parts of which are apparently drawn from Ellmann's work-in-progress, a full-scale biography of Wilde. There is one essay here, however, "Literary Biography," which helps to place his work thus far. Ellmann is suspicious of biographers (like Edel, Sartre or Erik Erikson) who look for one determining factor in an artist's life. Psychoanalysis and existentialism are established points of view, he admits, but "emphases are bound to change. Theories which once seemed to make everything clear will be brought into question." This implies a kind of safe, slightly cheap relativism and may explain why Ellmann has been unwilling to commit himself to a fixed set of causal principles. But he has no hesitation in asserting that biography, while inevitably a reflection of intellectual trends, may still be a humane and civilizing art:

We cannot know completely the intricacies with which any mind negotiates with its surroundings to produce literature. The controlled seething out of which great works come is not likely to yield all its secrets. Yet at moments, in glimpses, biographers seem to come close to it, and the effort to come close, to make out of apparently haphazard circumstances a plotted circle, to know another person who has lived as well as we know a character in fiction, and better than we know ourselves, is not frivolous. It may even be, for reader as for writer, an essential part of experience.

EMPSON, William.   British.   Born in Yokefleet, East Yorkshire, 27 September 1906. Educated at Winchester College, Hampshire; Magdalene College, Cambridge, B.A. in mathematics 1929, M.A. 1935. Married Hester Henrietta Crouse in 1941; two sons. Taught English Literature, Tokyo National University, 1931-34, and National University, Peking, 1937-39, 1947-52. Member of the Monitoring Service, 1940, and Chinese Editor, Far Eastern Section, 1941-46, BBC, London. Taught at Kenyon College, Gambier, Ohio, summers 1948, 1950, 1954. Professor of English Literature, Sheffield University, 1953-71; since 1971, Emeritus Professor. Recipient: Ingram Merrill Foundation Award, 1968. Litt.D.: University of East Anglia, Norwich, 1968; Bristol University, 1971; Sheffield University, 1974. Knighted, 1979. Address: Studio House, 1 Hampstead Hill Gardens, London N.W.3, England.

PUBLICATIONS

Criticism

Seven Types of Ambiguity: A Study of Its Effects on English Verse.   London, Chatto and Windus, 1930; New York, Harcourt Brace, 1931; revised edition, Chatto and Windus, and New York, New Directions, 1947; Chatto and Windus, 1953; New York, Noonday Press, 1955; London, Penguin-Chatto and Windus, 1963.

Some Versions of Pastoral.   London, Chatto and Windus, 1935; as *English Pastoral Poetry*, New York, Norton, 1938.

"The Best Policy" and "Timon's Dog," in *Shakespeare Survey*.   London, Brendin, 1937.

"Donne and the Rhetorical Tradition," in *Kenyon Review* (Gambier, Ohio), 11, 1949.

"Verbal Analysis," in *Kenyon Review* (Gambier, Ohio), 12, 1950.

The Structure of Complex Words.   London, Chatto and Windus, and New York, New Directions, 1951.

"Dover Wilson on *Macbeth,"* in *Kenyon Review* (Gambier, Ohio), 14, 1952.

"Hamlet When New," in *Sewanee Review* (Tennessee), 61, 1953.

"Falstaff and Mr. Dover Wilson," in *Kenyon Review* (Gambier, Ohio), 15, 1953.

"The Theme of *Ulysses,"* in *Kenyon Review* (Gambier, Ohio), 18, 1956.

"Donne and the Space Man," in *Kenyon Review* (Gambier, Ohio), 19, 1957.

"The Spanish Tragedy," in *English Critical Essays: Twentieth Century: Second Series*, edited by Derek Hudson.   London, Oxford University Press, 1958.

"Tom Jones," in *Kenyon Review* (Gambier, Ohio), 20, 1958.

Milton's God.   London, Chatto and Windus, 1961; New York, New Directions, 1962; revised edition, Chatto and Windus, 1965.

"Rhythm and Imagery in English Poetry," in *British Journal of Aesthetics* (London), 2, 1962.

"The Ancient Mariner," in *Critical Quarterly* (Hull, Yorkshire), 6, 1964.

"Volpone," in *Hudson Review* (New York), 21, 1969.
"The Alchemist," in *Hudson Review* (New York), 22, 1970.
"A Deist Tract by Dryden," in *Essays in Criticism* (Oxford), 25, 1975.

Verse

Letter IV. Cambridge, Heffer, 1929.
Poems. London, Chatto and Windus, 1935.
The Gathering Storm. London, Faber, 1940.
Collected Poems of William Empson. New York, Harcourt Brace, 1949; London, Chatto and Windus, 1955; revised edition, Harcourt Brace, 1961.

Other

"William Empson in Conversation with Christopher Ricks," in *The Modern Poet: Essays from "The Review,"* edited by Ian Hamilton. London, MacDonald, 1968.
"The Hammer's Ring," in *I.A. Richards: Essays in His Honor,* edited by Ruben Brower, Helen Vendler, and John Hollander. New York, Oxford University Press, 1973.

Editor, *The Outlook of Science,* by J.B.S. Haldane. London, Routledge, 1935.
Editor, *Science and Well-Being,* by J.B.S. Haldane. London, Routledge, 1935.
Editor, *Shakespeare's Poems.* New York, New American Library, 1969.
Editor, with David Pirie, *Coleridge's Verse: A Selection.* London, Faber, 1972; New York, Schocken Books, 1973.

CRITICAL STUDIES AND BIBLIOGRAPHY

Stanley Edgar Hyman, "William Empson and Categorical Criticism," in *The Armed Vision: A Study in the Methods of Modern Literary Criticism.* New York, Knopf, 1948; revised edition, 1955.
Elder Olson, "William Empson, Contemporary Criticism, and Poetic Diction," in *Critics and Criticism: Ancient and Modern,* edited by R.S. Crane. Chicago and London, University of Chicago Press, 1952.
Richard Sleight, "Mr. Empson's Complex Words," in *Essays in Criticism* (Oxford), 2 1952.
Hugh Kenner, "Alice in Empsonland," in *Gnomon: Essays on Contemporary Literature.* New York, McDowell Obolensky, 1958.
J.H. Wills, Jr., *William Empson.* New York and London, Columbia University Press, 1969.
Roger Sale, *Modern Heroism: Essays on D.H. Lawrence, William Empson, and J.R.R. Tolkien.* Berkeley and London, University of California Press, 1973.
Moira Megaw, "An Empson Bibliography," in *William Empson: The Man and His Work,* edited by Roma Gill. London and Boston, Routledge, 1974.
Christopher Norris, *William Empson and the Philosophy of Literary Criticism.* London, Athlone Press, 1978.

*   *   *

William Empson's long pursuit of a method which will describe "the exact shade of meaning a passage is meant to convey" begins in 1930, with *Seven Types of Ambiguity*, if not the best-known work of modern criticism then at least the work with the best-known title. Despite some cavalier remarks a number of years later to the effect that he had used the term to mean "anything I liked," Empson means something quite definite: "ambiguity" is a "phenomenon of compression" and as such is one of the "very roots of poetry": " 'Ambiguity' itself can mean an indecision as to what you mean, an intention to mean several things, a probability that one or other or both of two things has been meant, and the fact that a statement has several meanings." Thus an ambiguous piece of language requires that the mind hold in suspension alternate meanings which may complement, qualify or even contradict each other. So much is clear enough, but some of Empson's early critics felt that he had simply written himself a license to search for multiple meanings with no awareness of the controlling context in which the local ambiguity appears. No doubt many of Empson's readings are excessively ingenious; but as a theorist he is perfectly conscious of the need to see a word or image as part of a larger whole designed for a specific occasion. "Purpose, context and person," he maintains at the opening of *Seven Types*, constitute a major part of the "meaning" the critic wishes to determine. Moreover, the critic must also bear in mind the "critical principles of the author and of the public he is writing for." Thus in 1947 Empson looked back at his earlier reading of Shelley's "Skylark" and decided that he was wrong in "tackling it with so much effort and preparation"— wrong, that is, to assume that some sort of ambiguity *must* be present. And while he is willing to argue that ambiguity is a characteristic of all good poetry, he is far from claiming that ambiguity is automatically a virtue wherever it occurs; rather it must "in each case arise from, and be justified by, the peculiar requirements of the situation":

> In so far as an ambiguity sustains intricacy, delicacy, or compression of thought, or is an opportunism devoted to saying quickly what the reader already understands, it is to be respected.... It is not to be respected in so far as it is due to weakness or thinness of thought, obscures the matter at hand unnecessarily...or when the interest of the passage is not focussed upon it, so that it is merely an opportunism in the handlng of the material, if the reader will not understand the ideas which are being shuffled, and will be given a general impression of incoherence.

Readers unfamiliar with *Seven Types* will want an example of multiple meaning at this point, and the best brief instance one can provide is the passage usually produced for such occasions:

> To take a famous example, there is no pun, double syntax, or dubiety of feeling, in
>
> *Bare ruined choirs, where late the sweet birds sang,*
>
> but the comparison holds for many reasons; because ruined monastery choirs are places in which to sing, because they involve sitting in a row, because they are made of wood, are carved into knots and so forth, because they used to be surrounded by a sheltering building crystallised out of the likeness of a forest...because they are now abandoned by all but the grey walls coloured like the skies of winter, because the cold and Narcissistic charm suggested by choir-boys suits well with Shakespeare's feeling for the object of the Sonnets, and for various sociological and historical reasons (the protestant fear of monasteries; fear of puritanism), which it would be hard now to trace out in their proportions; these reasons, and many more relating the simile to its place in the Sonnet, must all combine to give the line its beauty, and there is a sort of ambiguity in not knowing which of them to hold most clearly in mind.

But this notorious example (which occurs at the beginning of the book and thus is one reason, apparently, it is so often quoted) gives no indication of how Empson can handle the incidental ambiguities as they contribute to a poetic whole. Here the reader should turn to his analysis of Herbert's "The Sacrifice" in a later chapter, or better yet, to his extraordinary reading of Shakespeare's Sonnet 94 in *Some Versions of Pastoral*.

As the title suggests, *Seven Types* deals systematically with different kinds of ambiguity in poetry; and although Empson admits that the types frequently overlap and generally refuse to stay put, there is a movement towards increasing complexity and "logical" disorder, from the second type, for example, which includes two or more alternative meanings fully resolved into one, to the seventh and most difficult type, which includes "two opposite meanings defined by the context, so that the total effect is to show a fundamental division in the writer's mind." The function of each type, however, remains the same—to cause a kind of pleasure we call "beauty." "Unexplained beauty," Empson confesses, "arouses an irritation in me, a sense that this would be a good place to scratch; the reasons that make a line of verse likely to give pleasure, I believe, are like the reasons for anything else." Thus *Seven Types* is primarily an exercise intended to help the reader who has already felt the pleasure understand the nature of his response. As for Empson's method, the unfolding of multiple meanings, it is "scientific," but not naïvely so:

> In wishing to apply verbal analysis to poetry the position of the critic is like that of a scientist wishing to apply determinism to the world. It may not be valid everywhere; though it be valid everywhere it may not explain everything; but in so far as he is to do any work he must assume it is valid where he is working, and will explain what he is trying to explain.

By calling attention to the multiple meanings of words and images Empson is aware that he is not doing anything new—as he states at one point, most of what he has to say about Shakespeare comes from the notes to the Arden texts. His distinction is rather that he welcomes such disclosures while conventional editors usually wish to play down the presence of ambiguities or deny that the poet meant them to be there:

> The conservative attitude to ambiguity is curious and no doubt wise; it allows a structure of associated meanings to be shown in a note, but not to be admitted; the reader is encouraged to swallow the thing by a decent reserve; it is thought best not to let him know that he is thinking in such a complicated medium.

In short, Empson is interested in increasing our conscious awareness of the devices which give us pleasure; and the relationship between such pleasure and the ultimate purpose of art leads directly to one of the most complicated issues his criticism raises.

While he gives Robert Graves credit for the method of sorting out meanings, Empson's heaviest debt is to his former teacher, I.A. Richards. Very briefly, Richards had argued that poetic language is valuable because it calls forth, in a fit reader, certain complex adjustments or "attitudes" toward experience which help him to cope more adequately with a bewildering "reality." Ideally, poetic statements bring about a condition of poise and readiness, so that the loss of poetry would be nothing less than a "biological calamity" for the human race. Empson would not go this far, perhaps, but he is still able to assert that

> many works of art give their public a sort of relief and strength, because they are independent of the moral code which their public accepts and is dependent upon; relief, by fantasy gratification; strength, because it gives you a sort of equilibrium within your boundaries to have been taken outside them, however secretly, because you know your own boundaries better when you have seen them from both sides.

The influence of Richards is even more apparent in Empson's crucial claim that "the object of life, after all, is not to understand things, but to maintain one's defences and equilibrium and live as well as one can." Again, he observes (in a note to one of his own poems, "Bacchus"), "the notion is that life involves maintaining oneself between contradictions that can't be solved by analysis." Analysis may not "solve" anything, yet the more one understands one's own reactions, "the less one is at their mercy." Critical understanding is particularly important just now

> because it gives one a certain power of dealing with anything that may turn out to be true; and people have come to feel that that may be absolutely anything. I do not say that this power is of unique value...but it is widely and reasonably felt that those people are better able to deal with our present difficulties whose defences are strong enough for them to be able to afford to understand things; nor can I conceal my sympathy with those who want to understand as many things as possible, and to hang those consequences which cannot be foreseen.

Empson's passion for close reading may seem unrelated to questions of ultimate value and judgment, but in a brief later essay, "The Verbal Analysis," he states quite clearly that there is room for a great deal of exposition, in which the business of the critic is simply to show how the machine is meant to work, and therefore to show all its working parts in turn. This is the kind of criticism I am specially interested in, and I think it is often really needed. Anyone who objects to it because it does not give a Final Valuation of the work in relation to all other work seems to me merely irrelevant.... I do not mean to say, what would be a very foolish thing to say, that criticism has nothing to do with valuation. It has to do with it all the time, because you cannot even say just how one element works without suggesting how well it works. But to assess the value of the poem as a whole is not the primary purpose of this kind of criticism, or at any rate ought only to emerge from the analysis as a whole.

And he concludes that "the kind of criticism that most interests me, verbal analysis or whatever one calls it, is concerned to examine what already goes on in the mind of a fit reader." Of course as a fit reader himself, Empson frequently sharpens his readers' awareness of something they may have felt vaguely, if at all; at his best, as Roger Sale has noted, Empson makes us feel that we have never read properly or fully before.

In *The Structure of Complex Words* Empson continues to explore the problem of meaning and implications, still accepting Richards' general theory of value (although now on grounds somewhat different from Richards') but rejecting the distinction Richards makes between emotive language (the pseudo-statements of poetry) and cognitive language (the referential language of science). Empson argues at length, and convincingly, that there is finally "no use trying to chase belief-feelings out of poetry altogether" and then proceeds to develop his own "little bits of machinery" for describing both the emotive and cognitive aspects of a given utterance. Hugh Kenner's admirable summary of the dense first two chapters will give some indication of what Empson is attempting here:

> In *Complex Words*, therefore, we get an atomic theory of language, with symbols for the components of the atom. Words carry Emotions, and Doctrines. Emotions in words are on the whole perfectly analyzable, whether or not they are in life.... Taking A for the Sense under discussion, the emotive components are: A/1, its main "implication" or "association" or "connotation"; (A), a sense held at the back of the mind, so that A (B) means the sense A secretly bolstered by the sense B;—A, a sense deliberately excluded in a given usage; A + , the sense made "warmer and fuller"; A -, the sense made more astringent; A £ 1, the first Mood of Sense A (a mood conveys the speaker's relation to an audience or context); 'A,' the mood conveyed by quotes; either "What *I* call A, but *they* don't," or "What *they* call A but *I* don't": A? the sense used of oneself under cover of using it of someone else, more commonly—A?...and finally A!1, the primary Emotion associated with sense A when all the above have been eliminated.... Doctrines are conveyed in words mainly by what Mr. Empson calls Equations; an Equation ties two senses together and implies that they have an intrinsic connection (A = B). The equations go into four classes: I Context-meaning implies dictionary-meaning; II. Major sense implies connotation (A = A/1); III. Head-meaning implies context meaning; IV. Neither meaning can be regarded as dominant.

Empson then examines a number of particular complex key words—"wit" in Pope's "Essay on Criticism," "all" in *Paradise Lost*, "fool" in *Lear*, "sense" in *The Prelude*, and so on. Kenner's patient summary is fair and accurate but his general verdict is harshly negative; another patient reader, however, Richard Sleight, claims that *The Structure of Complex Words* is "unquestionably the most important contribution to critical theory since *The Sacred Wood*." Fit readers will have to make up their own minds, but at least one important question should be raised here. Can other readers actually employ Empson's machinery with comparable results? After all, the machinery can only describe what has already been perceived or felt—to which the retort might be simply that no method has ever made a reader more intelligent. Sleight comments that

> we are not asked to surrender to a soulless machinery. My complaint is against the technique's demand, in its early stages of operation, for more discrimination than the use of symbols warrants. On the other hand, the compensating advantage is a lack of

dogmatism and the consequent freedom to work in a wider field. Nevertheless the equations are perplexing at first because their terms are not completely defined. They perhaps need a special type of mind to handle them adequately.

Demanding as *The Structure of Complex Words* is, most readers should have the feeling that they could master the machinery if they worked hard enough. *Some Versions of Pastoral*, however, is difficult in an entirely different way, and here readers, even very fit ones, may feel that the arguments are often so subtle and elliptical that it is impossible to say what, on the whole, Empson is driving at. "Pastoral," he tells us, puts "the complex into the simple"; a pastoral work may be "about" the "people," but it is certainly not "by" or "for" them. As an example of putting the complex into the simple, perhaps, we may take this stanza from Gray's *Elegy*:

> Full many a gem of purest ray serene
> The dark, unfathomed caves of ocean bear;
> Full many a flower is born to blush unseen
> And waste its sweetness on the desert air.

Empson discloses some unsuspected social implications here ("what this means, as the context makes clear, is that the eighteenth-century had no scholarship system or *carrière ouverte aux talents*") but then concludes

> And yet what is said is one of the permanent truths; it is only in degree that any improvement of society could prevent wastage of human power; the waste even in a fortunate life, the isolation even of a life rich in intimacy, cannot but be felt deeply, and is the central feeling of tragedy.

The essential trick of the old pastoral was "to imply a beautiful relation between rich and poor [and] to make simple people express strong feelings...in learned and fashionable language (so that you wrote about the best subject in the best way)":

> From seeing the two sorts of people combined like this you thought better of both; the best parts of both were used. The effect was in some degree to combine in the reader or author the merits of the two sorts; he was made to mirror in himself more completely the effective elements of the society he lived in.

And "trick" does seem to be a key word here:

> The feeling that life is essentially inadequate to the human spirit, and yet that a good life must avoid saying so, is naturally at home with most versions of pastoral; in pastoral you take a limited life and pretend it is the full and normal one, and a suggestion that one do this with all life, because the normal is itself limited, is easily put into the trick though not necessary to its power.

Thus "the poetic statements of human waste and limitation, whose function is to give strength to see life clearly and so to adopt a fuller attitude to it, usually bring in, or leave room for the reader to bring in, the whole set of pastoral ideas." Finally, pastoral seems to have something to do with preserving the unity of a healthy society, or at least preserving the illusion of unity, helping to reconcile some conflict between the parts of the society: "literature is a social process, and also an attempt to reconcile the conflicts of an individual in whom those of society will be mirrored." In *Modern Heroism*, Roger Sale has made his own valiant attempt to grasp *Some Versions of Pastoral* as a unified work with a continuous argument: "its subject," he asserts, "is the collapse of the old pastoral relation of the swain-hero to the sheep-people and the consequences of that collapse in the period between the end of the sixteenth and the beginning of the nineteenth century"; as modern readers

> we live in a world where the magical relation of hero to people has been lost so that the people have become a mob and the hero painfully alienated.... Empson puts his unifying

figure in the background, a metaphoric hero-swain-Christ, and then begins at the end of the sixteenth century and tells his stories of those swains, heroes, and Christ figures who are only *versions* of the old pastoral figures because the disintegrating motions of history prevented their being more than this.

This is a brave attempt, but as Sale admits, "maddeningly, Empson never says this or anything like this"; and without the kind of frame Sale has provided it is often difficult to "believe that more is happening than the chatter of an intellectual raconteur." Once again, the reader willing to work hard will have to form his own conclusions; he may agree with Sale or discover his own organizing principle; or he may settle, as most readers have, for the brilliant passages on Marvell, *The Beggars' Opera* and *Alice in Wonderland*.

Unfortunately there is nothing in the least obscure or indirect about *Milton's God*. It is essentially a diatribe against Christianity, which Empson feels has had a monopoly on torture-worship, sexual repression and hypocrisy. The basis of the argument is thoroughly naturalistic—at one point Empson admits that "I am still inclined to the theory of Bentham which was in favour when I was a student at Cambridge; that the satisfaction of any impulse is in itself an elementary good, and that the practical ethical question is merely how to satisfy the greatest number." As a humane naturalist, then, he is horrified at the sacrifices Christianity imposes on its followers and the atrocities it asks them to condone. "The Christian God," he observes, "the Father, the God of Tertullian, Augustine and Aquinas, is the wickedest thing yet invented by the black heart of man." If Christians have often been decent in the past it is simply because people with "civilized consciences" have managed to keep the doctrine at bay. Since the cruelty of the Christian God could never be admitted, "the horrible doctrine has gone on doing harm for two thousand years, with brave and intelligent men incessantly struggling either to stave it off or to drive themselves into facing its logical consequences."

The book is also about Milton, and it is Empson's point that Milton "is struggling to make his God appear less wicked...and does succeed in making him noticably less wicked than the traditional Christian one": Milton has "cut out of Christianity both the torture-horror and the sex-horror, and after that the monster seems almost decent." He carefully traces what he feels to be Milton's "large minded" account of the temptation and fall of Lucifer, Adam and Eve, and places a good deal of weight, finally, on the very remote possibility that Milton's God intends to "abdicate":

> When Milton made God the Father plan for his eventual abdication, he ascribed to him in the high tradition of Plutarch the noblest sentiment that could be found in an absolute ruler; and could reflect with pride that he had himself seen it in operation [in Cromwell], though with a tragic end. Milton's God is thus to be regarded as like King Lear and Prospero, turbulent and masterful characters who are struggling to become able to renounce their power and enter peace; the story makes him behave much worse than they do, but the author allows him the purifying aspiration.

In short, *Milton's God* is also a partial defence of Milton's essential humanity and thus stands in sharp opposition to the orthodox interpretations of "neo-Christian" critics such as C.S. Lewis and E.M.W. Tillyard.

Like Kenneth Burke, Empson resists summary and defeats any attempt at just paraphrase; and like Burke, he is so complex and demanding a writer that his full influence and value have yet to be estimated. Whatever the eventual verdict, Empson has been one of the essential figures of modern criticism, and it should be noted that any fair verdict will have to take into account the later essays on Donne, Jonson and Fielding, among others, which have yet to be collected.

ENRIGHT, D(ennis) J(oseph). British. Born in Leamington, Warwickshire, 11 March 1920. Educated at Leamington College; Downing College, Cambridge, B.A. (honours) in English 1944, M.A. 1946; University of Alexandria, Egypt, D.Litt. 1949. Married Madeleine Harders in 1949; one daughter. Lecturer in English, University of Alexandria, 1947-50; Extra Mural Lecturer, Birmingham University, England, 1950-53; Visiting Professor, Konan University, Kobe, Japan, 1953-56; Gastdozent, Free University, West Berlin, 1956-57; British Council Professor of English, Chulalongkorn University, Bangkok, 1957-59; Professor of English, University of Singapore, 1960-70. Temporary Lecturer in English, University of Leeds, Yorkshire, 1970-71. Since 1975, Professor of English, University of Warwick, Coventry. Co-Editor of *Encounter* magazine, London, 1970-72. Editorial Advisor, 1971-73, and since 1973, Member, Board of Directors, Chatto and Windus, publishers, London. Recipient: Cholmondeley Award, 1974; Society of Authors Travelling Fellowship, 1981. Fellow, Royal Society of Literature, 1961. Address: Chatto and Windus Ltd., 40-42 William IV Street, London WC2N 4DF, England.

PUBLICATIONS

Criticism

A Commentary on Goethe's "Faust". New York, New Directions, 1949.
Literature for Man's Sake: Critical Essays. Tokyo, Kenkyusha, 1955.
The Apothecary's Shop. London, Secker and Warburg, 1957; Chester Springs, Pennsylvania, Dufour, 1959.
Robert Graves and the Decline of Modernism. Singapore, Craftsman Press, 1960; Folcroft, Pennsylvania, Folcroft Editions, 1974; reprinted in *Conspirators and Poets*, 1966.
"The Literature of the First World War," in *The Pelican Guide to English Literature 7*, edited by Boris Ford. London, Penguin, 1961; revised edition, 1963, 1973.
Conspirators and Poets. London, Chatto and Windus, and Chester Springs, Pennsylvania, Dufour, 1966.
Shakespeare and the Students. London, Chatto and Windus, 1970; New York, Schocken Books, 1971.
Man Is an Onion: Essays and Reviews. London, Chatto and Windus, 1972; La Salle, Illinois, Library Press, 1973.

Verse

The Laughing Hyena and Other Poems. London, Routledge, 1953.
Bread Rather Than Blossoms. London, Secker and Warburg, 1956.
Some Men Are Brothers. London, Chatto and Windus, 1960.
Addictions. London, Chatto and Windus, 1962.
The Old Adam. London, Chatto and Windus, 1965.
Unlawful Assembly. London, Chatto and Windus, and Middletown, Connecticut, Wesleyan University Press, 1968.
Selected Poems. London, Chatto and Windus, 1969.
The Typewriter Revolution and Other Poems. New York, Library Press, 1971.
In the Basilica of the Annunciation. London, Poem-of-the-Month Club, 1971.
Daughters of Earth. London, Chatto and Windus, 1972.
Foreign Devils. London, Convent Garden Press, 1972.
The Terrible Shears: Scenes from a Twenties Childhood. London, Chatto and Windus, 1973; Middletown, Connecticut, Wesleyan University Press, 1974.
Rhymes Times Rhyme (for children). London, Chatto and Windus, 1974.
Sad Ires and Others. London, Chatto and Windus, 1975.

Penguin Modern Poets 26, with Dannie Abse and Michael Longley.   London, Penguin, 1975.

Novels

Academic Year.   London, Secker and Warburg, 1955.
Heaven Knows Where.   London, Secker and Warburg, 1957.
Insufficient Poppy.   London, Chatto and Windus, 1960.
Figures of Speech.   London, Heinemann, 1965.

Other

Memoirs of a Mendicant Professor.   London, Chatto and Windus, 1969.

Editor, *Poetry of the 1950's: An Anthology of New English Verse*.   Tokyo, Kenkyusha, 1955.
Editor, with Takamichi Ninomiya, *The Poetry of Living Japan*.   London, Murray, and New York, Grove Press, 1957.
Editor, with Ernst de Chickera, *English Critical Texts: 16th Century to 20th Century*. London and New York, Oxford University Press, 1962.
Editor, *A Choice of Milton's Verse*.   London, Faber, 1975.
Editor, *The History of Rasselas, Prince of Abbisinia*, by Johnson.   London, Penguin, 1976.
Editor, *The Oxford Book of Contemporary Verse*.   London and New York, Oxford University Press, 1980.

*   *   *

Like many good poets and novelsts who are also part time critics, D.J. Enright has healthy misgivings about the claims of modern criticism. We live in an age of criticism, he admits, but too often it is "yesterday's criticism, ornamented, petrified, both attenuated and constricted, and trivialized." But there are, or were, important exceptions:

In the seminal works of modern literary criticism (such as Eliot's earlier essays and Leavis's *Revaluation*) new techniques of evaluation were accompanied by the older conceptions of literature's *human* meaningfulness. A little later, however, and the ingenious hunts for "extra" significance began to obscure that meaningfulness. The type of search which started (with Empson's *Seven Types of Ambiguity*) as light thrown upon dark places soon turned into a piecemeal darkness. Where reading had previously been too, too easy, it now became impossible. Modern criticism, for all its appearance of sophistication, has really proved rather ingenuous. It repeated, more crudely, what was happening in poetry: in short, the turning upside-down of Romanticism, whereby the Heart was relegated to the bottom of the class and the Brain was promoted to the top. One form of tyranny was replaced by another.

This says a good deal about Enright's criticism and about his poetry as well. Trained by F.R. Leavis, he absorbed many of this teacher's best qualities (or perhaps had them to begin with, since Leavis needn't be given full credit for every humane student to emerge from Downing College) and somehow managed to avoid the irritability which often marks those associated with *Scrutiny*. The virtues he admires in Goethe are in fact the virtues of his own work:

What is rarely perceived is that Goethe does take a side, that he does commit himself, and with a loving whole-heartedness that has become increasingly uncommon among writers. He accepts, above all other considerations, the prime value of being alive; from this acceptance follows the conclusion that, however wrongly a man is living his life, it can only be taken away from him for the strongest and most practical of reasons. It is the sin against life that is dreadful, not the sin against ideas.

Again, the novels of Thomas Mann,

in spite of their apparent preoccupation with disease...are full of athletic vigor and enthusiasm for things human. Unlike much of our most brilliant modern writing, they send us back into life, not terrified into despair or dullness or quiescence by the sight of others' follies, but cheerfully prepared to commit our own.

By the same token Enright is suspicious of a self-regarding artist such as Nabokov and impatient with modish pessimism, while still recognizing that "a chastened humanism is the only sort of humanism our age can allow." In "On Not Teaching *The Cocktail Party*: A Professional Dialogue," his spokesman complains

It's all the fashion these days to turn up the nose at the merely human. Look at the writers making good money out of showing a sentimental public how rotten the heart of the matter is and how sordidly the affair is bound to end. If we don't stop soon we shall become extinct out of sheer self-disgust. There is a middle way between the concentration camp and the monastery, and I still think it's a decent way, and by no means stale and unprofitable.

The question posed by another essay, "To the Lighthouse or to India?" is a rhetorical one; of course we should prefer Forster's solidity and guarded optimism to Virginia Woolf's pale symbols and inner worlds which are "finally stifling." In short, critics must be concerned with values and ideas (although Enright wisely grants that an idea inside a work of art is not quite the same as an idea in its native habitat):

Pure objectivity doesn't exist, except perhaps among the angels and the beasts.... [The critic] will certainly not be a person who is unaffected by his own beliefs or immune to those of others. On the contrary, let him not refrain from showing his beliefs (as clearly as Leavis shows his moral concerns), without "inhibitions" and without exhibitions. And then, whatever our own beliefs may be, he will have helped us to understand the work he is criticizing.

Thus Enright is almost never preoccupied with matters of technique or formal excellence. What matters is the author's plain humanity.

These broad democratic values may sometimes have to be inferred but there is no question about the things Enright dislikes. He brings up Shakespeare's phrase, "Art made tongue-tied by authority," and admits that "Authority, when it is kindly, achieves [stability] by fighting our battles for us, by providing us not only with social welfare—no one can decently object to that—but also spiritual welfare." The problem is that Authority is likely to be abused; and hence Enright's frequent attacks on the "critocracy," on the fetish that has been made of Eliot's insistence on the importance of "tradition," and on totalitarianism in general. "Art will not thrive," he warns, "in any society which is run in the style of a children's nursery, whether the role of nanny is taken by a set of well-read dons or by a government department."

This same mistrust of control by specialists governs his scene-by-scene commentaries on *Lear, Macbeth, Antony and Cleopatra* and *The Winter's Tale* in *Shakespeare and the Students*. There must be other teachers, he complains,

who feel that we have been rescued from the smoke and fire of romanticism only to be dropped into the hygienic incinerators of symbolism, imagery-computation, a curiously trite moralising, and philosophising of a sort so primitive as undoubtedly to have contributed to the discredit which literature has fallen into among the serious-minded. If in the heat of his excitement A.C. Bradley occasionally gets between us and Shakespeare, yet he never obscures for long what he purposes to reveal; he sometimes expands the text into thin air, but he doesn't reduce it; he may distort, but never belittles, for his commentary invariably makes you feel that at least the text is worth reading.

Enright is clearly on Bradley's side. His approach is commonsensical, his psychologizing plain but shrewd, and his primary concern with things more universal than textual problems, stage conventions or image clusters. William Walsh has observed that "if the limitations of Enright's treatment is to underemphasize the magnificence and the terrible in the characters, as it does the gorgeousness of the rhetoric, its advantage is to stress the reality, sometimes the quite homely and freckled reality, of the characters." This might be put more strongly: granted that Enright is a relief after too much G. Wilson Knight, a little of the latter may also be a relief after so much straightforwardness.

"Humanism" is a broad and easy badge that has to be earned, as in fact Enright does earn it in essay after essay. If there is anything to regret here it is simply that he usually restricts himself to short pieces and reviews, often of trivial or bad books. What he has to say about even the worst, however, is never dull.

ESSLIN, Martin (Julius).   British.   Born in Hungary, 8 June 1918; naturalized British subject, 1947. Educated at the University of Vienna; attended Rinehardt Seminar of Dramatic Arts, Vienna. Married Renate Gerstenberg in 1947; has 1 child. Producer and Scriptwriter, European Division, 1941-55, Assistant Head of European Productions Department, 1955, Assistant Head of Drama, 1961-63, and Head of Drama (Sound), 1963-77, B.B.C., London. Visiting Professor of Theatre, Florida State University, Tallahassee, 1969. Member (Chairman, 1976), Drama Panel, Arts Council of Great Britain. Since 1977, Professor of Drama (two quarters each year), Stanford University, California. Since 1978, Drama Editor, *Kenyon Review* (Gambier, Ohio), and Dramaturg, Magic Theatre, San Francisco. Awarded the title of Professor by the President of Austria, 1967. O.B.E. (Officer, Order of the British Empire), 1972. Address: January to June—Department of Drama, Stanford University, Stanford, California 94305, U.S.A.; July to December—64 Loudoun Road, London NW8, England.

PUBLICATIONS

Criticism

Brecht: A Choice of Evils: A Critical Study of the Man, His Work, and His Opinions. London, Eyre and Spottiswoode, 1950; as *Brecht: The Man and His Work*, New York, Doubleday, 1960.

The Theatre of the Absurd.   New York, Doubleday, 1961; London, Eyre and Spottiswoode, 1962; revised edition, London, Penguin, 1968; Doubleday, 1969.

Harold Pinter.   Velber bei Hanover, Friedrich Verlag, 1967.

Bertolt Brecht.   New York, Columbia University Press, 1969.

Reflections: Essays on Modern Theatre.   New York, Doubleday, 1969; enlarged edition as *Brief Chronicles; Essays on Modern Theatre*, London, Temple Smith, 1970.

The Peopled Wound: The Work of Harold Pinter.   New York, Doubleday, 1970; as *The Peopled Wound: The Plays of Harold Pinter*, London, Methuen, 1970; as *Pinter: A Study of His Plays*, Doubleday, and London, Methuen, 1973.

An Anatomy of Drama.   London, Temple Smith, 1976; New York, Hill and Wang, 1977.

Artaud.   London, Calder, 1976; as *Antonin Artaud*, New York, Penguin, 1977.

Mediations: Essays on Brecht, Beckett, and the Media.   Baton Rouge, Louisiana State
University Press, and London, Eyre Methuen, 1980.
"A Search for Subjective Truth," in *What Is Criticism?* edited by Paul Hernadi.   Bloom-
ington and London, Indiana University Press, 1981.

Other

Editor, with others, *Sinn oder Unsinn? Das Groteske im Modernen Drama.*   Basel,
Basilius, 1962.
Editor, *Samuel Beckett: A Collection of Critical Essays.*   Englewood Cliffs, New Jersey,
Prentice Hall, 1965.
Editor, *Absurd Drama.*   London, Penguin, 1965.
Editor, *The Genius of the German Theater.*   New York, New American Library, 1968.
Editor, *The New Theatre of Europe*, vol. 4.   New York, Dell, 1970.
Editor, *Illustrated Encyclopaedia of World Theatre*, by Karl Gröning and Werner Kliess,
translated by Estella Schmid.   London, Thames and Hudson, and New York,
Scribner, 1977.

Translator, with Renate Esslin and Herb Greer, *All Change and Other Plays*, by Wolfgang
Bauer.   London, Boyars, 1973.

*   *   *

For good or ill, the phrase Martin Esslin coined in the early 1960's, "the theatre of the
absurd," has stuck fast. Like some other phrases, the Angry Young Men, for example, or the
Beat Generation, it is an attractive label: it seems to locate something new and interesting and
possibly important—and to some extent it excuses further thought or analysis, although it is
obviously unfair to blame Esslin for the abuse it has suffered by now. The term "absurd,"
however, does not originate with Esslin. Camus borrowed it from Malraux, apparently, and
used it in *The Myth of Sisyphus* to characterize the sense of frustration the intellect experiences
when it confronts a universe which does not answer to human expectations and desires:

A world that can be explained by reasoning, however faulty, is a familiar world. But in a
universe that is suddenly deprived of illusions and of light, man feels a stranger. He is an
irremediable exile, because he is deprived of memories of a lost homeland as much as he
lacks the hope of a promised land to come. This divorce between man and his life, the
actor and his setting, truly constitutes the feeling of Absurdity.

The "theatre of the absurd," Esslin argues, should be seen as a reflection of "what seems to be
the attitude most genuinely representative of our own time":

The hallmark of this attitude is its sense that the certitudes and unshakable basic
assumptions of former ages have been swept away, that they have been tested and found
wanting, that they have been discredited as cheap and easy and somewhat childish
illusions. The decline of religious faith was masked until the end of the Second World
War by the substitute religion of faith in progress, nationalism, and various totalitarian
fallacies...[The] sense of metaphysical anguish at the absurdity of the human condition
is, broadly speaking, the theme of the plays of Beckett, Ionesco, Genet, and the other
writers discussed in [*The Theatre of the Absurd*].

In *The Theatre of the Absurd* and *Reflections* Esslin works hard to demonstrate to an intrigued
but suspicious audience that these playwrights are not only comprehensible but have a valuable
service to perform in the modern world.
    The theatre of the absurd is not to be defined, however, merely by the presence of this
particular kind of existentialism as a "subject" to be conveyed; it is quite possible, as some of
Kafka's work indicates, to embody the "absurd" point of view in a work which is fully and

conventionally organized. The true theatre of the absurd "strives to express its sense of the senselessness of the human condition...by the open abandonment of rational devices and discursive thought." Firmly constructed plots, clearly and consistently motivated characters— judged by these standards the plays Esslin has selected are not good plays at all. The question thus becomes: what is to be gained by this defiance of naturalistic expectations?

Basically Esslin seems to agree that the absurdist view is not only characteristic of our time but also *true*—or at least truer than the ordered views of past philosophy and religion. Oddly enough his final appeal is to "the modern scientific attitude" which

> rejects the postulates of a wholly coherent and simplified explanation that must account for all phenomena, purposes, and moral rules of the world. In concentrating on the slow, painstaking exploration of limited areas of reality by trial and error...the scientific attitude cheerfully accepts the view that we must be able to live with the realization that large segments of knowledge and experience will remain for a long time, perhaps forever, outside our ken; that ultimate purposes cannot, and never will be, known; and that we must therefore be able to accept the fact that much that earlier metaphysical systems, mythical, religious, or philosophical, sought to explain must forever remain unexplained.

Thus the theatre of the absurd at least displays a kind of courage in refusing to evade the uncomfortable truths of the human condition. But more important, Esslin argues, the theatre of the absurd has a therapeutic function:

> the spectator is confronted with the madness of the human condition, is enabled to see his situation in all its grimness and despair. Stripped of illusions and vaguely felt fears and anxieties, he can face his situation consciously...[and] by facing up to anxiety and despair and the absence of divinely revealed alternatives, anxiety and despair can be overcome.

This seems a noble hope rather than a logical or convincing proposition. At the conclusion of *The Theatre of the Absurd* Esslin simply *asserts* that "the dignity of man lies in his ability to face reality in all its senselessness; to accept it freely, without fear, without illusions—and to laugh at it."

Whatever the therapeutic possibilities involved, there are serious aesthetic problems left to deal with. The issue is basically that of the fallacy of imitative form, the term Yvor Winters uses to characterize that procedure in which "form succumbs to the raw material of the poem." Commenting on the implications of this position Cleanth Brooks observes that

> the modern poet would justify the formlessness of his poem by saying that he is writing about a chaotic and disordered age. But on the basis of such reasoning as this one could argue that the proper way to write a poem about madness is to make the poem itself insanely irrational, and the proper way to write about dullness is for the poet to make his *Dunciad* as dull and sleep-provoking as possible.

Esslin seems to recognize what is at stake but tends to evade the critical consequences. Or it may be simply that for him the truth-value of the absurdist vision is sufficient to outweigh any purely "aesthetic" shortcomings. Nevertheless he does propose two formal standards of his own: complexity of poetic image, which is relatively easy to recognize if not to define, and "quality of invention," which remains vague at best:

> Here we have one of the real hallmarks of excellence in the Theatre of the Absurd. Only when its invention springs from the deep layers of profoundly experienced emotion, only when it mirrors real obsessions, dreams, and valid images in the subconscious mind of its author, will such a work of art have that quality of truth...as distinct from...the delusions of the mentally afflicted. This quality of depth and unity of vision is instantly recognizable and beyond trickery.

The purely descriptive chapters in *The Theatre of the Absurd* and *Reflections* are of genuine value, whatever theoretical questions remain unanswered; the historical chapter of the former work, however, "The Tradition of the Absurd," is less useful because it becomes increasingly general and all-inclusive: at times Esslin seems to welcome into the tradition *any* departures from conventional naturalism. In his full-length study of Harold Pinter Esslin does an admirable job of demonstrating the indeterminacy of Pinter's plots and once again suggests that they are justified because Pinter's view of the world is the right one:

> for after all, the opaqueness, the impenetrability of other people's lives, their feelings, their true motivations, is, precisely, an essential figure of the true quality of the world and of our own experience of the world.... [Pinter's plays raise] metaphors of the fact that life itself consists of a succession of such questions that cannot, or will not, be capable of an answer.

As for the presence of shape or artistic form:

> The external world, objectively and meticulously recorded, must, of necessity, be fragmentary, disconnected, unmotivated, and without a clearly discernible structure; segments of reality are like that. But because these fragments have been noted down by a highly individual personality whose very act of perception must be an expression of his individual mode of experiencing the world around him, simply because certain objects or images will touch him more than others, the disconnected ingredients will coalesce into an organic structure, expressing its own inner consistencies—obeying its own inner law as an individual's personal vision of his own personal world.

But will fragments of perception necessarily "coalesce into an organic structure" just because one individual perceiver has been at work? And are "inner consistencies" different from the usual kind? The real issues disappear in a verbal haze not at all typical of Esslin when he deals patiently with specific works—perhaps too patiently. In the end there may be something wrong with wanting to domesticate these enigmatic writers, some of whom, at least, are clearly rejecting the entire humanistic tradition.

———————————————

FERGUSSON, Francis (De Liesseline).   American.   Born in Albuquerque, New Mexico, 21 February 1904. Educated at Harvard University, Cambridge, Massachusetts, 1921-23, and Queens College, Oxford (Rhodes Scholar), B.A. 1926. Married Marion Crowne in 1931 (died, 1959), two children; Peggy Watts, 1962. Associate Director, American Laboratory Theater, New York, 1927-30; Drama Critic, *The Bookman*, New York, 1930-32; Lecturer, New School for Social Research, New York, 1932-34; Member of the Humanities and Drama Faculty, Bennington College, Vermont, 1934-47; Member, Institute for Advanced Study, Princeton University, Princeton, New Jersey, 1947-49; Director, Princeton Seminars in Criticism, 1949-52; Professor of Comparative Literature, Rutgers University, New Brunswick, New Jersey, 1952-69. Since 1973, Professor, Princeton University. Visiting Professor, Indiana University, Bloomington, 1952-53. Member, Editorial Board, *Comparative Literature*, 1952-60. Member, Editorial Board, *The Sewanee Review*, Tennessee. Member, National Institute of Arts and Letters, and American Academy of Arts and Sciences; Fellow, School of Letters, Indiana University. Recipient: National Institute of Arts and Letters award, 1953; Phi Beta Kappa Christian Gauss Prize, 1954. D.Litt.: University of New Mexico, Albuquerque, 1955. Address: Box 143, Kingston, New Jersey 08528, U.S.A.

PUBLICATIONS

Criticism

Introduction to *Exiles*, by James Joyce, edited by Francis Fergusson.   New York, New
Directions, 1945.
The Idea of a Theater: A Study of Ten Plays: The Art of Drama in Changing Perspective.
Princeton, New Jersey, Princeton University Press, 1949.
Introduction to *Plays of Molière*.   New York, Modern Library, 1950.
Dante's Drama of the Mind: A Modern Reading of the Purgatorio.   Princeton, New
Jersey, Princeton University Press, 1953.
The Human Image in Dramatic Literature.   New York, Doubleday, 1957.
Introduction to *Plays*, by Paul Valéry.   New York, Pantheon, and London, Routledge,
1960.
Introduction to *Aristotle's Poetics*.   New York, Hill and Wang, 1961.
Dante Alighieri: Three Lectures.   Washington, D.C., Library of Congress, 1965.
Dante.   New York, Macmillan, and London, Weidenfeld and Nicolson, 1966.
Shakespeare: The Pattern in His Carpet.   New York, Delacorte Press, 1970.
Literary Landmarks: Essays on the Theory and Practice of Literature.   New Brunswick,
New Jersey, Rutgers University Press, 1976.
Trope and Allegory: Themes Common to Dante and Shakespeare.   Athens, University
of Georgia Press, 1977.

Verse

Poems: 1929-1961.   New Brunswick, New Jersey, Rutgers University Press, 1962.

Plays

*Sophocles' Electra: A Version for the Modern Stage with Notes on Production and
Critical Bibliography.*   New York, William B. Scott, 1938.
The King and the Duke (play with music, 1938), in *From the Modern Repertoire: Series
Two*, edited by Eric Bentley.   Denver, University of Denver Press, 1952.

Other

Editor, "Dante Alighieri: A Symposium of Modern Criticism," in *Kenyon Review*
(Gambier, Ohio), 14, 1952.
General Editor, *The Laurel Shakespeare*.   New York, Dell, 1958-68.

*   *   *

Admired as he has been by a generation or two of new critics, Francis Fergusson is not really
of their party, at least if we expect a new critic to be more concerned with verbal intricacies than
with the cultural forces which shape works of art. "The analysis of the art of drama," he insists,
"leads to the idea of a theater which gives it its sanction, and its actual life in its time and place";
and this principle in turn leads Fergusson to practice the kind of myth criticism now associated
with Maud Bodkin or Northrop Frye. The Greek and Elizabethan theaters held the mirror up
to nature, with memorable results, because these theaters themselves "had been formed at the
center of the culture of [their] time, and at the center of the life and awareness of the
community." And he continues:

We know that such a mirror is rarely formed. We doubt that our time has an age, a body, a form, or a pressure; we are more apt to think of it as a wilderness which is without form. Human nature seems to us a hopelessly elusive and uncandid entity, and our playwrights (like hunters with camera and flash-bulbs in the depths of the Belgian Congo) are lucky if they can fix it, at rare intervals, in one of its momentary postures, and in a single, bright, exclusive angle of vision. Thus the very *idea* of a theater, as Hamlet assumed it, gets lost; and the art of drama, having no place of its own in contemporary life, is confused with lyric poetry or music on the one side, or with editorializing and gossip on the other.

Thus in the first sections of *The Idea of a Theater* Fergusson examines the theater of *Hamlet* and *Oedipus Rex* as instances of cultural situations in which the artist and his audience shared a comprehensive grasp of human life as a whole. But capacious as the visions of Sophocles and Shakespeare may be, it is Dante who is the supreme artist for Fergusson. The *Divine Comedy* presents "the most developed idea of the theater of human life to be found in the [Western] tradition"; the *Purgatorio*, in particular, is "the most highly developed presentation of the tragic rhythm of human action we possess." The terms "action" and "tragic rhythm" take us to the center of Fergusson's critical thinking and require some definition, for while he agrees with Aristotle that art imitates life as it takes the form of action, he makes a further distinction between plot and action. "Plot" refers to the actual sequence of events the artist presents, whereas "action" refers to a larger context which the literal events may only suggest or imply; and this larger context is that of myth and ritual:

> We grasp the stagelife of a play through the plot, characters and words which manifest it; and if we are successful we can then act it, on the stage, or privately and silently. By such make-believe we come to understand the theater which the genius of the playwright has used to fix his vision. Beyond that we more vaguely discern the further mysteries: the picture of the human situation which the whole culture embodies and which the stage life itself represents. At this point the studies of historians, theologians, and anthropologists are useful, for they may help to free us from some of our provincial habits of mind.

The theater of Sophocles and Shakespeare must be understood, finally, as resting upon the fundamental truths (or at least coherence) defined by ritual. In *Hamlet* and *Oedipus Rex* the protagonists may suffer undeservedly as individuals, but their ordeals are part of a larger pattern of regeneration and continuity and would be understood as such by audiences whose "ritual expectancy" the artist was able to take for granted. The sources of pollution in Thebes and Denmark are uncovered and purged; the "precarious life of the human City" is maintained, although modern audiences may fail to grasp the intended emphasis and concentrate on preoccupations of their own. But properly grasped, Fergusson argues, the figure of Oedipus "fulfills all the requirements of the scapegoat, the dismembered king or god figure" of primitive myth; and whatever else we may make of *Hamlet*, "we are certainly intended to feel that Hamlet, however darkly and uncertainly he worked, had discerned the way to be obedient to his deepest values, and accomplished some sort of purgatorial progress for himself and Denmark."

These references to scapegoat and god figure indicate a conception of myth and ritual which Fergusson takes over from the Cambridge anthropologists. We may imagine a circle representing the course of the sun, the corresponding cycle of the seasons, and the life of the individual thrust into a pattern he must try to control or at least understand. The movement from birth to death, from dawn to midnight, from spring to winter, is "tragic," but there is also the countermovement of romance and comedy, to use Northrop Frye's terms, in which new life returns. The cycle persists and is celebrated in myth and ritual and later, however partially, in more "sophisticated" literature. Thus Fergusson's term "tragic rhythm" is partly misleading, since he means not only the tragic descent of the hero, but the implied (or dramatized) restoration as well. There is a tragic rhythm in Dante, but the *Divine Comedy* is just that, a comedy and not a tragedy; *Oedipus Rex* also exhibits the tragic rhythm, but the Oedipus "action" is not tragic. What Fergusson has attempted to do, then, is to join some of the principles of Aristotle's *Poetics* with the principles of modern myth criticism. This is clearly not the Aristotle of R.S. Crane or Elder Olson, and if the reader objects that Aristotle has little or nothing to say about ritual in the *Poetics*, Fergusson's answer is simply that the text of the work is notoriously incomplete.

Fergusson is indebted to Aristotle and to one school of cultural anthropology, and in later sections of *The Idea of a Theater* to T.S. Eliot as well. Early in his criticism Eliot had postulated the idea of a "unified sensibility" as a way of explaining the power of the Elizabethan dramatists and the Metaphysicals. The great poets (and the great periods of human culture) possess the ability to think and feel at the same moment. Browning and Tennyson are poets, Eliot argues, and they think,

> but they do not feel their thought as immediately as the odor of a rose. A thought to Donne was an experience; it modified his sensibility. When a poet's mind is perfectly equipped for its work, it is constantly amalgamating disparate experience; the ordinary man's experience is chaotic, irregular, fragmentary. The latter falls in love, or reads Spinoza, and these two experiences have nothing to do with each other, or with the noise of the typewriter or the smell of cooking; in the mind of the poet these experiences are always forming new wholes....The poets of the seventeenth century, the successors of the dramatists of the sixteenth, possessed a mechanism of sensibility which could devour any kind of experience....In the seventeenth century a dissociation of sensibility set in, from which we have never recovered.

The clear implication, of course, is that when a culture no longer possesses a common, unified grasp of human experience as a whole, the work of the artist is made extremely difficult or impossible. Fergusson sees a kind of dissociation of sensibility at work in the history of the drama as well. Unlike the theater of Sophocles, he maintains, the theater of Racine concentrates on one and only one dimension of human life, the moment of moral resolution:

> In Racine's dramaturgy, the situation, static in the eye of the mind, and illustrating the eternal plight of reason, is the basic unit of composition; in Sophocles' the basic unit is the tragic rhythm in which the mysterious human essence, never completely or fully realized, is manifested in successive and varied modes of action.

Just as fragmentary is the theater of Wagner's *Tristan*, in which not reason, but only passion is to be obeyed. In the last chapters of *The Idea of a Theater* Fergusson examines some of the leading but still partial perspectives of modern drama—the "realism" of Ibsen and Chekov, the deliberate theatricality of Shaw and Pirandello, and the "poetry" of more recent dramatic experiments. But once again he is forced to conclude that when the idea of a theater is lacking or inadequate,

> we are reduced to speculating about the plight of the whole culture. Unless the demoralizing power of modern industry is understood in some perspective, how can human life itself be seen as anything more than a by-product (marketable or unmarketable) of its developing and collapsing machinery? Unless the cultural components of our melting-pot are recognized, evaluated, and understood in some sort of relationship—our religious, racial, and regional traditions, and our actual habits of mind derived from applied science and practical politics, seen as mutually relevant—how can we get a perspective on anything?...The ultimate questions about the theater of human life in our time, and the drama of the modern world , are interdependent, theoretical and practical at once; and therefore unanswerable. We do not have a theater in the classic sense nor do we see how we could have one.

Unlike Eliot, however, Fergusson is patient, tolerant, even generous as he looks at the condition of modern art. "We do not blame the poets, playwrights and novelists for the confusion of the modern world," he observes in the preface to *The Human Image in Dramatic Literature*:

> We no longer believe that the poets are the unacknowledged legislators of the race; we do not know whom to accuse. We do not demand that the writer show us an order in the tradition as it reaches us, for order may be lost. We hold a poet responsible only for what he really and intimately sees, and are duly grateful for such harmonies as he does make, limited as they are by what he can hear where he sits, and by what his own sensibility can

catch....The authentic life of Humane Letters is to be found, now, in the diverse achievements of individual artists rather than in any common, central vision.

"What does it take to revive Humane Letters?" he asks in a splendid essay on Erich Auerbach:

> Is a love and understanding of Humane Letters themselves enough, or would it require a faith beyond them to make them sprout once more, like the withered tree in Dante's Paradiso Terrestre, which puts forth foliage when Christ's tear touches it?...*Lentement les temps se divident*: our children's children may see what the fate of Humane Letters is be.

The tone of this dying fall is quite different from the tone of Eliot, at least the intransigent Eliot of *After Strange Gods*, so bitterly critical of the heresy and "diabolism" in modern literature.

Predictably enough, Fergusson has written at length about Dante and Shakespeare. "His two books on Dante," Allen Tate has observed, "are expository masterpieces" (and he adds generously, "I have no reason [not] to believe that the professional Dantisti, here and abroad, have seen in Francis Fergusson their superior"). That the *Divine Comedy* rests upon a totally unified view of human life is beyond dispute, but the unity of Shakespeare's vision is a much more problematic issue. Fergusson, at least, is convinced that there is a coherent pattern in Shakespeare's carpet from beginning to end:

> Shakespeare's first concern was to make his stories credible....[His] "realism" is based ultimately on the faith that God Himself speaks through the visible world and all that occurs there. The poet's task, therefore, is first of all to reflect God's world with pious accuracy, and then to interpret correctly the meaning—God's truth—which it embodies. Whatever Shakespeare's formal belief may have been, he inherited from the Middle Ages this conception of poetry, and the medieval habits of allegorical interpretation that go with it....In dramatizing his old stories Shakespeare took full responsibility for embodying their true moral and religious meanings.

After noting the unified "world picture" of the Elizabethans Fergusson continues:

> I find no evidence that Shakespeare ever rejected, or even altered, this great underlying vision of man's life on earth, but of course he did not realize it fully until experience and thought had ripened it for him. And in the course of his career different aspects of it preoccupied him: in his youth, the promises of felicity; in the middle of the journey, its dark and terrifying depths; near the end of his career, its ancient signs of the natural sequence from cradle to grave.

This reference to the grave, however, should be taken in conjunction with his view of the last plays:

> The same sequence from innocence, to experience, to innocence regained underlies all four late plays. It resembles ancient parabolic representations of the course of human life, as a number of students of Shakespeare have pointed out in recent years: initiation ceremonies, rites of passage, myths of religious quests and ordeals of "culture heroes"; Dante's *Purgatory*, in which so many versions of this "timeless theme" (as Colin Still called it) are combined.

"Myth criticism" is sometimes a disparaging term, partly because myth critics are often reductive in their search for common denominators and indifferent to purely aesthetic matters. It would be hard to imagine a critic more sensitive or flexible than Francis Fergusson, however, or one who is so truly self-effacing, in the best sense of that word, when he examines a particular work or the efforts of his fellow-critics.

FIEDLER, Leslie A(aron).   American.   Born in Newark, New Jersey, 8 March 1917. Educated at New York University, B.A. 1938; University of Wisconsin, Madison, M.A. 1939, Ph.D. 1941; Harvard University, Cambridge, Massachusetts (Rockefeller Fellow), 1946-47. Served in the United States Naval Reserve, 1942-46: Lieutenant. Married 1) Margaret Ann Shipley in 1939 (divorced, 1973), six children; 2) Sally Smith Andersen, 1973, two foster children. Assistant Professor, 1947-48, Associate Professor, 1948-52, Professor of English, 1953-64, and Chairman of the Department, 1954-56, Montana State University, Missoula. Since 1965, Professor of English, currently Samuel Clemens Professor, State University of New York at Buffalo. Fulbright Lecturer, University of Rome, 1951-52, University of Bologna and Ca Foscari University, 1952-53, and University of Athens, 1961-62; Gauss Lecturer in Criticism, Princeton University, New Jersey, 1956-57; Lecturer, University of Sussex, Brighton, and University of Amsterdam, 1967-68; Visiting Professor, University of Vincennes, Paris, 1970-71. Fellow, Indiana University School of Letters, Bloomington, 1953; Associate Fellow, Calhoun College, Yale University, New Haven, Connecticut, 1969. Advisory Editor, *Ramparts* magazine, New York, 1958-61. Recipient: *Furioso* poetry prize, 1951; *Kenyon Review* Fellowship, for non-fiction, 1956; American Academy grant, 1957; American Council of Learned Societies grant, 1960, 1961; Guggenheim Fellowship, 1970. Address: 154 Morris Avenue, Buffalo, New York 14214, U.S.A.

PUBLICATIONS

Criticism

An End to Innocence: Essays on Culture and Politics.   Boston, Beacon Press, 1955; reprinted in *Collected Essays*, vol. 1, 1971.
The Jew in the American Novel.   New York, Herzl Press, 1959; reprinted in *Collected Essays*, vol. 2, 1971.
Love and Death in the American Novel.   New York, Criterion Books, 1960; London, Secker and Warburg, 1961; revised edition, New York, Stein and Day, 1966; London, Cape, 1967.
No! In Thunder: Essays on Myth and Literature.   Boston, Beacon Press, 1960; London, Eyre and Spottiswoode, 1963; reprinted in *Collected Essays*, vol. 1, 1971.
The Riddle of Shakespeare's Sonnets.   New York, Basic Books, 1962.
Waiting for the End.   New York, Stein and Day, 1964; as *Waiting for the End: The American Literary Scene from Hemingway to Baldwin*, London, Cape, 1965.
The Return of the Vanishing American.   New York, Stein and Day, and London, Cape, 1968.
The Collected Essays of Leslie Fiedler.   New York, Stein and Day, 2 vols., 1971.
The Stranger in Shakespeare.   New York, Stein and Day, 1972; London, Croom Helm, 1973.
To the Gentiles.   New York, Stein and Day, 1972.
Cross the Border, Close the Gap.   New York, Stein and Day, 1972.
The Inadvertant Epic: From Uncle Tom's Cabin to Roots.   Toronto, Canadian Broadcasting Corporation, 1979; New York, Simon and Schuster, 1980.

Novels

The Second Stone: A Love Story.   New York, Stein and Day, 1963; London, Heinemann, 1966.
Back to China.   New York, Stein and Day, 1965.
The Messengers Will Come No More.   New York, Stein and Day, 1974.

Short Stories

Pull Down Vanity and Other Stories. Philadelphia, Lippincott, 1962; London, Secker and Warburg, 1963.
The Last Jew in America. New York, Stein and Day, 1966.
Nude Croquet and Other Stories. New York, Stein and Day, 1969; London, Secker and Warburg, 1970.

Other

Being Busted. New York, Stein and Day, and London, Secker and Warburg, 1970.
A Fiedler Reader. New York, Stein and Day, 1977.
Freaks: Myths and Images of the Secret Self. New York, Simon and Schuster, 1978.

Editor, *The Art of the Essay.* New York, Crowell, 1958; revised edition, 1969.
Editor, *Selections from "Leaves of Grass,"* by Walt Whitman. New York, Dell, 1959.
Editor, with J. Vinocur, *The Continuing Debate: Essays on Education.* New York, St. Martin's Press, 1965.
Editor, with A. Zager, *O Brave New World.* New York, Dell, 1968.
Editor, with Houston A. Baker, Jr., *English Literature: Opening Up the Canon.* Baltimore, Maryland, Johns Hopkins University Press, 1981.

*   *   *

Despite his well-known preoccupation with social and psychological issues, Leslie Fiedler regards himself as *"primarily* a literary person, though one whose interest in works of art is dictated by a moral passion rather than a cooler technical concern." In fact, he insists, "there is no 'work itself,' no independent formal entity which is its own sole context; the poem is the sum total of many contexts, all of which must be known to know it and evaluate it. 'Only connect!' should be the motto of all critics and teachers." And in the preface to *Love and Death in the American Novel* he concludes that

> the best criticism can hope to do is to set the work in as many illuminating contexts as possible: the context of the genre to which it belongs, of the whole body of work of its author, of the life of the author and of his times. In this sense, it becomes clear that the "text" is merely one of the contexts of a piece of literature, its lexical or verbal one, no more or less important than the sociological, psychological, historical, anthropological or generic.

Thus in theory, at least, Fiedler is a kind of pluralist, though he tends to be impatient with formal, academic criticism. His own readers, he goes on, will recognize that he usually concentrates on "the mythic element...which is to say on an element which is indifferent to medium, rather than on those formal elements which distinguish one medium from another." All of these quotations help to locate Fiedler's basic critical position, but for the clearest possible statement of his commitments readers should consult the two essays which make up the last section of the first volume of his *Collected Essays* and the introduction to *No! In Thunder.*

For Fiedler, human awareness begins as *mythos,* that is, the intuitive perception of the archetypes of experience, "those archaic and persisting clusters of image and emotion which at once define and attempt to solve what is most pertinent in the human predicament." Archetype, like myth, comes to mean "any of the immemorial patterns of response to the human situation in its most permanent aspects: death, love, the biological family, the relationship with the Unknown, etc." Myth expresses the archetypal situations of life, then (in which case it is difficult to think of any imaginative literature which is *not* "mythic") and also retains, as science does not, the element of emotion proper to those occasions, particularly the emotions of wonder and love:

Certainly, it is in the power of scientific discourse to specify archetypal intuitions of man's relation to his own existence, his death and the universe around him, so that they are more viable for healing and social control and even the encouragement of civic virtue; so that, in short, they *work*. What is lost, however, is the sense of reverence and astonishment...which alone breeds *pietas*—not religion, for even science can be a religion; but that natural piety without which we can approach the given world only as an enemy or a bore....

The world has not abandoned us, but we it; for only as we love it can we know it, and the scientific knowing is a knowledge without love, a rape of nature.

With the rise of philosophy and science there is an inevitable "fall from intuition into idea" ("*Logos*," as Fiedler calls it) and a consequent loss of feeling. Imaginative literature preserves the intuition and the emotion but of course is not simply "mythic": it also bears the stamp of history and the artist's own individual concerns and powers, or "Signature." The true critic, then, is alert to both Myth and Signature: far from being irrelevant to the final act of judgment, "the consideration of the archetypal content of works of art is essential to it!" This is a crucial point, but like many myth critics, Fiedler evades its implications. Myth becomes a kind of privileged subject matter whose relationship to conventional aesthetic standards is unclear. The reader may wonder whether (and why) some myths are more significant than others and how their significance varies from one culture to another.

Once he moves beyond primitive myth, however, Fiedler is on familiar ground. Art is moral activity or it is nothing, he asserts; men will always pay handsomely to be lied to, to be distracted from the painful issues of life, but the great artist has a responsibility to say no, in thunder, as Melville did, to the conventional pieties:

Insofar as a work of art is, as art, successful, it performs a negative critical function: for the irony of art in the human situation lies in this: that man—or better, some men—are capable of achieving in works of art a coherence, a unity, a balance, a satisfaction of conflicting impulses which they cannot (but which they desperately long to) achieve in love, family relations, politics. Yet works of art are *about* love, family relations, politics, etc; and to the degree that these radically imperfect human activities are represented in a perfectly articulated form, they are revealed in all their intolerable inadequacy. The image of man in art, however magnificently portrayed—indeed, precisely when it is most magnificently portrayed—is the image of a failure. There is no way out....Especially in recent times, when the obligations of self-consciousness are imposed on us with a rigor unheard of in the past, the writer becomes aware that his Muse is more like the *Daimon* of Socrates (who appeared only to say No!) or the God of Job than like any of those white-draped Ladies of the genteel mythologists.

"Moral ambiguity" (by which Fiedler seems to mean moral complexity) is also something we expect of the modern artist:

The conventional definitions of the comic and the tragic strike him as simplifications, falsifications of human life, appropriate to a less complex time. To insist that we regard man, even for the space of three acts or five, as *either* horrible or funny; to require of us, through four or five hundred pages, *either* to laugh or to cry we find offensive in an age when we can scarcely conceive of wanting to do one without the other.

There is nothing new here, of course, save perhaps the energy of Fiedler's style. The satisfaction of conflicting impulses strongly suggests Richards, while the moral demands are simply a restatement of Arnold's slogan that at bottom, art is a criticism of life.

Yet on more than one occasion Fiedler has deprecated these "theoretical" essays and implied that it might be more profitable to approach his practical criticism in terms of the various stages of development he has passed through—although his vantage point, he insists, has always been that of "a liberal, intellectual, writer, American, and Jew." And he adds, "I do not mind, as some people apparently do, thinking of myself in such categorical terms; being representative of a class, a generation, a certain temper seems to me not at all a threat to my individuality." But like many other intellectuals who started out in the 'thirties, Fiedler explains, he has been thrice-born. His first position was that of "radical dissent" (this apparently predates any of his published criticism). A period of "radical disillusion" followed—disillusionment, that is, with the oversimplifications of dogmatic liberalism—and is the driving force behind many of the best essays in his first collection, *An End to Innocence* (the essays, for example, on Hiss, McCarthy and the Rosenbergs). A third stage, which moves uncertainly into "whatever it is that lies beyond both commitment and disaffection" brings us up to date.

The second stage is literary as well as political. Fiedler's approach in *Love and Death in the American Novel* is mythic, that is, concerned with the archetypes of American fiction, and "disillusioned"—though the term is no doubt too dramatic—to the extent that he refuses to accept the genteel literary commonplaces which deny the darker issues of American life and literature. The determining premise here is psychological rather than purely "literary": "The failure of the American fictionalist to deal with adult heterosexual love," Fiedler asserts bluntly, "and his consequent obsession with death, incest and homosexuality are not merely matters of historical interest or literary relevance. They affect the lives we live from day to day and influence the writers in whom the consciousness of our plight is given clarity and form." The failure of our fiction is rooted in "the regressiveness, in a technical sense, of American life, its implacable nostalgia for the infantile." Fiedler admits that it is difficult to determine whether "the fear of sex, a strange blindness to the daily manifestations of sex, or the attenuation of sexuality itself drove the American novel back over the lintel of puberty"; but that American sexuality is, or was, deficient or regressive, he has no doubts. Because of this our classic novels "turn away from society to nature or nightmare out of a desperate need to avoid the facts of wooing, marriage and child-bearing." Thus the American artist is unable to imagine "the confrontation of man and woman which leads to the fall of sex, marriage, and responsibility." We are still waiting, he complains in an earlier essay, for the American writer "who can render as successfully as, say, any second-rate French novelist of the nineteenth century the complexities and the ambiguities of sexual passion, of—(how absurdly hard it is for the American writer to say simply "love") of *love*." Fiedler traces the American translations of available European fictional models—particularly the sentimental novel and the historical romance—but maintains that it was the Gothic Romance which had the decisive influence on our fiction, since "the primary meaning of the gothic romance...lies in its substitution of terror for love." Guilt (over our assault on the virgin land and our oppression of Indians and Blacks), terror and idealized homoeroticism fill the vacuum left by the fear of "adult sex."

If all of this is true, then there are some very troubling implications. If we assume, for example, that American life is to some extent pathological, our writers must seem like disturbed patients caught up in a kind of determinism which denies them the freedom and mastery we usually believe are the artist's greatest gifts. Thus Fiedler can confidently asert that had she lived, Catherine (the doomed heroine of *A Farewell to Arms*) "could only have turned into a bitch; for this is the fate in Hemingway's imagination of all Anglo-Saxon women." And if our strongest writers are still victims of our culture, then they can hardly rise to the responsibilities Fiedler clearly insists upon in *No! In Thunder*; their best work, like Poe's, may seem "symptoms rather than achievements." But Fiedler rushes to the rescue at the very end of *Love and Death*. He asserts—it would be difficult to say that he proves or argues—that it is the gothic element itself which saves American fiction:

> All fictionalists are committed, surely, whatever their other concerns, to revealing the inevitable discrepancy between what life at any moment is imagined and what it is, between what man dreams and what he achieves, between what he would like to believe and what he fears is true. But the "what he fears is true" is the subject par excellence of the gothic, when it is more than mere trifling and titillation.
>
> Nowhere in the world does the writer feel more deeply than in the United States the secret appeal of the community at large that he deny their publicly asserted orthodoxies, expose their dearly preserved deceits.

Fiedler is now confident that *Love and Death* and his other related works "have become for a new generation of teachers in universities, colleges and high schools, the basis for a new understanding of our classic books and of our culture in general, as well as the model for critical studies which do not even bother to acknowledge their source," but the outcry they occasioned from conservative critics may be imagined. Yet one recurring criticism—that Fiedler had been "too psychological"—seems oddly beside the point. It would make more sense to object that he has not been psychological enough. When bits of Freud and Jung appear and disappear so quickly, alone or in uneasy conjunction, the reader may well want to ask questions about the kind of psychology Fiedler practices. Clearly, some version of Freudianism is at work most of the time and raises other problems. If the covert theme of a work is the truly important element (Shakespeare's "anti-feminism," for example, which Fiedler explores in *The Stranger in Shakespeare*), is our failure to respond to it a symptom of our own psychological distress? And if so, does a proper reading, in Fiedler's terms, "correct" our rationalizations? The reader may find himself in the position of the defensive patient who insists that he just doesn't see things that way. That *proves* I'm right, the critic-analyst can reply easily enough. Certain kinds of Freudianism offer splendid examples of what Kenneth Burke calls heads-I-win, tails-you-lose tactics.

As for the most recent stage of Fiedler's development: for some time now he has been asserting that modernism is dead, that the age of Eliot and Mann and Joyce is over, and that the elitist criticism their work fostered is no longer relevant to writers who are "turning away after nearly half a century from sophisticated literary cosmopolitanism; and...returning—with extraordinary ferocity and what can only be called a willing suspension of intelligence—to the crassest kind of nationalism, nativism, and primitivism: back to Caliban, in short." Thus a truly up-to-date criticism

> certainly will no longer be formalist or intrinsic; it will be contextual rather than textual, not primarily concerned with structure or diction or syntax, all of which assume that the work of art "really" exists on the page rather than in a reader's passionate apprehension and response. Not words-on-the-page but words-in-the-world or rather words-in-the-head, which is to say, at the private juncture of a thousand contexts, social, psychological, historical, biographical, geographical, in the consciousness of the lonely reader (delivered for an instant, but an instant only, from all of those contexts by the *ekstasis* of reading): this will be the proper concern of the critics to come.

This program for the Newest Criticism is anything but clear (but perhaps it can't be, dealing as it must with mutant anti-literature).

Fiedler's critical method requires some comment. His manner is oracular; he rarely proves or demonstrates, preferring to depend on the force of an unexpected generalization. Sometimes the generalizations are shrewd and genuinely arresting; sometimes they are vacant gestures ("Though the novel marks the entrance of the libido onto the stage of European art, in it the libido enters with eyes cast down and hands clasped—in the white garments of a maiden"). He strives for somehow profound similarities and strains for size and significance ("In his relationship to his lot, his final resolve to accept what is called these days his 'terrible freedom,' Huck Finn seems the first Existentialist hero..."). Still, there are readers who find passages such as this exciting:

> Desdemona dreams, or rather Shakespeare dreams through her, a symbolic marriage of all that Europe and Africa mythically mean: civilization and barbarism, courtesy and strength, belonging and freedom, Beauty and the Beast; or, in classical terms, Diana and Ares, which is to say, the virgin and the warrior, the absolute poles of masculinity and femininity. So long as the marriage holds, it signifies a miracle, a *discordia concors* in the flesh. And when it fails, it represents, by the same token, the eternal impossibility of the union that man eternally dreams: the reuniting of the original bisexual self, sundered by the wrath of the gods (as in the myth Plato attributes in the *Symposium* to Aristophanes).

Critics who assume the role of oracle are in a difficult position: they have to be right. But if they are confident of their vision (and Fiedler is supremely self-confident: how could everyone *else* be so square and unadult, his essays keep implying), they apparently feel that humble matters of argument and proof can be left to the faithful.

FISH, Stanley E(ugene).   American.   Born in Providence, Rhode Island, 19 April 1938. Educated at University of Pennsylvania, Philadelphia, B.A. 1959; Yale University, New Haven, Connecticut, M.A. 1960, Ph.D. 1962. Married Adrienne A. Aaron in 1959; one daughter. Instructor, 1962-63, Assistant Professor, 1963-67, and Associate Professor, 1967-74 (Humanities Research Professorship, 1966 and 1970), University of California, Berkeley; Leonard S. Bing Visiting Professor, University of Southern California, Los Angeles, 1973-74. Visiting Professor, 1971, and since 1974 Professor of English, Johns Hopkins University, Baltimore, Maryland. Member of the Editorial Board, *Milton Quarterly, Milton Studies*, and *Medievalia et Humanistica*. Recipient: American Council of Learned Societies Fellowship, 1966; Guggenheim Fellowship, 1969. Address: Department of English, Johns Hopkins University, Baltimore, Maryland 21218, U.S.A.

PUBLICATIONS

Criticism

> *John Skelton's Poetry.*   New Haven, Connecticut, and London, Yale University Press, 1965.
> *Surprised by Sin: The Reader in Paradise Lost.*   London, Macmillan, and New York, St. Martin's Press, 1967.
> "Literature in the Reader: Affective Stylistics," in *New Literary History* (Charlottesville, Virginia), 2, 1970; reprinted in *Self-Consuming Artifacts*, 1972, and *Is There a Text in This Class?* 1980.
> *Self-Consuming Artifacts: The Experience of Seventeenth-Century Literature.*   Los Angeles and London, University of California Press, 1972.
> "What Is Stylistics and Why Are They Saying Such Terrible Things about It?" in *Approaches to Poetics*, edited by Seymour Chatman.   New York, Columbia University Press, 1973; reprinted in *Is There a Text in This Class?* 1980.
> "How Ordinary Is Ordinary Language?" in *New Literary History* (Charlottesville, Virginia), 3, 1973; reprinted in *Is There a Text in This Class?* 1980.
> "Facts and Fictions," A Reply to Ralph Rader," in *Critical Inquiry* (Chicago), 1, 1975; reprinted in *Is There a Text in This Class?* 1980.
> "Interpreting the *Variorum*," in *Critical Inquiry* (Chicago), 2, 1976; reprinted in *Is There a Text in This Class?* 1980.
> "Interpreting 'Interpreting the *Variorum*,' " in *Critical Inquiry* (Chicago), 3, 1976; reprinted in *Is There a Text in This Class?* 1980.
> "How to Do Things with Austin and Searle: Speech Act Theory and Literary Criticism," in *Modern Language Notes* (Baltimore), 91, 1976; reprinted in *Is There a Text in This Class?*, 1980.
> "Normal Circumstances, Literal Language, Direct Speech Acts, the Ordinary, the Everyday, the Obvious, What Goes Without Saying, and Other Special Cases," in *Critical Inquiry* (Chicago), 4, 1978; reprinted in *Is There a Text in This Class?*, 1980.
> *The Living Temple: George Herbert and Catechizing.*   Berkeley and Los Angeles, University of California Press, 1978.
> "What Is Stylistics and Why Are They Saying Such Terrible Things About It?—Part II," in *Boundary 2* (Binghamton, New York), 7, 1979; reprinted in *Is There a Text in This Class?*, 1980.
> *Is There a Text in This Class? The Authority of Interpretive Communities.*   Cambridge, Massachusetts, and London, Harvard University Press, 1980.
> "*Lycidas*: A Poem Finally Anonymous," in *Glyph* (Baltimore), 8, 1981.

CRITICAL STUDIES

> Ralph W. Rader, "Fact, Theory, and Literary Explanation," in *Critical Inquiry* (Chicago), 1, 1974.

Douglas Bush, "Professor Fish on the Milton *Variorum*," in *Critical Inquiry* (Chicago), 3, 1976.

Steven Mailloux, "Stanley Fish's 'Interpreting the *Variorum*': Advance or Retreat?" in *Critical Inquiry* (Chicago), 3, 1976.

M.H. Abrams, "How to Do Things With Texts," in *Partisan Review* (Boston), 46, 1979.

Joseph F. Graham, "Critical Persuasion: In Response to Stanley Fish," in *Boundary 2* (Binghamton, New York), 7, 1979.

Jonathan Culler, "Stanley Fish and the Righting of the Reader," in *The Pursuit of Signs: Semiotics, Literature, Deconstruction.* Ithaca, New York, Cornell University Press, 1981.

*   *   *

"Conservative" critics and readers as Stanley Fish now characterizes them—with just a trace of amused disdain—are almost by definition bound to agree upon one crucial principle: it is possible, and highly desirable, to have rational consensus about the often complex but ultimately fixed, determinate meaning of a literary text. We can say that one interpretation is better than another because, by means of sensitivity and scholarship, we can determine the author's intended meaning and as responsible readers honor it. This is the position taken by M.H. Abrams, E.D. Hirsch, Wayne Booth and a good many other common readers and critics. Fish would also agree that such consensus is possible, indeed inevitable, but he operates from a vantage point which separates him radically from the opposition. For him (to oversimplify for the moment), we do not recover embedded authorial meanings, we create them ourselves, using the interpretive strategies we bring to our extremely loaded "perception" of a text; literature is not essentially different from ordinary discourse, it is merely a conventional category ("What will, at any time, be recognized as literature is a function of the communal decision as to what will count as literature"). And if we think we have consensus about what we naïvely take to be the meaning of a text, it is simply because, and only insofar as, we happen to belong to the same interpretive community. Not that Fish has always challenged the establishment so directly: in 1967, for example, he flatly asserted that "there is only one true interpretation of *Paradise Lost*" which is the "reward" for those readers who have the capacity to become one with "Milton's spirit." The stages Fish has gone through during the past fifteen or so years are complex and instructive.

In his first book, *Surprised by Sin*, Fish argues very persuasively that *Paradise Lost* is a poem "about how its readers came to be the way they are," that is, fallen creatures, temptation-ridden but capable of learning and thus still candidates for redemption. Time and time again, as Fish demonstrates, Milton "entangles" rather than merely teaches his readers. By means of complex syntax and imagery and every other stylistic device at his command, he leads us down the same dangerous paths Adam and Eve and Satan took, only to obstruct or reverse our course and thus correct our errors: "Milton compels the sense of Christian obedience by fitting temptations to our inclinations and then confronting us immediately with the evidence of our fallibility. And in the process, he fosters the intense self-consciousness which is the goal of spiritual self-examination." Unlike some of his students, Fish does not suggest that all poems be read in his way; he admits, however, that he is "drawn to works which do not allow the reader the security of his normal patterns of thought and belief," and in *Self-Consuming Artifacts* distinguishes these "dialectical" works from those which are merely "rhetorical":

> A presentation is rhetorical if it satisfies the needs of its readers. The word "satisfies" is meant literally here; for it is characteristic of a rhetorical form to mirror and present for approval the opinions its readers already hold.... A dialectical presentation, on the other hand, is disturbing, for it requires of its readers a searching and rigorous scrutiny of everything they believe in and live by.

All of this depends upon a sophisticated conception of the reading process itself which Fish did not make explicit until 1970, in his influential essay "Literature in the Reader: Affective Stylistics." The act of reading, he maintains here, is precisely that, an *act*, a "kinetic process," a "temporal experience" criticism falsifies by turning into a "spatial experience," from which a "message" is then extracted. Genuine criticism, as Fish defines it, is a "language-sensitizing" device which allows us to understand meaning properly as an "event," and involves "an analysis of the developing responses of the reader in relation to the words as they succeed one another in time." For example, the meaning of Milton's line, "Nor did they not perceive the evil plight," experienced in context as an unfolding and then modification of expectations, is quite different from the meaning of the line recollected and paraphrased after the act of reading. But since all reading is activity, are all readings equally interesting or relevant? The answer of course is no, they are not; and Fish is able to escape relativism by positing a reader who has "literary competence," a skill analogous to what Chomsky calls "linguistic competence": in each case the terms refer to the capacity we have to understand utterances and to learn the ways in which they can be used for various effects. The "temporal flow" of reading is "monitored and structured by everything the reader brings with him," and among the things the competent reader brings with him is the learned ability to be an "informed reader" whose mind is now the repository of the "potential responses a given text may call out." In operation, then, this method

> will obviously be radically historical. The critic has the responsibility of becoming not one but a number of informed readers, each of whom will be determined by a matrix of political, cultural, and literary determinants. The informed reader of Milton will not be the informed reader of Whitman, although the latter will necessarily comprehend the former.

In "How To Do Things With Texts" M.H. Abrams has raised some important questions about the adequacy of Fish's model of reading, calling it an artificial, after-the-fact "stop-start" device which allows him to find exactly what he wants to find—something Fish now cheerfully admits. But even if the model needs modification (psycholinguists would probably be able to help here), the valuable conception of meaning as event remains. We might go further, however, and raise an issue which may or may not constitute an objection. If Fish is correct about the temporal nature of understanding and about literary competence, then the fullest and most powerful aesthetic experience is a fragile and unrepeatable affair. The real force, at least of dialectical works, can be felt only when the competent reader first encounters the text, with no prior knowledge of where it will take him (if he is incompetent, the effect will be lost on him; if he has experienced the work before, the effect is certain to be diminished). Possibly Fish would be willing to admit this, and to recognize the sad implications it has for competent tourists, competent lovers, competent consumers of any sort. The burden of familiarity, in short.

In any event, despite his apparent emphasis on "the role of the reader," Fish had not yet abandoned the notion of a fixed text and the possibility of one correct interpretation. The competent reader *is* active, but he is not the instigator of the action; he follows where the entangling text leads him. A few years later, however, Fish saw matters differently. He gave up the "enabling assumptions" of his reader-oriented position and demonstrated that in his own criticism "the formal features with which I began [were] the product of the interpretive principles for which they are supposedly evidence." Thus

> I did what critics always do: I "saw" what my interpretive principles permitted or directed me to see and then I turned around and attributed what I had "seen" to a text and an intention...This would mean, for example, that the moment crucial to my analysis of *Paradise Lost*, IV, 9-12, the moment when the reader mistakenly thinks that it is the loss of Eden of which Adam and Eve are declared innocent, is not discovered by the analytical method but produced by it.

It is not the text which sets interpretive strategies in motion. On the contrary, pre-existing strategies (which we often possess unconsciously or believe to be self-evident, objective truths) actively constitute the object of our interpretation. Why Fish made this startling shift is not entirely clear: perhaps it was the influence of John Searle or J.L. Austin or, more likely, Wittgenstein; perhaps it was his determination to discover what there was of value behind the nihilism and jargon of Derrida and his American followers; or it might simply be the result of his rigor and unwillingness to take anything on faith. For whatever reasons, Fish now argues from a position firmly grounded in what historians of philosophy usually refer to as "critical realism."

For naïve realists, according to Fish,

> it is possible to specify a level at which language correlates with the objective world and
> from which one then builds up to contexts, situations, emotions, biases, and finally, at
> the outermost and dangerous limits, to literature. The claim is a far-reaching one,
> because to make it is at the same time to make claims about the nature of reality, the
> structure of the mind, the dynamics of perception, the autonomy of the self, the ontology
> of literature, the possibility and scope of formalization, the stability of literary (and
> therefore of nonliterary) texts, the independence of fact from value, and the independence
> of meaning from interpretation. It is not too much to say that everything I write is
> written against that claim, in all of its consequences and implications.

For Fish, as for all critical realists, nothing is "given." There are no pure acts of perception, that
is, acts which are disinterested or separate from complex tissues of assumptions, expectations
and goals. We never know what is "really out there"; we know only the reports of our senses, out
of which we actively *make* a picture of reality. That picture may be consoling or beneficial but it
is a picture nonetheless, and we have no right to claim any one-to-one relationship between
what we "know" and what is really out there. Taking up a well-known example from Austin's
How To Do Things With Words, the "truth value" of a statement such as "France is
hexagonal," Fish maintains that

> There are a great many things one can say about France, including that it is or is not
> hexagonal, but the felicity of whatever one says will be a function of its relation to some
> dimension of assessment or other—whether that dimension is military, geographical,
> culinary, or economic—and moreover, the France one is saying it about will be
> recognizable, and therefore describable, *only* within that dimension. In short, the one
> thing you can never say about France is what it is *really* like, if by "really" you mean
> France as it exists independently of any dimension of assessment whatsoever. The
> France you are talking about will always be the product of the talk about it, and will
> *never* be independently available.
>   What the example of France shows is that all facts are discourse specific...and that
> therefore no one can claim for any language a special relationship to the facts as they
> "simply are," unmeditated by social or conventional assumptions.

All our knowledge, therefore, is, as another critical realist, Santayana, puts it, "fictive." We live
not in the world but inside a fictive version of the world which Fish calls the "standard story."
John Searle's argument in *Speech Acts*, Fish continues, at first seems "so obviously right":

> But its rightness is a function of the *extra-theoretical* stipulation of the standard story as
> uniquely true. That is, I am not denying that what will and will not be accepted as true is
> determined by the standard story. I am only pointing out that its being (or telling: it
> comes to the same thing) the truth is not a matter of a special relationship it bears to the
> world (the world does not impose it on us) but of a special relationship it bears to its
> users.
>   In large part, my argument follows from Wittgenstein's notion of a "language game"
> in which words are responsible not to what is real but to what has been laid down as real
> (as pickoutable) by a set of constitutive rules; the players of the game are able to agree
> that they mean the same things by their words not because they see the same things, in
> some absolute phenomenal sense, but because they are predisposed by the fact of being
> in the game (of being parties to the standard story) to "see them," to pick them out.

The conclusion, then, is that "all objects are made and not found, and that they are made by the
interpretive strategies we set in motion." But even the phrase itself, "set in motion," is
misleading. Usually it is we who are set in motion by the language games and interpretive
strategies which permeate our culture and education:

> The self is constituted, no less than the texts it constitutes in turn, by conventional ways
> of thinking...[The] thoughts an individual can think and the mental operations he can

perform have their source in some or other interpretive community...[He] is as much a product of that community (acting as an extension of it) as the meanings it enables him to produce.

The consequences for the interpretation of literary texts is no less decisive. Just as there are, from this point of view, no brute facts, no knowledge of what France is really like, so there is no simple text called *Paradise Lost* or *Surprised by Sin*. We see only what our strategies allow us to see and are rarely if ever in control of the cultural perspective which generates the strategies in the first place. Has Fish therefore condemned himself to a thinly disguised form of solipsism? He is aware of the problem but so far has not formally taken it up (he might easily do so, however. There are arguments available—Santayana's powerful arguments, for example, in *Skepticism and Animal Faith*). Finally, is he able to account for change? Why is it that some strategies flourish at the expense of others? How are new strategies brought into being? Again, Fish has not taken up these questions, but there is nothing in his system which would prevent him or anyone else from doing so.

"For brilliance and forcefulness in argumentation and for sheer boldness of mind and spirit," Barbara Herrnstein Smith observed recently, Fish "has no match." This is extravagant but not unreasonable praise. At the very least Fish has made some of us uncomfortable. It is not as easy as it once was to believe texts and readers lead independent lives in a world of hard facts and self-evident truths.

FORSTER, E(dward) M(organ). British. Born in London, 1 January 1879. Educated at Tonbridge School, and at King's College, Cambridge, B.A. 1901, M.A. 1910. Lived in Greece and Italy, 1901-07; helped found, and contributed to, the *Independent Review*, London, 1903; lectured at the Working Men's College, London, 1907; visited India, 1912; Red Cross Volunteer Worker in Egypt, 1914-18; Literary Editor, *The Daily Herald*, London, 1920-21; Private Secretary to the Maharajah of Dewas, India, 1922; Fellow of King's College, Cambridge, and Clark Lecturer, Trinity College, Cambridge, 1927; Honorary Fellow of King's College, 1946, until his death. Vice-President, London Library; Member, General Advisory Council, BBC; President, Cambridge Humanists. Recipient: Black Memorial Prize, 1925; Prix Femina Vie Heureuse, 1925; Royal Society of Literature Benson Medal, 1937, and Companion of Literature, 1961. LL.D.: University of Aberdeen, 1931; Litt.D.: University of Liverpool, 1947; Hamilton College, Clinton, New York, 1949; Cambridge University, 1950; University of Nottingham, 1951; University of Manchester, 1954; Leyden University, Holland, 1954; University of Leicester, 1958. Honorary Member, American Academy and Bavarian Academy of Fine Arts. Companion of Honour, 1953; Order of Merit, 1968. *Died 7 June 1970.*

PUBLICATIONS

Criticism

Anonymity: An Enquiry. London, Hogarth Press, 1925; reprinted in *Two Cheers for Democracy*, 1951.
Aspects of the Novel. London, Arnold, and New York, Harcourt Brace, 1927.
Sinclair Lewis Interprets America. Privately printed, 1932; reprinted in *Abinger Harvest*, 1936.
Abinger Harvest. London, Arnold, and New York, Harcourt Brace, 1936.
Reading as Usual (radio talk). London, Tottenham Public Libraries, 1939.

Virginia Woolf (lecture).   Cambridge, University Press, and New York, Harcourt Brace, 1942; reprinted in *Two Cheers for Democracy*, 1951.
The Development of English Prose Between 1918 and 1939 (lecture).   Glasgow, University Press, 1945; reprinted in *Two Cheers for Democracy*, 1951.
Two Cheers for Democracy.   London, Arnold, and New York, Harcourt Brace, 1951.
Desmond MacCarthy.   Privately printed, 1952.
Aspects of the Novel and Related Writings, edited by Oliver Stallybrass.   London, Arnold, 1974.

Novels

Where Angels Fear to Tread.   Edinburgh, Blackwood, 1905; New York, Knopf, 1920.
The Longest Journey.   Edinburgh, Blackwood, 1907; New York, Knopf, 1922.
A Room with a View.   London, Arnold, 1908; New York, Putnam, 1911.
Howards End.   London, Arnold, 1910; New York, Putnam, 1911.
A Passage to India.   London, Arnold, and New York, Harcourt Brace, 1924.
Maurice.   London, Arnold, and New York, Norton, 1971.

Short Stories

The Celestial Omnibus and Other Stories.   London, Sidgwick and Jackson, 1911; New York, Knopf, 1923.
The Story of the Siren.   Richmond, Surrey, Hogarth Press, 1920.
The Eternal Moment and Other Stories.   London, Sidgwick and Jackson, and New York, Harcourt Brace, 1928.
The Collected Tales of E.M. Forster.   New York, Knopf, 1947; as *The Collected Short Stories of E.M. Forster*, London, Sidgwick and Jackson, 1948.
The Life to Come and Other Stories.   London, Arnold, 1972; New York, Norton, 1973.
Arctic Summer and Other Fiction.   London, Arnold, 1980; New York, Holmes and Meier, 1981.

Plays

England's Pleasant Land: A Pageant Play (produced Westcott, Surrey, 1938).   London, Hogarth Press, 1940.
Billy Budd, with Eric Crozier, music by Benjamin Britten, adaptation of the story by Herman Melville (produced London and Bloomington, Indiana, 1952).   London and New York, Boosey and Hawkes, 1951; revised version (produced London, 1964; New York, 1966), Boosey and Hawkes, 1961.

Screenplay: *A Diary for Timothy* (documentary), 1945.

Other

Egypt.   London, Labour Research Department, 1920.
Alexandria: A History and a Guide.   Alexandria, Whitehead Morris, 1922; New York, Doubleday, 1961; revised edition, Whitehead Morris, 1938.
Pharos and Pharillon.   Richmond, Surrey, Hogarth Press, and New York, Knopf, 1923.
A Letter to Madan Blanchard.   London, Arnold, and New York, Harcourt Brace, 1932.

Goldsworthy Lowes Dickinson (biography).   London, Arnold, and New York, Harcourt Brace, 1934.

What I Believe.   London, Hogarth Press, 1939.

Nordic Twilight.   London, Macmillan, 1940.

The New Disorder.   New York, privately printed, 1949.

The Hill of Devi, Being Letters from Dewas State Senior.   London, Arnold, and New York, Harcourt Brace, 1953.

I Assert That There Is an Alternative in Humanism.   London, Ethical Society, 1955.

Battersea Rise.   New York, Harcourt Brace, 1955.

Marianne Thornton, 1797-1887: A Domestic Biography.   London, Arnold, and New York, Harcourt Brace, 1956.

Albergo Empedocle and Other Writings, edited by George H. Thomson.   New York, Liveright, 1971.

E.M. Forster's Letters to Donald Windham.   Privately printed, 1976.

Commonplace Book (facsimile edition).   London, Scolar Press, 1978.

Only Connect: Letters to Indian Friends, edited by Syed Hamid Husain.   New Delhi, Arnold Heinemann, 1979.

CRITICAL STUDIES, BIOGRAPHY, AND BIBLIOGRAPHY

Lionel Trilling, *E.M. Forster*.   New York, New Directions, 1943; as *E.M. Forster: A Study*, London, Hogarth Press, 1944; revised edition, New Directions, 1965, Hogarth Press, 1967.

B.J. Kirkpatrick, *A Bibliography of E.M. Forster*.   London, Hart Davis, 1965.

Wilfred Stone, *The Cave and the Mountain: A Study of E.M. Forster*.   Stanford, California, Stanford University Press, and London, Oxford University Press, 1966.

Alfred Borrello, *E.M. Forster: An Annotated Bibliography of Secondary Materials*.   Metuchen, New Jersey, Scarecrow Press, 1973.

P.N. Furbank, *E.M. Forster: A Life*.   London, Secker and Warburg, 2 vols., 1977-79; New York, Harcourt Brace, 1 vol., 1979.

Frederick F.W. McDonald, *E.M. Forster: An Annotated Bibliography of Writings About Him*.   DeKalb, Northern Illinois University Press, 1978.

*   *   *

Anyone familiar with modern criticism is likely to know at least something about *Aspects of the Novel*. It is not only well-known, it is generally admired, even held in affection, although often for the wrong reason. Those who do not really trust criticism as a discipline take some comfort in Forster's gentle hesitations ("Yes—oh dear yes—the novel tells a story") and apparent unwillingness to make firm definitions (the novel, as Chevally tells us, is "a fiction in prose of a certain extent." And that, Forster, comments, "is quite good enough for us"). If so fine a novelist and so perceptive an essayist can do without theory, then perhaps it is alright for us to be impressionistic too. But in fact *Aspects of the Novel* is a good deal more thoughtful and consistent than its admirers usually realize; and to do it full justice we should approach it in terms of the larger context established by the essays which make up the "Art in General" section of *Two Cheers for Democracy*.

In one of these pieces, "The Raison d'Etre of Criticism in the Arts," Forster asserts that music is the "deepest of the arts" and "lies deep" beneath the other arts as well. For him, as for Pater, all art aspires to the condition of music, to the complete fusion of form and content and the self-sufficiency possible in a mode of expression which seems to "imitate" nothing beyond itself. The other arts must refer to something beyond themselves if they are to move us—the verbal arts, for example, depend on the two primary functions of words to convey information and "create atmosphere." In "Anonymity: An Enquiry" Forster asks us to imagine a continuum lying between two points: at one extreme is the language of prose, in which words refer to real, existing facts and situations; at the other is the language of poetry, in which words refer to nothing "real" but exist to evoke a certain kind of effect in the reader. The distinctions Forster proposes here owe something to Valéry and possibly something to I.A. Richards' discussion of poetry as "emotive language" as well. In any event, poetic statements are valuable because they can arouse emotion and—a point as old as the argument of *On the Sublime*—because they make the reader feel as if he were the creator. "What is wonderful about great literature," Forster maintains, is that "it transforms the man who reads it towards the condition of the man who wrote, and brings to birth in us also the creative impulse." Music has the same power:

> We are rapt into a region near to that where the artist worked, and like him when we return to earth we feel surprised. To claim we actually entered his state and became co-creators with him there is presumptuous. However much excited I am by Brahms' Fourth Symphony I cannot suppose I feel Brahms' excitement....But there has been an infection from Brahms through his music to myself. Something has passed. I have been transformed towards his condition, he has called me out of myself, he has thrown me into a sublunary dream: and when the passacaglia has been trodden out, and the transformation closed, I too feel surprise.

In his most important critical essay, "Art for Art's Sake," Forster completes his defense of creativity, maintaining that

> A work of art—whatever else it may be—is a self-contained entity, with a life of its own imposed on it by its creator. It has internal order....it is the only material object in the universe which may possess internal harmony....The work of art stands up by itself, and nothing else does. It achieves something that has often been promised by society, but always delusively. Ancient Athens made a mess—but the *Antigone* stands up. Renaissance Rome made a mess—but the ceiling of the Sistine Chapel got painted. James I made a mess—but there was *Macbeth*. Louis XIV—but there was *Phèdre*. Art for art's sake? I should just think so, and more so than ever at the present time. It is the one orderly product which our muddling race has produced. It is the cry of a thousand sentinels, the echo from a thousand labyrinths; it is the lighthouse which cannot be hidden: *c'est le meilleur témoignage que nous puissons donner de notre dignité.*

Why is "order" so important? The question may be redundant, or it may be unanswerable: "In this pertinacity there seems to me, as I grow older, something more and more profound, something which does in fact concern people who do not care about art at all." Art is a refuge, a consolation, the only access to timelessness, perhaps, which mortal creatures may have— unless, as Forster characteristically adds, we allow the claims of mystics.

Criticism has its place, Forster concludes: the critic "helps to civilise the community, builds up standards, forms theories, stimulates, dissects, encourages the individual to enjoy the world into which he has been born; and on its destructive side criticism exposes fraud and pretentiousness and checks conceit." Yet the gap between creativity and criticism is so "grotesque," finally, that "the claim of criticism to take us to the heart of the Arts must therefore be disallowed." Nevertheless, *Aspects of the Novel* is clearly a work of criticism, and it clearly rests on the notion of the imaginary continuum connecting prose and poetry. The novel is a mixed form, lying ambiguously between history and "factual" prose on the one hand, and pure lyric poetry on the other. Obviously we can learn something of the "real" world by reading *Julius Caesar* or Proust; to some extent novels do convey information. But the novel also has the obligation to strive for the order which poetry and music realize more fully. After reading a novel, if it is a fine novel, we may sense the existence of a whole, suspended in our minds, similar to the sense of wholeness and completion we feel after the music has died away:

> Is there any effect in novels comparable to the effect of the Fifth Symphony as a whole, where, when the orchestra stops, we hear something that has never actually been played? The opening movement, the andante, and the trio-scherzo-trio-finale-trio-finale that composes the third block, all enter the mind at once, and extend one another into a common entity. This common entity, this new thing, is the symphony as a whole, and it has been achieved mainly (though not entirely) by the relations between the three big blocks of sound which the orchestra has been playing. I am calling this relation

"rhythmic." If the correct musical term is something else, that does not matter; what we have now to ask ourselves is whether there is an analogy to it in fiction.

But the argument breaks off here: "I cannot find any analogy. Yet there may be one; in music fiction is likely to find its nearest parallel." And although fiction can never achieve the purity and self-sufficiency of music, it can achieve something else—and what that something else is forms the real subject of *Aspects of the Novel*.

It may distress some readers to do so, but *Aspects of the Novel* can be regarded as a poetics of fiction, similar in some general ways to Aristotle's poetics of tragedy. Like the drama, fiction represents or "imitates" life in order to evoke a particular response in the audience. For Aristotle the dramatist has at his disposal several constituent elements—primarily plot, character and diction; for Forster the novelist has "aspects"—people, plot, fantasy, prophecy, pattern and rhythm. For Aristotle the intended effect determines the kind of plot the dramatist will construct, and plot in turn determines the moral and intellectual qualities necessary in his agents or characters. Forster accepts the principle of hierarchy implied here but argues that while action may be of primary importance in the drama, in the novel it is the revelation of character which determines how the artist shall proceed. The novelist has direct access to our hidden inner life, the dramatist does not. But the revelation of character is not, finally, an end in itself:

> Suppose I suddenly altered my voice...and [said] to you, "Look out—I can see Moll [Flanders] in the audience"...well, you would know at once that I was wrong, that I was sinning against not only probabilities, which does not signify, but against daily life and books and the gulf that divides them. If I said, "Look out, there's some one like Moll in the audience," you might not believe me but you would not be annoyed at my imbecile lack of taste: I should only be sinning against probability....She cannot be here because she belongs to a world where the narrator and the creator are one. And now we can get a definition as to when a character in a book is real: it is real when the novelist knows everything about it. He may not choose to tell us all he knows—many of the facts, even of the kind we call obvious, may be hidden. But he will give us the feeling that though the character has not been explained, it is explicable, and we get from this a reality of a kind we can never get in daily life.
>
> For human intercourse, as soon as we look at it for its own sake and not as a social adjunct, is seen to be haunted by a spectre. We cannot understand each other except in a rough and ready way; we cannot reveal ourselves, even when we want to; what we call intimacy is only a makeshift; perfect knowledge is an illusion. But in the novel we can know people perfectly, and, apart from the general pleasure of reading, we can find here a compensation for their dimness in life....That is why Moll Flanders cannot be here, that is one of the reasons why Amelia and Emma cannot be here. They are people whose secret lives are visible or might be visible: we are people whose secret lives are invisible.
>
> And that is why novels, even when they are about wicked people, can solace us; *they suggest a more comprehensible and thus a more manageable human race; they give us the illusion of perspicacity and power*. (my italics)

"Compensation," "solace," "illusion": each of these words carries implications the reader must ponder carefully if he is to understand Forster's view of the novel—or his fiction.

As for the other constituent parts or aspects: the story is fundamental in the sense that it engages our interest on the most primitive level and makes us want to know what happened next; when the story makes or implies causal connections between events, it becomes a "plot." The story reveals life as it unfolds in time, but

> there seems to be something else in life besides time, something which may conveniently be called "value," something which is measured not by minutes or hours, but by intensity....So daily life, whatever it may be really, is practically composed of two lives—the life in time and the life by values—and our conduct reveals a double allegiance. "I only saw her for five minutes, but it was worth it." There you have both allegiances in a single sentence. And what the story does is to narrate the life in time. And what the entire novel does—if it is a good novel—is to include the life by values as well.

Obviously "life by values" cannot be conveyed by events alone; we must care about the characters in one way or another if we are to value them, and we are back once again to the primacy of "people" for Forster. Furthermore, there are two kinds of characters: they may be "round," capable of growth, of change, of surprising us at times, or they may be "flat," that is, fixed and unchanging throughout (a flat character is not to be understood as a failed round character, however: most novels require the presence of both types).

Prophecy and Fantasy are rather hard to define precisely. The latter seems to refer to any departure from our normal sense of the probable and the necessary, but Forster is not clear what the gain may be. After quoting a passage from *Zuleika Dobson* with obvious approval he asks, "Has not a passage like this a beauty unattainable by serious literature?" Apparently it has, but the point is dropped without further explanation. Prophecy seems to refer to the symbolic use of character to serve some other end. Thus a scene in *Adam Bede* is "penetrated with Christianity"; in Dostoevsky "the characters and situations always stand for more than themselves"—Mitya (in *The Brothers Karamazov*) "becomes real through what he implies" and Melville "reaches straight back into the universal." These chapters are sketchy compared to the earlier discussion of plot and character but it is clear that Forster has relatively little taste for prophecy (which, among other things, requires "humility...a quality for which I have only a limited admiration") or fantasy.

The novel may also strive for the kind of symmetry or pattern we find in the visual arts, but if it does so at the expense of creating and revealing character, then the price is too high (hence Forster's devastating appraisal of *The Ambassadors* and the late James in general). The final aspect, rhythm, has been mentioned before: it refers to that mysterious sense of a completed whole which lingers in the mind. But while the novel may at times move towards the condition of music, its very impurity is the source of its unique value. Fiction gives us something the other arts can never provide: "The intense, stiflingly human quality of the novel is not to be avoided; the novel is sogged with humanity....Human beings have their great chance in the novel."

FRANK. Joseph (Nathaniel).   American. Born in New York City, 6 October 1918. Educated at New York University, 1937-38; University of Wisconsin, Madison, 1941-42; University of Paris, 1950-51 (Fulbright Scholar); University of Chicago, 1952-54 (Rockefeller Fellow, 1952-53, and Rockefeller and University of Chicago Fellow, 1953-54), Ph.D. 1960. Married Marguerite J. Straus in 1953; has two daughters. Editor, Bureau of National Affairs, Washington D.C. 1942-50; Special Researcher, American Embassy, Paris, 1951-52; Christian Gauss Lecturer, 1954-55, and Lecturer, 1955-56, Princeton University, New Jersey; Assistant Professor, University of Minnesota, Minneapolis, 1958-61; Associate Professor and Professor of Comparative Literature, Rutgers University, New Brunswick, New Jersey, 1961-66; Visiting Professor, Harvard University, Cambridge, Massachusetts, Spring 1965. Since 1966, Professor of Comparative Literature and Director of Christian Gauss Seminars in Criticism, Princeton University. Recipient: Guggenheim Fellowship, 1956-57; National Institute of Arts and Letters Award, 1958; American Council of Learned Societies Grant, 1961-62, 1964-65, 1967-68, 1970-71; Bollingen Grant-in-Aid, 1962; James Russell Lowell Prize, 1977; Christian Gauss Award, Phi Beta Kappa, 1977; Research Grant, Rockefeller Foundation, 1979-80. Fellow, American Academy of Arts and Sciences, 1969. Address: Department of Comparative Literature, Princeton University, Princeton, New Jersey 08544, U.S.A.

PUBLICATIONS

Criticism

"Spatial Form in Modern Literature," in *Sewanee Review* (Tennessee), 53, 1945; revised
version in *The Widening Gyre*, 1963.
The Widening Gyre: Crisis and Mastery in Modern Literature.   New Brunswick, New
Jersey, Rutgers University Press, 1963.
"Spatial Form: An Answer to Critics, " in *Critical Inquiry* (Chicago), 4, 1977.
"Spatial Form: Some Further Reflections," in *Critical Inquiry* (Chicago), 5, 1978.
"Lionel Trilling and the Conservative Imagination," in *Salmagundi* (Saratoga Springs,
New York), 41, 1978; reprinted from *The Widening Gyre*, 1963, with a new Appendix.

Other

Dostoevsky: The Seeds of Revolt 1821-1849.   Princeton, New Jersey, Princeton University Press, 1976: London, Robson, 1977.

Editor, with others, *Horizons of a Philosopher: Essays in Honor of David Baumgardt.*
Leiden, E.J. Brill, 1963.
Editor, *A Primer of Ignorance*, by R.P. Blackmur.   New York, Harcourt Brace, 1967.

CRITICAL STUDIES

G. Giovannini, "Method in the Study of Literature and Its Relation to the Other Fine
Arts," in *Journal of Aesthetics and Art Criticism* (Cleveland), 8, 1950.
Walter Sutton, "The Literary Image and the Reader, " in *Journal of Aesthetics and Art
Criticism* (Cleveland), 16, 1957.
Philip Rahv, "The Myth and the Powerhouse," in *Literature and the Sixth Sense*.   Bos-
ton, Houghton Mifflin, 1969; London, Faber, 1970.
Eric S. Rabkin, "Spatial Form and Plot," in *Critical Inquiry* (Chicago), 4, 1977.
William Holtz, "Spatial Form in Modern Literature: A Reconsideration," in *Critical
Inquiry* (Chicago), 4, 1977.
Frank Kermode, "A Reply to Joseph Frank," in *Critical Inquiry* (Chicago), 4, 1978.
W.J.T. Mitchell, "Spatial Form in Literature: Toward a General Theory," in *Critical
Inquiry* (Chicago), 6, 1980.

*   *   *

For more than twenty years Joseph Frank has devoted himself primarily to a massive
biography of Dostoevsky, the first highly praised volume of which appeared in 1976 (three
more volumes are scheduled to follow); in 1963 he published his only collection of critical pieces
thus far, *The Widening Gyre*. And yet despite his long absence from the critical scene, Frank
continues to be regarded as an important figure, partly because of his pioneering essays on
Malraux and Mann's *Dr. Faustus*, but mainly because of his influential, widely anthologized
"Spatial Form in Literature." Even if that essay has not quite assumed the status of a "modern
classic," William Holtz observed recently, "it is at least among the canon of critical essays that
deal with the fundamental nature of literature."
The "fundamental" issue here is the distinction between the spatial and temporal arts: a
painting hangs before us in space, seemingly complete in the instant it takes us to perceive it,
whereas a novel or poem, like a piece of music, gradually unfolds before us, grows, changes, and
is finally completed only in the world of time and memory. The history of the distinction is a

long and fairly complex matter, but not, it seems, a point of contention or even of much theoretical interest until Lessing and the middle of the eighteenth century. "Ut pictura poesis," Horace maintains in the *Ars Poetica* ("as in painting, so in poetry"), thus providing a memorable phrase for what was already a critical commonplace. "Painting," Plutarch had observed, "is mute poetry and poetry a speaking picture." And for all their radical différences about the value of music, painting and literature, Plato and Aristotle agree that the arts are essentially imitative: whether by means of color and lines or tones or sequences of words, artists depict the natural world and the world of human actions and feelings. The break with this tradition which emphasizes similarity rather than difference comes with Lessing, who (in Frank's summary)

> analyzes the laws of aesthetic perception; shows how they prescribe necessary limitations to literature and the plastic arts; and then demonstrates how Greek writers and painters, especially his cherished Homer, created masterpieces in obedience to these laws.

Lessing's argument starts from the simple observation that literature and the plastic arts, working through different sensuous mediums, must differ in the fundamental laws governing their creation. "If it is true," Lessing wrote in *Laocoön*, "that painting and poetry in their imitations make use of entirely different means or symbols...[and] if these symbols indisputably require a suitable relation to the thing symbolized, then it is clear that symbols arranged in juxtaposition can only express objects of which the wholes or parts exist in juxaposition; while consecutive symbols can only express subjects of which the wholes or parts are themselves consecutive.

By means of this distinction Lessing was able to "attack two artistic genres highly popular in his day: pictorial poetry and allegorical painting." Both were doomed to failure because "their aims were in contradiction to the fundamental properties of their mediums." What Lessing proposed, in effect, was "a new approach to aesthetic form." Frank's use of Lessing, it should be noted, is heuristic, nothing more. A modern follower of Lessing, if one could be imagined, would be distressed by the mingling of temporal and spatial effects which Frank finds in some key works of modern literature. Frank himself is not distressed; he merely finds it useful to apply Lessing's distinction for descriptive purposes. His aim, as he puts it, is

> to trace the evolution of form in modern poetry and, more particularly, in the novel. For modern literature, exemplified by such writers as T.S. Eliot, Ezra Pound, Marcel Proust, and James Joyce, is moving in the direction of spatial form; and this tendency receives an original development in Djuna Barnes' remarkable book, *Nightwood*. All these writers ideally intend the reader to apprehend their work spatially, in a moment of time, rather than as a sequence. And since changes in aesthetic form always involve major changes in the sensibility of a particular cultural period, an effort will be made to outline the spiritual attitudes that have led to the predominance of spatial form.

Locating the chief impetus behind modern poetry in the early work of Pound and Eliot, Frank is able to make a striking case for his thesis. Pound made the "image" the primary vehicle of poetic expresion, and in doing so had used visual or spatial terms ("an 'Image'," he wrote, "is that which presents an intellectual and emotional complex in an instant of time"). What Pound was doing (and what Eliot was to do shortly with his doctrine of the "objective correlative") was to "spatialize" the perception of a literary whole. To be properly understood, Frank maintains, the "word-groups" which make up Pound's *Cantos* and Eliot's "The Waste Land"

> must be juxtaposed with one another and perceived simultaneously. Only when this is done can they be adequately grasped; for, while they follow one another in time, their meaning does not depend on this temporal relationship.... Aesthetic form in modern poetry, then, is based on a space-logic that demands a complete reorientation in the reader's attitude towards language.... Instead of the instinctive and immediate reference of words and word-groups to the objects or events they symbolize and the construction of meaning from the sequence of these references, modern poetry asks its readers to suspend the process of individual reference temporarily until the entire pattern of internal references can be apprehended as a unity.

Frank discovers the same tendency in Flaubert (at least in parts of *Madame Bovary*), in Mallarmé, in Proust and in Joyce. In *Ulysses*, for example, Joyce tries to achieve the "unified impact...the sense of simultaneous activity occurring in different places":

> Joyce frequently makes use of the same method as Flaubert...and he usually does so to obtain the same ironic effect. But Joyce faced the additional problem of creating this impression of simultaneity for the life of a whole teeming city, and of maintaining it—or rather of strengthening it—through hundreds of pages that must be read as a sequence. To meet this problem Joyce was forced to go far beyond what Flaubert had done.

And in *Nightwood* (to which Frank devotes nearly a third of his essay), Djuna Barnes "carries the evolution of spatial form in the novel forward to a point where it is practically indistinguishable from modern poetry."

In the final section of his essay, Frank boldly uses Wilhelm Worringer's arguments in *Abstraction and Empathy* (first published in 1908) as a way of explaining why modern writers have tended to spatialize what had always seemed to be an essentially temporal art. Throughout the history of the arts, Worringer maintains, there has been "a continual alternation between naturalistic and non-naturalistic styles" (from the conventional point of view, of course, spatial form in literature does seem "non-naturalistic"). Summarizing Worringer, Frank points out that

> Naturalism...always has been created by cultures that have achieved an equilibrium between man and the cosmos. Like the Greeks of the classical period, man feels himself at one with organic nature; or, like modern man from the Renaissance to the close of the nineteenth century, he is convinced of his ability to dominate and control natural forces. In both these periods man has a relationship of confidence and intimacy with a world in which he feels at home; and he creates a naturalistic art that delights in reproducing the forms and appearances of the organic world....On the other hand, when the relationship between man and the cosmos is one of disharmony and disequilibrium, we find that nonorganic, linear-geometric styles are always produced.

The *Cantos*, "The Waste Land" and *Ulysses* are works in which "disharmony and disequilibrium" play a major part, thus reflecting the spirit of the times:

> If there is one theme that dominates the history of modern culture since the last quarter of the nineteenth century, it is precisely that of insecurity, instability, the feeling of loss of control over the meaning and purpose of life amidst the continuing triumphs of science and technics. Artists are always the most sensitive barometers of cultural change; and it is hardly surprising that the stylistic evolution of modern art, when viewed as a whole, would reveal the effects of this spiritual crisis.

The tendency of such works is to escape not only "the times" but time itself by retreating to abstraction and spatialization, in short to become "mythic and "ahistoric":

> What has occurred, at least so far as literature is concerned, may be described as the transformation of the historical imagination into myth—an imagination for which historical time does not exist, and which sees actions and events of a particular time only as the bodying forth of eternal prototypes.... [Mircea Eliade has noted that] "the work of two of the most significant artists of our day--T.S. Eliot and James Joyce--is saturated with nostalgia for the myth of eternal repetition and, in the last analysis, for the abolition of time."

It would be unfair to force all of the essays in *The Widening Gyre* into a rigid pattern, but the recurring theme here is in fact the despair and rebelliousness of modern literature, the "rejection of humanism and liberalism, and a preference--both formally and ideologically--for the primitive, the mythic, and the irrational." In his Preface Frank notes that

> It is a dilemma to which I return constantly in the course of these essays--the dilemma of

a culture whose creations more and more tend to deny or negate some essential aspect of the human agency at their source and to escape from its control.

In 1977 and again in 1978, Frank had occasion to defend his conception of spatial form in literature and to define its relationship to some recent developments in literary theory. In the first of these essays, "Spatial Form: An Answer to Critics," he deals with the objections raised over the years by four writers, the first of whom, G. Giovannini, he dismisses fairly enough as having misunderstood the argument. A second critic, Walter Sutton, had complained that "the 'spatialization' of literature can never be entirely achieved." Frank concedes this—in fact had conceded this in 1963:

> [Sutton's]major argument is that, since reading is a time-act, the achievement of spatial form is really a physical impossibility. I could not agree more. But this has not stopped modern writers from working out techniques to achieve the impossible—as much as possible.

Some writers may have attempted the impossible, in which case it is still the responsibility of the critic to chart the course of their experiments. Another critic, Philip Rahv, "was greatly incensed by the rise in prestige of myth as a focus of cultural attention." Yet Rahv also admitted that Frank's conception of spatial form was "extremely plausible." What Rahv did "was not so much to attack 'spatial form' as to articulate his dislike of the negative responses to history that it expresses"; and Frank quite rightly notes that Rahv's "commitment to history" derives from his "residual Marxism" (the Marxist mission, of course, is to change, not to escape from history). Finally there is a more formidable opponent: in a private letter to the writer of an unpublished dissertation (the plot thickens), Frank Kermode had referred to the theory of spatial form as a relic of the past, "an outmoded period aesthetic". It is impossible to summarize fairly Frank's reply, Kermode's reply to that reply, and Frank's final remarks; but very briefly, Frank objects to Kermode's linking of spatial form with a preference (in the writers, not the critics) for authoritarian forms of control. And yet, Frank continues, in *Romantic Image* and *The Sense of an Ending* Kermode himself is very much concerned with something analogous to the desire to escape from time and history.

Kermode concludes *his* reply with a telling point which indicates the chief weakness in the entire conception of spatial form. Frank, he observes sharply, "cannot rid himself of the notion that whatever is not temporal is spatial." At crucial points Frank does indeed assume that what is not temporal must be spatial and thereby traps himself unnecessarily in a false, either-or position. Why the position is false, Kermode does not pause to demonstrate; but this is precisely what W.J.T. Mitchell does in his rigorous essay, "Spatial Form in Literature: Toward a General Theory." The fact is, Mitchell argues, "that spatial form is the perceptual basis of our notion of time, that we literally cannot 'tell time' without the mediation of space." And his conclusion is one which properly brooded upon would make further controversy pointless: "Instead of viewing space and time as antithetical modalities, we ought to treat their relationship as one of complex interconnection, interdependence and interpenetration."

In his 1978 essay, "Spatial Form: Some Further Reflections," Frank continues to defend his position, this time by relating spatial form to the important distinction linguists now make between the diachronic and synchronic dimensions of language. It is true that languages change with the passage of time (this is the diachronic dimension) but it is equally true that at any given moment (this is the synchronic dimension) a language is also a complete system of interlocking parts. Thus there is some similarity between synchronicity and spatialization—both prove to be useful descriptive terms. Two further points might be raised, one of which Frank had touched upon briefly in his 1977 essay: thirty-two years earlier he had been characterizing as "modernism" what now appears to have been only one manifestation of that elusive phenomenon. There are, or were, other forms, just as there are now enough forms of post-modernism to tax the ingenuity of any descriptive critic. Finally, and quite oddly, Frank and his critics have never cared to take up, even in passing, what still seems to some readers the most intriguing part of the whole enterprise, the matter of a causal explanation for one important kind of modernism. In all the local skirmishes and critical cross-fire, what's become of Worringer?

FRASER, G(eorge) S(utherland). British. Born in Glasgow, Scotland, 8 November 1915. Educated at Glasgow Academy; Aberdeen Grammar School; St. Andrews University, M.A. 1937. Served in the Middle East, 1939-45. Married Eileen Lucy Andrew in 1946; two daughters and one son. Journalist, Aberdeen *Press and Journal*, 1937-39. Free-lance Journalist, 1946-59. Cultural Adviser to the UK Liaison Mission in Japan, 1950-51. Regular Reviewer and Lea-derwriter, *Times Literary Supplement*, London. Reviewer, *New Statesman*, London, and "New Poetry" broadcaster on BBC radio, in the 1950's. Lecturer, 1959-63, and Reader in Modern English Literature, 1964-79, University of Leicester. Visiting Professor, Rochester University, New York, 1963-64. Recipient: Hodder and Stoughton bursary, 1946. *Died 3 January 1980.*

PUBLICATIONS

Criticism

Post-War Trends in English Literature. Tokyo, Hokuseido Press, 1950.
The Modern Writer and His World: Continuity and Innovation in Twentieth-Century English Literature. London, Verschoyle, 1953; New York, Criterion Books, 1955; revised edition, London, Deutsch, 1964; New York, Praeger, 1965.
W.B. Yeats. London, Longman, 1954; revised edition, 1962, 1965.
Dylan Thomas. London, Longman, 1957; revised edition, 1964.
Vision and Rhetoric: Studies in Modern Poetry. London, Faber, 1959; New York, Barnes and Noble, 1960.
Ezra Pound. Edinburgh, Oliver and Boyd, 1960; New York, Grove Press, 1961.
Lawrence Durrell: A Critical Study. London, Faber, 1968; New York, Dutton, 1969.
Lawrence Durrell. London, Longman, 1970.
Metre, Rhythm, and Free Verse. London, Methuen, 1970.
Introduction to *The Poetry of Louis MacNeice*, by Donald B. Moore. Leicester, Lei-cester University Press, and New York, Humanities Press, 1972.
P.H. Newby. London, Longman, 1974.
Essays on Twentieth-Century Poets. Leicester, Leicester University Press, and Tot-owa, New Jersey, Rowman and Littlefield, 1977.
Alexander Pope. London, Routledge, 1978.
A Short History of English Poetry. London, Open Books, 1979.

Verse

The Fatal Landscape and Other Poems. London, Editions Poetry, 1943.
Home Town Elegy. London, Editions Poetry, 1944.
The Traveller Has Regrets and Other Poems. London, Harvill Press-Editions Poetry, 1948.
Leaves Without a Tree. Tokyo, Hokuseido Press, 1956.
Conditions: Selected Recent Poetry. Nottingham, Byron Press, 1969.

Other

Vision of Scotland. London, Elek, 1948.
News from South America (travel). London, Harvill Press, 1949; New York, Library Publishers, 1952.
Scotland. London, Thames and Hudson, and New York, Studio Publications, 1955.

Editor, with John Waller, *The Collected Poems of Keith Douglas*.   London, Editions
   Poetry, 1951; revised edition, with J. Waller and J.C. Hall, London, Faber, 1966; New
   York, Chilmark Press, 1967.
Editor, with Ian Fletcher, *Springtime: An Anthology of Young Poets and Writers*.
   London, Peter Owen, 1953.
Editor, *Poetry Now: An Anthology*.   London, Faber, 1956.
Editor, *Selected Poems of Robert Burns*.   London, Heinemann, and New York, Mac-
   millan, 1960.
Editor, *Vaughan College Poems*.   Leicester, Leicester University Press, 1963.
Editor, with J. Waller and J.C. Hall, *Allamein to Zem Zem*, by Keith Douglas.   London,
   Faber, 1966; New York, Chilmark Press, 1967.
Editor, with others, *Workshop* 8 (London), 1969.

Translator, *The Dedicated Life in Poetry, and the Correspondence of Lauren de Cayeux*,
   by Patrice de la Tour du Pin.   London, Harvill Press, 1948.
Translator, *The Mystery of Being*, by Gabriel Marcel.   London, Harvill Press, 1950.
Translator, *Men Against Humanity*, by Gabriel Marcel.   London, Harvill Press, 1952.
Translator, *Pascal: His Life and Works*, by Jean Mesnard.   London, Harvill Press,
   1952.
Translator, with E. de Mauny, *Béla Bartók*, by S. Moreux.   London, Harvill Press,
   1953.
Translator, with others, *Dante's Inferno*.   London, BBC Publications, 1966.

*   *   *

Sympathy, tolerance, flexibility—the very qualities which make G.S. Fraser so attractive a
critic also make it difficult to pin him down to any fixed set of standards. "I have never had the
time to think out a theory of poetics," he observes in the preface to *Vision and Rhetoric*,

and, indeed, I doubt if my gifts lie that way.... A Jungian psychologist who is also a
literary critic once told me, very gently, that I had no intuitions and that I could not
think, but that my faculty of feeling was so strongly developed and, he flatteringly said,
so nicely discriminative that it did duty for thinking, for all practical purposes....
Certainly I would describe my primary approach to any work of literature as being made
through a kind of groping tact; confronted with a new book, as with a new social
atmosphere, I put out my hands and see what I can feel through my finger-tips.
   Mr. F.W. Bateson was making the same sort of point as my Jungian psychologist
when he described me once, with kindly humour, as the typical lively journalist who gets
on very well without principles.

More important than principles for Fraser seems to be the ability to give his readers a vivid,
immediate sense of the writer under consideration. Thus he remarks quite characteristically,
after examining Durrell's *Tunc*, "I have given what Durrell himself would call a 'character
squeeze' of the novel rather than a properly objective critical analysis of it. But I hope I have at
least conveyed the *feel* of the book."
   The Modern Writer and His World, first published in 1953 for Japanese students and
extensively rewritten in 1964, is a thoroughly sensible guide to its subject, British poetry, fiction
and drama (with a glance at criticism) since 1880. "The topic which gives this book such unity as
it has," he maintains, "is the writer's relation to his age." Nevertheless, historical generalizations
and sweeping literary judgments are kept to a minimum. For Fraser modernity is not primarily
a historical phenomenon; rather it refers to qualities which can appear at any time, so that we
may find Catullus, Donne and Clough—but not Virgil, Spenser or Tennyson—"modern." He
then proceeds to discuss realism and the rise of psychological analysis in the novel, and
"complexity, allusiveness, irony and obscurity" in modern poetry. Like most general guides to a
particular period, *The Modern Writer and His World* soon turns into a writer-by-writer
descriptive summary, and as such is remarkably fair-minded—perhaps too much so at times.
On the other hand it is refreshing to find a critic who confesses that he has never been able to
read more than a few pages of any Beckett novel and who complains (gently, in a footnote) that

227

there is a coarse, bullying tone in much of C.S. Lewis' fiction. Fraser is sympathetic when he discusses Angus Wilson, Iris Murdoch and other writers who came into their own in the 1950's, but his most helpful chapter is the one devoted primarily to Leavis and Richards, "Critics from Cambridge."

The opening and closing sections of *Vision and Rhetoric* suggest a more openly evaluative attitude towards modern British poetry. By "rhetoric" Fraser means intentional didacticism, the use of poetry as "a mode of moral discourse, directed at the feelings, and providing rational motives for the feelings it seeks to evoke." This position is put forward most emphatically by the American critic Yvor Winters, but Fraser believes that a number of younger British poets have come to accept it as well; and he adds,

> My objection to this theory, which is so much more easily defensible than any romantic theory of poetry, is both that in the end it does not wholly square with my personal experience of what writing a poem involves and that, if it does not produce so many bad poems as a romantic attitude does, it does not produce so many genuinely exciting poems either. There are many poems, for instance, of Dylan Thomas's which can hardly be defended as efficient communicative instruments and there is perhaps hardly any poem of his which could be put forward as a mature criticism of life. All Mr. Philip Larkin's poems are efficient communicative instruments; a poem like "Church Going," of his, is an extremely sensitive, sane, and mature "criticism of life." It is relevant to the deep and central problems of modern life in a way which Dylan Thomas's poetry is not. And yet Mr. Larkin's poetry lacks something which Thomas's poetry possesses, at its best, and that something I would call vision.

Fraser's best book to date is his "little plain man's guide to Pound," published in 1960, when hostility to Pound was stronger than it now seems to be. Defending him is still a hard task, as Fraser realizes; but by using some of the distinctions Hannah Arendt proposes in *The Human Condition* he is able to find a coherent, humane pattern in Pound's work and make what is probably the best case we have for its saving virtues. Fraser's final remarks are worth quoting in full, for their own sake and for what they reveal about his admirable fair-mindedness:

> I think myself that he is an innovator of the utmost importance, a superlative verse technician, a poet with from the beginning to the end of his work an impeccable ear; an explorer of genius; a man bitterly and exactly sensitive to the pressures in a democratic society that kill instinctual life, rather as D.H. Lawrence was; a man, in all his personal relationships, of the utmost generosity of heart; a poet more splendidly and largely concerned than any poet of our time with the disparate yet similar essences of human civilization: the poet, perhaps, as cultural anthropologist. I think also that the great strength, and the great weakness, of all his writing stems from his Odyssean life, from having known·so many men and cities, and having never really "belonged" anywhere; and from that, too, comes one of the vulnerable elements in him, the staginess, the show-off side.... Ruin and failure and waning away are around him from his beginnings, but surmounting them, more importantly, the basic creative impulse and the basic creative power: "Make it new."

FRYE, (Herman) Northrop. Canadian. Born in Sherbrooke, Quebec, 14 July 1912. Educated at the University of Toronto, B.A. 1933; Merton College, Oxford, M.A. 1940; ordained to the ministry, United Church of Canada, 1936. Married Helen Kemp in 1937. Lecturer in English, 1939-47, Professor, 1947-67, and Principal, 1957-67, Victoria College, University of Toronto, and since 1967 University Professor, University of Toronto. Editor, *Canadian Forum*, 1948-52; Member, Executive Council, Canadian Radio and TV Commission, 1958-61.

Recipient: Guggenheim Fellowship, 1950; President's Medal, University of Western Ontario, 1954; Lorne Pierce Medal, 1958. LL.D.: Carleton University, Ottawa, 1957; Queen's University, Kingston, Ontario, 1962; University of Saskatchewan, Saskatoon, 1968; Franklin and Marshall College, Lancaster, Pennsylvania, 1968; Victoria College, British Columbia, 1969; D.D.: University of Winnipeg, 1958; Dr. Lett.: University of New Brunswick, Fredericton, 1960; Mount Allison University, Sackville, New Brunswick, 1962; University of British Columbia, Vancouver, 1963; University of Manitoba, Winnipeg, 1964; St. Lawrence University, Canton, New York, 1966; Dartmouth College, Hanover, New Hampshire, 1967; D.H.L.: Princeton University, New Jersey, 1966; University of Chicago, 1967; D.Litt.: Acadia University, Wolfville, Nova Scotia, 1969; University of Western Ontario, London, 1969; York University, Downsville, Ontario, 1969; Middlebury College, Vermont, 1969; University of Windsor, Ontario, 1970; University of Waterloo, Ontario, 1972; Harvard University, Cambridge, Massachusetts, 1972; L.H.D.: University of California at Irvine, 1969; Boston College, 1972. Companion, Order of Canada, 1972; Honorary Fellow, Merton College, Oxford, 1973, and American Academy of Arts and Sciences. Address: Department of English, Massey College, University of Toronto, 4 Devonshire Place, Toronto, Ontario M5S 2E1, Canada.

PUBLICATIONS

Criticism

Fearful Symmetry: *A Study of William Blake*.   Princeton, New Jersey, Princeton University Press, 1947.
Anatomy of Criticism: *Four Essays*.   Princeton, New Jersey, Princeton University Press, 1957.
The Educated Imagination.   Toronto, Canadian Broadcasting Corporation, 1963; Bloomington, Indiana University Press, 1964.
Fables of Identity: *Studies in Poetic Mythology*.   New York, Harcourt Brace, 1963.
"Literary Criticism," in *The Aims and Methods of Scholarship in Modern Languages and Literatures*, edited by James Thorpe.   New York, Modern Language Association, 1963.
T.S. Eliot.   New York, Grove Press and Edinburgh, Oliver and Boyd, 1963; revised edition, Oliver and Boyd, 1968, and New York, Putnam, 1972.
The Well-Tempered Critic.   Bloomington, Indiana University Press, 1963.
A Natural Perspective: *The Development of Shakespearean Comedy and Romance*. New York, Columbia University Press, 1965.
The Return of Eden: *Five Essays on Milton's Epics*.   Toronto, University of Toronto Press, 1965; as *Five Essays on Milton's Epics,* London, Routledge, 1966.
"Reflections in a Mirror," in *Northrop Frye in Modern Criticism*, edited by Murray Krieger.   New York, Columbia University Press, 1966.
Fools of Time: Studies in Shakespearean Tragedy.   Toronto, University of Toronto Press, 1967; London, Oxford University Press, 1968.
"Literature and Myth," in *Relations of Literary Study: Essays on Interdisciplinary Contributions*, edited by James Thorpe.   New York, Modern Language Association, 1967.
The Modern Century.   Toronto, Oxford University Press, 1967; London, Oxford University Press, 1969.
A Study of English Romanticism.   New York, Random House, 1968.
"The Critical Path: An Essay on the Social Context of Literary Criticism," in *Daedalus* (Cambridge, Massachusetts), 99, 1970: revised and expanded edition as *The Critical Path*, Bloomington, Indiana University Press, and Don Mills, Ontario, Fitzhenry and Whiteside, 1971.
The Stubborn Structure: *Essays on Criticism and Society*.   Ithaca, New York, Cornell University Press, and London, Methuen, 1970.
The Bush Garden: *Essays on the Canadian Imagination*.   Toronto, Anansi, 1971.

On Teaching Literature.   New York, Harcourt Brace, 1972.
"The Search for Acceptable Words," in Daedalus (Cambridge, Massachusetts) 102, 1973.
"Expanding Eyes," in Critical Inquiry (Chicago), 2, 1975.
The Secular Scripture: A Study of the Structure of Romance.   Cambridge, Massachu-
    setts, and London, Harvard University Press, 1976.
Spiritus Mundi: Essays on Literature, Myth and Society.   Bloomington, Indiana Uni-
    versity Press, 1977.
Northrop Frye on Culture and Literature: A Collection of Review Essays, edited by
    Robert Denham.   Chicago and London, University of Chicago Press, 1978.
Creation and Recreation.   Toronto and London, University of Toronto Press, 1980.
"Literary History," in New Literary History (Baltimore), 12, 1981.

Other

Culture and the National Will (lecture).   Ottawa, Carleton University, 1957.
By Liberal Things (lecture).   Toronto, Clarke Irwin, 1959.
Silence in the Sea (lecture).   St. John's, Newfoundland, Memorial University, 1968.

Editor, Across My Path, by Pelham Edgar.   Toronto, Ryerson Press, 1952.
Editor, Selected Poetry and Prose, by William Blake.   New York, Modern Library,
    1953.
Editor, I Brought the Ages Home, by C.T. Currelly.   Toronto, Ryerson Press, 1956.
Editor, Sound and Poetry.   New York, Columbia University Press, 1957.
Editor, The Collected Poems of E.J. Pratt.   Toronto, Macmillan, 1958.
Editor, The Valley of Vision: Blake as Prophet and Revolutionary, by Peter F. Fisher.
    Toronto, University of Toronto Press, 1961.
Editor, Romanticism Reconsidered.   New York, Columbia University Press, 1963.
Editor, Blake: A Collection of Critical Essays.   Englewood Cliffs, New Jersey, Prentice
    Hall, 1966.
Editor, with James V. Logan and John E. Jordan, Some British Romantics: A Collection
    of Essays.   Columbus, Ohio State University Press, 1966.
Editor, with Sheridan Baker, Practical Imagination.   New York, Harper, 1980.

CRITICAL STUDIES AND BIBLIOGRAPHY

John Holloway, "The Critical Zodiac of Northrop Frye," in Colours of Clarity: Essays on
    Contemporary Literature and Education.   London, Routledge, 1964.
Northrop Frye in Modern Criticism, edited by Murray Krieger.   New York, Columbia
    University Press, 1966.
John Casey, "A 'Science' of Criticism: Northrop Frye," in The Language of Criticism.
    London, Methuen, 1966.
Pauline Kogan, Northrop Frye: The High Priest of Clerical Obscurantism.   Montreal,
    Progressive Books and Periodicals, 1969.
Walter Jackson Bate, "Northrop Frye," in Criticism: The Major Texts.   New York,
    Harcourt Brace, 1970.
René Wellek, "The Poet as Critic, the Critic as Poet, the Poet-Critic," in Discriminations:
    Further Concepts of Criticism.   New Haven, Connecticut, and London, Yale Uni-
    versity Press, 1970.
Ronald Bates, Northrop Frye.   Toronto, McClelland and Stewart, 1971.
William Righter, "Myth and Interpretation," in New Literary History (Charlottesville,
    Virginia), 3, 1972.
Robert D. Denham, Northrop Frye: An Enumerative Bibliography.   Metuchen, New
    Jersey, Scarecrow Press, 1974.

Angus Fletcher, "Northrop Frye: The Critical Passion," in *Critical Inquiry* (Chicago), 1, 1975.

Robert D. Denham, *Northrop Frye and Critical Method*.   University Park, Pennsylvania, and London, Pennsylvania State University Press, 1978.

Richard Kostelanetz, "The Literature Professors' Literature Professor," in *Michigan Quarterly Review* (Ann Arbor), 17, 1978.

Frank Lentricchia, "The Place of Northrop Frye's 'Anatomy of Criticism,' " in *After the New Criticism*.   Chicago and London, University of Chicago Press, 1980.

*   *   *

Comprehensive as it seems to be, the theory of literature Northrop Frye develops in *Anatomy of Criticism* is apparently not intended to prescribe only one proper critical approach. In a typical extended simile Frye proposes that

> In looking at a picture we may stand close to it and analyse the details of brush work and palette knife. This corresponds roughly to the rhetorical analysis of the new critics in literature. At a little distance back, the design comes into clearer view, and we study rather the content represented: this is the best distance for realistic Dutch pictures, for example, where we are in a sense reading the picture. The further back we go, the more conscious we are of the organizing design. At a great distance from, say, a Madonna, we can see nothing but the archetype of the Madonna, a large centripetal blue mass with a contrasting point of interest at its center. In the criticism of literature, too, we often have to "stand back" from the poem to see its archetypal organization. If we "stand back" from Spenser's *Mutabilitie Cantoes*, we see a background of ordered circular light and a sinister black mass thrusting up into the lower foreground—much the same archetypal shape we see in the opening of the Book of Job. If we "stand back" from the beginning of the fifth act of *Hamlet*, we see a grave opening on the stage, the hero, his enemy, and the heroine descending into it, followed by a fatal struggle in the upper world. If we "stand back" from a realistic novel such as Tolstoy's *Resurrection* or Zola's *Germinal*, we can see the mythopoeic designs indicated by those titles.

Carried out logically this figure would lead to the kind of critical pluralism recommended by R.S. Crane: the subject matter criticism deals with is too complex to be exhausted by a single frame of reference; therefore we need—and should welcome— a multiplicity of critical languages, each with its own concern, powers and limitations. But while there is a genuinely pluralistic element in Frye's thinking it is also clear that he regards archetypal criticism as prior in importance to any other method.

When we consider a given work we soon become aware that it bears some striking resemblances to other works; and like an experienced naturalist, Frye argues, we should therefore try to place our specimen in the broader context of related species, genera, and finally the entire range of organic life. The obvious similarities between works lead Frye to make a fundamental assumption that there is a "total coherence" to be investigated and described. Without such an assumption criticism is at best a "discrete series of analyses based on the mere existence of the literary structure" and is thus unable to explain "how the structure came to be what it [is] and what its nearest relatives are." In short, what criticism has lacked thus far is a "coordinating principle, a central hypothesis which, like the theory of evolution in biology, will see the phenomena it deals with as parts of a whole." Rather than struggle with Frye's elaborate descriptions of the "total structure" of literature in the *Anatomy*, however, readers will do better to start with the *Fables of Identity* and *The Educated Imagination*. And following Frye's own suggestion in "The Archetypes of Literature" (the first essay of the *Fables*), we may outline his basic position by using the Aristotelian conception of the four causes. Very briefly, we will grasp a work fully only when we consider its efficient cause (the artist), its material and formal causes (the material from which it has been made and the recognisable shape imposed upon that material), and the final cause (the purpose for which it has been made). Frye handles efficient, formal and final causes clearly enough but his one reference to material cause (the "social conditions and cultural demands which produced...the work of art") is too vague to be of any use. For an Aristotelian, of course, words are the material cause of the poem.

Frye has relatively little interest in the efficient cause of literature. What makes a man a poet is the faculty which all men possess to some extent, the imagination. But, Frye asserts,

> the unity of a work of art, the basis of structural analysis, has not been produced solely by the unconditioned will of the artist.... The fact that revision is possible, that the poet makes changes not because he likes them better but because they are better, means that poems, like poets, are born and not made. The poet's task is to deliver the poem in as uninjured a state as possible, and if the poem is alive, it is equally anxious to be rid of him, and screams out to be cut loose from his private memories and associations, his desire for self-expression, and all the other navelstrings and feeding tubes of his ego. The critic takes over where the poet leaves off, and criticism can hardly do without a kind of literary psychology connecting the poet with the poem. Part of this may be a psychological study of the poet, though this is useful chiefly in analysing the failures in his expression, the things in him which are still attached to his work. More important is the fact that every poet has his private mythology, his own spectroscopic band or peculiar formation of symbols.

In preparing his book on Blake, however, Frye tells us that he began by studying the entire "mental landscape" of that poet, only to discover that a supposedly "private" system of imagery revealed an "increasing number of similarities to the structures of other poets."

The formal cause of literature is myth, and to understand fully what Frye means by myth we must turn to *The Educated Imagination* and another elaborate simile. If we imagine ourselves in the position of a man shipwrecked alone on an island, Frye proposes, we will be able to repeat the development of human consciousness itself. Thrust suddenly into a world "without human shape or human meaning," we feel "lonely and afraid." Our reason "feels curious" about the world; it accepts the facts of nature as it finds them and we have the beginnings of primitive "science." But our emotions are "unreasonable": for them "it's what they like and don't like that comes first." The imagination, which we call upon to "assimilate nature to human forms," is thus a constructive power, a primitive artistic faculty which conjures up new possibilities for a more congenial existence. And when we attempt to put ourselves into some sort of intelligible relationship with nature we seize first upon the recurring patterns of the solar year, night and day, and human growth itself:

> the poet thinks in terms of likeness and identity. And what likeness and identity suggest is adding to the cycle of nature the rhythm of life, with human life at its center, moving from birth and death and back again to new life. But this step gets our emotions immediately involved with the cycle. And as poetry continues to express not merely the rhythm of what we see around us but what we feel as a part of ourselves, a second principle begins to operate, a principle which tends to separate what we hate or fear from what we want or love. Out of this cycle of death and renewal, and out of the separation of our feelings about the cycle, there gradually emerge four fundamental types of imaginative experience in literature.

Myth is therefore the primitive imaginative structure which "provides the main outlines and the circumference of a verbal universe which is later occupied by literature" and is thus the "matrix" to which "major poetry keeps returning":

> In every age poets who are thinkers (remembering that poets think in metaphors and images, not in propositions) and are deeply concerned with the origin or destiny or desires of mankind—with anything that belongs to the larger outlines of what literature can express—can hardly find a literary theme that does not coincide with a myth.

The four different types of imaginative experience become the four major genres of Frye's system: romance, tragedy, comedy and irony. We may imagine the great encompassing myth of mankind as a circle, with noon, summer and youth at the zenith, and night, winter and death at the nadir: those myths and later stories which dramatize part of the downward movement are tragic or ironic; those which dramatize part of the upward movement towards spring, dawn and rebirth are comic.

In myth, then, Frye believes he has an intelligible principle which will explain the appearance of basic plots and characters in cultures widely separated in time. As humanizing imaginative constructs, myths persist in one form or another and will continue to persist as long as men have needs and dreams. Our own sophisticated literature rarely seems "mythic," but if we know enough about the structure of mythologies we can see how a myth has been "displaced" or covered over with a veneer of surface realism, making the "new" work "credible, logically motivated or morally acceptable" to a modern audience. A good myth critic will have no trouble finding the archetypal patterns beneath the surface of *Pride and Prejudice* or *Tom Jones* or *Lycidas*—or for that matter any work.

For Frye art does not imitate life directly, since "a writer's desire to write can only come from his previous experience of literature": in effect, art imitates art. The point is less paradoxical than it may seem at first and will be verified quickly enough by anyone who has had any experience with "creative writing" programs. We are born into a society which is organized around some encompassing mythology (the "myth of concern" as Frye calls it) and we experience "reality" only as it has been conditioned by those who came before us. Thus when a young writer begins to write he consciously or unconsciously uses as a model some pre-existing imaginative version of experience. "Our principle, then," Frye asserts,

> is that literature can derive its forms only from itself; they can't exist outside literature, any more than musical forms like the sonata and fugue can exist outside music.... I'm not saying that there's nothing new in literature; I'm saying that everything is new and yet recognizably the same kind of thing as the old, just as a new baby is a genuinely new individual, although it's also an example of something very common, which is human beings, and it's also lineally descended from the first human beings that ever were.

Therefore "allusiveness runs through all our literary experience. If we don't know the Bible and the central stories of Greek and Roman literature, we can still read books and see plays, but our knowledge of literature can't grow, just as our knowledge of mathematics can't grow if we don't learn the multiplication tables."

But obviously imaginative transformations of nature and experience are not always visionary or consoling, as Frye recognizes. Artists spend much of their time depicting

> the misery, frustration and absurdity of human experience. In other words literature leads us not only towards the regaining of identity, but it also separates this state from its opposite, the world we don't like and want to get away from.

The effect of such cautionary works is "ironic" and the purpose of irony is to

> enable us to see over the head of a situation...and so detach us, at least in imagination, from the world we'd rather not be involved with.... There are two halves of literary experience, then. The imagination gives us both a better and a worse world than the one we usually live in, and demands that we keep looking steadily at both.... Literature then is not a dream world: it's two kinds of dreams, a wish-fulfillment dream and an anxiety dream, that are focussed together, like a pair of glasses, and become a fully conscious vision.

This last passage leads directly to Frye's conception of the purpose or final cause of literature. By imagining what we want—and don't want—we move closer to the goal of life, which for Frye is the free, humane community of men. The ethical goal of liberal education (education, that is, which gives proper emphasis to man's imaginative constructions)

> is to liberate, which can only mean to make one capable of conceiving society as free, classless, and urbane. No such society exists, which is one reason why a liberal education must be deeply concerned with works of imagination. The imaginative element in works of art, again, lifts them clear of the bondage of history. Anything that emerges from the total experience of criticism to form part of a liberal education becomes, by virtue of that fact, part of the emancipated and humane community of culture, whatever its original reference.

The myths of a given culture, including our own, are always incomplete and tend to make us intolerant of differing imaginative visions. Thus by teaching imaginative works from the past and from different cultures we not only keep our students' imaginations open and flexible, we also "teach the ability to be aware of one's imaginative social vision, and so escape the prison of social conditioning." What we teach in the humanities, properly conceived of, is "some aspect of the freedom of man." No social vision is definitive, Frye concludes: "there is always more outside it." And therefore the proper experience of literature helps us to be "continually expanding and reshaping that vision."

The function of criticism follows naturally from all of this. The critic is a kind of cultural anthropologist, and expert at detecting the presence of mythic patterns in their variously displaced and fragmented forms (to see how adroitly Frye can apply these principles the reader might well start with the handling of Shakespearian romance in *A Natural Perspective*). The critic will describe and classify as precisely as possible—but he will *not* evaluate. In "Literary Criticism" Frye makes his notorious distinction between the kind of criticism just mentioned, which he calls "academic" criticism, and "judicial" criticism, which does make value judgments and is the province not of cumulative learning or science, but of "book reviewing":

> I am aware of the weight and influence of critics today who insist that criticism is primarily evaluative, and my next sentence, whether right or wrong, has been carefully considered. The metaphor of the judge, and in fact the whole practice of judicial criticism, is entirely confined to reviewing, or surveying current literature or scholarship: all the metaphors transferred from it to academic criticism are misleading and all the practices derived from it are mistaken. The reviewer of a current book, whatever its content, is expected to lead up to a value judgment, to give a clear indication of whether or not he thinks the book worth reading. But an academic critic, concerned with the scholarly organization of literature, is never in this judicial position.

Value judgments are based on "taste" and are in themselves "individual, unpredictable, variable, incommunicable, indemonstrable, and mainly intuitive reactions to knowledge." We may express our taste or values, but when we do so we are usually speaking only for the taste of our time (Edmund Wilson, for example, is "perhaps the finest judicial critic of our time, with an academic orbit of about a century or so, and it is instructive to see how his judgment goes out of focus when dealing with anything outside that orbit"). Frye's conclusion is blunt and unequivocal: "criticism as knowledge is one thing, and value judgments informed by taste are another."

The *Anatomy of Criticism* appeared in 1956 and has had so many enthusiastic supporters ever since that a few words about the limitations of Frye's system will not be out of place (for a sustained and generally devastating attack on Frye the reader should consult W.K. Wimsatt's "Northrop Frye: Criticism as Myth," printed in *Northrop Frye in Modern Criticism*). Frye's "method"—his constant dependence on simile and analogy to make his main points—raises some serious questions. The analogies are often striking, but whether or not they have much logical validity is another matter. Nor can Frye tell us anything about individual excellence: why is it, for example, that one work with a mythic theme will move us while an inferior work with the same theme does not? Yet the very sweep of Frye's system has proved irresistible to many academic critics, perhaps because it is secular and value-free (unlike the criticism, for example, of Eliot and Winters) and still proclaims that the study of literature is of great human importance. The system also has the advantage of being "open"—or simply vague—at certain crucial points. Unlike Richards or Burke, Frye will not make a clear commitment to any school of psychology (he warns us, for example, that his use of the terms "myth" and "archetype" should not be taken as indications that he is a Jungian like Maud Bodkin, "whom...I resemble about as much as I resemble the late Sarah Bernhardt"). When the generalizations are so attractively broad and the real commitments so few, there is little to argue firmly against.

In short, the system is safe; it is an educationist's dream come true.

GARDNER, Helen (Louise). British. Born in England, 13 February 1908. Educated at North London Collegiate School; St. Hilda's College, Oxford, B.A. 1929, M.A. 1935. Assistant Lecturer, 1930-31, and Lecturer, 1934-41, University of Birmingham; Assistant Lecturer, Royal Holloway College, University of London, 1931-43. Tutor, 1941-54, and Fellow, 1942-66, St. Hilda's College, Oxford, and Reader in Renaissance English Literature, Oxford University, 1954-66; Fellow of Lady Margaret Hall, Oxford, and Merton Professor of English Literature, Oxford University, 1966-75; now Honorary Fellow of Lady Margaret Hall and St. Hilda's College. Delegate, Oxford University Press, 1959-75; Member, Robbins Committee on Higher Education, 1961-63; Member, National Council for Academic Awards, 1964-67. Since 1968, Trustee, National Portrait Gallery, London. Ewing Lecturer, University of California at Los Angeles, 1954; Riddell Memorial Lecturer, University of Durham, 1956; Alexander Lecturer, University of Toronto, 1962; Messenger Lecturer, Cornell University, Ithaca, New York, 1967; T.S. Eliot Memorial Lecturer, University of Kent, Canterbury, 1968. D.Litt.: University of Durham, 1960; Oxford University, 1963; University of East Anglia, Norwich, 1967; University of London, 1969; University of Birmingham, 1970; Harvard University, Cambridge, Massachusetts, 1971; LL.D.: University of Aberdeen, 1967. C.B.E. (Commander, Order of the British Empire), 1962; D.B.E. (Dame Commander, Order of the British Empire), 1967. Fellow of the Royal Academy, 1958, and of the Royal Society of Literature, 1962. Address: Myrtle House, 12 Mill Street, Eynsham, Oxford OX8 1JS, England.

PUBLICATIONS

Criticism

"Walter Hilton and the Mystical Tradition in England," in *Essays and Studies of the English Association 22*. Oxford, Clarendon Press, 1937.
"Milton's 'Satan' and the Theme of Damnation in Elizabethan Tragedy," in *English Studies*, new series 1. London, Murray, 1948; reprinted in *A Reading of Paradise Lost*, 1965.
The Art of T.S. Eliot. London, Cresset Press, 1949; New York, Dutton, 1950.
"Milton's Firt Illustrator," in *English Studies*, new series 9. London, Murray, 1956.
"The Noble Moor," in *Proceedings of the British Academy 41*. London, Oxford University Press, 1956.
The Limits of Literary Criticism: Reflections on the Interpretation of Poetry and Scripture. London, Oxford University Press, 1956; reprinted in *The Business of Criticism*, 1959.
The Business of Criticism. Oxford, Clarendon Press, 1959.
Edwin Muir (lecture). Cardiff, University of Wales Press, 1961.
A Reading of Paradise Lost. Oxford, Clarendon Press, 1965.
T.S. Eliot and the English Poetic Tradition. Nottingham, Nottingham University, 1965.
Literary Studies (lecture). Oxford, Clarendon Press, 1967.
King Lear (lecture). London, Athlone Press, 1967.
Religion and Literature. London, Faber, and New York, Oxford University Press, 1971.
The Waste Land 1972 (lecture). Manchester, Manchester University Press, 1972.
Poems in the Making (lecture). Southampton, University of Southampton Press, 1972.
The Composition of "Four Quartets." London, Faber, 1977; New York, Oxford University Press, 1978.

Other

Editor, *The Divine Poems*, by John Donne. Oxford, Clarendon Press, 1952.
Editor, *The Metaphysical Poets*. London, Penguin, 1957.
Editor, with G.M. Story, *The Sonnets of William Alabaster*. London, Oxford University Press, 1959.

Editor, with Herbert Davis, *Elizabethan and Jacobean Studies Presented to Frank Percy Wilson in Honour of His Seventieth Birthday.* London, Oxford University Press, 1959.

Editor, *The Metaphysical Poets.* London, Oxford University Press, 1961.

Editor, *John Donne: A Collection of Critical Essays.* Englewood Cliffs, New Jersey, Prentice Hall, 1962.

Editor, *The Elegies and the Songs and Sonnets*, by John Donne. Oxford, Clarendon Press, 1965.

Editor, with Timothy Healy, *Selected Prose*, by John Donne. London, Oxford University Press, 1967.

Editor, *Shakespearian and Other Studies*, by F.P. Wilson. Oxford, Clarendon Press, 1969.

Editor, *Shakespeare and the New Bibliography*, by F.P. Wilson. Oxford, Clarendon Press, 1970.

Editor, *The Faber Book of Religious Verse.* London, Faber, 1972; as *A Book of Religious Verse*, New York, Oxford University Press, 1972.

Editor, *The New Oxford Book of English Verse 1250-1950.* Oxford, Clarendon Press, and New York, Oxford University Press, 1972.

*   *   *

Dame Helen Gardner is a distinguished scholar whose approach to criticism, as one would expect, involves serious attention to the proper relationship between historical awareness and the final act of judgment. Psychologically, judgment seems to come first, since criticism begins with the sense that a work has "value":

> The primary critical act is a judgment, the decision that a certain piece of writing has significance and value. It asserts a hold in some way upon my intellect, which entertains the propositions which it makes. It appeals through my senses and imagination to my capacity to recognize order and harmony and so be delighted by them. It appeals also to my experience as a human being, to my conscience and moral life.

Since the impressions of a trained sensibility are different from those of the amateur, the critic's job is "to assist his readers to find the value which he believes the work to have." His aim should be to illuminate what is there, not to legislate (to decide what *should* have been there) or to make comparative value judgments:

> The attempt to measure the amount of value, to declare or attempt to demonstrate that this poem is more valuable than that, or to range writers in an order of merit does not seem to me to be the true purpose of criticism. Such attempts ignore the nature of taste and the nature of values. Good taste is not an absolute....Statements about relative values are unnecessary...or else they are rationalizations of personal and temporary tastes and prejudices.

For Dame Helen art is both temporal and timeless. The work exists first of all as an embodied meaning, intended by the author to be grasped in a determinate way:

> If this is to be guilty of "the intentional heresy" I am quite content to be excommunicated for it. A poem is not whatever I choose to make of it. It is something which its author has made with deliberation, choosing that it should say this and not that. Whether he made it with ease, so that it "came right," or with great labour...he made it, as far as he was able, to his own satisfaction, recognizing, when it was finished: "This is what I meant to say."...The power to recognize this conception, which is the source of the poem's life in all its parts, and to read the poem in its light, is what I mean by true judgment in a critic.

But the work also exists for future audiences as well, and although Dame Helen does not use the terms "meaning" and "significance" in their restricted hermeneutic senses, the distinction is basic to her argument. "Meaning" refers to the complex sense (and implications) of an utterance, while "significance" refers to the way in which we relate that meaning to our own concerns and values. Interpretation is the recovery of meaning, criticism is the assertion of significance. Both activities are valid, but unless we are content to use the work as a kind of Rorschach blot criticism depends on the valid determination of meaning. The responsible critic, in the broad sense, knows how the author expected to be understood:

> The beginning of the discipline of literary criticism lies in the recognition of the work of art's objective existence as the product of another mind, which exists not to be used but to be understood and enjoyed. Its process is the progressive correction of misconception, due to ignorance, personal prejudice, or temperamental defects, the setting of the work at a distance, the disentangling it from my personal hopes, fears, and beliefs, so that the poem which my mind re-creates in the reading becomes more and more a poem which my own mind would never have created.

Yet important as this historical awareness is, Dame Helen is suspicious of any claims that the scholar has recaptured the perspective of an earlier age:

> The "Elizabethan World Picture" tidily presented to us as a system of thought cannot tell us how much of that picture had truth and meaning for any single Elizabethan. And even if we could discover a kind of highest common factor of contemporary beliefs and attitudes, it could not tell us what any individual believed, and certainly not what Shakespeare believed....Our sense of a period is far too arbitrary, unstable and conjectural to provide us with an objective field of reference by which we can assert, "This is what the work of art must have meant."

Even if it were possible to transform the modern reader into Donne or Shakespeare's ideal contemporary, there is still an area which criticism should not presume to command:

> This is the area of aesthetic experience, which must, of its nature, be personal, conditioned by the individual's experience of life and art. The critic's task is to assist his readers to read for themselves, not to read for them. He must respect their sensibilities by not obtruding his own.

Equally important, a true work of art generates new values as it moves through time:

> The historical approach takes us toward the meaning and can explain much; but the value of the poem does not lie in its power to tell us how men once thought and felt. It has an extra-historical life, which makes what had significance, beauty, and meaning in its own age have significance, beauty, and meaning now. The total meaning of a work of art cannot be analysed or treated historically, though I believe we cannot approach it except through history as we ourselves meet it in history.

At its best, then, criticism prepares us to enjoy the value of a work; and when she makes pleasure the end of art, Dame Helen has in mind the classical conception of exercising and satisfying those capacities which characterize man at *his* best:

> A critic's attitude to works of art must depend ultimately on his conception of the nature of man. Those who hold seriously to enjoyment as the true end of reading speak from within the Greek tradition which rates the life of contemplation above the life of action and holds that man's destiny is to enjoy the vision of truth, beauty, and goodness or, to use the Christian formulation, to "glorify God and enjoy Him for ever."

A Reading of Paradise Lost clearly illustrates these principles (drawn from *The Business of Criticism*) in action. Here Dame Helen is concerned to protect the poem from the wrong kinds of questions. "With both Donne and Milton," she observes, "a modern critic has to steer a course between two extremes: the attempt to interpret their poetry solely in terms of their own age, and the attempt to interpret it solely in terms of ours." In practical terms, criticism means knowing enough to know what the right questions are. But finally the reader may wonder if all perspectives are of equal value: isn't there a vantage point, which is somehow of primary importance when we make final judgments of significance? For Dame Helen personally, there is: a work is best apprehended from the Christian point of view. But true to her own principles, she never insists upon doctrinal interpretation.

The Art of T.S. Eliot is considerably more than a simple commentary, since Dame Helen has two claims to put forward: first, that Eliot is a major poet, and second, that in *Four Quartets* he manages to solve "the problem of communication for a religious poet in an age where his religious beliefs are not widely held." The latter claim she argues convincingly, making a number of subtle and original observations about Eliot's metrics and diction which other critics have been borrowing, usually without acknowledgement, ever since. But as for Eliot's stature as a major poet, readers may be less convinced, particularly if they accept Dame Helen's own definition of a major poet as one who creates "an idiom and a rhythm which are new and individual but which become classic," thus giving to later poets "a form they can use for their own purposes." So far *Four Quartets* seems to be a work without heirs (and to be just, fifteen years after writing *The Art of T.S. Eliot* Dame Helen admitted that "Pound and Eliot are no longer important influences on young writers"). But if we have learned anything from *The Business of Criticism*, it is to be wary of sweeping judgments.

"Religion and Tragedy," (the first part of *Religion and Literature*), takes on the ambitious problem of isolating a valid common element in the definitions of tragedy which have been proposed since Aristotle. After surveying some of the most influential attempts at definition Dame Helen concludes that "one note is always struck: that tragedy includes, or reconciles, or preserves in tension, contraries." This tension (and it is usually tension rather than reconciliation) springs from a basic ambiguity, much like the ambiguity of those gestalt psychology illustrations in which a geometric figure first seems to move forward, then to recede in space. A tragedy such as *Oedipus* or *Hamlet*, for example, may pose the question, is man free or are his actions predetermined? But there is no "right" way to read the illustration, or the tragedy: mystery is an intended part of the design:

> In tragic art, the imagination, the power that reveals itself as Coleridge declared in the balance and reconcilement of contraries, is seen at its greatest, since the elements it balances and reconciles are so sharply opposed and so harshly discordant. Most writers on tragedy stress the close as the source of the tragedy's power to satisfy and console. But the pleasure, delight, satisfaction, consolation are surely felt throughout in the tension between the design and what the design strives to include, in the justice that is done to what baffles our understanding as well as to our understanding. Even at the close, in some form or other, there remain unanswerable questions. The design has to be strong. There must be a logic of events, not a mere sequence of distressing accidents, in order that the sense of ultimate mystery may be felt with its full power. Because we understand so much, we realize we understand so little.

Shakespearian tragedy is mysterious in this sense, she argues, and fundamentally "Christian":

> And when I call Shakespearian Tragedy "Christian Tragedy" I do not mean that I think of it as expounding analogically or otherwise the Christian scheme of Redemption, or as in any way concerned, in Miltoh's words, with "praising God aright and Godlike man, the Holiest of Holies and his Saints." I mean that the mysteries it exposes are mysteries that arise out of Christian conceptions and out of Christian formulations, and that some of its most characteristic features are related to Christian religious feeling and Christian apprehensions....I think of Shakespearian tragedy as "Christian" when contrasted with classical tragedy and with tragedies modelled on or attempting to rival ancient tragedy. But going beyond these generalities, I find also a relation between the tragic balance of protest and acceptance in Shakespearian tragedy and mysteries that particularly oppress a Christian consciousness in the dialectic between faith and experience.

While the Christian perspective allows for mystery and the inexplicable, it still assumes that the world is coherent and man responsible for his actions; but when these assumptions give way, as they have in the modern world, tragedy becomes impossible. "Because our age is peculiarly aware of the irrational, of the incoherence of our lives, sees sin as a sickness rather than the willed choice of wrong, and is unsympathetic to the idea of the heroic," Dame Helen maintains, "our response to Shakespearian Tragedy is different from the response of Johnson or of Coleridge or of Bradley." It is not merely our powers of response that are affected, of course, but our powers of creation as well. Her concluding remarks illustrate that fine balance between historical concern and aesthetic sensitivity which is characteristic of all her work:

> We rightly object to the Christian, the Marxist, or the Freudian who reduces works of imagination and power to exemplifications of the doctrine he holds. We should equally protest against "Shakespeare our Contemporary," and the fashionable attempt to present Shakespeare as an existentialist. To make the tragedies of Shakespeare conform to our idea of "the tragic" as "the meaningless," to sacrifice Shakespeare the poet to our desire for spectacle and violence, is outrageous arrogance. A false concept of progress is at work here, which imprisons us in the contemporary, in our own anxieties and problems. The humble and reverent contemplation of great works of the past can release us from the prison of present fears and anxieties and, in so releasing us, give us new understanding of them.

GEISMAR, Maxwell (David).   American.   Born in New York City, 1 August 1909. Educated at Columbia University, New York, B.A. 1931, M.A. 1932; Teaching Fellow, Harvard University, Cambridge, Massachusetts, 1932-33. Married Anne Rosenberg in 1932; three children. Member of the Literature Department, Sarah Lawrence College, Bronxville, New York, 1933-44. From 1945, Free-lance writer, editor and lecturer. Contributing Editor, *The Nation*, New York, 1945-50; Senior Editor, *Ramparts* magazine, 1966; Founding Editor, *Scanlon's Monthly*. Recipient: Guggenheim Fellowship, 1943; National Institute of Arts and Letters award, 1950. *Died 24 July 1979.*

PUBLICATIONS

Criticism

Writers in Crisis: The American Novel, 1925-1940.   Boston, Houghton Mifflin, 1942; London, Secker and Warburg, 1943.
The Last of the Provincials: The American Novel, 1915-1925.   Boston, Houghton Mifflin, and London, Secker and Warburg, 1947.
Rebels and Ancestors: The American Novel, 1890-1915.   Boston, Houghton Mifflin, 1953.
American Moderns: From Rebellion to Conformity.   New York, Hill and Wang, and London, W.H. Allen, 1958.
Henry James and the Jacobites.   Boston, Houghton Mifflin, 1963; as *Henry James and His Cult*, London, Chatto and Windus, 1964.
Mark Twain: An American Prophet.   Boston, Houghton Mifflin, 1970.
Ring Lardner and the Portrait of Folly.   New York, Crowell, 1972.

Other

The Higher Animals: A Mark Twain Bestiary.   New York, Crowell, 1976.

Editor, *The Portable Thomas Wolfe*. New York, Viking Press, 1946.
Editor, *Sister Carrie*, by Theodore Dreiser. New York, Pocket Books, 1949.
Editor, *Moby Dick*, by Herman Melville. New York, Washington Square Press, 1949.
Editor, *Selections from the Works of Thomas Wolfe*. London, Heinemann, 1952.
Editor, *Whitman Reader*. New York, Pocket Books, 1955.
Editor, *Short Stories*, by Jack London. New York, Hill and Wang, and London, Paterson, 1960.
Editor, *Short Stories of Sherwood Anderson*. New York, Hill and Wang, 1962.
Editor, *The Ring Lardner Reader*. New York, Scribner, 1963.
Editor, *Emile Zola: The Naturalist Novel*. Montreal, Harvest House, 1964.
Editor, *Benito Cereno and Billy Budd*, by Herman Melville. New York, Limited Editions Club, 1965.
Editor, *Unfinished Business*, by James Rosenberg. Mamaroneck, New York, Marasia Press, 1967.
Editor, *Mark Twain and the Three R's: Race, Religion, Revolution—and Related Matters*. Indianapolis, Bobbs Merrill, 1973.

*   *   *

"I am a literary critic of the historical school," Maxwell Geismar explained to his *Saturday Review* audience in 1949:

> As it happens, I am interested in our social patterns, and especially in what has happend to the national character during the last fifty years of industrial concentration and corporate capitalism. I am engaged in a project which is trying to evaluate the kind of life we have lived in the past through the major figures in our literature: a literary record which may well turn out to be either a tribute to our hopes or an epitaph of our decline.

And he continues:

> Now I agree that a work of art is a separate identity, a particular and unique crystallization of experience achieved through a specific technique. But I see a supplementary, not a contradictory meaning in the fact that it is also the expression of a personality and the highest mark of an environment.

This seems judicious enough, but when a critic spends so much time treating literature as a kind of social document it suggests that while all approaches may be equal, some are more equal than others.

The considerable enterprise Geismar undertook is a history of the American novel from 1860 to 1940. The "crisis" of the first volume, *Writers in Crisis*, is the threat to democracy posed by the Crash of 1929 and the Depression which followed. The unbridled individualism and corporate capitalism which led to the Depression were for Geismar a kind of wrong turning, but his faith in the future of democracy remained strong: "The basis of this book is democratic," he maintained, "its belief is the potential of democratic society, and especially American society, as the only mature form of our communal life." Thus he discusses Ring Lardner, Hemingway, Faulkner, Dos Passos, Wolfe and Steinbeck in terms of their responses to problems of the 1930's. Lardner dramatizes the hollowness of America's "commercial supermen, enthusiastic visionaries of the pocketbook," while Faulkner ominously represents that "descending spiral of isolation, rebellion and denial" which ends in a kind of negation favorable to fascism:

> I have used the title of Maurice Samuel's penetrating study of the Fascist superstitions, "The Great Hatred," to best describe Faulkner's work as a whole. For it is in the larger tradition of reversionary, neo-pagan, and neurotic discontent (from which Fascism stems) that much of Faulkner's writing must be placed—the anti-civilizational revolt which has caught so many modern mystics, the revolt rising out of modern social evils, nourished by ignorance of their true nature, and which succumbs to malice as their solution.

240

But the other writers are capable of growth and the reaffirmation of our true communal life, or so it seemed to Geismar in 1942:

> Our studies of these major novelists, in fact, will reveal that the depression of the nineteen-thirties, seemingly so destructive and despairing, was actually a time of regeneration for the writer....[The] social crisis of the thirties brought to the writers a spiritual positive based, as it were, on the actual collapse of their society. The conversion, however late or imperfect, of Hemingway [in *To Have and to Have Not*], the fusing of Dos Passos's "two nations," the astonishing development of Thomas Wolfe, and the typical evolution of John Steinbeck all point this up....In crisis the writer may find courage. In the recognition of his social usefulness, his belonging, the writer may gain a conviction he has too often lacked in the past, a faith in his cultural function which was previously denied him by a boom-time America that considered the writer, if at all, a sort of exotic excrescence.

The optimistic note is missing in *The Last of the Provincials*, inevitably, perhaps, since Geismar is now dealing with the "Middle Generation" of American novelists who responded in their various ways as America changed from an agrarian, provincial society to "an industrialized urban world power: the U.S.A." This is a period of "dry rot" for Geismar:

> The history of the American literary spirit during these years is the history of a spiritual constriction—of a survival struggle, as in the case of both Mencken and Cather, which very often omitted the elements that makes survival pleasant or even probable....The voices of communal aspiration have become those of solitary bitterness, of evasion and fantasy, of a desperate hedonism.

Rebels and Ancestors traces the rise of nationalism in similar terms, while *American Moderns* is an unhappy postscript, a disillusioned look at what became of the writers whose rebirth Geismar had hoped for and those new writers who settled for bleak conformity after the second World War. "There were no new intellectual or literary trends in general," he observes; and in an aside which reveals a good deal about his conception of literature he adds, "It was not a fresh period; but then, how could it be? The social atmosphere was so heavy, dense, oppressive. The aesthetic air was so thin, pure and abstract."

The limitations of Geismar's historical approach are obvious. No doubt fiction is in part a socially determined phenomenon, but this particular kind of historical reductiveness robs the artist of that freedom and objectivity which can make a work something more than a reflection of its times. It is unfair to blame Geismar for the uses to which his history may be put, but a troubling question remains: whom are these books intended for? Too often the projected reader seems to be an amateur social historian who wants to be spared the trouble of reading a particular class of documents. Like many literary historians, Geismar has no way of distinguishing artistic value from social significance.

In his *Who's Who* entry Geismar announced that he despised and detested "all literary fabrications (and there are many), fads, hoaxes, etc., and all writers who know but do not reveal the truth about their world and their times." This is admirable, if a little self-righteous, but what are we to make of *Henry James and the Jacobites*? Here the argument is simply the old Van Wyck Brooks line, slightly modernized, dishonest rather than uninformed and crudely abusive of its subject matter. Since these are unpleasant charges, an example is in order. In the early James story, "The Madonna of the Future," the narrator, an American visiting Florence, meets an expatriate painter who cries out that Americans are the "disinherited of art":

> We are condemned to be superficial! We are excluded from the magic circle. The soil of American perception is a poor little barren deposit. Yes! We are wedded to imperfection. An American, to excel, has just ten times as much to learn as a European....Our crude and garish climate, our silent past, our deafening future, the constant pressure about us of unlovely circumstances, are as void of all that nourishes and prompts and inspires the artist as my sad heart is void of bitterness in saying so!

So much—and so much only—Geismar quotes as proof as James' supposed snobbery. If we read the story James wrote, however, and not the story Geismar has edited into being, we soon discover that the narrator, after listening to this self-indulgent outburst, replies:

> Nothing is so idle as to talk about our want of a nutritive soil, of opportunity, of inspiration, and all the rest of it. The worthy part is to do something fine! There is no law in our glorious Constitution against that. Invent, create, achieve! No matter if you've to study fifty times as much as one of these! What else are you an artist for? Be your own Moses...and lead us out of the house of bondage!

In short, the narrator provides that balance Geismar accuses James of lacking, and other examples of misreading and misrepresentation might be multiplied almost indefinitely. Geismar's deviousness was a matter for his own conscience, but the critical mistake involved here is simply the antique blunder of assuming that the author is always on the side of his central character. And Geismar was just as disturbed by the critical reputation James enjoyed during the 1940's and 50's, since it all seemed to have something to do with paleface snobbery, cultural insularity, McCarthy and Eisenhower. The period of James' ascension, he contended, was one of "conformity and sterility":

> The Jamesian esthetics was the perfect register, reverberator, mirror, reflector, for changing and distorting, or for eliminating, the realities of world history which a large sector of American intellectuals no longer wished to understand and deal with. Henry James was the symbol of national make-believe on the highest level of intellectual or cultural status and respectability.

Thus Geismar yearned disconsolately for "the voice of an Emerson, or a Thoreau, very different indeed; or of a Melville, a Whitman, a Howells, a Mark Twain, a Dreiser!" This is all very confusing and troubling, but the reader who has reached Geismar's final chapter has already left reason far behind. Only one mildly interesting question remains: where did Geismar get the strength to push through the complete works of a writer he so obviously detests? *Henry James and the Jacobites* is an unparalleled instance of literary masochism.

GOODMAN, Paul. American. Born in New York City, 9 September 1911. Educated at the City College of New York, B.A. 1931; University of Chicago, Ph.D. 1940 (received, 1954). Married twice; two daughters. Reader for Metro-Goldwyn-Mayer, 1931; Instructor, University of Chicago, 1939-40; Teacher of Latin, physics, history and mathematics, Manumit School of Progressive Education, Pawling, New York, 1942; also taught at New York University, 1948; Black Mountain College, North Carolina, 1950; Sarah Lawrence College, Bronxville, New York, 1961; Knapp Professor, University of Wisconsin, Madison, 1964; taught at the Experimental College of San Francisco State College, 1966; University of Hawaii, Honolulu, 1969, 1971. Formerly, Editor, *Complex* magazine, New York; Film Editor, *Partisan Review*, New Brunswick, New Jersey; Television Critic, *New Republic*, Washington, D.C.; Editor, *Liberation* magazine, New York, 1962-70. Recipient: American Council of Learned Societies Fellowship, 1940; Harriet Monroe Memorial Prize (*Poetry*, Chicago), 1949; National Institute of Arts and Letters grant, 1953. Fellow, New York Institute for Gestalt Therapy, 1953; Institute for Policy Studies, Washington, D.C., 1965. *Died 3 August 1972.*

Criticism

Art and Social Nature.   New York, Vinco Publishing Company, 1946.
Kafka's Prayer.   New York, Vanguard Press, 1947.
The Structure of Literature.   Chicago, University of Chicago Press, and London, Cambridge University Press, 1954.
Speaking and Language: Defence of Poetry.   New York, Random House, 1972.
Creator Spirit Come! The Literary Essays of Paul Goodman, edited by Taylor Stoehr.   New York, Free Life Editions, 1977.

Verse

Ten Lyric Poems.   New York, 5 x 8 Press, 1934.
12 Ethical Sonnets.   New York, 5 x 8 Press, 1935.
15 Poems with Time Expressions.   New York, 5 x 8 Press, 1936.
Homecoming and Departure.   New York, 5 x 8 Press, 1937.
Childish Jokes: Crying Backstage.   New York, 5 x 8 Press, 1938.
A Warning at My Leisure.   Harrington Park, New Jersey, 5 x 8 Press, 1939.
Pieces of Three, with Meyer Liben and Edouard Roditi.   Harrington Park, New Jersey, 5 x 8 Press, 1942.
Five Young American Poets, with others.   New York, New Directions, 1942.
The Copernican Revolution.   Saugatuck, Connecticut, 5 x 8 Press, 1946.
Day and Other Poems.   New York, privately printed, 1954.
Red Jacket.   New York, privately printed, 1955.
Berg Goodman Mezey: Poems.   Philadelphia, New Ventures Press, 1957.
The Well of Bethlehem.   New York, privately printed, 1957.
Ten Poems.   Privately printed, 1961.
The Lordly Hudson: Collected Poems of Paul Goodman.   New York, Macmillan, 1962.
Hawkweed.   New York, Random House, 1967.
North Percy.   Los Angeles, Black Sparrow Press, 1968.
Homespun of Oatmeal Gray.   New York, Random House, 1970.
Two Sentences.   Toronto, Coach House Press, 1970.
Collected Poems, edited by Taylor Stoehr.   New York, Random House, 1974.

Novels

The Grand Piano; or, The Almanac of Alienation.   San Francisco, Colt Press, 1942.
The State of Nature.   New York, Vanguard Press, 1946.
The Dead of Spring.   Glen Gardner, New Jersey, Libertarian Press, 1950.
Parents Day.   Saugatuck, Connecticut, 5 x 8 Press, 1951.
Empire City.   Indianapolis, Bobbs Merrill, 1959; London, Wildwood House, 1978.
Making Do.   New York, Macmillan, 1963.
Don Juan; or, The Continuum of the Libido, edited by Taylor Stoehr.   Los Angeles, Black Sparrow Press, 1979.

Short Stories

The Facts of Life.   New York, Vanguard Press, 1945; London, Editions Poetry London, 1946.

The Break-Up of Our Camp and Other Stories.   New York, New Directions, 1949.
Our Visit to Niagara.   New York, Horizon Press, 1960.
Adam and His Works: Collected Stories.   New York, Random House, 1968.
"The Writings of Paul Goodman: 'Johnson' and Other Stories," edited by David Ray and
   Taylor Stoehr, in *New Letters* (Kansas City), 42, 1976.
The Collected Stories and Sketches of Paul Goodman, edited by Taylor Stoehr.   Los
   Angeles, Black Sparrow Press, 4 vols., 1978-80.

Plays

The Tower of Babel, in *New Directions in Prose and Poetry 5.*   New York, New
   Directions, 1940.
2 Noh Plays (produced New York, 1950).   Included in *Stop-Light*, 1941.
Stop-Light (5 Noh plays: *Dusk: A Noh Play, The Birthday, The Three Disciples, The
   Cyclist, The Stop Light*).   Harrington Park, New Jersey, 5 x 8 Press, 1941.
Theory of Tragedy, in *Quarterly Review of Literature* (Annandale-on-Hudson, New
   York), v, 4, 1940.
Jonah (produced New York, 1950).   Included in *Three Plays*, 1965.
Faustina (produced New York, 1952).   Included in *Three Plays*, 1965.
Abraham (cycle of Abraham plays; produced New York, 1953).   *Abraham and Isaac*
   published in *Cambridge Review* (Cambridge, Massachusetts), November 1955.
The Young Disciple (produced New York, 1955).   Included in *Three Plays*, 1965.
Little Hero (produced New York, 1957).   Included in *Tragedy and Comedy: 4 Cubist
   Plays*, 1970.
The Cave at Machpelah (produced New York, 1959).   Published in *Commentary* (New
   York), June 1958.
Three Plays: The Young Disciple, Faustina, Jonah.   New York, Random House, 1965.
Tragedy and Comedy: 4 Cubist Plays (includes *Structure of Tragedy, After Aeschylus*;
   Structure of Tragedy, After Sophocles; *Structure of Pathos, After Euripides*; *Little
   Hero, After Molière*).   Los Angeles, Black Sparrow Press, 1970.

Other

Communitas: Means of Livelihood and Ways of Life, with Percival Goodman.   Chicago,
   University of Chicago Press, and London, Cambridge University Press, 1947; revised
   edition, New York, Knopf, 1960.
Gestalt Therapy: Excitement and Growth in the Human Personality, with Frederick Perls
   and Ralph Hefferline.   New York, Julian Press, 1951.
*Censorship and Pornography on the Stage, and Are Writers Shirking Their Political
   Duty?*   New York, Living Theatre, 1959.
Growing Up Absurd: Problems of Youth in the Organizational Society.   New York,
   Random House, 1960; London, Gollancz, 1961.
Drawing the Line.   New York, Random House, 1962.
The Community of Scholars.   New York, Random House, 1962.
Utopian Essays and Practical Proposals.   New York, Random House, 1962.
The Society I Live in Is Mine.   New York, Horizon Press, 1963.
Compulsory Mis-Education.   New York, Horizon Press, 1964; revised edition, London,
   Penguin, 1971.
People or Personnel: Decentralizing and the Mixed System.   New York, Random
   House, 1965.   .
The Moral Ambiguity of America (lecture).   Toronto, CBC Publications; revised version
   as *Like a Conquered Province: The Moral Ambiguity of America.*   New York,
   Random House, 1967.

The Open Look. New York, Funk and Wagnalls, 1969.
New Reformation: Notes of a Neolithic Conservative. New York, Random House, 1970.
Little Prayers and Finite Experience. New York, Harper, 1972.
Drawing the Line: The Political Essays of Paul Goodman, edited by Taylor Stoehr. New York, Free Life Editions, 1977.
Nature Heals: The Psychological Essays of Paul Goodman, edited by Taylor Stoehr. New York, Free Life Editions, 1977.
The Black Flag of Anarchism. London, Kropotkin's Lighthouse Publications, 1978.

BIBLIOGRAPHY

Tom Nicely, *Adam and His Work: A Bibliography of Sources by and about Paul Goodman (1911-1972).* Metuchen, New Jersey, Scarecrow Press, 1979.

*   *   *

While *Art and Social Nature* has relatively little to say about art itself, it does illustrate clearly that radical, utopian and finally romantic conception of human nature and freedom which is central to Goodman's thinking in every area. "By 'revolutionary,'" he explains, "I here refer to the heirs of Rousseau and the French Revolution: the conviction that man is born free and is in institutional chains, that fraternity is the deepest political force and the fountain of social invention; and that socialism implies the absence of state or other coercive power." Of course Goodman himself is one of these heirs: for him the natural life of the instincts is essentially good and any coercion wrong if it "prevents the ego from realizing the living power of interpreting and defending the most original instinctual demands." What keeps him from totally anarchic individualism is his strong belief in the natural tendency towards social cooperation and his conviction that "the society we want is universally present in the heart, tho now generally submerged." Modern corporate capitalism thwarts the individual in several important respects: it often stifles natural impulses; it alienates the worker from his work; and it creates those false "needs" which are characteristic of affluence and the consumer mentality which Marxism failed to anticipate. It is probably fair enough to deduce from this that art should be on the side of individualism and the true community, but Goodman's remarks are limited to a few brief speculations about the ways in which a writer's social position may influence his choice of techniques.

Kafka's Prayer is a full-scale study in every sense, however, and one of the most remarkable of Goodman's many remarkable books. Troubled by Kafka's apparent inability to finish many of his works, Goodman assets that "incompleteness is a biographical fact, to be explained psychologically or some other way; it is not a predicate of poetics." However free-wheeling his thinking may have been in other respects, Goodman never wavered in his conviction that "categorically the wholeness of a work of art is the same as its being art." Yet Kafka is obviously a moving and powerful artist. Goodman explores this paradox by distinguishing between art as "prayer" (Kafka's own terms) or the expression of need and guilt, and art as "dream" or the temporary solution of some psychic conflict which the artist relieves by projection (here Goodman is at least as much indebted to Otto Rank as to Freud). There is an implication that art may have a similar therapeutic function for the audience, but Goodman does not make this point explicit until later, in *The Structure of Literature*, when he observes that since the writer "solves an inner conflict" and "rids himself of the neurotic symptom by turning it outward," the audience also "shares his deep experience with him":

> To the extent that art-working *solves* the "inner" conflict, it does so, like any other activity, by changing the environment to express the repressed need; this the artist does by spontaneous action in his public medium. Thus, if we want psychologically to explain the artist's success rather than his failure, we analyze the art-working itself and its completion in the work itself, for this is how the old-fashioned business is finished at last in the open.

There is a tension or conflict which interrupts Kafka's work, a fundamental opposition between "writing as dream, escape from father, and...writing as prayer: humility, imploring father." The successful work is the one which manages (in some undefined way) to be both prayer and dream; the Kafka Goodman admires is the Kafka who speaks up for community and the rightness of the instincts. At his best Kafka vividly portrays "an ego closed against the instincts, narcissistically binding their energy but so aware of itself that it does not misjudge, rationalize or condemn the things of this world, but can contemplate them as they are." This is a highly personal reading of Kafka, as Goodman admits: "Obviously I would not have spent so much time with an author unless I felt that here in a special way was *my* truth; but more important, that here was also something challenging my truth, so that either I must change or be refuted." The despairing side of Kafka is "refuted," but Goodman also recognizes the importance of the energy with which Kafka expresses his hopelessness. Still, moving as his work often may be, Kafka is not one of the great creators:

> The sense of the infinite, of what our theologians call the Crisis, is nothing obscure: it is the sense of two of several incompatible fundamental evaluations each absolutely affirmed. Kafka was a master of literary devices to express this sentiment.... His devices of infinity reduce infinity to *trompe-l'oeil*. *Trompe-l'oeil* is the trivial surprise that two incompatible constructions exist in one appearance; it is a gay and empty journey.

The Structure of Literature is an ambitious but far less convincing book. Evidently impressed by the pluralism of R.S. Crane and Richard McKeon, Goodman begins by arguing that the formalist approach to literature—the approach which seeks to answer the question, "How do the parts imply one another to make this whole?"—is only one of the several valid approaches a critic may use. *The Structure of Literature* is formalistic in this sense, then, concerned with "certain combinations of literary parts, ways of modifying the rhythms, different repetitions and returns, kinds of sequence in the plot, and exhaustion or expansion of the possibilities of combination." But Goodman complicates matters by insisting "I do not mean that the events in the work are the causes of which the feeling of the audience are the effects (I take this to be the position of I.A. Richards)" and dodging certain crucial questions (" 'What *is* a unifying relation and what kind of unity does a work of art have'—this question belongs to metaphysics and epistemology and will get no answer here.") Even within the terms of his limited framework Goodman fails to be helpful, mainly because he is vague about the question of final causes (in Aristotelian thinking the purpose or reason why a certain form has been used). Thus he talks about "serious" plots in the drama but never manages to define "serious" with sufficient precision. *Oedipus* and *Philoctetes* are both serious, but as the analysis soon indicates, they are so different in their final effects that the category "serious," if indeed it can be called a category, has little value. Goodman's treatment of comic dramatic plots is more to the point, but his discussion of "novelistic plots" is, once again, confusing:

> Novels of the sentimental kind are sequences of occasions for sentiment, leading to abiding attitudes or active commitments. Unlike serious poems, the actions of the persons do not essentially engage them; that is, formally, the persons have a scope and career greater than these particular actions; the persons respond to the events rather than being completely in them. And yet...these actions and other occasions of response do make a difference; the responses add up; disposition is fixed into character.

The distinctions proposed between characters in a novel and characters in a drama will simply not hold up, as any experienced reader can demonstrate easily enough. And if tight organic unity is still a primary virtue, then novelistic plots are inherently inferior to tragic and comic drama—but by this time it is impossible to distinguish between "plot," "kind," and "structure." Readers who wish to see what can be done with the Aristotelian method would do far better to consult R.S. Crane and Elder Olson. In his final remarks about lyric "forms" Goodman settles for the usual commonplaces about the interdependence of diction, imagery, meter and so forth in a successful poem.

Goodman's stubborn individualism is the motive force behind *Speaking and Language*, in which he attacks the tendency of modern linguists to ignore context and to reduce language to a univocal "code," thus sacrificing the "immediacy, feelingfulness, and concrete reality that alone give speech its human meaning." His concern is basically political:

> Why am I so polemical about recent language theory?... Why don't I let those scholars do their thing, while I, as a man of letters, do mine? Frankly I am made politically uneasy by it, by the thrust of cultural anthropology, Basic languages, scientific linguistics, communications engineering, and the Theory of Communications. They usually treat human communication as far more mechanistic than it is, they are technological in an antihumanistic sense.... My own bias, to be equally frank, is to play up the animal, spontaneous, artistic, and populist forces in speech. These forces are both agitational and deeply conservative—as I think good politics is. And as a writer, I want to defend literature and poetry as the indispensable renovators of dessicated and corrupt language.

Goodman goes on to argue that poetry at its best is never far from the immediacy of living language (he may owe something here to Alfred North Whitehead's defense of Romantic poetry in *Science and the Modern World*); he also makes some interesting observations about style as "hypothesis" or way of seeing the world—and then soon wanders off into other areas. Here, as in *The Structure of Literature*, Goodman reveals a passion for systematic thought but very little real aptitude for it. One settles for those sudden, sharp insights which often seem to be the special province of the poet and born outsider.

GRAVES, Robert (Ranke).   British.   Born in London, 24 July 1895. Educated at Charterhouse School, Surrey; St. John's College, Oxford, B. Litt. 1926. Served with the Royal Welch Fusiliers in World War I; was refused admittance into the armed forces in World War II. Married 1) Nancy Nicholson; 2) Beryl Pritchard; seven children. Professor of English, Egyptian University, Cairo, 1926. Settled in Deyá, Majorca in 1929; with the poet Laura Riding established the Seizin Press and *Epilogue* magazine. Left Majorca during the Spanish Civil War; settled in Glampton-Brixton, Devon during World War II; returned to Majorca after the war. Clark Lecturer, Trinity College, Cambridge, 1954; Professor of Poetry, Oxford University, 1961-66; Arthur Dehon Little Memorial Lecturer, Massachusetts Institute of Technology, Cambridge, 1963. Recipient: Bronze Medal for Poetry, Olympic Games, Paris, 1924; Hawthornden Prize, for fiction, 1935; Black Memorial Prize, for fiction, 1935; Femina Vie Heureuse-Stock Prize, 1939; Russell Loines Poetry Award, 1958; National Poetry Society of America Gold Medal, 1960; Foyle Poetry Prize, 1960; Arts Council Poetry Award, 1962; Italia Prize, for radio play, 1965; Queen's Gold Medal for Poetry, 1968; Gold Medal for Poetry, Cultural Olympics, Mexico City, 1968. M.A.: Oxford University, 1961. Honorary Member, American Academy of Arts and Sciences, 1970. Address: c/o A.P. Watt and Son, 26-28 Bedford Row, London W.C. 1, England.

PUBLICATIONS

Criticism

On English Poetry: Being an Irregular Approach to the Psychology of This Art, from Evidence Mainly Subjective.   New York, Knopf, and London, Heinemann, 1922.
"Dreams and Poetry," in *The Meaning of Dreams.*   London, Cecil Palmer, 1924; New York, Greenberg, 1925; later incorporated in *The White Goddess*, 1948.
Poetic Unreason and Other Studies.   London, Cecil Palmer, 1925.

Contemporary Techniques of Poetry: A Political Analogy. London, Hogarth Press, 1925.

Another Future of Poetry. London, Hogarth Press, 1926.

The English Ballad: A Short Critical Survey. London, Benn, 1927; revised edition, as *English and Scottish Ballads*, London, Heinemann, and New York, Macmillan, 1957.

A Survey of Modernist Poetry, with Laura Riding. London, Methuen, 1927; New York, Doubleday, 1928.

A Pamphlet Agianst Anthologies, with Laura Riding. London, Cape, and New York, Doubleday, 1928.

Epilogue: A Critical Summary, vols. 1, 2 and 3, with Laura Riding and others. Deyá, Majorca, Seizin Press, and London, Constable, 1935-37.

The White Goddess: A Historical Grammar of Poetic Myth. London, Faber, and New York, Creative Age Press, 1948; revised edition, Faber, and New York, Knopf, 1958.

The Common Asphodel: Collected Essays on Poetry, 1922-1949. London, Hamish Hamilton, 1949.

The Crowning Privilege: The Clark Lectures, 1954-55; Also Various Essays on Poetry and Sixteen New Poems. London, Cassell, 1955; New York, Doubleday, 1956.

Five Pens in Hand. New York, Doubleday, 1958.

Steps: Stories, Talks, Essays, Poems, Studies in History. London, Cassell, 1958.

Food for Centaurs: Stories, Talks, Critical Studies, Poems. New York, Doubleday, 1960.

Oxford Addresses on Poetry. London, 1961; New York, Doubleday, 1962.

Mammon and the Black Goddess. London, Cassell, and New York, Doubleday, 1965.

Poetic Craft and Principle. London, Cassell, 1967.

The Crane Bag and Other Disputed Subjects. London, Cassell, 1969.

On Poetry: Collected Talks and Essays. New York, Doubleday, 1969.

Difficult Questions, Easy Answers. London, Cassell, 1972; New York, Doubleday, 1973.

Verse

Over the Brazier. London, Poetry Bookshop, 1916; New York, St. Martin's Press, 1975.

Goliath and David. London, Chiswick Press, 1916.

Fairies and Fusiliers. London, Heinemann, 1917; New York, Knopf, 1918.

Treasure Box. London, Chiswick Press, 1919.

Country Sentiment. London, Secker, and New York, Knopf, 1920.

The Pier-Glass. London, Secker, and New York, Knopf, 1921.

Whipperginny. London, Heinemann, and New York, Knopf, 1923.

The Feather Bed. Richmond, Surrey, Hogarth Press, 1923.

Mock Beggar Hall. London, Hogarth Press, 1924.

Welchman's Hose. London, The Fleuron, 1925; Folcroft, Pennsylvania, Folcroft Editions, 1971.

(Poems). London, Benn, 1925.

The Marmosite's Miscellany (as John Doyle). London, Hogarth Press, 1925.

Poems (1914-1926). London, Heinemann, 1927; New York, Doubleday, 1929.

Poems (1914-1927). London, Heinemann, 1927.

Poems 1929. London, Seizin Press, 1929.

Ten Poems More. Paris, Hours Press, 1930.

Poems 1926-1930. London, Heinemann, 1931.

To Whom Else? Deyá, Majorca, Seizin Press, 1931.

Poems 1930-1933. London, Barker, 1933.

Collected Poems. London, Cassell, and New York, Random House, 1938.

No More Ghosts: Selected Poems. London, Faber, 1940.

(Poems). London, Eyre and Spottiswoode, 1943.

Poems 1938-1945. London, Cassell, and New York, Creative Age Press, 1946.

Collected Poems (1914-1947). London, Cassell, 1948.

Poems and Satires 1951.   London, Cassell, 1951.
Poems 1953.   London, Cassell, 1953.
Collected Poems 1955.   New York, Doubleday, 1955.
Poems Selected by Himself.   London, Penguin, 1957; revised edition, 1961, 1966, 1972.
The Poems of Robert Graves.   New York, Doubleday, 1958.
Collected Poems 1959.   London, Cassell, 1959.
More Poems 1961.   London, Cassell, 1961.
Collected Poems.   New York, Doubleday, 1961.
New Poems 1962.   London, Cassell, 1962; as *New Poems*, New York, Doubleday, 1963.
The More Deserving Cases: Eighteen Old Poems for Reconsideration.   Marlborough, Marlborough College Press, 1962; Folcroft, Pennsylvania, Folcroft Editions, 1978.
Man Does, Woman Is 1964.   London, Cassell, and New York, Doubleday, 1964.
Love Respelt.   London, Cassell, 1965.
Collected Poems 1965.   London, Cassell, 1965.
Seventeen Poems Missing from "Love Respelt".   Privately printed, 1966.
Collected Poems 1966.   New York, Doubleday, 1966.
Colophon to "Love Respelt".   Privately printed, 1967.
(*Poems*), with D.H. Lawrence, edited by Leonard Clark.   London, Longman, 1967.
Poems 1965-1968.   London, Cassell, 1968; New York, Doubleday, 1969.
Poems about Love.   London, Cassell, and New York, Doubleday, 1969.
Love Respelt Again.   New York, Doubleday, 1969.
Beyond Giving.   Privately printed, 1969.
Poems 1968-1970.   London, Cassell, 1970.
Advice from a Mother.   London, Poem-of-the-Month Club, 1970.
The Green-Sailed Vessel.   Privately printed, 1971.
Corgi Modern Poets in Focus 3, with others, edited by Dannie Abse.   London, Corgi, 1971.
Poems 1970-1972.   London, Cassell, 1972; New York, Doubleday, 1973.
Deyá.   London, Motif Editions, 1973.
Timeless Meeting: Poems.   London, Bertram Rota, 1973.
At the Gate.   London, Bertram Rota, 1974.
Collected Poems 1975.   London, Cassell, 2 vols., 1975.
New Collected Poems.   New York, Doubleday, 1977.

Recordings: *Robert Graves Reading His Own Poems*, Argo and Listen, 1960; *Robert Graves Reading His Own Poetry and the White Goddess*, Caedmon; *The Rubaiyat of Omar Khayyam*, Spoken Arts.

Plays

John Kemp's Wager: A Ballad Opera.   Oxford, Blackwell, and New York, T.B. Edwards, 1925

Radio Play: *The Anger of Achilles*, 1964.

Novels

No Decency Left, with Laura Riding (as Barbara Rich).   London, Cape, 1932.
The Real David Copperfield.   London, Barker, 1933; as *David Copperfield by Charles Dickens, Condensed by Robert Graves*, edited by Merrill P. Paine, New York, Harcourt Brace, 1934.
I, Claudius: From the Autobiography of Tiberius Claudius, Emperor of the Romans, Born B.C. 10, Murdered and Deified A.D. 54.   London, Barker, and New York, Smith and Haas, 1934.

Claudius the God and His Wife Messalina: The Troublesome Reign of Tiberius Claudius Caesar, Emperor of the Romans (Born B.C. 10, Died A.D. 54), As Described by Himself; Also His Murder at the Hands of the Notorious Agrippina (Mother of the Emperor Nero) and His Subsequent Deification, As Described by Others. London, Barker, 1934; New York, Smith and Haas, 1935.

"Antiqua, Penny, Puce." Deyá, Majorca, Seizin Press, and London, Constable, 1936; as The Antigua Stamp, New York, Random House, 1937.

Count Belisarius. London, Cassell, and New York, Random House, 1938.

Sergeant Lamb of the Ninth. London, Methuen, 1940; as Sergeant Lamb's America, New York, Random House, 1940.

Proceed, Sergeant Lamb. London, Methuen, and New York, Random House, 1941.

The Story of Marie Powell: Wife to Mr. Milton. London, Cassell, 1943, as Wife to Mr. Milton: The Story of Marie Powell, New York, Creative Age Press, 1944.

The Golden Fleece. London, Cassell, 1944; as Hercules, My Shipmate, New York, Creative Age Press, 1945.

King Jesus. New York, Creative Age Press, and London, Cassell, 1946.

Watch the North Wind Rise. New York, Creative Age Press, 1949; as Seven Days in New Crete, London, 1949.

The Islands of Unwisdom. New York, Doubleday, 1949; as The Isles of Unwisdom, London, Cassell, 1950.

Homer's Daughter. London, Cassell, and New York, Doubleday, 1955.

Short Stories

The Shout. New York, Creative Age Press, and London, Cassell, 1946.

¡Catacrok! Mostly Stories, Mostly Funny. London, Cassell, 1956.

Collected Short Stories. New York, Doubleday, 1964; London, Cassell, 1965; as The Shout and Other Stories, London, Penguin, 1978.

Other

My Head! My Head! Being the History of Elisha and the Shumanite Woman; with the History of Moses as Elisha Related It, and Her Questions to Him. London, Secker, and New York, Knopf, 1925.

Lars Porsena; or, The Future of Swearing and Improper Language. London, Kegan Paul Trench Trubner, and New York, Dutton, 1927; revised edition, as The Future of Swearing and Improper Language, Kegan Paul Trench Trubner, 1936.

Lawrence and the Arabs. London, Cape, 1927; as Lawrence and the Arabian Adventure, New York, Doubleday, 1928.

Mrs. Fisher; or, The Future of Humour. London, Kegan Paul Trench Trubner, 1928; New York, Haskell House, 1974.

Goodbye to All That: An Autobiography. London, Cape, 1929; New York, Cape and Smith, 1930; revised edition, New York, Doubleday, and London, Cassell, 1957, London, Penguin, 1960.

T.E. Lawrence to His Biographer Robert Graves. New York, Doubleday, 1938; London, Faber, 1939.

The Long Week-end: A Social History of Great Britain 1918-1939, with Alan Hodge. London, Faber, 1940; New York, Macmillan, 1941.

Work in Hand, with others. London, Hogarth Press, 1942.

The Reader over Your Shoulder: A Handbook for Writers of English Prose, with Alan Hodge. London, Cape, 1943; New York, Macmillan, 1944.

Occupation: Writer. New York, Creative Age Press, 1950; London, Cassell, 1951.

The Nazarene Gospel Restored, with Joshua Podro. London, Cassell, 1953; New York, Doubleday, 1954.

Adam's Rib and Other Anomalous Elements in the Hebrew Creation Myth: A New View. London, Trianon Press, 1955; New York, Yoseloff, 1958.
The Greek Myths. London, and Baltimore, Penguin, 2 vols., 1955.
Jesus in Rome: A Historical Conjecture, with Joshua Podro. London, Cassell, 1957.
They Hanged My Saintly Billy. London, Cassell, 1957; as *They Hanged My Saintly Billy: The Life and Death of Dr. William Palmer*, New York, Doubleday, 1957.
The Penny Fiddle: Poems for Children. London, Cassell, 1960; New York, Doubleday, 1961.
Greek Gods and Heroes. New York, Doubleday, 1960; as *Myths of Ancient Greece*, London, Cassell, 1961.
Selected Poetry and Prose, edited by James Reeves. London, Hutchinson, 1961.
The Siege and Fall of Troy (juvenile). London, Cassell, 1962; New York, Doubleday, 1963.
The Big Green Book. New York, Crowell Collier, 1962.
Nine Hundred Iron Chariots: The Twelfth Arthur Dehon Little Memorial Lecture. Cambridge, Massachusetts Institute of Technology, 1963.
Hebrew Myths: The Book of Genesis, with Raphael Patai. New York, Doubleday, and London, Cassell, 1964.
Ann at Highwood Hall: Poems for Children. London, Cassell, 1964.
Majorca Observed. London, Cassell, and New York, Doubleday, 1965.
Two Wise Children (juvenile). New York, Harlin Quist, 1966; London, W.H. Allen, 1967.
Spiritual Quixote. London, Oxford University Press, 1967.
The Poor Boy Who Followed His Star (juvenile). London, Cassell, 1968; New York, Doubleday, 1969.
Poems: Abridged for Dolls and Princes (juvenile). London, Cassell, 1971.

Editor, with Alan Porter and Richard Hughes, *Oxford Poetry 1921*. Oxford, Blackwell, 1921.
Editor, *John Skelton (Laureate), 1460 (?)-1529*. London, Benn, 1927.
Editor, *The Less Familiar Nursery Rhymes*. London, Benn, 1927.
Editor, *English and Scottish Ballads*. London, Heinemann, and New York, Macmillan, 1957.
Editor, *The Comedies of Terence*. New York, Doubleday, 1962; London, Cassell, 1963.

Translator, with Laura Riding, *Almost Forgotten Germany*, by George Schwartz. Deyá, Majorca, Seizin Press, London, Constable, and New York, Random House, 1936.
Translator, *The Transformation of Lucius, Otherwise Known as The Golden Ass*, by Apuleius. London, Penguin, 1950; New York, Farrar Straus, 1951.
Translator, *The Cross and the Sword*, by Manuel de Jesus Galvan. Bloomington, Indiana University Press, 1955; London, Gollancz, 1956.
Translator, *The Infant with the Globe*, by Pedro Antonio de Alarcon. London, Trianon Press, 1955; New York, Yoseloff, 1958.
Translator, *Winter in Majorca*, by George Sand. London, Cassell, 1956.
Translator, *Pharsalia: Dramatic Episodes of the Civil Wars*, by Lucan. London, Penguin, 1956.
Translator, *The Twelve Caesars*, by Suetonius. London, Penguin, 1957.
Translator, *The Anger of Achilles: Homer's Iliad*. New York, Doubleday, 1959; London, Cassell, 1960.
Translator, with Omar Ali-Shah, *Rubaiyyat of Omar Khayaam*. London, Cassell, 1967.
Translator, *The Song of Songs*. New York, Clarkson Potter, and London, Collins, 1973.

CRITICAL STUDIES AND BIBLIOGRAPHY

Robert Hayman, "Robert Graves," in *Essays in Criticism* (Oxford), 5, 1955.

George Steiner, "The Genius of Robert Graves," in *Kenyon Review* (Gambier, Ohio), 22, 1960.

Douglas Day, *Swifter Than Reason: The Poetry and Criticism of Robert Graves.* Chapel Hill, University of North Carolina Press, 1963; London, Oxford University Press, 1964.

Fred H. Higginson, *A Bibliography of the Works of Robert Graves.* London, Nicholas and Vane, 1966.

Randall Jarrell, "Graves and the White Goddess," in *The Third Book of Criticism.* New York, Farrar Straus, 1969; London, Faber, 1974.

Laura Riding Jackson, "Some Autobiographical Corrections of Literary History," in *Denver Quarterly* (Colorado), 8, 1974.

A Gathering in Celebration of the Eightieth Birthday of Robert Graves, edited by Robin Skelton and William David Thomas, in *The Malahat Review* (Victoria, British Columbia), 35, 1975 (contains "Robert Graves: A Checklist of His Publications, 1965-74," edited by A.S.G. Edwards and Diane Tolomeo).

*   *   *

Looking back in 1949 at the four short books on poetry he had written between 1922 and 1926, Robert Graves recalls that he was "still in a neurasthenic state from my own war experiences.... My hope was to help the recovery of public health of mind, as well as my own, by the writing of 'therapeutic' poems." In the first of these books. *On English Poetry*, Graves took over a version of Freudianism he had discovered in the work of W.H.R. Rivers and argued that

> There are two meanings of Poetry as the poet himself has come to use the word:—first, Poetry, the unforeseen fusion in his mind of apparently contradictory emotional ideas; and second, Poetry, the more-or-less deliberate attempt, with the help of a rhythmic mesmerism, to impose the illusion of actual experience on the minds of others.... Poetry as the Greeks knew...is a form of psychotherapy. Being the transformation into dream symbolism of some disturbing emotional crisis in the poet's mind...poetry has the power of homeopathically healing other men's minds similarly troubled, by presenting them under the spell of hypnosis with an allegorical solution of the trouble. Once the allegory is recognized by the reader's unconscious mind as applicable the affective power of his own emotional crisis is diminished.

But from the very beginning of his own career Graves also seems to have felt the limitations of a therapeutic conception of poetry: if poems are curative, if their efficacy is relative to the particular psychological needs of the poet and his audience at a given moment, then it becomes difficult to make any absolute claims for the value of poetry. Thus he confessed (again in 1949) that

> The difficulty lay in my attempt to satisfy myself by satisfying everyone as if myself. I was trying to reconcile the psychological view with my own poetic conscience; the relativist view of good and bad with a strong personal bias towards the good; and a sentimental love of humanity with an unappeasable mistrust of the individuals that composed humanity.... The answers I gave [in *Poetic Unreason*] were: that the psychological view could be challenged by postulating true poetry as a post-Classical Romanticism...and that the personal bias towards good could be excluded as a human limitation which the assiduous practice of poetry might in time remove. But these conclusions were not confidently drawn.

About one issue, however, Graves has never changed his mind: the need for the poet to be an expert craftsman. "The art of poetry," he maintains, "consists in taking a poem through draft after draft, without losing its inspirational magic; [the poet] removes everything irrelevant or distracting, and tightens up what is left." True poetic statements thus differ from prose statements in several crucial respects:

> Prose is the art of manifest statement: the periods and diction may vary with the

emotional mood, but the latent meanings of the words that compose it are largely disregarded. In poetry a supplementary statement is framed by a precise marshalling of these latent meanings; yet the reader would not be aware of more than the manifest statement were it not for the heightened sensibility induced in him by the rhythmic intoxication of verse.

And while every good poem for Graves is "economical," the economy is always a function of the total verbal complexity the poet intends. Examining Shakespeare's sonnet. "Th' expence of Spirit," in *A Survey of Modernist Poetry* (written in collaboration with Laura Riding), Graves asserts that modern habits of punctuation rob the poem of its proper richness:

> The effect of this amended punctuation has been to restrict meanings to special interpretations of special words. Shakespeare's punctuation allows the variety of meanings he actually intends; if we must choose any one meaning, then we owe it to Shakespeare to choose at least one he intended and one embracing as many meanings as possible, that is, the most difficult meaning. It is always the most difficult meaning which is the most nearly final.... Making poetry easy for the reader should mean showing clearly how difficult it really is.

It is this theory of latent meanings and its detailed application to the Shakespeare sonnet which William Empson admits was the starting point of his own complex investigations in *Seven Types of Ambiguity*.

The true poet faces the problem of remaining faithful to his original inspiration and the standards of his craft. The public, on the other hand, thinks and feels in terms of stereotypes and will pay the anthology-poets handsomely to confirm those stereotypes. The true poet "must write in a new way if he is to evoke fresh responses in his readers," but most readers do not *want* the challenge of seeing things afresh and therefore complain about the "obscurity" of modern poetry:

> the quarrel is between the larger reading public and the modernist poet over the definition of clearness. Both agree that perfect clearness is the end of poetry; but the larger reading public insist that no poetry is clear unless it can be understood at a glance, whereas the modernist poet insists that the clearness of which the poetic mind is capable demands thought and language of a far greater sensitivity and complexity than the reading public permits it to use.

Yet since most men remain "unaware of the universe," they constantly depend on the poet for "a second-hand sense of the universe through language." Graves made these assertions in 1926, but in 1928 (and this time without the help of Miss Riding) he apparently discarded the romantic and therapeutic conceptions of poetry he had been developing:

> When I write now, I write only to please one thing, and that is the sense of what the poem I am writing ought to be intrinsically, and I don't care at all whether you, the aggregate public, like it or not.... The aggregate public is an aggregate disorder without seriousness or truth—its members are concerned only in *doing the right thing*.

"I should define a good poem," Graves announced in a 1957 lecture, "as one that makes complete sense; and says all it has to say memorably and economically; and has been written for no other than poetic reasons." If we are looking for some continuity in Graves' thinking, then the problem is to define "poetic reasons," particularly if they are no longer the reasons he had proposed in the 1920's. And the proper motives for writing a poem now turn out to be the recognition and worship of the "White Goddess," the archetypal fertility goddess, common to all primitive matriarchal cultures, in her three-fold identity as mother, sexual companion, and the "old Crone who presides over [the male's] burial." Graves provides a very useful summary of his contentions in an Oxford address, "The Personal Muse," in which he explains that the theme of his mammoth anthropological-historical study, *The White Goddess*,

> is the birth, life, death and resurrection of the Demigod of the Waxing Year; the central

chapters concern his losing fight against the Demigod of the Waning Year, his rival for love of the all-powerful and inscrutable Threefold Goddess, their mother, bride and layer-out. The poet identifies himself with the Demigod of the Waxing Year; the rival is his twin, his second self, his weird. All true poetry—true by A.E. Housman's practical razor test: "Does it make the hairs of one's chin bristle if one repeats it silently while shaving?"—celebrates some incident or other of this ancient story; and the three main characters are so much a part of our racial legacy that they also assert themselves in dreams and paranoiac visions.... Housman offered an alternative test of true poetry: whether it matches a phrase of Keats', "everything that reminds me of her goes through me like a spear." This has equal pertinence to the Theme: Keats was writing under the shadow of death about his personal Muse, Fanny Brawne; and "the spear that roars for blood" is the traditional weapon of the dark executioner and supplanter.

And in another of his lectures Graves observes that

My conclusions have not been condemned at universities; but neither have they been approved.... Don't mistake this for a grievance.... Granted, I seem to have stumbled on the cental secret of neolithic and Bronze Age religious faith, which makes sense of many otherwise inexplicable myths and religious customs; but this discovery is not essential to my central theme—namely the persistent survival of this faith among what are loosely called "romantic poets." Their imagery, I have shown, is drawn either consciously or unconsciously from the cult of the White Goddess, and the magic their poems exert largely depends on its closeness to her mysteries.
The most important single fact in the early history of Western religion and sociology was undoubtedly the gradual suppression of this Lunar Mother-goddess's inspiratory cult, and its supersession...by the busy, rational cult of the Solar God Apollo, who...initiated European literature and science.
This general view led me to differentiate between Muse poetry and Apollonian poetry: written respectively by those who rely on inspiration, checked by commonsense, and those who rely on intellectual verse decorated by the artificial flowers of fancy.

"No Muse-poet can grow conscious of the Muse except by experience of some woman in whom the Muse-power is to some degree or other resident": thus just as Graves is able to suggest that Fanny Brawne was Keats' *sunsum* or Goddess-representative, so Randall Jarrell argued, much to Graves' disgust, that the whole White Goddess business was a peculiar rationalization on Graves' part of his relationship with Laura Riding. But regardless of this possibility, Graves is well aware that a modern audience is bound to ask if he is speaking literally or metaphorically. His answer is a little evasive:

Some of you are looking queerly at me. Do I think that poets are literally inspired by the White Goddess? That is a improper question. What would you think, should I ask you if, in your opinion, the Hebrew prophets were literally inspired by God? Whether God is a metaphor or a fact cannot be reasonably argued; let us likewise be discreet on the subject of the Goddess. All we can know for sure is that the Ten Commandments, said to have been promulgated by Moses in the name of a Solar God, still carry religious force for those hereditarily prone to accept them; and that scores of poems written in the Muse-tradition still carry the authentic moon-magic for those hereditarily prone to accept that.... Since the source of creative power in poetry is not scientific intelligence, but inspiration—however this may be scientifically accounted for—why not attribute inspiration to the Lunar Muse, the oldest and most convenient European term for the source in question?

In *Mammon and the Black Goddess* Graves suddenly introduces another deity, the Black Goddess, who may appear to the true servant of the White Goddess and give him what the latter has withheld, "certitude in love." But Graves warns, "She is hardly more than a word of hope whispered among the few who have served their apprenticeship to the White Goddess."
In the essays and lectures which follow *The White Goddess* Graves elaborates and illustrates his distinction between the true, Muse-dedicated poet, like Skelton, whose "crowning privi-

lege" it is to serve the Goddess, and the Apollonian poet, like Virgil, who is all craft and no inspiration. Graves' discussion of a brief passage from Virgil provides a good example of his critical method in action:

> Euryalus rolls over in death. Athwart his lovely limbs runs the blood—and his drooping neck sinks on his shoulder. As when a purple flower lopped by the plough-share droops in death, or as when poppies with weary neck bow the head when weighted by some chance shower....

> I find this much-admired passage poetically inept. Poetry must be practical. Once blood has suffused Euryalus' limbs, the purple or scarlet colour of the flower should not be stressed; after all, Euryalus' head was uninjured, and would have grown pallid in comparison with his bloody limbs. Also, the simile is false: when the root of a plant has been sliced by a plough-share, its flower gradually droops; a lopped flower, however, has no chance to do so. The alternate simile of the poppy weighted down by rain comes straight from the *Iliad*, but Virgil spoils it, changing "poppy" to "poppies," which scan better.

Graves' attacks on Milton, Pope, Wordsworth (and so on: for Graves there have been very few English Muse-dedicated poets) are as amusing as they are unfair. Douglas Day's comment, in his very helpful study of Graves, *Swifter Than Reason*, is to the point: such analyses

> are ideal weapons for destruction, but useful for little else: *any* poem, when its every detail is scrutinized sardonically and negatively, is likely to appear ludicrous and sloppily contrived...and Graves frequently leaves himself open to charges of malice and narrowness when he employs it—which he does frequently.

In effect, Graves is defending only one kind of poetry and the plain style (much like his own) which still allows for important latent meanings.

The true poem seems to have become for Graves a kind of private ceremony, and act of homage, a dialogue in which, to quote Day once more, "the reader can only be an eavesdropper." Nevertheless, in "The Personal Muse" Graves comes close to implying a conception of poetry which is at least partly "therapeutic" in its suggestion that the poet may help to restore the proper balance between male and female principles:

> A tremendous effort of will freed early historic man from subservience to a matriarchate. Breaking the female monopoly of arts, sciences, and religious ritual, he consolidated his gains by a development of intellect, until he had made women his chattels. By a tremendous effort of intellect he achieved the power of personal choice. Modern men cannot be expected to renounce this hardly won power, and sell themselves back into collective slavery. But they can perhaps be persuaded that the a-moral exercise of intellect has created institutions hostile to human happiness —total wars, uncontrolled money, denatured food, soul-destroying machines, academicism, commercialized entertainment—which is no great advance on prehistoric savagery.

"Genius," he concludes in *Difficult Questions, Easy Answers*, "not only diagnoses the situation but supplies the answer."

HARDING, D(enys) (Clement) W(yatt). British. Born in Lowestoft, Suffolk, 13 July 1906. Educated at Lowestoft Secondary School; Emmanuel College, Cambridge, B.A. 1928, M.A. 1930. Married Jessie Muriel Ward in 1930. Investigator and Member of the Research Staff, National Institute of Industrial Psychology, London, 1928-33; Assistant, later Lecturer in Social Psychology, London School of Economics, 1933-38; Senior Lecturer in Psychology, University of Liverpool, 1938-45; Part-time Lecturer in Psychology, University of Manchester, 1940-41, 1944-45; Professor of Psychology, Bedford College, University of London, 1945-68, now Emeritus. Member, Editorial Board, *Scrutiny*, Cambridge, 1933-47; Honorary General Secretary, British Psychological Society, 1944-48; Editor, *British Journal of Psychology* (Central Section), London, 1948-54; Clark Lecturer, Trinity College, Cambridge, 1971-72. Address: Ashbocking Old Vicarage, near Ipswich, Suffolk IP6 9LG, England.

PUBLICATIONS

Criticism

"Evaluations (1): I.A. Richards," in *Scrutiny* (Cambridge), 1, 1933.
"The Work of L.H. Myers," in *Scrutiny* (Cambridge), 3, 1935.
"Psychology and Criticism: A Comment," in *Scrutiny* (Cambridge), 3, 1935.
"Regulated Hatred: As Aspect of the Work of Jane Austen," in *Scrutiny* (Cambridge), 8, 1940.
"The Rhythmical Intention in Wyatt's Poetry," in *Scrutiny* (Cambridge), 14, 1947.
"Scott Fitzgerald," in *Scrutiny* (Cambridge), 18, 1952.
"Shelley's Poetry," in *The Pelican Guide to English Literature 5*, edited by Boris Ford. London, Penguin, 1957.
"Psychological Processes in the Reading of Fiction," in *The British Journal of Aesthetics* (London), 2, 1962.
Experience into Words: Essays on Poetry. London, Chatto and Windus, 1963; New York, Horizon Press, 1964.
"What the Thunder Said," in *"The Waste Land" in Different Voices*, edited by A.D. Moody. London, Arnold, and New York, St. Martin's Press, 1975.
Words into Rhythm: English Speech Rhythm in Verse and Prose. London, Cambridge University Press, 1976.

Other

The Impulse to Dominate. London, Allen and Unwin, 1941.
Social Psychology and Individual Values. London, Hutchinson, 1953; revised edition, 1966.

Editor, with Gordon Bottomley, *The Collected Works of Isaac Rosenberg*. London, Chatto and Windus, 1937.
Editor, with Gordon Bottomley, *The Collected Poems of Isaac Rosenberg*. London, Chatto and Windus, 1949.
Editor, *Persuasion*, by Jane Austen. London, Penguin, 1965.

Translator, with Erik Mesterton, *The Eternal Smile*, by Pär Lagerkvist. Cambridge, Gordon Fraser, 1934.
Translator, with Erik Mesterton, *Guest of Reality*, by Pär Lagerkvist. London, Cape, 1936.

*   *   *

For one reason or another, collaborations between modern psychological theory and literary theory seldom have the results we might hope for. Psychologists seem happy to dismiss overt meaning and artistic control in favor of "real" latent meanings, just as critics are often content with a handful of terms detached from Freud and Jung. D.W. Harding, however, is a rare and welcome exception. His sensitivity to recurring patterns in a writer's work (and it is usually a body of work which interests him rather than a single text) is acute: his essays on the moral function of Jane Austen's "regulated hatred," for example, or Donne's habit of anticipating experience as a means of psychological defense, or on the nature of the guilt Coleridge appears to be struggling with in the *Ancient Mariner*—these are models of their kind. But good as these pieces are, it is the last two chapters of *Experience into Words* which other critics are likely to find of most value.

In the first of these chapters, "Reader and Author," Harding argues that authors intend a meaning and take pleasure or "satisfaction" in the expression of their intentions. In turn the reader experiences the embodied meaning and also shares vicariously in the artist's creative satisfaction. Thus Harding observes that

> a first principle of criticism might seem to be, then, that the reader is concerned only with two things: the piece of writing as it is and his own mental processes in the face of it. Knowing either of these things accurately is difficult enough, let alone making out what was in the author's mind. Attractive as that principle is, it has to be qualified if it is not to mislead. For to the extent to which either the author or the reader interprets the work in a private, idiosyncratic way, they have lost the implicit social link between them. This probably matters to the author; it certainly affects the reader who has come to suspect it. If what he enjoys in a work of art is unconnected with the artist's satisfaction, the work becomes an unintended feature of the world, non-social, like a sunset or a canyon, beautiful perhaps, but not mediating contact with a human maker. The social aspects of our enjoyment of any pleasing object matter all the time.

Suppose we discover that Shakespeare did not say of the dying Falstaff, "his nose was sharp as a pen, and a babbl'd of green fields":

> there would be a disappointment. The phrase would still be there, as fine as ever; but the sense of communication with Shakespeare through a shared satisfaction in it would be lost. Similarly with the modern cleaning of Canaletto's paintings: the revelation of sugary pinks and blues spoil [sic]—for those who find them disappointing—not only the cleaned pictures but the uncleaned ones too, for we have to recognize that our satisfaction in the subtler greyed colours may not have been a satisfaction Canaletto shared. What matters, for the social relation between the author and reader, is the author's satisfaction in his work, not his intention.

To take another example: the critic who "interprets" Don Quixote's windmills as symbols of modern industrialization is importing a meaning Cervantes obviously could not have intended; and Harding comments once again:

> This breadth of interpretive sweep holds a danger. When it goes so far that the attributed accretions of meaning are altogether beyond what the author could possibly have been aware of, we have lost the social relation between ourselves and him. Instead of feeling that when we contemplate the work of art we share in the author's satisfaction that it was as it was and not otherwise, we now have to recognize that he was only the initiator of a group process and that what we enjoy is a much later stage of that process.

When the reader engages in this kind of interpretation, he fails in his responsibility to the author; but by the same token the author may fail his readers: the social relationship of art is reciprocal. Thus Harding maintains that Blake's "obscurity" comes about in part because he "had no adequate reading public whose adverse criticism or lack of comprehension he could have taken seriously":

> He wanted to be understood, but not at the cost of trimming down his meaning to the

assimilative capacity of conventional minds....The miracle is that he produced such work at all. He represents a tremendous opportunity in English literature that was largely wasted owing to the reading public's restricted capacities for response.

The blame here is mutual, a point Harding makes again in his discussions of Shelley.

In his final and most important chapter, "The Hinterland of Thought," Harding takes issue with those psychologists who assert that thinking or mental activity in general is always somehow verbal or imagistic, whereas in fact

> both the emergent impulses and the processes that modify them exist in modes far different from words or imagery, these latter forming a late stage of their definition ....There can be no reason to doubt that interaction between the perceptual response with its emotion and the modifying mood or trait (the anxiety state, for example, or the courage given by trust in one's companions) may begin at the physical level. If we really believe in the organism as a psycho-physical whole and not as a body bossed by a mind we can hardly deny that a great deal of organization and mutual modification of impulse can go on in bodily terms whether or not it eventually appears as cognitive experience.

Words are not simply the outer clothing of thought: they are rather the tip of the iceberg of meaning, the "presentational symbols" which are "not merely a way of expressing these incipient attitudes and ideas but an indication that they had come into relation with one another long before they reached articulate thought." If the social relation between reader and author is to be preserved, of course the reader must be adept in sensing what lies behind the presentational symbols of the work. By attending closely to the verbal intricacies of "Adonais," for example, Harding is able to demonstrate the complexity of Shelley's attitude towards death. "When we speak or write," he concludes, "experience in some way merges with, and emerges in the form of, patterns of language. But in some minds the language processes reflect not only the main experience, in statements that could be more or less paraphrased, but also much subtler features of the non-verbal experience." What Harding has done, then, is to provide a psychological explanation of the ways in which ambiguity, paradox and multiple meanings may get into words. In a sense this concern is pre-critical and has little bearing on literary excellence, yet at the end of *Experience into Words* Harding observes that "the creative writers provide examples of nominally discursive statement which shows on inspection some of the characteristics of presentational symbolism and at times traces of a richer matrix, perhaps more confused, perhaps more complex, from which their words and images have emerged." These phrases— "perhaps more confused, perhaps more complex"—are not merely descriptive. They suggest a critical attitude which is in fact present in Harding's discussions of the occasional incoherence of Blake and Shelley. But poetic complexity may also be of great value: after examining a passage from "Burnt Norton" Harding observes that

> one could say, perhaps, that the poem takes the place of the ideas of "regret" and "eternity." Where in ordinary speech we would have to use those words, and hope by conventional trial-and-error to obviate the grosser misunderstandings, this poem is a newly created concept, equally abstract but vastly more exact and rich in meaning. It makes no statement...it is a linguistic creation....And the creation of a new concept, with all the assimilation and communication of experience that that involves, is perhaps the greatest of linguistic achievements.

The critic will have to judge each instance of complexity in its own terms; and like any other responsible reader he will have to make certain he is honoring that social bond which is basic to aesthetic experience.

Harding deliberately excluded any consideration of the rhythmic dimension of words and phrases in *Experience into Words*, but takes up this notoriously elusive issue in *Words into Rhythm*, based on his 1971 Clark Lectures at Cambridge. This is a less interesting study—or to put it more fairly, a less conclusive one—in large part because the relationship between rhythm and emotional affect is so extraordinarily difficult to generalize about. Harding's most important contribution here, then, is to discredit those theories which generalize too quickly and too broadly. "It is impossible to believe," he maintains, "that rhythms in themselves can make such fine discriminations as words can, in all their subtlety of sense and association." A more accurate approach, he suggests, would be one which considered the rhythmic movement of verse lines as units of "energy expenditure":

> It seems to me probable that, rather than according directly with particular emotional states, rhythm reflects—or, more properly, is itself part of—the energy conditions that accompany emotion. The characteristics of our imagined energy expenditure—our readiness to exert much or little of our available strength, and to exert it in specifiable ways, for instance stealthily or jauntily...boldly or hesitantly, restlessly, steadily—these are the features of our total state that are likeliest to be reflected in rhythm. They are, of course, closely bound up with emotional states: mournful sadness usually goes with a low level of energy release and heavy, plodding rhythms of movement; more frantic grief with impetuous or perhaps jagged rhythms; anger with abrupt and hammering stresses; delight with crisp, quick movement. But these are crudities of correspondence. The achievement of gifted writers is to manage infinitely subtler shades of emotional and energy states, with delicate and complex mergings that justify themselves by the very fact of defying paraphrase.

"Just as there are innumerable ways of mobilizing, withholding and releasing our energy," he cautions, "so the movement of verse has an indefinite range of resources for suggesting these possibilities." Rhythm does not "express" modes of energy expenditure, "it is part of them." Thus the total configuration of the individual poem is finally what should direct critical analysis: "It is not 'rhythm' or 'metre' that matters, but the unique rhythm of the unique poem":

> the possibilities of rhythmical movement are innumerable, and their effects are part of the literary critic's concern, and any reader's concern, with particular works; and—it scarcely needs saying—the rhythm has always to be viewed in relation with all the other factors at work.

Harding is much too sensitive and discriminating a reader of verse rhythms and emotional nuances to press much further than this.

HARDY, Barbara (Gladys). Born Barbara Nathan. British. Educated at Swansea High School for Girls; University College, University of London, B.A. 1947, M.A. 1949. Married; has two children. Professor, Royal Holloway College, University of London, 1965-70; since 1970, Professor of English, Birkbeck College, University of London. Recipient: British Academy Rose Mary Crawshay Prize, 1962. Address: Birkbeck College, Malet Street, London WC1E 7HX, England.

PUBLICATIONS

Criticism

> *The Novels of George Eliot: A Study in Form.*   London, Athlone Press, 1959.
> *Twelfth Night.*   Oxford, Blackwell, 1962.
> *Wuthering Heights.*   Oxford, Blackwell, 1963; New York, Barnes and Noble, 1964.
> *The Appropriate Form: An Essay on the Novel.*   London, Athlone Press, 1964; Evanston, Illinois, Northwestern University Press, 1971.

Jane Eyre. Oxford, Blackwell, 1964; New York, Barnes and Noble, 1965.

"Towards a Poetics of Fiction: (3) An Approach Through Narrative," in *Novel* (Providence, Rhode Island), 2, 1969.

Charles Dickens: The Later Novels. London, Longman, 1968.

Forms and Feelings in the Sonnets of Gerard Manley Hopkins (lecture). Douglas, Isle of Man, Island Development Company, 1970.

The Moral Art of Dickens. London, Athlone Press, and New York, Oxford University Press, 1970.

The Exposure of Luxury: Radical Themes in Thackeray. London, Owen, 1972.

Rituals and Feeling in the Novels of George Eliot (lecture). Swansea, University College of Swansea, 1973.

Tellers and Listeners: The Narrative Imagination. London, Athlone Press, 1975; New York, Humanities Press, 1976.

A Reading of Jane Austen. London, Owen, 1976; New York, New York University Press, 1979.

The Advantage of Lyric: Essays on Feeling in Poetry. London, Athlone Press, and Bloomington, Indiana University Press, 1977.

Other

Editor, *Middlemarch: Critical Approaches to the Novel*. London, Athlone Press, and New York, Oxford University Press, 1967.

Editor, *Daniel Deronda*, by George Eliot. London, Penguin, 1967.

Editor, *Critical Essays on George Eliot*. London, Routledge, and New York, Barnes and Noble, 1970.

Editor, *The Trumpet Major*, by Thomas Hardy. London, Macmillan, 1974.

*   *   *

Criticism of the novel does not begin with Henry James—it merely seems that way to most of us, and with good reason. Readers of Miriam Allott's invaluable *Novelists on the Novel* will recall that the quotations begin with Richardson and Rousseau, but as for sustained criticism, there is virtually nothing before James and the start of the modern period. The novel was a relatively new form, if in fact it is a form, without the prestige of tragedy or the epic; and it was essentially a popular form. When a subject matter is not taken seriously it is seldom speculated about: thus James observed in the early 1880's that until recently there was a "comfortable, good-humoured feeling abroad that a novel is a novel, as a pudding is a pudding, and that our only business ·with it could be to swallow it." But more important, perhaps, there may be something inherent in the novel which resists theory and generalization. In *The Rise of the Novel* Ian Watt argues that since Descartes "the pursuit of truth [has been] conceived of as a wholly individual matter, logically independent of the tradition of past thought, and indeed as more likely to be arrived at by departure from it":

> The novel is the form of literature which most fully reflects this individualistic and innovating reorientation. Previous literary forms had reflected the general tendency of their cultures to make conformity to a traditional practice the major test of truth....This literary traditionalism was first and most fully challenged by the novel, whose primary criterion was truth to individual experience—individual experience which is always unique and therefore new.... What is often felt as the formlessness of the novel, as compared, say, with tragedy or the ode, probably follows from this: the poverty of the novel's formal conventions would seem to be the price it must pay for its realism.

As Aristotle observed, there can be no science of particulars.

Barbara Hardy's most interesting book thus far, *The Appropriate Form*, is basically a development of Watt's suggestive remarks (although she does not mention Watt, or Forster's

Aspects of the Novel, to which she is more clearly indebted). She admits that the art of fiction is "the most various and least aesthetic moral art," but is still convinced that it is an art and thus will reward formal analysis. By "form," however, she seems to mean something analogous to the devices of symmetry, repetition, variation and so on in music and visual arts; certainly she does not have in mind anything like the classical differentiation of forms according to different intended effects. The novel gains our attention, she states, by means of plot; it informs us by moral argument; and it moves us by the convincing presentation of "individual presences and moments." *The Appropriate Form* is not really polemical, but as the reader follows Mrs. Hardy's argument he soon realizes that while "form" must always be appropriate to a given view of life, and that views naturally differ, she prefers the large, loose forms of Tolstoy and George Eliot to the tight economy and "total relevance" of the Jamesian novel. The capaciousness of *Middlemarch* and *Anna Karenina* allows the writer to "report more truthfully and fully the quality of the individual moment, the loose end, the doubt and contradiction and mutability. James was wrong to call such novels 'fluid puddings' but we might do worse than keep his adjectve while rejecting his noun." Thus after examining the "inconclusive" ending of *Women in Love* she maintains

> Lawrence is doing something very rare in art. He is not achieving impersonality and psychical distance, not externalizing his ideas and experiences, but writing out of doubt and failure, expressing ideas in which he has only uncertain faith. This is the untidiness and uncertainty of incomplete and fumbling human experience, usually inappropriate material for art, which we expect to provide an ordered version even of disordered experience. It records a failed experiment, in living and in thinking, and it is as far removed as art can be from the blueprint which projects an ideal form on the mutability and incompleteness of experience. To deny its power is, I suggest, to have rigid canons of art and insufficient respect for the kind of honesty which can admit despair and doubt, not just in art, but in living too.

This is not simply an argument about "form": life *is* mutable and incomplete; in his efforts to render life with its "individual presences and moments," it is better for the artist to risk what Yvor Winters calls the "fallacy of imitative form" than to falsify or distort for the sake of a pleasing aesthetic pattern. In the first part of *The Appropriate Form* Mrs. Hardy discusses James' "aesthetic obsession" and "sacrifice of human complexity"; in her later chapters she discusses another kind of distortion (in the work of Defoe, Charlotte Brontë, Hardy and Forster) whereby the artist subordinates "plausible action and psychology to an ideological pattern."

Mrs. Hardy's full-length study of George Eliot rests on the same assumptions and preferences and provides detailed, convincing demonstrations of George Eliot's "power of form," hidden though it often is by her realism and "human fullness." As for George Eliot's "moral vision" (and it should be remembered that for Mrs. Hardy the novel is always a moral art, in the broadest sense):

> She is insistently didactic, but her morally unequivocal world is never a tightly contracted one....She shows all the human variables: the successes as well as the failures, the mixed cases, even the unacted possible lives that haunt all our commitments. The result is moral definiteness, maybe, but it is also human movement. We are left with the impression, after reading one of her novels, that this is as close as the novelist can get to human multiplicity—that here form has been given to fluidity and expansiveness. We can trace the form as we can trace a diagram but the form is always there in the interest of the human picture.

Once again, form and "life" seem somehow separate, though no doubt they shouldn't be; and if the choice must be made, it is life that matters in the novel.

It seems to be "life" that matters most to Mrs. Hardy in poetry as well—the "life of unique feeling" which constitutes, for her, "the advantage of lyric." She might not be willing to generalize as rashly as Poe did, that a long poem is a contradiction in terms, but it is clear that she places almost unqualified value on the condensing powers of the short lyric: "Lyric poetry isolates feeling in small compasses and so renders it at its most intense." After examining a Shakespeare sonnet briefly, she maintains the poem

> is typical of lyric poetry in that it creates and discovers feeling under the guise of affirming it, and does not have to discuss, analyse, explain or imitate it....The advantage of lyric poetry comes from its undiluted attention to feeling and feeling alone, and its articulateness in clarifying that feeling, in attesting conviction or what may somewhat misleadingly be called sincerity, and transferring this from privacy to publicity.

As for the function of lyric poetry,

> Our need for this kind of lucid and intense expression of feeling need not be laboured. We have insufficient time and scope for feeling, surrounded as we are by all the business, all the classifying, judging, and analysing apparatus, of an environment where even introverts have not time to be anything but extroverts....If a more ethical or educational metaphor seemed necessary, we could propose catharsis....Reading and writing the poetry of feeling is plainly a valuable means of achieving what Proust speaks of as sentimental honesty.

Mrs. Hardy is sensitive and discerning when she examines moments of lyric intensity in the poems she selects (she is particularly good on the mixture of reticence and emotion in some of Auden's poetry), but her simplistic distinction between thought and feeling makes for some extremely awkward moments as well—in her discussion of Hopkins, for example. Here she argues that while "In the Valley of the Elwy" and "Spring" begin well enough, with "powerful, passionate and sensuous rendering," they lapse into "the reduction of allegory, of dogma, of message." In short, "thought" of any kind becomes a kind of impurity in poetry at its most intense. A theory such as this, it might be argued, which in practical application forces Mrs. Hardy to reject "Spring" and welcome an oddity like "The Shepherd's Brow" is a burden, finally, rather than an advantage. If she pushed the distinction a bit further—which she wisely does not do—it would be vulnerable to all the devastating criticism which has been rightly aimed at I.A. Richards' once popular distinction between emotive and referential language.

HARTMAN, Geoffrey H.   American.   Born in Germany, 11 August 1929; emigrated to the United States, 1946: naturalized, 1946. Educated at Queens College, New York, B.A. 1949; University of Dijon, France (Fulbright Fellow), 1951-52; Yale University, New Haven, Connecticut (Sterling Fellow, 1952-53), Ph.D. in comparative literature 1953. Served in the United States Army, 1953-55. Married Renee Gross in 1956; has two children. Instructor, 1955-60, Morse Faculty Fellow, 1958, and Assistant Professor, 1961-62, Yale University; Visiting Assistant Professor, University of Chicago, 1960-61; Associate Professor, 1962-64, and Professor, 1964-65, University of Iowa, Iowa City: Professor, Cornell University, Ithaca, New York, 1966-67. Since 1967, Professor of English and Comparative Literature, Yale University. Visiting Fellow, 1963, Christian Gauss Lecturer, 1967, and Visiting Professor, 1971, Princeton University, New Jersey; Visiting Professor, University of Zurich, 1966-67, and summer 1973; Mellon Visiting Professor, University of Pittsburgh, 1972; Visiting Fellow, Wesleyan University, Middletown, Connecticut, 1972; Director, School of Criticism and Theory, Northwestern University, Evanston, Illinois, 1981. Recipient: American Council of Learned Societies Fellowship, 1963; Phi Beta Kappa Christian Gauss Award, 1965; Guggenheim Fellowship, 1969; Distinguished Alumnus Award, Queens College, 1971; National Endowment for the Humanities Fellowship, 1976. Member, American Academy of Arts and Sciences. Address: 260 Everit Street, New Haven, Connecticut 06511, U.S.A.

PUBLICATIONS

Criticism

The Unmediated Vision: An Interpretation of Wordsworth, Hopkins, Rilke, and Valéry. New Haven, Connecticut, Yale University Press, and London, Oxford University Press, 1954.
André Malraux. New York, Hillary House, and London, Bowes and Bowes, 1960.
Wordsworth's Poetry: 1787-1814. New Haven, Connecticut, and London, Yale University Press, 1964.
Beyond Formalism: Literary Essays, 1958-1970. New Haven, Connecticut, and London, Yale University Press, 1970.
The Fate of Reading and Other Essays. Chicago and London, University of Chicago Press, 1975.
"Literary Criticism and Its Discontents," in *Critical Inquiry* (Chicago), 3, 1976; as "Past and Present" in *Criticism in the Wilderness,* 1980.
"Preface" and "Words, Wish, Worth: Wordsworth," in *Deconstruction and Criticism: Harold Bloom, Paul de Man, Jacques Derrida, Geoffrey Hartman, J. Hillis Miller.* New York, Seabury Press, 1979.
Criticism in the Wilderness: The Study of Literature Today. New Haven, Connecticut, and London, Yale University Press, 1980.
"The Poetics of Prophecy," in *High Romantic Argument: Essays for M.H. Abrams,* edited by Lawrence Lipking. Ithaca, New York, and London, Cornell University Press, 1981.
Saving the Text: Literature/Derrida/Philosophy. Baltimore and London, Johns Hopkins University Press, 1981.

Verse

Akiba's Children. Emory, Virginia, Iron Mountain Press, 1978.

Other

Editor, *Hopkins: A Collection of Critical Essays.* Englewood Cliffs, New Jersey, Prentice Hall, 1966.
Editor, *Selected Poetry and Prose of William Wordsworth.* New York, New American Library, 1970.
Editor, *New Perspectives on Coleridge and Wordsworth.* New York, Columbia University Press, 1972.
Editor, with David Thorburn, *Romanticism: Vistas, Instances, Continuities.* Ithaca, New York, Cornell University Press, 1973.
Editor, *Psychoanalysis and the Question of the Text: Selected Papers from the English Institute 1976-77.* Baltimore, Johns Hopkins University Press, 1978.

*   *   *

During the past few years a number of younger American critics have expressed their dissatisfaction with the heritage of the New Criticism and its narrow emphasis on the pure "literariness" of imaginative works. Some of this discontent—the impatient cry for "relevance" at the close of the 1960's, for example, or the unrealistic efforts to make the humanities somehow competitive with sociology and the hard sciences—has been futile at best; but the complaints of a few other critics, chiefly Frederick Crews, Harold Bloom and Geoffrey Hartman, are too well-founded to dismiss without careful consideration.

Whatever incidental difficulties Hartman presents (and they are usually formidable) his clear primary aim has always been to defend the creative imagination against certain kinds of reductive formalism and inadequate literary history. In the Introduction to his first book, *The Unmediated Vision*, he insists that we "have barely started to attempt to understand literature as a distinctive mode of knowledge in which the processes, or better, the desires of the human mind find their clearest expressions." The argument which follows is not easy to trace, but basically Hartman believes that the function of imaginative literature, especially poetry, is to confront and represent experience without taking refuge in simplifying abstractions: "Great poetry...is written by men who have chosen to stay bound by experience, who would not—or could not—free themselves by an act of knowledge from the immediacy of good and evil." Here, as elsewhere, Hartman assumes that the mind is driven by a rage for order and a passion to make sense of the world. Only such knowledge can bring that "unconditioned continuity of the mind" which is apparently the greatest good we can achieve. Hartman does not define "continuity" here but seems to mean that poise, balance, and informed competence in the face of whatever experience offers which I.A. Richards also maintains is the great gift of the imagination. This ideal of a "perfect reciprocity" between the mind and nature has always haunted Hartman and is best summarized, perhaps, in a passage he quotes (in "I.A. Richards and the Dream of Communictation") from E.H. Gombrich:

> It is the ego that acquires the capacity to transmute and canalize the impulses from the id, and to unite them in these multiform crystals of miraculous complexity we call works of art. They are symbols, not symptoms, of such control. It is *our* ego which, in resonance, receives from these configurations the certainty that the resolution of conflict, the achievement of freedom without threat to our inner security, is not wholly beyond the grasp of the aspiring human mind.

Yet to say that poetry simply represents experience verbally is misleading. The problem is that the welter and endless particularity of experience constantly threaten to overwhelm the mind: thus "reality" must be represented or "mediated" by words and symbols which do not impoverish our sense of the world outside (here Hartman may well have in mind something akin to what Coleridge calls the "abridgment of nature"). The goal, then, is "pure representation," in which the poet

> represents the mind as knowing without a cause from perception, and so in and from itself; or he will represent the mind as no less real than the objects of its perceiving. For the mind that perceives, and accepts this fact, since it can never know the objects of perception entirely in themselves, would know itself in itself—free of the irreducible, objective, and inevitable cause of perception. However, since it can never know itself entirely in itself, it is seized by an infinite desire for the very externality perceived.

When Hartman refers to the mind "knowing without a cause from perception" he probably means that the mind is no longer the passive victim of an endless cycle of stimulus and response : the mind now commands its own knowledge—intuition may be a better term—and in the process of knowing comes to know itself as the knower. The danger here of total solipsism apparently troubles Hartman as little as it does most essentially Romantic theorists of the self.

Obviously nature is often indifferent or hostile to our dream of reciprocity. The function of myth, then, as the great collective imaginative enterprise which has fundamental similarities to the activity of the individual artist, is to "mediate a discontinuity—winter, death, paradise lost, *temps perdu*." Human life itself is

> an indeterminate middle between overspecified poles always threatening to collapse it. The poles may be birth and death, father and mother, mother and wife, love and judgment, heaven and earth, first things and last things. Art narrates that middle region and charts it like a purgatory, for only if it exists can life exist; only if imagination presses against the poles are life and illusion—all those things which Shelley called "generous superstitions"—possible. The excluded middle is a tragedy also for the imagination.

Even the language here is reminiscent of Wallace Stevens, who is, for Hartman and his colleague Harold Bloom, the great Romantic poet of our time. "The mind," Stevens observes (in "The Noble Rider and the Sound of Words")

> has added nothing to human nature. It is a violence from within that protects us from a violence without. It is the imagination pressing back against the pressure of reality. It seems, in the last analysis, to have something to do with our self-preservation; and that, no doubt, is why the expression of it, the sound of its words, helps us to live our lives.

In short, we need our illusions, those necessary fictions without which we can know neither the world nor our own deeper natures. As Hartman points out in the Preface to *Beyond Formalism,*

> Illusions can be of many kinds. Shelley suggests that there are "generous superstitions," and perhaps it is art that makes them generous. If we denominate as Romance the field of all strong illusions—of all myths that have charmed, for good or bad, the mind of man—then art cultivates that field.... With the Romantic poets the purification of Romance moves into the center of the literary enterprise. Though they belong to the Enlightenment and believe in a progress of consciousness, they were not for bigger and better minds but for a finer magic, a more liberal participation of all in the imaginative life. Without imagination, no soul-making. When we are young we have projects for sun and moon, as for everything. Born into romance, we replace one illusion with another, until the pain of being is the pain of imagination. Only one myth, perhaps, proves inexhaustible. A poet, says Keats, "has no identity; he is continually in for—and filling—some other Body." There will always be an Other, or the dream of Otherness. Literature is the form that dream takes in an enlightened mind.

There was a time when the Judaeo-Christian tradition provided the necessary fiction, but with the decline of religious belief it was left to the poets to mediate experience for us. Thus the four poets Hartman discusses in *The Unmediated Vision* have in common the task of "pure representation." In Wordsworth, for example, we discover a

> constant concern with denudation, stemming from both a fear of visual reality and a desire for physical indestructibility. And the fine image [in *The Prelude*] of the mind turned by the spectacle as if with the might of waters, refers to that vast identity established throughout the poems of Wordsworth, an identity against sight, its fever and triviality, and making all things tend to the sound of universal waters; subduing the eyes by a power of harmony, and the reason by the suggestion of a Final Judgment which is God's alone. The intuition of indestructibility in the midst of decay, and the identity of the power in light with the power of sound...are the two modes of a vision in which the mind knows itself almost without exterior cause or else as no less real, no less indestructible than the object of its perceptions.

Wordsworth, Hopkins, Rilke and Valéry—each of these poets "has tried to conceive a pure representation distinguished from that of Jewish or medieval Christian thought in that its motive and terminal object is identified not wih the God of the Testaments, but with Nature, the body, or human consciousness." The poet's personal experience now becomes that shield of Perseus which makes reality—the inevitable "shock of life"—endurable for the rest of us. For Hartman poetry is thus of supreme importance: if books are not prophetic, he concludes, then they are expendable.

In his later and more difficult essays Hartman is primarily concerned with the tendency of modern academic criticism, or formalism, to rob poetry of its sustaining power and in effect to sever art from life. "Formalism" is any method which seeks to reveal the human content of art "by a study of its formal properties" and makes the perception of literature largely an affair of the classroom ("as if the world has to pass through that needle's eye"). There is good reason, he argues,

> why many in this country, as well as in Europe, have voiced a suspicion of Anglo-Saxon

formalism. The dominion of Exegesis is great: she is our Whore of Babylon, sitting robed in Academic black on the great dragon of Criticism, and dispensing a repetitive and soporific balm from the pedantic cup. If our neo-scriptural activity of explication were as daring as it used to be when Bible texts had to be harmonized with strange or contrary experience, i.e., with history, no one could level this charge of puerility. Yet our present explication-centered criticism is indeed puerile, or at most pedagogic: we forget its merely preparatory function, that it stands to a mature criticism as pastoral to epic. Explication is the end of criticism only if we succumb to what Trotsky called the formalist's "superstition of the word." To redeem the word from the superstition of the word is to humanize it, to make it participate once more in a living concert of voices, and to raise exegesis to its former state by confronting art with experience as searchingly as if art were scripture.

Predictably enough then, Hartman is much more responsive to Northrop Frye, Barthes, Lévi-Strauss and other critics who are interested in relating literature to the greater imaginative structures which govern societies.

At the same time Hartman is by no means uncritical of these attempts to go beyond formalism. In 1966 he observed that his tentative conclusion had to be a "sceptical one, or else critical in Kant's sense: to go beyond formalism is as yet too hard for us and may even be, unless we are Hegelians believing in an absolute spirit, against the nature of understanding"; and as late as 1975 he was still forced to admit that he had not found "a method to distinguish clearly what is formal and what is not, or what is figurative and what is not, or what is the reader's share in 'producing' the complex understanding which surrounds a literary work." Still, the attempt must be made, and whatever form it takes, criticism which successfully goes beyond formalism will have two general characteristics: it will consider literature in the light of larger symbol-systems and it will give far greater emphasis to the active interpreting presence of the critic himself:

Can we not...fifty years after the new chastity of Eliot and Richards, and a hundred years after Pater and Ruskin, afford a détente? The more "creative writing" runs amuck in fiction, the more we find ourselves indecisive before it: now stupidly admiring, now donnishly supercilious. The literary essay can avoid that split; it knows itself as both creative and receptive, a part of literature as well as about literature. True, we can't go back to Pater or Ruskin, or the best Hazlitt and Coleridge; the amount of positive historical knowledge we are expected to carry along is too great. But they gave the essay a dignity which it need not lose in its more specialized and burdened form.

Mightn't it be possible for the critic to be faithful to the text and to "interpret himself as well as the work of art?"

We do not ask for personality in the critic any more than in the artist. Nor do we ask him to suppress it. We ask him not to hide behind his text. The writer of fiction has his persona, a face wrought from life to look at life with, and often more than one face. Should not the interpreter have personae? Is it not his strength to be as deeply moved by works of the imagination as by life itself? Interpreter: define thyself.

Jacques Derrida writing on Rousseau, Hartman maintains, "is almost as interesting as Rousseau." But the burden here will be great, as Hartman probably would admit. The critic will have to be almost as interesting as his subject, and so far Harold Bloom is not as interesting as Shelley or Stevens, nor Hartman himself as interesting as Keats or Virginia Woolf or even Pater.

Criticism in the Wilderness is something of a miscellany in which many of these same themes appear again, but with new force and, at times, considerable eloquence. A number of the essays are totally embedded in the language and perspectives of Heidegger, Derrida, Walter Benjamin, among others—all writers, as Hartman notes, who usually inspire a kind of xenophobic dread in American and British critics. But there are at least three pieces here (the Introduction, "Past and Present" and "A Short History of Practical Criticism") which are of troubling importance to anyone who cares about the future of criticism. The wilderness American universities now find themselves in, Hartman argues, is largely of their own making. The assumptions of what is loosely called the New Criticism, of critics, that is, like Richards, Empson, Eliot, Ransom and Cleanth Brooks, were few, relatively simple and not given to self-questioning. They were enormously influential, but they also encouraged what Hartman calls a servile attitude towards literature: the function of criticism was simply to prepare the way for the clearest possible understanding or passive reception of complex but determinate texts from a canonized "tradition." Firmly established in the university teaching of English (at least in America, where it was highly successful in meeting important short-term educational needs and, later, narrow professional interests), this servility developed into a kind of arrogance, self-protective and deeply suspicious of "creative" critics, especially if they were caught flirting with disruptive "Continental" thought. The results, Hartman goes on, have been fatal to criticism, and this is one of the reasons why literature departments lose good students, productive contact with other university departments and finally with society itself. Moreover, this provincialism denies the fact that "each work of art, and each work of reading, is potentially a demonstration of freedom." Nietzsche's question, "What does the interpreter *want*?" needs a firm answer:

> To an extent what is involved is the right to one's own tongue. We wish to have our say despite or within authoritative pressures coming from the great writers of the past, institutions asking us to conform to a community model, politics that limit subtly or by force what can be said or written.

What Hartman wants, then, is the cosmopolitan atmosphere which will nourish the creative freedom of the true readers and writers—the same atmosphere, he implies, which helped to produce some of the great works of our time which cannot easily be classified as either "creative" or "critical": Valéry's dialogues, Borges' *Inquisitions*, Virginia Woolf's *A Room of One's Own*, D.H. Lawrence's study of American writers, Walter Benjamin's *Baudelaire*, Charles Olson's *Call Me Ishmael* (and one might just as well add a text Hartman now seems obsessed with, Jacques Derrida's wild deconstructionist romp through Hegel and Genet, *Glas*). In a rather less formal setting, a short column for the *New York Times Book Review* for 5 April 1981, Hartman observed

> The critical essay is prose above all, is an essay above all: a literary and experimental work rather than a dogmatic pronouncement. I do not mean, of course, that everyone should purple his prose or load it with literary ornament. But if we are indeed in an Age of Criticism, and if indeed a "literature of criticism" now exists, then criticism, too, will have to be read closely. It should not be fobbed off as a secondary activity, as a handmaiden to more "creative" thinking like poems or novels.

Hartman, it should be emphasized, is not a deconstructionist, although he is sometimes assumed to be one. In the Preface to *Deconstruction and Criticism* he explains that

> Deconstruction, as it has come to be called, refuses to identify the force of literature with any concept of embedded meaning and shows how deeply such logocentric or incarnationist perspectives have influenced the way we think about art. We assume that, by the miracle of art, the "presence of the word" is equivalent to the presence of meaning. But the opposite can also be urged, that the word carries with it a certain absence or indeterminacy of meaning.

But while Paul de Man, Jacques Derrida and J. Hillis Miller (other contributors to this anthology) are indeed "boa-deconstructors," Hartman warns the reader that he and Harold Bloom are not; in fact they often "write against" deconstruction. (The whole issue is complex and still developing. For a start, readers will find a lucid but hardly non-partisan account of the problems involved, in Denis Donoghue's essay, "Deconstructing Deconstructionism," in the *New York Review of Books* for 12 June 1980.) Criticism at its best should not be regarded as a rival of literature; it is a kind of literature itself, speculative and creative. And in the Introduction to *Criticism in the Wilderness* Hartman provides a resounding statement about the affirmative nature of literature which puts him squarely in line with the classical critical tradition:

> [art]...shapes my consciousness as if that were as material as language and makes my eyes and ears brood. It relieves the shift between work and leisure, or the vacancy and elation of great thought. It gives words and takes them away. Through it I can feel in touch with myself, and sometimes with others. It is blind, as Kant said of the imagination; yet one often feels a higher reason in it, which not only literary theory but the sciences of man, such as anthropology, psychology, and semiotics try to grasp.

HASSAN, Ihab (Habib).   American.   Born in Cairo, Egypt, 17 October 1925; emigrated to the United States, 1946; naturalized 1956. Educated at Cairo University, B.Sc. 1946; University of Pennsylvania, Philadelphia (Egyptian Educational Mission fellow, 1946-48; Harrison Fellow, 1949-50; University Scholar, 1950-51), M.S. 1948, M.A. 1950, Ph.D. 1953. Married Alida Koten in 1949 (divorced), one son; Sarah Margaret Green, 1966. Instructor, Rensselaer Polytechnic Institute, Troy, New York, 1952-54; Assistant Professor, 1954-58, Associate Professor, 1958-62, Professor, 1962-63, Benjamin L. Waite Professor of English, 1963-70, Chairman of the Department of English, 1961-64, 1968-69, Director of the College of Letters, 1964-66, and Director of the Center for the Humanities, 1969-70, Wesleyan University, Middletown, Connecticut. Since 1970, Vilas Research Professor of English and Comparative Literature, University of Wisconsin at Milwaukee. Fellow, School of Letters, Indiana University, Bloomington, 1964; Tutor, Salzburg Seminar in American Studies, 1965; Fulbright Lecturer, Grenoble, France, 1966-67, 1974-75; Lecturer, United States Information Agency, France, Belgium, Holland and Germany, 1966-74; Lecturer, Kyoto Seminars in American Studies, 1974. Recipient: Guggenheim Fellowship, 1958, 1962; Camargo Foundation Fellowship, 1974. Address: 2137 North Terrace Avenue, Milwaukee, Wisconsin 53202, U.S.A.

PUBLICATIONS

Criticism

> *Radical Innocence: Studies in the Contemporary American Novel.*   Princeton, New Jersey, Princeton University Press, 1961.
> *Littérature Américaine*, with Russell B. Nye and Georges-Albert Astre.   Paris, Minard, 1961.
> *Crise du Héros dans le Roman Américaine Contemporain.*   Paris, Minard, 1963.
> *The Literature of Silence: Henry Miller and Samuel Beckett.*   New York, Knopf, 1968.
> *The Dismemberment of Orpheus: Toward a Postmodern Literature.*   New York, Oxford University Press, 1971.
> *Contemporary American Literature: An Introduction.*   New York, Ungar, 1973.
> "The New Consciousness" and "Fiction," in *Literary History of the United States*, edited by Robert E. Spiller and others, revised edition.   New York, Macmillan, and London, Collier Macmillan, 1974.
> *Paracriticisms: Seven Speculations of the Times.*   Urbana, University of Illinois Press, 1975.
> "Parabiography: The Varieties of Critical Experience," in *Georgia Review* (Athens), 34, 1980.

Other

The Right Promethean Fire: *Imagination, Science, and Cultural Change*.   Urbana and
London, University of Illinois Press, 1980.
Editor, *Liberations*: *New Essays on the Humanities in Revolution*.   Middletown, Con-
necticut, Wesleyan University Press, 1971.

*   *   *

Despite occasional obscurities the critical position of Ihab Hassan is a fairly simple one,
governed primarily by a conception of modern (or "post-modern") literature as radically
nihilistic and at the same time somehow affirmative as well. "For almost two hundred years
now," Hassan argues, "a particular kind of literature has made itself by denying the assumptions of art, form and language." This is the "literature of silence" which "turns against itself"
and gives us "intimations of outrage and apocalypse," expressing something like a "total
rejection of Western history...and the image of man as the measure of all things." The term
"silence" is partly misleading, since the writers Hassan deals with are voluable and energetic in
making their various denials; nevertheless this is the metaphor he depends upon in three of the
four longer critical works he has published to date. And for a clear understanding of what
Hassan means by "the literature of silence" the reader should turn first to the "Prelude" which
opens *The Dismemberment of Orpheus*.
Here Hassan summarizes the main characteristics of the tendency he sees beginning with
Sade and extending past Barth and Beckett. The literature of silence "implies alienation from
reason, society, and history, a reduction of all engagements in the created world of men"; it
exploits "extreme states of mind" and frequently involves "separation from nature, a perver-
sion of vital and erotic responses." It dislocates the language of ordinary speech and subverts
conventional notions of form, opposing "control, closure, stasis, telos, and historic pattern."
Such art, Hassan concludes, "pretends to become anti-art...till nothing—or so it seems—
remains." "Pretends" and "seems" are key words since Hassan goes on to argue that even the
most nihilistic visions are paradoxically still in the service of "humanism." Thus in *Radical
Innocence* he takes over D.H. Lawrence's claim that "To be alive, to be the whole man alive:
that is the point.... And at its best, the novel, and the novel supremely, can help you. It can help
you not to be a dead man in life" (or in Hassan's own typically inflated language, the novel
"explores and enlarges the modalities or our *being*"). The modern world is an "affront" to man's
traditional conception of himself; it hurls its scientific, economic and psychological denials at
humanity but humanity responds with imaginative literature which seems nihilistic even as it
conspires with the older forms of humanism to make the continuance of life possible. The
argument implied here is a familiar one: the true nihilist does not write books or paint pictures;
unlike Beckett, for example, the unequivocal nihilist does not write plays, much less translate
them from one language into another or supervise their production. There is a poem by Wallace
Stevens which begins

> After the final no there comes a yes
> And on that yes the future world depends

and concludes

> It can never be satisfied, the mind, never.

—never satisfied, that is, with denial and negation. To my knowledge Hassan has never referred
directly to this poem ("The Well Dressed Man with a Beard") but it epitomizes as well as
anything could the main concern of his criticism.
In *Radical Innocence* Hassan maintains that the modern world has reduced the traditional
hero of fiction to the role of rebel or victim ("The rebel denies without saying No to life, the
victim without saying Yes to oppression. Both acts are, in a sense, identical: they affirm the
human against the nonhuman"). The modern novel depicts the Self recoiling from the world,
but to recoil is in itself a resource of the spirit, "a strategy of its *will*." "Radical innocence" is the
basic attitude of a Self which "refuses to accept the immitigable rule of reality, including

death"and whose freedom "cannot be stifled." Hassan then traces these recoils of the spirit and gradually expands his two initial categories of rebel and victim. Using the mythic approach of Frye, Joseph Campbell and Maud Bodkin, he finds that there are really three kinds of modern heroes, each corresponding to three kinds of mythic quests for regeneration. The basic pattern is that of the eternal cycle of day and night, the seasons, and the life of the individual. We may imagine a circle with noon, summer and young manhood at the zenith, and night, winter and death at the nadir. The descent from light to darkness is the subject of tragedy; the ascent towards the light is the subject of comedy. Since the tendency of the modern American novel can hardly be called comic, Hassan settles for three modified versions of the tragic and comic pattern. The new hero appears first in the guise of "a victim or scapegoat, *pharmakos*. He enjoys little or no freedom of action: he is ruled, that is, by necessity. The ironic mode borders here on tragedy. The form of fiction is *closed* to any real change in the life of the hero, any self-renewal." To illustrate this mode Hassan discusses novels by Styron, Swados and Mailer. The hero may also appear "primarily in the guise of the self-deprecating *eiron*. He enjoys a limited degree of freedom.... The ironic mode, hovering between comedy and tragedy, may touch on romance." Here Hassan turns to novels by Buechner, Malamud and Ellison. Finally, the hero may appear as a "rebel, rogue, or self-inflating *alazon*. He enjoys considerable freedom, and gives the illusion of escaping from necessity. The ironic mode veers toward comedy." And to illustrate this mode Hassan considers novels by Gold, Cheever and Donleavy. Essentially the same kind of argument—identification of theme would be a better term—supports *The Dismemberment of Orpheus*, in which Hassan simply switches myths: Orpheus, the traditional figure of the poet, is torn apart by the Maenads of modern life, yet his head goes on singing. After discussing Sade, Hemingway, Kafka, Genet and Beckett, Hassan ends with the tentative hope that "after self-parody, self-subversion, and self-transcendence, after the pride and revulsion of anti-art will have gone their way, art may move toward a redeemed imagination, commensurate with the full mystery of human consciousness."

In *Radical Innocence, The Literature of Silence* and *The Dismemberment of Orpheus* Hassan is concerned with affirmations of post-modern literature; in *Paracriticisms* he is concerned with the responsibilities of the critic in dealing with these strange new forms of humanism. Like some other recent critics, Hassan is impatient with the limitations of formal academic criticism. It is not simply that the systems which derive basically from Eliot or Richards might be extended to encompass the work of Burroughs or Genet:

> I would plead for a more radical view. From Kant to Cassirer, from Coleridge to Croce and down to the New Critics, the idea of organic form has been a touchstone of value and a cornerstone of theory in literary study. We assume, and indeed we believe, that the imagination incarnates itself only as an aesthetic order, and that such an order is available to the analytic mind. We believe more: that aesthetic order defines the deepest pleasures of literature and conveys its enduring attractions. I am not at all secure in these beliefs. Indeed, I am willing to take the devil's part and entertain the notion that "structure" is not always present or explicable in literary works; and that where it reveals itself, it is not always worth the attention we give it. Such works as *Hamlet* and *Don Quixote* are not diminished by the discovery that their form, whatever it may be, is less organic than we expect the form of great works to be. Even that supreme artifact of our century, that total structure of symbols, puns, and cross-references, that city of words full of secret alleys and connecting catacombs, even Joyce's *Ulysses*, may prove to the keen, fresh eye of a critic more of a labyrinth, dead ends and ways without issue, than Dublin itself, which encloses the nightmare of history. This is precisely what Robert Martin Adams concludes in his fascinating study *Surface and Symbol....*Nothing catastrophic to the future of criticism is presaged by [his conclusions]. Quite the contrary: criticism may derive new vitality from some attention to the unstructured and even random element in literature. For is not form, after all, best conceived as a mode of awareness, a function of cognition, a question, that is, of epistemology rather than ontology? Its objective reality is qualified by the overpowering reality of human *need*. In the end, we perceive what we need to perceive, and our sense of patterns as of relation is conditioned by our deeper sense of relevance. This is why the aesthetic of the future will have to reckon with Freud, Nietzsche, and even Kierkegaard, who have given us, as well as Marx, compelling economies of human needs.

At its best this aesthetic of the future

> should learn about playful discontinuity and become itself less than the sum of its parts. It should offer the reader empty spaces, silences, in which he can meet himself in the presence of literature. This is paracriticism: an attempt to recover the art of multivocation. Not the texts and its letters but metaphors thereof. Not a form strictly imposed but the tentativeness between one form and another. In old dreams—the testament of our broken lives—begin our new responsibilities. Shatter the mirrors.

Paracriticisms is playful, in a ponderous kind of way (trendy typographical experiments, interrupted self-interviews and so on), but merely repeats many of the arguments of the earlier books. Again Hassan rejects "traditional" modern criticism; Barthes, Blanchot, Poulet, and especially Buckminster Fuller and Norman O. Brown—these are the new prophets and interpreters.

Hassan is one of those writers whose idea of criticism differs so radically from my own that I may be unable to represent him fairly. His style is a formidable obstacle as well, although there are readers who will find a passage such as this genuinely exciting:

> Primitivism proposes the candor of the naked emotion rather than the naked fact. Under its influence, the novel sets itself to explore those instinctual gestures and primary sensations which adolescents have long favored before black leather jackets and tight jeans came into vogue, or Brando and James Dean scowled and muscled their way into our communal heart. The caged sensitivity, the lurid restraint often portrayed by these actors on the screen, find a more responsible antecedent in Hemingway's Nick Adams; and who knows but that they may ultimately derive from the frenzied image of Rimbaud's life? But more relevant than Rimbaud's brand of romantic primitivism is Bergson's subjectivist philosophy. As Justin O'Brien noted in his study, *The Novel of Adolescence in France*, the literary adherents of Bergson considered adolescent initiation a phase of human development in which society had not yet succeeded in separating the "real I" from the "symbolic representations." To the evocation of the "real I" by the printed word, Gertrude Stein gave her most scrupulous attention. Some years later, when the impact of Freud began to be felt in America, Sherwood Anderson applied his awkward intuition to the same end.

It is hard to trust these sweeping generalizations when Hassan's particular observations often seem so out of proportion to their subject matter—

> Daisy Miller is an "initiate" of a different kind. It is by conscious choice rather than necessity that she immolates herself to her innocence. Huck...[pursues] the process of initation in fits and starts; James's heroine rejects it point blank. She will accept life only on its own terms, and will not compromise her innocence or ignorance or conscience— call it what you like—even for the sake of love. When she fails to win the unconditioned love or trust of Winterbourne, she dies of Roman fever....[In her refusal to behave as society dictates] she affirms her faith in the autonomy of candor, in the rights of the individual against those of the group, in Protestant conscience against Catholic form. She is, in short, a rebel, and the price of her rebellion is death.

—or so abysmally wrong, as when he refers, for example, to the "refined hypocrisy of the chorus in a Greek play." Given the kind of critical language Hassan has decided upon, all he can do is point to recurrent themes; and the implication seems to be, the more Theme, the better (thus Faulkner receives a dozen scattered pages in *Radical Innocence* while Truman Capote is scrutinized in a respectful twenty-eight page essay). John Holloway's sharp general comment about thematic criticism is very much to the point here: "The mere presence of a thing is without interest, unless it can be shown that its presence makes the work better. The whole problem lies there." And again, the themes themselves are so vast that nothing seems irrelevant. As another old-style modern critic, R.S. Crane, has observed, "What we are committed to, if we want to write this kind of criticism, is the discovery of conceptual equivalents of the concrete relationships of elements discernible in poems....It requires no great insight to find an inner dialectic of

271

order and disorder or a struggle of a good and evil in any serious plot." Fair-minded readers had better go directly to Hassan and make up their own minds. It would be foolish to deny that the established modern critical systems do not have their own considerable limitations: but whether or not paracriticism is a valid alternative—if it means anything at all—is another matter.

HEILMAN, Robert B(echtold). American. Born in Philadelphia, Pennsylvania, 18 July 1906. Educated at Lafayette College, Pennsylvania, B.A. 1927; Tufts University, Medford, Massachusetts, 1927-28 (Teaching Fellow); Ohio State University, Columbus, M.A. 1930; Harvard University, Cambridge, Massachusetts, M.A. 1931, Ph.D. 1935. Married Ruth Dela-van Champlin in 1935; has one child. Instructor in English, University of Maine, Orono, 1931-35; Instructor, 1935-36, Assistant Professor, 1936-42, Associate Professor, 1942-46, and Professor of English, 1946-48, Louisiana State University, Baton Rouge. Professor of English (Chairman of the Department, 1948-71), 1948-1977, and since 1977, Professor Emeritus, University of Washington, Seattle. Arnold Professor, Walla Walla, Washington, 1977. President, Philological Association of the West Coast, 1959; Member of the Executive Council, American Association of University Professors, 1962-65, and Modern Language Association of America, 1966-69. Reviewer, Phi Beta Kappa *Key Reporter*; since 1967 Senator, and since 1973 Member of the Executive Committee, Phi Beta Kappa. Member of the Editorial Board of *Poetry Northwest*, since 1962; *Studies in the Novel*, since 1966; *Shakespeare Studies*, since 1966; *Modern Language Quarterly*, 1973-77, *Sewanee Review*, since 1974. Recipient: *Arizona Quarterly* Essay Prize, 1956; *Explicator* Award, 1957; Huntington Library Grant, 1959; Longview Foundation Essay Award (*Texas Quarterly*), 1960. Recipient: Guggenheim Fellowship, 1964 and 1976; National Endowment for the Humanities Grant, 1971; Christian Gauss Prize, Phi Beta Kappa, 1979. LL.D.: Grinnell College, Iowa, 1971; L.H.D.: Kenyon College, Gambier, Ohio, 1973; HH.D.: Whitman College, Walla Walla, Washington; Litt.D.: University of the South, Sewanee, Tennessee, 1978. Address: Department of English, University of Washington, Seattle, Washington 98195, U.S.A.

<small>PUBLICATIONS</small>

Criticism

> *America in English Fiction, 1760-1800: The Influences of the American Revolution.* Baton Rouge, Louisiana State University Press, 1937.
> *This Great Stage: Image and Structure in "King Lear."* Baton Rouge, Louisiana State University Press, 1948.
> "*The Turn of the Screw* as Poem," in *University of Kansas City Review*, 14, 1948.
> *Magic in the Web: Action and Language in "Othello."* Lexington, University of Kentucky Press, 1956.
> *Tragedy and Melodrama: Versions of Experience.* Seattle and London, University of Washington Press, 1968.
> *The Ghost on the Ramparts, and Other Essays in the Humanities.* Athens, University of Georgia Press, 1973.
> *The Iceman, The Arsonist, and the Troubled Agent: Tragedy and Melodrama on the Modern Stage.* Seattle, University of Washington Press, and London, Allen and Unwin, 1973.

The Ways of the World: Comedy and Society.   Seattle and London, University of
   Washington Press, 1978.
"Robespierre and Santa Claus: Men of Virtue in Drama," in Southern Review (Baton
   Rouge, Louisiana), 14, 1978.
"Farce Transformed: Plautus, Shakespeare, and Unamuno," in Comparative Literature
   (Eugene, Oregon), 31, 1979.
" 'Losing Battles' and Winning the War," in Eudora Welty: Critical Essays, edited by
   Peggy Whitman Prenshaw.   Jackson, University of Mississippi Press, 1980.

Other

Understanding Drama, with Cleanth Brooks.   New York, Holt, 1945; London, Harrap,
   1947; revised edition, Holt Rinehart, 1960.

Editor, Aspects of Democracy.   Baton Rouge, Louisiana State University Press, 1941.
Editor, Gulliver's Travels, A Tale of a Tub, The Battle of the Books, by Jonathan
   Swift.   New York, Modern Library, 1950.
Editor, Modern Short Stories: A Critical Anthology.   New York, Harcourt Brace, 1950.
Editor, An Anthology of English Drama Before Shakespeare.   New York, Rinehart,
   1952.
Editor, Lord Jim, by Joseph Conrad.   New York, Rinehart, 1957.
Editor, The Mayor of Casterbridge, by Thomas Hardy.   Boston, Houghton Mifflin,
   1962.
Editor, Silas Marner, by George Eliot.   Boston, Houghton Mifflin, 1962.
Editor, with others, Essays on Shakespeare.   Princeton, New Jersey, Princeton Univer-
   sity Press, 1965.
Editor, Jude the Obscure, by Thomas Hardy.   New York, Harper, 1966.
Editor, The Taming of the Shrew, by Shakespeare.   New York, New American Library,
   1966.
Editor, The Turn of the Screw, by Henry James.   New York, Oxford University Press,
   1967.

CRITICAL STUDY

W.R. Keast, "The 'New Criticism' and King Lear," in Critics and Criticism, Ancient and
   Modern, edited by R.S. Crane.   Chicago and London, University of Chicago Press,
   1952.

*   *   *

This Great Stage and Magic in the Web both depend upon the argument that verse drama is
essentially different from drama in prose, since verse does much more than simply enhance
effects equally available to prose. For Heilman, as for many other modern critics, the distinguishing characteristic of verse is its imagistic nature, or more precisely, its metaphoric powers.
The metaphors a character uses must of course have a literal function and propriety—they must
contribute to the action and be appropriate to the character employing them; but more
important, metaphor is a primary means of extending relevant implications. By exploiting
suggestive comparisons, by placing particulars in new fields of association, the poet is able to
gain a "generalizing force" which achieves meaning "far in excess of the minimal requirements
of the occasion." For example,

When Iago calls his false statements to Othello "poison," he exhibits the intellectual
clarity required for self-identification and the moral callousness necessary to accept the
identification. But when he calls what he has told Othello "medicine," he uses a much

more vibrant and exciting metaphor, one by which the author "says" vastly more to the reader: aside from expressing Iago's sardonic delight in an action which seems to be one thing but is another, it brings into focus the vast irony of Iago's frequent resemblance to the physician in his dealings with others, and the general state of affairs so often set forth in images of disease and disability; thus it is part of a "poetic" construction that deals vividly with the theme of evil. Suppose Iago had spoken only of his "tales" or "lies."

Thus when we "follow up mimesis far enough, we come to archetype and symbol.... We cannot have the multidimensionalism of poetic language—not to mention the barrier-breaking tendency of the verbal drama generally—without constantly being pushed beyond the bare action into all the reaches of meaning possible to literary art." In the theater, when we witness an actual performance, we respond mainly to the immediate plot and characters; but later, when we have the desire to brood upon the implications of essentially symbolic language, we move closer to "metaphysical" conclusions. We come to recognize, for example, that *Othello*, like the *Divine Comedy* is "about" the nature of love and evil. Othello himself, like the protagonist of some morality plays, is "torn between two versions of love." The plot becomes an extended metaphor (Heilman owes a great deal to G. Wilson Knight at this point); and if we ask metaphor for what, the answer is: for the largest possible set of generalizations about human life. *Oedipus* is about "appearance and reality"; *Lear*, finally, is "about the ways of looking at and assessing the world of human experience." Since the structure of a work reveals itself "in its fullness...only by means of the pattern of imagery," Heilman traces these patterns and their complex interconnections in full, usually tedious detail.

Shortly after *The Great Stage* appeared the neo-Aristotelian critic W.R. Keast made it the object of a devastating attack in "The 'New Criticism' and *King Lear*." As an Aristotelian Keast argued that Heilman has inverted the proper causal relationships which govern dramatic construction: it is overall effect which determines the kind of plot an artist selects, and plot in turn determines suitable agents who use suitable diction to advance the plot and reveal suitable moral and intellectual qualities. Metaphors are simply devices of diction; in no sense do they form independent structures of meaning. Keast also pointed out that Heilman's primary emphasis on imagery "results in a construction that resembles a great play much less than it does an inferior philosophic dialogue," for when we consider the "philosophic yield" of *Lear* it turns out to be "pitifully meager—a poor thing by comparison, say, with...the *Novum Organum* or the *Laws of Ecclesiastical Polity*." Finally, we have no warrant to assume that the proper reading of a play like *Lear* must be symbolic:

> Nothing in the text of the play, nothing in Shakespeare's habits as a dramatist, nothing in the circumstances of its composition and production, nothing in Elizabethan dramatic practice in general, nothing in the dramatic criticism of Shakespeare's day—nothing, in short, internal or external, suggests, or has been thought until recent years to suggest, that a literal reading of *King Lear* will fail to account for essential features of the play and that the tragedy must be interpreted, therefore, as an organized body of symbols. Anyone who wishes to take this position is, of course, free to do so; but he must discharge the initial critical and logical responsibility of showing his assumption to be needful and relevant, by making it clear that an interpretation of the play as a literal action is inadequate to the author's intention as revealed in the details of the work.

In his later books, *Tragedy and Melodrama* and *The Iceman, The Arsonist, and the Troubled Agent* (the title refers to three kinds of protagonists in modern drama), Heilman is primarily interested in establishing generic distinctions. Tragedy and melodrama both deal with the terrible in human affairs, but not all terrible things are tragic. For his differentiating principle Heilman relies on a brief observation by Camus: "Melodrama could...be summed up by saying: 'Only one is just and justifiable,' while the perfect tragic formula would be: 'All can be justified, no one is just.' " In melodrama the conflict between good and evil is external, divided according to opposing forces or sides, one of which is clearly "just"; in tragedy the conflict is within the heart and mind of a central character, who is therefore not perfectly "just" (although the universe itself is governed by moral forces and is therefore "justifiable"). "In sum," Heilman concludes,

I would use the word *tragedy* only to describe the situation in which the divided human being faces basic conflicts, perhaps rationally insoluble, of obligations and passions; makes choices, for good or for evil; errs knowingly or involuntarily; accepts consequences; comes into a new, larger awareness; suffers or dies, yet with a larger wisdom.

There are times when the broad simplifications of melodrama are proper: "it is not meretricious when it portrays recognizable evil—as in Renaissance revengers or Count Cenci or Brecht's Nazis or Koestler's Gletkin—or plausible courage and fidelity, as in the Talbots in *Henry VI*." But tragedy is the more enduring form because it allows for growth and is, in the long run, more faithful to the complexities of existence. This distinction between forms is as reductive as it is derivative, but it has a certain heuristic value: it keeps Heilman away from hopelessly large generalizations (*Oedipus* may be about appearance and reality, but so is every other dramatic plot, tragic or comic) and allows him to make a number of useful observations about a great many individual plays.

Having worked for so long with tragedy, which explores the conflict within the moral nature of man, and melodrama, which is concerned with external conflicts between men and groups of men, it was impossible, Heilman observes, not to "develop some ideas about the territory of comedy in the wide human terrain occupied by these dramatic types." What he hopes to establish in *The Ways of the World: Comedy and Society* is "a middle ground between a relentlessly logical and limiting formula for comedy...and a lax permissiveness which despairs of discovering a basic comic form and lets the genre become endlessly capacious." "Comedy," he maintains, is

affirmative, conciliatory, less given to position-taking than to living with different positions as inevitable rather than improvable, as bearable if not always lovable, as amusing rather than contemptible, as expectably imperfect rather than destructive or fatal....[The comic] can be adequately, indeed profoundly, described as a mode of rational accommodation, in which drives demanding aggression are more than balanced by a communal sense leaning toward survival by adjustment.

It is possible to imagine a solitary tragic figure (given Heilman's definition of tragedy as the exploration of a moral conflict within a man), but comedy seems to demand a sense of man in his social setting; and therein lies its particular virtue:

What survives in comedy is the human quality by which man acknowledges the nature of life in the immediate world; he understands the claims of others and the limits in himself rather than romantically mistakes both as symbols of an oppression that he must rebel against or escape from into utopia or solitude; the comic continuity, which depends upon a nonsentimental mutuality, is essentially social. The manners that we can hardly dissociate from comedy...symbolize concessions to others, curbings of the native aggressiveness that is inimical to social existence.

Satire rejects things as they are; comedy accepts things as they are—though not uncritically—and recognizes that they must be as they are, or are unlikely to change.

In the sections which follow Heilman provides a shrewd account of other theories of tragedy, from Aristotle through Bergson and Elder Olson, and applies his own definition to an astonishing number of particular works. But as Kenneth Muir pointed out in a sympathetic review of *The Ways of the World*, Heilman's catholicity has its drawbacks: there are a great many plays here whose chief claim to distinction lies in the fact that Heilman has paused to consider them. Heilman's kind of criticism, that is, can tell us very little about how well a writer succeeds in carrying out a comic design. For that kind of criticism, Heilman might well reply, look elsewhere.

HICKS, Granville.   American.   Born in Exeter, New Hampshire, 9 September 1901. Educated at Harvard University, Cambridge, Massachusetts, A.B. 1923, M.A. 1929. Married
Dorothy Dyer in 1925; has one child. Instructor in Biblical Literature, Smith College, Nor-
thampton, Massachusetts, 1925-28; Assistant Professor of English, Rensselaer Polytechnic
Institute, Troy, New York, 1929-35; Counselor in American Civilization, Harvard University,
1938-39; Lecturer, Pacific Northwest Writers' Conference, Seattle, 1948; Instructor in Novel
Writing, New School for Social Research, New York, 1955-58; Berg Visiting Professor, New
York University, 1959; Visiting Professor, Syracuse University, Syracuse, New York, 1960;
McGuffey Visiting Professor, Ohio University, Athens, 1967-68, and Chatham College, Pitts-
burgh, 1973. Literary Adviser, The Macmillan Company, New York, 1930-65; Member,
Editorial Staff, *New Masses*, New York, 1934-39; Chairman, "Speaking of Books" radio
program, 1941-43; Literary Consultant, *The New Leader*, New York, 1951-58; Contributing
Editor, *Saturday Review*, New York, 1958-69. Since 1973; Books Editor, *The American Way*
magazine, San Antonio, Texas. Acting Executive Director, Corporation of Yaddo, Saratoga
Springs, New York, 1970-71. Recipient: Guggenheim Fellowship, 1936; Rockefeller Fellow-
ship, 1945; American Library Association Clarence Day Award, 1968. D.H.L.: Skidmore
College, Saratoga Springs, New York, 1968; Ohio University, Athens, 1969; Litt.D.: Siena
College, Loudonville, New York, 1971. Address: Box 144, Grafton, New York 12082, U.S.A.

PUBLICATIONS

Criticism

The Great Tradition: An Interpretation of American Literature since the Civil War.
    New York, Macmillan, 1933; London, Macmillan, 1934; revised edition, New York,
    Macmillan, 1935; Chicago, Quadrangle, 1969.
*Figures of Transition: A Study of British Literature at the End of the Nineteenth
    Century.*   New York, Macmillan, 1939.
James Gould Cozzens.   Minneapolis, University of Minnesota Press, 1958.
Literary Horizons: A Quarter Century of American Fiction, with the assistance of Jack
    Alan Robbins.   New York, New York University Press, 1970.
Granville Hicks in "The New Masses," edited by Jack Alan Robbins.   Port Washington,
    New York, Kennikat Press, 1974.

Novels

The First to Awaken, with Richard M. Bennett.   New York, Modern Age, 1940.
Only One Storm.   New York, Macmillan, 1942.
Behold Trouble.   New York, Macmillan, 1944.
There Was a Man in Our Town.   New York, Viking Press, 1952.

Verse

New Light, with Stuart B. Hoppin.   Boston, Birchard, 1932.

Other

Eight Ways of Looking at Christianity.   New York, Macmillan, 1926.
One of Us: The Story of John Reed.   New York, Equinox Press, 1935.

John Reed: The Making of a Revolutionary, with John Stuart.   New York, Macmillan, 1936.
I Like America (social commentary).   New York, Modern Age, 1938.
Small Town (social commentary).   New York, Macmillan, 1946.
Where We Came Out (social commentary).   New York, Viking Press, and London, Gollancz, 1954.
Part of the Truth (autobiography).   New York, Harcourt Brace, 1965.

Editor, with others, *Proletarian Literature in the United States: An Anthology*.   New York, International Publishers, 1935; London, Lawrence, 1936.
Editor, with Ella Winter, *The Letters of Lincoln Steffens*.   New York, Harcourt Brace, 2 vols., 1938.
Editor, *The Living Novel: A Symposium*.   New York, Macmillan, 1957.

BIBLIOGRAPHY

Robert J. Bicker, *Granville Hicks: An Annotated Bibliography, February, 1927 to June, 1967, with a Supplement to June, 1968*.   Emporia, Kansas, Emporia Research Series, 1968.

*   *   *

Early in 1931 Granville Hicks began work on what was to become his best-known book, *The Great Tradition*. "I proposed to study American literature since the Civil War," he recalls in his 1965 autobiography, *Part of the Truth*,

with a view to discovering what writers had been able to make of the industrial revolution and its consequences. I had stated the problem...in an article called "Industry and the Imagination," and I had dealt with a related problem, the impact of science on poetry, in the paper I had written [at Harvard] for John Livingston Lowes. The great changes that had taken place in American life in the second half of the nineteenth century seemed to me to challenge all writers, and I wanted to see how the challenge had been met.

"I passed for a radical," he adds, "because I disliked Roosevelt and had no respect for a business civilization, but I had become largely nonpolitical.... I was not a Communist at the time, even though I was willing to concede that Communism might some day triumph." By the end of the year, however, Hicks found it increasingly difficult to remain "unpolitical":

As I walked up the street, I was saying to myself, "This is it. If the most liberal intelligent businessman you have ever known or known anything about is helpless in this crisis, what hope is there that the business community can save us?" And there was instantly a voice that said, "Why not Communism?"
   Communism was in the air, at least in the air that I was breathing that fall. Lincoln Steffens, who had said in his autobiography that a reformed capitalism might work, was now insisting that only the Communists were proposing a real solution for the depression. Edmund Wilson had published an article in the *New Republic* in which he urged us to adopt the program of Communism while rejecting the Communist Party. All sorts of people were convinced that the capitalist system had collapsed.

While such contact as he had with Communists did not inspire him with confidence in their intelligence or integrity, his resistance to the Party, he goes on,

was slowly being worn away, chiefly by what I was seeing with my own eyes.... Often I went by train from Troy to Albany, to work in the library there, and I would stare with dismay at the Hooverville that had grown up by the tracks, wondering what life could be

like in those shacks made of packing boxes and hunks of corrugated iron and odds and
ends of cardboard and cloth. When I was in New York, and had been to the theatre or to
a party, I would see men sleeping in the subway entrances, on and even under the
newspapers they had managed to salvage. I knew as well as I had ever known anything
that I could not ignore all this. Something had to be done, and the voices were asking,
more and more insistently, "Why not Communism?"

By the time Hicks had finished *The Great Tradition* his commitment to the Marxist
interpretation of history was complete and unqualified. The primary function of the artist is to
understand and express his times, which in Marxist terms means that the American artist after
the Civil War must understand the accelerated growth of capitalism and the miseries it
brings—war, periodic depressions and, for the exploited workers, dehumanizing alienation. It
is the responsibility of the writer to make others aware of this oppression and to create that
sense of solidarity which must precede the inevitable proletarian revolution and the establishment of a just, classless society. Thus the question Hicks asks about each writer he considers is
always the same: to what degree did he understand the economic conditions of this time and
their social consequences? Most of the verdicts are predictably harsh: there were writers like
Henry James, who isolated himself from the realities of his time, and writers like Mark Twain,
who compromised his genuine gifts for the easy rewards of a popular entertainer; there were
regionalists locked nostalgically into the past and writers who cultivated a life-denying aestheticism or took refuge in a class-protected Genteel Tradition. As industrialism became more and
more important,

> the implications of capitalism grew clearer and clearer, the lines of the class struggle were
> drawn more and more sharply, and consequently the cost of evasion grew greater and
> greater. Comparing Edith Wharton with Henry James, or Willa Cather with Sarah Orne
> Jewett, or Robert Frost with Emily Dickinson, we have realized that it has been
> increasingly difficult for those who ignore industrialism to create a vital literature.

Yet on the other hand there was a saving remnant of writers who had tried to understand
American life: Emerson and Whitman with their confidence in the common man, Thoreau and
his rebellion against organized society, and in their own ways and with varying degrees of
success such writers as Howells, Garland, Norris, Sinclair, London and Dos Passos—these are
the creators of a "great tradition" in American literature which has been critical of "greed,
cowardice, and meanness":

> How can authors refuse to strike at the sources of the evils they so constantly attacked? It
> has also been a hopeful literature, touched again and again with a passion for brother-
> hood, justice, and intellectual honesty. How can authors refuse to struggle against an
> order based on falsehood, oppression, and the division of mankind into exploiters and
> exploited? The issue is now so clearly drawn that evasion is almost impossible: on the one
> hand lies repudiation of the best in the American literary past, on the other the
> fulfillment of all that was dreamed of and worked for in the past and the beginning of a
> struggle for more than the past could ever have hoped.

But as the 1930's came to a close, Hicks displayed the now-familiar symptoms of the
intellectual's disillusionment with Communism. *The Great Tradition* represents, in retrospect,
what he now calls a "hopelessly narrow way of judging literature"—hopelessly narrow or
simply wrong to begin with. Marx had "important insights into historical processes," but his
predictions have not come true:

> Capitalism had not collapsed as a result of the contradictions he had pointed out, but, in
> most countries, had been modified in ways that he said were impossible. Where a
> backward capitalism had collapsed, in Russia, power had not been assumed by the
> proletariat but by a small group of professional and mostly middle-class revolutionaries.
> And the socialization of the means of production had not resulted in the establishment of
> a classless society but in a cruel dictatorship.

It is only fair to mention the classic Marxist rejoinder here: it is too soon to tell. Capitalism seems to have a genius for postponing the logical consequences of its inherent contradictions. In any event, Hicks' own final attitude is a curious mixture of compromise, tolerance and gentle self-interest:

> If I had had my years of comforting certainty, when Marxism seemed to answer every question, I had long since had to learn how to live with doubts of every kind. I was agnostic in much more than the theological sense. I was reasonably sure that the universe was not organized for the benefit of the human race, but beyond that I could make few generalizations. It was clear to me that my life had grown constantly more complicated during my lifetime, and it seemed likely to continue to do so for as long as our civilization endured. That that civilization might end at any moment was obvious, and it seemed probable that, even if the peril of nuclear destruction could be eliminated, the future would offer some tough problems.
>
> On the other had, the contemporary American scene did not appear so black to me as it did to many people. Whatever false values prosperity might be fostering, it was in itself a good thing, and I could not see how anyone who remembered the depression could believe otherwise.... That the fruits of prosperity were not equitably distributed was certain, and there was poverty enough to war on, but millions of people were better off than they had ever been....
>
> If there was one virtue I had acquired over the years, it was tolerance.... My disillusionment with Communism; my fallibility; Grafton [Hicks' home town] taught me that people of many sorts could be right in their own ways, even when their ways were not my ways. I knew that tolerance had its dangers, that there were things of which one should not be tolerant, that tolerance could be cowardice, but, within proper limits, it was a virtue.
>
> I had decided some time before that I was not personally responsible for saving the world; now it became clear that I could not save the world even if I put my mind to it. I had learned to adapt myself to disabilities of various kinds, and I realized that, whether I liked it or not, the remainder of my life would have to be largely self-centered. I had only a limited amount of energy, and although I could spend some of it in causes in which I believed, I should have to think first of my own needs.

For Hicks himself then, and probably for most of his readers, *The Great Tradition* and the *New Masses* articles are based on fundamental misapprehensions about the nature of literature and society. The selected reviews which make up *Literary Horizons* are too ephemeral to be of much interest now, but they have an attractive openness one would never have predicted in the 1930's. A sensibility which can take genuine pleasure in Barth or Nabokov is one which has continued to grow and prosper.

HIRSCH, E(ric) D(onald), Jr. American. Born in Memphis, Tennessee, 22 March 1928. Educated at Cornell University, Ithaca, New York, B.A. 1950; Yale University, New Haven, Connecticut, M.A. 1953, Ph.D. 1957. Served in the United States Navy, 1950-52. Married Mary Monteith Pope, 1958; has three children. Instructor in English, 1956-60, Assistant Professor, 1960-63, and Associate Professor, 1963-66, Yale University. Professor, 1966-73, Chairman of the Department, 1968-71, and since 1973 Kenan Professor, University of Virginia, Charlottesville. Recipient: Fulbright Fellowship, 1955; Morse Fellowship, 1960; Guggenheim Fellowship, 1964; *Explicator* Prize, 1965; National Endowment for the Arts Fellowship, 1970; Wesleyan University Center for the Humanities Fellowship, 1973. Fellow in the Humanities, Princeton University, New Jersey, 1977; Fellow, Center for Advanced Study in the Behavioral Sciences, Stanford University, California. Address: Department of English, University of Virginia, Charlottesville, Virginia 22901, U.S.A.

PUBLICATIONS

Criticism

>*Wordsworth and Schelling*: *A Typological Study of Romanticism.*   New Haven, Con-
>necticut, and London, Yale University Press, 1960.
>*Innocence and Experience*: *An Introduction to Blake.*   New Haven, Connecticut, and
>London, Yale University Press, 1964.
>"Byron and the Terrestrial Paradise," in *From Sensibility to Romanticism*: *Essays
>Presented to Frederick A. Pottle*, edited by Harold Bloom and Frederick W. Hilles.
>New York, Oxford University Press, 1965.
>"Truth and Method in Interpretation," in *Review of Metaphysics* (New Haven, Connec-
>ticut), 18, 1965.
>*Validity in Interpretation.*   New Haven, Connecticut, and London, Yale University
>Press, 1967.
>*The Aims of Interpretation.*   Chicago and London, University of Chicago Press, 1976.
>"Faulty Perspectives," in *Essays in Criticism* (Oxford), 26, 1976.
>"What Isn't Literature?" in *What Is Literature?* edited by Paul Hernadi.   Bloomington
>and London, Indiana University Press, 1978.
>"The Well-Read Urn: A Thought Experiment," in *History as a Tool in Critical Interpre-
>tation*: *A Symposium*, edited by Thomas F. Rugh and Erin R. Silva.   Provo, Utah,
>Brigham Young University Press, 1978.

Other

>*The Philosophy of Composition.*   Chicago and London, University of Chicago Press,
>1977.

CRITICAL STUDIES

>William E. Cain, "Authority, 'Cognitive Atheism,' and the Aims of Interpretation," in
>*College English* (Chicago), 39, 1977.
>Frank Lentricchia, "E.D. Hirsch: The Hermeneutics of Innocence," in *After the New
>Criticism*.   Chicago and London, University of Chicago Press, 1980.

                              *   *   *

E.D. Hirsch's aim in *Validity in Interpretation* is nothing less than to establish the right of
interpretation to "claim as its object genuine knowledge"; or to put it more specifically, to raise
our interpretive guesses (that is, our hypotheses as to the meaning of the kinds of utterances we
encounter in literature) to the level of explicit understanding which can be confirmed by other
rational interpreters. To appreciate all this implies, however, we need to consider Hirsch's
conception of the relationship which exists between author and reader inside the larger context
of a shared language system.

All languages are "culture-bound" or made up of potentially sharable sets of symbols
determined and limited by certain linguistic norms. Furthermore, every individual utterance
must be, by definition, an instance of a prior type of utterance (or possibly a new combination
of existing types): if meaning were really unique, then obviously it could communicate nothing
to the reader or listener. Thus utterances are counters in the various subsets or games which
make up the language as a whole; and just as types have traits, expressed or implicit, so
meanings will carry implications. To take Hirsch's own example:

if we consider a very simple type such as a right triangle, we can say that the type contains
the implication stated in the Pythagorean theorem.... But why is it that the type "right
triangle" contains the implication, the square of the hypotenuse equals the summed
squares of the other two sides? If one answers, "because that is the nature of a right
triangle," one simply begs the question. If one answers, "because part of the meaning of a
right triangle is the Pythagorean theorem," that would be more descriptive, but it would
not explain how "right triangle" can contain "Pythagorean theorem," particularly if one
did not explicitly attend to the theorem when one intended the type. "But the theorem
applies to all right triangles so it must apply here." This begins to be more illuminating,
though we may still wonder how one meaning "contains" the other. "Since I have heard,
thanks to Pythagoras, that his theorem applies to all right triangles, and since almost
everybody else has learned this too, it is possible to mean 'Pythagorean theorem' as *part*
of what I mean when I say 'right triangle.' *If nobody had ever heard of the theorem it
would not be possible to have it as part of my verbal meaning.* Not only does the theorem
apply to all members of the type, but it is also something that is known by others to
belong. Because of *their* knowledge, the theorem is contained in the meaning of 'right
triangle.' They are able to fill out the implications because they are familiar with the type.
If they were not familiar with it they could not do so, and I could not convey the
implication."

For communication to take place the reader must understand the *kind* of utterance he is dealing
with and the range of implications it necessarily or probably carries.

The author or speaker uses language to convey an intended type-meaning which, while it may
be complex, is also determinate, reproducible, and again, has implications: the utterance is an
instance of a particular genre, to be understood, interpreted, "re-cognized," by the reader. Thus
Schleiermacher summarized the hermeneutic ideal when he stated that "Everything in a given
text which requires fuller explanation must be explained and determined exclusively from the
linguistic domain common to the author and his original public." It is vital to recognize that
there can be no a priori laws for the right reconstruction of an author's meaning, no method, as
Hirsch points out, for making the correct interpretive hypothesis: "the act of understanding is
at first a genial (or a mistaken) guess, and there are no methods for making guesses, no rules for
generating insights." Transcending the hermeneutic circle (the problem of how we can know the
parts without first identifying the whole and how, conversely, we can know the whole without
first recognizing the parts) depends upon "divination" or intuition; but fortunately initial
intuitions can be, and often must be, discarded or revised.

Hirsch is now able to make the crucial distinction between meaning and significance:

Meaning is that which is represented by a text; it is what the author meant by his use of a
particular sign sequence; it is what the signs represent. *Significance*, on the other hand,
names a relationship between that meaning and a person, or a conception, or a situation,
or indeed anything imaginable. Authors, who like everyone else change their attitudes,
feelings, opinions, and value criteria in the course of time, will obviously in the course of
time tend to view their own work in different contexts. Clearly what changes for them is
not the meaning of the work, but rather their relationship to that meaning. Significance
always implies a relationship, and one constant, unchanging pole of that relationship is
what the text means. Failure to consider this simple and essential distinction has been the
source of enormous confusion in hermeneutic theory.

When we recover the determinate meaning of an author's statement, we interpret; when we
relate that meaning to our own on-going scheme of values (or indeed to anything else, as Hirsch
remarks), we criticize: thus interpretation is to criticism as meaning is to significance. To take
another of Hirsch's examples:

A colleague once pointed out to me that Simone Weil could not have written so
brilliantly on the way *The Iliad* disclosed the role of brute force in human life if she had
not passed through the horrors of Nazism, and, furthermore, that her emphasis on this
aspect of *The Iliad* would not have struck a responsive chord in her readers if they had
not also witnessed those times. In this observation we can see how closely connected in

practice are understanding [grasping the intended meaning], interpretation, and criticism, and how necessary it is to distinguish them in theory. Surely Simone Weil's
emphasis on the role of force in *The Iliad* brilliantly exploited the experiences she shared
with her audience, and probably she did not overemphasize the role of force within
Homer's imagination. The element of *criticism* in her commentary was her implication
that Homer was right—human life is like that, and we, in this age, know it. The element
of *interpretation* in her commentary was her laying out in an ordered way Homer's
implications about the role of force in life. But we do not respond to her interpretation
just because we live in a violent age; we agree with it because we too have read *The Iliad*
and have perceived that same meaning—even if we have not perceived it so explicitly. I
cannot imagine any competent reader of any past age who did not implicitly grasp this
meaning in *The Iliad*, though I can certainly imagine a time when readers did not feel this
meaning to be a comment on life worthy of a special monograph.

Obviously there can be intelligent consensus about the *probable* meaning the author intended
(we can never have absolute certainty) by his use of particular type-utterances and their
implications, although it is equally obvious that the recovery of meaning may be a difficult
undertaking which requires all of the resources of scholarship and historical sophistication. But
there can never be consensus about significance as long as there are two readers left on earth
who hold different values. An enormous amount of futile controversy could be avoided in
literary discussions if we would only be properly aware of what kind of statement, critical or
interpretive, we are making or responding to at any given moment. And properly understood,
the distinction between meaning and significance is by no means a restriction or prohibition;
rather it is

> a charter of freedom to the critic...for the liberty of the critic to describe the countless
> dimensions of a text's significance is closely dependent on his not being constricted by a
> confusion between meaning and significance.... If he recognizes that verbal meaning is
> determinate, whereas significance and the possibilities of legitimate criticism are bound-
> less, he will have overcome a confusion that has, ironically, inhibited critical freedom.

Hirsch further distinguishes between two kinds of criticism: intrinsic, which is "founded
entirely on the author's aims and norms and is nowadays too frequently underrated as an
important form of judgment," and extrinsic, in which the critic judges the work by criteria other
than the author's. Next, there is *appropriate* extrinsic criticism, which is

> always close to intrinsic criticism in one respect: the critic may disagree with the author's
> purposes and hierarchy of purposes, with his taste and methods, but always takes those
> purposes into consideration. That is to say, he judges with respect to *some* of the
> purposes and values entertained by the author and does not simply ignore the conven-
> tions, aims, and systems of expectations under which the work was composed. Approp-
> riate extrinsic criticism differs from intrinsic criticism primarily in weighing the author's
> values and aims differently from the author. Such criticism is extrinsic because the
> critic's hierarchy of aims and values is different from the author's, but it is appropriate
> because many of the critic's criteria are the same as the author's even though they are
> weighed or valued differently. Pope, for instance, implied that dramatic effectiveness
> and the evocation of awe should have been more important aims in Milton's portrayal of
> God than rational theological justification. Certainly Milton did aim at dramatic
> effectiveness and the evocation of awe in Book III, but he valued theological justification
> more than Pope. While critic and author are in disagreement over relative values, they
> do at least have a common foundation for their disagreement.

Finally, "judicial criticism" is appropriate extrinsic criticism which is based on valid interpretation of the author's probable intended meaning and rests ultimately on the correct discrimination of type-trait relationships. Such discrimination should lead to an interpretive hypothesis
which will make "more functional" the parts of the whole (the crucial assumption here is of
course the traditional one that a work of art always strives for some kind of organic shape or
maximum part-whole relationship).

As a simple example of valid or probably correct interpretation—and it is perhaps too simple for what Hirsch has in mind—we might take these lines by Herrick:

> Here a pretty baby lies
> Sung asleep with lullabys:
> Pray be silent, and not stirre
> Th' easie earth that covers her.

The phrase, "Here a pretty baby lies," might at first seem to refer to a sleeping child, or it might suggest to a more "informed" reader the type-utterance "epitaph." Once we make our decision and examine the parts in terms of an hypothesized whole we soon discover that the "epitaph" interpretation is more valid; it activates more details of the poem: this is a *Christian* epitaph, the soul of the child is merely asleep, and so on.

In an important later essay, "Three Dimensions of Hermeneutics" (now reprinted in *The Aims of Interpretation*), Hirsch clarifies the ultimately ethical basis of his argument. As interpreters we are concerned with the re-cognition of "original" meaning; but obviously other constructions of meaning are possible too: the medieval commentators who found in Vergil an allegorized body of Christian doctrine were constructing what Hirsch calls "anachronistic" meaning. The problem for critical theory is important: to what extent are we constrained by original meaning? To what extent and under what circumstances is anachronistic meaning permissible or even superior to original meaning—the Christian readings of Vergil exist, and so do *Shelley's Mythmaking, Love and Death in the American Novel*, and G. Wilson Knight's studies of Shakespeare. If we wish to defend original meaning as the proper goal of interpretation we can do so only on ethical grounds. "There is a fundamental ethical maxim for interpretation," Hirsch maintains, "that claims no privileged sanction from metaphysics or analysis, but only from general ethical tenets, generally shared":

> *Unless there is powerful overriding value in disregarding an author's intention (i.e., original meaning), we who interpret as a vocation should not disregard it.* Mere individual preference would not be such an overriding value, nor would be the mere preferences of many persons. The possible exception is mentioned only because every ethical maxim requires such an escape clause. (Example: unless there is a powerful overriding value in lying, a person should tell the truth. Yet there are times when a lie is ethically better than to tell the truth so the maxim cannot be an absolute one.) Similarly, one might fudge on original meaning for the sake of young, impressionable children, and so on. But except in these very special cases there is a strong ethical presumption against anachronistic meaning. When we simply use an author's words for our own purposes without respecting his intention, we transgress what Charles Stevenson in another context called "the ethics of language," just as we transgress ethical norms when we use another person merely for our own ends. Kant held it to be a foundation of moral action that men should be conceived as ends in themselves, and not as instruments of other men. This imperative is transferable to the words of men because speech is an extension and expression of men in the social domain, and also because when we fail to conjoin a man's intentions to his words we lose the soul of speech, which is to convey meaning and to understand what is intended to be conveyed.... The peculiarly modern anarchy of every man for himself in matters of interpretation may sound like the ultimate victory of the Protestant spirit. Actually, such anarchy is the direct consequence of transgressing the fundamental ethical norms of speech and its interpretation.

Many of these propositions are not, of course, new or startling, but Hirsch has the ability to support them with a compelling logical force and cogency which no summary can begin to suggest. *Validity in Interpretation* provides an indispensable foundation for anyone who wants to understand and go beyond what I.A. Richards once called the "chaos of critical theories."

HOLLAND, Norman (Norwood, Junior).   American.   Born in New York City, 19 September 1927. Educated at Massachusetts Institute of Technology, Cambridge, S.B. 1947; Harvard University, Cambridge, Massachusetts, L.L.B. 1950, Ph.D. 1956; Resident, Boston Psychoanalytic Institute, 1960-66. Married; has 2 children. Teaching Fellow and Tutor, Harvard University, 1953-55; Instructor, Assistant Professor and Associate Professor of English, Massachusetts Institute of Technology, 1955-66. Since 1966, Professor of English (Chairman of the Department, 1966-68) and Director, Center for the Psychological Study of the Arts, State University of New York at Buffalo. Visiting Professor of English, University of Paris, 1971-72. American Council of Learned Societies Fellow, 1974-75. Address: Center for the Psychological Study of the Arts, 409 Samuel Clemens Hall, State University of New York, Amherst, New York 14260, U.S.A.

PUBLICATIONS

Criticism

>   *The First Modern Comedies*: *The Significance of Etherege, Wycherley and Congreve.*
>   Cambridge, Massachusetts, Harvard University Press, 1959.
>   *The Shakespearean Imagination.*   New York, Macmillan, 1964.
>   *Psychoanalysis and Shakespeare.*   New York, McGraw Hill, 1966.
>   *The Dynamics of Literary Response.*   New York, Oxford University Press, 1968.
>   "Why Organic Unity?" in *College English* (Chicago), 30, 1968.
>   "Prose and Minds: A Psychoanalytic Approach to Non-Fiction," in *The Art of Victorian Prose*, edited by George Levine and William Madden.   New York, Oxford University Press, 1968.
>   *Poems in Persons*: *An Introduction to the Psychoanalysis of Literature.*   New York, Norton, 1973.
>   "A Touching of Literary and Psychiatric Education," in *Seminars in Psychiatry* (New York), 5, 1973.
>   "Defense, Displacement and the Ego's Algebra," in *International Journal of Psycho-Analysis* (London), 54, 1973.
>   *5 Readers Reading.*   New Haven, Connecticut, and London, Yale University Press, 1975.
>   "Unit Identity Text Self," in *Publications of the Modern Language Association* (New York), 90, 1975.
>   "Literary Interpretation and Three Phases of Psychoanalysis," in *Critical Inquiry* (Chicago), 3, 1976.
>   "The New Paradigm: Subjective or Transactive?" in *New Literary History* (Charlottesville, Virginia), 7, 1976.
>   "Gothic Possibilities," with Leona F. Sherman, in *New Literary History* (Charlottesville, Virginia), 8, 1977.
>   "Identity: An Interrogation at the Border of Psychology," in *Language and Style* (Flushing, New York), 10, 1977.
>   "What Can a Concept of Identity Add to Psycholinguistics?" in *Psychoanalysis and Language*, edited by Joseph H. Smith.   New Haven, Connecticut, and London, Yale University Press, 1978.
>   "How Can Dr. Johnson's Remarks on Cordelia's Death Add to My Own Responses?" in *Psychoanalysis and the Question of the Text*, edited by Geoffrey Hartman.   New York, Columbia University Press, 1978.
>   "Literature as Transaction," in *What Is Literature?* edited by Paul Hernadi.   Bloomington and London, Indiana University Press, 1978.
>   "Human Identity," in *Critical Inquiry* (Chicago), 4, 1978.
>   "Re-covering 'The Purloined Letter': Literature as Personal Transaction," in *The Reader in the Text*: *Essays on Audience and Interpretation*, edited by Susan R. Suleiman and Inge Crossman.   Princeton, New Jersey, Princeton University Press, 1980.

"Why Ellen Laughed," in *Critical Inquiry* (Chicago), 7, 1980.

*   *   *

The great "defining event" of the twentieth century, Norman Holland maintains at the start of his 1966 study, *Shakespeare and Psychoanalysis*, was Freud's "inconspicuous discovery of the unconscious mind at the end of the nineteenth century." The recognition of that "unknown" part of the mind which had so much influence over our conscious life profoundly affected every dimension of human activity, of course, including literature and criticism:

> Quite simply, it has become possible in this century to answer with some certianty the traditional puzzles about literature: What is the nature of inspiration? The creative process? How do we respond to literature? How does form work in our response? Meaning? Identification?...in every case the answers can make a stronger claim on our belief than mere tradition or opinion would, a claim, in fact, approaching that of science.

"Freudian psychology" and "psychoanalysis" are misleading terms, however, if they suggest a static body of principles and methods—in the 1920s; Freud himself made radical changes in his thinking about the dynamics of the mind—and thus Holland's recent essay "Literary Interpretation and Three Phases of Psychoanalysis" is particularly valuable: it provides an informed account of what has happened to orthodox Freudian psychology over the past seventy years and also gives us a convenient way of classifying Holland's own work. The first phase

> grew out of Freud's discoveries of latent and manifest content in a variety of settings: dreams, neurotic symptoms, jokes, forgetting, and slips of all kinds. As he realized this polarity applied in so many different spheres of mental activity, he understood that he had arrived at a general psychological principle, the polarity between conscious and unconscious, thought of as systems or even as places.

At this stage psychoanalytic criticism amounted to little more than a kind of reductive decoding: the events of everyday life and the objects and events depicted in works of art were to be interpreted as more or less invariant "symbols" for the "real" unconscious meaning. The procedure gave psychoanalytic criticism the bad name it still has in some circles, but it was not a stage which Holland himself had to pass through. The second phase represents a considerable advance:

> We can date it from Freud's positing a superego, an ego, and an id in 1923. We can identify its basic polarity as between ego and non-ego, that is, between the mind's synthesizing functions and either external reality or another internal psychic structure. Where therapy in the first phase tried to make the unconscious conscious, therapy in the second aimed at enlarging and strengthening the ego.

By strengthening our awareness of the ego-functions, this phase made criticism "less bizarre":

> It relates to other ways of thinking and reading. We are able to integrate an unconscious content for the [work]—some of which is available to us through the translation methods of the first phase—with conscious themes and the [work's] repertoire of formal devices as discovered by regular literary criticism.

This is the stage Holland uses in *The Dynamics of Literary Response*, which requires some separate comment before we move on to the third phase, "identity psychology," and the use Holland has made of that in *Five Readers Reading* and his most recent essays.

At the opening of the *Dynamics*, Holland asks why it is that busy, active creatures are so willing to suspend their disbelief and open themselves to obviously artificial things like plays and poems and novels. The answer, he asserts in very orthodox Freudian tems, is that "we must approach literature as we approach just about everything else in life, with a wish for pleasure." The particular kind of pleasure art affords and our susceptibility to it are Holland's primary concerns here, and they depend completely on Freud's view of the development of the personality. We enter the world as bundles of instinctual demands for gratification, which means we must very quickly focus on the primary family group: on the mother as the source of satisfaction and sustenance, and, in a quite different way, on the authority of the father. The young child learns quickly that his demands must often be radically modified or repressed altogether. They are not put aside, however, and continue to be active in our private fantasy-lives, in which we act out our intimate fears and hopes. (Holland does not presuppose any great familiarity with Freud, by the way, but readers coming to these matters for the first time—if there are any left—should probably try a little straight Freud as well: the early lectures on psychoanalysis and certainly the magnificent late essay, *Civilization and Its Discontents*, in which Freud eloquently examines the tragic impasse between society's demands and the individual's desire for happiness.) Society has very little use for the anarchic world of impulse and desire, and it is here that art becomes important: "Literature transforms our primitive fears and wishes into significance and coherence, and this transformation gives us pleasure." At this point Holland relies heavily on Ernst Kris, for whom art is "regression in the service of the ego." That is, art dramatizes primitive fantasies, though often in disguised or displaced forms, and at the same time offers us defenses against them; it enables us to re-enact our primal battles and transform them into adult "ego" terms:

> a psychoanalytic reading will arrive at a central or nuclear fantasy, known from clinical evidence, in which all the separate elements of the text play a role. Because we know these fantasies clinically, because they have to do with the primitive, unconscious part of our mental life, we can safely say they are what give literature its astonishing power over us. Literature transforms these nuclear fantasies toward meaningfulness and thereby allows them to elude the censoring part of our minds and achieve an oblique expression and gratification. In effect, a literary text has implicit in it two dimensions: one reaches "up," toward the world of social, intellectual, moral and religious concerns; the other reaches "down," to the dark, chthonic, primitive, bodily part of our mental life.

We take particular pleasure in the experience of transformation; the meaning of a literary work is not in a generalized point or message, but in the activity of stimulus, mastery and control. Literary value is therefore determined by how well the work lets us dramatize, defend ourselves against, and transform fantasy material: "The 'better' poem offers a defense which is more complex, reaching to higher levels of moral and intellectual life, and more likely to be culturally accepted. The 'less good' poem offers a less complex defense and one more likely to be associated with guilt." For an extended example of how an analysis of a "good poem" works, readers should consider Holland's discussion of "Dover Beach" in section four of the *Dynamics*.

Thus literature may be seen as a powerful tool in the civilizing process, intimate, formative and yet more "permissive" than parental authority and social forces often can afford to be. But in fact Holland is remarkably cautious in the claims he makes for literature:

> perhaps it also opens up possibilities of growth once we have put the text aside. Whether growth will in fact come is questionable—unless we make the quite unwarranted assumption that a momentary loosening of boundaries during reading will carry over to other activities. And even if growth comes, it will very likely come from quite unliterary sources.... [Given] the firmness of cultural structures and individual character, it is very hard to see how the effects of literature can be more than small, local and transient.... Without experimental evidence, the best information we have suggests that we should make no claim of a long-term moral effect for literature.

This will be troublesome for those of us who have continued to value literature long after childhood years when our reading, as Bruno Bettleheim has demonstrated, had an obvious relationship to our fears and desires. We can remember, we like to think, when we were powerfully seized by a new work and forced, often painfully, to look at ourselves afresh. Rilke tells us all great works demand that we change our lives. But this is the sort of experience which Holland cannot deal with, or might possibly classify as an illusion. It may be that we cannot change our lives to any real degree—but who, precisely, "we" are takes us into the third phase of psychoanalytic theory.

The *Dynamics* was an application of the second stage, in which we dealt with general patterns of human defense and response. Yet we are also individuals, with different life-histories and different character shapes or "identities." The great achievement of the third phase, "Identity Theory," now enables us, according to Holland, "to understand that interaction of firm critical hypotheses with exciting, shimmering fields of personal knowledge"; here "criticism risks intimacy in order to restore individuality." *5 Readers Reading* is a massive exploration of the ways in which five young American college students (some of them graduate students in literature) responded, in conversation with Holland, to a few selected texts and thereby revealed their own special identities. Here Holland relies upon the concept of identity as it has been developed by Heinz Lichtenstein, Erik Erikson and others. In Fenichel's words, "the ego's habitual modes of adjustment to the external world, the id, and the superego, and the characteristic types of combining these modes with one another, constitute character."

5 Readers Reading is a powerful reminder of how subjective and at times tyrannical the reading process can be. Holland's quite "normal" students insisted on imposing their own identities as they "interpreted" the texts or quite simply rejected the texts which offered them no space for introjection. Conventional criticism, Holland maintains, is therefore unrealistic in its assumption that we passively submit to the determinate meaning of a text: "Such a view subordinates the lively and human appreciation of human achievement to something transhuman. It puts literature on a pedestal." To replace this inadequate model Holland suggests that we see the reading process as "transactive": "I am advocating a criticism in which we consciously recognize that we re-create literature for ourselves, just as the transactive psychologists have shown we create the colors, shapes, and directions of the world we perceive."

Once again, many readers are likely to have questions, or, in the heads-I-win-tails-you-lose rhetoric of psychoanalysis, "defenses." To what extent are our identities totally formed by the time we reach the age of, say, Holland's young respondents? For all of his flexibility elsewhere, Holland is adamant. In a 1978 essay, "Human Identity," he agrees completely with Heinz Lichtenstein:

> Lichtenstein comes closer [than Erikson] to the problem in his concept of a *primary identity*: something that develops in each of us in the first year of life as mother and infant mutually fulfill needs through each other. A mother has a style of need and relation. An infant also brings to their relation a style that began in the genes. The two styles must, for the child's survival, mesh, and that meshing creates a primary identity "in the infant," "a zero point which must precede all other mental developments," "an invariant whose transformations would provide the developmental sequences with an unchanging core or form."

In a striking passage Holland concludes that "we are seduced into becoming ourselves by the love and nurture we receive in infancy." In short, he is speaking on behalf of a radically deterministic view of human identity, disagreeable to those of us who feel we can sometimes will a change in our lives and look to literature not as a kindly prison-keeper but as an ally. Readers—of this last remark—will have to make up their own minds; and as they do so they might take some indirect consolation in thinking about the progress of Norman Holland himself, the writer of a completely conventional study of Restoration comedy, then of *The Dynamics of Literary Response*, and then, as the occasion arose, of *5 Readers Reading*.

HOLLOWAY, (Christopher) John. British. Born in London, 1 August 1920. Educated at County School, Beckenham, Kent; New College, Oxford (Open History Scholar), M.A. 1945, D.Phil. 1947. Served in the British Army, 1941-45. Married 1) Audrey Gooding in 1946, two children; 2) Joan Black in 1978. Temporary Lecturer in Philosophy, New College, 1945, Fellow, All Souls College, 1946-60, and John Locke Scholar, 1947, Oxford; Lecturer in

English, Aberdeen University, 1949-54. University Lecturer in English, 1954-66, Fellow of Queens' College, 1955, Reader in Modern English, 1966-72, and since 1972, Professor of Modern English, Cambridge, Byron Professor, University of Athens, 1961-63; Alexander White Professor, University of Chicago, 1965; Hinkley Professor, Johns Hopkins University, Baltimore, 1972. Litt.D.: Aberdeen University 1954; Cambridge University, 1969. Fellow, Royal Society of Literature, 1956. Address: Queens' College, Cambridge, England.

PUBLICATIONS

Criticism

> *The Victorian Sage: Studies in Argument.* London, Macmillan, and New York, St. Martin's Press, 1953.
> "The Literary Scene," in *The Pelican Guide to English Literature 7,* edited by Boris Ford. London, Penguin, 1961.
> *The Charted Mirror: Literary and Critical Essays.* London, Routledge, 1960; New York, Horizon Press, 1962.
> *The Story of the Night: Studies in Shakespeare's Major Tragedies.* London, Routledge, 1961; Lincoln, University of Nebraska Press, 1963.
> *The Colours of Clarity: Essays in Contemporary Literature and Education.* London, Routledge, and Hamden, Connecticut, Shoe String Press, 1964.
> *The Lion Hunt: A Pursuit of Poetry and Reality.* London, Routledge, and Hamden, Connecticut, Shoe String Press, 1964.
> *Widening Horizons in English Verse.* London, Routledge, 1966; Evanston, Illinois, Northwestern University Press, 1967.
> *Blake: The Lyric Poetry.* London, Arnold, 1968.
> *The Establishment of English.* London, Cambridge University Press, 1972.
> *The Proud Knowledge: Poetry, Insight, and the Self, 1620-1920.* London, and Boston, Routledge, 1977.
> *Narrative and Structure: Exploratory Essays.* London, and New York, Oxford University Press, 1979.

Verse

> *(Poems).* Oxford Fantasy Press, 1954.
> *The Minute and Longer Poems.* Hessle, Yorkshire, Marvell Press, 1956.
> *The Fugue and Shorter Pieces.* London, Routledge, 1960.
> *The Landfallers: A Poem in Twelve Parts.* London, Routledge, 1962.
> *Wood and Windfall.* London, Routledge, 1965.
> *New Poems.* New York, Scribner, 1970.
> *Planet of the Winds.* London, Routledge, 1977.

Other

> *Language and Intelligence.* London, Macmillan, 1951; Hamden, Connecticut, Shoe String Press, 1974.
> *A London Childhood* (autobiography). London, Routledge, 1966; New York, Scribner, 1968.

Editor, *Poems of Mid-Century.* London, Harrap, 1957.

Editor, *Selected Poems*, by Percy Bysshe Shelley.   London, Heinemann, 1959; New
    York, Macmillan, 1960.
Editor, *Little Dorrit*, by Charles Dickens.   London, Penguin, 1967.
Editor, with Joan Black, *Later English Broadside Ballads*.   London, Routledge, 2 vols.,
    1975-79.

*   *   *

Because he recognizes that different aims and subject matters necessarily entail different
procedures—especially if the critic really knows what he is trying to do—it is impossible to
place John Holloway in terms of any one fixed critical position. In this respect he comes very
close to the kind of pluralism defended by R.S. Crane, whose work he had discussed, with
guarded admiration, in the late 1950's. The question of influence is not the issue here; what
matters is that some understanding of Crane's argument will help readers to see more clearly the
scope and value of Holloway's criticism thus far.

Very briefly, Crane points out that a literary work is something in itself—a formed whole of a
certain kind—and something which exists in a complex series of relationships with other
phenomena. Ideally, he concludes (in *The Languages of Criticism and the Structure of Poetry*),
we ought to have as many modes of criticism as there are "distinguishable major aspects in the
construction, appreciation and use of literary works." Thus a critic may wish to investigate the
literal meaning and form of a particular work; he may wish to examine it as a manifestation of
the artist's sensibility or as it is determined, in part, by the conventions of the time; and finally,
he may judge its significance according to the values he holds. All of these lines of inquiry are
perfectly valid, but the crucial point is that no one critical framework or language can possibly
do justice to each of these aspects. By definition a critical system is a kind of discourse whose
range is limited by its assumptions and implied methodology. In practice, however, a critic is
quite likely to assume that his system can answer all the relevant questions, or worse, come to
believe that the only important questions are those his preferred language allows him to deal
with. How close Holloway is to this kind of critical pluralism is apparent in the preface to his
first collection of essays, *The Charted Mirror*:

> The multiplicity of tasks which critical discussion can undertake, and the always decisive
> importance of what is distinctive in the particular case, mean that to think of "putting
> theories into practice" would be out of place. Rather, it is a question of exploring, in
> particular or in general, how any guiding idea with which the critic may equip himself,
> any question which he comes recurrently to ask about what he reads, is likely to open up
> certain parts of his particular subject, but certain parts only. Illumination is always from
> a certain angle, and of a certain kind. It cannot easily throw one thing into relief, without
> throwing another into shadow. In part, the mirror which the critic must "chart" is that in
> himself which forms an image of the work he studies. It is no unrelieved or flawless plane,
> but complex and partly personal, both magnifying and diminishing, in accordance with
> all that makes up his outlook, guiding ideas, and general approach.... [The essays in this
> book] seek to explore their subject from the standpoint of an idea which is often
> neglected. This is an idea of the *variety* in the questions which a critic may put about a
> work: the variety, on different occasions, of the paths he must pursue, or the factors he
> must consider, if the final picture is to emerge truly into focus.

One of the critic's tasks, then, is to "locate the deeper qualities of something which could be
praised or condemned for what it seems on the surface." For examples of this mode of criticism
Holloway directs readers to his essays on Skelton and on Patmore and Donne, both of which
make two further points which have remained central to his critical thinking. In "Skelton" he
accepts the principle of generic differences and warns against the fallacy of approaching a work
with the wrong set of expectations; and in "Patmore, Donne, and the 'Wit of Love' " he assumes
that the ultimate value of a work lies in the degree of its "felt contact" with the diversity of life
itself. Thus the difference between Patmore's verse and the more powerful verse of Donne is
that the latter is "almost always creating in the reader's mind a profound impression that behind
it there is a rich and wide and sensitive contact with reality." Holloway develops this conception
of "contact" at much greater length in his mannered, eloquent lyrical meditation on poetry, *The
Lion Hunt*.

At other times the critic may wish to "trace closely how what can be known of a writer's life lights up that exact feature and quality of what he wrote" or to see how "the literary interest of a work is made clearer when its reflections of an age, or resumption of an historical continuity, is also made clearer." The essay on Keats' Odes illustrates the former kind of criticism while the essays on Wyndham Lewis, *Tess* and *The Awkward Age*, and on the Angry Young Men of the 1950's illustrate the historical approach, as does the valuable longer study of Blake's lyric poetry and its relationship to certain eighteenth-century traditions of thought and feeling. And in *Widening Horizons in English Verse* Holloway considers still another kind of historical problem. In the time of Spenser and Shakespeare, he observes,

> men had no idea that all the languages of Europe belonged to one large family. They knew nothing about the techniques for assessing the reliability of chronicles and other historical documents. They had virtually no access to any English documents from before medieval times, except the Anglo-Saxon Chronicle. Few could read Anglo-Saxon, and none could read Old Norse. No one in Europe, let alone England, could read the Runic alphabet; and the great literature of Iceland was unknown even to the Icelanders themselves.

His aim here is "to give a picture...of some of the stages by which this ignorance was replaced by knowledge; and more particularly, some of the ways in which this kindled the interest of writers and poets, and entered into their work." Or leaving biographical and historical questions aside, the critic may wish to demonstrate (as Holloway does in his essay on Swift's satire) that "in a distinctive kind of writing...the local texture of language may operate quite differently from what we have learnt to look for in 'practical criticism' of lyrical verse." Finally, the critic may turn directly to the significance—the human value—of different poetic forms (*The Story of the Night* provides the clearest example of this mode of criticism).

It would not be difficult to translate these concerns into Crane's "aspects" and their corresponding modes of criticism, but what is important here is that Holloway has seen the need for a pluralistic approach and has the learning and sensitivity to move convincingly from one mode of criticism to another. In this respect—and in his concern to reason with his readers and not merely to settle for blank assertions—he is probably the most sophisticated British critic now at work.

In *The Charted Mirror* and *The Colours of Clarity* Holloway develops an important argument concerning the "essential" quality of longer narrative and dramatic forms and at the same time exposes the weaknesses of certain modern critical assumptions. He points out that it is senseless to value such works for their "informativeness" or supposed revelation of universals and confirmation of moral truths: the mere presence of a theme "is without interest, unless it can be shown that its presence makes the work better." Again,

> Is the theme of a work, then, some statement—implicit, needless to say; some point of view embodied in the work? Sometimes the critics are cautious, and they talk about "vital problems" or "obstinate questionings"; as if the great masterpieces went in for these things, but not the answers to them. When they do come out into the open and do indicate the main point of view which they detect as theme, I cannot help thinking that, normally, the result is disastrous. For example, one critic says that for Shakespeare the chief meaning of the history plays was "that political capacity and moral sensibility tend necessarily to diverge." We do not need Shakespeare to convey the truth of this, because we know from history and experience that it is false: sometimes those two things diverge, sometimes they converge.

The conclusion of this remarkable essay ("The New 'Establishment' in Criticism," in *The Charted Mirror*) is worth quoting in full:

> Sometimes we tell an anecdote which is meant for typical. "Here is a case," we say; "this kind of thing goes on every day." At other times we tell a story because it is not typical but the opposite; because it is amazing and exceptional. Nor does that make it any the less informative. Life is not chemistry: being informed about it is not knowing the general nature of man, or life's necessary tendencies, or what, according to the natural

order, is the consequence of what. Men whose knowledge is only of this kind live in shells. Besides all this, real knowledge of life is knowledge of the exceptional: of how near the exceptional always is; of how easily it can come; and if it does come, how elaborate, or astonishing, or disastrous it may very well be.

There is no elementary parallel to this in the physical or social sciences; though there are, I believe, some fairly recondite ones. But this is the way in which many, perhaps most, literary masterpieces extend and enrich the reader's grasp of life. Seldom or never in experience does one encounter a divergence from the norm, an aberration of nature, which is as fully developed in every detail, and above all as complete, as what is depicted in the literary work at its most ambitious. Which is not to deny that such works have a universal relevance, nor that we can sense a norm within the extraordinary; but to come closer to how this universality and normality really enter our experience as we read.

It is this completeness through to the end with which a particular case is depicted that distinguishes imaginative writing; this is what it does that no other kind of writing begins to do, and is thus what makes it irreplaceable. There is a speech by Anna Karenina which brings this out with beautiful exactness. She is half-way through her disastrous affair with Count Vronsky. In speaking of it to her brother she says: "No, Stiva; I'm lost: worse than lost: I'm not lost *yet*—I can't say that all is over: on the contrary, I feel that it's not ended. I'm like an overstrained violin string that must snap. But it's not ended yet...and the end will be terrible." Anna's was, we might say, the perfect case of the disease, wonderfully complete and intensified—which is to say highly exceptional—and she had to go right through to the end of it: there is its completeness and finality.

This "going right through to the end," neglected as it is, seems the central feature of imaginative literature in the full-length work. Which brings me back to current critical establishment. A pattern of imagery, a set of interdependent themes, could run through a group of unrelated short stories; or a discursive work like an essay by Montaigne or a long selection of *pensées* from Pascal. We do not, by these means, even glimpse the really decisive quality of the play or novel; or, in general, of the work which is a unity in the imaginative order. What is that decisive quality? It is what demands that the work be read and seen from beginning to end as a single organic thing: something that, as we read it, pervades and controls and extends our whole experience throughout a period of time; and that, whenever we recall it, lives in our minds again with that unique temporal coherence. In most cases (though not in all) what is really distinctive of this kind of writing, what it does that nothing else does, is start off with a narrative, a story, and carry it through to a point where that narrative appears to complete itself, to run decisively to a halt.

Thus Holloway has very sharp things to say about critics who reduce literature to some kind of "informativeness" or who neglect "the contours of the whole" and concentrate, in a pseudo-scientific manner, on details of language, close reading and explication. I.A. Richards, for example, reveals his "scientific" bias not only in his denial that poetic statements have any truth value but also

in what he tried to provide as the proper method of criticism; a poem, for example, being rather like a scientific specimen, the complex structure of which needs to be laid bare, and a critic requiring the detachment, fine discrimination, patience, persistence, and sharp cutting-edge of a biologist—with the suggestion that *that is all*. For under his progressive dissection, the good poem turns out to have a delicate and subtle organization, and the bad one to have, not another kind of organization, but no organization whatever. Evaluation need not take place. Analysis veritably disintegrates the bad; the good is proved by standing up to it.

The basis of Holloway's objections here lead directly to his own belief that criticism must never divorce itself from larger questions of human values. In "Matthew Arnold and the Modern Dilemma" he concludes that

Modern criticism, if it rejects Arnold's opinion that the critic is essentially a winnower, separating wheat and chaff, tends to run in a quite contrary direction. It holds instead that criticism is sensitive and sympathetic interpretation, and that selecting among what is actually good is a kind of impoverishment. To think this the staple of criticism is to make one of two assumptions: that there is no hierarchy within what is good, or that the hierarchy is so easily and familiarly known to all that it need not be insisted upon. The point is less that the first assumption is false, as that unfortunately the second is false too; and that because of this the criticism of sensitive interpretation is unduly optimistic. It is criticism for readers in Heaven.... The attempt to assess [literature] *fully* in abstraction from what it says is another attempt to evaluate without making value judgments; it tempts us today because we handle values uneasily. Arnold is perfectly clear that no work of literature can be fully assessed save by reference, in part, to the insights into life which are to be found in it, as well as to the organization which these receive, because literature is art. He makes both demands. In the end no one, unless confused either by timidity or by language, can do anything else.

And in *The Story of the Night*, Holloway provides the clearest statement thus far of the value of tragedy—and of art in general, as he sees it:

The outcome of reading (or watching) the whole work may indeed be that we are left with many new ideas about what life is or may be like, and that our own perception of life may prove to have been made larger and keener in many directions. But there is also a quite distinctive emotional condition in which most (not, I think, all) great works leave us. It is a condition at once exuberant and reposed: the sense of having passed through a great experience, one which testifies (as do great experiences of any kind) to the superb wealth and range of life, and to the splendid rather than the disastrous powers of man.

The great work is a "source of *power*," a "*momentous and energizing experience*:"

The work's essential interest will be to have added a great new item to the furniture of the world; to have become a thing; a fount of experience. It is precious to individuals because, over centuries or over millennia, it thus enhances the life, and the capacity for life, of society's members.

The recognition and elucidation of these qualities, then, form "the nerve and life of the critic's task," his "deepest and most creative concern." Holloway's own criticism has never been easy—he is a professionally trained philosopher and, of course, a distinguished poet, whose mind often works by compression and indirection—but even by his high standards for attentive reading, *Narrative and Structure* is a demanding book. His basic concern, however, is clear enough (and would have been clearer still had he defined it in his first rather than his last chapter here). Following Aristotle closely, Holloway argues that modern criticism has often paid too much attention to language (Aristotle's "diction") and not enough to narrative structure (the plot which is for Aristotle the "soul" of any mimetic work). In the *Poetics* Aristotle assumes that the work of art is a complex whole, made up of constituent parts, whose end or purpose is to move us in a certain way. The major constituent parts are the plot, the characters, with their differing intellectual and moral qualities, and the diction they use. The crucial point is that Aristotle has constructed a hierarchy of parts: overall intended effect dictates the kind of plot the artist will select; the plot, in turn, will dictate the appropriate characters to enact the plot; and the nature of the characters will determine the kind of diction or language they will use. Holloway's objection to the emphasis on language in modern criticism is thoroughly Aristotelian, then, and in kind not really different from, say, Elder Olson's objections to William Empson's emphasis on matters of language. Plot or narrative modes, Holloway maintains, "have access to the most powerful forces and drives in life because of the 'what' that [they] imitate, the 'things' that make up [their] subject-matter." Moreover— and here he follows Kant—narrative structures have an inherent appeal to the nature of the human mind itself:

There is a general connection between the degree to which structure in a literary work can connect with the deepest terrors and desires or embody and so evoke the mind's reverent openness before life, and the degree to which experience and consciousness are seen in something like Kantian terms. To think of "Kantian terms" in this context means simply the fundamental idea that the forms and structures of experience are not imposed wholesale on the mind from the reality which lies outside it, but at least in part represent the mind's own permanent nature and what in consequence are the standing possibilities of our consciousness. If those aspects of experience have the form, or the structure, that they do have, because those forms and structures represent something deep and permanent within ourselves that enters into our experiences and moulds those experiences into the general patterns that it has of itself, then it is simple enough to see how those forms and structures can embody and therefore evoke the most alive and creative part of the mind.

"What this means," Holloway concludes, "is that narrative structure, being essentially about changes and resolutions, must essentially be also about what releases, and manifests, and finally orders, some of the greater or perhaps the greatest energies of the work." All of this is clear enough, but what makes *Narrative and Structure* such a formidable book is Holloway's analysis and tentative classification of various narrative forms and devices in the texts he examines, from the *Decameron* through Henry James, Muriel Spark, and Christopher Isherwood. He is clearly dissatisfied with the "inadequate" descriptions provided by Propp, Todorov and other Structuralists, and in an attempt to work out more precise tools and categories has recourse to "certain mathematical ideas." He presupposes that his readers will be able to handle such matters as Boolean algebra and Hesse Diagrams, and will be familar with Chomsky and a number of other modern linguists. He also admits that these essays are "exploratory," however, and modestly hopes that "others, better qualified than I, may see possibilities of advance far beyond what I have attempted."

The Proud Knowledge is a much more conventional but hardly less impressive book. Holloway is interested here in characterizing some of the major modes of poetry which have come into being in English literature since the eighteenth century, and diverse as they may seem, the common element which unites them, "the powers and potentialities of the individual and the self":

> this conception of the individual as having the power, the right, and perhaps the duty to engage upon a solitary and more or less unaided journey of intellectual or spiritual exploration towards the terms of life and the status of man, is one of the most imaginative and ambitious intellectual achievements of the past five centuries.... One after another, the outstanding minds show themselves as having, in one medium or another, embarked upon the search for an independent fundamental insight; and the means towards it has been the individual's relying upon his own inner powers.

But the "aspiring mind" has its dark side as well, the temptation of pride and, when quests fail, "uncertainty, bafflement, isolation and near-despair": part of the "price paid by the dedicated spiritual pilgrim is [a] kind of estrangement from all the less dedicated of mankind." The fears which these quests entail have also given rise to another kind of poetry and a deep concern for the opposite cases, the unassuming, simple "zero lives" of the ordinary man which poets like Hardy and Wordsworth treat so memorably. In a brief "Postscript" Holloway suggests that there is now some reason to believe that the belief in man and the importance of his proud knowledge is on the wane. He finds in Yeats, for example, a "revulsion against the life of enquiry and intellect," but quickly breaks off and remarks that this is a topic for another book. The problem of man's aspiring mind and the attendant dangers is not of course a new one, nor does Holloway pretend that it is. What gives *Proud Knowledge* its value is what at first glance might seem a trivial gift, a genius for quotation. But it is hardly a trivial gift: Holloway has what most critics usually lack, a loving attentiveness to the poems he examines (and not merely "uses") and a total familiarity with the range of English verse. Perhaps more than any other critic at work just now, Holloway has the ability to go to the heart of the poem and make poem and critical comment enhance and mutually illuminate each other.

HOUGH, Graham (Goulder). British. Born in Great Crosby, Lancashire, 14 February 1908. Educated at Prescot Grammar School; University of Liverpool; Queens' College, Cambridge. Served as a volunteer in the Singapore Royal Artillery, 1942-45. Married Rosamund Oswell in 1942 (marriage dissolved), two children; Ingeborg Neumann, 1952. Lecturer in English, Raffles College, Singapore, 1930; Professor of English, University of Malaya, 1946; Visiting Lecturer, Johns Hopkins University, Baltimore, 1950; Visiting Professor, Cornell University, Ithaca, New York, 1958; Fellow, 1950-66, and Tutor, 1955-60, of Christ's College, Praelector and Fellow of Darwin College, 1966-75, University Reader in English, 1965-66, and Professor of English, 1966-75, Cambridge University. D.Litt.: University of Malaya, 1955; Litt.D.: Cambridge University, 1961. Address: The White Cottage, Grantchester, Cambridge, England.

PUBLICATIONS

Criticism

The Last Romantics. London, Duckworth, 1949; New York, Barnes and Noble, 1961.
The Romantic Poets. London, Hutchinson, 1953.
The Dark Sun: A Study of D.H. Lawrence. London, Duckworth, 1956; New York, Macmillan, 1957.
Image and Experience: Reflections on a Literary Revolution. Washington, D.C., Catholic University of America Press, and London, Duckworth, 1960.
A Preface to "The Faerie Queene." London, Duckworth, 1962; New York, Norton, 1963.
The Dream and the Task: Literature and Morals in the Culture of Today. London, Duckworth, 1963; New York, Norton, 1964.
An Essay on Criticism. London, Duckworth, and New York, Norton, 1966.
Style and Stylistics. London, Routledge, and New York, Humanities Press, 1969.
Selected Essays. London, Cambridge University Press, 1978.

Verse

Legends and Pastorals: Poems. London, Duckworth, 1961.

Other

Editor, *Orlando Furioso*, by Ariosto, Sir John Harrington's translation. Carbondale, Southern Illinois University Press, 1962; London, Centaur Press, 1963.
Editor, *Selected Poems of George Meredith.* London, Oxford University Press, 1962.
Editor, *Poems of Samuel Taylor Coleridge.* London, Folio Society, 1963.
Editor, *Edmund Spenser: The Faerie Queene 1596.* London, Scolar Press, 2 vols., 1976.

CRITICAL STUDY

Frank Kermode, "Counter-Revolution," in *Puzzles and Epiphanies: Essays and Reviews 1958-1961.* London, Routledge, and New York, Chilmark Press, 1962.

*   *   *

If he hopes to be taken seriously, any critic who questions the established academic belief in "modernism" as a fertile literary tradition needs more than sheer nerve: he needs precisely the kind of sceptical intelligence and independence Graham Hough displays in his most important book, *Image and Experience*. The founding fathers of modern poetry were right, Hough concedes, to be weary of "Dover Beach" and the worn-out rhetoric of the late Victorians. Poetic progress has always depended upon periodic rebellion against "clichés of feeling and expression." But Hough also contends that the tactics of the Imagists, whose ideas are "at the centre of the characteristic poetic procedures of our time," should never have been erected into first principles for poetry in general.

Traditionally, poetry has always been regarded as an attempt by the writer to move his readers by the imitation of fundamental human experiences. As a man speaking to other men he has at his disposal various possibilities for the creation of plot and character; to embody his subject as fully as possible he has the resources of language, one of which is the making of apt analogies or, in the broadest sense of the term, "images." In their rejection of conventional nineteenth-century rhetoric, however, Hulme, Pound, Eliot and Stevens made the image into the primary and sometimes the exclusive vehicle of poetic communication. Thus poetry in their hands became "the art of making equations for emotions" and "the unit of poetry [becomes] the pictograph, the record of a significant glimpse." Hough argues that imagery alone cannot serve as the basis for more ambitious works, and thus the procedure of *The Waste Land* and Pound's *Cantos* "forbids that most ancient recipe for a poem—the poem in which first a natural object is presented, and then some reflection on human experience that arises from it, or is in some way parallel to it." By disregarding or inverting the hierarchy of parts—plot, character and diction—in their relationship to a moving whole these poets have radically limited the power of their work to touch the common reader. Dr. Johnson's phrase is crucial here, as it is elsewhere in Hough's criticism. If we accept Johnson's claim that the ultimate appeal must always be to the "common sense of readers uncorrupted with literary prejudices," then we are in trouble; for these are words, Hough argues,

> that no one who cares about poetry in our century can read without a twinge. The appeal to a body of readers who are not specialists or eccentrics, who are merely representative of the common sentiment and intelligence of human kind, is one we feel ourselves so little able to make, one that we know so well, if we are honest, ought to be made—that we can think of it only with a feeling of distress. Where is contemporary poetry read, and where is it written? In the universities. Who is it read by? Students; professional students of literature mostly, and professors, who expect to write papers on it, or to lecture on it—to "explicate" it, in the current cant. What has become (not to go back to some prelapsarian Eden) of the kind of public that even so recent a poet as Tennyson could enjoy? It has been warned off; it has been treated to sneers, threats and enigmas. It has been told so often that it has no status and no business in the sacred wood, and it has found the business actually being transacted there so remote from its ordinary apprehension, that it has turned away, in indifference, or disgust, or despair....The wilful Alexandrianism, the allusiveness and multiplicity of reference, above all, the deliberate cultivation of modes of organization that are utterly at variance with those of ordinary discourse—these are the main reasons for the disappearance of Johnson's common reader. It is hard to say this, for to say it lines one up with the hostile, the malicious and the Philistine, with all those who hate and suspect the exploring sensibility and have never made the effort to penetrate into the imaginative life of their time. But it is sometimes necessary to risk being put in bad company for the sake of saying what seems to be true. One can only hope that one has better reasons for saying it.

The Waste Land, the *Cantos*, the longer poems, apparently, of Thomas and Stevens, are spectacular monuments to nothing but themselves, unique experiments which, if they are to survive, will do so "not assisted by their structure, but in spite of it." And Hough concludes that

> If we are to use metaphors, mine [for much modern poetry] would not be a cul-de-sac but a détour, a diversion from the main road. Traffic along the main road has been proceeding all the time, and we do not sufficiently remember this. In talking of modern poetry we ought to recall more often than we do that Hardy was writing till 1926, and

that among the poets of our century are Robert Frost, Robert Graves, John Crowe Ransom, Edwin Muir and John Betjeman. But the détour has been considerable, and most of the heavy traffic has chosen to travel on it. It is probably time it rejoined the main highway. But, to abandon the metaphor, which is becoming inconvenient, it is no use imagining that things will ever be the same again....All we can say is that some of the most brilliant poetic innovations of the most original poetic talents of our day are probably inimitable and unrepeatable. They cannot be developed any farther, and they have been of a kind from which it is very difficult to learn. Yet they cannot be forgotten or ignored. This I believe is the difficult situation that poetry finds itself in today.

With the exception of Yeats, the "important" modern poets have not been men talking to other men, at least not in any very intelligible fashion: it seems hard to deny this assertion. The common reader has vanished, or has turned from poetry to novels and from novels to history and sociology. But does it really matter? Hough believes it does, for reasons he makes explicit in a later work, *The Dream and the Task*. Here he argues effectively that while "culture" can never be made into a substitute for religion or morals, imaginative literature still provides us with a kind of vital knowledge not available from other sources:

> Literature can do very little to alter the brute facts of power and history. Its capacities in this respect have been generally exaggerated; for this we need to call on other energies; and no amount of literary culture can excuse us from employing them. But it can knock a window in the subtopian fall-out shelter to which contemporary politics and economics seem bent on condemning us. With its aid we have continually before us a view of other possibilities....Knowledge acquired only through these channels [history and anthropology] can too easily remain inert and dead. It is mainly through the arts that these vicarious expansions of our experience can become not mere possessions or accomplishments but a part of our living tissue.

Yet if we are to benefit fully from this vicarious experience we must keep ourselves open to the full range of literature. In a passage very reminiscent of Northrop Frye, Hough concludes that

> Literature is the total dream of man. I used the word dream not sentimentally but advisedly; for literature is not the record of man's doings; that is history; it is not his formal speculation; that is philosophy; literature is man's vision of his condition and his destiny....But one thing seems certain—that if literature is not to fail us in its enormously extended role, we must make use of the whole of literature. Nothing else will do. It must be the whole of man's recorded imaginative experience, not some section of it, selected to agree with some temporary social or moral prejudice. And if a note of asperity has crept into my condemnation of restrictive practices in criticism and education, it is because I believe profoundly that the allegiance of any man who proposes to build his life, or a large part of his life, on literature, must be impartial, all-embracing—it must in principle be an allegiance to the whole.

It follows naturally, then, that criticism should be as open and flexible as Hough's own practical criticism has always managed to be. He is an expert guide to Spenser and the problem of defining allegory and symbolism, to the complexities of D.H. Lawrence, and particularly to the emergent aestheticism of nineteenth-century British poetry and criticism. In *The Last Romantics* Hough typically suggests rather insists upon the value of a Jungian approach to Ruskin, the Pre-Raphaelites, Morris, Pater and Yeats. These were artists who were in "general melancholy agreement that art and the sense of beauty have a rougher time in the modern world than they ever had before" and who sought, in their different ways, a "special artistic point of view" which would justify the cultivation of sensuous perception and the power of imagination to recreate a world which was steadily growing uglier. These are commonplaces by now, but Hough goes further and raises the possibility that these figures were not mere dreamers or escapists. For Jung, art is not simple wish-fulfillment; at its best it is curative, one of the means nature employs to restore balance to a culture which has become one-sided. Hough implies much of this but is curiously reticent in his use of the psychologist "who has done most justice to the depth and variety of human experience." There is no reason why the reader should not be bolder, however, and turn directly from *The Last Romantics* to the essays on literature and psychology in Jung's *Modern Man in Search of a Soul*.

By any standards *An Essay on Criticism* is a depressing performance. Very briefly, Hough argues here that despite their apparent diversity, critical systems are always either "formal" or "ethical": formal criticism is concerned with what literature *is*, ethical criticism asks what literature is *for*. This distinction is so reductive that it can only mislead students and dismay more experienced readers. And having made this simplistic division Hough then predictably argues that criticism ought to be dialectical:

> The enquirer into what literature is for seeks to complete his enquiry by moving inwards towards the centre—what it is. The enquirer into what literature is seeks to complete his enquiry by moving outwards toward the totality of human experience—what it is for. This is a dialectical relation. It should result in a critical synthesis by which it is possible to discuss, in the same discourse and in compatible terms, both the essence of literature and its function, both what it is and what it is for.

Anyone who thinks the fundamental problems of critical methodology can be solved so easily should read Richard P. McKeon and R.S. Crane. From the fragmentary sections which conclude the *Essay* it is hard not to suspect that Hough has grown tired of the entire critical enterprise. If this is true it is of course a pity; but it in no way diminishes the achievement of *The Last Romantics* and *Image and Experience*.

HOWE, Irving. American. Born in New York City, 11 June 1920. Educated at City College of New York, B.Sc. 1940; Brooklyn College, New York. Served in the United States Army, 1942-45. Married Arien Hausknecht; has two children. Associate Professor, and Professor of English, Brandeis University, Waltham, Massachusetts, 1953-61; Christian Gauss Lecturer, Princeton University, New Jersey, 1953; Professor of English, Stanford University, California, 1961-63. Professor of English, 1963-70, and since 1970 Distinguished Professor, Hunter College of the City University of New York. Since 1954, Editor, *Dissent*, New York. Formerly, Visiting Professor, University of Vermont, and University of Washington; Judge, National Book Awards, 1969. Recipient: *Kenyon Review* Fellowship in Criticism, 1953; Longview Foundation prize for literary criticism; Bollingen Award, 1959; National Institute for Arts and Letters Award, 1960; Guggenheim Fellowship, 1964, 1971. Address: Department of English, Hunter College, New York, New York 10021, U.S.A.

PUBLICATIONS

Criticism

Sherwood Anderson: A Critical Biography. New York, Sloane, 1951; London, Methuen, 1952.
William Faulkner: A Critical Study. New York, Random House, 1952; revised edition, 1962.
Politics and the Novel. New York, Horizon Press, 1957; London, Stevens, 1961.
A World More Attractive: A View of Modern Literature and Politics. New York, Horizon Press, 1963.
Thomas Hardy. New York, Macmillan, 1967; London, Weidenfeld and Nicolson, 1968.
Decline of the New. New York, Harcourt Brace, 1970; London, Gollancz, 1971.

The Critical Point: On Literature and Culture.   New York, Horizon Press, 1973.
Celebrations and Attacks: Thirty Years of Literary and Cultural Commentary.   New York, Horizon Press, 1978; London, Deutsch, 1979.

Other

The U.A.W. and Walter Reuther, with B.J. Widick.   New York, Random House, 1949.
The American Communist Party: A Critical History, 1919-1957, with Lewis Coser.   Boston, Beacon Press, 1957.
Steady Work: Essays in the Politics of Democratic Radicalism, 1953-1966.   New York, Harcourt Brace, 1966.
The New Conservatives: A Critique from the Left, with Lewis Coser.   New York, Quadrangle Books-New York Times, 1974.
World of Our Fathers.   New York, Harcourt Brace, 1976; as *The Immigrant Jews of New York 1881 to the Present*, London, Routledge, 1976.
Leon Trotsky.   New York, Viking Press, and London, Fontana, 1978.
How We Lived: A Documentary History of Immigrant Jews in America 1880-1930, with Kenneth Libo.   New York, Marek, 1979.

Editor, *The Essence of Judaism*, by Leo Baeck.   New York, Schocken Books, 1948.
Editor, with Eliezer Greenberg, *A Treasury of Yiddish Stories.*   New York, Viking Press, 1954; London, Deutsch, 1955.
Editor, *Modern Literary Criticism: An Anthology 1919-1957.*   Boston, Beacon Press, 1958.
Editor, *The House of Mirth*, by Edith Wharton.   New York, Holt Rinehart, 1962.
Editor, *Edith Wharton: A Collection of Critical Essays.*   Englewood Cliffs, New Jersey, Prentice Hall, 1962.
Editor, *New Grub Street*, by George Gissing.   Boston, Houghton Mifflin, 1962.
Editor, *Nineteen Eighty-Four: Text, Sources, Criticism*, by George Orwell.   New York, Harcourt Brace, 1963.
Editor, *Basic Writings*, by Leon Trotsky.   New York, Random House, 1963; London, Secker and Warburg, 1964.
Editor, *The Radical Papers.*   New York, Doubleday, 1966.
Editor, *Selected Short Stories*, by Isaac Bashevis Singer.   New York, Modern Library, 1966.
Editor, *Selected Writings: Stories, Poems, and Essays*, by Thomas Hardy.   Greenwich, Connecticut, Fawcett, 1966.
Editor, *The Radical Imagination: An Anthology from Dissent Magazine.*   New York, New American Library, 1967.
Editor, *Student Activism.*   Indianapolis, Bobbs Merrill, 1967.
Editor, *Literary Modernism.*   Greenwich, Connecticut, Fawcett, 1967.
Editor, *The Idea of the Modern in Literature and the Arts.*   New York, Horizon Press, 1968.
Editor, *Classics of Modern Fiction: Eight Short Novels.*   New York, Harcourt Brace, 1968; revised edition, 1972.
Editor, with Jeremy Larner, *Poverty: Views from the Left.*   New York, Morrow, 1968.
Editor, *A Dissenter's Guide to Foreign Policy.*   New York, Praeger, 1968.
Editor, with Eliezer Greenberg, *A Treasury of Yiddish Poetry.*   New York, Holt Rinehart, 1969.
Editor, *Beyond the New Left: A Confrontation and Critique.*   New York, McCall, 1970.
Editor, *Essential Works of Socialism.*   New York, Holt Rinehart, 1970; as *A Handbook of Socialist Thought*, London, Gollancz, 1972.
Editor, *The Literature of America: Nineteenth Century.*   New York, McGraw Hill, 1970.
Editor, *The Blue Collar Worker.*   New York, Quadrangle Books, 1972.
Editor, with Eliezer Greenberg, *Voices from the Yiddish: Essays, Memoirs, Diaries.*   Ann Arbor, University of Michigan Press, 1972.

Editor, with Carl Gershman, *Israel, The Arabs, and the Middle East*. New York, Quadrangle Books, 1972.

Editor, with Michael Harrington, *The Seventies: Problems and Proposals*. New York, Harper, 1972.

Editor, with Eliezer Greenberg, *Yiddish Stories: Old and New*. New York, Holiday House, 1974.

Editor, *Herzog*, by Saul Bellow. New York, Viking Press, 1976.

Editor, with Eliezer Greenberg, *Ashes Out of Hope: Fiction by Soviet-Yiddish Writers*. London and New York, Schocken, 1978.

Editor, *Fiction as Experience: An Anthology*. New York, Harcourt Brace, 1978.

Editor, with Ruth Wisse, *The Best of Sholem Aleichem*. Washington, D.C., New Republic Books, and London, Weidenfeld and Nicolson, 1979.

Editor, *Twenty-Five Years of "Dissent": An American Tradition*. London, Methuen, 1979.

*   *   *

For Irving Howe the responsibilities of criticism, at least of modern literary criticism, have always been closely related to the peculiar nature of "modernism" itself. "The kind of literature called modern," he observes in an early essay,

is almost always difficult; indeed, that is a sign of its modernity. To the established guardians of culture, the modern writer seems wilfully inaccessible. He works with new and unfamiliar forms; he chooses subjects that disturb the audience and lead it to suppose that he is trying to violate its most cherished feelings; he provokes traditionalist critics to such epithets as "unwholesome," "coterie," and "decadent."

At certain points in the development of a culture, usually points of dismay and restlessness, writers find themselves *affronting* their audience; and not from decision or whim but from some deep moral and psychological necessity....Why does this clash arise? Because, for one thing, the modern writer can no longer accept the formal claims of society. When he does try to acquiesce in the norms of the audience, he finds himself depressed or outraged. The usual morality seems to him counterfeit; taste, a genteel indulgence; tradition, a wearisome fetter.

However destructive modernism may seem to be, it has a positive contribution to make to our well-being; and thus Howe quotes—with guarded approval—Eugene Zamiatin's claim that

harmful literature is more useful than useful literature: because it is anti-entropic, militates against calcification, sclerosis, encrustedness, moss, peace. It is utopian and ridiculous. Like Babeuf, in 1797, it is right one hundred and fifty years later.

When modernism is a vital force criticism may therefore take on a "unique importance"; and Howe continues:

To indulge in a useful simplification: the more problematic modern literature seems, the more does criticism need to rehearse the nature of the problem. And that, in response to the growth during the present century of a distinctively modern literature, is what criticism has for the most part been doing.

Some of the critics, usually the younger ones, welcome the new writers and become their champions....These younger critics have as their main purpose the exploration of a new sensibility, and with time they become the mediators between the modern writers and that section of the public which is able, perhaps a bit too late, to respond to such writers.

But during periods of stasis and decadence criticism finds itself without a cause to champion:

Started early in the present century, [modernism] had come to an end by the mid-fifties. The *avant garde* has now disappeared almost entirely, and the enormous impetus—the zest, animation, and self-confidence—it had imparted to criticism has also largely disappeared....[If] criticism now finds itself in a state of uncertainty and perhaps even exhaustion, one reason must surely be that it has lost the buoying sense of purpose that had come from the *avant garde* experience.

Yet even at such times criticism may still have an honorable mission to carry out: "The preservation of taste in a time of mass-produced vulgarity; the defense of literacy against its systematized public abuse; a restatement of faith in the power of the private imagination—these were among the tasks that modern critics set for themselves."

What Howe meant by the exhaustion of the *avant garde* was not clear, however, until his later essays, "The Culture of Modernism" (reprinted in *Decline of the New*) and "What's the Trouble?" (the important opening essay of *The Critical Point*). Modernism is still defined as a movement "committed to the view that the human lot is inescapably problematic," but there are two basic reasons why its energies have been dissipated. In the first place it is hard to maintain the stance of the rebel: "this commitment to the problematic...requires nerves of iron; and even as the great figures of modernism sense that for them everything depends on keeping a firm grip on the idea of the problematic, many of them cannot resist completely the invading powers of ideology and system." And in the second place modernism paradoxically found itself courted and rewarded by bourgeois culture:

> Bracing enmity has given way to wet embraces, the middle class has discovered that the fiercest attacks upon its values can be transposed into pleasing entertainments, and the avant garde writer or artist must confront the one challenge for which he has not been prepared: the challenge of success. Contemporary society is endlessly assimilative, even if it vulgarizes what it has learned, sometimes foolishly, to praise. The avant garde is thereby no longer allowed the integrity of opposition or the cosiness of sectarianism; it must either watch helplessly its gradual absorption into the surrounding culture or try to preserve its distinctiveness by continually raising the ante of sensation and shock—itself a course leading, perversely, to a growing popularity with the bourgeois audience.

"What's the Trouble?" completes the argument and brings it up to date. In "The Culture of Modernism" Howe had remarked, rather cryptically, that "the terror which haunts the modern mind is that of a meaningless and eternal death." But as he explains in the later essay it is not simply death which terrifies us; it is the feeling that without some transcendental sanctions life itself is meaningless. While we may know that science is correct in denying our hopes of transcendence, the desire nevertheless remains unconquerable; and if thwarted in one area of life it will reappear in distorted form somewhere else:

> By an irony too painful to underscore, it is only in Eastern Europe that intellectuals have come to appreciate the value of liberal institutions. In the West, a mere three decades after the ravages of totalitarianism, there is again visible a strident contempt for the ethic of liberal discourse and the style of rationality. In part this arises from the mixed failings and successes of the welfare state, but in part from an upswell of unacknowledged and ill-understood religious sentiments that, unable to find a proper religious outlet, become twisted into moral and political absolutism, a hunger for total solutions and apocalyptic visions. Impatience with the sluggish masses, burning convictions of righteousness, the suffocation of technological society, the boredom of over-crowded cities, the yearning for transcendent ends beyond the petty limits of group interest, romantic-sinister illusions about the charismatic virtues of dictatorship in under-developed countries—all these tempt young people into apolitical politics, at best communes and at worst bombs, but both sharing an amorphous revulsion from civilization itself.

Howe has always been explicit about his own values: he is a socialist, an intellectual who believes in "democractic radicalism" but who has never denied the rich heritage of liberalism or doubted the importance of rational discourse. What is new in his later work is the forcefulness with which he identifies the enemies—on the Left as well as on the Right—of liberal humanism. Yet necessary as the values of humanism are, Howe also recognizes that no political program can meet the demands which a thwarted hope for ultimate explanations provokes:

The question that must then follow, and which it would be foolish to try to answer, is this: can a reasonably decent society, liberal in its political style and egalitarian in its socioeconomic outlook, survive in the conditions likely to exist during the next fifty or sixty years?...[There] is a problem here of the gravest difficulty through one that has come to seem acute only recently. Such a liberal or social democratic society may well provide the best conditions for human beings to live in; but insofar as it comes closer to realization, it may not provide spiritual or psychic goals that will satisfy the people who live in it, at least those most inclined to sentience and restlessness.

It may already be too late to establish such a society, whatever its inadequacies. The drift towards conservativism may bring us to a "half welfare and half garrison society in which the population grows passive, indifferent and atomized...and in which man becomes a consumer, himself mass-produced like the products, diversions and values that he absorbs." We may be moving towards "a quiet desert of moderation where men will forget the passion of moral and spiritual restlessness that has characterized Western society." Nor does the New Left and the literature it inspires offer any greater hope for the preservation of liberal humanism:

> We are confronting, then, a new phase in our culture, which in motive and spring represents a wish to shake off the bleeding heritage of modernism and reinstate one of those periods of the collective naïf which seems endemic to American experience. The new sensibility is impatient with ideas. It is impatient with literary structure of complexity and coherence, only yesterday the catchwords of our criticism. It wants instead works of literature—though literature may be the wrong word—that will be as absolute as the sun, as unarguable as orgasm, and as delicious as a lollipop. It schemes to throw off the weight of nuance and ambiguity, legacies of high consciousness and tired blood. It is weary of the habit of reflection, the making of distinctions, the squareness of dialectic, the tarnished gold of inherited wisdom. It cares nothing for the haunted memories of old Jews. It has no taste for the ethical nail-biting of those writers of the left who suffered defeat and could never again accept the narcotic of uncertainty. It is sick of those magnifications of irony that Mann gave us, sick of those visions of entrapment to which Kafka led us, sick of those shufflings of daily horror and grace that Joyce left us. It breathes contempt for rationality, impatience with mind, and a hostility to the artifices and decorums of high culture. It despises liberal values, liberal cautions, liberal virtues. It is bored with the past: for the past is a fink.

(These words were written at the end of the sixties, when the New Left seemed to have some political vitality. A few years later Howe observed that he now found little comfort in the early death of the movement, "for together with the gross delusions...there were genuine stirrings of moral outrage, creditable impulses of social rebelliousness and idealism.") Yet despite his pessimism concerning the forces which now threaten liberalism, Howe has never doubted that "freedom is our signature" or that

> the obligation to defend and extend freedom in its simplest and most fundamental aspects is the sacred task of the intellectual, the one task he must not compromise even when his posture seems intractable, or unreasonable, or hopeless, or even when it means standing alone against fashionable shibboleths like Revolution or The Third World.

Nor has he lost his faith that the artist—and his critics—have always stood, in Trotsky's words, for "a world more attractive than any other."

All these excursions into social history may seem far removed from the actual business of literary criticism, but it should be clear by now that it is impossible to separate Howe the critic from Howe the cultural historian and liberal humanist. He is a prolific, often repetitious and sometimes derivative critic, but always animated by a shrewd sense of how society may shape and limit an artist (*Sherwood Anderson*), of how an artist may both recreate and criticize his social myths (*William Faulkner*, for example, or the essays on Edith Wharton), of how artists befriend or betray liberalism and reason, and of how, finally (in *Politics and the Novel*), overtly ideological issues enter into the fabric of literature. Still, Howe's firm sense of values has never dictated a fixed critical "method." At its best criticism is a "personal art" in which the power of insight counts far more than allegiance to a critical theory or position....The best method could not make a mediocre man into a good critic; the worst can do a sensitive critic harm but not, I think, suppress his gifts indefinitely. And no method can give the critic what he needs most: knowledge, disinterestedness, love, insight, style. "The only method," Eliot once wrote, "is to be very intelligent." He might have added that it is also the hardest method.

For some critics a professed suspicion of method can be an easy excuse for random impressionism, but it would be a mistake to put Howe in their company. Rarely as "intelligent" as, say, Edmund Wilson or Alfred Kazin, he is still something more than a mere literary journalist.

HYMAN, Stanley Edgar. American. Born in New York City, 11 June 1919. Educated at Syracuse University, New York, B.A. 1940. Married the novelist Shirley Jackson in 1940 (died, 1965), four children; Phoebe Pettingell, 1966, one child. Editorial Assistant, *The New Republic*, New York, 1940; Staff Writer, *The New Yorker*, 1940-70; Literary Critic, *The New Leader*, New York, 1961-65. Member of the Literature Faculty, Bennington College, Vermont, 1945-46, 1952-70. Visiting Professor, State University of New York at Buffalo, 1969-70. Recipient: American Council of Learned Societies Fellowship, 1959; National Institute of Arts and Letters Award in Criticism, 1967; Guggenheim Fellowship, 1969. *Died 29 July 1970.*

PUBLICATIONS

Criticism

The Armed Vision: A Study in the Methods of Modern Literary Criticism. New York, Knopf, 1948; revised edition, 1955.
Poetry and Criticism: Four Revolutions in Literary Taste. New York, Atheneum, 1961.
Nathanael West. Minneapolis, University of Minnesota Press, 1962.
The Tangled Bank: Darwin, Marx, Frazer and Freud as Imaginative Writers. New York, Atheneum, 1962.
The Promised End: Essays and Reviews, 1942-1962. Cleveland, World, 1963.
Standards: A Chronicle of Books for Our Time. New York, Horizon Press, 1966.
Flannery O'Connor. Minneapolis, University of Minnesota Press, 1966.
Iago: Some Approaches to the Illusion of His Motivation. New York, Atheneum, 1970; London, Elek, 1971.
The Critic's Credentials: Essays and Reviews, edited by Phoebe Pettingell. New York, Atheneum, 1978.

Other

Editor, *The Critical Performance: An Anthology of American and British Literary Criticism of Our Century.* New York, Knopf, 1956.
Editor, *Darwin for Today: The Essence of His Works.* New York, Viking Press, 1963.
Editor, with Barbara Karlmiller, *Perspectives by Incongruity* and *Terms for Order* (selections from the work of Kenneth Burke). Bloomington, Indiana University Press, 2 vols., 1964.

Editor, *The Magic of Shirley Jackson*. New York, Farrar Straus, 1966.
Editor, *Selected Essays*, by William Troy. New Brunswick, New Jersey, Rutgers University Press, 1967.
Editor, *Come Along with Me*, by Shirley Jackson. New York, Viking Press, 1968.

CRITICAL STUDY

Howard Nemerov, "A Survey of Criticism," in *Poetry and Fiction: Essays*. New Brunswick, New Jersey, Rutgers University Press, 1963

*   *   *

However obvious its limitations seem now, *The Armed Vision* was widely read and generally admired for a number of years after its first appearance. Stanley Edgar Hyman was a guide who had read everything, who was undaunted by Burke and Empson, and who confidently offered, on his opening page, an italicized reason for the extraordinary vitality of Anglo-American criticism between the two World Wars. Modern criticism, Hyman proposed, is characterized primarily by "*the organized use of non-literary techniques and bodies of knowledge to obtain insights into literature.*" The past thirty years had been years of growth and achievement not because of a sudden proliferation of new Aristotles and Coleridges, but because non-literary disciplines (sociology, psychology, cultural anthropology and in fact any investigation of "man functioning in the group") provided a firm basis for the collective efforts of modestly gifted critics. The analogy to science is important here: for Hyman literature is an object of definite if not precisely scientific knowledge, once fundamental principles have been established. Thus the superiority which John Crowe Ransom claimed for the criticism of our own times rests on the new understanding of human behavior provided by four authentic masters, Darwin, Marx, Frazer and Freud. From Darwin, Hyman argues, we derive

the view of man as part of the natural order, and of culture as an evolutionary development. From Marx, the concept of literature as reflecting, in however complex and indirect a fashion, the social and productive relations of its time. From Freud, the concept of literature as the disguised expression and fulfillment of repressed wishes, on the analogy of dreams, with these disguises operating in accord with known principles; and underlying that, the even more basic assumptions of mental levels beneath consciousness and some conflict between an expressive and a censorship principle. From Frazer, the view of primitive magic, myth, and ritual underlying the most transcendent literary patterns and themes.

(A number of years later, in *The Tangled Bank*, Hyman provided a useful popularization of these four figures, but in *The Armed Vision* their commanding importance is simply taken for granted).

Hyman devotes a chapter to each of twelve influential critics (and those more or less associated with their points of view) but warns that his approach is not merely descriptive or explanatory; it is, rather, "both biased and opinionated." Thus he begins his survey with Yvor Winters, T.S. Eliot and Van Wyck Brooks (who represent, respectively, "evaluation in criticism," "tradition in criticism," and "biographical criticism") and makes it clear that he has little sympathy with their values—particularly the "reactionary-aristocratic-religious" values of Winters and Eliot. His treatment of Winters in this respect is typical: while modern criticism might profitably adopt his "vigor and boldness of evaluation," it should also strive for "sounder evaluations than his." Winters is finally "an excessively irritating and bad critic of some importance." Hyman is much more sympathetic to the folk criticism of Constance Rourke, the Jungian criticism of Maud Bodkin, the scholarly criticism of Caroline Spurgeon and the exegetical criticism of R.P. Blackmur (these crude classifications prevent him from seeing that Blackmur's criticism, for example, is at least as evaluative as Winters'). Hyman's greatest approval, however, is reserved for Empson, Richards and Burke, all of whom approach literature in a "scientific" manner and hold values he has no difficulty accepting. The omission of Ransom (referred to only in passing) and F.R. Leavis (referred to briefly and inappropriately in the chapter on Empson) is a serious drawback, and since the book was published in 1948 it could not take into account later important work by Richards, Empson and Burke.

In his final chapter, "Attempts at Integration," Hyman argues that the ideal critic would be that paragon who combined the virtues of all the critics just discussed. This ideal synthesis is probably impossible, however—especially now:

> our best critics never seem to have enough time or space to go as far as they would like, and the demand on their learning is formidable. In the future we can expect that the burden of having a working command of every field of man's knowledge applicable to literary criticism will grow increasingly difficult to bear, and eventually simply become impossible. With the tremendous growth of the social sciences in particular, sooner or later knowing enough of any one of them to turn it fruitfully on literature will demand a life study, leaving no time for anything else except some acquaintance with the corpus of literature itself.

But there is another, more fundamental reason why this composite critic is an impossibility. R.S. Crane has argued convincingly (in *The Languages of Criticism and the Structure of Poetry* and elsewhere) that since the reality criticism investigates is too complex to be encompassed by any one frame of reference, we need a multiplicity of separate methods, each with its own proper aim, powers and limitations. The simplistic eclecticism proposed by Hyman is a logical as well as a practical impossibility. And there is a final difficulty with *The Armed Vision* which Howard Nemerov emphasized in a sharp early review of the book:

> At last, who is to read this work, and what is he to read it for? Do we envision the tired businessman getting around the problem of "modern poetry" by reading a highly rational account of what some people have said about it? Or the undergraduate, cramming for that quiz on the fallacy of expressive form? Or the graduate student, for whose proposed teaching career the book may represent almost the entire critical equipment? Or perhaps the full professor, whose relation with modern criticism will not run to marriage but may include this brief liaison? For if you haven't read the major texts with which the book works you are reading a popularization, of a very educational sort, of course (somehow these doctrines are always considerably easier in Mr. Hyman's version than in the originals, where the train of thought is always being interrupted by the consideration of a poem); if you have read them and studied them you may be charmed with Mr. Hyman or alarmed at him...but you probably will not be instructed by him.

As a practicing critic, Hyman is usually disappointing. His reviews for *The New Yorker* and *The New Leader* (now collected in *Standards* and *The Promised End*) are too brief and topical to be of much interest now, and a more ambitious undertaking, *Poetry and Criticism*, fails because of its depressingly reductive "theory." The true relationship between poetry and criticism, Hyman asserts, lies in the fact that

> revolutions in criticism follow after revolutions in poetry, sometimes long after, codifying and consolidating them. When a critic makes a general statement about all poetry, he tends to have some particular poetry in mind, which he takes to be the ideal. We can best see this by reducing the multiplicity of literature in any given period to four representative specimens. A is the original poem, which we will call the *standard*. B is the criticism which erects the A poem's formal organization into general principles, the *poetics*. C is the new or deviant work that cannot be accommodated to the critical principles of B, and we will call it the *challenge*. D is the new critical generalization that arises out of and justifies C, and it might be called the *sanction*.

Thus in his first chapter Hyman finds that while Aristotle's *Poetics* is the perfect sanction for a tragedy like *Oedipus*, it cannot deal with a play like *Medea*. The challenge of that play is met only by Longinus. Shakespeare's *Antony and Cleopatra* was exalted by one generation but challenged by Dryden in the next; *The Rape of the Lock* is challenged by *Resolution and*

Independence, Arnold's defense of the Grand Style by Eliot's theory and practice, and so on. Hyman never speculates about the more interesting question of why these revolutions occur in the first place: it all seems as pointless and mechanical as the endless swing of a pendulum.

JARRELL, Randall.   American.   Born in Nashville, Tennessee, 6 May 1914. Educated at Vanderbilt University, Nashville, B.S. (Phi Beta Kappa) in psychology 1936, M.A. in English 1939. Served as a celestial navigation tower operator in the United States Army Air Corps, 1942-46. Married Mary Eloise von Schrader in 1952. Instructor in English, Kenyon College, Gambier, Ohio, 1937-39, University of Texas, Austin, 1939-42, and Sarah Lawrence College, Bronxville, New York, 1946-47; Associate Professor, 1947-58, and Professor of English, 1958-65, Women's College of the University of North Carolina (later, University of North Carolina at Greensboro). Lecturer, Salzburg Seminar in American Civilization, 1948; Visiting Fellow in Creative Writing, Princeton University, New Jersey, 1951-52; Fellow, Indiana School of Letters, Bloomington, Summer 1952; Visiting Professor of English, University of Illinois, Urbana, 1953; Elliston Lecturer, University of Cincinnati, Ohio, 1958. Acting Literary Editor, *The Nation*, New York, 1946-47; Poetry Critic, *Partisan Review*, New Brunswick, New Jersey, 1949-53, and *Yale Review*, New Haven, Connecticut, 1955-57; Member of the Editorial Board, *American Scholar*, Washington, D.C., 1957-65. Consultant in Poetry, Library of Congress, Washington, D.C., 1956-58. Recipient: *Southern Review* Prize, 1936; Jeanette Sewell Davis Prize, 1943, Levinson Prize, 1948, and Oscar Blumenthal Prize, 1951 (*Poetry*, Chicago); J.P. Bishop Memorial Literary Prize (*Sewanee Review*), 1946; Guggenheim Fellowship, 1946; National Institute of Arts and Letters grant, 1951; National Book Award, 1961; Oliver Max Gardner Award, University of North Carolina, 1962; American Association of University Women Juvenile Award, 1964; Ingram Merrill Award, 1965. D.H.L.: Bard College, Annandale-on-Hudson, New York, 1962. Member, National Institute of Arts and Letters; Chancellor, Academy of American Poets, 1956. *Died 14 October 1965.*

PUBLICATIONS

Criticism

> *Poetry and the Age.*   New York, Knopf, 1953; London, Faber, 1955.
> *Poets, Critics, and Readers.*   Charlottesville, University of Virginia Press, 1959; reprinted in *A Sad Heart at the Supermarket*, 1962.
> *A Sad Heart at the Supermarket: Essays and Fables.*   New York, Atheneum, 1962; London, Eyre and Spottiswoode, 1965.
> *The Third Book of Criticism.*   New York, Farrar Straus, 1969; London, Faber, 1974.
> *Kipling, Auden & Co.: Essays and Reviews 1935-1967.*   New York, Farrar Straus, 1980; Manchester, Carcanet Press, 1981.

Verse

Five Young American Poets, with others.   New York, New Directions, 1940.
Blood for a Stranger.   New York, Harcourt Brace, 1942.
Little Friend, Little Friend.   New York, Dial Press, 1945.
Losses.   New York, Harcourt Brace, 1948.
The Seven-League Crutches.   New York, Harcourt Brace, 1951.
Selected Poems.   New York, Knopf, 1955; London, Faber, 1956.
Uncollected Poems.   Privately printed, 1958.
The Woman at the Washington Zoo: Poems and Translations.   New York, Atheneum, 1960.
Selected Poems.   New York, Atheneum, 1964.
The Lost World: New Poems.   New York, Macmillan, 1965; London, Eyre and Spottiswoode, 1966.
The Complete Poems.   New York, Farrar Straus, 1969; London, Faber, 1971.
The Achievement of Randall Jarrell: A Comprehensive Selection of His Poems with a Critical Introduction, by Frederick J. Hoffman.   Chicago, Scott Foresman, 1970.
Jerome: The Biography of a Poem.   New York, Grossman, 1971.

Novel

Pictures from an Institution: A Comedy.   New York, Knopf, and London, Faber, 1954.

Play

The Three Sisters, adaptation of a play by Chekov (produced New York, 1964).   New York, Macmillan, 1969.

Other

The Gingerbread Rabbit (juvenile).   New York, Macmillan, and London, Collier Macmillan, 1964.
The Bat-Poet (juvenile).   New York, Macmillan, 1964; London, Collier Macmillan, 1966.
The Animal Family (juvenile).   New York, Pantheon, 1965; London, Hart Davis, 1967.

Editor, *The Anchor Book of Stories*.   New York, Doubleday, 1958.
Editor, *The Best Short Stories of Rudyard Kipling*.   New York, Hanover House, 1961; as *In the Vernacular: The English in India* and *The English in England*, New York, Doubleday, 2 vols., 1963.
Editor, *Six Russian Short Novels*.   New York, Doubleday, 1963.

Translator, with Moses Hadas, *The Ghetto and the Jews of Rome*, by Ferdinand Gregorovius.   New York, Schocken, 1948.
Translator, *The Rabbit Catcher and Other Fairy Tales of Ludwig Bechstein*.   New York, Macmillan, and London, Macmillan, 1962.
Translator, *The Golden Bird and Other Fairy Tales by the Brothers Grimm*.   New York, Macmillan, 1962.
Translator, *Snow White and the Seven Dwarfs: A Tale from the Brothers Grimm*.   New York, Farrar Straus, 1972; London, Penguin, 1974.
Translator, *The Juniper Tree and Other Tales by the Brothers Grimm*.   New York, Farrar Straus, 1973.

306

Translator, *Goethe's Faust, Part One*.   New York, Farrar Straus, 1976; London Faber, 1978.

CRITICAL STUDIES AND BIBLIOGRAPHY

Charles M. Adams, *Randall Jarrell: A Bibliography*.   Chapel Hill, University of North Carolina Press, and London, Oxford University Press, 1958; supplement in *Analects* (Greensboro, North Carolina), 1, 1961.
Randall Jarrell, 1914-1965, edited by Robert Lowell, Peter Taylor and Robert Penn Warren.   New York, Farrar Straus, 1967.
Frederick J. Hoffman, introduction to *The Achievement of Randall Jarrell: A Comprehensive Selection of His Poems with a Critical Introduction*.   Chicago, Scott Foresman, 1970.
Suzanne Ferguson, *The Poetry of Randall Jarrell*.   Baton Rouge, Louisiana State University Press, 1971.

*   *   *

In one of his best-known essays, "The Obscurity of the Poet," Randall Jarrell argues that art matters

not only because it is the most magnificent ornament and the most clearly unfailing occupation of our lives, but because it is life itself. From Christ to Freud we have believed that, if we know the truth, the truth will set us free: art is indispensable because so much of this truth can be learned through works of art and through works of art alone—for which of us could have learned for himself what Proust and Chekov, Hardy and Yeats and Rilke, Shakespeare and Homer learned for us? and in what other way could they have made us see the truths which they themselves saw, those differing and contradictory truths which seem nevertheless, to the mind which contains them, in some sense a single truth? And all these things, by their very nature, demand to be shared; if we are satisfied to know these things ourselves and to look with superiority and indifference at those who do not have that knowledge, we have made a refusal that corrupts us as surely as anything can....One of the oldest, deepest, and most nearly conclusive attractions of democracy is manifested in our feeling that through it not only material but also spiritual goods can be shared; that in a democracy bread and justice, education and art, will be accessible to everybody.

And he concludes that the only way in which we can come to terms with the power of art is the way of "love." The function of the critic follows naturally from all of this: since the truths of art "demand to be shared," since democracy must provide spiritual as well as material goods, and since there are forces at work in modern society which degrade the imagination, the critic must serve the works he has come to love, mediating between them and the public.

In "Poets, Critics, and Readers" Jarrell continues

All of us have read criticism in which the critic takes it for granted that what he writes about comes first, and what he writes comes second—takes it for granted that he is writing as a reader to other readers, to be of use to them; criticism in which the critic works, as far as he is able, in the spirit of Wordsworth's "I have endeavored to look steadily at my subject." All of us have some favorite, exceptional critic who might say, with substantial truth, that he has not set up rigid standards to which a true work of art must conform, but that he has tried instead to let many true works of art—his experience of them—set up the general expectation to which his criticism of art conforms; that he has tried never to see a work of art as mere raw material for criticism, data for generalization; that he has tried never to forget the difference between creating a work of art and criticizing a work of art.

This is also true of Jarrell's own best criticism. He obviously loves the poetry of Marianne Moore, Frost and Whitman, among others, and manages to convey that love in a felicitious and convincing way. And since he is also a "sensitive empiricist," to use a phrase of Goethe's he was fond of quoting, it would be impossible to reduce his discussions of poetry or fiction to a fixed method. He has a positive genius for finding the exact quotation which will bring to life his often quite ordinary generalizations; he happily makes substantial lists for his readers, telling them exactly which poems to read and in what order; and like many lovers, he frequently goes on for far too long (his effusive fifty-page appreciation of Christina Stead's *The Man Who Loved Children*, for example, or his interminable analysis of Frost's "Home Burial," that moving but after all not very obscure poem).

Since Jarrell favors lists as a means of criticism it may not be completely unfair to propose a list of what seems most valuable in his own books of criticism: from *Poetry and the Age*, two essays on Frost which did yeoman service when that poet was admired for the wrong reasons, and an equally fine pair of essays on Marianne Moore; from *A Sad Heart at the Supermarket*, marred as that collection is by shrill protests against the anti-intellectualism of American life, a convincing essay on Kipling's powerful short fiction, and a devastating account of the glories and fatuities of Malraux's *The Voices of Silence*; and from *The Third Book of Criticism*, an examination of the weakness of middle-period Auden, a handsome tribute to Wallace Stevens, and a genuinely helpful essay on the hard-to-place virtues of Robert Graves (and the White Goddess in his career, Laura Riding). "In place of a hermeneutics of art," Susan Sontag maintains in *Against Interpretation*, "we need an erotics of art": we need the sort of critic who will supply "a really accurate, sharp, loving description of the appearance of a work of art." And when called upon to name a critic who could do just that, she quite rightly chose Randall Jarrell.

KAZIN, Alfred.   American.   Born in Brooklyn, New York, 5 June 1915.   Educated at the City College of New York, B.S.S. 1935 (Phi Beta Kappa); Columbia University, New York, M.A. 1938. Married Natasha Kazin; Caroline Bookman in 1947 (divorced), one son; Ann Birstein, 1952, one daughter. Literary Editor, 1942-43, and Contributing Editor, 1943-45, *The New Republic*, New York; Contributing Editor, *Fortune*, New York, 1943-44. Tutor in Literature, City College of New York, 1937-42; Lecturer, Black Mountain College, North Carolina, ·1944; Visiting Professor, University of Minnesota, Minneapolis, Summers 1946, 1950; Fulbright Lecturer, Cambridge University, 1952; Lecturer, Harvard University, Cambridge, Massachusetts, 1953; William Allan Neilson Research Professor, Smith College, Northampton, Massachusetts, 1954-55; Professor of American Studies, Amherst College, Massachusetts, 1955-58; Berg Professor of Literature, City College of New York, 1957; Visiting Professor, University of Puerto Rico, Rio Piedras, 1959; Christian Gauss Lecturer, Princeton University, New Jersey, 1961; Buell Gallagher Professor, City College of New York, 1962; Beckman Professor, University of California, Berkeley, 1963; Distinguished Professor of English, State University of New York at Stony Brook, 1963-73. Since 1973, Professor of English, Hunter College, New York City. Senior Fellow, Center for Advanced Study in the Behavioral Sciences, Stanford, California, 1977-78; Visiting Professor, Notre Dame University, South Bend, Indiana, 1978-79. Recipient: Guggenheim Fellowship, 1940, 1947; Rockefeller Fellowship, 1945; George Polk Memorial Prize for Criticism, 1966; Brandeis University Creative Arts Award, 1973. D.Litt: Adelphi University, Garden City, New York, 1965. Member, National Institute of Arts and Letters; American Academy of Arts and Sciences. Address: Department of English, City University of New York, 33 West 42nd Street, New York, New York 10036, U.S.A.

PUBLICATIONS

Criticism

> *On Native Grounds*: *An Interpretation of Modern American Prose Literature*.   New
> York, Reynal, 1942; London, Cape, 1943.
> *The Inmost Leaf*: *A Selection of Essays*.   New York, Harcourt Brace, 1955.
> *Contemporaries*.   Boston, Little Brown, 1962; London, Secker and Warburg, 1963.
> *Bright Book of Life: American Novelists and Storytellers from Hemingway to Mailer*.
> Boston, Little Brown, 1973; London, Secker and Warburg, 1974.
> "On Modernism," in *New Republic* (New York), 17 January 1976.

Other

> *A Walker in the City* (autobiography).   New York, Harcourt Brace, 1951; London,
> Gollancz, 1952.
> *Starting Out in the Thirties* (autobiography).   Boston, Little Brown, 1965; London,
> Secker and Warburg, 1966.
> *New York Jew* (autobiography).   New York, Knopf, and London, Secker and Warburg,
> 1978.
>
> Editor, *The Portable Blake*.   New York, Viking Press, 1946; as *The Essential Blake*,
> London, Chatto and Windus, 1968.
> Editor, *F. Scott Fitzgerald: The Man and His Work*.   Cleveland, World, 1951.
> Editor, with Charles Shapiro, *The Stature of Theodore Dreiser*: *A Critical Study of the
> Man and His Work*.   Bloomington, Indiana University Press, 1955.
> Editor, *Moby Dick*, by Herman Melville.   Boston, Houghton Mifflin, 1959.
> Editor, with Ann Birstein, *The Works of Anne Frank*.   New York, Doubleday, 1959.
> Editor, with Daniel Aaron, *Emerson*: *A Modern Anthology*.   Boston, Houghton
> Mifflin, 1959.
> Editor, *Sister Carrie*, by Theodore Dreiser.   New York, Dell, 1960.
> Editor, *The Financier*, by Theodore Dreiser.   New York, Dell, 1961.
> Editor, *The Open Form*: *Essays for Our Time*.   New York, Harcourt Brace, 1961; revised
> edition, 1965.
> Editor, *Selected Short Stories*, by Nathaniel Hawthorne.   Greenwich, Connecticut,
> Fawcett, 1966.
> Editor, *Writers at Work*: *The Paris Review Interviews*, *Third Series*.   New York, Viking
> Press, 1967.
> Editor, *The Ambassadors*, by Henry James.   New York, Bantam Books, 1969.

*   *   *

A few years ago Alfred Kazin complained about editors who were indifferent to his values
and readers who "come up to say how much they 'enjoyed' a piece but who never discuss the
argument in it." Since the argument is a serious and disturbing one no doubt Kazin's disappointment is real enough; but his readers are not entirely at fault here. "No critic who is any
good," he continues, "sets out deliberately to enlighten someone else; he writes to put his own
ideas in order." And in fact it would have taken an unusually devoted reader, prior to *Bright
Book of Life*, to piece together the argument Kazin has been developing in scores of reviews and
brief essays over the past thirty-five years.

In the mid-thirties, Kazin recalls, "I thought of Socialism as orthodox Christians might think
of the Second Coming—a wholly supernatural event which one might await with perfect faith."
He began *On Native Grounds* shortly after this, in 1938, and as he explored the "dark seedtime"
of modern American letters he came to feel as if he were living

in the dark revolutionary time of the Eighties and Nineties, with "the struggle for realism" and the Knights of Labor, and that everything was about to flower in the revolutionary *avant-garde* of Greenwich Village. When I read Randolph Bourne and the young Van Wyck Brooks of *America's Coming of Age*, I could not feel that 1938 was so far from 1912. Like so many writers who came of age in the Thirties, I took for granted the continuing spirit of the Twenties that I knew from *Winesburg, Ohio* and *Prejudices* and *The Sun Also Rises*. I was sure that we of the revolutionary Thirties would retain what was vital in the great books of the Twenties and direct it toward a more hopeful outlook, a fraternal society. We would improve on the nihilism of Hemingway, the callousness of Mencken, the frivolity of Sinclair Lewis. Like so many literary radicals who were becoming interested in American literature, I thought I could see across the wasteland of the Twenties to our real literary brethren in the utopians and Socialist bohemians of 1912. I felt connected to the Socialist Van Wyck Brooks, the libertarian and revolutionary pacifist Randolph Bourne, the Edmund Wilson who in *Axel's Castle* had described the great twentieth-century writers as breaking down the wall of the present. My mind was full of Taine and Brandes and Sainte-Beuve and Francisco De Sanctus and Renan, with their comprehensive sense of literature and their organic vision of history that seemed to unite man to his proper destiny. Working on my book, I felt radicalism as a spiritual passion; I was helping to direct a new impulse into the future. We were in revolution, prodigiously on the move again, as in that glorious season before the First World War, whose greatest spirits everywhere had been *literary* radicals, the *avant-garde* in every department of life. The young Van Wyck Brooks had affirmed that literary criticism "is always impelled sooner or later to become social criticism...because the future of our literature and art depends upon the wholesale reconstruction of a social life all the elements of which are as if united in a sort of conspiracy against the growth and freedom of the spirit." *There* was the voice I recognized, the vocation I loved; I wanted to see a radical slashing insurgency of spirit to take over in everything, so that life would be purified and beautiful and everyone would live as Natasha [Kazin's first wife] and I lived in the radiance of cultural truth.

But by the time Kazin finished the book in 1942, the Spanish Civil War was over, Stalin had signed the non-aggression pact with Hitler ("'No!' I shouted at the radio. 'It's not true!'"), and America had gone to war. What would never come back, Kazin concludes, was "the faith in a wholly new society that had been implicit in the revolutionary ideal." Yet at the same time he and his friends from the *Nation, New Republic* and *Partisan Review* managed to share a "fundamental realism about our society and obstinate hopes for mankind." Whatever disappointments Kazin experienced during the forties and fifties, he never seems to have waivered in his conviction that "the eventual vindication of life by the imagination is what gives meaning to every great artist's life, and it is the critic's job to support this belief, to delineate it, fight for it."

Had Kazin completed *On Native Grounds* before the Second World War, it might have been a different book, more programatic, more confident that America was fulfilling the dream of a fraternal society. As it is, however, *On Native Grounds* hovers between optimism and doubt. Kazin is an expert at tracing the rise of social realism but recognizes that the great American books have always been marked by "tragic complexity":

it was this same conviction that American "modernism" grew principally out of its surprise before the forces making a new world that led me to understand a little better what is for me the greatest single fact about our modern American writing—our writers' absorption in every last detail of their American world together with their deep and subtle alienation from it.

There is a terrible estrangement in this writing, a nameless yearning for a world no one ever really possessed, that rises above the skills our writers have mastered and the famous repeated liberations they have won to speak out plainly about the life men lead in America. All modern writers, it may be, have known that alienation equally well, and for all the reasons that make up the history of the modern spirit; have known it and learned to live with what they have and what they are. But what interested me here was our alienation *on* native grounds....

No one, he admits, can tell us *why* Fitzgerald was so profoundly right when he said that "there are no second acts in American lives"

> or why we have been so oppressed by the sense of time, or why our triumphs have been so brittle. We can only feel the need of a fuller truth then we possess, and bring in our fragment and wait. So is this book only a panel in the larger story, and not merely because it is limited to prose. It is in part an effort at moral history, which is greater than literary history, and is needed to illuminate it.

"Alienation" is to be understood here in the usual Marxist sense and the "fuller truth" probably refers to revolutionary goals, but Kazin does not press the point and *On Native Grounds* is a better book because of his hesitation to do so (in this respect he is a far more sophisticated critic than, say, Granville Hicks, who "wrote as if history—even literature—consisted in coherent answers to sensible questions"). He loves the activity of describing books, even awful ones if they can tell us something interesting about life in America, and he has always had the gift of gathering up details lucidly and compactly, like a man, as he once said of Edmund Wilson, "whose life hangs on the rightness of every sentence."

By 1955 the argument had taken a darker turn. The burst of creative energy set loose around 1914 appeared to be spent: "No one knows what the times are like any longer," Kazin now concluded: "step by step the great confidence that man could understand his time and build from it...has gone from us." Thus *Bright Book of Life* is a kind of summing up, in part an elegy for the passing of modernism and in part a troubled, authoritative survey of American writers who had come into their own since 1945 (always excluding the poets and dramatists, who have never really engaged Kazin's attention). Hemingway and Faulkner, the two lonely moderns who lived on into the fifties and sixties, receive their tributes as the last members of a generation for whom true style could still be an act of affronting the "falseness and inconsequence of the world." Hemingway "came...to identify literature with the act of writing, writing as the word-for-word struggle against the murkiness of death":

> Hemingway's was the perfect reduction, the ultimate logic, of this modernist faith: what was unmistakable would be indestructible. Immortality existed, for artists. Dos Passos, with the same esthetic, was able to organize this special gift for one-to-one definition in the mechanics of *U.S.A.* The same urgency of form explains the felt excitement behind Fitzgerald's fiction—"that stamp that goes into my books so that people can read it blind like Braille."...As a style in the largest sense, a way of putting everything into succession, this dream of literature as perfect order was to show itself in the design-typography with which E.E. Cummings's lines fell into place, in the excision of whatever was "vague," "religious," "shadowy," like Kafka, from Edmund Wilson's admiration. These writers were the last embodiment and justification of their fathers' rugged individualism. They had class in both senses of the word, and they had social confidence, for they still believed in civilization—a community of mind with their adoring readers.... This severe modernist esthetic, this faith in a conscious perfectibility through the ordering of words, was the property of rebellious privileged children of the upper middle class.

The greatness of Faulkner reveals itself in the kind of growth which is "possible only when the chronicle of man's past lives in a man's mind as if he had lived all of it and were now responsible to all of it":

> Surely this explains the attempt, in " The Bear, " to make a single sentence out of so many pages. This is the most famous instance of what Faulkner described as "my ambition to put everything into one sentence—not only the present but the whole past on which it depends and which keeps overtaking the present." He was accountable only to the laws of his own thought, and there are single units in his writing—sentences, paragraphs, pages, whole narrative sections—which are great waves of passion, recrimination, anguish and doubt, beating against the rock of man's past. There *was* a great guilt incurred in the South, a curse *was* put on the land that was given to all men freely to enjoy. Faulkner does not excuse this guilt, he does not apologize for it, he does not evade it. He is a Southerner and has a great story to tell.... In no other American writer is this

obligation to the past so complex as in this greatest Southern writer—who more than most writers has interrogated the past and has not been able to escape it in one moment of thought.

Once the elegies are over Kazin scrutinizes the ways in which the postmoderns have tried to cope with the disorienting fury of American life. There is a handsome tribute to the other Southern writers who have fought to go on believing that the world is "moral, historical, meaningful" and a chapter on the professional observers of American life, O'Hara, Updike, Salinger and Cheever. There is a splendid account of Katherine Anne Porter, Susan Sontag, Joan Didion and Joyce Carol Oates; a predictably earnest examination of Roth, Malamud, Bellow and Singer; a little about Ellison and Baldwin; and an acute appraisal of Capote's and Mailer's excursions into the limbo between journalism and fiction. And there is, not quite finally, a penetrating set of observations on the end of the postmodern road in Barth, Pynchon, Burroughs and Vonnegut. Kazin concludes with an odd chapter, dense and ambiguous at several points, on Nabokov, and propels himself towards an affirmative ending by an act of sheer will. That arrogant master illusionist would seem to be the last novelist Kazin could admire, yet he maintains that Nabokov's exuberance and spectacular display of self-sufficiency, which is for our time "a major form of freedom," may save us from being too much at the mercy of our age.

For Kazin this spontaneity and individuality have always been essential characteristics of modernism: "Whatever modernism means, it does not mean a fear of freedom." But from the vantage point of the mid-seventies, modernism looks more and more like the privileged gesture of an historical moment which is nearly over. Thus in an important essay, "On Modernism," Kazin reaches what may be the end of his long critical argument:

> Ours is a world of incessant nationalistic, tribal wars and revolutionary disruptions, a slavish culture organized not only through the "media" but somehow *for* them. We are getting farther and farther away from the world in which a self-centered, white, individualistic, still "elitist" culture thought of itself as the center of existence.

In some ways the founders of modernism are still our guides,

> but modernism was and remains an upper-class revolution, a necessary perception of the radical forms necessary to guarantee the continuity of our traditional culture. That culture is no longer believed in by those who still live in it. The masses still have no access to it and can hardly have a reason for finding one now. The present age has shown itself all too revolutionary, disruptive and uncontainable to be "modernist."...Against this background of prodigious social destruction and human manipulation [in fascist Germany and now in China], the 1920s, especially in America, now seem the last word in the innocence of the pleasure principle. All those delightful young people finally making their way to the big city from the small town! All that romantic jazz! It belongs to another world. But it was a world in which a few with better eyes than most saw that one day the whole gorgeous machine could go smash. Or as Henry Adams put it, America was the perfect subject for "scientific history, for here man was at last in sight of his own end."

A chronological sketch such as this, while it may be useful for understanding Kazin's career, does nothing to convey how brilliantly he writes or how sane his judgments have been over the years. What Edmund Wilson accomplished for American literature during the twenties and thirties, Kazin has done and continues to do, despite his mounting pessimism, for the decades following. Yet even with the best critics—or perhaps especially with them—the habit of being so right, even about one's mistakes, can turn into a kind of self-righteousness. And this may be what John Updike had in mind when he complained recently about the American literary establishment—or for that matter "any literary establishment":

> If a harsh Providence were to obliterate, say, Alfred Kazin, Richard Gilman, Stanley Kauffmann, and Irving Howe, tomorrow new critics would arise with the same worthy intelligence, the same complacently agonized humanism, the same inability to read a

book except as a disappointing version of one they might have written, the same deadly "auntiness."

KENNER, (William) Hugh. Canadian. Born in Peterborough, Ontario, 7 January 1923. Educated at the University of Toronto, B.A. 1945, M.A. 1946; Yale University, New Haven, Connecticut (Porter Prize, 1950), Ph.D. 1950. Married Mary Josephine Waite in 1947 (died, 1964), five children; Mary Anne Bittner, 1965, two children. Assistant Professor, Assumption College, Windsor, Ontario, 1946-48; Instructor, 1950-51, Assistant Professor, 1951-56, Associate Professor, 1956-58, Professor of English, 1958-73, and Chairman of the Department, 1956-62, University of California at Santa Barbara. Professor of English, 1973-75, and since 1975 Andrew W. Mellon Professor in Humanities, Johns Hopkins University, Baltimore. Visiting Professor, University of Michigan, Ann Arbor, Summer 1956, University of Chicago, Summer 1962, and University of Virginia, Charlottesville, Autumn 1963. Recipient: American Council of Learned Societies Fellowship, 1949; Guggenheim Fellowship, 1956, 1964; American Philosophical Society Grant, 1956; Phi Beta Kappa Christian Gauss Prize, 1972. D.H.L.: University of Chicago, 1976; Trent University, Peterborough, Ontario, 1977. Fellow, Royal Society of Literature. Address: 103 Edgevale Road, Baltimore, Maryland 21210, U.S.A.

PUBLICATIONS

Criticism

> *Paradox in Chesterton*.   New York, Sheed and Ward, 1947; New York, Sheed and Ward, 1948.
> *The Poetry of Ezra Pound*.   New York, New Directions, and London, Faber, 1951.
> *Wyndham Lewis*.   New York, New Directions, and London, Methuen, 1954.
> *Dublin's Joyce*.   London, Chatto and Windus, 1955; Bloomington, Indiana University Press, 1956.
> *Gnomon: Essays on Contemporary Literature*.   New York, McDowell Obolensky, 1958.
> "Words in the Dark," in *Essays by Divers Hands* (London), 29, new series, 1958.
> *The Invisible Poet*: *T.S. Eliot*.   New York, McDowell Obolensky, 1959; London, W.H. Allen, 1960.
> *Samuel Beckett:A Critical Study*.   New York, Grove Press, and London, John Calder, 1962; revised edition, Berkeley, University of California Press, 1968.
> *Flaubert, Joyce and Beckett: The Stoic Comedians*.   Boston, Beacon Press, 1962; London, W.H. Allen, 1964.
> *The Counterfeiters*: *An Historical Comedy*.   Bloomington, Indiana University Press, 1968.
> *The Pound Era*.   Berkeley, University of California Press, 1971; London, Faber, 1972.
> *A Reader's Guide to Samuel Beckett*.   New York, Farrar Straus, and London, Thames and Hudson, 1973.
> "The Urban Apocalypse," in *Eliot in His Time*, edited by A. Walton Litz.   Princeton, New Jersey, Princeton University Press, and London, Oxford University Press, 1973.
> "Some Post-Symbolist Structures," in *Literary Theory and Structure*: *Essays Presented to William K. Wimsatt*, edited by Frank Brady, John Palmer and Martin Price.   New Haven, Connecticut, and London, Yale University Press, 1973.
> *A Homemade World: The American Modernist Writers*.   New York, Knopf, 1975; London, Marion Boyars, 1977.

"Reflections on the Foregoing,' in *Denver Quarterly* (Colorado), 12, 1977.
Joyce's Voices.   Berkeley, University of California Press, and London, Faber, 1978.
"Sincerity Kills," in *Sylvia Plath: New Views on the Poetry*, edited by Gary Lane.   Baltimore and London, Johns Hopkins University Press, 1979.
"Machinespeak," in *The State of the Language*, edited by Leonard Michaels and Christopher Ricks.   Berkeley and London, University of California Press, 1980.
Ulysses.   London, and Winchester, Massachusetts, Allen and Unwin, 1980.

Other

Bucky: A Guided Tour of Buckminster Fuller.   New York, Morrow, 1973.
Geodesic Math and How to Use It.   Berkeley and London, University of California Press, 1976.

Editor, *The Art of Poetry*.   New York, Rinehart, 1959.
Editor, *T.S. Eliot: A Collection of Critical Essays*.   Englewood Cliffs, New Jersey, Prentice Hall, 1962.
Editor, *Seventeenth Century Poetry: The Schools of Donne and Jonson*.   New York, Holt Rinehart, 1964.
Editor, *Studies in Change: A Book of the Short Story*.   Englewood Cliffs, New Jersey, Prentice Hall, 1965.

CRITICAL STUDIES

Lawrence Lipking, "kenner," in *Denver Quarterly* (Colorado), 12, 1977.
Cary Nelson, "Allusion and Authority: Hugh Kenner's Exemplary Critical Voice," in *Denver Quarterly* (Colorado), 12, 1977.

*   *   *

"The function of criticism," Hugh Kenner proposes (in his Foreword to *Gnomon*) "is 'the elucidation of works of art'; from this follows 'the correction of taste.'" These familiar phrases from Eliot are clear enough in a general way, and unexceptionable; the real problems begin when we try to determine precisely what the foundations of true "taste" are for Kenner. Thus the reader who turns to *The Poetry of Ezra Pound* for an expert elucidation of, say, the *Homage to Sextus Propertius* is magisterially told that Pound has been undervalued because of certain false expectations which have prevailed "since the overt collapse, contemporary with Shakespeare, of the moral and political structure of western Europe." This sounds very serious, but Kenner does not stop for patient explanation—he rarely does, yet the information is not gratuitous. For Kenner, as for Eliot, elucidation and criticism rest upon a much more complex theory of cultural, or rather spiritual, decline; but for some reason, Kenner, unlike Eliot, has been unwilling to make explicit the religious convictions which finally govern his thinking.
Proper judgment, like art itself, is a kind of moral activity which depends upon the accurate perception of particulars. True art—in Kenner's words—is always "the process of compelling out of mute particulars, by their electric juxtaposition, traces, intelligible patterns, of an intense, clear, luminous intellective world." Rightly apprehended the particulars of this world testify to an intelligible order of being which empiricism, in science or philosophy, can never hope to grasp. The artist moves us, Kenner maintains, by that "clarity" of perception which was once the chief artistic resource of pre-Cartesian Europe:

Descartes' distrust of language as an autonomous matrix, his dialectician's confidence that language provides at best a desperate, deceptive and (from the enlightened thinker's point of view) ignoble shorthand has introduced into the channels of communication a vehement determination to effect between poet and audience a transfusion of personality rather than of perception.... [In] Tennyson as much as in Housman (a much more naive and anxious person) or Shelley (a self-consciously primitive, vehement person) there is visible an identical distrust of the possibility of any communication, especially of emotion states, without constant comment, constant overt appeal to the reader's experience, habits, and day-dreams. Poetic, that is, has given way to rhetoric. The poet in a dialectical milieu is conscious of an audience to be influenced rather than of a poem to be made. And the quality of what is communicated suffers in consequence, so that technical judgments are inseparable from moral.

Pound, Eliot, Joyce, and Yeats mark by contrast a return to the Aristotelian benison.... A poem is an *imitation* in the sense that it offers an image, an action, a chain of events, such as, on contemplation, may yield the intelligible species proper to the initial experience.

For "Aristotelian" it may be more appropriate to read "Thomist" here, but in any event there can be no true communciation for Kenner, no poetic *style* worthy of the name, unless we maintain "a real and supple relation between the world consisting of a congeries of intelligible things, and language considered as a structure of directed perceptions." With the rise of empirical science (and, one has to infer, the loss of religious faith), the process of decay was already well advanced by the early 18th century. Pope, however, was still able to rely upon

such minimal and cliché-ridden orderliness as can still be evoked; he postulates the intelligibility of created things, the normality of their symbolic functions, the rationality of poetic images. We hear much about the aptness of his literary parody; but the literary order upon the prestige of which Pope depends for so many of this literary effects isn't to his mind venerable because it happens to exist, but radiant because sanctioned by those very analogies between a divine and human inteligence which permit and render fructive the ready resemblances between wise men and seamarks, light and intelligence, the Playwright and God; which enable the writer to see in ordonnance an image of order, to co-operate with his material rather than fight it, and make with ease intelligible statements about the intelligible: which in short reveal a world interesting enough to write about.

If we have eyes to see, our world is a created world of ordered relationships, of hierarchy, in short, which should also support our social structures. And it is this further, unstated principle which may explain Kenner's conservatism and his high tolerance—to put it gently—for the politics of Eliot, Pound and Wyndham Lewis.

For Kenner, as for Eliot once again, the chief literary manifestation of this general decline is the dissociation of sensibility—that fatal separation of thought from feeling which characterizes, for these critics, the poetry of the 19th century. But with the recovery of accurate perception and the refashioning of poetic language which was the major achievement of Hulme, Pound, Eliot and the other "men of 1914," we have access once more to a universe "where intelligibility does not need to be imposed by the mind: Pope's universe, and Chaucer's, as well as Shakespeare's." The distinction between perceiving and inventing an order of intelligibility is crucial here. "The poet projects an intelligible world": but this act of projection is not an act of original creation. The point is difficult to illustrate concisely, but Kenner's discussion of William Carlos Williams in *Gnomon* is useful:

Neither does some familiar modus of meaning inform the novel materials of *Paterson*, nor is it the poet-physician's "view of life" that we are to listen for as we turn its pages. This is writing that by a Jacob's wrestle with words *gets down what happens*—

                they coalesce now
        glass-smooth with their swiftness,
        quiet or seem to quiet as at the close
        they leap to the conclusion and
        fall, fall in air! as if
        floating, relieved of their weight,
        split apart, ribbons; dazed, drunk

> with the catastrophe of the descent
> floating unsupported
> to hit the rocks; to a thunder,
> as if lightning had struck

—the language never reaching out of its proper dimension, level and solid as ice a foot thick, but buoyed up by the whole depth and weight of the profound reality with which it is in contact, and whose contours it holds fast.

And Kenner concludes that

an image which Dr. Williams doesn't use [in *Paterson*] but which his whole career as a physician and poet urges on the attention, recommends itself as the most adequate basis for summary and praise: the obstetrician devoting in a few critical moments his every wile, his concentration, so far as his capacity allows, of the entire tradition of medical science since Hippocrates, to the deliverance, with his bare hands, into independent life of something he did not make, the identity of which he unshakeably respects, and which but for his ministrations would die voiceless.

At the risk of laboring the obvious, then: the poet is the obstetrician, delivering, not creating, an existing order or "life"; the "tradition of medical science" is the tradition of Dante and Shakespeare, revived in our time by the heroes of the Pound era.

The triumph of empiricism has had other consequences as well. Having destroyed the traditional "hierarchies of knowledge" and rearranged the "things we know" for the sake of convenience, science now offers us the behaviorist's model of human nature, a kind of "counterfeit man" whose essence is reduced to a matter of mechanics. But the arts can still enlighten us "precisely as they enlighten us about the nature of counterfeiting"—as Swift does, for example, in his parable of those two equal counterfeits, Gulliver and the Houyhnhnms; they can rescue us from "debility among the conventions of empiricism" (that game whose "central rule forbids you to understand what you are talking about") and so help us to find "equilibrium in a universe wholly constituted out of facts."

With these distinctions in mind readers may be able to approach *The Pound Era*, that *Finnegans Wake* of modern criticism, with a little more confidence. To oversimplify radically: Pound, Eliot, Joyce, Lewis and the other artists Kenner associates with the "Vortex" are responsible for a "second Renaissance" which made available, for the discerning artist, a usable past, a means of moving beyond the rhetoric of the 19th century. It is true that after the First World War the Vortex was dissipated: "the age was divisive" and each of these artists went his separate way. Nevertheless,

The gods have never left us. Nothing we know the mind to have known has ever left us. Quickened by hints, the mind can know it again, and make it new. Romantic Time no longer thickens our sight, time receding, bearing visions away. Our books of cave paintings are the emblems of its abolition, and the literary consolidation of that theme stands as the era's achievement.... We read differently now, though the only possible evidence is the way we write. So reading [as Pound and the others have taught us to do], we have kept the classics alive. Whereas 30 years ago the classical languages were near death, undergraduates today demand to be taught Greek to read a Homer they first glimpsed in some version read, maybe, at the behest of *Ulysses* or the *Cantos*. And poetic language characteristically strives today for intricacy and immediacy together, and often prose does too.

The men of the Vortex achieved all that and more. We will never know how much of our minds they prepared.

In *A Homemade World* Kenner takes up those artists who stayed in America—William Carlos Williams once again, Wallace Stevens, Marianne Moore, Hemingway, Fitzgerald and Faulkner—and "grouped together under the banner of Dedalus, to practice art as though its moral commitments were like technology's." The poets hammered out a poetic "as American as the Kitty Hawk plane, not really in the debt of the international example, austere and astringent":

> They shared hidden sources of craftsmanship, hidden incentives to rewrite a page, which we can trace to a doctrine of perception—the world valued both in itself and in its power to denote—very evident when we watch a second generation of poets (Oppen, Zukofsky) work out themes that seem shared by both Hemingway and Williams. That doctrine of perception, like general semantics, seems peculiarly adapted to the American weather, which fact helps explain why, from Pound's early days until now, modern poetry in whatever country has borne so unmistakably American an impress.

And Kenner concludes, in a passage whose meaning is at best problematic,

> For the language flattened, the language *exhibited*, the language staunchly condensing information while frisking in enjoyment of its release from the obligation to do no more than to inform: these are the eleménts of a twentieth-century American poetic, a pivotal discovery of our age.

A Homemade World is a thesis-ridden book, astonishingly unfair at times (especially to Stevens) and astonishingly enthusiastic about the later "Objectivists."

Some years ago, and with no apparent irony, Kenner observed that Mr. Pound's Chinese emperors were sounding more and more like Mr. Pound. True enough: but a creative liberty is not necessarily a critical virtue, and over the years Kenner himself has tended to sound more and more like his dogmatic mentors. If criticism means an attempt to argue and not merely to pronounce, then Kenner is something other than a critic; he is, or has become, a preacher preaching to the converted. A few examples will have to suffice here. On the first page of *Wyndham Lewis* we are advised that Lewis is "one of the great painters of the twentieth century," that his novel, *The Revenge for Love*, is "a twentieth century classic," and that *Time and Western Man* is "one of the key books for the student of modern thought." This is criticism by assertion, nothing more. To take another example from *Wyndham Lewis* (a crude one but of the same type that Kenner uses much more complexly in *The Pound Era*), here is Lewis' judgment of Henry James: "Henry James: Ghost psychology of New England old maid: stately maze of imperturbable analogies." This is dead wrong, cheap and easy (anyone can play the assertion game) but let us suppose there is a writer who answers to this description. Kenner's "analysis" of the passage is instructive:

> Every word attaches itself to Henry James; but it was Lewis who attached them alchemically to one another. It isn't the maze that is stately, nor the analogies that are imperturbable; but by unhooking each of these words from its appointed object and joining them instead to each other, Lewis, in setting his signature on the combination, releases magnetisms that makes its elements seem, once so joined, inseparable. The phrases thus arrived at are so condensed that their rightness grows wonderfully persuasive. Assonance and rhythm—not meaning—cause this particular ordering of the terms to snap together like a clock spring: any other arrangement, once we have seen this one, would hang open in flaccid incompetence. In this universe of words—precisely the "finely sculptured surface of sheer words" Lewis much later suggested discriminating readers should hunger for—we soon stop worrying about the mere reality.

Mere reality? To what extent does this self-intoxicated reading of Lewis' gawky prose actually make any mere sense? In an angry review of *Gnomon* some years ago, Steven Marcus asked

> What is all this? Is it, as crusty Christopher once said, "a narcotic dose administered by a crazy charlatan?" It's hardly that simple. Praising Lessing as a critic, Kierkegaard remarked that he possessed "an exceedingly uncommon gift of explaining what he himself had understood. There he stopped. In our age people go further and explain more than they have understood." Mr. Kenner's special genius lies in explaining more than he has understood in ways few others will ever care to understand. He is more like an alchemist or a mathematician than a critic; in his most typical essays he does nothing

less than conjure up an autonomous, self-referring universe, whose terms have virtually nothing to do with experience, and which functions according to some arcane concoction of rules whose unintelligibility is the safeguard of their inconsequence.

And of course things have not been getting any clearer since *Gnomon*.

KERMODE, (John) Frank. British. Born in Douglas, Isle of Man, 29 November 1919. Educated at Douglas High School; University of Liverpool, B.A. 1940, M.A. 1947. Served in the Royal Navy, 1940-46; Lieutenant. Married Maureen Eccles in 1947 (divorced, 1970); has two children; Anita Van Vactor, 1976. Lecturer, King's College, Newcastle upon Tyne (University of Durham), 1947-49, and University of Reading, 1949-58; John Edward Taylor Professor of English Literature, University of Manchester, 1958-65; Winterstoke Professor of English, University of Bristol, 1965-67; Lord Northcliffe Professor of Modern English Literature, University College, University of London, 1967-74. Since 1974, Fellow of King's College, Cambridge, and King Edward VII Professor of English Literature, Cambridge University. Visiting Professor, Harvard University, Cambridge, Massachusetts, Summer 1961; Warton Lecturer, British Academy, 1962; Mary Flexner Lecturer, Bryn Mawr College, Pennsylvania, 1965; Charles Eliot Norton Professor of Poetry, Harvard University, 1977-78. Co-Editor, *Encounter*, London, 1966-67. Member, Arts Council, 1968-71. Chairman, Poetry Book Society, London, 1968. General Editor, Modern Masters, Viking Press, New York, and Collins-Fontana, London. Recipient: Wesleyan University Center for Advanced Study Fellowship, 1962. D.H.L.: University of Chicago, 1975; D.Litt.: University of Liverpool, 1981. Fellow of the Royal Society of Literature, 1958; Fellow of the British Academy, 1973; Officier de l'Ordre des Arts et des Sciences. Address: King's College, Cambridge CB2 1ST, England.

PUBLICATIONS

Criticism

Romantic Image. London, Routledge, and New York, Macmillan, 1957.
John Donne. London, Longman, 1957; reprinted in *Shakespeare, Spenser, Donne: Renaissance Essays*, 1971.
Wallace Stevens. Edinburgh, Oliver and Boyd, 1960; New York, Grove Press, 1961; revised edition, 1967.
The Banquet of Sense. Manchester, John Rylands Library, 1961; reprinted in *Shakespeare, Spenser, Donne: Renaissance Essays*, 1971.
"Spenser and the Allegorists," in *Proceedings of the British Academy 48.* London, Oxford University Press, 1961; reprinted in *Shakespeare, Spenser, Donne: Renaissance Essays*, 1971.
Puzzles and Epiphanies: Essays and Reviews 1958-1961. London, Routledge, and New York, Chilmark Press, 1962.
William Shakespeare: The Final Plays. London, Longman, 1963; reprinted in *Shakespeare, Spenser, Donne: Renaissance Essays*, 1971.
The Faerie Queen, I and V. Manchester, John Rylands Library, 1964; reprinted in *Shakespeare, Spenser, Donne: Renaissance Essays*, 1971.
The Patience of Shakespeare. New York, Harcourt Brace, 1964; reprinted in *Shakespeare, Spenser, Donne: Renaissance Essays*, 1971.
On Shakespeare's Learning. Middletown, Connecticut, Wesleyan University Press, 1965; reprinted in *Shakespeare, Spenser, Donne: Renaissance Essays*, 1971.

The Sense of an Ending: Studies in the Theory of Fiction.   New York, Oxford University
    Press, 1967.
Continuities.   London, Routledge, and New York, Random House, 1968.
"Novel, History, and Type," in *Novel* (Providence, Rhode Island), 1, 1968.
"The Structure of Fictions," in *Modern Language Notes* (Baltimore) 84, 1969.
Modern Essays.   London, Fontana, 1971.
Shakespeare, Spenser, Donne: Renaissance Essays.   London, Routledge, and New
    York, Viking Press, 1971.
Novel and Narrative (lecture).   Glasgow, University of Glasgow Press, 1972.
D.H. Lawrence.   London, Fontana, and New York, Viking Press, 1973.
"The Use of the Codes," in *Approaches to Poetics*, edited by Seymour Chatman.   New
    York, Columbia University Press, 1973.
The Classic.   London, Faber, and New York, Viking Press, 1975.
"Novels: Recognition and Deception," in *Critical Inquiry* (Chicago), 1, 1975.
"Can We Say Absolutely Anything We Like?" in *Art, Politics, and Will: Essays in Honor
    of Lionel Trilling*, edited by Quentin Anderson, Stephen Donadio and Steven Marcus.
    New York, Basic Books, 1977.
The Genesis of Secrecy: On the Interpretation of Narrative.   Cambridge, Massachusetts,
    Harvard University Press, 1979.
"Institutional Control of Interpretation," in *Salmagundi* (Saratoga Springs, New York),
    43, 1979.
"Secrets and Narrative History," in *Critical Inquiry* (Chicago), 7, 1980.
"Dwelling Poetically in Connecticut," in *Wallace Stevens: A Celebration*, edited by Frank
    Doggett and Robert Buttel.   Princeton, New Jersey, Princeton University Press, 1980.

Other

Editor, *English Pastoral Poetry: From the Beginnings to Marvell.*   London, Harrap, and
    New York, Barnes and Noble, 1952.
Editor, *The Tempest*, by Shakespeare.   London, Methuen, 1954.
Editor, with J.P. Cutts, *Seventeenth Century Songs.*   London, Oxford University Press,
    1956.
Editor, *The Living Milton: Essays by Various Hands.*   London, Routledge, 1960; New
    York, Macmillan, 1961.
Editor, *Discussions of John Donne.*   Boston, Heath, 1962.
Editor, *Spenser: Selections from the Minor Poems and the Faerie Queene.*   London,
    Oxford University Press, 1965.
Editor, *Four Centuries of Shakespearian Criticism.*   New York, Avon, 1965.
Editor, *The Metaphysical Poets: Essays on Metaphysical Poetry.*   Greenwich, Connec-
    ticut, Fawcett, 1969.
Editor, *King Lear: A Casebook.*   London, Macmillan, 1969; Nashville, Aurora Pub-
    lishers, 1970.
Editor, with Richard Poirier, *The Oxford Reader: Varieties of Contemporary Discourse.*
    New York, Oxford University Press, 1971.
General Editor, with others, *The Oxford Anthology of English Literature.*   New York,
    Oxford University Press, 2 vols., 1973.
Editor, *Selected Prose of T.S. Eliot.*   London, Faber, and New York, Harcourt Brace,
    1975.

*   *   *

Frank Kermode's aim in his first critical work, *Romantic Image*, is "the commendable one of
revising historical categories," in this case the popular—and misleading—distinction between
Romanticism and the apparently anti-Romantic poetics of Hulme, Eliot and Pound. "I here
use 'Romantic' in a restricted sense," he explains, "as applicable to the literature of one epoch,
beginning in the late years of the eighteenth century and not yet finished, and as referring to the

high valuation placed upon the image-making powers of the mind at the expense of its rational powers, and to the substitution of organicist for mechanical modes of thinking about art." Despite superficial differences, both Romanticism and Modernism see the artist as an isolated, estranged figure and the work of art itself as a "symbol" or "aesthetic monad"

> utterly original and not in the old sense "imitated"; "concrete," yet fluid and suggestive; a means of truth, a truth unrelated to, and more exalted than, that of positivist science, or any observation depending upon the discursive reason; out of the flux of life, and therefore, under one aspect, dead; yet uniquely alive because of its participation in a higher order of existence, and because it is analogous not to a machine but an organism; coextensive in matter and form; resistant to explication; largely independent of intention, and of any form of ethical utility; and itself emblematised in certain recurring images.... These formulae involve certain apparent contradictions.... Yet some such conception of the Image as that given [here] animates much of the best writing between Coleridge and Blake at the outset and Pound and Eliot in our own time.

Romanticism so defined does not, of course, run directly from Blake to Eliot; it re-enters modern English poetic theory and practice with Hulme's "secularization" of the Symbolist doctrine of the Image as "a radiant truth out of time":

> One might summarise it in this way. Hulme hands over to the English tradition a modernised, but essentially traditional, aesthetic of Symbolism. It would have made ground here in any case, but Hulme gave it a form which has persisted into modern thought, a form which for various reasons offers an acceptable version of the magic Image, or Romantic anti-positivism, and of the excluded artist.

And while Kermode admits that the doctrine of the Image and the closely related doctrine of the dissociation of sensibility were necessary supports for the kind of poetry Eliot and Pound wanted to write—as Eliot himself emphasized a few years later in "To Criticize the Critic"—he also argues that there have been certain harmful consequences. *Romantic Image* is a sophisticated exercise in descriptive literary history, but in his brief final chapter Kermode maintains that what we need now is a "corrective to the Symbolist theory of language" which will "restore the long poem to the centre of activity":

> For the English this means Milton; and this fact alone justifies any attempt to kill the Symbolist historical doctrine of dissociation of sensibility as publicly as possible.... The time will come when [*Paradise Lost*] will be read once more as the most perfect achievement of English poetry, perhaps the richest and most intricately beautiful poem in the world. When it does, poets will marvel that it could have been done without so long; as easy, they will say, to image a Greek literature which abjured Homer.

For a polemical extension of this argument against "imagism" in this broad sense, readers should consult Graham Hough's *Image and Experience.*

In *The Sense of an Ending, The Classic* and the important first section of *Continuities* Kermode is primarily interested in developing and testing a conception of modernism and its relationship to imaginative fictions in general. The "Moderns" of the seventeenth century, Kermode observes (in *Continuities*), "created a climate in which hypothesis and fiction replace myth, in which the nature of ideologies is to undergo rapid alteration and fragmentation, as ours do." And in *The Classic* he concludes that "secularization multiplies the world's structures of probability." These remarks are compressed, even for Kermode; but properly understood, his emphasis upon "secularization" will explain much of what is central to his thinking thus far. The moving spirit here seems to be Wallace Stevens; or, more accurately, Stevens is Kermode's poetic spokesman, since Kermode is familiar not only with Santayana, as Stevens was, but also with a more complicated line of philosophic thought running from Kant through Vaihinger and beyond. Very briefly, the human mind demands a comprehensive, unified view of the world it inhabits. In Stevens' well-known phrase, we are driven by a "blessed rage for order" ("biology and cultural adaptation require it," Kermode asserts in *The Sense of an Ending*). We insist upon a view of existence which puts man into some intelligible, if often tragic, relationship to the natural order of things:

> whether you think that time will have a stop or that the world is eternal...there is still a need to speak humanly of a life's importance in relation to it—a need in the moment of existence to belong, to be related to a beginning and an end...to imagine a significance for [ourselves]....

Kermode accepts without question the proposition that all human knowledge is by definition "poetic," that is, "fictive," or humanly constructed and radically conditioned by our perceptual limitations and inspired by our emotional needs. The theology of Aquinas, the poetry of Dante, the world-view of modern physics—there are all equally fictive accounts of reality.

At the same time our fictions must be forged from a tough sense of the world as it actually appears in daily experience: "fictions too easy we call 'escapist'; we want them not only to console but to make discoveries of the hard truth here and now, in the middest." (Thus Kermode provides a brilliant reading of *La Nausée*, in *The Sense of an Ending*, in which he demonstrates that Sartre's form here is "an instructive dissonance between humanity and contingency; it discovers a new way of establishing a concord between the human mind and things as they are.") The pressures of reality pose a constant threat to the stability of the larger imaginative paradigms which maintain a culture or an epoch. At the turn of the century Santayana—perhaps recalling the old Chinese curse, May you live in interesting times—asserted that we do in fact live in interesting times: the shell of Christendom has been broken, the old consolations and sanctions are gone, and we need a new "supreme fiction" if we are to continue to make sense of our lives. The term "supreme fiction" is of course Stevens'; and Stevens knew as well as anyone else that we actually live amid a welter of conflicting ideologies. With secularization, then, came those competing "structures of probability" Kermode refers to, shifting, complex, and asserted, as Stevens saw, with "ever increasing incoherence."

The fictions of Apocalypse which Kermode exmines in *The Sense of an Ending* are merely one kind of fiction, but they are crucial since only a projected "end" can give intelligible shape to our conceptions of meaning and purpose:

> What it seems to come to is this. Men in the middest make considerable imaginative investments in coherent patterns which, by the provision of an end, make possible a satisfying consonance with the origins and with the middle. That is why the image of the end can never be *permanently* falsified. But they also, when awake and sane, feel the need to show a marked respect for things as they are.

With a good deal of subtlety Kermode attempts to relate "the theory of literary fictions to the theory of fictions in general" and traces the fate of various apocalyptic fictions, with their characteristic categories of empire, decadence, renovation, progress and catastrophe. Thoroughly secularized by now, of course, we live with a perpetual sense of uncertainty, haunted by the kind of anxiety which is nearly synonymous with modernity. And finally Kermode distinguishes between two kinds of modernism, each of which "reacts to a 'painful transitional situation,' one in terms of continuity and the other in terms of schism":

> The point is simply this: whereas such a poem as *The Waste Land* draws upon a tradition which imposes the necessity of form, though it may have none that can be apprehended without a disciplined act of faith, a new modernism prefers and professes to do without the tradition and the illusion.

Of course it is impossible for an artist to reject completely the form-making activities of the past and the inherent structures of language, but to the extent that he attempts to do so—to experiment, for example, with pure randomness—he runs the risk of sinking into "noncommunicative triviality."

In what sense, then, can an earlier text survive as a classic or continuing source of meaning?

There are, to speak very broadly, two ways of maintaining a classic, of establishing its access to a modern mind. The first of these depends on philology and historiography—it asks what the text *meant* to its author and his best readers, and may still mean to those who have the necessary knowledge and skill. The second is the method of accommodation, by which I mean any method by which the old document may be induced to signify what it cannot be said to have expressly stated. The chief instrument of accommodation is allegory, if we use the word in a sense wide enough to include prophecy.

A valuable fiction like the *Aeneid* can be allegorized and extended, but the time may finally come when the process of accommodation can go no further, when Vergil may be "handed over from the allegorists to the philologists." The text then is "closed"—but if a text *can* be closed completely, it is not a "classic":

> It seems that on a just view of the matter the books we call classics possess intrinsic qualities that endure, but possess also an openness to accommodation which keeps them alive under endlessly varying dispositions.... In fact, the only works we value enough to call classics are those which, [as] they demonstrate by surviving, are complex and indeterminate enough to allow us our necessary pluralities.... It is in the nature of works of art to be open, in so far as they are "good"; though it is in the nature of authors, and of readers, to close them.

For Kermode there are really two kinds of classics, the older ones, which had to be allegorized, and "consciously modern" ones, "carefully unauthoritative, open to multiple interpretation because the modern world is so." Hawthorne's texts, for example, "with all their varying, fading voices, their controlled lapses into possible inauthenticity, are meant as invitations to co-production on the part of the reader." The modern classic

> offers itself only to readings which are encouraged by its failure to give a definitive account of itself. Unlike the old classic, which was expected to provide answers, this one poses a virtually infinite set of questions. And when we have learnt how to ask some of the questions we may discover that the same kinds of question can also be put to the old classic. The modern classic, and the modern way of reading the classic, are not to be separated.

At this point Kermode turns for support to Roland Barthes, who argues that our conventional criticism is the victim of *asymbolie*, or the inability to cope with any text whose language "exceeds narrow rationalism":

> But the moment one begins to consider a work as it is in itself, symbolic reading becomes unavoidable. You may be able to show that the reader has made his rules wrong or applied them wrongly, but errors of this kind do not invalidate the principle. [In *Critique et Vérité*] Barthes explains that in his usage a symbol is not an image but a plurality of senses; the text will have many, not through the infirmity of readers who know less history than Professor Picard [Barthes' chief critic], but in its very nature as a structure of signifiers. "L'oeuvre propose, l'homme dispose." Multiplicity of readings must result from the work's "constitutive ambiguity," an expression Barthes borrows from Jakobson. And if that ambiguity itself does not exclude from the work the authority of its writer, then death will do so: "By erasing the author's signature, death establishes the truth of the work, which is an enigma."

The problems such assertions raise are as crucial as they are obvious: is there *no* privileged reading? Are all individual readings equally valuable—or valueless—to someone else? "Within certain limits," Kermode admits, "we make the book according to the order or disorder of our own imagination." But what *are* these limits? Kermode is well aware of the difficulties involved, of course:

> Barthes denies the charge that on his view of the reading process one can say absolutely anything one likes about the work in question, but he is actually much less interested in defining constraints than in asserting liberties. There are some suggestive figures in his recent book *Le Plaisir du texte* (1973) from which we gather that authorial presence is

somehow a ghostly necessity, like a dummy at bridge, or the shadow without which Die Frau ohne Schatten must remain sterile; and there are hints that diachrony, a knowledge of transient dispositions, may be necessary even to the *nouvelle critique* completely practiced. Such restrictions on criticism *à outrance* can perhaps only be formulated in terms of a theory of competence and performance analogous to that of linguistics.

Again, what, specifically, will constitute "competence"? The argument stops at this tantalizing point, however, to be taken up later, perhaps, or perhaps simply left for the reader to ponder. Kermode is fond of quoting Wolfgang Iser's "neat formula" that " 'the repair of indeterminacy' is what gives rise to 'the generation of meaning.' " The same might be said of Kermode's own best criticism (as distinct, of course, from his expert traditional scholarship, the *Renaissance Essays*, for example, or his edition of *The Tempest*): it stimulates, in the truest sense of that abused term. Stevens may have the last word here: "It is necessary to propose an enigma to the mind. The mind always proposes a solution."

The Genesis of Secrecy is an elegant, subversive book which raises once again the problem of radical subjectivity mentioned above in connection with Kermode's interest in Barthes and now, it seems, Jacques Derrida. We approach a text, Kermode argues, as we approach the world itself, with high hopes of finding coherence, order and fixed meanings. Modern philosophy and modern science, however, have undermined the old certainties and forced us to recognize that in large part we create the world we perceive, and create it according to our own needs and desires:

> And we interpret always as transients...both in the book and in the world which resembles the book. For the world is our beloved codex. We may not see it, as Dante did, in perfect order, gathered by love into one volume, but we do, living as reading, like to think of it as a place where we can travel back and forth at will, divining congruences, conjunctions, opposites; extracting secrets from its secrecy, making understood relations, an appropriate algebra. This is the way we satisfy ourselves with explanations of the unfollowable world—as if it were a structured narrative, of which more might always be said by trained readers of it, by insiders. World and book, it may be, are hopelessly plural, endlessly disappointing; we stand alone before them, aware of their arbitrariness and impenetrability, knowing that they may be narratives only because of our impudent intervention, and susceptible of interpretation only by our hermeneutic tricks. Hot for secrets, our only conversation may be with guardians who know less and see less than we can; and our sole hope and pleasure is in the perception of a momentary radiance, before the door of disappointment is finally shut on us.

The consequences of this modish pessimism for literary interpretation are clear. Like the world, texts are opaque and thus have "inexhaustible hermeneutic potential"; that is, they are open to an infinite number of readings or interpretations—or rather an *almost* infinite number, since here Kermode, like Stanley Fish, draws back sharply from Derrida. For both critics institutional constraints are decisive. We may seem to have consensus about literary meaning at times, and we seem able to talk to each other about texts, but this is so only when we happen to belong to what Fish calls the same "interpretive community." Once an institution (the church, influential university circles, and so on) has defined a text as valuable, it becomes the object of respectful scrutiny and interpretation; and once it enters by this means into a world of shifting values and perspectives, it is subject to endless re-readings and reinterpretations. But because meanings are generated by historical processes (that is, they are not "intrinsic" to texts), our efforts to establish a fixed, authoritative meaning are doomed to end in disappointment. Using Kafka's parable of the man who is perpetually denied access to the Law and the "radiance" of full understanding, Kermode concludes that

> No one, however special his point of vantage, can get past all those doorkeepers into the shrine of the single sense. I make an allegory, once more, of Kafka's parable; but some such position is the starting point of all modern hermeneutics except those which are consciously reactionary. The pleasures of interpretation are henceforth linked to loss and disappointment, so that most of us will find the task too hard, or simply repugnant;

and then, abandoning meaning, we slip back into the old comfortable fictions of transparency [recoverable meaning], the single sense, the truth.

In *The Genesis of Secrecy* Kermode refers at times to "naive" and "reactionary" theories of interpretation which assume that we can "re-cognize" original authorial meaning and which also argue that interpretive differences are not differences about such meanings but only about "significance," or the ways in which we then relate meaning to our own ongoing concerns which are, of course, deeply rooted in our own personal and historical circumstances. This is the position held by E.D. Hirsch at present, and by critics such as Wayne Booth and M.H. Abrams; and thus it is not surprising to find Hirsch responding sharply to Kermode's arguments. In a review of *The Genesis of Secrecy* published in the *New York Review of Books* for 14 June 1979, Hirsch comments

> To be blunt, I find this an unconvincing show of epistemological handwringing. It is *not* the way we interpret the world we live in. It might have some plausibility if Kermode were saying that we cannot solve the big mysteries such as "Is there a God?" "Is mind distinct from matter?" "How did the world begin?" or "What is the meaning of life?" If that is what Kermode means by "impenetrability," then of course we accept that he is right. But everything in Kermode's book points to a much more radical skepticism. For him even the smallest mysteries remain mysteries; and only our fictions—which we know to be arbitrary and artificial—allow us respite from uncertainty and incoherence...[his] words illustrate a tendency of post-Heideggerian hermeneutic theory to partition off the realm of literary speculation from the rest of life, and thus to trivialize literary specula-tion. Kermode does *not* ask himself each day, "Shall I part my hair behind?" "Do I dare to eat a peach?" "Am I still a professor of English?" "Is this the same tooth brush that I used last night?"... Such epistemological uncertainty may offer a momentary *frisson*, but not even literary theorists inhabit such a consistently arbitrary and impenetrable world.

The debate goes on and shows no signs of coming to a conclusion. In fact, given such mutually exclusive conceptions of words, the world and the status of understanding, it cannot come to an end. Even the word "debate" seems foolishly hopeful.

KETTLE, Arnold (Charles).   British.   Born in London, 17 March 1916. Educated at Mer-chant Taylors' School, London, 1928-34; Pembroke College, Cambridge, B.A., Ph.D. Served in the British Army, 1942-46: Captain. Married Marguerite Gale in 1946; has two children. Lecturer, then Senior Lecturer in English Literature, University of Leeds, 1947-67; Professor of Literature, University of Dar es Salaam, Tanzania, 1967-70. Since 1970, Professor of Litera-ture (Pro-Vice-Chancellor Academic, 1973-75), The Open University, Milton Keynes. Address: The Open University, Walton Hall, Milton Keynes MK7 6AA, England.

PUBLICATIONS

Criticism

An Introduction to the English Novel.   London, Hutchinson, 2 vols., 1951-1953.
"The Early Victorian Social-Problem Novel," in *The Pelican Guide to English Literature 6,* edited by Boris Ford.   London, Penguin, 1958.

"What Is Kim?" in *The Morality of Art: Essays Presented to G. Wilson Knight by His Colleagues and Friends*, edited by D.W. Jefferson.   London, Routledge, 1959.
"The Consistency of James Joyce," in *The Pelican Guide to English Literature 7*, edited by Boris Ford.   London, Penguin, 1961.
Hardy the Novelist: A Reconsideration.   Swansea, University College of Swansea, 1967.
Man and the Arts: A Marxist Approach, with V.G. Hanes.   New York, American Institute for Marxist Studies, 1968.

Other

Karl Marx: Founder of Modern Communism.   London, Weidenfeld and Nicolson, 1963; New York, Roy, 1964; revised edition Weidenfeld and Nicolson, 1968.
Communism and the Intellectuals.   London, Lawrence and Wishart, 1965.

Editor, *Shakespeare in a Changing World*.   London, Lawrence and Wishart, and New York, International Publishers, 1964.
Editor, *Tess of the D'Urbervilles*, by Thomas Hardy.   New York, Harper, 1966.
Editor, *The Nineteenth-Century Novel: Critical Essays and Documents*.   London, Heinemann, 1972.

*   *   *

The questions a critic asks about his subject matter are usually a reliable guide to the very foundations of his thinking. Thus when Arnold Kettle asserts that the *essential* questions about the novel are why it arose at all, and why it arose when it did, the reader may well suspect that some kind of historical determinism is at work—and of course he will be right. In this case the conception of history also happens to be thoroughly Marxist. "We shall not understand the rise of the English novel," Kettle maintains, "unless we understand the meaning and importance of the English revolution of the seventeenth century." The earlier feudal period, which was marked by a rigid class structure and "intellectual conservatism," generated a literature appropriate to its needs and values:

> Romance was the non-realistic, aristocratic literature of feudalism. It was nonrealistic in the sense that its underlying purpose was not to help people cope in a positive way with the business of living but to transport them to a world different, idealized, *nicer* than their own. It was aristocratic because the attitudes it expressed and recommended were precisely the attitudes the ruling class wished...to encourage in order that their privileged position might be perpetuated.

The revolutionary bourgeois class which "organized the remarkable, democratic New Model Army, cut off the King's head and established the republican Commonwealth" in turn produced its characteristic literature:

> literature to the bourgeois writers of this period was, above all, a means of taking stock of the new society. A medium which could express a realistic and objective curiosity about man and his world, this was what they were after. It was the search for such a medium that led Fielding to describe *Joseph Andrews* as "a comic epic poem in prose." Their task was not so much to adapt themselves to a revolutionary situation as to cull and examine what the revolution had produced...they were more free and therefore more realistic than their predecessors to just the extent and in just those ways that the English bourgeois revolution involved in fact an increase in human freedom.

But sometimes writers do more than merely "express" their age and its economic foundations. Faced with the inhuman consequences of established capitalism, "honest writers" of the nineteenth century "were bound to feel a deep revulsion against the underlying principles and the warped relationships of the society they lived in":

> after Jane Austen, the great novels of the nineteenth century are all, in their differing ways, novels of revolt. The task of the novelists was the same as it had always been—to achieve realism, to express (with whatever innovations of form and structure they needs must discover) the truth about life as it faced them. But to do this, to cut through the whole complex structure of unhumanity and false feeling that ate into the consciousness of the capitalist world, it was necessary to become a rebel.

Readers familiar with George Lukács and Christopher Caudwell know what comes next. The late Victorian period, whatever else it may have been, was also "an era of desperation—of a hectic and bloody imperial race against new upstart competitors, of the first modern economic slump, of the rise of the Labour movement as we know it," and so on. Butler and Hardy, for example, are "rebels and critics, crying out...against the sanctities and ethics of the Victorian bourgeois world." The first twenty five years of our century are marked by "uncertainty and tension":

> In the greatest writers of the age—Conrad, Lawrence, Joyce—the battle of the novelist with his raw material tends to be an unequal one. None of these writers tamely accepts the decadent aspects of the society in which they all find themselves, yet not one of them is able to achieve a philosophy and hence an artistic vantage point from which he is able quite satisfactorily to cope with and subjugate the world he tackles.

As for the second quarter of the century:

> The two qualities which strike one most, perhaps, as one surveys the period, are narrowness and pessimism. Both are, of course, quite understandable in their historical context, nor are they quite separable. The narrowness is to a considerable degree a by-product of the pessimism. Writers who feel unable to come to terms with the world at large tend to retreat to the only corner they can feel reasonably sure of—their own spiritual predicament and that of a few people like themselves.

And he concludes:

> The point is not merely that the material with which these writers are concerned is unsympathetic, that they write about a society which manifests all the classic aspects of decadence; what is significant is that the writers themselves partake overwhelmingly in the values of the society they depict. They are not simply writers describing decadence, they are decadent writers.

For Kettle, as for most orthodox Marxists, history is essentially the record of a dialectical struggle for human freedom. *Middlemarch* is in many ways a great novel, but finally it is unsatisfactory because "George Eliot's view of society is in the last analysis a mechanistic and determinist one....It is the very inadequacy of her mechanistic philosophy, its failure to incorporate a dialectical sense of contradiction and motion, that drives [her] to treat the aspirations of Dorothea idealistically." Marxism may be materialistic but it is not deterministic in George Eliot's sense. The distinction is, emotionally, a very real one:

> Life develops through struggle and change. The particular struggle is solved, another emerges. The particular tragedy is solved, but we are faced with our own tragic dilemma. This will be solved in turn, though not perhaps by us, and the experience of the past will help to solve it. Just as life though it involves tragedy, is not tragic (or it would not have gone on for thousands of years), so art, though it springs from its own time and situation, is not merely transient and relative in value.

And Kettle concludes that while we must "see each novel as a part of history and its value as the quality of its contribution to the achievement of man's freedom, yet it is important to remember that it is the book *itself* we are judging, not its intention, nor the amount of 'social significance' to be got out of it, nor even its importance as a measurable historical influence."

This dialectical view of history, however, is not the only critical tool Kettle uses in his history of the English novel. In his opening chapter he also makes a simplistic distinction between novels which are primarily interested in rendering the surface of life realistically and those "moral fables" which are primarily dramatizations of an ethical or philosophical point of view. The realists will tend to write books which are "amorphous and unorganized," the writers of moral fables will tend towards a certain "rigidity." Armed with these two sets of related principles—the Marxist conception of history and the distinction between realism and fable—Kettle then traces the growth of the English novel from the early eighteenth century to 1950, quite sensibly limiting himself to a few representative works from each major period. The quotations above are drawn mainly from the historical interchapters of the *Introduction* and thus may be misleading, since Kettle's discussions of individual novels are often sensitive and flexible (readers who feel that Marxist criticism is necessarily dogmatic should read Kettle's chapter on Bunyan or his eloquent essay on *Portrait of a Lady*). Since there is no reason to believe that Kettle has abandoned Marxism, it would be interesting to see how he might account for the course of British fiction since 1950.

KITTO, H(umphrey) D(avy) F(indley). British. Born in Stroud, Gloucestershire, 6 February 1897. Educated at Crypt Grammar School, Gloucestershire; St. John's College, Cambridge, B.A. 1920. Married Ann Kraft in 1928; has two children. Assistant, then Lecturer in Greek, University of Glasgow, 1921-44; Professor of Greek, University of Bristol, 1944-62 (now Emeritus). Visiting Professor, Cornell University, Ithaca, New York, 1954; Brandeis University, Waltham, Massachusetts, 1959, 1962-63 (Ziskind Professor); Sather Professor, University of California, Berkeley, 1960-61; Regents Professor, University of California at Santa Barbara, 1963-64. Docteur-és-lettres, University of Aix-Marseille, 1961. Fellow of the British Academy, 1955; Fellow of the Royal Society of Literature, 1957. Address: 9 Southfield Road, Bristol BS6 6AX, England.

PUBLICATIONS

Criticism

Greek Tragedy: A Literary Study. London, Metheun, 1939; revised edition, 1950, 1961; New York, Barnes and Noble, 1952, 1966.
Form and Meaning in Drama: A Study of Six Greek Plays and of "Hamlet." London, Methuen, 1956; New York, Barnes and Noble, 1957.
Sophocles, Dramatist and Philosopher. London and New York, Oxford University Press, 1958.
"Tragic Drama and Intellectualism," in *Essays by Divers Hands 31.* London, Oxford University Press, 1963.
Poiesis: Structure and Thought. Berkeley and Los Angeles, University of California Press, and London, Cambridge University Press, 1966.

Other

In the Mountains of Greece. London, Methuen, 1933.
The Greeks. London, Penguin, 1951; revised edition, 1961.

Translator, *Three Tragedies*, by Sophocles. London and New York, Oxford University Press, 1962.

*   *   *

In America at least, generations of young instructors recruited from their various departments to teach introductory courses in "the humanities" have turned with relief and gratitude to H.D.F. Kitto's *Greek Tragedy.* Without promising to turn well-meaning amateurs into competent classicists, Kitto still offers an approach which is of great value because it is so consistently sensible. "Sensible" is not a glamorous word, perhaps, but the kind of good sense Kitto offers is in the long run far more useful than the "grand manner," as he calls it, which permits a critic to say "almost anything" about a work of art, "according to his own sympathies and preposessions."

Kitto states his basic position most clearly in the first section of a later study, *Poiesis* (the title of his opening chapter here, "Chaos and Criticism," may well be intended to remind readers of a similar argument in "The Chaos of Critical Theories," the opening chapter of I. A. Richards' *Principles of Literary Criticism*). He points out that what we have in discussions of Greek tragedy is not intelligent consensus but a bewildering variety of conflicting "interpretations." "Either criticism has no discipline," he asserts, "or if there is one, it is not sufficiently understood." The proper discipline of criticism, then, is the real subject of *Greek Tragedy, Form and Meaning in Drama*, and *Poiesis.* What Kitto does in each of these studies is to "confront Chaos with Aristotle: to take up his doctrine of poiesis and see if it works, to see if the way in which a writer first chooses his material can do anything to reveal the true unity of his work and thereby facilitate our contact with his mind and enable us to escape from our own *idées reçues*." Poiesis means making—not the making of poetry rather than prose, but the making of a particular form by a particular disposition of material. Kitto assumes, as does Aristotle, that the poet is first of all a craftsman, and warns us against the belief that the Greek dramatists were somehow more "primitive" than Greek sculptors or architects. Like any other craftsman, the poet strives to create an organic whole which, regardless of its subject matter, will please us by its beauty—its order and magnitude, in Aristotelian terms. The chaos of critical interpretations comes about because we are unable or unwilling to see what the artist has made, what he has included and excluded and why. Thus Kitto observes that the Romantics made Prometheus into a symbol of revolt against tyranny—as they had every right to do; the troubles begin when we assume that Aeschylus and Shelley must have shared the same artistic intention:

> [The Romantics] were doing what their predecessors had done: refashioning the myth in order to say through it something that they wanted to say. We can have no quarrel with Goethe or Shelley on that score; but an existing play is another matter. Aeschylus, constructing *his* play out of the myth, *meant* something, and if an interpreter, for any reason, makes him to have said something else, then he has failed in his duty as a critic: for the major task of criticism is to promote the meeting of minds—the reader's with the writer's.

That the artist is a craftsman who consciously intends a meaning, that a work must be unified, with each part contributing to a determinate effect—these are empty commonplaces unless the critic is able to make them come alive and illuminate particular works of art: and this is exactly what Kitto does so well in his painstaking examinations of individual Greek tragedies, *Hamlet* and *Coriolanus*. As for the purpose of those earlier tragedies, Kitto asks his readers to remember that for the Greeks the poet was a teacher, whereas

> our more elusive, suggestive, individual conception of poetry is natural in a culture that has an abundance of prose forms for the public communication of ideas which are

important to the community and the human race, but is not natural to one in which poetry is the only medium. In a society that has no prose literature, poetry naturally attracted, and discharged, wider and heavier responsibility that it does today. Painting, today, can perhaps afford the luxury of being only fascinating...but those who painted for the Medieval Church, though they could indeed be fascinating, had as their first responsibility the duty of saying simple and important things.... When Poetry stood alone, it could not afford to be only an aesthetic luxury.

This Aristotelian conception of tragedy as a closed form with a determinate, specific effect may of course be extended to other forms from other periods, but Kitto proposes a basic distinction between the Elizabethan drama, which is "representational," and Greek drama, which is primarily "constructive." Like the Greek philosophers, the Greek poets

looked out on their Universe of human action and suffering, and saw unending variety— and they saw it with that quickness and sharpness in which the Greek was seldom wanting. But it was not his habit to represent this directly. He sought rather to apprehend the unifying simplicity, the fundamental laws; and these, once apprehended, became the framework of his drama. The immediate objects of his observation—the characters, actions, experiences of men—became, so to speak, his raw material, and out of it, discarding and rearranging, he built his new completely intelligible structure. From the material he selected only what was immediately relevant to his purpose, and the purpose was not to represent a typical human situation, but to recreate the inner reality. Such, after all, is the very meaning of...poiesis, which has become our word "poetry"; quite literally it means "construction." Let it be said again that of course the English dramatic poets also did this, as any artist must, but the balance between the constructive and representational activities in the Greek and the Elizabethan respectively is considerable, and explains, to a very great extent, the differences in form and style.

"The exciting thing in Shakespeare," he continues,

apart from his poetry, is the delight—or it may be the revulsion—with which he seizes one character or one situation after another and puts its essence before us. The exciting quality in Aeschylus and Sophocles, apart from their poetry, is the imaginative and intellectual control with which they make every detail a significant part of one illuminating design.

Thus Greek tragedy is didactic, or essentially "religious," but Kitto is prepared to argue that at least one major Elizabethan play is religious in this sense as well. Like the controversies about *Oedipus*, the conflicting interpretations of *Hamlet* come about because we use the wrong assumptions and pose the wrong questions. But, Kitto asks, "what if *Hamlet* is a play which it is reasonable to call 'religious drama'...? what if the ingrained individualism of the last two centuries—to say nothing of romanticism—has blinded us to one aspect of the play without which it cannot possibly appear as a firm and coherent structure?" That is, if we shift the emphasis from a concern for the intricacies of Hamlet the individual character to a concern for certain principles of "Nature" or order, the pieces suddenly fit:

we should not try to consider everything in the play as something that reveals or influences the mind and the fate of one tragic hero, Hamlet; rather should we contemplate the characters as a group of people who are destroyed, and work each other's destruction, because of the evil influences with which they are surrounded. Hamlet is not the centre of the play; he is the epicentre.

At the end of *Hamlet* and at the end of *Oedipus* the source of evil has been removed and the principle of general order reaffirmed, although the cost in terms of individual suffering has been great.

This Aristotelianism may not be indefinitely extendable, however, as Kitto clearly recognizes: modern denials of universal order and changing conceptions of character and fate will radically affect our conceptions of what a work of art should be and do. But *Hamlet* and

Oedipus, Prometheus Bound and *Coriolanus* remain what their creators worked to make them be, and not simply what we may be free to make of them now. Responsible criticism is dedicated to the best possible understanding of what the artist meant.

KNIGHT, G(eorge Richard) Wilson. British. Born in Sutton, Surrey, 19 September 1897. Educated at Dulwich College, London; St. Edmund Hall, Oxford, B.A. 1923, M.A. 1931. Served in the Royal Engineers, Signal Service, 1916-20. Master, Seaford House, Littlehampton, Sussex, 1920, St. Peter's School, Seaford, Sussex, 1921, Hawtreys School, Westgate-on-Sea, Kent, 1923-25, and Dean Close School, Cheltenhem, 1925-31; Chancellors' Professor of English, Trinity College, University of Toronto, 1931-40; Assistant Master, Stowe School, Buckinghamshire, 1941-46; Reader in English Literature, 1946-56, and Professor of English Literature, 1956-62 (now Emeritus), University of Leeds. Visiting Lecturer, University of the West Indies, 1951, and University of Cape Town, 1952; Byron Foundation Lecturer, University of Nottingham, 1953; Clark Lecturer, Trinity College, Cambridge, 1962; Visiting Professor, University of Chicago, 1963. Shakespearean actor and producer, Hart House Theatre, Toronto, 1931-40, Westminster Theatre, London, 1941, and University of Leeds, 1946-60. Litt.D.: University of Sheffield, 1966; University of Exeter, 1968. Fellow, Royal Society of Literature; Honorary Fellow, St. Edmund Hall, Oxford, 1965; Vice-President, Spiritualist Association of Great Britain, 1965; C.B.E. (Commander, Order of the British Empire), 1968. Address: Caroline House, Streatham Rise, Exeter, Devon EX4 4PE, England.

PUBLICATIONS

Criticism

Myth and Miracle: An Essay on the Mystic Symbolism of Shakespeare. London, Edward J. Burrow, 1929; reprinted in *The Crown of Life,* 1947.
The Wheel of Fire: Essays in Interpretation of Shakespeare's Sombre Tragedies. London, Oxford University Press, 1930; revised editon, London, Methuen, 1949.
The Imperial Theme: Further Interpretations of Shakespeare's Tragedies, Including the Roman Plays. London, Oxford University Press, 1931; New York, Oxford University Press, 1961.
The Shakespearian Tempest. London, Oxford University Press, 1932; New York, Barnes and Noble, 1960.
The Christian Renaissance, with Interpretations of Dante, Shakespeare and Goethe and a Note on T.S. Eliot. Toronto, Macmillan, 1933; revised editon, London, Methuen, and New York, Barnes and Noble, 1962.
Principles of Shakespearian Production, with Especial Reference to the Tragedies. London, Faber, and New York, Macmillan, 1936; revised version as *Shakespearian Production,* London, Faber, and Evanston, Illinois, Northwestern University Press, 1964.
The Burning Oracle: Studies in the Poetry of Action. London, Oxford University Press, 1939.
This Sceptred Isle: Shakespeare's Message for England at War. Oxford, Blackwell, 1940.
The Starlit Dome: Studies in the Poetry of Vision. London, Oxford University Press, 1941; New York, Barnes and Noble, 1960.

Chariot of Wrath: *The Message of John Milton to Democracy at War*.   London, Faber, 1942; Folcroft, Pennsylvania, Folcroft Editions, 1969; condensed version, in *Poets of Action*, 1967.

The Olive and the Sword: *A Study of England's Shakespeare*.   London, Oxford University Press, 1944; reprinted in part in *The Sovereign Flower*, 1958, and *Shakespeare and Religion*, 1967.

The Crown of Life: *Essays in Interpretation of Shakespeare's Final Plays*.   London and New York, Oxford University Press, 1947.

Christ and Nietzsche: *An Essay in Poetic Wisdom*.   London and New York, Staples Press, 1948.

Lord Byron: *Christian Virtues*.   London, Routledge, 1952; New York, Oxford University Press, 1953.

Laureate of Peace: *On the Genius of Alexander Pope*.   London, Routledge, 1954; as *The Poetry of Pope*, London, Routledge, and New York, Barnes and Noble, 1965.

The Mutual Flame: *On Shakespeare's Sonnets and "The Phoenix and the Turtle."*   London, Methuen, and New York, Macmillan, 1955.

Lord Byron's Marriage: *The Evidence of Asterisks*.   London, Routledge, and New York, Macmillan, 1957.

The Sovereign Flower: *On Shakespeare as the Poet of Royalism Together with Related Essays and Indexes to Earlier Volumes*.   London, Methuen, and New York, Macmillan, 1958.

Ibsen.   London, Oliver and Boyd, 1962; as *Henrik Ibsen*, New York, Grove Press, 1963.

The Golden Labyrinth: *A Study of British Drama*.   London, Phoenix House, and New York, Norton, 1962.

The Saturnian Quest: *A Chart of the Prose Works of John Cowper Powys*.   London, Methuen, and New York, Barnes and Noble, 1964.

Byron and Shakespeare.   London, Routledge, and New York, Barnes and Noble, 1966.

Shakespeare and Religion: *Essays of Forty Years*.   London, Routledge, and New York, Barnes and Noble, 1967.

Poets of Action.   London, Methuen, and New York, Barnes and Noble, 1967.

Neglected Powers: *Essays on Nineteenth and Twentieth Century Literature*.   London, Routledge, and New York, Barnes and Noble, 1971.

"Thoughts on *The Waste Land*," in *Denver Quarterly*, 7, 1972.

Shakespeare's Dramatic Challenge: *On the Rise of Shakespeare's Tragic Heroes*.   London, Croom Helm, 1977.

Symbol of Man: *On Body-Soul for Stage and Studio*.   London, Regency Press, 1979.

Verse

Gold-Dust with Other Poetry.   London, Routledge, and New York, Barnes and Noble, 1968.

Play

The Last of the Incas: *A Play on the Conquest of Peru* (produced Sheffield, 1954).   Leeds, privately printed, 1954.

Other

Atlantic Crossing: *An Autobiographical Design*.   London, Dent, 1936.
The Dynasty of Stowe (autobiography).   London, Fortune Press, 1945.
Hiroshima: *On Prophecy and the Sun-Bomb*.   London, Dakers, 1946.

Jackson Knight: A Biography.   Oxford, Allen and Mowbray, 1975.

Editor, *Elysion: On Ancient Greek and Roman Beliefs Concerning a Life after Death*, by
    W.F. Jackson Knight.   London, Rider, and New York, Barnes and Noble, 1970.

Critical Studies and Bibliography

F.R. Leavis, review of *The Christian Renaissance*, in *Scrutiny* (Cambridge), 2, 1933.
John E. Van Domelen, "A Select List of the Published Writings of George Wilson
    Knight," in *The Morality of Art: Essays Presented to G. Wilson Knight by His
    Colleagues and Friends*, edited by D.W. Jefferson.   London, Routledge, 1959.
Roger Sale, "G. Wilson Knight," in *Modern Language Quarterly* (Seattle), 29, 1968.

*   *   *

Since Lessing the distinction between "temporal" and "spatial" arts has been a commonplace
if not exactly a received truth of aesthetics. We experience a Bach fugue or James novel as a
sequence unfolding before us, but we experience a Cezanne still-life in what seems to be, by
comparison, an instant of time. In the visual or spatial arts we are pleased by the "content"
represented and by those elements of balance, order and closure which allow us to grasp a work
as a completed whole, suspended in time. But obviously fugues and narratives also have a kind
of spatial dimension: because we have what E.M. Forster calls (in *Aspects of the Novel*)
"memory and intelligence" we can hold sequences in our minds and perceive something which
has formal coherence analogous to that of a painting or piece of sculpture. Thus Forster is able
to discuss, for example, the "hourglass" patten of *The Ambassadors*, a novel whose "architectural competence" James himself was proud of.

This spatial dimension of literature is of fundamental importance to G. Wilson Knight. He
recalls that when he went up to Oxford after the First World War he was troubled by the
apparent inability of criticism to fathom Shakespeare's essential meaning or "secret":

> I had grown dissatisfied with the usual division of Shakespeare's art into "characters"
> and "poetry": surely the dramatic people were themselves poetic, and if so they should be
> understood in that light. Shakespearian study in the 1920's was clouded by what has
> become known as "realistic" criticism, a term which covered some fine scholarly virtues
> and a yet greater number of scholarly vices. By "vices" I refer to the kind of study which
> appeared to believe, and made wide sections of the public believe, that a proper
> understanding of the Elizabethan stage and Elizabethan prompt books and printing
> would serve if driven far enough to render up the Shakespearian secret.... From an
> imaginative, and also from a commonsense, standpoint Shakespearian studies were in a
> state of chaos.

If we are to experience the plays properly we must be able to see them in space:

> It is natural in analysis to pursue the steps of the tale in sequence, noticing the logic that
> connects them, regarding those essentials that Aristotle noted: beginning, middle, and
> end. But by giving supreme attention to this temporal nature of drama we omit what, in
> Shakespeare, is at least of equal importance. A Shakespearian tragedy is set spatially as
> well as temporally in the mind. By this I mean that there are throughout the play a set of
> correspondences which relate to each other independently of the time-sequence which is
> the story.... Now if we are prepared to see the whole play laid out, so to speak, as an area,
> being simultaneously aware of these thickly-scattered correspondences in a single view
> of the whole, we possess the unique quality of the play in a new sense. "Faults" begin to
> vanish into thin air. Immediately we begin to realize necessity where before we saw
> irrelevance and beauty dethroning ugliness.

We can now begin to understand the plays as "expanded metaphors," as "visionary wholes" or patterns of recurring images; but the term "spatial." Knight warns us, "must not be allowed to suggest the static: what I have called the 'fiery' significances starting from the page were anything but that. The truth is, they [have] a vertical rather than a horizontal activity." In short, Shakespeare's plays are "symbolic," but Shakespeare's symbolism, unlike that of Blake or Yeats, is not esoteric: we recognize, for example, "the power of Shakespeare's tempest-symbol as suggesting human tragedy, or his use of jewel-metaphors to embody the costly riches of love. In ages hence, when perhaps tempests are controlled by science and communism has replaced wealth, then the point of Shakespeare's symbolism may need explanation." By symbols Knight does not, of course, mean conventional signs; rather, symbols exist to give "sensory form to values and powers not otherwise easy to express; at the limit, to extra-sensory dimensions of being and spirit realities."

In an early essay, *Myth and Miracle*, Knight lays the foundation for the long series of symbolic readings of Shakespeare now published in *The Wheel of Fire, The Imperial Theme, The Shakespearian Tempest, The Crown of Life* and *The Mutual Flame*:

> Let me recall the outline of the Shakespearian progress. In the problem plays there is mental division: on the one side an exquisite appreciation of the spiritual—beauty, romance, poetry; on the other, the hate-theme—loathing of the impure, aversion from the animal kinship of man, disgust at the decaying body of death. This dualism is resolved in the tragedies; the hate-theme itself is finely sublimated in *Timon* by means of the purification of great passion, human grandeur, and all the panoply of high tragedy. The recurrent poetic symbol of tragedy in Shakespeare is "storm" or "tempest." The third group outsoars the intuition of tragedy and gives us plays whose plots explicate the quality of immortality: the predominating symbols are loss in tempest and revival to the sounds of music.

The late plays, with their mythic patterns of reunion and rebirth, must be taken "as seriously in their own right as the tragedies":

> When in *Pericles* Thaisa is restored from the dead by the saintly Cimon and when at the conclusion to *The Winter's Tale* that statue of the supposedly dead Hermione warms to life, what [is needed is] a simple, child-like response to the miraculous, such as we accord to similar events in the New Testament. We [see] a mystical or miraculous statement pushing through the form and structure of a conventional play. Everything at once [falls] into place: questions of authorship settle themselves. We [have] no reason to suppose that the greater part of *Pericles* or the Vision of Jupiter in *Cymbeline* [is] spurious.

Myth and Miracle and the essays which followed in quick succession are interpretive rather than critical, as Knight was careful to point out:

> "Criticism" to me suggests a certain process of deliberately objectifying the work under consideration; the comparison of it with other similar works in order especially to show in what respects it surpasses, or falls short of, those works; and, finally, a formal judgment as to its lasting validity. "Interpretation," on the contrary, tends to merge into the work it analyses; it attempts, as far as possible, to understand its subject in the light of its own nature.... Thus criticism is active and looks ahead, treating past work often as material on which to base future standards and canons of art; interpretation is passive, and looks back, regarding only the imperative challenge of a poetic vision. Criticism is a judgment of vision; interpretation a reconstruction of vision.

Knight's straightforward, often incredibly careful tracing out of image patterns won the approval, at least for a while, of Eliot and Leavis, and had considerable influence on such critics as L.C. Knights, R.B. Heilman (at a later date), and—it is reasonable to guess—Knight's younger Canadian friend, Northrop Frye. But by the mid-1930's it was clear that Knight had been moving in a direction few others could take seriously. To put it as briefly and neutrally as possible: Knight believes in the immortality of the soul and in a spiritual "beyond" which has little in common with orthodox Christian doctrine. Art is quite literally revelation, the

333

"extroverted expression of the creative imagination which, when introverted, becomes religion":

> From the ancient world down, from Homer and Aeschylus to Byron and Hardy, the business of great literature may be defined as the interweaving of human affairs with spiritualistic appearances, phantasms of the dead, resurrections and visitations; or, if they are not present, with symbols of eternal suggestions of atmospheric effects which may be called "numinous."

Thus art is, or strives to be, a kind of white magic; it aims at "control and transmutations"; it exists in order to "enlarge our experience" and is "active, as wisdom and mysticism by themselves, are not." "We need to listen," Knight concludes, "to the positive powers impinging on our present society from beyond."

What Knight has undertaken is nothing less than to rewrite the history of English poetry and drama from the point of view of Spiritualism. In *The Starlit Dome*, for example, he examines the spirit intuitions of Keats, Coleridge, Wordsworth and Shelley. These rambling essays are not easy to describe, but fortunately Knight's brother, the classicist W.F. Jackson Knight, has provided a convenient summary:

> The poetry of these "romantic" poets is very highly symbolic; and this symbolic language urgently needed to be explained. How it is worked out is very impressive.
>
> The "dome" itself may fairly claim the chief importance. A "dome" had become a frequent symbol before the Romantic Period, and in that period became more frequent still. A dome is sometimes what we now understand by a dome, but the word is cognate with other words conveying other meanings, for example, "cathedral" or merely "house." Now the poets regularly introduce an edifice of some sort when they are thinking about aspiration generated in human life. Human life flows onwards, but it is not content with the horizontal flow. We aspire to a reality more high, and more stable and permanent; that is, to an eternity. How neat, and how satisfying, these identifications can be is shown...by the interpretation of *Kubla Khan*, which is probably the clearest and most quickly convincing example of the method and its results so far published.... [The] poem is at last known for what it is, a well-formed and comprehensive, though concise, solution to an important, if not the most important problem, and not at all the unintelligible fragment which it used to be considered.... *Kubla Khan* reveals a pattern which all the four poets examined [here] followed in their life-work. Wordsworth spent about the first half of his [poetic career] on the visible nature in which life is lived, and the other half, approximately, on the other sphere of being which is symbolized in domes and other edifices. Shelley's aspiration towards the eternal world is so passionate that in one of his characteristic figures his rivers actually appear to flow uphill into mountains on which, finally, edifices are found. Keats' symbols are as clear as anyone's, but all the way along he notably blends all the opposites together, nature and art, the temporal and spatial, life as it is and aspiration, and indeed time and eternity. Once his "dome" becomes a Grecian urn, with ardent living still pictured on it in eternal permanence.

To take one more example: in his "comprehensive account" of English drama, *The Golden Labyrinth*, Knight claims that he has "established the close relation in all periods between drama and the occult, and showed how, since the Spiritualistic movement started in the last century, the emphasis has become more emphatic than ever." If we object that these poets and dramatists never intended the spirit-messages Knight decodes, the answer is simply that writers are inspired creatures, merely the vessels through which the truth may flow; as Socrates pointed out—in a rather different context—in their prosaic moments they usually have no comprehension of what their lines mean.

From the point of view of critical theory it is futile to comment in any detail on Knight's later work: his exhaustive treatment of Byron, his insistence on the prophetic strain in Milton's "nationalism," on bisexual idealism and the erotic core of creativity—these and a dozen other matters belong more properly to the history of modern Spiritualism. Yet anyone who looks into these strange books will find it impossible to doubt Knight's sincerity or sense of urgency.

In a long retrospective essay, "Poetry and Magic" (printed in *Neglected Powers*), he quotes a passage from Mrs. Radcliffe's *The Italian*:

> The elder brothers of the convent said that he had talents, but denied him learning; they applauded him for the profound subtlety which he occasionally discovered in argument, but observed that he seldom perceived truth when it lay on the surface; he could follow it through all the labyrinths of disquisition, but overlooked it when it was undisguised before him. In fact he cared not for truth, nor sought it by bold and broad argument, but loved to exert the wily cunning of his nature in hunting it through artificial perplexities. At length, from a habit of intricacy and suspicion, his vitiated mind could receive nothing for truth which was simple and easily comprehended.

and observes that "this critique may be applied to our culture at the present time" and "our supposedly 'Christian' era":

> In a speech...on the occasion of my retirement at the University of Leeds, I asserted that there lies, ready to hand, the *resolving* factor. Spiritualism touches each of our academic disciplines.... A brief glance at the monthly syllabus of the Spiritualist Association of Great Britain...indicates the barrier which must, and eventually will, be broken. There are, as I see it, only two promising ways open: one is the Churches' Fellowship for Psychical and Spiritual Studies; the other is literature.

Christianity has become so rigid, so much a matter of "faith" (whereas psychic research now offers us "evidence"), that literature and Spiritualism must take on the burdens of prophecy and revelation.

From beginning to end Knight's criticism has been "thematic": literature matters because of what it reveals; *how* it does so is of less importance. Or to be more precise, Knight uses a kind of critical language which can tell us nothing at all about artistic excellence or relative virtues— unless, of course, we are content to award the prizes to works which contain the most domes or other right symbols. As early as 1933, when Knight still seemed to be a fairly conventional critic, F.R. Leavis pointed out the dangers of this approach to literature in a way which can hardly be improved upon:

> He explicitly exempts himself from critical discipline, the plea being that to analyse and check scrupulously would baulk and hamper the swift play of intuition, the immediate sensitive response, on which the virtue of his work depends. And one must admit that, in *The Wheel of Fire*, all qualifications being made, he is justified. But the plea is a dangerous one. Shakespeare's text he knows intimately, and it is a text potent enough to keep the interpreter's "romantic consciousness" under some control. But with other texts he pays little heed to the "poetry itself": it becomes quickly plain that the "creative vision" we are most concerned with is rarely that of the poet specified.... Professor Knight shows not the least sign of uneasiness at having to rely on Cary's *Divine Comedy* and Professor Latham's *Faust*. In the poetry of his own language his procedure its truly shocking: any text will do so long as it yields a congenial or convenient explicit "content."... He seems, in fact, completely indifferent about quality—realized value: the general paraphrasable meaning, if it fits the argument, is good enough.

What Leavis observes about *The Christian Renaissance*—that it is "neither criticism nor poetry"—may seem to most readers a just comment on all of Knight's later work as well. And yet, Leavis concludes,

> there is something admirable about the very extravagance of Professor Knight's ambition. One cannot imagine [another critic] proposing to regard "the whole New Testament as a single art-form of Shakespearian quality" or prophesying the "advent of a newly Christianized literature and a newly poetic Christianity." The courage and the energy are magnificent: is refusal of discipline their essential condition?

KNIGHTS, L(ionel) C(harles). British. Born in Grantham, Lincolnshire, 15 May 1906. Educated at Selwyn College and Christ's College, Cambridge (Charles Oldham Shakespeare Scholar, 1938; Members' Prize, 1929), B.A. 1928, M.A. 1931, Ph.D. 1936. Married Elizabeth Mary Barnes in 1936; has two children. Lecturer in English, University of Manchester, 1933-34, 1935-47; Professor of English, University of Sheffield, 1947-52; Winterstoke Professor of English, University of Bristol, 1953-64; Fellow of Queens' College, Cambridge, and King Edward VII Professor of English Literature, Cambridge University, 1965-73, now Emeritus. Andrew Mellon Visiting Professor, University of Pittsburgh, 1961-62, 1966; Beckman Visiting Professor, University of California, Berkeley, 1970. Member, Editorial Board, *Scrutiny* magazine, Cambridge, 1932-53. Docteur de l'Université de Bordeaux, 1964; D.Univ.: University of York, 1969; D.Litt.: University of Manchester, 1974; University of Sheffield, 1978; University of Warwick, 1979. Honorary Fellow, Selwyn College, Cambridge, 1974. Foreign Honorary Member, American Academy of Arts and Sciences, 1981. Address: 57 Jesus Lane, Cambridge CB5 8BS, England.

PUBLICATIONS

Criticism

> *How Many Children Had Lady Macbeth? An Essay in the Theory and Practice of Shakespeare Criticism.* Cambridge, Gordon Fraser The Minority Press, 1933; Folcroft, Pennsylvania, Folcroft Editons, 1970; reprinted in *Explorations*, 1946.
> *Drama and Society in the Age of Jonson.* London, Chatto and Windus, 1937; New York, George Stewart, 1947.
> *Explorations: Essays in Criticism, Mainly on the Literature of the Seventeenth Century.* London, Chatto and Windus, 1946; New York, George Stewart, 1947.
> *Literature and the Study of Society.* Sheffield, University of Sheffield, 1948.
> *Poetry, Politics and the English Tradition.* London, Chatto and Windus, 1954; Folcroft, Pennsylvania, Folcroft Editions, 1973.
> *Shakespeare's Politics, with Some Reflections on the Nature of Tradition.* London, Oxford University Press, 1957; Folcroft, Pennsylvania, Folcroft Editons, 1969.
> *Some Shakespearean Themes.* London, Chatto and Windus, 1959; Stanford, California, Stanford University Press, 1960.
> *An Approach to Hamlet.* London, Chatto and Windus, 1960; Stanford, California, Stanford University Press, 1961.
> *William Shakespeare: The Histories: Richard III, King John, Richard II, Henry V.* London, Longman, 1962; reprinted in *Explorations 3*, 1976.
> *Further Explorations.* London, Chatto and Windus, and Stanford, California, Stanford University Press, 1965.
> *Some Shakespearean Themes and An Approach to Hamlet.* Stanford, California, Stanford University Press, 1966.
> *Public Voices: Literature and Politics with Special Reference to the Seventeenth Century.* London, Chatto and Windus, 1971; Totowa, New Jersey, Rowman and Littlefield, 1972.
> *Explorations 3.* London, Chatto and Windus, and Pittsburgh, University of Pittsburgh Press, 1976.
> *Hamlet and Other Shakespearean Essays.* London, Cambridge University Press, 1979.
> *Selected Essays in Criticism.* London, Cambridge University Press, 1981.

Other

> Editor, with Basil Cottle, *Metaphor and Symbol.* London, Butterworth, 1960.

Editor, with others, *Myth and Symbol: Critical Approaches and Applications.*   Lincoln, University of Nebraska Press, 1964.

*   *   *

L.C. Knights is a consistently sensible critic (no one familiar with modern criticism will regard this as faint praise) but not an especially original one, nor has he ever pretended to be. He indicates his debt to I.A. Richards in the Preface to *Explorations* and tells readers of *Drama and Society in the Age of Jonson* that another debt, to F.R. Leavis, is "altogether too large for public acknowledgement." If we add to the list the more elusive influence of Marx, or some aspects of Marxist economic determinism, then we have the boundaries within which Knights has been content to work.

Well over forty years ago Knights established the critical principle which, at least as a theory, he has never abandoned. A Shakespeare play, he maintained in *How Many Children Had Lady Macbeth?* is a "dramatic poem" and must be apprehended as such if its value is to be realized. And by "poetry" Knights clearly had in mind the conception of imaginative activity which I.A. Richards had been developing a few years before, in *Principles of Literary Criticism* and *Practical Criticism.* In a later essay, "The Interaction of Words" (an essay which Knights refers to in *Explorations*), Richards maintains that in Donne's *Anatomy of the World*

> there is a prodigious activity between the words as we read them. Following, exploring, realizing, *becoming* that activity is, I suggest, the essential thing in reading the poem. Understanding it is not a preparation for reading the poem. It is itself the poem. And it is a constructive, hazardous, free creative process, a process of conception through which a new being is growing in the mind.

This "new being," brought about if the reader rightly attends to the complex interaction of words in a successful poem, is a more highly organized awareness of life, an increased competence for dealing with experience, a kind of informed poise or equilibrium which is central to Richards' thoroughly naturalistic position. Very briefly: as struggling creatures beset by drives and impulses, we will "prefer to satisfy a greater number of equal appetencies rather than a less": thus "the conduct of life throughout is an attempt to organize impulses so that success is obtained for the greater number or mass of them, for the most important and weightiest set." In the *Principles* Richards concludes that the arts

> are our storehouse of recorded values. They spring from and perpetuate hours in the lives of exceptional people, when their control and command of experience is at its highest...when the varying possibilities of existence are most clearly seen and the different activities which may arise are most exquisitely reconciled.... Subtle or recondite experiences are for most men incommunicable or indescribable, though social conventions or the terror of the loneliness of the human situation may make us pretend the contrary. In the arts we find the record in the only form in which these things can be recorded of the experiences which have seemed most worth having to the most sensitive and discriminating people.... It should be unnecessary to insist upon the degree to which high civilization, in other words, free, varied and unwasteful life, depends upon them in a numerous society.

The loss of poetry, that is, the ability to read poetry properly, would be nothing less than a "biological calamity" for the human race. How close Knights is to this position may be seen in the following passage from *Some Shakespearean Themes*:

> *King John* is a good play, containing some admirably vigorous poetry; but the kind of attention its poetry demands is qualitatively different from the kind of attention demanded by the poetry of *Macbeth*. And the level at which meaning takes place in poetry is determined by the kind and degree of activity that the poetry—the whole play—calls for on the part of the reader. Not only is the verse of *Macbeth* more fluid, more vivid and compressed than the verse of *King John*, the mind of the reader or spectator is more fully activated, and activated in different ways. The compression, the

337

thick cluster of imagery (with rapidly changing metaphors completely superseding the similes and drawn-out figures to be found in the earlier plays), the surprising juxtapositions, the over-riding of grammar, and the shifts and overlappings of meanings—all these, demanding an unusual liveliness of attention, force the reader to respond with the whole of his active imagination.

and in this passage from "The University Teaching of English and History":

The reading of literature, in so far as it is anything more than a pastime, involves the continuous development of the power of intelligent discrimination. Literature, moreover, is simply the exact expression of realized values—and these values are never purely personal.... The discipline of strict literary criticism is the only means we have of apprehending those embodied values with sureness and subtlety.

To return to *How Many Children Had Lady Macbeth?*: Knights is less interested in giving a full poetic analysis of *Macbeth* than in pointing out how an overemphasis on "character" may prevent or inhibit full response to the play. "In the mass of Shakespeare criticism," he concludes (the reader should bear in mind this is 1933),

there is not a hint that "character"—like "plot," "rhythm," "construction" and all our other critical counters—is merely an abstraction from the total response in the mind of the reader or spectator, brought into being by written or spoken words; that the critic therefore—however far he may ultimately range—begins with the words of which the play is composed. This applies equally to the novel or any other form of art that uses language as its medium.

Total response—response, in other words, which raises the mind of the reader to the level of the controlling, ordering mind of the artist—is possible only by "an exact and sensitive study of the quality of the verse, of the rhythm and imagery, of the controlled associations of the words and their emotional and intellectual force."

In light of this argument, Knights' extended treatment of Shakespeare elsewhere in *An Approach to Hamlet* and *Some Shakespearean Themes*, raises some questions, since—to put the matter in rather unfairly simplified terms—the former is primarily a study of "character" and the latter primarily of "thought" (Shakespeare's thought, that is, and not the intellectual characteristics of the agents depicted in the plays). In *An Approach to Hamlet* Knights proposes that Hamlet is one of those Shakespearean "fools of time"

not because there is something hostile to men's hopes and aspirations in the very nature of things, so that "checks and disasters" necessarily "grow in the veins of actions highest reared" [but] because of some failure of reason or of the imagination.

Like Othello, Hamlet is "self-dramatizing and self-regarding" and thus erects a "barrier against the knowledge that would bring freedom"; Hamlet is "immature," "regressive," incapable of true growth, as we see if we compare him with Lear:

In each of these plays—I have named *Othello, Timon,* and some others—there is an exploration of the ways in which "being" and "knowing" are related, so that failure in being, the corruption of consciousness, results either in a false affirmation, as with Othello, or in an inability to affirm at all, as with Hamlet. In *King Lear,* where so many lines of Shakespeare's thought converge, Lear only comes to "see better" through a purgatorial process of self-knowledge which enables him finally to respond to love. Perhaps we may say that Hamlet's consciousness is not unlike the consciousness of the unregenerate Lear, full of the knowledge of bitter wrong, of evil seemingly inherent in human nature. But Hamlet, unlike Lear—even if, initially, he is less greatly sinning— cannot break out of the closed circle of loathing and self-contempt, so that his nature is "subdued to what it works in, like the dyer's hand." The awareness that he embodies is at best an intermediate stage of the spirit, at worst a blind alley. Most certainly Hamlet's way of knowing the world is not Shakespeare's own.

(This last sentence indicates that *An Approach to Hamlet* is in part an extended reply to T.S. Eliot's well-known charge that *Hamlet* is an inadequate "objective correlative" of Shakespeare's own problems: for Knights the play is a splendidly-realized depiction of a *character* who has not attained "maturity.") *Some Shakespearean Themes* is "based on the belief that Shakespeare's plays form a coherent whole, that they stem from and express a developing 'attitude to life'—which does not mean that individually they were not also a response to outside demands, such as those of a particular audience." But by Shakespeare's "thought" Knights does not mean some accumulation of maxims that can be abstracted from the plays:

> The reader knows that what he has to deal with is not statement poetically embellished, from which the metaphors could be subtracted leaving the meaning more or less intact, but with a poetry which is profoundly exploratory, that evokes what it seeks to define, and in which the implicit evaluation of experience is entirely dependent on the fullness of evocation.... In responding to that poetry we find that we are dealing with certain themes that shape themselves into a developing pattern. These are not "abstract themes," "philosophical concepts," or "bare general propositions"; they represent a set or slant of interest that springs from and engages the concern of the personality as a whole; and although that, in turn, is far from being simply a concern for *this* man in *this* action—for it has to do with fundamental and lasting aspects of the human situation that are focussed in a given case—it is only through the particular action, the precise articulation of a work of art, that it can be clarified and brought to expression.... [The plays] point towards...an organization of experience so living and complex when we are engaged in it, living it to the full extent of our powers, we have no need of token definitions.... Great poetry has this in common with great moral teaching. "The wisest of the Ancients," said Blake in his famous letter to Dr. Trusler, "consider'd what was not too Explicit as the fittest for Instruction, because it rouzes the faculties to act."

To summarize Shakespeare's "philosophy," then, is to translate it into a different kind of language and diminish its force. But at the risk of doing so, Knights argues that the early plays depict a "public world" which is "keenly observed" but not "felt from within," as the later plays are. *Lear* is a "great exploratory allegory to which so many of the earlier plays lead and on which the later plays depend":

> Those written before *Lear* stand firmly enough in their own right, but behind some of the most significant of them there is an insistent and unresolved questioning.... Why do both the public world and the world of intense subjective experience seem somehow flawed and unsatisfactory? Is there any escape from appearance and illusion? What is the status of human values in a world dominated by time and death? On what, in the world as we know it, can man take his stand? In *King Lear* Shakespeare discovered an answer to these questions not in terms of copy-book maxims but in terms of intense living experience. The resulting freedom from inner tensions is seen alike in the assured judgment and magnificent vitality of *Macbeth, Antony and Cleopatra* and *Coriolanus*, in each of which qualities making for wholeness and essential life are glimpsed through the perversion or entanglement of energies and passions deeply rooted in human nature. In the latest plays, without discarding or ignoring the experience of the tragic period, Shakespeare puts in the forefront of his drama "the possible other case," and directly bodies forth experiences in which not only does good triumph but the energies of "nature" themselves contribute to the sense of renewed life.

An Approach to Hamlet and *Some Shakespearean Themes* are valuable, often suggestive works, but in neither of them is Knights as attentive as one might expect him to be to the "interaction of words."

The influence of F.R. Leavis is pervasive but much more difficult to demonstrate briefly: a few examples here of the familiar concern with "maturity," "values" and "tradition" will have to suffice. Hamlet, as we saw before, is "immature" whereas the poetry of George Herbert reveals a "mature 'acceptance' of life" and an "integration of attitude." Restoration comedy is "trivial, gross and dull." About Jonson's poetry Knights observes that "the important question is, What values do these poems embody and help to keep alive?" Herbert's poetry is "an integral part of the great English tradition." And again,

> the possibilities of living at any moment are not merely an individual matter; they depend on physical circumstances and (what is less of a commonplace) on current habits of thought and feeling, on all that is implied by "tradition"—or the lack of it. The poet who is able to draw on a living tradition embodies it in a particular, comprehensible form; and for us to grasp that form is to work our way into those extra-personal conditions which combined with the writer's genius to make his work.

In "The University Teaching of English and History" Knights suggests that the two disciplines could be "brought into profitable correlation and directed towards education for living in the twentieth century" but warns that a "radical overhauling of present educational methods is involved" and that his own contribution will be small. This was in 1939; when the essay was reprinted in the 1945 *Explorations* Knights was happy to add a footnote directing his readers to Leavis' recently published *Education and the University*.

As for the "Marxist" influence, it is worth noting that on several occasions Knights has made use of a passage from Engels,

> We make our own history but in the first place under very different presuppositions and conditions. Among these the economic ones are finally decisive.

and another passage from Marx:

> The methods of production in material life determine the general character of the social, political and spiritual processes of life. It is not the consciousness of men that determines their being, but, on the contrary, their social being determines their consciousness.

Although far from being an orthodox Marxist, Knights attempts to explore, tentatively, in *Drama and Society in the Age of Jonson*, "a few of the intercommunications between economic and social conditions and one of the cultural forms of the period." The artist does much more, however, than merely "express" the economically determined attitudes of his time:

> if this book establishes anything it should be that the reactions of a genuine poet to his environment form a criticism of society at least as important as the keenest analysis in purely economic terms; that the intelligence and perception that help to make great poetry do not function in a special "poetic" sphere, but are immediately relevant to all questions of "the good life."

This raises a problem for Marxism and indeed for any form of determinism: how is it possible to rise above the limitations of a determining environment and make an objective analysis of one's situation? How is economic determinism any less "conditioned" than apologies for competition and free enterprise? Knights recognizes the difficulty when he asks, "In what ways was the dominant moral code of the period *merely* 'the product, in the last analysis, of the economic stage which society had reached at that particular epoch,' and in what ways was it (to use another phrase from Engels) 'a really human morality,' i.e., a code which supported and enriched ways of thinking, feeling and behaving to which we can still respond?" That there can be a "really human morality" remains a matter of faith, or perhaps of hope. Knights does not press further, just as he has always stopped short of endorsing the extremes which Richards, Leavis and the Marxists have sometimes embraced.

KRIEGER, Murray. American. Born in Newark, New Jersey, 27 November 1923. Educated at Rutgers University, New Brunswick, New Jersey, 1940-42; University of Chicago, M.A. 1948; Ohio State University, Columbus, Ph.D. 1952. Served in the United States Army, 1942-46. Married Joan Stone in 1947; has two children. Instructor, Kenyon College, Gambier, Ohio, 1948-49; Assistant Professor, 1952-55, and Associate Professor, 1955-58, University of Minnesota, Minneapolis; Professor of English, University of Illinois, Urbana, 1958-63; M.F. Carpenter Professor of Literary Criticism, University of Iowa, Iowa City, 1963-66. Since 1967, Professor of English, University of California at Irvine (Co-Director, 1975-77, and Director, 1977-79, School for Criticism and Theory); since 1973, Professor of English, and since 1974, University Professor, University of California at Los Angeles. Associate Member, University of Illinois Center for Advanced Study, 1961-62; Regents' Lecturer, University of California at Davis, 1966. Recipient: Guggenheim Fellowship, 1956, 1961; American Council of Learned Societies Postdoctoral Fellowship, 1966; National Endowment for the Humanities Grant, 1971; Rockefeller Humanities Research Fellowship, 1978. Address: Department of English and Comparative Literature, University of California, Irvine, California 92664, U.S.A.

PUBLICATIONS

Criticism

The New Apologists for Poetry. Minneapolis, University of Minnesota Press, 1956.
Visions of Extremity in Modern Literature:
   1. *The Tragic Vision: Variations on a Theme in Literary Interpretation.* New York, Holt Rinehart, 1960; as *The Tragic Vision: The Confrontation of Extremity*, Baltimore, Johns Hopkins University Press, 1973.
   2. *The Classic Vision: The Retreat from Extremity in Modern Literature.* Baltimore, Johns Hopkins University Press, 1971; as *The Classic Vision*, 1974.
A Window to Criticism: Shakespeare's Sonnets and Modern Poetics. Princeton, New Jersey, Princeton University Press, 1964.
The Play and Place of Criticism. Baltimore, John Hopkins University Press, 1967.
"Fiction, History, and Empirical Reality," in *Critical Inquiry* (Chicago), 1, 1974.
Theory of Criticism: A Tradition and Its System. Baltimore, Johns Hopkins University Press, 1976.
Poetic Presence and Illusion: Essays in Critical History and Theory. Baltimore, and London, Johns Hopkins University Press, 1979.
"Criticism as a Secondary Art," in *What is Criticism?* edited by Paul Hernadi. Bloomington and London, Indiana University Press, 1981.
Arts on the Level: The Fall of the Elite Object. Knoxville, University of Tennessee Press, 1981.

Other

Editor, with Eliseo Vivas, *The Problems of Aesthetics: A Book of Readings.* New York, Rinehart, 1953.
Editor, *Northrop Frye in Modern Criticism.* New York, Columbia University Press, 1966.
Editor, with L.S. Dembo, *Directions for Criticism: Structuralism and Its Alternatives.* Madison, University of Wisconsin Press, 1977.

CRITICAL STUDY

> Frank Lentricchia, "Murray Krieger's Last Romanticism," in *After the New Criticism*. Chicago and London, University of Chicago Press, 1980.

*   *   *

The New Apologists for Poetry, The Tragic Vision, The Classic Vision and *The Play and Place of Criticism* are difficult texts, more difficult than they needed to be for at least two reasons. In the first place Murray Krieger's key terms, tragic, vision, thematic, contextual and "ethical" (with quotation marks to indicate Kierkegaard's special sense of that word), do not mean what they usually mean in ordinary discourse; and in the second place Krieger has what is probably the worst prose style of any critic worth taking seriously. Four brief examples from *The Tragic Vision* should support this unpleasant charge:

> Perhaps it was not for the Greek theoretical consciousness—even in as late a representative as Aristotle—to be as self-consciously aware of the disturbing implications of the tragic mentality as it was of the formal requirements which transcended, or rather absorbed, this mentality and restored order to the universe threatened by it.

> For the cheerfully naturalistic vision, which, pampering its security, denies itself nothing despite the fearsome implications of its own metaphysical denials, which existentially shirks the void it must rationally insist upon, is a pre-crisis vision, an illusion of ethical man demanded by his comfort, but one the stricken man can no longer afford.

> The autonomy of poetry they [the new critics] must assert since only as autonomous can its revelations be those which poetry can uniquely afford.

> As we saw with Gide, he does not exhaust himself even in his most intensely created character but creates such a character as but one extreme of the dialogue the self conducts with the soul, an extreme that the very act of dialogue—so long as it is a disciplined act—manages partly to tame?

But since Krieger is not the only modern critic who writes badly, and since it is possible to use a kind of verbal algebra when dealing with his arguments ("Let 'vision' equal...," and so on), he is not, strictly speaking, unreadable.

Whatever important differences there may be between Eliot, Richards, Ransom and some other "New Critics," Krieger maintains that they have one thing in common. In *The New Apologists for Poetry* he is concerned primarily with those critics "who are trying to answer the need, forced on them by historical pressures, to justify poetry by securing for it a unique function for which modern scientism cannot find a surrogate." These new apologists are determined to prove that poetry is "autonomous" and that poetry can do something important for us that science cannot do. But the claims are irreconcilable, at least given Krieger's reductive, either-or mode of reasoning:

> The poem must in one sense, as a special form of discourse, be nonreferential, even as it must be referential to be any form of discourse at all. It must, as organic, be autonomous, even as it illuminates human experience. If it is to be on the ground of the integrated, disinterested, even selfless experience I would denominate as aesthetic, the poem must be distinguished by what have been termed "immanent meanings," even though these cannot be discovered if I do not bring to the poem clearly specified meanings from the outside.

From the point of view of formal aesthetics—from the point of view, that is, of a branch of philosophy in which strict internal consistency is essential—most modern poetic theories do in fact turn out to be somewhat muddled and contradictory. Eliot's confusing discussion of "creativity" is a case in point, yet Krieger's victory here is a peculiarly empty one, since Eliot himself warned readers that his statements about poetry should be understood as "by-products of my private poetry work-shop," of primary value to scholars "interested in the mind of my generation." In one sense Krieger's objections are perfectly justified; in another, and for most readers far more important sense, they are largely irrelevant. It is more realistic to argue as M.H. Abrams does in his important essay, "What's the Use of Theorizing about the Arts?" that "once a concept or assertion has been adopted as the basis of a critical theory, its origin or truth-claim, whether empirical or metaphysical, ceases to matter, for its validity in this context is to be determined by its power of illumination when brought to bear in the scrutiny of works of art." Historical importance and heuristic value, not philosophical purity, are the qualities which really matter.

In *The Tragic Vision* and *The Classic Vision* (which should be considered as parts of one argument) and the title essay of *The Play and Place of Criticism* Krieger attempts to construct a theory which will do justice to poetry as a special mode of perception. Reality is a welter of particulars, or irreducibly individual occasions and conflicting forces which the philosopher approaches by means of propositional discourse; his account of reality will therefore be "generic, conceptual, mediate." The poet, however, approaches reality with a different kind of discourse, capable of expressing the fullness of actual experience:

> Experience, always unique, is never to be seen as common, is unapproachable except by poetry; and poetry, in order to keep itself eligible to approach, resists all non-poetic sense. Life in its phenomenological fullness is the reality behind the universals that as rationalists we insist upon, though these are the veil, only the construct of our social necessities, as poetry exists to remind us when we can afford to free our vision to look. Poetry breaks through because it alone dares construct itself in freedom from the equally false, equally comforting, veils of stock forms of language. Poetry is the only object, fixed in a final form, that does not objectify and destroy—that embodies to preserve—the object as universal subject by refusing itself to be universal.

But if criticism is necessarily a form of propositional discourse, how can it hope to convey the uniquely valuable nature of poetic contexts? In terms of either-or logic the problem cannot be resolved: the critic's procedure is "muddy and self-defeating"—and yet obviously he must go on, "doggedly and with a clumsy pragmatism that is his response to what is theoretically denied him." "Pragmatism" is the key word here, since the critic does after all have an important role to play:

> the critic can tell us what the poem is *not* as he seeks to protect it from non-poetic systems. So he can speak negatively of what it is not and what it does not mean. But can he speak positively of what the poem is and means? Clearly, in spite of all he argues he cannot, he must speak to this purpose. And he must speak in a way that, cautious and distrustful of itself and its imprisonings, yet imposes discursive system, however tentatively, sporadically, sloppily. Otherwise, for all its superb functioning, the poem may have no more than aesthetic effects on us, may be prevented from shaping our vision of the world. Of course, the great poems have always managed to have more than aesthetic effects and to help shape the vision of their culture, but not so many as might have—and those not so profoundly and as immediately as they might have—if each had its critic, at once diffident and daring, at once imposing discursive categories and forcing these to vibrate to the poem's destruction of categories. The critic, then, must make the thematic plunge as he forces his fidelity to the poem to give way in part to his responsibility to history and his ambition for himself.

The moral is that criticism must recognize its limitations and know its "place." What Krieger proposes here is convincing enough, but by the standards of *The New Apologists for Poetry* his own approach is finally as "impure," as contradictory and instrumental, as the theories he had taken to task in that earlier book.

For Krieger reality is a mass of "raging particulars," "befuddling" in their intractability, "fearfully and maddeningly Manichaean." To recognize this is to attain the "tragic vision" of the existentialists which is the great denier, the negation of all order—cosmic, moral, and aesthetic. As the outlawed and solitary, unabsorbed Dionysian, as unrelieved Kierkegaardian despair, it can affirm only the denial, only chaos; and this is the self-denying contradiction in that it precludes the order needed to affirm anything, even the existence of the tragic state itself as an entity. So the tragic is not really a state so much as it is power—raw, nay-saying, destructive power—the release of naked force, the flow of self-governing sensation. It is an unmediated embrace of the extremity that the existent has confronted and which, simultaneously, has stricken him.

The person who has been forced to look into the abyss can no longer affirm what Kierkegaard calls the "ethical" order of existence, that is, the conventional, utilitarian codes which deny the abyss and the uniqueness of the individual; if he does try to discount what he has seen his life becomes "inauthentic." And of course we no longer live in the world of Sophocles, or even of Hegel, in which we could face disorder and still affirm a larger, universal order. The question is therefore whether art is possible in a world which by definition seems to deny form and purpose; what shapes *can* contain the tragic vision without becoming—as ordered acts—inauthentic as well?

In *The Tragic Vision* Krieger examines a number of modern works in which the protagonist is forced to gaze into the heart of darkness. But since he is destroyed or paralyzed by the experience, his vision must usually be conveyed by a narrator-observer: Kurtz has his Marlow and Ahab his Ishmael. This tactic is still something of an evasion and compromise, however. There is no solution; if life is to go on we must make some "retreat from extremity":

> we can with our Marlows and our Ishmaels turn to the example and the hope of Lena Grove and Byron in *Light in August*: the hope of common mankind for a retreat from extremity, from the demands of purity and integrity, to the homely sanctity of the commonplace, where there can be an acceptance of the imperfection of all things, human action chief among them. It is what the Melville of *Pierre* would term the cultivation of the catnip to the neglect of the amaranth. This is not to deny the Manichaean face of reality so much as to deny the need to confront it.

In *The Classic Vision* Krieger takes up in detail the kinds of retreat from extremity which somehow avoid the inauthentic "ethical":

> This volume is written to demonstrate that there is an authentic classic—as well as the cheaper ethical—affirmation, and that our profoundest authors have attained it. It will claim that the tragic visionary has too simple a dialectic—leading to too limited a dialogue—if his antagonist to the tragic existent is only the easily assailed straw man composed of unyielding universals drawn from the Babbitt-like ethical realm.... A less parochial view of our literature reveals alternatives to the tragic other than the ethical: it reveals ways of returning to the living without denying all that the tragic has revealed, without yielding up the primacy of the uniquely particular that was established by the existential trauma which led to the tragic.

But *how* can we "earn the right to affirm" without denying the truth of tragic vision?

> the classic visionary moves, not to an acceptance of the ethical, but to the acceptance of something more catholic—embracing the entire race—and less doctrinal: the very opposite of the persistent, aggressive puritanical commitment to righteousness that is at the heart of ethical imposition. And somehow its very catholicity is not, in any binding sense, universal. There is always, in the classic visionary, an underlying assumption of the barnyard imperfection of the race. But instead of trying to subdue the stinking animal (in himself as well as others) by organizing the race in accordance with ethical universals, he suffers imperfection to be lived with in rejection of the "either-or" considerations that could drive it, and him, and us all, into the extremity that sanctions demonism.

More specifically, there are four "overlapping grounds for this acceptance":

(1) the rejection of extremity through the worship of bloodless abstractions, (2) the rejection of extremity through the embrace of the natural human community, (3) the rejection of extremity through reconciliation with the depths of the human barnyard, and (4) the rejection of extremity through the posing of an alternative to sainthood.

And all of this leads, finally, to Krieger's justification of the existential basis of the tragic and classic visions:

> literature gives us vicarious breadth, both existential and visionary, as it undoes our fanaticisms. We ourselves, even less bold than our cautious literary visionaries, dare not give up the ethical as our order of existence; but we are forever newly broadened by our dialogistic visions and the dialogue *we* conduct among them. As we return to walk our ethical path, we walk the more tentatively as our sadness becomes the more certain: our forbearance rises as our expectations fall. Softened by vision, we tread with a light foot and a heavy heart.

This is Pop Existentialism of a fairly rudimentary sort, but the real objection is the one prompted by any version of thematic criticism (using that term in the ordinary way and not in Krieger's own rather mysterious sense). As John Holloway has observed. "The mere presence of the thing is without interest, unless it can be shown that its presence makes the work better." In itself, then, the depiction of existential awareness or resigned acceptance has no necessary relationship to literary excellence. And as for the critical task of calling attention to such themes, R.S. Crane put the matter with typical severity: "It requires no great insight to find an inner dialectic of order and disorder...in any serious plot."

In *Theory of Criticism* and *Poetic Presence and Illusion* Krieger explicitly takes up the problems of aesthetic experience and the peculiar reality or "presence" of the poem as an aesthetic object (by "poem" Krieger means all verbal artifacts which have an aesthetic dimension). Aesthetic experience is essentially different from other forms of perceptual and cognitive activity and involves our wrapt attention, our recognition, for its own pleasing sake, of the interrelationship among the parts which constitute a unified whole:

> Looking upon an object—say, a configuration of clouds in the sky—would lead us, as cognitive creatures, to consequences beyond this experience that various hypotheses about the interrelations among elements within the object would enable us to postulate (even if we were no fancier a cognitive creature than a weather forecaster). Looking at the same objects morally, we can infer certain practical consequences for human weal or woe that the elements within the object suggest (as, for example, the need to warn people in the valley below of imminent danger). By contrast to both of these, looking at the object aesthetically would require that we be locked into the rapturous exploration of its discernible elements as they relate to each other. What would characterize the experience as aesthetic rather than either cognitive or moral would be its self-sufficiency, its capacity to trap us within itself, to keep us from moving beyond it to further knowledge or to practical effects.

The kind of reading Krieger favors, then, is the reading which sees the poem as establishing its own unique configuration or "context" (hence his typically idiosyncratic use of yet another term, "contextualism," to designate proper aesthetic response). This would obviously commit Krieger to an extreme aestheticism if he did not believe that the aesthetic object is also of use in the practical world of action. *How* this can also be the case is the source of most of the problems his system entails, but to oversimplify a bit, Krieger regards the poem as an object in itself and as a guide or source of enlightenment about the perilous world outside:

> But in tending to its own completeness the poem does not, in the end, turn its back on reality. Instead, it subverts our normal ways of meaning because *those ways lead to the dead universals that must also be subverted if we are to break through to the throbbing existence beyond*. The poem becomes almost a microcosm of the particularizations that existence offers so profusely (*and these particularizations are all that existence offers*) but that normal language, as generic, must ignore even while it absorbs them.

345

The passages I have emphasized clearly indicate that Krieger's basic view of life remains existential: we live in a world of maddening contingencies and particulars which make our attempts at order as "absurd" as they are necessary (this is of course the world Krieger characterizes in some detail in *The Tragic Vision*). The poem is not essentially "referential" and yet it manages to "exemplify." In his essay on Northrop Frye (in *The Play and Place of Criticism*), Krieger says flatly that "the ultimate function of a contextual poetry is to provide existential revelation."

The true poem provides revelation and "somehow keeps its inviolate aesthetic nature as a veritable "presence." Krieger's use of the term "presence" is a deliberate attempt to separate his thinking from that of Jacques Derrida, for whom all discourse is marked by "absence," by a fatal distance, that is, between words and what they seem to represent. Krieger's answer to this claim is simply to assert that poetry is not continuous with other forms of discourse. Derrida may "deconstruct" metaphysics if he wishes, but he cannot deconstruct poetry, since it belongs to another order of being. The argument, if it is an argument at all, is obviously circular, as Krieger himself seems to admit at times.

On what grounds then can we believe in this unique kind of discourse? We can do so only on the basis of accepting it as a "fiction," and here Krieger aligns himself directly with Santayana and Wallace Stevens. From this point of view there is a crucial difference between believing a fiction or myth *is* a reality and believing it while also recognizing it is a fiction. To believe in the dignity of our own constructs is to affirm the dignity of man as a form-making creature:

> It may seem that I am doing little more than, in a retrograde neo-Kantian fashion, raising the ghost of Ernst Cassirer against the living, though negative, power of Derrida. But, unlike an idealist, I do insist that one must see around the categories of vision to existential fact, since it is fact that wins in the end. It *is* man's humanistic triumph that he is a myth maker—so long as he sees the myth as myth and does not so reify it that he makes it his only reality.

If we press further and ask again why this should be so, the answer seems to be merely that such myths or fictions are consoling and inspiring (here again Krieger is following Santayana and Stevens). In other words, Krieger's final court of appeals is a kind of humane, chastened pragmatism. A brief summary such as this is perhaps unfair, but it should at least indicate the full range of philosophic problems Krieger's thinking raises. In a long, basically unsympathetic chapter of his recent book, *After the New Criticism*, Frank Lentricchia examines the logic of Krieger's position and concludes that he is really the "last romantic" among contemporary critics, that is, the last of the critics who try in desperation to rescue poetry as a unique form of discourse. To put it more crudely still—to demythify if not deconstruct Krieger's elaborate enterprise—he is the supreme example of an insatiable reader who wants to eat his poems and have them too.

LANGBAUM, Robert (Woodrow).   American.   Born in New York City, 23 February 1924. Educated at Cornell University, Ithaca, New York, B.A. 1947; Columbia University, New York, M.A. 1949, Ph.D. 1954. Served in the United States Army Military Intelligence Service, 1942-46: First Lieutenant. Married Francesca Vidale in 1950; has one child. Instructor in English, 1950-55, and Assistant Professor, 1955-60, Cornell University. Associate Professor, 1960-63, Professor, 1963-67, and since 1967 James Branch Cabell Professor of English and American Literature, University of Virginia, Charlottesville. Visiting Professor, Columbia University, 1965-66; Harvard University, Cambridge, Massachusetts, Summer 1965. Member,

Editorial Board, *Victorian Poetry*, since 1963, *Style*, since 1967, and *New Literary History*, since 1969. Recipient: Ford Foundation Fellowship, Center for Advanced Study, Stanford, California, 1961; Guggenheim Fellowship, 1969; National Endowment for the Humanities Senior Fellowship, 1972; American Society for Learned Studies Grant, 1975-76. Address: Department of English, University of Virginia, Charlottesville, Virginia 22901, U.S.A.

PUBLICATIONS

Criticism

> *The Poetry of Experience: The Dramatic Monologue in Modern Literary Tradition.* New York, Random House, and London, Chatto and Windus, 1957.
> *The Gayety of Vision: A Study of Isak Dinesen's Art.* London, Chatto and Windus, 1964; New York, Random House, 1965.
> *The Modern Spirit: Essays on the Continuity of Nineteenth and Twentieth-Century Literature.* New York, Oxford University Press, and London, Chatto and Windus, 1970.
> "New Modes of Characterization in *The Waste Land*," in *Eliot in His Time*, edited by A. Walton Litz. Princeton, New Jersey, Princeton University Press, and London, Oxford University Press, 1973.
> *The Mysteries of Identity: A Theme in Modern Literature.* New York, Oxford University Press, 1977; London, Oxford University Press, 1978.

Other

> Editor, *The Tempest*, by Shakespeare. New York, New American Library, 1964.
> Editor, *The Victorian Age: Essays in History and in Social and Literary Criticism.* Greenwich, Connecticut, Fawcett, 1967.

*   *   *

While he freely admits the virtues of the "New Criticism" and its emphasis on verbal complexities, Robert Langbaum also contends (in "The Function of Criticism Once More," printed in *The Modern Spirit*) that it is an "incomplete criticism":

> Let me sketch out briefly the sort of thing a complete criticism might do. In addition to explaining texts, a complete criticism would go on to explore the questions that inevitably occur to the serious reader who has understood a text. Such a reader wants to know how this particular work relates to and modifies the literary tradition, and how it relates to and modifies other branches of knowledge. He wants to understand the relevance of the work to its time and to him and his time, the reasons he likes or dislikes the work, and what his liking or disliking tells him about himself and his time....A complete criticism, I would say, completes the literary process by dealing not only with the text, the part of the literary process over which the author has control, but also by dealing with that part of the literary process over which the author has little control—the part that takes place before the author begins to write and after he finishes, the part that takes place before the reader opens the book and after he closes it.

The Poetry of Experience is an ambitious essay in "complete criticism" in which Langbaum attempts to construct a theory which will "connect the poetry of the nineteenth and twentieth centuries, to connect romanticism with the so-called reactions against it." Basically his argument rests on familiar principles drawn from Whitehead's *Science and the Modern World*: whatever the differences, the nineteenth century poet and his modern counterpart both confront a scientific world view in which fact and value have been separated. These poets (in Langbaum's words) "are connected by their view of the world as meaningless"—that is, by a world which seems devoid of firm, objective, validating principles. "Reality" has been reduced to a random collection of colorless vibrating masses extended in space; whatever values or goods we envision are simply projections of our own needs and desires. In short, science has given us a world in which fact is a "measurable quantity while value is man-made and illusory. Such a world offers no objective verification for just the perceptions by which men live, perceptions of beauty, goodness and spirit." The Romantic poets and their modern heirs place their faith in a purely human faculty, the imagination, and its power to reintegrate fact and value. Romantic poetry, Langbaum argues, is not self-indulgent but "reconstructive"; the imagination is creative, illuminating what it seeks to know with its own light. Hence when it seeks to know the world it also comes to know itself: "The process of experience is for the romanticist a process of self-realization, of a constantly expanding discovery of the self through discoveries of its imprint on the external world." At the heart of romantic theory and practice is the belief that "imaginative apprehension gained through immediate experience is primary and certain, whereas the analytic reflection that follows is secondary and problematical."

In many ways, then, reliance on personal, imaginative perception and the consequent importance of the dramatic monologue as a key poetic mode are both the result of a skeptical, even, paradoxically, a scientific view of the world. We confront *all* experience openly now, with curiosity and sympathy; categorical moral judgments have been replaced by the desire to explore and understand extreme states of consciousness:

> We are dealing, in other words, with empiricism in literature. The pursuit of all experience corresponds to the scientific pursuit of all knowledge; while the sympathy that is a condition of the dramatic monologue corresponds to the scientific attitude of the mind, the willingness to understand everything for its own sake and without consideration of practical or moral value. We might even say that the dramatic monologue takes toward its material the literary equivalent of the scientific attitude—the equivalent being, where men and women are the subject of investigation, the historicizing and psychologizing of judgment.

If this is true, is moral judgment—which has always been regarded as fundamental to literary response and judgment—irrelevant? Langbaum admits the importance of the question and seems to move in the direction of complete relativism:

> There is judgment all right among modern empiricists, but it follows understanding and remains tentative and subordinate to it....We adopt a man's point of view and the point of view of his age in order to judge him—which makes the judgment relative, limited in applicability to the particular conditions of the case. This is the kind of judgment we get in the dramatic monologue, which is for this reason an appropriate form for an empiricist and relativist age, an age which has come to consider values as an evolving thing dependent upon the changing individual and social requirements of the historical process. For such an age judgment can never be final, it has changed and will change again; it must be perpetually checked against fact, which comes before judgment and remains always more certain.

At the end of this central chapter, "The Dramatic Monologue: Sympathy versus Judgment," readers may want to pause and check Langbaum's argument against their own responses. Is it really true, for example, that as we encounter the Duke in Browning's "My Last Duchess" we "allow him to have his way with us...[and] subordinate all other considerations to the business of understanding?"

Inevitably, psychological sophistication and the increased importance of direct experience seem to undermine the classical foundations of imitative art. In Aristotle's *Poetics*—and in the *Ethics*—the end is always action of a certain kind. Character portrayal is a means of implementing action; and action, properly represented and understood, reveals the fixed order of things: art is "more philosophic than history." But when conceptions of truth and order change, the relationship of action or plot to character may be inverted. We now value character for its own interesting sake; action is subordinate:

For Wordsworth and Coleridge, then, as for Nietzsche, the poem exists not to imitate or describe life but to make it manifest. It is this purpose of evocation that united the poetry of experience—from the romantic poems of Wordsworth and Browning, with their individualized speakers and objects, to the symbolist poems of Yeats and Eliot, with their archetypal speakers and objects....In all cases we know the poem through sentience, *and the poem's meaning is the sentience which it calls into awareness.* (My italics)

What Langbaum tries to establish, finally, is a basic distinction between the older "poetry of meaning," in which a fixed conception of order is revealed through action, and our modern "poetry of experience."

At this point two important questions seem inescapable. First, does *The Poetry of Experience* give us any *literary* means of distinguishing a good dramatic monologue from a poor one? The answer here may be simply that no single critical approach can do everything—other critics can help us separate "My Last Duchess" from, say, "Fifine," and *The Poetry of Experience* may have its greatest value as a contribution to cultural history, as Langbaum himself seems to suggest at one point:

Since a new culture, like a new art, looks disorderly until we discover its principle of order, and since the principle which gives order to a culture is intimately related to the principle which gives order to its art, the critic who finds the latter principle is by implication at least helping to find the former.

The second question is more difficult: isn't the "poetry of experience" *too* broad and inclusive a term to be of much use? Again Langbaum admits this may be the case: "The question even arises whether in the post-Enlightenment world, in a scientific and democratic age, literature, whatever its program, can be anything but romantic in the sense I mean." But having raised this issue Langbaum does nothing more with it and passes on to his main concern, the growth of the dramatic monologue from Wordsworth, Browning and Tennyson, through Eliot and Pound.

The Modern Spirit is something of a miscellany, but the best essays here are still concerned with the problem of continuity. Clearly Langbaum himself is, by his own definition, "modern": he seems to be a thorough-going naturalist, mistrustful of dogmatic moral assertions and properly suspicious of any naive distinctions between "subjective" and "objective" knowledge. In short, he is an advocate for the romantic view of the self and an admirer of those modern artists who attempt to heal the breach between the fact and value. As one might expect, then, he is critical of anything suggesting solipsism or nihilism:

It is perhaps appropriate that the current loss-of-self writers live in Paris; for they have, in their disillusionment with the high nineteenth-century claims for the self, fallen back upon attitudes of the French Enlightenment. Robbe-Grillet gives us the self as a mechanical recorder of sensations. Sarraute gives us something like La Rochefoucauld's brilliantly comic reduction of motives to an automatic pursuit of a nasty, piddling kind of self-interest. Beckett returns to Descartes' idea of the self as a locked-up thinking box cut off not only from other selves but from its own body as well. To avoid phoniness, these writers have, as an ironical comment on the nineteenth-century ideal, reduced the self to a mere twitch.

"Our best writers," he maintains, are

twentieth-century romanticists who have managed to sustain the potency of the self by joining it to powerful outside forces—by recognizing, for example, that the self is not, as the nineteenth-century romanticists tended to think, opposed to culture, but that the self is a cultural achievement....When writers are as deliberate and self-conscious as this, however, in bridging the gap between the individual and the culture that seemed to make tragedy impossible, the art they come out with may have or suggest the richness, depth and complexity of tragedy, but it must be in its final effect comic or rather tragicomic. That is why tragicomedy would seem to be the characteristically modern style in literature.

This explains, in part, why Langbaum admires Isak Dinesen, who, like "Rilke, Kafka, Mann, Joyce, Eliot, Lawrence, Yeats...takes off from a sense of individuality developed in the course of the nineteenth-century to the point of morbidity, and leads that individuality where it wants to go. She leads it back to a universal principle and a connection with the external world."

Langbaum's reference to "tragicomedy" in the important passage quoted above needs an additional word of explanation. He has in mind here Northrop Frye's use of the term as a means of placing various kinds of plots. If we imagine a circle representing the cyclic processes of day and night, the seasons, and human life itself, then those plots which follow the downward movement, from dawn, spring and youth to night, winter and death are "tragic"; and those plots which trace the countermovement from darkness to light and renewed life are "comic." By encompassing both parts of the cycle works such as *The Tempest* and *The Divine Comedy* are "tragicomedies." And it is finally this form which Langbaum values most, since it has most to say to a world which is irretrievably "modern," that is, naturalistic in its outlook. For the individual life is inevitably tragic; but even so, that same individual, by contemplating the cyclic movement of life, may sense the vital continuity of experience and of existence itself. It seems to be one of the primary functions of art, for Frye and Langbaum and other critics of this persuasion, to remind us of the eternal renewal of experience.

In his most recent book, *The Mysteries of Identity*, Langbaum takes up another of the big issues which he is always attracted to, the problem of selfhood as it is reflected in the work of six romantic and modern writers. When the self was regarded as a soul created by God, and when what Langbaum calls "social imperatives" embodied the sense of hierarchy and obligations which traditional religion authorized, there was little difficulty in knowing what an authentic self or "identity" entailed. With the decline of religion, however, and the rise of romantic individualism, achieving selfhood became increasingly problematic. In his moral, even slightly moralistic introduction, Langbaum agrees with Christopher Lasch's facile indictment of narcissism in modern society and the failure to attain maturity as Martin Buber and Erik Erikson, among others, define it. What passes for identity now is usually an endless series of assumed "roles" or a kind of infantile, grasping egotism which may be inevitable when "no values or persons seem real enough to be worth the sacrifice or even postponement of one's own gratification":

> The solipsist-narcissist syndrome defines the main problem of identity treated by literature since the romanticists. On the one hand, there is the need for a strong individuality that can reject old values and create new ones, that can create its own organization of the world. On the other hand, there is the danger that such an individuality will make a world of itself. The solution, as formulated by Lawrence and Erik Erikson, is to maintain a strong ego open to connections.

In the opening section of *The Mysteries of Identity*, Langbaum explains,

> I shall show how, after the Enlightenment attack on a God-created identity, Wordsworth asserted a new romantic self that drew sufficient vitality from an organic connection with nature to project into nature, to find itself out there and nature within itself, and thus bridge the Enlightenment split between subject and object, value and fact. I shall then...trace the steady decline in the organizing and projective vitality of the romantic self through Arnold, early Eliot and Beckett. The declining vitality of the self in literature has accompanied a declining confidence in society, in the spiritual power of nature, and in the organic connection of self with nature. It has accompanied a loss of confidence in the individual and individual effort due to mass production, mass markets, mass media, to increasing urbanization, industrialization, specialization, and to the increasing alienation of the self, according to Marx's analysis, from all its specialized functions. Nietzsche calls such specialized men "inverse cripples"; worse off than ordinary cripples, whole men without a leg, these modern men "are nothing but a big eye or a big mouth or a big belly."...The declining vitality of the self in literature reaches its low point in my model with Beckett, whose characters dwell so entirely within their skulls ...that they are alienated not only from society and nature but from their own bodies. I shall in the concluding chapters discuss the attempts of Yeats and Lawrence to reconstitute the self by drawing upon and helping to create two modern secular religions: Yeats draws upon the religion of art, Lawrence upon the religion of love.

Langbaum's discussions of Arnold, Eliot and Beckett are fairly routine affairs, but in his long essays on Yeats and Lawrence he makes an impressive case for the ways in which these writers dramatically worked out the basis for a new individualism. Langbaum is not offering them as models, however, and he seems pessimistic about the future (in his introduction he admits "the fact that Beckett follows Yeats and Lawrence in time leaves it doubtful whether the latter are prophets of a new reconstituted ego open to connections or simply, as Yeats put it, 'the last romantics.' ") Yeats has been dead for more than forty years, Lawrence for more than fifty. There have of course been writers like Eliot and Auden who have solved the mystery of identity by returning to a pre-romantic conception of the self. But with the possible exception of Wallace Stevens, there are few if any major modern "secular" writers Langbaum might point to who have continued to believe that authentic selfhood is still possible.

LEAVIS, F(rank) R(aymond).   British.   Born in Cambridge, 14 July 1895. Educated at the Perse School, Cambridge; Emmanuel College, Cambridge. Married Queenie Dorothy Roth in 1929; had three children. Founding Editor, *Scrutiny*, Cambridge, 1932-53. Fellow, Downing College, Cambridge, 1936-62; Lecturer in English, 1937-60, and Reader in English, 1960-62, Cambridge University (Clark Lecturer, 1965). Visiting Professor of English, University of York, 1965-68; Cheltenham Lecturer, 1968; Visiting Professor, University of Wales, 1969; Churchill Visiting Professor, University of Bristol, 1970. D.Litt.: University of Leeds, 1965; University of York, 1967; Queen's University of Belfast, 1973; University of Delhi, 1973; LL.D.: University of Aberdeen, 1970. Honorary Fellow, Downing College, Cambridge, 1962-64. Honorary Member, American Academy of Arts and Sciences, 1963. C.H. (Companion of Honour), 1978. *Died 14 April 1978.*

PUBLICATIONS

Criticism

> *Mass Civilization and Minority Culture.*   Cambridge, Gordon Fraser, 1930; reprinted in *For Continuity*, 1933.
> *D.H. Lawrence.*   Cambridge, Gordon Fraser, 1930; reprinted in *For Continuity*, 1933.
> *New Bearings in English Poetry: A Study of the Contemporary Situation.*   London, Chatto and Windus, 1932; revised edition, 1950; New York, Stewart, 1950.
> *How to Teach Reading: A Primer for Ezra Pound.*   Cambridge, Gordon Fraser, 1932; Folcroft, Pennsylvania, Folcroft Editions, 1969; reprinted in *Education and the University*, 1943.
> *For Continuity.*   Cambridge, Minority Press, 1933; Freeport, New York, Books for Libraries, 1968.
> *Culture and Environment: The Training of Critical Awareness*, with Denys Thompson.   London, Chatto and Windus, 1933; New York, Barnes and Noble, 1964.
> Introduction to *Towards Standards of Criticism: Selections from "The Calendar of Modern Letters" 1925-1927*, edited by F.R. Leavis.   London, Wishart, 1933; Folcroft, Pennsylvania, Folcroft Editions, 1969; reprinted in *Anna Karenina and Other Essays*, 1967.
> *Revaluation: Tradition and Development in English Poetry.*   London, Chatto and Windus, 1936; New York, Stewart, 1947.
> "Arnold as Critic," in *Scrutiny* (Cambridge), 7, 1938; reprinted in *A Selection from Scrutiny*, 1968.

"Coleridge in Criticism," in *Scrutiny* (Cambridge), 9, 1940; reprinted in *A Selection from Scrutiny*, 1968.

Education and the University: A Sketch for an "English School." London, Chatto and Windus, 1943; New York, Stewart, 1948.

" 'Thought' and Emotional Quality" and "Imagery and Movement," in *Scrutiny* (Cambridge), 13, 1945; reprinted in *The Living Principle*, 1975.

The Great Tradition: George Eliot, Henry James, Joseph Conrad. London, Chatto and Windus, and New York, Stewart, 1948.

Introduction to *Mill on Bentham and Coleridge.* London, Chatto and Windus, 1950; New York, Stewart, 1951.

The Common Pursuit. London, Chatto and Windus, and New York, Stewart, 1952.

"Reality and Sincerity," in *Scrutiny* (Cambridge), 19, 1952-53; reprinted in *The Living Principle*, 1975.

"The Responsible Critic; or, The Function of Criticism at Any Time," in *Scrutiny* (Cambridge), 19, 1953; reprinted in *A Selection from Scrutiny*, 1968.

D.H. Lawrence, Novelist. London, Chatto and Windus, 1955; New York, Knopf, 1956.

Scrutiny: A Retrospect. London, Cambridge University Press, 1963.

Anna Karenina and Other Essays. London, Chatto and Windus, 1967; New York, Pantheon Books, 1968.

English Literature in Our Time and the University. London, Chatto and Windus, 1969.

Lectures in America, with Q.D. Leavis. London, Chatto and Windus, and New York, Pantheon Books, 1969.

Dickens the Novelist, with Q.D. Leavis. London, Chatto and Windus, 1970; New York, Pantheon Books, 1971.

Letters in Criticism, edited by John Tasker. London, Chatto and Windus, 1974.

The Living Principle: "English" as a Discipline of Thought. London, Chatto and Windus, and New York, Oxford University Press, 1975.

Thought, Words, and Creativity: Art and Thought in Lawrence. London, Chatto and Windus, and New York, Oxford University Press, 1976.

Other

Two Cultures? The Significance of C.P. Snow. London, Chatto and Windus, 1962; New York, Pantheon Books, 1963; reprinted in *Nor Shall My Sword*, 1972.

Nor Shall My Sword: Discourses on Pluralism, Compassion and Social Hope. London, Chatto and Windus, and New York, Barnes and Noble, 1972.

Editor, *Towards Standards of Criticism: Selections from "The Calendar of Modern Letters," 1925-1927.* London, Wishart, 1933; Folcroft, Pennsylvania, Folcroft Editions, 1974.

Editor, *Determinations: Critical Essays.* London, Chatto and Windus, 1934.

Editor, *A Selection from Scrutiny.* London, Cambridge University Press, 2 vols., 1968.

CRITICAL STUDIES AND BIBLIOGRAPHY

René Wellek, "Literary Criticism and Philosophy," in *Scrutiny* (Cambridge), 6, 1937; reprinted in *The Importance of Scrutiny*, edited by Eric Bentley, New York, Stewart, 1948.

Eric Bentley, Introduction to *The Importance of Scrutiny: Selections from Scrutiny, A Quarterly Review, 1932-1948.* New York, Stewart, 1948.

Martin Jarrett-Kerr, "The Literary Criticism of F.R. Leavis," in *Essays in Criticism* (Oxford), 2, 1952.

Bernard C. Heyl, "The Absolutism of F.R. Leavis," in *Journal of Aesthetics and Art Criticism* (Cleveland), 13, 1954.

L.D. Lerner, "The Life and Death of *Scrutiny*," in *London Magazine*, 2, 1955.

Vincent Buckley, *Poetry and Morality: Studies on the Criticism of Matthew Arnold, T.S. Eliot, and F.R. Leavis.* London, Chatto and Windus, 1959.

René Wellek, "The Literary Criticism of Frank Raymond Leavis," in *Literary Views: Critical and Historical*, edited by Carroll Camden. Chicago, University of Chicago Press, 1964.

Lionel Trilling, "Science, Literature and Culture: The Leavis-Snow Controversy," in *Beyond Culture: Essays on Literature and Learning.* New York, Viking Press, 1965; London, Secker and Warburg, 1966.

D.F. McKenzie and M.-P. Allum, *F.R. Leavis: A Checklist, 1924-1964.* London, Chatto and Windus, 1966.

W.W. ·Robson, "Mr. Leavis on Literary Studies," in *Critical Essays.* London, Routledge, 1966.

R.P. Bilan, "The Basic Concepts and Criteria of F.R. Leavis' Novel Criticism," in *Novel* (Providence, Rhode Island), 9, 1976.

Ronald Hayman, *Leavis.* London, Heinemann, 1976; Totowa, New Jersey, Roman and Littlefield, 1977.

F.W. Bateson, "The *Scrutiny* Phenomenon," in *Sewanee Review* (Tennessee), 85, 1977.

Robert Boyers, *F.R. Leavis, Judgment and the Discipline of Thought.* Columbia, University of Missouri Press, 1978.

Donald Davie, "Winters and Leavis: Memories and Reflections," in *Sewanee Review* (Tennessee), 87, 1979.

R.P. Bilan, *The Literary Criticism of F.R. Leavis.* London, Cambridge University Press, 1979.

Robert Byrne, "Leavis, Literary Criticism, and Philosophy," in *British Journal of Aesthetics* (London), 19, 1979.

Glenn W. Most, "Principled Reading," in *Diacritics* (Ithaca, New York), 9, 1979.

William Walsh, *F.R. Leavis.* London, Chatto and Windus, and Bloomington, Indiana University Press, 1980.

Francis Mulhern, *The Moment of "Scrutiny."* London, New Left Books, 1980.

Denis Donoghue, "Leavis and Eliot," in *Raritan* (New Brunswick, New Jersey), 1, 1981.

René Wellek, "The Later Leavis," in *Southern Review* (Baton Rouge, Louisiana), 17, 1981.

*   *   *

It was René Wellek, apparently, who first raised the charge of tacit assumptions and undefined terms which has always troubled the readers of F.R. Leavis. After praising the many "acute critical observations" and "brilliant interpretations" of individual texts in *Revaluation*, the second of Leavis' three sustained attempts to establish the "great tradition" of English poetry and fiction, Wellek went on to express his disappointment that

> you [have not] stated your assumptions more explicit and defended them systematically. I do not doubt the value of these assumptions and, as a matter of fact, I share them with you for the most part, but I would have misgivings in pronouncing them without elaborating a specific defence or a theory in their defence. Allow me to sketch your ideal of poetry, your "norm" with which you measure every poet: your poetry must be in serious relation to actuality, it must have a firm grasp of the actual, of the object, it must be in relation to life, it must not be cut off from direct vulgar living, it should not be personal in the sense of indulging in personal dreams and fantasies, there should be no emotion for its own sake in it, no afflatus, no mere generous emotionality, no luxury in pain or joy, but also no sensuous poverty, but a sharp, concrete realization, a sensuous particularity....You will recognize, of course, in this description tags from your book chosen from all chapters, and the only question I would ask you is to defend this position more abstractly and to become conscious that large ethical, philosophical, and, of course, ultimately also *aesthetic* choices are involved.

In his prompt rejoinder Leavis explained that these were the objections of a "philosopher" and that literary criticism and philosophy were "quite different and distinct kinds of disciplines":

> Philosophy, we say, is "abstract"...and poetry "concrete." Words in poetry invite us not to "think about" and judge, but to "feel into" or "become"—to realize a complex experience that is given in the words. They demand not merely a fuller-bodied response, but a completer responsiveness—a kind of responsiveness that is incompatible with the judicial, one-eye-on-the-standard approach suggested by Dr. Wellek's phrase: "your 'norm' with which you measure every poet." The critic—the reader of poetry—is indeed concerned with evaluation, but to figure him as measuring with a norm which he brings up to the object and applies from the outside is to misrepresent the process.

If he avoided those generalizations Wellek abstracted from *Revaluation*, Leavis went on, it was because "they seemed too clumsy to be of any use":

> I thought I had provided something better. My whole effort was to work in terms of concrete judgements and particular analyses: "This—doesn't it?—bears such a relation to that: this kind of thing—don't you find it so?—wears better than that," etc....I feel that by my own methods I have attained a relative precision that makes [Wellek's] summarizing seem intolerably clumsy and inadequate....I do not, again, argue in general terms ...but by choice, arrangement, and analysis of concrete examples I give those phrases (in so far, that is, as I have achieved my purpose) a precision of meaning they couldn't have got in any other way. There is, I hope, a chance that I may in this way have advanced theory, even if I haven't done the theorizing. I know that the cogency and precision I have aimed at are limited; but I believe that any approach involves limitations, and that it is by recognizing them and working with them that one may hope to get something done.

Wellek, however, remained unconvinced. Nearly thirty years later he was to repeat many of his earlier charges and to conclude, much more harshly now, that

> Leavis's gravest failing seems to me his distrust and even hatred for theory: his resolute, complacent, nominalistic empiricism, his worship of the concrete and particular at any price. This allows him to leave his norms unexamined....I recognize that [his terms] assume their proper meaning only in a context, but they do represent implicit norms, an underlying scheme or pattern which is discoverable in every critic and which it is the business of the historian of criticism to describe and judge. The refusal to theorize has a paralyzing effect on Leavis's practice; it makes him reject the tools and concepts of technical analysis and be content with impressions or dogmatically stated feelings.

The debate was necessarily inconclusive since neither party spoke to the real issue: it is one thing to maintain that poetry and philosophy are different kinds of discourse with different privileges (Wellek could hardly dispute this) and quite another to imply, as Leavis has always done, that criticism, or discourse *about* poetry, enjoys some of the same privileges—the same "concreteness," for example—as poetry itself.

As a matter of fact, Leavis' criticism, even before *Revaluation*, had always been governed by assumptions about the nature of language which would have lost nothing by being made explicit—as he himself may finally have decided. In any event, he published two crucial essays in 1945 (" 'Thought' and Emotional Quality" and "Imagery and Movement") and a third in 1952 ("Reality and Sincerity") which make it possible to state clearly enough the "underlying scheme or pattern" of his thought. This is not to say that certain problems do not remain: they do, but they are not quite the same problems which Wellek and other readers have complained about.

In a very early pamphlet, *Mass Civilization and Minority Culture*, Leavis asserted that in any period,

> it is upon a very small minority that the discerning appreciation of art and literature depends: it is...only a few who are capable of unprompted, first-hand judgment. They are still a small minority, though a larger one, who are capable of endorsing such first-hand

judgment by genuine personal response. The accepted valuations are a kind of paper currency based upon a very small proportion of gold.

What is at stake, however, is not simply "discerning appreciation" of the great works of the past, as Leavis makes clear when he supports his assertions with a well-known passage from *Principles of Literary Criticism* in which I.A. Richards argued that the artist is "the point at which the growth of the mind shows itself." The arts, Richards went on,

> are our storehouse of recorded values. They spring from and perpetuate hours in the lives of exceptional people when their control and command of experience is at its height...when the varying possibilities of existence are most clearly seen and the different activities which may arise are most exquisitely reconciled.... Subtle or recondite experiences are for most men incommunicable or indescribable....In the arts we find the record in the only form in which these things can be recorded of the experiences which have seemed most worth having for the most sensitive and discriminating people....It should be unnecessary to insist upon the degree to which high civilization, in other words, free, varied, and unwasteful life, depends upon them in a numerous society.

Leavis' debt to Richards is even clearer in *New Bearings in English Poetry*, published four years before *Revaluation*:

> Poetry matters because of the kind of poet who is more alive than other people, more alive in his own age. He is, as it were, the most conscious point of the race in his time....The potentialities of human experience in any age are realized only by a tiny minority, and the important poet is important because he belongs to this (and has also, of course, the power of communication). Indeed, his capacity for experiencing and his power of communicating are indistinguishable....He is unusually sensitive, unusually aware, more sincere and more himself than the ordinary man can be. He knows what he feels and knows what he is interested in. He is a poet because his interest in his experience is not separable from his interest in words; because, that is, of his habit of seeking by the evocative use of words to sharpen his awareness of his way of feeling, so making these communicable.

The great artists are significant, he was to maintain much later (in *The Great Tradition*), "in terms of the human awareness they promote; awareness of the possibilities of life." They are distinguished by their "vital capacity for experience"; in their best work "certain human potentialities are nobly celebrated." In short, as Lawrence put it in an assertion Leavis is fond of quoting, "One must speak for life and growth, amid all this mass of destruction and disintegration."

Contrary to what these exalted phrases may suggest, Leavis is not interested in the artist himself, save insofar as his character is embodied in the very texture of the words he uses—and here it is best to turn to Leavis' fullest discussion of language itself, in *The Living Principle* (the first half of which reprints, with some revisions, the 1945 and 1952 essays mentioned before). The art of literature, Whitehead proposed, is to adjust the language so that words "embody what they signify": to my knowledge Leavis has never referred to this statement, but it comes very close to his principle that in a successful poem words "enact" what they mean or "signify." Thus he argues that Johnson, for example, was wrong to think that Shakespeare merely stated a moral position in *Macbeth* ("Johnson cannot understand that works of art enact their moral valuations") and that Santayana is wrong, in his discussion of the same play, to regard Shakespeare's language as simply the "medium" in which pre-existing thoughts and feelings might be expressed. Poetic language, or better "creative language" (since the power to enact meaning is not limited to verse alone), is a kind of "third thing":

> [poems come] somewhere between full concrete actuality and merely "talking about."
> ...In reading a successful poem it is as if, with the kind of qualification intimated, one were living that particular action, situation, or piece of life; the qualification representing the condition of the peculiar completeness and fineness of art. The "realization" demanded of the poet, then, is not an easily definable matter: it is one kind of thing in this

poem and another in that, and, within a poem, the relation of imagery to the whole involves complex possibilities of variety.

As an example of what he means Leavis takes a passage from Donne:

> On a huge hill,
> Cragged, and steep, truth stands, and hee that will
> Reach her, about must, and about must goe;
> And what the hills suddenness resists, winne so...

and comments:

> Here the line-end imposes on the reader as he passes from the "will" to the "Reach" an analogical enactment of meaning.
>
> We might perhaps say a "metaphorical enactment," though what we have here wouldn't ordinarily be called a metaphor. The important point is that it provides the most obvious local illustration of a pervasive action of the verse—or action in the reader as he follows the verse: as he takes the meaning, re-creates the organization, responds to the play of the sense-movement, makes the succession of efforts necessary to pronounce the organized words, he performs in various modes a continuous analogical enactment. Such an enactment is apparent in
>
> > about must, and about must goe;
>
> and, if less obvious, sufficiently apparent in
>
> > what the hills suddenness resists, winne so
>
> and where the sense-movement is brought up abruptly as by a rock-face at "resists," and then, starting on another track, comes to a successful conclusion.

To what extent is prose, which is much less free to exploit the resources of rhythm and metaphor, also capable of such "enactment"? Leavis recognizes the question and deals with it in the last section of the essay "Judgment and Analysis" (in *The Living Principle*), but his examples there are so oddly chosen and his demonstrations so badly strained that few readers will be convinced. In any event, creative language is not simply a means of expression:

> it is the heuristic conquest won out of representative experience, the upshot or precipitate of immemorial human living, and embodies values, distinctions, identifications, conclusions, promptings, cartographical hints and tested potentialities. It exemplifies the truth that life is growth and growth change, and the condition of these is continuity. It takes the individual being, the particularizing actuality of life, back to the dawn of human consciousness, and beyond, and does this in fostering the *ahnung* [which Leavis states elsewhere is the equivalent of Polanyi's "anticipatory intuition"] in him of what is not yet—the as yet unrealized, the achieved discovery of which demands creative effort.

Moreover, the creative use of language is the highest manifestation of our basic ability to create and sustain a truly human world:

> the creativity of the artist [is] continuous with the general human creativity that, having created the human world we live in, keeps it renewed and real. This day-to-day work of collaborative creation includes the creation of language, without which there couldn't have been a human world. In language, as I have said, the truth I will refer to as "life and lives," the basic unstatable which, lost to view and left out, disables any attempt to think radically about human life, is most open to recognition and invites it.

The function of literature follows from all of this: the job of the great artist is to promote "sincerity" (the "elimination of ego-interested distortion and all impure motives"); and to promote sincerity is to promote nothing less than full realization of our proper place in a human world. In "Tragedy and the 'Medium' " Leavis observes that the experience of tragedy

> is constructive or creative, and involves a recognition of positive values as in some way defined and vindicated by death. It is as if we are challenged at the profoundest level by the question, "In what does the significance of life reside?" and found ourselves contemplating, for answer, a view of life, and of the things giving it value, that makes the valued appear unquestionably more important than the valuer, so that significance lies, clearly and inescapably, in the willing adhesion of the individual self to something other than itself.

It would be a mistake to interpret this cryptic reference to "something other" as the sign of a commitment to anything more than the human community, here, now, and in the future (since future possibilities depend upon present awareness), and to "Life" itself, the "basic unstable" and ultimate ground of all Leavis' appeals. On a number of occasions he has referred—with obviously complete approval—to one of Lawrence's last pronouncements, "One writes out of one's moral sense—for the race, as it were." Thus we call a writer "major," he concludes in *The Living Principle*, "when we judge that his wisdom, more deeply and robustly rooted, represents a more securely poised resultant, one more fully comprehensive and humanly better centered— considerations bearing crucially on future growth—than any that any ordinarily brilliant person could offer us."

By now it should be apparent that one vital "logical" step is missing in Leavis' defense of the great tradition of creative language which makes "Life" a continuing possibility, even in an Americanized age of semi-literacy, mass production and generally debased standards. The writer does not simply enact a pre-existing situation; he does that, of course, but he also enacts the "mature" moral judgment appropriate to it (for a concise illustration of what Leavis means here, readers should consult his discussion of Lawrence's "Piano," in which a "regressive" attitude is vividly enacted and at the same time judged by the poet to be immature). In the language of Yvor Winters, who is very close to Leavis on this point, criticism involves a judgment of the judgment made by the artist himself. If the responsible critic turns to Shelley, for example, he will find himself, Leavis argues, "passing, by inevitable transitions, from describing characteristics to making adverse judgments about emotional quality; and so to a kind of discussion in which, by its proper methods and in pursuit of its proper ends, literary criticism becomes the diagnosis of what, looking for an inclusive term, we can only call spiritual malady." The problem is that Leavis has never made clear what particular kind of ethical philosophy the standards of "maturity" and "human potentialities" are to be based upon. Yvor Winters very properly and very emphatically tells his readers that his judgments rest on the Aristotelian moral tradition as restated by Aquinas, who "composed...the most thorough and defensible moral and philosophical system, in all likelihood, that the world has known." Winters does not spend his time demonstrating how his judgment of Hart Crane or Emerson may be derived from this tradition, but the reader who is interested has the proper clue and can work from that, agreeing or disagreeing as he will. What is missing in Leavis is just this necessary clue. The basis of his moral sentiment is apparently not religious, it is probably pragmatic and thoroughly naturalistic—but it is impossible to speculate much further, especially since Leavis has been highly critical of the utilitarian ethics which seem to be the logical consequence of naturalism. As long as they are left unattached to a clearly defined ethical point of view, "maturity" and all the other endlessly invoked terms are hortatory, empty, and a little self-congratulating.

With these discriminations in mind it is easy enough to follow Leavis' moralized history of English poetry and fiction. In *Revaluation* he attempts to establish the tradition of mature poetry which starts in the seventeenth century, disappears in the Romantic and Victorian periods, and is renewed by Hopkins, Pound, and Eliot, who are the chief subjects of *New Bearings in English Poetry*. With few exceptions Leavis endorses the verdicts Eliot had laid down in the 1920's: Shakespeare and the Metaphysicals are given first place, Milton's greatness severely questioned, and nineteenth century poetry largely dismissed because of the "dissociation of sensibility," that fatal split between thinking and feeling supposed to be characteristic of the Romantics and Victorians (as for the exceptions: Leavis' appreciation of Pope and the Augustans is more sensitive than Eliot's, or so it might be argued, and he has a higher opinion of the best in Wordsworth). In the 1940's Leavis shifted his attention from poetry to fiction for reasons which were not entirely clear until *D.H. Lawrence, Novelist*: in Jane Austen, George Eliot, Dickens (with important qualifications), James, Conrad and Lawrence, he asserts,

> we have the successors of Shakespeare; for in the nineteenth century and later the strength—the poetic and creative strength—of the English language goes into prose fiction. In comparison the formal poetry is a marginal affair. And the achievement of T.S. Eliot, remarkable as it was, did not reverse the relation.

In *The Great Tradition* Leavis examines George Eliot, James and Conrad in detail; Mrs. Leavis had written about Jane Austen at some length in *Scrutiny*; and Lawrence, of course, is the subject of a separate study—a magically reconstituted Lawrence with all the despair and equivocations swept out of sight.

Since inherited standards and the supports of a traditional, organic culture have been destroyed, everything now depends upon the cultivation of "the individual sensibility." Thus for well over forty years Leavis has been active as a teacher and has written extensively about University "English" as a discipline increasingly necessary in a "technologico-Benthamite" society which looks up to C.P. Snow, reads the *New States-man*, and listens to the BBC. And for the small minority capable of endorsing the first-hand valuations of an even smaller minority, there was, for twenty years, *Scrutiny*. How important all of this has been in England it is virtually impossible for an American to determine.

What can be said against Leavis is familiar enough by now: he has been unable or unwilling to read sympathetically anything written after 1930 (with the possible exception of *Four Quartets*); he has defended, with brutal zeal, an important but limited group of writers; he is a moralist whose moral assumptions are, at best, vague. And finally, if prose enacts a quality of mind, what is one to make of his style—of this passage, for example, from that apparent *summa, The Living Principle*?

> What we have to get essential recognition for is that major creative writers are concerned with a necessary kind of thought. To such recognition the climate of our age is hostile, the hostility being a measure of the importance that is denied. Where the hostility prevails, thought is disabled for the performance of an indispensable function, the central one. The slighted truths are implicit in my insistence that "English" should represent, and be recognized to represent, a discipline *sui generis*—a discipline of intelligence. There will be no neat and final account of the distinctive discipline, but the need and the challenge to define and re-define will always be there. For the problems—decidedly in the plural here—that present themselves in so formidable a way and so inexorably as practical ones involve tentativeness, incompleteness and compromise so inescapably that the ends ("the living principle") that, together with the *ahnung* implicit in them, should give the defects their meaning will be lost if practice is not associated with thought that renews and reformulates. By slipping in after "ends" that brief parenthetic phrase I meant to intimate that what one for this, for that or for the other directing purpose necessarily emphasizes as an end in view gets its full significance from a totality of apprehension and concern, and that the complex totality is a vital unity.

Even an American may suspect that something is very wrong here.

LEAVIS, Q(ueenie) D(orothy). British. Born Queenie Dorothy Roth, in London, 7 December 1906. Married F.R. Leavis in 1929; three children. Educated at Cambridge University, Ph.D. Ottilie Hancock Research Fellow, Girton College, Cambridge, 1929-32; worked with F.R. Leavis on *Scrutiny*, Cambridge, 1932-53. *Died 17 March 1981.*

PUBLICATIONS

Criticism

"Lady Novelists and the Lower Orders," in *Scrutiny* (Cambridge), 4, 1935.
"The Critical Writings of George Santayana," in *Scrutiny* (Cambridge), 4, 1935.
"Henry James' Heiress: The Importance of Edith Wharton," in *Scrutiny* (Cambridge), 7, 1938; reprinted in *A Selection from Scrutiny*, edited by F.R. Leavis, London, Cambridge University Press, 1968.
"Leslie Stevens: A Cambridge Critic," in *Scrutiny* (Cambridge), 7, 1939; reprinted in *A Selection from Scrutiny*, edited by F.R. Leavis, London, Cambridge University Press, 1968.
"A Critical Theory of Jane Austen's Writings," in *Scrutiny* (Cambridge), 10, 1941-42, and 12, 1944; reprinted in *A Selection from Scrutiny*, edited by F.R. Leavis, London, Cambridge University Press, 1968.
"A Fresh Approach to *Wuthering Heights*," in *Lectures in America*, with F.R. Leavis. London, Chatto and Windus, and New York, Pantheon Books, 1969.
"Dickens and Tolstoy: The Case for a Serious View of *David Copperfield*," "*Bleak House*: A Chancery World," "How We Must Read *Great Expectations*" and "The Dickens Illustrations: Their Function," in *Dickens the Novelist*, with F.R. Leavis. London, Chatto and Windus, 1970; New York, Pantheon Books, 1971.

Other

Fiction and the Reading Public.   London, Chatto and Windus, 1932; New York, Russell and Russell, 1965.
"The Discipline of Letters: A Sociological Note," in *Scrutiny* (Cambridge), 13, 1943; reprinted in *A Selection from Scrutiny*, edited by F.R. Leavis, London, Cambridge University Press, 1968.
"Henry Sidgwick's Cambridge," in *Scrutiny* (Cambridge), 15, 1947; reprinted in *A Selection from Scrutiny*, edited by F.R. Leavis, London, Cambridge University Press, 1968.
"Professor Chadwick and English Studies," in *Scrutiny* (Cambridge), 14, 1947; reprinted in *A Selection from Scrutiny*, edited by F.R. Leavis, London, Cambridge University Press, 1968.

Editor, *Mansfield Park*, by Jane Austen.   London, Macdonald, 1957.
Editor, *Jane Eyre*, by Charlotte Brontë.   London, Penguin, 1966.
Editor, *Sila Marner*, by George Eliot.   London, Penguin, 1967.

CRITICAL STUDIES AND BIBLIOGRAPHY

Bibliography in *Scrutiny* (Cambridge), 20, 1963.
William Walsh, "The Principal Collaborator," in *F.R. Leavis*.   London, Chatto and Windus, and Bloomington, Indiana University Press, 1980.

*   *   *

Although Q.D. Leavis wrote only a small number of critical essays, her standards are clear enough—and virtually identical, as one might reasonably expect, with those of her husband and occasional collaborator, F.R. Leavis. For both critics the great tradition of English poetry and fiction is made up of works in which language "enacts" or "incarnates" a worthy subject and the moral valuation appropriate to it. A great writer's judgments are "mature": his use of "creative language" helps to sustain and to renew that "living principle" on which a truly human community depends. Mrs. Leavis maintains, for example, that in his novels E.M. Forster has never shown "a capacity for such an ironical achievement as *Cakes and Ale*, which, side by side with a sardonic criticism of the writer's environment, exhibits positive values convincingly incarnated." Or again, in her essay on Edith Wharton, she observes that

> In *Bunner Sisters, Summer,* and some other places Mrs. Wharton rests upon the simple goodness of the decent poor, as indeed George Eliot and Wordsworth both do in part, that is, the most widespread common factor of moral worth. But beyond that Mrs. Wharton has only negatives, her values emerging, I suppose, as something other than what she exposes as worthless. This is not very nourishing, and it is on similar grounds that Flaubert, so long admired as the ideal artist of the novel, has begun to lose esteem. It seems to be the fault of the disintegrating and spiritually impoverished society she analyses....She has none of that natural piety, that richness of feeling and sense of moral order, of experience as a process of growth, in which George Eliot's local criticisms are embedded and which give the latter her large stature.

Criticism too is ultimately a moral activity, since the critic's job is to judge properly the moral judgment already embodied in the work under consideration. The "self-indulgent" impressionistic criticism of a Desmond MacCarthy is therefore an evasion of an important responsibility:

> Let us recapitulate the grounds of dispute between Mr. MacCarthy and Leslie Stephen. Stephen, misguided man, thought the critic should confine himself to what is discussible about a work of art instead of recording his thrill at experiencing it: the youngest hand will have the answer ready that it is the critic's business to advance the profitable discussion of literature, substitute-creation ("transmitting the emotions derived from literature") being indefensible egotism. His detailed analyses of writings, focusing on the writer's idiom and technical devices, do not help us to decide whether the work is good or bad, says Mr. MacCarthy; we, on the contrary, who believe that literary criticism can be demonstrated and so argued about find Stephen's procedure—starting from the surface and working inwards to radical criticism—obviously right and convincing. We believe with Stephen that literary criticism is not a mystic rapture but a process of the intelligence.

Leslie Stephen, she concludes, "was the type of critic who makes no parade of personality, has no studied attitudes, whose manner consists of an absence of manner but is felt as the presence of a mature personality."

Mrs. Leavis' essays on *Wuthering Heights* and on Dickens are unmistakably "moral" exercises in the familiar *Scrutiny* pattern (this is less true, however, of her early and by now rather dated essays on Jane Austen, in which her primary aim is to trace that novelist's developing craftsmanship, "from the simple technique of *Lady Susan* to the final, complicated, laboriously achieved *Mansfield Park*." Even so, Mrs. Leavis' interest here is not exclusively technical: in her last novels Jane Austen proves herself to be an artist "like Henry James and Joseph Conrad"—a worthy member, in short, of the great tradition). Mrs. Leavis admits that *Wuthering Heights* "certainly isn't a seamless 'work of art,' " but she is unwilling to accept the verdict of another *Scrutiny* critic that "because the author's preferences are not shown...it is not a moral tale." "I shall argue," she goes on, that

> the author's preferences *are* shown, Catherine is judged by the author in the parallel but notably different history of the daughter who, inheriting her mother's name, and likenesses both physical and psychological, is shown by deliberate choice, and trial and error, developing the maturity and therefore achieving the happiness, that her mother failed in, whereas we have seen the mother hardening into fatal immaturity which destroys herself and those...involved with her. Nor is the author's impersonality...inconsistent with a moral intention. That is, the reader is obliged to draw moral conclusions, from the very nature of the scenes and actors in whose lives he is involved by sympathy and compassion or horror and repulsion.

The argument is a very long and closely detailed one, but in order to establish her claim that the novel is in fact "a moral tale," Mrs. Leavis must pick and choose carefully at points. The important general human truths of *Wuthering Heights* are, she concedes, "obscured in places and to varying degrees by discordant trimmings or leftovers from earlier writings or stages of its conception; for these, stylistic and other evidence exists in the text." Thus it is necessary "to distinguish what is genuine complexity from what is mere confusion." And the problem, obviously, then becomes *how* we are to make the proper distinctions. Frank Kermode has praised the essay generously (its "mature authority"—magical phrase!—"dwarfs" all the competition) but continues, very shrewdly (in *The Classic*),

> It seems very clear to me that the "real novel" Mrs. Leavis describes *is* there, in the text. It is also clear that she is aware of the danger in her own procedures, for she explains how easy it would be to account for *Wuthering Heights* as a sociological novel by discarding certain elements and concentrating on others, which, she says, would be "misconceiving the novel and slighting it." What she will not admit is that there is a sense in which all these versions are not only present but have a claim on our attention. She creates a hierarchy of elements, and does so by a peculiar archaeology of her own, for there is no *evidence* that the novel existed in the earlier forms which are supposed to have left vestiges in the only text we have, and there is no reason why the kind of speculation and conjecture on which her historical argument depends could not have been practised with equal right by proponents of quite other theories. Nor can I explain why it seemed to her that the only way to establish hers as the central reading of the book was to explain the rest away; for there, after all, the others *are*. Digging and carbon-dating simply have no equivalents here; there is no way of distinguishing old signs from new; among readings which attend to the text it cannot be argued that one attends to a truer text than all the others.

Mrs. Leavis' reading is, in short, "privileged." But again, on what grounds and by what authority?

Both the Leavises are members of what C.S. Lewis has called—without naming names—the "Vigilant" school of criticism. For these critics, he argues (in *An Experiment in Criticism*),

> criticism is a form of social and ethical hygiene. They see all clear thinking, all sense of reality, and all fineness of living [Richards' phrase, it should be noted, later adopted by F.R. Leavis], threatened on every side by propaganda, by advertisement, by film and television. The hosts of Midian "prowl and prowl around." But they prowl most dangerously in the printed word. And the printed word is most subtly dangerous, able "if it were possible, to deceive the very elect," not in obvious trash beyond the pale but in authors who appear (unless you know them better) to be "literary" and well within the pale. Burroughs [a primary target in Mrs. Leavis' *Fiction and the Reading Public*] and the Westerns will snare only the mob; a subtler poison lurks in Milton, Shelley, Lamb, Dickens, Meredith, Kipling, or De La Mare. Against this the Vigilant school are our watchdogs or detectives. They have been accused of acrimony, of Arnold's "obduracy and over-vehemence in liking and disliking—a remnant, I suppose, of our insular ferocity." But this is perhaps hardly fair. They are entirely honest, and wholly in earnest. They believe they are smelling out and checking a very great evil....They labour to promote the sort of literary experience that they think is good; but their conception of what is good in literature makes a seamless whole with their total conception of the good life. Their whole scheme of values, though never, I believe, set out *en règle*, is engaged in every critical act....Nothing for them is a matter of taste. They admit to no such realm of experience as the aesthetic. There is for them no specifically literary good. A work, or a single passage, cannot for them be good in any sense unless it is good simply, unless it reveals attitudes which are essential elements in the good life. You must therefore accept their (implied) conception of the good life if you are to accept their criticism. That is, you can admire them as critics only if you revere them as sages. And before we revere them as sages we should need to see their whole system of values set out, not as an instrument of criticism but standing on its own feet and offering its credentials—commending itself to its proper judges, to moralists, moral theologians, psychologists, sociologists or philo-

sophers. For we must not run round in a circle, accepting them as sages because they are good critics and believing them good critics because they are sages.

The conclusion is inevitable: since these critics never have set out their "whole scheme of values," it is impossible to accept them as sages; or if not impossible, then at least a risky act of faith. For whatever reasons, the Leavises have been unwilling to attach their favorite terms of approval—and contempt—to any clearly defined ethical point of view. And if readers think that Lewis' description of the Leavises' *tone* is unfair, they should consult the first paragraph of the joint-preface to *Dickens the Novelist*. (As for Mrs. Leavis' own contributions to that volume, they raise, rather less severely, the same problem of selection and privileged reading discussed above.)

Some mention should be made of *Fiction and the Reading Public*, although it is not, strictly speaking, a "critical" work. Mrs. Leavis' approach here is, as she calls it, "anthropological" and her aim is to demonstrate that "the general reading public of the twentieth century is no longer in touch with the best literature of its own day or of the past." During the great period of the Elizabethan drama, for example, there was no important separation between "the life of the cultivated and the life of the generality: the artist and the ordinary citizen felt and thought in the same idiom, there was a way of communication open between them." Or again, for the discerning common readers of Johnson's day, "Life was not...a series of frivolous stimuli as it now is for the suburban dweller, and there was time for the less immediate pleasures." Because of a complex series of social changes, "the important poets of the twentieth century, like its novelists, are unknown to and hopelessly out of reach of the common reader; and so are most of the artists of the past." And the prognosis, even in 1932, was not encouraging:

> The temptation to accept the cheap and easy pleasures offered by the cinema, the circulating library, the magazine, the newspaper, the dance-hall, and the loudspeaker is too much for almost every one. To refrain would be to exercise a severer self-discipline than even the strongest-minded are likely to practise, for only the unusually self-aware could perceive the necessity of doing so.

It is not Mrs. Leavis' concern here to define what the "best" or "important" in literature means, but much more than the simple preservation of past greatness is at stake. It seems reasonable to understand her argument in terms of the context developed by F.R. Leavis two years before, in *Mass Civilization and Minority Culture*, and based finally on I.A. Richards' work, a few years before that. The arts, Richards had argued,

> are our storehouse of recorded values. They spring from and perpetuate hours in the lives of exceptional people when their control and command of experience is at its height...when the varying possibilities of existence are most clearly seen and the different activities which may arise are the most exquisitely reconciled....In the arts we find the record in the only form in which these things can be recorded of the experiences which have seemed most worth having to the most sensitive and discriminating people....It should be unnecessary to insist upon the degree to which high civilization, in other words, free, varied, and unwasteful life, depends upon them in a numerous society.

The loss of poetry, of the arts in general, would be nothing less than a "biological calamity" for the human race.

LEVIN, Harry (Tuchman). American. Born in Minneapolis, Minnesota, 18 July 1912. Educated at Harvard University, Cambridge, Massachusetts, B.A. 1933; University of Paris, 1934. Married Elena Zarudnaya in 1939; has one child. Junior Fellow, 1934-39, Senior Fellow, 1947-66, and Acting Chairman, 1964-65, Society of Fellows, Instructor and Tutor in English, 1939-44, Associate Professor, 1944-48, Chairman of Comparative Literature 1946-51, 1953-54, 1960-61, 1962-69, 1977-78, Chairman of the Division of Modern Languages, 1951-52, 1955-61, and since 1954 Professor, and since 1960 Irving Babbitt Professor of Comparative Literature, Harvard University. Lowell Lecturer, Harvard University, 1952; taught at the Salzburg Seminar in American Studies, 1953; Exchange Professor, University of Paris, 1953; Visiting Professor, Tokyo University, 1955; Beckman Professor, University of California, Berkeley, 1957; Alexander Lecturer, University of Toronto, 1958; Christian Gauss Lecturer, Princeton University, New Jersey, 1961; Patten Lecturer, University of Indiana, Bloomington, 1967; Overseas Fellow, Churchill College, Cambridge, 1967. Chairman, English Institute, 1957; Vice-President, 1963-65, and President, 1965-68, American Comparative Literature Association; Vice-President, International Comparative Literature Association, 1964-67. Recipient: Guggenheim Fellowship, 1943; National Institute of Arts and Letters Award, 1948; American Council of Learned Societies Award, 1962; Huntington Library Fellowship, 1966. Litt.D.: Syracuse University, New York, 1952; LL.D.: St. Andrews University, Scotland, 1962; L.H.D.: Union College, Schenectady, New York, 1968; Clarkson College, Potsdam, New York, 1970; Dr. honoris causa, The Sorbonne, University of Paris, 1973. Fellow of the American Academy of Arts and Sciences, National Institute of Arts and Letters, and the American Philosophical Society. Address: 14 Kirkland Place, Cambridge, Massachusetts 02138, U.S.A.

PUBLICATIONS

Criticism

> *The Broken Column: A Study in Romantic Hellenism* (undergraduate essay). Cambridge, Massachusetts, Harvard University Press, 1931.
> *James Joyce: A Critical Introduction.* New York, New Directions, 1941; London, Faber, 1944; revised edition, 1960.
> *Toward Stendhal.* New York, New Directions, 1945.
> *Toward Balzac.* New York, New Directions, 1948.
> *The Overreacher: A Study of Christopher Marlowe.* Cambridge, Massachusetts, Harvard University Press, 1952; London, Faber, 1954.
> *Contexts of Criticism.* Cambridge, Massachusetts, Harvard University Press, 1957.
> *The Power of Blackness: Hawthorne, Poe, Melville.* New York, Knopf, and London, Faber, 1958.
> *The Question of Hamlet.* New York and London, Oxford University Press, 1959.
> *The Gates of Horn: A Study of Five French Realists.* New York and London, Oxford University Press, 1963.
> *Symbolism and Fiction* (lecture). Charlottesville, University of Virginia Press, 1965.
> "Wonderland Revisited," in *Kenyon Review* (Gambier, Ohio), 27, 1965.
> *Refractions: Essays in Comparative Literature.* New York, Oxford University Press, 1966; London, Oxford University Press, 1969.
> *Why Literary Criticism Is Not an Exact Science.* Cambridge, Heffer, and Cambridge, Massachusetts, Harvard University Press, 1967; reprinted in *Grounds for Comparison*, 1972.
> *The Myth of the Golden Age in the Renaissance.* Bloomington, Indiana University Press, 1969; London, Faber, 1970.
> *Grounds for Comparison.* Cambridge, Massachusetts, Harvard University Press, 1972.
> "The Waste Land from Ur to Echt," in *Plural* (Mexico City) 1972; New York, New Directions, 1972.
> *Shakespeare and the Revolution of the Times: Perspectives and Commentaries.* New York and London, Oxford University Press, 1976.
> *Memories of the Moderns.* New York, New Directions, 1980; London, Faber, 1981.

Other

Editor, *Selected Works*, by Ben Jonson.   New York, Random House, 1938; introduction reprinted in *Grounds for Comparison*, 1972.

Editor, *A Satire against Mankind and Other Poems*, by John Wilmot, Earl of Rochester. New York, New Directions, 1942; introduction reprinted in *Grounds for Comparison*, 1972.

Editor, *The Portable James Joyce*.   New York, Viking Press, 1947; as *The Essential James Joyce*, London, Cape, 1948.

Editor, *Perspectives of Criticism*.   Cambridge, Massachusetts, Harvard University Press, and London, Oxford University Press, 1950.

Editor, *Coriolanus*, by Shakespeare.   London, Penguin, 1956.

Editor, *The Scarlet Letter*, by Nathaniel Hawthorne.   Boston, Houghton Mifflin, 1960; introduction reprinted in *Grounds for Comparison*, 1972.

Editor, *The Comedy of Errors*, by Shakespeare.   New York, New American Library, 1965.

Editor, *Veins of Humor*.   Cambridge, Massachusetts, Harvard University Press, 1972.

Editor, with G.B. Evans and others, *The Riverside Shakespeare*.   Boston, Houghton Mifflin, 1974.

*   *   *

Looking back over his career, Harry Levin observed recently that "I seem to have started out as a young critic who had a certain amount of scholarly background. Nowadays I am likely to be viewed—if at all—as an elder scholar who has, or else had, certain critical interests." In light of the considerable body of work Levin has produced over the past forty-five years it now seems possible to divide these "critical interests" into two fairly distinct categories: he has been intent on exploring the relationships between realism and romance, especially in fiction, and he has been equally concerned with the need to compare the themes of literary works, or, indeed, of whole bodies of literature.

"It has long been recognized," he asserts (in *The Gates of Horn*), "that the ways of the imagination are bifurcated":

Alfred de Vigny...distinguished two perennial needs of the human heart, seemingly opposed yet intermingled: "one is a love of the true, the other a love of the fabulous." Insofar as the former dominates the latter, we might add, a work of art is realistic. But the sense of wonder is at least as fundamental as the zeal for truth, and when it dominates we have what Vigny terms "the fable." He does not mean that the fabulous is wholly untrue, or that the fictitious is necessarily false; fact, not truth, is the opposite of fiction. He means that, although the fable may deviate from factual truth, it may still be true in its own way. It is never created out of nothing, and the psychologists would agree with Vigny that subconscious fantasy often reveals as much as conscious realism.

In Greek myths and the classical literature based upon them we are told that the dreams and visions sent to mankind from the underworld must pass through the gates of transparent horn or the gates of opaque ivory. According to Homer, in the eleventh book of *The Odyssey*,

Two gates for ghostly dreams there are: one gateway
of honest horn, and one of ivory.
Issuing by the ivory gates are dreams
of glimmering illusion, fantasies,
but those that come through solid polished horn
may be borne out, if mortals only know them.
(Fitzgerald translation, my italics)

These two gates serve as Levin's metaphor for the opposition between realistic art (realistic means of presentation as well as realistic "content") and romance or fantasy, with its usual reliance on symbolism rather than direct representation. And the metaphor also suggests, indirectly, that we need the dreams and visions which artists can give us. Here Levin seems willing to settle for a very broad conception of the purpose of art derived from Bergson:

> The habit of fabulation, as Bergson described it, is instinctive and therefore must be universal. Its function, as he saw it, is to meditate between the ego and society. More explicitly to our purpose, it preserves continuities; it envisages possibilities; it projects ideals; it sums up conditions; it determines man's conception of himself. Though its basic materials are unchanging, they have been and will be subjected to endless permutations.

At its best, art offers us a distinct and valuable kind of knowledge:

> Into that bleak and incomplete state of affairs [modern "specialization"] art brings the possibility of enlargement. The kind of experience it offers, to be sure, is not the real thing; if we want to be ontological about it, we must admit, it is notoriously second-hand. But reality is also many-faceted, and our apprehension of it so single-minded, that we are lucky to have this intersubjective means of keeping in touch with the curiosities and the sympathies of our fellow men. Every mode of inquiry is symbolic, in that it faces particular complexities and reduces them to a quantitative, syllogistic, linguistic, or graphic generalizations; for an intractable and elusive whole it substitutes some convenient and typical part. But artistic symbols—being at once less rigorous and less arbitrary than other types—are all the more significant, in that they connote personalities and situations which have the widest appeal and the most immediate meaning. Although universality is itself a relative concept, here it may help to distinguish the esthetic from the more technical phases of experience. The latter may be valid or not, as the appropriate specialists determine, according to their objective criteria and independently of what others may think. The former owes its degree of validity to the reactions of whoever is willing to participate in it, on a basis of nothing more nor less than common humanity.

In "A Personal Retrospect," the opening essay of *Grounds for Comparison*, Levin provides a very useful summary of his long preoccupation with realism and romance:

> [Joyce's] *Ulysses* was so paradigmatic because, as Eliot had noted in relating it to his own work and that of Yeats, it so magisterially handled the parallelism between the mythic and the realistic. But the observation could be generalized and applied to the whole of literature—or rather, to the imaginative process that brings it into being—inasmuch as all fiction must combine, though in widely varying proportions, symbolism with realism.
>
> Joyce the modernist pointed back to the *Odyssey*, which had outlined the situation in parable. Yet those two metaphorical gates...coexisted not merely as alternatives but as poles at the ends of a sliding scale. In recounting men's actions and projecting their values by means of fabulation...narrative has fluctuated between the poles, depending at every stage on social conditions and modes of communication. The novel from Cervantes onward has been increasingly rigorous in its observation of life, habitually tending toward the realistic pole; and there my theorizing found rich confirmation in the stylistic studies of Erich Auerbach. Style was the immediate vehicle for a changing world-view, not least in that explicit repudiation of literary artifice which I have come to call the Quixote principle; but, along with the texture, one also had to consider the structure of the critique that the realists were involved in, to compare their versions of actuality with the historical ways in which it might be documented. France was the exemplary terrain for such a demonstration, as Babbitt had affirmed, even though he had not cared for this part of its literary history.... [Paris] had furnished the books and men, from Stendhal to Proust, for the central movement in the history of realistic fiction.

Thus in *The Gates of Horn* Levin discusses in great detail the realism of Stendhal, Balzac, Flaubert, Zola and Proust. There is, of course, an immediate problem: "if art were simply the mirror of reality, then realism would be a constant"—that is, we would have one fixed realistic style running from Cervantes through Proust. But obviously this is not the case; what we have are different kinds of "realisms" with their own artistic conventions; and we can discriminate among them only by investigating the conceptions of reality which particular artists held. These conceptions, finally, are "social" in the broadest sense of the term (here Levin is indebted to the Marxists, or at least to Georg Lukács). The great French realists reflect—and criticize—the rise of the French *bourgeoisie* after the Revolution, just as the epic and romance once spoke for earlier stages of social organization:

> In his illuminating study, *Epic and Romance*, W.P. Ker analyzed these two forms by referring them back to their respective states of society, to the heroic and the chivalric ages. An analysis of the third significant form of fiction, the novel, should be no less dependent on the continued cross-reference to the bourgeois age, and to our own state of social organization. Epic, romance, and novel are the representatives of three successive estates and styles of life: military, courtly, and mercantile.

But Levin's contrast between romance and realism is not simply historical. He clearly prefers the great achievement of the realists, as the reductive metaphor of the gates suggests (after all, it is "glimmering illusions" which pass through the ivory gates). The realists belong

> to that world which is inhabited by the greatest writers of all time; for all great writers, in so far as they are committed to a searching and scrupulous critique of life as they know it, may be reckoned among the realists.

So much for, say, Dante. And again,

> The ivory gate has always been the one surrounded by welcoming crowds, since its apparitions are so attractive and easy. To stand at the hornéd gate is an anxious and difficult vigil, since it is conceived as *our only means of access to the portents of reality*....There are many windows in the house of fiction, as we should always be glad to hear James remind us; but few of them are wider or clearer than these [the realist's], and none has let in more light on the darker places of time and fate and human will. (my italics)

And so much, apparently, for Kafka, Nabokov and Borges.

In *The Power of Blackness* Levin examines the essentially romantic or symbolic nature of nineteenth century American fiction:

> This was primarily a study in literary iconology, in the adaptation of archetypal themes to given circumstances close at hand. It emphasized the obverse side of the story-telling faculty, its deep immersion in myth, as opposed to its sharp confrontation with actuality.

More specifically, he is concerned with the contrast between the affirmative public philosophy of American life and the darker insights of her artists:

> Wanting to believe in a national credo, we have found ourselves declining to accept one that seems more and more self-evidently composed of eupeptic half-truths. Consequently, our most perceptive minds have distinguished themselves from our popular spokesmen by concentrating upon the dark other half of the situation, and their distinctive attitude has been introspection, dissent, or irony. Where the voice of the majority is by definition affirmative, the spirit of independence is likeliest to manifest itself by employing the negative: by saying *no* in thunder—as Melville wrote to Hawthorne—though bidden by the devil himself to say yes.

As these brief summaries should begin to suggest, it is not possible, finally, to make any absolute separations between modes of representation and the themes they convey. In any event, Levin argues in an important essay, "Thematics and Criticism" (reprinted in *Grounds for Comparison*), that "culture provides [the artist] with a sequence of themes to which he responds according to his imaginative bent; and when we are fully aware of them and can trace their projection through the minds of other writers, we may then be in a position to gauge both the individual quality of that response and the functioning of the collective imagination" (*how* we may move from recognition of a given "theme" to right judgment of "individual quality" is left unexplained). Further, themes, like symbols,

are polysemous: that is, they can be endowed with different meanings in the face of different situations. This is what makes an inquiry into their permutations an adventure in the history of ideas (see Don Cameron Allen on Noah or George K. Anderson on the Wandering Jew). Our knowledge can be enriched by finding out why certain themes have been chosen at certain periods (the Wagnerian resurrection of the *Nibelungenlied*) or in certain localities (the Vergilian linkage of Rome with Troy) or by certain authors— why should the saintly figure of Joan of Arc have impressed such skeptics as Mark Twain, Bernard Shaw, and Anatole France, while failing to win the sympathy of Shakespeare? Themes, like biological entities, seem to have their cycles, phases of growth, of heyday, and of decline, as with Troilus and Cressida. It is not surprising, in our latter day, that so many of them seem to have reached a state of exhaustion. Audiences get tired of hearing the same old names, and writers find it harder and harder to compete with their illustrious forerunners. But motifs seem inexhaustible. As long as man's aspirations and limitations are what they have been, his journey through life will be envisioned as an intercepted quest, like that of *Moby-Dick*. He will sooner or later find himself located somewhere, and place will be sublimated by dream. His ego will invoke its alter ego, it double or *Doppelgänger*, whether in reflection of the author's intimate bond with his protagonist or with his reader ("mon semblable, mon frère") or by the sort of optical illusion that projects a fabric by our fantasies.

All of this raises a final important question. The academic mind thrives on the possibility that everything may be compared with everything else: comparisons often lead to major discoveries. But to make a possibility into a moral imperative—everything *ought* to be compared with everything else—is another matter. One or two illustrations from Levin's work will have to suffice. In *The Question of Hamlet*, Levin pauses to discuss the relationships among characters in Acts IV and V and observes that

In the duel of mighty opposites, Claudius is represented by deputies, who defend him by parrying Hamlet's thrusts. Of these, Laertes, who has public support for the kingship, is the last and most formidable....Claudius...fans the flames of competition, by falsely reporting that Hamlet is envious of Laertes' chivalric accomplishments. Flattery is reinforced by a testimonial from another man of parts, a gentleman of Normandy, so skilled in horsemanship that he has seemed "incorps'd and deminatur'd / With the brave beast" (iv.vii 88-9). Claudius digresses to such an extent, in citing this shadowy witness, that we may wonder what ulterior purpose he—or Shakespeare—had in introducing him. Do we perceive, in the centaur-like description, another emblem of man in his animal guise? Or may we take a hint from the Quarto reading, where the Frenchman's name—Lamound in the Folio—is spelled Lamord? Could that have been, by an easily possible slip of typography or pronounciation, La Mort? And could that equestrian stranger be a premonitory vision of Death on a pale horse, heralding the outcome of the duel? That vision appears unexpectedly in familiar places; in the squares of Paris, as Rilke imagined them, Madame Lamort, the fateful dressmaker, winds and binds the restless ways of world.

But do these "suggestive parallels" between Shakespeare and Rilke serve any clear purpose? Or again, in the last two paragraphs of *The Overreacher* we have references to Spengler, Mann, Valéry, Flaubert's St. Anthony, Goethe, Mallarmé's *Prose pour des Esseintes*, F.M. Cornford, Joyce, Icarus, Eliot, Drayton, Lucretius and Epicurus, Ovid, Lucan and Bacon. To what end? These displays may reveal nothing more than the extraordinarily well-stocked interior of Levin's mind; they are dazzling, or boring, depending on one's taste. As Lincoln observed about something else, people who like this sort of thing will find this the sort of thing they like. In the preface to *Contexts of Criticism* Levin claims that "Relativity, if not relativism, conceived not as the disappearance of standards but as the discernment of relationships, must be a premise whenever we consider literature, if we would trace any order in its complexities." To put the question in its proper form, then: *what is* this "order" which seems to underlie the complexity of literary phenomena? Is it, for example, anything like the great mythic structure Northrop Frye sees informing all literary plots? Unfortunately Levin has never really faced the question.

LEWIS, C(live) S(taples).   British.   Born in Belfast, Northern Ireland, 29 November 1898. Educated at Wynyard School, Hertfordshire, 1908-10; Campbell College, Northern Ireland, 1910; Cherbourg School, Malvern, 1911-13; privately 1914-17; University College, Oxford (Scholar; Chancellor's English Essay Prize, 1921), 1917, 1919-23, B.A. (honours) 1922. Served in the Somerset Light Infantry, 1917-19; First Lieutenant. Married Joy Davidman Gresham in 1956 (died, 1960). Philosophy Tutor, 1924, and Lecturer in English, 1924, University College, Oxford; Fellow and Tutor in English, Magdalen College, Oxford, 1924-54; Professor of Medieval and Renaissance English, Cambridge University, 1954-63. Riddell Lecturer, University of Durham, 1943; Clark Lecturer, Cambridge University, 1944. Recipient: Gollancz Prize for Literature, 1937; Library Association Carnegie Medal, 1957. D.D.: University of St. Andrews, Scotland, 1946; Docteur-ès-Lettres, Laval University, Quebec, 1952; D.Litt.: University of Manchester, 1959; Hon. Dr.: University of Dijon, 1962; University of Lyon, 1963. Honorary Fellow, Magdalen College, Oxford, 1955; University College, Oxford, 1958; Magdalene College, Cambridge, 1963. Fellow of the Royal Society of Literature, 1948; Fellow of the British Academy, 1955. *Died 22 November 1963.*

PUBLICATIONS

Criticism

> *The Allegory of Love: A Study in Medieval Tradition.*   Oxford, Clarendon Press, and New York, Oxford University Press, 1936.
> *Rehabilitations and Other Essays.*   London and New York, Oxford University Press, 1939; reprinted in part in *Selected Literary Essays,* 1969.
> *The Personal Heresy: A Controversy,* with E.M.W. Tillyard.   London and New York, Oxford University Press, 1939.
> *A Preface to "Paradise Lost."*   London and New York, Oxford University Press, 1942.
> Preface to *George Macdonald: An Anthology.*   London, Bles, 1946; New York, Doubleday, 1962.
> Commentary in *Arthurian Torso, Containing the Posthumous Fragment of "The Figure of Arthur,"* by Charles Williams.   London and New York, Oxford University Press, 1948.
> *English Literature in the Sixteenth Century, Excluding Drama.*   Oxford, Clarendon Press, 1954. (Vol. 3 of The Oxford History of English Literature)
> *De Descriptione Temporum* (lecture).   London, Cambridge University Press, 1955; reprinted in *Selected Literary Essays,* 1969.
> *Studies in Words.*   London, Cambridge University Press, 1960; revised edition, 1967.
> *An Experiment in Criticism.*   London, Cambridge University Press, 1961.
> *They Asked for a Paper: Papers and Addresses.*   London, Bles, 1962; reprinted in part in *Selected Literary Essays,* 1969.
> "The English Prose *Morte*," in *Essays on Malory,* edited by J.A.W. Bennett.   Oxford, Clarendon Press, 1963.
> Introduction to *Selections from Layamon's "Brut,"* edited by G.L. Brook.   Oxford, Clarendon Press, 1963.

The Discarded Image: An Introduction to Medieval and Renaissance Literature. London, Cambridge University Press, 1964.
Studies in Medieval and Renaissance Literature, edited by Walter Hooper. London, Cambridge University Press, 1966.
"Christianity and Literature," in *Christian Reflections*, edited by Walter Hooper. London, Cambridge University Press, 1967.
Spenser's Images of Life, edited by Alastair Fowler. London, Cambridge University Press, 1967.
Selected Literary Essays, edited by Walter Hooper. London, Cambridge University Press, 1969.

Verse

Spirits in Bondage: A Cycle of Lyrics (as Clive Hamilton). London, Heinemann, 1919.
Dymer (as Clive Hamilton). London, Dent, and New York, Macmillan, 1926.
Poems, edited by Walter Hooper. London, Bles, 1964; New York, Harcourt Brace, 1965.
Narrative Poems, edited by Walter Hooper. London, Bles, 1969; New York, Harcourt Brace, 1972.

Novels

Out of the Silent Planet. London, Lane, 1938; New York, Macmillan, 1943.
Perelandra. London, Lane, 1943; New York, Macmillan, 1944; as *Voyage to Venus*, London, Pan, 1960.
That Hideous Strength: A Modern Fairy-Tale for Grown-Ups. London, Lane, 1945; New York, Macmillan, 1946; abridged edition as *The Tortured Planet*, New York, Avon, 1958.
The Lion, the Witch, and the Wardrobe (juvenile). London, Bles, and New York, Macmillan, 1950.
Prince Caspian: The Return to Narnia (juvenile). London, Bles, and New York, Macmillan, 1951.
The Voyage of the "Dawn Treader" (juvenile). London, Bles, and New York, Macmillan, 1952.
The Silver Chair (juvenile). London, Bles, and New York, Macmillan, 1953.
The Horse and His Boy (juvenile). London, Bles, and New York, Macmillan, 1954.
The Magician's Nephew (juvenile). London, Lane, and New York, Macmillan, 1955.
The Last Battle (juvenile). London, Lane, and New York, Macmillan, 1956.
Till We Have Faces: A Myth Retold. London, Bles, and New York, Harcourt Brace, 1957.

Short Stories

Of Other Worlds: Essays and Stories, edited by Walter Hooper. London, Collins, 1966; New York, Harcourt Brace, 1967.
The Dark Tower and Other Stories, edited by Walter Hooper. London, Collins, and New York, Harcourt Brace, 1977.

Other

The Pilgrim's Regress: An Allegorical Apology for Christianity, Reason and Romanti-
  cism. London, Dent, 1933; New York, Sheed and Ward, 1935; revised edition,
  London, Bles, 1943; Sheed and Ward, 1944.
The Problem of Pain. London, Bles, 1940; New York, Macmillan, 1943.
The Weight of Glory. London, S.P.C.K., 1942.
The Screwtape Letters. London, Bles, 1942; New York, Macmillan, 1944; revised edi-
  tion, Bles, 1961.
Broadcast Talks: Right and Wrong: A Clue to the Meaning of the Universe, and What
  Christians Believe. London, Bles, 1942; as The Case for Christianity, New York,
  Macmillan, 1943; reprinted in Mere Christianity, 1952.
Christian Behaviour: A Further Series of Broadcast Talks. London, Bles, and New
  York, Macmillan, 1943; reprinted in Mere Christianity, 1952.
The Abolition of Man; or, Reflections on Education with Special Reference to the
  Teaching of English in the Upper Forms of Schools. London, Oxford University
  Press, 1943; New York, Macmillan, 1947.
Beyond Personality: The Christian Idea of God. London, Bles, 1944; New York,
  Macmillan, 1945; reprinted in Mere Christianity, 1952.
The Great Divorce: A Dream. London, Bles, 1945; New York, Macmillan, 1946.
Miracles: A Preliminary Study. London, Bles, and New York, Macmillan, 1947.
Vivisection. London, Anti-Vivisection Society, 1948.
Transpositions and Other Addresses. London, Bles, 1949; as The Weight of Glory and
  Other Addresses, New York, Macmillan, 1949.
The Literary Impact of the Authorized Version (lecture). London, Athlone Press, 1950;
  Philadelphia, Fortress Press, 1963.
Mere Christianity. London, Bles, and New York, Macmillan, 1952.
Hero and Leander (lecture). London, Oxford University Press, 1952.
The Voyage of the "Dawn Treader" (juvenile). London, Bles, and New York,
  Macmillan, 1952.
Surprised by Joy: The Shape of My Early Life. London, Bles, 1955; New York, Har-
  court Brace, 1956.
Reflections on the Psalms. London, Bles, and New York, Harcourt Brace, 1958.
Shall We Lose God in Outer Space? London, S.P.C.K., 1959; reprinted in The World's
  Last Night and Other Essays, 1960.
The Four Loves. London, Bles, and New York, Harcourt Brace, 1960.
The World's Last Night and Other Essays. New York, Harcourt Brace, 1960.
A Grief Observed (as N.W. Clerk; autobiography). London, Faber, 1961; Greenwich,
  Connecticut, Seabury Press, 1963.
Beyond the Bright Blue (letters). New York, Harcourt Brace, 1963.
Letters to Malcolm, Chiefly on Prayer. London, Bles, and New York, Harcourt Brace,
  1964.
Screwtape Proposes a Toast and Other Pieces. London, Collins, 1965.
Of Other Worlds: Essays and Stories, edited by Walter Hooper. London, Bles, 1966;
  New York, Harcourt Brace, 1967.
Letters, edited by W.H. Lewis. London, Bles, and New York, Harcourt Brace, 1966.
Christian Reflections, edited by Walter Hooper. London, Bles, and Grand Rapids,
  Michigan, Eerdmans, 1967.
Letters to an American Lady, edited by Clyde S. Kilby. Grand Rapids, Michigan,
  Eerdmans, 1967; London, Hodder and Stoughton, 1969.
Mark vs. Tristam: Correspondence Between C.S. Lewis and Owen Barfield, edited by
  Walter Hooper. Cambridge, Massachusetts, Lowell House Printers, 1967.
A Mind Awake: An Anthology of C.S. Lewis, edited by Clyde S. Kilby. London, Bles,
  1968; New York, Harcourt Brace, 1969.
God in the Dock: Essays on Theology and Ethics, edited by Walter Hooper. Grand
  Rapids, Michigan, Eerdmans, 1970; as Undeceptions: Essays on Theology and Ethics,
  London, Bles, 1971.

The Humanitarian Theory of Punishment. Abingdon, Berkshire, Marcham Books Press, 1972.

Fern-Seed and Elephants and Other Essays on Christianity, edited by Walter Hooper. London, Fontana, 1975.

The Joyful Christian: 128 Readings, edited by William Griffin. New York, Macmillan, 1977.

They Stand Together: The Letters of C.S. Lewis to Arthur Greeves 1914-1963, edited by Walter Hooper. London, Collins, and New York, Macmillan, 1979.

Editor, *Arthurian Torso, Containing the Posthumous Fragment of "The Figure of Arthur,"* by Charles Williams. London and New York, Oxford University Press, 1948.

Editor, *George MacDonald: An Anthology.* London, Bles, 1946; New York, Macmillan, 1962.

BIOGRAPHY, CRITICAL STUDIES AND BIBLIOGRAPHY

Chad Walsh, *C.S. Lewis: Apostle to the Sceptics.* New York, Macmillan, 1949.

S.L. Goldberg, "C.S. Lewis and the Study of English," in *Melbourne Critical Review*, 5, 1962.

Walter Hooper, "A Bibliography of the Writings of C.S. Lewis," in *Light on C.S. Lewis*, edited by Jocelyn Gibb. London, Bles, 1965.

W.W. Robson, "The Romanticism of C.S. Lewis," in *Critical Essays.* London, Routledge, 1966.

P.S. Sundaram, "C.S. Lewis: Literary Critic," in *Quest* (Bombay), 60, 1969.

James Como, "The Critical Principles of C.S. Lewis," in *Bulletin of the New York C.S. Lewis Society* (Ossining), 2, 1971.

Roger Lancelyn Green and Walter Hooper, *C.S. Lewis: A Biography.* London, Collins, 1974.

Joe R. Christopher and Joan K. Ostlin, *C.S. Lewis: An Annotated Checklist of Writings about Him and His Works.* Kent, Ohio, Kent State University Press, 1975.

Paul L. Holmer, *C.S. Lewis: The Shape of His Faith and Thought.* London, Sheldon Press, 1977.

Lionel Adey, *C.S. Lewis's "Great War" with Owen Barfield.* Victoria, British Columbia, English Literature Studies, 1978.

Humphrey Carpenter, *The Inklings: C.S. Lewis, J.R.R. Tolkien, Charles Williams and Their Friends.* New York, Houghton Mifflin, 1979.

Chad Walsh, *The Literary Legacy of C.S. Lewis.* New York, Harcourt Brace, 1979; London, Sheldon Press, 1980.

Gilbert Meilander, *The Taste for the Other: The Social and Ethical Thought of C.S. Lewis.* Grand Rapids, Michigan, Eerdmans, 1979.

C.S. Lewis at the Breakfast Table and Other Reminiscences, edited by James T. Como. New York, Macmillan, 1979; London, Collins, 1980.

*   *   *

Early in the 1940's, C.S. Lewis warned a Westfield College audience that psychoanalysis, whatever its therapeutic claims, was one of those disciplines which easily distracts us from facing the "genuinely critical question, 'Why, and how, do we read this?' " He went on to describe as fairly as anyone ever has the limitations of the psychoanalytic approach to literature but said nothing more, except by implication, about the nature of proper criticism; nor was he to develop his position fully until much later, in *An Experiment in Criticism.*

Some familiarity with hermeneutic theory should make it easier to place Lewis' conception of poetry—of imaginative literature, that is, in the broadest sense—and the responsibilities of criticism. For the classical tradition which hermeneutics presupposes, literature is essentially a public activity: the poet intends to inform and move his readers and can do so only by using the range of meanings and implications permitted by the language they have in common. Authorial or "original" meaning may be complex, but it is willed, determinate and sharable, as E.D. Hirsch has demonstrated in *Validity in Interpretation*. Thus Schleiermacher stated the interpretive or hermeneutic ideal when he maintained, at the end of the eighteenth century, that "Everything in a given text which requires fuller interpretation must be explained and determined exclusively from the linguistic domain common to the author and his original public." It is important to keep in mind here the crucial distinction between meaning, or what the text says and implies, and significance, or the way in which we relate that meaning to our other concerns: proper interpretation is therefore limited to the re-cognition of original meaning; and about this rational consensus is possible, if often difficult. But clearly other constructions of meaning are possible too: when medieval commentators found an allegorized body of Christian prophecy in Vergil they were constructing what Hirsch calls "anachronistic meaning." The problem for critical theory is obvious: to what extent are we constrained by original meaning? To what extent and under what conditions is anachronistic meaning permissible and perhaps even superior to original meaning? There is nothing necessary or logically compelling about original meaning—the Christian readings of Vergil exist, and so do *Shelley's Mythmaking, Love and Death in the American Novel* and G. Wilson Knight's books on Shakespeare. If we wish to defend original meaning as the goal of interpretation we can do so only on *ethical* grounds. There is a fundamental ethical maxim for interpretation, Hirsch maintains (in *The Aims of Interpretation*), "that claims no privileged sanction from metaphysics or analysis, but only from general ethical tenets, generally shared":

> *Unless there is a powerful overriding value in disregarding an author's intention (i.e., original meaning), we who interpret as a vocation should not disregard it.* Mere individual preference would not be such an overriding value, nor would be the mere preferences of many persons. The possible exception is mentioned only because every ethical maxim requires such an escape clause. (Example: unless there is a powerful overriding value in lying, a person should tell the truth. Yet there are times when a lie is ethically better than to tell the truth, so the maxim cannot be an absolute one.) Similarly, one might fudge on original meaning for the sake of young, impressionable children, and so on. But except in these very special cases there is a strong ethical presumption against anachronistic meaning. When we simply use an author's words for our own purposes without respecting his intention, we transgress what Charles Stevenson in another context called "the ethics of language," just as we transgress ethical norms when we use another person merely for our own ends. Kant held it to be a foundation of moral action that men should be conceived as ends in themselves, and not as instruments of other men. This imperative is transferable to the words of men because speech is an extension and expression of men in the social domain, and also because when we fail to conjoin a man's intentions to his words we lose the Soul of Speech, which is to convey meaning and to understand what is intended to be conveyed.... The peculiarly modern anarchy of every man for himself in matters of interpretation may sound like the ultimate victory of the Protestant spirit. Actually, such anarchy is the direct consequence of transgressing the fundamental ethical norms of speech and its interpretation.

For Lewis too, criticism is, or should be, a body of knowledge which "enables the reader to enter more fully into the author's intentions," as he puts it in "The Anthropological Approach" (reprinted in *Selected Literary Essays*): the justification here is ethical as well, and specifically Christian, as we can see by tracing the rather indirect argument of *The Personal Heresy* and *An Experiment in Criticism*. In the latter work Lewis proposes that we discriminate not between good and bad texts, but between good and bad reading. The good reader receives the text, the bad reader uses it:

> A work of (whatever) art can be either "received" or "used." When we "receive" it we exert our sense and imagination and various other powers according to a pattern invented by the artist. When we "use" it we treat it as an assistance for our own activities....The "uses" which [unliterary readers] make of the arts may or may not be intrinsically vulgar, depraved, or morbid. That's as may be. "Using" is inferior to "reception" because art, if used rather than received, merely facilitates, brightens,

relieves or palliates our life, and does not add to it....The "user" wants to use [literary] content—as pastime for a dull or torturing hour, as a puzzle, as a help to castle-building, or perhaps as a source for "philosophies of life." The "recipient" wants to rest in it. It is for him, at least temporarily, an end. That way, it may be compared (upward) with religious contemplation or (downward) with a game.

A literary text is both *logos*, or something said, and *poiema*, or something made; the good reader is sensitive to and takes pleasure in a harmonious, well-made whole; the bad reader attends only to the *logos* or content, particularly as it reflects or confirms his own individual interests. Thus good and bad readings are really analogous to proper responses in other areas of life. It is natural, Lewis goes on,

that when we have gone through the ordered movements which a great play or narrative excites in us—when we have danced that dance or enacted that ritual or submitted to that pattern—it should suggest to us many interesting reflections. We have "put on mental muscle" as a result of this activity. We may thank Dante or Shakespeare for that muscle, but we had better not father on them the philosophical or ethical use we make of it. For one thing, this use is unlikely to rise very much—it may rise a little—above our own ordinary level. Many of the comments of life which people get out of Shakespeare could have been reached by very moderate talents without his assistance. For another, it may well impede further receptions of the work itself. We may go back to it chiefly to find further confirmation for our belief that it teaches us this or that, rather than for a fresh immersion in what it is. We shall be like a man poking his fire, not to boil the kettle or warm the room, but in hope of seeing in it the same picture he saw yesterday. And since a text is "but a cheverel glove" to a determined critic—since everything can be a symbol, or an irony, or an ambiguity—we shall easily find what we want. The supreme objection to this is that which lies against the popular use of all the arts. We are so busy doing things with the work that we give it too little chance to work on us. Thus increasingly we meet only ourselves.

But one of the chief operations of art is to remove our gaze from that mirrored face, to deliver us from that solitude.

Or again, in *A Preface to "Paradise Lost"*:

I had much rather know what I should feel like if I adopted the beliefs of Lucretius than how Lucretius would have felt if he had never entertained them. The possible Lucretius in myself interests me more than the possible C.S. Lewis in Lucretius. There is in G.K. Chesterton's *Avowals and Denials* a wholly admirable essay called *On Man: Heir of All the Ages*. An heir is one who inherits and "any man who is cut off from the past...is a man most justly disinherited." To enjoy our full humanity we ought, so far as is possible, to contain within us potentially at all times, and on occasion to actualize, all the modes of feeling and thinking through which man has passed. You must, so far as in you lies, become an Achaean chief while reading Homer, a medieval knight while reading Malory, and an eighteenth century Londoner while reading Johnson. Only thus will you be able to judge the work "in the same spirit that its author writ" and to avoid chimerical criticism.

The ethical implications here should now be apparent: in proper reading we exercise that power of sympathetic understanding which transcends self-interest and thus helps to strengthen one of the noblest and most difficult of human capacities. The argument here is Aristotelian in form (an activity is "good" when it actualizes the highest capacities of the agent) and Christian in spirit (the moral virtue analogous to good reading is, of course, compassion or disinterested love). As Lewis puts it at the end of the *Experiment*:

Good reading, therefore, though it is not essentially an affectional or moral or intellectual activity, has something in common with all three. In love we escape from our self into one another. In the moral sphere, every act of justice or charity involves putting ourselves in the other person's place and thus transcending our own competitive particularity. In coming to understand anything we are rejecting the facts as they are for us in favour of the facts as they are. The primary impulse of each is to maintain and aggrandise himself. The secondary impulse is to go out of the self, to correct its provincialism and heal its loneliness. In love, in virtue, in the pursuit of knowledge, and in the reception of the arts, we are doing this. Obviously this process can be described either as an enlargement or as a temporary annihilation of the self. But that is an old paradox; "he that loseth his life shall save it."

And he concludes,

> This, so far as I can see, is the specific value or good of literature considered as Logos; it admits us to experiences other than our own....Those of us who are true readers seldom fully realise the enormous extension of our being which we owe to authors. We realise it best when we talk with an unliterary friend. He may be full of goodness and good sense but he inhabits a tiny world. In it, we should be suffocated....Literary experience heals the wound, without undermining the privilege, of individuality. There are mass emotions which heal the wound; but they destroy the privilege. In them our separate selves are pooled and we sink back into sub-individuality. But in reading great literature I become a thousand men and yet remain myself. Like the night sky in the Greek poem, I see with a myriad eyes, but it is still I who see. Here, as in worship, in love, in moral action, and in knowing, I transcend myself; and am never more myself than when I do.

In *The Personal Heresy* Lewis argues against the popular belief that poetry is "an expression of personality" and that we read chiefly to attain "a certain contract with the poet's soul." When we read properly we read not to gain access to the poet's consciousness but rather to what that consciousness has seen and felt. "Let it be granted that I do approach the poet," Lewis admits,

> at least I do it by sharing his consciousness, not by studying it. I look with his eyes, not at him. He, for the moment, will be precisely what I do not see.... The poet is not a man who asks me to look at *him*; he is a man who says "look at that" and points; the more I follow the pointing of his finger the less I can possibly see of *him*. To be sure there are all sorts of difficult questions hanging over us. But for the moment let us thrust them aside.... To see things as the poet sees them I must share his consciousness and not attend to it; I must look where he looks and not turn round to face him; I must make of him not a spectacle, but a pair of spectacles; in fine, as Professor Alexander would say, I must *enjoy* him and not *contemplate* him.

The next step of the argument is crucial: "It cannot...have escaped anyone's attention," he goes on, "that there is a whole class of poetical experiences in which the consciousness that we share cannot possibly be attributed to any single human individual." After examining the first draft of some lines from *Hyperion* Lewis demonstrates that Keats had to search for the rich, embodied meaning of the revision:

> Keats lacked this perception when he began to write. It was therefore no permanent element in his psychology, nor even in his poetic psychology. He had to bring it into existence; and what created it in him was the very same cause that creates it in us—the words, incarnating common experiences and juxtaposed so as to make new experience. Both for Keats and for us the heightened consciousness is *something foreign, something won from without, from the boundless ocean of racial, not personal perception....* Let us remember that...poethood consists not in the fact that each [poet] approached the universal world from his own angle (all men do that), but in their power of telling us what things are severally to be seen from those angles.... If he remains at his [individual] starting-point he is no poet; as long as he is (like the rest of us) a mere personality, all is still to do. It is his business, starting from his own mode of consciousness, whatever that may happen to be, to find *that arrangement of public experiences, embodied in words*, which will admit him (and incidentally us) to a new mode of consciousness.... (italics mine)

374

The great poet's consciousness, in other words, reflects his consciousness of tradition and public meaning, the accumulated sensitivity and wisdom of the race and not simply the idiosyncratic vision of an isolated individual trying to devise his own private poetic language (this explains, in part, Lewis' disdain for modern poetry).

This does not imply that while there may be good and bad reading there are no bad texts. Obviously we may learn a great deal by sharing, for the moment, the perspective of a corrupted consciousness—of Milton's Satan, for example; but obviously there are texts which disclose *only* a limited or corrupted consciousness. The question thus becomes, on what ground do we separate worthy from unworthy literary experiences? Quite simply, there are no special aesthetic standards to be invoked here:

> Whether we regard it as fortunate or unfortunate, the fact is that there is no *essential* qualification for criticism more definite than general wisdom and health of mind.... That is interesting *simpliciter* which interests the wise man.

Lewis does not pause to define "general wisdom" or "health" in his criticism, although much of his position might be deduced from *A Preface to "Paradise Lost"*. The reader interested in understanding Lewis' ultimate standards should turn to the various ethical and religious essays (preferably to *The Abolition of Man*, at least to start with, rather than the popular theology of *The Screwtape Letters* or *Mere Christianity*). Finally, while literature may contribute to the right conduct of life, increasing our capacity to understand and sympathize, Lewis, like Eliot and Auden, warns against any substitution of aesthetics for ethics or religion. He makes this clear in an indispensable essay, "Christianity and Literature" (unfortunately not reprinted in the *Selected Literary Essays*):

> The Christian will take literature a little less seriously than the cultured Pagan: he will feel less uneasy with a purely hedonistic standard for at least many kinds of work. The unbeliever is always apt to make a kind of religion of his aesthetic experiences; he feels ethically irresponsible, perhaps, but he braces his strength to receive responsibilities of another kind which seem to the Christian quite illusory. He has to be "creative"; he has to obey a mystical amoral law called his artistic conscience; and he commonly wishes to maintain his superiority to the great mass of mankind who turn to books for mere recreation. But the Christian knows from the outset that the salvation of a single soul is more important than the production or preservation of all the epics and tragedies in the world; and as for superiority, he knows that the vulgar since they include most of the poor probably include most of his superiors.... The real frivolity, the solemn vacuity, is all with those who make literature a self-existent thing to be valued for its own sake. Pater prepared for pleasure as if it were martyrdom.

If we keep all of these discriminations in mind we should appreciate the extraordinary acuteness of Kathleen Raine's brief tribute to Lewis as a critic: "What was best of all in his immense learning was that it had an orientation; almost—not quite—alone in the Cambridge of [his] time he understood that poetry and the other arts are the language of tradition, and exist to serve ends which are not literary."

It follows from all this that good criticism is criticism which encourages good reading of worthy texts; it prevents us from using literature as a means of indulging our private interests and it prevents us, insofar as possible, from merely enjoying the possession of another ego. Thus Lewis is able to propose a hierarchy of four different kinds of critical activity. At the top comes textual criticism:

> Obviously I have owed, and must continue to owe, far more to editors, textual critics, commentators, and lexicographers than to anyone else. Find out what the author actually wrote and what the hard words meant and what the allusions were to, and you have done far more for me than a hundred new interpretations or assessments could ever do.

Below this comes "that despised class, the literary historians":

I mean the really good ones like W.P. Ker or Oliver Elton. These have really helped me, first of all, by telling me what works exist. But still more by putting them in their setting; thus showing me what demands they were meant to satisfy, what furniture they presupposed in the minds of their readers. They have headed me off from false approaches, taught me what to look for, enabled me in some degree to put myself into the frame of mind of those to whom they were addressed.

Below the historians come the various "emotive critics who, up to a certain age, did me very good service by infecting me with their own enthusiasms and thus not only sending me but sending me with a good appetite to the authors they admired. I should not enjoy rereading most of these critics now, but they were useful for a while." And at the very bottom come the evaluative critics, even the great ones:

Can I, honestly and strictly speaking, say with any confidence that my appreciation of any scene, chapter, stanza or line has been improved by my reading of Aristotle, Dryden, Johnson, Lessing, Coleridge, Arnold himself (a practising critic), Pater, or Bradley? I am not sure that I can.

And how indeed could it be otherwise since we invariably judge a critic by the extent to which he illuminates reading we have already done? Brunetière's *aimer Montaigne, c'est aimer soi meme* seems to me as penetrating a remark as I have ever read. But how could I know it was penetrating unless I saw that Brunetière had laid his finger on an element in my enjoyment of Montaigne which I recognise as soon as it is mentioned but had not sufficiently attended to? Therefore my enjoyment of Montaigne comes first.... The truth is not that we need the critics in order to enjoy the authors but that we need the authors in order to enjoy the critics.... I am far from suggesting that a retrospective light on literary experiences we have already had is without value.... We love to hear exactly how others enjoy what we enjoy ourselves. It is natural and wholly proper that we should especially enjoy hearing how a first-class mind responds to a very great work. That is why we read the great critics with interest (not often with any great measure of agreement). They are very good reading; as a help to the reading of others their value is, I believe, overestimated.

And there is another reason why we should be wary of evaluative criticism; it is usually adverse criticism: and as Auden also contended, it is generally bad for the character; it brings out the worst in a man. As Lewis puts it, "the difficulty lies within."

All of Lewis' criticism is designed to enable the reader to "enter more fully into the author's intentions" (with the possible exception of *English Literature in the Sixteenth Century*, parts of which are surprisingly, aggressively "evaluative"). In *Studies in Words* he is concerned with the accurate meaning of certain key words at various times in the past: if we don't know what Shakespeare or Pope meant by "nature" and "wit" we are likely to create our own anachronistic meaning. In *A Preface to "Paradise Lost"* he demonstrates exactly what kind of poem Milton attempted to write, and this involves him in some extremely valuable general discussions of primary and secondary epics, the epic style, and Milton's theology. *The Allegory of Love* is, in Chad Walsh's concise summary,

an essay in social history and at the same time a treatment of the evolution of a particular literary genre. The social history has to do with the astonishing rise and development of "courtly love," which sprang up almost full-blown in Southern France during the eleventh century and quickly spread into other parts of Western Europe. Courtly love was a highly stylized form of romantic love, the goal being adultery not marriage. As such, it formed a world apart from Christian morality and sometimes became almost a rival religion. But adulterous though it was, it introduced a tenderness and consideration into the relations of men and women which had been conspicuously lacking from the ancient idea of marriage.

The literary genre studied by Lewis is the allegory. He traces it back to late Roman times, and shows how it became the favorite form of writing about courtly love.... The book culminates in the treatment of Spenser, for with him the English allegory reaches its fullest development, and at the same time the idea of courtly love definitely emerges from its adulterous associations and passes into marriage. Modern romantic love, with marriage as its normal goal, has become a part of the social pattern; Christianity and the religion of love have made peace.

And in *The Discarded Image* Lewis patiently reconstructs the world view of the late medieval period. As he argued in *De Descriptione Temporum*, his brilliant inaugural address as Professor of Medieval and Renaissance Literature at Cambridge, it is becoming more and more difficult for modern readers to understand the texts of the "Old Western Order." The great break in western cultural history occurred not between antiquity and the coming of Christianity or the dark ages and the Renaissance but, for various social, political and religious reasons, between the present age and "the age of Jane Austen and Scott." His conclusion deserves to be quoted in full:

> I myself belong far more to that Old Western Order than to yours. I am going to claim this, which in one way is a disqualification for my task, yet in another a qualification. The disqualification is obvious. You don't want to be lectured on Neanderthal Man by a Neanderthaler, still less on dinosaurs by a dinosaur. And yet, is that the whole story? If a live dinosaur dragged its slow length into the laboratory, would we not all look back as we fled? What a chance to know at last how it really moved and looked and smelled and what noises it made! And if the Neanderthaler could talk, then, though his lecturing technique might leave much to be desired, should we not almost certainly learn from him some things about him which the best modern anthropologist could never have told us? He would tell us without knowing he was telling. One thing I know: I would give a great deal to hear any ancient Athenian, even a stupid one, talking about Greek tragedy. He would know in his bones so much that we seek in vain. At any moment some chance phrase might, unknown to him, show us where modern scholarship has been on the wrong track for years. Ladies and gentlemen, I stand before you somewhat as that Athenian might stand. I read as a native texts that you must read as foreigners. You see why I said that the claim was not really arrogant; who can be proud of speaking fluently his mother tongue or knowing his way about his father's house? It is my settled conviction that in order to read Old Western Literature aright you must suspend most of the responses and unlearn most of the habits you have acquired in reading modern literature. And because this is the judgement of a native, I claim that, even if the defence of my conviction is weak, the fact of my conviction is a historical *datum* to which you should give full weight. That way, where I fail as a critic, I may yet be useful as a specimen. I would even dare to go further. Speaking not only for myself but for all other Old Western men whom you may meet, I would say, use your specimens while you can. There are not going to be many more dinosaurs.

It is one thing to trace Lewis' general conception of literature and criticism and quite another, obviously, to pretend to pass judgment on how well he reconstructs the original meaning of the authors he deals with. The subjects he chose, as Nevill Coghill observed, "have generally been of intrinsic greatness and difficulty"; and while Coghill believes that Lewis' achievements have been "magistral," there have been some dissenters (readers may consult the convenient Christopher and Ostlin *Checklist* for the controversy which surrounds, for example, *English Literature in the Sixteenth Century*). What one needs here is not simply another expert or team of experts in various specialized fields, but an expert judge of experts. For many of us admitted amateurs who are deeply and permanently indebted to Lewis' criticism precisely because it is so useful in the truest sense of the term, the best reply to his detractors—whose motives, incidentally, are not always above suspicion—may be the crudely challenging one: show us *better* work.

LEWIS, R(ichard) W(arrington) B(aldwin).   American.   Born in Chicago, Illinois, 1 November 1917. Educated at Phillips Exeter Academy, New Hampshire; Harvard University, Cambridge, Massachusetts, B.A. 1935, M.A. 1939; University of Chicago, Ph.D. 1953. Served in the United States Army, 1942-46. Married Nancy Lindau in 1950; has two children. Taught at Bennington College, Vermont, 1948-50; Dean, Salzburg Seminar in American Studies, 1950-51; Visiting Professor, Smith College, Northampton, Massachusetts, 1951-52; Hodder Fellow, 1952-53, and Resident Fellow in Creative Writing, 1953-54, Princeton University, New Jersey; Associate Professor, and Professor, Newark College, Rutgers University, New Jersey, 1954-59; Fulbright Lecturer, University of Munich, 1957-58. Visiting Lecturer, 1959-60, and since 1960 Professor of English and American Studies and Fellow of Calhoun College, Yale University, New Haven, Connecticut. Fellow, 1957-66, and since 1966 Senior Fellow, School of Letters, University of Indiana, Bloomington. Since 1966, Literary Consultant for Universal Pictures. Recipient: *Kenyon Review* Fellowship in Criticism, 1954-55; National Institute of Arts and Letters Award, 1958; Bancroft Prize, 1976; Pulitzer Prize, 1976. Litt.D.: Wesleyan University, Middletown, Connecticut, 1961. Address: Department of English, Yale University, New Haven, Connecticut 06520, U.S.A.

PUBLICATIONS

Criticism

The American Adam: *Innocence, Tragedy and Tradition in the Nineteenth Century*. Chicago, University of Chicago Press, 1955.
The Picaresque Saint: *Representative Figures in Contemporary Fiction*.   Philadelphia, Lippincott, 1959; London, Gollancz, 1960.
Trials of The Word: *Essays in American Literature and the Humanistic Tradition*.   New Haven, Connecticut, and London, Yale University Press, 1965.
The Poetry of Hart Crane: *A Critical Study*.   Princeton, New Jersey, Princeton University Press, 1967.

Other

Edith Wharton: *A Biography*.   New York, Harper, 1975.

Editor, *Herman Melville*.   New York, Dell, 1962.
Editor, *The Presence of Walt Whitman*.   New York, Columbia University Press, 1962.
Editor, *The House of Mirth*, by Edith Wharton.   Boston, Houghton Mifflin, 1963.
Editor, *Malraux*: *A Collection of Critical Essays*.   Englewood Cliffs, New Jersey, Prentice Hall, 1964.
Editor, *The Confidence Man*, by Herman Melville.   New York, New American Library, 1964.
Editor, *The Collected Short Stories of Edith Wharton*.   New York, Scribner, 2 vols., 1968.
Editor, *The Power and the Glory*, by Graham Greene.   New York, Viking Press, 1970.
Editor, with Cleanth Brooks and Robert Penn Warren, *American Literature*: *The Makers and the Making*.   New York, St. Martin's Press, 2 vols., 1973.

*   *   *

The American Adam and *The Picaresque Saint* are sophisticated examples of what is usually called, for want of a better term, thematic criticism, or criticism in which the critic, while not necessarily indifferent to questions of literary value, is primarily interested in representative plot and character types. Properly interpreted, that is, symbolically interpreted, the types we can abstract from a wide variety of particular works may tell us something important about large cultural and philosophical issues. Thus at a certain level of generalization the figure of Adam, the uncorrupted man of the future encountering a new world of complex experiences, has obvious implications for the history of American self-consciousness. "A century ago," Lewis argues, "the image contrived to embody the most fruitful contemporary ideas was that of the authentic American as a figure of heroic innocence and vast potentialities poised at the start of a new history." Every culture, he goes on,

> as it advances toward maturity [seems] to produce its own determining debate over the ideas that preoccupy it: salvation, the order of nature, money, power, sex, the machine, and the like. The debate, indeed, may be said to *be* the culture, at least on its loftiest levels; for a culture achieves identity not so much through the ascendancy of one particular set of convictions as through the emergence of its peculiar and distinctive dialogue.... [The] historian looks not only for the major terms of discourse, but also for major pairs of opposed terms which, by their very opposition, carry discourse forward.

In short, the historical process is dialectical; but dialectical forces, like magnetic fields, can be grasped only by discovering the impact they have on concrete phenomena. And whatever else works of art may be, they are also like iron filings: they reveal the lines of force we want to understand. Imaginative works are especially useful here since they seem to have a greater capacity than other forms of discourse to encompass the contending attitudes which shape a culture. In particular, narrative art "dramatizes as human conflict what is elsewhere a thoughtful exchange of ideas; and art projects—in a single packed dramatic image—conflicting principles which the discursive mind must contemplate separately and consecutively." The elegaic tones of the *Aeneid*, for example, "reflect Virgil's poetic ambivalence toward the Roman ideals that his poem nonetheless affirmed."

The figure of Adam is so overdetermined, however, that it was bound to provoke quite different responses from what Emerson called the parties of Hope and Memory. For the party of Hope—for Emerson, Whitman and Thoreau—the emerging American character represented what was best and most promising in human nature, "a clear conscience unsullied by the past"; but for the party of Memory, as Lewis points out, "the sinfulness of man never seemed so patent as currently in America. As the hopeful expressed their mounting contempt for the doctrine of inherited sin, the nostalgic intoned on Sundays the fixed legacy of corruption in ever more emphatic accents; and centers of orthodox Calvinism, like Andover and Princeton, became citadels of the old and increasingly cheerless theology." By themselves, however, these two parties cannot account for the full dialectic of American history, and thus Lewis postulates a third force—for which there is no proper name "unless we call it the party of Irony"—and argues that American culture "has traditionally consisted of the productive and lively interplay" of all three parties. The ironic point of view is characterized by "tragic optimism" and "a sense of the tragic collisions to which innocence [is] liable" and is in effect a version of the Fortunate Fall of Christian doctrine: experience and the knowledge of evil inevitably bring suffering, but in turn suffering may lead to "heightened perception" and the growth of "moral intelligence." Therefore the terms of Lewis' argument are not merely descriptive: the party of irony, of Hawthorne, Melville, and Henry James, knows more and sees more and deserves to be recognized as the source of our mature or "authentic" cultural awareness:

> The isolated hero "alone in a hostile, or at best a neutral universe" begins to replace the Adamic personality in the New World Eden. The essential continuity of American fiction explains itself through this historical transformation whereby the Adamic fable yielded to what I take to be the authentic American narrative: the individual going forth toward experience, the inventor of his own character and creator of his personal history; the self-moving individual who is made to confront that "other"—the world of society, the element which provides experience. But as we move from Cooper to Hawthorne, the situation very notably darkens; qualities of evil and fear and destructiveness have entered; self-sufficiency is questioned through terrible trials; and the stage is set for tragedy.

And finally,

It has been said that America is always coming of age; but it might be more fairly maintained that America has come of age in sections, here and there—whenever its implicit myth of the American Adam has been a defining part of the writer's consciousness. When this has happened, the emergent mythology of the new world has been recognized and exploited as a stable resource; the writer has found means, at hand and at home, for a fresh definition of experience and a fresh contribution to culture. This is what is meant, I take it, by cultural maturity.

Of course irony may also lead to skepticism and despair, and in fact this is what happens in later generations of American writers. The figure of Adam has been "frowned quite out of existence"—inevitably, perhaps, but also at some real cost:

> The contemporary view [of the "hopelessness of the human condition"] is not a dishonest one. It contains many remarkable and even irreversible psychological, sociological, and political insights. It seems to be the picture most clearly warranted by public and private experience in our time. But it remains curiously frozen in outline; it is anything but dialectical and contains within it no opposite possibilities on which to feed and fatten. Irony is fertile and alive; the chilling skepticism of the mid-twentieth century represents one of the modes of death. The new hopelessness is, paradoxically, as simple minded as innocence; and it is opposed only by that parody of hope which consists in an appeal for "positive thinking"—a wilful return to innocence based upon a wilful ignorance, momentarily popular in the market place of culture but with no hold at all upon the truth known of experience.

Lewis takes up the fate of the Adamic figure again in a long and brilliant essay, "Days of Wrath and Laughter" (reprinted in *Trials of the Word*), and demonstrates that the dominant tone of American literature is now "apocalyptic": "time present in the contemporary American novel is precisely the moment of the last loosening of Satan," the seventh of the ten stages predicted by *Revelation* and other apocalyptic books. The last stage promises a new heaven and earth but Lewis is unwilling to push his metaphor that far; he is also unwilling, however, to believe that the essential spirit of modern American literature is as nihilistic as it often appears to be:

> one does sometimes feel the way Satan himself was said to feel some years ago in the jauntily ironic ballad by John Crowe Ransom, "Armageddon": "The immortal adversary shook his head:...'These Armageddons weary me much,' he said." But in a sense these are just the attitudes implicit in the fiction I have been primarily concerned with. West, Ellison, and the others have without a doubt kept us well informed about everything that is cruel, deadly, inhuman, hate-filled, disruptive, congealing, and in general chaotic and destructive on our modern American scene. The apprehension of immense catastrophe is close to the heart of their imagination. But at the heart itself is a humane perspective rooted not quite in hope but in a hope about hope. The sense of the comic is at once the symptom and the executive agency of that root sensibility. For if there is a large portion of bitterness in the laughter, and if laughter sometimes seems the only response still possible in a radically graceless world, it has served nonetheless to define, to measure and to assess the horror, to reveal its sources and make visible its shape. To do this is to reassert the human. The apocalyptic visions indeed are offered as weapons for averting the catastrophe.

The modern preoccupation with apocalypse, or simply with death and absurdity, is equally important in *The Picaresque Saint*:

> Death is the beginning, often it is the middle, and sometimes, as in [Joyce's] "The Dead," it seems to be the end of the century's most splendid works of the literary art. We hardly need ask why this should be so. It is still the business of the artist (in the words of Hamlet's advice to the players) to show the age and body of his time its form and pressure; and the first fact of modern historic life is the death that presses in on it from all sides: death in battle, death in prison, death in the pit of the soul and the very heart of the culture. Death is the word we use for all those tendencies and events that led so vibrant a

spirit as Antoine de St-Exupéry to exclaim "I hate my epoch!" And on the basis of death Camus can write, with cold accuracy, that the secret of modern Europe is that it no longer loves life. America no longer loves it either, though only its harried artists dare to say so.

But once again, Lewis is unwilling to accept the nihilistic implications of this obsession with death and failure:

And yet, after all, death is *not* the end, in the masterpieces of our time, when we look at the matter more closely. The true artist is constantly seeking ways to confound death. Indeed, the best way to distinguish the two or three literary generations of our century is in the manner of their responding to the fact of death—that is, in the manner of somehow getting beyond it.

Proust, Joyce, and Mann, the members of the first great generation of modern novelists, turned to art as a refuge from or alternative to the nightmare of modern history; Moravia, Silone, Camus, Graham Greene, and Faulkner make up the second generation (this list is obviously more debatable) and have responded quite differently:

With an unconsciously common impulse, the writers of this generation have resorted to a rather desperate strategy. They have been forced to find, or try to find, certain grounds for living *in life itself*. In order to write at all, they must continue to live.... And indeed, if we reach for a single phrase to explain the basis for the renewed sense of life, discovered in most, if not all of these [writers], the one that comes to mind is the seemingly tame one: human companionship. Mild as it sounds, and dangerously close as it comes to fashionable piety, the phrase is perhaps more accurate than that ambiguous vocable "love".... Companionship, as dramatized in the contemporary novel, should suggest in its prefix the idea of sharing; but it echoes in its syllables the matter whose sharing it requires—by echoing the note of compassion (that is, literally and etymologically, of *suffering with*). The key impulse I am describing requires the sharing of pain; but the word itself also retains its own root meaning of the sharing of bread—of *panis* broken in common.

The archetypal hero of these novels is "the apprentice saint or the saint *manqué*"; the archetypal plot is episodic or picaresque since its looseness, compared to the finely wrought structures of Proust, Joyce, and Mann, "engages perhaps a more recognizable chunk of humanity"; and if there is one writer who sums up the tendencies of the entire second generation, it is Malraux, in whom

we confront a familiar Gallic phenomenon, the French talent for moving directly to the point and from one point to the next, displaying each of them in what is offered as its universal aspect. If, in the generation-wide struggle to come alive, Moravia represents the erotic motif; if Camus represents human reason in its compassionate workings: if Silone represents the conversion of the political ambition into the charitable urge, and Faulkner the conversion of darkness into light and the old into the new; if Greene represents the interplay of more than human with the less than human—then Malraux may be said to represent all of these things or versions of them. Thus, he may be said to typify the strongly marked evolution of the whole second generation.

Lewis' repeated use of Christian symbols suggests that for him they may be more than convenient expository metaphors. In the Preface to *Trials of the Word* he admits that he tends "to focus upon those phases of a work of literature in which what have to be called religious considerations are overtly or secretively paramount." Moreover, "to be concerned with modern literature is, I believe, to be deeply concerned with the devious ways in which the irrepressible religious consciousness finds expression in the midst of its resolutely secular and frequently very ordinary materials." *Trials of the Word* is something of a miscellany, but if there is one thematic concern here it is the tension in American literature between the desire for transcendence and the equally strong desire to master the hard facts of daily reality. When we think about our literature, Lewis suggests, we should keep in mind "the remark made to Emerson by an old Boston lady who, talking about the extreme religious sensibility of an earlier generation, said about those pious folk that 'they had to hold on hard to the huckleberry bushes to hinder themselves from being translated.'" And their instinct, Lewis concludes, "was as sound as their impulse was proper." But if his personal beliefs are involved here, he does not make an issue of them. The reader is perfectly free to take Adam and the Fortunate Fall, the apprentice saints, the Apocalypse and the huckleberry bushes as metaphors and to judge them as such. The important question is the one thematic criticism always raises: are the broad generalizations it offers interesting and valuable enough to conpensate for the inability to say much about literary worth? John Holloway puts the matter concisely in *The Charted Mirror*:

> Every intelligible work, however abysmally bad, has several or many themes in this sense, and they probably cannot help becoming interrelated unless it is a very short work indeed. Could one not, if one tried, be sure of finding interrelated themes in the first story in the pile of magazines at the dentist's?...The mere presence of the thing is without interest unless it can be shown that its presence makes the work better. The whole problem lies there.

Some mention should be made here of *Edith Wharton*, which is arguably the best biography we have of any recent American writer, and *The Poetry of Hart Crane*, a minutely detailed reading of Crane's work in which biographical information, while plentiful, never becomes an end in itself. If there is anything to regret here it is simply that Lewis, who is one of the most interesting American critics now writing (regardless of what one feels about thematic criticism), has lavished so much time and sensitivity on two writers who are not quite first-rate.

LIDDELL, (John) Robert. British. Born in Tunbridge Wells, Kent, 13 October 1908. Educated at Haileybury College, Hertford, 1922-27; Corpus Christi College, Oxford (Passmore Edwards Scholar, 1933), 1927-33, B.A. (lst class honours) 1931, B.Litt. 1933, M.A. 1935. Senior Assistant, Department of Western Manuscripts, Bodleian Library, Oxford, 1933-38. Lecturer, University of Helsingfors, Finland, 1939, and Farouk I University, Alexandria, 1941-46; Lecturer, 1946-51, and Assistant Professor, 1951-52, Fuad I University, Cairo. Since 1953, British Council Lecturer in Athens. Head of the English Department, Athens University, 1963-68. Fellow, Royal Society of Literature, 1964. Address: c/o Barclays Bank, High Street, Oxford, England.

PUBLICATIONS

Criticism

A Treatise on the Novel. London, Cape, 1947; Bloomington, Indiana University Press, 1948; reprinted with *Some Principles of Fiction* as *Robert Liddell on the Novel*, Chicago, University of Chicago Press, 1969.

Some Principles of Fiction. London, Cape, 1953; Bloomington, Indiana University Press, 1954; reprinted with *A Treatise on the Novel* as *Robert Liddell on the Novel*, Chicago, University of Chicago Press, 1969.

The Novels of I. Compton-Burnett. London, Gollancz, 1956; Folcroft, Pennsylvania, Folcroft Editions, 1975.

The Novels of Jane Austen. London, Longman, and New York, Barnes and Noble, 1963.

"Percy Lubbock," in *Kenyon Review* (Gambier, Ohio), 29, 1967.
Cavafy: A Critical Biography.   London, Duckworth, 1974; New York, Schocken Books, 1976.
The Novels of George Eliot.   London, Duckworth, and New York, St. Martin's Press, 1977.

Novels

The Almond Tree.   London, Cape, 1938.
Kind Relations.   London, Cape, 1939; as *Take This Child*, New York, Greystone Press, 1939.
The Gantillons.   London, Cape, 1940.
The Last Enchantments.   London, Cape, 1948; New York, Appleton Century Crofts, 1949.
Unreal City.   London, Cape, 1952.
The Rivers of Babylon.   London, Cape, 1959.
An Object for a Walk.   London, Longman, 1966.
The Deep End.   London, Longman, 1968.
Stepsons.   London, Longman, 1969.

Short Stories

Watering Place.   London, Cape, 1945.

Play

Radio Play: *A Lesson from the Master*, 1966.

Other

Aegean Greece.   London, Cape, 1954.
Byzantium and Istanbul.   London, Cape, and New York, Macmillan, 1956.
The Morea (travel).   London, Cape, 1958; Mystic, Connecticut, Verry, 1964.
Mainland Greece.   London, Longman, 1965.

Translator, *Old and New Athens*, by Demetrios Sicilianos.   London, Putnam, 1960; Chester Springs, Pennsylvania, Dufour, 1962.
Translator, *A History of Modern Greek Literature*, by Linos Politis.   London, Oxford University Press, 1973.
Translator, *The Fall of the Shah*, by Fereydoun Hoveyda.   London, Wyndham, 1980.

*   *   *

In his helpful introduction to the American edition of *A Treatise on the Novel* and *Some Principles of Fiction* Wayne Booth suggests that perhaps Robert Liddell's criticism has been neglected beause of

his aggressive lack of system, his casual way of ignoring problems of logic and method that many American critics would worry over for hundreds of pages. No coherent theory of the novel is stated openly in these books, and I doubt that one could be extracted. No rules of technique are here, and if there is something like an implied great tradition of Novelists Who Matter, it is so broad and eclectic as to disappoint those who have found the simple canon of Leavis reassuring.

This does not sound promising; yet Booth also maintains that "few pages ever written about fiction are so stimulating as these," and that "by a steady habit of looking at his own experience as novelist and reader rather than at abstract rules about what a novel ought to be, he produces an astonishingly concentrated list of provocations to thought about fiction."

While Liddell's flexibility makes it impossible to summarize his position, there are some general principles which seem to direct most of his thinking. "The history of the Drama," he observes, "is the pre-history of the Novel"; when English theatre died, the English novel was born. George Eliot restored "Unity of Action" to the novel, and

> without being pedantic about Unity of Action, without having what Jane Austen called "starched notions"about the Novel and while admitting a degree of legitimate difference in taste, it is reasonable to claim that such structurally perfect novels as *Emma, Madame Bovary* and *The Ambassadors*, whose underlying principle is dramatic rather than epic, belong to a higher artistic order than the more rambling of the Waverley novels or *Martin Chuzzlewit*.

Thus Liddell prefers the fully rendered "Scene" to authorial summary or "telling": "the most vital part of a novel is always in the form of Scene, and Scene is the condition to which narrative always seems to aspire." And as for a broad definition of what the novel should be and do, Liddell is quite willing to settle for Jane Austen's defense of the form as one in which "the most thorough knowledge of human nature, the happiest delineation of its varieties, the liveliest effusions of wit and humour are conveyed to the world in the best chosen language."

Liddell's treatment of "values" in the novel is rather more complicated. He argues that the artist's primary motive is to *make* something: "no good writer ever directly aims at self-expression, or the criticism of life, when engaged in creative work—he wants to make a definite work, through which he may indeed be found to have expressed himself, and to have commented on the world around him." The poet and the historian "pass judgment on a finished action"; the novelist simply shows an action taking place. He is concerned with "particular manifestations of life, for which he requires very sharp eyes, but not with life in general." Yet there is a magical "if" involved which turns the craftsman into a kind of moralist:

> The moral is this—and it is both edifying and beautiful—if a novelist refuses to be seduced by the clamour of contemporary fashion into a dissertation upon economics, politics, the philosophy of history or the like, and if he is true to his calling, which is the study of human nature, then all these other things will be given to him. He will inevitably be a social critic, a philosopher of history.

As for the particular kind of values the novelist should hold, Liddell summarizes them under the general heading "Humanism":

> if [the novelist] accepts a definite system or belief, then it must be a system or belief in itself not incompatible with humanist standards, and he must not accept it with an anti-humanist fanaticism—an attitude which can, unhappily, be applied to systems of belief which do not require it, and which are not in themselves opposed to humanism. [The novelist] may not have an angry conviction. He must be able to understand and to sympathize with views he does not share.... If Humanism makes for breadth, tolerance, equilibrium and sanity, then the humanist virtues will be Justice, and its better part, Mercy.

Liddell shrewdly demonstrates some lapses in E.M. Forster's "humanism" and is equally convincing when he praises Jane Austen's values and the moral dimensions of Ivy Compton-Burnett's fiction (his study of the latter is in fact a model of the kind of generous tribute one artist may pay to another).

Thus fiction is a "rhetorical art," though not insistently so. Liddell makes use of I.A.

Richards' general conception of meaning and his argument that we need to examine any statement, literary or otherwise, in terms of its Sense, Feeling (the author's attitude towards his subject matter), Tone (his attitude towards his audience), and Intention (the emotional or intellectual response he is trying to evoke). But to suggest that Liddell really has much taste for such theorizing is, once again, misleading. Like the novelists he admires most, he is a stylish moralist in his own right. An example will probably do more than any generalization might do to give the reader a sense of the pleasures he may expect from *A Treatise on the Novel* and *Some Principles of Fiction*:

> If we think that it does not matter what happens to the individual, then we have no reason to think that it matters what happens in the world, for it is the individual who feels what happens to the world.
>
> If we think that individuals matter, then our sympathy can as easily be extended to the imaginary individual—for other people are to us for the most part imaginary individuals. And if the novelist seems to be fiddling while Rome is burning, it may be a useful service to play to the firemen while they have their luncheon.
>
> St. Augustine says that he could not weep for his sins, which might plunge him into Hell, but he could weep for Dido's unhappy love. He thought this a sign of his own perversity, but we may also regard it as sign of Vergil's artistry: Vergil made him weep for Dido. A novelist may still hope to make us weep for his heroine, and to forget for a while the things that may plunge us into ruin; but his Dido, if she is a woman living in the world of today, will have a shakier throne to sit on, and a more unstable background than that of the Queen of Carthage. This is one of the things that will make her story more dificult to tell. The novelist not only has to keep his eye on his character, and no interesting characters keep still for very long—he has also to keep his eye upon a surrounding world that will not keep still, as it kept (comparatively) still for Jane Austen or for Trollope—to see steadily what is, itself, unsteady.

LODGE, David (John). British. Born in London, 28 January 1935. Educated at St. Joseph's Academy, London; University College, London, 1952-55, 1957-59, B.A. (honours) in English 1955, M.A. 1959; University of Birmingham, Ph.D. 1967. Served in the Royal Armoured Corps, 1955-57. Married Mary Frances Jacob in 1959; two sons and one daughter. Assistant, British Council, London, 1959-60. Assistant Lecturer, 1960-62, Lecturer, 1963-71, Senior Lecturer, 1971-73, Reader, 1973-76, and since 1976, Professor of Modern English Literature, University of Birmingham. Visiting Associate Professor, University of California, Berkeley, 1969. Recipient: Harkness Commonwealth Fellowship, 1964; *Yorkshire Post* Award, 1975; Hawthornden Prize, 1976; Whitbread Award, for fiction and for book of the year, 1980. Fellow, Royal Society of Literature, 1976. Address: Department of English, University of Birmingham, Birmingham B15 2TT, England.

PUBLICATIONS

Criticism

Language of Fiction.   London, Routledge, and New York, Columbia University Press, 1966.
Graham Greene.   New York and London, Columbia University Press, 1966.

The Novelist at the Crossroads and Other Essays on Fiction and Criticism.   London,
    Routledge, and Ithaca, New York, Cornell University Press, 1971.
Evelyn Waugh.   New York and London, Columbia University Press, 1971.
The Modes of Modern Writing: *Metaphor, Metonymy and the Typology of Modern
    Literature.*   London, Arnold, 1977.
"Where It's At: California Language," in *The State of the Language*, edited by Leonard
    Michaels and Christopher Ricks.   Berkeley and Los Angeles, University of California
    Press, 1980.
"The Realist Text: Hemingway," in *Poetics Today* (Tel Aviv), 1, 1980.
Working with Structuralism: *Essays and Reviews on Nineteenth and Twentieth-Century
    Literature.*   London, Routledge, 1981.

Novels

The Picturegoers.   London, MacGibbon and Kee, 1960.
Ginger, You're Barmy.   London, MacGibbon and Kee, 1962; New York, Doubleday,
    1965.
The British Museum Is Falling Down.   London, MacGibbon and Kee, 1965; New York,
    Holt Rinehart, 1967.
Out of the Shelter.   London, Macmillan, 1970.
Changing Places: *A Tale of Two Campuses.*   London, Secker and Warburg, 1975; New
    York, Penguin, 1979.
How Far Can You Go?   London, Secker and Warburg, 1980.

Plays

Between These Four Walls, with Malcolm Bradbury and James Duckett (produced
    Birmingham, 1963).
Slap in the Middle, with others (produced Birmingham, 1965).

Other

About Catholic Authors (juvenile).   London, St. Paul Publications, 1958.

Editor, *Jane Austen*: "*Emma*": *A Casebook.*   London, Macmillan, 1968; Nashville,
    Aurora, 1970.
Editor, *Emma*, by Jane Austen.   London, Oxford University Press, 1971.
Editor, *Twentieth Century Literary Criticism*: *A Reader.*   London, Longman, 1972.
Editor, *Scenes of Clerical Life*, by George Eliot.   London, Penguin, 1973.
Editor, *The Woodlanders*, by Thomas Hardy.   London, Macmillan, 1974.

*   *   *

In the opening section of *Language of Fiction* and a companion piece, "Towards a Poetics of
Fiction: An Approach Through Language" (now reprinted in *The Novelist at the Crossroads*),
David Lodge attempts to justify "on theoretical grounds" the importance of language *in* the
novel and hence for criticism *of* the novel as well. His job is not an easy one, since the novel was
not taken seriously until fairly late in the history of criticism and since such criticism as it has
received usually rests on some version of the Aristotelian conception of a hierarchy of
constituent parts. Very briefly, the Aristotelian approach makes over-all emotional effect the
final cause or purpose of imitative works: the dramatist constructs a line of action which will
achieve that effect and then devises agents who will advance the action by the moral and

intellectual qualities they reveal in "diction," or the words they use. Effect determines plot, plot determines character, character determines diction, the least important of the parts which make up a dramatic whole. Thus it is possible (or so the argument runs) to have a play which is powerfully effective, regardless of its weak diction, because it has a well-made plot and suitable characters; conversely, superb diction will not save a play which has a weak plot and poorly realized characters. Moreover, the resources of poetic language (rhythm, euphony, and sustained imagery) are obviously greater than the resources of language which must be kept appropriate to a "realistic" form such as the novel. Thus we have come to believe that the language of poetry is somehow essentially different from the plain language of prose and requires a degree of attention which would be wasted on novels.

Lodge is one of the very few younger British critics with a taste and talent for theoretical speculation and does his best to deal wih these problems. As for the belief that the language of poetry is unique, it simply will not withstand logical examination: Lodge demonstrates convincingly that a passage from Proust does in fact lose a good deal when translated into English. Even "prose," it seems, is untranslatable, if by translation we mean exact equivalence. At most there seems to be a continuum extending from the purely "emotive" language of lyric poetry to the purely referential language of utilitarian prose reporting. As for the hierarchy of constituent parts, Lodge argues that this is a critic's model which bears very little relationship to the ways in which artists actually work (or the way the rest of us usually think). In *Language of Fiction* he admits that to some limited degree artistic planning may be prior to verbal embodiment:

> It is true that the successful writing of fiction depends on the novelist's prior possession of certain "gifts" or faculties, such as: precise visual and aural recall, ability to project hypothetical events and their consequences, perception of the representative and expressive possibilities in what is observed in human behaviour of the natural world, honest introspection, curiosity, wisdom, intelligence, a sense of humour...one could go on adding to the list. And though it would be false to hold that these faculties operate independently of language (since they are forms of consciousness which depend upon verbal concepts) it could be said that their operation is *up to a certain point* independent of "art language"—the concretely particularized, deliberately ordered language of imaginative lierature.

But in "Towards a Poetics of Fiction: An Approach Through Language" he is less willing to make any concessions:

> What I am denying is that these things [plot, character and so on] have any substantive existence somehow "outside" language.... Fundamentally my position rests on the assumption that consciousness is essentially conceptual, i.e., verbal. There is of course such a thing as non-verbal or pre-verbal *experience*—the whole life of sensation, for example—but we cannot be conscious of that experience without verbal concepts. This position would only imply solipsism if language was a private and arbitrary affair. It is not, but the notion that, in Wittgenstein's words, "the limits of my language are the limits of my world" is apt to be resented because it seems to deny the reality of non-verbal experience. In this latter view meaning resides in experience, in things, in "life," which we use language merely to refer to. But this is to confuse meaning with reference, it is, as Wittgenstein says, to confound the *meaning* of a name with the *bearer* of a name. Meaning, we might risk saying, resides in the application of a concept to a thing in particular circumstances. [As Wittgenstein points out] "Just as a move in chess doesn't consist merely in moving a piece in such and such a way on the board—nor yet in one's feelings or thoughts as one makes the move: but in the circumstances that we call 'playing a game of chess,' 'solving a chess problem,' and so on."
>
> It is true that this leaves us problematically situated in relation to "reality." We "know" that there is a reality outside language, but we have no means of describing it except through language: language, as someone succinctly put it, is an experiment without a control. This makes the practice of criticism particularly difficult, but it is evidently the price we pay for being human.
>
> It follows from what I have been saying that there is no mental act involved in the creation of a novel, however far one projects back, which is not conducted in language.

By this time certain questions are bound to occur to the reader. Granted that creation may begin with words and certainly terminates in words, and granted that no critic ought to overlook the importance of these words, still, isn't a novelist's diction a means to the more important ends of plot, character and theme? John Holloway's argument in "The New 'Establishment' in Criticism" (reprinted in *The Charted Mirror*) is very much to the point. Holloway cites L.C. Knights' statement that "the total response to a play can only be obtained by...an exact and sensitive study of Shakespeare's language," and comments:

> Here we are, back at linguistic texture again; and I entirely agree. But the question is: would this kind of approach, studying the language, exclude *anything* from our consideration of a play; or would it even tell us that some things were unimportant, others specially important? Certainly not: there is nothing whatever in a play—not plot, not characterization, not the girlhood of Shakespeare's heroines, even, which we could conceivably study in any way save by a study of the language of the play. There is nothing else to study. Whatever aspect of a play we study—relevant or irrelevant to true criticism—where we have to study it is in the language. If we study the language loosely and vaguely, our results will be loose and vague; an exact and sensitive study gives exact and sensitive results. So this general principle gives no guide at all as to what things will be important in a play. It leaves every question completely open. In fact, it is a truism.

These objections may be less damaging than they seem to be at first glance. Lodge would probably reply that language is most "important" in the sense of being the first and only means we have of moving on to other obviously important matters of plot and character. Holloway's observation that "exact and sensitive study gives exact and sensitive results" is crucial: the real test is how well a critic uses his awareness of language, and here Lodge is on very firm ground. He may well start, for example, with painstaking attention to the "vocabulary" of *Mansfield Park* but he hardly stops there. The essays in practical criticism in *Language of Fiction* and *The Novelist at the Crossroads* are sharp, genuinely helpful and finally concerned with much more than questions of diction.

The "crossroads" which the modern novelist faces refers to his choice between conventional naturalism and the various escapes from realism which Robert Scholes calls "fabulations." Lodge is aware that some of the most gifted modern novelists have turned to the "problematic novel" (in which the novelist's hesitation about his means is built into the novel itself), largely because of an increasing "impatience with the literary decorums of the 'well-made' realistic novel, combined with an inability to commit oneself wholeheartedly to any radical alternative...." But he is still able to make "a modest affirmation of faith in the future of realistic fiction. In part this is a rationalization of a personal preference. I like realistic novels, and I tend to write realistic fiction myself." And he concludes

> The realist—and liberal—answer to this case [that modern reality, being so extreme and violent, naturally forces writers to be experimental and apocalyptic] must be that while many aspects of contemporary experience encourage an extreme, apocalyptic response, most of us continue to live most of our lives on the assumption that the reality which realism imitates actually exists. History may be, in a philosophical sense, a fiction, but it does not feel like that when we miss a train or somebody starts a war. We are conscious of ourselves as unique, historic individuals, living together in societies by virtue of certain common assumptions and methods of communication; we are conscious that our sense of identity, of happiness and unhappiness, is defined by small things as well as large: we seek to adjust our lives, individually and communally, to some order or system of values which, however, we know is always at the mercy of chance and contingency. It is this sense of reality which realism imitates; and it seems likely that the latter will survive as long as the former.

Lodge begins his impressive recent book, *The Modes of Modern Fiction*, with the paralyzing question, "what is literature?" After a shrewd survey of recent criticism he concludes that nothing has really changed. Now, as always, critics fall into two groups. On one side are those who maintain that literature is primarily an imitative art, and as such has an obligation to tell us something about the nature of the world it reflects; on the other side are the "aesthetic" critics who maintain that the referential value of literature is unimportant. What matters for them is the pleasure we take in experiencing a unified structure. Both points of view make sense—and are mutually exclusive. What Lodge wishes to establish, then, is a way of talking about literature which will go beyond these limiting contradictions; and to do so he turns to the work of the formidable Czech structuralists, Jan Mukarovsky and Roman Jakobson, who define literature in terms of "foregrounding" and "deviance". To oversimplify a bit, "foregrounding" refers to the pointed emphasis which one constituent part of an utterance—an image, for example, or a rhythmic cadence—receives. As Lodge explains it, "any item in discourse that attracts attention to itself for what it *is*, rather than acting merely as a vehicle for information, is foregrounded. Foregrounding depends upon a 'background' of 'automatized' components— that is, language used in customary and predictable ways so that it does *not* attract attention." In Ruqaiva Hasan's summary statement,

> In poetic language foregrounding achieves maximum intensity to the extent of pushing communication into the background as the objective of expression and of being used for its own sake; it is not used in the services of communication, but in order to place in the foreground the act of expression, the act of speech itself.

It is important to remember, of course, that here, as in *Languages of Fiction*, Lodge refuses to make any essential, qualitative distinction between poetry and prose: both may be used in "literary" or "non-literary" ways. The foregrounding a component part receives makes it "deviate" or depart from the expectations we have for discourse in which what is said matters, not how it is said. The best term we have for such deviance, Lodge argues, is "fictionality": literary discourse is "either self-evidently fictional or may be treated as such, and...what compels or permits such reading is the structural organization of its component parts, its systematic foregrounding." He then proceeds to demonstrate the ways in which such "fictionality" marks the difference between Orwell's well-known essay, "A Hanging," and a routine newspaper account of a similar event. "A Hanging"

> may be completely factual, it may be partly based on experience, or partly on the reported experience of others, or partly fictional, or wholly fictional—though the last possibility seems to me the least likely. The point I wish to make is that it doesn't really matter. As a text, 'A Hanging' is self-sufficient, self-authenticating—autotelic, to use the jargon word. The internal relationships of its component parts are far more significant than their external references.

He is thus in substantial agreement with the Russian Formalist Victor Shklovsky, who asserts that "in art, it is our experience of the process of construction that counts, not the finished product." And at the same time Lodge is able to maintain an admirable flexibility:

> Literature is an open category in the sense that you can, in theory, put any kind of discourse into it—but only on condition that such discourse has something in common with the discourse you cannot take out of it: that something being a structure which indicates the fictionality of a text or enables a text to be read as if it were fictional.

Of course "A Hanging" tells us something about the real world, but that is not what makes it "literature" for Lodge.

What we naively and often pejoratively call "realistic" fiction, then, is just as "literary" as the novels of Joyce or Virginia Woolf. Bennett's *The Old Wives' Tale*, for example, and *Ulysses* and *Mrs. Dalloway* are all literary works because they depend vitally upon foregrounding—on artful selection and emphasis, in short. Yet they are obviously very different kinds of books, so the problem becomes one of finding appropriate sub-categories within the major category, "literature." Lodge does this by turning once again to an unexpected source, this time Jakobson's elliptical distinction between the metaphoric and metonymic poles of language. All discourse is "temporal," that is, it moves and unfolds, unsually to some end. The crucial point is *how* an utterance guides the mind: the process involved in grasping "the ship ploughed the sea" (Lodge's example) is quite different from the process involved in grasping "the ship sailed the sea" or "the vessel sailed the sea." The first expression is metaphoric and requires us to perceive the relevant likeness between "ship" and "plough" in this context; the latter expression is metonymic because ships and vesels are, in Jakobson's rather unhelpful term, "contiguous," that is, they have roughly interchangeable meanings within a given system or "code," whereas plough and ship do not. The development of discourse, Jakobson states,

> may take place along two different semantic lines: one topic may lead to another either through their similarity or their contiguity. The metaphorical way would be the more appropriate term for the first case, and the metonymic for the second, since they find their most condensed expression in metaphor and metonymy respectively.

Metonymy, the mode which expreses contiguity, is clearly the natural mode for realistic novels, in that it satisfies the normal expectations we have for things which go together, for logical sequences and causal relationships. In the metaphoric mode, however, whether in fiction or verse, this is not the case:

> To illustrate the point...we might cite the "Unreal city" sequence of *The Waste Land*, which, beginning with a deceptively metonymic description of London commuters, in which there is a submerged analogy with Dante's *Inferno*

> > Under the brown fog of a winter dawn,
> > A crowd flowed over London bridge, so many
> > I had not thought death had undone so many

> suddenly explodes into metaphor:

> > 'Stetson!
> > You who were with us in the ships at Mylae!
> > 'That corpse you planted last year in the garden
> > 'Has it begun to sprout? Will it bloom this year?
> > 'Or has the sudden frost disturbed its bed?'

> There is no contextual support for these remarks, which would explain them or supply links between them. They are intelligible only as metaphorical articulations of motifs already introduced elsewhere in the poem...*The Waste Land* is indeed a prime example of metaphorical discourse, since it is structured almost exclusively on the principle of similarity and contrast, dislocating and rupturing relationships of contiguity and combination.

In summary, this may sound like a very roundabout way of restating a commonplace, but what Lodge has done, with a great deal of ingenuity, is to ground that commonplace in an interesting, suggestive distinction. The term "metonymy" is troublesome, however, so that Graham Hough's comment is very much to the point:

> The terminology is unfortunate; "metaphoric" is all right, and is more or less self-explanatory—the axis of analogy, resemblance; transferred to literature, the realm of allegory, symbolism, archetype. What Jakobson obscurely and misleadingly calls the "metonymic" *actually* means the sequential—the axis of language along which a sentence is constructed, a story is told, an object described, or an argument carried on.

In the third section of *The Modes of Modern Writing*, Lodge demonstrates brilliantly and convincingly how useful the distinction can be when applied to a variety of modern British novelists. If Lawrence, Virginia Woolf, Joyce and other metaphoric writers receive most of his attention, it is simply because in the first part of the century the metaphorical mode was dominant. But why should this be so? Why is it that at any given period one mode seems to overshadow the other? Here Lodge is less convincing. At one point he observes "1930s writing was, characteristically, antimodernist, realistic, readerly and metonymic. In the 1940s the pendulum of literary fashion swung back—not fully, but to a perceptible degree—towards the pole we have designated as modernist, symbolist, writerly and metaphoric." Again, near the end of the book, concludes that

> The history of modern English literature...can be seen as an oscillation in the practice of writing between polarized clusters of attitudes and techniques...What looks like innovation—a new mode of writing foregrounding itself against the background of the received mode when the latter becomes stale and exhausted—is also therefore in some sense a reversion to the principles and procedures of an earlier phase.

"Oscillation" and "pendulum" are crude and reductive images for a critic of Lodge's skill, but when he turns to particular cases, he is once more sensitive and penetrating. Graham Greene, for example, is not left to oscillate or ride the wave of fashion:

> Greene has reacted against the modernist or symbolist mode of writing for two quite independent reasons.... One reason was literary and was shared in common by most writers of his generation: they deplored the emphasis on individual consciousness and sensibility in modernist writing because it seemed to dissolve and deny the empirical reality of "the visible world"...The other set of reasons was moral and religious and was largely peculiar to Greene.... He thought the methods of the modernist novel were incompatible with the expression of a Christian world-view. One can see why: Christianity is based on a linear concept of time extending from Genesis to the Last Day...whereas modernist writing is strongly attracted to pagan or neo-Platonic forms of religion, cyclic theories of history and the idea of reincarnation.

In the last part of the book Lodge takes a quick, slightly uneasy look at "post modernist" fiction—novels, that is, which seem neither metonymic nor metaphoric. Works like Nabokov's *Pale Fire*, for example, or John Barth's *Lost in the Funhouse* are not only artificial—all works are—but insist on displaying their artificiality to the reader and deliberately frustrate expectations of form and order. Such fiction, Lodge suggests, is parasitic and depends for its vitality on the negative energy of defiance:

> many of these books and stories are imaginatively liberating to a high degree, and have done much to keep the possibilities of writing open in the very process of asserting that the most familiar ones are closed. If this assertion were really made good, however—if postmodernism really succeeded in expelling the idea of order (whether expressed in metonymic or metaphoric form) from modern writing, then it would truly abolish itself, by destroying the norms against which we perceive its deviations. A foreground without a background inevitably becomes the background for something else. Postmodernism cannot rely upon the historical memory of modernist and antimodernist writing for its background, because it is essentially a rule-breaking kind of art, and unless people are still trying to keep the rules there is no point in breaking them, and no interest in seeing them broken.

LUBBOCK, Percy. British. Born in London, 4 June 1879. Educated at Stone House, Broadstairs, Kent; Eton College, Buckinghamshire; King's College, Cambridge, 1898-1901. Married Lady Sybil Cuffe in 1926 (died, 1943). Member, Board of Education, London, and journalist, 1904-06; Librarian, Bibliotheca Pepsyiana, Magdalene College, Cambridge, 1906-08; British Red Cross Worker during World War I. Recipient: James Tate Black Prize, 1922; *Fémina-Vie Heureuse* Prize, 1923; Royal Society of Literature Benson Medal, 1926. C.B.E. (Commander, Order of the British Empire), 1952. *Died 1 August 1965.*

PUBLICATIONS

Criticism

The Craft of Fiction.   London, Cape, and New York, Scribner, 1921.

Novels

Roman Pictures.   London, Cape, and New York, Scribner, 1923.
The Region Cloud.   London, Cape, and New York, Scribner, 1925.

Other

Elizabeth Barrett Browning in Her Letters.   London, Smith Elder, 1906.
Samuel Pepys.   London, Hodder and Stoughton, and New York, Scribner, 1909.
George Calderon: A Sketch from Memory.   London, Richards, 1921.
Earlham (history and autobiography).   London, Cape, and New York, Scribner, 1922.
Mary Cholmondeley: A Sketch from Memory.   London, Cape, 1928.
Shades of Eton (autobiography).   London, Cape, and New York, Scribner, 1929.
Portrait of Edith Wharton.   London, Cape, and New York, Appleton Century, 1947.
Percy Lubbock Reader, edited by Marjory Gane Harkness.   Freeport, Maine, Bond Wheelright, 1957.

Editor, *A Book of English Prose.*   London, Cambridge University Press, 2 vols., 1913.
Editor, *The Ivory Tower*, by Henry James.   New York, Scribner, and London, Collins, 1917.
Editor, *The Middle Years*, by Henry James.   New York, Scribner, and London, Collins, 1917.
Editor, *The Sense of the Past*, by Henry James.   New York, Scribner, and London, Collins, 1917.
Editor, *The Letters of Henry James.*   New York, Scribner, and London, Macmillan, 2 vols., 1920.
Editor, *The Novels and Stories of Henry James.*   London, Macmillan, and New York, Scribner, 35 vols., 1921-23.
Editor, *The Diary of Arthur Christopher Benson.*   London, Hutchinson, and New York, Longman, 1926.

CRITICAL STUDIES

Robert Liddell, "Percy Lubbock," in *Kenyon Review* (Gambier, Ohio), 29, 1967.
Ashley Brown, "Hommage to Percy Lubbock," in *Southern Review* (Baton Rouge, Louisiana), 15, 1979.

*   *   *

While *The Craft of Fiction* makes perfectly good sense in its own terms, Percy Lubbock is so deeply indebted here to Henry James that readers will do well to keep in mind that writer's principal assertions about the art of novel. For James, "the only reason for the existence of a novel is that it does attempt to represent life." When it gives up this attempt, James goes on (in "The Art of Fiction"),

> the same attempt that we see on the canvas of the painter, it will have arrived at a very strange pass. It is not expected of the picture that it will make itself humble in order to be forgiven; and the analogy between the art of the painter and the art of the novelist is, so far as I can see, complete. Their inspiration is the same, their process (allowing for the different quality of the vehicle) is the same, their success is the same...[Just as] the picture is reality, so the novel is history. That is the only general description (which does it justice) that we may give of the novel.

Art is a matter of craft, of deliberate choosing and making, but before that it is also a matter of inspiration and native ability. "It goes without saying,"James warns, "that you will not write a good novel unless you possess the sense of reality; but it will be difficult to give you a recipe for calling that sense into being." And in addition to needing this "sense of reality," the novelist must also have the gift of locating a potential subject in the welter of ordinary experience (as Lubbock puts it, "the power that recognizes the fruitful idea and seizes it is a thing apart. For this reason we judge the novelist's eye for a subject to be his cardinal gift"). Once the artist has his subject, his *donnée*, to use James' term, everything then becomes a matter of conscious selection, of weighing various possibilities and alternatives. Finally, the novelist faces the eternal problem of giving us a vivid sense of life and at the same time satisfying our desire for shape or form without falsifying our sense of the way things "really" are. For James, once again,

> Catching the very note and trick, the strange irregular rhythm of life, that is the attempt whose strenuous force keeps Fiction upon her feet. In proportion as is what she offers us we see life *without* rearrangement do we feel that we are touching the truth; in proportion as we see it *with* rearrangement do we feel that we are being put off with a substitute, a compromise and convention.

But of course "rearrangement" is necessary; selection and composition are the very conditions of art, whereas in life, "really, universally, relations stop nowhere"—relationships, that is, between one event and another. Thus the "exquisite problem of the artist is but to draw, by a geometry of his own, the circle within which they shall happily appear to do so. He is in the perpetual predicament that the continuity of things is never for the space of an instant or an inch broken." There is no "solution" to his problem, however; art is a kind of confidence game which gives us the illusion of a completed whole. And since the great gift of the novel is that "extension of consciousness" which we gain from a vivid recreation of reality, the artist must be careful not to intrude in such a way as to suggest that that whole affair is, after all, only a "fiction":

> Certain accomplished novelists have the habit of giving themselves away which must often bring tears to the eyes of people who take their fiction seriously. I was lately struck, in reading over many pages of Anthony Trollope, with his want of discretion in this particular. In a digression, a parenthesis or an aside, he concedes to the reader that he and his trusting friend are only "making believe." He admits that the events he narrates have not really happened, and that he can give his narrative any turn the reader may like best. Such a betrayal of a sacred office seems to me, I confess, a terrible crime....

Despite his insistence that criticism must not lay down rules in advance (we must grant the artist his *donnée*: "our criticism is applied only to what he makes of it"), James' own preference is for dramatic representation rather than authorial narration and description. There is a revealing passage in *A Small Boy and Others* which suggests why this may be so: after recalling a childhood incident during which he heard a spoiled young cousin warned not to "make a scene," he reflects that

> the note was...epoch-making. The expression, so vivid, so portentous, was one I had never heard—it had never been addressed to us at home; and who should say now what a world one mightn't at once read into it. Life at these intensities clearly became "scenes";

but the great thing, the immense illumination, was that we could make them or not as we chose.... The mark had been made for me and the door flung open; the passage, gathering up *all* the elements of the troubled time, had been itself a scene, quite enough of one, and I had become aware with it of a rich accession of possibilities.

At moments of intensity life does become "scene"; hence it is the job of the novelist to present his scenes directly, as James does in much of *The Awkward Age*, or at one remove, as they register on the consciousness of a central character (this is the method of *The Ambassadors*, of course, and many other later stories and novels).

Not all of these principles appear explicitly in *The Craft of Fiction*, but anyone familiar with that book will recognize at once how deeply Lubbock depends on Jamesian assumptions. For Lubbock, as for James, the novel exists primarily to represent life; but equally important, the novel must give form to the reality it depicts. The novel must have "ideal shape," though we can discuss "shape" only by drawing upon the vocabularies of the other arts, particularly painting and architecture. And while James states that the analogy between painting and fiction is "complete," Lubbock is unwilling to go quite this far. In more formal terms, Lubbock is wrestling, gently, with the problem of the spatial arts as opposed to the temporal arts: the novel unfolds in time, building in the reader's mind the sense of a completed whole which has form and symmetry—but how are we to describe the shape, or even be sure we recall it correctly, once we put the novel down? James proudly calls attention to the "architectural competence" of *Portrait of a Lady* and *The Ambassadors*, Lubbock is less certain of these analogies. Total grasp of form may be a "forlorn enterprise" for criticism. Nevertheless, there are "degrees of unsuccess," and having made this tentative qualification, Lubbock proceeds in a thoroughly Jamesian manner.

It is not quite accurate to say that for Lubbock form is *as* important as the sense of life a novel provides. If we had to make a choice betweeen a sprawling mass which gives a vivid sense of reality and a perfectly shaped but lifeless whole, we should naturally choose the former. Lubbock admits that *War and Peace* presents "a picture of life that has never been surpassed for its grandeur and its beauty." Does it matter, then, that it is formally impure or confused? The business of the novelist, Lubbock goes on, "is to create life, and here is life created indeed; the satisfaction of a clean, coherent form is wanting, and it would be well to have it, but that is all. We have a magnificent novel without it." But magnificent as it is, *War and Peace* would be more magnificent still "with the addition of another excellence, a comeliness of form." Lubbock then contrasts Tolstoy's novel with the perfectly finished and unified *Madame Bovary*.

At this point in *The Craft of Fiction* there is a shift away from the problem of form to that of point of view (it may be simply that Lubbock expects the reader to make the right connection here: one of the novelist's chief formal resources has always been a controlling point of view). How is the subject to be conveyed to the reader? By what agency does the reader come to know what he needs to know? Like James, Lubbock asserts rather than argues for the superiority of the dramatic method, the unmediated rendering of scene, over "picture" or authorial description. As E.M. Forster and Wayne Booth have pointed out, however, this preference for showing rather than telling is a good deal more complicated than most Jamesians are willing to admit. But for Lubbock, "there is no doubt that the scene holds the place of honour, that it is the readiest means of starting an interest and raising a question":

As for intensity of life...the novelist has recourse to his other arm, the one that corresponds with the single arm of the dramatist. Inevitably, as the plot thickens and the climax approaches—inevitably, whenever an impression is to be emphasized and driven home—narration gives place to enactment, train of events to the particular episode, the broad picture to the dramatic scene.

At this point the reader may wonder if the novel is not by definition a lower form, constantly aspiring to the condition of drama. But of course this is not the case. Lubbock, like Forster after him, sees the great advantage of the novel as its power to move directly into the consciousness of its characters and to reveal what Foster calls the "hidden life."

In his later chapters Lubbock traces the progress novelists have made in their capacity to turn picture into scene. His view of the novel, in short, is an evolutionary one. At first the novelist simply told his story in his own voice; but for Lubbock, as for James, the presence of the author commenting on his subject may fatally impair the necessary illusion of reality. By incorporating himself as a character inside his fiction, the novelist took a step in the right direction:

> This, then, is the readiest means of dramatically heightening a reported impression, this device of telling a story in the first person, in the person of somebody in the book; and large in our fiction the first person accordingly bulks. The characterized "I" is substituted for the loose and general "I" of the author; the loss of freedom is more than repaid by the more salient effect of the picture. Precision, individuality is given to it by this pair of eyes, known and named, through which the reader sees it; instead of drifting in space above the spectacle he keeps his allotted station and contemplates a delimited field of vision.

There were still problems, as Lubbock argues in his discussion of the first-person narrator of Meredith's *Harry Richmond*.

> What it was like to *be* Harry, with all that action and reaction of character and fortune proceeding within him—that is the question, the chief question; and since it is the most important affair in the book, it should obviously be rendered as solidly as possible, by the most emphatic method that the author can command. But Harry, speaking of himself, can only report; he can only recall the past and tell us what he was, only *describe* his emotion; and he may describe very vividly, and he does, but it would necessarily be more convincing if we could get behind his description and judge for ourselves. Drama we want, always drama, for the central, paramount affair, whatever it is.

The solution is to dramatize the consciousness of a fixed, central character, as James does with Strether in *The Ambassadors*: Strether "may stand as a living demonstration of all that autobiography cannot achieve"; James does not tell us the story of Strether's mind, "he makes it tell itself, he dramatizes it." Lubbock's final justification of James' mature method needs to be quoted in full:

> *The Ambassadors*, then, is a story which is seen from one man's point of view, and yet a story in which that point of view is itself a matter for the reader to confront and to watch constructively. Everything in the novel is now dramatically rendered, whether it is a page of dialogue or a page of description, because even in the page of description nobody is addressing us, nobody is reporting his impression to the reader. The impression is enacting itself in the endless series of images that play over the outspread expanse of the man's mind and memory. When the story passes from these to the scenes of dialogue— from the silent drama of Strether's meditation to the spoken drama of men and women—there is thus no break in the method.... And yet *as a whole* the book is all pictorial, an indirect impression received through Strether's intervening consciousness, beyond which the story never strays. I conclude that on this paradox the art of dramatizing the picture of somebody's experience—the art I have been considering in these last chapters—touches its limit. There is indeed no further for it to go.

Understandably enough, Lubbock has sometimes been criticized for being more Catholic than the Pope, but the accusation is not really justified—it is clear, for example, that Lubbock enjoys the Russian novelists much more than James ever could, and for the right reasons. But more important there is a kind of flexibility in parts of *The Craft of Fiction* which looks forward to the sophistication of Wayne Booth's *Rhetoric of Fiction*. Lubbock is more willing than James ever was, *in practice*, to follow the injunction that questions of criticism must be questions of execution only. Near the end of *The Craft of Fiction*, after praising the dramatic method in predictable terms, Lubbock draws back for a moment and remarks

> Such is the progress of the writer of fiction towards drama; such is his method of evading the drawbacks of a mere reporter and assuming the advantages, as far as possible, of a dramatist. *How far he may choose to push the process in his book—that is a matter to be decided by the subject; it entirely depends upon the kind of effect that the theme*

demands. It may respond to all the dramatization it can get, it may give all that it had to give for less. The subject dictates the method. (my italics).

Observations such as this encourage genuine critical speculation and make *The Craft of Fiction* much more than an apology for the late Jamesian manner.

MATTHIESSEN, F(rancis) O(tto). American. Born in Pasadena, California, 19 February 1902. Educated at the Hackley School, Tarrytown, New York, 1914-18; Yale University, New Haven, Connecticut, B.A. 1923; Oxford University, B.Litt. 1925; Harvard University, Cambridge, Massachusetts, M.A. 1926, Ph.D. 1927. Instructor and Tutor, 1929-30, Assistant Professor, 1930-34 (Chairman, Board of Tutors in History and Literature, 1931-48), Associate Professor, 1934-42, and Professor of English, 1942-50, Harvard University. Alexander Lecturer, University of Toronto, 1944; Visiting Professor, Charles University, Prague, 1947; Senior Fellow, Kenyon School of English, Gambier, Ohio, 1948-50. Member, Editorial Board of *The New England Quarterly*, 1937-40; Member, Executive Committee, Massachusetts Civil Liberties Union; President, Harvard Teachers Union, 1940-42, 1946-47. Member, National Institute of Arts and Letters. D.Litt.: Princeton University, New Jersey, 1947. *Died in 1950.*

PUBLICATIONS

Criticism

Sarah Orne Jewett. Boston, Houghton Mifflin, 1929.
Translation: An Elizabethan Art. Cambridge, Massachusetts, Harvard University Press, and London, Oxford University Press, 1931.
The Achievement of T.S. Eliot: An Essay on the Nature of Poetry. Boston, Houghton Mifflin, and London, Oxford University Press, 1935; revised edition, New York, Oxford University Press, 1947; with additional material by C.L. Barber, 1958.
American Renaissance: Art and Expression in the Age of Emerson and Whitman. New York and London, Oxford University Press, 1941.
Henry James: The Major Phase. New York, Oxford University Press, 1944.
Introduction to *Stories of Writers and Artists*, by Henry James. New York, New Directions, 1944.
"Edgar Allan Poe" and "Poetry," in *Literary History of the United States*, edited by Robert E. Spiller and others. New York, Macmillan, 1948.
Theodore Dreiser. New York, Sloane, and London, Methuen, 1951.
The Responsibilities of the Critic: Essays and Reviews by F.O. Matthiessen, edited by John Rackliffe. New York, Oxford University Press, 1952.

Other

Russell Cheney, 1881-1945: A Record of His Work. New York, Oxford University Press, 1947.
The James Family: Including Selections from the Writings of Henry James, Senior, William, Henry, and Alice James. New York, Knopf, 1947.
From the Heart of Europe (journal). New York, Oxford University Press, 1948.

Rat and the Devil: Journal Letters of F.O. Matthiessen and Russell Cheney, edited by
   Louis K. Hyde.   Hamden, Connecticut, Archon Books, 1978.

Editor, *Stories of Writers and Artists*, by Henry James.   New York, New Directions,
   1944
Editor, *Herman Melville: Selected Poems*.   New York, New Directions, 1944.
Editor, *The American Novels and Stories of Henry James*.   New York, Knopf, 1947.
Editor, with Kenneth Murdock, *The Notebooks of Henry James*.   New York, Oxford
   University Press, 1947.
Editor, *The Oxford Book of American Verse*.   New York, Oxford University Press,
   1950.

CRITICAL STUDIES AND BIBLIOGRAPHY

"F.O. Matthiessen (1902-1950): A Collective Portrait," edited by Paul Sweezy and Leo
   Huberman, in "Matthiessen Memorial Issue" of *Monthly Review* (New York), 2,
   1950-51;   reprinted, New York, Schuman, 1959.
George Abbot White, "Ideology and Literature: *American Renaissance* and F.O. Matth-
   iessen," in *Tri-Quarterly* (Evanston, Ilinois), 23-24, 1972.
Giles B. Gunn, *F.O. Matthiessen: The Critical Achievement*.   Seattle and London,
   University of Washington Press, 1975 (includes bibliography).

*   *   *

As a friend, colleague, and teacher, F.O. Matthiessen has been praised so often, so lavishly, and with such obvious sincerity by so many distinguished men that it may seem outrageous to offer a dissenting opinion about the value of his published work. But for those who did not know Matthiessen personally there are real problems: for this reader, at least, *American Renaissance* and the studies of James and Eliot are inevitably dated, oddly contradictory at points, and fundamentally confused.

Ironically enough, the best things in *Henry James: The Major Phase* and *The Achievement of T.S. Eliot* are the most dated. In 1935, as C.L. Barber has observed, Matthiessen was "locating Eliot's achievement as well as describing it, and his essay has the vitality of discovery: a new major writer's position is just being made out and the whole landscape is being reordered in consequence." Eliot is now such an established part of that landscape that it is probably impossible to appreciate just how useful Matthiessen's interpretive comments must have been at the time; nevertheless, he was not the first critic to see what Eliot was doing (F.R. Leavis' fine essay in *New Bearings in English Poetry*, for example, had appeared two years earlier), and whatever its original value, *The Achievement of T.S. Eliot* has long since been superseded by the more precise and informed work of Helen Gardner, George Williamson and Grover Smith. More serious is Matthiessen's failure to realize the two goals he sets up in his preface: "my double aim," he asserts there, "is to evaluate Eliot's method and achievement as an artist, and in so doing to emphasize certain of the fundamental elements in the nature of poetry which are in danger of being obscured by the increasing tendency to treat poetry as a social document and to forget that it is an art." But there is nothing in the least "evaluative" about his discussion of Eliot's poetry and criticism: as Giles Gunn concedes (and Gunn is one of Matthiessen's ablest supporters), the book is "so dependent upon Eliot's own standards for a critical evaluation of his poetry that it never quite escapes from the shadow cast by its subject or attains a genuine authority of its own." Nor does Matthiessen have much to say about any "fundamental elements in the nature of poetry." Gunn, once again, admits that Matthiessen

   makes it difficult to follow the thread of unity which winds its way throughout his
   criticism, because, in spite of his absorption with religious concerns, he assiduously
   avoided extensive systematic treatments of most of the issues that mattered to him. One
   looks in vain for a clear statement not only of his religious position but also of his theory
   of literature or his view of criticism.

Finally, to judge from Matthiessen's commentaries, Eliot had written one long poem, any part of which could be compared profitably with any other part. There is little sense here of different poems with different shapes and purposes.

In the preface to *Henry James: The Major Phase*, Matthiessen announces that he intends to concentrate on "what interests me most...the great works of [James'] final maturity," that is, on *The Ambassadors*, *The Wings of the Dove*, and *The Golden Bowl*. Yet in his chapter on *The Ambasador* he concludes that

> fond as James is of [Strether], we cannot help feeling his relative emptiness. At times...it is forced upon us that, despite James' humorous awareness of his hero's adventures, neither Strether nor his creator escape a certain soft fussiness.

And as for *The Golden Bowl*, he maintains that because James has failed to provide any sense of the "larger society" to which his characters belong, it is

> finally a decadent book, in the strict sense in which decadence was defined by [A.R.] Orage, as "the substitution of the part for the whole."...*The Golden Bowl* forces upon our attention too many flagrant lapses in the way things happen both in the personal and in the wider social sphere. With all its magnificence, it is almost as hollow as the châteaux that had risen along Fifth Avenue and that had crowded out the old Newport world that James remembered.

In his preface Matthiessen asserts that "*The Wings of the Dove* searches as deeply into the American consciousness as *Winesburg, Ohio*," but in his chapter on the former novel he observes that "neither Adams nor James could be said to have remotely understood that American world of their maturity."

A simple discrepancy between proposed and achieved intentions is not in itself very important: if the individual chapters are valuable it is easy enough to disregard the preface. In his discussions of particular works, however, Matthiessen is guilty of a more serious error, that of confusing the works themselves with James' own announced intentions in his notebooks and prefaces to the New York edition. About "The Figure in the Carpet," for example, Matthiessen maintains that here is an instance

> where James' curiosity...has run into the ground. All of the characters of that story are so obsessed with pursuing the hidden meaning of Hugh Vereker's novels that their criticism turns into a nightmarish game as the very issues of life and death are engulfed in their excessive and finally futile ingenuity. But James' intention was fresher than his effect....

Matthiessen misses the point of the story partly because he places too much importance on James' musings *about* it. To take a clearer and more important example: from the notebooks, letters and other biographical sources Matthiessen became aware of James' love—if that is the right word—for his doomed young cousin, Minny Temple, who served as the model for Milly Theale in *The Wings of the Dove*. But in fact Milly is not the primary figure in that novel; and if we read it as Matthiessen does, as a long, sustained elegy for Minny Temple, then we cannot account for the importance of Kate Croy and, especially, Merton Densher. The reason for Matthiessen's misplaced emphasis may be simple enough: as one of the first critics to read through James' notebooks (and the first, to my knowledge, to be permitted to quote from them), he was understandably excited by James' apparent willingness to "explain" his work. It now seems wiser to concentrate on the *differences* between James' first reflections and the finished work (if the reader is skeptical here he should consult Wayne Booth's *Rhetoric of Fiction*).

It is not difficult to isolate several promising-sounding statements from the opening of *American Renaissance*:

> my main subject [is] the conception held by five of our major writers [Emerson, Thoreau, Hawthorne, Melville and Whitman] concerning the function and nature of literature, and the degree to which their practice bore out their theories.... It has seemed to me that the literary accomplishment of [these] years could be judged most adequately if

approached in the light of its authors' purposes and in that of our own developing conception of literature.... Emerson's theory of expression was that on which Thoreau built, to which Whitman gave extension, and to which Hawthorne and Melville were indebted by being forced to react against its philosophical assumptions.

The one common denominator of my five writers, uniting even Hawthorne and Whitman, was their devotion to the possibilities of democracy.... Their tones were sometimes optimistic, sometimes blatantly, even dangerously expansive, sometimes disillusioned, even despairing, but what emerges from the total pattern of their achievement—if we will make the effort to repossess it—is literature for our democracy. In reading the lyric, heroic, and tragic expression of our first great age, we can feel the challenge of our still undiminished resources.

works of art can be best perceived if we do not approach them only through the influences that shaped them, but if we also make use of what we invariably bring from our own lives.

But it is virtually impossible to trace any clear or coherent exposition of any of these propositions in the 650 pages which follow. A sympathetic reader of the book, George Abbot White, has commented recently that "to the reader in 1941 *without* an ideological orientation, *American Renaissance* must have seemed a maddening array of authors, works, and themes; a vaguely-chronological linkage of sixty-four quite separate essays." The problem is that even with some knowledge of Matthiessen's Christian-socialist "ideology" (a matter which both White and Giles Gunn labor to define), the book still seems hopelessly diffuse. It may be significant that Matthiessen could not decide upon a title for the completed manuscript ("American Renaissance" is Harry Levin's contribution). Yet the book had considerable impact when it first appeared and seems to have been influential on the subsequent development of "American Studies" programs at the university level. Gunn suggests that we cannot understand the importance of the book

without taking into account the state of mind that prevailed among many liberal intellectuals at the time of its publication. The late 1930s and early 1940s were an era of considerable disillusionment in which the generous hopes first awakened by the uneasy peace following World War I and then by Roosevelt's first term following the Great Depression had slowly eroded, leaving in their place a sense of confusion and defeat. The rise of fascism in Europe, Stalin's purges in Russia, the massacre of the Republicans in Spain, the collapse of the Popular Front in America, Stalin's nonaggression pact with Hitler, the German blitz into Poland—these were only a few of the blows suffered by the cause of democratic liberalism during those years. Many people, of course, were quickly caught up again in war fever, once America declared war against the Axis powers, and thus found their faith restored as The Allies united to stem the spread of tyranny. But others remained badly shaken at the roots and would not soon recover until they had found some tradition, some defining intellectual and spiritual heritage, to which they could appeal for explanation of the present state of crisis. And that is exactly what Matthiessen's book provided them: a distinctively American tradition founded upon liberal and democratic impulses which at the same time explained how those impulses could go awry and why they were so vulnerable in the first place. As a genuinely native tradition, therefore, it was all the more valuable and all the more usable, just because it carried within itself its own elements of self-criticism. In the novels of Hawthorne and Melville, democratic humanism was tempered by what Melville called "the fine hammered steel of woe" and emerged perhaps no less vigorous but considerably tougher, soberer, and more tragic.

If this is true, then *American Renaissance*, like the studies of James and Eliot, has historical rather than intrinsic importance. Fair-minded readers will have to judge for themselves, but it may turn out that the proper monument to Matthiessen is that impressive body of personal tributes his friends provided in the "Collective Portrait" of 1950.

McCARTHY, Mary (Therese). American. Born in Seattle, Washington, 21 June 1912. Educated at Forest Ridge Convent, Seattle; Annie Wright Seminary, Tacoma, Washington; Vassar College, Poughkeepsie, New York, A.B. 1933 (Phi Beta Kappa). Married 1) Harold Johnsrud in 1933; 2) the writer Edmund Wilson in 1938, one son; 3) Bowden Broadwater in 1946; 4) James Raymond West in 1961. Editor, Covici Friede, publishers, New York, 1936-38; Editor, 1937-38, and Drama Critic, 1937-62, *Partisan Review*, New York; Instructor, Bard College, Annandale on Hudson, New York, 1945-46, and Sarah Lawrence College, Bronxville, New York, 1948. Northcliffe Lecturer, University College, London, 1980. Recipient: Guggenheim Fellowship, 1949, 1959; *Horizon* prize, 1949; American Academy grant, 1957. Member, American Academy. D.Let.: Syracuse University, New York, 1973; D.Litt.: University of Hull, Yorkshire, 1974; LL.D.: Aberdeen University, 1979. Address: Castine, Maine 04421, U.S.A.

PUBLICATIONS

Criticism

> *Sights and Spectacles, 1937-56.* New York, Farrar Straus, 1956; as *Sights and Spectacles: Theatre Chronicles, 1937-58*, London, Heinemann, 1959; augmented edition, as *Mary McCarthy's Theatre Chronicles, 1937-62*, New York, Farrar Straus, 1963.
> *On the Contrary.* New York, Farrar Straus, 1961; London, Heinemann, 1962.
> *The Writing on the Wall.* New York, Harcourt Brace, and London, Weidenfeld and Nicolson, 1970.
> *Can There Be a Gothic Literature?* (lecture). Amsterdam, Harmonie, 1975.
> *Ideas and the Novel.* New York, Harcourt Brace, 1980; London, Weidenfeld and Nicolson, 1981.

Novels

> *The Company She Keeps.* New York, Simon and Schuster, 1942; London, Weidenfeld and Nicolson, 1957.
> *The Oasis.* New York, Random House, 1949; as *A Source of Embarrassment*, London, Heinemann, 1950.
> *The Groves of Academe.* New York, Harcourt Brace, 1952; London, Heinemann, 1953.
> *A Charmed Life.* New York, Harcourt Brace, 1955; London, Weidenfeld and Nicolson, 1956.
> *The Group.* New York, Harcourt Brace, and London, Weidenfeld and Nicolson, 1963.
> *Birds of America.* New York, Harcourt Brace, and London, Weidenfeld and Nicolson, 1971.
> *Cannibals and Missionaries.* New York, Harcourt Brace, and London, Weidenfeld and Nicolson, 1979.

Short Stories

> *Cast a Cold Eye.* New York, Harcourt Brace, 1950; London, Heinemann, 1952.

Other

> *Venice Observed: Comments on Venetian Civilization.* New York, Reynal, and London, Zwemmer, 1956.

Memories of a Catholic Girlhood.   New York, Harcourt Brace, and London, Heinemann, 1957.
The Stones of Florence.   New York, Harcourt Brace, and London, Heinemann, 1959.
Vietnam.   New York, Harcourt Brace, and London, Weidenfeld and Nicolson, 1967.
Hanoi.   New York, Harcourt Brace, and London, Weidenfeld and Nicolson, 1968.
Medina.   New York, Harcourt Brace, 1972; London, Wildwood House, 1973.
The Mask of State: Watergate Portraits.   New York and London, Harcourt Brace, 1974.
The Seventeenth Degree.   New York, Harcourt Brace, 1974; London, Weidenfeld and Nicolson, 1975.

Translator, *The Iliad; or, The Poem of Force*, by Simone Weil.   New York, Politics, 1948.
Translator, *On the Iliad*, by Rachel Bespaloff.   New York, Pantheon Books, 1948.

CRITICAL STUDIES AND BIBLIOGRAPHY

Barbara McKenzie, *Mary McCarthy*.   New York, Twayne, 1966.
Irvin Stock, *Mary McCarthy*.   Minneapolis, University of Minnesota Press, 1968.
Sherli Goldman, *Mary McCarthy: A Bibliography*.   New York, Harcourt Brace, 1968.

*   *   *

Looking back on the theatre reviews and essays now collected in *Sights and Spectacles*, Mary McCarthy notes that in the earliest of these pieces what one hears is the voice of "a young, pedantic, pontificating critic." Unlike her editors at the *Partisan Review*, she was not a Communist but she took her line from them as well as she could:

> We automatically suspected any *succes d'estime*; this, I fear, was my guiding critical principle. I remember how uneasy I felt when I decided that I *liked* Thornton Wilder's *Our Town*. Could this mean there was something the matter with me? Was I starting to sell out? Such haunting fears, like the fear of impotence in men, were common in the avant-garde of those days. The sagest position was to remain always on the attack....Knowing our readers' interests, I tried to show a play in its social context, to smoke out its latent tendencies. This begins to disappear toward the end of the war, though by then I had become more skillful at obliging a play to "tell something" about the society that was paying to see it.

Her tone may have been "insufferably patronizing" at times, but on the whole she remains content with the judgments themselves:

> The hostility to existing values that bristled in my theatre chronicles did not have a foundation in theory, but it had an emotional truth. I hated the plays most people liked or permitted themselves to be satisfied by. I demanded something better, which was what I had in common with the radical demand for a better world. Neither of these demands has been satisfied. The theatre is perhaps a little better than it was in 1937; the world is probably worse.

In addition to being the driving force behind Miss McCarthy's fiction, this "hostility to existing values" may also explain why, as a critic, she has always been concerned with the fate of realism; for it is realism (or so it might be argued) which is best able to document the falsity of current values. As she remarks in one of her best essays, "The American Realist Playwrights," realism is "a deprecation of the real." Ibsen's characters, for example,

> complain that they are "stifling"; in the airless hypocrisy of the puritan middle-class parlor, people were being poisoned by the dead gas of lies. Hypocrisy is the cardinal sin of the middle class, and the exposure of a lie is at the center of all Ibsen's plots. The

strength and passion of realism in his indictment of society avoids the old method of satire with its delighted exaggeration.

In one sense art can never be entirely "realistic": the artist cannot duplicate reality, therefore he must decide what to include and what to leave out. "The details that are not eliminated," Miss McCarthy explains in "Settling the Colonel's Hash," "have to stand as symbols of the whole, like stenographic signs, and of course there is an art of selection, even in a newspaper account: the writer, if he has any ability, is looking for the revealing detail that will sum up the picture for the reader in a flash of recognition." This is "natural symbolism," which has a "centripetal intention":

> It hovers over an object, an event, or series of events and tries to declare what it is. Analogy (that is, comparison to other objects) is inevitably one of its methods. "The weather was soupy," i.e., like soup. "He wedged his way in," i.e., he had to enter, thin edge first, as a wedge enters, and so on. All this is obvious. But these metaphorical aids to communication are a far cry from literary symbolism, as taught in the schools and practiced by certain fashionable writers. Literary symbolism is centrifugal and flees from the object, the event, into the incorporeal distance, where concepts are taken for substance and floating ideas and archetypes assume a hieratic authority.

Despite *Pilgrim's Progress* and *Moby Dick*, "the great body of fiction contains only...natural symbolism"; and this, of course, is the main point of Miss McCarthy's argument. The distinctive characteristic of the novel *is* its "concern with the actual world, the world of fact, of the verifiable, of figures, even, and statistics." The true novelist has a passion for "fact in a raw state":

> You remember how in *The Brothers Karamazov* when Father Zossima dies, his faction (most of the sympathetic characters in the book) expects a miracle: that his body will stay sweet and fresh because he died "in the odor of sanctity." But instead he begins to stink. The stink of Father Zossima is the natural, generic smell of the novel.

The problem is that the "facts" of modern life resist representation. "We know that the real world exists," Miss McCarthy explains in "The Fact in Fiction," "but we can no longer imagine it":

> That is, the existence of Highbury or the Province of O------ is rendered impossible, unveracious, by Buchenwald and Auschwitz, the population curve of China, and the hydrogen bomb....The coexistence of the great world and us, when contemplated, appears impossible....And here is the dilemma of the novelist, which is only a kind of professional sub-case of the dilemma of everyone: if he writes about his province, he feels its inverisimilitude; if he tries, on the other hand, to write about people who make lampshades of human skin, like the infamous Ilse Koch, he feels still more the inverisimilitude of what he is asserting. His love of truth revolts. And yet this love of truth, ordinary common truth recognizable to everyone, is the ruling passion of the novel. Putting two and two together, then, it would seem that the novel, with its common sense, is of all forms the least adapted to encompass the modern world, whose leading characteristic is irreality.

Moreover, because he has been caught up in the experimental movements of "sensibility" and "sensation," the modern novelist is unable to create memorable characters. The school of sensibility ("Virginia Woolf, Katherine Mansfield, Dorothy Richardson, Elizabeth Bowen, Forster") "annihilates the sense of character": the "perambulating sensibility of Mrs. Dalloway," for example, "cannot fix for us Mrs. Dalloway as a person; she remains a palpitant organ, like the heroine of a pornographic novel." For the school of sensation ("Hemingway and his imitators") "violence becomes a substitute for action." Both movements "have the effect of abolishing the social," the only medium in which a character can live and grow. The only alternative is to imitate one's characters "from within," and here Miss McCarthy's argument takes a very curious turn. "There is something burglarious," she ventures, "about these silent entries into a private or alien consciousness":

> Or so I feel when I do it myself....I cannot know, really, what it feels like to be a vindictive man professor [in *The Groves of Academe*], any more than a young man can know what it is to be an old man or Faulkner can know what it is to be a feeble-minded adult who had his balls cut off. All fictions, of course, are impersonations, but it seems to me somehow less dubious to impersonate the outside of a person, say Mrs. Micawber with her mysterious "I will never leave Mr. Micawber," than to claim to know what it feels like to *be* Mrs. Micawber.

No doubt Miss McCarthy means what she says here; but she is on firmer ground, or at least will make more sense to more readers of modern fiction, when she takes up, briefly but very acutely, the problem of what Wayne Booth calls the "unreliable narrator." After making some observations about *The Adventures of Augie March, Henderson the Rain King, The Catcher in the Rye, Lolita*, and two of her own novels, she concludes that these books are "dramatic monologues or a series of monologues":

> The reader, tuned in, is left in no doubt as to where he is physically, and yet in many of these books he finds himself puzzled by the very vocal consciousness he has entered: is it good or bad, impartial or biased? Can it be trusted as Huck Finn or Marcel or David Copperfield could be trusted? He senses the author, cramped inside the character like a contortionist in a box, and suspects (often rightly) some trick. In short, it is not at all straight shooting, as it was with the old novelists.

What we have lost is "the power of the author to speak in his own voice or through the undisguised voice of an alter ego, the hero, at once a known and an unknown, a bearer of human freedom." Is it still possible to write novels at all? "The answer," she concludes, "is certainly not yes and perhaps, tentatively, no."

Only a year or two later Miss McCarthy startled us with her dazzling essays on *Pale Fire* and *Naked Lunch*, and on Ivy Compston-Burnett and Nathalie Sarraute (all reprinted in *The Writing on the Wall*). It is impossible to tell just what happened—perhaps reality itself had somehow shifted ("although the national novel, like the nation-state [is] dying," she remarks, "a new kind of novel [is] being written"). About *Pale Fire* (by that well-known straight-shooter Vladimir Nabokov) she writes that while pretending to be a "curio," it "cannot disguise the fact that it is one of the very great works of art of this century, the modern novel that everyone thought was dead and that was only playing possum." Nathalie Sarraute's shadowy novel, *The Golden Fruits*, is "an heroic book" and therefore "merits not fame but glory." These are remarkable claims, but Miss McCarthy supports them with incomparable skill and a kind of loving attentiveness which no one familiar with her earlier criticism—let alone her fiction— could possibly have anticipated.

Ideas and the Novel, based on Miss McCarthy's Northcliffe Lectures for 1980, is a rather slapdash affair which contains the makings of two interesting, loosely related books about the current state of fiction. Her primary aim here is to argue that the modern novelist has been impoverished by his refusal to deal with "ideas," by which she usually means the intellectual consideration of important social issues. The villain here is Henry James (although she observes, rather oddly, that "no Jamesian novels are being produced any more—if they ever were, apart from the Master's own.") The Jamesian model "remains a standard, an archetype, against which contemporary impurities and laxities are measured." T.S. Eliot's well-known remark—that James "had a mind so fine no idea could violate it"—is for Miss McCarthy symptomatic:

> The young Eliot's epigram summed up with cutting brevity a creed that for modernists appeared beyond dispute. Implicit in it is the snubbing notion, radical at the time [1918] but by now canon doctrine, of the novel as a fine art and of the novelist as an intelligence superior to mere intellect. In this patronizing view, the intellect's crude apparatus was capable only of formulating concepts, which then underwent the process of diffusion, so that by dint of repetition they fell within anybody's reach....The power of the novelist

insofar as he was a supreme intelligence was to free himself from the work-load of commentary and simply, awesomely, to show: his creation was beyond paraphrase or reduction. As a pure work of art, it stood beautifully apart, impervious to the dry rot affecting the brain's constructions and the welter of factuality.... James etherialized the novel beyond its wildest dreams and perhaps etherized it as well.

One might argue that this is not quite true—that *Portrait of a Lady*, for example, is a powerful implicit dramatization of the Puritan "idea" of duty and its consequences, or that *Jacob's Room* (which Miss McCarthy calls Virginia Woolf's "position paper for the reform of the novel") is an equally powerful dramatization of the idea that we can never truly know another person. But Miss McCarthy sticks to her simplistic distinction between thought and feeling, between the "novel of ideas" and "the novel of images." In any event, something important has been lost, she goes on, and implies that her own work has been affected as well:

> [today] ideas are held not to belong to the novel; in the art of fiction we are beyond such simplicities. The doctrine of progress in the arts is a hard doctrine, imposing itself even on those who are fervent non-believers. The artist is an imitative beast, and, being of my own place and time, I cannot philosophize in a novel in the good old way, any more than I can write "We Mortals." A novel that has ideas stamps itself as dated; there is no escape from that law.

But self-pity never has been Miss McCarthy's strong suit: *Birds of America* is nothing if not a novel of ideas, *The Group*—in her own words—is about the idea of progress, and so on. Miss McCarthy's fiction is saturated with ideas. Some other novelists have escaped as well: there is the "brilliant example" of J.G. Farrell's *The Siege of Krishnapur*, there is John Updike's *The Coup*, there is Robert Pirsig's *Zen and the Art of Motorcycle Maintenance*—and then Miss McCarthy adds that "a special license has always been allowed to the Jewish novel, which is free to juggle ideas in full view of the public." Bellow, Malamud, Philip Roth (Miss McCarthy always surprises) "still avail themselves of the right, which is never conceded to us goys." Miss McCarthy's purpose is to contrast all this with the classic nineteenth century novel, particularly in France. A novel by Stendhal, Balzac or Hugo was "so evidently an idea-carrier that the component of overt thought in it must have been taken for granted by the reader as an ingredient as predictable as a leavening agent in bread....So intrinsic to the novelistic medium were ideas and other forms of commentary, all tending to 'set' the narration in a general scheme, that it would have been impossible in former days to speak of 'the novel of ideas.' It would have seemed to be a tautology."

Miss McCarthy's concern for ideas leads directly to her second, much subtler and more interesting line of argument, that the great novelists of the nineteenth century were passionately attracted to ideas but also ambivalent about them: they were aware, that is, that ideas can possess a man and have disastrous consequences for himself and for others. Dostoievsky provides a clear example of this paradox:

> It is clear that Dostoievsky stood in awe of the power of ideas. The most fearful, evidently, in his eyes were socialistic ideas with their humanitarian tinge. And here, at any rate, he could speak from experience: his having belonged to a group—the Petrashevsky circle—that engaged in discussion of Utopian socialism had taken him to Siberia and nearly to the firing squad. Yet this experience, he believed, had not only taught him a lesson in the ordinary way ("Stay out of discussion groups"), but had brought about a spiritual rebirth. His dread of the power of ideas combined with a fatal attraction to them; like so many Russian writers then and now, he was drawn to ideas as if to a potent drug. In Geneva, long after he had returned, a new man, from Siberia, he could not resist going to hear Bakunin expound his theories, and he expressed disappointment that Bakunin was not more constructive. In Dostoievsky, ideas may lead those they fasten on to extreme suffering, but they can also be bringers of redemption, the one in fact leading to the other, as had happened in his own case.

The great English novelists of the nineteenth century were also attracted to ideas but with the exception of Dickens, tended, like George Eliot, to treat them as the source of "wholesome moral reflections" ("If George Eliot fails, even in *Middlemarch*, to be a very great writer, this, I think, is because of an intellectual deficiency.") The argument might very well be extended. In fiction—perhaps in all art—there is a necessary and beneficial tension between indispensable abstractions and an equally necessary awareness of the world of contingent particulars. Miss McCarthy does not go this far, however, and simply concludes with the implication that the modern novelist would be a good deal better off, and so would we, if he did not have a fashionable contempt for ideas.

MILES, Josephine (Louise).   American.   Born in Chicago, Illinois, 11 June 1911. Educated at the University of California, Los Angeles, A.B. 1932 (Phi Beta Kappa); University of California, Berkeley, M.A. 1934, Ph.D. 1938. Since 1940, Member of the English Department, and since 1973, University Professor, University of California, Berkeley. Recipient: Shelley Memorial Award, 1936; Phelan Award, 1937; American Association of University Women fellowship, 1939; Guggenheim Fellowship, 1948; National Institute of Arts and Letters grant, 1956; Oscar Blumenthal Prize (*Poetry*, Chicago), 1959; American Council of Learned Societies Fellowship, 1965; National Endowment for the Arts grant, 1967; James Russell Lowell Prize, 1975; Academy of American Poets Award, 1978. D.Litt.: Mills College, Oakland, California, 1965. Fellow, American Academy of Arts and Sciences. Address: 2275 Virginia Street, Berkeley, California 94709, U.S.A.

PUBLICATIONS

Criticism

Wordsworth and the Vocabulary of Emotion.   Berkeley and Los Angeles, University of California Press, 1942.
Pathetic Fallacy in the 19th Century: A Study of the Changing Relation Between Object and Emotion.   Berkeley and Los Angeles, University of California Press, 1942.
The Vocabulary of Poetry: Three Studies.   Berkeley and Los Angeles, University of California Press, 1946.
The Continuity of Poetic Language: Studies in English Poetry from the 1540's to the 1940's.   Berkeley, University of California Press, 1951.
  I. *The Primary Language of Poetry in the 1640's.*   Berkeley, University of California Press, 1948.
  II. *The Primary Language of Poetry in the 1740's and 1840's.*   Berkeley, University of California Press, 1950.
  III. *The Primary Language of Poetry in the 1940's.*   Berkeley, University of California Press, 1951.
Eras and Modes in English Poetry.   Berkeley, University of California Press, 1957; revised edition, 1964.
Renaissance, Eighteenth-Century and Modern Language in English Poetry: A Tabular View.   Berkeley, University of California Press, 1960.
Ralph Waldo Emerson.   Minneapolis, University of Minnesota Press, 1964.
Style and Proportion: The Language of Prose and Poetry.   Boston, Little Brown, 1967.
Poetry and Change: Donne, Milton, Wordsworth, and the Equilibrium of the Present. Berkeley, University of California Press, 1974.
"Values in Language, or, Where Have *Goodness, Truth,* and *Beauty* Gone?" in *Critical Inquiry* (Chicago), 3, 1976.

Working Out Ideas: Predication and Other Essays.   San Francisco, Bay Area Writers Project, 1979.

Verse

Lines at Intersection.   New York, Macmillan, 1939.
Poems on Several Occasions.   New York, New Directions, 1941.
Local Measures.   New York, Reynal, 1946.
After This Sea.   San Francisco, Book Club of California, 1947.
Prefabrications.   Bloomington, Indiana University Press, 1955.
Poems 1930-1960.   Bloomington, Indiana University Press, 1960.
Civil Poems.   Berkeley, California, Oyez, 1966.
Bent.   Santa Barbara, California, Unicorn Press, 1967.
Kinds of Affection.   Middletown, Connecticut, Wesleyan University Press, 1967.
Saving the Bay.   San Francisco, Open Space, 1967.
Fields of Learning.   Berkeley, California, Oyez, 1968.
American Poems.   Berkeley, California, Cloud Marauder Press, 1970.
To All Appearances: New and Selected Poems.   Urbana, University of Illinois Press, 1974.
Coming to Terms.   Urbana, University of Illinois Press, 1979.

Recording: *Today's Poets 2*, with others, Folkways, 1968.

Play

House and Home (produced Berkeley, California, 1960).   Published in *First Stage* (Lafayette, Indiana), Fall 1965.

Other

Editor, with Mark Schorer and Gordon McKenzie, *Criticism: The Foundations of Modern Literary Judgment.*   New York, Harcourt Brace, 1948; revised edition, 1958.
Editor, with others, *Idea and Experiment.*   Berkeley, University of California Press, 1950.
Editor, *The Poem: A Critical Anthology.*   Englewood Cliffs, New Jersey, Prentice Hall, 1959; revised edition, as *The Ways of the Poem*, 1973.
Editor, *Classic Essays in English.*   Boston, Little Brown, 1961; revised edition, 1965.

CRITICAL STUDY

Denis Donoghue, "The Habits of the Poet," in *The Times Literary Supplement* (London), 25 April 1975.

*   *   *

As Josephine Miles points out, we often want to consider a poem as a unique verbal context which significantly "conditions its own language" by the arrangement of its constituent parts. We want to find out, for example, how a word or phrase which is fairly "neutral" in ordinary discourse suddenly becomes charged with new meanings when it enters the poem, how it comes to life, phonetically and imagistically, and contributes to a particular kind of complexity and poetic pleasure. But at the same time

> we must remember that the language which the poem selects as well as arranges is already conditioned in structure and emphasis by the beliefs of its general users. Language is not a raw and amorphous material, but individually and socially shaped, and contains within it, at least in the Indo-European forms that we know, all the working characteristics which have from time to time been attributed to poetry alone or prose alone.

The two approaches are complementary, but no one critical framework or "language," as R.S. Crane calls it, can do justice to the poem as individual context *and* type or example of a "shared way of poetizing." Thus we may be able to learn something valuable from Miss Miles' pioneering, unfashionable efforts to establish a set of descriptive principles which will account for "period sequences" in English verse. The crucial assumption here, of course (and it is hard to disagree with it), is that no matter how individual a given poem may seem to us, it also has affinities with other poems—particularly with other poems written around the same time. Properly understood the following passage from *Eras and Modes in English Poetry* will explain the connections between Miss Miles' essentially quantitative approach to poetic style and large questions of continuity and change which we usually feel lie beyond the reach of descriptive techniques:

> If it is possible for us to conceive of continuities of usage, from parts of speech to sentence structures, to extensions by figure, norm and symbol, to modes, styles, eras, and beliefs, in certain recurrent configurations of language in poetry, then we may be persuaded to ask certain questions about poetry as history. Perhaps poetry gives us history in an intensive form—the shape of values selected and stressed by artistic forces. Perhaps the terms and structures which a poet most cares about tend to be those which a group, even an era, most cares about, as they represent the basic choices of the time. The language we speak, and even more the language we versify, may seem to be a loaded language, carrying the weight of chosen values.

Miss Miles has been tabulating and describing these "continuities of usage" for over thirty years. She has paid little attention to metrics as a source of discrimination among styles (perhaps because careful metrical studies are not uncommon), but she has examined poetic vocabularies in detail and devoted a great deal of attention to the three basic grammatical sentence patterns available to writers of English:

> The distinction which I have found pertinent in kinds of sentence structure is between the sort which emphasizes substantial elements—the phrasal and coördinative modifications of subject and object—and the sort which emphasizes clausal coördination and complication of the predicate. The first or phrasal type employs an abundance of adjectives and nouns, in heavy modifications and compounding of subjects, in a variety of phrasal constructions, including verbs turned to participles; it is a cumulative way of speaking. The second or clausal type emphasizes compound or serial predicates, subordinate verbs in relative and adverbial clauses, action, and rational subordination; it is a discursive way of speaking. The first might say, "Rising and soaring, the golden bird flies into the stormy night of the east"; the second if given the same terms would say, "The golden bird rises and soars; it flies into the night which storms in the east." The motion and concept both differ;. and, indeed, the discursive type is less apt to be speaking of "golden birds" at all than to be dealing with abstractions or complex events.
>
> Theoretically, there might be a third type between these two: not merely a scale of degrees between extremes, but a mode of statement characterized by a balance between clausal and phrasal elements. And actually, just as we do in fact find kinds of poetry which are dominantly phrasal or dominantly clausal, so we find a kind of poetry in which sentence structure is balanced between the two. We have, then, three modes technically describable in terms of dominant sentence structure and emphasized by usage in meter

and vocabulary; these I call provisionally the clausal, the phrasal, and the balanced modes of poetic statement.

Classifying the poetry written from 1500 to 1900 in accordance with this distinction, we discover a sequence which runs as follows: clausal, clausal, balanced; clausal, clausal, balanced; phrasal, phrasal, balanced; clausal, clausal, balanced. In other words, there are four groups, one in each century, each begun by an extreme and terminated by a balance. No periods of extreme come immediately together, because each is followed by moderation in a balanced form.

Moreover, choices among grammatical structures are usually accompanied by other patterns of artistic choice which can be counted and described:

> One is not surprised to learn that reference and sound work closely with sentence [structure]; that the language of poetry is integral in its characteristics. Which moves first, which new sound makes for new sense, or new structure for new sound, is a question needing more than the evidence available. At least, in generational stages, we can see that the three phases move together, though not with equal force, vocabulary the least likely, structure the most, to return to old stages. All work as one poetic unit: the relational pattern of clausal sentence with stanzaic sound and with conceptual vocabulary; or the cumulative pattern of phrasal sentence with internal onomatopoetic sound and sublime vocabulary; or the distinct, not merely transitional, balanced patterns of structure, line, and human nature in nature which we call classical. Here, in this nucleus of language properties, we may find some of the basis for a definition of modes; and in modes, of styles; and in styles, of eras.

Denis Donoghue has provided a very useful summary of the "history" of English verse which emerges from Miss Miles' painstaking studies:

> The main tradition of English poetry...is based upon the clausal mode which Miss Miles finds at work in Chaucer, Wyatt, Donne, Jonson, Herbert, in its early phase, and later in Coleridge, Byron, Landor, Browning, Hardy, Frost, and Auden. This tradition uses substantives (nouns and adjectives) in proportion to predicates (verbs) in a ratio of two to one. In the phrasal mode, the poets beginning with Spenser, Quarles, Crashaw and Milton use a ratio of three to one, and for Thomson, Akenside, the Whartons, an extreme of four to one. The phrasal tradition is maintained by Blake, Keats, Tennyson, Whitman, and many American poets, including Hart Crane. This mode accommodates much of the feeling which we describe as Whig, Protestant, enthusiastic, or sublime. Miss Miles finds the balanced mode in Dryden, Marvell, Goldsmith, Crabbe, Wordsworth, Hopkins, Stevens, Eliot, and Yeats: its great master is Wordsworth, whose special concern is with "the process of the reception and interpretation of sensation by feeling, in verbs of perception, in adjectives of size, scope, age, and affection, and in nouns of bodily and emotional sense half combined with concepts and atmosphere."

The Continuity of Poetic Language is likely to prove hard going for non-specialists, but the brilliant, though often elliptical summary essays and essays in application which make up *Eras and Modes* and *Poetry and Change* are designed for a wider audience. "A history of values," Miss Miles asserts, "resides in the history of poetic recurrences and repetitions"; and it is these questions of value, particularly of changing values, which the wider audience will find more interesting. Here, however, Miss Miles is usually less willing to generalize or speculate. "One may ask the Why of this discoverable pattern," she admits at one point in *Eras and Modes*, "but I have no idea of the Why, and am indeed still much concerned with the details of How":

> It may be simply that artists, like others, are intensely aware of living and working in a beginning or ending century, and so suit their tones and structures. It may be some repetition we have been caught up in, as many cyclical theorists suggest. Curt Sachs in *The Commonwealth of Art*, Francois Mentré in *Les Générations sociales*, and Max Förster in "The Psychological Basis of Literary Periods" (*Studies for Wm. A. Read*) are three, for example, who suggest pendular swings. Agnes Young in *Recurring Cycles of*

Fashion finds three eras of dress fashion in each sequence. Dialectics, whether idealist or materialist, suggest a clash of opposites and then a resolution. But the poetic patterns seems rather a matter of mediation between opposites, a pendular swing but not a smooth one, in stages, not a continuous arc. Perhaps the stages are a matter of generations, as Mentré suggests, with epochs of rebellion, transition, and reconciliation; at least, the consciousness of era seems to be part of the problem.

In the last essay of *Eras and Modes* Miss Miles offers a few more tantalizing suggestions:

> Reference, even in its barest selection, rests in belief; so that before we even look at patterning, at the complications of theme and tone in the full arrangements of style, we may see in the simplest presences of terms themselves, in their proportioning and their various possibilities of intensification, some of the bases of their use in some of our assumptions about value and reality. Our native active and thoughtful mode is visible at once in lively verbs and in metaphorical extensions, that is, both clausal and figurative subordinations which rest in the belief of metaphysically subordinate and microcosmic man. Our sublime and rare extremes of the eternal, as distinct from the temporal, are visible at once in our epithets of cosmos and seer, in our images which are symbols of the ineffable, and rest in the belief of a receptive and prophetic man. Our classical essentializing of human situations is visible at once in the balances of human terms and norms, the structure between clausal and phrasal, the location between microcosm and macrocosm in the level world, and rests in our belief in man as able to achieve his own balances.

In short, poetic continuities may reflect the image of man which a culture accepts at any given time. If this is true, then perhaps poets never legislate (or perhaps the question is simply too broad to be of any use): the impetus for change comes from "outside" poetry. But again, Miss Miles is reluctant to speculate much further; and again, Denis Donoghue's summarizing remarks are extremely useful:

> Miss Miles writes of these matters with impeccable grace. If she has an axe to grind, I cannot hear the noise. She attends upon her three modes with such generosity in each case that I have to invoke her own poems as evidence that she favors the clausal or predicative mode when it comes to a choice between her first two, and would favour the balanced mode if she could have one of the three for the asking. I infer that if she could have her wish as a poet she would begin like Donne with the poetry of a thinking process and achieve at length the structures of deliberation which she admires in Wordsworth....Speaking of the contemporary situation in poetry, she says that "we are turning away from comparison and contrast of qualitative bases toward the synapses of juxtaposition, Charles Olson's sparks of energies jumping across chasms of disrelation," but I do not think she is content with that programme. If poetry is moving away from "values of objectivity" to "values of immediacy and impact," there is evidence that she would urge a further move into "human validation." She wonders "how our systems-civilization will make its way into value; how laws, plans, committees, bureaucracies, machines, will find some human validation."

Donoghue then moves on to Miss Miles' poetry, and the necessity to do so at this point clearly suggests that as a critic Miss Miles prefers to document rather than evaluate. But it would be a great mistake to conclude that because her approach is quantitative she is merely a cool statistician or relativist.

MILLER, J(oseph) Hillis. American. Born in Newport News, Virginia, 5 March 1928. Educated at Oberlin College, Ohio, B.A. 1948; Harvard University, Cambridge, Massachusetts, M.A. 1949, Ph.D. 1952. Married Marian Dorothy Jones in 1940; has three children. Instructor, Williams College, Williamstown, Massachusetts, 1952-53; Assistant Professor, 1953-59, Associate Professor, 1959-63, Professor of English, 1967-72, and Professor of English and Humanistic Studies, 1968-72, Johns Hopkins University, Baltimore, Maryland. Professor of English, 1972-75, Gray Professor of Rhetoric, 1975-76, Frederick W. Hilles Professor of English and Professor of Comparative Literature (Chairman, Department of English, 1976-79), Yale University, New Haven, Connecticut. Visiting Professor of English, University of Hawaii, Honolulu, Summer, 1956; Harvard University, 1962 and 1973; Ward-Philips Lecturer, Notre Dame University, Indiana, 1967; Visiting Professor, University of Virginia, Charlottesville, 1969; University of Washington, Seattle, 1971; University of Zurich, 1972 and 1978; Princeton University, New Jersey, 1974; Fellow, Wesleyan Center for the Humanities, Middletown, Connecticut, 1971; Phi Beta Kappa Lecturer, 1977-78; Professor at the School of Criticism and Theory, University of California at Irvine, 1979; Carnegie Fellow, University of Edinburgh, 1981. Editor, *Modern Language Notes*, 1953-61. Since 1953, Editor, *English Literature History*. Trustee, Keuka College, Keuka Park, New York, 1971-80. Recipient: Guggenheim Fellowship, 1959, 1965; Harbison Distinguished Teaching Award, Danforth Foundation, 1968. H.D.L.: University of Florida, Gainesville, 1980. Address: The Literature Major, Yale University, Box 3010 Yale Station, New Haven, Connecticut 06520, U.S.A.

PUBLICATIONS

Criticism

> *Charles Dickens: The World of His Novels.* Cambridge, Massachusetts, Harvard University Press, 1958.
> *The Disappearance of God: Five Nineteenth-Century Writers.* Cambridge, Massachusetts, Harvard University Press, 1963.
> *Poets of Reality: Six Twentieth-Century Writers.* Cambridge, Massachusetts, Harvard University Press, 1965; London, Oxford University Press, 1966.
> "Literature and Religion," in *Relations of Literary Study: Essays in Interdisciplinary Contributions*, edited by James Thorpe. New York, Modern Language Association, 1967.
> "The Geneva School: The Criticism of Marcel Raymond, Albert Béguin, Georges Poulet, Jean Rousset, Jean-Pierre Richard, and Jean Starobinski," in *Virginia Quarterly Review* (Charlottesville), 43, 1967.
> "The Problem of Form: First-Person Narration in *David Copperfield* and *Huckleberry Finn*," in *Experience in the Novel*, edited by Roy Harvey Pearce. New York, Columbia University Press, 1968.
> *The Form of Victorian Fiction: Thackeray, Dickens, Trollope, George Eliot, Meredith, and Hardy.* Notre Dame, Indiana, and London, University of Notre Dame Press, 1968.
> *Thomas Hardy: Distance and Desire.* Cambridge, Massachusetts, Harvard University Press, and London, Oxford University Press, 1970.
> "Williams' *Spring and All* and the Progress of Poetry," in *Daedalus* (Cambridge, Massachusetts), Spring 1970.
> "The Interpretation of *Lord Jim*," in *The Interpretation of Narrative*, edited by Morton W. Bloomfield. Cambridge, Massachusetts, Harvard University Press, 1970.
> "The Still Heart: Poetic Form in Wordsworth," in *New Literary History* (Charlottesville), 2, 1971.
> *Charles Dickens and George Cruikshank.* Los Angeles, University of California William Andrews Clark Memorial Library, 1971.
> "Georges Poulet's 'Criticism and Identification,'" in *The Quest for Imagination*, edited by O.B. Hardison, Jr. Cleveland, Ohio, Case Western Reserve University Press, 1971.

"Tradition and Difference," in *Diacritics* (Ithaca, New York), 2, 1972.

"Optic and Semiotic in *Middlemarch*," in *The Worlds of Victorian Fiction*, edited by Jerome H. Buckley.   Cambridge, Massachusetts, Harvard University Press, 1975.

"Fiction and Repetition: *Tess of the d'Urbervilles*," in *Forms of Victorian Fiction*, edited by Alan Warren Friedman.   Austin, University of Texas Press, 1975.

"Ariadne's Thread: Repetition and the Narrative Line," in *Critical Inquiry* (Chicago), 3, 1976.

"Stevens' Rock as Criticism and Cure I and II," in *Georgia Review* (Athens), 30, 1976.

"Walter Pater: A Partial Portrait," in *Daedalus* (Cambridge, Massachusetts), 105, 1976.

"The Linguistic Moment in 'The Wreck of the Deutschland,' " in *The New Criticism and After*, edited by Thomas Daniel Young.   Charlottesville, University of Virginia Press, 1976.

"The Limits of Pluralism III: The Critic as Host," in *Critical Inquiry* (Chicago), 3, 1977; reprinted in *Deconstruction & Criticism: Harold Bloom, Paul de Man, Jacques Derrida, Geoffrey Hartman, J. Hillis Miller*.   New York, Seabury Press, 1979; London, Routledge, 1980.

"Nature and the Linguistic Moment," in *Nature and the Victorian Imagination*, edited by U.C. Knoepflmacher and G.B. Tennyson.   Berkeley, University of California Press, 1977.

"Ariachne's Broken Woof," in *Georgia Review* (Athens), 31, 1977.

"The Problematic of Ending in Fiction," in *Nineteenth Century Fiction*, (Berkeley, California), 33, 1978.

"On Edge: The Crossways of Contemporary Criticism," in *Bulletin of the American Academy of Arts and Sciences* (Boston), 32, 1979.

"A Buchstäbliches Reading of Elective Affinities," in *Glyph* (Baltimore), 6, 1979.

"Theory and Practice: Response to Vincent Leitch," in *Critical Inquiry* (Chicago), 6, 1980.

"The Figure in the Carpet," in *Poetics Today* (Tel Aviv), 1, 1980.

"Theoretical and Atheoretical," in *Wallace Stevens: A Celebration*, edited by Frank Doggett and Rober Buttel.   Princeton, New Jersey, Princeton University Press, 1980.

Other

Editor, with Roy Harvey Pearce, *The Act of the Mind: Essays on the Poetry of Wallace Stevens*.   Baltimore, Johns Hopkins University Press, 1965.

Editor, *William Carlos Williams: A Collection of Critical Essays*.   Englewood Cliffs, New Jersey, Prentice Hall, 1966.

Editor, *Aspects of Narrative*.   New York, Columbia University Press, 1971.

Editor, *The Well-Beloved*, by Thomas Hardy.   London, Macmillan, 1976.

Critical Studies

Sarah Lawall, *Critics of Consciousness*.   Cambridge, Massachusetts, Harvard University Press, 1968.

Vincent B. Leitch, "The Lateral Dance: The Deconstructive Criticism of J. Hillis Miller," in *Critical Inquiry* (Chicago), 6, 1980.

*   *   *

For J. Hillis Miller during the first part of his critical career, for his former mentor, Georges Poulet, and for the other "Geneva" critics (the group also includes Marcel Raymond, Albert Béguin, Jean Rousset, Jean-Pierre Richard, and Jean Starobinski), literature is primarily a "form of consciousness." As Miller points out in his very useful essay, "The Geneva School," Poulet and Raymond regard literature as neither an objective structure of meanings residing in the words of a poem or novel, nor the tissue of self-references of a "message" turned in on itself, nor the unwitting expression of the hidden complexes of a writer's unconscious, nor a revelation of the latent structures of exchange or symbolization which integrate a society. Literature, for them, is the embodiment of a state of mind. In the language of a text from Rousseau's "Rêveries," or a poem by Hugo, or a novel by Balzac a certain mode of consciousness has been brought into the open in a union of mind and words. This union incarnates the consciousness and makes it available to others.

Most modern British and American critics have tended to locate the essential character of literature—especially of poetry—in the kind of statement the poet makes ("emotive" as opposed to "referential" statements, for example), in the rhetorical devices he uses (irony, ambiguity, and so on), in the intrinsic power of certain kinds of "themes," or in the effects possible in different kinds of imitative works. The Geneva critics, however, "are relatively without interest in the external form of individual works of literature"; they "replace a concern for the objective structure of individual works with a concern for the subjective structure of the mind revealed by *the whole body of an author's writings*" (my italics). But they differ among themselves as to the nature of consciousness:

> Poulet's commitment to the idea that consciousness is the living source of literature distinguishes his work from all that criticism which presupposes a Husserlian conception of consciousness. For Husserl, for Martin Heidegger, for Maurice Merleau-Ponty, for Gaston Bachelard, for Jean-Pierre Richard, and for many other contemporary thinkers and artists, consciousness is always consciousness *of* something or other. For such men there is never an act of self-consciousness in which the mind is never aware of anything but its own native affective tone. However far back one goes, however seemingly far away from the world, no state of mind can be encountered which is not already an interpenetration of subject and object, mind and things. This categorical rejection of any complete division of consciousness and the world, so fecund in recent developments in philosophy and art, is fundamentally anti-Cartesian. It rejects the idea of a *Cogito* in which the mind knows nothing but itself. Poulet, on the other hand, maintains the traditional dualism and affirms the priority of consciousness as the genetic energy in literature .... [He] rejects all that modern tradition of thought which may be called phenomenological and [maintains] his allegiance to the tradition of Descartes ....

This distinction between "consciousness" and "consciousness of" is puzzling, at least to an outsider. It is difficult to think of consciousness as an empty "form"—as a system of innate laws, perhaps, or categories—and just as difficult to think of it as simply a receptacle filled with impressions from the outside world. And when both alternatives seem unsatisfactory, there may be something wrong with the way the problem has been formulated in the first place. But in any event, the nature of criticism follows naturally enough from all of this:

> Poulet thinks of criticism as beginning and ending in a coincidence of the mind of the critic and the mind of the author. There must be what he called an "absolute transparency" with the soul of the other. Poulet differs from [the other Geneva critics] in his unwillingness to use this transparency as a means to reach some further end. His "criticism of pure identification" is an end in itself.... The aim of each of his critical essays is to re-create as precisely as possible the exact tone which persists in a given writer throughout all the variety of his work.

In short, criticism becomes *"consciousness of consciousness, literature about literature."*
How closely Miller follows Poulet here is best illustrated by a passage from the Preface to *Thomas Hardy: Distance and Desire*:

> Literary criticism is language about language, or, to put it another way, a re-creating in the mind of the critic of the consciousness inscribed in the texts studied, generated there by the words. To say this is to put in question certain habitual metaphors for what happens in the act of criticism. Among these are all those visual metaphors which set the

critic over against the text as a spectator who surveys the literary work as a scientist is
sometimes thought to survey the thing he investigates dispassionately and objectively.
Illicit also are the metaphors for the criticism which propose to explain the text by
something extralinguistic which precedes it and which is its generative source—the life
or psychology of the author, historical conditions at a certain time, some event which is
the model "imitated" or "reflected" or "represented" in the poem or story. The centuries-
old metaphors of mimesis obscure the nature of literary language. The pre-text of a given
text is always another text open in its turn to interpretation. There is never an
extralinguistic "origin" by means of which the critic can escape from the labyrinthine
wanderings within the complexities of relationship among words. The critic, moreover,
does not possess a power of looking from the outside in a sovereign view which sees all
the text at once as a spatial design. To understand the text he must be inside it. The
means of his entry is language, a medium within which he already dwells. He can insert
himself into the text because both he and it are already interpenetrated by their common
language. The means of his interpretation is also language, those words of his which even
in the most passive act of reading he adds to the text as he understands it. If there is no
escape outside the text, if language is as much the source of consciousness or of history as
consciousness or history is the source of language, then far better than any visual
metaphor for what happens in criticism is that image employed by Thomas Hardy in *The
Dynasts* and elsewhere, the image of the text of history as a woven cloth. A literary text is
a texture of words, its threads and filaments reaching out into the pre-existing warp and
woof of the language. The critic adds his weaving to the Penelope's web of the text, or
unravels it so that its structuring threads may be laid bare, or reweaves it, or traces out
one thread in the text to reveal the design it inscribes, or cuts the whole cloth to one shape
or another. In some way the critic necessarily does violence to the text in the act of
understanding it or of interpreting it. There is no innocent reading, no reading which
leaves the work exactly as it is.

To pursue the total form of a writer's consciousness means, as Miller recognizes, "necessarily
having to forego full interpretation of the richness and complexity of any single work." The
same goal (the "absolute transparency with the soul of the other") and the same limitation, if
one regards it as such (the unwillingness or inability to deal with individual works), characterize
Miller's other important studies, *Charles Dickens, The Disappearance of God,* and *Poets of
Reality.*

In *Charles Dickens: The World of His Novels* Miller is primarily interested in describing the
"assimilative" consciousness of Dickens and the final pattern that consciousness creates:

Dickens wanted to absorb the city [that is, the plenitude of life itself] into his imagination
and present it again in the persons and events of his novels. But how could he reach the
real city, the city hidden from all the people who are distorting the world by interpreting
it in terms of their fears and fancies and opinions? Perhaps he could transcend the
limitations of any single point of view by presenting as many as possible of the limited
persons, and of the new aspects which the city gets when seen through their eyes. The
truth thus reached would be Dickens' own truth too, the truth of his deepest sense of the
nature of the world. From novel to novel throughout his career Dickens sought an ever
closer approach to the truth hidden behind the surface appearance of things. But he
sought the truth not so much by going behind the surface as by giving an exhaustive
inventory of the surface itself. For the truth behind appearances is unavailable by any
direct approach. And to reveal the secrets in the hearts of his characters is not to
approach any closer to the truth of the unknown city, for the city is hidden from each of
them too. The special qualty of Dicken's imagination is his assumption that he can get
behind the surface by describing all of it bit by bit.

As for the completed "pattern," it may be understood—very fancily indeed—as a kind of
"negative transcendence" and acceptance of the ordinary world:

[The typical Dickens hero] is alienated from himself and views his own consciousness as
something mysterious and separated from himself. Beginning in isolation, each protag-

onist moves through successive adventures... [which are] essentially attempts to understand the world, to integrate himself in it, and by that integration to find a real self. In this interchange between mind and world there is in Dickens' characters and in the novels themselves as wholes a constant attempt to reach something transcendent, something more real than one's own consciousness or than the too solid everyday material world. This supra-reality is perhaps caught in fleeting glimpses at the horizon of the material world, or in the depths beneath the upper layers of consciousness. In those depths are the regions of dreams, or of that hallucinated vision of things and people which is so characteristic of Dickens.... Dickens' protagonists, initially creatures of poverty and indigence, are constantly in search of something outside the self, something other than the self, and even something other than human, something which will support and maintain the self without vaporizing and engulfing it. Dickens' novels...form a unified whole, a unified totality. Within this whole a single problem, the search for viable identity, is stated and restated with increasing approximation to the hidden center, Dickens' deepest apprehension of the nature of the world and of the human condition within it.

Finally, in *Our Mutual Friend* and *The Mystery of Edwin Drood*, we encounter

a new notion that the transcendent spiritual power glimpsed at the margins or in the depths of the material world is not really a positive support for human values, even for good ones, but is the negation and reduction to nothing of all the human world indiscriminately. And it is a belief, deriving from this new vision of transcendence, that the human condition, with all its sufferings and unreality, can in no way be completely escaped, as long as life lasts. The human world is itself the only real support for human values. There is only one world for man. Dickens' last heroes and heroines come back to life after a purifying descent into dark waters of death, but they come back to assume just that situation which was their given one in society. The difference is that their contact with the negative transcendence has liberated them to a new attitude toward their situation... The terminal point of *Our Mutual Friend*, as of the world of Dickens as a whole, is man's reaffirmation, after a withdrawal, of his particular, limited engagement in the world and in society.

The Disappearance of God and *Poets of Reality* may be taken as parts of one continuous argument in which Miller maintains that the "gradual withdrawal of God from the world" is one of the major concerns of "post-medieval" literature. The disappearance of God, however, does not necessarily mean the death of God. He may still exist, but by the nineteenth century,

The lines of connection between us and God have broken down, or God himself has slipped away from the places where he used to be. He no longer inheres in the world as the force binding together all men and all things. As a result the nineteenth and twentieth centuries seem to many writers a time when God is no more present, and can only be experienced negatively, as a terrifying absence.... Only if God would return or if we could somehow reach him might our broken world be unified again. But this has not yet happened. God keeps himself hidden. There seems to be no way to re-establish connection.

But as for the reasons for this withdrawal, Miller bluntly and rather surprisingly refuses to speculate further:

The history of modern literature is in part the history of the splitting apart of this communion [between God and man]. This splitting apart has been matched by a similar dispersal of the cultural unity of man, God, nature, and language. It is not possible to explain why this fragmentation has come about. A great historical transformation remains mysterious, just as does the homogeneity of the culture of a single age. We can neither explain why people stop feeling and believing in an old way, nor why a new way of feeling and believing appears simultaneously in widely separated cultures.

Whatever the hidden causes may be, however, there are several clearly definable ways in which human consciousness may respond to God's "absence":

> Humanism, perpectivism, nihilism, pious acceptance—each of these has been a possible reaction to the absence of God. But the five writers studied here [De Quincey, Browning, Emily Brontë, Arnold, and Hopkins] all belong to another tradition: romanticism. The romantics still believe in God, and they find his absence intolerable. At all costs they must attempt to re-establish communication. They too begin in destitution, abandoned by God. All the traditional means of mediation have broken down, and romanticism therefore defines the artist as the creator or discoverer of hitherto unapprehended symbols which establish a new relation, across the gap, between man and God. The artist is the man who goes out into the empty space between man and God and takes the enormous risk of attempting to create in that vacancy a new fabric of connections between man and the divine power. The romantic artist is a maker or discoverer of the radically new, rather than the imitator of what is already known.

The troublesome problem of "consciousness" as opposed to "consciousness of" returns here, as it does elsewhere in Miller's criticism—at least if we assume that he is trying to remain faithful to Poulet's adherence to the Cartesian rather than the phenomenological tradition. On the one hand Miller maintains that "Every poetic universe is unique and ultimately incommensurable with any other"; on the other hand he also seems intent on proposing a broad history of modern consciousness as consciousness *of* the disappearance and death of God, that is, of transcendent sanctions and authority. Either the problem is insoluble or Miller may be implying that while true criticism can provide history with important materials, literary history itself can never be truly critical.

In any event, the language of Miller's later criticism *sounds* increasingly "historical." At the beginning of *Poets of Reality* he proposes that "A new kind of poetry has appeared in our day, a poetry which grows out of romanticism, but goes beyond it." If the Victorians he examined earlier had presupposed the disappearance of God, "the death of God is the starting point for many twentieth-century writers." Conrad "explored nihilism to its depths" and Yeats, Eliot, Thomas, Stevens, and Williams have "played important roles in this twentieth-century revolution in man's experience of existence":

> Each begins with an experience of nihilism or its concomitants, and each in his own way enters the new reality: Yeats by his affirmation of the infinite richness of the finite moment; Eliot by his discovery that the Incarnation is here and now; Thomas by an acceptance of death which makes the poet an ark rescuing all things; Stevens by his identification of imagination and reality in the poetry of being; Williams by his plunge into the "filthy Passaic."...The unity of twentieth-century poetry is suggested by the fact that these authors are in the end poets not of absence but of proximity.

The unity is very loose if it can include both Eliot *and* Williams, or so one might object; "reality" seems to mean, finally, *any* kind of sanction for living. For Miller, Stevens and Williams represent the triumphant capacity of human consciousness to go beyond nihilism and to establish an essentially post-romantic understanding of man's proper place in the world:

> To walk barefoot into reality [an adaptation of Stevens' phrase, "to step barefoot into reality"] means abandoning the independence of the ego. Instead of making everything an object for the self, the mind must efface itself before reality, or plunge into the density of an exterior world, dispersing itself in a milieu which exceeds it and which it has not made. The effacement of the ego before reality means abandoning the will to power over things. This is the most difficult of acts for a modern man to perform. It goes counter to all the penchants of our culture.... When man is willing to let things be, then they appear in a space which is no longer that of an objective world opposed to the mind. In this new space the mind is dispersed everywhere in things and forms one with them.

Apparently Miller agrees with Williams; no poetry—at least no poetry now—but "in things." This kind of criticism obviously raises some difficult questions. Given Miller's approach, is it really possible to say why one consciousness is more valuable than another? Is there some special kind of quality of consciousness which distinguishes the artist from the non-artist and the good poet from the bad? If so, what is it and how do we talk about it? Clearly Miller feels that some writers are more worth thinking about than others, but on what grounds? So far the only answer he provides is the one implied in a passage from the Preface to *The Disappearance of God*:

> The structure of consciousness expressed in a poem or novel is like that "inscape" which Gerard Manley Hopkins says is present in every example of a given species, but usually "detached to the mind" only through repetition. Repetition "gives the visible law: looked at in any one instance it flies."...My presupposition is that all an author's writings form a living unity, just as each individual work is a life within that larger life, and my method is the one recommended by Proust and Hopkins: the juxtaposition of diverse works in order to identify the "novel and unique beauty" which is their common essence.

The problem is, of course, that Miller's particular critical language gives us no way of handling "novel and unique beauty."

No modern literary critic has made quite so abrupt and decisive a break with his earlier thinking than Miller was to shortly after 1970. Poulet disappears completely as a guiding influence and is unequivocally replaced by Jacques Derrida. The crucial document, as Vincent Leitch demonstrates in his careful essay on Miller's later development, is the 1971 review of M.H. Abrams' *Natural Supernaturalism* ("here,"Leitch observes, "the rift in contemporary critical theory, opened by deconstructive criticism, emerges in public for the first time in America"). Miller begins by praising Abrams' massive study as a work "in the grand tradition of modern humanistic scholarship, the tradition of Curtius, Auerbach, Lovejoy, and C.S. Lewis"—and then goes on to assert that the very foundations of that tradition are misguided, based as they are on the assumption that words are referential and meanings determinable and recoverable. "The notion of a literal or referential use of language," Miller continues,

> is only an illusion born of the forgetting of the metaphorical "roots" of language. Language is from the start fictive, illusory, displaced from any direct reference to things as they are. The human condition is to be caught in a web of words which weaves and reweaves for man through the centuries the same tapestry of myths, concepts, and metaphorical analogies, in short, the whole system of Occidental metaphysics.

The "Occidental" or Western belief in a philosophic center and fixed meanings is in Derrida's terms simply the "desire" for certainty which, after Nietzsche, Marx and Freud, we should have the courage to recognize does not exist. "The concepts of origin, end, and continuity," Miller asserts, "are replaced by the categories of repetition, of difference, of discontinuity, of openness, and of the free and contradictory struggle of individual human energies, each seen as a center of interpretation, which means misinterpretation, of the whole." Thus in Leitch's summary, "Miller undermines traditional ideas and beliefs about language, literature, truth, meaning, consciousness, and interpretation. In effect, he assumes the role of unrelenting destroyer—or nihilistic magician—who dances demonically upon the broken and scattered fragments of the Western tradition."

Miller provided a full-dress "deconstructive" reading of Wallace Stevens' "The Rock" in 1976. In this poem, he argues,

> The multiple meanings of the word "cure," like the meanings of all key words and figures in "The Rock" are incompatible, irreconcilable. They may not be followed, etymologically, to a single root which will unify or explain them, explicate them in a single source. They may not be folded together in a unified structure, as of leaves, blossom and fruit from one stem. The origin rather is bifurcated, even trifurcated, a forking root which leads the searcher for the ground of the word into labyrinthine wanderings in the forest of words.... However hard...[we] try to fix the word in a single sense it remains indeterminable, uncannily resisting...[our] attempts to end its movement. Cover the abyss, or open it up, or find the bottom, the ground of the rock, and make a solid base on which to build—which is it? How could it be all three at once? Yet it is impossible to

decide which it is. To choose one is to be led to the others and so to be led by the words of the poem into a blind alley of thought.

As a result, criticism or interpretation must give up its traditional goal of recovering authorial meaning; there can be no accurate readings of texts, only the creative "free play" of words about other words. Readings, according to Paul de Man (with whom Miller seems to be in complete agreement at nearly every point), are either "wrong" or "valid" (or "good") misreadings: "By a good misreading," de Man explains, "I mean a text that produces another text which can itself be shown to be an interesting misreading, a text which engenders additional texts. If you have a poor text, you cannot make up a very rewarding construction." By the late 1970's, the lines were firmly drawn: on one side there are the conservative critics, such as M.H. Abrams, Wayne Booth and E.D. Hirsch, who continue to argue that there can be rational consensus about the meaning of literary works; on the other side, Derrida, de Man, Miller, Geoffrey Hartman (to a limited extent), and operating from a rather different set of principles, Stanley Fish and Harold Bloom. For an expert account of the invasion of the deconstructionists, readers should consult Chapter 5, "History or the Abyss: Poststructuralism," of Frank Lentricchia's *After the New Criticism*.

Since all language by definition falsifies, it follows that the language of the deconstructionists can itself be deconstructed—a fact which Derrida and his followers cheerfully admit ("Deconstructive discourse can never reach a clarity," Miller concedes, "which is not vulnerable to being deconstructed in its turn"). For this reason M.H. Abrams had called the whole enterprise "suicidal," and in fact it is difficult to see how deconstructionism might institutionalize itself in any productive way. Nevertheless, in his temperate reply to Leitch's essay, Miller seems optimistic about the future:

> it would be a mistake to underestimate the changes that deconstruction would make and has already begun making in the institution of literary studies in America. These would include more or less radical changes within the institution, changes in the content and style of teaching, changes in the organization of courses, curricula, and department.... [The] orderly making of these changes and the assimilation of the implications of the new methods of literary study seem to me the major tasks facing departments of English, comparative literature, and foreign languages today.... The conflicts between different attitudes towards literature, the resistance to theory, the nostalgia for old "certainties," the exhilaration of insights coming from newer strategies of interpretation, are, in their most important forms, not so much externalized as quarrels between this group of critics and that as internalized within individual teachers and critics. In work I am now doing I am trying to think through these inner conflicts in terms of what I call "the ethics of reading."

MUIR, Edwin. British. Born in Pomona, Orkney, Scotland, 15 May 1887. Educated at Kirkwall Burgh School, Orkney. Married Willa Anderson in 1919; one child. Worked in various commercial and ship building offices in Glasgow, 1901-18, and as a journalist and translator. Staff Member, *New Age*, London, 1919-21; worked for the British Council in Edinburgh 1942-45, and for the British Council in Prague, 1945-48, and in Rome, 1948-50: Director of the British Institute, Rome, 1949. Warden of Newbattle Abbey College, Dalkeith, 1950-55; Norton Professor of Poetry, Harvard University, Cambridge, Massachusetts, 1955-56; Visiting Winston Churchill Professor, University of Bristol, 1958. Ph.D.: Charles University, Prague, 1947; LL.D.: University of Edinburgh, 1947; Docteur-ès-Lettres: University of Rennes, 1949; Litt.D.: Leeds University, 1955; Cambridge University, 1958. Recipient: Foyle Prize, 1950; Heinemann Award, 1953; Frederick Niven Literary Award, 1953; Russell Loines Award, 1957; Saltire Society Prize, 1957. Fellow of the Royal Society of Literature, 1953. C.B.E. (Commander, Order of the British Empire), 1953. *Died 3 January 1959.*

PUBLICATIONS

Criticism

We Moderns: *Enigmas and Guesses* (as Edward Moore).   London, Allen and Unwin, 1918; New York, Knopf, 1920.
Latitudes.   London, Andrew Melrose, and New York, Huebsch, 1924.
Transition: *Essays on Contemporary Literature*.   London, Hogarth Press, and New York, Viking Press, 1926.
The Structure of the Novel.   London, Hogarth Press, 1928; New York, Harcourt Brace, 1929.
The Present Age, from 1914.   London, Cresset Press, 1939; New York, McBride, 1940.
The Politics of King Lear (lecture).   Glasgow, University Press 1947; reprinted in *Essays on Literature and Society*, 1949.
Essays on Literature and Society.   London, Hogarth Press, 1949; augmented edition, Hogarth Press, and Cambridge, Massachusetts, Harvard University Press, 1965.
The Estate of Poetry (lectures).   London, Hogarth Press, and Cambridge, Massachusetts, Harvard University Press, 1962.

Verse

First Poems.   London, Hogarth Press, and New York, Huebsch, 1925.
Chorus of the Newly Dead.   London, Hogarth Press, 1926.
Six Poems.   Warlingham, Surrey, Samson Press, 1932.
Variations on a Time Theme.   London, Dent, 1934.
Journeys and Places.   London, Dent, 1937.
The Narrow Place.   London, Faber, 1943.
The Voyage and Other Poems.   London, Faber, 1946.
The Labyrinth.   London, Faber, 1949.
Collected Poems 1921-1951, edited by J.C. Hall.   London, Faber, 1952; New York, Grove Press, 1953; revised edition, as *Collected Poems 1921-1958*, edited by J.C. Hall and Willa Muir, Faber, 1960, 1963; with a preface by T.S. Eliot, New York, Oxford University Press, 1965.
Prometheus.   London, Faber, 1954.
One Foot in Eden.   London, Faber, and New York, Grove Press, 1956.
Selected Poems, with a preface by T.S. Eliot.   London, Faber, 1965.

Novels

The Marionette.   London, Hogarth Press, and New York, Viking Press, 1927.
The Three Brothers.   London, Heinemann, and New York, Doubleday, 1931.
Poor Tom.   London, Dent, 1932.

Other

John Knox: *Portrait of a Calvinist*. .   London, Cape, and New York, Viking Press, 1929.

Scottish Journey.   London, Heinemann-Gollancz, 1935.
Social Credit and the Labour Party: An Appeal.   London, Nott, 1935.
Scott and Scotland: The Predicament of the Scottish Writer.   London, Routledge, 1936;
   New York, Robert Speller, 1938.
The Story and the Fable: An Autobiography.   London, Harrap, 1940; revised edition, as
   An Autobiography, London, Hogarth Press, and New York, Sloane, 1954.
The Scots and Their Country.   London, Longman, 1946.
Selected Letters of Edwin Muir, edited by P.H. Butter.   London, Hogarth Press, 1974.

Translator, with Willa Muir, *Poetic Dramas*, by Gerhart Hauptmann.   London, Secker,
   and New York, Huebsch, 1925.
Translator, with Willa Muir, *The Island of the Great Mother*, by Gerhart Hauptmann.
   London, Secker, and New York, Viking Press, 1925.
Translator, with Willa Muir, *Jew Süss*, by Lion Feuchtwanger.   London, Secker, and
   New York, Viking Press, 1926.
Translator, with Willa Muir, *The Ugly Duchess*, by Lion Feuchtwanger.   London,
   Secker, 1927; New York, Viking Press, 1928.
Translator, with Willa Muir, *Two Anglo-Saxon Plays: The Oil Islands and Warren
   Hastings*, by Lion Feuchtwanger.   New York, Viking Press, 1928; London, Secker,
   1929.
Translator, with Willa Muir, *Veland*, in *Historical and Legendary Dramas*, by Gerhart
   Hauptmann.   London, Secker, and New York, Viking Press, 1929.
Translator, with Willa Muir, *War*, by Ludwig Renn.   London, Secker, and New York,
   Dodd Mead, 1929.
Translator, with Willa Muir, *Class of 1902*, by Ernest Glaeser.   London, Secker, and
   New York, Viking Press, 1929.
Translator, with Willa Muir, *The Castle*, by Franz Kafka.   London, Secker, and New
   York, Knopf, 1930.
Translator, with Willa Muir, *The Life of Eleonora Duse*, by Emil Alphons Rheinhardt.
   London, Secker, 1930.
Translator, with Willa Muir, *Success*, by Lion Feuchtwanger.   London, Secker, and
   New York, Viking Press, 1930.
Translator, with Willa Muir, *After War*, by Ludwig Renn.   London, Secker, and New
   York, Dodd Mead, 1931.
Translator, with Willa Muir, *Inner Journey*, by Kurt Heuser.   London, Secker, 1932; as
   Journey Inward, New York, Viking Press, 1932.
Translator, with Willa Muir, *The Sleepwalkers*, by Hermann Broch.   London, Secker,
   and Boston, Little Brown, 1932.
Translator, with Willa Muir, *Josephus*, by Lion Feuchtwanger.   London, Secker, and
   New York, Viking Press, 1932.
Translator, with Willa Muir, *The Great Wall of China and Other Pieces*, by Franz
   Kafka.   London, Secker, 1933.
Translator, with Willa Muir, *Little Friend*, by Ernest Lothar.   London, Secker, and New
   York, Putnam, 1933.
Translator, with Willa Muir, *Three Cities*, by Shalom Asch.   London, Gollancz, and
   New York, Putnam, 1933.
Translator, with Willa Muir, *Hill of Lies*, by Heinrich Mann.   London, Jarrolds, 1934;
   New York, Dutton, 1935.
Translator, with Willa Muir, *Salvation*, by Shalom Asch.   London, Gollancz, and New
   York, Putnam, 1934.
Translator, with Willa Muir, *Mottke the Thief*, by Shalom Asch.   London, Gollancz,
   and New York, Putnam, 1935.
Translator, with Willa Muir, *The Unknown Quantity*, by Hermann Broch.   London,
   Collins, and New York, Viking Press, 1935.
Translator, with Willa Muir, *The Mills of God*, by Ernst Lothar.   London, Secker, 1935;
   as *The Loom of Justice*, New York, Putnam, 1935.
Translator, with Willa Muir, *The Jew of Rome*, by Lion Feuchtwanger.   London,
   Hutchinson, 1935; New York, Viking Press, 1936.

Translator, with Willa Muir, *Night over the East*, by Erik Maria von Kühnelt-Leddihn.   London, Sheed and Ward, and New York, Oxford University Press, 1936.

Translator, with Willa Muir, *The Queen's Doctor*, by Robert Neumann.   London, Gollancz, and New York, Knopf, 1936.

Translator, with Willa Muir, *Calf of Paper*, by Shalom Asch.   London, Gollancz, 1936; as *War Goes On*, New York, Putnam, 1936.

Translator, with Willa Muir, *False Nero*, by Lion Feuchtwanger.   London, Hutchinson, 1937; as *Pretender*, New York, Viking Press, 1937.

Translator, with Willa Muir, *The Trial*, by Franz Kafka.   London, Gollancz, and New York, Knopf, 1937.

Translator, with Willa Muir, *A Woman Screamed*, by Robert Neumann.   London, Cassell, and New York, Dial Press, 1938.

Translator, with Willa Muir, *Enigmatic Czar*, by Georges Maurice Paléolgue.   London, Hamish Hamilton, and New York, Harper, 1938.

Translator, with Willa Muir, *America*, by Franz Kafka.   London, Routledge, 1938; New York, New Directions, 1940.

Translator, with Willa Muir, *Richelieu*, by Carl Jakob Burckhardt.   London, Allen and Unwin, and New York, Nelson, 1940.

Translator, with Willa Muir, *Through a Woman's Eyes*, by Zsolt Harsányi.   New York, Putnam, 1940; as *Through the Eyes of a Woman*, London, Routledge, 1941.

Translator, with Willa Muir and Paul Tabor, *Lover of Life*, by Zsolt Harsányi.   New York, Putnam, 1942.

Translator, with Willa Muir and Clement Greenberg, *Parables, In German and English*, by Franz Kafka.   New York, Schocken Books, 1947.

Translator, with Willa Muir, *In the Penal Settlement: Tales and Short Pieces*, by Franz Kafka.   London, Secker and Warburg, and New York, Schocken Books, 1948.

BIOGRAPHY, CRITICAL STUDIES AND BIBLIOGRAPHY

P.H. Butter, "The Critic: of Literature and Society," in *Edwin Muir*.   Edinburgh, Oliver and Boyd, 1962.

Elgin W. Mellown, *Bibliography of the Writings of the Edwin Muir*.   University, Alabama, University of Alabama Press, 1964; revised edition, London, Nicholas Vane, 1966.

P.H. Butter, *Edwin Muir: Man and Poet*.   Edinburgh, Oliver and Boyd, 1966; New York, Barnes and Noble, 1967.

Peter C. Hoy and Elgin W. Mellown, *A Checklist of Writings about Edwin Muir*.   Troy, New York, Whitston, 1971.

*   *   *

Edwin Muir's biographer, P.H. Butter, observes that *The Structure of the Novel* is a "concentrated" study which "demands to be read as a whole and with care"; it is the one critical book in which Muir was "able to develop a sustained argument at length, and makes one wish that he had had the leisure to do so more often." This is fair enough, but prospective readers should also be advised to bear with the rather desultory opening chapters for the sake of the interesting arguments which follow, and that those arguments, interesting as they may by, are not fully intelligible without some knowledge of Muir's other criticism.

For Muir there are three major novelistic forms or "structures" (the early romances and novels of action which were designed mainly to let the reader "escape from the uninteresting prosaic limitations of ordinary life" are not really forms at all). The first form, the "novel of character," is "one of the most important divisions in prose fiction." In *Vanity Fair*, for example, the characters are not subservient to the action, as they are in a primitive novel of action like *The Famous History of Doctor Faustus*, but "exist independently, and the action is subservient to them." Since the primary aim 'of this form is the revelation of human nature, the characters are usually "flat' (here Muir uses Forster's term in Forster's own rather special sense:

a flat character is simply one who does not change or develop as the novel progresses). In the second major form, the "dramatic novel," the distinction between plot and character disappears:

> The characters are not part of the machinery of the plot; nor is the plot merely a rough framework round the characters. On the contrary, both are knit together. The given qualities of the characters determine the action, and the action in turn progressively changes the characters, and thus everything is borne forward to an end. At its greatest the affinity of the dramatic novel is with poetic tragedy, just as that of the novel of character is with comedy.

"Strict internal causation" is vital here (*Pride and Prejudice* is Muir's chief example), since one of the functions of the dramatic novel is to reflect the complex interplay of freedom and necessity which characterizes our lives in the "real" world. These distinctions, however, are not meant to suggest that one form is superior to the other:

> Keeping our eyes on those two divisions of the novel as they are, we must needs believe that neither could give us its characteristic sense of human variety if it did not observe its limitations. Without its shut-in arena the one could not evoke such a range and absoluteness of experience in its figures. Without the unchangeability of its types the other could not show us a clear-cut diversity of character and manners. It is here the static definition, the completeness of every character at every moment, that points the diversity and makes it self-evident. To see sharply the difference between a multitude of living things we must arrest their movement. They must not change while we look, or the change will confuse our sense of distinction; difference will merge at times into identity, to disentangle itself and to merge again. By the same analogy, to produce a sense of diversity of character with the maximum effect, the same figures must be rendered static, or rather must be seen as static, as certain types of imagination in fact see them. If all this is so, however, the limitations of the dramatic and the character novel, in appearance arbitrary, are in reality reasonable and necessary, for only by observing them can the writer get his effect and externalise his peculiar vision of life.

Muir's discussion of the third form, the "chronicle novel," is considerably more original. The special province of the dramatic novel is "time," in which the plot must be carried forward; the special province of the novel of character is "space," in which the novelist places his portraits; but the chronicle novel is limited by neither time nor space:

> When we have closed *War and Peace*...we feel that "time goes on." The process, ten, twenty, thirty, forty, fifty, and all the people by means of whose lives we count it, remain in our minds and in the world. "The cycle of birth and growth, death and birth again"; this has been the pattern of the story; but this is the pattern of life too. So that, finished, the chronicle releases an echo which wanders in larger spaces than those in which it has just been confined, spaces, moreover, which repeat on an unimaginably vaster scale the proportions of their original, and respond to the same tones. Tolstoy describes only a few generations, but the emphasis of his imagination makes the endless cycles of generations unroll in our imagination; and we see human life as birth, growth, and decay, and process perpetually repeated. This then is the framework, ideal and actual, of the chronicle; its framework of universality.

Thus it soon becomes apparent that the three primary structures of the novel reflect the very categories of the mind itself:

> We see things in terms of Time, Space and Causality; and only the Supreme Being, Kant affirmed, can see the whole unity from beginning to end. Yet the imagination desires to see the whole unity, or an image of it; and it seems that the image can only be conceived when the imagination accepts certain limitations, or finds itself spontaneously working within them. If the matter could be pursued to the end, then I hold that it would be found that those limitations determine the principle of structure in the various types of

imaginative creation; in the dramatic novel, for example, the character novel, and the chronicle.

But whatever structure the novelist is drawn to, he must produce

> an image of life, not a mere record of experience; but being an image it will inevitably observe the conditions which alone make the image complete, and universal, and those...reduce themselves to a representation of action predominantly in time or predominantly in space. Seeing life in time, or seeing it in space, the writer can work out the relations, the dynamic values, of his plot satisfactorily and to an end, and transform his vague and contingent sense of life into a positive image, an imaginative judgment. We have the same right to demand this imaginative judgment from a novel as we have to demand it from the poetic tragedy and the epic; for the novel is a form of art, like these, or it is nothing.

To understand what Muir means by "imaginative judgment" (this crucial term is never defined in *The Structure of the Novel*), one must turn to the later essays, "The Decline of the Novel" and "The Poetic Imagination," now reprinted in *Essays on Literature and Society*. In the former Muir argues that "the characteristic modern novel is a story without an ending," and that this is so because "our own order is not a classical order; we have a grasp of origins but not of ends; our existence, like our works, is an unfinished sentence":

> A comprehensive and widely accepted conception of human life produces good imaginative art; a tentative and partially accepted conception of life, unsatisfactory imaginative art. In an age when such a conception prevails the subject-matter of the artist will not mould itself into a form; every image of human existence will have the mark of organic imperfection.... Seen against eternity the life of man is a complete story. Seen against time it is an unfinished one.... When [religious belief] partially fails, imagination suffers an eclipse, and art becomes a problem rather than a function.

According to P.H. Butter there were two crucial stages in Muir's spiritual development: by 1924 he had become convinced that (in his own words) "the life of every man is an endlessly repeated performance of the life of man"; by 1935 he had accepted fully the Christian conception of the timeless pattern inside of which every individual "performance" is acted out and takes on meaning. *The Structure of the Novel* is a transitional work (it first appeared in 1928), and this may explain the incompleteness of Muir's argument; but, in any event, it now seems clear that by "judgment" he means the ability to perceive the life of the individual against the pattern of eternity. And it is the imagination, as Muir defines it in "Poetry and Imagination," which allows the artist to penetrate the lives of others; it is "the faculty by which life is grasped in its individual forms":

> Hugo von Hofmannsthal once said that great imagination is always conservative. By this he may have meant that it keeps intact the bond which unites us with the past of mankind, so that we can still understand Odysseus and Penelope and the people of the Old Testament. Or he may have meant something more: that imagination is able to do this because it sees the life of everyone as the endless repetition of a universal pattern. It is hard to explain how we can enter into the lives of people long dead, if this is not so. Imagination tells us that we become human by repetition, that our life is a rehearsal of lives that have been lived over and over, and that this act, with all that is good and evil in it, is a theme for delighted and awed contemplation.... We can feel but not see life whole until it has been placed [by the artist] in some kind of past where it discovers its true shape.

In *The Estate of Poetry* Muir is primarily concerned with the disappearance in modern times of the poet's audience. Men are no longer moved by poetry as the Greeks were by their rhapsodes or even as Muir and his family and friends had been at the turn of the century by Burns and the Scottish ballads. New means of communication have given our minds and feelings a certain predilection for the abstract and the cliché; and the cliché is the popular expression of the abstract. It tends to make us view life impersonally, as third parties and onlookers, and it inclines us to use, even when we are strongly moved, a kind of language which is suited only for general ideas and newspaper reports, or even for headlines. The public, which has its genuine function, in this way insinuates itself into our private lives. And that is a matter of importance, for the language we use colors and circumscribes our feelings, our thoughts, and our image of the world.

Returning to the poet, the idea of confronting him with the public, if this is what it is, appears strangely anomalous. He cannot speak its language, which is the language of the third party and the onlooker. He abhors the cliché. He is not concerned with life in its generality, but in its immediacy and its individuality. His object is to see into the life of the people, to enter into their feelings and thoughts, good and bad. What can he say to the public, or the public to him?

Ironically enough, criticism has increased the distance between the poet and his audience, "or perhaps one should rather say that [modern critical] method legalizes the divorce as a settled and normal state." After discussing Cleanth Brooks' analysis of "Tears, Idle Tears" (in *The Well Wrought Urn*), Muir concludes that this kind of criticism seems to him "of very little use to any reader" and gives him, personally,

> a faint touch of claustrophobia, the feeling that I am being confined in a narrow place with the poet and the critic, and that I shall not get away until all three of us are exhausted. The great danger of this kind of criticism is that it shuts the poem in upon itself an an object, not of enjoyment but of scrutiny, and cuts it off from the air which it should breathe and its spontaneous operation on those who are capable of receiving it. Everything is slowed down or arrested; the poem cannot get on; the movement, and the movement of a poem is an essential part of it, is held up, while we examine its parts in isolation. One thinks of a laboratory; and indeed the analysis of poetry, pushed to this length, resembles a scientific test.

Muir ends with the hope—and it is only a faint hope—that the poet will be able to see past the public to "men and women, with their individual lives."

The responsibilities of the critic follow naturally from all of this. Just as the poet uses his imagination to grasp the lives of others, so the critic must use his powers of sympathetic understanding to grasp the particular "image" or vision of the artist he is considering; for the critic poetry is, or should be, the "starting point for an enquiry into the human spirit." The reviews and occasional pieces which make up *Transition, Latitudes* and *Essays on Literature and Society* are often disappointingly brief and fragmentary, but even the slightest of them are marked by the sense of common humanity which will be familiar to readers who know Muir's moving *Autobiography* and his magnificent later poetry.

OLSON, Elder (James). American. Born in Chicago, Illinois, 9 March 1909. Educated at the University of Chicago, B.A. 1934 (Phi Beta Kappa), M.A. 1935, Ph.D. 1938. Married 1) Ann Elizabeth Jones in 1937 (divorced, 1948); 2) Geraldine Louise Hays in 1948; four children. Instructor, Armour Institute of Technology, Chicago, 1938-42. Assistant Professor, 1942-48, Associate Professor, 1948-53, and since 1954, Professor of English, University of Chicago. Visiting Professor, University of Puerto Rico, Rio Piedras, 1952-53; University of Frankfurt; Powell Professor of Philosophy, 1955, Visiting Professor of Literary Criticism, 1958-59, and Patten Lecturer, 1964, University of Indiana, Bloomington; Rockefeller Visiting Professor, University of the Philippines, Quezon City, 1966-67. Recipient: Witter Bynner Award, 1927; Guarantors Prize, 1931, and Eunice Tietjens Memorial Prize, 1953 (*Poetry*, Chicago); Poetry

Society of America Chap-Book Award, 1955; Academy of American Poets Award, 1956; Longview Foundation Award, 1958; Balch Award (*Virginia Quarterly Review*, Charlottesville), 1965; Quantrell Award, University of Chicago, 1966. Address: Department of English, University of Chicago, Chicago, Illinois 60637, U.S.A.

PUBLICATIONS

Criticism

"A Symbolic Reading of the 'Ancient Mariner,'" in *Critics and Criticism: Ancient and Modern*, edited by R.S. Crane and others. Chicago, University of Chicago Press, 1952.
"Criticism" and "Verse," in *Encyclopaedia Britannica*. Chicago, Encyclopaedia Britannica, 1952, and later editions.
The Poetry of Dylan Thomas. Chicago, University of Chicago Press, 1954.
Tragedy and the Theory of Drama. Detroit, Wayne State University Press, 1961.
The Theory of Comedy. Bloomington, Indiana University Press, 1968.
On Value Judgments in the Arts and Other Essays. Chicago and London, University of Chicago Press, 1976.
"A Conspectus of Poetry I and II," in *Critical Inquiry* (Chicago), 4, 1977.

Verse

Thing of Sorrow: Poems. New York, Macmillan, 1934.
The Cock of Heaven. New York, Macmillan, 1940.
The Scarecrow Christ and Other Poems. New York, Noonday Press, 1954.
Poems and Plays 1948-58. Chicago, University of Chicago Press, 1958.
A Crack in the Universe (verse drama), in *First Stage* (Lafayette, Indiana), Spring 1962.
The Abstract Universe: A Comedy of Masks (verse drama), in *First Stage* (Lafayette, Indiana), Summer 1963.
Collected Poems. Chicago, University of Chicago Press, 1963.
Olson's Penny Arcade. Chicago and London, University of Chicago Press, 1976.

Other

Editor, *American Lyric Poems: From Colonial Days to the Present*. New York, Appleton Century Crofts, 1963.
Editor, *Aristotle's "Poetics" and English Literature: A Collection of Critical Essays*. Chicago, University of Chicago Press, 1965.
Editor, *Major Voices: 20 British and American Poets*. New York, McGraw Hill, 1973.

CRITICAL STUDY

Thomas E. Lucas, *Elder Olson*. New York, Twayne, 1972.

*   *   *

There are good reasons why R.S. Crane and his students and colleagues at the University of Chicago, Elder Olson and Wayne Booth, are often referred to as "Neo-Aristotelians," and even better reasons why they prefer to be called critical pluralists. Crane and Olson (and to a lesser degree Booth) are both critics and "metacritics"; that is, as critics of criticism they are pluralists, but as practical critics they have chosen—for a variety of reasons—to investigate the ways in which the principles of the *Poetics* may be interpreted and applied to a specific range of problems which existing literary works present. There are important connections between "Aristotelianism," in this narrower sense, and pluralism, but the topics must be considered separately.

These critics begin with certain crucial premises concerning the nature of art (or any other subject matter) and the discourse which attempts to describe it. Questions such as "What is poetry?" or "Why is there so little agreement among literary critics?" are false questions in the sense of being misleadingly reductive. As Crane observes in *The Languages of Criticism and the Structure of Poetry*, the phenomena which the critic is concerned with are too complex to be encompassed by any one intellectual framework or "language." A work of art is both a unique entity and an object or force existing in a complex series of relationships with "nature," the artist and his time, different audiences, and so on. In "Questions and Answers in the Teaching of Literary Works" Crane recognizes five major distinguishable aspects the critic may attend to; in "An Outline of Poetic Theory" Olson argues that critical discourse may consider art variously

> as a product; as an activity or passivity of the artist; as certain faculties or as a certain character of the artist; as a certain activity or passivity of the audience; as an instrument; or as a sign, either of certain characteristics of the artist or his audience or of something else involved in art, e.g., its means, subject, etc.

The important point here is that one cannot discuss all the aspects of a work using only one critical language. Every conceptual scheme is limited by its assumptions, terms, and methodology. Thus Olson concludes (in "The Poetic Method of Aristotle") that by this point in intellectual history, we

> should have learned a few things about philosophy, and about criticism too, since that is also philosophy. We should have learned...that every philosophy is limited by the problems which it raises and that every philosophic problem is limited by the terms in which it is couched. We should have learned, after all the labors of logicians, that there are many different ways of making propositions and that there are many senses of the terms "truth" and "falsity." We should have learned, after the many kinds of proofs and demonstrations offered to us, that there are many kinds of valid logics, as there are many valid geometries and algebras; and we should be wise enough to conclude that perhaps there are many "valid" philosophies. We should be too wise to accept any one philosophy as exhausting the whole of truth, and too wise to conclude that therefore every philosophy is false or that we must make a patchwork of philosophies without consideration of the diverse methods which they entail. We should, in short, be wise enough consider the diverse valid philosophies as instruments, all with various powers and limitations, and valuable relative to the kinds of questions to which they are directed.

In short, critical pluralism is by no means a form of relativism.

Crane and Olson agree about the way in which a given critical language delimits its subject matter. And they also agree about the importance of a second limiting factor, the critic's method, his "dialectic," in Olson's terms, or the ways in which he is able to make inferences and build his argument. Here both Olson and Crane are indebted to Richard P. McKeon's distinction between literal and analogical modes of discourse: in "The Philosophic Bases of Art and Criticism," which is in many ways the cornerstone of "Chicago" criticism, McKeon observes that the basic question which divides apparently opposed systems is:

> whether one discusses art adequately by discussing something else or by discussing art, for, in the former case, oppositions turn on what precise subject other than art should be discussed and, in the latter case, on what art itself is. The theories which have been based on the assumption that the meaning of art is explained best, or solely, by means of other phenomena have recently, as in the past, borrowed the principles and terminology of

aesthetics and criticism from some fashionable science, from semantics, psychoanalysis, or economics, from sociology, morals or theology, The art object and the art experience are then nothing in themselves, since they are determined by circumstances and require, like the circumstances which determine them, biological, social, psychological, or historical principles of explanation. The theories which have been based on the assumption that aesthetic phenomena should be analyzed separately, whatever the complexities of the relations in which the aesthetic object of experience is involved, has sought principles in the construction and unity of the art object viewed in terms of expression (in which experience and intention are matched by form), composition (in which details are organized in form), or communication (in which emotion is evoked by form).

Each mode—the literal, which discusses the nature of the object itself, and the analogical, which discusses the object in its various ralationships—has inherent powers and limitations; and therefore McKeon concludes that "in application and precept, modes of criticism thus differently oriented select different points of excellence in the work of the artist and indicate different objectives to be urged on his attention." In "The Dialectical Foundations of Critical Pluralism" Olson uses McKeon's basic distinction and goes on to identify seven types of dialectic and eight fundamental kinds of criticism. Further summary is impossible, however—and impertinent. This extraordinarily complex and rewarding essay displays a kind of thinking about thinking which has rarely been attempted by any critic, modern or otherwise.

As a practical critic—that is, as a critic using a particular framework to examine existing works and *types* of works—Olson is firmly Aristotelian in his conception of poetic wholes and the function of art. He is not interested in a work as the manifestation of an individual sensibility, as an example of "diction" which is somehow inherently different from the diction of other kinds of discourse, or as an instance of the general symbolic processes which govern the life of a society. "I am concerned with the product," he asserts in *Tragedy and the Theory of Drama*, "and with the principles which make it what it is." What "it is," of course, is an arrangement of constituent parts to form an imitative whole. Not all works are primarily "imitative" (nor did Aristotle say they were), but Olson limits himself to clearly imitative works and the relationships between the simpler forms of the lyric and the "maximal" forms of tragedy and comedy. These works imitate or represent human action and character; and whatever particular situation they imitate, they all have a basic responsibility to please us by their beauty, or orderly arrangement of parts. In the *Poetics* Aristotle defines beauty as "an affair of order and magnitude"; in "An Outline of Poetic ·Theory" Olson explains,

> By "beauty" I mean the excellence of perceptible form in a composite continuum which is a whole; and by "excellence of perceptible form" I mean the possession of perceptible magnitude in accordance with a mean determined by the whole as a whole of such-and-such quality.... The constituents of beauty are, therefore, definiteness, order, and symmetry; the last being such commensurability of the parts as renders a thing self-determined, a measure to itself, as it were; for example, a plot is symmetrical when complication and denouement are commensurate. As a thing departs from its proper magnitude, it is either spoiled (i.e., retains its nature but loses its beauty) or is destroyed (i.e., loses even its nature). Compare a drawing of a beautiful head: alter its definitive magnitude to a degree, and the beauty is lost; alter it still further, and it is no longer recognizable as a head.

But the most important pleasures we take in experiencing imitative works are those caused by the emotions the objects of imitation arouse; and thus for an Aristotelian it is the overall *effect* of the work which matters most. ("We have talked a good deal about that 'effect'; we have assumed, and will continue to assume, that it is precisely to achieve this effect that the whole work is organized and that it is this effect which gives the work its value.") Emotions belong to the genus pleasure and pain and play a crucial role in the Aristotelian conception of virtue and the good life: education means training the young to take pleasure in the right things, to feel as well as to know the appropriate responses to the serious issues of life. The good man is the man who takes pleasure in or has the right emotional response to the right object, in the right way and for the right reasons. All such responses, then, depend upon a prior value judgment: we cannot feel anger or pity or fear or any of the other primary emotions unless we have already estimated the worth of what is being depicted: "Every emotional experience," Olson goes on, "must either confirm or alter in some way our system of values: and in altering it, make it better or worse whenever it affects a moral value." Thus the purpose of art is to evoke, confirm and intensify the proper sort of emotional reaction and therefore move us toward the *habit* of right response: in art and life we should feel pity for the undeserved misfortune of the tragic hero. But in life we often fail to grasp the true character of others or to respond to them apart from our own immediate self-interest:

> Thus far we have proceeded on the supposition that the imitative poetic arts have as their ends certain pleasures, produced through their play upon our emotions. Certainly, these are ends of art and such as any consideration of art must embrace; but to suppose that art has no further effect and that it may have no further ends relative to these is vastly to underestimate the powers of art. It exercises, for example, a compelling influence upon human action—individual, social, or political—for among the causes of the misdirection of human action are the failure to conceive vividly and the failure to conceive apart from self-interest; and these are failures which art above all other things is potent to avert, since it vivifies, and since in art we must view man on his merits and not in relation to our private interest. It is not that art teaches by precept, as older generations thought, nor that it moves to action; but clearly it inculcates moral attitudes; it determines our feelings towards characters of a certain kind for no other reason than that they are such characters. The ethical function of art, therefore, is never in opposition to the purely artistic end; on the contrary, it is best achieved when the artistic end has been best accomplished, for it is only a further consequence of the power of art. The same is true of any political or social ends of art provided that the state be a good state or the society a moral society. To reflect on these things is to realize the importance and value of art, which, excellent in itself, becomes ever more excellent as we view it in ever more general relations.

The ultimate responsibility of the artist, then, is to bring us closer to the condition of Aristotle's *phronesis*, or practical wisdom:

> I shall say, therefore, that a work possesses significance or meaning as it promotes perceptions—perceptions based on feelings—which are conducive to practical wisdom; which would, if acted upon, eventuate in such wisdom. The condition of mind which it immediately promotes is a temporary alignment of passion, emotion, and desire with right principle.

Thus there are two kinds of value judgment the critic makes: he judges the suitability of the means the artist has employed to reach his end, or effect, and he judges the value of that effect itself on ethical grounds which are, of course, prior to questions of skill or technique (here the reader should consult the splendid recent essay, "On Value Judgments in the Arts"). As we might expect, Olson is not happy with modern "realism," since it usually has as its subject situations which by definition cannot evoke the worthiest emotions; or to be more precise, he is unhappy with the fact that this kind of realism seems to dominate the modern theatre. And he is even more unhappy with those works which have no determinate effect and therefore prevent stable response of any sort. This "suspense of form" is a "distinctively modern device...[which] consists in keeping the audience uncertain as to *what kind of play* they are witnessing; is it comic, or serious, farce or tragedy, realism or fantasy?" Furthermore,

> suspense of form implies a systematic attack upon all the conventional—that is habitual—emotional and moral responses of the audience, a breaking up of established emotional and moral associations to replace them with new ones...it undermines the very foundation of [the audience's] emotions and moral judgments.

Olson's position here may be compared to Booth's similar uneasiness with "unreliable narrators" and "unstable ironies."

With these distinctions and standards in mind, we may turn briefly to Olson's classification of poetic forms. In two relatively early essays, " 'Sailing to Byzantium': Prolegomena to a

Poetics of the Lyric" and "An Outline of Poetic Theory," he seemed about to undertake a full poetics of the lyric: in Yeats' poem he finds a kind of "argument" which is analogous to the unifying force of "plot" in larger dramatic wholes; and he concludes that the effect of the poem is "something that, in the absence of a comprehensive system of the emotions, we can only call a kind of noble joy or exaltation." Later on he seems to have abandoned the attempt to build a total poetics, for reasons which are not entirely clear. It may be simply that without such a "comprehensive system of the emotions" the task would be impossibly difficult. Clearly Olson feels (in "Art and Science") that modern psychology is of little use:

> You will remember that I spoke of the dependency of poetic sciences on other branches of learning; very unfortunately, some of these have developed in directions utterly useless to art, while failing to supply things that are necessary. I have psychology particularly in mind. I do not mean at all, let me say, that I want more of Freud on Da Vinci and Dostoevsky, more Ernest Jones on Hamlet, more Jung on archetypes.... But all of the arts operate on man, affect man, and it is crucial to have, for instance, a theory of the emotions which completely sets out the various families of emotion in all their degrees with all their causes. Modern psychology seems to have reduced them to as few as possible—so that I myself have had to go back to earlier systems which discriminated among them.

Since all knowledge depends upon an intelligent division of labor, in theory there is no reason why an Aristotelian critic might not take over a fully developed system of the emotions and use them for his own purposes. But in a more recent essay, "The Lyric," Olson concludes that

> A further thing is clear—that it is futile to attempt a definition of the lyric, if we mean by a definition a statement of the nature or essence of something; for things of different natures cannot have one nature or definition. A corollary of this is that it is also futile to attempt to define poetry in general; for the same principle applies, and if lyric cannot be defined, neither can poetry.

What Olson settles for, then, is something less ambitious: a charting of the boundaries of lyric forms or kinds, based not on effect, but on the complexity of the subject matter or, in Aristotelian terms, the "object of imitation." The simplest kind is the lyric of personal expression, provided by one character in a "closed situation" ("O Westron Wind," for example, "involves a single wish for spring"). Next we have a verbal act of "address"—persuading, beseeching, commanding, informing, betraying, and so on"—again provided by a particular character in a particular situation ("To His Coy Mistress," for example). But if the mistress were to respond, we would have a more complex type, a "colloquy" or expression of "interaction" ("The Nut-Brown Maid," for example). And there is one final possibility, in which (as in Meredith's sequence, "Modern Love") "a framework of action—some sort of general action not serving as a plot" becomes the *occasion* for lyric poems. And Olson concludes that

> In the lyric of mental experience or activity, that experience or activity is primary. In the lyric of the verbal act, it is no longer primary but merely a factor of the act. In the lyric of colloquy, the verbal act is no longer primary but a factor in the colloquy. And so on: each is sublated in the next.

We are now approaching those imitative works based upon a *system* of actions, in other words the "maximal forms" of tragedy and comedy.

Tragedy and the Theory of Drama and *The Theory of Comedy* are "poetics" in the full sense of the term, since they rest on definitions which discriminate among emotional effects. (The argument of the book on tragedy is the familiar Aristotelian one, expanded and extended, but constructed from the point of view of "the working dramatist.") Comedy, like tragedy, depends upon a system of actions producing a determinate effect, but the effect of comedy, of course, is quite different. Here the end is that kind of laughter which is evoked when we experience the "ridiculous," and the ridiculous, in turn, is the name we give to those situations in which an initial estimation of seriousness is reversed: "In other words, when we see something as ridiculous after having taken it seriously, we learn not merely that we were mistaken in taking it seriously, that there was inadequate ground for doing so; we are also impelled to take the contrary view of it, because of a *manifest* absurdity." The emotion proper to comedy, then, is

> a relaxation, or as Aristotle would say, a *katastasis*, of concern due to a manifest absurdity of the grounds for concern.... We can see now why this is a pleasant emotion, for concern of any kind involves tension; the relaxation of concern involves...the settling of the soul into its natural or normal condition, which is always pleasant.... Tragedy endows with worth; comedy takes worth away. Tragedy exhibits life as directed to important ends; comedy as either not directed to such ends, or unlikely to achieve them.

For over forty years Elder Olson has been making a sustained case for a way of thinking about the arts and their moral powers which begins with Plato and Aristotle, for all their differences, but is no longer fashionable. It may never be fashionable again; and if this is the case, then it says something troubling about the world we think we want to live in (for an eloquent examination of *that* problem, readers should turn to Booth's *Modern Dogma and the Rhetoric of Assent*). What we may be in danger of losing is a generous view of the arts and at the same time a controlling sense that pleasing, complex and valuable as they may be, they exist to serve other ends. In "On Value Judgments in the Arts" Olson concludes that there are

> values and kinds and degrees and quantities and orders of values, and we come to know the *Summum Bonum* in each art as we do the *Summum Bonum* in life. We come to know more about art as we come to know more about life, and we begin to realize its true importance only when we realize that, important as art is, it would not be so important if other things were not *more* important. And our conception of art and its values must be qualified always by the reflection that we shall never know all about them, but that neither this fact nor the inexactness of the subject gives us license for imprecision. We shall never know all about art or the values of art until all art is at an end; meanwhile, artists will continue to instruct us.

PEARCE, Roy Harvey. American. Born in Chicago, Illinois, 2 December 1919. Educated at the University of California at Los Angeles, B.A. 1940 (Phi Beta Kappa), M.A. 1942; Johns Hopkins University, Baltimore, Ph.D. 1945. Married Marie Jeanette Vandenberg in 1947; has two children. Instructor, 1945-46, and Associate Professor, 1949-54, Ohio State University, Columbus; Assistant Professor, 1946-49, and Professor, 1954-63, University of California, Berkeley. Since 1963, Professor of American Literature, University of California at San Diego; also, Associate Dean of Graduate Studies and Research, 1968-71, and Dean of Graduate Studies, 1971-75. Visiting Professor, Johns Hopkins University, Salzburg Seminar in American Literature, 1954, and Claremont Graduate School, California, Summer 1960; Fulbright Lecturer, University of Bordeaux, 1961-62; Visiting Professor, Columbia University Teachers College, New York, 1963. Member of the Committee, International Exchange of Persons, 1963-66. Since 1946, Member of the Editorial Board, *English Literary History*; since 1962, Editor, with others, Centenary Edition of the Works of Nathaniel Hawthorne. Recipient: American Council of Learned Societies Resident Fellowship, 1947, 1958, 1959, 1977, and Faculty Study Fellowship, 1950; Committee for Midwestern Studies Fellowship, 1950; Fund for the Advancement of Education Fellowship, 1953; Poetry Society of America Poetry Chap Book Award, 1962; Guggenheim Fellowship, 1975. Fellow of the American Anthropological Association and the American Academy of Arts and Sciences. Address: Office of Graduate Studies and Research, University of California at San Diego, La Jolla, California 92037, U.S.A.

PUBLICATIONS

Criticism

Introduction to *Dissertation on the Progress of the Fine Arts*, by John Robert Scott. Los Angeles, University of California William Andrews Clark Memorial Library, 1954.
The Growth of American Literature, with E.H. Cady and Frederick J. Hoffman. New York, American Book Company, 1956.
The Continuity of American Poetry. Princeton, New Jersey, Princeton University Press, 1961.
Introduction to *Leaves of Grass* (facsimile edition), by Walt Whitman. Ithaca, New York, Great Seal Books, 1961.
Historicism Once More: Problems and Occasions for the American Scholar. Princeton, New Jersey, Princeton University Press, 1969.
"The Cry and the Occasion: 'Chocorua to Its Neighbor,' " in *Southern Review* (Baton Rouge, Louisiana), 15, 1979.
"Toward Decreation: Stevens and the 'Theory of Poetry,' " in *Wallace Stevens: A Celebration*, edited by Frank Doggett and Robert Buttel. Princeton, New Jersey, Princeton University Press, 1980.

Other

The Savages of America: A Study of the Indian and the Idea of Civilization. Baltimore, Johns Hopkins University Press, 1953; revised edition as *Savagism and Civilization: A Study of the Indian and the American Mind*, 1967.

Editor, with William Matthews, *American Diaries: An Annotated Bibliography of American Diaries Written Prior to the Year 1861*. Berkeley and Los Angeles, University of California Press, 1945.
Editor, *Colonial American Writing*. New York, Rinehart, 1950; revised edition, Holt Rinehart, 1969.
Editor, *Whitman: A Collection of Critical Essays*. Englewood Cliffs, New Jersey, Prentice Hall, 1962.
Editor, *Hawthorne Centenary Essays*. Columbus, Ohio State University Press, 1964.
Editor, with J. Hillis Miller, *The Act of the Mind: Essays on the Poetry of Wallace Stevens*. Baltimore, Johns Hopkins University Press, 1965.
Editor, *Experience in the Novel*. New York, Columbia University Press, 1968.

*   *   *

Borrowing a phrase from Melville, Roy Harvey Pearce calls *The Continuity of American Poetry* an "inside narrative" whose "real subject" is "the dignity of man in the United States." The special achievement of American poetry, he proposes,

is a good measure of the achievement of American culture as a whole. The poet's particular relation to his culture—his self-imposed obligation to make the best possible use of the language he is given—is such as to put him at the center of the web of communications which gives his culture its characteristic spirit and style. He asks— above all, in the United States he has asked—how much it has cost to achieve them. And he measures the cost in terms of something as simple, and as difficult, as his sense of the dignity of man.

The best American poets have always defended what Pearce calls elsewhere our *"humanitas"*;

like Hawthorne, they have said "NO! in thunder" to the conventional pieties and compromises and insisted that freedom is the essential condition of dignity:

> The conditions of modern life, of nineteenth- and twentieth-century life, have in the United States as elsewhere brought the poet to discover in the antinomian impulse a necessary means to the freedom without which there could not be a full sense of that sort of community in which men may realize the dignity that makes them human. The American poet...has had as his abiding task the reconciliation of the impulse to freedom with the impulse to community, as the use of language in poetry may help bring it about.

In poetry above all, language "transmits *values*" and

> an awareness of the infinite degree of choice involved in being "for" or "against" something; of wanting or not wanting it, of desiring or fearing it, and also the means of knowing, projecting, and judging that awareness. Poetry is thus a means whereby...we may be made aware of the values of a culture as they have (and have not) made possible the communal life of the individuals of whom it is composed. A history of poetry so conceived is necessarily an "inside narrative." Inside the narrative, if only we will read it carefully enough, we may yet find ourselves as we were: as we might well have been were we not as we are, living now instead of then.

For Pearce there are really two traditions or lines of continuity in American poetry:

> Its denouement, then, is bound up in the fact of that insistent opposition: the egocentric as against the theocentric, man without history as against history without man, the antinomian as against the orthodox, personality as against culture, the Adamic as against the mythic.

Eliot represents the extreme development of the mythic view of man; Stevens represents the extreme development of the Adamic view and seems to bear the greater burden: "The terrible predicament of the writer in the egocentric tradition is that he must, by his own definition of his task, take all forms of knowledge as his province and is therefore driven to set himself in opposition to those who say, by a definition they derive from their sense of tradition, that this is impossible." As readers we "want it both ways," but from the seventeenth century onwards our best poets "have said that we can have it only one way or the other." Yet Pearce uses the term "denouement" and presumably accepts its implications; and he also speaks of establishing a "proper balance" between the Adamic and the mythic perspectives. *How* this is to be accomplished he never indicates: if there can be no common ground between the poet who wrote "Sunday Morning" and the poet who wrote *Ash Wednesday* it is difficult to see how there can be any common ground between readers who take these poets seriously. In his disconcerting last chapter Pearce seems to beg—or simply to erase—the question of opposing perspectives:

> In the long run, the grounds for the defense [of man]—radically humanistic as in the Adamic tradition, ultimately Christian as in the mythic tradition—really do not matter. For, defending man, they have defended the idea of poetry. That is to say, they have defended the idea of man as maker....

In any event and by whatever logic, Pearce somehow envisions a synthesis between the Adamic and mythic traditions which will do justice to individual "men" and not merely to the abstract concept "man." The achievements of these two traditions are real enough, but they were gained "at a great sacrifice":

> For *men*, the whole texture of relationships which ineluctably goes with the idea of *men*, have had in the course of that triumph no major defender—at least among poets. Men cannot be defended until the sense of the Adamic and the mythic have been restored to their proper balance, until the ground of poetry is taken to be not only the poet but the very history which, with his poems, he helps make and the community he helps build.

431

The opposition between Stevens and Eliot can be repeated endlessly but permits no further development: with these poets "we have come to the end of a line." And at this crucial point Pearce becomes vague once again. There are poets writing now, he suggests, who "do try unashamedly to comprehend love, family, and community, do try to proclaim the brotherhood of man" and who "want to make poetry once more something that is spoken and heard, not just read and meditated." But he gives no names (the book was written in 1961 and comes from California: is it possible he had some of the Beats in mind? If not—if the possibility is embarrassing—he should have been more specific).

Except for its puzzling last chapter, *The Continuity of American Poetry* is intelligible enough in its own terms and frequently helpful. If readers want an explicit defense of the method Pearce uses here, they should turn to the title-essay of *Historicism Once More*. What Pearce argues for in this long and often tedious defense of historicism is essentially what critics in the hermeneutic tradition refer to, very concisely, as the distinction between "original" and "anachronistic" meaning. Whatever we make of a text now, we should be aware of and respect the meaning it had for the writer and his original audience. The New Critics, Pearce asserts, tended to isolate literature and to dismiss the matrix of values it sprang from and in turn preserved or modified. But for the properly "historical" critic,

> Pastness in a literary work is an aspect—a vital, authentic aspect, a *sine qua non*—of presentness. The work of art may well live forever as the creation of a man like other men before and after him. But an integral part of its life, of its formal quality, will derive from the fact that it was created at a time, and for and of a time. Thus, and thus only, is literature possible. Thus, and thus only, does it become what it is.

And finally,

> The value of a literary work, we can conclude, may be measured precisely as it is a whole structure whose very ordering into wholeness is set by its realization of its potential of *humanitas*. Literature is not an expression of (or above) history, but rather an expression *in* history. The greatness of a literary work is an index and an assessment of the possibilities for greatness of the culture out of which it has come. Literature is for both writer and reader—although in different measure and to differing immediate ends—an act of commitment to, and a full and humble acknowledgment of, that possibility.... All cultures, thus, through their great writers, manifest the *possibility* of greatness. What art teaches us is the degree to which that possibility has been realized.

PECKHAM, Morse. American. Born in Yonkers, New York, 17 August, 1914. Educated at the University of Rochester, New York, B.A. 1935; Princeton University, New Jersey, M.A. 1938, Ph.D. 1947. Served in the United States Army Air Force, 1941-46: Bronze Star. Assistant Professor, The Citadel, Charleston, South Carolina, 1938-41; Instructor, 1946-47, and Assistant Professor, 1948-49, Rutgers University, New Brunswick, New Jersey; Assistant Professor, 1949-52, Associate Professor, 1952-61, Director of the Institute for Humanistic Research, 1953-54, and of the University Press, 1953-55, and Professor, 1961-67, University of Pennsylvania, Philadelphia. Since 1967, Distinguished Service Professor of English and Comparative Literature, University of South Carolina, Columbia. Address: Department of English, University of South Carolina, Columbia, South Carolina 29208, U.S.A.

Publications

Criticism

Man's Rage for Chaos: Biology, Behavior, and the Arts. Philadelphia, Chilton, 1965.
Art and Pornography: An Experiment in Explanation. New York, Basic Books, 1969.
The Triumph of Romanticism: Collected Essays. Columbia, University of South Carolina Press, 1970.
Romanticism and Behavior: Collected Essays II. Columbia, University of South Carolina Press, 1976.
"The Infinitude of Pluralism," in *Critical Inquiry* (Chicago), 3, 1977.
" 'Literature': Disjunction and Redundancy," in *What Is Literature?* edited by Paul Hernadi. Bloomington and London, Indiana University Press, 1978.
"The Intentional Fallacy," in *New Orleans Review* (Louisiana), 1, 1979.
"Three Notions About Criticism," in *What Is Criticism?* edited by Paul Hernadi. Bloomington and London, Indiana University Press, 1981.

Other

A Humanistic Re-education for the Corporation Executive. White Plains, New York, Fund for Adult Education, 1957.
Humanistic Education for Business Executives: An Essay in General Education. Philadelphia, University of Pennsylvania Press, 1960.
Beyond the Tragic Vision: The Quest for Identity in the Nineteenth Century. New York, Braziller, 1962.
Victorian Revolutionaries: Speculation on Some Heroes of a Culture Crisis. New York, Braziller, 1970.
Explanation and Power: The Control of Human Behavior. New York, Seabury Press, 1979.

Editor, *The Origin of Species: A Variorum Text*, by Charles Darwin. Philadelphia, University of Pennsylvania Press, 1959.
Editor, with Seymour Chatman, *Word, Meaning, Poem: An Anthology of Poetry.* New York, Crowell, 1961.
Editor, *Romanticism: The Culture of the Nineteenth Century.* New York, Braziller, 1965.
Editor, *Paracelsus*, by Robert Browning. Athens, Ohio State University Press, 1969.
Editor, *Poems and Ballads* and *Atalanta in Calydon*, by Swinburne. Indianapolis, Bobbs Merrill, 1970.
Editor, with Philip McFarland and Sharon Breakstone, *Reflections in Literature.* Boston, Houghton Mifflin, 1972.

*   *   *

"For years," Morse Peckham explained in 1967, "I have been engaged in an effort to introduce into the study of literature the instability of scientific theory." Properly understood, this summary statement (which Peckham makes in "Literary Interpretation as Conventionalized Verbal Behavior," now reprinted in *The Triumph of Romanticism*) will account for his elaborate arguments in *Man's Rage for Chaos*, his persistent—and influential—interest in "Romanticism," and the important connection between these two concerns.

"Instability" is not a perjorative term here. Science has made phenomenal progress because it recognizes, as Darwin put it, that a natural law is a mental convenience, nothing more. That is, "laws" are not facts of nature or disclosures of fixed, objective attributes, but rather human constructions, hypotheses, or "orientations," which may be revised or discarded as new situations and needs arise. Any discipline which is not self-correcting or "unstable" in this special sense is doomed to triviality and irrelevance. Thus like medieval science, traditional aesthetics, with its inflexible assumptions and categories, is "bankrupt"; whether we like it or not, Peckham asserts, the empirical and experimental methods of modern science constitute the "recognized model for meaningful and valid interpretations of the world in which we find ourselves." And sooner or later, he concludes, "it will be recognized that the study of literature belongs to the behavioral sciences."

The particular behavioral model which governs *Man's Rage for Chaos* is that of the organism trying to adapt itself to a purely natural environment: to maintain ourselves we modify our behavior or, sometimes, the environment itself. The ideal condition is homeostasis—the only sin, as Santayana once observed, is "the original sin of unfitness." But of course something is always going wrong in the environment. We approach new situations in terms of strategies for coping derived from earlier, similar (or similar-seeming) situations. And since no two experiences are ever exactly the same, there is often bound to be a gap or "mismatch" between the new data and the old orientation. The result is "cognitive tension," which, if endured, may lead to a new, more encompassing orientation. Peckham summarizes his position conveniently in "Art and Disorder" (also reprinted in *The Triumph of Romanticism*):

> Perception, then, selects, simplifies, reduces, and organizes. That such behavior is adaptational, or biologically functional, is obvious. But on the other hand, the very character of perception, which enables us successfully to find our way about in the world, is the element of our behavior which disqualifies us for successful adaptation. The reason is that the perceptual model must eliminate data which are essential to successful situational adaptation. The hunter concentrating on spearing a charging lion ignores the tickling of the poisonous spider; the man with a fear of all authority misses the data which if properly observed would have shown him how to defeat the authority, when it was to his interest to do so. The very aspect of our behavior which qualifies us to deal with the environment disqualifies us. Functional perception is dysfunctional as well ....Given this condition, there must be some form of human activity which is devoted to the practice or rehearsal of the endurance of cognitive tension; and this rehearsal must occur in situations in which nothing is at stake, in which the appearance or nonappearance of a genuine problem is a matter of indifference. That activity is, I believe, artistic behavior....

In the last chapter of *Man's Rage for Chaos* he writes

> Man desires above all a predictable and ordered world, a world to which he is oriented, and this is the motivation behind the role of the scientist. But because man desires such a world so passionately, he is very much inclined to ignore anything that intimates that he does not have it. And to anything that disorients him, anything that requires him to experience cognitive tension he ascribes negative value. Only in protracted situations, characterized by high walls of psychic insulation, can he afford to let himself be aware of the disparity between his interests, that is, his expectancy or set or orientation, and the data his interaction with the environment actually produces.

Art offers "precisely this kind of experience":

> Art tells us nothing about the world that we cannot find elsewhere and more reliably. Art does not make us better citizens, or more moral, or more honest. It may conceivably make us worse. It is easy to become addicted to art; it can be as dangerous as any drug. Art is something of a nuisance; it has certainly ruined the teakettle and, on the whole, the house. The great poetry of the past, if we take it too seriously, is capable of teaching us the most revolting nonsense. Dante is a prime example. Clearly the perception of art and the affective response to its signs and its discontinuities prepare us for no mode of behavior, no role, no pattern, no style. But it *is* preparation. Of the various possibilities of the dramatic metaphor, art fits most easily into rehearsal.
>
> We rehearse for various roles all our lives, and for various patterns of behavior. We rehearse our national, our local, and our personal styles. These things we rehearse so that

we may participate in a predictable world of social and environmental interaction. But we must also rehearse the power to perceive the failure, the necessary failure, of all those patterns of behavior. Art, as an adaptational mechanism, is reinforcement of the ability to be aware of the disparity between behavioral pattern and the demands consequent upon the interaction with the environment. Art is rehearsal for those real situations in which it is vital for our survival to endure cognitive tension, to refuse the comforts of validation by affective congruence when such validation is inappropriate because too vital interests are at stake; art is the reinforcement of the capacity to endure disorientation so that a real and significant problem may emerge. Art is the exposure to the tensions and problems of a false world so that man may endure exposing himself to the tensions and problems of the real world....Art offers man an entry into a fraudulent and deceiving world, but it is necessary. Art is an expensive nuisance, but it is necessary. It is a biological adaptation which serves to keep man alive, capable of perceiving that he is neither adequate nor inadequate but a perilous mixture of the two, capable of innovation. Art is rehearsal for the orientation which makes innovation possible....Of all man's burdens, art is one of the most terrible and certainly the most necessary. Without it he would not, he could not be human. But of that burden, with effort, with skill, with intelligence, and above all with luck, it is perhaps possible—at least for the very old—to be free.

Niels Bohr once observed that "the opposite of a correct statement is a false statement. But the opposite of a profound truth may well be another profound truth." If we accept the traditional view that art is primarily an affair of order, then Peckham's claim that it is equally an affair of disorder may be, if not another profound truth, at least a complementary truth worth thinking about seriously. The problem here may be partly rhetorical: in his enthusiasm Peckham often talks as though disorder rather than order were the primary characteristic of art; in moments of moderation, however, he seems willing to accept what most of us have never doubted, namely, that all works of art establish a pattern of expectations ("tonality" in music, for example, or "iambic pentameter" in serious verse) and then, for good reasons, vary or depart from that pattern. But without a governing background of order we could hardly perceive disorder—or anything else, for that matter. Thus Peckham's discussion of rhythmic discontinuities in poetry are not convincing because he deliberately isolates metrical effects from other large controlling devices. (See, for example, his analysis of the opening lines of *Paradise Lost*. Granted that there are departures from the iambic pentameter pattern here, there are also important generic understandings here which maintain "order.") Peckham's claims are sweeping: at his worst he is an arrogant dilettante whose arguments concerning music and the visual arts readers will have to watch carefully. (For a masterful example of what an expert critic of this persuasion *can* accomplish, readers should investigate Leonard Meyer's *Emotion and Meaning in Music*).

Once the reader has understood Peckham's basic position he is almost certain to be troubled by a wide range of unanswered questions. Let me raise only two here. If we agree that a work of art involves a cunning interplay between satisfying and frustrating tendencies, then clearly the work should have its greatest—and most beneficial—impact when we experience it for the first time. After that the discontinuities themselves become predictable and the work will wear out for us (as Peckham seems close to admitting at points). How then are we to account for the fact that for many trained readers and listeners even fairly uncomplicated works are often the source of increasing pleasure and satisfaction? More important, perhaps: it takes an experienced listener to perceive the "disorder" of a Bach fugue, a more experienced listener to "hear" the music of Schönberg properly, and a still more expert listener to hear the music of, say, Elliott Carter. As Nabokov once said, his ideal audience would be a lot of little Nabokovs. In other words, real perception of order and disorder is often limited to a very small elite. The average listener will find Bach "monotonous"; the average reader will find *Pale Fire* unintelligible. For most men art has never been as crucially important as Peckham seems to assume. And yet he clearly believes that the loss of art would be nothing less, as I.A. Richards once put it, than a "biological calamity" for the human race—and not merely for a sophisticated elite.

As for "Romanticism," Peckham confidently asserts that this nineteenth century movement was "the profoundest cultural transformation in human history since the invention of the city." In his first and most influential essay on Romanticism ("Toward a Theory of Romanticism," first published in 1950), he defines that transformation as essentially the substitution of one model of the cosmos for another. The "mighty, static metaphysic" of nature as a perfectly ordered machine "collapsed of its own internal inconsistencies in the late eighteenth century— or collapsed for some people." The metaphor of the faultless machine was replaced by the more adequate metaphor of a developing organism:

> What then is Romanticism? Whether philosophic, theologic, or aesthetic, it is the revolution in the European mind against thinking in terms of static mechanism and the redirection of the mind to thinking in terms of dynamic organicism. Its values are change, imperfection, growth, diversity, the creative imagination, the unconscious.

And to account for such "failed" Romantics as Byron, Peckham devises the term "Negative Romanticism." Fully developed Romantic works such as "The Rime of the Ancient Mariner," *The Prelude*, and *Sartor Resartus* are about

> spiritual death and rebirth, or secular conversion. In its baldest form, such an experience amounts to this: A man moves from a trust in the universe to a period of doubt and despair of any meaning in the universe, and then to a reaffirmation of faith in cosmic meaning and goodness, or at least meaning. The transition from the first stage to the second we may call spiritual death; from the second to the third we may call spiritual rebirth.

Negative Romanticism on the other hand, is "the expression of the attitudes, the feelings, and the ideas of a man who has left static mechanism but has not yet arrived at a reintegration of his thought and art in terms of dynamic organicism."

In his later essays on Romanticism Peckham makes several modifications of his basic definition, the most important of which concerns the nature of values. What seems most important to him now is the growing realization on the part of many nineteenth-century artists and philosophers that values are neither transcendental nor immanent, but essentially human constructions. He divides the search for identity and validation into four major stages, the last of which culminates in Nietzsche's discovery that the only "reality" is human history:

> And so Nietzsche's work is the triumph of Romanticism, for he solved the problem of value and returned the Romantic to history, by showing that there is no ground to value and no escape from history. As the Romantic had always known but had never, until Nietzsche, been able to believe, reality is history, and only the experience of reality has value, an experience to be achieved by creating illusions so that we may live and by destroying them so that we may recover our freedom. Value is process, a perpetual weaving and unweaving of our own identities. Sorrow is a sentimental lust for finality: joy is the penetration beyond that sentimentality into the valuelessness of reality, into its freedom, the achievement of which is inevitably its loss. Joy is the eternal recurrence of the same problem, forever solved and forever unsolvable. Nietzsche found what the Romantics had sought for a hundred years, a way of encompassing, without loss of tension, the contrarieties and paradoxes of human experience.

The crucial connection between *Man's Rage for Chaos*, *Beyond the Tragic Vision*, and *The Triumph of Romanticism* may now be a little clearer. "My whole argument," Peckham admits, "amounts, one way or another, to the assertion that the Romantics discovered [the human imposition of values] to be the center of the human position, and that modern perceptual theory has confirmed their discovery over and over again, as well as much modern philosophy." Romanticism rests on the most adequate model of human behavior we have yet devised; as the remarks about Nietzsche suggest, Romanticism carries within itself the self-correcting principle of "instability" and thus has proved to be remarkably durable:

> modern culture, in its vital areas, is a Romantic culture, and...nothing has yet replaced it. Since the logic of Romanticism is that contradictions must be included in a single orientation, but without pseudo-reconciliations, Romanticism is a remarkably stable and fruitful orientation. For the past 175 years the Romantic has been the tough-minded

man, determined to create value and project order to make feasible the pure assertion of identity, determined to assert identity in order to engage with reality simply because it is there and because there is nothing else, and knowing eventually that his orientations are adaptive instruments and that no orientation is or can be final. The Romantic artist does not escape from reality; he escapes into it.

Of course it is hardly surprising that Romanticism has been so durable if we define it as a kind of tough-minded naturalism which insists that man is the creator of his own values: it could be threatened only by an unlikely revival of some form of transcendentalism or by those thoroughly irrational, nihilistic works Peckham has considered briefly in some of his later essays. In any event, the lesson for prospective critics is clear. Like any other inflexible discipline, criticism is useless unless it becomes contextual and "behavioral" by incorporating the instability principle which has been the salvation of science and Romanticism.

Obviously, everything Peckham has to say about literature finally depends upon his conception of human behavior, a matter he has now taken up at great length in *Explanation and Power*. The argument here is long and complex, but basically comes down to something like this: society demands for its survival the control of individual human behavior, and controls this behavior largely by endorsing and institutionalizing certain kinds of "meanings." These meanings, however, are not inherent in language itself; statements are not primarily referential but really exist as implied commands. The "true" meaning of an utterance is contextual and must be understood in terms of the *results* it engenders. In " 'Literature': Disjunction and Redundancy," a short essay which repeats many of the central points of *Explanation and Power*, Peckham maintains that

> Culture, in the full, anthropological, sense, consists of sets of directions for a performance, and language is subsumed by culture. Even "descriptive" statements—such as, "There is a mouse in the corner over there"—are in their full form instructions for a performance: "If you look in the corner over there, you will see a mouse—if he's still there."

But how is it that society is able to "direct" our performances so successfully so much of the time?

> Why is there not far greater deviance than there is? In any society there is, statistically speaking, only very little. (Wealthier societies can tolerate far more than can poor societies.) The answer, I believe, lies in the phenomenon of redundancy, the endless repetition of the same verbal (and non-verbal, under the control of the verbal) instructions in various verbal and non-verbal semiotic modes.

Thus society will sanction many kinds of literary or "fictive" utterances precisely because they are redundant and thereby reinforce desirable meanings, that is, controlled behavior. And yet at the same time, the human brain has as its "most remarkable product" the capacity for "randomness," for "deviance, innovation, creativity [and] imagination"; and it is precisely this capacity which literature may also embody. In periods of social change ("economic disengagement," as Peckham calls it), such literature has its great chance:

> The justification for the teaching of literature is that, by providing exemplifications of a variety of ideologies, it modifies the overall behavior of the student in the direction of flexibility. As situations change, patterns of economically engaged behavior must change. A certain portion of society, gradually sifted for decisions at a higher socio-economic level, is trained by the literature of high culture in perceiving the possibilities of alternative modes of behavior and alternative ideologies, and in randomness and innovation.

Literature thus has a double capacity: it can maintain the redundancies of a culture and it may also be able to change them: "Thus it has the power to support the economic interactional patterns of its culture, to modify them, and to destroy them." In *Explanation and Power* Peckham asserts that the only fruitful ideological commitment is a commitment to an ideology of noncommitment. Were that established, then a truly democratic social situation might emerge—not one that is free of hierarchy, for institutional hierarchy is no more than explanatory regression, and that is the condition of human existence—but rather a social situation in which throughout all institutions negative feedback could be fed upward with impunity or at least with greater impunity than is now the circumstance for all of us.

Presumably it is the function of literature and of criticism to keep open those channels of "negative feedback" and thus counteract oppressive social control. Peckham is not particulary hopeful about the future, however, and for a basic reason which takes us back to the argument of *Man's Rage for Chaos*. As individuals we are creatures for whom total control and blank freedom are equally intolerable extremes. At the conclusion of *Explanation and Power* Peckham observes sadly that

> Truly the individual is catch-22, for there is nothing but the individual organism, behaving, and by that device we call semiosis turning behavior into performance. The behavioral individual is the precipitate of semiosis and culture and redundancies and institutions and ultimate sanctions; he is the irreducible surd of existence, the fundamental incoherence of human life, for he cannot but strive with all his might, with all his aggressiveness, for stability; and yet at the same time he is the only source of that randomization from which issue emergent innovations—which if they cannot eliminate can at least modify, and not infrequently for the better, our fictive and normative absurdities of explanation.

POIRIER, Richard (William). American. Born in Gloucester, Massachusetts, 9 September 1925. Educated at the University of Paris, 1944-45; Amherst College, Massachusetts, B.A. 1949 (Phi Beta Kappa); Yale University, New Haven, Connecticut, M.A. 1951; Cambridge University (Fulbright Scholar), 1952-53; Harvard University, Cambridge, Massachusetts, Ph.D. 1959. Served in the United States Army, 1943-45. Instructor, Williams College, Williamstown, Massachusetts, 1950-52. Instructor, 1958-60, and Assistant Professor, 1960-63, Harvard University. Distinguished Professor of English, 1963-77, and since 1977 Marius Bewley Professor of English, Rutgers University, New Brunswick, New Jersey (Chairman, Department of English, 1963-72, and Director of Graduate Studies, 1972-80). Editor, *Partisan Review*, 1963-73, and since 1981, *Raritan Review*, New Brunswick. Recipient: Bollingen Foundation Fellowship, 1962; Guggenheim Fellowship, 1974-75; National Endowment for the Humanities Fellowship, 1978-79; Achievement Award, American Academy of Arts and Letters, 1979. D.H.L.: Amherst College, Massachusetts, 1978. Member, American Academy of Arts and Sciences, 1979. Address: Department of English, Rutgers University, New Brunswick, New Jersey 08903, U.S.A.

PUBLICATIONS

Criticism

The Comic Sense of Henry James: A Study of the Early Novels. New York, Oxford University Press, and London, Chatto and Windus, 1960.
A World Elsewhere: The Place of Style in American Literature. New York, Oxford University Press, 1966; London, Chatto and Windus, 1967.

The Performing Self: Compositions and Decompositions in the Languages of Contemporary Life.   New York, Oxford University Press, 1971.
Norman Mailer.   New York, Viking Press, and London, Fontana, 1972.
The Aesthetics of Contemporary American Radicalism (lecture).   Leicester, Leicester University Press, and New York, Humanities Press, 1972.
Robert Frost: The Work of Knowing.   New York, Oxford University Press, 1977; London, Oxford University Press, 1978.
"The Difficulties of Modernism and the Modernism of Difficulty," in *Images and Ideas in American Culture: The Function of Criticism: Essays in Memory of Philip Rahv*, edited by Arthur Edelstein.   Hanover, New Hampshire, Brandeis University Press, 1979.
"Correcting the Record," in *Salmagundi* (Saratoga Springs, New York), 52-53, 1981.
"Writing Off the Self," in *Raritan Review* (New Brunswick, New Jersey), 1, 1981.

Other

Editor, with Reuben A. Brower, *In Defense of Reading.*   New York, Dutton, 1962.
Editor, with W.L. Vance, *American Literature.*   Boston, Little Brown, 1970.
Editor, with Frank Kermode, *The Oxford Reader.*   New York, Oxford University Press, 1971.
Editor, *Prize Stories 1961-64: The O. Henry Awards.*   New York, Doubleday, 4 vols., 1961-64.
Editor, with William Abrahams, *Prize Stories 1965-66: The O. Henry Awards.*   New York, Doubleday, 2 vols., 1965, 1966.

*   *   *

In the first and most conventional of his critical studies, Richard Poirier argues that by using certain comic devices Henry James was able to heighten the dramatic opposition between "free" and "fixed" characters which is one of his primary concerns. Poirier limits himself to six relatively early novels, only one of which, *Confidence*, is comic in the traditional sense of having a fully resolved happy ending. He does not define comedy, however, nor does he indicate clearly the principle which makes these oppositions amusing at times, rather than tragic or simply ironic: in fact, since three of the novels are serious (*Roderick Hudson, The American*, and *Washington Square*), and since another of them at least verges on the tragic (*The Portrait of a Lady*), Poirier is dealing here with the tricky business of comic devices in the service of far from comic ends. *The Comic Sense of Henry James* is innocent of theory— disappointingly so—but from his commentaries on the individual novels and from a few brief references to Fielding, we can deduce the general characteristics of what Poirier probably means by the "comic."

For Fielding the source of comedy or laughter is the disclosure of the "ridiculous," specifically that kind of "affectation" which comes from "vanity or hypocrisy." Fielding's partial definition comes, in turn, from Aristotle (whom Poirier does not mention) and that passage in the *Poetics* in which he observes that comedy imitates or represents men

worse than average; worse, however, not as regards any and every sort of fault, but only as regards one particular kind, the Ridiculous, which is a species of the Ugly. The Ridiculous may be defined as a mistake or deformity not productive of pain or harm to others; the mask, for instance, that excites laughter, is something ugly and distorted without causing pain.

This "ugliness" is usually a kind of moral flaw or shortcoming, though one which, like the tragic flaw, falls short of true depravity or viciousness. Our response to comedy, then, presupposes a prior value judgment; and value judgments presuppose the existence of a standard or norm of desirable human characteristics. We admire those people whose qualities place them above the norm; we laugh at those who inhabit or slip into the world below—but not too far below—the norm. As Poirier's references to Fielding imply, it is also possible to locate and define the Jamesian "norm." The Jamesian hero or heroine is the "free" person who has the ability to develop a full and discriminating consciousness: James' method, Poirier goes on, "is to have all the characters measured by their relationship to an ideal of awareness and selflessness." The "fixed" characters fail to live up to this ideal and are therefore a source of comedy in some of the novels and a suitable foil for their "free" superiors. James' comedy thus "exposes and evaluates the difference between the 'free' and 'fixed' characters":

> Considering this aspect of comedy in James, we come to recognise features of his style that are seldom noticed: the witty and pointed verbal play, the exaggerated expression, the hyperbole in description by which...he satirizes all those who are not capable of reverence for impractical aspiration. Encouraged by James himself, we have been calling these characters "fixed," and we are not allowed to find extenuations for their inadequacies. They may amuse and even please, but they are wholly incapable of those evidences of feeling and intelligence which would direct us to probe beyond their loudly apparent grotesqueness....And finally, even the irony expended upon the heroic figures themselves tends to be affectionately partial to their aspiring habits of mind....It can be said that all of the novelistic devices of comic entertainment are used in these works to show the beauty of people who are intensely conscious and who desire much that cannot be satisfied by practical social means.

The *fate* of these vessels of consciousness is never, of course, comic: James' heroes and heroines grow, suffer and sacrifice; by refusing to become "fixed," they lose mere vulgar happiness and sometimes a good deal more. That James makes these distinctions, that his fine characters are often used and betrayed by their companions, that the opposition between them is sometimes sadly amusing (the contrast, for example, between Isabel Archer and Henrietta Stackpole)—none of this is new. But what gives Poirier's book its very real value is his close and sensitive readings of individual scenes and passages. He rightly points out that thematic and "symbolic" readings of James usually ignore the splendid surfaces of these novels. If the critic is "sophisticated enough" he may provide "that dizzying substitute for critical effort—a pattern of images, soon related to an abstraction and moulded into a dazzlingly efficient key, as the saying goes, to the meaning":

> But if such procedures save us labour, they also cheat us of our pleasure. To turn the pages of *The Europeans*, a consistently ignored masterpiece, and to experience the poised and resonant clarity of its style, to discover the variety of one's particular dramatic relationships to the narrative voice or the excitement of overhearing some of the wittiest dialogue in James's fiction—what has this to do with those mechanical schematizations about Europe and America which have inevitably obscured the understanding of this sophisticated and urbanely comic book?

Poirier's own commentaries on these early novels help to correct the situation he deplores here—particularly his long concluding chapter on *The Portrait of a Lady*, which is arguably the finest and most comprehensive essay we have on that novel. By this time, of course, he has gone far beyond his rather ordinary and loosely-defined conception of "comic" devices.

Freedom and the full development of the self are also the subject of Poirier's more complex second book, *A World Elsewhere*. Here he is interested in the ways in which the styles of a number of American novelists reflect the typically American desire to "create...an environment in which the inner consciousness of the hero-poet can freely express itself, an environment in which he can sound publicly what he privately is." But once again definitions prove to be something of a problem. "Style," Poirier explains, "refers to grammar, syntax, and tropes only by way of defining those more significant aspects of style: the sounds, identities, and presences shaped by these technical aspects of expression." Style, as he reminds us, is the man. But if we use "style" to mean "sounds, identities, and presences," then there is nothing in the writer which is *not* his style. Thus everything Poirier wishes to say about Emerson, Hawthorne, Twain, James, Dreiser and Edith Wharton (and others in passing) becomes a consideration of "style."

Only the sharpness of his individual commentaries makes up for the diffuseness of his general terms.

In any event, one of the chief tendencies of American novelists has been to make their characters (and thus themselves and their readers), in Santayana's words, "citizens, by anticipation, in the world we crave." It might be argued (as in fact Santayana does argue in *Interpretations of Poetry and Religion*) that it always has been the function of the imagination to project a better world and that unhampered freedom of being which the "real" world denies. Poirier seems willing to concede this, and to grant that the American desire for a world more suited to our egotistical yearnings is an obsessive development of a desire which characterizes all art, or at least all "Romantic" art: "All we can say is that American literature does offer us the most persistent, the most poignantly heroic example of a recurrent literary compulsion, not at all confined to our literature, to believe in the possibilities of a new style." "The greatest American authors really do try," he continues, "against the perpetually greater power of reality, to create an environment that might allow some longer existence to the hero's momentary expansions of consciousness." But unlimited freedom and development are impossible goals: sooner or later these writers are "forced to return their characters to prison"—the "prison," that is, of social and historical reality. And the unhappy returns are part of an even unhappier general movement in American literature as Poirier reads it:

> Not even a novelist so consciously protective of his characters' freedom as James could fail to give enormous weight to environmental forces antagonistic to it. The weight is proportionately heavier in Dreiser, Edith Wharton, and Fitzgerald, however, because their heroes are often anxious to surrender themselves to the powers that destroy them. The vision of the Self joining the formative processes of Nature, of the Self believing that it can contend for dominance with the forces of Nature, of the Self believing merely that it can define what it is—these notions give way, as literary situations, to an essentially twentieth-century vision of the Self enthralled (and destroyed) by the power and wealth of the City.

Still, Poirier is able to end on a tentative note of optimism:

> In Faulkner and Fitzgerald, in Nabokov and Mailer is a resurgence of the Emersonian dream of possibly "building" a world out of the self in a style that is that self. The effort in *Lolita* to preserve an "intangible island of entranced time" succeeds no more than did the efforts in [Cooper's] *The Crater*, over a hundred years before, to preserve an island paradise from the contaminations of modern democratic America. But such efforts are celebrated by these and by the other American writers perhaps because success *is* forbidden them by realities other than style, by exigencies of time and space. The effort is celebrated because even out of the perverse design of Nabokov's hero there emerges those marvels of human ingenuity, those exuberances of imagination, those extravagances of yearning that create the objects they yearn for—these are the evidences still in American literature of the continuing struggle toward some further created being and some other world.

Poirier's remarks about individual novels and writers are, as always, highly sophisticated—so much so that we are left wondering if he regards expansion of the self as an unqualified good. Is it too stuffy to suggest that Humbert Humbert *should* be talking to us from his "prison"?

In 1960 Poirier conducted a remarkable interview with Robert Frost, during which the poet recalled something he had said (or rather paraphrased from Horace) many years before: "No tears in the writer, no tears in the reader": if the writer wishes to move us, he must first be genuinely moved. In the interview Frost went on to make "another distinction":

> However sad, no grievance, grief without grievance. How could I, how could anyone have a good time with what cost me too much agony, how could they? What do I want to communicate but what a *hell* of a good time I had writing it? The whole thing is performance and prowess and feats of association. Why don't critics talk more about those things—what a feat it was to turn that away, and what a feat it was to remember that, to be reminded of this by that? Why don't they talk about that? Scoring. You've got

to score. They say not, but you've got to score, in all the realms—theology, politics, astronomy, history, and the country life around you.

This same concern with art as performance rather than artifact, and with criticism as a recreation of process rather than exploration of fixed structures, is at the heart of Poirier's collection of essays, *The Performing Self.* "The kind of writer or personality or group I most admire," he admits, "displays an unusual and even arduous energy of performance." Writing is a "form of energy" and should be experienced as such:

> The gap between the completed work, which is supposed to constitute the writer's vision, and the multiple acts of performance that went into it is an image of the gap between the artist's self as he discovered it in performance and the self, altogether less grimy, discovered afterward in the final shape and the world's reception of it. The question, responded to quite differently by the writers I'll be looking at, is simply this: which kind of power—of performance or of the contemplatable visions that can be deduced from their end results—is the more illusory when it comes to understanding a literary work? There is no answer to this question. Rather, it posits a condition within which any writer, and any critic, finds himself working. It is a question not of belief in meanings but in belief in one kind of power or energy and another—one kind in the supposed act of doing, the other in the supposed result.

Too much modern criticism has been concerned with books, he argues, rather than with "those manifestations of energy one might call *écriture*." It will be "terribly hard," he admits, "to make this shift of muscularity of mind and spirit from one allegedly elevated mode of expression, where the muscles can be most conveniently developed, to another mode of expression both more inaccessible and considered so ordinary, so natural as to be beyond inquiry." "And yet," he concludes, "in this transfer of activity and in the reciprocations that would follow from it, is the promise of some genuine interplay between different and multiplying cultural traditions." One might object that all expert teaching and criticism is "terribly hard": the question is whether or not the shift Poirier has in mind is even possible. What would this kind of criticism look like? His own discussion of the Beatles, for example, is not all that different from the kind of discussion we would expect from a conventional critic intent on understanding poetry. Nevertheless, Poirier's discontent with the limitations of modern academic criticism in America is genuine and justified. *The Performing Self* is a painful and restless book, provoked at least in part by America's involvement in Vietnam and the student unrest of the late 1960's. But the war stopped as it had begun, unaided by wisdom or compassion, and the administrators very easily regained control of the campuses. In retrospect Poirier's work suggests that by failing to explore new kinds of freedom, however hard they are to define, we may have lost something valuable.

Given Poirier's interest in the active performance a good work of literature embodies—and forces its readers to re-enact—it is not surprising that he should eventually turn to a major study of Robert Frost (who had of course provided the motto Poirier used before: "The whole thing is performance and prowess and feats of association"). As late as 1977 Poirier still felt it was necessary to tell readers that Frost is as difficult and subtle a poet as Yeats or Eliot—in a sense *more* difficult because of the deceptively simple surfaces which some of his most complex poems present ("All the fun," Frost once observed, "is outside, saying things that suggest formulae but don't quite formulate. I should like to be so subtle at this game as to seem to a casual person altogether obvious"). Compared to Eliot, Pound and Yeats, who are "difficult" but usually quite consistent and even doctrinaire once the reader knows the various religious, political and mythic perspectives they employ, Frost is often genuinely elusive and enigmatic. Poirier maintains that

> [Frost's] reiterations about the limits of metaphor and the boundaries of form are evidences not of fastidiousness or fear...so much as an effort to promote in writing and in reading an inquisitiveness about what cannot quite be signified.

Truth, William James proposed, is not the passive possession of a fixed vision: "Truth," he insisted, "is not a stagnant property....Truth is *made*, just as health, wealth and strength are made, in the course of experience." Thus once again, the emphasis is on performance, or to use the word Poirier prefers here, "work," the dynamic process by which, in the course of particular experiences, one comes to know as much as can be known about the nature of things. After a sensitive reading of Frost's sonnet, "She is as in a field a silken tent," Poirier concludes

> The whole poem is a performance, a display for the beloved while also being an exemplification of what it is like for a poem, as well as a tent or a person, to exist within the constrictions of space ("a field") and time ("at midday") wherein the greatest possible freedom is consistent with the intricacies of form and inseparable from them.

It would be unfair to insist that Poirier use only the kind of critical approach he had outlined in *The Performing Self*. Quite sensibly he uses whatever tools will work, and has produced what is certainly the best book we have on Frost, and possibly the best book we have on any major American poet. Poirier gives close readings when they are called for, is able to support generalizations which at first seem unwarranted ("Frost is a great poet of marriage, maybe the greatest since Milton"), and also uses larger organizing schemes to illustrate recurring issues in the poetry (the opposition, for example, between Frost's poetry of "home" and "extravagance," those periods of solitude and departure which can be dangerous—or enhancing. "Frost's poetry of home," he concludes, "is a dramatization of the human costs and human benefits of decorum"). For all his uncertainties, however, Frost is for Poirier finally a reassuring poet:

> Frost's poetry can therefore be said to include terror without itself being terrified; it is for the most part reassuring in that it leaves us feeling more rather than less confident about our capacities. His is unlike the poetry of most of his contemporaries, except Lawrence and Stevens, because while you may make your life more complicated by reading it, you do not make your life more unmanageable. You are not led to believe that life is unintelligible or that your capacity to make sense of it merely proves your triviality.

At the same time Poirier is able to be sharply critical of those poems in which Frost does "sell out" to his popular audience and has the courage to point out that "Directive," a poem which has been the object of uncritical awe ever since Randall Jarrell singled it out as a masterpiece, is really "a tricky and devious poem not because it has a lot to say but because it is not sure of what it does want to say, or do."

For any serious admirer of Frost one vexing problem remains: why is it that there is so little memorable verse after, say, 1935? Poirier does his best to call attention to what there is worth reading in the later poetry, but suggests that Frost's decline was the result of his own ambivalence about the times and the kind of reputation he had achieved:

> No matter how many honors he received from universities, no matter four Pulitzer Prizes...or the appreciation of distinguished fellow poets like Edward Thomas, Edwin Muir, Auden, Graves, Robert Penn Warren, and, later, Randall Jarrell, Robert Lowell, and Richard Wilbur, Frost in his lifetime was somehow denied the status accorded to Eliot by the consensus of the most respected kind of criticism. Like many other American writers who have been particularly successful, Frost never quite made his mark where it eventually came to matter most to him. What such writers finally want is the kind of sustained critical attention that will establish them securely within the academic curricula and at a central intersection on the literary-historical map.

Furthermore,

> In the thirties Frost began to suspect that the metaphors, including that of *laissez-faire*, which governed his thinking and his poetry were being substantially displaced within that national consciousness by two others. On the one hand, there were metaphors of "wasteland," or apocalyptic disillusion, against which individual resistance was presumably useless; and on the other, the metaphor of "planning," of the New Deal, of provision, which, as Frost saw it, was designed to relieve the individual of responsibility for his own fate.

Frost's insecurity may have led him into a kind of brash and self-indulgent assertiveness:

> when he becomes defensively explicit about [his politics and poetics] he reveals the cost of having spent a lifetime with mostly second-rate literary minds, or with academics, some of them brilliant men and women, who were bound to be deferential to the great man on campus, or with people ignorant of social theory....I am talking about his decisions, in specific poems, to propose himself to us as a poet whose thinking should matter, who chose to display a cogitating mind in verse, and was unembarrassed by the sometimes trivial results.

Poirier himself is being a bit defensive here, perhaps, but it hardly matters. His book is indispensable reading for anyone who cares about Frost, modern poetry, or the workings of the imagination.

POUND, Ezra (Weston Loomis). American. Born in Hailey, Idaho, 30 October 1885. Educated at Hamilton College, Clinton, New York, Ph.B. 1905; University of Pennsylvania, Philadelphia, M.A. 1906. Travelled in Spain, Italy and France, 1906-07; lived in London, 1908-20, in Paris, 1920-24, then in Italy until the end of World War II. One of the creators of the Imagist movement. English Editor of *Poetry*, Chicago, 1912-19; Founder, with Wyndham Lewis, of *Blast*, 1914; English Editor of *The Little Review*, 1917-19; Paris Correspondent of *The Dial*, 1922; Founder and Editor of *The Exile*, 1927-28. Broadcast over Italian Radio to the United States after 1941, and was arrested and jailed for these broadcasts by the United States Army in 1945; imprisoned near Pisa, found unfit to stand trial for treason, and committed to St. Elizabeth's Hospital, Washington, D.C.; released in 1958 and returned to Italy. Recipient: Dial Award, 1928; Academy of American Poets Fellowship, 1963. *Died 1 November 1972.*

PUBLICATIONS

Criticism

The Spirit of Romance. London, Dent, and New York, Dutton, 1910; revised edition, London, Peter Owen, and New York, New Directions, 1953.
"Noh" or Accomplishment: A Study of the Classical Stage of Japan, with Ernest Fenollosa. London Macmillan, 1916; New York, Knopf, 1917; as *The Classical Noh Theatre of Japan*, New York, New Directions, 1959.
Pavannes and Divisions. New York, Knopf, 1918.
Instigations. New York, Boni and Liveright, 1920.
Indiscretions; or, Une Revue de Deux Mondes. Paris, Three Mountains Press, 1923.
Imaginary Letters. Paris, Black Sun Press, 1930.
How to Read. London, Desmond Harmsworth, 1931; reprinted in *Literary Essays of Ezra Pound*, 1954.
ABC of Reading. London, Routledge, and New Haven, Connecticut, Yale University Press, 1934.
Make It New: Essays. London, Faber, 1934; New Haven, Connecticut, Yale University Press, 1935.
Polite Essays. London, Faber, 1937; New York, New Directions, 1940.
Literary Essays of Ezra Pound, edited by T.S. Eliot. London, Faber, and New York, New Directions, 1954.

Pavannes and Divagations.   New York, New Directions, 1958; London, Peter Owen, 1960.

Verse

A Lume Spento.   Venice, printed for the author by A. Antonini, 1908.
A Quinzaine for This Yule.   London, Pollock, 1908.
Personae.   London, Elkin Mathews, 1909.
Exultations.   London, Elkin Matthews, 1909.
Provença: Poems Selected from Personae, Exultations, and Canzoniere.   Boston, Small Maynard, 1910.
Canzoni.   London, Elkin Mathews, 1911.
Ripostes.   London, Stephen Swift, 1912; Boston, Small Maynard, 1913.
Lustra.   London, Elkin Mathews, 1916.
Lustra, with Earlier Poems.   New York, privately printed, 1917.
Quia Pauper Amavi.   London, The Egoist, 1919.
The Fourth Canto.   London, privately printed, 1919.
Umbra: The Early Poems.   London, Elkin Mathews, 1920.
Hugh Selwyn Mauberley.   London, Ovid Press, 1920.
Poems, 1918-21, Including Three Portraits and Four Cantos.   New York, Boni and Liveright, 1921.
A Draft of XVI Cantos.   Paris, Three Mountains Press, 1925.
Personae: The Collected Poems of Ezra Pound.   New York, Boni and Liveright, 1926; revised edition, New York, New Directions, 1949; as *Personae: Collected Shorter Poems*, London, Faber, 1952; as *Collected Shorter Poems*, Faber, 1968.
Selected Poems, edited by T.S. Eliot.   London, Faber and Gwyer, 1928.
A Draft of the Cantos 17-27.   London, John Rodker, 1928.
A Draft of XXX Cantos.   Paris, Hours Press, 1930; New York, Farrar and Rinehart, and London, Faber, 1933.
Homage to Sextus Propertius.   London, Faber, 1934.
Eleven New Cantos: XXXI-XLI.   New York, Farrar and Rinehart, 1934; as *A Draft of Cantos XXXI-XLI*, London, Faber, 1935.
Alfred Venison's Poems, Social Credit Themes (as The Poet of Titchfield Street).   London, Nott, 1935.
The Fifth Decad of Cantos.   London, Faber, and New York, Farrar and Rinehart, 1937.
A Selection of Poems.   London, Faber, 1940.
Cantos LII-LXXI.   London, Faber, and New York, New Directions, 1940.
The Pisan Cantos.   New York, New Directions, 1948; London, Faber, 1949.
The Cantos.   New York, New Directions, 1948; revised edition, 1965; revised edition, as *Cantos No. 1-117, 120*, 1970.
Selected Poems.   New York, New Directions, 1949.
Seventy Cantos.   London, Faber, 1950; revised edition, as *The Cantos*, 1954, 1964, 1976.
Section: Rock-Drill: 86-95 de los cantares.   Milan, All'Insegna del Pesce d'Oro, 1955; New York, New Directions, 1956; London, Faber, 1957.
Thrones: 96-109 de los Cantares.   Milan, All'Insegna del Pesce d'Oro, and New York, New Directions, 1959; London, Faber, 1960.
A Lume Spento and Other Early Poems.   New York, New Directions, 1965; London, Faber, 1966.
Canto CX.   Cambridge, Massachusetts, Sextant Press, 1965.
Selected Cantos.   London, Faber, 1967; New York, New Directions, 1970.
Cantos, 110-116.   New York, F.U. Press, 1967.
Drafts and Fragments, Cantos CX-CXVII.   New York, New Directions, 1968; London, Faber, 1970.
Selected Poems 1908-1959.   London, Faber, 1975.
Collected Early Poems, edited by Michael John King.   New York, New Directions, 1976; London, Faber, 1977.

Other

Gaudier-Brzeska: A Memoir. London and New York, Lane, 1916; revised edition, Hessle, Yorkshire, Marvell Press, 1960; New York, New Directions, 1961.

Antheil and The Treatise on Harmony. Paris, Three Mountains Press, 1924; Chicago, Covici, 1927.

ABC of Economics. London, Faber, 1933; New York, New Directions, 1940.

Social Credit: An Impact. London, Nott, 1935.

Jefferson and/or Mussolini. London, Nott, 1935; New York, Liveright, 1936; revised edition, as *Jefferson e Mussolini*, Venice, Casa Editrice delle Edizioni Popolari, 1944.

Guide to Kulchur. London, Faber, 1938; as *Culture*, New York, New Directions, 1938.

What Is Money For? London, Greater Britain Publications, 1939.

Carta da Visita. Rome, Edizioni di Lettere d'Oggi, 1942; translated by John Drummond, as *A Visiting Card*, London, Peter Russsell, 1952.

L'America, Roosevelt, e le Cause della Guerra Presente. Venice, Casa Editrice delle Edizioni Popolari, 1944; translated by John Drummond, as *America, Roosevelt, and the Causes of the Present War*, London, Peter Russell, 1951.

Oro e Lavoro. Rapallo, Tip. Moderna, 1944; translated by John Drummond, as *Gold and Labour*, London, Peter Russell, 1952.

Introduzione alla Natura Economica degli S.U.A. Venice, Casa Editrice delle Edizioni Popolari, 1944; translated by Carmine Amore, as *An Introduction to the Economic Nature of the United States*, London, Peter Russell, 1950.

Orientamenti. Venice, Casa Editrice delle Edizioni Popolari, 1944.

If This Be Treason. Siena, Olga Rudge, 1948.

The Letters of Ezra Pound, 1907-1941, edited by D.D. Paige. New York, Harcourt Brace, 1950; London, Faber, 1951.

Patria Mia. Chicago, Seymour, 1950; as *Patria Mia and The Treatise on Harmony*, London, Peter Owen, 1962.

The Translations of Ezra Pound, edited by Hugh Kenner. London, Faber, and New York, New Directions, 1953; revised edition, Faber, 1970.

Impact: Essays on Ignorance and the Decline of American Civilization, edited by Noel Stock. Chicago, Regnery, 1960.

EP to LU: Nine Letters Written to Louis Untermeyer by Ezra Pound, edited by J. Albert Robbins. Bloomington, Indiana University Press, 1963.

Pound/Joyce: The Letters of Ezra Pound to James Joyce, edited by Forrest Read. New York, New Directions, 1967; London, Faber, 1968.

Redondillas: or, Something of That Sort. New York, New Directions, 1967.

The Caged Panther: Ezra Pound at St. Elizabeths (includes 53 letters), by Harry M. Meachum. New York, Twayne, 1967.

Selected Prose 1909-1965, edited by Wiliam Cookson. London, Faber, and New York, New Directions, 1973.

Editor, *Des Imagistes: An Anthology* . New York, Boni, and London, Poetry Bookshop, 1914.

Editor, *Catholic Anthology, 1914-1915.* London, Elkin Mathews, 1915.

Editor, *Poetical Works of Lionel Johnson.* London, Elkin Mathews, 1915.

Editor, *Passages from the Letters of John Butler Yeats.* Dublin, Cuala Press, 1917.

Editor, *Profile: An Anthology.* Milan, Scheiwiller, 1932.

Editor, *Rime*, by Guido Cavalcanti. Genoa, Edizioni Marsano, 1932.

Editor, *Active Anthology.* London, Faber, 1933.

Editor, *The Chinese Written Character as a Medium for Poetry: An Ars Poetica*, by Ernest Fenollosa. London, Nott, and New York, Arow Editions, 1936.

Editor, *De Moribus Brachmanorum, Liber Sancto Ambrosio Falso Adscriptus.* Milan, Scheiwiller, 1956.

Editor, with Marcelia Spann, *Confucius to Cummings.* New York, New Directions, 1964.

Translator, *The Sonnets and Ballate of Guido Cavalcanti*.   Boston, Small Maynard, and London, Stephen Swift, 1912; as *Ezra Pound's Cavalcanti Poems*, New York, New Directions, 1966.

Translator, *Cathay: Translations*.   London, Elkin Mathews, 1915.

Translator, with Ernest Fenollosa, *Certain Noble Plays of Japan*.   Dublin, Cuala Press, 1916.

Translator, *Dialogues of Fontenelle*.   London, The Egoist, 1917.

Translator, *The Natural Philosophy of Love*, by Rémy de Gourmont.   New York, Boni and Liveright, 1922; London, Casanova Society, 1926.

Translator, *The Call of the Road*, by Edouard Estaunié.   New York, Boni and Liveright, 1923.

Translator, *Ta Hio: The Great Learning*, by Confucius.   Seattle, University of Washington Book Store, 1928; London, Nott, 1936.

Translator, *Digest of the Analects*, by Confucius.   Milan, Scheiwiller, 1937.

Translator, *Italy's Policy of Social Economics 1939-1940*, by Odon Por.   Bergamo, Istituto Italiano d'Arti Grafiche, 1941.

Translator, with Alberto Luchini, *Ta S'en Dai Gaku, Studio Integrale*, by Confucius.   Rapallo, Scuola Tipografica Orfanotrofio Emiliani, 1942.

Translator, *Ciung Iung, l'Asse che non Vacilla*, by Confucius.   Venice, Casa Editrice delle Edizioni Popolari, 1945.

Translator, *The Unwobbling Pivot and The Great Digest*, by Confucius.   New York, New Directions, 1947; London, Peter Owen, 1952.

Translator, *Confucian Analects*.   New York, Square $ Series, 1951; London, Peter Owen, 1956.

Translator, *The Classic Anthology Defined by Confucius*.   Cambridge, Massachussetts, Harvard University Press, 1954; London, Faber, 1955.

Translator, *Women of Trachis*, by Sophocles.   London, Spearman, 1956; New York, New Directions, 1957.

Translator, *Moscardino*, by Enrico Pea.   Milan, All'Insegna del Pesce d'Oro, 1956.

Translator, *Rimbaud* (5 poems).   Milan, All'Insegna del Pesce d'Oro, 1957.

Translator, with Noel Stock, *Love Poems of Ancient Egypt*.   New York, New Directions, 1962.

CRITICAL STUDIES AND BIBLIOGRAPHY

Hugh Kenner, *The Poetry of Ezra Pound*.   New York, New Directions, and London, Faber, 1951.

T.S. Eliot, Introduction to *Literary Essays of Ezra Pound*.   London, Faber, and New York, New Directions, 1954.

Donald Gallup, *A Bibliography of Ezra Pound*.   London, Hart Davis, 1963; revised edition, 1969.

N. Christoph De Nagy, *Ezra Pound's Poetics and Literary Tradition: The Critical Decade*.   Berne, Switzerland, Francke Verlag, 1966.

Hugh Kenner, *The Pound Era*.   Berkeley and Los Angeles, University of California Press, 1971.

Donald Davie, *Ezra Pound*.   London, Fontana, 1975; New York, Viking Press, 1976.

*   *   *

Commenting on the *Pisan Cantos*, Noel Stock, Pound's sympathetic biographer, admits that

If at times the verse is silly, it is because in himself Pound was often silly; if at times it is firm, dignified and intelligent, it is because in himself Pound was often firm, dignified and intelligent; *if it is fragmentary and confused, it is because Pound was never able to think out his position and did not know how the matters with which he dealt were related.* (my italics)

This is probably true for the *Cantos* and perhaps true for all of Pound's later poetry; it is certainly true, especially the passage I have emphasized, for the mass of assertions, admonitions, slogans, battle-cries and "excernments" which make up his criticism. Nevertheless, there are "matters" here which can be identified and are worth trying to group together if only because of Pound's reputation as a poet and the apparent extent of his influence.

"It is tremendously important that great poetry be written," Pound announced early in his career, "it makes no jot of difference who writes it." To understand why this is so for Pound and the implications it has for the only kinds of criticism he felt had much value, we have to turn to his theory of language, or rather to those scattered remarks about thought and language which appear in *How to Read* (now reprinted in *Literary Essays of Ezra Pound*) and the *ABC of Reading*. "Precision" is the keyword here; and as Christoph De Nagy has pointed out, Pound's insistence that "words" must always conform to "things" derives from Flaubert's contention that

> il y a un rapport nécessaire entre le mot musical et le mot juste. Il n'y a qu'un seul mot qui puisse parfaitement et complètement exprimer une chose ou une idée et c'est le mot qu'il faut trouver, dût-on passer huit jours à le chercher...le mot est consubstantiel à l'idée.

But for Pound the quest for the right word is not merely an aesthetic adventure: the very health and stability of a culture depend upon its "literature," taken in the broadest sense. Clear thinking and precise expression are inseparable parts of the same process, and both are determined, finally, by the accurate perception of particulars. There is a magical relationship between a thing and its correct name, which like a Chinese ideograph, should be the "picture of the thing." The besetting vice of much European thought is its tendency to depart from the concrete and the particular ("In Europe, if you ask a man to define anything, his definition moves away from the simple things that he knows perfectly well, it recedes into an unknown region that is a region of remoter and progressively remoter abstraction"). Pound never indicates, however, that he recognizes the problem this kind of realism raises: in effect we are left with a fragmented world of objects and their signs; we have no way of knowing how to move from the precise naming of particulars to the formation of adequate universals (Pound remarks simply that "an abstract or general statement is GOOD if it be ultimately found to correspond to the facts"—and lets it go at that). His failure to define the exact relationship between perception, word and thought is typical of his failure to think out his position, but this is not to say that some of his assertions are not capable of intelligent development. The interested reader might consider, for example, what Pound's most fanatic admirer, Hugh Kenner, does with the doctrine of "luminous particulars."

But having moved somehow from words and objects to the verbal rendering of complex feelings and situations, Pound maintains that the art of literature lies in the precise embodiment of its subject matter ("When Shakespeare talks of the 'Dawn in russet mantle clad' he presents something which the painter does not present. There is in this line of his nothing that one can call description; he presents"). In *How to Read* he gives what is probably his clearest statement of the purpose of literature:

> Has literature a function in the state, in the aggregation of humans, in the republic, in the *res publica*, which ought to mean the public convenience (despite the slime of bureaucracy, and the execrable taste of the populace in selecting its rulers)? It has.
>
> And this function is *not* the coercing or emotionally persuading, or bullying or suppressing people into the acceptance of any one set or any six sets of opinions as opposed to any other set or half-dozen sets of opinions.
>
> It has to do with the clarity and vigour of "any and every" thought and opinion. It has to do with maintaining the very cleanliness of the tools, the health of the very matter of thought itself. Save in the rare and limited instances of invention in the plastic arts, or in mathematics, the individual cannot think and communicate his thought, the governor and legislator cannot act effectively or frame his laws, without words, and the solidity and validity of these words is in the care of the damned and despised *litterati*. When their work goes rotten—by that I do not mean when they express indecorous thoughts—but when their very medium, the very essence of their work, the application of word to thing goes rotten, i.e., becomes slushy and inexact, or excessive and bloated, the whole

machinery of social and individual thought and order goes to pot. This is a lesson of history, and a lesson not yet half learned.

The great writers need no debunking.

The pap is not in them, and doesn't need to be squeezed out. They do not lend themselves to imperial and sentimental exploitations. A civilization was founded on Homer, civilization not a mere bloated empire. The Macedonian domination rose and grew after the sophists. It also subsided.

Further, it appears to him "quite tenable"

that the function of literature as a generated prize-worthy force is precisely that it does incite humanity to continue living; that it eases the mind of strain, and feeds it. I mean definitely as *nutrition of impulse*.

And finally (in "The Serious Artist"), Pound asserts that the arts furnish "data for ethics":

It is obvious that ethics are based on the nature of man, just as it is obvious that civics are based upon the nature of men when living together in groups.

It is obvious that the good of the greatest number cannot be attained until we know in some sort of what that good must consist. In other words we must know what sort of animal man is, before we can contrive his happiness, or before we can decide what percentage of that happiness he can have without causing too great a percentage of unhappiness to those about him.

The arts, literature, poesy, are a science, just as chemistry is a science. Their subject is man, mankind and the individual. The subject of chemistry is matter considered as to its composition.

The arts give us a great percentage of the lasting and unassailable data regarding the nature of man, of immaterial man, of man considered as a thinking and sentient creature. They begin where the science of medicine leaves off or rather they overlap that science. The borders of the two sciences cross...if any science save the arts were able more precisely to determine what the individual does not actually desire, then those sciences would be of more use in providing the data for ethics.

For these reasons, then, great literature, and particularly great poetry, is of "tremendous importance." It is "news that stays news"—that is, it incarnates those truths which are always valid and hence always "new."

Prose and poetry both have important psychological and ethical functions to discharge, but it is in poetry, of course, that language is "charged with meaning to the utmost possible degree." And there are three ways in which this "charging" may be accomplished:

That is to say, there are three "kinds of poetry":

MELOPOEIA, wherein the words are charged, over and above their plain meaning, with some musical property, which directs the bearing or trend of that meaning.

PHANOPOEIA, which is a casting of images upon the visual imagination.

LOGOPOEIA, "the dance of the intellect among words," that is to say, it employs words not only for their direct meaning, but it takes count in a special way of habits of usage, of the context we expect to find with the word, its usual concomitants, of its known acceptances, and of ironical play. It holds the aesthetic content which is peculiarly the domain of verbal manifestation, and cannot possibly be contained in plastic or in music. It is the latest come, and perhaps most tricky and undependable mode.

The *melopoeia* can be appreciated by à foreigner with a sensitive ear, even though he be ignorant of the language in which the poem is written. It is practically impossible to transfer or translate it from one language to another, save perhaps by divine accident, and for half a line at a time.

Phanopoeia can, on the other hand, be translated almost, or wholly, intact. When it is good enough, it is practically impossible for the translator to destroy it save by very cross bungling, and the neglect of perfectly well-known and formulative rules.

Logopoeia does not translate; though the attitude of mind it expresses may pass through a paraphrase. Or one might say, you can *not* translate it "locally," but having determined the original author's state of mind, you may or may not be able to find a derivative or an equivalent.

Pound never defines *logopoeia* any more precisely than this, save to remark that it involves "irony" (later he adds that unless he is right in discovering it in Propertius, "we must almost say that Laforgue invented *logopoeia*"). The importance of *phanopoeia* for the exact rendering of emotion explains in large part Pound's early interest in "images." In a well-known section of "A Retrospect" he asserts that

> An "Image" is that which presents an intellectual and emotional complex in an instant of time.... It is the presentation of such a "complex" instantaneously which gives that sense of sudden liberation; that sense of freedom from time limits and space limits; that sense of sudden growth, which we experience in the presence of the greatest works of art.

But it is *melopoeia* which Pound seems to have cared most about and which accounts for his long devotion to the Troubadours, Arnaut Daniel and Cavalcanti, since it is in these poets that he finds the maximum conjunction of meaning and musical phrasing. As for the poets themselves, Pound sets up six main groups: the inventors (the "discoverers of a particular process or of more than one mode and process"); the masters (those inventors who "are able to assimilate and co-ordinate a large number of preceding inventions...[and] either start with a core of their own and accumulate adjuncts, or...digest a vast mass of subject-matter, apply a number of known modes of expression, and succeed in pervading the whole with homogeneous fullness"); the diluters (who follow the great writers and "produce something valid"); the nameless group which "always produces the great bulk of all writing" and does "more or less good work in the more or less good style of a period"); the *Belles Lettres* ("Longus, Prévost, Benjamin Constant, who are not exactly 'great masters,' who can hardly be said to have originated a form, but who nevertheless have brought some mode to a very high development"); and finally the "starters of crazes, the Ossianic MacPhersons, the Gongoras whose wave of fashion flows over writing for a few centuries or a few decades, and then subsides, leaving things as they were."

The responsibilities of the critic follow naturally enough from all of this. In his earliest and most influential criticism Pound was writing primarily for those of his contemporaries who were dissatisfied with the heritage of the nineteenth century ("a rather blurry, messy sort of period, a rather sentimentalistic, mannerish sort of period") and who needed to establish connections with the vital inventors and masters of the past ("a man feeling the divorce of life and his art may naturally try to resurrect a forgotten mode if he finds in that mode some leaven, or if he thinks he sees in it some element lacking in contemporary art which might unite that art again to its sustenance, life"). In his generous introduction to Pound's *Literary Essays*, T.S. Eliot maintains that

> Much of the *permanence* of Mr. Pound's criticism is due simply to his having seen so clearly what needed to be said at a particualar time; his occupation with his own moment and its needs has led him to say many things which are of permanent value, but the value of which may not be immediately appreciated by later readers who lack the sense of historical situation.
>
> Inevitably, after the passage of time, such a critic as Mr. Pound (who has never been afraid of his own insights) will appear to have exaggerated the importance of some principles, or of some authors, and to have unjustly depreciated others. He has enlarged criticism by his interpretation of neglected authors and literatures, and by his rehabilitation of misesteemed authors. As for the reputations that he has attacked, we must recall the reaction against the Augustan Age initiated by the Lake Poets. Any pioneer of a revolution in poetry—and Mr. Pound is more responsible for the XXth Century revolution in poetry than is any other individual—is sure to attack some venerated names. For the real point of attack is the idolatry of a great artist by unintelligent critics, and his imitation by uninspired practitioners.... [Pound] has always been, first and foremost, a teacher and a campaigner. He has always been impelled, not merely to find out for himself how poetry should be written, but to pass on the benefit of his discoveries

to others; not simply to make these benefits available, but to insist upon their being received. He would cajole, and almost coerce, other men into writing well; so that he often presents the appearance of a man trying to convey to a very deaf person the fact that the house is on fire. Every change he has advocated has always struck him as being of instant urgency. This is not only the temperament of the teacher; it represents also, with Pound, a passionate desire, not merely to write well himself, but to live in a period in which he could be surrounded by equally intelligent and creative minds.

"What does seem to me true, and necessary to say," Eliot concludes, "is that Pound's critical writings, scattered and occasional as they seem to have been, form the *least dispensable* body of critical writing in our time."

Pound himself concludes (in "Date Line") that so far as he has been able to discover, criticism has two functions:

> 1.   Theoretically it tries to forerun composition, to serve as a gunsight, though there is, I believe, no recorded instance of the foresight having EVER been of the slightest use save to actual composers....
> 2.   Excernment. The general ordering and weeding out of what has actually been performed. The elimination of repetitions. The work analogous to that which a good hanging committee or a curator would perform in a National Gallery or in a biological museum;
>   The ordering of knowledge so that the next man (generation) can most readily find the live part of it, and waste the least possible time among obsolete issues.

Keeping all of these considerations in mind, then, we may divide Pound's criticism into four main categories: there are those essays in *The Spirit of Romance* (and the scattered pieces which Eliot groups together in *Literary Essays* under the general heading "The Tradition") in which Pound seeks to re-define the living continuity of poetry; there are those instances—the most spectacular of which is his editing of *The Waste Land*—in which he tries to "forerun composition"; there are the "exhibits" and excernments" which make up the second half of the *ABC of Reading*; and finally there are the brief but important early pieces (on Frost, for example, and Joyce) in which he calls attention to something which is truly new and valuable.

How just is Eliot's astonishing conclusion that Pound's criticism forms the *"least dispensable"* body of criticism in our time? Obviously it depends upon the standards we apply. If we expect a critic to "know how the matters with which he dealt are related" (and in this brief sketch I have only been able to suggest that this is not the case with Pound), if we expect him to reason with his readers and not merely to cajole or bully, then most of Pound's criticism seems virtually useless. But if we accept Eliot's proposition that more than any other figure Pound was responsible for the "XXth Century revolution in poetry," then his criticism has real historical importance. Every poet-critic, Allen Tate observes, is programmatic; that is, like Pound, he writes the kind of criticism which will define and justify the kind of poetry he wants to write. In 1961 (in "To Criticize the Critic") Eliot confessed that in his own early criticism he was "implicitly defending the sort of poetry that I and my friends wrote" and went on to say that some of his best-known phrases should be interpreted as "conceptual symbols for emotional preferences." This applies with equal truth to Pound. And Eliot concludes, even more strikingly, that while his poetry and the poetry of his friends was congenial to the age, he wonders "if that age is not coming to an end." The age has come to an end, and the issue now is the significance of the poetry itself. A critical generation or two ago none of us would have doubted that Eliot, Pound and Joyce were unquestionably the inventors and masters of modern poetry; more recently, however, such thoughful critics as Graham Hough, Frank Kermode and Donald Davie have been calling for a reassessment of what Hugh Kenner calls so confidently "the Pound era." In *Image and Experience* Graham Hough argues that the *Cantos* and *The Waste Land* are monuments only to themselves, unique experiments which will survive, if at all, "not assisted by their structure, but in spite of it." No serious student of modern literature can afford to dismiss his conclusions:

> If we are to use metaphors, mine [for much modern poetry in the "Imagist" tradition] would not be cul-de-sac but a détour, a diversion from the main road. Traffic along the

main road has been proceeding all the time, and we do not sufficiently remember this. In talking of modern poetry we ought to recall more often that we do that Hardy was writing in 1926, and that among the poets of our century are Robert Frost, Robert Graves, John Crowe Ransom, Edwin Muir and John Betjeman. But the détour has been considerable, and most of the heavy traffic has chosen to travel on it. It is probably time it rejoined the main highway. But, to abandon the metaphor, which is becoming inconvenient, it is no use imagining that things will ever be the same again.... All we can say is that some of the most brilliant poetic innovations of the most original poetic talents of our day are probably inimitable and unrepeatable. They cannot be developed any farther, and they have been of a kind from which it is very difficult to learn. This I believe is the difficult situation that poetry finds itself in today.

PRITCHETT, V(ictor) S(awdon). British. Born in Ipswich, Suffolk, 16 December 1900. Educated at Alleyn's School, Dulwich, London. Married Dorothy Rudge Roberts in 1936; has one son and one daughter. Worked in the leather trade in London, 1916-20, and in the shellac, glue, and photographic trade in Paris, 1920-32; Correspondent in Ireland and Spain for the *Christian Science Monitor*, Boston, 1923-26; Critic from 1926, Permanent Critic from 1937, and Director, 1946-78, *New Statesman*, London. Christian Gauss Lecturer, Princeton University, New Jersey, 1953; Beckman Professor, University of California, Berkeley, 1962; Writer-in-Residence, Smith College, Northampton, Massachusetts, 1966, 1970-72; Visiting Professor, Brandeis University, Waltham, Massachusetts, 1968; Clark Lecturer, Cambridge University, 1969; Visiting Professor, Columbia University, New York, 1972. President, P.E.N. Club, English Centre, 1970, and President of International P.E.N., 1974-76. Recipient: Heinemann Award, for non-fiction, 1969; P.E.N. Award, for non-fiction, 1974. D.Lit.: University of Leeds, 1972; D.Litt.: Columbia University, 1978; University of Sussex, Brighton, 1980. Fellow, Royal Society of Literature, 1969. Honorary Member, American Academy, 1971. C.B.E. (Commander, Order of the British Empire), 1968. Knighted, 1975. Address: 12 Regent's Park Terrace, London N.W. 1, England.

PUBLICATIONS

Criticism

In My Good Books. London, Chatto and Windus, 1942; Port Washington, New York, Kennikat Press, 1977.
The Living Novel. London, Chatto and Windus, 1946; New York, Reynal, 1947; revised edition, New York, Random House, 1964.
Why Do I Write: An Exchange of Views Between Elizabeth Bowen, Graham Greene, and V.S. Pritchett. London, Marshall, 1948; New York, Haskell House, 1976.
Books in General. London, Chatto and Windus, and New York, Harcourt Brace, 1953.
The Working Novelist. London, Chatto and Windus, 1946.
George Meredith and English Comedy. London, Chatto and Windus, and New York, Random House, 1970.
Balzac: A Biography. London, Chatto and Windus, and New York, Knopf, 1973.
The Gentle Barbarian: The Life and Work of Turgenev. London, Chatto and Windus, and New York, Random House, 1977.
Autobiography (address). London, English Association, 1977.
The Mythmakers: Essays on European, Russian, and South American Novelists. London, Chatto and Windus, and New York, Random House, 1979.

The Tale Bearers: Essays on English, American and Other Writers.   London, Chatto and Windus, and New York, Random House, 1980.

Novels

Clare Drummer.   London, Benn, 1929.
Shirley Sanz.   London, Gollancz, 1932; as *Elopement into Exile*, Boston, Little Brown, 1932.
Nothing like Leather.   London, Chatto and Windus, and New York, Macmillan, 1935.
Dead Man Leading.   London, Chatto and Windus, and New York, Macmillan, 1937.
Mr. Beluncle.   London, Chatto and Windus, and New York, Harcourt Brace, 1951.

Short Stories

The Spanish Virgin and Other Stories.   London, Benn, 1930.
You Make Your Own Life.   London, Chatto and Windus, 1938.
It May Never Happen and Other Stories.   London, Chatto and Windus, 1945; New York, Reynal, 1947.
Collected Stories.   London, Chatto and Windus, 1956.
The Sailor, The Sense of Humour, and Other Stories.   New York, Knopf, 1956.
When My Girl Comes Home.   London, Chatto and Windus, and New York, Knopf, 1961.
The Key to My Heart.   London, Chatto and Windus, 1963; New York, Random House, 1964.
The Saint and Other Stories.   London, Penguin, 1966.
Blind Love and Other Stories.   London, Chatto and Windus, 1969; New York, Random House, 1970.
Penguin Stories 9, with others.   London, Penguin, 1971.
The Camberwell Beauty and Other Stories.   London, Chatto and Windus, and New York, Random House, 1974.
Selected Stories.   London, Chatto and Windus, and New York, Random House, 1978.
On the Edge of the Cliff.   New York, Random House, 1979; London, Chatto and Windus, 1980.

Plays

The Gambler (broadcast, 1947).   Published in *Imaginary Conversations*, edited by Rayner Heppenstall.   London, Secker and Warburg, 1948.

Screenplays: *Essential Jobs* (documentary), 1942; *The Two Feathers*, with Anthony Asquith, 1944.

Radio Play: *The Gambler*, 1947.

Other

Marching Spain (travel).   London, Benn, 1928.
The Spanish Temper (travel).   London, Chatto and Windus, and New York, Knopf, 1954.
London Perceived.   London, Chatto and Windus, and New York, Harcourt Brace, 1962.

Foreign Faces.   London, Chatto and Windus, 1964; as *The Offensive Traveller*, New York, Knopf, 1964.
New York Proclaimed.   London, Chatto and Windus, and New York, Harcourt Brace, 1965.
Dublin: A Portrait.   London, Bodley Head, and New York, Harper, 1967.
A Cab at the Door: Childhood and Youth, 1900-1920.   London, Chatto and Windus, 1968; as *A·Cab at the Door: A Memoir*, New York, Random House, 1968.
Midnight Oil (autobiography).   London, Chatto and Windus, 1971; New York, Random House, 1972.
Great American Families, with others.   New York, Norton, and London, Times Books, 1977.

Editor, *This England.*   London, New Statesman and Nation, 1938.
Editor, *Novels and Stories*, by Robert Louis Stevenson.   London, Pilot Press, 1945; New York, Duell, 1946.
Editor, *Turnstile One: A Literary Miscellany from the New Statesman.*   London, Turnstile Press, 1948.
Editor, *The Oxford Book of Short Stories.*   London and New York, Oxford University Press, 1981.

*   *   *

In *Midnight Oil* V.S. Pritchett describes—with typical modesty—the conditions under which "a critic emerged from the hack" during the early days of World War Two. Since many younger contributors to *The New Statesman* had been called into government service, it became his job to write "the leading literary article for the paper, almost every week." And since few new books were being published, his editors decided that the articles must "deal with a re-reading of the classics":

So, one week the subject might be Sir Walter Scott, the next Dostoevsky, after that Benjamin Constant, George Fox, Zola, Gil Blas and so on. When I look now upon the long list of such essays, they seem to fly about or drop like washing on a clothes line. Two thousand words was the limit. In the first year the tone was nervous: my writing is filled in with hesitant or forensic phrases; I was writing against time. I had read widely but I had never "done" Eng. Lit., French Lit., or Russian Lit. I had no critical doctrine—a shock later on to the platoons of New Critics and later regiments—for critical doctrine is of little interest to the novelist, though it may mean something to the poet. The tendencies of the thirties persuaded me to the situation of the writer who was being enjoyed first and *then* examined....I was moved by attitudes to social justice; but presently I saw that literature grows out of literature as much as out of a writer's times. A work of art is a deposit left by the conflicts and contradictions a writer has in his own nature. I am not a scholarly man; and I am not interested for very long in the elaborate super-structures of criticism. Some of my critics speak of insights and intuitions; the compliment is often left-handed for these are signs of the amateur's luck; I had no choice in the matter. Anyone who has written a piece of imaginative prose knows how much a writer relies on instinct and intuition. The war had added to my knowledge of human nature. I appear as a disarranged stoic, a humanist with one wall of his room missing— an advantage there, I think, for all writing has one of its sources in the sense of a moral danger to which the writer is sensitive....I attained a reputation in England and America and found that I was seriously split in two. I had the advantage of being an heir to the long and honourable tradition of serious periodical journalism; and of having, in a minor way, written imaginatively: I am aware of the novelist's methods. I cannot help putting myself in his position as he faces the empty page. I have always thought of myself—and therefore of my subjects—as being "in life," indeed books and life have always seemed to be a form of life, and not a distraction from it. I see myself as a practising writer who gives himself to a book as he gives himself to any human experience.

Pritchett's limitations may be obvious enough: apparently he has never cared to give himself to poetry or the drama, nor has he ever hesitated to spend a good deal of his time on clearly minor writers. But he is a shrewd and humane moralist with a positive genius for compression (as he remarks about the challenge of short-story writing, "there is the fascination of packing a great deal into very little space"), and as soon as one starts to read him on the British, French and Russian novelists he knows and loves so well, the limitations cease to matter.

Although Pritchett is not a systematic critic, his prefaces to *The Living Novel* and *In My Good Books* provide some indication of what he looks for in fiction:

> Let us admit that changes in style, method and belief often stand between us and the immediate enjoyment of many of the great novelists; but these barriers become unimportant when we perceive that the great are the great, not only because of their inherent qualities, but because they were the writers who were most sensitive to the situation of their time. They are in the finer sense, contemporary. I do not mean that they explicitly responded to external events, though they often did; evidently even bad writers reflect the age in which they live; I mean that they are sensitive to an intrinsic situation. We say that we are living in an age of transition, "between two worlds"; the lesson of the master is that human life is always in transition; an essential part of his excellence is that he brings this clearly out in his work.

The masters of the novel "have a direct apprehension of life"; they put "intensity of experience before everything else." The true classic "comes to life in our hands, raw, unfinished, questioning and restless with its own disturbance":

> We hold up the crystal sphere; we see ourselves in miniature reflection and, perhaps, if our minds are not too literal, we may also see our future....We look back from Hemingway to Defoe, from modern non-attachment to the dynamic quietism of George Fox. In the middle of the eighteenth century Fielding draws a Fuehrer. I do not suggest that such comparisons will always be found in these essays; but in numerous cases of wide difference, in Le Sage, Synge or Zola, to take random examples, the differences take on meaning when we turn from literary criticism to a consideration of the social background of the authors. Our pleasure in literature is increased by knowing that a book is the fruit of living in a certain way.

The truly "living novel" offers an implied criticism of the way we live now; and thus after a penetrating discussion of *Germinal* Pritchett observes that one may of course read the novel and

> think that its philosophic background is as dated as the bestial conditions it describes; the mines are no longer brothels; people no longer starve at work; they starve for lack of it. War has become the crux of the social problem. But the greatness of *Germinal* lies in the exalted thoroughness of its exposure of the situation as it was during Zola's time, and equally in the mastery of its story. Its lesson to English novelists is that their education is incomplete and sterile if it does not apply itself to reinterpreting contemporary history.

Again, after an equally acute discussion of Lermontoff's *A Hero of Our Times*, Pritchett concludes that "it is the measure of the failure of modern novelists that they have not observed and defined a characteristic man of these years; and the explanation of the failure is our lack of moral and political perceptiveness. Our novels would be shorter, more readable and more important if we had one or two more ideas about our times and far fewer characters."

There are no prefaces to *Books in General* or *The Working Novelist*, however, which may be a sign that the reader should stop trying to find any grand unifying concerns. What Pritchett cares about, in the friends and relatives he describes so vividly in *A Cab at the Door* and *Midnight Oil* or in the characters he conjures up in his own splendid stories, is simply experience in its immediacy and the ways in which a small gesture can sum up a man and catch what Henry James called "the strange, irregular rhythm of life." But since these will be empty generalizations for anyone who has not had the pleasure of reading Pritchett, the best thing to do is to quote. Here, for example, is the opening paragraph of his essay on *Oblomov*:

If literature were to follow the excellent custom of the Catholic Church which adds a new saint to the calendar in every generation, and with more than half an eye on the needs of the time, it is easy to see which character in fiction is now ripe for canonisation. Not the propaganding figure of Don Quixote; not the innocent Pickwick; certainly not Robinson Crusoe, that too industrious town-planner knocking up a new society. The function of the saints is to assuage the wishes of the unconscious, to appeal to that part of a man which is least apparent to himself, and to-day we must turn away from the heroic, the energetic, expansive and productive characters. Falstaff the coward, Oblomov the sublime sluggard and absentee, seem to me our natural candidates. Oblomov above all. In a world of planners he plans himself to sleep. In a world of action he discovers the poetry of procrastination. In a world of passion he discovers the delicacies of reluctance. And when we reject his passivity he bears our secret desire for it like a martyr. For us he sleeps, for us he lies in bed day-dreaming, for us his mind goes back to the Arcadia of his childhood, drinking the opiate of memory. For our sakes who live in clean rooms and jump out of bed when the alarm clock goes, Oblomov lies among his cobwebs and his fleas, his books unread, his ink dry in the bottle, his letters unanswered. While we prosper, he is cheated. And at the end of our racketing day we see his face—the moon-like face of the obese and the slack, and with that wry kink of fret and faint madness which the moon sometimes has on it—we see his face looking upon us with the penetrating, disturbing criticism of the incurable, the mysterious reproach of the man who is in the wrong. Slowly, guiltily, his foot comes out of the bedclothes and dangles furtively above the slipper on the floor and then, with a tremor of modesty before the implications of an act so obscenely decisive, the foot is withdrawn. Who knows what valuable grains of sensibility are lost to the soul when man is persuaded to stand upright?

Compared to the best of Pritchett's essays and reviews, *George Meredith and English Comedy* is something of a disappointment, partly, perhaps, because the wider spaces of these Clark Lectures fail to provide the usual challenge to compress and epitomize. The opening lecture, however, is promising. Pritchett tells us that he has chosen Meredith for his subject because "we learn so much from writers who have either got into difficulties or who have a certain vanity in creating them." By taking on nothing less than the "Idea of absolute Comedy" Meredith had to deal with a major tradition in our literature:

> Now the comic tradition in the English novel is a powerful one; it is an alternative to the Puritan tradition; it inspects as it alleviates or makes finer the demands of moral seriousness. Meredith who was a great adapter from the past can tell us a good deal about our comic tradition. What he was trying to do was to conceptualise—which is not a common English habit; and he was conceptualising a dominant tradition of the English novel. In comic irony our novelists have been pre-eminent. It is their most militant and graceful gift. It has modified or refined their didactic habit and drawn them closer to nature.

Pritchett then goes on to define the three main streams of the comic tradition which Meredith draws upon. There is the "masculine" tradition which runs from Fielding through Anthony Powell:

> It is sanguine, positive, morally tough, believes in good sense, even in angered good sense and suspects sensibility. These novelists have paid their dues to society or a moral order. They are on the whole generous, though they have their acerbities. They are robust and hard-headed. They know that, in the long run, feeling must submit to intelligence.

There is the "feminine" tradition which runs from Sterne through Beckett:

> ...suppose you reject the Way, the belief in habit and behaviour. Suppose you rely on your own mind and not on society's. Suppose you value your privacy, value imagination and sensibility more than common sense. Suppose you live not by clock time, but by the uncertain hours of your feeling. Suppose you live by your imagination or your fantasies. Suppose, with Gray, you think that all you have is your own "pleasing anxious being"

and are, perhaps, liable to fright, illness, egocentricity and sin. Then you will be with Sterne in the disorderly, talkative, fantasticating tradition. I call it the feminine, the affectable. It is wayward.

And finally there is the "mythic" tradition, which Pritchett never really defines, save by way of a not very clear example:

> I have called the third strain in our comic tradition mythic or fantastic and this is so adjacent to Sterne's habit that I hesitate over the distinction. But it has to be made because the comedy of Dickens stands a great deal on its own because his genius belongs to a century of violent revolution....In the last twenty years or so great stress has been put on the serious socially conscious Dickens, the poetic symbolist, the often melodramatic and violent enemy of social injustice; and the effect of this stress has been to make us treat his comedy as comic relief....I do not believe that Dickens can be split in two in this way: one part reformer, the other part original English humorist. He represents, for me, his century's release of an important psychological force.
>
> In Dickens we are faced with a vast Gothic structure, a mixture of sprawling Parliament and sinister, often blood-and-thunder theatre. After the pragmatism of the eighteenth century, we have a myth-maker.

Dicken's characters are "actors"; "they are strange, even mad, because they speak as if they were the only persons in the world." Pecksniff, for example, draws on "his sense of himself as a walking history or legend."

But after this promising start, Pritchett retreats to rather general commentaries on five of Meredith's novels and finds there a common pattern of "spiritual ordeal":

> The soul has to pass through fire. And what has to be burned away? Pride above all and self-delusion. The business of comedy is ruthlessly to expose the false emotions and the false image of oneself and the purpose of comedy is to establish sanity. This is the theme that dominates all Meredith's novels; it is his only important theme. His hero should emerge at the end, fitted at last to face life. By nature his heroes are honourable but wilful extremists. They live in the imagination, which gives them a tremendous energy.

What Pritchett has to say about the individual novels, and about Meredith's poetic style and use of romance, is never commonplace; but the larger issues raised in the first lecture tend to disappear. In the end one is left with the sense of an unsolved puzzle: *is* Meredith really worth bothering about? He was "rich in verbal imagination" but "impotent when it comes to creating something new out of life." And finally, his "moral range is too personal":

> Like James he is morally a tourist. His positive contribution is that, in our comic and romantic tradition, he is a storehouse of ways and means, a fine diagnostician in his field as a poet will be; and rather hard and intelligently merciless—which is refreshing in the nineteenth century. And if he looks askance at many pretended virtues, the virtues he preaches (and happily by implication) are truthfulness and fortitude in the romantic disaster. He is a hot-house stoic and perhaps we should look upon him, first and last, as one of the startling temperaments of a very temperamental age.

RAHV, Philip. American. Born in Kupin, the Ukraine, 10 March 1908. Emigrated to the United States in 1922. Lived in New York City and contributed to *The Nation*, *The New Republic*, *The New Masses*, *The New Leader*, *The Southern Review* and other periodicals. Joined the John Reed Club in 1933. Founding co-editor, with William Phillips, *Partisan*

Review, New York, 1934-69. Professor of English, Brandeis University, Waltham, Massachusetts, 1957-73. Founding Editor, *Modern Occasions*, 1970. *Died 23 December 1973.*

PUBLICATIONS

Criticism

Image and Idea: Fourteen Essays on Literary Themes. New York, New Directions, 1949; enlarged edition, as *Image and Idea: Twenty Essays on Literary Themes*, 1957; London, Weidenfeld and Nicolson, 1957; reprinted in *Literature and the Sixth Sense*, 1969.
The Myth and the Powerhouse. New York, Farrar Straus, 1965; reprinted in *Literature and the Sixth Sense*, 1969.
Literature and the Sixth Sense. Boston, Houghton Mifflin, 1969; London, Faber, 1970.
Essays on Literature and Politics 1932-72, edited by Arabel J. Porter and Andrew J. Dvorsin, with a memoir by Mary McCarthy. Boston, Houghton Mifflin, 1978.

Other

Editor, *The Great Short Novels of Henry James.* New York, Dial Press, 1944.
Editor, *The Bostonians*, by Henry James. New York, Dial Press, 1945.
Editor, *The Short Novels of Tolstoy*, translated by Aylmer Maude. New York, Dial Press, 1946.
Editor, with William Phillips, *The Partisan Reader: Ten Years of the Partisan Review, 1934-1944.* New York, Dial Press, 1946.
Editor, *Discovery of Europe: The Story of American Experience in the Old World.* Boston, Houghton Mifflin, 1947; revised edition, New York, Doubleday, 1960.
Editor, *Great Russian Short Novels.* New York, Dial Press, 1951.
Editor, with William Phillips, *The New Partisan Reader, 1945-1953.* New York, Harcourt Brace, 1953.
Editor, with William Phillips, *The Avon Book of Modern Writing 1-2.* New York, Avon, 2 vols., 1953.
Editor, with William Phillips, *The Berkley Book of Modern Writing.* New York, Berkley, 1953.
Editor, *Literature in America: An Anthology of Literary Criticism.* New York, Meridian Books, 1957.
Editor, *The Partisan Review Anthology.* New York, Holt Rinehart, and London, Macmillan, 1962.
Editor, *Eight Great American Short Novels.* New York, Berkley, 1963.
Editor, *Modern Occasions.* New York, Farrar Straus, 1965; London, Weidenfeld and Nicolson, 1967.
Editor, *Modern Occasions 2.* Port Washington, New York, Kennikat Press, 1974.

CRITICAL STUDIES

Milton Hindus, "Philip Rahv," in *Images and Ideas in American Culture: The Function of Criticism: Essays in Memory of Philip Rahv*, edited by Arthur Edelstein. Hanover, New Hampshire, Brandeis University Press, 1979.
Alan Lelchuk, "Philip Rahv: The Last Years," in *Images and Ideas in American Culture*, 1979.

Christopher Lasch, "Modernism, Politics and Philip Rahv," in *Partisan Review* (Boston), 47, 1980.

*   *   *

"Though Rahv was inherently one of the narrowest men I knew," Alfred Kazin recalls (in *Starting Out in the Thirties*), "he was vividly authentic and stimulating as a critic of literature in society....Literature for him came out of social tension, and to social tension it had to contribute—and Rahv's ideal aim was to add to it." And in a brief tribute published shortly after Rahv's death. Mary McCarthy commented on some of the same strengths and limitations. In many ways he was "narrow":

> He was a resolute modernist, which made him in these recent days old-fashioned. It was as though he came into being with the steam engine: for him, literature began with Dostoevsky and stopped with Joyce, Proust and Eliot; politics began with Marx and stopped with Lenin. He was not interested in Shakespeare, the classics, Greek city states; and he despised most contemporary writing and contemporary political groups....Late in his life, serendipity introduced him to the word "swingers," which summed up everything he was against. With sardonic relish he adopted it as his personal shorthand. If he came down from Boston to New York and went to a *literary* party and you asked him, "Well, how was it?" he would answer "Nothing but swingers!" and give his short bark of a laugh.

But at the same time he was a superb editor. He had a gift for finding new writers (Miss McCarthy names Elizabeth Hardwick, Bellow, Jarrell, Berryman and Malamud, and adds "there were many others"); he had a "powerful intellect," and he was passionately devoted to certain kinds of "ideas"; "'He has no *ideas*,' he would declare, dismissing some literary claimant; to be void of ideas was, for him, the worst disaster that could befall an intellectual."

Rahv's passion for ideas, or more accurately ideologies, is the chief characteristic of many of the best essays and reviews he brought together in *Literature and the Sixth Sense*. As he was preparing the volume he confesses that he "was struck...by the way in which my own strong interest in historical reality as well as historical reason has in the long run affected my literary attitudes and judgments" (the "sixth sense" of the title refers to the mind's awareness of itself as at least partly an historical product, an awareness that Rahv, following Nietzsche, finds peculiarly "modern"). The ideas which concern him are those which either block or advance the revolutionary movement towards freedom and what Marx called "the first truly human culture":

> I think that the origins of my predilection for a heightened form of historical awareness can be traced primarily though not exclusively to my early training in Marxism. Even if through the years I have pulled back from a good deal that was implicit in that training at its very inception...I have nonetheless retained from it a certain approach, a measure of social and intellectual commitment and, I make bold to say, a certain kind of realism, not untouched with hope and expectancy, in my outlook on society and the human potential as articulated in the constructs of the imagination.

The value of his work, he goes on, "might well lie in the implicit summons [it contains] to recognize and in that sense restore a proper perspective on what has transpired in American literary culture during the past thirty years." And he then summarizes very conveniently what he sees as the three chief tendencies of this period:

> The first is that of the socially oriented thirties and the entanglement of many radical writers of that time with the Soviet version of Communism. The second, which lasted till nearly the end of the fifties, was fundamentally conservative in nature, taking form among the then dominant group of "new critics" in a perfervid adherence to "tradition" as well as the onset of a peculiarly belated and shallow kind of religiosity among literary intellectuals. The prevailing mood was one of total revulsion from all political activity and ideas that smacked in any way of the old Leninism. The third and present period,

that of the "swinging" sixties, is still with us. It is a period exhibiting very little cohesion—a mere jumble of mutually contradictory trends....[Its] spokesmen retain nothing more than the cultish mannerisms of the classic avant-garde; they ape its dissidence and revolt while actually constituting themselves as a veritable academy, and a ruling academy at that, fawned upon in the most respectable quarters even as it turns out art objects as consumer goods.

Literature and the Sixth Sense is by no means a tightly organized book, but Rahv's quick historical sketch does provide a way of grouping these essays and reviews. The "entanglement" of radical writers with Soviet Communism is the subject of "Proletarian Literature: A Political Autopsy," "Koestler and Homeless Radicalism," and, to a lesser extent, "Notes on the Decline of Naturalism." The ascendancy of the New Criticism and its reactionary worship of "tradition" is the subject of "Criticism and the Imagination of Alternatives," "Fiction and the Criticism of Fiction," and one of Rahv's finest essays, "The Myth and the Powerhouse," in which he argues that the renewed interest in myth represents another reactionary inability to face the "power-house" of social change. This "fear of history"

is at bottom the fear of the hazards of freedom. Insofar as man can be said to be capable of self-determination, history is the sole sphere in which he can conceivably attain it....In literature the withdrawal from historical experience and creativeness can only mean stagnation. For the creative artist to deny time in the name of the timeless and immemorial [i.e., the "mythic"] is to misconceive his task. He will never discover a shortcut to transcendence. True, in the imaginative act the artist does indeed challenge time, but in order to win he must also be able to meet *its* challenge; and his triumph over it is like that blessing which Jacob exacted from the angel only after grappling with him till the break of day.

Finally there are two essays, "Crime Without Punishment" (on Mailer) and "On Pornography, Black Humor, Norman Mailer, Etc.," in which Rahv attacks the swingers and the nihilists.

There are other essays, however, which cannot be so easily categorized. Unfortunately the best-known of them, "Paleface and Redskin," is one of his weakest. Here Rahv divides American writers into two groups, the palefaces (like James and Hawthorne), who are cultivated and self-conscious but who tend towards an "estrangement from reality," and the redskins (like Cooper, Whitman and Dreiser), who revel in "reality" but who are often vulgarly anti-intellectual, "combining aggression with conformity and reverting to the crudest forms of frontier psychology." In short, the creative mind in America is "fragmented" and "one-sided":

For the process of polarization has produced a dichotomy between experience and consciousness—a dislocation between energy and sensibility, between conduct and theories of conduct, between life conceived as an opportunity and life conceived as a discipline.

What American literature has lacked is that rich balance between mind and energy which Rahv believes is the most valuable characteristic of "mature" European writing (in a companion essay, "The Cult of Experience in American Writing," for example, he observes that "whereas Europeans like Malraux and Silone enter deeply into the meaning of political ideas and beliefs, Americans touch only superficially on such matters..."). The terms "paleface" and "redskin" caught on all too quickly, and for the wrong reasons. They are attractively reductive but they do contain a small element of truth; and thus they seem to be saying something important but in effect offer an excuse for not having to make finer discriminations and distinctions.

There are a few essays, however, which are not concerned with politics or ideologies, and here Rahv is at his very best. He loved Gogol, Dostoevsky, and especially Tolstoy, and wrote about them appreciatively, in the true sense of that abused term. He has little to say about form or style in these writers—he has no critical vocabulary for that—but his enthusiasm is irresistible. What Kazin once said about Malraux is also true of these essays: "the critic aroused the reader in behalf of the imagination that had aroused him."

RANSOM, John Crowe. American. Born in Pulaski, Tennessee, 30 April 1888. Educated at Vanderbilt University, Nashville, Tennessee, A.B. 1909 (Phi Beta Kappa); Christ Church, Oxford (Rhodes Scholar) B.A. 1913. Served in the United States Army, 1917-19. Married Robb Reavill in 1920; three children. Assistant in English, Harvard University, Cambridge, Massachusetts, 1914. Member of the Faculty, 1914-27, and Professor of English, 1927-37, Vanderbilt University; Carnegie Professor of Poetry, 1937-58, and Professor Emeritus, 1958-74, Kenyon College, Gambier, Ohio. Visiting Lecturer in English, Chattanooga University, Tennessee, 1938; Visiting Lecturer in Language and Criticism, University of Texas, Austin, 1956. Member of the Fugitive Group of Poets: Founding Editor, with Allen Tate, *The Fugitive*, Nashville, 1922-25; Editor, *Kenyon Review*, Gambier, Ohio, 1937-59. Formerly, Honorary Consultant in American Letters, Library of Congress, Washington, D.C. Recipient: Guggenheim Fellowship, 1931; Bollingen Prize, 1951; Loines Award, 1951; Brandeis University Creative Arts Award, 1958; Academy of American Poets Fellowship, 1962; National Book Award, 1964; National Endowment for the Arts award, 1966; Emerson-Thoreau Medal, 1968; National Institute of Arts and Letters Gold Metal, 1973. Member, American Academy of Arts and Letters, and American Academy of Arts and Sciences. *Died 3 July 1974.*

PUBLICATIONS

Criticism

The World's Body. New York, Scribner, 1938; revised edition, Baton Rouge, Louisiana State University Press, 1968.
"Yeasts and His Symbols," in *Kenyon Review* (Gambier, Ohio), 1, 1939.
The New Criticism. New York, New Directions, 1941.
"Criticism as Pure Speculation," in *The Intent of the Critic*, edited by Donald A. Stauffer. Princeton, New Jersey, Princeton University Press, 1941.
"The Inorganic Muses," in *Kenyon Review* (Gambier, Ohio), 5, 1943.
"The Bases of Criticism" in *Sewanee Review* (Tennessee), 52, 1944.
"Poetry I: The Formal Analysis," and "Poetry II: The Final Cause," in *Kenyon Review* (Gambier, Ohio), 9, 1947.
"The Understanding of Fiction," in *Kenyon Review* (Gambier, Ohio), 12, 1950.
"The Poetry of 1900-1950," in *Kenyon Review* (Gambier, Ohio), 13, 1951.
Poems and Essays. New York, Knopf, 1955.
"The Strange Music of English Verse," in *Kenyon Review* (Gambier, Ohio), 18, 1956.
"New Poets and Old Muses," in *American Poetry at Mid-Century*. Washington D.C., Library of Congress, 1958.
Introduction to *Selected Poems of Thomas Hardy*. New York, Macmillan, 1960.
"The Planetary Poet," in *Kenyon Review* (Gambier, Ohio), 26, 1964.
Beating the Bushes: Selected Essays 1941-1970. New York, New Directions, 1972.
"Art as Adventure in Form: Letters of John Crowe Ransom, 1923-1927" (letters to Allen Tate), edited by Thomas Daniel Young and George Core, in *Southern Review* (Baton Rouge, Louisiana), 12, 1976.

Verse

Poems about God. New York, Holt, 1919.
Armageddon, with *A Fragment*, by William Alexander Percy, and *Avalon*, by Donald Davidson. Charleston, Poetry Society of South Carolina, 1923.
Chills and Fevers: Poems. New York, Knopf, 1924.
Grace after Meat. London, Hogarth Press, 1924.
Two Gentlemen in Bonds. New York, Knopf, 1927.

Selected Poems.   New York, Knopf, 1945; London, Eyre and Spottiswoode, 1947; revised edition, 1963, 1969.

Other

God Without Thunder: An Unorthodox Defense of Orthodoxy.   New York, Harcourt Brace, 1930; London, Gerald Howe, 1931.
A College Primer of Writing.   New York, Holt, 1943.
Exercises on the Occasion of the Dedication of the New Phi Beta Kappa Hall....   Williamsburg, Virginia, College of William and Mary, 1958.

Editor, *Topics for Freshman Writing: Twenty Topics for Writing, with Appropriate Material for Study.*   New York, Holt, 1935.
Editor, *The Kenyon Critics: Studies in Modern Literature from the "Kenyon Review".*   Cleveland, World, 1951.
Editor, *Selected Poems,* by Thomas Hardy.   New York, Macmillan, 1961.

BIOGRAPHY, CRITICAL STUDIES AND BIBLIOGRAPHY

Yvor Winters, "John Crowe Ransom; or, Thunder Without God," in *In Defense of Reason.*   New York, Swallow Press and Morrow, 1947.
John Crowe Ransom: Critical Essays and a Bibliography, edited by Thomas Daniel Young.   Baton Rouge, Louisiana State University Press, 1968.
James E. Magner, Jr., *John Crowe Ransom: Critical Principles and Preoccupations.*   The Hague, Mouton, 1971.
René Wellek, "John Crowe Ransom's Theory of Poetry," in *Literary Theory and Structure,* edited by Frank Brady, John Palmer, and Martin Price.   New Haven, Connecticut, and London, Yale University Press, 1973.
George Core, "Mr. Ransom and the House of Poetry," in *Sewanee Review* (Tennessee), 82, 1974.
Marcia McDonald, "The Function of the Persona of Ransom's Critical Prose," in *Mississippi Quarterly* (University Park), 30, 1976-77.
Thomas Daniel Young, "John Crowe Ransom: A Checklist, 1967-76,"in *Mississippi Quarterly* (University Park), 30, 1976-77.
Thomas Daniel Young, *Gentleman in a Dustcoat: A Biography of John Crowe Ransom.*   Baton Rouge, Louisiana State University Press, 1976.

*   *   *

No one since Coleridge—and perhaps not even Coleridge himself—has pursued more intently than John Crowe Ransom the essential distinction between "poetry" and other forms of discourse and the relationship of this distinction to the justification of art in general as "the fullest and freest and most sympathetic image of the human experience" that we have. For Ransom we live in a realm of particular objects and occasions which make up "the world's body." But our need to abstract and form concepts, if we are to survive, makes us "predatory" and all too ready to "devour" particulars as a means to some utilitarian end. "The fierce drives of the animals," he observes in an early piece ("Forms and Citizens"),

whether human or otherwise, are only towards a *kind* of thing, the indifferent instance of a universal, and not some private and irreplaceable thing. All the nouns at this stage are common nouns. But we, for our curse or our pride, have sentiments; they are directed towards persons and things; and a sentiment is the totality of love and knowledge which we have of an object that is private and unique.

That is (as he states in a later essay on Aristotle), "a particular always qualitatively exceeds the universal." The emphasis here on quality is crucial, since for Ransom, if not for Aristotle (and certainly not for those existentialists who are repelled by the thing-ness of this world), particulars are a primary source of value: we should cherish them, we must "bless what there is for being," as Auden says, for only here do we have the opportunities for love and the disinterested contemplation of the fulness of being which complete our humanity. The more "Platonizing" or "universalizing" we become, the more we separate ourselves from these proper activities:

> In [practical] labor we sacrificed nearly everything, and naturally the reward is as tenuous as the labor. Where is the body and solid substance of the world? It seems to have retired into the fulness of memory, but out of this we construct the fulness of poetry, which is counterpart to the world's fulness.
>
> The true poetry has no great interest in improving or idealizing the world, which does well enough. It only wants to realize the world, to see it better. Poetry is the kind of knowledge by which we must know what we have arranged that we shall not know otherwise. We have elected to know the world through our science, and we know a great deal, but science is only the cognitive department of our animal life, and by it we know the world only as a scheme of abstract conveniences. What we cannot know constitutionally as scientists is the world which is made of whole and indefeasible objects, and this is the world which poetry recovers for us. Men become poets, or at least they read poets, in order to atone for having been hard practical men and hard theoretical scientists.

In short, we have two faculties: the reason, which abstracts for practical purposes, and the imagination, an "organ of knowledge" whose technique employs "images." Whenever we encounter a relatively simple two-term dialectic such as this (reason and imagination, science and poetry) we usually suspect that some proposed "synthesis" may be waiting in the wings. But this is not the case with Ransom, who never forgets the fundamental opposition between his terms. In his excellent essay on Ransom, George Core maintains

> it should be remembered that John Crowe Ransom was a dualist. That is what he meant once in saying to Robert Penn Warren that he thought man was a kind of "oscillating mechanism." Robert Buffington has framed this well: "Man, he believes, must be as content as he can with a dual citizenship, living now in one country, now in the other, never enjoying a permanent home; it is his lasting temptation, and the deadliest error, to try to renounce one or the other for the simplicity of one allegiance." In other words man cannot reconcile the conflicts between head and heart, soul and body.

Art keeps this oscillation in motion, and since the particular occasions of value for an individual are fleeting, the true poem becomes in Ransom's words, a "desperate ontological or metaphysical manoeuvre":

> The poet himself, in the agony of composition, has something like this sense of his labors. The poet perpetuates in his poem an order of existence which in actual life is constantly crumbling beneath his touch. His poem celebrates the object which is real, individual, and qualitatively infinite.

But how does poetry keep the predatory tendencies of the poet himself at bay and transform "instinctive experience" into "aesthetic experience"? in *The World's Body* Ransom proposes that the formal requirements of verse, particularly its metrical conventions, hold the poet at an aesthetic distance from his object, much as the rituals of courtship once kept the lover at a respectful distance. The analogy in this case is "strict":

> Our terms now are Artist, Object, and Form. Confronting his object, the artist is tempted to react at once by registering just that aspect of the object in which he is practically "interested." For he is originally, and may at any moment revert to, a natural man, having a predatory and acquistitive interest in the object, or at best looking at it

with a "scientific" curiosity to see if he cannot discover one somewhere in it. Art has a canon to restrain this natural man. It puts the object out of his reach; or more accurately, removes him to where he cannot hurt the object, nor disrespect it by taking his practical attitude towards it, exchanging his actual station, where he is too determined by proximity to the object, and contemporaneity with it, for the mere ideal station furnished by the literary form.... [The] intention of art is one that is particulary hard to pursue steadily, because it goes against the grain of our dominant and carefully instructed instincts; it wants us to enjoy life, to taste and reflect as we drink; when we are always tending as abstract appetites to proceed, by a milder analogue, to the cold fury of "disinterested" science. A technique of art must, then, be unprepossessing, and look vain and affected, and in fact look just like the technique of fine manners, or of ritual. Heroic intentions call for heroic measures.... The formal tradition, as I have said, lays upon the poet evidently a double requirement. One is metrical or mechanical; but the measured speech is part of the logical identity of the poem; it goes into the "character" which it possesses as an ideal creation, out of the order of the actual. The other requirement is the basic one of the make-believe, the drama, the specific anonymity or pseudoanonymity, which defines the poem as poem; when that goes we may also say that the poem goes; so that there would seem to be taking place in the act of poetry a rather unprofitable labor if this anonymity is not clearly conceived when a poet is starting upon his poem, and a labor lost if the poet, who has once conceived it and established it, forgets to maintain it.

There are problems here: how is it, for example, that restraint does not merely whet the acquisitive appetite? But Ransom's arguments are so gracious and his intentions so benign that one invariably wants him to be *right* as well. In any event, from the beginning of his career Ransom was uneasy with poetry which seems to be romantically self-assertive or dispenses with the discipline of meter.

Once again, Ransom's dualism is apparent in his conception of the poem itself, which is by no means a "pure" transformation of practical interest. In "Criticism, Inc.," the important final essay of *The World's Body*, he anticipates his most important later concerns:

> The critic should find in the poem a total poetic or individual object which tends to be universalized, but is not permitted to suffer this fate. His identification of the poetic object is in terms of the universal or commonplace to which it tends, and of the tissue, or totality of connotation, which holds it secure.

Three years later, in *The New Criticism*, Ransom was quite explicit about the "mixed" nature of poetry: a poem consists of a logical core, a "structure" or a paraphrasable content which runs in a certain argumentative direction, and a tissue of local "irrelevancies" or "texture," the particular details and "totality of connotation" which keep the poem close to the contingent world of individual occasions and values. Parenthetically it is worth noting that readers who often have never seen this book—it has been a scarce item for a good many years—simply assume that Ransom's intention here is to praise Eliot, Richards, Empson, and Yvor Winters. This is not the case, however. Ransom praises their seriousness but finds that each of these critics fails to do justice to the complex nature of poetry: Richards reduces poetry to affective states, Winters reduces it to simple moral argument, and so on. In his final chapter, "Wanted: An Ontological Critic," which *has* been reprinted and is widely known, Ransom develops his own proposal for a more adequate poetics. (Most of the quotations immediately following are drawn from this chapter.) The texture of the poem preserves the "qualitative density, or value density" of particulars; the structure keeps the poem intelligible and gives us a degree of "objective knowledge." The symbols of the art work are therefore "iconic" symbols and not merely the referential signs of prose discourse. Meter is of central importance in regulating the relationship between structure and texture, but Ransom's argument is too complex to be summarized here (the interested reader should consult sections six through ten of "Wanted: An Ontological Critic" and then turn to the later essay, "Why Critics Don't Go Mad," in which Ransom makes his strongest case for meter: it now seems as important to him as texture and structure themselves. "The poem," he concludes, "assumes the form of a trinitarian existence").

Ransom's claim that the particularity of a poem is maintained by a texture of "local irrelevancies" is the source of a good many difficulties. The details are not irrelevant in the usual, pejorative sense of that term: they somehow "depend" upon the logical argument, though they are "not closely determined by it." After discussing the fairly commonplace argument of "To His Coy Mistress," Ransom cites the last lines and praises their "brilliance." The details here "luxuriate" and "display energy in unpredictable ways," so that "we have got a good deal more than we had hoped for." The details may be surprising, one might object at this point, but they are hardly "irrelevant." With his unerring sense of logical tangles, W.K. Wimsatt remarks (in "The Concrete Universal," now reprinted in *The Verbal Icon*) that for Ransom

> The argument [structure] ...is the prose or scientific meaning, what the poem has in common with other kinds of writing. The irrelevance is a texture of concreteness which does not contribute anything to the argument, but is somehow enjoyable or valuable for its own sake, the vehicle of a metaphor which one boards heedless of where it runs, whether crosstown or downtown—just for the ride. So Ransom nurses and refines the argument, and on one page he makes the remark that the poet searches for "suitability" in his particular phrases, and by suitability Ransom means "the propriety which consists in their denoting the particularity which really belongs to the logical object." But the difference between "propriety" and relevance in such a context is not easy to see. And the relevance is logic.

And he concludes—unanswerably, it seems to me—that Ransom's doctrine of argument and local irrelevance is simply "a version of the theory of ornamental metaphor." Ransom takes up Wimsatt's objections in his second essay on the concrete universal, published in 1970, but fails to come to terms with the real issue here.

Ransom's 1955 essay, "The Concrete Universal: Observations on the Understanding of Poetry," completes his long defense of the dual nature of poetry. A concrete universal is rather like the blueprint of a bridge: when the bridge is built the original plan and the concrete manifestation or embodiment of it overlap at every point. But the basic concerns of poetry are "moral universals" and we call a poem "beautiful" when we see that the universal does not completely use up the details by which it manifests itself. This is beauty in Kant's sense:

> Kant cites readily an instance or so of natural beauty. In a garden the foliage or the blossoms of the plants will answer insofar as the general profile is concerned to the gardener's geometrical Universal, yet the configuration in its profuse detail is much too intricate, and spontaneous-looking, to account for, and implies energies not used up by the Universal. It is as if the plants obey the law of their placement only to exhibit their own freedom beneath it the more luxuriantly. We have learned to think that this is just the right condition in which they will manifest their grace, or their beauty. And Kant has supplied the paradigm of natural beauty. (If there was anticipation of this paradigm, it was not on radical or philosophical grounds.) Nature seems to have no inclination to reject or even to resent the human Universal, for now obtains the condition of "freedom under the law," and its consequence of beauty. In these or similar terms the paradigm is recited nearly everywhere.... Poetry is the representation of natural beauty. The spectacular faculty of Imagination is its agent.

Ransom's argument in this long, dense and brilliant essay is so attractive that once again one likes to accept it without qualification. But there is an indication here of what may be an important limitation of sensibility. What about those deeply tragic works which seem to make affirmation impossible? The poet's faith, Ransom concludes,

> is that this is "the best of all possible worlds"; inasmuch as it is not possible for imagination to acquaint us with any other world. It is a horrid as well as a beautiful world, but without the horror we should never focus the beauty; without death there would be no relish for life; without danger, no courage; without savagery, no gentleness; and without the background of our frequent ignominy, no human dignity and pride. (These are excellent and rather Hegelian commonplaces.)

But is this the only "faith" which can produce great poetry? For Ransom true poetry always turns out to be poetry of a very special and limited kind: like the metaphysical verse of the seventeenth century it must display a particularly rich relationship between structure and texture. Moreover, Ransom gives us no way of talking about extended poems or poetic drama and has virtually nothing to say about the possible greatness of prose works, in which meter, of course, cannot be present.

In any event, the function of criticism is clear enough. The questions which the poet asks himself as he creates the work are the questions the critic asks once the poem has been written:

> when do we have a structure which will hold up the poem we have started to write? How should we develop the structure we have in mind so that its unfolding will consist with a successful poem? Where in this development must we enforce the logic and where may we relax it and incorporate pure texture? What are the sorts of texture which will go along with a given structure? And what structure permits a given texture?

The critic must also inquire into the ways in which the metrical pattern of a given poem completes its "trinitarian existence." And these are precisely the questions which Ransom consistently raises in his own practical criticism, from his famous dissenting view of Shakespeare's sonnets, in *The World's Body*, through the late, magnanimous essays on Hardy and Stevens. When Ransom is writing about the relatively narrow range of poetry he values most, he is a superb critic. It is something of a scandal that his many distinguished friends and students have let most of these pieces languish in the back files of *The Kenyon Review*.

RICHARDS, I(vor) A(rmstrong).   British.   Born in Sandbach, Cheshire, 26 February 1893. Educated at Clifton College; Magdalene College, Cambridge, B.A. 1914, M.A. 1918, D.Litt. 1932. Married Dorothy Eleanor Pilley in 1926. Lecturer in English, Cambridge University, 1919; Fellow, Magdalene College, 1926; Visiting Professor, Tsing Hua University, Peking, 1929-30. Visiting Lecturer, 1931, University Lecturer, 1939, University Professor, 1943-63, and Professor Emeritus, 1963-79, Harvard University, Cambridge, Massachusetts. Director, the Orthological Institute of China, 1936-38. Corresponding Fellow, British Academy, 1959; Honorary Fellow, Magdalene College, 1964. Recipient: Loines Award, 1962; Companion of Honour, 1964; Emerson-Thoreau Medal, 1970; Brandeis University Creative Arts Medal, 1972. Litt.D.: Harvard University, 1944. Honorary Member, American Academy of Arts and Letters. *Died 7 September 1979.*

PUBLICATIONS

Criticism

> *The Foundations of Aesthetics*, with C.K. Ogden and James Wood.   London, Allen and Unwin, 1922; New York, Lear, 1925.
> *The Principals of Literary Criticism.*   London, Kegan Paul Trench Trubner, 1924; New York, Harcourt Brace, 1925.
> *Science and Poetry.*   London, Kegan Paul Trench Trubner, 1926; revised edition, 1935; as *Poetries and Sciences*, London, Routledge, and New York, Norton, 1970.
> *Practical Criticism: A Study of Literary Judgment.*   London, Kegan Paul Trench Trubner, 1929; New York, Harcourt Brace, 1950.
> *Coleridge on Imagination.*   London, Paul Trench Trubner, 1934; New York, Harcourt Brace, 1935.

Speculative Instruments.   Chicago, University of Chicago Press, and London, Routledge, 1955.
Coleridge's Minor Poems (lecture).   Missoula, Montana State University Press, 1960; reprinted in *Poetries*, 1974.
Poetries: Their Media and Ends, edited by Trevor Eaton.   The Hague, Mouton, 1974.
Beyond.   New York, Harcourt Brace, 1974.
Complementarities: Uncollected Essays and Reviews, edited by John Paul Russo. Cambridge, Massachusetts, Harvard University Press, 1976; Manchester, Carcanet Press, 1977.
Verse and Prose (address).   London, English Association, 1978.

Verse

Goodbye Earth and Other Poems.   New York, Harcourt Brace, 1958; London, Routledge, 1959.
The Screens and Other Poems.   New York, Harcourt Brace, 1960; London, Routledge, 1961.
Internal Colloquies: Poems and Plays.   New York, Harcourt Brace, 1971; London, Routledge, 1972.
New and Selected Poems.   Manchester, Carcanet Press, 1978.

Other

The Meaning of Meaning, with C.K. Ogden.   London, Kegan Paul Trench Trubner, 1923; New York, Harcourt Brace, 1956.
Mencius on the Mind: Experiments in Multiple Definition.   London, Paul Trench Trubner, and New York, Harcourt Brace, 1932.
Basic Rules of Reason.   London, Paul Trench Trubner, 1933.
Basic in Teaching: East and West.   London, Paul Trench Trubner, 1935.
The Philosophy of Rhetoric.   New York and London, Oxford University Press, 1936.
Interpretation in Teaching.   New York, Harcourt Brace, and London, Paul Trench Trubner, 1938.
How to Read a Page: A Course in Effective Reading, with an Introduction to a Hundred Great Words.   New York, Norton, 1942; London, Paul Trench Trubner, 1943.
Basic English and Its Uses.   New York, Norton, and London, Paul Trench Trubner, 1943.
A World Language: An Address.   New York, New York Herald Tribune, 1944.
The Pocket Book of Basic English: A Self-Teaching Way into English with Directions in Spanish, French, Italian, Portuguese, German, with Christine M. Gibson.   New York, Pocket Books, 1945; revised edition, 1946; as *English Through Pictures*, 1952.
Learning Basic English: A Practical Handbook for English-Speaking People, with Christine Gibson.   New York, Norton, 1945.
Nations and Peace.   New York, Simon and Schuster, 1947.
The Republic of Plato: A Version in Simplified English.   London, Paul Trench Trubner, 1948.
French Self-Taught with Pictures, with M.H. Ilsley and Christine Gibson.   New York, Pocket Books, 1950.
Spanish Self-Taught Through Pictures, with Ruth C. Metcalf Romero and Christine Gibson.   New York, Pocket Books, 1950.
The Wrath of Achilles: The Iliad of Homer, Shortened.   New York, Norton, 1950; London, Routledge, 1951.
German Through Pictures, with others.   New York, Pocket Books, 1953.
Hebrew Through Pictures, with David Weinstein and Christine Gibson.   New York, Pocket Books, 1954.

Italian Through Pictures, with Italo Evangelista and Christine Gibson. New York, Pocket Books, 1955.
First Steps in Reading English, with Christine Gibson. New York, Pocket Books, 1957.
French Through Pictures, with M.H. Ilsley and Christine Gibson. New York, Pocket Books, 1959.
A First Workbook of French, with M.H. Ilsley and Christine Gibson. New York, Washington Square Press, 1960.
Russian Through Pictures, with Evelyn Jasiulko Harden and Christine Gibson. New York, Pocket Books, 1961.
Design for Escape: World Education Through Modern Media. New York, Harcourt Brace, 1968.
So Much Nearer: Essays Towards a World English. New York, Harcourt Brace, 1968.

Editor, with C.K. Ogden, *The Times of India Guide to Basic English.* Bombay, Times of India Press, 1938.
Editor, *The Portable Coleridge.* New York, Viking Press, 1950; London, Penguin, 1977.
Editor and Translator, *Republic*, by Plato. Cambridge, University Press, 1966.

CRITICAL STUDIES AND BIBLIOGRAPHY

F.R. Leavis, "Dr. Richards, Bentham and Coleridge," in *Scrutiny* (Cambridge), 3, 1935.
John Crowe Ransom, "I. A. Richards: The Psychological Critic," in *The New Criticism.* New York, New Directions, 1941.
R.S. Crane, "I. A. Richards on the Art of Interpretation," in *Critics and Criticism: Ancient and Modern.* Chicago, University of Chicago Press, 1952.
W.H.N. Hotopf, *Language, Thought, and Comprehension: A Case Study in the Writings of I.A. Richards.* Bloomington, Indiana University Press, and London, Routledge, 1965.
René Wellek, "On Rereading I.A. Richards," in *Southern Review* (Baton Rouge, Louisiana), 3, 1967.
Jerome P. Schiller, *I.A. Richards' Theory of Literature.* New Haven, Connecticut, and London, Yale University Press, 1969 (contains a selective bibliography of works by and about Richards).
John Paul Russo, "Richards and the Search for Critical Instruments," in *Twentieth-Century Literature in Retrospect*, edited by Reuben A. Brower. Cambridge, Massachusetts, Harvard University Press, 1971.
John Paul Russo, "A Bibliography of the Books, Articles, and Reviews of I.A. Richards," in *I.A. Richards: Essays in His Honor*, edited by Helen Vendler, Reuben Brower, and John Hollander. New York, Oxford University Press, 1973.
John Paul Russo, "A Study in Influence: The Moore-Richards Paradigm," in *Critical Inquiry* (Chicago), 5, 1979.

*   *   *

Poetry, perhaps even art itself, "may very possibly decline and...disappear," I.A. Richards warned his readers in 1924, but if they do, "a biological calamity of the first order will have occurred." Properly understood, this extraordinary contention accounts for much of Richards' thinking during the 1920's and at least helps to explain the two paradoxes which must strike anyone interested in his work. How is it that this most positivistic of critics ("naturalistic" may be a safer term) could place such enormous value on the "pseudo-statements" of poetry? And why did the "Guru of Cambridge," as Basil Willey once called him, leave Cambridge—and literary criticism? "Fame found him early in the 1920's," Dudley Young observed in a review of *Beyond* (a review Richards was not happy with):

[He] dazzled Cambridge University with a unique combination of Arnoldian high seriousness, philosophic rigor, a timely awareness of the rising importance of psychology, and a rare inwardness with poetry.... In the thirties, however, his career took a strange turn. From the commanding heights, the very center of the cultural debate, he gradually wandered away—first to China and then to Harvard to work on primary education and linguistics.

To deal with the first paradox, we have to take up the argument of *Principles of Literary Criticism* in some detail. Richards begins by virtually dismissing the entire critical tradition:

> A few conjectures, a supply of admonitions, many acute isolated observations, some brilliant guesses, much oratory and applied poetry, inexhaustible confusion, a sufficiency of dogma, no small stock of prejudices, whimsies and crochets, a profusion of mysticism, a little genuine speculation, sundry stray inspirations, pregnant hints and *aperçus*; of such as these, it may be said without exaggeration, is extant critical theory composed.

As R.S. Crane pointed out, there are several ways of responding to this indictment. We may become completely sceptical about criticism as a branch of knowledge; we may try to patch together a system, picking and choosing where we will; or we may become dogmatic and assert that only a new approach can set things straight and make criticism into a genuine discipline. Richards, of course, is a dogmatist; to put it very briefly, in the *Principles* he builds (or borrows) a purely naturalistic theory of value which will account for the importance of art, while in *Practical Criticism* he isolates those factors in the reader which prevent a full response to the value of art, or at least of poetry.

For Richards aesthetic experience is in no sense different from our other experiences. The belief in a "special" aesthetic state is one of the causes of the "chaos of critical theories," but the real source of error lies in our habitual appeal to some "metaphysical" grounds for a definition of value. Here it would be impossible to imagine a more thoroughly "scientific" approach: "With the underpinning of a solid British empiricism," John Paul Russo explains, "[Richards] built a model on the best strictly neurological principles in postwar England" (specifically, the model Sir Charles Sherrington proposes in *Intergrative Action of the Nervous System*). At any given moment the human organism is an incredibly complex system of physiochemical events whose primary function is to direct our transactions with a constantly shifting environment. From this point of view, whatever facilitates our better adjustment to the environment is a "good" and "has value": "Among those who reject any metaphysical view of value it has become usual to define value as a capacity for satisfying feeling and desire in various intricate ways." Further, "apart from circumstances, anyone *will actually prefer* to satisfy a greater number of equal appetencies rather than a less." And finally, "that organisation which is least wasteful of human possibilities is...the best." (Richards is well aware of the ethical question this kind of neurological utilitarianism raises: "It may very well be the case that a person's own interests are such that, *if he understood them,* were well organised, in other words, he would be a useful and charming member of the community, but so long as there are people about who are not well organised, communities must protect themselves.") In short, Richards relies on the familiar and unfashionable principle of the greatest happiness for the greatest number of inner and outer relations; and since this position may seem hopelessly outmoded to many readers, it is worth quoting William Empson's defense of the matter:

> The idea of making a calculation to secure the greatest happiness for the greatest number is perhaps inherently absurd, but it seems the only picture we can offer. Sensible people have long been accustomed to consider what would be "for the best," bearing in mind the whole situation, and have often emerged from this effort with sensible answers. To claim that God has told you to act for the general harm would surely be blasphemous if made quite specific. Short of that, the only alternatives to Bentham are arty and smarty moralising; giving unreasoned importance either to a whim of one's own or to the whim of a social clique.

In any event, for Richards morals are "purely prudential," and "the conduct of life is throughout an attempt to organise impulses so that success is obtained for the greatest number of them, for the most important and weightiest set."

The arts are supremely valuable as stimuli, as preparations for more competent living:

> The arts are our storehouse of recorded values. They spring from and perpetuate hours in the lives of exceptional people when their control and command of experience is at its highest, hours when the varying possibilities of experience are most clearly seen and the different activities which may arise are most exquisitely reconciled.... [The arts] record the most important judgements we possess as to the values of experience.... But subtle or recondite experiences are for most men incommunicable and indescribable.... In the arts we find the record in the only form in which these things can be recorded of the experiences which have seemed most worth having to the most sensitive and discriminating persons.

Every experience affects us and alters, however slightly, the possibilities for action and the formation of a more complex "attitude." One of Richards' examples makes the point very nicely:

> every perception probably includes a response in the form of incipient action. We constantly overlook the extent to which all the while we are making preliminary adjustments, getting ready to act in one way or another. Reading Captain Slocum's account of the centipede which bit him on the head...the writer has been caused to leap right out of his chair by a leaf which fell upon his face from a tree. Only occasionally does some such accident show how extensive are the adjustments made in what appear to be the most unmuscular occupations.

The modified organization may remain at the level of attitude or incipient action, but this in no way reduces the value of the experience for useful response in the future.

The problems readers have had with Richards' model are as serious as they are predictable. John Crowe Ransom, for example, complained that we simply cannot examine these delicate interior and exterior adjustments—to which the best reply would be that Richards realizes how insuperably difficult it is to build an accurate model of the "mind." The final test for the value of art has to be pragmatic. And it is here that a more serious objection is inevitable. If we accept Richards' model thus far, it should follow that the greatest artists have been the most competent of men in at least some other important areas of life, and that their best audiences follow them at one or two removes: Richards proposes that "if the artist's organisation is such as to allow him to live a fuller life than the average, with less unnecessary interference between its component impulses, then plainly we should do well to be more like him...." But is this actually the case? The lives of the poets (and the painters and the composers) do not offer encouraging evidence, while from the point of view of the audience even the most valuable works can be *used*, to borrow C.S. Lewis' terms, rather than *received*. Richards' attempts to counter these objections (in Chapter 24 of the *Principles*) are not very convincing.

But most troublesome of all have been the issues raised by Richards' distinction between emotive and referential language. As a thorough-going naturalist he has to maintain that "the bulk of poetry consists of statements which only the very foolish would think of attempting to verify" (the "very foolish" here are those, for example, who believe that the *Divine Comedy* and the *Phaedo* are "true" in the usual, empirical sense of the term). Yet he has also made the highest possible claims for poetry as an aid to living. Dealing with this paradox in the *Principles*, he argues that

> Fictions whether aroused by statement or by analogous things in other arts may be used in many ways. They may be used, for example, to deceive. But this is not a characteristic use in poetry. The distinction which needs to be kept clear does not set up fictions in opposition to verifiable truths in the scientific sense. A statement may be used for the sake of the *reference*, true or false, which it causes. This is the scientific use of language. But it may also be used for the sake of the effects in emotion and attitude produced by the reference it occasions. This is the *emotive* use of language. The distinction once clearly grasped is simple. We may either use words for the sake of the references they promote, or we may use them for the sake of attitudes and emotions which ensue. Many arrangements of words evoke attitudes without any reference being required *en route*. They

operate like musical phrases.... It matters not at all in such cases whether the references are true or false. Their sole function is to bring about and support the attitudes which are the further response.

Science makes statements which are "true" in the sense that they point to something beyond themselves, to real, existing situations in which empirical demonstration is both possible and necessary. But poetry gives us statements which are, in Richards' unhappy phrase, "pseudo-statements": The *Divine Comedy* points to nothing in the world of fact. Richards is in the very difficult position of maintaining that "untrue," that is, non-referential statements, properly received, are among the most potent devices we have for arousing attitudes which allow us to function with maximum efficiency in the eminently referential world outside the arts. Thus he is able to conclude that "it should be unnecessary to insist upon the degree to which high civilization, in other words, free, varied and unwasteful life, depends upon [the arts]"; their loss would be nothing less than a "biological calamity" for the race. Richards has insisted upon maintaining this distinction over the years (see *Sciences and Poetries*, "Emotive Meaning Still" in *Speculative Instruments*, and Chapter 1 and 16 of *Poetries: Their Media and Ends*), just as his critics have never tired of asserting that his position is too paradoxical to be tenable. Not all paradoxes involve irreconcilable contradictions, however; and the reader who is willing to grant this much will recognize that the whole question soon leads to one of the most difficult issues aesthetics has to confront, the problem of belief. The best place to begin *here*—and it is by no means a mere "introduction" to the problem—is M.H. Abrams' beautifully reasoned essay, "Belief and the Suspension of Disbelief."

We are now in a better position to understand Richards' distinction between good art and bad. "Badness" in poetry means the failure of the work to provide adequate or worthy stimuli; bad poetry simply repeats and thus tends to confirm those *clichés* and stereotypes which interfere with flexible living: "Only for those who make certain conventional, stereotyped maladjustments does the magic of [the bad poem] work." The man who lives by means of stock responses cannot adjust to the demands of a rapidly changing world; he is able only to "face fictions," and this in turn leads to "not only an acceptance of the mediocre in ordering life, but a blurring and confusion of impulses and a very widespread loss of value." The mind of the average, technically literate person is becoming "of inferior shape—thin, brittle and patchy" (and Richards adds in an ominous aside, "As to the less 'well-educated'—genius apart—they inhabit chaos." This was in 1929: can teachers today be more optimistic?). The greatest works of art are those which are most "inclusive":

> There are two ways in which impulses may be organised; by exclusion and by inclusion, by synthesis and by elimination. Although every coherent state of mind depends upon both, it is permissable to contrast experiences which win order and stability through a narrowing of the response with those which widen it. A very great deal of art is content with the full, ordered development of comparatively special and limited experiences, with a definite emotion, for example, Sorrow, Joy, Pride, or a definite attitude, Love, Indignation, Admiration, Hope, or with a specific mood, Melancholy, Optimism or Longing. And such art has its own value and place in human affairs. No one will quarrel with "Break, break, break," or with the *Coronach* or with *Rose Aylmer*, or with *Love's Philosophy*, although clearly they are limited and exclusive. But they are not the greatest kind of poetry; we do not expect from them what we find in the *Ode to a Nightingale*, in *Proud Maisie*, in *Sir Patrick Spens*, in *The Definition of Love* or in the *Nocturnall upon S. Lucie's Day*.
>
> The structures of these two kinds of experience are different, and the difference is not one of subject but of the relations *inter se* of the several impulses active in the experience. A poem of the first group is built out of sets of impulses which run parallel, which have the same direction. In a poem of the second group the most obvious feature is the extraordinary heterogeneity of the distinguishable impulses. But they are more than heterogeneous, they are opposed. They are such that in ordinary, non-poetic, non-imaginative experience, one or another set would be suppressed to give as it might appear freer development to the others.

The great inclusive works lead to "the equilibrium of opposed impulses, which we suspect to be the ground-plan of the most valuable aesthetic experiences" and bring into play "far more of our personality than is possible in experiences of a more defined emotion." For Richards the chief resource the poet has to achieve this equilibrium is, of course, metaphor, "the supreme agent by which disparate and hitherto unconnected things are brought together in poetry for the sake of the effects upon attitudes and impulses which spring from their collocation and from the combinations which the mind then establishes between them." Again, the finest works "will withstand the test of irony," whereas lesser works "will not bear an ironical contemplation":

> We have only to read *The War Song of Dinas Vawr* in close conjunction with the *Coronach*, or to remember that unfortunate phrase "Those lips, O slippery blisses!" from *Endymion*, while reading *Love's Philosophy*, to notice this. Irony in this sense consists in the bringing in of the opposite, the complementary impulses: that is why poetry which is exposed to it is not of the highest order, and why irony itself is so constantly a characteristic of poetry which is.

Finally, it is in tragedy that we have the most valuable examples of what Coleridge called "the balance or reconciliation of opposed or discordant qualities."

Anyone familiar with the development of modern criticism in the 1930's and 40's will recognise at once how influential this distinction between the poetry of inclusion and exclusion has been. In England William Empson (who had been Richards' student) demonstrated the multivalent power of individual words and images in "inclusive" poems. (It is no accident that most of Empson's illustrations in *Seven Types of Ambiguity* come from Shakespeare. And while Richards himself had not used the word "ambiguity," Empson's special sense of the term is clearly derived from the argument outlined above: our ability to keep multiple meanings and their implications in mind has an important bearing on our ability to maintain ourselves in a complex world.) In America the same distinction seems to have determined much of Cleanth Brooks' critical thinking, and Brooks in turn had an extraordinary influence on the teaching of literature in the universities. Many of the terms (and implied standards) which Brooks and Warren popularized in *Understanding Poetry*—tension, irony, paradox, and so on—have their origins in Chapter 23 of the *Principles*.

In the *Principles* Richards also makes a distinction between "technical" and "critical" remarks:

> in a full critical statement which states not only that the experience is valuable, but also that it is caused by certain features in a contemplated object, the part which describes the value of the experience we call the *critical part*. That which describes the object we shall call the *technical* part.

Richards has made relatively few "technical" observations over the years, but what he does say in *Practical Criticism* is important. We cannot grasp any utterance fully, he argues, unless we understand the writer's *sense* (his paraphrasable meaning), his *feeling* (his attitude towards his subject), his *tone* (his attitude towards his audience) and his overall purpose or *intention*. Ideal understanding of what is in the "contemplated object" would involve "not only an accurate direction of thought, a correct evocation of feeling, an exact apprehension of tone and a precise recognition of intention, but further it would get these contributory meanings in their right order and proportion to one another, and seize—though not in terms of explicit thought—their interdependence upon one another." Thus in *Practical Criticism* Richards' primary aim is to diagnose the causes of imperfect understanding: obviously if we cannot grasp the meaning of a text we cannot receive the value which he had been at such pains to define in the *Principles*.

The experiments in understanding which Richards conducted at Cambridge form the basis of *Practical Criticism*. During 1925 and 1927 he had his students respond to four or five poems a week. The students were "exceptionally miscellaneous," Joan Bennett recalls in her splendid essay, "How It Strikes a Contemporary" (printed in *I.A. Richards: Essays In His Honor*). Of the sixty or so who attended each session, "Probably two thirds...were undergraduates, most of them studying for the English Tripos. The remaining third included young graduates in their twenties, most of them doing some teaching for their colleges." The students were not told (and rarely guessed) the authors of the poems, which ranged from the very good to the very bad; they had a week in which to record their judgments, and at the next session, Mrs. Bennett goes on, Richards discussed the results:

> Comments which illustrated types of misreading and consequent misjudgment were read out, also some that expressed valuable insights. As can be imagined there could be painful moments for some members of the audience, caught out in careless reading, even though no one but themselves could know of their failure. On the whole however, those hours in the lecture room were hilarious, salutary and revealing. Except where a comment was as arrogant as it was absurd, Richards skilfully steered us towards mutual tolerance and shared amusement, as well as towards greater humility, and above all towards more alert attention to the words on the page.
>
> The most startling and inescapable result of this experiment was the discovery of widespread incomprehension of meaning at the most elementary level.

Richards devotes the greater part of *Practical Criticism* to a devastating analysis of the causes of misreading (ten in number, ranging from simple failure to construe the literal meaning of the text to various kinds of affective failures and preconceptions as to what a poem should be and do). The evidence for blocked understanding is overwhelming, and in the concluding section of the book Richards repeats the lesson of the *Principles*: if we cannot read we cannot experience the value of art; we cannot achieve what he now calls "self-completion," that level of organization in which "no disorder, no mutual frustration of impulses remains."

The nature of criticism follows logically enough from Richards' definition of value and self-completion: the critic is as much concerned with the health of the mind as the physician is with bodily health; he must be "adept at experiencing, without eccentricities, the state of mind relevant to the work of art he is experiencing," and he must be "a sound judge of values":

> The critical act is the starting-point, not the conclusion, of an argument. The personality stands balanced between the particular experience which is the realised poem and the whole fabric of its past experiences and developed habits of mind. What is being settled is whether this new experience can or cannot be taken into the fabric with advantage. Would the fabric afterwards be better or worse?

Five years later, in *Coleridge on Imagination*, Richards offered an eloquent summary statement of the value of poetry and the responsibilities of criticism:

> To free [us] from distracting trivialities, from literary chit-chat, from discussion of form which does not ask what has the form, from flattering rationalization, from the clouds of unchecked sensibility and unexamined interpretations is a minor duty of criticism. But there is a more positive task: to recall that poetry is the supreme use of language, man's chief co-ordinating instrument, in the service of the most integral purposes of life; and to explore, with thoroughness, the intricacies of the modes of language as working modes of the mind.

To return, finally, to the second of our two opening paradoxes: how is it that Richards was soon to leave "literary criticism" in the usual sense of the term? In a recent interview with Reuben Brower, Richards recalls that after he had finished *Interpretation in Teaching* (in which he diagnoses the misunderstanding of prose) he made his "big transition":

> Actually, those two books [*Philosophy of Rhetoric* and *Interpretation in Teaching*] sickened me for life of trying to read examination papers fairly. It's too hard to judge how foolish a comment really is and there are too many, too big a proportion of foolish comments. Do you know when I decided to back out of literature, as a subject, I learnt something? I learnt where the academic railway tracks are. I was crossing the railway tracks in a most sinister fashion, I was told so again and again. [Bertrand] Russell had tried to do it, you know. He'd founded a school and written a book on education. And people had said, "No wonder. He hadn't anything more to say." There's a very severe penalty attaching to going the wrong way across the railway tracks.

And in the foreword to *Speculative Instruments* he remarks, sadly, "No one, I imagine, migrates from Literature to Education for fun, but through a feeling as to what will happen if we do not develop improved teaching soon enough." It seems, then, that Richards' encounters with misreading among the "well-educated" convinced him that if there is to be any improvement, it must begin at far more elementary levels, just as the spectre of international misunderstanding may account for his vigorous efforts on behalf of Basic English.

Richards' criticism seems to be wholly out of favor at the moment. His curious mixture of positivism and high Arnoldian seriousness may never be in fashion again, but this is not to say that his methods were wrong or his hopes foolish. It may be simply that he arrived too late on the scene, and that in any event neither he nor anyone else could have prevented the erosion, quick and perhaps inevitable, of our faith in high culture to form and sustain a fully human world.

RICKS, Christopher (Bruce).   British.   Born in London, 18 September 1933. Educated at King Alfred's School, Wantage, Berkshire; Balliol College, Oxford (Andrew Bradley Junior Research Fellow, 1957), B.A. 1956, B.Litt. 1958, M.A. 1960. Served as 2nd Lieutenant, Green Howards, 1952. Married Kirsten Jensen in 1956 (marriage dissolved); Judith Aronson in 1977. Fellow of Worcester College, Oxford, 1958-68; Professor of English, University of Bristol, 1968-75. Since 1975, Professor of English, Cambridge University. Visiting Professor, Stanford University, California, and University of California, Berkeley, 1965; Smith College, Northampton, Massachusetts, 1967; Harvard University, Cambridge, Massachusetts, 1971; Wesleyan University, Middletown, Connecticut, 1974; Brandeis University, Waltham, Massachusetts, 1977, 1981. Co-Editor, *Essays in Criticism*, Oxford. Vice-President, Tennyson Society. Recipient: George Orwell Memorial Prize, 1979. Fellow of the British Academy, 1975. Address: Christ's College, Cambridge, England.

PUBLICATIONS

Criticism

Milton's Grand Style: A Study of Paradise Lost.   Oxford, Clarendon Press, 1963.
"Wordsworth: 'A Pure Organic Pleasure from the Lines,' " in *Essays in Criticism* (Oxford), 21, 1971.
Tennyson: A Biographical and Critical Study.   New York, Macmillan, 1972.
Keats and Embarrassment.   Oxford, Clarendon Press, 1974.
"Empson's Poetry," in *William Empson: The Man and His Work*, edited by Roma Gill.   London and Boston, Routledge, 1974.
"Lies," in *Critical Inquiry* (Chicago), 2, 1975.
"Geoffrey Hill and the Tongue's Atrocities" (lecture).   Swansea, University College, 1978.
"Clichés," in *The State of the Language*, edited by Leonard Michaels and Christopher Ricks.   Berkeley and London, University of California Press, 1980.

Other

Editor, with Harry Carter, *A Dissertation upon English Typographical Founders and Foundries, 1788*, by Edward Rowe Mores.   London, Oxford University Press, 1961.

Editor, *Poems and Critics: An Anthology of Poetry and Criticism from Shakespeare to Hardy.* London, Collins, 1966; New York, Harper, 1972.

Editor, *A.E. Housman: A Collection of Critical Essays.* Englewood Cliffs, New Jersey, Prentice Hall, 1968.

Editor, *Poems of 1842*, by Alfred Lord Tennyson. London, Collins, 1968.

Editor, *Paradise Lost and Paradise Regained*, by John Milton. New York, New American Library, 1968.

Editor, *The Poems of Tennyson.* London, Longman, 1969.

Editor, *The Brownings: Letters and Poetry.* New York, Doubleday, 1970.

Editor, *English Poetry and Prose, 1540-1674* (essays). London, Barrie and Jenkins, 1970.

Editor, *English Drama to 1710* (essays). London, Barrie and Jenkins, 1971.

Editor, *A Collection of Poems by Alfred Lord Tennyson.* New York, Doubleday, 1972.

Editor, *Poems of Tennyson.* New York, Norton, 1972.

Editor, with Leonard Michaels, *The State of the Language.* Berkeley and London, University of California Press, 1980.

*   *   *

In the Introduction to his useful anthology, *Poems and Critics*, Christopher Ricks asserts—with rather untypical directness—that Dr. Johnson's definition of literary criticism is still the best we have:

> It is...the task of criticism to establish principles; to improve opinion into knowledge; and to distinguish those means of pleasing which depend upon known causes and rational deduction, from the nameless and inexplicable elegancies which appeal wholly to the fancy, from which we feel delight, but know not how to produce it, and which may well be termed the enchantresses of the soul. (*The Rambler* No. 92)

Thus the critic, Ricks goes on, "will hope to extend the area where rational argument about literature is possible" and has three chief responsibilities. First, he will try to determine the relationship, in a given work, between those "antithetical" qualities, the "natural" and the "novel":

> In Dr. Johnson's terms, we ask of a work of literature that it be both natural and novel. Natural, in that it will relate recognizably to the world and will deal, in some fashion and with whatever stylization, with what is certainly true to human life. Novel, in that it will do so in some new way, so that we are grateful that this particular work has been added to those that exist already.... The greatest poems will weld together novelty and naturalness, just as they will weld together sound and sense, form and content, the particular and the universal, the personal and the impersonal, fidelity to the disorder of life with fidelity to the order of art. And of course every term of praise which we might wish to use—which indeed we have no choice but to use—simply has blame on the other side of the coin. We want a poem to be economical, but not cramped. We want it to be fluent, but not diffuse. Strong, but not brutal. Sensitive, but not spineless. Personal, but not eccentric. We want it to be both masculine and feminine, and able to do justice to antithetical abilities and habits of mind. Which is why everything depends on the particular words, on the niceties of phrasing, of rhythm, of sound, of structure.

Second, the critic will try to determine the kind and degree of success which is "internal" to the poem: he must

> understand and judge the poem in its own terms, to be confident that he understands just what the poem is trying to do and then to judge the extent to which it has succeeded.... You must know whether you are confronted by a hymn or a limerick, otherwise both your praise and your blame will be irrelevant. Often there will be no difficulty in deciding what kind of poem you are faced with; until the middle of the eighteenth century, poets were very conscious of writing in kinds of genres...and they expected their readers to

understand the terms on which the poem was being set before them. Since Romanticism, the system of genres has proved inadequate to cover all the various shades which differentiate one poem from another (though the system has not been superseded or discarded), but we still need some idea of what sort of poem we are dealing with.

"Analysis and comparison," as Eliot calls them, are the tools the critic has for this task. And finally, the critic must also judge the work by "external" standards:

> The dangers of this external judgment are obvious. It can be inflexible and so allow insufficiently for the variety within a kind. It can lend itself to the mechanical application of a rule-of-thumb. But whatever the dangers, there is no doing without some such judgment. Otherwise, if you judge a poem solely by the internal criterion of its "success" and leave out altogether the question of what it is succeeding *at*, you have no way at all of judging between, say, Milton and Matthew Prior. Prior was an excellent epigramatist, and he wrote many epigrams that are flawless in their tiny wit. Milton's epic, despite everything that is sublime and astonishing about it, has terrible flaws—as all critics have recognized. So that if we judge by the internal criterion alone...we will have no choice but to conclude that Prior is a greater poet than Milton. Which is absurd, as any reader of the two poets will know.... [Two] opposite critical principles brace against each other.... The critical terms for the external judgment are likely to be words that stand back and speak of size, scope, range, and centrality. Large words, that make large judgments, and which must always be tested against the more particular terms appropriate to the internal judgment that is achieved by analysis rather than by comparison.

Thus the responsible critic will enhance our sense of the insights a work of literature gives us into the past and the insights it gives us into our own condition now. Criticism is not a substitute for literature—the experience of reading the poem will always be primary and there will always be some "inexplicable elegancies"—but it can prepare us to receive the gifts that only art can bestow: "Literature appeals to the mind as well as the heart, the intelligence as well as the emotions—or rather, in its unity and harmony it appeals to a whole person who is released for the moment from any such divisions." Art also has the power, Ricks continues (in *Keats and Embarrassment*), to enlarge our human sympathies and "make us more alive to things" when we return to the world outside the poem. Art is "generous" and consoling: it is this sense, that

> the deep and true consolations of art are made possible by a relationship that is indeed not mutual or reciprocal as are the deep and true consolations of human relationships, which animates one of the greatest passages that Keats ever wrote:

> But for her eyes I should have fled away.
> They held me back, with a benignant light,
> Soft-mitigated by divinest lids
> Half-closed, and visionless entire they seem'd
> Of all external things—they saw me not,
> But in blank splendor beam'd like the mild moon,
> Who comforts those she sees not, who knows not
> What eyes are upward cast.

> (*The Fall of Hyperion*, I. 264-71)

The blank splendour of the moon is a type of the blank (not empty) splendour of art, which comforts those she sees not, and knows not what eyes are upward cast. The consolation which Keats here imagines, he at the same time provides; he comforts those he sees not, and this is of the essence of art.

Ricks' own critical method is that kind of close verbal analysis which "now seems one of the most important and useful ways of approaching literature." "My own general position," he admits, "is very like Mr. Empson's." The danger of Empsonian criticism, of course, is the temptation it offers an imaginative reader to use the poem as a point of departure for his own ingenuity and supersubtlety—as Empson himself realizes in *Milton's God*:

> If one view makes a bit of poetry very good, and another makes it very bad, the author's intention is inherently likely to be the one that makes it good; especially if we know that he writes well sometimes.... To try to make a printed page mean something good is only fair. There is a question for a critic at what point this generous and agreeable effort of mind ought to stop, and with an old text (the *Hamlet* of Shakespeare for example) it is no use to impute a meaning which the intended readers or audience could not have had in mind, either consciously or unconsciously.

After quoting this passage Ricks observes that

> Though the following pages owe everything to Empsonian criticism, they try to slow down the process in which Mr. Empson is so agonizingly nimble. They try to offer, wherever possible, some kind of substantiation. That is why I have made so much use of Milton's earliest commentators. And if I too am sometimes anxious about the "more the merrier" critics (and about my own leaning) the school seems to me preferable to the one whose dusty answer seems to be "the *less* the merrier," and which takes a lugubrious relish in trying to scotch any close criticism which might suggest that a poet's use of words is subtle, delicate, ingenious, or new.

The thesis of *Milton's Grand Style* is a fairly simple one: while critics have never denied the power and sweep of Milton's style in *Paradise Lost* or its appropriateness for an epic form, they have failed to see that this same style is also capable of the subtleties we usually associate with intimate lyric poetry. Ricks argues that "without abandoning epic grandeur," Milton is still able to draw upon "the infinite suggestiveness of word-order and words"; there is nothing in the grand style which is incompatible, in Leavis' words, with "sharp, concrete realization." Generalizations of the sort I am about to offer are always risky and vulnerable, but it seems to me that there is nowhere in modern criticism a finer example of what disciplined, close verbal analysis can accomplish. It is impossible to illustrate briefly Ricks' apparently endless sensitivity and, at the same time, his unerring sense of when not to go too far, but if the reader can imagine Empson's best qualities combined with the firm sense of overall purpose which distinguishes C.S. Lewis' brief discussion of Milton's style in *A Preface to Paradise Lost*, then he will have some idea of the strength of this wonderfully good book.

Keats and Embarrassment is a quirky essay which often does go too far in directions which were never very clear in the first place. Once again, Ricks' general argument is easy enough to summarize: Keats is "probably more widely and subtly gifted with powers of empathy than any other English poet." The sign of this empathy is his sensitivity to potentially embarrassing situations, and embarrassment itself is "very important" in life. By "recognizing, refining, and putting [embarrassment] to good human purposes," art, "in its unique combination of the private and the public, offers us a unique kind of human relationship freed from the possibility, which is incident to other human relationships, of an embarrassment that clogs, paralyses, or coarsens." The problem is that Ricks never defines with sufficient explicitness what he means by embarrassment: it is impossible to discriminate here between embarrassment and shame, embarrassment for oneself and for others, and all the subtle interconnections between these feelings. Perhaps Ricks assumes that his nimble readers will make the right adjustments at the right moment and will follow with no difficulty his ingenious readings of individual passages (but never, unfortunately, whole poems). If so, the assumption is not always warranted (here readers might consider his justification of Keats' notorious phrase, "slippery blisses"). Nevertheless, there are pages in *Keats and Embarrassment* in which Ricks displays the kind of sympathetic understanding which only a first rate critic can command:

> Though many kinds of hero, Keats was no kind of saint. When the sour Hodgkinson (partner of Keats's guardian, Richard Abbey) came to grief, Keats wrote to his sister Fanny: "No one can regret Mr. Hodgkinson's ill fortune: I must own illness has not made such a Saint of me as to prevent my rejoicing at his reverse." Yet his apprehension of life's pain was profound: "However among the effects this breathing is father of is that

tremendous one of sharpening one's vision into the heart and nature of Man—of convincing one's nerves that the World is full of Misery and Heartbreak, Pain, Sickness and oppression—" It is "convincing one's nerves" which is so authentically Keats; to convince one's reason, and to stir one's nerves, these are valuable enough, but the fusion in Keat's best poetry and letters, his essential ambition, was to convince one's nerves— his own and ours. Yet I think that his greatness as a man and as a writer has less to do with "convincing one's nerves that the World is full of Misery and Heartbreak, Pain, Sickness and oppression," than with convincing one's nerves that the world is full of delight, health, and liberation—all of which are sometimes ours, and needing to be achieved rather than sure to drop into our hands, and all of which are other people's all around us. All this makes up the "*physique* of our pleasures," the pleasures being necessarily mostly others' and not ours (there being more others). To convince one's nerves of others' happiness, and then without perfunctoriness, embarrassment, cynicism, or dismay to rejoice at it, is Keats's central moral impulse and especial verbal power. Keats's most truly illuminating epithet for "light" was "generous": "generous light" (*Endymion*, I. 154).

RICKWORD, (John) Edgell. British. Born in Colchester, Essex, 22 October 1898. Educated at Colchester Grammar School; Pembroke College, Oxford, 1919-20. Served in the Royal Berkshire Regiment during World War I: Military Cross. Reviewer for *New Statesman, London Mercury* and *Times Literary Supplement*, 1920-25; Editor, *Calendar of Modern Letters*, 1925-27; Reviewer, *Sunday Referee*, 1928-31; Associate Editor, *Left Review*, 1934-38; Editor, *Our Time*, 1944-47. Recipient: Arts Council Prize, 1966; D.Litt.: University of Essex, Colchester, 1978. Address: 2 Hopping Lane, London, N1 2NJ, England.

PUBLICATIONS

Criticism

> *Rimbaud: The Boy and the Poet.* London, Heinemann, and New York, Knopf, 1924; revised edition, Castle Hedingham, Essex, Daimon Press, 1963; partly reprinted in *Essays and Opinions*, 1974.
> *William Wordsworth 1770-1850.* London, Bureau of Current Affairs, 1950; reprinted in *Literature in Society*, 1978.
> *Gilray and Cruikshank*, with Michael Kantanka. Aylesbury, Buckinghamshire, Shire, 1973; reprinted in *Literature in Society*, 1978.
> *Essays and Opinions 1921-1931*, edited by Alan Young. Cheadle, Cheshire, Carcanet, 1974.
> *Literature in Society: Essays and Opinions (II) 1931-1978*, edited by Alan Young. Manchester, Carcanet, 1978.

Verse

> *Behind the Eyes.* London, Sidgwick and Jackson, 1921.
> *Invocations to Angels, and The Happy New Year.* London, Wishart, 1928.

Twittingpan and Some Others.   London, Wishart, 1931.
Collected Poems.   London, Lane, 1947.
Fifty Poems.   London, Enitharmon Press, 1970.
Behind the Eyes: Selected Poems and Translations.   Manchester, Carcanet Press, 1976.

Short Stories

Love One Another: Seven Tales.   London, Mandrake Press, 1929.

Other

Editor, *Scrutinies by Various Writers.*   London, Wishart, 2 vols., 1928-31; Folcroft, Pennsylvania, Folcroft Editions, 1976.
Editor, with Jack Lindsay, *A Handbook of Freedom: A Record of English Democracy Through Twelve Centuries.*   London, Lawrence and Wishart, and New York, International, 1939.
Editor, *Soviet Writers Reply to English Writers' Questions.*   London, Society for Cultural Relations with the U.S.S.R., 1948.
Editor, *Further Studies in a Dying Culture*, by Christopher Caudwell.   London, Lane, 1949; New York, Dodd Mead, 1958.
Editor, *Radical Squibs and Loyal Ripostes: Satirical Pamphlets of the Regency Period, 1819-1821.*   Bath, Adams and Dart, 1971.

Translator (as John Mavin), with Douglas Mavin Garman, *Charles Baudelaire: A Biography*, by François Porché.   London, Wishart, 1928.
Translator, *Poet under Saturn: The Tragedy of Verlaine*, by Marcel Coulin.   London, Toulmin, 1932.
Translator, *La Princesse aux Soleils, and Harmonie* (bilingual edition), by Ronald Firbank.   London, Enitharmon Press, 1974.

*   *   *

The hundred and fifty or so brief essays and reviews collected in *Essays and Opinions* and *Literature in Society* cover a period of nearly sixty years, making Edgell Rickword probably the most durable literary journalist of his time (only V.S. Pritchett and Malcolm Cowley have anything like comparable track records). Given this extraordinary span, it would be unreasonable not to expect developments and second thoughts, and in fact around 1934 Rickword did make a decisive change in his approach to literature—as a glance at his shifting attitudes toward T.S Eliot will indicate. In 1923 he reviewed "The Waste Land" for the *Times Literary Supplement*, a daunting enough assignment for a critic of twenty-five. But unlike many of his more experienced elders, Rickword responded to the poem in an objective, unhysterical manner: he compared it to a dazzling magic-lantern show, made some shrewd remarks about a poetic style which depends so heavily on allusiveness and observes that despite some fine effects, the poem declines to a "mere notation, the result of an indolence of the imagination." "Always evasive of the grand manner," he concludes, "Mr. Eliot has reached a stage at which he can no longer refuse to recognize the limitations of his medium; he is sometimes walking close to the very limits of coherence." Two years later, in a penetrating review of *Poems, 1909-1925*, Rickword maintains that "by his struggle with technique Mr. Eliot has been able to get closer than any other poet to the physiology of our sensations...to explore and make palpable the more intimate distress of a generation for whom all the romantic escapes have been blocked." Eliot has "now achieved things which make it impossible for the poet who has read them to regard his own particular problems of expression in the same way." In 1933 Rickword squarely faced the problems which Eliot's religious commitments now raised for secular readers, at least of his criticism. It was at this time, of course, that Eliot was making some of his most uncompromising declarations. (In "Thoughts after Lambeth," for example, he had just observed cooly that "The World is trying the experiment of attempting to form a civilized but non-Christian mentality. The experiment will fail; but we must be very patient in awaiting its collapse; meanwhile redeeming the time so that the Faith may be preserved alive through the dark age before us.") Rickword himself was a thoroughgoing naturalist—as early as 1924 he had concluded that "enormous cycles of years must have evolved before primitive man conceived the idea of God"—but he is remarkably fair to Eliot:

> Mr. Eliot is not outstanding as a 'thinker' as he is a literary critic. His thinking is adequate to his emotional needs, as a good poet's always is, but it has not much extra-personal validity.... [Nevertheless] if Mr. Eliot has for the time being gone outside literature, the loss is very much to literature.... If literary criticism is not one of the means Mr. Eliot envisages of redeeming the time, nothing can obscure the value of his example. As our writings are, so are our feelings, and the finer the discrimination as to the value of those writings, the better chance we have of not being ashamed of being human.

And then one year later Rickword has this to say in passing about Eliot's recent church pageant, *The Rock*:

> Since the economics of Fascism inevitably leads to want, the ideology of its literature is full of eulogies to the beauties of sacrifice (in a world overstocked with everything) and the superiority of spiritual to material enjoyment. 'None of you is without a 'ome,' the 'serio-comic' workman exhorted us in Eliot's *The Rock*, 'but God 'as no 'ome. Build 'Im one.' And this was at Sadler's Wells, within two minutes' walk of some of the most abominable slums.

What happened is that between 1933 and 1934 Rickword committed himself totally to a doctrinaire Marxist view of society and the function of literature. The change is so fundamental that it is really necessary to treat Rickword as two or possibly even three separate critics.

From the early pieces it is possible to deduce a sketchy theory of literature, or at least of poetry, which is anything but socially oriented. Rickword is relentless in his attack upon poets who "treat language not as a habit of thought but as a lifeless substance which can be built up into patterns independent of the rhythm of contemporary life," and this is in part a social standard; but when it comes to the poet ("the most star-like of men") and the function of literature, he is resolutely sceptical and individualistic. The aim of writing, he maintains, "is not to convince someone else...but to satisfy oneself." The profit to the audience is something of a side-effect, although an important one:

> Perhaps there are not so many individuals as there are men and women with names and addresses. Perhaps the streams of people in the street are no more dissimilar than autumn leaves, manure for next summer's generations. The artist, who can differ only in degree and function from the rest of men, by revealing differences, creates realities. It is through him we can perfect our individuality, our own shape, which under the comparatively crude strokes of actual experience might remain only roughly chipped out on the surface of that rock of ages, the folk-mind.

We may need and long for such an enabling "heroic" artist, but in fact

> The age of idols is past, for an idol implies a herd...and for the modern mind the age of herds is past. For some time after the breakdown of the Victorian religion of great men, disconsolate worshippers sought refuge from the rigour of solitary conviction in a succession of literary chapels, each of which claimed its patron as the most efficacious to salvation. Scepticism as to the validity of choice has destroyed the comfort of this 'exclusiveness' except for a few simple souls.

Therefore although "a Hero would seem to be due," he will have to be

> an exhaustively disillusioned Hero (we could not put up with another new creed) who

has yet so much vitality that his thoughts seize all sorts of analogies between apparently unrelated objects and so create an unbiased but self-consistent, humorous universe for himself.... So long as the social mind has no coherent expression like that given it by a supernatural explanation of the universe, the fantastic and the comic, disintegrating forces, will continue to be the most reputable of styles.

The second primary concern of these early pieces is with the sluggishness of British criticism and the mindless tendency to accept without question the "greatness" of such writers as Galsworthy, Bennett, Masefield and Kipling. In the late 'twenties and early 'thirties Rickword and some of his friends ("a sort of discontented club," he called them) conducted a series of attacks on these established figures in *The Calendar of Modern Letters* and *Scrutinies*. The results are often lively, as this passage from Rickword's own essay on Sir James Barrie illustrates:

The nearest thing to a villain Barrie has ever dared to imagine is Captain Hook, and because his existence is admitted, even though merely a fantastic shadow derived from Stevenson's romantic shadow, *Peter Pan* has a sort of vitality that the plays of experience lack. In the language of psychoanalysis, Peter Pan is the symbol of the libido wandering in the infantile world from which it has always been denied an outlet into actuality. For it would be absurd to accept Peter as a symbol of joy. He is a dwarfed and clammy imago, the *alter ego* of an adult who has grown up in spite of himself, physically, while his mind messes about among shadows. Children may get something out of the play, for they get something out of almost anything, but it is to be hoped that it is not the same thing as their elders get, which is a middle-aged person's idea of their own childish innocence. And that would not be a very good idea on which to bring up a child.

The *Times Literary Supplement* complained about the "low standard of literary courtesy" in the *Scrutinies*, to which Rickword merely replied that "To a paralytic, I suppose, any man who walks with ordinary freedom must seem to be executing a violent and gratuitously offensive gesture." The influence of the *Calendar* and *Scrutinies*, Alan Young has observed,

cannot be overestimated. When, in 1933, F.R. Leavis presented his selection of critical essays and reviews from *The Calendar* he suggested that the periodical's greatest achievement had been to bring to life and to sustain a spirit of open critical intelligence in response to literature. This response had been a cultural landmark in a period of intellectual disintegration, a time when the taste of the English reading public was being seriously misled and even increasingly undermined by many established literary pundits.

Rickword's departure from this sceptical, highly individual view of literature and society is as abrupt as it is complete, and his Marxism of the plainest and most strident sort: capitalist society has produced intolerable social conditions and must be swept away by radical, revolutionary action. Old-fashioned liberal humanitarianism is merely "an age-old sentiment reaching at its farthest utopian socialism, and certainly a factor in the disintegration of the bourgeois ideology, but powerless in the absence of a revolutionary class theory." Shaw, for example, does not go far enough: the Prefaces to his plays are "an object lesson in the futility of any but a revolutionary solution to the problems they raise." Rickword now has harsh words for many of the writers he was able to praise a few years before:

In literature it is not merely the technical superiority of such writers as Joyce, Eliot, Huxley or Virginia Woolf, which ensures that they shall be treated as 'representative' writers. Their various degrees of pessimism, of confusion, the very skill with which they represent life as a skein of infinitely interwoven sensations and motives and emotions whose 'meaning' can no more be consciously grasped than the exact colour of a mist at sunrise, suggest to the reader a feeling of impotence faced with the complexity of life, and leave him, if with any certainty, then the certainty that no line of behaviour is any better than any other.

Even the best-intentioned intellectuals "fall victim when they live in an atmosphere where the basic reasons of existence, food and shelter and love, are no longer realized in their origin as solely the emanations of human labour." Bourgeois education in England has produced a false set of values which leads men to praise art which merely "deodorizes the ideology of the ruling class." It is only in the Soviet Union where

> the problem of giving a meaning to art has ceased to exist. By their understanding of the work of Socialist construction, the writers, musicians, painters and poets have found all the inspiration they need for works which satisfy the highest ambitions and appeal to the masses of the people.

In short, Rickword was now quite as dogmatic as Eliot ever was, though of course their aims as writers could hardly be more opposed.

This dogmatic tone continues in Rickword's criticism throughout most of the second World War—and then seems to vanish as suddenly as it had appeared. The final section of *Literature in Society* is called "English Radicals," but there is nothing in these relaxed, slightly nostalgic essays on Milton, Wordsworth, Cruikshank and others which would trouble even the most conservative critic or historian. For whatever reason—the progress of Russian Communism, the rise of the Welfare State, the unforseen tenacity of capitalism—the revolutionary ardor is gone. "Nothing," Rickword observes here, "can negate Milton's testimony to his belief that men can construct a society for themselves in which a reasoned and conscious discipline will liberate the active virtue in each individual." Why then did such a society not come about? His answer is blunt: "History played Milton a dirty trick." The same might be said about British Marxists in the 'thirties, but of course it was not on them alone that history had dirty tricks to play.

SCHORER, Mark. American. Born in Sauk City, Wisconsin, 17 May 1908. Educated in Sauk City public schools; at the University of Wisconsin, Madison, 1925-29, 1931-36, A.B. 1929, Ph.D. 1936; Harvard University, Cambridge, Massachusetts, 1929-30, M.A. 1930. Married Ruth Tozier Page in 1936; two children. Instructor in English, 1937-40, and Briggs-Copeland Faculty Instructor, 1940-45, Harvard University. Associate Professor, 1945-47, and Professor of English, 1947-77, University of California, Berkeley: Chairman of the English Department, 1960-65. Christian Gauss Seminarian, Princeton University, New Jersey, 1949; Visiting Professor, Harvard University, 1952, and University of Tokyo, 1956; Fulbright Professor, University of Pisa, 1952-53, and University of Rome, 1964. Fellow, Indiana University School of Letters, Bloomington, from 1947. Member, Board of Directors, American Council of Learned Societies, New York, from 1965; West Coast Adviser, Executive Council, Authors' Guild, from 1966. Recipient: Guggenheim Fellowship, 1941, 1942, 1948; Center for Advanced Study in the Behavioral Sciences Fellowship, Stanford, California, 1958-59; Bollingen Fellowship, 1960. D.Litt.: University of Wisconsin, 1962. Member, American Academy of Arts and Sciences, 1962. *Died 11 August 1977.*

PUBLICATIONS

Criticism

> *William Blake: The Politics of Vision.* New York, Holt, 1946.
> *Sinclair Lewis.* Minneapolis, University of Minnesota Press, 1963.

The World We Imagine: Selected Essays.   New York, Farrar Straus, 1968; London, Chatto and Windus, 1969.
D.H. Lawrence.   New York, Dell, 1968.

Novels

A House Too Old.   New York, Reynal, 1935.
The Hermit Place.   New York, Random House, 1941.
The Wars of Love.   New York, McGraw Hill, and London, Eyre and Spottiswoode, 1954.

Short Stories

The State of Mind: Thirty-Two Stories.   Boston, Houghton Mifflin, 1947.
The State of Mind: Twenty-Two Stories.   London, Eyre and Spottiswoode, 1956.
Colonel Markesan and Less Pleasant People, with August Derleth.   Sauk City, Wisconsin, Arkham House, 1966.
Pieces of Life.   New York, Farrar Straus, 1977.

Other

Sinclair Lewis: An American Life.   New York, McGraw Hill, 1961; London, Heinemann, 1963.

Editor, with others, *Criticism: The Foundations of Modern Literary Judgment.*   New York, Harcourt Brace, 1948; revised edition, 1958.
Editor, *The Story: A Critical Anthology.*   New York, Prentice Hall, 1950; London, Bailey Brothers and Swinfen, 1955; revised edition, Englewood Cliffs, New Jersey. Prentice Hall, 1967.
Editor, *Society and Self in the Novel.*   New York, Columbia University Press, and London, Oxford University Press, 1956.
Editor, with Philip Durham and Everett L. Jones, *Harbrace College Reader.*   New York, Harcourt Brace, 1959; revised edition, 1968.
Editor, *Modern British Fiction.*   New York, Oxford University Press, 1961.
Editor, *Sinclair Lewis: A Collection of Critical Essays.*   Englewood Cliffs, New Jersey, Prentice Hall, 1962.
Editor, *Selected Writings*, by Truman Capote.   New York, Modern Library, and London, Hamish Hamilton, 1963.
Editor, with others, *American Literature.*   Boston, Houghton Mifflin, 1965.
Editor, *Galaxy: Literary Modes and Genres.*   New York, Harcourt Brace, 1967.
Editor, *The Literature of America: Twentieth Century.*   New York, McGraw Hill, 1970.
Editor, *Sons and Lovers: A Facsimile of the Manuscript*, by D.H. Lawrence.   Berkeley and London, University of California Press, 1977.

*   *   *

Mark Schorer wrote a number of moving short stories and one remarkable novel, *The Wars of Love*; he was an even abler biographer (of Lawrence and Sinclair Lewis) and he wrote briefly, yet as well as anyone ever has, on the complex relations between fiction and biography. On a number of occasions he also turned his attention to more speculative criticism, but here the results were less impressive.

"Technique as Discovery" first appeared in 1947 and has been anthologized and alluded to ever since, although the reader coming to it now for the first time may wonder why. Here (and in a less well-known essay, "Fiction and the 'Analogical Matrix' ") Schorer argues quite sensibly that fiction deserves the same scrutiny, the same close attention to diction and metaphor, that the New Critics had been lavishing on poetry. Such criticism has shown us that "to speak of content as such is not to speak of art at all, but of experience." Only when we discuss *achieved* content, the form, the work of art as a work of art," do we speak as critics. This is true enough: but Schorer then goes on to say that "the difference between content, or experience, and achieved content, or art, is technique": thus when we discuss technique, "we speak of nearly everything." "Nearly everything" is not a useful critical category, however, and Schorer soon—and surprisingly—limits his meaning of technique to moral evaluation (the novelist's evaluation, that is, of his "content"). In *Moll Flanders*, for example, we have "our classic revelation of the mercantile mind" and "the morality of measurement"—a morality which Defoe himself has "completely neglected to measure." In other words, Defoe has failed to judge his material properly (there are strong echoes here of Yvor Winters, for whom criticism is the act of judging, by one's own austere standards, the judgment the artist has made of his material). Again, in *Sons and Lovers* there are troublesome paradoxes (the sudden, slightly affirmative conclusion, for example, and Paul's ambivalent attitude towards his father): for Schorer these are *technical* failures, which means only that he is unwilling to accept suspended or ambiguous judgments (compare Yvor Winters' discussion of James in *Maule's Curse*). In *Wuthering Heights*, however, Emily Brontë is able to make the *right* judgment (unmoral passion comes to grief) because of her complex use of narrative perspective; and in *Portrait of the Artist* Joyce is able to make the *right* judgment (Stephen's ambition is "illusory") by his use of contrasting prose styles at the very end of that novel. These are sincere and perfectly reasonable moral judgments on Schorer's part—but they are just that: moral judgments; and to call them questions of technique is to put unnecessary strain on an already overburdened term. Anyone familiar with Wayne Booth's superb discussions of technique and valuation, or even with David Lodge's *Language of Fiction*, is likely to find Schorer's arguments of very little interest.

SCHWARTZ, Delmore. American. Born in Brooklyn, New York, 8 December 1913. Educated at the University of Wisconsin, Madison, 1931; New York University (Editor, *Mosaic* magazine), 1933-35, B.A. in philosophy 1935; Harvard University, Cambridge, Massachusetts, 1935-37. Married 1) Gertrude Buckman (marriage dissolved); 2) Elizabeth Pollet in 1949. Briggs-Copeland Instructor, 1940, Instructor, 1941-45, and Assistant Professor of English, 1946-47, Harvard University. Fellow, Kenyon School of English, Gambier, Ohio, Summer 1950; Visiting Professor at New York University, Indiana School of Letters, Bloomington, Princeton University, New Jersey, and University of Chicago. Editor, 1943-47, and Associate Editor, 1947-55, *Partisan Review*, New York; associated with *Perspectives*, New York, 1952-53; Literary Consultant, New Directions, publishers, New York, 1952-53; Poetry Editor and Film Critic, *New Republic*, Washington, D.C., 1955-57. Recipient: Guggenheim Fellowship, 1940; National Institute of Arts and Letters grant, 1953; *Kenyon Review* Fellowship, 1957; Levinson Prize (*Poetry*, Chicago), 1959; Bollingen Prize, 1960; Shelley Memorial Award, 1960. *Died 11 July 1966.*

PUBLICATIONS

Criticism

The Selected Essays of Delmore Schwartz, edited by Donald A. Dike and David H.
Zucker.   Chicago and London, University of Chicago Press, 1970 (incudes bibliography).

Verse

In Dreams Begin Responsibilities (includes short story and play).   New York, New
Directions, 1938.
Genesis: Book One (includes prose).   New York, New Directions, 1943.
Vaudeville for a Princess and Other Poems (includes prose).   New York, New Directions,
1950.
Summer Knowledge: New and Selected Poems, 1938-1958.   New York, Doubleday,
1959.
Last and Lost Poems of Delmore Schwartz, edited by Robert Phillips.   New York,
Vanguard Press, 1979.

Play

Shenandoah; or, The Naming of the Child.   New York, New Directions, 1941.

Short Stories

The World Is a Wedding and Other Stories.   New York, New Directions, 1948; London,
Lehmann, 1949.
Successful Love and Other Stories.   New York, Corinth Books, 1961.

Other

Editor, *Syracuse Poems 1964.*   Syracuse, New York, Syracuse University Department of
English, 1965.

Translator, *A Season in Hell* (bilingual edition), by Rimbaud.   New York, New Directions, 1939.

CRITICAL STUDY AND BIOGRAPHY

Richard McDougall, *Delmore Schwartz.*   New York, Twayne, 1974.
James Atlas, *Delmore Schwartz: The Life of an American Poet.*   New York, Farrar
Straus, 1977; London, Faber, 1979.

*   *   *

Writing about Edmund Wilson's achievements as a critic, Delmore Schwartz observed that *Axel's Castle*

> suffers from the virtue of being addressed...to an audience which is vague in extent, but is certainly constituted for the most part of readers who would like to be helped to read the difficult new authors. The essays are good introductions for such readers...but for the reader who has mastered Proust and Joyce there is little which he really needs.

This verdict applies with equal force to much of Schwartz' own intelligent criticism during the 1930's and 40's. As a teacher and later as an editor of the *Partisan Review* during its most influential years, Schwartz happily accepted the role of an explainer of complex, demanding modern writers, many of whose careers were far from over; his audience consisted of what he was to call later that "critical nonconformist intelligentsia" whose taste and convictions determine the health of a culture at any given time. What inevitably happened, of course, is that these introductions have long since outlived their usefulness: Schwartz' basic insights are often sound enough, but the "critical nonconformist intelligentsia" now has an extensive body of considered criticism and painstaking scholarship to turn to for understanding the established writers of our time.

Like most good critics, Schwartz recognized that a work of art is both something in itself, a created shape which is a source of pleasure, *and* a statement about a reality which exists "outside" the work. As for the work itself, Schwartz argues that

> a poem is successful when its words represent its substance...a poet has feelings, observations, attitudes which are in him.... The poet wishes to establish these observations, feelings, etc. *outside* himself once and for all, in the full light, in a stadium from which the audience never goes home. The only way in which he can get his private possessions into that public place is by using words in certain formal ways, meter, metaphor, rhyme, etc., and by otherwise drawing upon what is the common property of all who can read the language. All of this and more is involved in the notion of representing a substance.

But sensitive as he often is to questions of poetic embodiment, Schwartz is more concered with the work as a statement. In an early essay on John Dos Passos, for example, he remarks that "we can say—and regard this as the best praise for anyone's intention—that his intention has been to tell the truth about the world in which he has had to exist." And since this "truth" is in part conditioned by social forces, Schwartz' general tactic as a critic is to look at the social context from the point of view of the writer and to summarize that point of view in terms more immediately accessible than the terms of the works themselves. The more precise and detailed Schwartz becomes, the more useful his criticism becomes: his essay on Faulkner is sound and convincing; his long essay on one particular novel, *A Fable*, is even more so.

It is as a critic of other critics, however, that Schwartz probably has his greatest value. He has an unerring sense of the limitations of Wilson, Trilling, Eliot, Blackmur and Winters, yet his discussions of these limitations are not merely destructive. He defines the strengths of each critic as well and reminds us that "it is a curious notion of the very good critic which supposes that he has no defects, nor serious limitations." The half-dozen or so essays which deal with these critics may still be read as generous appraisals of what Schwartz considered an honorable and important calling. If the intensity of this criticism of criticism now seems a little dated too, it is probably an indication that we have lost at least some of our faith in the power of high culture to form and sustain a genuinely humane society.

SHAPIRO, Karl (Jay). American. Born in Baltimore, Maryland, 10 November 1913. Educated at the University of Virginia, Charlottesville, 1932-33; Johns Hopkins University, Baltimore, 1937-39; Pratt Library School, Baltimore, 1940. Served in the United States Army, 1941-45. Married 1) Evelyn Katz in 1945 (divorced, 1967); 2) Teri Kovach in 1969; three children. Associate Professor, John Hopkins University, 1947-50; Visiting Professor, University of Wisconsin, Madison, 1948, and Loyola Univeristy, Chicago, 1951-52; Lecturer, Salzburg Seminar in American Studies, 1952; State Department Lecturer, India, 1955; Visiting Professor, University of California, Berkeley and Davis, 1955-56, and University of Indiana, Bloomington, 1956-57; Professor of English, University of Nebraska, Lincoln, 1956-66, and University of Illinois, Chicago Circle, 1966-68. Since 1968, Professor of English, University of California, Davis. Editor, *Poetry*, Chicago, 1950-56, *Newberry Library Bulletin*, Chicago, 1953-55, and *Prairie Schooner*, Lincoln, Nebraska, 1956-66. Consultant in Poetry, Library of Congress, Wahington, D.C., 1946-47. Recipient: Jeannette Davis Prize, 1942, Levinson Prize, 1942, Eunice Tietjens Memorial Prize, 1961, and Oscar Blumenthal Prize, 1963 (*Poetry*, Chicago); *Contemporary Poetry* prize, 1943; National Institute of Arts and Letters grant, 1944; Guggenheim Fellowship, 1944, 1953; Pulitzer Prize, 1945; Shelley Memorial Award, 1946; Kenyon School of Letters Fellowship, 1956, 1957; Bollingen Prize, 1969. D.H.L.: Wayne State University, Detroit, 1960; D.Litt.: Bucknell University, Lewisburg, Pennsylvania, 1972. Fellow in American Letters, Library of Congress. Member, American Academy of Arts and Sciences, and National Institute of Arts and Letters. Address: 1119 Bucknell Drive, Davis, California 95616, U.S.A.

PUBLICATIONS

Criticism

Beyond Criticism. Lincoln, University of Nebraska Press, 1953; as *A Primer for Poets*, 1965.
In Defense of Ignorance. New York, Random House, 1960; reprinted in part in *The Poetry Wreck*, 1975.
Start with the Sun: Studies in Cosmic Poetry, with James E. Miller, Jr., and Beatrice Slote. Lincoln, University of Nebraska Press, 1960.
The Writer's Experience, with Ralph Ellison. Washington, D.C., Library of Congress, 1964.
Randall Jarrell. Washington, D.C., Library of Congress, 1967; reprinted in *The Poetry Wreck*, 1975.
To Abolish Children and Other Essays. Chicago, Quadrangle Books, 1968.
The Poetry Wreck: Selected Essays 1950-1970. New York, Random House, 1975.

Verse

Poems. Baltimore, Waverly Press, 1935.
Five Young American Poets, with others. New York, New Directions, 1941.
Person, Place and Thing. New York, Reynal, 1942; London, Secker and Warburg, 1944.
The Place of Love. Melbourne, Comment Press, 1942.
V-Letter and Other Poems. New York, Reynal, 1944; London, Secker and Warburg, 1945.
Essay on Rime. New York, Reynal, 1945; London, Secker and Warburg, 1947.
Trial of a Poet and Other Poems. New York, Reynal, 1947.
Poems 1940-1953. New York, Random House, 1953.
The House. Privately printed, 1957.
Poems of a Jew. New York, Random House, 1958.
The Bourgeois Poet. New York, Random House, 1964.

Selected Poems.   New York, Random House, 1968.
White-Haired Lover.   New York, Random House, 1968.
Auden (1907-1973).   Davis, California, Putah Creek Press, 1973.
Adult Bookstore.   New York, Random House, 1976.
Collected Poems 1940-1977.   New York, Random House, 1978.

Play

The Tenor, music by Hugo Weisgall.   New York, Merion Music, 1956.

Novel

Edsel.   New York, Geis, 1971.

Other

English Prosody and Modern Poetry.   Baltimore, Johns Hopkins University Press, 1947.
A Bibliography of Modern Prosody.   Baltimore, Johns Hopkins University Press, 1948.
A Prosody Handbook, with Robert Beum.   New York, Harper, 1965.

BIBLIOGRAPHY

William White, *Karl Shapiro: A Bibliography*.   Detroit, Wayne State University Press, 1960.

*   *   *

Karl Shapiro is a distinguished poet; he is also one of the most exasperating of modern critics—of course, we already believe, as he so passionately does, that "the dictatorship of intellectual 'modernism,' the sanctimonious ministry of 'the Tradition,' [and] the ugly programmatic quality of twentieth-century criticism have maimed our poetry and turned it into a monstrosity of literature." As we near our "long-wished-for-*fin de siècle*," he asserts (in the Foreword to *The Poetry Wreck*),

> The hypercritical superconscious twentieth century awaits its own last judgment. It is a time of breathless anticipation, final solutions, Infernos, Purgatories, Paradises and Guinness Record Books. It is, one might add, the busiest time of literary criticism in history, for the poetry is almost all criticism. One poet [Randall Jarrell] called us the age of criticism, and did not live long enough to see us turn into the age of self-regard. Our trajectory has been millennial, a hysterical recapitulation of the centuries, ending in dissolution and the hungry death-wish.

And if modern poetry offers an accurate reflection of our culture, "then our century has much to answer for":

> The political simplemindedness and viciousness of the great trio of Pound, Eliot and Yeats incriminate the Academy and the literary establishment which have made them the touchstones of our age.... [These poets] defined an attitude toward literature and gave it an intellectual sanction. Sophisticated schools of criticism sprang up to defend

their aesthetic—the aesthetic of anti-humanism.... One can without stretching the point accuse the Trio of politicalizing poetry for our time. The abreaction to that eventuated in a poetry that was nothing but political, a poetry of the subjective revolution, of ego, of self-pity and of self-regard.

Like many polemicists, Shapiro is too often merely preaching to the converted; he rarely stops to demonstrate his assertions or to reason with his audience; moreover, his criticism is hurt by a weakness which he apparently senses himself: "The true critic," he admits (in "The Critic in Spite of Himself"), "has an obligation to affirmative judgment; I would go so far as to say that we cannot get a true work of criticism which has a coil of negative emotion lying at the bottom of it. A work of criticism may become a work of art only when the critic is in love with his subject and is carried away by it, exactly as the poet is carried away by his." Nevertheless, the dictatorship of Eliot, Pound and Yeats was bound to provoke powerful reactions, and whether or not we agree with Shapiro's specific indictments, we should be able to read *In Defense of Ignorance* and *The Poetry Wreck* with something more thoughtful than horrified fascination or amused contempt. What redeems these essays, at least in part, is his obvious sincerity: he cares deeply about the ways in which the official canons of modern poetry and criticism have made it almost impossibly difficult for some American poets to get on with their work.

For Shapiro the great enemy of true poetry (and criticism) is the "intellectual," the sort of man who, when he returns to find his house in flames,

might rush into the burning building to save his manuscripts or his record player or even his children (for intellectuals are frequently men of action), but he will be thinking all the time of the complexities of megalopolitan life or of Euripides' *Medea*, or something of that kind. The intellectual cannot experience anything without *thinking* about it. It was the intellectual whom Lawrence loathed above all modern creatures, and Lawrence was right. The Spanish intellectual Ortega once made the penetrating remark that the intellectual is not necessarily intelligent.

Why to think means to think badly or to embrace the wrong politics, Shapiro never explains; nor is he clear about the reasons why the poetry of our time has been overwhelmingly "intellectual" in this special sense. (Eliot and Pound, for example, "destroyed all emotion except emotion arising from ideas," while Auden's "retreat" from poetry to psychology involves "an almost total sacrifice of the poetic motive to the rational motive.") In any event, such poetry is not "true poetry"; it is "culture poetry," that is, poetry which attempts to "explain culture":

It can do this in the manner of the Metaphysical poets, who were troubled by scientific knowledge and who wished to compete with science; by rewriting history according to a plan; by tracing the rise and fall of a particular belief, and so forth. Culture poetry is always didactic, as indeed most modern poetry is. It is a means to an end, not an end, like art. Culture poetry is poetry in reverse; it dives back into the historical situation, into culture, instead of flowering from it. And there it remains to enrich the ground for criticism.

What Shapiro means by "true poetry" is somewhat harder to define. In "The Career of the Poem" he argues that

Science pursues demonstrable knowledge and calls itself the love of natural law. Religion pursues goodness and calls itself the love of God. And poetry pursues human personal knowledge and calls itself the love of beauty. With poetry, as with other forms of knowledge, there is no crossing the line, no violation of the nature of the thing, without contamination. All art that does so is marked by insincerity, whether intellectual insincerity...or emotional insincerity.... What claim, then, has the poet to any knowledge except the personal knowledge of truth or beauty?

Again, true poetry "springs from the love of personal truth" and "results in a thing of beauty." It is not intellectual, it is not "culture poetry"; indeed, by those standards it is "ignorant" (hence the title of the collection in which this essay appears):

> Imagine not having to write poems [as Auden does] about the Just City or to make definitions [as Eliot does] of Culture or to fret like poor Baudelaire about reducing the traces of Original Sin. No more theology, no more economic systems, no more psychology of depths, not even myth-making or the decline of the West! What a vacation for poetry! "But what else is there to write about?" cries the modern poet, dropping his *Explicator*. "You don't expect me to write about the birds and the bees, or flowers, or *people*! That's all been done, ages ago!"
>
> Yeats speaks somewhere of the fascination of what's difficult, and we all agree, but add: the difficult isn't the only thing that's fascinating. We do not find the difficulties of modern poetry and modern criticism particularly *intelligent* difficulties. Why make a fetish of difficulty-for-difficulty's sake? Is there no fascination for what's beautiful, or what's unknown, or what's innocent? Or are these things only the province of the "ignorant"?

Finally, true poetry is the poetry of "cosmic consciousness," by which Shapiro means "the capacity of the individual consciousness to experience a sense of total unity with all Nature, or the universe, or some degree of that experience." Unlike culture poetry, the poetry of cosmic consciousness embraces science ("I know nothing about science but it is apparent that underlying all scientific inquiry is the *belief* in this unity") and mysticism. Thus many of the writers who interest Shapiro, or who interested him in 1960 (for some reason he did not reprint "Poets of Cosmic Consciousness" in *The Poetry Wreck*), fall well outside the canon of official modernism; instead of Eliot, Pound, Yeats, Auden, and Freud, we have, among others, Jung, Reich, P.D. Ouspensky, Erwin Schrödinger, the *I Ching*, Robert Graves and Whitman.

Since modern poetry is mainly culture poetry or ideology masked as poetry, modern criticism has been preoccupied with paraphrase and explication. True poetry, however, resists such criticism; the real poem does not use words as words but builds a new complex of meaning and uses "language in a state of being, language trying to escape its condition" (that is, its limited, referential sense in ordinary discourse). The opening lines of *Paradise Lost*, for example, form

> one of the most extraordinary sentences ever written and worthy of the name of sublimity which Longinus gives to the creation in Genesis—what does it *mean*? It means that Milton has found the "poetry" of his immense theme, that he is caught up in the terror and splendor of his vision, which exists only in his expression of it. There is no way to say what these lines mean except by citing them. They mean what they mean; they are their own meaning. The modern critic reads a poem backwards; he does not want to know whether the vision is achieved or how well; he wants to know what went into the pudding. He want recipes.

True criticism, then, can only be "*a work of art about another work of art.*"

The culture poets, of course, are Eliot, Pound, Yeats, Auden, and their followers; the true poets are Whitman, William Carlos Williams, Lawrence, Henry Miller, Randall Jarrell, and—a hard case for Shapiro—Dylan Thomas (there seem to be no true critics around). The overwhelming prestige of the first group has made it difficult or impossible for the true poets and their would-be followers to confront American life directly, honestly, and without feeling that they must turn poetry into a surrogate for religion or politics. What would a genuine American poetry look like?

> It would be nonsensical, hilarious, and obscene like us. Absurd like us. It would be marked, as we are, by cultural forgetfulness and lack of principle. It would be void of values and ideas, sensual, joyous, bitter, curious, gossipy, knowledgeable to the last minute detail, ungrammatical, endlessly celebrating the faces, objects, neuroses, murders, love affairs, and vulgarities of America. Certainly it would develop favorite forms, but these would be soluble in prose. It would be comical and slack and full of junk; impure, generous, bookish, and cheap. It would be mystical, savage, drab, and as

hateful as Joyce Kilmer's "Trees." As sloppy as Whitman and—well, it would be like the great American novel which every American poet ends up writing as a tribute to "the diviner heaven" of prose.

But despite the great example of Whitman and the occasional, isolated successes of Williams and Jarrell, such poetry has yet to come into being. And by now it may be too late. It is hard not to be touched by the little parable Shapiro devises as the conclusion to a fairly recent essay, "Is Poetry an American Art?"

> Perhaps we should teach our children that once upon a time there was a thing called poetry, that it was very beautiful, and that people tried to bring it to our shores in boats but it died. And a few people couldn't live without it, so they went back to the Old World to see it. And others built elaborate greenhouses, called English Departments, where they kept it breathing. And they watered it with the most expensive electricity, but it didn't like it here and died anyhow. And some fractious students lost their tempers and began to smash the greenhouse windows. And then everybody started reading and writing prose.

As these remarks suggest, Shapiro indulges in overstatements when they suit his purposes (on Frost, for example: "I myself have never been able to see anything in the slightest American about [him]...he had to go to England for recognition and [until] the end, except for the great honor given him by Kennedy, his audience was English"); and he is untroubled by gross contradictions (in one essay we learn that Yeats is a "great genius," while in another Shapiro remarks "I am not trying to be witty when I say that the average graduate student who works a little can write a poem as well as Yeats"). But it is finally too easy to simplify a critic already given to so many oversimplifications of his own: Shapiro is a splendid prosodist and has a sharp ear for the strengths and weaknesses of versification in the poets he discusses; there are moments when it is clear that he admires, even loves what is best in Eliot and Auden, if not Pound; and there are moments when his judgments are so penetrating that they simply compel assent. Consider, for example, these remarks about Thomas:

> To talk about Thomas as a Symbolist is dishonest. Once in Hollywood Aldous Huxley introduced a Stravinsky composition based on a poem of Thomas'. Huxley quoted that line of Mallarmé's which says that poets purify the dialect of the tribe. This, said Huxley, was what Thomas did. Now anybody who has read Thomas knows that he did the exact opposite: Thomas did everything in his power to obscure the dialect of the tribe— whatever that high-and-mighty expression may mean. Thomas sometimes attempted to keep people from understanding his poems (which are frequently simple, once you know the dodges). He had a horror of simplicity—or what I consider to be a fear of it. He knew little except what a man knows who has lived about forty years, and there was little he wanted to know. There is a fatal pessimism in most of his poems, offset by a few bursts of joy and exuberance. The main symbol is masculine love, driven as hard as Freud drove it. In the background is God, hard to identify but always there, a kind of God who belongs to one's parents rather than to the children, who do not quite accept him.

Shapiro is right in one important respect: the hegemony of Pound, Eliot and Yeats and the criticism which sprang up to explain and praise their work had a deadening effect on many would-be poets during the 1930's and 40's. For something more than a cry of pain, however— for a saner account of why and how it all happened, readers should consult Graham Hough's *Image and Experience*, Donald Davie's *Articulate Energy*, and Frank Kermode's *Romantic Image*. In any event, time has a way of sorting things out. *Is* anyone reading the *Quartets* and *Cantos* these days, let alone trying to imitate them?

SISSON, C(harles) H(ubert). British. Born in Bristol, 22 April 1914. Educated at the University of Bristol, 1931-34, B.A. (honours) in philosophy and English literature 1934; University of Berlin and University of Freiburg, 1934-35; the Sorbonne, Paris, 1935-36. Served in the British Army Intelligence Corps, India, 1942-45. Married Nora Gilbertson in 1937; two children. Assistant Principal, 1935-42, Principal, 1945-53, Assistant Secretary, 1953-62, and Under Secretary, 1962-68, Ministry of Labour, London; Assistant Under Secretary of State, 1968-71, and Director of Occupational Safety and Health, 1971-73, Department of Employment, London. Since 1976, Co-Editor, *PN Review*. Recipient: Senior Simon Research Fellowship, University of Manchester, 1956. Agent: A.D. Peters and Company, 10 Buckingham Street, London WC2N 6BU. Address: Moorfield Cottage, The Hill, Langport, Somerset TA10 9PU, England.

PUBLICATIONS

Criticism

Art and Action. London, Methuen, 1965; partly reprinted in *The Avoidance of Literature*, 1978.
Essays. Sevenoaks, Kent, privately printed, 1967; partly reprinted in *The Avoidance of Literature*, 1978.
English Poetry 1900-1950: An Assessment. London, Hart Davis, 1971; partly reprinted in *The Avoidance of Literature*, 1978.
The Avoidance of Literature: Collected Essays, edited by Michael Schmidt. Manchester, Carcanet Press, 1978.

Verse

Versions and Perversions of Heine. London, Gaberbocchus, 1955.
Poems. Fairwarp, Sussex, Peter Russell, 1959.
Twenty-One Poems. Privately printed, 1960.
The London Zoo. London, Abelard Schuman, 1961.
Numbers. London, Methuen, 1965.
Catullus. London, MacGibbon and Kee, 1966; New York, Orion Press, 1967.
The Discarnation; or, How the Flesh Became Word and Dwelt among Us. Privately printed, 1967.
Metamorphoses. London, Methuen, 1968.
Roman Poems. Privately printed, 1968.
In the Trojan Ditch: Collected Poems and Selected Translations. Cheadle, Cheshire, Carcanet Press, 1974.
The Corridor. Hitchin, Hertfordshire, Mandeville Press, 1975.
Anchises. Manchester, Carcanet Press, 1976.

Novels

An Asiatic Romance. London, Gaberbocchus, 1953.
Christopher Homm. London, Methuen, 1965; Chester Springs, Pennsylvania, Dufour, 1975.

Other

The Curious Democrat, as Richard Ampers.   London, Peter Russell, 1950.
The Basis of Social Studies.   Amsterdam, North Holland Publishing Company, 1953.
The Spirit of British Administration and Some European Comparisons.   London, Faber, and New York, Praeger, 1959.
The Case of Walter Bagehot.   London, Faber, 1972.
David Hume.   Edinburgh, Ramsay Head Press, 1976.

Editor, *The English Sermon 1650-1750*.   Manchester, Carcanet Press, 1976.
Editor, *Poems of Jonathan Swift*.   Manchester, Carcanet Press, 1977.
Editor, *Jude the Obscure*, by Hardy.   London, Penguin, 1979.

Translator, *The Poetic Art: A Translation of Horace's Ars Poetica*.   Cheadle, Cheshire, Carcanet Press, 1975.
Translator, *The Poem on Nature: A Translation of Lucretius's De Rerum Natura*.   Manchester, Carcanet Press, 1976.
Translator, *Some Tales of La Fontaine*.   Manchester, Carcanet Press, 1979.
Translator, *The Divine Comedy: A New Translation of Dante*.   Manchester, Carcanet Press, 1979.

*   *   *

Shortly after his official conversion in 1928, T.S. Eliot announced that he was a "classicist in literature, royalist in politics, and [an] anglo-catholic in religion." He later came to regret the categorical flatness of these phrases—and their easy quotability—but they nevertheless provide a convenient summary of his basic concerns. And there is an important critical corollary here as well: just as the fallible individual needs the guidance of a strong, uncorrupted church and state, so the artist, if he is to mature and express anything more than mere personal emotions, needs the discipline provided by the Western literary tradition. C.H. Sisson's position as a critic is strikingly similar, but this claim requires some reasonable documentation since he has usually been guarded, and sometimes oddly hostile, when it comes to Eliot's prestige and influence. (In *English Poetry 1900-1950* he grudgingly concedes that like Pound and Yeats, Eliot is a major figure, but concludes that *Sweeney Agonistes* is probably his "best poem" and has nothing good whatsoever to say about the later plays and *Four Quartets*. It is hard not to suspect that the crux of the matter here lies in Sisson's resentment that an "imitation Englishman," as he calls Eliot, had assumed rather than inherited the Tory tradition—and by "Tory," incidentally, Sisson always means exactly what Dr. Johnson means by that term: "one who adheres to the ancient constitution of the state and the apostalic hierarchy of the church of England.")

From the very beginning of his career, Sisson was convinced that all government by definition represents the rule of authority as opposed to the intellectual freedom of the individual. In 1940 he proclaimed that "Government is a concentration of force, and to maintain itself it seeks to destroy the free person under it and the free state outside it." A year or so later, following Herbert Read, he argued that "the only society in which the individual can *be conceived* as being realized is an anarchist society"; but (unlike Read) he admits that an anarchist society is not a "practical possibility." Social restraints are necessary, although the agency which exercises those restraints is always suspect. Thus if an anarchist society is "unrealizable,"

it remains to discover in what sort of realizable society our ideals can most nearly be approached. The fantastic particularist Tory has much in common with the anarchist; both anarchist and Tory wish to restore our minds to a perception of the sensible realities. For the anarchist, however, the prospect of unlimited freedom of development is indispensable, and the Tory could only be one who believed that men can best develop within limits. The fantastic Tory would be even less easy to find at present than the perfect anarchist, but the establishment of a particularist society with a central authority armed with strong powers for limited purposes is, if unlikely to occur, at least not impossible.

Sisson himself, of course, was or was soon to become the very model of a "fantastic particularist Tory," deeply concerned with the true "sensible realities" of everyday living and the ways in which "modern lay states," be they democratic, socialist or fascist, have as their end the subservience of the individual. He had firsthand experience of German politics during the early 1930s; he came to detest his experience as a civil servant in an England where "the greatest social efforts [have] been to make dependence respectable"; and as for democracy, he maintains that the true Tory will have nothing but "contempt" for "those vulgar doctrines of our age which seek to derive rights from alleged personal merits or even from the meanest wants and appetites of the common man." In his revealing "Autobiographical Reflections on Politics," written in 1954 but not published until 1978 (in *The Avoidance of Literature*), he forthrightly states that

> The execution of Charles I was a blow to Christendom, and the Commonwealth prepared the way for the lay state of modern times which rests on the equality of all opinions and consequently can offer no ultimate justification for itself beyond the force that it is able to exercise. This characteristic of the modern state had been evident to me for too long to retain anything of the attractions of a discovery, and it repelled me for the brutal thing it is. The new if still somewhat dim perception of the nature of Christendom which my Asiatic residence [Sisson's army service in India] had given me no doubt made me readier than before to pursue the theological and ecclesiastical implications of what happened in the seventeenth century.

This last passage clearly reveals the basis of Sisson's "royalism." All governments may be oppressive, but the modern democratic or socialist state is the very embodiment of the kind of power which seeks to dominate the individual for the sake of its own preservation. The royalist is opposed to all of this and places his allegiance above mere "factions". Thus in "A Note on the Monarchy," published in 1953, Sisson maintains that

> the monarchic principle is not that the king should have all power, but that he is the legitimate source of all power.... We say...that the Queen rules through her Ministers, and that she does not rule any the less for that, just as Ministers are not less Ministers because they exercise their functions in the main through officials.... The Minister does not attend to the details of his Department's administration. It would be a true anachronism for him to do so. It would be a true anachronism for the Queen to express her preferences in the million and one topics that come before her government. The Minister has one inalienable function, which is to secure the coherence of her country. The Minister performs his function more by taking advice and bowing before facts than he does by giving advice and making the facts bow before him.... The maxim that the Queen's service must be carried on means, among other things, that it is of greatly more importance that there should be a government in England than that its complexion should be that of one or another party. It is of the nature of party politicians to exaggerate and exacerbate their differences. They present their policies, which are merely an aspect of things, as the thing itself. The thing itself is the great *res publica* whose continuance the Queen rules.... She wills the continuance of all those rights she has protected without enactment.

The final safeguard of liberty lies in "a point of unity in a single Person present on the throne by hereditary right and form of law." The ultimate justification for such a claim, of course, is religious:

> the sovereign of England is an Anglican, and only those ignorant of the superior force of a coherent and comprehensive body of ideas over an incoherent and partial, can suppose that this fact is without a national significance which will only end with the monarchy. The Queen adheres to the only religion possible in the West, and to that form of it which is most surely embedded in our millennial English traditions.

The similarities between Eliot and Sisson, then, should be apparent. If one had to press for a distinction between their positions, it would probably be that while Eliot derives his politics from his religious commitments, Sisson derives his religious commitments from his politics. In any event, there is a troubling passage at the conclusion of a 1977 review of a new edition of Coleridge's *On the Constitution of Church and State*:

> For my part, I shall prefer those who stay and fight their corner, content to be merely the Church in a place. This is partly because—perhaps it is wholly because—faced with the unintelligibility of the language the church speaks, I am of a religion in which—to use Coleridge's phrase—Christianity is an accident; the religion of our fathers, or the *mere patrie*, or the spirits buried in the ground, or the religion of England, I cannot help it. Of course, this in turn conceals a profound cynicism.

Or are readers supposed to find this admission "ironic"?

Sisson's literary judgments follow naturally enough from his religious and political commitments. Art is—or should be—devoted to the "sensible realities" of life which politics tries to obscure. "Art," he maintained in 1939, "and protest of the kind that is akin to it, are uses made of freedom." Literature is vigilant; it alerts us to the dangers which threaten liberty and strengthens the tradition which makes dissent possible. Genuine criticism, then, is itself a "protest" on behalf of freedom and insists on the distinction between good writing and bad:

> [the] distinction between public sentiments and private perceptions appears to me to be fundamentally the same as the distinction between good writing and bad. If this in fact is so, it may be said that bad writing is therefore any part of the system of force which is government. Good writing alone may be described as independent of government, and one has intellectual liberty just so far as one has the capacity to distinguish between valid work and invalid.

The great tradition of English literature for Sisson is therefore the tradition which directly or indirectly supports King and Country and thus speaks for "the source of the nation's persistent renewal." The voice of the writer, however, is not merely an individual voice:

> It is not the writer's function to invent anything in the nature of a programme.... What the writer proffers does not, in a healthy society, act on the statesman directly but by mingling with the ideas of thousands of other people, most of them dead.

"It is too readily supposed," he argues (in *Sevenoaks Essays*)

> that there is a "personal experience" which can be conveyed in words. In fact, the consciousness we have is a product of history, and we think we feel as we do as much as feel that way. We can only feel as we do, because only so will our forms of words and thoughts allow us to feel. There may be some uniformity between the feelings of men who have their legs cut off.... But when it comes to the feelings of a woman abandoned by her lover, the whole force of a civilization is in play. There is no original feeling in such a situation, and no overlay of tradition. The whole is an invention of thousands of years, places, times, religions, cultures. The individual variant which could be "expressed"—if we admit the conception—must be negligible by comparison.... In a sense [the artist] will be less concerned than other people to be original, because he will be seeking among forms of thought long current for the formulation which will apply most exactly to the new situation.

The principle of tradition here is of course the same principle which Eliot celebrates in his best-known essay, "Tradition and the Individual Talent," and also helps to explain the curious phrase, "the avoidance of literature," that Michael Schmidt uses as the title for his massive collection of Sisson's political and literary essays. In 1961 Sisson praised William Barnes, a writer deeply rooted in the traditions of his part of England, for escaping the "literary foibles of his time" and thus demonstrating that "the poet has to develop in a straight line from his origins, and that the avoidance of literature is indispensable for the man who wants to tell the truth." But the full meaning of the phrase becomes clear in a later essay on Ford Madox Ford. According to Ford, W.H. Hudson was "utterly undramatic in his methods":

When you read his books, you "forget the lines and the print. It is as if a remotely smiling face looked up at you out of the page and told you things." For the simple word he substituted the yet more simple word. There are no coruscating sentences. Hudson "builds up his atmosphere with such little, skilful touches that you are caught into his world before you are aware that you have even moved." This was what Ford himself aimed at, with immense patience over fifty years. With him the sentence ranks before the word, the page before the sentence, and the book before the page. So the whole thing is an exercise in forbearance, a quality much needed and neglected in the literature of the present day.

This is the true "avoidance of literature" (that is, the avoidance of an immature search for a merely personal voice or "style") which Sisson, once more like Eliot, values so highly. When he finds writers he can praise, he is often persuasive; when he deals with writers whose religious or social principles he cannot tolerate, the results are predictable. About Whitman, for example, he has this to say:

> One can see that this loud, untidy writer demands a place somewhere. He is a sinister portent of worse to come.... What a lout the man is! A lout of the western Protestant decadence, not of a civilization still refining itself. "I am the poet of the Body and I am the poet of the Soul"—but not to anyone who has read Dante.... All that, and much more, I can do without.

"Frost," he observes, "brought one certain aspects of the American scene, so autochthonous that one suspects an element of the phoney. For a proper evaluation his work needs to be set beside that of Edward Thomas, to whom he gave encouragement at the right moment." The necessity of placing Frost *beside* Thomas should remind readers of what can happen when literary judgments are made to conform to ideological passions.

SMITH, Barbara Herrnstein. American. Born Barbara Bernstein in New York City, 6 August 1932. Educated at City College, New York, 1951-52; Brandeis University, Waltham, Massachusetts, B.A. 1954, M.A. 1955, Ph.D. 1965. Married Richard Herrnstein, 1951 (divorced, 1961); Thomas H. Smith, 1964 (divorced, 1974); two daughters. Instructor, Sanz School of Languages, Washington, D.C., 1956-57; Teaching and Research Assistant, 1959-61, and Instructor, 1961-62, Brandeis University; Member, Literature Faculty, Bennington College, Vermont, 1962-74. Since 1974, Professor of English and Communications, University of Pennsylvania, Philadelphia. Visiting Lecturer, Annenberg School of Communications, University of Pennsylvania. Since 1974, Consultant, National Endowment for the Humanities. Member: Editorial Board, *Critical Inquiry*; Semiotic Society of America. Recipient: Huber Foundation Grant (Brandeis University), 1965, 1966; Ford Foundation Grant, 1968; Christian Gauss Award, 1968; *Explicator* Award, 1968. Address: Department of English, University of Pennsylvania, Philadelphia, Pennsylvania 19143, U.S.A.

PUBLICATIONS

Criticism

Poetic Closure: A Study of How Poems End. Chicago and London, University of Chicago Press, 1968.

496

On the Margins of Discourse: The Relation of Literature to Language.   Chicago and
   London, University of Chicago Press, 1978.
"Fixed Marks and Variable Constancies: A Parable of Literary Value," in *Poetics Today*
   (Tel Aviv), 1, 1979.
"Narrative Versions, Narrative Theories," in *Critical Inquiry* (Chicago), 7, 1980.

Other

   Editor, *Discussions of Shakespeare's Sonnets.*   Boston, Heath, 1964.
   Editor, *Sonnets*, by Shakespeare.   New York, New York University Press, 1969.

                          *   *   *

   What is time? Augustine asks in the *Confessions. He knows*, he tells us—until someone asks
him. It seems that the most pervasive aspects of existence are often the most difficult to grasp
and articulate; and in the realm of aesthetic experience, the nature of "beginnings" and
"endings," at first glance such commonsensical affairs, have raised particularly vexing questions. A few years ago, in *Beginnings*, Edward Said offered a meditation, as he calls it, on what
it means to project something new against the apparent continuity of existing things. A few
years before that, in 1968, Barbara Herrnstein Smith, in an even more remarkable book,
proposed a way of looking at "closure," or true endings as opposed to mere cessations. Both
studies are genuinely speculative, in the best sense of that worn adjective, and therefore
genuinely helpful.
   Although Ms. Smith does not allude to it, there is a classic statement about the problematic
nature of endings in Henry James' preface to his early novel, *Roderick Hudson*. "Really,
universally," James contends there, "relations stop nowhere, and the exquisite problem of the
artist is but to draw, by a geometry of his own, the circle within which they shall happily appear
to do so. He is in the perpetual predicament that the continuity of things is never for the space of
an instant or an inch broken" (by "relations" James means the interconnections which exist,
however faint, between all events, including human actions). Thus for James there is no
solution: art is a kind of confidence game, or better a contract into which we enter, for the sake
of gaining the "illusion of a completed whole." In turn that illusion contributes to the vicarious
knowledge and "extension of consciousness" which is the proper end of art. But if we finish, say,
Portrait of a Lady, wondering primarily what happened next to Isabel Archer, James has failed
to give us the necessary illusion. Solvable or not, the problems for the artist are at the very least
formidable. E.M. Forster once remarked that it if weren't for death and marriage, he didn't see
how the average novelist could get on.
   Ms. Smith does not pretend to solve these problems, but she manages to say a great many
illuminating things by examining them from the perspective of Gestalt psychology. There are
three relevant principles here, and one or two crucial underlying assumptions about the nature
of human perception. First of all, there is the "law of good continuation." In Leonard Meyer's
formulation, "a shape or pattern will, other things being equal, tend to be continued in its initial
mode of operation." Second, there is the "Law of Prägnanz," which states (in Ms. Smith's
words) that "whenever possible, we tend to perceive groups of stimuli as combining to form
simple, coherent and stable wholes." Finally there is the "saturation" principle or effect, which
specifies that while the repetition which is basic to patterning "tends to give stability to the
structure of which it is a part, the further it is extended the more desperate becomes our desire
for variation or conclusion." These principles are interlocking and depend upon the Gestalt
view of perception as a dynamic, unfolding process; they depend, even more fundamentally,
upon the belief that "we seek out 'enclosures': structures that are highly organized, separated as
if by an implicit frame from a background of relative disorder or randomness, and integral or
complete." We are gratified, therefore, when we experience completed wholes—but for maximum effect the gratification must not be too simple or come too directly:

   the most direct fulfillment of expectations is not, after all, as gratifying as something a
   little different. The most direct way of releasing the tension of being hungry is to eat a

square meal, but when we enter a restaurant with healthy appetites and begin by ordering an "appetizer," we obviously have some other route of gratification in mind. We enjoy, it seems, teasing our tensions, deferring the immediate fulfillment of our appetites and expectations.

Thus true closure offers a kind of gratification by releasing tensions and resolving extended expectations, and occurs when there is a modification of an ongoing pattern which "makes *stasis*, or the absence of further continuation, the most probably succeeding event" (it is not probable, for example, that a sonnet will have a fifteenth line). Closure is therefore quite different from cessation. A random series of noises stops; a well-made work achieves closure

> when the concluding portion of a poem creates in the reader a sense of appropriate cessation. It announces and justifies the absence of further development; it reinforces the feeling of finality, completion, and composure which we value in all works of art; and it gives ultimate unity and coherence to the reader's experience of the poem by providing a point from which all the preceding elements may be viewed comprehensively and their relations grasped as part of a significant design.

To return to James for a moment: the principles of Gestalt psychology as applied here may offer some explanation of the fact that we welcome the experience of completed wholes, even at the expense of our knowledge that life goes on after the hero dies or Isabel Archer returns to her wretched marriage. But why is the desire for closure so compelling? Ms. Smith is unwilling to go much further than this:

> The sources of our gratification in closure probably lie in the most fundamental aspects of our psychological and physiological organization, an area where speculation is attractive but ignorance keeps pulling us up short.... Perhaps all we can say, and even this may be too much, is that varying degrees or states of tension seem to be involved in all our experiences, and that the most gratifying ones are those in which whatever tensions are created are also released.

On what grounds, then, can Ms. Smith refer to the "appropriate cessation" of a poem? When she turns to poetry itself, she makes a basic distinction between the "formal" and the "thematic" (or "symbolic") properties of words. That is, words have formal characteristics, such as sound and stress values, apart from their meanings; but they have meanings, of course, and point to the world of objects and events outside the poem with which we are partly familiar. Moreover, we respond to these represented objects and events in terms of type-experiences and hence type-expectations, or, in Ms. Smith's terms, recurring "themes" of existence (courtships, quests and so on). Thus the formal effects of words depend upon our ability to hear patterning devices such as rhyme and rhythm, while thematic effects depend upon "the reader's responses to language as conditioned by his participation in [his] community" (courtships and quests work differently in different cultures). Closure occurs when formal and thematic expectations are aroused by patterning and the accompanying tensions are finally released. In practice, of course, the poet uses formal and thematic principles simultaneously; for the purpose of analysis, Ms. Smith separates them and provides an extensive catalogue of the resources the poet may draw upon. She also demonstrates the existence of a kind of proportional relationship between the devices: "in general, as the number of formal principles decreases, closural effects increasingly depend upon the thematic features of the work."

There are, then, degrees of closure, and this leads directly to the question of value—the value, that is, of works in which the artist provides weak rather than strong closure; and it is here that Ms. Smith has some penetrating things to say about modern art. While it is true that a good many modern artists rely just as heavily on formal and thematic principles as their predecessors did, it is also true that many of the most spectacular and influential modern works deny equilibrium and resist closure. Are such strategies justifiable, or do they push the work beyond the proper bounds of art as Gestalt psychology defines it? There are times, Ms. Smith argues, when weak closure may paradoxically be "the most successful kind of closure":

> thus, whereas the epigrammatic conclusion [an instance of very strong closure] will

convey authority, secure conviction, emotional containment, and brusque dismissal, the open-ended or anti-closural conclusion will convey doubt, tentativeness, an inability or refusal to make absolute and unqualified assertions. It affirms its own irresolution and compels the reader to participate in it. [Such works] ask, "What do we know? How can we be sure we know it?" They question the validity and even the possibility of unassail-able verities, the moral or intellectual legitimacy of final words.... We know too much and are sceptical of all that we know, feel, and say. All traditions are equally viable because all are equally suspect. Where conviction is seen as self-delusion and all last words are lies, the only resolution may be in the affirmation of irresolution, and conclusiveness may be seen as not only less honest but as *less stable* than inconclusiveness.

Here Ms. Smith relies explicitly on the way in which Leonard Meyer characterizes the major differences between traditional and avant-garde art, in an important essay, "The End of the Renaissance?" (now reprinted in his collection, *Music, the Arts, and Ideas*). In Meyer's summary,

> The denial of the reality of relationships and the relevance of purpose, the belief that only individual sensations and not the connections between them are real, and the assertion that predictions and goals depend not upon an order existing in nature, but upon the accumulated habits and preconceptions of men—all these rest upon a less explicit but even more fundamental denial: the denial of cause and effect.

Does this radical denial (and the works which dramatize it) constitute a gain or a loss? Ms. Smith cannily stops rather than closes her argument here: "We conclude, then, à la mode, with paradoxes.... Poetry ends in many ways, but poetry, I think, is not yet ended."

In *Poetic Closure*, Ms. Smith remarked in passing that "no sane man or woman engages for long in arguments regarding the proper definition of art." Perhaps not, but ten years later she was devoting herself, with splendid results, to the cognate problem of how we are to differen-tiate between the "fictive" utterances of verbal art and "natural" utterances or discourse. What are the essential differences between the speech of the Duke in Browning's "My Last Duchess" and a similar speech of implied warning uttered in the world of real, historical events and persons? If we cannot reasonably argue that the difference lies in the content of such utterances or the kinds of verbal devices they use (and such arguments go no place), how can we account for our persistent feeling that there *are* real and important differences?

Ms. Smith begins by drawing a distinction between natural and fictive utterances. The former, which take place in what she calls the "linguistic marketplace", are the utterances of real persons engaged in verbal transactions with each other. It is important to realize that for Ms. Smith, as for John Searle and J.L. Austin (and Kenneth Burke long before them), an utterance is a purposive act, situated in a context—and usually a self-interested act as well:

> what we communicate, when we do so and to whom, are always determined at least in part by the likelihood of the advantage we thereby derive for ourselves. Information is a commodity of some value, and we do not normally squander it or donate it *gratis* to whoever happens to be around. Rather, we exchange it for specific services, or invest it for long-term yield.

Gathering the full meaning of an utterance involves—to use I.A. Richards' formulation—the recognition of a speaker's literal sense, his "feeling" (his attitude towards that sense), his "tone" (his attitude towards his audience) and of course his intention or purpose. In this sense, we cannot understand the meaning of a speech act until we know the context in which it occurred; and even if we happen to be present, we still need to make inferences about total meaning from intonation, non-verbal gestures and so forth. Nevertheless, these aspects are "historical" and hence at least potentially recoverable.

Fictive discourse, on the other hand, is the *representation* of a natural utterance, offered by the writer to the reader in a quite special way. As the depiction of a natural utterance, a fictive utterance is also a fictive or imagined member of a real class or type-utterance (a promise, a command, a threat or whatever), and is to be grasped as such. To understand the fictive utterance, we must again infer the full meaning; but in fictive utterances the context does not exist apart from the work itself. The text must carry its own context, in other words, and the burden of inference-making is thereby increased. In reading a dramatic monologue the audience does not need historical knowledge, but rather "the capacity to conceive of the *kind* of situation which *might* lead a man to feel thus and to speak thus, and the reader can develop that capacity only out of his own experiences with men, their situations, their feelings, and especially their language." Furthermore, in fictive utterances the writer deliberately leaves "gaps" or psychological space, with the understanding that the reader will do the filling-in, creating a set of inferred data which never existed and is therefore not recoverable. (To take a simple example, what does Browning's Duke look like? No two readers will fill in that gap in exactly the same way). For Ms. Smith we cannot respond properly to (that is, profit from) a fictive utterance unless we *take* it to be one ("the classification of the utterance as fictive or natural will entail certain distinctive assumptions, expectations, and responses"). Of course it is quite possible to *mis*take the utterance: we may think that the Duke's speech is the record of an historically real event. The words remain the same, but our assumption that it is a natural and not a fictive utterance will destroy its effect or value.

The crucial question, then, concerns the value of fictive utterances, first for the writer, then for the reader. The fictive realm offers the writer a space where he can say things which in the linguistic marketplace (where different proprieties and conventions obtain) would be literally "unspeakable":

> we cannot really "speak" to dead friends, estranged lovers, sleeping babies, nightingales, or Grecian urns, although there may, in a sense, be things we wanted to say to them. And, of course, even when we do not require a particular listener, there are few occasions on which we can give unlimited expression to all our feelings, attitudes, and recognitions. Not even lovers or psychoanalysts can be enlisted as continuous audiences. Finally, even granted endlessly attentive analysts and lovers, our public voices are always dependent on our public roles, qualified as well as constrained by our relationships to our listeners. Consequently, there are always sentiments we could express, knowledge we could display, ways we could speak—possible utterances, in other words—for which there are no occasions, no audiences, or no available style. The conventions and assumptions of fictive discourse, however, may allow us to define the occasion, enlist the audience, and create or discover the necessary style.... What makes it worth the reader's while to heed the historically unspeakable utterance depends on the understanding that he shares with the "speaker" that it is not, in fact, historically spoken: that, insofar as it is being offered as fictive discourse, the reader and the author have entered a special relationship, one that is governed by assumptions, claims, and responsibilities quite different from those that obtain between the speaker and listener of a natural utterance.

As for the reader: once he recognizes that he is dealing with a fictive utterance, he can accept and enjoy what he could not enjoy or perhaps even tolerate in the linguistic marketplace. He will appreciate the stylistic skills of the writer (of course he can also appreciate the skills of a "real" speaker too), but the great value of fictive discourse, for Ms. Smith, lies in its capacity to stimulate what she calls "cognitive play," or the gathering of information and making of inferences for no immediate, practical end in the real world. Following Aristotle, Ms. Smith argues that all men by nature desire to know, and that gathering the meanings of things and thereby satisfying the desire is a source of positive and valuable pleasure:

> As creatures who must know our world in order to survive in it, we are engaged in almost continuous cognitive activity, scanning and exploring the environment, searching out principles of regularity and patterns of conformity, classifying and reclassifying phenomena, testing present against past experiences, examining and adjusting the categories or our knowledge. Indeed, we are probably creatures who have survived because of our epistemic hunger and irritability, our itch to know and our capacity to learn...it would seem that we...not only seek and value knowledge but find fundamentally gratifying the very process of *coming to know*.

And paradoxically enough, "it would seem that the pleasures of learning are maximal when the pressure to know is minimal": cognitive activity when we are students taking an important test or anxious travelers struggling with an unfamilar map is necessarily filled with tension. Those tensions are absent, however, when we are reading Keats or Virginia Woolf. The emphasis is therefore on cognitive *play*; fictive utterances become "the occasion for the exercise of the reader's own imaginative powers, specifically as the occasion for unusually creative cognitive activity."

This does not mean, in Ms. Smith's very carefully worked-out system, that the text is perilously close to being (as it is for a Freudian critic like Norman Holland) an Rorschach blot. The reader is not free to fill in the gaps any way he chooses:

> To the extent that the meanings of a poem are understood to be indeterminate [the Duke's age and appearance for example once again], we must supply meanings for it; and by obliging us to do so, the poem creates a need and therefore a use for knowledge that might otherwise remain unavailable to us. This is not to say, however, that a poem is a springboard for daydreaming. On the contrary, its value lies not simply in provoking that activity but also in shaping and, indeed, resisting it. Even as certain possibilities of interpretation are opened, they are also directed, lured, and redirected by the poet through the verbal structure he has designed.

There is still a contractual bond between the writer and the reader which must be honored if both parties are to profit.

Finally, the critic or interpreter of meaning has his responsibilities too:

> For the interpreter, if he speaks, speaks natural discourse. His utterances are therefore governed by the ethics of the linguistic marketplace, where the fundamental imperative for all speakers is that they mean what they say and take responsibility for having said it. For professional exegetes, this means, among other things, that they should acknowledge the nature, limits, motives, and consequences of their activities.

Yet at the same time, Ms. Smith is able to provide a place for the recent claims of Harold Bloom, Geoffrey Hartman, J. Hillis Miller and other followers of Jacques Derrida that all readings are necessarily misreadings, that criticism is a kind of "free play" and should be as creative as the texts it "deconstructs":

> In their most highly elaborated versions, the potential value and interest of such interpretations would consist not in the interpreter's putative identification of the historically determinate meanings of a work but, rather, in the intellectual subtlety and imaginative fertility that he displays in playing out various of its historically indeterminate meanings... [A] significant source of the pleasure and interest we take in our cognitive engagement with a poem is our presumption and projecting (or hypothesizing) of the artist's "design," and a corresponding source of interest and pleasure for the spectator of such a reported engagement—or reenacted "game"—is precisely its consequent quality of *inter-play*. This is a quality, it might be added, that extends to the transaction between the interpreter and his own audience, since the latter will inevitably "match" his own experience of the work against that represented by the offered "reading," and, to the extent that the interpreter's game thus *itself* becomes an occasion for cognitive play, it serves an "aesthetic" function.

We may very well be pleased, then, when we watch the inter-play of Hartman and Miller and their texts; it is simply a pleasure different from that we have in watching the performances of M.H. Abrams or Wayne Booth. And of course the virtuosity Ms. Smith displays in sorting out so many problems also provides a liberating pleasure of its own.

SMITH, James. British. Born in Batley, Yorkshire, 17 June 1904. Educated at Trinity College, Cambridge, B.A. (1st class honours) 1924; Princeton University, New Jersey (Jane Eliza Procter Visiting Fellow, 1928-39). Taught at Percival Whitley College of Further Education, Halifax, and King Edward VII School, Sheffield, 1931-33. Inspector of Schools, 1934-37. Examiner for the Cambridge Local Examinations Syndicate; Lecturer in English, Instituto Pedagógico, 1940, and Director of the British-Venezuelan Cultural Centre, Caracas. Professor of English, Roman Catholic University of Fribourg, Switzerland, 1947-69. *Died 1 August 1972.*

PUBLICATIONS

Criticism

"Alfred North Whitehead," in *Scrutiny* (Cambridge), 3, 1934.
"George Chapman," in *Scrutiny* (Cambridge), 3, 1934, and 4, 1935.
"Marlowe's 'Dr. Faustus,' " in *Scrutiny* (Cambridge), 8, 1939.
"The Tragedy of Blood," in *Scrutiny* (Cambridge), 8, 1939.
"Notes on the Criticism of T.S. Eliot," in *Essays in Criticism* (Oxford), 22, 1972.
"Chaucer, Boethius and Recent Trends in Criticism," in *Essays in Criticism* (Oxford), 22, 1972.
Shakespearian and Other Essays, edited by Edward M. Wilson. London, Cambridge University Press, 1974.
"Beowulf I and II," in *English* (London), 123-24, 1977-78.

CRITICAL STUDIES

F.W. Bateson, "Shakespeare under Scrutiny," in *Times Literary Supplement* (London), 30 August 1974.
Martin Dodsworth, "Classic Quality," in *Essays in Criticism* (Oxford), 26, 1976.

*   *   *

When James Smith died in 1972 he was completing a study of Shakespeare's comedies, one of two major projects he undertook after retiring from a teaching position which gave him, Edward Wilson recalls, "little happiness" or time for his own work. Of the dozen or so essays apparently intended for the book, seven have survived: four from the 1940's, two from the 50's, and one from 1972. In themselves the dates are not important, but they suggest something about the high standards Smith set for himself and something else, perhaps, about his curious reluctance to commit himself to a full critical point of view. Martin Dodsworth has claimed for these essays a certain "classic quality" because they "fundamentally question conventional readings of the comedies" and—surely more important—because they seem intent on "relating art to other human interests and activities." Yet these are not the qualities which first strike a reader: it is Smith's great sensitivity to individual passages and his closely reasoned arguments which are immediately impressive, and these are qualities not easily illustrated by brief quotation or summary.

There are some indications of the shape the completed study would probably have taken. At the start of his essay on *As You Like It* Smith remarks "I have begun to doubt whether not only *As You Like It* and *Hamlet,* but almost all the comedies and tragedies as a whole are not closely connected, and in a way which may be quite important." And he continues,

> I would venture to suggest that the essential difference between comedy and tragedy may perhaps be this sort of difference: not one of a kind, I mean, but of degree. As far as I can see it is possible and even probable that tragedy and comedy—Shakespearian comedy at any rate—treat of the same problems, comedy doing so...less seriously. And by "less

seriously,"...I mean that the problems are not forced to an issue: a lucky happening, a lucky trait of character (or what for the purposes of the play appears lucky) allowing them to be evaded. As, for example, conditions in Arden and conditions of his own temper preserve Jacques from fully realizing the nature and consequences of his scepticism: to Rosalind, to the reader, it is obvious that his interests are restricted, his vigour lessened, but he is never put to the test. Hamlet, on the other hand, in a similar spiritual state, is called upon to avenge a father, foil an uncle and govern a kingdom. And when at last chance forces him into action it is not only that he may slaughter but also that he may be slaughtered: in other words, not that in spite of his disability he may achieve his end, but that because of it he may fail.... In comedy the materials for tragedy are procured, in some cases heaped up; but they are not, so to speak, attended to, certainly not closely examined. And so what might have caused grief causes only a smile, or at worst a grimace.

The reader will naturally want and expect some further discussion of "luck." Is it related, for example, to conventional notions of "Fortune"? How does a departure from "inevitability" affect our overall responses to tragedy and comedy? Although Smith faintly suggests that there may be some connection between chance and grace, he does not really face these questions. There is only a brief indication that a core of common "problems" unifies Shakespeare's work taken as a whole, so that "the early comedies are a fitting preparation for the 'problem plays,' while from these to the tragedies is but a step."

In his acute review of *Seven Types of Ambiguity* Smith observes that a poem is "not a fragment of life, it is a fragment that has been detached, considered and judged by a mind." Yet a poem, or a drama at any rate, is not all-encompassing, and thus he argues (in his essay on *The Winter's Tale*) that

Souls so completely purged of pride are, in Lear's words, fit not to offer but to receive incense: fit, that is , to enter heaven—but hardly, alas! the fitter to hold their place in the world. Immured in his cell, however, Lear belongs to the world no longer, and that he should be removed from it by death is a matter of no concern to the play. What follows upon his exit to prison is irrelevant, and might with advantage be omitted.

"But what follows is so heart-rending!" Exactly: unless Aristotle and all reputable theorists of tragedy are at fault, words which merely rend the heart are not suitable for utterance on the public stage. Questions such as

> Why should a dog, a horse, a rat, have life
> And thou no breath at all?

—questions irrepressible and unanswerable as an agony: these are to be canvassed, if canvassed at all, only in the secret of the confessional or the closer secret of the heart. On pain of ceasing to discharge the function of alternative that, at its best, tragedy has always discharged, it needs to acknowledge a limit to its license to perturb; just as its partner, comedy, has never in effect put forward more than a limited pretension to soothe.... Not only are tragedy and comedy not the same as life but, no more than any other form of art, are they capable of digesting everything that insistently, persistently thrusts itself upon the living.

Basic issues are raised here but never pursued. How does tragedy change us? To what end does tragedy perturb and comedy console us? In a fragmentary essay on *Measure for Measure* Smith asserts that

The study of history, even the history of books which is bibliography, appears to me the idlest of occupations. If at times it may render aid, this can be of no more than a servile nature. Care must be taken lest history be allowed to rank alongside the study of the meaning of texts which, as it is the most difficult, is the most serious of occupations that can be pursued: for it imports the survival of humanity.

This may sound like I.A. Richards, for whom the loss of poetry would be a "biological calamity" for the race, but Smith's religious convictions make such an association unlikely. He is far closer to W.H. Auden's wary approval of art, and for the same fundamentally Christian motives. For Auden, we are commanded to "bless what there is for being," to regard this world "with a happy eye / But from a sober perspective," and there are indications Smith would agree. Thus at the end of his superb essay on *The Tempest* he maintains that that play, like Calderón's *La Vida Es Sueño*, is "a variation upon the argument that life is a dream":

> whereas in Calderón's play one character only is shown as dreaming, while the rest are wide awake and so have the opportunity of learning their lesson from him; in *The Tempest* all the characters are involved in the dream contemporaneously. All then must learn their lesson at their own expense; and even Prospero must relearn it, since he forgets it. Hence the realism of the play. It has no more and no less than the dreaminess of life. Hence reading it, the reader too must learn at his own expense. For he is no better off than the characters—and why should he be? Like them he is puzzled to know the qualities of the island; like them he will never be quite certain what behaviour to adopt towards Caliban. If he thinks it worthwhile to do so, he may ask himself a million times whether or not the spirits are real, whether Prospero really achieves anything with his conjuring. But his enjoyment of the play should thereby be not the less but the greater. He should enjoy it as he enjoys life, of which it is not a representation seen from a distance and therefore falsified, but the rarer perfume when life, because of its dreaminess, is seen to depend completely upon the supernatural. No desperation, no complacency; be cheerful! Tragicomedia?

The religious foundations of Smith's thinking are equally apparent in his comparison of *The Winter's Tale* with *King Lear*:

> The two plays, I would suggest, deal with the same topic, but under different aspects. The topic is *imbecillitas humana*: the folly or weakness because of which, unless men are prudent (and so few of them are), they begin to play fantastic tricks as soon as they have any authority to play with. In so far as they do so before high heaven they are unworthy of their theatre, and the likely result is tragedy. In so far as they are men, the tricks are inadequate to the ends they hope to gain: and so furnish promising material for comedy.

And he concludes that Camillo is not "perfectly prudent" but "well-nigh perfectly" so:

> Hence his part subjection to imbecility; hence the need of good fortune which is his no less than that of other men. How great must be our own need, who not only cannot benefit by the convention of comedy, but live in an age when imbecility of hitherto unknown proportions reigns over areas of an extent hitherto unknown. Watching a civilization sicker even than Lady Macbeth, we can only repeat with her physician: God, God forgive us all!

This *imbecillitas* is clearly related to the Christian conception of fallen human nature. In short, comedy is a deadly serious affair for Smith. He is an austere moralist, very much in the tradition of Dr. Johnson.

Remarkable as the Shakespeare essays are, "On Metaphysical Poetry," which first appeared in *Scrutiny* in 1933, is even finer, partly because of its greater generalizing force. Donne, Herbert and Marvell are the true metaphysical poets in English for Smith, but his careful definition has nothing to do with Johnson's complaints about obscure diction or far-fetched conceits. Donne and Lucretius may versify metaphysical doctrine at points, but the thought of the true metaphysical poet, like that of the metaphysician himself, is marked by a particular kind of tension:

> I am aware that at first sight there does not seem to be a great resemblance between Donne's turbulence, springing from his being full of problems, and what we may call Thomas's subtlety or elusiveness. Later I shall suggest that both spring from the same cause; and that the difference between the two, great as it is, is no greater than one would expect, given the very different aims that Donne and Thomas pursue. Here, leaving aside

for the moment profounder speculation, I wish to establish one point merely: that turbulence in Donne, elusiveness in Thomas—both are signs of something very different from the certainty to be found in Dante and Lucretius. Lacking such a certainty, Donne resembles Dante's master much more than does Dante himself; in one respect at least, therefore, he is, more properly than Dante, called "metaphysical." The question rises, whether this respect is important enough to merit consideration. And I think it is. For I am not suggesting a resemblance between Donne and Thomas in the possession of a negative quality merely. I do not believe that anyone who lacks certainty, who is puzzled and therefore in his account of his studies puzzling—for instance, the crossword fanatic or the half-wit—is for that reason to be called metaphysical. Metaphysics is "puzzling," if I may retain the homely word, in a peculiar way. It is not that, to the matters it studies, there is an abundance of clues, so that the mind is lost among them; or that there is a shortage of clues, so that the mind is left hesitant; but rather, that such clues as there are, while equally trustworthy, are contradictory. And again, I do not mean that they are contradictory as are, say, pleas in a law-court. A judge is puzzled if he has before him two chains of evidence, one tending to prove that a certain person was in a certain spot at a certain time, the other that he was not. In cases like this, the contradiction rests upon accidents merely: it is compatible with the nature of the person whose movements are being considered, either that he was, or that he was not, at the given spot. The contradictions in metaphysics, on the other hand, spring from essence. The very nature of things brings them forth. It seems impossible that the nature of things should possess either the one or the other of a pair of qualities; it seems impossible that it should possess both together: it seems impossible that it should not possess both. Concern with problems of this kind gives a quite peculiar air of being puzzled; it is only in possession of this air, and not of any other, that I wish to say Donne and Thomas resemble each other.

The great value of Smith's argument here—and it is precisely that, a true argument of compelling logical power—is that is can be extended to illuminate the work of poets from other periods. Smith himself suggests such an extension in the distinction he draws between closed and suspended conceits in one of his very last essays, "Notes on the Criticism of T.S. Eliot":

To the English language—to the English language in poetry, anyway—it would appear to be normal neither to close nor to thwart the conceit, but to suspend it: that is, to awaken or to keep awake a consciousness of the elements of a conceit, while avoiding the slightest attempt to bring them together. Always, these elements are those of what I once called a metaphysical conceit: persistent and perplexing opposites such as unity and multiplicity, death and life, flesh and spirit, time and eternity, the real and the ideal, and whatever falls under these or like pairs. The mind is made to savour more fully than usual the conditions under which it is required to operate—which may not mean of course that it relishes these conditions more fully, but rather the opposite. The mind desires, but cannot attain; or if it attains, does so by what the Greeks called a divine, and is certainly not a human chance. Stronger or more experienced spirits respond with something like a stoicism; the weaker and less prepared find themselves dazed, puzzled, held in suspense. But this is not the main reason why I give this form of conceit the name that I do; rather, it is because the conceit can be suspended over, may overarch and subtend, a whole poem, or one or more of the poem's considerable parts.

This essay on Eliot was to have been part of Smith's second project, a series of pieces, Edward Wilson informs us, "designed to establish an English literary tradition going back to *Beowulf*. He intended to start with T.S. Eliot and to work back through Henry James, Tennyson, Wordsworth, the metaphysicals, Chaucer, *Sir Gawain* and finally *Beowulf* itself." It is one of the few tragedies of modern criticism that Smith did not live to complete this project or to face more directly, as he might well have done in his revisions of the Shakespeare essays, the problems inherent in his earlier distinction between tragedy and comedy. As it is, Smith is still an extraordinary writer, a critic's critic, perhaps, and one of the small number of great stylists in criticism since Johnson.

SPENDER, Stephen (Harold).   British.   Born in London, 28 September 1909; son of the writer Harold Spender. Educated at University College School, London; University College, Oxford. Served as a fireman in the National Fire Service, 1941-44. Married 1) Agnes Marie Pearn in 1936; 2) Natasha Litvin in 1941; one son and one daughter. Editor, with Cyril Connolly, *Horizon* magazine, London, 1939-41; Co-Editor, 1953-66, and Corresponding Editor, 1966-67, *Encounter* magazine, London. Counsellor, UNESCO Section of Letters, 1947. Elliston Lecturer, University of Cincinnati, 1953; Beckman Professor, University of California, Berkeley, 1959; Visiting Professor, Northwestern University, Evanston, Illinois, 1963; Clark Lecturer, Cambridge University, 1966; Visiting Professor, University of Connecticut, Storrs, 1968-70; Mellon Lecturer, Washington, D.C., 1968; Northcliffe Lecturer, London University, 1969; Visiting Lecturer, University of Florida, Gainesville, 1976. Since 1970, Professor of English Literature, University College, London. Since 1975, President, English Centre, P.E.N. Consultant in Poetry in English, Library of Congress, Washington, D.C., 1965-66. Fellow of the Institute of Advance Studies, Wesleyan University, Middletown, Connecticut, 1967. Recipient: Queen's Gold Medal for Poetry, 1971; Companion of Literature, 1978. D.Litt.: University of Montpellier; Loyola University, Chicago. Honorary Member, American Academy of Arts and Letters, 1969. C.B.E. (Companion, Order of the British Empire), 1962. Address: 15 Loudoun Road, London N.W.8, England.

PUBLICATIONS

Criticism

> *The Destructive Element: A Study of Modern Writers and Beliefs.*   London, Cape, 1935; Boston, Houghton Mifflin, 1936.
> *Life and the Poet.*   London, Secker and Warburg, 1942; Folcroft, Pennsylvania, Folcroft Editions, 1974.
> *Poetry since 1939.*   London and New York, Longman, 1946.
> *Shelley.*   London, Longman, 1952.
> *The Creative Element: A Study of Vision, Despair, and Orthodoxy among Some Modern Writers.*   London, Hamish Hamilton, 1953.
> *The Making of a Poem.*   London, Hamish Hamilton, 1955; New York, Norton, 1962.
> *The Imagination in the Modern World: Three Lectures.*   Washington, D.C., Library of Congress, 1962.
> *The Struggle of the Modern.*   London, Hamish Hamilton, and Berkeley, University of California Press, 1963.
> *Chaos and Control in Poetry.*   Washington, D.C., Library of Congress, 1966.
> *Love-Hate Relations: A Study of Anglo-American Sensibilities.*   London, Hamish Hamilton , and New York, Random House, 1974.
> *Eliot.*   London, Fontana, 1975; as *T.S. Eliot*, New York, Viking Press, 1976.
> *The Thirties and After: Poetry, Politics, People (1933-1975).*   New York, Random House, and London, Macmillan, 1978.

Verse

> *Nine Experiments by S.H.S.: Being Poems Written at the Age of Eighteen.*   London, privately printed, 1928.
> *Twenty Poems.*   Oxford, Blackwell, 1930.
> *Poems.*   London, Faber, 1933; New York, Random House, 1934; revised edition, Faber, 1934.
> *Vienna.*   London, Faber, 1934; New York, Random House, 1935.
> *At Night.*   Cambridge, privately printed, 1935.
> *The Still Centre.*   London, Faber, 1939.

Selected Poems. London, Faber, 1940.
I Sit at the Window. Baltimore, Linden Press, n.d.
Ruins and Visions. London, Faber, and New York, Random House, 1942.
Spiritual Exercises (To Cecil Day Lewis). Privately printed, 1943.
Poems of Dedication. London, Faber, and New York, Random House, 1947.
Returning to Vienna 1947: Nine Sketches. Pawlet, Vermont, Banyan Press, 1947.
The Edge of Being. London, Faber, and New York, Random House, 1949.
Sirmione Peninsula. London, Faber, 1954.
Collected Poems 1928-1953. London, Faber, and New York, Random House, 1955.
Inscriptions. London, Poetry Book Society, 1958.
Selected Poems. New York, Random House, 1964; London, Faber, 1965.
The Generous Days: Ten Poems. Boston, Godine, 1969; augmented edition, as *The Generous Days*, London, Faber, and New York, Random House, 1971.
Descartes. London, Steam Press, 1970.
Art Student. London, Poem-of-the-Month Club, 1970.
Penguin Modern Poets 20, with John Heath-Stubbs and F.T. Prince. London, Penguin, 1971.
Recent Poems. London, Anvil Press Poetry, 1978.

Plays

Trial of a Judge (produced London, 1938). London, Faber, and New York, Random House, 1938.
Danton's Death, with Goronwy Rees, adaptation of a play by Georg Büchner (produced London, 1939). London, Faber, 1939; in *From the Modern Repertory*, edited by Eric Bentley, Bloomington, Indiana University Press, 1958.
To the Island (produced Oxford, 1951).
Mary Stuart, adaptation of the play by Schiller (produced New York, 1957; Edinburgh and London, 1958). London, Faber, 1959.
Lulu, adaptation of the play by Frank Wedekind (produced New York, 1958).
Rasputin's End, music by Nicholas Nabokov. Milan, Ricordi, 1963.

Novel

The Backward Son. London, Hogarth Press, 1940.

Short Stories

The Burning Cactus. London, Faber, and New York, Random House, 1936.
Engaged in Writing, and The Fool and the Princess. London, Hamish Hamilton, and New York, Farrar Straus, 1958.

Other

Forward from Liberalism. London, Gollancz, and New York, Random House, 1937.
The New Realism: A Discussion. London, Hogarth Press, 1939.
Jim Braidy: The Story of Britain's Firemen, with William Sansom and James Gordon. London, Drummond, 1943.
Citizens in War—and After. London, Harrap, 1945.
Botticelli. London, Faber, 1945; New York, Pitman, 1948.

European Witness. London, Hamish Hamilton, and New York, Reynal, 1946.
World Within World: The Autobiography of Stephen Spender. London, Hamish Hamilton, and New York, Harcourt Brace, 1951.
Europe in Photographs. London, Thames and Hudson, 1951.
Learning Laughter (on Israel). London, Weidenfeld and Nicolson, 1952; New York, Harcourt Brace, 1953.
Ghika: Paintings, Drawings, Sculpture, with Patrick Leigh Fermor. London, Lund Humphries, 1964; Boston, Boston Book and Art Shop, 1965.
The Magic Flute: Retold (juvenile). New York, Putnam, 1966.
The Year of the Young Rebels. London, Weidenfeld and Nicolson, and New York, Random House, 1969.
Letters to Christopher, edited by Lee Bartlett. Santa Barbara, California, Black Sparrow Press, 1981.

Editor, with Louis MacNeice, *Oxford Poetry 1929.* Oxford, Blackwell, 1929.
Editor, with Bernard Spencer, *Oxford Poetry 1930.* Oxford, Blackwell, 1930.
Editor, with John Lehmann and Christopher Isherwood, *New Writing, New Series I* and *II.* London, Hogarth Press, 1938, 1939.
Editor, with John Lehmann, *Poems for Spain.* London, Hogarth Press, 1939.
Editor, *A Choice of English Romantic Poetry.* New York, Dial Press, 1947.
Editor, *Selected Poems*, by Walt Whitman. London, Grey Walls Press, 1950.
Editor, with Elizabeth Jennings and Dannie Abse, *New Poems 1956: A P.E.N. Anthology.* London, Joseph, 1956
Editor, *Great Writings of Goethe.* New York, New American Library, 1958.
Editor, *Great German Short Stories.* New York, Dell, 1960.
Editor, *The Writer's Dilemma.* London, Oxford University Press, 1961.
Editor, with Donald Hall, *The Concise Encyclopedia of English and American Poets and Poetry.* London, Hutchinson, and New York, Hawthorn Books, 1963; revised edition, 1970.
Editor, with Irving Kristol and Melvin J. Lasky, *Encounters: An Anthology from Its First Ten Years of "Encounter" Magazine.* London, Weidenfeld and Nicolson, and New York, Basic Books, 1963.
Editor, *Selected Poems*, by Abba Kovner and Nelly Sachs. London, Penguin, 1971.
Editor, *A Choice of Shelley's Verse.* London, Faber, 1971.
Editor, *D.H. Lawrence: Novelist, Poet, Prophet.* London, Weidenfeld and Nicolson, and New York, Harper, 1973.
Editor, *The Poems of Percy Bysshe Shelley.* New York, Heritage Press, 1974.
Editor, *W.H. Auden: A Tribute.* London, Weidenfeld and Nicolson, and New York, Macmillan, 1975.

Translator, *Pastor Hall*, by Ernst Toller. London, Lane, 1939.
Translator, with J.L. Gili, *Poems*, by García Lorca. London, Dolphin, and New York, Oxford University Press, 1939.
Translator, with J.B. Leishman, *Duino Elegies*, by Rainer Maria Rilke. London, Hogarth Press, and New York, Norton, 1939; revised edition, Hogarth Press, 1948, Norton, 1963.
Translator, with J.L. Gili, *Selected Poems*, by García Lorca. London, Hogarth Press, 1943.
Translator, with Frances Cornford, *Le dur Désir de Durer*, by Paul Eluard. London, Faber, and New York, New Directions, 1950.
Translator, *The Life of the Virgin Mary* (*Das Marien-Leben*) (bilingual edition), by Rainer Maria Rilke. London, Vision Press, and New York, Philosophical Library, 1951.
Translator, with Frances Fawcett, *Five Tragedies of Sex* (includes *Spring's Awakening*, *Earth-Spirit*, *Pandora's Box*, *Death and Devil*, *Castle Wetterstein*), by Frank Wedekind. London, Vision Press, 1952.

BIBLIOGRAPHY

H.B. Kulkani, *Stephen Spender: Works and Criticism: An Annotated Bibliography.* New York, Garland Press, 1976.

*   *   *

In *Lord Jim* Conrad has one of his oracular characters warn us that we must "immerse" ourselves in "the destructive element," but even as we do so we must also "follow the dream, and again...follow the dream—and so—*ewig-usque ad finem.*" That is, we must confront an alien or hostile "reality" with no illusions as to our own importance or the objective worth of our "dreams" or values. As Robert Penn Warren has observed, for Conrad "the last wisdom is for man to realize that though his values are illusions, the illusion is necessary, is infinitely precious, is the work of his human achievement, and is, in the end, his only truth." How much of this Stephen Spender had in mind when he published *The Destructive Element* in 1935 is uncertain (he alludes to the passage from *Lord Jim* only as it occurs in a footnote to Richards' *Science and Poetry*), but what Conrad has to say about the precarious nature of human values and the forces which threaten them can help readers to follow the shifting pattern of Spender's criticism over the past forty years.

By the destructive element Spender means primarily the first World War, the economic miseries of the 1920's and 30's, the rise of fascism—in short the "political chaos," as he calls it, which capitalism and conventional liberalism fostered or at least were unable to prevent. The writers he discusses here (Henry James, Eliot, Yeats and Lawrence) were all "faced by the destructive element; that is, by the experience of an all-pervading Present": what they have in common, therefore, is "an intense dissatisfaction with modern political institutions." Given this collapse of values, Spender continues, several kinds of responses were possible. Henry James, for example, "retired more and more into the inventions of his own mind" (although Spender also contends that James' last great novels record "a profound indictment of our civilization"). Yeats did much the same thing when he retreated to a "magical system" which is "not socially constructive." Lawrence's sexual fantasies "enabled him to escape his real subject, which was modern civilization." Eliot, on the other hand, sought refuge in a real or imagined tradition and the church (but this, Spender concludes, "is a doctrine of Death"). Thus all of these writers "stood on the verge of the destructive element, but decided not to go in." The question, however, is "whether this despairing stage is now over, whether it is now possible for the artist to discover a system of values that are not purely subjective and individualistic, but objective and social; real in a world of society *outside* the artist in the same way as Nature is real." Spender ends *The Destructive Element* with a personal declaration:

> It is no use telling me...that I am a bourgeois-intellectual, that I know nothing, or next to nothing, of the proletariat. All that and a lot more may be true. The point is, though, that if I desire social justice I am not primarily concerned with myself, I am concerned with bringing into being a world quite external to my own interests....The Socialist artist is concerned with realizing in his own work the ideas of a classless society: that is to say, applying those ideas to the life around him, and giving them their reality. He is concerned with a change of heart.

That last phrase, "a change of heart," comes from Auden's early poem "Petition"; and for Spender, as for C. Day Lewis, it was Auden, with his political and psychological sophistication, who represented "a hope for poetry":

> In Auden's work...the interest is the relation of the individual to society, the individual who is not anti-social and a secret rebel, an anarchist, in the sense in which all the great aesthetes have been so, but who, if he is a rebel, is only that in conjunction with a social class.

But programmatic as this all seems to be, Spender was also careful to insist (a few years later, in *Life and the Poet*) that the artist must be allowed his freedom: to turn him into a propagandist is to rob him of that objectivity and power to criticize life which is his true calling.

509

In *The Creative Element*, which followed seventeen years later, Spender is somewhat more pessimistic:

> Thinking as I did [in *The Destructive Element*] that certain modern works stated— whether or not their writers knew it—social decay, I thought that the cure, not only for society but also for art, lay in social change which would remove the causes of the decay.... So at this time my mind was full of the idea that the greatness of the literature of the late nineteenth and early twentieth centuries was in its immersion in the "destructive element," which was the political doom of modern society. And beyond the "destructive element" lay a renewal of creativeness through the writer siding with those forces in society which would save it from destruction.

In retrospect, however, he now feels that he had "laid too much stress on the destructive forces in the novels of Henry James and much modern poetry, and not enough emphasis on the creative energy of the individual who confronted that destruction":

> The creative element is the individual vision of the writer who realizes in his work the decline of modern values while isolating his own individual values from the context of society. He never forgets the modern context, in fact he is always stating it, but he does so only to create the more forcibly the visions of his own isolation.... The main impulse of the whole great "modern movement" has been the individual vision of writers who, out of their intense realization of the destructive element of modern society, have isolated and perfected that vision.

Thus he concludes that there is a kind of exemplary heroism about the writers whom he earlier had called "the great aesthetes":

> the "destructive element" was not, as I thought, capitalism, fascism, the political mechanism which produced wars and unemployment. *It was simply society itself.* Genius had renounced, or moved outside, society, and any acceptance of a social concept which threatened individual isolation was destructive of its unique vision. (my italics)

Spender's argument is complicated, however, by his awareness that the age of heroic individualists is over and that the present return to orthodoxies of one sort or another (chiefly Marxism, the religious orthodoxy of Eliot, Auden, and Waugh, the Arts Council mentality of many recent British writers and artists, and the academic insularity of many American writers) was "inevitable." The visions of the great individualists were too private, their symbols too complex, to engage a wide audience. Thus the destructive element remains, while most of the sustaining "dreams" have faded away or become institutionalized (this is a much simplified version of Lionel Trilling's argument in *Beyond Culture*). At most there is the very faint hope that we will continue to "attach value to the idea of a life within a pattern of society where men respect the right to exist of their neighbours":

> Probably I shall be accused of writing that Christianity should become political. What I am trying to suggest is the reverse: that politics should become Christian. This, though, can only happen if the Christian accepts his responsibility within time and history. Such a responsibility would tell him that Marxism has been more successful than most philosophies in stating the problem of social justice within an industrial society.... The answer to Marxism is to accept the challenge of the necessity of worldwide social change, but at the same time to regard the individual with Christian charity and justice.

The Creative Element is something of an elegy, then, for the passing of modernism.

Twenty years later, in *Love-Hate Relations*, Spender was more pessimistic still. "Until quite recently," he asserts, "European civilization meant the extension into the present of the continuity of the past tradition." True civilization arises "only where there is a sense of the past as a vital force acting within the society." The destructive element now, the great enemy of tradition, is, of course, America, for whom the past is merely a museum or "a kind of vitamin which can be obtained by extracting it chemically from literature." Worse still, America, or rather Americanization,

> confronts the world and says: "This is your future." It converts all human requirements into problems which can be restated as ones in which the consumer meets a producer. Even mysterious and unexplained human aspirations—such as someone wishing to meet the right sexual partner—can ultimately be analyzed and reduced to the same terms of a supply meeting a demand.

The universities are the museum keepers, while the real—and fatally attractive—energy of America is "orgiastic," that is, concerned only with the intensity of each isolated moment. In this sense America represents nothing less than "death." The one remaining dream is that of an ideal community or, in Spender's latest vocabulary, "patria":

> The dramatization of choices between "life" and "death" occurs so often here that I should attempt now to explain the sense in which I employ the term "life." I do not mean the individual's awareness of being alive, nor the question mark poised above the phrases such as "the meaning of life." What I mean is the awareness felt particularly by writers...of the connection between their separate existence and their country, in its history, landscape and people. This awareness is of a life which is that of an ideal United States or England which the writer, if he is in correct relation to it, releases in his work. Unless he does have such an awareness, his work will be peripheral to that center or turned inward on himself. It follows that if the nation itself presents conditions which prevent the writer from identifying with it the ideal of the country in his mind, then he will find himself opposed to the official nation. His work will find its center in a patriotism against which he measures the surrounding public nation. To simplify my argument, let me call the idea of the true nation, the "patria."

But such an ideal seems almost impossible now. For America it is already too late; for England, however, "one quite justifiable reaction to the situation is to be nationalistic, idiomatic, concretely and stubbornly provincial." By developing a studied provincialism, by following the lines laid down by Hardy and, at the moment, by Philip Larkin, perhaps England may be able to "maintain distance and sanity." *Love-Hate Relations* is not literary criticism at all, nor does it pretend to be; at best it is an understandable if perhaps slightly vulgar cry of protest masquerading as literary history.

Of course it is possible that *Love-Hate Relations* may come to have the same sort of documentary value which still makes *The Destructive Element* and *The Creative Element* worth knowing about. And if there should be a revival of interest in Spender's poetry, then these studies may take on something more than historical interest. But the host of brief essays and reviews I have not mentioned here have not outlived their occasions: too often Spender has had an apparently irresistible urge to write instant literary history.

STEINER, (Francis) George. American. Born in Paris, France, 23 April 1929; emigrated to the United States, 1940, naturalized, 1944. Educated at the Sorbonne, Paris, Bachelier-ès-Lettres 1947; University of Chicago, B.A. 1948; Harvard University, Cambridge, Massachusetts (Bell Prize), M.A. 1950; Balliol College, Oxford (Rhodes Scholar; Chancellor's English Essay Prize, 1952), D.Phil. 1955. Married Zara Shakow in 1955; has two children. Staff Member, *The Economist*, London, 1952-56; Member, Institute for Advanced Study, 1957-59, and Gauss Lecturer in Criticism, 1959-60, Princeton University, New Jersey. Since 1961, Fellow, and since 1969, Extraordinary Fellow, Churchill College, Cambridge; since 1974, Professor of English and Comparative Literature, University of Geneva. Schweitzer Professor,

New York University, 1966-67; T.S. Eliot Lecturer, University of Kent, Canterbury, 1971; Regents Professor, University of California, 1974. President of the English Association, 1975-76. Recipient: O. Henry Award, 1958; *Jewish Chronicle* Book Award, 1968; National Institute of Arts and Letters Zabel Award, 1970; Guggenheim Fellowship, 1971; Cortine Ulisse Prize, 1972; Le Prix du Souvenir, 1974. Fellow, Royal Society of Literature, 1964. Address: 32 Barrow Road, Cambridge, England.

PUBLICATIONS

Criticism

> *Tolstoy or Dostoevsky: An Essay in the Old Criticism.*   New York, Knopf, 1959; as
>   *Tolstoy and Dostoevsky: An Essay in Contrast*, London, Faber, 1960.
> *The Death of Tragedy.*   New York, Knopf, and London, Faber, 1961.
> *Language and Silence: Essays on Language, Literature, and the Inhuman.*   New York,
>   Atheneum, and London, Faber, 1967.
> *Extraterritorial: Papers on Literature and the Language Revolution.*   New York, Athe-
>   neum, 1971; London, Faber, 1972.
> *In Bluebeard's Castle: Some Notes Towards the Redefinition of Culture.*   New Haven,
>   Connecticut, Yale University Press, and London, Faber, 1971.
> *After Babel: Aspects of Language and Translation.*   London and New York, Oxford
>   University Press, 1975.
> "Critic/Reader," in *New Literary History* (Charlottesville, Virginia), 10, 1979.
> *On Difficulty and Other Essays.*   London and New York, Oxford University Press, 1980.

Verse

> *(Poems).*   Oxford, Fantasy Press, 1953.

Novel

> *The Portage to San Cristobal of A.H.*   London, Faber, 1981.

Short Stories

> *Anno Domini: Three Stories.*   London, Faber, and New York, Atheneum, 1965.

Other

> *Malice: Chancellor's English Essay Prize, 1952.*   Oxford, Blackwell, 1952.
> *The Sporting Scene: White Knights of Reykjavik.*   London, Faber, 1973; as *Fields of
>   Force: Fischer and Spassky at Reykjavik*, New York, Viking Press, 1974.
> *Heidegger.*   Hassocks, Sussex, Harvester Press, 1978; as *Martin Heidegger*, New York,
>   Viking Press, 1979.
>
> Editor, with Robert Fagles, *Homer: A Collection of Critical Essays.*   Englewood Cliffs,
>   New Jersey, Prentice Hall, 1962.

Editor, *The Penguin Book of Modern Verse Translation.*   London, Penguin, 1966.

CRITICAL STUDIES

   John Simon, "The Theatre Critic and His Double," in *Acid Test.*   New York, Stein and
      Day, 1963.
   Irving Howe, "Auschwitz and High Mandarin," in *The Critical Point: On Literature and
      Culture.*   New York, Horizon Press, 1973.
   Kenneth Burke, "Above the Over-Towering Babel," in *Michigan Quarterly Review* (Ann
      Arbor), 15, 1976.
   Christopher Butler, "George Steiner and the Critical Performance," in *Sewanee Review*
      (Tennessee), 87, 1979.

                              *   *   *

"Literary criticism should arise out of a debt of love," George Steiner announces at the
beginning of *Tolstoy or Dostoevsky*, his first and in many ways his least typical book. The job
of the critic, he goes on, is to put his readers into a "responsive relationship with the work of art;
to do the job of the intermediary":

   Not to judge or to anatomize, but to mediate. Only through love of the work of art, only
   through the critic's constant and anguished recognition of the distance which separates
   his craft from that of the poet, can such mediation be accomplished.... These I take to be
   the tenets of what one might call "the old criticism" in partial distinction from that
   brilliant and prevailing school known as "the new criticism."

But these opening flourishes are a little disingenuous. Steiner is not a particularly modest or
self-effacing critic, and as his title implies, we may love both novelists but šooner or later must
choose between them—and for reasons which are by no means primarily critical or aesthetic.
   Both Dostoevsky and Tolstoy are "foremost among novelists" and both are essentially
"religious" writers. But the similarities end here for Steiner. Dostoevsky is the creator of
superbly concise melodramas—concise, that is, relative to the complexity of his aims—while
Tolstoy, "the Heraclitus of novelists," is an epic poet of Homeric amplitude (he is also a careful
craftsman and not merely the author of those vivid but "large loose baggy monsters" Henry
James complained about. Steiner is no more successful in handling this paradox than other
critics have been). Dostoevsky is a visionary, Tolstoy a rationalist; finally, Dostoevsky is
"Christian" while Tolstoy is "pagan." This last distinction clearly needs some supporting
arguments, and here Steiner is more convincing than one might have expected. Tolstoy's
ambivalent attitude toward the doctrines of personal immortality and the divinity of Christ
makes his apparently orthodox terminology, as Léon Shestov puts it, "dangerously fluid...God
is deliberately replaced by '*the Good*' and '*the Good*' is in turn replaced by brotherly love among
men. Actually, such a creed excludes neither complete atheism nor total disbelief." Shestov's
observations, Steiner continues, are "undeniably true":

   the defining conceptions are interchangeable and through a gradual process of equation
   we arrive at a theology without God. Or, rather, we arrive at an anthropology of mortal
   greatness in which men have created God in their own image. He is the utmost projection
   of their own nature; at times a titular guardian, at other times an enemy full of ancient
   cunning and sudden vengeance. Such a revision of God and the encounters between God
   and man which it entails are neither Christian nor athiest. They are pagan.... Where he
   did not envisage God as a metaphoric equivalent for a social and rational utopia, Tolstoy
   saw Him, through some covert blasphemy or solitude of love, as a being rather like
   himself.

In "utter contrariety" to Dostoevsky, Tolstoy "could not believe in a prophet who declared that
His Kingdom was not of the world."

                                                                                     513

At this point in Steiner's argument the reader suddenly realizes that he is being asked to choose between the two novelists, and for social rather than for religious or purely critical reasons. We have to decide whether Tolstoy or Dostoevsky gave "the truer image of human nature and the more prophetic account of history." By these standards, Dostoevsky is the greater writer: he is a tragic prophet who refused to settle for the comparatively easy and comfortable social meliorism of Tolstoy:

> The narrator of *Letters from the Underworld* expresses through his acts and language a final "No." When Tolstoy remarked to Gorky that Dostoevsky "ought to have made himself acquainted with the teachings of Confucius or the Buddhists; that would have calmed him down," the underground man must have howled derisively from his lair. Our times have given substance to his derision. The *univers concentrationnaire*—the world of the death camps—confirms beyond denial Dostoevsky's insights into the savagery of men, in their inclination, both as individuals and as hordes, to stamp out within themselves the embers of humanity. The subterranean narrator defines his species as "A creature which walks on two legs and is devoid of gratitude."

Thus Steiner is able to conclude that there is a natural affinity between Tolstoy and the Marxists and hence a potential threat to the true, "existential" individuality of man as Dostoevsky defines him:

> What the Marxists have discerned in Tolstoy is many of the elements which Dostoevsky imagined in the [Grand] Inquisitor: a radical belief in human progress through material means, a belief in pragmatic reason, a rejection of mystical experience, and a total absorption in the problems of this world to the near-exclusion of God. They have understood Dostoevsky, on the other hand, very much as the Inquisitor understands Christ, seeing in him the eternal "disturber," the disseminator of freedom and tragedy, the man to whom the resurrection of an individual soul was more important than the material progress of an entire society.

Tolstoy or Dostoevsky is not a simple exercise in criticism, old style or new, inspired by two equal debts of "love." Steiner's aim is polemical, although the basis of his concern here—his horror of the *univers concentrationnaire* and his regard for individual freedom—does not become fully clear until his later studies, *Language and Silence* and *In Bluebeard's Castle*.

The Death of Tragedy is a much less interesting book, chiefly because Steiner refuses to define his subject with any real precision. A "neat abstract definition" of tragedy, he claims, would "mean nothing"—and yet tragedies do have something in common: they give us representations of "personal suffering," although not all such representations are "tragic." The notion of "justice" gives Steiner his necessary (although largely unexamined) principle of differentiation here. Tragedy arises when an Oedipus, Lear or Pentheus is punished far in excess of his guilt. *King Lear* is tragic, the Book of Job is not, for in Job there is compensation, and where there is compensation, which is a form of justice, there can be no tragedy. Moreover,

> The Judaic vision sees in disaster a specific moral fault or failure of understanding. The Greek tragic poets [and the Elizabethans] assert that the forces which shape or destroy our lives lie outside the governance of reason or justice. Worse than that: there are around us daemonic energies which prey upon the soul and turn it to madness or which poison our will so that we inflict irreparable outrage upon ourselves and those we love.

But surely "justice" is a far more complex matter than Steiner seems willing to recognize here. Nor is he any more helpful when it comes to the purpose or function of tragedy. The Greeks and the Elizabethans give us "a terrible, stark insight into human life":

> Yet in the very excess of his suffering lies man's claim to dignity. Powerless and broken, a blind beggar hounded out of the city, [Oedipus] assumes a new grandeur. Man is ennobled by the vengeful spite or injustice of the gods. It does not make him innocent, but it hallows him as if he had passed through flame. Hence there is in the final moments

of great tragedy, whether Greek or Shakespearean or neo-classic, a fusion of grief and joy, a lament over the fall of man and of rejoicing in the resurrection of his spirit.

But are the spirits of Pentheus, Othello or Phèdre "resurrected"? "Dignity," "grandeur," "ennobled"—again Steiner fails to give these resounding terms the scrutiny they require (for an even harsher view of Steiner's reliability and inflated style, readers should consult John Simon's savage attack, now reprinted in *Acid Test*).

After this brief excursion into theory, Steiner begins his tedious survey of tragedies, near-tragedies and non-tragedies. Since the seventeenth century, he asserts, the writer of tragedy has had to face "a persistent conflict of ideals. Should he adopt the conventions which neo-classicism derived from Aeschylus, Sophocles, and Euripides, or should he turn to the Shakespearean tradition of open drama?" Dramatists since Racine have also had to face a series of circumstances which now make it virtually impossible to write tragedy at all. The "redemptive mythology" of Romanticism (and later of Marxism), the rise of the middle class and the increasing popularity of prose fiction: these are the familiar causes of the "death of tragedy" as a form. But near the end of the book, Steiner suddenly turns to a kind of argument which is very much his own:

> We cannot be certain that there is either in language or in the forms of art, a law of the conservation of energy. On the contrary, there is evidence to show that reserves of feeling can be depleted, that particular kinds of intellectual and physiological awareness can go brittle or unreal. There is a hardening of the arteries of the spirit as in those of the flesh. It is at least plausible that the complex of Hellenic and Christian values which is mirrored in tragic drama, and which has tempered the life of the western mind over the past two thousand years, is now in sharp decline. The history of modern Europe—the deportation, murder, or death in battle of some seventy million men, women, and children between 1914 and 1947—suggests that the reflexes by which a civilization alters its habits in order to survive mortal danger are no longer as swift or realistic as they once were....
> The political inhumanity of our time, moreover, has demeaned and brutalized language beyond any precedent. Words have been used to justify political falsehood, massive distortions of history, and the bestialities of the totalitarian state. It is conceivable that something of the lies and savagery has crept into their marrow. Because they have been useful to such base ends, words no longer give their full yield of meaning. And because they assail us in such vast, strident numbers, we no longer give them careful hearing. Every day we sup our fill of horrors...and thus we grow insensible to fresh outrage. This numbness has a crucial bearing on the possibility of tragic style. That which began in the romantic period, the inrush of current political and historical emotions on daily life, has become a dominant fact of our experience. Compared with the realities of war and oppression that surround us, the gravest imaginings of the poets are diminished to a scale of private or artificial terror.

For Steiner the atrocities of the first World War and the Holocaust—the world of Auschwitz, Belsen and Buchenwald—have threatened if not already destroyed the entire western tradition of "humane literacy" itself. In *Language and Silence* he asserts that

> The house of classic humanism, the dream of reason which animated Western society, have largely broken down. Ideas of cultural development, of inherent rationality held since ancient Greece and still immensely valid in the utopian historicism of Marx and stoic authoritarianism of Freud...can no longer be asserted with much confidence.... To think of literature, of education, of language, as if nothing very important had happened to challenge our very concept of these activities seems to me unrealistic.... We come after. We know now that a man can read Goethe or Rilke in the evening, that he can play Bach or Schubert, and go to his day's work at Auschwitz in the morning.

One of the alternatives for literature—one of the only decent responses possible—is silence, the tacit admission that the civilizing power of a culture based on "the word" is an illusion. As T.W. Adorno concluded, "No more poetry after Auschwitz." *In Bluebeard's Castle* completes Steiner's case against the modern world. Here his aim is to construct nothing less than a "theory

515

of culture" which will explain *why* the Holocaust could have taken place, and his explanation is an astonishing one. The Jews were responsible for "Monotheism at Sinai," with its intolerable moral imperatives, and for the hardly less demanding imperatives of primitive Christianity and messianic socialism ("Some political scientists put at roughly 80 percent the proportion of Jews in the ideological development of messianic socialism and communism"). Three times this lofty "insistence on the ideal" has come from "the same historical center":

> Three times, Judaism produced a summons to perfection and sought to impose it on the current and currency of Western life. Deep loathing built up in the social unconscious, murderous resentments. The mechanism is simple but primordial. *We hate most those who hold out to us a goal, an ideal, a visionary promise which, even though we have stretched our muscles to the utmost, we cannot reach, which slips, again and again, just out of the range of our racked fingers—yet, and this is crucial, which remains profoundly desirable, which we cannot reject because we fully acknowledge its supreme value.*

Thus by killing the Jews, western culture tried to annihilate those who had "invented God" or his secular moral equivalents; but by so doing, western culture has also condemned itself. We live in a doomed "post-culture"; we no longer believe in the future; our artists are no longer motivated by what Paul Eluard called "le dur desir de durer," that is, the hope of immortality through art. And yet with a smugness which is hardly less astonishing than his diagnosis of modern culture, Steiner is able to conclude that personally he is "drawn...to the conviction, irrational, even tactless as it may be, that it is enormously interesting to be alive at this cruel, late stage in Western affairs.... To be able to envisage possibilities of self-destruction, yet press home the debate with the unknown, is no mean thing." Understandably enough, Steiner's assumptions and the implications of his argument have provoked a good deal of angry debate (readers interested in pursuing the matter further should consider Irving Howe's reply to Steiner in *The Critical Point*). But to conclude that Steiner is simply "obsessed" or that *Language and Silence* and *In Bluebeard's Castle* have no bearing on "literary criticism" is to put oneself in the uncomfortable position of suggesting that one should not be appalled by the atrocities of recent history and that the humane powers of the written word have not somehow been diminished.

Could anyone who had followed Steiner's career up to this point have predicted the achievement of *After Babel*? Is it hopelessly crude to speculate that once Steiner had worked out his obsessions he was finally able to produce the book his admirers had always expected? In any event, for this writer *After Babel* is one of the important works of modern criticism. It is Steiner's longest book, and prodigiously learned; but for once everything is under control. The length is consistent with the major problems Steiner takes on here, the learning is unobtrusively at the service of his arguments—even the near-comic excesses of the prose in many of his earlier books have largely disappeared.

It is almost impossible to suggest the range of *After Babel*, but very briefly, and inadequately: Steiner begins his main argument with an innocent-seeming question: Why do men speak so many languages (between four and five thousand at present and as many as ten thousand in the past)? Why this "destructive prodigality"?—destructive, that is, if we believe that language is essentially "adaptive" behavior. What follows is a penetrating critique of current linguistic and philosophic approaches to "speech acts" and Steiner's own suggestions for a more adequate conception of language and the process of "translation" which is central to human communication. Steiner contends that neither of the two leading theories of language at the moment can account for the diversity and complex adaptive functions of speech. The "relativists"— Humboldt, Sapir, Whorf and their followers—see all language as culture-bound: we perceive and reason only in terms of the limited linguistic space our culture provides. The "universalists"—primarily Chomsky and his followers—have sought to "drive the very notion of grammar inward, to a specifically linguistic innate faculty of human consciousness." Both approaches, Steiner goes on, are reductive, and so too are the attempts by the followers of Wittgenstein to make philosophy into a kind of "speech therapy," that is, to "cure" language of its fictiveness and ambiguity. The "slippery, ambiguous, altering, subconscious or traditional contextual reflexes" of language are exactly what Steiner wishes to defend. He maintains that these maligned language functions are vital to our survival: "We are a mammal who can bear false witness. How has this potentiality arisen, what adaptive needs does it serve?"

My conviction is that we shall not get much further in understanding the evolution of language and the relations between speech and human performance so long as we see "falsity" as primarily negative, so long as we consider counter-factuality, contradiction, and the many nuances of conditionality as specialized, often logically bastard modes. *Language is the main instrument of man's refusal to accept the world as it is.* Without that refusal, without the unceasing generation by the mind of "counter-worlds"—a generation which cannot be divorced from the grammar of counter-factual and optative forms—we would turn forever on the treadmill of the present. Reality would be (to use Wittgenstein's phrase in an illicit sense), "all that is the case" and nothing more. Ours is the ability, the need, to gainsay or "un-say" the world, to image and speak it otherwise. In that capacity in its biological and social evolution, may lie some of the clues to the question of the origins of human speech and the multiplicity of tongues. It is not, perhaps, "a theory of information" that will serve us best in trying to clarify the nature of language, but a "theory of misinformation."

Language is essentially "fictive" because "the enemy is 'reality' ":

It is unlikely that man, as we know him, would have survived without the fictive, counter-factual, anti-determinist means of language, without the semantic capacity, generated and stored in the "superfluous" zones of the cortex, to conceive of, to articulate possibilities beyond the treadmill of organic decay and death. It is in this respect that human tongues, with their conspicuous consumption of subjunctive, future, and optative forms are a decisive evolutionary advantage. Through them we proceed in a substantive illusion of freedom. Man's sensibility endures and transcends the brevity, the haphazard ravages, the physiological programming of individual life because the semantically coded responses of the mind are constantly broader, freer, more inventive than the demands and stimulus of the material fact. "There is only *one* world," proclaims Nietzsche in the *Will to Power*, "and that world is false, cruel, contradictory, misleading, senseless.... We need lies to vanquish this reality, this 'truth,' we need lies *in order to live....* That lying is a necessity of life is itself a part of the terrifying and problematic character of existence." Through un-truth, through counter-factuality, man "violates" (*vergewaltigt*) an absurd, confining reality; and his ability to do so is at every point artistic, creative (*ein Künstler-Vermögen*). We secrete from within ourselves the grammar, the mythologies of hope, of fantasy, of self-deception without which we would have been arrested at some rung of primate behaviour or would, long since, have destroyed ourselves. It is our syntax, not the physiology of the body or the thermodynamics of the planetary system, which is full of tomorrows. Indeed, this may be the only area of "free will," of assertion outside direct neurochemical causation or programming. We speak, we dream ourselves free of the organic trap. Ibsen's phrase pulls together the whole evolutionary argument: man lives, he progresses by virtue of "the Life-Lie."

After Babel is about a good many other aspects of language as well. The long fifth chapter, for example, "The Hermeneutic Motion," offers a superbly illustrated theory of literary translations. But again, no brief summary can do justice to the book. What literary criticism has lacked, we are told often enough these days, is a properly sophisticated conception of language. Steiner has given us an immensely suggestive one.

TANNER, Tony.   British.   Born in Richmond, Surrey, in 1935. Educated at Jesus College, Cambridge, B.A. in English. Married. Fellow, King's College, Cambridge; Director of English Studies, King's College, 1964-76, and since 1977 Reader in American Literature, Cambridge University. Visiting Professor, Northwestern University, Evanston, Illinois; Emory University, Atlanta, Georgia; Stanford University, California. Recipient: Harkness Fellowship; American Council of Learned Societies Fellowship. Address: King's College, Cambridge CB2 1ST, England.

PUBLICATIONS

Criticism

 Conrad: Lord Jim.   London, Arnold, and Great Neck, New York, Barron's Educational Guide, 1963.
 The Reign of Wonder: Naivety and Reality in American Literature.   London and New York, Cambridge University Press, 1965.
 Saul Bellow.   Edinburgh, Oliver and Boyd, 1965; New York, Barnes and Noble, 1967.
 City of Words: American Fiction 1950-1970.   London, Cape, and New York, Harper, 1971.
 " 'Gnawed Bones' and 'Artless Tales'—Eating and Narration in Conrad," in *Partisan Review* (Boston), 65, 1978.
 Adultery in the Novel: Contract and Transgression.   Baltimore and London, Johns Hopkins University Press, 1979.

Other

 Editor, *Mansfield Park*, by Jane Austen.   London, Penguin, 1966.
 Editor, *Henry James: Modern Judgements.*   London, Macmillan, 1968.
 Editor, *Hawthorne*, by Henry James.   London, Macmillan, and New York, St. Martin's Press, 1968.

*   *   *

In *The Reign of Wonder*, the first of his two extended studies of American fiction, Tony Tanner proposes that our writers have been inclined to be more romantic than Rousseau himself, if by "romanticism" we mean a kind of passivity and unreflective delight—or horror—in the world around us. Rousseau, he reminds us, had emphasized the importance of "judgment," at least in the adult personality, whereas in American fiction the "reign of wonder" (the phrase is Carlyle's) has always been primary. "From the start," Tanner goes on, "wonder was put to much more far-reaching uses in American writing than in other literature":

> A major problem facing American writers was simply, overwhelmingly, the need to recognize and contain a new continent. The wondering vision was adopted as a prime method of inclusion and assimilation...[and] has *remained* a preferred way of dealing with experiences and confronting existence....

Tanner isolates the element of wonder in several American writers (mainly Emerson, Twain, Henry James, Gertrude Stein, Anderson and Hemingway); he attempts to describe the effect such naivety has had on American prose "style" (the "naive eye" prefers "the vernacular with its immediacy and concrete directness"); and he observes that the American writer has usually been "suspicious of unearned generalizations," a tendency which

 started with the fairly uncomplicated optimism of the Transcendentalists who could find

God in a stone, and...moved onto the unwilling scepticism of a Sherwood Anderson who found no manifest divinity or Law but only private consolation in the truth and beauty of a few pebbles. Where Emerson saw all fragments of concrete reality as being potentially transparent to some superior Reality, Hemingway saw only detached details of matter, marooned in a meaningless void.

The "wondering eye," which was once an "instrument of the orthodox," eventually becomes a "strategy for the alienated" ("Huck Finn lights out, Nick Adams makes a separate peace, Sherwood Anderson walks out of his business office and fills his work with an aching sense of lostness, exclusion and banishment—even Henry James is detached from the continent of contemporary reality and exists like a wise castaway on his island of wonder").

The reign of wonder has also affected the ability (and the willingness) of American writers to deal with the problem of literary form:

> once the hero (and this applies now to many American books) has opted for the stance of reverent wonder to the exclusion of all other forms of response, there is very little he can do except to reiterate this sense of wonder. This can lead only to the repetitious and ultimately boring, even unconvincing enthusiasm of a Jack Kerouac....Nearly all American writers have found it difficult to move beyond the first step, to find satisfactory forms....The passive wonder which constituted the preferred mode of vision of so many of the writers we have discussed is a valid strategy of assimilation, but of itself it can neither generate nor discover form.

Thus while American literature may be "rich and fertile,"

> it has often shown an inability to move beyond one particular syndrome of responses— wonder keeling over into horror, delight switching to disillusion, revulsion locked with awe. It has shown itself, perhaps, too suspicious of the analytical intellect, too disinclined to develop a complex reaction to society, too much given to extreme reaction, too hungry for metaphysics.

"And yet," he concludes (Tanner is nothing if not "fair"in the most academic sense of that term), these limitations are the deficiencies of notable virtues—"great personal integrity," a "noble refusal of complacency," "compassion and generosity and humour," and finally an "unremitting craving for reality and...reverent love for the world." At their best, American writers "replenish and vivify our vision of the world." This is the kind of weary, judicious critical prose which seems to write itself.

The Reign of Wonder is an earnest book, but like most thematic critics, Tanner is finally too reductive to be of much value. The more intricate the writer, the more Tanner has to stretch his simple terms (thus "Henry James was the first, and still by far the greatest, writer to inquire into the fate of wonder when it is introduced into the clotted complexities of society and the turbulence of time"). And like most thematic critics again, Tanner can tell us very little about the qualities for which most of us read or at least reread the American storytellers. In short, his thesis is neither complex nor new enough to warrant yet another trip through familiar territory.

City of Words is a much livelier book, largely because Tanner deals with quite recent writers (over twenty-five of them, ranging from such commanding figures as Nabokov and Bellow to the already vanishing Kesey and Brautigan: this is another peril of thematic criticism), and because his thesis this time is less restricting. American novelists of the 1950's and 60's, he argues, still cherish the dream that "an unpatterned, unconditioned life is possible, in which ...movements and stillnesses, choices and repudiations, are all [one's] own"; yet at the same time they also suffer from the "nightmare of being totally controlled by unseen agencies and powers." The great resource and refuge of these writers is a city of words, a purely verbal structure in which they can find "identity" and achieve "form." The basic problem, then, is to reconcile, somehow, freedom and form:

> We may say that a central concern of the hero of many recent American novels is this: can he find a freedom which is not a jelly, and can he establish an identity which is not a prison....[The] dilemma and quest of the hero are often analogous to those of the author.

Can he find a *stylistic* freedom which is not simply a meaningless incoherence, and can he find a stylistic form which will not trap him inside the existing forms of previous literature?

By the time Tanner completes his introductory chapter he has provided so many terms and touched on so many problems (freedom, form, identity, love of language, suspicion of language, what happens when we try to step "outside" society, and so on), that his original thesis—"style" as a kind of defensive strategy—has been expanded beyond recognition: almost anything he can say about any of these writers is bound to be "relevant" in one way or another. Nevertheless, he is often sharply perceptive about his authors, especially the less well-known ones, and never less than sensible.

Tanner's most recent book, *Adultery in the Novel*, is an extraordinary performance and may well be the most original contribution to British and American criticism in some time. At first glance the topic—adultery in the late eighteenth-century and nineteenth-century bourgeois novel—may not seem promising, especially when the reader learns that two of the novels Tanner will examine in minute detail, Rousseau's *Julie, or The New Eloise* and Goethe's *Elective Affinities*, are hardly well-known. Yet in treating these texts and *Madame Bovary*, Tanner manages to say a great many suggestive things about fiction, society and human nature. A short summary is damaging and unfair, but very briefly, he is concerned here with the novel as a "transgressive" form. It is no accident, he observes, that the protagonists of many novels are often "socially displaced or unplaced figures—orphans, prostitutes, adventurers, etc." Thus they

> represent or incarnate a potentially disruptive or socially unstabilized energy that may threaten, directly or indirectly, the organization of society, whether by the indeterminacy of their origins, the uncertainty of the direction in which they will focus their unbonded energy, or their attitude to the ties that hold society together and that they may choose to break.

Perhaps fiction and drama are always transgressive—after all, something has to *happen* to disrupt an initially stable situation; but as long as the marriage contract holds a central place in organized society, adultery is likely to be the enemy:

> [Indeed] we might suggest that it is the unstable triangularity, rather than the static symmetry of marriage, that is the generative form of Western literature as we know it....But it seems to me that adultery takes on a very special importance in the late-eighteenth- and nineteenth-century novel. Thus in this volume I am attempting to establish the groundwork for the kind of consideration of the topic that I consider most fruitful and rewarding.

And he adds in a footnote that he also has in mind a great many other works, ranging from Stendhal through Ford Madox Ford and Lawrence which he intends to discuss in a subsequent volume.

It is possible that the novel, in a society which is based on marriage and family stability, carries within itself the seeds of its own dissolution, and for a very interesting reason. That is, the novel may embody that destructive conflict between desire and the fulfillment of desire which is a fundamental part of human nature itself. Tanner supports his argument with an impressive range of authorities—Lacan, Foucault, Bataille and Horkheimer, among others—but surely the central document here (which of course he also uses) is Freud's paper, "The Most Prevalent Form of Degradation in Erotic Life." Here Freud maintains that

> It is easy to show that the value the mind sets on erotic need instantly sinks as soon as satisfaction becomes readily obtainable. Some obstacle is necessary to swell the tide of the libido to its height; and at all periods of history, wherever natural barriers in the way of satisfaction have not sufficed, mankind has erected conventional ones in order to enjoy love....In times during which no obstacles to sexual satisfaction existed, such as, may be, during the decline of the civilizations of antiquity, love became worthless, life

became empty, and strong reaction formations were necessary before the indispensable emotional value of love could be recovered.

Like men themselves, the novel "writes of contracts but dreams of transgressions, and in reading it, the dream tends to emerge more powerfully." The "real, if secret" energy of the novel, Tanner continues,

> has been aroused by the weak points in the family, the possible fissures, the breaches, the breakdowns. Which is why the novel tends to be drawn, all but irresistibly, to the problem of adultery....Both society and the novel, in their different ways, center on the family, and yet that binding, stabilizing unit turns out to contain potentially antagonistic and disruptive elements that make it a center that cannot hold, an illusory center, or perhaps not a center at all.

Where the second volume of Tanner's study may lead is not yet clear, of course, but at the end of *Adultery in the Novel* the reader has a disturbing sense that there may be a basic contradiction in fiction, perhaps in art itself as a mode of satisfying desire, and in life. When the book first appeared David Lodge hailed it as the first successful use of continental "deconstructionist" tactics. But the term is not really appropriate here. A true deconstructionist reading of these texts would "reveal" that they have no determinate meaning, whereas Tanner is doing something at once more old-fashioned and provocative: the texts he looks at do have meaning, or rather they have multiple meanings which are mutually opposed to each other. As one of the characters in Shaw's *Man and Superman* puts it, with devastating clarity, there are two tragedies in life: one is not to have your heart's desire, the other, to have it.

TATE, Allen, (John Orley).   American.   Born in Winchester, Kentucky, 19 November 1899. Educated at Georgetown Preparatory School, Washington, D.C.; Vanderbilt University, Nashville, Tennessee, B.A. 1922. Married the writer Caroline Gordon in 1924 (divorced, 1954); the poet Isabella Stewart Gardner, 1959; Helen Heinz, 1966; three children. Member of the Fugitive Group of Poets: Founding Editor, with John Crowe Ransom, *The Fugitive*, Nashvile, 1922-25. Editor, *Sewanee Review*, Tennessee, 1944-46; Editor, Belles Lettres series, Henry Holt and Company, New York, 1946-48. Lecturer in English, Southwestern College, Memphis, Tennessee, 1934-36; Professor of English, The Woman's College, Greensboro, North Carolina, 1938-39; Poet-in-Residence, Princeton University, New Jersey, 1939-42; Lecturer in the Humanities, New York University, 1947-51. From 1951, Professor of English, University of Minnesota, Minneapolis: Regents' Professor, 1966; Professor Emeritus, 1968. Visiting Professor in the Humanities, University of Chicago, 1949; Fulbright Lecturer, Oxford University, 1953, University of Rome, 1953-54, and Oxford and Leeds universities, 1958-59; Department of State Lecturer at the universities of Liège and Louvain, 1954, Delhi and Bombay, 1956, the Sorbonne, Paris, 1956, Nottingham, 1956, and Urbino and Florence, 1961; Visiting Professor of English, University of North Carolina, Greensboro, 1966, and Vanderbilt University, 1967. Phi Beta Kappa Orator, University of Virginia, Charlottesville, 1936, and University of Minnesota, 1952; Phi Beta Kappa Poet, College of William and Mary, Williamsburg, Virginia, 1948, and Columbia University, New York, 1950; Member, Phi Beta Kappa Senate, 1951-53. Fellow, 1948, and Senior Fellow, 1956, Kenyon School of English (now School of Letters, Indiana University, Bloomington). Consultant in Poetry, Library of Congress, Washington, D.C., 1943-44. Recipient: Guggenheim Fellowship, 1928, 1929; National Institute of Arts and Letters grant, 1948; Bollingen Prize, 1957; Brandeis University Creative Arts Award, 1960; Gold Medal of the Dante Society, Florence, 1962; Academy of American Poets Fellowship, 1963; Oscar Williams-Gene Derwood Award, 1975; National Medal for Literature, 1976. Litt.D.: University of Louisville, Kentucky, 1948; Coe College, Cedar Rapids, Iowa, 1955;

Colgate University, Hamilton, New York, 1956; University of Kentucky, Lexington, 1960; Carleton College, Northfield, Minnesota, 1963; University of the South, Sewanee, Tennessee, 1970. Member, American Academy of Arts and Letters. President, National Institute of Arts and Letters, 1968. Member, Board of Chancellors, Academy of American Poets. *Died 9 February 1979.*

PUBLICATIONS

Criticism

Reactionary Essays on Poetry and Ideas.   New York and London, Scribner, 1936.
Reason in Madness: Critical Essays.   New York, Putnam, 1941.
Invitation to Learning, with Huntington Cairns and Mark Van Doren.   New York, Random House, 1941.
On the Limits of Poetry: Selected Essays, 1928-1948.   New York, Swallow Press and Morrow, 1948.
The Hovering Fly and Other Essays.   Cummington, Massachusetts, Cummington Press, 1948.
The Forlorn Demon: Didactic and Critical Essays.   Chicago, Regnery, 1953.
The Man of Letters in the Modern World: Selected Essays, 1928-1955.   New York, Meridian, and London, Thames and Hudson, 1955.
Collected Essays.   Denver, Swallow, 1959.
Modern Literature and the Lost Traveller.   Nashville, Tennessee, George Peabody College for Teachers, 1969.
Essays of Four Decades.   Chicago, Swallow Press, 1969; London, Oxford University Press, 1970.
The Translation of Poetry.   Washington, D.C., Library of Congress, 1972.
The Literary Correspondence of Donald Davidson and Allen Tate, edited by John T. Fain and Thomas D. Young.   Athens, University of Georgia Press, 1974.
Memoirs and Opinions 1926-1974.   Chicago, Swallow Press, 1975; as *Memories and Essays: Old and New 1926-1974*, Manchester, Carcanet Press, 1976.
"Speculations," in *Southern Review* (Baton Rouge, Louisiana), 14, 1978.

Verse

The Golden Mean and Other Poems, with Ridley Wills.   Privately printed, 1923.
Mr. Pope and Other Poems.   New York, Minton Balch, 1928.
Three Poems: Ode to the Confederate Dead, Being the Revised and Final Version of a Poem Previously Published on Several Occasions: To Which Are Added Message from Abroad and The Cross.   New York, Minton Balch, 1930.
Poems: 1928-1931.   New York, Scribner, 1932.
The Mediterranean and Other Poems.   New York, Alcestis Press, 1936.
Selected Poems.   New York and London, Scribner, 1937.
Sonnets at Christmas.   Cummington, Massachusetts, Cummington Press, 1941.
The Winter Sea: A Book of Poems.   Cummington, Massachusetts, Cummington Press, 1944.
Poems, 1920-1945: A Selection.   London, Eyre and Spottiswoode, 1947.
Poems, 1922-1947.   New York, Scribner, 1948.
Two Conceits for the Eye to Sing, If Possible.   Cummington, Massachusetts, Cummington Press, 1950.
Poems.   New York, Scribner, 1960.
The Swimmers and Other Selected Poems.   London, Oxford University Press, 1970; New York, Scribner, 1971.

Collected Poems 1919-1976.   New York, Farrar Strauss, 1977.

Novel

The Fathers.   New York, Putnam, 1938; London, Eyre and Spottiswoode, 1939; revised
edition, Denver, Swallow, and Eyre and Spottiswoode, 1960.
The Fathers and Other Fiction.   Chicago, Swallow Press, 1976.

Play

The Governess, with Anne Goodwin Winslow (produced Minneapolis, 1962).

Other

Stonewall Jackson: The Good Soldier: A Narrative.   New York, Minton Balch, 1928;
London, Cassell, 1930.
Jefferson Davis: His Rise and Fall: A Biographical Narrative.   New York, Minton Balch,
1929.
Sixty American Poets, 1896-1944: A Preliminary Checklist.   Washington, D.C., Library
of Congress, 1945.
Christ and the Unicorn: An Address....   Iowa City, Cummington Press, 1966.

Editor, with others, *Fugitives: An Anthology of Verse.*   New York, Harcourt Brace,
1928.
Editor, with Herbert Agar, *Who Owns America? A New Declaration of Independence.*
Boston, Houghton Mifflin, 1936.
Editor, with A. Theodore Johnson, *America Through the Essay: An Anthology for
English Courses.*   New York, Oxford University Press, 1938.
Editor, *The Language of Poetry.*   Princeton, New Jersey, Princeton University Press,
1942.
Editor, *Princeton Verse Between Two Wars: An Anthology.*   Princeton, New Jersey,
Princeton University Press, 1942.
Editor, with John Peale Bishop, *American Harvest: Twenty Years of Creative Writing in
the United States.*   New York, Fischer, 1942.
Editor, *Recent American Poetry and Poetic Criticism: A Selected List of References.*
Washington, D.C., Library of Congress, 1943.
Editor, *A Southern Vanguard (The John Peale Bishop Memorial Volume).*   New York,
Prentice Hall, 1947.
Editor, *The Collected Poems of John Peale Bishop.*   New York, Scribner, 1948.
Editor, with Caroline Gordon, *The House of Fiction: An Anthology of the Short Story.*
New York, Scribner, 1950; revised edition, 1960.
Editor, with Lord David Cecil, *Modern Verse in English, 1900-1950.*   London, Eyre and
Spottiswoode, and New York, Macmillan, 1958.
Editor, with John Berryman and Ralph Ross, *The Arts of Learning.*   New York, Cro-
well, 1960.
Editor, *Selected Poems of John Peale Bishop.*   London, Chatto and Windus, 1960.
Editor, with Robert Penn Warren, *Selected Poems*, by Denis Devlin.   New York, Holt
Rinehart, 1963.
Editor, *T.S. Eliot: The Man and His Work.*   New York, Delacorte Press, 1966; London,
Chatto and Windus, 1967.
Editor, *The Complete Poems and Selected Criticism of Edgar Allan Poe.*   New York,
New American Library, 1968.

Editor, *Six American Poets*: *From Emily Dickinson to the Present*: *An Introduction.* London, Oxford University Press, 1972.

Translator, *The Vigil of Venus.* Cummington, Massachusetts, Cummington Press, 1943.

CRITICAL STUDIES AND BIBLIOGRAPHY

Willard Thorp, "Allen Tate: A Checklist," in *Princeton University Library Bulletin* (New Jersey), April 1942; reprinted with James Korges, "Allen Tate: A Checklist Continued," in *Critique* (Minneapolis), 10, 1968.

Monroe K. Spears, "The Criticism of Allen Tate," in *Sewanee Review* (Tennessee), 57, 1949; reprinted in *Allen Tate and His Work*: *Critical Evaluations*, 1972.

R.P. Blackmur, "San Giovanni in Venere: Allen Tate as Man of Letters," in *Sewanee Review* (Tennessee), 67, 1959; reprinted in *Allen Tate and His Work*: *Critical Evaluations*, 1972.

R.K. Meiners, *The Last Alternatives*: *A Study of the Works of Allen Tate.* Denver, Swallow, 1962.

Eliseo Vivas, "Allen Tate as Man of Letters," in *Creation and Discovery.* Chicago, Regnery, 1966; reprinted in *Allen Tate and His Work*: *Critical Evaluations*, 1972.

Ferman Bishop, *Allen Tate.* New York, Twayne, 1967.

George C. Core, "A Metaphysical Athlete: Allen Tate as Critic," in *Southern Literary Journal* (Chapel Hill, North Carolina), 2, 1969.

Marshall Fallwell, Jr., *Allen Tate*: *A Bibliography.* New York, David Lewis, 1969.

Radcliffe Squires, *Allen Tate*: *A Literary Biography.* Indianapolis, Bobbs Merrill, 1971.

Radcliffe Squires, editor, *Allen Tate and His Works*: *Critical Evaluations.* Minneapolis, University of Minnesota Press, 1972.

Cleanth Brooks, "Allen Tate and the Nature of Modernism," in *Southern Review* (Baton Rouge, Louisiana), 12, 1976.

Denis Donoghue, "Nuances on a Theme by Allen Tate," in *Southern Review* (Baton Rouge, Louisiana), 12, 1976.

"Writing in the South No. V: Allen Tate" issue of *Southern Review* (Baton Rouge, Louisiana), 12, 1976.

Robert Buffington, "Young Hawk Circling," in *Sewanee Review* (Tennessee), 87, 1979.

*   *   *

On a number of occasions Allen Tate expressed some surprise that he was regarded as a literary critic: "I am on record," he warns his readers, "as a casual essayist of whom little consistency can be expected." Even more pointedly (in the preface to *Essays of Four Decades*):

I am not alone in believing that "criticism" written by poets is "programmatic," and that criticism written by scholars is an effort to make the poets' intuited programs systematic and, further, to adjust all the programs of an age to one another and thus to reconstruct the "mind" of the age. But this is not the business of the poet-critic, who is not concerned with consistency and system, but merely with as much self-knowledge as he needs to write his own verse.

These apologies will seem a little disingenuous unless we speculate about what Tate may have had in mind when he made a distinction, very much in passing, between inconsistency and the "deeper fault" of incoherence. If by consistency we mean firm logical method, then he is not consistent (his essays often seem to exist in what one of his ablest supporters, R.K. Meiners, has to admit is "an argumentative void"). But he is by no mean incoherent, if by coherence we mean a fixed point of emotional and finally religious reference. What Tate says about the essays in *Reason in Madness*, that they have as a common theme "a deep illness of the modern mind," is true of everything he has written:

The point of view here...is that historicism, scientism, psychologism, biologism, in general the confident use of the scientific vocabularies in the spiritual realm, has created or is at any rate the expression of a spiritual disorder.... On the one hand we assume that all experience can be ordered scientifically, an asssumption that we are almost ready to confess has intensified if it has not actually created our distress; but on the other hand, this assumption has logically reduced the spiritual realm to irresponsible emotion, to what the positivists of our time see as irrelevant feeling; it is irrelevant because it cannot be reduced to the terms of positivist procedure. It is my contention here that the high forms of literature offer us the only complete, and thus the most responsible, versions of our experience. The point of view...[here] is the belief, philosophically tenable, in a radical discontinuity between the physical and the spiritual realms.

Properly understood, properly related to his later essays on Poe and the "Symbolic Imagination," this passage will reveal the genuine coherence of Tate's thinking over a long period of time.

By the "modern mind," Tate means the positivistic temper which separates the abstracting intellect from other modes of knowledge. Following Jacques Maritain, he argues that "when Descartes isolated thought from man's total being he isolated him from nature, including his own nature; and he divided man against himself.... The battle is now between the dehumanized society of secularism, which imitates Descartes' mechanized nature, and the eternal society of the communion of the human spirit." What we have on our hands now is a situation in which the vocabulary of stimulus and response has replaced the human vocabulary of "*end, choice, and discrimination*": we live in a society which believes in the perfectability of man and in which

means are divorced from ends, action from sensibility, matter from mind, society from the individual, religion from moral agency, love from lust, poetry from thought, communion from experience, and mankind in the community from men in the crowd. There is literally no end to this list of dissociations because there is no end, yet in sight, to the fragmenting of the western mind.

It is the function of literature to fight against these positivistic reductions, to give us a full report of experience, to restore us, in short, to a proper relationship with nature and the spiritual realm to which it bears a vital analogical relationship. The basis of Tate's argument here is, of course, Christian, and specifically Thomist: literature strengthens true culture, "the material medium through which men receive the one lost truth which must be perpetually recovered: the truth of what Jacques Maritain calls the 'supra-temporal destiny' of man":

It is the duty of the man of letters to supervise the culture of language, to which the rest of culture is subordinate, and to warn us when our language is ceasing to forward the end proper to man. The end of social man is communion in time through love, which is beyond time.

Like his mentor, John Crowe Ransom, Tate insists that it is the responsibility of literature, particularly of poetry, to remain true to the fullness of experience and the plenitude of "the world's body"; but Ransom, unlike Tate, offers no reason why we should strengthen this mode of perception—save, apparently, for the sake of the pleasure it can provide. For Tate, however, "Man is a creature that in the long run has got to believe in order to know, and to know in order to do." Literature is thus a form of knowledge and finally a means of revelation:

The human intellect cannot reach God as essence: only God as analogy. Analogy to what? Plainly analogy to the natural world; for there is nothing in the intellect that has not previously reached it through the senses. Had Dante arrived at the vision of God by way of sense? We must answer yes, because Dante's Triune Circle is light, which the finite intelligence can see only in what has already been seen by means of it... The reach of our imaginative enlargement is perhaps no longer than the ladder of analogy, at the top of which we may see all, if we still wish to *see* anything, that we have brought up with us from the bottom, where lies the sensible world.

And again (in "The Symbolic Imagination"):

> Catholic poets have lost, along with their heretical friends, the power to start with the "common thing": they have lost the gift for concrete experience. The abstraction of the modern mind has obscured their way into the natural order. Nature offers to the symbolic poet clearly denotable objects in depth and in the round, which yield the analogies to the higher syntheses. The modern poet rejects the higher synthesis, or tosses it into a vacuum of abstraction.

For Tate, Edgar Allan Poe becomes a symbol for our dehumanized condition ("what destroyed him is potentially destructive of us"). Poe's "failure to harmonize himself" resulted in the "hypertrophy of the three classical faculties: feeling, will, and intellect": he suffered from an "incapacity to represent the human condition in the central tradition of natural feeling"; he isolated his mind "from both love and the moral will"; and as a result of these failures, he "thrust [his] will beyond the human scale of action." He is therefore guilty of what Tate (again following Maritain) calls "the angelic fallacy." "The glory of man," Valéry observed in his essay on *Eureka*, "and something more than his glory, is to waste his powers on the void." For Tate that "something more" is closer to damnation than to glory:

> *The exhaustion of force as a consequence of his intellectual liberation from the sensible world*—that is my reading of Valéry as a gloss upon the angelism of Poe. The intellectual force is exhausted because in the end it has no real object.... Since he refuses to see nature, he is doomed to see nothing. He had overleaped and cheated the condition of man.... If we take nothing with us to the top [of the "ladder of analogy"] but our emptied, angelic intellects, we shall see nothing when we get there. Poe as God sits silent in darkness. Here the movement of tragedy is reversed: there is no action. Man as angel becomes a demon who cannot initiate the first motion of love, and we can feel only compassion with his suffering, for it is potentially ours.

The true poet, on the other hand, "is responsible for the virtue proper to him as a poet, for his special *arété* for the mastery of a disciplined language which will not shun the full report of the reality conveyed to him by his awareness." The poet achieves this condition by means of what Tate calls "tension":

> the meaning of poetry is its "tension," the full organized body of all the extension and intension that we can find in it. The remotest figurative significance that we can derive does not invalidate the extensions of the literal statement. Or we may begin with the literal statement and by stages develop the complications of metaphor: at every stage we may pause to state the meaning so far apprehended, and at every stage the meaning will be coherent.

By "extension" and "intension" Tate means, respectively, denotation (and the resources of logical argument) and connotation, with its affective powers to restore us to a fully human world: "our recognition of the action of this unified meaning is the gift of our experience, of culture, of, if you will, our humanism." Important as "tension" always was for Tate, however, there is a passage in his tribute to John Crowe Ransom (printed in *Memoirs and Opinions 1926-1974*) which suggests that he may later have had some misgivings:

> I have for years wondered how such an acute intelligence could seriously consider any formula for poetry, and I am still amazed that John Ransom, of all people, could come up with "structure" and "texture" as critical metaphors. After the elaborate essays in Kantian philosophical aesthetics, the simple structure-texture formula is a sad anticlimax—as sad as the late Yvor Winters' formula. Winters said, over some thirty years, that "the concept motivates the emotion." I can't pause here for a discussion of these two famous prescriptive shortcuts to the meaning of poetry; and I shall merely indicate their similarity to a somewhat less famous formula [Tate's own of course] that the single word "tension" conceals. It is not, of course, tension in the ordinary sense, though certain poems may be described as "*in*tense." What the inventor of poetic

"tension" had in mind was a pseudo-erudite pun; that is, he dropped the prefixes of the logical terms *extension* and *intension* and had tension derived from both, and containing both. Intension is connotation, or Ransom's structure, provided, of course, that the objects denoted are in an acceptable syntactical relation. May we say that Winters' concept is Ransom's structure, and his emotion, Ransom's texture? All these correspondences are only proximate, but they witness a remarkably similar critical impulse in men of different ages and backgrounds. I have no explanation of the astonishing fact that three Americans but no Europeans in the modern age tried to encapsulate poetry.

In any event, the failure to achieve such "tension" becomes Tate's version of Eliot's "dissociation of sensibility": "if...as in the great seventeenth-century poets, you find that exhaustive analysis applied to the texture of image and metaphor fails to turn up any inconsistency, and at the same time fails to get all the meaning of the poem into a logical statement, you are participating in a poetic experience." In Romantic poetry—and in a good deal of modern poetry—we have "the fallacy of mere denotation."

The duties of the literary critic—the "man of letters," to use Tate's own preferred term—are clearly implied in a number of the passages already cited. Specifically, the purpose of the arts is not only analogical revelation but "self-knowledge":

By these arts, one means the arts without which men can live, but without which they cannot live well, or live as men. To keep alive the knowledge of ourselves with which the literary arts continue to enlighten the more ignorant portion of mankind (among whom one includes oneself), to separate them from other indispensable modes of knowledge, and to define their limits, is the intellectual and thus the social function of the writer. Here the man of letters is the critic.

Tate's own "practical" criticism follows naturally from these considerations. As we might expect, he is particularly sensitive to the debilitating presence of any form of romanticism and to the difficult conditions under which the modern poet must work. (A unified sensibility depends upon a unified culture, and once more Tate is very close to Eliot. As R.K. Meiners observes, for Tate, "Order in poetry depends on an ordered mind; an ordered mind depends on a stable society; and the whole series finally depends on an ultimate unity of being, the *analogia entis*.")

It is easy enough to admire many of Tate's essays on individual writers (on Emily Dickinson in particular, and on Keats and Hart Crane) without sharing his religious convictions, just as it is possible, if a bit more difficult, to detach terms such as "tension" and "the symbolic imagination" from their proper contexts. But to do so, of course, is to give in to the same kind of "positivism" which Tate protested against so eloquently for so many years. Like Eliot once again, he was essentially and perhaps inevitably a critic without heirs.

TRILLING, Lionel. American. Born in New York City, 4 July 1905. Educated at Columbia University, New York, B.A. 1925, M.A. 1926, Ph.D. 1938. Married the writer Diana Rubin in 1929; one child. Instructor in English, University of Wisconsin, Madison, 1926-27, and Hunter College, New York, 1927-32; Instructor, 1932-39, Assistant Professor, 1939-45, Associate Professor, 1945-48, Professor of Engish 1948-70, Woodberry Professor of Literature and Criticism, 1965-70, University Professor 1970-74, and University Professor Emeritus, 1974-75, Columbia University. George Eastman Visiting Professor, Oxford University, 1964-65; Norton Visiting Professor of Poetry, Harvard University, Cambridge, Massachusetts, 1969-70; Visiting Fellow, All Souls College, Oxford, 1972-73. Founder, with John Crowe Ransom and F.O. Matthiessen, and Senior Fellow, Kenyon School of Letters, Kenyon College, Gambier, Ohio, later the Indiana University School of Letters, Bloomington. Recipient: Brandeis University

Creative Arts Award, 1968. D.Litt.: Trinity College, Hartford, Connecticut, 1955; Harvard University, 1962; Case-Western Reserve University, Cleveland, 1968; Durham University, 1973; Leicester University, 1973; L.H.D.: Northwestern University, Evanston, Illinois, 1963; Brandeis University, Waltham, Massachusetts, 1974; Yale University, New Haven, Connecticut, 1974. Member, National Institute of Arts and Letters, 1951; American Academy of Arts and Sciences, 1952. *Died 7 November 1975.*

PUBLICATIONS

Criticism

Matthew Arnold. New York, Norton, and London, Allen and Unwin, 1939; revised edition, New York, Columbia University Press, 1949.
E.M. Forster. New York, New Directions, 1943; as *E.M. Forster: A Study*, London, Hogarth Press, 1944; revised edition, New Directions, 1965, Hogarth Press, 1967.
The Liberal Imagination: Essays on Literature and Society. New York, Viking Press, 1950; London, Secker and Warburg, 1951.
The Opposing Self: Nine Essays in Criticism. New York, Viking Press, and London, Secker and Warburg, 1955.
A Gathering of Fugitives. Boston, Beacon Press, 1956; London, Secker and Warburg, 1957.
Beyond Culture: Essays on Literature and Learning. New York, Viking Press, 1965; London, Secker and Warburg, 1966.
Sincerity and Authenticity. Cambridge, Massachusetts, Harvard University Press, and London, Oxford University Press, 1972.
Mind in the Modern World. New York, Viking Press, 1973; reprinted in *The Last Decade*, 1979.
"Sincerity and Authenticity: A Symposium," with Irving Howe, Leslie H. Farber and William Hamilton, in *Salmagundi* (Saratoga Springs, New York), 41, 1978.
The Last Decade: Essays and Reviews, 1965-75, edited by Diana Trilling. New York, Harcourt Brace, 1979.
Speaking of Society and Literature, edited by Diana Trilling. New York, Harcourt Brace, 1980.

Novel

The Middle of the Journey. New York, Viking Press, 1947; London, Secker and Warburg, 1948.

Short Stories

Of This Time, Of That Place and Other Stories, edited by Diana Trilling. New York, Harcourt Brace, 1979.

Other

Freud and the Crisis of Our Culture. Boston, Beacon Press, 1956; revised version printed in *Beyond Culture*, 1965.

Editor, *The Portable Matthew Arnold*.   New York, Viking Press, 1949; as *The Essential Matthew Arnold*, London, Chatto and Windus, 1969.

Editor, *Selected Letters of John Keats*.   New York, Farrar Straus, 1951.

Editor, *Selected Short Stories of John O'Hara*.   New York, Modern Library, 1956.

Editor, with Steven Marcus, *The Life and Work of Sigmund Freud*, by Ernest Jones. New York, Basic Books, and London, Hogarth Press, 1961.

Editor, *The Experience of Literature: A Reader with Commentaries*.   New York, Holt Rinehart, 1967.

Editor, *Literary Criticism: An Introductory Reader*.   New York, Holt Rinehart, 1970.

Editor, with others, *The Oxford Anthology of English Literature*.   New York and London, Oxford University Press, 1972.

Critical Studies

Joseph Frank,"Lionel Trilling: and the Conservative Imagination," in *Sewanee Review* (Tennessee), 64, 1956; reprinted in *The Widening Gyre: Crisis and Mastery in Modern Literature*, New Brunswick, New Jersey, Rutgers University Press, 1963.

Nathan A. Scott, Jr., *Three American Moralists: Mailer, Bellow, Trilling*.   Notre Dame, Indiana, and London, University of Notre Dame Press, 1973.

Roger Sale, "Lionel Trilling," in *Hudson Review* (New York), 26, 1973.

Steven Marcus, "Lionel Trilling, 1905-75," in *The New York Times Book Review*, 8 February 1975.

Phillip Lopate, "Remembering Lionel Trilling," in *American Review 25* (New York), 1976.

Robert Boyers, *Lionel Trilling: Negative Capability and the Wisdom of Avoidance*. Columbia, University of Missouri Press, 1977.

David Kubal,"Lionel Trilling: The Mind and Its Discontents," in *Hudson Review* (New York), 31, 1978.

Robert Langbaum, "Lionel Trilling and His Time," in *Salmagundi* (Saratoga Springs, New York), 41, 1978.

Tom Samet, "The Modulated Vision: Lionel Trilling's 'Larger Naturalism,' " in *Critical Inquiry* (Chicago), 4, 1978.

Mark Schechner, "Psychoanalysis and Liberalism," in *Salmagundi* (Saratoga Springs, New York), 41, 1978.

Helen Vendler, "Lionel Trilling and the Immortality Ode," in *Salmagundi* (Saratoga Springs, New York), 41, 1978.

William M. Chace, *Lionel Trilling: Criticism and Politics*.   Stanford, California, Stanford University Press, 1980.

*   *   *

In his last and finest essay on Freud ("Freud; Within and Beyond Culture," now reprinted in *Beyond Cutlture*), Lionel Trilling maintains that "in its essence literature is concerned with the self; and the particular concern of the literature of the last two centuries has been with the self in its standing quarrel with culture":

We cannot mention the name of any great writer of the modern period whose work has not in some way, and usually in a passionate and explicit way, insisted on this quarrel, who has not expressed the bitterness of his discontent with civilization, who has not said that the self made greater legitimate demands than any culture could hope to satisfy. This intense conviction of the existence of the self apart from culture is, as culture well knows, its noblest and most generous achievement. At the present moment it must be thought of as a liberating idea without which our developing ideal of community is bound to defeat itself.

"We can speak no greater praise of Freud," he concludes, "than to say that he placed this idea at the very center of his thought." This is probably true of Freud; it is unquestionably true of Trilling himself: in each of his major collections of essays, *The Liberal Imagination, The Opposing Self*, and *Beyond Culture*, and in his final book, *Sincerity and Authenticity*, he is primarily interested in the conflict between the self and culture and in the power of art to "liberate the individual from the tyranny of his culture in the environmental sense and to permit him to stand beyond it in an autonomy of perception and judgment."

Like Matthew Arnold and E.M. Forster, both of whom he wrote about at length and with great persuasiveness, Trilling is a "liberal"; and like Arnold and Forster he is acutely aware of the ways in which even the most humane ideals may "deteriorate into ideology," that is, become dogmatic, rigid and exclusive. In the preface to *The Liberal Imagination* he defines liberalism in terms of its "vision of a general enlargement of [individual] freedom and rational direction of human life." But freedom of the self and individual happiness are emotional as well as political issues: the "moral passions" they generate have a paradoxical tendency to become "even more willful and imperious and impatient than the self-seeking passions," which in turn means that "we have to be aware of the dangers which lie in our most generous wishes." Thus it is "not conducive to the real strength of liberalism that it should occupy the intellectual field alone." The basic assumption here, of course, is that no single intellectual movement can possibly do justice to the richness and complexity of life. Like all such movements, liberalism tends to simplify the problems of existence,

> and this tendency is natural in view of the effort which liberalism makes to organize the elements of life in a rational way. And when we approach liberalism in a critical spirit, we shall fail in critical completeness if we do not take into account the value and necessity of its organizational impulse. But at the same time we must understand that organization means delegation, and agencies, and bureaus, and technicians, and that the ideas that can survive delegation...give up something of their largeness and modulation and complexity in order to survive. The lively sense of contingency and possibility, and of those exceptions to the rule which may be the beginning of the end of the rule—this sense does not suit well with the impulse of organization.

Thus it is the function of criticism, and more importantly, of literature itself,

> to recall liberalism to its first essential imagination of variousness and possibility, which implies the awareness of complexity and difficulty. To the carrying out of the job of criticizing the liberal imagination, literature has a unique relevance, not merely because so much of modern literature has directed itself upon politics, but...because literature is the human activity that takes the fullest and most precise account of variousness, possibility, complexity, and difficulty.

In *The Liberal Imagination* and *The Opposing Self* Trilling limits himself primarily— although by no means exclusively—to the ways in which some of the major nineteenth-century novelists kept alive the critical powers of the imagination. "For our time," he argues (in "Manners, Morals, and the Novel"),

> the most effective agent of the moral imagination has been the novel of the last two hundred years. It was never, either artistically or morally, a perfect form and its faults can be quickly enumerated. But its greatness and its practical usefulness lay in its unremitting work of involving the reader himself in the moral life, inviting him to put his own motives under examination, suggesting that reality is not as his conventional education has led him to see it. It taught us, as no other genre ever did, the extent of human variety and the value of this variety. It was the literary form to which the emotions of understanding and forgiveness were indigenous, as if by the definition of the form itself.

The novel is important for another reason as well. The appalling political events of the last fifty years have demoralized us and given us "desperate perceptions of life" and "visions of losses worse than that of existence—losses of civilization, personality, humanness." The "will of our

society" (that is, our ability to maintain the ideals of humanism) is "dying of its own excess."
And here, once again, the novel has a vital function to perform:

> The novel at its greatest is the record of the will acting under the direction of an idea,
> often an idea of will itself. All else in the novel is but secondary, and those examples
> which do not deal with the will in action are but secondary in their genre. Sensibility in
> the novel is but notation and documentation of the will in action.... To the restoration
> and reconstruction of the will thus understood the novelistic intelligence is most apt.

Art has the power to "prevent our being seduced by the godhead of disintegration."

The word "self" does not figure prominently in *The Liberal Imagination*, but the connection
between liberalism and this later key term is obvious enough: liberalism is concerned with the
freedom of the individual, that precious core of unconditioned being which Wordsworth means
when he refers to those "Points...all of us [have] within our souls / Where all stand single." The
authentic work of art, Trilling goes on, "instructs us in our inauthenticity," that is, in our failure
to maintain our uniqueness and autonomy against the levelling forces of culture. As modern
society grows stronger and more rigidly organized the self is increasingly characterized by "its
intense and adversary imagination of the culture in which it has its being." Matthew Arnold's
Scholar Gypsy, for example, "*is* poetry...*is* imagination, impulse and pleasure" (these are all
qualities which Trilling sees modern culture as tending to suppress or diminish):

> he is what virtually every writer of the modern period conceives, the experience of art
> projected into the actuality and totality of life as the ideal form of the moral life. His
> existence is intended to disturb us and make us dissatisfied with our habitual life in
> culture, whose nature his existence defines.

This "adversary culture," Trilling maintains, represents "a new idea in the world...[and] not in
literature alone." If the essays in *The Opposing Self* have any unity, he concludes, "it is because
they take notice of this idea, and of its vicissitudes, modulations, and negations."

While Trilling never seems to have lost faith in the power of art to sustain the self in society,
his later work is considerably more pessimistic. In *Beyond Culture* he is increasingly concerned
with the tendency even adversary culture itself has to deteriorate into ideology, to attract the
allegiance of a "class," and to find an ally in—of all places—the universities:

> we can say of it, as we say of any other class, that it has developed characteristic habitual
> responses to the stimuli of its environment. It is not without power, and we can say of it,
> as we can say of any other class with a degree of power, that it seeks to aggrandize and
> perpetuate itself. And, as with any other class, the relation it has to the autonomy of its
> members makes a relevant question, and the more, of course, by reason of the part that is
> played in the history of its ideology by the ideal of autonomy. There is reason to believe
> that the relation is ambiguous.

"My sense of this difficulty," he continues (in a passage which shocked a number of his
admirers),

> leads me to approach a view which will seem disastrous to many readers and which,
> indeed, rather surprises me. This is the view that art does not always tell the truth and
> does not always point out the right way, that it can even generate falsehood and
> habituate us to it, and that, on frequent occasions, it might well be subject, in the
> interests of autonomy, to the scrutiny of the rational intellect. The history of this faculty
> scarcely assures us that it is exempt from the influences of the cultures in which it has
> sought its development, but at the present juncture its informing purpose of standing
> beyond any culture, even an adversary one, may be of use.

Furthermore, to treat the great adversary works of the modern imagination as structures of
words, to put them into university courses, is to violate their essential spirit and intention; to
teach modern literature, as many of us now realize only too well, is to make it safe and
agreeable. Such institutionalizing of literature goes against the grain of the authors themselves:

structures of words they may indeed have created, but these structures were not pyramids or triumphal arches, they were manifestly contrived to be not static and commemorative but mobile and aggressive, and one does not describe a quinquereme or a howitzer or a tank without estimating how much *damage* it can do.

Modern criticism, he concludes (in "The Two Environments"), "has instructed us in an intelligent passivity before the beneficent aggression of literature. Attributing to literature virtually angelic powers, it has passed the word to readers of literature that the one thing you do not do when you meet an angel is to wrestle with him." Only readers familiar with Trilling's earlier work will be able to appreciate the honesty—the integrity, to use an unfashionable word—of these later pronouncements.

In short, the self still has to find a point of refuge and definition in the modern world, which leads to a final, desperate strategy: the tendency to identify the authentic self with madness, the most extreme gesture the individual can make against his culture:

> The position is grounded on two assumptive reasons. One is that insanity is a direct and appropriate response to the coercive inauthenticity of society. That is to say, insanity is not only a condition inflicted by the demands of society and passively endured; it is also an act, expressing the intention of the insane person to meet and overcome the coercive situation; and whether or not it succeeds in this intention, it is at least an act of criticism which exposes the true nature of society—thus interpreted, insanity is said to be a form of rationality and it is society itself that stands under the imputation of being irrational to the point of insanity. The second reason is that insanity is a negation of limiting conditions in general, a form of personal existence in which power is assured by self-sufficiency.

While Trilling is clearly sympathetic to the historical dilemmas the self has faced, it is also clear from his brief discussions of R.D. Laing, Michel Foucault, and Norman O. Brown, that he detests the glorification of irrationality:

> the doctrine that madness is health, that madness is liberation and authenticity, receives a happy welcome from a consequential part of the educated public. And when we give due weight to the likelihood that those who respond positively to the doctrine don't have it in mind to go mad...we must yet take it to be significant of our circumstances that many among us find it gratifying to entertain the thought that alienation is to be overcome only by the completeness of alienation, and that alienation completed is not a deprivation or deficiency but a potency. Perhaps exactly because the thought is assented to so facilely, so without what used to be called seriousness, it might seem that no expression of disaffection from the social existence was ever so extreme as this eagerness to say that authenticity of personal being is achieved through an ultimate isolatedness and through the power that this is presumed to bring. The falsities of an alienated social reality are rejected in favor of an upward psychopathic mobility to the point of divinity, each one of us a Christ—but with none of the inconveniences of undertaking to intercede, of being a sacrifice, of reasoning with rabbis, of making sermons, of having disciples, of going to weddings and to funerals, of beginning something and at a certain point remarking that it is finished.

The apparent conservatism of this concluding passage from *Sincerity and Authenticity* once again disappointed some of Trilling's earlier admirers, but at this level of seriousness terms such as "liberalism" and "conservatism" cease to have much value. For Trilling the authentic self finds its proper completion only when it accepts the responsibilities of living with other selves. True selfhood—and this is no facile paradox—may often demand self-sacrifice. And if this is conservatism, it is the conservatism of the *Nicomachean Ethics*.

Many of us who had the welcome opportunity of reading Trilling's essays as they appeared individually in the 1950's and 60's had very little sense of the emerging argument outlined above. His tone seemed to be primarily that of an elegant, dispassionate teacher, trying (in Arnold's phrase) to see the object as it truly is. Now that we have the completed work before us, however, the established view of Trilling as a genteel moralist, as an American Leavis with an infusion of manners, has to be revised. If he never achieved that "resolution" which he so admires in the later work of Arnold, it is another sign of his unwillingness to settle for inappropriate simplifications.

WAIN, John (Barrington).   British.   Born in Stoke-on-Trent, Staffordshire, 14 March 1925. Educated at the High School, Newcastle-under-Lyme, Staffordshire; St. John's College, Oxford, B.A. 1946, Fereday Fellow, 1946-49, M.A. 1950. Married Marianne Urmston in 1947 (divorced, 1956), and Eirian James in 1960; 3 children. Lecturer in English, University of Reading, Berkshire, 1947-55; Professor of Poetry, Oxford University, 1973-78. Churchill Visiting Professor, University of Bristol, 1967; Visiting Professor, Centre Universitaire Expér-imental, Vincennes, France, 1969. First Holder, Fellowship in Creative Arts, 1971-72, and since 1973, Supernumerary Fellow, Brasenose College, Oxford. Recipient: Maugham Award, 1958; Heinemann Award, 1975, and Black Memorial Award, 1975, both for non-fiction. Fellow, Royal Society of Literature, 1960; resigned, 1961. Address: c/o Macmillan and Company Ltd., 4 Little Essex Street, London WC2R 3LF, England.

PUBLICATIONS

Criticism

Preliminary Essays.   London, Macmillan, and New York, St. Martin's Press, 1957.
Gerard Manley Hopkins: An Idiom of Desperation.   London, Oxford University Press, and Folcroft, Pennsylvania, Folcroft Editions, 1959; reprinted in *Essays on Literature and Ideas*, 1963.
Essays on Literature and Ideas.   London, Macmillan, and New York, St. Martin's Press, 1963.
The Living World of Shakespeare: A Playgoer's Guide.   London, Macmillan, and New York, St. Martin's Press, 1964.
Arnold Bennett.   New York, Columbia University Press, 1967.
A House for the Truth: Critical Essays.   London, Macmillan, 1972; New York, Viking Press, 1974.
Professing Poetry.   London, Macmillan, 1977; New York, Viking Press, 1978.

Verse

Mixed Feelings.   Reading, Berkshire, Reading University School of Art, 1951.
A Word Carved on a Sill.   London, Routledge, and New York, St. Martin's Press, 1956.
Weep Before God: Poems.   London, Macmillan, and New York, St. Martin's Press, 1961.
Wildtrack: A Poem.   London, Macmillan, and New York, Viking Press, 1965.
Letters to Five Artists.   London, Macmillan, 1969; New York, Viking Press, 1970.
The Shape of Feng.   London, Covent Garden Press, 1972.
Feng.   London, Macmillan, and New York, Viking Press, 1975.
Poems for the Zodiac (12 booklets), illustrated by Brenda Stones.   London, Pisces Press, 1980.
Poems 1949-1979.   London, Macmillan, 1981.

Plays

Harry in the Night: An Optimistic Comedy (produced Stoke on Trent, 1975).

Radio Play: *You Wouldn't Remember*, 1978.

Novels

Hurry on Down.   London, Secker and Warburg, 1953; as *Born in Captivity*, New York, Knopf, 1954.
Living in the Present.   London, Secker and Warburg, 1955; New York, Putnam, 1960.
The Contenders.   London, Macmillan, and New York, St. Martin's Press, 1958.
A Travelling Woman.   London, Macmillan, and New York, St. Martin's Press, 1959.
Strike the Father Dead.   London, Macmillan, and New York, St. Martin's Press, 1962.
The Young Visitors.   London, Macmillan, and New York, Viking Press, 1965.
The Smaller Sky.   London, Macmillan, 1967.
A Winter in the Hills.   London, Macmillan, and New York, Viking Press, 1970.
The Pardoner's Tale.   London, Macmillan, 1978; New York, Viking Press, 1979.
Lizzie's Floating Ship.   London, Bodley Head, 1981.

Short Stories

Nuncle and Other Stories.   London, Macmillan, 1960; New York, St. Martin's Press, 1961.
Death of the Hind Legs and Other Stories.   London, Macmillan, and New York, Viking Press, 1966.
The Life Guard.   London, Macmillan, 1971; New York, Viking Press, 1972.
King Caliban and Other Stories.   London, Macmillan, 1978.

Other

Sprightly Running: Part of an Autobiography.   London, Macmillan, 1962; New York, St. Martin's Press, 1963.
Samuel Johnson (biography).   London, Macmillan, 1974; New York, Viking Press, 1975.
A John Wain Selection, edited by Geoffrey Halson.   London, Longman, 1977.

Editor, *Contemporary Reviews of Romantic Poetry.*   London, Harrap, and New York, Barnes and Noble, 1953.
Editor, *Interpretations: Essays on Twelve English Poems.*   London, Routledge, 1955; New York, Hillary House, 1957.
Editor, *International Literary Annual.*   London, John Calder, and New York, Criterion Books, 2 vols., 1959, 1960.
Editor, *Fanny Burney's Diary.*   London, Folio Society, 1960.
Editor, *Anthology of Modern Poetry.*   London, Hutchinson, 1963.
Editor, *Pope.*   New York, Dell, 1963.
Editor, *Selected Shorter Poems of Thomas Hardy.*   London, Macmillan, and New York, St. Martin's Press, 1966; revised edition, 1975.
Editor, *The Dynasts*, by Thomas Hardy.   London, Macmillan, and New York, St. Martin's Press, 1966.
Editor, *Selected Shorter Stories of Thomas Hardy.*   London, Macmillan, and New York, St. Martin's Press, 1966.

Editor, *Shakespeare: Macbeth: A Casebook*. London, Macmillan, 1968.
Editor, *Shakespeare: Othello: A Casebook*. London, Macmillan, 1971.
Editor, *Johnson as Critic*. London and Boston, Routledge, 1973.
Editor, *Lives of the English Poets: A Selection*, by Johnson. London, Dent, and New York, Dutton, 1975.
Editor, *Johnson on Johnson: A Selection of the Personal and Autobiographical Writings of Samuel Johnson*. London, Dent, and New York, Dutton, 1976.
Editor, *The Poetry of Thomas Hardy: A New Selection*. London, Macmillan, 1977.
Editor, *An Edmund Wilson Celebration*. Oxford, Phaidon Press, 1978.
Editor, *Personal Choice: A Poetry Anthology*. Newton Abbot, Devon, David and Charles, 1978.
Editor, *Everyman's Book of English Verse*. London, Dent, 1981.

BIBLIOGRAPHY

Dale Salwak, *John Braine and John Wain: A Reference Guide*. Boston, Hall, 1980.

*   *   *

The title "critic," John Wain asserts at the opening of *Preliminary Essays*, is one which must be earned. Criticism itself may not be a fine art, he concludes (in the final essay of the collection), but it is still a worthy undertaking, a "useful" art,

> and it can be carried on by anyone...who is prepared to put himself through a rather long training....Literary criticism is the discussion, between equals, of works of literature, with a view to establishing common ground on which judgements of value can be based....[The object of criticism] is the judgement of value, and the establishment of a hierarchy of quality...everything is *not* just a matter of "taste"; if we agree that I like *Hamlet* and you like Agatha Christie, we have *not* said the last significant word on the subject.

This is clear enough and unexceptionable: the problem is that Wain does virtually nothing here to establish such grounds or to defend an explicit "hierarchy of quality." His tone throughout is consistently personal ("I like *Pauline*") but modest (after referring to an obscure Restoration comedy he quickly adds, "I cannot claim great erudition, by the way, for digging up this kind of thing; it is all in one book, Professor Nell Wiley's *Rare Prologues and Epilogues, 1642-1700*"), and at times almost apologetic ("At any rate, here are a few notes on [Arnold Bennett], grouped into sections so that readers who find the whole too lengthy can skip any of the sections and still make sense of what they read....My main object is to try to engage the serious novel-reader's interest, leaving the final judgement to him, but I am afraid my enthusiasm will now and then bounce me into a 'value-judgment' "). His topics are usually interesting enough—the rise and fall of Ovid's reputation in English letters, the rehabilitation of Wordsworth, the intensity of Hopkins—but he seems unable to press hard or go very far or perhaps is unwilling to do so, simply because he means what he says in his preface:

> the book is called "Preliminary" because it takes a long time to learn to become a critic, and I have only been at it for ten years....These essays are the record of part of an apprenticeship; I cannot tell when, if ever, that apprenticeship will be over.

The rather grand title of Wain's second collection, *Essays on Literature and Ideas*, might suggest that the apprenticeship is over; but again, the essays are disappointing (a long opening piece, for example, "The Conflict of Forms in Contemporary English Literature," turns out to be just another survey of post-war fiction, poetry and drama, while "The Mind of Shakespeare" promises a good deal more than it delivers). Wain is quite frank, however, about his motives for writing criticism: he produces John Middleton Murry's confession that as he grew older he came to feel the truth of Anatole France's famous—or infamous—observation that criticism records the adventures of one's soul among masterpieces. Criticism of this kind, Murry goes on, "utterly absorbs me":

> There is a wall, as it were, of dense, warm darkness before me—a darkness which is secretly alive and thrilling to the sense. This, I believe, is the reflection in myself of the darkness which broods over the poet's creative mind. It forms slowly and gradually gathers while I read his work. The sense of mystery deepens and deepens; but the quality of the mystery becomes more plain. There is a moment when, as though unconsciously and out of my control, the deeper rhythm of a poet's work, the rise and fall of the great moods which determined what he was and what he wrote, enter into me also.

And this, Wain tells us, is exactly the kind of pleasure he takes in writing his own criticism. No doubt this is so, but the probable enjoyment of the reader who must follow such adventures at second hand is another question.

It is hard to make any excuses for the oversimplifications and insufferable condescension of *The Living World of Shakespeare*. The book is not for students with their New Ardens:

> No, the people I am more concerned with are those who fill the theatres in London and Stratford—and a hundred other places—where Shakespeare's plays are staged; and the actors and (dare I add?) producers responsible for that staging; and the radio and television staff who adapt Shakespeare to their own media now and again; and the amateur dramatic societies who undertake Shakespearean productions in village halls. (It is a heart-warming thought that every night of the year, somewhere, before an audience of some kind, Shakespeare is being played.) And beyond these I think of the man who sits down at his own fireside, after a day's work, to keep company with Shakespeare for an hour or two. What all these people need is a discussion of Shakespeare that will engage their interest as mature, imaginative, sensible men and women; an honest facing of the difficulties arising from the distance of time between Shakespeare's day and ours; and an "appreciation" not of the full-blown kind that tries to do their imagining for them, but of the more modest kind which points out a shade here, an opulence there, that might otherwise escape attention.

Wain's thesis here is simply an expansion of a remark he had made earlier (in *Essays on Literature and Ideas*), that the key to Shakespeare's work lies in recognizing "the combination of a world-view that called for unity and correspondence with a natural turn of mind that sought always to resolve discord into harmony and multiplicity into singleness." The plays are simply *there*, like mighty works of nature, to be admired and cherished; even their faults are natural and precious, "like knots in an oaken beam." Wain gives us 13 pages on *Lear* (Gloucester and Lear "have sinned against 'nature,' the vital principle in all things; and the revenge of nature will be a terrible one"), 12 pages on *Hamlet* (largely a simplified retelling of Eliot's view of that play), another 12 pages on *Othello* (Othello is a "kingly barbarian," Iago a "sharper with a dirty mind"), and so on, over the entire canon. There are no shades or opulences here—not even for the fireside readers and TV producers.

A House for the Truth is a better book in all respects (Raymond Chandler had observed that "the great critic builds a house for the truth": Wain hastens to add that while he does not regard himself as a great critic, he does believe that "in this throw-away age, the notion of building something as solid as a house seems...true and salutary"). If Orwell is "a moral hero for me," he goes on, "a hero in the Carlylean sense, so too are [Samuel] Johnson and Pasternak." His essays on these three writers (and on Flann O'Brien) are solid, salutary and convincing, perhaps because he is now arguing as a moralist. He is still far from having worked out a "common ground on which judgements of value can be based," but his own governing principle is clear and eloquent: he believes firmly in the abiding virtues of heroic individualism and integrity, and he is certain that an age of happenings, raw violence in the name of art, and irrationality in general urgently needs to listen to his heroes.

WALDOCK, A(rthur) J(ohn) A(lfred).   Australian.   Born in Hinton, New South Wales, 26 January 1898. Educated at Sydney Boys High School; University of Sydney (Coulson Scholar, 1917; Coutts Scholar, 1918; Frazer Scholar, 1918; University Medal, 1925), B.A. 1918, M.A. 1925. Instructor in English, Royal Australian Naval College, 1918; Lecturer, 1919-34, and Professor of English Literature, 1934-50, University of Sydney. *Died 14 January 1950.*

PUBLICATIONS

Criticism

> *William Lisle Bowles* (lecture).   Sydney, Australian English Association, 1928; reprinted in *James, Joyce, and Others*, 1937.
> *Hamlet: A Study in Critical Method.*   London, Cambridge University Press, 1931.
> *Thomas Hardy and "The Dynasts"* (lecture).   Sydney, Australian English Association, 1933; reprinted in *James, Joyce, and Others*, 1937.
> *Macbeth* (lecture).   Sydney, Australian English Association, n.d.; reprinted in *James, Joyce, and Others*, 1937.
> *Some Recent Developments in English Literature*, with others.   Sydney, Australian English Association, 1935.
> *James, Joyce, and Others.*   London, Williams and Norgate, 1937; Freeport, New York, Books for Libraries, 1967.
> *Paradise Lost and Its Critics.*   London, Cambridge University Press, 1947.
> *Sophocles the Dramatist.*   London, Cambridge University Press, 1951.

*   *   *

An early reviewer of *Paradise Lost and Its Critics* once complained that A.J.A. Waldock had confused the practice of criticism with the practice of law. The comparison is useful, even if the implied opposition between two "different" kinds of reasoning is not, for in each of his books Waldock clearly did enjoy playing the role of prosecuting attorney. He arraigns Sophocles, Shakespeare and Milton; he charges them with artistic malfeasance of one sort or another; he very effectively attacks the testimony of other critics—and then he suddenly appears to drop his case because the defendants are, after all, such remarkable creatures, so "human" and yet so "inimitable."

At the opening of his first book, *Hamlet: A Study in Critical Method*, Waldock advises us that some of the difficulties which have given rise to so much inconclusive speculation are "in the play." Even if this were not the case, however, Goethe, Coleridge and A.C. Bradley would still be wrong because their views of the play do not correspond to our immediate experience of it or to the text ("Now, of all such theories the first and final demand is that they shall be immediately demonstrated by the letter of the text"). Waldock himself comes close to accepting the Oedipal interpretation of *Hamlet* proposed by Robertson, Eliot and Ernest Jones: the play is a partial failure because Shakespeare cannot establish his primary effect (the spectacle of Hamlet suffering as a result of his mother's remarriage) by using the framework of earlier "revenge" stories (or plays, if they existed). But unlike these other critics, Waldock is not willing to conclude that Shakespeare too suffered from an unresolved Oedipal conflict. And while the play itself may be a partial failure, it is still "magnificently rugged." What would *Hamlet* be without its "puzzle" and "the external piquancy of its imperfection"? Finally, "there is no one, in history, or in literature, like Hamlet. All that humanity is, all that humanity might be, seem figured in him."

But why have so many sensitive and intelligent critics gone astray? We are bound to misread *Hamlet*, Waldock maintains, if we do not recognize that "a drama differs in several respects from a slice of actuality and is not amenable to quite the same handling." A play is not a "mine of secret motives," and if we persist in digging for them, what usually happens is that "our spade goes through the other side of the drama." Waldock drops the problem here but returns to it again in *Sophocles the Dramatist*, in which he argues that what matters most is our "natural

537

response" to a work of art. Again, we are sure to ask the wrong questions if we regard the work as a "document," as a "literal transcription" of facts, and believe that it "somehow records what, at [a] given time and place, an interlinked set of people said and did":

> What renders...every thesis of this nature ridiculous is the simple fact that a play is a work of art: a piece of writing most carefully put together in order that it may achieve a most carefully calculated effect. A play—or a novel, or any other creative work presenting an action—is by no means a flat documentary text; it is a complex of most subtle highlights and lowlights. It is compounded of shading and relief, its very being consists in intricate emphases and suppressions; and in a sense—unlike life—it has no depth. Literature operates on a thinnish crust. Any piece of fact has depth beyond depth underlying it. Our instruments of research may be weak, our discoveries, after all our efforts, meagre, but the depths are assuredly there. In literature, by contrast, *appearance* is everything, and there is no reality below the appearance.

The "*appearance*" exists entirely for the sake of a "most carefully calculated effect," and this emphasis upon effect places Waldock in the Aristotelian tradition: in life we might ask why a "real" Hamlet delays or pretends to be mad; in the play we keep such questions at their proper distance and respond primarily to the main issue, Hamlet's pain and the disaster it brings to others. Or again, if we ask detailed questions about Oedipus' "tragic flaw," we get nowhere:

> The play is not about the faults of Oedipus. It may be conceded that he has his failings, but these are merely incidental to the pattern. Bluntly, in the *Oedipus Tyrannus* the hero's faults are of little account. The play is too busy with another thing—with another all-powerful impression; and in the shadow of this other impression the hero's deficiencies fade into nothingness.

Then what is *Oedipus* about? Rejecting the conventional view, Waldock insists that it has no philosophic meaning in the sense of providing a universal statement (and here it should be noted that Waldock is in sharp opposition to Aristotle, who argues that the true work of art is "more philosophic than history" and that in *Oedipus* tragedy reached its final perfection as a form). To look for such meaning, Waldock goes on, is a "neat" but "illegitimate" manoeuvre:

> It is just one more way of smuggling significance into the *Oedipus Tyrannus*; just one more expression of the feeling that this work, by hook or by crook, must be made to mean something....But the action of this play is exceptional; no argument can alter that. Oedipus is a world-wonder in his suffering, in his peculiar destiny he is a freak. He is a man selected out of millions to undergo this staggering fate; that is why his story is so fascinating. It fascinates because it is rare; because on any rational assessment his story—as far as we are concerned—is impossible. We can imagine it all so vividly, we can live in every one of his emotions; yet we should as reasonably fear to be hit by a thunderbolt as to be embroiled in his particular set of misfortunes....Here the terror of sheer coincidence is vital....We have no feelings here of the nature of things; what we feel is an *interference* with nature. The play quintessentializes misfortune; it is an epigram in ill-luck....There is no meaning in the *Oedipus Tyrannus*; there is merely the terror of coincidence, and then, at the end of it all, our impression of man's power to suffer, and of his greatness because of this power.

Unfortunately Waldock does not explain why there is some kind of "greatness" in man's "power to suffer." He ends *Sophocles the Dramatist* with the same empty piety that closes the book on *Hamlet*. Despite its imperfections, *Oedipus Tyrannus* is still the "drama of dramas": "let us accept [it] with gratitude, as it is." And if there are even greater problems with the *Coloneus*, still we should not be sorry that Sophocles "relaxed," that he "brought us, this once, so close to himself; that he let us hear, beneath the words of the play, the beating of his own heart."

There are some important difficulties with the principle of "natural response" and Waldock's partial adherence to Aristotle, for whom the central effect of tragedy was the catharsis of pity and fear. Waldock can do nothing with this term, however, and suggests that Aristotle himself hardly knew what he meant (at which point readers should turn to Humphrey House's guide to the *Poetics* and Elder Olson's *Tragedy and the Theory of Drama*). But even if Waldock is right, even if we cannot assume that all tragedies have universal meaning and a common purpose or end, there is still the question of *whose* response is normative. Waldock laughs easily enough at those critics who assume that the Greek audience was an intensely serious one:

> This audience does not seem on enjoyment bent: its mood is much more serious and sombre. One suspects it of having brought along with it sets of Aristotle, Thucydides and Pindar; if not, it has arrived word-perfect in the works of those writers, and waits ready to make instant application of its knowledge. The dramatists must have hated this audience, for it is essentially an audience that nags. It is a terribly vigilant audience: an audience much given to "mistrusting," and to having doubts about the conduct of characters. It is an audience quite weighted down by its duties, an audience with a watching brief for the best standards in Athenian life. It is indeed in all respects so awkward an audience that the query is constantly occurring to one why the dramatists wrote so many plays for it. It is, in effect, so "unhistorical" an audience that we may feel quite sure that it never existed.

The "chief historical fact" for Waldock is that "man has remained much the same" over the centuries. But at what level of intelligence and beliefs? What is it that determines the ideal—yet "natural"—response to the Oedipus plays and *Hamlet*? Waldock's publishers tell us that he had "finished the manuscript only a few months before his death," but it is hard to believe that a critic so alert to so many problems and so unwilling to excuse evasiveness in others actually had finished with the problem of literary response.

In his earlier book on Milton, Waldock had asked, "what is really *happening* in *Paradise Lost*?" Why do critics—particularly modern critics—differ so greatly in their conclusions about the poem? Is Edwin Greenlaw right in emphasizing the "classical" virtues depicted in the poem at the expense of the virtues of piety and submission? Is E.M.W. Tillyard right when he argues that in order to understand the poem we must determine as precisely as possible Milton's state of mind when he wrote it? Waldock is more interested in developing his own reading of the poem, however, than in dealing specifically with these other critics. Not surprisingly he finds that poem badly flawed, for two reasons. In the first place, the material Milton had to work with, the scriptural account of the temptation and fall, would have been intractable material for any poet. There is no way, for example, in which the fall could be dramatized—it was impossible to make "the transition from sinlessness to sin perfectly intelligible":

> It was obvious that Adam and Eve must already have contracted human weaknesses before they can start on the course of conduct that leads to their fall: to put it another way, they must already be fallen (technically) before they can begin to fall. Nor, again, is it possible to see just how the change from love to lust came about, or what it was in the act of disobedience that necessitated it. There is no help for these matters.

And in the second place, even if he had been able to find artistic solutions to such problems, Milton really believed in his theme "much less intensely than he thought he did":

> In many senses *Paradise Lost* was his predestined theme, and yet in a sense it put him in a false position, cut clean against the grain of his nature. Believing rather more intensely than the average man that our dignity consists in independent and vigorous thought, and feeling with the same rather exceptional intensity that the essence of life is struggle, he must deplore the coming of thought into the world (for that is what it really amounts to) and represent man's best state as that original featureless blessedness. He was trapped, in a sense, by his theme, and from the trap there was no escape....[His] central theme denied him the fullest expression of his deepest interests. It was likely, then, that as his really deep interests could not find outlet in his poem in the right way they might do so in the wrong way. And to a certain extent they do; they find vents and safety valves often in inopportune places. Adam cannot give Milton much scope to express what he really feels about life: but Satan is there, Satan gives him scope. And the result is that the balance is

somewhat disturbed; pressures are set up that are at times disquieting, that seem to threaten more than once, indeed, the equilibrium of the poem.

And yet Waldock finds that the poem has moments of great power (the ending, for example, is "inimitable").

The final effect of these three energetic, closely reasoned studies is puzzling, even a little disturbing. Waldock had an unerring instinct for the crucial problems which even the greatest works present; point by point he is often brilliantly persuasive; but the reader may be left with the feeling that while C.S. Lewis loves *Paradise Lost* and (to exaggerate a bit) William Empson hates it, the real issues at stake mean very little to Waldock. The same holds true for his treatment of *Hamlet* and Sophocles: what engages him is the challenge of a debate and the *activity* of arguing. Once he feels he has scored his point, he seems to lose interest and settles for the nearest gentlemanly platitude. And if this is the case, then Waldock may be remembered only as a critic's critic.

WARREN, Austin. American. Born in Waltham, Massachusetts, 4 July 1899. Educated at Wesleyan University, Middletown, Connecticut, B.A. 1920; Harvard University, Cambridge, Massachusetts, M.A. 1922; Princeton University, Princeton, New Jersey, Ph.D. 1926. Married Eleanore Blake in 1941 (died, 1946); Antonia Keene, 1959. Instructor, University of Kentucky, Lexington, 1920-21, and the University of Minnesota, Minneapolis, 1922-24; Dean, St. Peter's School of Liberal and Humane Studies, Hebron, Connecticut, summers, 1922-30; Instructor, 1926-29, Assistant and Associate Professor, 1929-34, and Professor of English, 1934-39, Boston University; Professor of English, University of Iowa, Iowa City, 1939-48; Professor of English, University of Michigan, Ann Arbor, 1948-68. Berg Visiting Professor of American Literature, New York University, 1953-54. Associate Editor, *New England Quarterly*, 1937-40, 1942-46, *American Literature*, 1940-42, and *Comparative Literature*, 1948-50. Fellow, American Council of Learned Societies, 1930; Fellow, 1948-50, and since 1950, Senior Fellow, Kenyon School of English, Gambier, Ohio, later Indiana University School of Letters, Bloomington. Recipient: Guggenheim Fellowship, 1951; Award for Literature, American Academy of Arts and Letters, 1973. Litt.D.: Brown University, Providence, Rhode Island, 1974. Address: 90 Oriole Avenue, Providence, Rhode Island 02906, U.S.A.

PUBLICATIONS

Criticism

> *Alexander Pope as Critic and Humanist.* Princeton, New Jersey, Princeton University Press, 1929.
> *The Elder Henry James.* New York, Macmillan, 1934.
> *Richard Crashaw: A Study in Baroque Sensibility.* Baton Rouge, Louisiana State University Press, 1939; London, Faber, 1957.
> *Rage for Order: Essays in Criticism.* Chicago, University of Chicago Press, 1939.
> *Theory of Literature*, with René Wellek. New York, Harcourt Brace, and London, Cape, 1949.
> *New England Saints.* Ann Arbor, University of Michigan Press, 1956.
> *The New England Conscience.* Ann Arbor, University of Michigan Press, 1966.
> *Connections.* Ann Arbor, University of Michigan Press, 1970.

Teacher and Critic: Essays by and about Austin Warren, edited by Myron Simon and Harvey Gross.   Los Angeles, Plantin Press, 1976.
"The Quest for Auden," in *Sewanee Review* (Tennessee), 87, 1979.
"Carroll and His Alice Book," in *Sewanee Review* (Tennessee), 88, 1980.
"The Poetry of Auden," in *Southern Review* (Baton Rouge, Louisiana), 17, 1981.

Other

Editor, *Nathaniel Hawthorne: Representative Selections*.   New York, American Book Company, 1934.
Editor, *Letters*, by Thomas W. Parsons.   Privately printed, 1940.
Editor, *They Will Remain* (poems), by Susan Pendleton.   Ann Arbor, Michigan, Basil and Peters, 1966.

*   *   *

"As a literary critic," Austin Warren remarks in the preface to *Connections*, his most recent book of essays, "I have no 'method,' no speciality, but am what is called, in another discipline, a 'general practitioner' ":

> Literary theory and methodology have ever interested me; but, confronted with the situation of "practical criticism," I look through my repertory for the method and the mixture of methods appropriate to the case before me—in consequence of which the proportion of stylistic analysis to biographical, or biological to ideological, will be found to vary from essay to essay.

This modest statement describes his earlier criticism just as well: *Theory of Literature* is a formidable inquiry into "literary theory and methodology" (René Wellek is responsible for thirteen of the nineteen chapters, and although he and Warren describe this problematic book as "a real instance of a collaboration in which the author is the shared agreement between two writers," I have reserved comment about it for my discussion of Wellek); in *The Elder Henry James* and *Rage for Order*, Warren uses biographical material and stylistic analysis not as ends in themselves, but as a means of defining the "spiritual cosmos" of the writers under consideration; and in *New England Saints* and *The New England Conscience*, his aim is frankly rhetorical or "ideological." The title, *Connections*, comes from E.M. Forster ("Only Connect" is the motto of *Howards End*), but Warren means by this word, he tell us, something closer to what Henry James meant by "relations," that is, a "pervasive emphasis on attaching each particularity to as many other particularities as, by reasonable framing, is possible—the pervasive concern with 'interness.' " This holds true not only for *Connections* (and once again the two volumes on New England writers), but also for those studies, especially of Crashaw and some other seventeenth-century poets, in which Warren is interested in establishing what R.S. Crane once called "the sense of a period style."
    The title of Warren's best known collection, *Rage for Order*, makes another allusion, this time to Wallace Stevens' "The Idea of Order at Key West," in which the poet celebrates that "blessed rage for order," the "maker's rage to order words of the sea," the redemptive power of the human imagination to impose order on the disorder of everyday experience. A poem succeeds, Warren maintains, only when it achieves "an equilibrium which is also a tension, where there is a rage waiting to be ordered and a rage to find, or to make, that ordering." Creation thus involves both a technical discipline (the "deformation" or freshening of ordinary language) and a spiritual discipline (the discipline of "confronting disorder in one's self and in the world; of facing existentially, as a total human being living in time, the responsibility of vision and choice"). When the poet succeeds, he makes his work "a kind of cosmos; a concretely languaged, synoptically felt world; an ikon or image of the 'real world'...[which] cannot be abstracted from the language and the mythic structure in which it is incarnated." And the critic too, the ideal reader, is moved by a rage for order of his own:

a passionate desire to discover, by analysis and comparison, the systematic vision of the world which is the poet's construction, his equivalent of a philosophic or other conceptual system. He judges it a test of a mode of order that it be imaginable as well as conceivable. He hypothesizes that the cosmos of a serious poet is, intuitively and dramatically, coherent. He seeks to define the spiritual cosmos of each and the specifically literary structure which corresponds to it.

In each of the nine essays which make up *Rage for Order*, Warren considers a particular poet or novelist and examines the kind of "order" which he achieves and the various kinds of problems involved in the creation of an "equilibrium" which is also a "tension." (In *The Scarlet Letter*, for example, Hawthorne "does not wish to explain all at the end. He has two chief ways of giving a sense of the mysterious while offering a concurrent rationale." Or to take another example, for Hopkins, the difficult, perhaps impossible "ideal of poetry" was "to instress the inscapes without splintering the architecture of the universe and, expressionally, to make every word rich in a way compatible with a more than additively rich total poetic structure.") The essays here are fairly short and the principle terms, "order," "disorder," and "tension," so broad that they would be useless in the hands of a less acute critic. But Warren is so sympathetic to each of his authors—and writes so elegantly himself—that only the pieces on Yeats and Forster seem dated.

New England Saints is an even finer book, although one which is bound to appeal to a much smaller audience. "There are two strains in the New England character," Warren asserts here, "the Yankee trader and the Yankee saint (often a complex of scholar, priest, and poet)":

> This book is devoted to the saints. The Puritans, like St. Paul, used that term to designate members of their church, communicants, "the elect." I have used it more widely, but with a definite criterion. My saints are, none of them, canonized; but they are, whether priests, and of whatever "communion," men I recognize, and celebrate, as those to whom reality was the spiritual life, whose spiritual integrity was their calling and vocation. This is a hagiography, designed, like all hagiographies, for instruction, to be sure, but primarily for edification.

The scholars here are Bronson Alcott, Emerson, the elder Henry James, Charles Eliot Norton, and Warren's own teacher, Irving Babbitt; the priests are some of the early "orthodox parsons of Christ's Church" and the "Methodist saint," Edward Taylor; the poets include the *other* Edward Taylor, Anne Bradstreet and the Puritan elegiasts, and John Brooks Wheelwright, who was killed in 1940 and whose books, Warren believes, "will one day take their rightful place in American poetry and scripture." Warren means exactly what he says here: these essays are moving acts of piety, superbly written tributes to men and women who manifested and suffered *for* the power of the human conscience supported by Grace or inner light; the writers he examines in *The New England Conscience* are writers who suffered "*from* conscience" and thus illustrate the hypertrophy or "pathology" of that same moral power. Ranging from Roger Williams and Michael Wigglesworth, through Hawthorne, Henry James and Henry Adams, and extending down to Santayana's "last Puritan," Oliver Alden, these men suffer from the extremes of "scrupulosity" and self-examination which appear in their purest form as the nineteenth century draws to a close. By this time the Puritan conscience had survived its original purpose and virtue had become a burdensome end in itself:

> The things missing are pleasure, graciousness, joy, love. Neighbors and relatives do kind acts, give good gifts, but do and give so ungraciously that one wishes they wouldn't make the effort. The Lord loveth a cheerful giver. And how the heart of the recipient sinks when, trying to thank the donor, he is told, "I've done no more than my duty"—which turns one into an abstraction to whom an abstraction has been done for abstract motives.
> "Love is the fulfilling of the Law." How hard for a Yankee mind to take in. The Law is a duty; and now, instead of real love's taking its place, love is an additional duty.

Precisely because Warren is critical here rather than eulogistic, *The New England Conscience* will appeal to those readers for whom his study of the "saints" must seem a kind of radiant curiosity.

Obviously Warren has always felt free to use whatever approach his interests dictate. By the standards of *Theory of Literature*, which insists upon the purely "literary" study of literature, much of his most interesting work is not criticism at all. But it is a measure of his strength—or so it might be argued—that he has never been inhibited by the implications of his collaboration with Wellek.

WARREN, Robert Penn. American. Born in Guthrie, Kentucky, 24 April 1905. Educated at Guthrie High School; Vanderbilt University, Nashville, Tennessee, B.A. (summa cum laude) 1925; University of California, Berkeley, M.A. 1927; Yale University, New Haven, Connecticut, 1927-28; Oxford University (Rhodes Scholar), B.Litt. 1930. Married 1) Emma Brescia in 1930 (divorced, 1950); 2) the writer Eleanor Clark in 1952; two children. Assistant Professor, Southwestern College, Memphis, Tennessee, 1930-31, and Vanderbilt University, 1931-34; Assistant and Associate Professor, Louisiana State University, Baton Rouge, 1934-42; Professor of English, University of Minnesota, Minneapolis, 1942-50. Professor of Playwriting, 1950-56, Professor of English, 1962-73, and since 1973, Professor Emeritus, Yale University. Member of the Fugitive Group of poets: Co-Founding Editor, *The Fugitive*, Nashville, 1922-25. Founding Editor, *Southern Review*, Baton Rouge, Louisiana, 1935-42. Consultant in Poetry, Library of Congress, Washington, D.C., 1944-45. Recipient: Caroline Sinkler Award, 1936, 1937, 1938; Levinson Prize, 1936, Union League Civic and Arts Foundation Prize, 1953, and Harriet Monroe Prize, 1976 (*Poetry*, Chicago); Houghton Mifflin Literary Fellowship, 1939; Guggenheim Fellowship, 1939, 1947; Shelley Memorial Award, 1943; Pulitzer Prize, for fiction, 1947, for poetry, 1958, 1979; Robert Meltzer Award, Screen Writers Guild, 1949; Sidney Hillman Prize, 1957; Edna St. Vincent Millay Memorial Prize, 1958; National Book Award, for poetry, 1958; New York *Herald-Tribune* Van Doren Award, 1965; Bollingen Prize, for poetry, 1967; National Endowment for the Arts grant, 1968, and Lectureship, 1974; Henry A. Bellaman Prize, 1970; Van Wyck Brooks Award, for poetry, 1970; National Medal for Literature, 1970; Emerson-Thoreau Medal, 1975; Copernicus Award, 1976; Presidential Medal of Freedom, 1980; Common Wealth Award, 1981. D. Litt.: University of Louisville, Kentucky, 1949; Kenyon College, Gambier, Ohio, 1952; University of Kentucky, Lexington, 1955; Colby College, Waterville, Maine, 1956; Swarthmore College, Pennsylvania, 1958; Yale University, 1959; Fairfield University, Connecticut, 1969; Wesleyan University, Middletown, Connecticut, 1970; Harvard University, Cambridge, Massachusetts, 1973; Southwestern College, 1974; University of the South, Sewanee, Tennessee, 1974; Monmouth College, Illinois, 1979; LL.D.: Bridgeport University, Connecticut, 1965; University of New Haven, Connecticut, 1974; Johns Hopkins University, Baltimore, 1977. Member, American Academy, and American Academy of Arts and Sciences. Address: 2495 Redding Road, Fairfield, Connecticut 06430, U.S.A.

PUBLICATIONS

Criticism

"A Poem of Pure Imagination: An Experiment in Reading," in *The Rime of the Ancient Mariner*, by Samuel Taylor Coleridge. New York, Reynal and Hitchcock, 1946; reprinted in *Selected Essays*, 1958.

Selected Essays.   New York, Random House, 1958; London, Eyre and Spottiswoode, 1964.
A Plea in Mitigation: Modern Poetry and the End of an Era.   Macon, Georgia, Wesleyan College, 1966.
Homage to Theodore Dreiser.   New York, Random House, 1971.
John Greenleaf Whittier's Poetry: An Appraisal and a Selection.   Minneapolis, University of Minnesota Press, 1971.
Democracy and Poetry.   Cambridge, Massachusetts, Harvard University Press, 1975.

Novels

Night Rider.   Boston, Houghton Mifflin, 1939; London, Eyre and Spottiswoode, 1940.
At Heaven's Gate.   New York, Harcourt Brace, and London, Eyre and Spottiswoode, 1943.
All the King's Men.   New York, Harcourt Brace, 1946; London, Eyre and Spottiswoode, 1948.
World Enough and Time: A Romantic Novel.   New York, Random House, 1950; London, Eyre and Spottiswoode, 1951.
Band of Angels.   New York, Random House, 1955; London, Eyre and Spottiswoode, 1956.
The Cave.   New York, Random House, and London, Eyre and Spottiswoode, 1959.
Wilderness: A Tale of the Civil War.   New York, Random House, 1961; London, Eyre and Spottiswoode, 1962.
Flood: A Romance of Our Times.   New York, Random House, and London, Collins, 1964.
Meet Me in the Green Glen.   New York, Random House, 1971; London, Secker and Warburg, 1972.
A Place to Come To.   New York, Random House, and London, Secker and Warburg, 1977.

Short Stories

Blackberry Winter.   Cummington, Massachusetts, Cummington Press, 1946.
The Circus in the Attic and Other Stories.   New York, Harcourt Brace, 1947; London, Eyre and Spottiswoode, 1952.

Verse

Thirty-Six Poems.   New York, Alcestis Press, 1935.
Eleven Poems on the Same Theme.   New York, New Directions, 1942.
Selected Poems 1923-43.   New York, Harcourt Brace, 1944; London, Fortune Press, 1951.
Brother to Dragons: A Tale in Verse and Voices.   New York, Random House, 1953; revised edition, 1979; London, Eyre and Spottiswoode, 1954.
Promises: Poems 1954-1956.   New York, Random House, 1957; London, Eyre and Spottiswoode, 1959.
You, Emperors and Others: Poems 1957-1960.   New York, Random House, 1960.
Selected Poems: New and Old 1923-1966.   New York, Random House, 1966.
Incarnations: Poems 1966-1968.   New York, Random House, 1968; London, W.H. Allen, 1970.
Audubon: A Vision.   New York, Random House, 1969.
Or Else: Poem/Poems 1968-1974.   New York, Random House, 1974.

Selected Poems 1923-1975. New York, Random House, and London, Secker and
  Warburg, 1976.
Now and Then: Poems 1976-1978. New York, Random House, 1978.
Being Here: Poetry 1977-1980. New York, Random House, 1980.
Rumor Verified: Poems 1979-1980. New York, Random House, 1981.

Other

John Brown: The Making of a Martyr. New York, Payson and Clark, 1929.
I'll Take My Stand: The South and the Agrarian Tradition, with others. New York,
  Harper, 1930.
Understanding Poetry: An Anthology for College Students, with Cleanth Brooks. New
  York, Holt, 1938; revised edition, 1950, 1960.
Understanding Fiction, with Cleanth Brooks. New York, Crofts, 1943; revised edition,
  Appleton Century Crofts, 1959.
A Poem of Pure Imagination: An Experiment in Reading, in *The Rime of the Ancient
  Mariner*, by Samuel Taylor Coleridge. New York Reynal, 1946.
Modern Rhetoric: With Readings, with Cleanth Brooks. New York, Harcourt Brace,
  1949; revised edition, 1958, 1972.
Fundamentals of Good Writing: A Handbook of Modern Rhetoric, with Cleanth
  Brooks. New York, Harcourt Brace, 1950; London, Dobson, 1952; revised edition,
  Dobson,   1956.
Segregation: The Inner Conflict in the South. New York, Random House, 1956; Lon-
  don, Eyre and Spottiswoode, 1957.
Remember the Alamo! New York, Random House, 1958.
Selected Essays. New York, Random House, 1958; London, Eyre and Spottiswoode,
  1964.
The Gods of Mount Olympus (juvenile). New York, Random House, 1959; London,
  Muller, 1962.
How Texas Won Her Freedom. San Jacinto, Texas, San Jacinto Museum of History,
  1959.
The Legacy of the Civil War: Meditations on the Centennial. New York, Random
  House, 1961.
Who Speaks for the Negro? New York, Random House, 1965.
A Conversation with Robert Penn Warren, edited by Frank Gado. Schenectady, New
  York, The Idol, 1972.
Robert Penn Warren Talking: Interviews 1950-1978, edited by Floyd C. Watkins and
  John T. Hiers. New York, Random House, 1980.
Jefferson Davis Gets His Citizenship Back. Lexington, University of Kentucky Press,
  1980.

Editor, with Cleanth Brooks and J.T. Purser, *An Approach to Literature: A Collection of
  Prose and Verse with Analyses and Discussions.* Baton Rouge, Louisiana State
  University Press. 1936; revised edition, New York, Crofts, 1939, Appleton Century
  Crofts, 1952.
Editor, *A Southern Harvest: Short Stories by Southern Writers.* Boston, Houghton
  Mifflin, 1937.
Editor, with Cleanth Brooks, *Anthology of Stories from the Southern Review.* Baton
  Rouge, Louisiana State University Press, 1953.
Editor, with Albert Erskine, *Short Story Masterpieces.* New York, Dell, 1954.
Editor, with Albert Erskine, *Six Centuries of Great Poetry.* New York, Dell, 1955.
Editor, with Albert Erskine, *A New Southern Harvest.* New York, Bantam, 1957.
Editor, with Allen Tate, *Selected Poems*, by Denis Devlin. New York, Holt Rinehart,
  1963.
Editor, with Robert Lowell and Peter Taylor, *Randall Jarrell 1914-1965.* New York,
  Farrar Straus, 1967.

Editor, *Faulkner: A Collection of Critical Essays.*   Englewood Cliffs, New Jersey, Prentice Hall, 1967.

Editor, *Selected Poems of Herman Melville.*   New York, Random House, 1971.

Editor, *Selected Poems of John Greenleaf Whittier.*   New York, Random House, 1971.

Editor, with Cleanth Brooks and R.W.B. Lewis, *American Literature: The Makers and the Making.*   New York, St. Martin's Press, 2 vols., 1974.

Editor, *Katherine Anne Porter: A Collection of Critical Essays.*   Englewood Cliffs, New Jersey, Prentice Hall, 1979.

BIBLIOGRAPHY

Mary Nancy Huff, *Robert Penn Warren.*   New York, Lewis, 1968.

Neil Nakadate, *Robert Penn Warren: A Reference Guide.*   Boston, Hall, 1977.

*   *   *

"Pure and Impure Poetry" and "A Poem of Pure Imagination" (a long, "experimental" reading of Coleridge's *Ancient Mariner*) take up nearly half of Robert Penn Warren's *Selected Essays.* The first of these pieces, which appeared in 1943 and has been admired and widely anthologized ever since, is really nothing more than a genial popularization of the argument, borrowed from I.A. Richards, that the best poetry is always "ironic"—the same argument Warren and Brooks had made in their influential anthology-cum-commentary, *Understanding Poetry*, and which Brooks was to develop at greater length in *The Well Wrought Urn.* "Poetry wants to be pure," Warren begins, "but poems do not":

> At least most of them do not want to be too pure. The poems want to give us poetry, which is pure, and the elements of a poem, in so far as it is a good poem, will work together toward that end, but many of the elements, taken in themselves, may actually seem to contradict that end, or to be neutral toward the achieving of that end. Are we then to conclude that neutral or recalcitrant elements are simply an index to human frailty, and that in a perfect world there would be no dross in poems, which would, then, be perfectly pure?

Obviously we are to conclude nothing of the sort. For Warren, Brooks and Richards, pure poems are poems which simplify experience: at best they offer lyric embodiments of a single mood or perception. "The pure poem," Warren goes on, "tries to be pure by excluding, more or less rigidly, certain elements which might qualify or contradict its original impulse." Such poems are of relatively little value, of course, because they falsify the nature of experience itself. For Richards, successful living means the ability to synthesize the maximum number of relevant impulses into "attitudes" for competent response to the world. Richards argues that there are "two ways in which *impulses* may be organized":

> by *exclusion* and by *inclusion*, by *synthesis* and by elimination. Although every coherent state of mind depends upon both, it is permissible to contrast experiences which win stability and order through a narrowing of the response with those which widen it. A very great deal of poetry and art is content with the full, ordered development of comparatively special and limited experiences, with a definite emotion, for example, Sorrow, Joy, Pride, or a definite attitude, Love, Indignation, Admiration, Hope, or with a specific mood, Melancholy, Optimism or Longing. And such art has its own value and place in human affairs. No one will quarrel with "Break, break, break," or with the *Coronach* or with *Rose Aylmer* or with *Love's Philosophy*, although they are limited and *exclusive.* But they are not the greatest kind of poetry; we do not expect from them what we find in the *Ode to a Nightingale*, in *Proud Maisie*, in *Sir Patrick Spens*, in *The Definition of Love* or in the *Nocturnall upon S. Lucie's Day.*

The difference between the two kinds of poetry, Richards continues, are apparent

546

if we consider how comparatively unstable poems of the first kind are. They will not bear an ironical contemplation. We have only to read *The War Song of Dinas Vawr* in close conjunction with the *Coronach*, or to remember that unfortunate phrase "Those lips, O slippery blisses!" from *Endymion*, while reading *Love's Philosophy*, to notice this. Irony in this sense consists in the bringing in of the opposite, the complementary impulses; that is why poetry which is exposed to it is not of the highest order, and why irony itself is so constantly a characteristic of poetry which is.

Thus Warren gives as an example of "pure" (or exclusive) poetry a passage from Shelley in which "distinctions blur out in the 'purity' of the moment"; and as an example of "impure" poetry he offers (in token defiance of Richards) the apparently simple lyric in which Landor tells us that moved by grief as he is, he will consecrate *a* night of "memories and sighs" to Rose Aylmer. Warren advises us to "notice the understatement of '*a* night'":

> [the poet] says: "I know that life is a fairly complicated affair, and that I am committed to it and to its complications. I intend to stand by my commitment, as a man of integrity, that is, to live despite the grief. Since life is complicated, I cannot, if I am to live, spare too much time for indulging grief. I can give *a* night, but not all nights." The lover, like the hero of Frost's poem "Stopping by Woods on a Snowy Evening," tears himself from the temptation of staring into the treacherous, delicious blackness, for he, too, has "promises to keep." Or he resembles the Homeric heroes who, after they have beached their craft and eaten their meal, can then set aside an hour before sleep to mourn the comrades lost by the way—the heroes who, as Aldous Huxley says, understand realistically a whole truth as contrasted with a half-truth.

In other words, "impure" poetry is *mature* poetry: it expresses the complex balance of attitudes necessary for life itself, "outside" the poem. Although Richards is never mentioned in this essay, his influence is everywhere: a good poem, Warren concludes, is "a motion toward a point of rest, but if it is not a resisted motion, it is a motion of no consequence." This "point of rest" is simply Richards' "poise" or "equilibrium": the principle or source of resistance is "irony," the bringing to bear of precisely those opposing elements which perfect any attitude toward the world. Warren's essay is too casual to warrant further discussion, but for a thorough-going attack on Brooks and the principle of irony, readers should consult R.S. Crane's "The Critical Monism of Cleanth Brooks" (now reprinted in *Critics and Criticism: Ancient and Modern*).

In "A Poem of Pure Imagination" Warren attempts to defend the *Ancient Mariner* against charges that it is a meaningless dream, or worse, a meaningless dream with a moral awkwardly attached. It is, rather, precisely what Coleridge said it is, a poem of "pure imagination"; but if we are to understand what that means, we must turn to Coleridge's conception of the imagination as both aesthetic *and* moral activity. What Warren has to do, then, is to place the poem in the context of "Coleridge's basic theological and philosophical views." When we do so we see that the poem is "symbolic" in Coleridge's special sense of that term. In Warren's summary, for Coleridge,

> there is a God, and the creativity of the human mind, both in terms of the primary and in terms of the secondary imagination, is an analogue of Divine creation and a proof that man is created in God's image. Furthermore, the world of Nature is to be read by the mind as a symbol of Divinity, a symbol characterized by the "translucence of the eternal through and in the temporal," which "always partakes of the reality which renders it intelligible; and while it enunciates the whole, abides itself as a living part in that unity of which it is representative."

A true symbol, then as opposed to decorative similes or two-dimensional allegory, is "focal, massive and not arbitrary." Interpreted in this light, the *Ancient Mariner* becomes a poem about sin and regeneration: the Mariner's act represents man's "Original Sin," that "mystery of the corruption of the will, the mystery which is the beginning of the 'moral history of Man.' " The Mariner violates the "sacramental conception of the universe," but in the end comes to affirm it, so that "his will is released from its state of 'utmost abstraction' and gains the state of 'immanence' in wisdom and love." And finally, Warren concludes that "*in the poetic act as such...the moral concern and the aesthetic concern are aspects of the same activity, the creative activity, and...this activity is expressive of the whole mind... The Ancient Mariner* is, first, written out of this general belief, and second, written *about* this general belief." Warren's argument may seem plausible at first, but anyone familiar with recent Coleridge scholarship (particularly the work of Norman Fruman) will know how difficult it is to know with any certainty what Coleridge "meant." And as for Warren's reasoning, "A Poem of Pure Imagination" soon became the object of a devastating attack by Elder Olson, who concludes, correctly in this writer's opinion, that Warren makes his way "amid generous assumptions, undistributed middles, inconsistencies, misinterpretations, ignoraciones elenchi, post hoc propter hocs" and so on.

As Warren himself seems to recognize, the two Jefferson Lectures which in their expanded form make up *Democracy and Poetry* are difficult to classify:

> Certainly what I have written here may better be taken as "meditation" than "essays." Whatever they may be called, they do represent, in some degree, an utterance of a rather personal sort, a personal exploration, if you will. For all of my adult years, my central and obsessive concern has been with "poetry," and I scarcely find it strange that I should seek some connection between that concern and the "real" world.

For Warren, poetry, or imaginative literature in general, has both a "diagnostic" and a "therapeutic" role to play in modern life. Democracy, he maintains, is that program which envisions the full development of individual selves; but it also rests upon the principle that "the true self...can develop only in a vital relation between the unitary person and the group." Since the ideal of a democratic community is now being threatened by a number of forces it is the special function of our poets and novelists to remind us of what we are in danger of losing:

> They have faced, sometimes unconsciously, the tragic ambiguity of the fact that the spirit of the nation we had promised to create has often been the victim of our astonishing objective success, and that, in our success, we have put at pawn the very essence of the nation we had promised to create—that essence being the concept of the free man, the responsible self... [Our] poetry, in fulfilling its function of bringing us face to face with our nature and our fate, has told us, directly or indirectly, consciously or unconsciously, that we are driving toward the destruction of the very assumption on which our nation is presumably founded.

In this sense, then, poetry offers us a warning; and it is therapeutic in the sense that "the activity of making" involves, for Warren, "a dynamic affirmation of, as well as the image of, the self":

> "*Resistance to the organized mass*," Jung asserts (italics his), "*can be effective only by the man who is as well organized in his individuality as the mass itself*." And we may argue that the "made thing"—the poem, the work of art—stands as a "model" of the organized self.... The "made thing," the "formed thing," stands as a perennial possibility of experience, available whenever we turn to it; and insofar as we again, in any deep sense, open the imagination to it, it provides the freshness and immediacy of experience that returns us to ourselves and, as Nietzsche puts it, provides us with that "vision," that "enchantment," which is, for man, the "completion of his state" and an affirmation of his sense of life.

And because it demands the active participation of the reader, poetry "stirs the deepest recesses where life-will and values reside."

Warren obviously means what he says here, but *Democracy and Poetry* is a glib manifesto rather than an argument to be taken seriously. For a much more thoughtful analysis of many of the same problems, readers should turn to Lionel Trilling's *Sincerity and Authenticity*—a work which had appeared two years earlier and to which Warren makes a single, slighting reference, calling attention to one of Trilling's intellectual debts. But here as elsewhere it is Warren's own originality as a critic which might be questioned.

WATT, Ian (Pierre).   British.   Born in Windermere, Westmorland, 9 March 1917. Educated at St. John's College, Cambridge, B.A. 1938, M.A. 1946; Commonwealth Fellow, University of California at Los Angeles, and Harvard University, Cambridge, Massachusetts, 1946-48. Served in the British Army, 1939-46. Married Ruth Mellinkoff in 1947; has 2 children. Fellow, St. John's College, Cambridge, 1948-52; Assistant Professor, 1952-55, Associate Professor, 1955-58, and Professor of English, 1958-62, University of California, Berkeley; Dean, School of English Studies, University of East Anglia, Norwich, 1962-64. Since 1964, Professor of English, and since 1971, Eli Jackson Reynolds Professor of Humanities, Stanford University, California. Visiting Professor, University of Hawaii, Honolulu, 1967-68, Williams College, Williamstown, Massachusetts, 1970, and University of Paris and University of Nice, 1975-76; Alexander Lecturer, University of Toronto, 1974. Recipient: Guggenheim Fellowhship, 1959, 1972; Center for Advanced Studies in the Behavioral Sciences Fellowship, Stanford, California, 1966, 1976; American Council of Learned Societies Fellowship, 1966; National Endowment for the Humanities Fellowship, 1976. Fellow, American Academy of Arts and Sciences. Address: Department of English, Stanford University, Stanford, California 94305, U.S.A.

PUBLICATIONS

Criticism

> *The Rise of the Novel: Studies in Defoe, Richardson and Fielding.*   London, Chatto and Windus, and Berkeley, University of California Press, 1957.
> "The First Paragraph of *The Ambassadors*: an Explication," in *Essays in Criticism* (Oxford), 10, 1960.
> "The Recent Critical Fortunes of *Moll Flanders*," in *Eighteenth-Century Studies* (Davis, California), 1, 1967.
> "The Comic Syntax of *Tristram Shandy*," in *Studies in Criticism and Aesthetics, 1660-1800: Essays in Honor of Samuel Monk*, edited by Howard Anderson and John S. Shea.   Minneapolis, University of Minnesota Press, 1967.
> "Conrad, James, and Chance," in *Imagined Worlds: Essays in Some English Novels and Novelists in Honour of John Butt*, edited by Maynard Mack and Ian Gregor.   London, Methuen, 1968.
> "Serious Reflections on *The Rise of the Novel*," in *Novel* (Providence, Rhode Island), 1, 1968.
> "Two Historical Aspects of the Augustan Tradition," in *Studies in the Eighteenth Century: Papers Presented as the David Nicol Smith Memorial Seminar, 1966*, edited by R.F. Brissenden.   Canberra, Australian National University Press, 1968.
> "The Consequences of Literacy," with Jack Goody, in *Literature and Traditional Societies*, edited by Jack Goody.   London, Cambridge University Press, 1968.
> "The Ironic Tradition in Augustan Prose from Swift to Johnson," in *Stuart and Georgian Moments*, edited by Earl Miner.   Berkeley, University of California Press, 1972.
> *Conrad in the Nineteenth Century.*   Berkeley, University of California Press, 1979; London, Chatto and Windus, 1980.

Other

> Editor, *The Life and Opinions of Tristram Shandy, Gentleman*, by Sterne.   Boston, Houghton Mifflin, 1965.
> Editor, *Jane Austen: A Collection of Critical Essays.*   Englewood Cliffs, New Jersey, Prentice Hall, 1962.
> Editor, *The Victorian Novel: Essays in Criticism.*   New York, Oxford University Press, 1971.
> Editor, *Conrad's The Secret Agent.*   London, Macmillan, 1973.

*   *   *

The sophisticated historical explanation which Ian Watt gives for the "rise of the novel" in the early eighteenth century should not obscure the fact that he also has in mind a very definite critical notion of what a novel *ought* to be, not merely what it has been in the past. Since the novel is above all a "realistic" genre ("realism" is the "defining characteristic which differentiates the work of the early eighteenth-century novelists from previous fiction"), the successful novelist must provide "presentational realism," as Defoe does:

> At his best he convinces us completely that his narrative is occurring at a particular place and at a particular time, and our memory of his novels consists largely of these vividly realised moments in the lives of his characters, moments which are loosely strung together to form a convincing biographical perspective. We have a sense of personal identity subsisting through duration and yet being changed by the flow of experience.

At the same time the true novelist must also provide, as Defoe does not, an organic whole and exercise the kind of moral authority and control which Watt calls "realism of assessment." If the novel was to achieve "equality of status with other genres," he argues, "it had to be brought into contact with the whole tradition of civilised values." And finally, the novelist must give us these two kinds of realism without personally intruding into his fiction (as Fielding does) and avoid the risk of "diminishing the authenticity of his narrative." The novelist should dramatize or "render" his material. Watt does not announce these standards formally in *The Rise of the Novel*, but taken together and given due emphasis they reveal an "evolutionary" history of the novel and place him, as a critic, much closer to Henry James, F.R. Leavis and Wayne Booth than many of his readers seem to have noticed.

How are we to account for the rise of the novel? Assuming it was not an accident that Defoe, Richardson and Fielding appeared within a single generation, Watt begins, we have to seek an explanation in the "favourable conditions" of the time. Obviously there had to be a receptive, literate audience, a matter which Watt takes up in his second chapter; but what interests him much more is the emergence—and triumph—of "philosophical realism" which rejected the belief in fixed universals and unexamined deductive reasoning. The temper of such realism, Watt maintains, has always been

> critical, anti-traditional and innovating; its method has been the study of the particulars of experience by the individual investigator, who, ideally at least, is free from the body of past assumptions and traditional beliefs; and it has given a peculiar importance to semantics, to the problem of the nature of the correspondence between words and reality. All of these features of philosophical realism have analogies to the characteristic kind of correspondence between life and literature which has obtained in prose fiction since Defoe and Richardson.

The issue of these "analogies" is crucial to Watt's argument:

> just as there is a basic congruity between the non-realistic nature of the literary forms of the Greeks, their intensely social, or civic, moral outlook, and their philosophical preference for the universal, so the modern novel is closely allied on the one hand to the realist epistemology of the modern period, and on the other to the individualism of its social structure.

For Watt, however, these analogies do not "depend in any way on the presumption that the realistic tradition in philosophy was a cause of the realism of the novel":

> That there was some influence is very likely , especially through Locke, whose thought everywhere pervades the eighteenth-century climate of opinion. But if a causal relationship of any importance exists, it is probably much less direct: both the philosophical and literary innovations must be seen as parallel manifestations of a larger change—that vast transformation of Western civilisation since the Renaissance which has replaced the unified world picture of the Middle Ages with a very different one—one which presents

us, essentially, with a developing but unplanned aggregate of particular individuals having particular experiences at particular times and at particular places.

Defoe was eminently successful in giving his reader "presentational realism" of this sort; what he does not provide is a coherent whole which has been morally evaluated:

> Formal realism is only a mode of presentation, and it is therefore ethically neutral: all of Defoe's novels are ethically neutral because they make formal realism an end rather than a means, subordinating any ulterior significance to the illusion that the text presents the authentic lucubrations of an historical person. But the individual case-book is an arid study except in the hands of a skilled interrogator who can elicit the things we want to know, which are often the very things the person concerned does not know or is unwilling to admit: the problem of the novel was to discover and reveal those deeper meanings without any breach of formal realism.

Richardson gave his readers novels which have "intrinsic coherence" and offers startling glimpses into the inner lives of his individual characters; but in doing so, Watt argues, he gave the novel a "subjective direction" which has proved to be a dangerous legacy for later popular fiction:

> His attention was so largely focussed on developing a more elaborate representational technique than fiction had ever seen before that it was easy to overlook the content to which it was being applied—to forget that his narrative skill was actually being used to re-create the pseudo-realism of the daydream, to give an air of authenticity to a triumph against all obstacles and contrary to every expectation, a triumph which was in the last analysis as improbable as any in a romance.... [Such fiction] is fundamentally an unreal flattery of the reader's dreams.... For this reason, the popular novel is obviously liable to severe moral censure where the fairy story or romance is not: it pretends to be something else, and, mainly owing to the new power which accrued to formal realism as a result of the subjective direction which Richardson gave it, it confuses the differences between reality and dream more insidiously than any previous fiction.

It was Fielding, a few years later, who corrected this "subjective" tendency by returning to a classical concern for types rather than individuals:

> Fielding does not make any attempt to individualise his characters. Allworthy is sufficiently categorised by his name, while that of Tom Jones, compounded as it is out of two of the commonest names in the language, tells us that we must regard him as the representative of manhood in general, in accordance with his creator's purpose to show "not men, but manners; not an individual, but a species".... [If] as Johnson said, Fielding gives us the husk, it is because the surface alone is usually quite sufficient to identify the specimen—the expert does not need to assay the kernel.

Thus Fielding speaks on behalf of "civilised values" and helped the novel to achieve "equality of status with other genres":

> Fielding brought to the genre something that is ultimately even more important than narrative technique—a responsible wisdom about human affairs which plays upon the deeds and the characters of his novels.... [Fielding's] work serves as a perpetual reminder that if the new genre was to challenge the older forms it had to find a way of conveying not only a convincing impression but a wise assessment of life.

The problem is that Fielding achieves realism of assessment at the expense of presentational realism by intruding in his fictions as an authorial "voice". The effect is to "break the spell of the imaginary world represented in the novel":

> the main interference with the autonomy of this world comes from Fielding's introductory chapters, containing literary and moral essays, and even more from his frequent

discussions and asides to the reader within the narrative itself.... [His] interventions obviously interfere with any sense of narrative illusion, and break with almost every narrative precedent, beginning with that set by Homer.

It is only in the very brief last chapter of *The Rise of the Novel* that Watt's evolutionary view of fiction becomes quite apparent. His argument here, in fact, is not different in kind from the argument of the *Poetics*: just as Aristotle maintained that tragedy reached its full and proper form in Sophocles' *Oedipus the King*—a form which the experiments of earlier dramatists made possible—so Watt maintains that the novel reached its full and proper form, thanks to the efforts of Defoe, Richardson and Fielding, in Jane Austen:

> [Her] novels, in short, must be seen as the most successful solutions of the two narrative problems for which Richardson and Fielding had provided only partial answers. She was able to combine into a harmonious unity the advantages of both realism of presentation and realism of assessment, of the internal and of the external approaches to character; her novels have authenticity without diffuseness or trickery, wisdom of social comment without a garrulous essayist, and a sense of the social order which is not achieved at the expense of the individuality and autonomy of the characters.

The Rise of the Novel deserves the high reputation it has earned over the years but also poses some interesting questions, two of which are worth raising here. "Presentational realism" is a useful term, but a misleading one if taken too literally. That is, "realism" is never as "ethically neutral" as Watt assumes it to be: the selection of what matters to portray realistically and the omission of other matters are the deliberate acts, and usually judgmental acts, of what Wayne Booth calls "the implied author". (To be fair about this, Watt seems aware of the problem in an amiable 1968 essay, "Serious Reflections on *The Rise of the Novel*," where he concedes that there is a "continual interplay of presentation and assessment—explicit or tacit—in the larger compositional elements of all narrative." "Interplay," however, is not precise enough, since it seems to suggest that when it does appear, presentational realism is still somehow relatively "neutral.") Finally, if Watt remains committed to the view of fiction he presents in *The Rise of the Novel*, it is worth wondering what he might have to say about those modern (or "post-modern") novels which reject presentational realism and replace realism of assessment with ambiguity or mocking authorial silence. Watt has not discussed these matters, but on the available evidence it is hard not to conclude he would be as troubled as Wayne Booth has been by unreliable narrators, unstable ironies and deliberately fractured surfaces which force us to realize we are dealing with artifices, not with cunning illusions of life itself.

Twenty-five years after *The Rise of the Novel*, Watt published the first volume of a massive two volume study of Joseph Conrad. *Conrad in the Nineteenth Century* deals with the young Conrad's complex relationship to his Polish heritage, and with *Almayer's Folly*, *The Nigger of the "Narcissus,"* *Heart of Darkness* and *Lord Jim*; the second volume, Watt informs us, will take up "the short stories, the autobiographical writings, the last years, and seven of the novels: *Typhoon*, *Nostromo*, *The Secret Agent*, *Under Western Eyes*, *Chance*, *Victory*, and *The Shadow-Line*." Together the volumes are intended to provide "a comprehensive account of Conrad's literary career [in its] three main aspects: biographical, historical, and interpretative." The emphasis of the first volume is clearly "interpretative," once Watt has given his expert account of Conrad's formative years in Poland and the lasting effects they had on his fiction:

> Doomed resistance and heroic defeat constitute the sadly recurrent burden of Poland's history. The last two hundred years have done little but enact betrayal by foreign allies or through internal division; and this habituation has engendered a corresponding admiration for individual loyalty and group cohesion. These themes dominate Conrad's fiction; fidelity is the supreme value in Conrad's ethic, but it is always menaced and often defeated or betrayed. Conrad once insisted to Edward Garnett that he must be understood not as a Slav, but as a Pole, and specifically as a member of a nation which, for the last hundred years, had "been used to go to battle without illusions."

Watt provides the most extensive and sensible accounts of Conrad's fiction through 1900 that we have or are ever likely to have, but his aim is not merely to provide exhaustive accounts of these works, their origins in Conrad's personal experience, and their technical innovations. He is particularly concerned to demonstrate that Conrad is both a modern writer and a writer "whose basic intellectual assumptions were very similar to those of the most original and influential thinkers of the last decade of the nineteenth century" (Watt has in mind Carlyle, Spencer, Huxley, and above all, Nietzsche). He argues that Joyce, Lawrence, Pound and Eliot, like Conrad, see the world as a "panorama of chaos and futility, of cruelty, folly, vulgarity, and waste." But whereas these other writers invite us to "share the larger transcendental or private systems of order and value they have adopted or invented," Conrad was less convinced that such refuges were possible. In that sense he was more "contemporary" than they were; and yet at the same time he was also more "old-fashioned" because his "movement towards the ageless solidarities of human experience was much commoner among the Romantics and Victorians." Nevertheless, the Conrad who emerges from this masterful study is a despairing figure. The way in which Conrad did or not move beyond despair will presumably be the substantial issue of the second volume.

WELLEK, René. American. Born in Vienna, Austria, 22 August 1903; naturalized United States citizen, 1946. Educated at Charles University, Prague, Ph.D. 1926; Princeton University, New Jersey (Proctor Fellow), 1927-28. Married Olga Brodska in 1932 (died, 1967), one child; Nonna Shaw, 1968. Instructor in German, Smith College, Northampton, Massachusetts, 1928-29, and Princeton University, 1929-30; Privatdocent, Charles University, 1930-35; Lecturer in Czech, School of Slavonic Studies, University of London, 1935-39; Member of the Faculty, University of Iowa, Iowa City, 1939-41; Associate Professor, 1941-44, Professor of English, 1944-46, Professor of Slavic and Comparative Literature, 1946-72, Director of Graduate Studies, 1947-59, Fellow of Silliman College and Sterling Professor of Comparative Literature, 1950-72, Chairman of the Slavic Department, 1960-72, now Professor Emeritus, Yale University, New Haven, Connecticut. Visiting Professor, University of Minnesota, Minneapolis, 1947, Columbia University, New York, 1948, and Harvard University, Cambridge, Massachusetts, 1950, 1953-54; Lecturer in Criticism, 1950, and Visiting Professor of Comparative Literature, 1973, Princeton University; Visiting Professor, University of Hawaii, Honolulu, 1961, and University of California, Berkeley, 1963; Fulbright Professor, Florence and Rome universities, 1959-60, and Mainz University, 1969; Visiting Patten Professor of Comparative Literature, Indiana University, Bloomington, 1974. Associate Editor, *Philological Quarterly*, 1941-46; Member of the Editorial Board, *Comparative Literature*, *Slavic Review*, and *Studies in English Literature*. Fellow, Huntington Library, San Marino, California, 1942, and Kenyon School of English, Gambier, Ohio, later Indiana School of Letters, Bloomington, 1949-72. Member of the Editorial Board, 1946-50, 1953-59, and of the Executive Council, 1959, and Vice-President, 1964, Modern Language Association; President, International Association for Comparative Literature, 1961-64, American Association for Comparative Literature, 1962-65, Czechoslovak Society of Arts and Sciences in America, 1962-66, and Modern Humanities Research Association, 1974. Recipient: Guggenheim Fellowship, 1951, 1956, 1966; American Council of Learned Societies Prize for Distinguished Service to the Humanities, 1959; Bollingen Award, 1963; National Endowment for the Humanities Fellowship, 1972; Marjorie Peabody Waite Award, 1976, M.A.: Yale University, 1946; L.H.D.: Lawrence College, Appleton, Wisconsin, 1958; Litt.D.: Oxford University, 1960; Harvard University, 1960; University of Rome, 1961; University of Maryland, College Park, 1964; Boston College, 1966; Columbia University, 1968; University of Montreal, 1970; University of Louvain, 1970; University of Michigan, Ann Arbor, 1971; University of Munich, 1972; University of East Anglia, Norwich, 1975. Member of the American Academy of Arts and Sciences, Bavarian Academy, Royal Netherlands Academy of Sciences, and Italian National Academy. Address: Department of Comparative Literature, Yale University, New Haven, Connecticut 06520, U.S.A.

Publications

Criticism

"Literary Criticism and Philosophy," in *Scrutiny* (Cambridge), 6, 1937; reprinted in *The Importance of Scrutiny*, New York, Stewart, 1948.

Theory of Literature, with Austin Warren.   New York, Harcourt Brace, and London, Cape, 1949.

"The Criticism of T.S. Eliot," in *Sewanee Review* (Tennessee), 64, 1956.

The Concept of Realism in Literary Scholarship.   Groningen, J.B. Wolters, 1961.

Essays on Czech Literature.   The Hague, Mouton, 1963 (contains a bibliography of Wellek's writings in Czech through 1963).

Concepts of Criticism, edited by Stephen G. Nichols, Jr.   New Haven, Connecticut, and London, Yale University Press, 1963 (contains a bibliography of Wellek's writings in English through 1963).

Confrontations: Studies in the Intellectual and Literary Relations Between Germany, England, and the United States During the Nineteenth Century.   Princeton, New Jersey, Princeton University Press, 1965.

"On Rereading I.A. Richards," in *Southern Review* (Baton Rouge, Louisiana), 2, 1967.

Discriminations: Further Concepts of Criticism.   New Haven, Connecticut, and London, Yale University Press, 1970 (contains a bibliography of Wellek's writings through 1969).

"Kenneth Burke and Literary Criticism," in *Sewanee Review* (Tennessee), 79, 1971.

"R.P. Blackmur Re-Examined," in *Southern Review* (Baton Rouge, Louisiana), 7, 1971.

"John Crowe Ransom's Theory of Poetry," in *Literary Theory and Structure: Essays in Honor of William K. Wimsatt*, edited by Frank Brady, John Palmer, and Martin Price.   New Haven, Connecticut, and London, Yale University Press, 1973.

"Cleanth Brooks, Critic of Critics," in *Southern Review* (Baton Rouge, Louisiana), 10, 1974.

"Yvor Winters Rehearsed and Reconsidered," in *Denver Quarterly*, 10, 1975.

"The Literary Theory of William K. Wimsatt," in *Yale Quarterly Review* (New Haven, Connecticut), 66, 1976.

"Virginia Woolf as Critic," in *Southern Review* (Baton Rouge, Louisiana), 13, 1977.

"What Is Literature?" in *What Is Literature?* edited by Paul Hernadi.   Bloomington and London, Indiana University Press, 1978.

"The New Criticism: Pro and Contra," in *Critical Inquiry* (Chicago), 4, 1978.

"Literary History and Literary Criticism" and "Edmund Wilson (1895-1972)," in *History as a Tool in Critical Interpretation*, edited by Thomas F. Rugh and Erin R. Silva.   Provo, Utah, Brigham Young University Press, 1978.

"A Rejoinder to Gerald Graff," in *Critical Inquiry* (Chicago), 5, 1979.

"An End to Criticism,' in *Georgia Review* (Athens), 34, 1980.

"Prospect and Retrospect," in *Yale Review* (New Haven, Connecticut), 49, 1980.

"The Later Leavis," in *Southern Review* (Baton Rouge, Louisiana), 17, 1981.

Four Critics: Croce, Valéry, Lukács and Ingarden.   Seattle, University of Washington Press, 1981.

Other

Immanuel Kant in England 1793-1838.   Princeton, New Jersey, Princeton University Press, 1931.

The Rise of English Literary History.   Chapel Hill, University of North Carolina Press, 1941.

A History of Modern Criticism 1750-1950:
1. *The Later Eighteenth Century.* New Haven, Connecticut, Yale University Press, and London, Cape, 1955.
2. *The Romantic Age.* New Haven, Connecticut, Yale University Press, and London, Cape, 1955.
3. *The Age of Transition.* New Haven, Connecticut, Yale University Press, 1965; London, Cape, 1966.
4. *The Later Nineteenth Century.* New Haven, Connecticut, Yale University Press, 1965; London, Cape, 1966.

Editor, *Dostoyevsky: A Collection of Critical Essays.* Englewood Cliffs, New Jersey, Prentice Hall, 1962.
Editor, *The Meaning of Czech History*, by Thomáš G. Masaryk, translated by Peter Kussi. Chapel Hill, University of North Carolina Press, 1974.
Editor, with Alvaro Ribeiro, *Evidence in Literary Scholarship*: *Essays in Memory of James Marshall Osborne.* Oxford, Clarendon Press, 1979.

Translator, with Lowry Nelson, *Franz Kafka and Prague*, by Pavel Eisner. New York, Arts, 1950.

*   *   *

Theory of Literature is a difficult book, more difficult than it needed to be, perhaps, because of René Wellek's indirect handling of the "intrinsic" nature of literature, as he understands it, and his elliptical treatment of the relationship between the "subjective" and "objective" elements involved in the act of evaluation. (In these remarks I have assumed that Wellek was the moving force behind the *Theory*: he is responsible for thirteen of the nineteen chapters here and also, it appears, for the heavy debts to Kant, Roman Ingarden, and Jan Mukařovský. Nevertheless, in their preface, Wellek and Austin Warren state that the book is "a real instance of a collaboration in which the author is the shared agreement between two writers.")

The study of literature, Wellek maintains, should be "specifically literary"—a proposition which may have seemed more revolutionary in 1949 than it does now. Thus his program in the *Theory* is a double one: he attempts to discredit extrinsic studies and to develop an intrinsic approach which will do justice to the individuality of the work of literature and at the same time permit comparative judgments and serve as the basis for a genuinely "literary" history of literature. By "extrinsic," Wellek means simply those "widespread and flourishing methods of studying literature [which] concern themselves with its setting, its environment, its internal causes." These approaches—the approaches, that is, of the literary biographers, psychologists, sociologists, and philosophers—are "causal" in the sense of reducing the work to its origins, its effects, or its paraphrasable "content." But it is clear, Wellek objects, that "causal study can never dispose of the problems of description, analysis, and evaluation of an object such as a literary work of art. Cause and effect are incommensurate: the concrete result of these extrinsic causes—the work of art—is always unpredictable." Wellek's treatment of these reductive modes of criticism is convincing enough, but he is not above setting up straw men to argue against: very few biographers, psychologists, or social critics have ever maintained that the work was *nothing but* an act of self-expression, a stimulus for audience response, a conditioned part of the social superstructure, or whatever.

Wellek's development of a properly "intrinsic" method is harder to trace, partly because of the way he has organized the *Theory*. He devotes roughly one third of the book to his criticism of extrinsic approaches, but in each of these chapters he also isolates an element of truth which will eventually become part of the correct definition of the nature and function of literature. Readers must piece together this definition as they go along: in Chapter Two, for example, we learn that a literary work is a "highly complex organization of a stratified character with multiple meanings and relationships"; but it is not until Chapter Twelve that we learn the meaning of the key term, "stratification." In this same chapter we also learn that a work of literature is a "potential cause of experiences"; but it is not until Chapter Eighteen that we have a vital (though largely unexplained) qualification: the work of art is not only a potential cause of a certain kind of experience in the reader, but also a "specific, highly organized control of the reader's experience." In itself, Wellek asserts (again in Chapter Twelve), a work of art

> appears as an object of knowledge *sui generis* which has a special ontological status. It is neither real (like a statue) nor mental (like the experience of light or pain) nor ideal (like a triangle). It is a system of norms of ideal concepts which are intersubjective. They must be assumed to exist in collective ideology, changing with it, accessible only through individual mental experiences, based on the sound-structure of its sentences.

Although undefined here, a "system of norms" seems to mean something close to the Aristotelian conception of the "moral" basis of audience response: that is, the artist constructs a whole which will move us in a certain determinate way; our response depends on a prior judgment of worth—we cannot, for example, feel pity for a character we have been led to detest—and judgments of worth obviously presuppose some general, shared, or sharable ("intersubjective") code of values. As for the stratification of these complex wholes,

> Roman Ingarden, in an ingenious, highly technical analysis of the literary work of art, has employed the methods of Husserl's "Phenomenology" to arrive at such distinctions of strata. We need not follow him in every detail to see that his general distinctions are sound and useful: there is, first, the sound-stratum which is not, of course, to be confused with the actual sounding of the words.... [This] pattern is indispensable, as only on the basis of sounds can the second stratum arise: the units of meaning. Every single word will have its meaning, will combine into units in the context, into syntagmas and sentence patterns. Out of this syntactic structure arises a third stratum, that of the objects represented, the "world" of a novelist, the characters, the setting. Ingarden adds two other strata which may not have to be distinguished as separable. The stratum of the "world" is seen from a particular viewpoint, which is not necessarily stated but is implied.... And finally, Ingarden speaks of a stratum of "metaphysical qualities" (the sublime, the tragic, the terrible, the holy) of which art can give us contemplation. This stratum is not indispensable, and may be missing in some works of literature.

(Wellek acknowledges his debt to Ingarden again in "The Literary Theory and Aesthetics of the Prague School," an essay, now reprinted in *Discriminations*, which is indispensable reading for anyone who wants to make full sense of Wellek's criticism. In this same essay he also acknowledges an even more important debt to Jan Mukařovský's theory of literary history. *Theory of Literature*, Wellek goes on, is at least in part "a deliberate attempt to bring together the insights I had acquired as a junior member of the [Prague] Circle with my new knowledge of American criticism.") And finally, as for the function of art, Wellek follows Kant without any qualifications. In Chapter Eighteen of the *Theory* he concludes that "upon the character of the unique aesthetic experience, there is large agreement among philosophers":

> In his *Critique of Judgment*, Kant stresses the "purposiveness without purpose" (the purpose not directed toward action) of art, the aesthetic superiority of "pure" over "adherent" or applied beauty, the disinterestedness of the experiencer (who must not want to own or consume or otherwise turn into sensation or conation what is designed for perception). The aesthetic experience, our contemporary theorists agree, is a perception of a quality intrinsically pleasant and interesting, offering a terminal value and a sample and foretaste of other terminal values. It is connected with feeling...and the senses; but it objectifies and articulates feeling—the feeling finds, in the work of art, an "objective correlative," and it is distanced from sensation and conation by its object's frame of fictionality. The aesthetic object is that which interests me for its own qualities, which I don't endeavor to reform or turn into a part of myself, appropriate, or consume. The aesthetic experience is a form of contemplation, a loving attention to qualities and qualitative structures.

The fact that the reader has to gather these parts together for himself is relatively unimportant. The real problem is that while he can be tediously longwinded and obvious when dealing with his opponents, Wellek is unaccountably abrupt when it comes to his own Kantian principles. There is no discussion whatsoever of the "system of norms" referred to earlier, or of the way in which values inhere in literary works, or of the considerable range of problems involved in Kant's "purposiveness without purpose." Wellek seems to assume that these matters are self-explanatory, or that most of his readers already know a good deal about Kant and the neo-Kantian tradition. But neither assumption is warranted, and most readers will in fact have to turn elsewhere for help—to Wellek's own essay on Kant, for example (also reprinted in *Discriminations*), although even here Wellek is much less helpful than he might have been.

But suppose we agree that a literary work is a stratified, complex whole which arouses the reader's feelings and leads to a "form of contemplation." If the work is also a "system of norms," however, then it is crucial to decide what it is we are evaluating: the skill with which the object has been formed or the values it somehow manifests. Clearly we cannot be concerned with craftsmanship alone; but on the other hand, we know, as Wellek admits, that values change from one historical period to another. Must we limit criticism to judgments concerning the extent to which a work incorporates the values of its time? Wellek is well aware of this problem but provides no real answers. And in the end, he is unhelpfully dogmatic about the value of those works which seem to transcend historical conditioning:

> Does the *Weltanschauung* matter to the aesthetic judgment? The view of life presented in a poem, says Eliot, must be one which the critic can "accept as coherent, mature, and founded on the facts of experience." Eliot's dictum about coherence, maturity, and truth to experience, goes, in its phrasing, beyond any formalism: coherence, to be sure, is an aesthetic criterion as well as a logical; but "maturity" is a psychological criterion, and "truth to experience" an appeal to worlds outside the work of art, a call for the comparison of art and reality. Let us reply to Eliot that the maturity of a work of art is its inclusiveness, its awareness of complexity, its ironies and tensions; and the correspondence between a novel and experience can never be measured by any simple pairing off of terms: what we can legitimately compare is the total world of Dickens, Kafka, Balzac, or Tolstoy with our total experience, that is, our thought and felt "world." And our judgment of this correspondence registers itself in aesthetic terms of vividness, intensity, patterned contrast, width, or depth, static or kinetic.

Or again: "the aesthetic structures" of Chaucer, Spenser, Shakespeare and Milton are "so complex and rich that they can satisfy the sensibility of successive ages" *How*? Every phrase in these assertions raises a host of unanswered questions. It is not that terms such as vividness, complexity, intensity and richness are wrong or inherently suspect—it is simply that Wellek fails to define them with any precision. In short, at a number of crucial points in *Theory of Literature* he is as unspecific as he once accused F.R. Leavis of being (see Wellek's uncompromising "Literary Criticism and Philosophy," now reprinted in *The Importance of Scrutiny*).

For the past twenty-five years or so Wellek has been at work on a massive history of European criticism since 1750. His learning is astonishing—he is perfectly at ease in the critical literature of at least five languages—but what concerns us here is the relationship between criticism, literary criticism, and the history of criticism, as he uses these terms. Criticism is the act of evaluating individual works, but as the remarks above imply, for Wellek genuine criticism depends upon a grasp of the "system of norms" which exists outside the work as well as inside: criticism must be in a basic sense "historical" as well as aesthetic, just as the genuine literary history depends on a grasp of the "stratification" of individual works and genres. As for the history of criticism, it too must be evaluative as well as descriptive. In the important Postscript to volume four of the *History of Modern Criticism*, Wellek concludes that

> A history of criticism...cannot be narrative history in the way that a history of political or personal events can be. It is rather a description, analysis, and judgment of books or, more accurately, theories, doctrines, and opinions expounded in many books.... Sides have to be taken: the interlocutors have to be interrupted, perhaps rudely; questioned in turn; and called to account by the historian.

The basis for Wellek's own judgment of critical systems is of course the Kantian position outlined above. Quickly summarizing the argument of the *Theory of Literature* Wellek continues

> Criticism aims at a theory of literature, at a formulation of criteria, and standards of description, classification, interpretation, and finally judgment. It is thus an intellectual discipline, a branch of knowledge, a rational pursuit. If we want to arrive at a coherent theory of literature, we must do what all other disciplines do: isolate our object, establish our subject matter, distinguish the study of literature from other related pursuits. It seems obvious that the work of literature is the central subject matter of a theory of literature and not the biography or psychology of the author, or the social background, or the affective response of the reader.

As we might expect, Wellek is particularly critical of those systems which tend to "ignore or minimize the automony of art."

To date, Wellek has completed four of the projected five volumes of the *History*, bringing his account of literary theories up to 1900. Recently he has been publishing essays on a number of modern critics, and if anything has become more dogmatic than before (he is particularly contemptuous of Eliot, Auden, Tate, Ransom, and other amateur "poet-critics," as he calls them, who represent a fashionable "anticriticism.") By now it seems clear that Wellek is interested *only* in consistent theories of a quite limited kind; and although he maintains (in the Postscript) that "literary theory can thrive only in contact with works of art which initially at least demand sensitivity, enjoyment, and involvement," the *Theory* and *History* are arid books in which there is no sense of living contact with the works of literature which criticism is usually presumed to serve.

WEST, Paul.   British.   Born in Eckington, Derbyshire, 23 February 1930. Educated at the University of Birmingham, B.A. (1st class honours) 1950; Oxford University, 1950-52; Columbia University, New York, M.A. 1953. Served in the Royal Air Force, 1954-57: Flight Lieutenant. Assistant Professor, then Associate Professor of English, Memorial University of Newfoundland, St. John's, 1957-62. Associate Professor, 1962-68, and since 1968 Professor of English and Comparative Literature, and Senior Fellow, Institute for the Arts and Humanistic Studies, Pennsylvania State University, University Park. Visiting Professor of Comparative Literature, University of Wisconsin, Madison, 1965-66; Pratt Lecturer, Memorial University of Newfoundland, 1970; Crawshaw Professor of Literature, Colgate University, Hamilton, New York, Fall 1972; Virginia Woolf Lecturer, University of Tulsa, Oklahoma, 1974; Melvin Hill Visiting Professor, Hobart and William Smith Colleges, Geneva, New York, Fall 1974. Recipient: Canada Council Senior Fellowship, 1960; Guggenheim Fellowship, 1962; Aga Khan Prize (*Paris Review*), 1974; National Endowment for the Arts grant, 1975; Governor's Award for Excellence in the Arts, Pennsylvania, 1980. Address: 117 Burrowes Building, Pennsylvania State University, University Park, Pennsylvania 16802, U.S.A.

PUBLICATIONS

Criticism

> *The Fossils of Piety: Literary Humanism in Decline.*   New York, Vantage Press, 1959.
> *The Growth of the Novel.*   Toronto, Canadian Broadcasting Corporation, 1959.
> "Malraux's Genteel Humanism," in *Kenyon Review* (Gambier, Ohio), 21, 1959.

"Ortega and the Humanist Illusion," in *Twentieth Century* (London), 166, 1959.

"Symbol and Equivalent: The Poetry of Industrialism," in *Essays in Criticism* (Oxford), 9, 1959.

Byron and the Spoiler's Art.   London, Chatto, and Windus, 1960; New York, St. Martin's Press, 1961.

"'Myth Criticism' as a Humane Discipline," in *Wiseman Review* (London), 490, 1961-62.

The Modern Novel.   London, Hutchinson, 1963; New York, Hillary House, 1965.

"The Nature of Fiction," in *Essays in Criticism* (Oxford), 13, 1963.

"Eloquentia Standing Still: The Novel in Modern Spain," in *Kenyon Review* (Gambier, Ohio), 25, 1963.

"Respecting the Daedal Anonym," in *Journal of General Education* (University Park, Pennsylvania), 16, 1964.

Robert Penn Warren.   Minneapolis, University of Minnesota Press, 1964.

"Thor and Thaw: The Modern Russian Novel," in *Arizona Quarterly* (Tucson), 20, 1964.

"D.H. Lawrence: Mystic Critic, " in *Southern Review* (Baton Rouge, Louisiana), 1, new series, 1965.

The Wine of Absurdity.   University Park, Pennsylvania State University Press, 1966.

"Dylan Thomas: The Position in Calamity," in *Southern Review* (Baton Rouge, Louisiana), 3, new series, 1967.

"Thomas Mann and English Taste," in *Southern Review* (Baton Rouge, Louisiana), 5, new series, 1969.

"The Writer's Situation II," in *New American Review 10.*   New York, New American Library, 1970.

"Adam's Alembic, or Imagination versus mc²," in *New Literary History* (Charlottesville, Virginia), 2, 1970.

"Sheer Fiction: Mind and the Fabulist's Mirage," in *New Literary History* (Charlottesville, Viginia), 7, 1975-76.

"Enigmas of Imagination: Woolf's Orlando Through the Looking Glass," in *Southern Review* (Baton Rouge, Louisiana), 13, 1977.

Verse

The Spellbound Horses.   Toronto, Ryerson Press, 1959.

The Snow Leopard.   London, Hutchinson, 1964; New York, Harcourt Brace, 1965.

Novels

A Quality of Mercy.   London, Chatto and Windus, 1961.

Tenement of Clay.   London, Hutchinson, 1964.

Alley Jaggers.   London, Hutchinson, and New York, Harper, 1966.

I'm Expecting to Live Quite Soon.   New York, Harper, 1970; London, Gollancz, 1971.

Caliban's Filibuster.   New York, Doubleday, 1971.

Bela Lugosi's White Christmas.   London, Gollancz, and New York, Harper, 1972.

Colonel Mint.   New York, Dutton, 1972; London, Calder and Boyars, 1973.

Gala.   New York, Harper, 1976.

The Very Rich Hours of Count von Stauffenberg.   New York, Harper and Row, 1980.

Other

I, Said the Sparrow (autobiography).   London, Hutchinson, 1964.

Words for a Deaf Daughter.   London, Gollancz, 1969; New York, Harper, 1970.

Editor, *Byron*: *A Collection of Critical Essays*.   Englewood Cliffs, New Jersey, Prentice Hall, 1963.

*   *   *

Readers who have not always kept up with Paul West's fiction and criticism over the past fifteen years—and the pace he sets them is a brisk one—may sometimes have wondered about inconsistencies and shifts in judgment. How is it, for example, that he virtually dismisses *Orlando* in *The Modern Novel*, only to praise it enthusiastically in a recent essay on Virginia Woolf? In an important early piece, "The Nature of Fiction," he sounds rather like Wayne Booth, yet his own novels have become increasingly fantastic and "difficult." West himself admits that there have been some important changes. "Looking back," he writes (in *Contemporary Novelists*),

I see myself as a late starter who, between thirty and forty, in a sustained and intensive spell of application, set down half a lifetime's pondering and moved from a restless contentment with criticism and fairly orthodox fiction to an almost Fellini-like point of view.

Despite this admission, however, the changes in West's thinking have usually been more apparent than real. He has never abandoned the naturalism of *The Modern Novel* or *The Wine of Absurdity*, he has always recognized (and regretted) that art cannot wholly transcend or transform everyday experience—but what the imagination *can* do has become a growing source of delight and satisfaction for him. The Fellini-like point of view turns out to be the point of view of *The Clowns*, in which playful illusion is celebrated for what it is, rather than rejected for not being all that there is.

Sensibly enough, West has never proposed a formal definition of fiction: "The novel is whatever the novel does," he remarks in *The Modern Novel*. The most we can say, he suggests, is that like all works of art, the novel is "essentially artificial" and that it expresses (and in some way answers) our "curiosity" about man's inner nature as well as his social relationships and place in nature. Fiction is artificial, he argues (in "The Nature of Fiction"), because it records an individual and therefore partial impression of reality in words and syntactical patterns which are, in the last analysis, arbitrary. Fiction offers us a "deceit," but once we accept its limitations, that deceit may be both pleasing and instructive: a novel is something added to the sum of creation and thus becomes a possible object of pleasure and knowledge (after all, words may denote "universals"); it appeals to our desire for order and at its best gives us a "man-made counter- or substitute-world." The troubles begin only when we mistake the word for the thing, the fictive world for the real one, the artist's vision for an unmediated embodiment of experience. If we make these confusions, certain consequences follow: "disorder, flux and inarticulateness" challenge the rule of "plot, time and clarity"—the clarity, that is, provided by the controlling mind of the artist. Whether or not it was an inevitable result of the value we now place on consciousness in and of itself, many modern novelists have restricted themselves to the direct presentation of a limited mind as it confronts the world. The "reflective intelligence" of the author is minimized; the "semi-comprehending reader" becomes a tentative "explorer" rather than a poised observer; and thus West concludes, rather surprisingly, that the novel is in danger of turning into a form of symbolist poetry:

What has to be restored is the habit of generalizing about experiences which are exhaustively conveyed. And that, eventually, entails a return to form and structure—the emblems of the supervising narrator (the demiurge of fiction) even if he fails to appear in his own person.

It seems unlikely that West was directly indebted to Wayne Booth or Yvor Winters at this point, but his conclusions are not all that different from theirs.

For historical reasons, modern novelists "cannot escape the stream of consciousness," or at least it was impossible for them to do so at the beginning of this century. Before that, West explains (in *The Modern Novel*), "the inchoate had not had a run for its money in either abstract thought or the novel. No wonder the flux flooded over everything." Moreover, it had become more and more difficult to deny the primacy of human consciousness, now that religious supports had been questioned: we had only ourselves to depend upon; and this realization also had its consequences, for to recognize the lonely authority of our perceptions also meant to recognize our vulnerability. William James and Bergson, for example,

> overstress the streamingness of life; "duration" is held in the memory, it is true, but so are clear and abiding axioms. They both undervalue not the efficacy of the analytical intellect but its value as a comforter. Their theories celebrate impotence and passivity; here, perhaps, is the beginning of the unheroic hero who is no more than a full consciousness.

The history of the early modern novel, then, is the history of an excessive immersion in the "flux" of experience; but having exhausted itself in documenting the impressions of anti-heroes, the "cult of the flux" was followed by an equally incomplete "reflux" which "works private and abstract views of man against a view that is primarily social." For West, neither technique is sufficient: what we need, of course, is a synthesis of impression and analysis, however difficult that may be to achieve ("Perhaps only Dostoevsky got the proportions right"). West's penultimate view is "not heartening": the novelist (and the rest of us) live in a world

> divided between totalitarian and gentler societies, the one run by childishly closed-minded overseers, the other by demagogic manufacturers intent on keeping the majority of adults childishly fixated on advertised paraphenalia. For those who are allowed to write about it, and dare to, the bewildering and violent century is there; but one cannot be surprised if the best talents produce increasingly evasive parable-novels in which mid-century man prefers his cosmic and private doom to attrition by society. After the absurd universe the absurd society; and after that the absurdity of writing at all, save for oneself....[When] things get so bad that the medium of words cannot convey them or make them more palatable than they are, then the novelist might well say: "Enough. Let each man meet actuality for himself at first-hand; away with my kind of informative portrayal. I will amuse myself with fantasies, tricks and little noises."

And yet *The Modern Novel* ends in something less than despair. "My own belief," West concludes,

> is that we shall eschew fiction only when human society is too bad to know about or when it is too satisfactory to need art's rearrangements. Against infinity we have only human affinity, whether that is expressed in words or communal charity; and it is on such affinity that the novelist who communicates has to rest his case. He is unlikely, I think, to regard himself as an end in himself as long as most people are communicating in the known language.

There is no reason to doubt that West would agree with Henry James' eloquent profession of faith, "till the world is an unpeopled void, there will be an image in the mirror."

Of course it is possible to disregard the argument of *The Modern Novel* and respond to it as an expert reader's guide—the liveliest we have—to fiction since 1900 (in France, Germany, Italy, Russia and Spain, as well as in England and America); and it is possible to take the essays in *The Wine of Absurdity* on their own independent merits. But to do so is to miss the continuity of West's thinking. *The Wine of Absurdity* is not so much literary criticism as a chapter in West's intellectual autobiography in which he considers "some aspects of twentieth-century literary consolation" and examines the ways in which his authors have dealt with the problem of absurdity, that sense of "life's incomprehensiblity," the "division" (in Camus' words), between "the mind that desires and the world that disappoints." Each of these writers, West continues, "devises or accepts something that mitigates the absurdity of being human; and the wine of absurdity is the imaginative effort entailed, as well as the imaginative end product.... Such wine is a mea..s of accommodating ourselves to what seem immutable facts, and in the long run what orthodox religion and heretical literature have in common is imagination." Yeats and Lawrence "mythologize whatever is at hand in order to create a private religion which, as

561

they seek to demonstrate in sermons of messianic imprudence, bears also on the lives of all men." For Sartre, Camus and Malraux, "action [is] the means of self-definition." Eliot, Graham Greene and Simone Weil (here the argument is less convincing) are "three converts who also act heretically from within the established faith" and whose "deviations have as much to reveal...as have the more obvious ones of the writers already discussed." But it is Santayana, the last writer he discusses in detail, whose position West finds most congenial. Implicitly accepting the conclusions of *Interpretations of Poetry and Religion, The Life of Reason* and *Scepticism and Animal Faith*, he asserts "reason...tells us that we live in a semideterministic world which is also not always to be controlled and that men, when relegated to the condition of their animal needs alone, are just as compelled as beasts." Reason discloses and measures; the imagination, for Santayana and West, is a constructive power which proposes ideals to the reason or embodies traditional values in moving forms; it is

> the only restorative each man has that is entirely his own; it is the most benign form of anarchy and...the inevitable answer to the inevitable absurdity of man's not having created himself....To remain a coherent person entails always an effort of imagination, for imagination is the only means we have of going beyond minimal awareness....Life has no ready-made meaning but we can, if we wish, force meaning upon it or into it. And even the act of declaring life an absurd meander defeats absurdity by trapping it in words and thus humanizing it. Imagination, trite and presumptuous as it may seem to express the fact, is the only source of meaning our life can have.

Finally,

> If we respect man at all, it is for his capacity to live in tension without disintegrating; and Lawrence, Santayana and Camus, none of whom, of course, is perfect, display according to their emphases the strain and demands of being imaginatively heretical. Mix the best of the three and you have the makings of a tolerable humanism....

There is no compelling *logical* reason why these conclusions should support a "tolerable humanism" rather than tragic resignation: it is simply a temperamental fact that for Santayana, with some qualifications, and for West (and Wallace Stevens) with very few qualifications, there is more to admire than to despair of when we contemplate the human drive to resist the void. The ability to invent and imagine freely is finally what West now values most (in "Respecting the Daedal Anonym," for example, he remarks that "if, in the end, I am taken as pleading for [Shakespeare's] sheer vitality, then I shall be content"). Thus in his most recent essays he makes the best possible case for the pure energy of Lawrence and Dylan Thomas, and in his most remarkable piece of criticism to date, for Virginia Woolf's power to imagine how it feels to live in a "radiant" universe of quasars and curved space. "Who would settle for the Man of Property," he asks in "Sheer Fiction" (his own forceful manifesto as a novelist), "when he/she can have the universe?"

> It may be charming to pretend that Man has no cosmic context, or that art is not a product of mind, but it is also fatuous. A mobile collection of some 10^{14} cells, such as each of us is, in a universe whose particles total 10^{80}, has ample warrant for being inquisitive about the oldest subject matter of all.

WILLIAMS, Raymond (Henry). British. Born in Llanfihangel Crocorney, Wales, 31 August 1921. Educated at Abergavenny Grammar School, 1932-39; Trinity College, Cambridge, 1939-41, 1945-46, M.A. 1946, Litt.D. 1969. Served in the Anti-Tank Regiment, Guards Armoured Division, 1941-45: Captain. Married Joy Dalling in 1942; three children. Editor, *Politics and Letters*, 1946-47. Staff Tutor in Literature, Oxford University Delegacy for Extra-Mural Studies, 1946-61. Since 1961, Fellow of Jesus College, Cambridge; Reader, 1967-74, and since 1974 Professor of Drama, Cambridge University. Visiting Professor of Political Science, Stanford University, California, 1973. General Editor, New Thinkers Library, 1962-70. Reviewer for *The Guardian*, London. D. Univ.: Open University, Milton Keynes, Buckinghamshire, 1975; D.Litt.: University of Wales, Cardiff, 1980. Member of the Welsh Academy. Address: Jesus College, Cambridge CB5 8BL, England.

PUBLICATIONS

Criticism

> *Reading and Criticism.* London, Muller, 1950.
> *Drama from Ibsen to Eliot.* London, Chatto and Windus, 1952; New York, Oxford University Press, 1953; revised and expanded as *Drama from Ibsen to Brecht*, Chatto and Windus, 1968; Oxford University Press, 1969.
> *Drama in Performance.* London, Muller, 1954; Chester Springs, Pennsylvania, Dufour, 1961; revised edition, London, Watts, 1968.
> *Culture and Society, 1750-1950.* London, Chatto and Windus, and New York, Columbia University Press, 1958.
> *Modern Tragedy.* London, Chatto and Windus, and Stanford, California, Stanford University Press, 1958.
> *The English Novel from Dickens to Lawrence.* London, Chatto and Windus, 1970.
> *Orwell.* London, Fontana, 1971.
> *The Country and the City.* London, Chatto and Windus, 1973; New York, Oxford University Press, 1974.
> *Keywords: A Vocabulary of Culture and Society.* London, Croom Helm, and New York, Oxford University Press, 1976.
> *Marxism and Literature.* London and New York, Oxford University Press, 1977.

Novels

> *Border Country.* London, Chatto and Windus, 1960; New York, Horizon Press, 1962.
> *Second Generation.* London, Chatto and Windus, 1964; New York, Horizon Press, 1965.
> *The Volunteers.* London, Eyre Methuen, 1978.
> *The Fight for Manod.* London, Chatto and Windus, 1979.

Plays

> *Koba*, in *Modern Tragedy.* London, Chatto and Windus, and Stanford, California, Stanford University Press, 1958.
> *A Letter from the Country* (televised, 1966). Published in *Stand* (Newcastle upon Tyne), 1971.
> *Public Inquiry* (televised, 1967). Published in *Stand* (Newcastle upon Tyne), ix, 1, 1967.

Television Plays: *A Letter from the Country*, 1966; *Public Inquiry*, 1967; *The Country and the City* (documentary, *Where We Live Now* series), 1979.

Other

Preface to Film, with Michael Orrom.   London, Dobson, 1954.
The Long Revolution.   London, Chatto and Windus, and New York, Columbia University Press, 1961.
Communications.   London, Penguin, 1962; revised edition, London, Chatto and Windus, 1966; New York, Barnes and Noble, 1967.
Television: Technology and Cultural Form.   London, Fontana, 1974; New York, Schocken, 1975.
Politics and Letters: Interviews with New Left Review.   London, New Left Books, and New York, Schocken, 1979.
Problems in Materialism and Culture: Selected Essays.   London, New Left Books, 1980; New York, Schocken, 1981.
Culture.   London, Fontana, 1981.

Editor, *May Day Manifesto 1968*.   London, Penguin, 1968.
Editor, *The Pelican Book of English Prose: From 1780 to the Present Day*.   London, Penguin, 1970.
Editor, with Joy Williams, *D.H. Lawrence on Education*.   London, Penguin, 1973.
Editor, *George Orwell: A Collection of Critical Essays*.   Englewood Cliffs, New Jersey, Prentice Hall, 1974.
Editor, with Marie Axton, *English Drama: Forms and Development: Essays in Honour of Muriel Clara Bradbrook*.   London, Cambridge University Press, 1977.

*   *   *

"Literary theory," Raymond Williams observes in *Marxism and Literature*, "cannot be separated from cultural theory, though it may be distinguished within it." This is true enough— even critics who insist on divorcing art from politics are making an indirect political statement—and especially true of Williams himself. The problem confronting the reader coming to his work for the first time, particularly his most recent work, is that of discerning just what his "cultural theory" may be, and how it affects his conception of criticism and judgment. In a 1977 interview (now published in *Politics and Letters*), the editors of the *New Left Review* put the question directly to Williams:

> You argued very sharply [earlier in the interview and in *Keywords*] that the hypostatization of the reader as a judge is very damaging. On the other hand you stress that no one can go on for five minutes without making a judgment. Presumably these judgments are partisan, rather than judgments which are coming down from the chair of a magistrate. Yet in *Keywords* and *Marxism and Literature*, the partisan aspect of what you are saying is largely concealed from the reader.

Williams provides an answer of sorts here, but for a full understanding of what is involved, readers will have to turn not to *Culture and Society* or *The Long Revolution*, written when Williams' cultural theory was still in the process of development, but to his two books on dramatic theory, *Drama from Ibsen to Brecht* and *Modern Tragedy*.

Williams' subject in the first of these influential studies seems unpolitical enough: the development of serious drama during the past hundred years or so, from naturalism and expressionism to the theatre of the absurd and the experiments of Brecht. As a social or public art, the drama obviously has to take into account what the audience of a given period regards as the proper dramatic conventions. This body of attitudes and expectations is what Williams calls the prevailing "structure of feeling," and it soon becomes clear that this is not just a literary term: it refers, finally, to the whole world view of a society at a particular period in history, a view which is often so pervasive that it is held unconsciously and becomes an assumption about the way things "really" are. In short, "structure of feeling" means something quite close to what Marxists usually mean by "ideology". His own term is "difficult," Williams admits,

> but "feeling" is chosen to emphasize a distinction from more formal concepts of "world view" or "ideology." It is not only that we must go beyond formally held and systematic beliefs, though of course we always have to include them. It is that we are concerned with meanings and values as they are actively lived and felt, and the relations between these and formal or systematic beliefs...over a range from formal assent with private dissent to the more nuanced interaction between selected and interpreted beliefs and acted and justified experiences.... We are talking about characteristic elements of impulse, restraint, and tone; specifically affective elements of consciousness and relationships.... We are defining these elements as a "structure"; as a set, with specific internal relations, at once interlocking and in tension.

Serious drama reflects or embodies these structures of feeling—the Greek view, for example, of the relationship between men, the Gods, the Fate—but the point is that as material conditions change (in Marxist terms the social and economic "base"), so the structure of feeling changes as well, and it is the peculiar power of drama to express the often uneasy transition from one structure of feeling to another. Naturalism itself, Williams argues, constitutes "one of the great revolutions in the human consciousness," since it presents men in their everyday life without making any appeal to forces outside that life or determining environment. "The whole point of naturalism," Williams remarked on another occasion, "was its opposition to super-naturalism." Moreover, naturalism at its best is profoundly critical of the way the world is. In Ibsen and Chekov, for example, "the dramatic tension, again and again, is between what men feel themselves capable of becoming, and a thwarting, directly present environment." Naturalism "assumed an understandable, recognizable, manageable everyday world; the form, while linked to this, discovered a humanity which this same world was frustrating or destroying." It seems probable, Williams continues, that in the history of the drama "effective changes took place when there was already a latent willingness to accept them, at least among certain groups in society, from whom the artist drew his support"; and thus the tensions which the great naturalists explored reflected the tensions of society itself and prepared the way for Strindberg and expressionism. Here the scene changes from the world of libraries and drawing rooms to the consciousness of the individuals who are suffering from the limitations of that world. And it is this matter of "suffering" which Williams takes up in *Modern Tragedy* and which leads directly to the very heart of his "cultural theory."

Williams remarked to the *New Left Review* that he had been "appalled" at the academic attitude towards tragedy which he had encountered at Cambridge, and given his controlled and moving indignation in *Modern Tragedy*, that word is neither an exaggeration nor an affectation. In effect, the academic conception of tragedy, which simply enshrines the classical view of tragedy from Aristotle onwards, radically limits the range of human suffering (and its causes) which are considered worthy of dramatic representation. The fall of princes, the whims of the Gods and the decrees of Fate may be dealt with, but not, it seems, "a mining disaster, a burned-out family, a broken career, a smash on the road." Thus dramatic theory and practice blind us to whole areas of human concern and, even worse, make us feel that the causes of such suffering are beyond our control. The "external" causes of human suffering in classical and Renaissance tragedy are clear enough, and in naturalism "the suffering is passive because man can only endure and never really change his world":

> The endurance is given no moral or religious valuation; it is wholly mechanical, because both man and his world, in what is now understood as rational explanation, are the products of an impersonal and material process which though it changes through time has no ends. The impulse to describe and so change a human condition has narrowed to the simple impulse to describe a condition in which there can be no intervention by God or man, the human act of will being tiny and insignificant within the vast material process, universal or social, which at once determines and is indifferent to human destiny.

The crucial point for Williams is his conviction that we have reached a point in history where we can understand that a great deal of human suffering is in fact the quite unnecessary result of a social system which can be changed. "The sufferings of this man appall me," exclaims one of Brecht's characters, "because they are unnecessary." For Williams this response epitomizes the true aim of human history: at present, he continues, the "incorporation" of many men into society as "voters, as employees, or as persons entitled to education, legal protection, social services and so on" does represent a real gain; but in themselves they do not

> amount to that full membership of society which is the end of classes. The reality of full membership is the capacity to direct a particular society, by active mutual responsibility and co-operation, on a basis of full social equality. And while this is the purpose of revolution, it remains necessary in all societies in which there are, for example, subordinate racial groups, landless landworkers, hired hands, the unemployed, and suppressed or discriminate minorities of any kind. Revolution remains necessary, in these circumstances, not only because some men desire it, but because there can be no acceptable human order while the full humanity of any class of men is in practice denied.... This idea of "the total redemption of humanity" has the ultimate cast of resolution and order, but in the real world its perspective is inescapably tragic. It is born in pity and terror: in the perception of a radical disorder in which the humanity of some men is denied and by the fact that the idea of humanity itself is denied. It is born in the actual suffering of real men thus exposed, and in all the consequences of this suffering: degeneration, brutalisation, fear, hatred, envy. It is born in an experience of evil made the more intolerable by the conviction that it is not inevitable, but the result of particular actions and choices.

In this eloquent middle section of *Modern Tragedy* Williams speaks directly about the problem of social revolution and the necessary destruction of capitalism, and states that "in some Western societies we are engaged in the attempt to make total revolution without violence, by a process of argument and consensus." It is impossible, however, to "predict if we shall succeed. The arrest of humanity, in many groups and individuals, is still severe and seems often intractable." Whatever the outcome, the struggle will inevitably be "tragic," that is, full of suffering—but this time suffering for a true purpose.

In the last chapters of *Modern Tragedy* Williams takes up a number of important texts and in effect describes the "structure of feeling" they embody. In case after case the writers he examines are incapable of moving "beyond tragedy": Eliot and Pasternak, for example, end in sacrifice and resignation, while Chekov, Pirandello, Ionesco and Beckett end in "tragic deadlock and stalemate." And for all of their grasp of human suffering, Sartre and Camus remain locked in "tragic despair" and isolated, ineffectual gestures of "revolt." Only Brecht, as Williams interprets him, makes the necessary breakthrough and achieves a "very complex kind of seeing":

> Tragedy in some of its older senses is certainly rejected. There is nothing ennobling about this kind of failure [in *Mother Courage*]. It is a matter of human choice, and the choice is not once for all; it is a matter of continuing history. The major achievement of Brecht's mature work is this recovery of history as a dimension of tragedy. The sense of history becomes active through the discovery of methods of dramatic movement, so that the action is not single in space and time and certainly not "permanent and changeless."

In the 1960's Williams remained uncertain about the necessity of a violent "short revolution" against capitalism as a precondition for the "long revolution" involved in working out the actual structure of a just, classless society. Not surprisingly, the *New Left Review* pressed Williams on this point, and he reluctantly agreed that violence probably will be unavoidable:

> as an East European said to me after reading *The Long Revolution*: "We've had our short revolution, now we begin our long revolution." When I wrote the book I was mainly conscious of the immense length of the full social transformation, which has usually been under-played, yet which should be intrinsic to all strategic socialist thinking. I have no doubt now that the short revolution, to use that phrase, has also to occur.... So to make the theoretical position clear—I now believe, though I have not

always believed, that the condition for the success of the long revolution in any real terms is decisively a short revolution, which I would define not so much in terms of duration as of the loss by the state of its capacity for predominant reproduction of existing social relations.

This brief account of Williams' position make his "cultural theory" clear enough. What then about the issue of critical judgment? In *Keywords* he maintained:

The point would then be, not to find some other term to replace [criticism], while continuing the same kind of activity, but to get rid of the habit, which depends, fundamentally, on the abstraction of response from its real situation and circumstances: the elevation of judgment, and to an apparently general process, when what always needs to be understood is the specificity of the response, which is not a judgment but a practice, in active and complex relations with the situations and conditions of the practice, and, necessarily, with all other practices.

But as the interviewers suggested in 1977, doesn't this imply a kind of relativism? Williams responds that it does not:

The fact is that the abstraction of criticism, its supposed innocence as an activity solely concerned with judgment of our poets, is hypocrisy. You ask me: how can one retain the notion of what we are still calling judgment if we move through to say that no judgment is sufficient unless we know the conditions in which it has been made, the position from which it's been made? Doesn't that do away with judgment altogether, because then the judgment just dissolves into the conditions? I would agree that this is a danger, *but if we also judge the conditions in which the judgment was made, there is a protection against relativism.*

The crucial passage I have emphasized here is problematic, but on the basis of his books on the drama, *The English Novel from Dickens to Lawrence* and *The Country and City* it seems reasonable to conclude that criticism for Williams finally means judging structures of feeling, and judging them, of course, in terms of the meaning and purpose of human history. Williams, finally, is not a "literary critic" in the usual sense at all. "Great literature," he remarks in *The English Novel from Dickens to Lawrence*, "is indeed enriching, liberating and refining, but man is always and everywhere more than a reader, has indeed to be a great deal else before he can become an adequate reader."

WILSON, Edmund. American. Born in Red Bank, New Jersey, 8 May 1895. Educated at Hill School, Pottstown, Pennsylvania, 1909-12; Princeton University, New Jersey, 1912-16, A.B. 1916. Served in the United States Army, in the Intelligence Corps, 1917-19. Married Mary Blair in 1923; Margaret Candy, 1930; Mary McCarthy, *q.v.*, 1938; Elena Thornton, 1946; three children. Reporter, *New York Evening Sun*, 1916-17; Managing Editor, *Vanity Fair*, New York, 1922-23; Associate Editor, 1923-24, and Contributing Editor, 1925-31, *New Republic*, New York; Book Reviewer, *The New Yorker*, 1944-47, and occasionally thereafter. Recipient: Guggenheim Fellowship, 1935; National Institute of Arts and Letters Gold Medal, for non-fiction, 1955; Presidential Medal of Freedom, 1963; Edward MacDowell Medal, 1964;

Emerson-Thoreau Medal, 1966; National Book Committee's National Medal for Literature, 1966; Aspen Award, 1968; Golden Eagle Award, International Book Festival at Nice, 1971. *Died 12 June 1972.*

PUBLICATIONS

Criticism

Axel's Castle: A Study in the Imaginative Literature of 1870-1930. New York and London, Scribner, 1931.
The Triple Thinkers: Ten Essays on Literature. New York, Harcourt Brace, and London, Oxford University Press, 1938; enlarged edition as *The Triple Thinkers: Twelve Essays on Literary Subjects*, New York, Oxford University Press, 1948; London, Lehmann, 1952.
The Boys in the Back Room: Notes on California Novelists. San Francisco, Colt Press, 1941; reprinted in *Classics and Commercials*, 1950.
The Wound and the Bow: Seven Studies in Literature. Boston, Houghton Mifflin, 1941; London, Secker and Warburg, 1942.
Classics and Commercials: A Literary Chronicle of the Forties. New York, Farrar Straus, 1950; London, W.H. Allen, 1951.
The Shores of Light: A Literary Chronicle of the Twenties and Thirties. New York, Farrar Straus, and London, W.H. Allen, 1952.
Patriotic Gore: Studies in the Literature of the American Civil War. New York, Oxford University Press, and London, Deutsch, 1962.
The Bit Between My Teeth: A Literary Chronicle of 1950-1965. New York, Farrar Straus, 1965; London, W.H. Allen, 1966.
A Window on Russia for the Use of Foreign Readers. New York, Farrar Straus, 1972; London, Macmillan, 1973.
The Devils and Canon Barham: Ten Essays on Poets, Novelists, and Monsters. New York, Farrar Straus, and London, Macmillan, 1973.

Verse

The Undertaker's Garland, with John Peale Bishop. New York, Knopf, 1922.
Poets, Farewell! (poems and essays). New York, Scribner, 1929.
Note-Books of Night (poems, essays and stories). San Francisco, Colt Press, 1942; London, Secker and Warburg, 1945.
Three Reliques of Ancient Western Poetry Collected by Edmund Wilson from the Ruins of the Twentieth Century. Boston, Thomas Todd, 1951.
Wilson's Christmas Stocking: Fun for Young and Old. Boston, Thomas Todd, 1953.
A Christmas Delirium. Boston, Thomas Todd, 1955.
Night Thoughts. New York, Farrar Straus, 1961; London, W.H. Allen, 1962.
Holiday Greetings 1966. Boston, Thomas Todd, 1966.

Plays

The Crime in the Whistler Room (produced New York, 1924). Included in *This Room and This Gin and These Sandwiches*, 1937.
Discordant Encounters: Plays and Dialogues. New York, Boni, 1926.

This Room and This Gin and These Sandwiches: Three Plays (includes *The Crime in the Whistler Room, A Winter in Beech Street*, and *Beppo and Beth*).   New York, New Republic, 1937.
The Little Blue Light (produced Cambridge, Massachusetts, 1950; New York, 1951).   New York, Farrar Straus, 1950; London, Gollancz, 1951.
Five Plays: Cyprian's Prayer, The Crime in the Whistler Room, This Room and This Gin and These Sandwiches, Beppo and Beth, The Little Blue Light.   New York, Farrar Straus, and London, W.H. Allen, 1954.
The Duke of Palermo and Other Plays, with an Open Letter to Mike Nichols (includes *Dr. McGrath* and *Osbert's Career; or, The Poet's Progress*).   New York, Farrar Straus, and London, W.H. Allen, 1969.

Novels

I Thought of Daisy.   New York, Scribner, 1929; London, W.H. Allen, 1952; revised edition, with *Galahad*, New York, Farrar Straus, 1967.
Galahad, with I Thought of Daisy.   New York, Farrar Straus, 1967.

Short Stories

Memoirs of Hecate County.   New York, Doubleday, 1946; London, W.H. Allen, 1951.

Other

The American Jitters: A Year of the Slump (essays).   New York, Scribner, 1932; as *Devil Take the Hindmost*, London, Scribner, 1932.
Travels in Two Democracies (dialogues, essays, and story).   New York, Harcourt Brace, 1936.
To the Finland Station: A Study in the Writing and Acting of History.   New York, Harcourt Brace, and London, Secker and Warburg, 1940.
Europe Without Baedeker: Sketches among the Ruins of Italy, Greece, and England.   New York, Doubleday, 1947; London, Secker and Warburg, 1948; revised edition, as *Europe Without Baedeker: Sketches among the Ruins of Italy, Greece, and England, Together with Notes from a European Diary: 1963-64*, New York, Farrar Straus, 1966, and London, Hart Davis, 1967.
The Scrolls from the Dead Sea.   New York, Oxford University Press, and London, W.H. Allen, 1955.
Red, Black, Blond and Olive: Studies in Four Civilizations: Zuni, Haiti, Soviet Russia, Israel.   New York, Oxford University Press, and London, W.H. Allen, 1956.
A Piece of My Mind: Reflections at Sixty.   New York, Farrar Straus, 1956; London, W.H. Allen, 1957.
The American Earthquake: A Documentary of the Twenties and Thirties.   New York, Doubleday, and London, W.H. Allen, 1958.
Apologies to the Iroquois.   New York, Farrar Straus, and London, W.H. Allen, 1960.
The Cold War and the Income Tax: A Protest.   New York, Farrar Straus, 1963; London, W.H. Allen, 1964.
O Canada: An American's Notes on Canadian Culture.   New York, Farrar Straus, 1965; London, Hart Davis, 1967.
A Prelude: Landscapes, Characters and Conversations from the Earlier Years of My Life.   New York, Farrar Straus, and London, W.H. Allen, 1967.
The Fruits of the MLA.   New York, New York Review, 1968.

Upstate: Records and Recollections of Northern New York.   New York, Farrar Straus,
   1971; London, Macmillan, 1972.
The Twenties: From Notebooks and Diaries of the Period, edited by Leon Edel.   New
   York, Farrar Straus, and London, Macmillan, 1975.
Letters on Literature and Politics 1912-1972, edited by Elena Wilson and Daniel Aron.
   New York, Farrar Straus, and London, Routledge, 1977.
*The Nabokov-Wilson Letters: Correspondence Between Vladimir Nabokov and Edmund
   Wilson, 1940-1971*, edited by Simon Karlinsky.   New York, Harper, and London,
   Weidenfeld and Nicolson, 1979.
The Thirties: From Notebooks and Diaries of the Period, edited by Leon Edel.   New
   York, Farrar Straus, and London, Macmillan, 1980.

Editor, *The Last Tycoon: An Unfinished Novel by F. Scott Fitzgerald, Together with The
   Great Gatsby and Selected Stories.*   New York, Scribner, 1941.
Editor, *The Shock of Recognition: The Development of Literature in the United States
   Recorded by the Men Who Made It.*   New York, Doubleday, 1943; enlarged edition,
   New York, Farrar Straus, 1955; London, W.H. Allen, 1956.
Editor, *The Crack-Up: With Other Uncollected Pieces, Note-Books and Unpublished
   Letters...*, by F. Scott Fitzgerald.   New York, New Directions, 1945; London, Grey
   Walls Press, 1947.
Editor, *The Collected Essays of John Peale Bishop.*   New York and London, Scribner,
   1948.
Editor, *The Last Tycoon: An Unfinished Novel*, by F. Scott Fitzgerald.   London, Grey
   Walls Press, 1949.
Editor, *Peasants and Other Stories*, by Anton Chekhov.   New York, Doubleday, 1956.

CRITICAL STUDIES AND BIBLIOGRAPHY

Stanley Edgar Hyman, *The Armed Vision: A Study in the Methods of Modern Literary
   Criticism.*   New York, Knopf, 1948 (the chapter on Wilson is omitted in later editions).
Sherman Paul, *Edmund Wilson: A Study of the Literary Vocation in Our Time.*   Ur-
   bana, University of Illinois Press, 1965.
Charles P. Frank, *Edmund Wilson.*   New York, Twayne, 1970.
Leonard Kriegel, *Edmund Wilson.*   Carbondale, Southern Illinois University Press,
   1971.
Richard David Ramsey, *Edmund Wilson: A Bibliography.*   New York, David Lewis,
   1971.
René Wellek, "Edmund Wilson (1895-1972)," in *History as A Tool in Critical Interpreta-
   tion*, edited by Thomas F. Rugh and Erin R. Silva.   Provo, Utah, Brigham Young
   University Press, 1978.

*   *   *

"I never think of myself as a literary critic," Edmund Wilson remarked in 1959; "I think of
myself simply as a writer and as a journalist.... I'm as much interested in history as I am in
literature." On another occasion, and "with some vehemence," he complained to Leon Edel,
"Why do you speak to me always of my literary criticism?...I am a writer—a writer of many
things." A glance at the bibliography will explain Wilson's irritation quickly enough; it should
also suggest how difficult it is to generalize about this extraordinary man of letters—our only
complete man of letters, it seems, if, as we probably must, we let England claim T.S. Eliot.
Generalizations about Wilson's three or four "critical" books are difficult too, but properly
understood and qualified, his dedicatory note to the first of them, *Axel's Castle*, provides some
useful guidelines: here he expresses his gratitude to his Princeton mentor, Christian Gauss,
from whom he acquired his conception of "what literary criticism ought to be—a history of
man's ideas and imaginings in the setting of the conditions which have shaped them." Historical

explanations have always been of primary importance for Wilson: and early as this statement is, it clearly raises perhaps the most important question one can ask about his critical thinking: what *is* the relationship between historical explanations—which for Wilson usually mean causal explanations—and the act of literary evaluation?

The "Axel" of Wilson's title is the hero of Villiers de l'Isle-Adam's Symbolist play, *Axel*; but he is by no means the hero of *Axel's Castle*, since his mildly famous exclamation, "Live? Our servants will do that for us," epitomizes for Wilson the denial of social "reality" which characterizes an important development in late nineteenth and early twentieth-century literature. Wilson argues that Symbolism is essentially an "elaboration" of Romanticism, a "second flood of the same tide." Both movements were reactions against a dehumanizing view of man and nature: the early Romantics rebelled against the eighteenth-century conception of the universe as a faultless machine, while the French Symbolists of the late nineteenth century were rebelling against "naturalism":

> In the middle of the nineteenth century, science made new advances, and mechanistic ideas were brought back into fashion again. But they came this time from a different quarter—not from physics and mathematics, but from biology. It was the effect of the theory of Evolution to reduce man from the heroic stature to which the Romantics had tried to exalt him, to the semblance of a helpless animal, again very small in the universe and at the mercy of forces about him. Humanity was the accidental product of heredity and environment, and capable of being explained in terms of these. This doctrine in literature was called Naturalism, and it was put into practice by novelists like Zola....

When Wilson goes on to observe that "literature [was] rebounding again from the scientific-classic pole to the poetic-romantic one," he is implying, however tentatively, a theory of causation which Whitehead also implies in *Science and the Modern World* (to which Wilson acknowledges a major debt) and which Jung was to make explicit. It seems that the human spirit will not tolerate for long the extreme development of any one mode of thought or feeling. For Jung nature is purposeful and seeks completion in the fully developed consciousness of those men who seek to transcend the "one-sidedness" of the epoch they live in: nature literally uses the artist and his symbols to call attention to the imbalance of the moment. Thus the dynamic organicism of the Romantics corrects the reductive scientism of the late eighteenth-century, intuition and imagination correct the blank, colorless, abstract universe which pure reason offers as the true model of "reality," and so on—by now the argument is a very familiar one. But for Wilson there is also a major difference between Romanticism and Symbolism:

> Symbolism corresponds to Romanticism, and is in fact an outgrowth from it. But whereas it was characteristic of the Romantics to seek experience for its own sake—love, travel, politics—to try the possibilities of life; the Symbolists, although they also hate formulas, though they also discard conventions, carry on their experimentation in the field of literature alone; and although they, too, are essentially explorers, explore only the possibilities of imagination and thought. And whereas the Romantic, in his individualism, had usually revolted against or defied that society from which he felt himself at odds, the Symbolist has detached himself from society and schools himself in indifference to it: he will cultivate his unique personal sensibility even beyond the point to which the Romantics did, but he will not assert his individual will—he will end by shifting the field of literature altogether, as his spokesman Axel had done the arena of life, from an objective to a subjective world, from an experience shared with society to an experience savored in solitude.

The literary history of our time, Wilson maintains, is to be understood in terms of "the development of Symbolism and of its fusion or conflict with Naturalism." The modern heirs of the Symbolists, Proust, Yeats, Eliot, Valéry, Gertrude Stein, and (with important qualifications) Joyce, or at least many of the characters they create, are often "peculiarly maladjusted persons," in marked contrast to those writers "with a strong Romantic strain like H.G. Wells and Bernard Shaw [who] tried to promote through the new social sciences, in the teeth of the bourgeois world, the realization of these visions of universal happiness which had been cherished by some of the most individualistic of the Romantics, such as Shelley and Rousseau."

571

In short, the Symbolists and their heirs have "abandoned the detached study of human motives and the expression of those universal emotions which make all classes and people one, to become intolerant partisans." The modern writer—that is, the writer starting out in the 1930's—has "only two alternatives to follow—Axel's or Rimbaud's": Axel stands for the hermetic way which finally reduces art to an elegant private game; Rimbaud represents for Wilson the way of the deliberate, anarchic primitivist who "tries to leave the twentieth century behind—to find the good life in some country where modern manufacturing methods and modern democratic institutions do not present any problems to the artist because they haven't yet arrived":

> our cult...of more primitive places and people...—D.H. Lawrence's mornings in Mexico and his explorations of Sante Fé and Australia; Blaise Cendrars's negro anthology, the negro masks which bring such high prices in Paris, André Gide's lifelong passion for Africa which has finally led him to navigate the Congo, Sherwood Anderson's exhilaration at the "dark laughter" of the American South, and the fascination for white New Yorkers of Harlem; and even that strange fascination with the infantile...—all this has followed in the wake of Rimbaud.

Yet at the very end of *Axel's Castle*, Wilson seems to suggest that it is possible—somehow—for the modern artist to escape the oscillation between the "scientific-classic pole" and the "poetic-romantic one":

> as surely as Ibsen and Flaubert brought to their Naturalistic plays and novels the sensibility and language of Romanticism, the writers of a new reaction in the direction of the study of man in his relation to his neighbor and to society will profit by the new intelligence and technique of Symbolism. Or—what would be preferable and is perhaps more likely—this oscillation may finally cease. Our conceptions of objective and subjective have unquestionably been based on false dualisms; our materialisms and idealisms alike have been derived from mistaken conceptions of what the researches of science implied—Classicism and Romanticism, Naturalism and Symbolism are, in reality, therefore false alternatives. And so we may see Naturalism and Symbolism combine to provide us with a vision of human life and its universe, richer, more subtle, more complex and more complete than any that man has yet known—indeed they have already so combined, Symbolism has already rejoined Naturalism, in one great work of *Ulysses*.

In flat, summary form, and for the reader who has no first-hand familiarity with the book, *Axel's Castle* may sound like one more predictable, more or less Marxist complaint about the decadence of modern art; but in fact *Axel's Castle* is one of the secure classics of modern criticism, for reasons which hold true for all of Wilson's later work as well. When a reprint of the book appeared in England in 1961, Frank Kermode observed, very acutely, that its great strength derives from Wilson's "powerful primary, undogmatic, response to poetry":

> he can attach himself and then withdraw, and on withdrawal feels free to disapprove. In fact this is the whole method of *Axel's Castle*: passionate identification with the work under discussion; followed by detached appraisal; followed by historical inference, which does not neglect the primary response. Before asking whether the work is of any use to mankind, whether it will help us round the environmental obstacles, he proves that he has, in any case, responded to it.

One can go further: what always gives Wilson's criticism its vitality is his unerring ability to dramatize the movements and conflicts he sees in literary history writ large or writ small, in the lives of individual artists. In a 1959 essay, "A Modest Self-Tribute," he tells us that

> the primary key in my reading to my work as a literary critic [was] my finding in my father's library, at some point when I was about fifteen, the brilliant translation by H. van Laun of Taine's *History of English Literature*.... Later on, I read Taine in French, and on one occasion, when living in New York, I became so absorbed by the *coup de*

théâtre at the end of the final chapter by which Taine evokes Alfred de Musset in order to contrast him with Tennyson and leaves Musset with the moral advantage, that I continued to read it on the street all the way to some engagement. But in the meantime, while still at school, I had thus come under the influence of French criticism, and my whole point of view about literature was affected by Taine's methods of presentation and interpretation. He had created the creators themselves as characters in a large drama of cultural and social history, and writing about literature, for me, has always meant narrative and drama as well as the discussion of comparative values. I had also an interest in the biographies of writers which soon took the bit in its teeth.

Clearly *Axel's Castle* is both descriptive and evaluative; and while the source of Wilson's standards—his social idealism—is not exactly hidden there, it will be helpful to turn, however briefly and inadequately, to *To the Finland Station*. Wilson's aim here was not simply (as he explains in *The Bit Between My Teeth*) to "bring home to the 'bourgeois' intellectual world the most recent developments of Marxism in connection with the Russian Revolution"; his real intention, in Sherman Paul's words, was "to change the minds of Americans about the possibilities of socialism." *To the Finland Station*, Paul continues, "is a revolutionist's Plutarch's *Lives*, whose accurate subtitle would be " 'On Heroes, Hero-Worship and the Heroic in History.' " In his preface to the 1971 reissue of the book Wilson himself commented that he had been "assuming throughout that an important step in progress had been made, that a fundamental breakthrough had occurred, that nothing in our human history would ever be the same again." And he adds, sadly, "I had no premonition that the Soviet Union was to become one of the most hideous tyrannies that the world has ever known.... What was permanently valuable— whatever that implies—in the October Revolution I cannot pretend to estimate." The goal of the Revolution, of course, had been to establish what Trotsky called "the first truly human culture." And at the heart of Wilson's own idealism is his faith in the guiding power of a "republican" elite to maintain such a culture. In *A Piece of My Mind* he asserts that, "to simplify,"

> one can say that, on the one hand, you find in the United States the people who are constantly aware...that, beyond their opportunities for money-making, they have a stake in the success of our system, that they share the responsibility to carry on its institutions, to find expression for its new point of view, to give it dignity, to make it work; and, on the other hand, the people who are merely concerned with making a living or a fortune, with practicing some profession or mastering some skill, as they would in any other country, and who lack, or do not possess to quite the same degree, the sense of America's role.... Before the Civil War, this republican patriotism was shared by the North and the South.

"I do not mean to exalt this republican sense as the touchstone of the American spirit," he concludes: but of course he does do exactly that, not only for the "American spirit" (the subject of what he felt was his best book, *Patriotic Gore*), but for the human spirit generally. In the end America disappointed Wilson as tragically as Russia had (see *The Cold War and the Income Tax: A Protest* and the fairly brutal introduction to *Patriotic Gore*); but he never abandoned the ideal of a "truly human culture." Literature matters because it may help to establish that goal. But whether or not it is ever realized in fact, the idea of such a society is, as Socrates says at the end of the *Republic*, "a pattern laid up in our hearts."

To return to Wilson's "literary" criticism—and by now it should be obvious how inadequate this distinction is—there is a passage in his essay on Proust, in *Axel's Castle*, which provides the point of departure for *The Wound and the Bow* and many of the essays in *The Triple Thinkers*. Here he asserts that

> The real elements, of course, of any work of fiction, are the elements of the author's personality: his imagination embodies in the images of characters, situations and scenes the fundamental conflicts of his nature or the cycle of phases through which it habitually passes.

Wilson's method remains constant, then, if we extend the "conditions" which "shape men's

573

imaginings" to include the artist's personal psychological development. The basis of his explanations are now Freudian rather than Marxist, but they remain causal explanations all the same. To dramatize his thesis that "genius and disease, like strength and mutilation, may be inextricably bound up together," Wilson uses the myth of Philoctetes, which Sophocles had also used in one of his late plays. In the myth, Heracles, before he dies, gives his bow—the bow which "never misses its mark" and was in turn a gift from Apollo—to Philoctetes, who thereby becomes a valuable asset to the Greeks in their plan to siege Troy. But on their way to Troy, the Greeks (in Wilson's summary)

> had to stop off at the tiny island of Chrysè to sacrifice to the local deity. Philoctetes approached the shrine first, and he was bitten in the foot by a snake. The infection became peculiarly virulent; and the groans of Philoctetes made it impossible to perform the sacrifice...the bite began to suppurate with so horrible a smell that his companions could no longer bear to have him near them. They removed him to Lemnos, a neighbouring island which was much larger than Chrysè and inhabited, and sailed away to Troy without him.

Since the mysterious wound never healed, Philoctetes remained on Lemnos, nursing his hatred for the companions who had abandoned him. After ten years of unsuccessful efforts to take Troy, the Greeks learned from a soothsayer that they could never win "till they had sent for Neoptolemus, the son of Achilles, and given him his father's armour, and till they had brought Philoctetes and bow." Odysseus and Neoptolemus go to Lemnos to persuade—or trick—Philoctetes to join the Greeks. Disgusted by Odysseus' plan to use brute force, Neoptolemus does convince Philoctetes to return with them, and now

> Heracles suddenly appears from the skies and declares to Philoctetes that what [Neoptolemus] says is true, and that it is right for him to go to Troy. He and the son of Achilles shall stand together like lions and shall gloriously carry the day.—The *deus ex machina* here may of course figure a change of heart which has taken place in Philoctetes as the result of his having found a man who recognizes the wrong that has been done him and who is willing to champion his case.... The long hatred is finally exorcised.

"I should interpret the fable as follows," Wilson goes on:

> The victim of a malodorous disease which renders him abhorrent to society and periodically degrades him and makes him helpless is also the master of a superhuman art which everybody has to respect and which the normal man finds he needs. A practical man like Odysseus, at the same time coarse-grained and clever, imagines that he can somehow get the bow without having Philoctetes on his hands.... But the young son of Achilles knows better. It is at the moment when his sympathy for Philoctetes would naturally inhibit his cheating him...that it becomes clear to him that the words of the seer had meant that the bow would be useless without Philoctetes himself.... How then is the gulf to be got over between the ineffective plight of the bowman and his proper use of the bow, between his ignominy and his destined glory? Only by the intervention of one who is guileless enough and human enough to treat him, not as a monster, but simply as another man, whose suffering elicits his sympathy and whose courage and pride he admires.

In his essays on Dickens, Kipling, Casanova, Edith Wharton and Hemingway, in *The Wound and the Bow*, and in the essays on Jonson, Housman and Henry James, in *The Triple Thinkers*, Wilson tries to establish the crucial connection between the psychic wound which each of these artists appears to have suffered and the "gift"—the wisdom, insight and artistic power—which the wound made possible. Just as Wilson turns the Philoctetes myth into a parable of the artist and society, so readers may be tempted to see Wilson himself as a symbolic figure of the critic-as-Neoptolemus (Leon Edel makes this point very well in his introduction to *The Twenties*—and demonstrates that Wilson had his own personal "wound"). Both the public and the artist, with his often disturbing gift, need the mediating presence of the humane and understanding critic.

574

The objections to this linking of genius and psychological wound are predictable. In his otherwise patient and sympathetic study of Wilson, Charles Frank argues that "regardless of its validity as an explanation of the genesis of a work of art," the theory is "unnecessary and suspect in literary explication—and worthless in evaluation." When Wilson states that it is essential to see Dickens as a man in order to appreciate him as an artist he is "fundamentally wrong." "What is necessary to appreciate Dickens as an artist," Frank goes on, "is a willingness to see him *primarily* as an *artist*—an imitator, a fictionalist, a more or less detached craftsman." In other words Wilson is guilty of committing the genetic fallacy, or the error of judging a work in terms of its origins. In one respect Frank is right: it is possible for a naive reader or a determined Freudian to come away from these essays thinking that Wilson has reduced art to its causes; he does nothing to prevent such readers from making the reduction, although he does not do so himself (he does not argue that *all* disturbances eventuate in a work of art or that *all* works of art are caused by such disturbances). But to conclude that Wilson is unaware of the implications of his thesis would be a mistake; and here one has to turn to "Marxism and Literature" and "The Historical Interpretation of Literature" (both reprinted in *The Triple Thinkers*). In the first essay Wilson is careful to point out that regardless of what the work may have meant for the artist in terms of his own conflicts, the meaning of the work for the audience is by no means restricted in this way:

> In art...a sort of law of moral interchangeability prevails: we may transpose the actions and the sentiments that move us into terms of whatever we do or are ourselves. Real genius of moral insight is a motor which will start any engine. When Proust, in his wonderful chapter on the death of the novelist Bergotte, speaks of those moral obligations which impose themselves in spite of everything and which seem to come through to humanity from some source outside its wretched self (obligations "invisible only to fools—and are they really to them?"), he is describing a kind of duty which he felt only in connection with the literary work which he performed in his dark and fetid room; yet he speaks for every moral, esthetic or intellectual passion which holds the expediencies of the world in contempt.

And in "The Historical Interpretation of Literature" Wilson faces directly the problem of evaluation. The literary analyst and the literary critic have different aims: the analyst "is of course not concerned with the comparative values of his patients any more than the surgeon is":

> He cannot tell you why the neurotic Dostoevsky produces work of immense value to his fellows while another man with the same neurotic pattern would become a public menace. Freud himself emphatically states in his study of Leonardo that his method can make no attempt to account for Leonardo's genius. The problems of comparative artistic value still remain after we have given attention to the Freudian psychological factor just as they do after we have given attention to the Marxist economic factor and to the racial and geographical factors. No matter how thoroughly and searchingly we may have scrutinized works of literature from the historical and biographical points of view, we must be ready to attempt to estimate, in some such way as Saintsbury and Eliot do, the relative degrees of success attained by the products of the various personalities. We must be able to tell good from bad, the first-rate from the second-rate. We shall not otherwise write literary criticism at all, but merely social or political history as reflected in literary texts, or psychological case histories from past eras, or, to take the historical point of view in its simplest and most academic form, merely chronologies of books that have been published.

How then are we to tell good art from bad? Wilson's answer to this question is rather flat, rather disappointing, and quite possibly true: we follow the judgments of a sensitive, informed elite (their judgement in turn rests on an "emotional reaction"). How do we identify this elite?

> Well, it can only be said of them that they are self-appointed and self-perpetuating, and that they will compel you to accept their authority. Imposters may try to put themselves over, but these quacks will not last. The implied position of the people who know about literature (as is also the case in every other art) is simply that they know what they know,

and that they are determined to impose their opinions by main force of eloquence or assertion on the people who do not know.

The ultimate issue is thus the *cause* of the emotional response that determines our recognition—the recognition, that is, by the elite—of valuable works:

> In my view, all our intellectual activity, in whatever field it takes place, is an attempt to give a meaning to our experience—that is, to make life more practicable; for by understanding things we make it easier to survive and get around among them. The mathematician Euclid, working in a convention of abstractions, shows us relations between the distances of our unwieldy and cluttered-up environment upon which we are able to count. A drama of Sophocles also indicates relations between the various human impulses, which appear so confused and dangerous, and it brings out a certain justice of Fate...upon which we can also depend.... Some writers (as well as some scientists) have a different kind of explicit message beyond the reassurance implicit in the mere feat of understanding life or of moulding the harmony of artistic form. Not content with such an achievement as that of Sophocles...such writers attempt, like Plato, to think out and recommend a procedure for turning it into something better. But other departments of literature—lyric poetry such as Sappho's, for example—have *less* philosophical content than Sophocles. A lyric gives us nothing but a pattern imposed on the expression of feeling; but this pattern of metrical quantities and of consonants and vowels that balance has the effect of reducing the feeling, however unruly or painful it may seem when we experience it in the course of our lives, to something orderly, symmetrical and pleasing; and it also relates this feeling to the more impressive scheme, works it into the larger texture, of the body of poetic art. The discord has been resolved, the anomaly subjected to discipline. And this control of his emotion by the poet has the effect at second-hand of making it easier for the reader to manage his own emotions.

This important passage completes the argument begun in *The Wound and the Bow*: art is not merely the expression of psychological tensions; it may also help to relieve those tensions.

Wilson anticipates the objection which must be raised when one locates the sign of literary value in the emotional response of a particular group: "are not people often solaced and exhilarated by literature of the trashiest kind?"

> They are: crude and limited people do certainly feel some such emotion in connection with work that is limited and crude. The man who is more highly organized and has a wider intellectual range will feel it in connection with work that is finer and more complex.... When I was speaking...of the genuine connoisseurs who establish the standards of taste; I meant, of course, the people who can distinguish Grade A and who prefer it to other grades.

The flatness of this last point and the circularity of the argument will disappoint readers who feel that taste and judgment can be reduced to a method. But then, has method alone ever made anyone more sensitive or responsive? In any event, Wilson's "theory" of criticism is by no means the most interesting part of his work. What matters is the way in which he performed the duties of the critic as he saw them, forming and directing the taste of his readers, for over forty astonishingly productive years. Alfred Kazin's tribute to Malraux—that he "aroused the reader in behalf of the imagination that had aroused him"—is supremely true of Wilson as well. In this respect he is the finest critic America has yet produced.

WIMSATT, W(illiam) K(urtz), Jr. American. Born in Washington, D.C., 27 November 1907. Educated at Georgetown University, Washington, D.C., B.A. 1928, M.A. 1929; Catholic University, St. Louis, 1935-36; Yale University, New Haven, Connecticut, Ph.D. 1939. Married Margaret Elizabeth Hecht in 1944; two children. Head of the Department of English, Portsmouth Priory School, Rhode Island, 1930-35; Instructor, 1939-42, Fellow of Silliman College, 1941-75, Assistant Professor, 1943-49, Associate Professor, 1949-55, Professor, 1955-65, Frederick Clifford Ford Professor, 1965-75, and Sterling Professor of English, 1975, Yale University. Chairman of the English Institute, 1954; Member of the Executive Council, Modern Language Association, 1955-58; Chairman of the Catholic Commission on Intellectual and Cultural Affairs, 1964; President of the Connecticut Academy of Arts and Sciences, 1969-70. Recipient: Guggenheim Fellowship, 1946; Fund for the Advancement of Learning Fellowship, 1953; Yale University Senior Faculty Fellowship, 1960. Litt.D.: Villanova University, Pennsylvania, 1962; Notre Dame University, Indiana, 1963; LL.D.: St. Louis University, 1964; D.H.L.: LeMoyne College, Syracuse, New York, 1965; Kenyon College, Gambier, Ohio, 1970. *Died 17 December 1975.*

PUBLICATIONS

Criticism

The Prose Style of Samuel Johnson. New Haven, Connecticut, Yale University Press, 1941.

Philosophic Words: A Study of Style and Meaning in the "Rambler" and "Dictionary" of Samuel Johnson. New Haven, Connecticut, Yale University Press, 1948.

The Verbal Icon: Studies in the Meaning of Poetry, with two preliminary essays written in collaboration with Monroe C. Beardsley. Lexington, University of Kentucky Press, 1954; London, Methuen, 1970.

Literary Criticism: A Short History, with Cleanth Brooks. New York, Knopf, and London, Routledge, 1957.

Hateful Contraries: Studies in Literature and Criticism, with an essay on English meter written in collaboration with Monroe C. Beardsley. Lexington, University of Kentucky Press, 1965.

The Portraits of Alexander Pope. New Haven, Connecticut, Yale University Press, 1965.

Day of the Leopards: Essays in Defense of Poems. New Haven, Connecticut, Yale University Press, 1976.

Other

How to Compose Chess Problems and Why. New Haven, Connecticut, privately printed, 1966.

Editor, *Alexander Pope: Selected Prose and Poetry.* New York, Rinehart, 1951; revised edition, 1972.

Editor, *English Stage Comedy: Six Essays.* New York, Columbia University Press, 1955.

Editor, *Parodies of Ballad Criticism 1711-1787.* Los Angeles, Augustan Reprint Society, 1957.

Editor, with F.A. Pottle, *Boswell for the Defense, 1769-1774.* New York, McGraw Hill, and London, Heinemann, 1959.

Editor, *Samuel Johnson on Shakespeare.* New York, Hill and Wang, 1960; as *Dr. Johnson on Shakespeare,* London, Penguin, 1969.

Editor, *Explication as Criticism: Selected Papers from the English Institute, 1941-1952.* New York, Columbia University Press, 1963.

Editor, *The Idea of Comedy: Essays in Prose and Verse, Ben Jonson to George Meredith.* New York, Prentice Hall, 1969.

Editor, *Versification: Major Language Types.* New York, Modern Language Association, 1972.

Editor, *Literary Criticism: Idea and Act: Selected Essays from the English Institute 1939-1972.* Berkeley and Los Angeles, University of California Press, 1974.

Editor, with Frank Brady, *Samuel Johnson: Selected Poetry and Prose.* Berkeley and London, University of California Press, 1977.

CRITICAL STUDY

René Wellek, "The Literary Theory of W.K. Wimsatt," in *Yale Quarterly Review* (New Haven, Connecticut), 66, 1976.

*   *   *

The most intelligent (and surely the subtlest) of the American New Critics of poetry, W.K. Wimsatt, still seems to be best-known for two 1946 essays, "The Intentional Fallacy" and "The Affective Fallacy," written in collaboration with Monroe Beardsley. The Intentional Fallacy begins, the authors explain, by "trying to derive the standards of criticism from the *causes* of the poem and ends in biography and relativism," whereas the Affective Fallacy

> is a confusion between the poem and its *results* (what it *is* and what it *does*), a special case of epistemological skepticism, though usually advanced as if it had far stronger claims than the overall forms of skepticism. It begins by trying to derive the standards of criticism from the psychological effects of the poem and ends in impressionism and relativism. The outcome of either Fallacy, the Intentional or the Affective, is that the poem itself, as an object of specifically critical judgment, tends to disappear.

Anyone familiar with modern criticism will recognize that Wimsatt and Beardsley are not setting up phantom opponents: critics dealing with Henry James, for example, often rely heavily on biographical material and on what James said *about* a given work—about his aim, that is, or "intentions"—in his letters, journals or prefaces. And as for the Affective Fallacy, Wimsatt and Beardsley have in mind, if not always Richards himself, then at least those who follow him in one way or another and argue enthusiastically for the "therapeutic" powers of poetry. Influential as these essays have been, however, they represent only a small part of Wimsatt's total position. No brief discussion can do justice to the complexity of that position, but for the purposes of summary, we may use the diagram he provides in "Horses of Wrath: Recent Critical Lessons" (reprinted in *Hateful Contraries*), in which the five Roman numerals refer to different ways of describing and evaluating poetry:

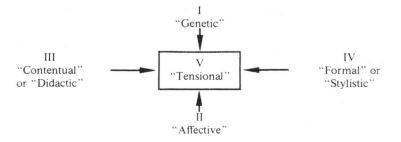

The Genetic and Affective approaches are simply versions of the Fallacies referred to above; the

Contentual approach tends to reduce the poem to its paraphrasable "wisdom," while the Formalist approach, which tends to concentrate on purely structural matters, is unable to deal satisfactorily with the referential dimensions of the language which the poem uses.

The fifth or "Tensional" approach is designed to overcome these limitations, but in order to understand fully what Wimsatt means by "tension," we have to take into account his deeply Christian view of the "mixed" nature of moral experience. "Let us say," he continues in "Horses of Wrath,"

> that we recognize the fact of material concreteness in human experience, and though matter itself be not evil...yet it does seem the plausible enough ground for some kind of dualism, division, tension, and conflict, the clash of desires, and evil and pain. Spirit and matter, supernatural and natural, good and evil, these tend to line up as parallel oppositions.... We say that art ought to have the concreteness of recognition and inclusion; it ought to have tension, balance, wholeness.... Of course we will say that we don't call evil itself, or division, or conflict, desirable things. We only call facing up to them, facing up to the human predicament, a desirable and mature state of soul and the right model and course of a mature poetic art.

Like any other Christian, the Christian critic will maintain that "the human condition is intrinsically a material and mixed condition, where faith and love of God and fellow man can scarcely occur except in a milieu that is full of the possibility of their opposites." Thus "if verbal art has to take up the mixed matter of good and evil, its most likely way of success, and its peculiar way, is a mixed way." And the "mixed" way of presentation refers, in turn, to the "iconic" nature of rhythmic and analogical language, which is why Wimsatt places so much emphasis on the role of metaphor in poetry. "Metaphor," he argues, "is the holding together of opposites" (not, it should be noted, the "reconciliation" of opposites) and therefore can reflect the complex nature of experience itself; it is a device by which the poet is able to reveal the differences as well as the likenesses between tenor and vehicle (that is, between his primary subject and the term of comparison). In grasping metaphorical language properly, Wimsatt observes (in another important essay, "Symbol and Metaphor," reprinted in *The Verbal Icon*), "we are often required to consider now how B (vehicle) explains A (tenor), but what meanings are generated when A and B are confronted or seen each in the light of the other." Moreover, this "new meaning" is often a meaning which brings together the general and the particular—a claim which Wimsatt illustrates most clearly in "The Concrete Universal" (also reprinted in *The Verbal Icon*):

> Even the simplest form of metaphor or simile ("My love is like a red, red rose") presents us with a special and creative, in fact a concrete kind of abstraction different from that of science. For behind a metaphor lies a resemblance between two classes, *and hence a more general third class*. This class is unnamed and most likely remains unnamed and is apprehended only through the metaphor. It is a new conception for which there is no other expression. Keats discovering Homer is like a traveller in the realms of gold, like an astronomer who discovers a planet, like Cortez gazing at the Pacific. The title of the sonnet, "On First Looking into Chapman's Homer," seems to furnish not so much the subject of the poem as a fourth member of a central metaphor, the real subject of the poem being an abstraction, a certain kind of thrill in discovering, for which there is no name and no other description, only the four members of the metaphor pointing, as to the center of their pattern. The point of the poem seems to lie outside both vehicle and tenor. (My emphasis)

In other words, metaphor is the means the poet uses to embody the complexity of experience in the texture of the poem *and* a means of extending the range of his implications, without lapsing into the flatly "symbolic" or the purely "representational." In his own fashion, then, Wimsatt has attempted to demonstrate the way in which, as Aristotle asserted, poetry may be "more philosophic than history."

Metaphor, however, is not the only means the poet has for achieving a "fullness of actually presented meaning." He also has the resources of word sounds and rhythm, and it is the successful exploitation of all these resources which makes a poem "iconic." As Wimsatt explains, an icon is not a mere sign or symbol but rather a participant in the qualities of the process or situation it also "represents." Poetic structure, he argues (in "Romantic Nature Imagery," also reprinted in *The Verbal Icon*),

> is always a fusion of ideas with material, a statement in which the solidity of symbol and the sensory verbal qualities are somehow not washed out by the abstraction. For this effect the iconic or directly imitative powers of language are important—and of these the well known onomatopoeia or imitation of sound is only one, and one of the simplest. The "stiff twin compasses" [of Donne's "A Valediction: forbiding Mourning"] have a kind of iconicity in the very stiffness and the odd emphasis of the metrical situation.... [In] Shelley's "Ode to the West Wind" the shifts in imagery of the second stanza, the pell-mell raggedness and confusion of loose clouds, decaying leaves, angels and Maenads with hair uplifted, the dirge, the dome, the vapors, and the enjambment from tercet to tercet combine to give an impression beyond statement of the very wildness, the breath and power which is the vehicle of the poem's radical metaphor.

All of this leaves us wondering, of course, if fiction or non-poetic drama can also attain "iconicity." Prose may often be metaphorical, and tension may be embodied at the level of character and action as well as diction; but without the resources of emphatic sound and rhythm, prose may be by definition a lesser medium of expression. In any event, Wimsatt never seems to have been interested enough in the novel or prose drama to have pursued these questions.

In summary definition, then (to return to "Horses of Wrath"), poetry is "the expression of a relation between subject and object: dramatic, metaphoric, involving complexity of values. Poetry is more than beautiful language, *and less than (or at least different from) religious, moral, and social truth.*" The slightly equivocal passage which I have emphasized here raises what is probably the most important problem in Wimsatt's critical system. In the "Epilogue" to *Literary Criticism: A Short History*, Wimsatt and his collaborator, Cleanth Brooks, conclude that

> The patristic idea of the "Fortunate Fall," variously expressed by Ambrose, by Augustine, by Gregory the Great, and in the liturgy ("*O felix culpa, quae talem ac tantum meruit habere Redemptorem*") is probably a closer analogue to an adequate literary theory than such neo-Platonic ideas as Augustine entertained about the beauty of the triangle or the circle. The writers of the present history have not been concerned to implicate literary theory with any kind of religious doctrine. It appears to us, however, relevant, as we near our conclusion, at least to confess an opinion that the kind of literary theory which seems to us to emerge the most plausibly from the long history of [critical] debates is far more difficult to orient within any of the Platonic or Gnostic ideal world views, or within the Manichaean full dualism and strife of principles, than precisely within the vision of suffering, the optimism, the mystery which are embraced in the religious dogma of the Incarnation.

But in what ways is successful poetry "less than or at least different from" the revealed truth of religion? In "Poetry and Christianity," the final essay in *The Verbal Icon*, Wimsatt himself seems uncertain:

> What then is an adequately serious view of poetry? I submit that this has always been, and remains, difficult if not impossible to define with any rigor. What is the formula by which we shall recognize the metaphoric capacities of language and the moral importance of valid linguistic expression without surrendering our conception of truth as a thing beyond language, without yielding to the lead of the idealistic symbolists, the ritualists, and the myth-makers? I confess that I do not clearly see the answer. I have not found the book in which the answer is permanently and canonically formulated.

In view of the later essays in *Hateful Contraries* and *Day of the Leopards*, however, it is tempting to speculate (and it is nothing more than speculation) that he would have to accept W.H. Auden's formulation of the problem in "The Virgin and the Dynamo":

a poem is beautiful or ugly to the degree that it succeeds or fails in reconciling contradictory feelings in an order of mutual propriety. Every beautiful poem presents an analogy to the forgiveness of sins; an analogy, not an imitation, because it is not evil intentions which are repented of and pardoned but contradictory feelings which the poet surrenders to the poem in which they are reconciled.

The effect of beauty, therefore, is good to the degree that, through its analogies, the goodness of created existence, the historical fall into unfreedom and disorder, and the possibility of regaining paradise through repentence and forgiveness are recognized.

"Reconciled" may be too strong a term for Wimsatt—"balanced in opposition" would be more precise—but for both writers the key, ambiguous word is "analogue." It is necessary for Auden to insist (and the logic of Wimsatt's position would force him to agree) that aesthetic experience cannot be the same as religious experience or revelation: aesthetic experience may be somehow "like" but not connatural with such experience. For both Auden and Wimsatt the danger of an iconic view of art is quite simply idolatry, the confusion of aesthetic and religious value. In any event, the function of poetry follows from all of this, and the function of criticism as well. The successful poem, Wimsatt concludes, gives us, precisely because of its "tensional"quality, a "fresh vision of reality, a fullness, completeness, concreteness of experience. It will be an experience that includes pain as well as pleasure, evil and ugliness as well as beauty and good, an experience where the tragic and comic can be discriminated but where they show a complementary and an easily mixed relationship." Thus while art and religion must be held separate, it seems that aesthetic perception and creation may be forms of moral activity. So too with criticism, which aims to keep us aware of the tensional reality of poetry: "Religious thinkers," Wimsatt concludes, "should be sympathetic to criticism because it is a branch of philosophy; it is an effort to get at certain truths about signs, knowledge, and reality."

Despite this, René Wellek states that "it is sometimes difficult to see what the function of poetry could be in Wimsatt's scheme." But in all probability Wellek understands Wimsatt only too well, and like many readers finds it impossible to accept the Christian foundations of Wimsatt's "scheme." Thus Wellek concludes (in "The Literary Theory of William K. Wimsatt") that

> Wimsatt has to assume an ultimately mystical view of the universe, one that sees analogies and metaphors in reality, a language of meanings in nature and society "incarnate" in poetry. This is the *signatura rerum* embraced by a Crashaw or even by the Schlegels, Novalis, and Coleridge, but it seems unacceptable in the present situation of thinking about such matters.

To what extent can Wimsatt's criticism be detached from its proper foundation in Christian doctrine? Here again, many readers may want to agree with Wellek:

> A phenomenological approach...would obviate an appeal to the mystery of the Incarnation and an emblematic view of the universe. But this is an ultimate philosophical or religious decision. An answer differing from Wimsatt's should not, however, obscure the value of his literary theory: its focus on the object, his analysis of its features, his polemical successes against fashionable rival views such as the Chicago Aristotelians or the myth critics, his excursions into the history of poetry and criticism, his resolute defense of evaluation in criticism, and his never misplaced plea for the meaning of literature as "being" something in its own right but also "saying" something about man and the universe, in many and often discordant voices.

As Wellek's tribute suggests, Wimsatt's criticism is never doctrinal in any crucial sense: his best essays—the essays on the relationship of meter and rhyme to sense, for example, or the essays on Pope and Johnson—are conducted at a level of argumentation rarely equalled by any other modern critic.

If it means anything at all, the "New Criticism" refers to the effort to keep discussions of poetry "pure"—uncontaminated, that is, by any of the fallacies and misguided approaches mentioned earlier. And for these critics, for Wimsatt, Cleanth Brooks, Allen Tate, John Crowe Ransom and (a more difficult case) Robert Penn Warren, it also means emphasizing the tensional aspects of poetic diction (irony, paradox, and ambiguity) first suggested by the resolutely un-Christian I.A. Richards. The interplay of sacred and profane motives in modern criticism is something for future historians to ponder, but Wimsatt's conclusion to "Horses of Wrath" is worth repeating here in full:

> I think one might summarize the best poetic debates of the past thirty years in America with the observation that the theory of poetic tension is likely to be involved in difficulties with two main kinds of simplification: on the one hand, with the simplifications of hedonistic and utilitarian science and sociology, and on the other with the simplifications of theological and moral doctrine. For the fact is that, no matter how correct anyone may conceive a given doctrine to be, it is still an abstraction and a simplification. At the same time, the religious doctrines have a backing of depth and substantial mystery—whereas the naturalistic are in the end phenomenological, sensate, and flat. So the religious mind would seem, in the end, to be more hospitable to the tension and metaphysical view of poetry than the naturalistic mind is able to be. And this is borne out in recent history. The metaphysical criticism which was "new" is the 1940's (working by the norms of wit, irony, metaphor, drama, tension) has some of its strongest champions among poets and critics of the Anglican school and has enjoyed for the most part at least a friendly reception in Roman Catholic schools and journals. The same school of criticism has met with strong disapproval from Marxist and other socially oriented thought and in general from the naturalistic Saturday and Sunday popular presses.

This passage dates from 1962 and may imply some of Wimsatt's uneasiness with the naturalistic "simplifications" of modern life. By 1975, the year of his death, that uneasiness had turned into a kind of bitter dismay at "the intoxication of the contemporary elite with destructive symbols" and the surrender to unreason in academic criticism (he saw and clearly did not like the conclusions Frye, Harold Bloom, J. Hillis Miller and Geoffrey Hartman, among many others, would be drawn to). The particular circumstances which provoked "Day of the Leopards"— social and academic rebellion in America during the late 1960's—may have passed without bringing the consequences Wimsatt feared, but in one important sense he was right: The New Criticism has had its day. In a late essay ("I.A.R.: What to Say about a Poem") he confesses that despite his mistrust of "affective" criticism,

> The critical thinking of Richards has always cut close to the quick of poetic interest. It has been exciting. It has generated a world of ideas favorable to a general excitement with criticism. And for that reason I see it as a better kind of critical thinking than most of the now emergent vogues:—the boundless expansions of the schools of "consciousness," the self-justifying apparatuses of transformational grammar, the neutralisms of historical hermeneutics, the despairs of the tropes of "silence," the "aleatory" assemblage of *textes* from newspaper, dictionary, or telephone directory, the celebrations of the "death of literature," the various other attempts to play midwife to the "post-modern imagination."

The various tendencies which he lists here are those which in the language of another late essay, "batter the object," that is, the iconic nature of the poem. But to deny iconicity, of course, is to deny that criticism is an objective discipline and to attack, if not reason and faith themselves, at least the most important analogues we have of those threatened virtues.

WINTERS, (Arthur) Yvor.   American.   Born in Chicago, Illinois, 17 October 1900. Educated at the University of Chicago, 1917-18; University of Colorado, Boulder, B.A., M.A. 1925;
Stanford University, California, Ph.D. 1935. Married the writer Janet Lewis in 1926; two
children. Instructor in French and Spanish, University of Idaho, Pocatello, 1925-27; Member
of the English Department, 1927-48, Professor, 1948-51, and Albert Guerard Professor,
1961-66, Stanford University. Founding Editor, *The Gyroscope*, Los Altos, California, 1929-
30; Regional Editor, *The Hound and Horn*, 1932-34. Fellow, Kenyon School of English,
Gambier, Ohio, 1948-50. Recipient: Oscar Blumenthal Prize (*Poetry*, Chicago), 1945; National
Institute of Arts and Letters grant, 1952; Brandeis University Creative Arts Award, for Poetry,
1959; Harriet Monroe Poetry Award, 1960; Guggenheim Fellowship, 1961; Bollingen Award,
1961; National Endowment for the Arts grant, 1967. Member, American Academy of Arts and
Sciences. *Died 25 January 1968.*

PUBLICATIONS

Criticism

Primitivism and Decadence: A Study of American Experimental Poetry.   New York,
   Arrow Editions, 1937; reprinted in *In Defense of Reason*, 1947.
Maule's Curse: Seven Studies in the History of American Obscurantism.   New York,
   New Directions, 1938; reprinted in *In Defense of Reason*, 1947.
The Anatomy of Nonsense.   New York, New Directions, 1943; reprinted in *In Defense of
   Reason*, 1947.
Edwin Arlington Robinson.   New York, New Directions, 1946; revised edition, 1971.
In Defense of Reason.   Denver, Swallow, 1947; revised edition, 1960; London, Rout-
   ledge, 1960.
The Function of Criticism: Problems and Exercises.   Denver, Swallow, 1957; London,
   Routledge, 1962.
On Modern Poets.   New York, Meridian, 1959; London, Routledge, 1960.
The Poetry of W.B. Yeats.   Denver, Swallow, 1960.
The Poetry of J.V. Cunningham.   Denver, Swallow, 1961.
*Forms of Discovery: Critical and Historical Essays on the Forms of the Short Poem in
   English.*   Denver, Swallow, 1967.
Uncollected Essays and Reviews, edited by Francis Murphy.   Chicago, Swallow Press,
   1976.

Verse

The Immobile Wind.   Evanston, Illinois, Monroe Wheeler, 1921.
The Magpie's Shadow.   Chicago, Musterbookhouse, 1922.
The Bare Hills: A Book of Poems.   Boston, Four Seas, 1927.
The Proof.   New York, Coward McCann, 1930.
The Journey and Other Poems.   Ithaca, New York, Dragon Press, 1931.
Before Disaster.   Tryon, North Carolina, Tryon Pamphlets, 1934.
Poems.   Los Altos, California, Gyroscope Press, 1940.
The Giant Weapon.   New York, New Directions, 1943.
To the Holy Spirit: A Poem.   San Francisco, California Poetry Folios, 1947.
Three Poems.   Cummington, Massachusetts, Cummington Press, 1950.
Collected Poems.   Denver, Swallow, 1952; revised edition, 1960; London, Routledge,
   1963.
The Early Poems of Yvor Winters 1920-28.   Denver, Swallow, 1966.
The Collected Poetry of Yvor Winters, edited by Donald Davie.   Manchester, Carcanet
   Press, 1978; Chicago, Swallow, 1980.

Short Story

The Brink of Darkness.   Denver, Swallow, 1932.

Other

"Notes on the Mechanics of the Poetic Image: The Testament of a Stone," in *Secession* (New York), 8, 1924.
The Case of David Lamson: A Summary, with Frances Theresa Russell.   San Francisco, Lamson Defense Committee, 1934.
Hart Crane and Yvor Winters: Their Literary Correspondence, edited by Thomas Parkinson.   Berkeley and London, University of California Press, 1978.

Editor, *Twelve Poets of the Pacific*.   New York, New Directions, 1937.
Editor, *Selected Poems*, by Elizabeth Daryush.   New York, Swallow Press-Morrow, 1948.
Editor, *Poets of the Pacific, Second Series*.   Stanford, California, Stanford University Press, 1949.
Editor, with Kenneth Fields, *Quest for Reality: An Anthology of Short Poems in English*. Chicago, Swallow Press, 1969.

CRITICAL STUDIES AND BIBLIOGRAPHY

John Crowe Ransom, "Yvor Winters: The Logical Critic," in *The New Criticism*.   New York, New Directions, 1941.
Stanley Edgar Hyman, "Yvor Winters and Evaluation in Criticism," in *The Armed Vision: A Study in the Methods of Modern Literary Criticism*.   New York, Knopf, 1948; revised edition, 1955.
Kenneth A. Lohf and Eugene P. Sheehy, *Yvor Winters: A Bibliography*.   Denver, Swallow, 1959.
Keith F. McLean, *The Moral Measure of Literature*.   Denver, Swallow, 1961.
Richard Sexton, *The Complex of Yvor Winters' Criticism*.   The Hague, Mouton, 1974.
Denis Donoghue, "The Will to Certitude," in *Times Literary Supplement* (London), 30 August 1974.
René Wellek, "Yvor Winters Rehearsed and Reconsidered," in *Denver Quarterly*, 10, 1975.
Grosvenor Powell, "Being, Poetry, and Yvor Winters' Criticism," in *Denver Quarterly*, 10, 1975.
W.W. Robson, "Yvor Winters: Counter-Romantic," in *Essays in Criticism* (Oxford), 25, 1975.
David Levin, "Yvor Winters at Stanford," in *Virginia Quarterly Review* (Charlottesville), 54, 1978.
Donald Davie, "Winters and Leavis: Memories and Reflections," in *Sewanee Review* (Tennessee), 87, 1979.

*   *   *

Yvor Winters' theory of poetry is easy enough to summarize; the ethical system it rests upon, however, is somewhat more complicated. For Winters, any "statement" (and all works of literature are primarily "statements about human experience") is both conceptual and emotive: the artist uses words to generate referential meanings, but he also uses the emotional connotations which have become associated with these words. The referential sense of any statement is its "motive"; the connotations form its "emotion" (Winters' terms here are virtually identical with the usual meaning of denotation and connotation and are quite similar as well to Allen Tate's "extension" and "intension"). Thus the poet

> makes his statement in such a way as to employ both concept and connotation as efficiently as possible. The poem is good in as far as it makes a defensible rational statement about a given human experience...and at the same time communicates the emotion which ought to be motivated by that rational understanding of that experience. This notion of poetry, whatever its defects, will account both for the power of poetry and of artistic literature on its readers and for the seriousness with which the great poets have taken their art.

All literature, of course, makes use of motive and emotion, but poetry has the additional resource of rhythm and various metrical effects:

> Rhythm, for reasons which I do not wholly understand, has the power of communicating emotion; and as a part of the poem it has the power of qualifying the total emotion.... [The] poem exists in time, the mind proceeds through it in time, and if the poet is a good one he takes advantage of this fact and makes the progression rhythmical. These aspects of the poem will be efficient in so far as the poet subordinates them to the total aim of the poem.

Rhythm is just as important as motive and intention, but Winters' only theoretical discussion of the problems involved here ("The Influence of Meter on Poetic Convention," in *Primitivism and Decadence*) is disappointingly general and vague at certain crucial points.

The question is *how* we are to determine what emotion a given motive should arouse: by what principle are we to decide that the poet has made the proper adjustment between these two aspects of language? In a brief but very useful essay Denis Donoghue rightly calls attention to an early piece, "Notes on Contemporary Criticism," in which Winters asserts that

> The basis of Evil is emotion; Good rests in the power of rational selection in action, as a preliminary to which the emotion in any situation must be as far as possible eliminated, and, in so far as it cannot be eliminated, understood. I say "as far as possible" advisedly, for such an elimination can never be complete; and the irreducible emotion, if properly evaluated, may even function on the side of Good. If the subsisting emotion in any situation is genuinely irreducible, there is at least the possibility of a sound moral evaluation of its character on the part of the person experiencing it; and if such an evaluation is made, right action becomes highly probable even though the emotion be definitely aligned with the forces of Evil.... If it be objected that I propose no end for which a man should reduce his emotion to a minimum and then, if need be, thwart that minimum, I answer with the Stoics that the end is a controlled and harmonious life.

In themselves the emotions are not evil, but to the extent that they threaten the rule of right reason, they are by far the greatest source of error in human behavior. The reference to the Stoics, however, is misleading, as is any attempt to turn Winters into a Platonist of some sort because he is a moral absolutist and has a dread of emotional indulgence. The basis of his thinking is firmly Thomistic, and finally Aristotelian, as his later work makes quite clear (between them, Aquinas and Aristotle have provided "the most thorough and defensible moral and philosophical system, in all likelihood, that the world has known"). Although Winters does not use Aristotle's specific terms, what he has in mind is the Aristotelian conception of a mean between responses which are deficient or excessive with respect to the attitudes which various situations provoke—a mean which it is the task of practical wisdom to discover. For Aristotle, the man of practical wisdom determines and does the right thing, in the right way, for the right reasons, and takes pleasure in doing so. The pleasures which accompany the exercise of the moral and intellectual virtues constitute that happiness which is the end of life for man *qua* man. Winters' version of all this appears in the opening section of *The Anatomy of Nonsense*:

> The relationship in the poem of rational meaning to feeling...must be a satisfactory relationship. How do we determine whether such a relationship is satisfactory? We

determine it by an act of moral judgment.... If morality can be considered real, if a theory of morality can be said to derive from reality, it is because it guides us toward the greatest happiness which the accidents of life permit; that is, towards the fullest realization of our nature, in the Aristotelian or Thomistic sense.... We can guide ourselves toward such an adjustment in life, as in art, by means of theory and the critical examination of special instances; but the final act of judgment is in both life and art a unique act—it is a relationship between two elements, the rational understanding and the feeling, of which only one is classifactory and of which the other has infinite possibilities.

Determining the mean, making the proper judgment, is in no sense a compromise: it is, rather, the ideal goal of right action and is therefore rarely achieved. Like anyone else, the poet will be deficient in his responses—or excessive (as Hopkins is, for Winters, or to take another example, Wordsworth and Shelley: "One cannot believe...that Wordsworth's passions were charmed away by a look at the daffodils, or that Shelley's were aroused by the sight of the leaves blown about in the autumn wind"). But when a great poet has made the proper adjustment of emotion to motive his work will have a powerful moral impact:

> Poetry, if pursued either by the poet or the reader, in the manner which I have suggested, should offer a means of enriching one's awareness of human experience and of so rendering greater the possibility of intelligence in the course of future action; and it should offer likewise a means of inducing certain more or less constant habits of feeling, which should render greater the possibility of one's acting, in a future situation, in accordance with the findings of one's improved intelligence.... If the poetic discipline is to have steadiness and direction, it requires an antecedent discipline of ethical thinking and at least some ethical feeling, which may be in whole or in part the gift of religion or of a social tradition, or which may be largely the result of individual acquisition by way of study. The poetic discipline includes the antecedent discipline and more: it is the richest and most perfect technique of contemplation.

As Winters points out in the 1947 Forward to *In Defense of Reason*, his theory of poetry is sharply opposed to didactic theories (which neglect the role of properly adjusted emotions), hedonistic theories (which make pleasure the end of art and therefore lead, as hedonism always does, to exhaustion and ennui), and especially "Romantic" theories of one sort or another. In a passage which sounds very much like Hulme or Irving Babbitt, he maintains that the Romantics

> offer a fallacious and dangerous view of the nature both of literature and of man. The Romantic theory assumes that literature is mainly or even purely an emotional experience, that man is naturally good, that man's impulses are trustworthy, and that the rational faculty is unreliable to the point of being dangerous or possibly evil.... Literature thus becomes a form of what is known popularly as self-expression. It is not the business of man to understand and improve himself, for such an effort is superfluous: he is good as he is, if he will only let himself alone, or, as we might say, let himself go. The poem is valuable because it enables us to share the experience of a man who has let himself go, who has expressed his feelings, without hindrance, as he has found them at a given moment.

His definition of criticism follows naturally enough from these moral considerations. The critic is primarily a judge: by adjusting motive to emotion the poet has made a judgment of the experience he depicts; the critic then judges that judgment. The critic's final judgment is a "unique" act ("particular" would be a more accurate word here than "unique"), "the general nature of which can be indicated, but which cannot be communicated precisely, since it consists in receiving from the poet his own final and unique judgment of his matter and in judging that judgment."

These convictions make it possible for Winters to erect an uncompromising hierarchy of literary forms. In *The Function of Criticism* he returns to the distinction between poetry and prose and argues that because of the mysterious power of rhythm, verse can express a stronger emotion than prose, and, within the limits proper to it, can express emotion more precisely than prose, even if the emotion is not strong. But it has a different range of emotion than that of a prose: the total range of verse is higher, although the two ranges overlap perhaps half of the time. Thus there are subjects which verse can treat with greater power than prose; there are many subjects which prose can treat with propriety and which verse cannot treat without a somewhat embarrassing exaggeration. The problem with any particular work in hand is to decide which of the two mediums will be more effective the greater part of the time and in general: the decision may be far from an easy one, but one should never forget that the power of truly great prose is far from contemptible—the fact is, that truly great prose is great, although we have not seen much prose of this kind in the past one hundred years.

But it is still poetry, of course, which at its best remains man's "richest and most complete technique of contemplation." Winters then proceeds to make an important distinction between "mimetic" prose and poetry, in which the artist limits himself to the representation of particular characters in particular situations, and the "lyric" or philosophic poem, in which the poet is free to speak in his own voice and express as completely as possible the degree of understanding he commands. By definition, then, mimetic works are inferior to this kind of lyric poetry: in most dramas and novels (and in many dramatic poems) the characters do not fully understand the situations in which they are involved and therefore cannot judge them properly. Shakespeare understands Hamlet's position better than Hamlet does, but he cannot transcend Hamlet's understanding without violating the limitations of mimetic art. Shakespeare cannot be more intelligent than Macbeth (though Macbeth is more intelligent than Hamlet: he understands that he has "murdered his own soul"); nor can Henry James, Virginia Woolf, and James Joyce be more intelligent than Lambert Strether, Clarissa Dalloway, or Leopold Bloom. For many readers this will probably seem the weakest part of Winters' approach, since it is possible to argue that in mimetic works, even those which keep close to the consciousness of one character, it is still possible for the artist to provide clues which allow the reader to understand the characters better than they understand themselves. Winters seems completely unaware of the subtle devices Wayne Booth has explored in *The Rhetoric of Fiction*.

In his last major work, *Forms of Discovery*, Winters literally rewrites the history of English verse in accordance with the principles outlined above, and finds, of course, that there has been a progressive deterioration in the quality of that verse since the late sixteenth century. There are two chief reasons for the decline: the rise of various forms of Romanticism already referred to, and the triumph of "associationist" psychologies—a matter which he summarizes most succinctly in *The Function of Criticism*:

> For the past two hundred and fifty years it has been common to assume that abstract language is a dead language, that poetry must depict particular actions, or if it be "lyric" that it must be revery over remembered sensory impressions, according to the formula of the associationists. But these assumptions are false. They are our heritage of confusion from Hobbes and Locke, by way of Addison, Hartley, and Alison—and more recently by way of Ezra Pound. A race that has lost the capacity to handle abstractions with discretion and dignity may do well to confine itself to sensory impression, but our ancestors were more fortunate, and we ought to labor to regain what we have lost. The language of metaphysics from Plato onward is a concentration of the theoretical understanding of human experience; and that language as it was refined by the great theologians is even more obviously so. The writings of Aquinas have latent in them the most profound and intense experiences of our race. It is the command of scholastic thought, the realization in terms of experience and feeling of the meaning of scholastic language, that gives Shakespeare his peculiar power among dramatists, and Fulke Greville his peculiar power among the English masters of the short poem.

In *Maule's Curse* Winters examines eight American writers from this special point of view (in what ways were they infected by some form of Romanticism or associationism?). In *Primitivism and Decadence* he is concerned with modern American "experimental" verse (which plays dangerously with "free verse" and thus often loses the disciplining power of rhythm). And in

The Anatomy of Nonsense and *The Function of Criticism* he completes his sweeping history of poetry with essays on Hopkins, Eliot, Frost and Stevens.

This outline of Winters' position gives no sense whatsoever of what is best and worst in his criticism. The lunacy of some of his particular judgments is only too well-known: F.G. Tuckerman's "The Grasshopper" is the greatest poem written during the nineteenth century; Elizabeth Daryush is "the finest British poet since T. Sturge Moore"; Moore is vastly superior to Hopkins, and so on. But it would be a serious mistake to conclude that these verdicts follow necessarily from Winters' premises. They represent spectacular lapses of taste, nothing more. Winters is an austere moralist and is bound to seem narrow—at least as narrow as Aristotle and Aquinas—to an essentially Romantic and anti-rational age. But within his chosen limits, narrow or not, he has a kind of integrity and moral grandeur which no other modern critic can touch. His best prose (which I have not been able to illustrate here) has a Johnsonian power which is equally beyond the reach of any modern critic. Readers who are tempted to find these claims as eccentric as some of Winters' own verdicts should suspend judgment until they have considered, say, the essay on James in *Maule's Curse* or the opening section of *The Function of Criticism*.

WOOLF, (Adeline) Virginia.   British.   Born in London, 25 January 1882; daughter of the writer Leslie Stephen. Educated privately. Married the writer Leonard Woolf in 1912. Reviewer, *Times Literary Supplement*, London. Founder, and Editor, with Leonard Woolf, The Hogarth Press, Richmond, Surrey, later London, 1918-41. *Died 28 March 1941.*

PUBLICATIONS

Criticism

> *Mr. Bennett and Mrs. Brown.*   London, Hogarth Press, 1924; in *Hogarth Essays*, New York, Doubleday, 1928; reprinted in *Collected Essays*, 1967.
> *The Common Reader.*   London, Hogarth Press, and New York, Harcourt Brace, 1925.
> *The Common Reader: Second Series.*   London, Hogarth Press, and New York, Harcourt Brace, 1932.
> *A Letter to a Young Poet.*   London, Hogarth Press, 1932; reprinted in *The Death of the Moth and Other Essays*, 1942.
> *Reviewing.*   London, Hogarth Press, 1939; reprinted in *The Captain's Death Bed and Other Essays*, 1950.
> *The Death of the Moth and Other Essays.*   London, Hogarth Press, and New York, Harcourt Brace, 1942.
> *The Moment and Other Essays.*   London, Hogarth Press, 1947; New York, Harcourt Brace, 1948.
> *The Captain's Death Bed and Other Essays.*   New York, Harcourt Brace, and London, Hogarth Press, 1950.
> *Hours in a Library.*   New York, Harcourt Brace, 1958; reprinted in *Granite and Rainbow: Essays*, 1958.
> *Granite and Rainbow: Essays.*   London, Hogarth Press, and New York, Harcourt Brace, 1958.
> *Contemporary Writers*, edited by Jean Guiguet.   London, Hogarth Press, 1965; New York, Harcourt Brace, 1966.

Collected Essays, edited by Leonard Woolf.   London, Hogarth Press, and New York, Harcourt Brace, 4 vols., 1967.
Books and Portraits: Some Further Selections from the Literary and Biographical Writing of Virginia Woolf, edited by Mary Lyon.   London, Hogarth Press, 1977; New York, Harcourt Brace, 1978.

Play

Freshwater, edited by Lucio P. Ruotolo.   London, Hogarth Press, and New York, Harcourt Brace, 1976.

Novels

The Voyage Out.   London, Duckworth, 1915; New York, Doran, 1920.
Night and Day.   London, Duckworth, 1919; New York, Doran, 1920.
Jacob's Room.   Richmond, Hogarth Press, 1922; New York, Harcourt Brace, 1923.
Mrs. Dalloway.   London, Hogarth Press, and New York, Harcourt Brace, 1925.
To the Lighthouse.   London, Hogarth Press, and New York, Harcourt Brace, 1927.
Orlando: A Biography.   New York, Crosby Gaige, and London, Hogarth Press, 1928.
The Waves.   London, Hogarth Press, and New York, Harcourt Brace, 1931.
Flush: A Biography.   London, Hogarth Press, and New York, Harcourt Brace, 1933.
The Years.   London, Hogarth Press, and New York, Harcourt Brace, 1937.
Between the Acts.   London, Hogarth Press, and New York, Harcourt Brace, 1941.
The Waves: The Two Holograph Drafts, edited by J.W. Graham.   London, Hogarth Press, 1976.
The Pargiters: The Novel-Essay Portion of The Years, edited by Mitchell Leaska.   London, Hogarth Press, and New York, Harcourt Brace, 1978.

Short Stories

Two Stories, with Leonard Woolf.   Richmond, Hogarth Press, 1917.
Kew Gardens.   Richmond, Hogarth Press, 1919.
Monday or Tuesday.   Richmond, Hogarth Press, and New York, Harcourt Brace, 1921.
A Haunted House and Other Short Stories.   London, Hogarth Press, and New York, Harcourt Brace, 1944.
Mrs. Dalloway's Party: A Short Story Sequence, edited by Stella McNichol.   London, Hogarth Press, 1973; New York, Harcourt Brace, 1975.

Other

A Room of One's Own.   New York, Fountain Press, and London, Hogarth Press, 1929.
Street Haunting.   San Francisco, Westgate Press, 1930.
On Being Ill.   London, Hogarth Press, 1930.
Beau Brummell.   New York, Rimington and Hooper, 1930.
Walter Sickert: A Conversation.   London, Hogarth Press, 1934.
The Roger Fry Memorial Exhibition: An Address.   Privately printed, 1935.
Three Guineas.   London, Hogarth Press, and New York, Harcourt Brace, 1938.
Roger Fry: A Biography.   London, Hogarth Press, and New York, Harcourt Brace, 1940.

A Writer's Diary, Being Extracts from the Diary of Virginia Woolf, edited by Leonard Woolf.   London, Hogarth Press, 1953; New York, Harcourt Brace, 1954.
Virginia Woolf and Lytton Strachey: Letters, edited by Leonard Woolf and James Strachey.   London, Hogarth Press-Chatto and Windus, and New York, Harcourt Brace, 1956.
Nurse Lugton's Golden Thimble (juvenile).   London, Hogarth Press, 1966.
The Letters of Virginia Woolf, edited by Nigel Nicolson and Joanne Trautmann.   London, Hogarth Press, and New York, Harcourt Brace, 6 vols., 1975-80.
Moments of Being: Unpublished Autobiographical Writings, edited by Jeanne Schulkind.   Brighton, University of Sussex Press, 1976; New York, Harcourt Brace, 1977.
The Diary of Virginia Woolf, edited by Anne Olivier Bell.   London, Hogarth Press, and New York, Harcourt Brace, 5 vols., 1977-82.

Translator, with S.S. Koteliansky, *Stavrogin's Confession...*by Dostoevsky.   Richmond, Hogarth Press, 1922.
Translator, with S.S. Koteliansky, *Tolstoi's Love Letters...*   Richmond, Hogarth Press, 1923.
Translator, with S.S. Koteliansky, *Talks with Tolstoy*, by A.D. Goldenveizer.   Richmond, Hogarth Press, 1923.

BIOGRAPHY, CRITICAL STUDIES AND BIBLIOGRAPHY

Bernard Blackstone, "Criticism and Biography," in *Virginia Woolf: A Commentary*.   London, Hogarth Press, 1949.
B.J. Kirkpatrick, *A Bibliography of Virginia Woolf*.   London, Hart Davis, 1957; revised edition, 1967.
Joan Bennett, "Virginia Woolf as Critic," in *Virginia Woolf: Her Art as a Novelist*.   London, Cambridge University Press, revised edition, 1964.
Jean Guiguet, *Virginia Woolf and Her Works*, translated by Jean Stuart.   New York, Harcourt Brace, 1966.
Quentin Bell, *Virginia Woolf: A Biography*.   London, Hogarth Press, 2 vols., 1972; New York, Harcourt Brace, 1972.
Barbara Currier Bell and Carol Ohmann, "Virginia Woolf's Criticism: A Polemical Introduction," in *Critical Inquiry* (Chicago), 1, 1974.
René Wellek, "Virginia Woolf as Critic," in *Southern Review* (Baton Rouge, Louisiana) 13, 1977.

*   *   *

In their lively defence of Virginia Woolf as a practical critic—the best defense she has had so far, although still not good enough—Barbara Currier Bell and Carol Ohmann attempt to disarm the opposition at once by cheerfully admitting that yes, Woolf was "defiantly feminine"; even worse, she was "creative, appreciative, and subjective." (These are not fashionable claims, of course: a good many modern critics have worked hard to discredit the belief that one should be intuitive and creative, rather than coolly analytical, detached, and interested only in what is "in the text.") No other twentieth century critic, Bell and Ohmann go on, "approached literature with less explicit 'system' and more sympathy." Thus Woolf is "truly revolutionary" and "offers a highly attractive alternative to conventional literary criticism":

The features of Woolf's criticism...are all...strategies in a single campaign: an effort to take books down from library shelves and put them into the hands of her ideal community, the common readers. And to talk about them outside the walls of lecture rooms. And to talk about them, finally, in such a way that they matter, not in literary history, but in our lives.

To succeed in talking about books this way, they conclude, helps us to "humanize our lives" and attain a "liberation and wholeness of self."

"Sympathy" is a crucial word here, and so too is the more problematic word, "creative." "Do not dictate to your author," Woolf urges in "How Should One Read a Book?" "Try to become him. Be his fellow worker and accomplice." But this advice is not revolutionary: it is at least as old as Pope ("A perfect judge will read each work of wit/ With the same spirit that its author writ")—and as up to date as Georges Poulet's arguments that criticism is "the consciousness of consciousness" and should strive for the perfect coincidence of the mind of the critic with the mind of the creator. Woolf is "creative," Bell and Ohmann insist, because she "invents 'the common reader' and employs that persona convincingly." But again, this is misleading: Woolf did not invent the common reader any more than she invents the texts whose accomplice she tries to be. The notion of the common reader comes, of course (as Bell and Ohmann know), from Dr. Johnson. In the opening essays of the first *Common Reader* Woolf observes that

> There is a sentence in Dr. Johnson's Life of Gray which might well be written up in all those rooms, too humble to be called libraries, yet full of books, where the pursuit of reading is carried on by private people. "...I rejoice to concur with the common reader; for by the common sense of readers, uncorrupted by literary prejudices, after all the refinements of subtilty and the dogmatism of learning, must be finally decided all claim to poetical honours." It defines their qualities; it dignifies their aims; it bestows upon a pursuit which devours a good deal of time, and is yet apt to leave behind it nothing very substantial, the sanction of the great man's approval.

The common reader, she continues, "reads for his own pleasure rather than to impart knowledge or correct the opinions of others":

> Above all, he is guided by an instinct to create for himself, out of whatever odds and ends he can come by, some kind of whole—a portrait of a man, a sketch of an age, a theory of the art of writing. He never ceases, as he reads, to run up some rickety and ramshackle fabric which shall give him the temporary satisfaction of looking sufficiently like the real object to allow of affection, laughter, and argument.

In essay after essay, then, Woolf attempts to approach her author with self-effacing sympathy and to give her readers a sense of, say, Crabbe, or Jane Austen, or the world of the Russian novelists; she presupposes, as Dr. Johnson did, the existence of the common reader (although no critic can afford to do so now). Such sympathetic recreation is, in the best sense of that abused term, "appreciative." And to enter appreciatively into the world of another writer or period does extend and thus "humanize" our lives: the act of reading, Poulet maintains (in "The Phenomenology of Reading"), "has delivered me from my egocentricity." This is true for Woolf as well (it is worth noting that she has a special sympathy for the small, neglected, often grotesque figures who are not immediately attractive to readers); but to understand fully why sympathetic criticism is so important to her, we have to consider, as Bell and Ohmann do not, her conception of the novel itself and the function of art.

Probably the easiest way to do so is to contrast her position with that of E.M. Forster. In an early pamphlet, *Anonymity: An Enquiry* (first published by the Woolfs at the Hogarth Press), Forster asks us to imagine two poles or extremes of language functions; at one pole lies scientific, informative, denotative, purely referential language; at the other, purely poetic language, which is connotative (it "creates atmosphere") and may be used to build up non-referential structures which have "internal order" and stability (an important matter which Forster hints at here and develops at length in a later essay, "Art for Art's Sake"). Forster continues his argument in *Aspects of the Novel*, in which he maintains that the novel is by definition a "mixed" form: it may be patterned, but its primary function is to inform us, to give us a sense of the "hidden lives" of characters such as we never get in real life and thus suggest "a more comprehensible and...a more manageable human race." The best novels create "the illusion of perspicacity and power"; they are "sogged with humanity." And while the novel may rely on pattern as a source of order, Forster often seems to regard pattern as a menace rather than a challenge: in Henry James, for example, the sacrifices made for the sake of order are too great ("most of human life has to disappear before he can do us a novel").

In her deceptively sympathetic review of *Aspects of the Novel* Woolf complains that Forster is defending the "human as opposed to the aesthetic view of fiction." He argues that if the novelist neglects life, he will perish. But at this point, she objects,

> the pertinacious pupil may demand: "What is this 'Life' that keeps cropping up so mysteriously and so complacently in books about fiction? Why is it absent in a pattern and present in a tea party? Why is the pleasure that we get in the pattern of *The Golden Bowl* less valuable than the emotion which Trollope gives us when he describes a lady drinking tea in a parsonage? Surely the definition of life is too arbitrary, and requires to be expanded." To all of this Mr. Forster would reply, presumably, that he lays down no laws; the novel somehow seems to him too soft a substance to be carved like the other arts; he is merely telling us what moves him and what leaves him cold.... [The] assumption that fiction is more intimately and humbly attached to the service of human beings than the other arts leads to a further position.... It is unnecessary to dwell upon [the novel's] aesthetic functions because they are so feeble that they can be safely ignored. Thus, though it is impossible to imagine a book on painting in which not a word should be said about the medium in which a painter works, a wise and brilliant book, like Mr. Forster's, can be written about fiction without saying more than sentence or two about the medium in which a novelist works. Almost nothing is said about words. One might suppose, unless one had read them, that a sentence means the same thing and is used for the same purpose by Sterne and Wells. One might conclude that *Tristram Shandy* gains nothing from the language in which it is written. So with the other aesthetic qualities. Pattern...is recognised, but savagely censured for her tendency to obscure human features. Beauty occurs but she is suspect.... [Fiction] is treated as a parasite which draws sustenance from life and must in gratitude resemble life or perish. In poetry, in drama, words may excite and stimulate and deepen without this allegiance; but in fiction they must first and foremost hold themselves at the service of the teapot and the pug dog, and to be found wanting is to be found lacking.

Can the novel be a work of art? Woolf closes her review on a tentative note:

> In England at any rate the novel is not a work of art.... In France and Russia they take fiction seriously. Flaubert spends a month seeking a phrase to describe a cabbage. Tolstoy writes *War and Peace* seven times over. Something of their pre-eminence may be due to the pains they take, something to the severity with which they are judged. If the English critic were less domestic, less assiduous to protect the rights of what it pleases him to call life, the novelist might be bolder too. He might cut adrift from the eternal tea-table and the plausible and preposterous formulas which are supposed to represent the whole of our human adventure. But then the story might wobble; the plot might crumble; ruin might seize upon the characters. The novel, in short, might become a work of art.

In any event, by emphasizing the importance of order, Woolf clearly intends to move the novel closer than Forster will permit to the realm of poetry. She develops the point at length in "Phases of Fiction" (reprinted in *Granite and Rainbow*) and exemplifies it, of course, in her own practice as a novelist.

What this experience of order can provide she describes unforgettably in the most complex of her novels, *The Waves*. Listening to a string quartet performing Mozart, Rhoda feels how "There is a square; there is an oblong":

> The players take the square and place it upon the oblong. They place it very accurately; they make a perfect dwelling-place. Very little is left outside. The structure is now visible; what is inchoate is now stated; we are not so various or so mean; we have made oblongs and stood them upon squares. This is our triumph; this is our consolation.

But art offers us more than "consolation": it may provide a way of sustaining ourselves against the disorder of ordinary life. Thus when the music is finished, Rhoda feels that "the sweetness of this content overflowing runs down the walls of my mind, and liberates understanding":

Wander no more, I say; this is an end. The oblong has been set upon the square; the spiral is on top. We have been hauled over the shingle, down to the sea. The players come again. But they are mopping their faces. They are no longer so spruce or so debonair. I will go...I will fling myself fearlessly into trams, into omnibuses. As we lurch down Regent Street, and I am flung upon this woman, this man, I am not injured. I am not outraged by the collision. A square stands upon an oblong. Here are mean streets where chaffering goes on in street markets, and every sort of iron rod, bolt and screw is laid out, and people swarm off the pavement, pinching raw meat with thick fingers. The structure is visible. We have made a dwelling-place.

To make this experience of order more available to the common reader is therefore one of Woolf's chief aims in her critical essays.

But to conclude that she was more interested in pattern and order than in "life" would be a mistake. It is more accurate to say that she objects to Forster's position because he emphasizes the humane view of fiction *at the expense of* the aesthetic view. How much value she too attaches to life and the revelation of character is abundantly clear in her best-known essay, *Mr. Bennett and Mrs. Brown*. Novelists, she observes here,

> differ from the rest of the world because they do not cease to be interested in character when they have learnt enough about it for practical purposes. They go a step further, they feel that there is something permanently interesting in character in itself. When all the practical business of life has been discharged, there is something about people which continues to seem to them of overwhelming importance, in spite of the fact that it has no bearing whatever upon their happiness, comfort, or income. The study of character becomes to them an absorbing pursuit; to impart character is an obsession.... I believe that all novels, that is to say, deal with character, and that it is to express character...that the form of the novels, so clumsy, verbose, and undramatic, so rich, elastic, and alive, has been evolved.

Arnold Bennett, she reminds us, says that no novel can survive if its characters are not "real." But, she asks, what is this "reality"? She evades the question here but turns to it directly in "Modern Fiction" (reprinted in the first *Common Reader*):

> Look within and life, it seems, is very far from being "like this" [life, that is, as the conventional realists present it]. Examine for a moment an ordinary day. The mind receives a myriad impressions—trivial, fantastic, evanescent, or engraved with the sharpness of steel. From all sides they come, an incessant shower of innumerable atoms; and as they fall, as they shape themselves into the life of Monday or Tuesday, the accent falls differently from of old; the moment of importance came not here but there; so that, if a writer were a free man and not a slave, if he could write what he chose, not what he must, if he could base his work upon his own feeling and not upon convention, there would be no plot, no comedy, no tragedy, no love interest or catastrophe in the accepted style, and perhaps not a single button sewn on as the Bond Street tailors would have it. Life is not a series of gig lamps symmetrically arranged; life is a luminous halo, a semi-transparent envelope surrounding us from the beginning of consciousness to the end. Is it not the task of the novelist to convey this varying, this unknown and uncircumscribed spirit, whatever aberration or complexity it may display, with as little mixture of the alien and external as possible?

The connection between "character," then, and "reality," is simply this: the novelist can render reality only as he shows it impinging on the consciousness of his characters. And again, our participation in the artist's sense of reality may be of great value. Whatever this sense touches, she maintains (in *A Room of One's Own*), "it fixes and makes permanent":

> Now the writer, as I think has the chance to live more than other people in the presence of this reality. It is his business to find it and collect it and communicate it to the rest of us. So at least I infer from reading *Lear* or *Emma* or *La Recherche du Temps Perdu*. For the reading of these books seems to perform a curious couching operation on the senses; one

sees more intensely afterwards; the world seems bared of its covering and given an intenser life. Those are the enviable people who live at enmity with unreality; and those are the pitiable who are knocked on the head by the thing done without knowing or caring.

Thus, once again, appreciative criticism can help us to see what the artist saw, and through his own eyes (hence the odd image of the "couching operation," a procedure for removing cataracts).

These remarks may be of some help to readers unfamiliar with the conception of fiction implicit in Woolf's criticism, but they give very little sense of the extraordinary beauty of her prose, or of its imaginative power. For there are times, of course, when the novelist takes the place of the critic. A few years ago, Geoffrey Hartman remarked that reading Derrida on Rousseau was almost as interesting as reading Rousseau. One can go further: reading Woolf *on* Hakluyt or Gissing is much more interesting than reading Hakluyt or Gissing themselves. And if she occasionally invents authors who turn out to be as fascinating as any of the imaginary artists conjured up by Borges or Nabokov, it seems foolish to deny oneself these pleasures in the name of "criticism." There are times when criticism does become a work of art about another work of art—the only mistake lies in believing that this will happen very often, or with writers less gifted than Virginia Woolf.

YOUNG, Philip (Pratt).   American.   Born in Boston, Massachusetts, 26 May 1918. Educated a. Amherst College, Massachusetts, B.A. 1940; Harvard University, Cambridge, Massachusetts 1940-41; University of Iowa, Iowa City, Ph.D. 1948. Served in the United States Army 1942-46: First Lieutenant, Air Medal. Married Caroline Anderson in 1944 (died); Katharine Garner, 1968; has four children. Graduate Assistant and Instructor in English, University of Iowa, 1946-48; Instructor, 1948-50, and Adjunct Assistant Professor, 1952-53, New York University; Associate Professor, Kansas State University, Manhattan, 1953-59. Professor of American Literature, 1959-66, and since 1966, Research Professor and Fellow in the Institute for Arts and Humanistic Studies, Pennsylvania State University, University Park. Visiting Lecturer, University of Minnesota, Minneapolis, 1955-56; United States State Department American Specialist in India, 1957; Fulbright Lecturer in France and Italy, 1962-63. Recipient: American Council of Learned Societies Fellowship, 1950. D.H.L.: Westminster College, New Wilmington, Pennsylvania, 1971. Address: Department of English, Pennsylvania State University, University Park, Pennsylvania 16802, U.S.A.

PUBLICATIONS

Criticism

"The Early Psychologists and Poe," in *American Literature* (Durham, North Carolina), 22, 1951.
Ernest Hemingway.   New York, Rinehart, 1952; London, G. Bell, 1953; revised edition as *Ernest Hemingway: A Reconsideration*, University Park, Pennsylvania State University Press, 1966.
"Scott Fitzgerald's Waste Land," in *Kansas Magazine* (Manhattan), 1958.
Ernest Hemingway.   Minneapolis, University of Minnesota Press, 1959.
"The Assumptions of Literature," in *College English* (Chicago), 24, 1963.

"To Have Not: Tough Luck," in *Tough Guy Writers of the Thirties*, edited by David Madden.   Carbondale, Southern Illinois University Press, 1968.

Commentaries in *By-Line: Ernest Hemingway: Selected Articles and Dispatches of Four Decades*, edited by William White.   New York, Scribner, 1967; London, Collins, 1968.

Three Bags Full: Essays in American Fiction.   New York, Harcourt Brace, 1972.

"Big World out There: The Nick Adams Stories," in *Novel* (Providence, Rhode Island), 6, 1972.

"The Story of the Missing Man," in *Directions in Literary Criticism*, edited by Stanley Weintraub and Philip Young.   University Park, Pennsylvania State University Press, 1973.

"For Malcolm Cowley, Critic, Poet, 1898— ," in *Southern Review* (Baton Rouge, Louisiana), 9, 1973.

"Posthumous Hemingway, and Nicholas Adams," in *Hemingway in Our Time*, edited by R. Astro and J. Nenson.   Corvallis, Oregon State University Press, 1974.

"In Search of a Lost Generation," in *Kansas Quarterly* (Manhattan), 7, 1975.

"Born Decadent: The American Novel and Charles Brockden Brown," in *Southern Review* (Baton Rouge, Louisiana), 17, 1981.

Other

The Hemingway Manuscripts: An Inventory, with Charles W. Mann.   University Park and London, Pennsylvania State University Press, 1969.

"Of Strength and Vulnerability: An Interview wih Philip Young," in *Dialogue* (Bradford, Pennsylvania), 1, 1973.

"Iowa City and After," in *Teacher and Critic: Essays by and about Austin Warren*, edited by Myron Simon and Harvey Gross.   Los Angeles, Plantin Press, 1976.

Revolutionary Ladies.   New York, Knopf, 1977.

Editor, *The House of the Seven Gables*, by Nathaniel Hawthorne.   New York, Rinehart, 1957; revised edition, 1970.

Editor, *Typee*, by Herman Melville.   London, Cassell, 1967.

Editor, *The Nick Adams Stories*, by Ernest Hemingway.   New York, Scribner, 1972.

Editor, with Stanley Weintraub, *Directions in Literary Criticism: Contemporary Approaches to Literature.*   University Park, Pennsylvania State University Press, 1973.

*   *   *

No one familiar with the competition is likely to object to a flat assertion that Philip Young's *Ernest Hemingway: A Reconsideration* is the definitive study of that writer. But quite apart from the fact that a word like "definitive" is often nothing more than a pleasant emotive noise, to make such an assertion raises, for the last time in these essays, the crucial point of the hermeneutical distinction between meaning and significance recently introduced into American criticism by E.D. Hirsch.

As Hirsch presents the argument (in *Validity in Interpretation*), "meaning" refers to "that which is represented by the text"; it is "what the author meant by a particular sign sequence." "Significance," on the other hand, "names a relationship between meaning and a person, a conception, a situation, or indeed anything imaginable" (for all practical purposes, of course, determining the significance of literary text usually involves naming the relationship between authorial or "original" meaning and the reader's own set of values). Thus as long as a verbal utterance is, as Hirsch demonstrates, determinate, reproducible, and hence sharable, there can be (and ought to be) consensus, if never absolute certainty, about the probable intended meaning. But even though they might be in perfect agreement about meaning, as long as there are two readers left who hold differing values, there cannot be consensus about significance (nor should there be, unless we feel that everyone should hold the same values). Interpretation is the act of recovering the author's original meaning; criticism is the act of determining the significance of that meaning: and thus a good many apparent disputes are really nothing more than the result of failure to recognize what kind of statement, critical or interpretive, we happen to be making or responding to. And in this sense criticism can never be "definitive."

Twenty-five years have passed since Young published the first version of the *Reconsideration*; but despite that, and despite the posthumous work and the new biographical material which has become available, his interpretation of Hemingway's fiction taken as a coherent whole has never been seriously challenged or even seriously questioned—save by Hemingway himself:

> Writing is very tough work, [Hemingway] said, yet it requires mechanisms as delicate as the most delicate mechanisms imaginable. If someone comes along, not himself an expert, and takes the machine apart for his own benefit, it's all very well to say that he has a right to take any old machine apart, but Hemingway did not feel the right existed while the mechanisms were still in good running order.

If Hemingway meant what he said here (Young is paraphrasing a letter which he had no permission to quote directly), then of course he would have objected to any interpretation of his work made while he was still writing, and not merely to the interpretation Young was proposing. In any event, Young was the first critic to see how the early stories and sketches fitted together and to illuminate the obsessive pattern which runs through Hemingway's work from the Nick Adams stories through *The Old Man and the Sea*. And in order to do this, Young admits that while his interest in Hemingway was not primarily biographical, he did have to draw upon "enough biography to reveal that the experience of the [Hemingway] hero was typically a refraction or projection of the author's": as Young presents him, the Hemingway hero is "pretty close to being Hemingway himself." Again Hemingway was bound to object and managed to have publication of the book delayed for some time. Young's own fascinating and cheerful account of the whole affair (he won) now appears as the first chapter of the *Reconsideration*.

Like Hemingway himself, the Nick Adams of *In Our Time* returns to America from the first War badly wounded in mind and body. But the atrocities they were exposed to during the War were by no means a first introduction to a world of violence and apparently pointless suffering. That process had begun earlier for both of them, during adolescence: "Indian Camp," for example, is based upon one of Hemingway's own experiences and also serves as Nick's "initiation to pain, and to the violence of birth and death." As a boy and later as a man, Nick

has been coming into contact with "life" in our time. Each of these contacts has been in some way violent, evil, or unsettling in that no ready answers are available. They have complicated and damaged the man who, when an ex-infantryman, is a very unwell soldier. He cannot sleep at night; when he can sleep he has nightmares. He has seen a great deal of unpleasantness, not only in the war but earlier up in Michigan as well; and he has been wounded by these experiences in a physical way and...also in a psychical way.... Here is a sensitive, humorless, honest, rather passive male. He is the outdoor man who revels in the life of the senses, loves to hunt and fish and takes pride in his knowledge of how to do such things. He is virile even as an adolescent, and very conscious of his nerve; maturity has forced a reckoning with his nerves as well. Once grown he is a man who knows his way around but he is superstitious too, and is developing a complex ritual whereby thinking can be stopped, the evil spirits placated and warded off...Nick *is* the Hemingway hero, the first one. The drawing of him is very sketchy as yet, but it is true and Hemingway never takes it back to cancel half a line: the experiences of childhood, adolescence and young manhood which shape Nick shaped as well Lt. Henry, Jake Barnes, Col. Cantwell, and several other heroes.... [The] Hemingway hero, the big, tough, outdoor man, is also the wounded man, and descriptions of certain scenes in the life of Nick Adams explain how he got that way. The man will die a thousand times before his death, but from his wounds he would never recover as long as Hemingway lived and recorded his adventures.

Nick is the archetypal Hemingway hero, the "first leading actor" in the repeated drama to which Hemingway "dedicated nearly four decades of his life."

Another survivor, Lt. Henry (in *A Farewell to Arms*), observes that "The world breaks everyone and afterwards many are strong at the broken places." They may be "many," but they are still special enough to form the elect in Hemingway's best stories and novels. The Hemingway hero is the man who suffers but endures and now lives by a "code" and shows "grace under pressure":

> [The "code"] is made of the controls of honor and courage which in a life of tension and pain make a man a man and distinguish him from the people who follow random impulses, let down their hair, and are generally messy, perhaps cowardly, and without inviolable rules for how to live holding tight.

However admirable they may be in life, stoicism and courage are not in themselves artistically moving attitudes, as Young recognizes. "To have the skill, then, to convince others that this is a valid vision," he goes on, "is Hemingway's achievement"; and the means of this achievement, of course, is verbal style, the perfect adjustment, in Hemingway's best work, between words and cadences and the view of life they embody. Hemingway's prose is "easily recognized":

> The typical sentence is a simple declarative one, or a couple of these joined by a conjunction. The effect is of crispness, cleanness, clarity, and a scrupulous care.... It is a remarkably unintellectual style.... The things that Hemingway's style most conveys are the very things he says outright. His style is as communicative of the content as the content itself, and is a large and inextricable part of the content. The strictly disciplined controls exerted over the hero and his nervous system are precise parallels to the strictly disciplined sentences. The "mindlessness" of the style is a reflection and expression of the need to "stop thinking" when thought means remembering the things that upset. The intense simplicity of the prose is a means of saying that things must be *made* simple, or the hero is lost, and in "a way you'll never be." The economy and narrow focus of the prose controls the little that can be absolutely mastered. The prose is tense because the atmosphere in which the struggle for control takes place is tense, and the tension in the style expresses that fact.

(For the sake of conciseness I have drawn these passages from Young's University of Minnesota pamphlet on Hemingway. Readers who quite properly want the demonstration and not merely the conclusions should turn to the fifth chapter of the *Reconsideration*, which is one of the best examples of stylistic analysis modern criticism has to offer).

If this were all, the *Reconsideration* would be primarily an interpretative study. Of course it is more than that; but given Young's patience and ingenuity up to this point, readers may be surprised that he finds Hemingway an influential and "unmistakably major" writer, but also a "limited" one. It is easy enough to protest against Hemingway's world, he admits, for it is a world "seen through a crack in the wall by a man who is pinned down by gunfire, who can move outside to look around only on penalty of the death he seeks out but also seeks to stay"; it is a world (to quote once more from the Minnesota pamphlet)

> in which things do not grow and bear fruit, but explode, break, decompose, or are eaten away. It is saved from total misery by visions of endurance, competence, and courage, by what happiness the body can give when it is not in pain, by interludes of love that cannot outlast the furlough, by a pleasure in the countries one can visit, or fish and hunt in, and the cafés one can sit in, and by very little else. Hemingway's characters do not "mature" in the ordinary sense, do not become "adult." It is impossible to picture them in a family circle, going to the polls to vote, or making out their income tax returns. It is a very narrow world.

Nevertheless, Hemingway's view of life may not be as radically limited as we might like to believe:

> We may argue the utter inadequacy of the world Hemingway has refracted and

597

re-created; indeed we should protest against it.... But if we choose to look back over our time, what essential facts can we stack against the facts of violence, evil, and death? We remember countless "minor" wars, and two tremendous ones, and prepare for the day when we may be engaged in a holocaust beyond which we cannot see anything. We may argue against Hemingway's world, but we should not find it easy to prove that it is not the world we have been living in.

Thus Hemingway is valuable for Young at least in part because he dramatizes and confirms the testimony of modern history. Readers may agree or disagree, but one further point should be raised: granted that Hemingway and modern history both tell us about an appalling amount of evil in our time, they do so in quite different ways. They differ, that is, in the accounts they give of the *causes* of suffering. For Hemingway evil is usually somehow "out there"; he shows very little understanding, especially in his early (and best) work, of wilful aggression, of the ways in which men decide to wage wars and systematically torture each other. And surely we have some reason to believe that human virtue is something complex and problematical—that courage, for example, is something more than the capacity to suffer manfully. But to argue in such terms is to begin a genuinely critical debate which rests upon rather than questions the authoritative interpretation of Hemingway's vision of life which Young has provided.

Young has not limited himself to this one writer. Several of the essays in *Three Bags Full* suggest that given the time or inclination, he might do for Hawthorne what he has done for Hemingway; but the most important pieces in this collection are two virtuoso excursions into myth criticism, "The Mother of Us All: Pocahontas," and "Fallen from Time: Rip Van Winkle." Like a number of critics who have been interested in myth, however, Young is wary about committing himself to any one causal explanation as to *why* we are moved by certain recurring narrative lines. The problem had come up earlier, in the *Reconsideration*: speculating briefly about the haunting appeal of the river interludes in *Huckleberry Finn*, Young remarks

> There must be Freudians who, with a suggestion of knowing smiles on their lips, would leap to "explain" this mystery. These gliding escapes into the silent darkness are simply lyrical expressions of the "death instinct," or of that desire to "return to the womb" which is about the same thing as dying, with an added advantage in the possibility of being reborn.

At the same time,

> There must also be Jungians who would be quick to explain what is going on in this flight, for here seems to be a perfect example of a psychic reaction in readers which is out of proportion to its exciting cause, and must therefore...lead us to suspect the presence of an "archetype," a pattern in the "collective unconscious" of the race, which has been stirred. Huck's escapes by water are vastly more suggestive than some of the *Archetypal Patterns in Poetry* investigated by Maud Bodkin. Here is one of those downward movements "towards quiescence or toward disintegration and death" that she wrote about. Or, not much different, here is a repetition of the archetype of rebirth, which she found in night journeys.

But Young goes on, "Of course there is no conclusive evidence for such claims as these.... There is no more need to accept the existence of a collective unconscious than of a death instinct in order understand that the dream of a final flight from a very imperfect life could powerfully attract us." This is a little evasive: if we want to understand the appeal of such patterns and not merely note their various disguises, then of course it is necessary to endorse some causal model. Still, for certain purposes it may not matter all that much. "As literary people," Young remarks (in "The Assumptions of Literature"), "the problem is not so much where the [mythic] sounds come from as what they are saying."

In actual practice, Young does base his argument on an assumption broad enough to permit what he calls "amateur liftings" from both Freud and Jung (and to assume as they do a loose but vital connection between dream, myth and art). "Nothing survives indefinitely," he maintains, "without filling some function." Thus he is intent on establishing the psychological usefulness of the Pocahontas and Rip Van Winkle themes in literature and myth, and he does so with the dramatic skill of an expert detective re-enacting the solution of an elusive mystery. As for the Pocahontas motif, the enduring stories of a native princess who saves the heroic intruder but does not become part of his later life are in part wish-fulfillment fantasies and thus subject to Freudian interpretation:

> In our fondness of Pocahontas can we make out a longing that is buried somewhere below even the affection we bear for our fair selves and white causes? This yearning might be for another kind of love entirely, a love that has forever been hidden under the differences that set countries, creeds, and colors against each other. From the freedom and noble impracticality of childhood, we as a people have taken this Indian girl to heart. Could we be hinting at a wish for a love that would really cross the barriers of race? When the beautiful brown head comes down, does a whole nation dream this dream?

But these stories also provide a kind of warning or concealed moral and are thus subject to Jungian analysis, which stresses the importance of "corrective" images. The dream of union is only a dream:

> And that fact helps to explain why it is that from the very beginning the story has what looks like the wrong ending, why the wedding of the protagonists remains a symbol that was never realized.... We sense that the adventure has to end the way it does partly because we know the difference between what we dream and what we get. We are not particularly happy with the denouement, but we feel its correctness, and with it we acknowledge that this is all just make-believe.

In short, Young has conflated the two models: the wishful fantasy may also serve the reality principle, the everyday needs of the collective psyche to face things as they are.

This fusion of Freud and Jung is even more effective when applied to the Rip Van Winkle motif. In Washington Irving's tale, the Freudian possibilities seem dominant: the weak yet attractively childish Rip has been exposed to certain rites of initiation (he participates in a "nearly forgotten ceremony in the worship of Thor for the production of rain"), but after his miraculous sleep he is neither wiser nor more effective than before. Unlike the archetypal hero of the monomyth Joseph Campbell defines in *The Hero with a Thousand Faces*, he does not come back to his fellow men bearing special gifts. Irving's use of the myth is therefore "ironic," but the irony is not a pointless sophistication. "To be technical for a moment," Young argues, Rip "represents the ego arrested at the infantile level in an Oedipal situation; under pressure he reverts all the way back to the sleep of the womb." In its unironic versions, the myth depends upon a theory of personality development which Freudians accept; but the ironic version also has a cautionary dimension which Jungians will find more important:

> We know perfectly well that as an adult this darling of generations of Americans will not entirely do. But if he does seem, finally, meek, blessed, pure in heart, and if we mock him for what he has missed we do it tenderly—partly because it is something hidden in ourselves we mock. And this is not just our own hidden childishness. It is all our own lost lives and roles, the lives and roles that once seemed possible and are possible no more. In twenty years all springs are over; without mockery it might be too sad to bear. Today would grieve, and tomorrow would grieve; best cover it over lightly.

Taken together, these two essays offer a kind of mythic interpretation which makes the efforts of Richard Chase and Leslie Fiedler—and even much of Northrop Frye—seem thin and arbitrary. But for Young, as for most myth critics, there is a point at which uncovering a mythic pattern is virtually indistinguishable from making a critical judgment. However weak their aesthetic embodiments may be at times, the presence of these wishes and warnings gives a literary work some unforgettable overtones and lasting appeal. Myth criticism may become a "minor industry," Young concludes (in "The Assumptions of Literature"), but "the procedure continues to seem profitable":

> And so it is with a great deal of the very best fiction.... Because at its best it engages life, which is inexhaustibly rich, at its deepest levels, it has reserves of suggestion and mystery

which are themselves inexhaustible. This is the kind of fiction which is most worth teaching, and worth critical attention; and bring all the disciplines to bear on it we will, the essential mysteries remain because of the essential mysteriousness of life.